The University of Chicago Spanish–English Dictionary

Diccionario Universidad de Chicago Inglés–Español

The University of Chicago Spanish–English Dictionary

Diccionario Universidad de Chicago Inglés–Español

Originally Compiled by Carlos Castillo and Otto F. Bond

Compilación original de Carlos Castillo y Otto F. Bond

SIXTH EDITION · *SEXTA EDICIÓN*

David A. Pharies
Editor in Chief · *Director*

María Irene Moyna
Editor · *Editora*

Gary K. Baker
Assistant Editor · *Redactor*

Meagan M. Day
Editorial Assistant · *Redactora*

POCKET BOOKS

NEW YORK LONDON TORONTO SYDNEY NEW DELHI

Pocket Books
A Division of Simon & Schuster, Inc.
1230 Avenue of the Americas
New York, NY 10020

Published by arrangement with The University of Chicago Press

First Pocket Books paperback printing of this revised edition July 2012

POCKET and colophon are registered trademarks of Simon & Schuster, Inc.

For information about special discounts for bulk purchases, please contact Simon &
Schuster Special Sales at 1-866-506-1949 or business@simonandschuster.com

The Simon & Schuster Speakers Bureau can bring authors to your live event. For
more information or to book an event contact the Simon & Schuster Speakers
Bureau at 1-866-248-3049 or visit our website at www.simonspeakers.com.

Manufactured in the United States of America

10 9 8 7 6 5 4 3 2 1

ISBN 978-1-4516-9828-2

Contents

Preface to the Sixth Edition

The *University of Chicago Spanish–English Dictionary* has been compiled for the general use of Spanish-speaking learners of American English and American English-speaking learners of Spanish. In step with the rapid pace of cultural and linguistic change at the beginning of the twenty-first century, we have thoroughly revised the *Dictionary* for its sixth edition to reflect the most current vocabulary and usage in both languages.

Since our goal is to ensure that users will always find the words and phrases they seek, the greatest change for this new edition is the addition of some six thousand words and meanings. In choosing among possible additions, we have paid particular attention to frequency of use in written and spoken contexts, since a user is more likely to seek a word that appears frequently (e.g., *libertad* 'liberty', number 540 in frequency according to the extensive list available at www.wordfrequency.info) than one that appears infrequently (e.g., *verdolaga* 'purslane', number 19,705).

Frequency of use cannot serve as the sole criterion for new material, however, for three reasons. First, some words become current so quickly that no frequency list can possibly capture them. Digital terminology offers good examples of this trend, such as the word *app*, which has risen from obscurity to universal acceptance in very little time. Second, some of the changes that a dictionary should reflect occur at a semantic or phrasal level not captured by frequencies. Current expressions such as *to go off on* 'to scold' and *to be down with* 'to be in agreement with' consist of extremely frequent words used in novel ways. Finally, a word can be essential without being frequent. Medical terms, for example, can be vitally important to anyone negotiating another nation's health system, even if they are used infrequently outside of medical contexts.

Medicine is in fact one of four cultural and technical areas of increasing global importance for which we have specially enhanced our coverage for this edition. Along with the 600 new words and meanings that have been added in this field, the sixth edition incorporates 750 new items from the field of business, 500 relating to digital technology, and over 400 relating to the terminology of several globally popular sports, including basketball, baseball, soccer, tennis, and golf.

In many cases, the additions in these four areas warranted completely new entries, as in the case of *allergen* (Sp. *alérgeno*), *auditing* (*auditoría*), *adapter* (*adaptador*), and *unplayable* (*injugable*). In many others, we added a meaning or an equivalent to an existing entry, as in the case of *pinza* (to whose entry was added Eng. [*medical*] *clamp*), *fraudulento* (adding *bogus*), *descifrar* (*to decrypt*), and *abanicar* (*to swing and miss*). On the English side, many additions take the form of compounds attached to existing entries—for example, *clubfoot* (*pie zambo*), added to the *club* entry; *business agreement* (*con-*

venio comercial), added to the *business* entry; *copy protection* (*protección contra copias*) added to *copy*; and *corner kick* (*córner*) added to *corner*.

To further increase the utility of the *Dictionary* for beginning learners of both Spanish and English, we have added "blind" or reference entries for irregular verb forms that differ markedly from their citation forms. These entries take the following form: *quepa, quepo*: ver *caber* (Spanish–English) and *frozen*: see *freeze* (English–Spanish).

Finally, we have invested considerable effort in expanding and perfecting the already well-developed set of semantic delimiters or disambiguators whose purpose is to help users differentiate among meanings in polysemic words. The English word *easy*, for example, has different Spanish equivalents according to whether it means 'simple' (*fácil, sencillo*), 'compliant' (*fácil*), 'comfortable' (*cómodo*), 'informal' (*desenvuelto*), or 'unworried' (*tranquilo*). Similarly, the Spanish word *gusto* has different equivalents for its several meanings: 'sentido', 'sabor', 'sentido estético' (*taste*), 'agrado' (*pleasure*), and 'preferencia personal' (*like*).

Preámbulo a la sexta edición

El *Diccionario Universidad de Chicago Inglés-Español* se ha compilado para el uso general de estudiantes hispanoparlantes que aprenden el inglés de los Estados Unidos y para estudiantes angloparlantes de los Estados Unidos que estudian español. Para acompasarse a los rápidos cambios culturales y lingüísticos que se vienen sucediendo desde comienzos del siglo XXI, se ha hecho una revisión profunda del *Diccionario* con el fin de reflejar el vocabulario y los usos más actualizados en ambas lenguas.

Ya que nuestro propósito es asegurar que los usuarios siempre encuentren los términos y expresiones que buscan, el cambio más sustancial de esta nueva edición es la inclusión de unos seis mil términos y significados nuevos. Para elegir entre las muchas posibles adiciones, se le prestó mucha atención a la frecuencia de uso en el medio escrito y oral, ya que es más probable que un usuario se encuentre con una palabra que aparece con frecuencia (v.g., *libertad*, que ocupa el puesto 540 en frecuencia según la exhaustiva lista de frecuencias disponible en www.wordfrequency.info) que con otra palabra que aparece con baja frecuencia (v.g., *verdolaga*, que ocupa el puesto 19.705 en la misma lista).

Sin embargo, la frecuencia de uso no puede ser el único criterio empleado para incluir material nuevo, por tres razones. En primer lugar, algunas palabras se generalizan tan rápidamente que no alcanzan a ser incluidas en listas de frecuencia. Un buen ejemplo de esta tendencia lo constituye la terminología digital; considérese la palabra inglesa *app* 'aplicación informática', que en muy poco tiempo ha pasado de ser casi desconocida a tener aceptación general. En segundo lugar, algunos de los cambios que debe reflejar un diccionario suceden al nivel de la frase, y estos cambios no se pueden registrar meramente a partir de las frecuencias de los términos. Algunas expresiones actuales tales como *to go off on* 'regañar' y *to be down with* 'estar de acuerdo con' están constituidas por palabras de alta frecuencia empleadas en combinaciones novedosas. Por último, una palabra puede ser esencial sin por ello ser muy frecuente. Por ejemplo, la terminología médica puede ser de importancia vital para alguien que está tratando de resolver un problema de salud mientras se encuentra en un país extranjero. Por lo tanto, esas palabras deben figurar en el *Diccionario* aunque sean de poca frecuencia fuera de los contextos médicos.

De hecho, la medicina es una de las cuatro áreas culturales y técnicas cuya cobertura se ha aumentado en esta edición, debido a su importancia cada vez mayor en el contexto internacional. Además de 600 nuevos términos y significados del área médica, la presente edición incorpora 750 nuevos términos del campo de los negocios, 500 relacionados con el mundo de la informática y la tecnología digital y más de 400 relacionados con varios deportes de popularidad mundial, incluyendo el baloncesto, el béisbol, el fútbol, el tenis y el golf.

En muchos casos, las incorporaciones a estos cuatro campos nos llevaron a crear entradas completamente nuevas, como es el caso de *alérgeno* (ing. *allergen*), *auditoría* (*auditing*), *adaptador* (*adapter*) e *injugable* (*unplayable*). En muchos otros casos, se agregó un significado o un equivalente nuevo a una entrada preexistente. Tal es el caso de *pinza* (a cuya entrada se le agregó el significado inglés de [*medical*] *clamp*), *fraudulento* (*bogus*), *descifrar* (*decrypt*) y *abanicar* (con el significado en béisbol de *to swing and miss*). En el lado inglés, se incorporaron muchos términos compuestos a entradas ya existentes, tales como *clubfoot* (*pie zambo*), que fue agregado a la entrada de *club*; *business agreement* (*convenio comercial*), que fue agregado a la entrada de *business*; *copy protection* (*protección contra copias*) agregado a *copy*; y *corner kick* (*córner*) agregado a *corner*.

Para hacer todavía más útil el *Diccionario* para los estudiantes principiantes tanto de español como de inglés, se han agregado entradas "ciegas" o de referencia, para las formas verbales irregulares que son muy diferentes de sus formas infinitivas. Estas entradas tienen la siguiente estructura: *quepa*, *quepo*: ver *caber* (español−inglés) y *frozen*: see *freeze* (inglés−español).

Por último, se ha hecho un esfuerzo considerable para expandir y perfeccionar todavía más los delimitadores semánticos o desambiguadores, que tienen como propósito asistir a los usuarios a distinguir entre los diversos significados de palabras polisémicas. Por ejemplo, la palabra inglesa *easy* tiene diferentes equivalentes en español según signifique 'simple' (*fácil* o *sencillo*), 'compliant' (*fácil*), 'comfortable' (*cómodo*), 'informal' (*desenvuelto*) o 'unworried' (*tranquilo*). Del mismo modo, la palabra española *gusto* tiene diferentes equivalentes ingleses para sus múltiples significados: *taste* para 'sentido', 'sabor', 'sentido estético', *pleasure* para 'agrado' y *like* para 'preferencia personal'.

How to Use *The University of Chicago Spanish–English Dictionary*

Order of Entries

Alphabetical order is observed irrespective of hyphens or spaces, such that *air conditioner* precedes *aircraft* and *middle school* precedes *middle-sized*. Homographs are placed under a single entry (*lie* 'to prevaricate', *lie* 'to recline', both pronounced [laɪ]), unless they are pronounced differently (e.g., *bow* [baʊ] 'forward end of a vessel', *bow* [bo] 'bend, curve'). Regarding Spanish, according to the current policy of the Spanish Royal Academy,[1] *ch* and *ll* are no longer recognized as separate letters, such that *ch* now follows *ce* and precedes *ci*, and *ll* follows *li* and precedes *lo* in alphabetization.

Compounds listed within entries are also alphabetized. However, the need to list compounds under their first element sometimes interferes with alphabetization, as when *slumlord*, a compound listed under *slum*, comes before the next headword, *slumber*, even though strict alphabetization would require the reverse.

Spelling

Spelling of English words reflects common American usage, variants being noted where applicable (*ax*, *axe*; *sulfur*, *sulphur*; *stymie*, *stymy*). The spelling of Spanish words, where possible, follows the conventions of the Spanish Royal Academy. For the orthography of problematic Spanish words such as recent borrowings (*escáner*, *scooter*), country names (*Malí*, *Irak*) and adjectives of nationality (*zimbabuo*), a variety of authorities were consulted, including the *Diccionario del español actual*, the *Diccionario de dudas*, the *Libro de estilo* published by the Madrid newspaper *El País*, and various Internet sources.[2] It should be noted that there is vacillation in some cases, such as *Bahrain*, which is listed as *Bahrein* in the *Libro de estilo* and as *Bahráin* or *Bahréin* in the *Diccionario de dudas*. In these cases, we either opt for the form that appears to be most generally accepted or provide multiple equivalents.

---

1. Real Academia Española, *Ortografía de la lengua española* (Madrid: Espasa-Calpe, 1999), 2.

2. Manuel Seco, Olimpia Andrés, and Gabino Ramos, *Diccionario del español actual* (Madrid: Aguilar, 1999); Manuel Seco, *Diccionario de dudas y dificultades de la lengua española*, 10th ed. (Madrid: Espasa-Calpe, 1998); *El País: Libro de estilo*, 9th ed. (Madrid: Ediciones El País, 1990).

Omissions

Some categories of words are systematically omitted from the vocabulary entries. Adverbial forms ending in *-ly* (English) and *-mente* (Spanish) are included only when their usage and meaning are not transparently derivable from their adjectival bases. Thus, *clearly* is omitted, as its usage is predictable from its adjectival base ('in a clear way'), while *surely* is included, since in addition to 'in a sure way', it means 'undoubtedly' or 'without fail'. Similarly, *claramente* 'clearly' is omitted, while *atentamente* is retained, since the latter, in addition to meaning 'in an attentive manner', is used as a farewell, equivalent to 'yours truly'. Also, English nouns ending in *-ing* and adjectives in *-ed*, which may appear as glosses of Spanish words, are not always accorded separate entries on the English–Spanish side, due to their derivational regularity and to considerations of space.

Structure of Entries

1. HEADWORD. Spelling variants, if any, follow the most frequent form, which appears first. In Spanish, occupational designations, titles, and kinship terms are shown in both masculine and feminine forms, as in *abogado -da.*

2. PRONUNCIATION. Pronunciation of English words is indicated through a modified version of the International Phonetic Alphabet, whose conventions are explained on pp. 292–93. No individual transcription of Spanish words is required, given the simplicity and consistency of the Spanish orthographic system. See "The Spanish Spelling System and the Sounds Represented" (p. 2) for an explanation.

3. GRAMMATICAL CATEGORY. Meanings are marked according to whether they reflect usage as a noun (N), adjective (ADJ), adverb (ADV), conjunction (CONJ), preposition (PREP), pronoun (PRON), interjection (INTERJ), transitive verb (VT), or intransitive verb (VI). The exception to this rule is that nouns on the Spanish–English side are marked only by gender, M (masculine noun) or F (feminine noun).

    Order of meanings within an entry reflects frequency of usage. Where more than one grammatical category can be rendered by the same gloss, the two are listed together, cf. Eng. *red*, which can be glossed as Sp. *rojo* in both its adjective and noun meanings.

    Traditionally, Spanish adjectives are listed in their masculine form only. However, where the adjective normally functions as a noun as well, it is shown with both masculine and feminine forms if both are possible, cf. the case of *africano -na*, which can mean *African* in the adjectival sense as well as *African* (*man*) and *African* (*woman*).

    Special mention must be made of the combination "VI/VT." Occasionally, a single verb form may function both transitively and intransitively, e.g., both *to eat* and its Spanish equivalent *comer*. Not infrequently, however, Spanish glosses of English intransitives require the addition of the pronominal particle *-se*. Thus, in cases such as *to bathe*, marked "VI/VT" and glossed *bañar(se)*, it should be understood that the bare form is transitive and the -*se* form intransitive. Finally, where transitivity differs between a headword and its equivalent in the second language, particles must be added to reflect this, as in the case of the transitive English verb *to regret*, which is glossed in Spanish as *arrepentirse de*, since *arrepentirse* alone is intransitive. Where an English verb can be used both transitively and intransitively and its Spanish equivalent is only intransitive, the latter may sometimes be made transitive through the addition of a preposition, which appears in brackets. Thus, English *fight* is glossed as *pelear* [*con*] to show that its intransitive equivalent is *pelear*, whereas its transitive equivalent is *pelear con*.

Again for reasons of economy, pronominal forms of Spanish verbs are omitted in two cases: first, when the particle -*se* functions as a direct object, either reflexive or reciprocal, cf. *mirarse*, which can mean both *to look at oneself* and *to look at each other*, and second, when the addition of -*se* does not affect the English translation, cf. *bañar*(*se*), glossed in both meanings as *to bathe*. In contrast, pronominal forms of verbs are included when they differ substantially in meaning from the bare forms, cf. *ir*, glossed as *to go*, vs. *irse*, which means *to leave*.

4. DELIMITERS. Whenever a word, within a grammatical category, is considered to have two or more meanings, these are differentiated by means of delimiters, that is, explanatory markers. Most commonly, synonyms are used, cf. *retort*, which in the meaning 'reply' is glossed as *réplica* and in the meaning 'vessel' as *retorta*. On occasion, however, other strategies may be adopted. Thus, transitive verbs are sometimes best differentiated according to the objects they take, cf. *to negotiate* (a contract), which is glossed *negociar*, while *to negotiate* (an obstacle) is glossed *salvar*. Similarly, adjectives may be most easily distinguished by showing the referents to which they regularly apply, cf. *refreshing*, which applied to drink is *refrescante*, to sleep is *reparador*, and to honesty is *amable*. Not infrequently, a single equivalent covers almost all meanings of a headword in a single grammatical category. In such cases, only the "exceptional" meaning, placed second, is delimited. For example, the equivalent of Eng. *net* in almost all its meanings is Sp. *red*, but when it refers specifically to a hairnet it is *redecilla*. Although delimiters typically precede the gloss they are meant to distinguish, occasionally they are placed afterward. In these cases they are meant to erase doubts about the applicability of a given gloss in a specific secondary context, cf. *site*, whose gloss *sitio* is followed by the delimiter "also Internet."

5. GLOSSES. Insofar as is possible, glosses are intended to match the headword in terms of meaning, register, and frequency. Thus, *cop* is glossed as *poli* rather than the more formal *policía*. Similarly, *orinar* is glossed as *to urinate* rather than the informal and vulgar *to pee*. Glosses separated by a comma are to be considered interchangeable, if not perfectly synonymous. Semicolons, on the other hand, indicate separate meanings.

6. REGIONAL USAGE. No systematic attempt has been made to reflect regional usage in either English or Spanish, since in the great majority of cases a word of more general currency is available as a gloss. Thus, among the many Spanish equivalents of Eng. *peasant*, Sp. *campesino* is understood everywhere, even where a local term also exists, such as Puerto Rican *jíbaro*, Cuban *guajiro*, and Chilean

guaso. However, Spanish regional usage is marked where any of the following conditions are met: (1) there is no term of international currency, or it might not be understood in a given location (cf. the various regional Spanish equivalents of Eng. *bean*) or (2) a specific regionalism is known throughout the Spanish-speaking world to be typical of a given dialect, cf. River Plate *che* 'hey!', Mexican *ándale* 'come on!', *cuate* 'pal'.

7. STYLISTIC MARKERS. Because, as mentioned earlier, equivalents are chosen in order to match headwords in all aspects of their meaning, including register and frequency, stylistic markers are only infrequently employed. For example, there is no need to mark the Spanish gloss *tonto* as familiar, since it is meant to be equivalent to the equally familiar Eng. *fool*. Only five register markers are employed: literary (*lit*), which also includes poetic and formal language; familiar (*fam*), which designates words used among family and friends; vulgar (*vulg*), for words whose use is socially censured; pejorative (*pej*), which implies a negative evaluation; and *offensive* (not abbreviated), for words meant to insult people.

8. COMPOUNDS. Ease of usage would dictate that each lexical item receive its own entry, but for reasons of economy this is not possible in a concise dictionary. This explains why compound words, which are composed of two or more preexisting words, are listed in almost all cases under the entry of their initial constituent, at the end of the corresponding grammatical category. Thus, *doghouse* is listed as —*house*, under *dog*. There are certain exceptions to this convention, however. First, compounds are listed under the headword of their second constituent when the first is extremely frequent, as are the so-called empty verbs such as Eng. *keep*, *take*, *turn*, Sp. *hacer*, *tener*, *tomar*. Thus, *to have a good time*, glossed *divertirse*, is listed under *time* rather than *have*, and *tener paciencia*, glossed *to be patient*, is under *paciencia* rather than *tener*. Second, English compounds whose first element is a preposition (*offsides*, *outcast*, *overcome*) are listed as separate headwords, chiefly because of their frequent grammatical complexity, cf. *overhead*, which can be an adverb (*it flew overhead*), an adjective (*overhead projector*), or a noun (*overhead from grant money*). Conversely, derived words, that is, words that contain one or more affixes (e.g., *antiabortion*, composed of the prefix *anti*- plus *abortion*, and *kingdom*, composed of *king* plus the suffix -*dom*), are listed as separate headwords.

9. ILLUSTRATIVE PHRASES. Appearing together with the compound words pertinent to any given grammatical category are illustrative phrases, a category defined so as to include idioms, collocations, proverbs, and, especially, sentences required to clarify usage in some way, as when the usage of *gustarle a uno* as a gloss of *to like* is illustrated by the phrase *he likes dogs*, with the translation *le gustan los perros*.

Cómo usar el *Diccionario Universidad de Chicago Inglés–Español*

Orden de las entradas

Se respeta el orden alfabético, independientemente de la presencia de guiones o espacios, de tal manera que *air conditioning* precede a *aircraft* y *middle school* precede a *middle-sized*. Los homógrafos se ubican en una sola entrada (*lie* 'mentir' y *lie* 'yacer', ambos con la pronunciación [laɪ]), a no ser que se pronuncien de forma diferente (e.g., *bow* [baʊ] 'proa' y *bow* [bo] 'curva'). En cuanto al español y siguiendo la política oficial de la Real Academia Española,[1] *ch* y *ll* ya no se reconocen como letras independientes, de tal manera que *ch* ahora sigue a *ce* y precede a *ci*, y *ll* sigue a *li* y precede a *lo* en el orden alfabético.

Asimismo, los compuestos incluidos dentro de una entrada determinada aparecen en orden alfabético a continuación de su primer elemento, lo cual a veces interfiere con el orden alfabético general. Así, por ejemplo, *rompeolas* aparece a continuación de *romper*, porque se trata de un compuesto de dicho verbo, si bien el orden alfabético requeriría lo contrario.

Ortografía

La ortografía de los vocablos ingleses refleja el uso general en inglés americano, y las variantes se incluyen en los casos pertinentes (*ax, axe; sulfur, sulphur; stymie, stymy*). La ortografía española sigue las convenciones de la Real Academia Española. Para la grafía española de palabras problemáticas, tales como préstamos recientes (*escáner, scooter*), nombres de países (*Malí, Irak*) y gentilicios (*zimbabuo*), se consultaron fuentes tales como el *Diccionario del español actual*, el *Diccionario de dudas*, el *Libro de estilo* de *El País* de Madrid y varios sitios en el internet.[2] Corresponde hacer notar que la grafía de algunos términos vacila entre varias posibles, cf. la versión española de *Bahrain*, que aparece como *Bahrein* en el *Libro de estilo* y como *Bahráin* o *Bahréin* en el *Diccionario de dudas*, en cuyo caso damos la forma que parece más generalmente aceptada u ofrecemos varias.

---

1. Real Academia Española, *Ortografía de la lengua española* (Madrid: Espasa-Calpe, 1999), 2.

2. Manuel Seco, Olimpia Andrés y Gabino Ramos, *Diccionario del español actual* (Madrid: Aguilar, 1999); Manuel Seco, *Diccionario de dudas y dificultades de la lengua española*, 10ª ed. (Madrid: Espasa-Calpe, 1998); *El País: Libro de estilo*, 9ª ed. (Madrid: Ediciones El País, 1990).

Omisiones

Algunas categorías de palabras se omiten sistemáticamente de las entradas del diccionario. Las formas adverbiales que terminan en -*mente* (español) y en -*ly* (inglés) se incluyen solamente cuando su uso y significado no pueden deducirse claramente de sus bases adjetivas. De esta forma, *claramente* se omite, ya que su significado es predecible a partir de su base adjetiva ('de manera clara'), mientras que *atentamente* se incluye, ya que además de significar 'de manera atenta', también se usa como fórmula de despedida epistolar. Del mismo modo, se omite *clearly*, porque su equivalente, 'de manera clara', se deduce de su base adjetiva, mientras que se incluye *surely* porque además de significar 'de forma segura' también quiere decir 'sin duda'. Debe notarse también que los sustantivos ingleses terminados en -*ing* y los adjetivos en -*ed*, que pueden aparecer como traducción de palabras españolas en la parte español–inglés, no figuran siempre como cabezas de artículo en la parte inglés–español debido a la total regularidad de su formación y a consideraciones de espacio.

Estructura de las entradas

1. PALABRAS CABEZA DE ARTÍCULO. Las variantes ortográficas, si las hay, siguen a la forma más frecuente, que aparece en primer término. En español, las designaciones de profesiones y oficios, los títulos y las relaciones de parentesco aparecen tanto en la forma masculina como en la femenina, como por ejemplo, *abogado -da*.
2. PRONUNCIACIÓN. La pronunciación de las palabras inglesas se indica mediante una versión modificada del Alfabético Fonético Internacional, cuyas convenciones se explican en las pgs. 292–93. No se requiere transcripción individual de las palabras españolas, gracias a la simplicidad y sistematicidad de la ortografía española. Para detalles, ver la sección titulada "The Spanish Spelling System" en la p. 2.
3. CATEGORÍA GRAMATICAL. Los significados se marcan según reflejen el uso de la palabra como sustantivo masculino (*m*), sustantivo femenino (*f*), adjetivo (*adj*), adverbio (*adv*), conjunción (*conj*), preposición (*prep*), pronombre (*pron*), interjección (*interj*), verbo transitivo (*vt*) o verbo intransitivo (*vi*). En inglés, en cambio, los sustantivos se marcan con *n*, abreviación de *noun*.

    Los significados dentro de una entrada aparecen ordenados de manera que el más frecuente figure primero. Cuando la misma traducción cubre el significado de dos categorías gramaticales, ambas aparecen juntas, cf. el inglés *red*, que puede traducirse como *rojo* tanto en su significado sustantivo como en el adjetivo.

    Siguiendo la tradición, los adjetivos españoles aparecen exclusivamente en su forma masculina. Sin embargo, cuando el adjetivo frecuentemente funciona además como sustantivo, se muestra tanto en la forma masculina como en la femenina si ambas son posibles, cf. el caso de *africano -na*, traducido al inglés como *African*, forma adecuada para todos sus usos.

    La combinación *vi/vt* merece mención especial. En ocasiones, una única forma verbal funciona tanto transitiva como intransitivamente, v.g., tanto *comer* como su equivalente inglés *to eat*. Sin embargo, es también frecuente que las traducciones españolas de verbos intransitivos ingleses requieran el agregado de una partícula pronominal *-se*. Así, en casos tales como *to bathe*, que se marca "vi/vt" y se traduce como *bañar(se)*, debe entenderse que la forma no pronominalizada es transitiva y la forma con *-se* es intransitiva. En aquellos casos cuando la palabra cabeza de artículo y su equivalente en la otra lengua difieren en transitividad, se deben agregar partículas para reflejar esta diferencia. Tal es el caso del verbo *aprobar*, que se traduce al inglés como *to approve of* en algunos de sus significados, ya que *to approve* es intransitivo si no va acompañado de preposición. Finalmente, en los casos en los que un verbo español puede usarse tanto intransitiva como transitivamente y su equivalente inglés es exclusivamente intransitivo, este último puede a veces volverse transitivo mediante el agregado de una preposición entre corchetes. Así, el esp. *chivar* se traduce como *to snitch* [*on*] para mostrar que su forma intransitiva en inglés es *to snitch* mientras que el equivalente transitivo es *to snitch on*.

Por razones de espacio se omiten las formas pronominales de los verbos españoles en dos casos. En primer lugar, se omiten si la partícula pronominal hace las veces de complemento directo reflexivo o recíproco, cf. *mirarse* (a sí mismo o el uno al otro). En segundo lugar no se incluyen tampoco si la partícula pronominal no afecta la traducción al inglés, como en el caso de *bañar* y *bañarse*, ambos *to bathe*. Sí se incluyen aquellas formas pronominales que difieren semánticamente de sus verbos de base, cf. *ir* vs. *irse*.

4. INDICADORES SEMÁNTICOS. En aquellos casos en los que una palabra, dentro de una misma categoría gramatical, tiene dos o más acepciones, estas se distinguen por medio de indicadores semánticos, o sea, explicaciones parentéticas. Lo más frecuente es que se empleen sinónimos, cf. *arco*, que se traduce *arc* cuando se trata de una curva, como *arch* cuando se refiere a una estructura arquitectónica, y como *bow* cuando se trata de un arma, aunque en otras ocasiones se adoptan otras estrategias. Así, los verbos transitivos a veces se distinguen con mayor facilidad mediante los tipos de complementos directos que los acompañan, cf. *acordonar* (un zapato) *to lace*, (un lugar) *to rope off*, (una moneda) *to mill*, mientras que la forma más sencilla de distinguir adjetivos es mostrar los tipos de referentes a los cuales se aplican con mayor frecuencia, cf. *inseguro*, que aplicado a una persona se traduce por *insecure*, a un vehículo por *unsafe*, y al andar por *unsteady*. Es frecuente que un único equivalente abarque casi todas las acepciones de una palabra cabeza de artículo dentro de una categoría gramatical determinada. En esos casos, solamente el significado "excepcional", que aparece en segundo lugar, se acompaña de un indicador semántico. Por ejemplo, el equivalente de *acceso* en casi todas sus acepciones es *access*, excepto cuando se refiere a un ataque de tos o rabia, en cuyo caso se traduce como *fit*. Aunque los indicadores semánticos normalmente preceden a la traducción que les corresponde, en ocasiones se ubican después. En estos casos tienen como objetivo eliminar dudas acerca del empleo de una traducción determinada en un contexto secundario específico, cf. *acompañar*, cuya traducción *to accompany* va seguida de un indicador semántico "también en música" para confirmar al lector su aplicación a ese contexto.

5. TRADUCCIONES. En la medida de lo posible, se ha tratado de que las traducciones sean equivalentes a la palabra cabeza de artículo en cuanto a su significado, registro y frecuencia. Así, *poli* se traduce como *cop* y no como *policeman*, palabra más formal. De la misma forma, *to urinate* se traduce como *orinar* y no como *hacer pipí*, palabra más familiar. Las traducciones separadas por una coma deben considerarse equivalentes, aunque no sean exactamente sinónimas. El uso del punto y coma indica acepciones distintas.

6. USO REGIONAL. No se ha hecho ningún esfuerzo sistemático por reflejar usos regionales, ni en inglés ni en español, ya que en la gran mayoría de los casos existe una palabra de uso general. Así, entre los muchos equivalentes españoles de la palabra inglesa *peasant*, su equivalente español *campesino* se entiende en todo el mundo de habla hispana, aun cuando existan términos locales, tales como *jíbaro* en Puerto Rico, *guajiro* en Cuba y *guaso* en Chile. Sin embargo, el uso regional se indica para el español en tres casos específicos. En primer lugar se encuentran los casos en los que una palabra determinada podría resultar desconocida en una región dada, como los varios equivalentes españoles del ingl. *bean*. En segundo término, se han incluido regionalismos que se reconocen en todo el mundo de habla hispana como típicos de un dialecto determinado, cf. español rioplatense *che*, mexicano *ándale, cuate*.

7. INDICADORES DE ESTILO. Ya que, como se mencionó anteriormente, los equivalentes se eligen para que correspondan a las palabras cabeza de artículo en todos los aspectos de su significado, incluyendo nivel de lengua y frecuencia, los indicadores de estilo se usan poco. Por ejemplo, no hay necesidad de indicar que la palabra inglesa *fool* es familiar, ya que figura como equivalente del español *tonto*. Se han empleado cinco indicadores de estilo: literario (*lit*), que incluye lenguaje poético y formal, familiar (*fam*), que designa palabras que se usan en situaciones de intimidad, vulgar (*vulg*), que designa términos cuyo uso está censurado socialmente, peyorativo (*pey*), que designa palabras que tienen una carga connotativa negativa hacia el referente, y *ofensivo* (sin abreviar), que designa insultos.

8. COMPUESTOS. El criterio de facilidad de uso requeriría que cada palabra recibiera su propia entrada, pero por razones de economía de espacio esto no es posible en un diccionario conciso. Por lo tanto, las palabras compuestas, formadas por dos o más vocablos preexistentes, aparecen en casi todos los casos en la entrada de su primer constituyente, al final de la categoría gramatical correspondiente. De tal forma, *hombre rana* aparece como — *rana*, en la entrada de *hombre*. Hay ciertas excepciones a esta regla, sin embargo. En primer lugar, los compuestos aparecen bajo la cabeza de artículo de su segundo constituyente cuando el primero es extremadamente frecuente, tal como lo son los verbos semánticamente "vacíos" como el español *hacer, tener, tomar* y el inglés *to keep, to take, to turn*. De este modo, *tener paciencia* aparece en la entrada de *paciencia* y no en la de *tener*, y *to have a good time* figura bajo *time* y no bajo *to have*. En segundo lugar, los compuestos ingleses cuyo primer elemento es una preposición (*offsides, overcome, outcast*) aparecen como cabezas de artículo independientes, sobre todo debido a su complejidad gramatical, cf. *overhead*, que puede ser adverbio (*it flew overhead*, que equivale a *voló en lo alto*), adjetivo (*overhead projector*, es decir, *retroproyector*) y sustantivo (*overhead from*

grant money, o sea, *gastos generales de una subvención*). No obstante, las palabras derivadas, i.e., aquellas que contienen uno o más afijos (e.g., *anticuerpo*, compuesta del prefijo *anti-* y *cuerpo*, y *cabezón*, compuesta por *cabeza* y el sufijo *-ón*), figuran como cabezas de artículo independientes.

9. FRASES ILUSTRATIVAS. Junto con las palabras compuestas de una determinada categoría gramatical figuran las frases ilustrativas, una categoría que incluye expresiones idiomáticas, colocaciones típicas, refranes y, especialmente, oraciones necesarias para aclarar el uso de alguna palabra, como cuando el uso de *like* como traducción de *gustar* se ilustra con la frase *he likes dogs*, que se traduce *le gustan los perros*.

Spanish–English · Español–Inglés

List of Abbreviations / Lista de abreviaturas

adj	adjective	adjetivo
adv	adverb, adverbial	adverbio, adverbial
Am	America	América
art	article	artículo
Carib	Caribbean	Caribe
conj	conjunction	conjunción
def	definite	definido
dem	demonstrative	demostrativo
Esp	Spain, Spanish	España, español
f	feminine	femenino
fam	familiar	familiar
indef	indefinite	indefinido
interj	interjection	interjección
interr	interrogative	interrogativo
inv	invariable	invariable
lit	literary	literario
loc	locution	locución
m	masculine	masculino
Méx	Mexico	México
num	numeral	numeral
pej, pey	pejorative	peyorativo
pers	personal	personal
pl	plural	plural
pos	possessive	posesivo
prep	preposition, prepositional	preposición, preposicional
pron	pronoun	pronombre
rel	relative	relativo
RP	River Plate	Río de la Plata
sg	singular	singular
Sp	Spain, Spanish	España, español
v aux	auxiliary verb	verbo auxiliar
vi	intransitive verb	verbo intransitivo
vt	transitive verb	verbo transitivo
vulg	vulgar	vulgar

Spanish Pronunciation

Spanish orthography very closely mirrors Spanish pronunciation, much more so than is the case in English. This explains why, in bilingual dictionaries such as this, each English entry must be accompanied by a phonetic representation, while Spanish pronunciation may be presented in synoptic form.

This synopsis is meant only as an introduction, however. In spite of the clarity of the orthographical system of Spanish, the individual sounds of the language are difficult for adult native speakers of English to pronounce, and this difficulty is compounded by the syllabic structure of the language. For these reasons, readers who wish to perfect their pronunciation of Spanish are strongly advised to seek the help of a competent teacher.

To say that orthography mirrors pronunciation means that there is a close correlation between letters and sounds. Thus, most Spanish letters correspond to a single sound, or to a single family of closely related sounds, as is the case for all vowels and the consonants *f*, *l*, *m*, *n*, *p*, *t*, and *s*. In a few cases a single letter represents two very different sounds, as *c*, which is pronounced as *k* before *a*, *o*, and *u*, but *th* (as in *thin*, in parts of Spain, or as *s* in America) before *e* or *i*. Rarely, two letters represent a single sound, as in the case of *ch*.

The overarching differences between Spanish and English pronunciation are tenseness of articulation and syllabification within the breath group. Due to the tenseness of their articulation, for example, all Spanish vowels have a clear nondiphthongal character, unlike English long vowels, which tend to be bipartite (e.g., *late*, pronounced [leⁱt]). Syllabification is a problem for English speakers because in Spanish, syllables are formed without respect to word boundaries, such that *el hado* 'fate' and *helado* 'ice cream' are both pronounced as e-la-do, and the phrase *tus otras hermanas* 'your other sisters' is syllabified as tu-so-tra-ser-ma-nas. In fast speech, vowels may combine, as in *lo ofendiste* 'you offended him', pronounced lo-fen-dis-te. Finally, when Spanish consonants occur in clusters, very often the articulation of the second influences that of the first, as when *un peso* 'one peso' is pronounced um-pe-so, and *en que* 'in which' is pronounced eŋ ke, where ŋ represents the sound of the letters *ng* in English.

The Spanish Spelling System and the Sounds Represented

I. VOWELS

i as a single vowel always represents a sound similar to the second vowel of *police*. Examples: **hilo, camino, piso.** As a part of a diphthong, it sounds like the *y* of English *yes, year*. Examples: **bien, baile, reina.**

e is similar to the vowel of *late* ([leⁱt]), but without the diphthong. Examples: **mesa, hablé, tres.**

a is similar to the vowel of *pod*. Examples: **casa, mala, América.** Notably, **a** is always pronounced this way, even when not stressed. This contrasts with the English tendency to reduce unstressed vowels to schwa ([ə]), as in *America*, pronounced in English as [ə-mέ-rɪ-kə].

o has a value similar to that of the vowel in Eng. *coat* [koʷt], but without the diphthong. Examples: **no, modo, amó.**

u has a value similar to that of English *oo*, as in *boot* [buʷt], but without the diphthong. Examples: **cura, agudo, uno.** Note that the letter **u** is not pronounced in the syllables **qui, que, gui,** and **gue** (unless spelled with dieresis, as in *bilingüe*). When **u** occurs in diphthongs such as those of **cuida, cuento, deuda,** it has the sound of *w* (as in *way*).

II. CONSONANTS

b and **v** represent the same sounds in Spanish. At the beginning of a breath group or when preceded by the *m* sound (which may be spelled *n*), they are both pronounced like English *b*. Examples: **bomba, en vez de, vine, invierno.** In other environments, especially between vowels, both letters are pronounced as a very relaxed *b*, in which the lips do not completely touch and the air is not completely stopped. This sound has no equivalent in English. Examples: **haba, uva, la vaca, la banda.**

c represents a *k* sound before **a, o, u, l,** and **r.** However, this sound is not accompanied by a puff of air as it is in Eng. *can* and *coat* (compare the *c* in *scan*, which is more similar to the Spanish sound). Examples: **casa, cosa, cuna, crudo, aclamar.** In contrast, when appearing before the vowels **e** and **i, c** is pronounced as *s* in Spanish America and the southwest of Spain, and as *th* (as in *thin*) in other parts of Spain (see **s** for more information).

ch is no longer considered to be a separate letter in the Spanish alphabet. However, it represents a single sound, which is similar to the English *ch* in *church* and *cheek*. Examples: **chato, chaleco, mucho.**

d is phonetically complex in Spanish. In terms of articulation, it is pronounced by the tongue touching the teeth rather than the alveolar ridge as in English. Second, it is represented by two variants. The first of these, which is similar to that of English *dame* and *did*, occurs at the beginning of breath groups or after **n** and **l.** Examples: **donde, falda, conde.** In all other situations the letter represents a sound similar to the *th* of English *then*. Examples: **hado, cuerda, cuadro, usted.** This sound tends to be very relaxed, to the point of disappearing in certain environments, such as word-final and intervocalic.

f is very similar to the English *f* sound. Examples: **faro, elefante, alfalfa.**

g is phonetically complex. Before the vowels **e** and **i**, it is pronounced as *h* in many American dialects, while in northern Spain it is realized like the *ch* in the German word *Bach*. Examples: **gente, giro**. At the beginning of breath groups and after nasals before the vowels **a, o, u**, and the consonants **l** and **r**, it is pronounced like the **g** of English *go*. Examples: **ganga, globo, grada**. In all other environments it is pronounced as a very relaxed *g*. Examples: **lago, la goma, agrado**.

h is silent. Examples: **hoja, humo, harto**.

j is realized in most American dialects as *h*, while in northern Spain it is pronounced like the *ch* in the German word *Bach*. Examples: **jamás, jugo, jota**.

k sounds like Eng. *k*, but without the accompanying puff of air. Examples: **kilo, keroseno**.

l is pronounced forward in the mouth, as the *l* in *leaf, leak*, never in the back, as in *bell, full*. Examples: **lado, ala, sol**.

ll is no longer considered to be a separate letter in the Spanish alphabet. However, it does represent a single sound, which differs widely in pronunciation throughout the Spanish-speaking world. In most areas, it is pronounced like the *y* of Eng. *yes*, though with greater tension. In extreme northern Spain and in parts of the Andes, it sounds like the *lli* in Eng. *million*. In the River Plate area it is pronounced like the *g* in *beige* or the *sh* in *ship*. Examples: **calle, llano, olla**.

m is essentially the same as in English. Examples: **madre, mano, cama**. However, in final position, as in **álbum** 'album', it is pronounced as [ŋ], the final sound of Eng. *sing*.

n is normally pronounced like Eng. *n*. Examples: **no, mano, hablan**. There are exceptions, however. For example, before **b, v, p**, and **m**, it is pronounced *m*, as in **en Barcelona, en vez de, un peso**, while before **k, g, j, ge-**, and **gi-**, it is realized as [ŋ], the final sound of Eng. *sing*, as in **anca, tengo, naranja, engendrar**.

ñ is similar to but more tense than the *ny* of Eng. *canyon*. Examples: **cañón, año, ñato**.

p is like English *p* except that it is not accompanied by a puff of air, as it is in Eng. *pill* and *papa* (compare the *p* in *spot*, which is more similar to the Spanish sound). Examples: **padre, capa, apuro**.

q combined with **u** has the sound of *k*. Examples: **queso, aquí, quien**.

r usually represents a sound similar to that of the *tt* in Eng. *kitty* and the *dd* in *ladder*. Examples: **caro, tren, comer.** In contrast, at the beginning of words and after **n, l, s,** the letter **r** is realized as a trill, as in **rosa, Enrique, alrededor, Israel.** The double letter **rr** always represents a trill, as in **carro, correr, guerrero.**

s is pronounced the same as in standard American English in most parts of Spanish America and in parts of southern Spain. In most of Spain, in contrast, it is realized with the tip of the tongue against the alveolar ridge, producing a whistling sound that is sometimes heard in southern dialects of American English. Examples: **solo, casa, es.** In the Caribbean and in coastal Spanish generally, there is a strong tendency to pronounce **s** in certain environments (usually preconsonantal) as *h*, or to eliminate it entirely. In these dialects, *esta* may be pronounced as *ehta* or *eta*.

t differs from English *t* in two respects: first, it is articulated by the tongue touching the teeth rather than the alveolar ridge, and second, it is not accompanied by a puff of air, as it is in English *too* and *titillate* (compare the *t* in *stop*, which is more similar to the Spanish sound). Examples: **tela, tino, tinta.**

x has a wide range of phonetic realizations. Between vowels, it is usually pronounced *ks* or *gs* (but never *gz*), as in **examen, próximo,** though in a few words it is pronounced as *s*, e.g., *exacto, auxilio*. Before a consonant, **x** is almost always pronounced *s*, as in **extranjero, experiencia.** In many Mexican and Central American words of indigenous origin, **x** represents *h*, as in **México.**

y varies regionally in its pronunciation. In most areas it is pronounced like the *y* of Eng. *yes*, though with greater tension. In the River Plate area it is pronounced like the *g* in *beige* or the *sh* in *ship*. Examples: **yo, ayer.**

z is subject to dialectal variation as well. In most parts of Spain, except the southwest, it is pronounced as the *th* in Eng. *thin, cloth*. In southwestern Spain and all of Spanish America, in contrast, it is pronounced *s*. Examples: **zagal, hallazgo, luz.**

Stress Assignment in Spanish and the Use of the Written Accent

Spanish words are normally stressed on the next-to-last syllable when they end in a vowel or the consonants **n** or **s.** Examples: <u>**me**sa</u>, <u>za**pa**to</u>, <u>aconteci**mien**to</u>, <u>**hab**lan</u>, <u>mu**je**res</u>. Words whose pronunciation does not conform to this rule are considered exceptions, and their stressed syllable is indicated with an accent mark. Examples: <u>**lám**para</u>, <u>es**tó**mago</u>, <u>**gé**nero</u>, <u>a**cá**</u>, <u>va**rón**</u>, <u>ade**más**</u>.

Conversely, Spanish words are normally stressed on the final syllable when they end in a consonant other than **n** or **s.** Examples: <u>mu**jer**</u>, <u>actuali**dad**</u>, <u>pe**dal**</u>, <u>vo**raz**</u>. Words whose pronunciation does not conform to this rule are considered exceptions, and their stressed syllable is indicated with an accent mark. Examples: **nácar, volátil, lápiz.**

For the purposes of stress assignment, diphthongs are considered the same as simple vowels. Thus, **arduo** and **industria** are considered to have two and three syllables respectively, with regular stress on the penultimate syllable. However, some sequences of vowels are not considered diphthongs. For example, **alegría** and **continúo** are both considered to have four syllables, with the stress mark indicating the absence of a diphthong.

Until recently certain words received written accents in order to differentiate functions, even though they are pronounced identically (this is still true in certain cases, such as **de** 'of', **dé** 'give'). Thus, the orthography **esta** was assigned to the demonstrative adjective ('this', fem.), while the demonstrative pronoun ('this one', fem.) was written **ésta.** This convention is no longer observed by most writers.

Notes on Spanish Grammar

The Noun

Gender. All Spanish nouns, not just those that denote male or female beings, are assigned either masculine or feminine gender. As a general rule, male beings (**muchacho** 'boy', **toro** 'bull') and all nouns ending in -o (**lodo** 'mud') are assigned masculine gender (exceptions: **mano** 'hand', **foto** 'photo', both feminine). Similarly, female beings (**mujer** 'woman', **vaca** 'cow') and nouns ending in -a (**envidia** 'envy') tend to be assigned feminine gender (exceptions: **mapa** 'map', **drama** 'drama', **día** 'day', all masculine). In addition, nouns ending in **-ción, -tad, -dad, -tud,** and **-umbre** are always feminine: **canción** 'song', **facultad** 'college', **ciudad** 'city', **virtud** 'virtue', and **muchedumbre** 'crowd'. Otherwise, nouns ending in consonants and vowels other than -o and -a are of unpredictable gender. Some are feminine (**barbarie** 'savagery', **clase** 'class', **nariz** 'nose', **tribu** 'tribe'), while others are masculine (**antílope** 'antelope', **corte** 'cut', **mesón** 'lodge', **nácar** 'mother of pearl').

Nouns in -o that denote human beings (and to some extent, animals) form the feminine by replacing -o with -a, as in **tío** 'uncle' / **tía** 'aunt', **niño** 'boy' / **niña** 'girl', **oso** 'bear' / **osa** 'she-bear'. Where the masculine noun does not end in -o, the rules of formation are more complex. For example, nouns ending in **-ón, -or,** and **-án** require the addition of -a, as in the pairs **patrón / patrona** 'patron', **pastor / pastora** 'shepherd', **holgazán / holgazana** 'lazy person'. In other cases the difference is more unpredictable: **emperador** 'emperor' / **emperatriz** 'empress', **abad** 'abbot' / **abadesa** 'abbess'.

Some nouns have different genders according to their meanings: **corte** (m) 'cut', (f) 'court', **capital** (m) 'money capital', (f) 'capital city', while others have invariable endings which are used for both the masculine and the feminine: **artista** 'artist' (and all nouns ending in **-ista**), **amante** 'lover', **aristócrata** 'aristocrat', **homicida** 'murderer', **cliente** 'customer'. Finally, some words vacillate as to gender, e.g., **mar** 'sea', which is normally masculine but is feminine in certain expressions (**en alta mar** 'on the high seas') and in poetic contexts, and **arte,** which is masculine in the singular but feminine in the plural. Some words, such as **armazón** and **esperma,** can be both masculine and feminine.

Pluralization. Nouns ending in an unaccented vowel and **-é** add **-s** to form the plural: **libro / libros, casa / casas, café / cafés.** Nouns ending in a consonant, in **-y,** or in an accented vowel other than **-é** add **-es: papel / papeles, canción / canciones, ley / leyes, rubí / rubíes.** Exceptions to this rule include the words **papá / papás** and **mamá / mamás,** as well as the small group of nouns ending in unaccented **-es** or **-is,** which do not change in the plural: **lunes** 'Monday', 'Mondays', **tesis** 'thesis', 'theses'.

Articles

Definite Article. The equivalent of English **the** is as follows: masculine singular, **el;** feminine singular, **la;** masculine plural, **los;** feminine plural, **las.** Feminine words beginning with stressed **a** or **ha** take **el** in the singular and **las** in the plural: **el alma** 'the soul' / **las almas** 'the souls', **el hacha** 'the hatchet' / **las hachas** 'the hatchets'. In spite of this, these nouns remain feminine in the singular, as shown by adjective agreement: **el alma bendita** 'the blessed soul'. When preceded by the prepositions **a** and **de,** the masculine singular article **el** forms the contractions **al** and **del.**

Indefinite Article. The equivalent of English **a, an** is as follows: masculine singular, **un;** feminine singular, **una.** In the plural, masculine **unos** and feminine **unas** are equivalent to English **some.** Feminine words beginning with stressed **a** or **ha** take **un** in the singular and **unas** in the plural: **un alma** 'a soul' / **unas almas** 'some souls', **un hacha** 'a hatchet' / **unas hachas** 'some hatchets'.

Adjectives

Agreement. The adjective in Spanish agrees in gender and number with the noun it modifies: **el lápiz rojo** 'the red pencil', **la casa blanca** 'the white house', **los libros interesantes** 'the interesting books', **las flores hermosas** 'the beautiful flowers'.

Formation of the Plural. Adjectives follow the same rules as nouns for the formation of the plural: **pálido, pálidos** 'pale', **fácil, fáciles** 'easy', **cortés, corteses** 'courteous', **capaz, capaces** 'capable'.

Formation of the Feminine. Adjectives ending in **-o** change to **-a: blanco, blanca** 'white'. Adjectives ending in other vowels are invariable: **verde** 'green', **fuerte** 'strong', **indígena** 'indigenous, native', **pesimista** 'pessimistic', **baladí** 'trivial', as are adjectives ending in a consonant: **fácil** 'easy', **cortés** 'courteous', **mayor** 'older', 'larger'. Some cases are more complex: (a) adjectives ending in **-ón, -án, -or** (except comparatives like **mayor**) add **-a** to form the feminine: **holgazán, holgazana** 'lazy', **preguntón, preguntona** 'inquisitive', **hablador, habladora** 'talkative'; (b) adjectives of nationality ending in a consonant add **-a** to form the feminine: **francés, francesa** 'French', **español, española** 'Spanish', **alemán, alemana** 'German'.

Adverbs

Most adverbs are formed by adding **-mente** to the feminine form of the adjective: **clara** 'clear' / **claramente** 'clearly', **fácil** 'easy' / **fácilmente** 'easily'.

Comparison of Inequality in Adjectives and Adverbs

The comparative of inequality is formed by placing **más** or **menos** before the positive form of the adjective or adverb: **más rico que** 'richer than', **menos rico que** 'less rich than', **más tarde** 'later', **menos tarde** 'less late'. The superlative is formed by placing the definite article **el** before the comparative: **el más rico** 'the richest', **el menos rico** 'the least rich'.

The following adjectives and adverbs have irregular forms of comparison:

Positive	Comparative	Superlative
bueno	mejor	el (la) mejor
malo	peor	el (la) peor
grande	mayor	el (la) mayor
pequeño	menor	el (la) menor

Common Spanish Suffixes

-aco   is a pejorative suffix: **pajarraco** 'ugly bird' (from **pájaro** 'bird'), **libraco** 'large, bulky book' (**libro** 'book')

-ada   *a.*   attaches to verbal stems to indicate an action: **mirada** 'look' (**mirar** 'to look'), **empujada** 'push' (**empujar** 'to push')

    b.   attaches to noun stems to indicate a blow: **cachetada** 'blow on the cheek' (**cachete** 'cheek'), **puñalada** 'stab with a dagger' (**puñal** 'dagger')

    c.   attaches to nominal stems to indicate an action characteristic of a person or group: **bobada** 'foolish act' (**bobo** 'fool'), **niñada** 'childish act' (**niño** 'child')

-al, -ar   attach to nouns indicating trees to form nouns that denote a grove: **naranjal** 'orange grove' (from **naranjo** 'orange tree'), **pinar** 'pine grove' (**pino** 'pine tree')

-azo   attaches to noun stems, forming nouns that indicate

    a.   augmentation: **hombrazo** 'big man' (**hombre** 'man'), **marranazo** 'large hog' (**marrano** 'hog')

	b. a blow or explosion: **porrazo** 'blow with a club' (**porra** 'club'), **cañonazo** 'cannon shot' (**cañón** 'cannon')
-cito	is a diminutive suffix: **cochecito** 'a little car' (**coche** 'car'), **mujercita** 'little woman' (**mujer** 'woman')
-dor	forms agent nouns from verbs: **hablador** 'talker' (**hablar** 'to talk'), **regulador** 'regulator' (**regular** 'to regulate'), which are sometimes used as adjectives: **hablador** 'talkative', **regulador** 'regulating'
-ejo	is a pejorative suffix: **librejo** 'worthless book' (**libro** 'book'), **lugarejo** 'Podunk' (**lugar** 'place')
-ería	attaches to noun stems to denote

a. a place where something is made or sold: **zapatería** 'shoestore' (**zapato** 'shoe'), **pastelería** 'pastry shop' (**pastel** 'pastry')

b. a profession, business, or occupation: **carpintería** 'carpentry' (**carpintero** 'carpenter'), **ingeniería** 'engineering' (**ingeniero** 'engineer')

c. a group: **chiquillería** 'bunch of children' (**chiquillo** 'little kid')

-ero *a.* attaches to nouns to indicate a person who makes, sells, or is in charge of something: **librero** 'bookseller' (**libro** 'book'), **zapatero** 'shoemaker' (**zapato** 'shoe'), **carcelero** 'jailer' (**cárcel** 'jail')

b. attaches to nominal stems to form adjectives: **guerrero** 'warlike' (**guerra** 'war'), **conejero** 'for hunting rabbits' (**conejo** 'rabbit')

-ez, -eza are used to make abstract nouns from adjectival bases: **vejez** 'old age' (**viejo** 'old'), **niñez** 'childhood' (**niño** 'child'), **grandeza** 'greatness' (**grande** 'large, great'), **rareza** 'rarity' (**raro** 'rare')

-ía forms abstract nouns from adjectival bases: **valentía** 'courage' (**valiente** 'brave'), **cobardía** 'cowardice' (**cobarde** 'coward')

-ico is a diminutive suffix: **ratico** 'little while' (**rato** 'while'), **momentico** 'brief moment' (**momento** 'moment')

-(i)ento attaches to adjectives to indicate attenuation, as in **amarillento** 'yellowish' (**amarillo** 'yellow'), or an undesirable quality, as in **hambriento** 'hungry' (**hambre** 'hunger')

-illo is sometimes a diminutive suffix: **politiquillo** 'insignificant politician' (**político** 'politician'), **chiquillo** 'little kid' (**chico** 'child')

-ísimo attaches to adjectives to indicate an extreme degree of a quality: **hermosísimo** 'very beautiful' (**hermoso** 'beautiful')

-ito	is a diminutive suffix: **librito** 'small book' (**libro** 'book'), **casita** 'little house' (**casa** 'house')
-izo	forms adjectives from nominal stems, indicating a tendency or attenuation: **rojizo** 'reddish' (**rojo** 'red'), **olvidadizo** 'forgetful' (**olvidar** 'to forget')
-mente	is the adverbial ending attached to the feminine form of the adjective: **generosamente** 'generously' (**generoso** 'generous'), **claramente** 'clearly' (**claro** 'clear')
-ón *a.*	is an augmentative adjectival suffix: **barrigón** 'potbellied' (**barriga** 'belly'), **cabezón** 'large-headed' (**cabeza** 'head')
b.	attaches to verb stems to denote sudden actions: **tirón** 'pull, jerk' (**tirar** 'to pull'), **apretón** 'push' (**apretar** 'to push')
-oso	forms adjectives from nouns, indicating abundance or character: **rocoso** 'rocky' (**roca** 'rock'), **tormentoso** 'stormy' (**tormenta** 'storm')
-ote, -ota	is an augmentative and pejorative suffix attached to nouns: **discursote** 'long, boring speech' (**discurso** 'speech'), **narizota** 'big ugly nose' (**nariz** 'nose')
-udo	forms adjectives from nouns, indicating an excess: **peludo** 'hairy' (**pelo** 'hair'), **panzudo** 'big-bellied' (**panza** 'belly')
-ura	forms abstract nouns from adjectives: **negrura** 'blackness' (**negro** 'black'), **altura** 'height' (**alto** 'high')
-uzco	forms adjectives from other adjectives, indicating attenuation: **blancuzco** 'whitish' (**blanco** 'white'), **negruzco** 'blackish' (**negro** 'black')

Spanish Regular Verbs

First Conjugation

infinitive	**hablar**
pres. indic.	hablo, hablas, habla, hablamos, habláis, hablan
pres. subj.	hable, hables, hable, hablemos, habléis, hablen
pret. indic.	hablé, hablaste, habló, hablamos, hablasteis, hablaron
imp. indic.	hablaba, hablabas, hablaba, hablábamos, hablabais, hablaban

imp. subj.	hablara, hablaras, hablara, habláramos, hablarais, hablaran, *or*
	hablase, hablases, hablase, hablásemos, hablaseis, hablasen
fut. indic.	hablaré, hablarás, hablará, hablaremos, hablaréis, hablarán
cond.	hablaría, hablarías, hablaría, hablaríamos, hablaríais, hablarían
imper.	habla (tú), hable (usted), hablemos (nosotros), hablad (vosotros), hablen (ustedes)
pres. part.	hablando
past part.	hablado

Second Conjugation

infinitive	**comer**
pres. indic.	como, comes, come, comemos, coméis, comen
pres. subj.	coma, comas, coma, comamos, comáis, coman
pret. indic.	comí, comiste, comió, comimos, comisteis, comieron
imp. indic.	comía, comías, comía, comíamos, comíais, comían
imp. subj.	comiera, comieras, comiera, comiéramos, comierais, comieran, *or*
	comiese, comieses, comiese, comiésemos, comieseis, comiesen
fut. indic.	comeré, comerás, comerá, comeremos, comeréis, comerán
cond.	comería, comerías, comería, comeríamos, comeríais, comerían
imper.	come (tú), coma (usted), comamos (nosotros), comed (vosotros), coman (ustedes)
pres. part.	comiendo
past part.	comido

Third Conjugation

infinitive	**vivir**
pres. indic.	vivo, vives, vive, vivimos, vivís, viven
pres. subj.	viva, vivas, viva, vivamos, viváis, vivan
pret. indic.	viví, viviste, vivió, vivimos, vivisteis, vivieron
imp. indic.	vivía, vivías, vivía, vivíamos, vivíais, vivían
imp. subj.	viviera, vivieras, viviera, viviéramos, vivierais, vivieran, *or*
	viviese, vivieses, viviese, viviésemos, vivieseis, viviesen
fut. indic.	viviré, vivirás, vivirá, viviremos, viviréis, vivirán
cond.	viviría, vivirías, viviría, viviríamos, viviríais, vivirían
imper.	vive (tú), viva (usted), vivamos (nosotros), vivid (vosotros), vivan (ustedes)
pres. part.	viviendo
past part.	vivido

Spanish Irregular and Orthographic Changing Verbs

The superscript number or numbers listed as part of a verb entry indicate that the verb is to be conjugated like the model verb in this section that has the corresponding number. Only the tenses that have irregular forms or spelling changes are given, and these irregular forms and spelling changes are shown in boldface type.

1. **pensar**
   pres. indic. **pienso, piensas, piensa,** pensamos, pensáis, **piensan**
   pres. subj. **piense, pienses, piense,** pensemos, penséis, **piensen**
   imper. **piensa** (tú), **piense** (usted), pensemos (nosotros), pensad (vosotros), **piensen** (ustedes)

2. **perder**
   pres. indic. **pierdo, pierdes, pierde,** perdemos, perdéis, **pierden**
   pres. subj. **pierda, pierdas, pierda,** perdamos, perdáis, **pierdan**
   imper. **pierde** (tú), **pierda** (usted), perdamos (nosotros), perded (vosotros), **pierdan** (ustedes)

3. **discernir**
   pres. indic. **discierno, disciernes, discierne,** discernimos, discernís, **disciernen**
   pres. subj. **discierna, disciernas, discierna,** discernamos, discernáis, **disciernan**
   imper. **discierne** (tú), **discierna** (usted), discernamos (nosotros), discernid (vosotros), **disciernan** (ustedes)

4. **adquirir**
   pres. indic. **adquiero, adquieres, adquiere,** adquirimos, adquirís, **adquieren**
   pres. subj. **adquiera, adquieras, adquiera,** adquiramos, adquiráis, **adquieran**
   imper. **adquiere** (tú), **adquiera** (usted), adquiramos (nosotros), adquirid (vosotros), **adquieran** (ustedes)

5. **contar**
   pres. indic. **cuento, cuentas, cuenta,** contamos, contáis, **cuentan**
   pres. subj. **cuente, cuentes, cuente,** contemos, contéis, **cuenten**
   imper. **cuenta** (tú), **cuente** (usted), contemos (nosotros), contad (vosotros), **cuenten** (ustedes)

6. **volver**
   pres. indic. **vuelvo, vuelves, vuelve,** volvemos, volvéis, **vuelven**
   pres. subj. **vuelva, vuelvas, vuelva,** volvamos, volvéis, **vuelvan**

	imper.	**vuelve** (tú), **vuelva** (usted), volvamos (nosotros) volved (vosotros), **vuelvan** (ustedes)
	past part.	**vuelto**

7. **dormir**

	pres. indic.	**duermo, duermes, duerme,** dormimos, dormís, **duermen**
	pres. subj.	**duerma, duermas, duerma, durmamos, durmáis, duerman**
	pret. indic.	dormí, dormiste, **durmió,** dormimos, dormisteis, **durmieron**
	imp. subj.	**durmiera, durmieras, durmiera, durmiéramos, durmierais, durmieran,** or **durmiese, durmieses, durmiese, durmiésemos, durmieseis, durmiesen**
	imper.	**duerme** (tú), **duerma** (usted), **durmamos** (nosotros), dormid (vosotros), **duerman** (ustedes)
	pres. part.	**durmiendo**

8. **sentir**

	pres. indic.	**siento, sientes, siente,** sentimos, sentís, **sienten**
	pres. subj.	**sienta, sientas, sienta, sintamos, sintáis, sientan**
	pret. indic.	sentí, sentiste, **sintió,** sentimos, sentisteis, **sintieron**
	imp. subj.	**sintiera, sintieras, sintiera, sintiéramos, sintierais, sintieran,** or **sintiese, sintieses, sintiese, sintiésemos, sintieseis, sintiesen**
	imper.	**siente** (tú), **sienta** (usted), **sintamos** (nosotros), sentid (vosotros), **sientan** (ustedes)
	pres. part.	**sintiendo**

9. **pedir**

	pres. indic.	**pido, pides, pide,** pedimos, pedís, **piden**
	pres. subj.	**pida, pidas, pida, pidamos, pidáis, pidan**
	pret. indic.	pedí, pediste, **pidió,** pedimos, pedisteis, **pidieron**
	imp. subj.	**pidiera, pidieras, pidiera, pidiéramos, pidierais, pidieran,** or **pidiese, pidieses, pidiese, pidiésemos, pidieseis, pidiesen**
	imper.	**pide** (tú), **pida** (usted), **pidamos** (nosotros), pedid (vosotros), **pidan** (ustedes)
	pres. part.	**pidiendo**

10. **reír**

	pres. indic.	**río, ríes, ríe,** reímos, reís, **ríen**
	pres. subj.	**ría, rías, ría, riamos, riáis, rían**
	pret. indic.	reí, reíste, **rió,** reímos, reísteis, **rieron**

imp. subj.	**riera, rieras, riera, riéramos, rierais, rieran,** or **riese, rieses, riese, riésemos, rieseis, riesen**
imper.	**ríe** (tú), **ría** (usted), **riamos** (nosotros), reíd (vosotros), **rían** (ustedes)
pres. part.	**riendo**
past part.	**reído**

11. **reñir**

pres. indic.	**riño, riñes, riñe,** reñimos, reñís, **riñen**
pres. subj.	**riña, riñas, riña, riñamos, riñáis, riñan**
pret. indic.	reñí, reñiste, **riñó,** reñimos, reñisteis, **riñeron**
imp. subj.	**riñera, riñeras, riñera, riñéramos, riñerais, riñeran,** or **riñese, riñeses, riñese, riñésemos, riñeseis, riñesen**
imper.	**riñe** (tú), **riña** (usted), **riñamos** (nosotros), reñid (vosotros), **riñan** (ustedes)
pres. part.	**riñendo**

12. **seguir**

pres. indic.	**sigo, sigues, sigue,** seguimos, seguís, **siguen**
pres. subj.	**siga, sigas, siga, sigamos, sigáis, sigan**
pret. indic.	seguí, seguiste, **siguió,** seguimos, seguisteis, **siguieron**
imp. subj.	**siguiera, siguieras, siguiera, siguiéramos, siguierais, siguieran,** or **siguiese, siguieses, siguiese, siguiésemos, siguieses, siguiesen**
imper.	**sigue** (tú), **siga** (usted), **sigamos** (nosotros), seguid (vosotros), **sigan** (ustedes)
pres. part.	**siguiendo**

13. **erguir**

pres. indic.	**yergo, yergues, yergue,** erguimos, erguís, **yerguen** or **irgo, irgues, irgue,** erguimos, erguís, **irguen**
pres. subj.	**yerga, yergas, yerga, irgamos, irgáis, yergan** or **irga, irgas, irga, irgamos, irgáis, irgan**
pret. indic.	erguí, erguiste, **irguió,** erguimos, erguisteis, **irguieron**
imp. subj.	**irguiera, irguieras, irguiera, irguiéramos, irguierais, irguieran,** or **irguiese, irguieses, irguiese, irguiésemos, irguieseis, irguiesen**
imper.	**yergue** or **irgue** (tú), **yerga** or **irga** (usted), **irgamos** (nosotros), erguid (vosotros), **yergan** or **irgan** (ustedes)
pres. part.	**irguiendo**

14. **elegir**

pres. indic.	**elijo, eliges, elige,** elegimos, elegís, **eligen**
pres. subj.	**elija, elijas, elija, elijamos, elijáis, elijan**

pret. indic.	elegí, elegiste, **eligió,** elegimos, elegisteis, **eligieron**
imp. subj.	**eligiera, eligieras, eligiera, eligiéramos, eligierais, eligieran,** or **eligiese, eligieses, eligiese, eligiésemos, eligieseis, eligiesen**
imper.	**elige** (tú), **elija** (usted), **elijamos** (nosotros), elegid (vosotros), **elijan** (ustedes)
pres. part.	**eligiendo**

15. **tañer**

pret. indic.	tañí, tañiste, **tañó,** tañimos, tañisteis, **tañeron**
imp. subj.	**tañera, tañeras, tañera, tañéramos, tañerais, tañeran,** or **tañese, tañeses, tañese, tañésemos, tañeseis, tañesen**
pres. part.	**tañendo**

16. **bullir**

pret. indic.	bullí, bulliste, **bulló,** bullimos, bullisteis, **bulleron**
imp. subj.	**bullera, bulleras, bullera, bulléramos, bullerais, bulleran,** or **bullese, bulleses, bullese, bullésemos, bulleseis, bullesen**
pres. part.	**bullendo**

17. **gruñir**

pret. indic.	gruñí, gruñiste, **gruñó,** gruñisteis, **gruñeron**
imp. subj.	**gruñera, gruñeras, gruñera, gruñéramos, gruñerais, gruñeran,** or **gruñese, gruñeses, gruñese, gruñésemos, gruñeseis, gruñesen**
pres. part.	**gruñendo**

18. **creer**

pret. indic.	creí, creíste, **creyó,** creímos, creísteis, **creyeron**
imp. subj.	**creyera, creyeras, creyera, creyéramos, creyerais, creyeran,** or **creyese, creyeses, creyese, creyésemos, creyeseis, creyesen**
pres. part.	**creyendo**
past part.	**creído**

19. **huir**

pres. indic.	**huyo, huyes, huye,** huimos, huís, **huyen**
pres. subj.	**huya, huyas, huya, huyamos, huyáis, huyan**
pret. indic.	hui, huiste, **huyó,** huimos, huisteis, **huyeron**
imp. subj.	**huyera, huyeras, huyera, huyéramos, huyerais, huyeran,** or **huyese, huyeses, huyese, huyésemos, huyeseis, huyesen**

imper.		**huye** (tú), **huya** (usted), **huyamos** (nosotros), huid (vosotros), **huyan** (ustedes)
pres. part.		**huyendo**

20. **argüir**

pres. indic.	**arguyo, arguyes, arguye,** argüimos, argüís, **arguyen**
pres. subj.	**arguya, arguyas, arguya, arguyamos, arguyáis, arguyan**
pret. indic.	argüí, argüiste, **arguyó,** argüimos, argüisteis, **arguyeron**
imp. subj.	**arguyera, arguyeras, arguyera, arguyéramos, arguyerais, arguyeran,** or **arguyese, arguyeses, arguyese, arguyésemos, arguyeseis, arguyesen**
imper.	**arguye** (tú), **arguya** (usted), **arguyamos** (nosotros), argüid (vosotros), **arguyan** (ustedes)
pres. part.	**arguyendo**

21. **errar**

pres. indic.	**yerro, yerras, yerra,** erramos, erráis, **yerran**
pres. subj.	**yerre, yerres, yerre,** erremos, erréis, **yerren**
imper.	**yerra** (tú), **yerre** (usted), erremos (nosotros), errad (vosotros), **yerren** (ustedes)

22. **oler**

pres. indic.	**huelo, hueles, huele,** olemos, oléis, **huelen**
pres. subj.	**huela, huelas, huela,** olamos, oláis, **huelan**
imper.	**huele** (tú), **huela** (usted), oled (vosotros), **huelan** (ustedes)

23. **avergonzar**

pres. indic.	**avergüenzo, avergüenzas, avergüenza,** avergonzamos, avergonzáis, **avergüenzan**
pres. subj.	**avergüence, avergüences, avergüence, avergoncemos, avergoncéis, avergüencen**
pret. indic.	**avergoncé,** avergonzaste, avergonzó, avergonzamos, avergonzasteis, avergonzaron
imper.	**avergüenza** (tú), **avergüence** (usted), **avergoncemos** (nosotros), avergonzad (vosotros), **avergüencen** (ustedes)

24. **degollar**

pres. indic.	**degüello, degüellas, degüella,** degollamos, degolláis, **degüellan**
pres. subj.	**degüelle, degüelles, degüelle,** degollemos, degolléis, **degüellen**
imper.	**degüella** (tú), **degüelle** (usted), degollemos (nosotros), degollad (vosotros), **degüellen** (ustedes)

25. **averiguar**
    pres. subj.   **averigüe, averigües, averigüe, averigüemos, averigüéis, averigüen**
    pres. indic.   **averigüé,** averiguaste, averiguó, averiguamos, averiguasteis, averiguaron
    imper.   averigua (tú), **averigüe** (usted), **averigüemos** (nosotros), averiguad (vosotros), **averigüen** (ustedes)

26. **continuar**
    pres. indic.   **continúo, continúas, continúa,** continuamos, continuáis, **continúan**
    pres. subj.   **continúe, continúes, continúe,** continuemos, continuéis, **continúen**
    imper.   **continúa** (tú), **continúe** (usted), continuemos (nosotros), continuad (vosotros), **continúen** (ustedes)

27. **reunir**
    pres. indic.   **reúno, reúnes, reúne,** reunimos, reunís, **reúnen**
    pres. subj.   **reúna, reúnas, reúna,** reunamos, reunáis, **reúnan**
    imper.   **reúne** (tú), **reúna** (usted), reunamos (nosotros), reunid (vosotros), **reúnan** (ustedes)

28. **enviar**
    pres. indic.   **envío, envías, envía,** enviamos, enviáis, **envían**
    pres. subj.   **envíe, envíes, envíe,** enviemos, enviéis, **envíen**
    imper.   **envía** (tú), **envíe** (usted), enviemos (nosotros), enviad (vosotros), **envíen** (ustedes)

29. **prohibir**
    pres. indic.   **prohíbo, prohíbes, prohíbe,** prohibimos, prohibís, **prohíben**
    pres. subj.   **prohíba, prohíbas, prohíba,** prohibamos, prohibáis, **prohíban**
    imper.   **prohíbe** (tú), **prohíba** (usted), prohibamos (nosotros), prohibid (vosotros), **prohíban** (ustedes)

30. **buscar**
    pres. subj.   **busque, busques, busque, busquemos, busquéis, busquen**
    pret. indic.   **busqué,** buscaste, buscó, buscamos, buscasteis, buscaron
    imper.   busca (tú), **busque** (usted), **busquemos** (nosotros), buscad (vosotros), **busquen** (ustedes)

31. **trocar**
    pres. indic.   **trueco, truecas, trueca,** trocamos, trocáis, **truecan**
    pres. subj.   **trueque, trueques, trueque, troquemos, troquéis, truequen**
    pret. indic. **troqué,** trocaste, trocó, trocamos, trocasteis, trocaron
    imper.   **trueca** (tú), **trueque** (usted), **troquemos** (nosotros), trocad (vosotros), **truequen** (ustedes)

32. **convencer**
    pres. indic.   **convenzo,** convences, convence, convencemos, convencéis, convencen
    pres. subj.   **convenza, convenzas, convenza, convenzamos, convenzáis, convenzan**
    imper.   convence (tú), **convenza** (usted), **convenzamos** (nosotros), convenced (vosotros), **convenzan** (ustedes)

33. **esparcir**
    pres. indic.   **esparzo,** esparces, esparce, esparcimos, esparcís, esparcen
    pres. subj.   **esparza, esparzas, esparza, esparzamos, esparzáis, esparzan**
    imper.   esparce (tú), **esparza** (usted), **esparzamos** (nosotros), esparcid (vosotros), **esparzan** (ustedes)

34. **cocer**
    pres. indic.   **cuezo, cueces, cuece,** cocemos, cocéis, **cuecen**
    pres. subj.   **cueza, cuezas, cueza, cozamos, cozáis, cuezan**
    imper.   **cuece** (tú), **cueza** (usted), **cozamos** (nosotros), coced (vosotros), **cuezan** (ustedes)

35. **conocer**
    pres. indic.   **conozco,** conoces, conoce, conocemos, conocéis, conocen
    pres. subj.   **conozca, conozcas, conozca, conozcamos, conozcáis, conozcan**
    imper.   conoce (tú), **conozca** (usted), **conozcamos** (nosotros), conoced (vosotros), **conozcan** (ustedes)

36. **placer**
    pres. indic.   **plazco,** places, place, placemos, placéis, placen
    pres. subj.   **plazca, plazcas, plazca, plazcamos, plazcáis, plazcan**
    imper.   place (tú), **plazca** (usted), **plazcamos** (nosotros), placed (vosotros), **plazcan** (ustedes)

37. **yacer**

pres. indic.	**yazco** or **yazgo** or **yago,** yaces, yace, yacemos, yacéis, yacen
pres. subj.	**yazca, yazcas, yazca, yazcamos, yazcáis, yazcan,** or **yazga, yazgas, yazga, yazgamos, yazgáis, yazgan** or **yaga, yagas, yaga, yagamos, yagáis, yagan**
imper.	yace or **yaz** (tú), **yazca** or **yazga** or **yaga** (usted), **yazcamos** or **yazgamos** or **yagamos** (nosotros), yaced (vosotros), **yazcan** or **yazgan** or **yagan** (ustedes)

38. **conducir**

pres. indic.	**conduzco,** conduces, conduce, conducimos, conducís, conducen
pres. subj.	**conduzca, conduzcas, conduzca, conduzcamos, conduzcáis, conduzcan**
pret. indic.	**conduje, condujiste, condujo, condujimos, condujisteis, condujeron**
imp. subj.	**condujera, condujeras, condujera, condujéramos, condujerais, condujeran,** or **condujese, condujeses, condujese, condujésemos, condujeseis, condujesen**
imper.	conduce (tú), **conduzca** (usted), **conduzcamos** (nosotros), conducid (vosotros), **conduzcan** (ustedes)

39. **lucir**

pres. indic.	**luzco,** luces, luce, lucimos, lucís, lucen
pres. subj.	**luzca, luzcas, luzca, luzcamos, luzcáis, luzcan**
imper.	luce (tú), **luzca** (usted), **luzcamos** (nosotros), lucid (vosotros), **luzcan** (ustedes)

40. **llegar**

pres. subj.	**llegue, llegues, llegue, lleguemos, lleguéis, lleguen**
pret. indic.	**llegué,** llegaste, llegó, llegamos, llegasteis, llegaron
imper.	llega (tú), **llegue** (usted), **lleguemos** (nosotros), llegad (vosotros), **lleguen** (ustedes)

41. **negar**

pres. indic.	**niego, niegas, niega,** negamos, negáis, **niegan**
pres. subj.	**niegue, niegues, niegue, neguemos, neguéis, nieguen**
pret. indic.	**negué,** negaste, negó, negamos, negasteis, negaron
imper.	**niega** (tú), **niegue** (usted), **neguemos** (nosotros), negad (vosotros), **nieguen** (ustedes)

42. **colgar**

pres. indic.	**cuelgo, cuelgas, cuelga,** colgamos, colgáis, **cuelgan**
pres. subj.	**cuelgue, cuelgues, cuelgue, colguemos, colguéis, cuelguen**
pret. indic.	**colgué,** colgaste, colgó, colgamos, colgasteis, colgaron
imper.	**cuelga** (tú), **cuelgue** (usted), **colguemos** (nosotros), colgad (vosotros), **cuelguen** (ustedes)

43. **jugar**

pres. indic.	**juego, juegas, juega,** jugamos, jugáis, **juegan**
pres. subj.	**juegue, juegues, juegue, juguemos, juguéis, jueguen**
pret. indic.	**jugué,** jugaste, jugó, jugamos, jugasteis, jugaron
imper.	**juega** (tú), **juegue** (usted), **juguemos** (nosotros), jugad (vosotros), **jueguen** (ustedes)

44. **distinguir**

pres. indic.	**distingo,** distingues, distingue, distinguimos, distinguís, distinguen
pres. subj.	**distinga, distingas, distinga, distingamos, distingáis, distingan**
imper.	distingue (tú), **distinga** (usted), **distingamos** (nosotros), distinguid (vosotros), **distingan** (ustedes)

45. **coger**

pres. indic.	**cojo,** coges, coge, cogemos, cogéis, cogen
pres. subj.	**coja, cojas, coja, cojamos, cojáis, cojan**
imper.	coge (tú), **coja** (usted), **cojamos** (nosotros), coged (vosotros), **cojan** (ustedes)

46. **dirigir**

pres. indic.	**dirijo,** diriges, dirige, dirigimos, dirigís, dirigen
pres. subj.	**dirija, dirijas, dirija, dirijamos, dirijáis, dirijan**
imper.	dirige (tú), **dirija** (usted), **dirijamos** (nosotros), dirigid (vosotros), **dirijan** (ustedes)

47. **abrazar**

pres. subj.	**abrace, abraces, abrace, abracemos, abracéis, abracen**
pret. indic.	**abracé,** abrazaste, abrazó, abrazamos, abrazasteis, abrazaron
imper.	abraza (tú), **abrace** (usted), **abracemos** (nosotros), abrazad (vosotros), **abracen** (ustedes)

48. **empezar**

pres. indic.	**empiezo, empiezas, empieza,** empezamos, empezáis, **empiezan**
pres. subj.	**empiece, empieces, empiece, empecemos, empecéis, empiecen**
pret. indic.	**empecé,** empezaste, empezó, empezamos, empezasteis, empezaron
imper.	**empieza** (tú), **empiece** (usted), **empecemos** (nosotros), empezad (vosotros), **empiecen** (ustedes)

49. **forzar**

pres. indic.	**fuerzo, fuerzas, fuerza,** forzamos, forzáis, **fuerzan**
pres. subj.	**fuerce, fuerces, fuerce, forcemos, forcéis, fuercen**
pret. indic.	**forcé,** forzaste, forzó, forzamos, forzasteis, forzaron
imper.	**fuerza** (tú), **fuerce** (usted), **forcemos** (nosotros), forzad (vosotros), **fuercen** (ustedes)

50. **asir**

pres. indic.	**asgo,** ases, ase, asimos, asís, asen
pres. subj.	**asga, asgas, asga, asgamos, asgáis, asgan**
imper.	ase (tú), **asga** (usted), **asgamos** (nosotros), asid (vosotros), **asgan** (ustedes)

51. **bendecir**

pres. indic.	**bendigo, bendices, bendice,** bendecimos, bendecís, **bendicen**
pres. subj.	**bendiga, bendigas, bendiga, bendigamos, bendigáis, bendigan**
pret. indic..	**bendije, bendijiste, bendijo, bendijimos, bendijisteis, bendijeron**
imp. subj.	**bendijera, bendijeras, bendijera, bendijéramos, bendijerais, bendijeran** or **bendijese, bendijeses, bendijese, bendijésemos, bendijeseis, bendijesen**
fut. indic.	bendeciré, bendecirás, bendecirá, bendeciremos, bendeciréis, bendecirán
cond.	bendeciría, bendecirías, bendeciría, bendeciríamos, bendeciríais, bendecirían
imper.	**bendice** (tú), **bendiga** (usted), **bendigamos** (nosotros), bendecid (vosotros), **bendigan** (ustedes)
pres. part.	**bendiciendo**
past part.	bendecido

52. **caer**

pres. indic.	**caigo,** caes, cae, caemos, caéis, caen
pres. subj.	**caiga, caigas, caiga, caigamos, caigáis, caigan**

	pret. indic.	caí, caíste, **cayó,** caímos, caísteis, **cayeron**
	imp. subj.	**cayera, cayeras, cayera, cayéramos, cayerais, cayeran,** or **cayese, cayeses, cayese, cayésemos, cayeseis, cayesen**
	imper.	cae (tú), **caiga** (usted), **caigamos** (nosotros), caed (vosotros), **caigan** (ustedes)
	pres. part.	**cayendo**
	past part.	**caído**

53. **decir**[1]

	pres. indic.	**digo, dices, dice,** decimos, decís, **dicen**
	pres. subj.	**diga, digas, diga, digamos, digáis, digan**
	pret. indic.	**dije, dijiste, dijo, dijimos, dijisteis, dijeron**
	imp. subj.	**dijera, dijeras, dijera, dijéramos, dijerais, dijeran,** or **dijese, dijeses, dijese, dijésemos, dijeseis, dijesen**
	fut. indic.	**diré, dirás, dirá, diremos, diréis, dirán**
	cond.	**diría, dirías, diría, diríamos, diríais, dirían**
	imper.	**di** (tú), **diga** (usted), **digamos** (nosotros), decid (vosotros), **digan** (ustedes)
	pres. part.	**diciendo**
	past part.	**dicho**

54. **hacer**

	pres. indic.	**hago,** haces, hace, hacemos, hacéis, hacen
	pres. subj.	**haga, hagas, haga, hagamos, hagáis, hagan**
	pret. indic.	**hice, hiciste, hizo, hicimos, hicisteis, hicieron**
	imp. subj.	**hiciera, hicieras, hiciera, hiciéramos, hicierais, hicieran,** or **hiciese, hicieses, hiciese, hiciésemos, hicieseis, hiciesen**
	fut. indic.	**haré, harás, hará, haremos, haréis, harán**
	cond.	**haría, harías, haría, haríamos, haríais, harían**
	imper.	**haz** (tú), **haga** (usted), **hagamos** (nosotros), haced (vosotros), **hagan** (ustedes)
	past part.	**hecho**

55. **oír**

	pres. indic.	**oigo, oyes, oye,** oímos, oís, **oyen**
	pres. subj.	**oiga, oigas, oiga, oigamos, oigáis, oigan**
	pret. indic.	oí, oíste, **oyó,** oímos, oísteis, **oyeron**

1. The compound verbs of *decir* have the same irregularities with the exception of the following: The future and conditional forms of the compound verbs *contradecir, desdecir,* and *predecir* are used interchangeably in both their irregular and regular forms (see 51 **bendecir**). However, their past participles are always irregular (see 74 **Irregular Past Participles**).

imp. subj.	**oyera, oyeras, oyera, oyéramos, oyerais, oyeran,** or **oyese, oyeses, oyese, oyésemos, oyeseis, oyesen**
imper.	**oye** (tú), **oiga** (usted), **oigamos** (nosotros), oíd (vosotros), **oigan** (ustedes)
pres. part.	**oyendo**
past part.	**oído**

56. **poner**

pres. indic.	**pongo,** pones, pone, ponemos, ponéis, ponen
pres. subj.	**ponga, pongas, ponga, pongamos, pongáis, pongan**
pret. indic.	**puse, pusiste, puso, pusimos, pusisteis, pusieron**
imp. subj.	**pusiera, pusieras, pusiera, pusiéramos, pusierais, pusieran,** or **pusiese, pusieses, pusiese, pusiésemos, pusieseis, pusiesen**
fut. indic.	**pondré, pondrás, pondrá, pondremos, pondréis, pondrán**
cond.	**pondría, pondrías, pondría, pondríamos, pondríais, pondrían**
imper.	**pon** (tú), **ponga** (usted), **pongamos** (nosotros), poned (vosotros), **pongan** (ustedes)
past part.	**puesto**

57. **salir**

pres. indic.	**salgo,** sales, sale, salimos, salís, salen
pres. subj.	**salga, salgas, salga, salgamos, salgáis, salgan**
fut. indic.	**saldré, saldrás, saldrá, saldremos, saldréis, saldrán**
cond.	**saldría, saldrías, saldría, saldríamos, saldríais, saldrían**
imper.	**sal** (tú),[2] **salga** (usted), **salgamos** (nosotros), salid (vosotros), **salgan** (ustedes)

58. **tener**

pres. indic.	**tengo, tienes, tiene,** tenemos, tenéis, **tienen**
pres. subj.	**tenga, tengas, tenga, tengamos, tengáis, tengan**
pret. indic.	**tuve, tuviste, tuvo, tuvimos, tuvisteis, tuvieron**
imp. subj.	**tuviera, tuvieras, tuviera, tuviéramos, tuvierais, tuvieran,** or **tuviese, tuvieses, tuviese, tuviésemos, tuvieseis, tuviesen**
fut. indic.	**tendré, tendrás, tendrá, tendremos, tendréis, tendrán**

2. The compound *sobresalir* is regular in the familiar imperative: *sobresale.*

cond.	**tendría, tendrías, tendría, tendríamos, tendríais, tendrían**
imper.	**ten** (tú), **tenga** (usted), **tengamos** (nosotros), tened (vosotros), **tengan** (ustedes)

59. **traer**

pres. indic.	**traigo,** traes, trae, traemos, traéis, traen
pres. subj.	**traiga, traigas, traiga, traigamos, traigáis, traigan**
pret. indic.	**traje, trajiste, trajo, trajimos, trajisteis, trajeron**
imp. subj.	**trajera, trajeras, trajera, trajéramos, trajerais, trajeran,** or **trajese, trajeses, trajese, trajésemos, trajeseis, trajesen**
imper.	trae (tú), **traiga** (usted), **traigamos** (nosotros), traed (vosotros), **traigan** (ustedes)
pres. part.	**trayendo**
past part.	**traído**

60. **valer**

pres. indic.	**valgo,** vales, vale, valemos, valéis, valen
pres. subj.	**valga, valgas, valga, valgamos, valgáis, valgan**
fut. indic.	**valdré, valdrás, valdrá, valdremos, valdréis, valdrán**
cond.	**valdría, valdrías, valdría, valdríamos, valdríais, valdrían**
imper.	**val** or **vale** (tú), **valga** (usted), **valgamos** (nosotros), valed (vosotros), **valgan** (ustedes)

61. **venir**

pres. indic.	**vengo, vienes, viene,** venimos, venís, **vienen**
pres. subj.	**venga, vengas, venga, vengamos, vengáis, vengan**
pret. indic.	**vine, viniste, vino, vinimos, vinisteis, vinieron**
imp. subj.	**viniera, vinieras, viniera, viniéramos, vinierais, vinieran,** or **viniese, vinieses, viniese, viniésemos, vinieseis, viniesen**
fut. indic.	**vendré, vendrás, vendrá, vendremos, vendréis, vendrán**
cond.	**vendría, vendrías, vendría, vendríamos, vendríais, vendrían**
imper.	**ven** (tú), **venga** (usted), **vengamos** (nosotros), venid (vosotros), **vengan** (ustedes)
pres. part.	**viniendo**

62. **dar**

pres. indic.	**doy,** das, da, damos, dais, dan

pres. subj.	**dé**, des, **dé**, demos, deis, den
pret. indic.	**di, diste, dio, dimos, disteis, dieron**
imp. subj.	**diera, dieras, diera, diéramos, dierais, dieran**, or **diese, dieses, diese, diésemos, dieseis, diesen**
imper.	da (tú), **dé** (usted), demos (nosotros), dad (vosotros), den (ustedes)

63. **estar**

pres. indic.	**estoy, estás, está**, estamos, estáis, **están**
pres. subj.	**esté, estés, esté**, estemos, estéis, **estén**
pret. indic.	**estuve, estuviste, estuvo, estuvimos, estuvisteis, estuvieron**
imp. subj.	**estuviera, estuvieras, estuviera, estuviéramos, estuvierais, estuvieran**, or **estuviese, estuvieses, estuviese, estuviésemos, estuvieseis, estuviesen**
imper.	**está** (tú), **esté** (usted), estemos (nosotros), estad (vosotros), **estén** (ustedes)

64. **ir**

pres. indic.	**voy, vas, va, vamos, vais, van**
pres. subj.	**vaya, vayas, vaya, vayamos, vayáis, vayan**
imp. indic.	**iba, ibas, iba, íbamos, ibais, iban**
pret. indic.	**fui, fuiste, fue, fuimos, fuisteis, fueron**
imp. subj.	**fuera, fueras, fuera, fuéramos, fuerais, fueran**, or **fuese, fueses, fuese, fuésemos, fueseis, fuesen**
imper.	**ve** (tú), **vaya** (usted), **vayamos** (nosotros), id (vosotros), **vayan** (ustedes)
pres. part.	**yendo**

65. **ser**

pres. indic.	**soy, eres, es, somos, sois, son**
pres. subj.	**sea, seas, sea, seamos, seáis, sean**
imp. indic.	**era, eras, era, éramos, erais, eran**
pret. indic.	**fui, fuiste, fue, fuimos, fuisteis, fueron**
imp. subj.	**fuera, fueras, fuera, fuéramos, fuerais, fueran**, or **fuese, fueses, fuese, fuésemos, fueseis, fuesen**
imper.	**sé** (tú), **sea** (usted), **seamos** (nosotros), sed (vosotros), **sean** (ustedes)

66. **andar**

pret. indic.	**anduve, anduviste, anduvo, anduvimos, anduvisteis, anduvieron**

imp. subj.	**anduviera, anduvieras, anduviera, anduviéramos, anduvierais, anduvieran,** or **anduviese, anduvieses, anduviese, anduviésemos, anduvieseis, anduviesen**

67. caber

pres. indic.	**quepo,** cabes, cabe, cabemos, cabéis, caben
pres. subj.	**quepa, quepas, quepa, quepamos, quepáis, quepan**
pret. indic.	**cupe, cupiste, cupo, cupimos, cupisteis, cupieron**
imp. subj.	**cupiera, cupieras, cupiera, cupiéramos, cupierais, cupieran,** or **cupiese, cupieses, cupiese, cupiésemos, cupieseis, cupiesen**
fut. indic.	**cabré, cabrás, cabrá, cabremos, cabréis, cabrán**
cond.	**cabría, cabrías, cabría, cabríamos, cabríais, cabrían**
imper.	cabe (tú), **quepa** (usted), **quepamos** (nosotros), cabed (vosotros), **quepan** (ustedes)

68. haber

pres. indic.	**he, has, ha, hemos,** habéis, **han**
pres. subj.	**haya, hayas, haya, hayamos, hayáis, hayan**
pret. indic.	**hube, hubiste, hubo, hubimos, hubisteis, hubieron**
imp. subj.	**hubiera, hubieras, hubiera, hubiéramos, hubierais, hubieran,** or **hubiese, hubieses, hubiese, hubiésemos, hubieseis, hubiesen**
fut. indic.	**habré, habrás, habrá, habremos, habréis, habrán**
cond.	**habría, habrías, habría, habríamos, habríais, habrían**

69. poder

pres. indic.	**puedo, puedes, puede,** podemos, podéis, **pueden**
pres. subj.	**pueda, puedas, pueda,** podamos, podáis, **puedan**
pret. indic.	**pude, pudiste, pudo, pudimos, pudisteis, pudieron**
imp. subj.	**pudiera, pudieras, pudiera, pudiéramos, pudierais, pudieran,** or **pudiese, pudieses, pudiese, pudiésemos, pudieseis, pudiesen**
fut. indic.	**podré, podrás, podrá, podremos, podréis, podrán**
cond.	**podría, podrías, podría, podríamos, podríais, podrían**
pres. part.	**pudiendo**

70. **querer**

pres. indic.	**quiero, quieres, quiere,** queremos, queréis, **quieren**
pres. subj.	**quiera, quieras, quiera,** queramos, queráis, **quieran**
pret. indic.	**quise, quisiste, quiso, quisimos, quisisteis, quisieron**
imp. subj.	**quisiera, quisieras, quisiera, quisiéramos, quisierais, quisieran,** or **quisiese, quisieses, quisiese, quisiésemos, quisieseis, quisiesen**
fut. indic.	**querré, querrás, querrá, querremos, querréis, querrán**
cond.	**querría, querrías, querría, querríamos, querríais, querrían**
imper.	**quiere** (tú), **quiera** (usted), queramos (nosotros), quered (vosotros), **quieran** (ustedes)

71. **saber**

pres. indic.	**sé,** sabes, sabe, sabemos, sabéis, saben
pres. subj.	**sepa, sepas, sepa, sepamos, sepáis, sepan**
pret. indic.	**supe, supiste, supo, supimos, supisteis, supieron**
imp. subj.	**supiera, supieras, supiera, supiéramos, supierais, supieran,** or **supiese, supieses, supiese, supiésemos, supieseis, supiesen**
fut. indic.	**sabré, sabrás, sabrá, sabremos, sabréis, sabrán**
cond.	**sabría, sabrías, sabría, sabríamos, sabríais, sabrían**
imper.	sabe (tú), **sepa** (usted), **sepamos** (nosotros), sabed (vosotros), **sepan** (ustedes)

72. **ver**[3]

pres. indic.	**veo,** ves, ve, vemos, veis, ven
pres. subj.	**vea, veas, vea, veamos, veáis, vean**
pret. indic.	**vi, viste, vio, vimos, visteis, vieron**
imp. indic.	**veía, veías, veía, veíamos, veíais, veían**
imp. subj.	**viera, vieras, viera, viéramos, vierais, vieran** or **viese, vieses, viese, viésemos, vieseis, viesen**
imper.	ve (tú), **vea** (usted), **veamos** (nosotros), ved (vosotros), **vean** (ustedes)
past part.	**visto**

---

3. The verb *prever* differs orthographically in the second- and third-person forms of the present indicative (*prevés, prevéis, prevé, prevén*), the first- and third-person singular forms of the preterit indicative (*preví, previó*), and the familiar imperative form (*prevé*).

73. Defective Verbs

The following verbs are used only in the forms that have an **i** in the ending: **abolir, agredir, aterirse, empedernirse, transgredir.**

The verb **atañer** is used only in the third person, most frequently in the present indicative: atañe, atañen.

The verb **concernir** is used only in the third person of the following tenses:

pres. indic.	**concierne, conciernen**
pres. subj.	**concierna, conciernan**
imp. indic.	concernía, concernían
imp. subj.	concerniera or concerniese, concernieran or concerniesen
fut. indic	concernirá, concernirán
cond.	concerniría, concernirían

The verb **roer** (also **corroer**) has three forms in the first person of the present indicative: **roo, royo, roigo,** all of which are infrequently used. In the present subjunctive the preferable form is **roa, roas, roa,** etc., although the forms **roya** and **roiga** are found.

The verb **soler** is used most frequently in the present and imperfect indicative. It is less frequently used in the present subjunctive.

pres. indic.	**suelo, sueles, suele,** solemos, soléis, **suelen**
pres. subj.	**suela, suelas, suela,** solamos, soláis, **suelan**
imp. indic.	solía, solías, solía, solíamos, solíais, solían

74. Additional Irregular Past Participles
absolver—**absuelto**
abrir—**abierto**
anteponer—**antepuesto**
circunscribir—**circunscrito**
componer—**compuesto**
contradecir—**contradicho**
cubrir—**cubierto**
decir—**dicho**
deponer—**depuesto**
descomponer—**descompuesto**
describir—**descrito**
descubrir—**descubierto**
desdecir—**desdicho**
desenvolver—**desenvuelto**
deshacer—**deshecho**
devolver—**devuelto**
disolver—**disuelto**

disponer—**dispuesto**
encubrir—**encubierto**
entreabrir—**entreabierto**
entrever—**entrevisto**
envolver—**envuelto**
escribir—**escrito**
exponer—**expuesto**
freír—**frito** (often regular, **freído**)
hacer—**hecho**
imponer—**impuesto**
imprimir—**impreso** (often regular, **imprimido**)
indisponer—**indispuesto**
inscribir—**inscrito**
interponer—**interpuesto**
morir—**muerto**
oponer—**opuesto**
poner—**puesto**
posponer—**pospuesto**
predecir—**predicho**
predisponer—**predispuesto**
prescribir—**prescrito**
presuponer—**presupuesto**
prever—**previsto**
proponer—**propuesto**
proscribir—**proscrito**
proveer—**provisto** (often regular, **proveído**)
pudrir—**podrido**
reabrir—**reabierto**
recubrir—**recubierto**
reescribir—**reescrito**
rehacer—**rehecho**
reponer—**repuesto**
resolver—**resuelto**
revolver—**revuelto**
romper—**roto**
satisfacer—**satisfecho**
sobreponer—**sobrepuesto**
suscribir—**suscrito**
superponer—**superpuesto**
suponer—**supuesto**
transcribir—**transcrito**
trasponer—**traspuesto**
ver—**visto**
volver—**vuelto**
yuxtaponer—**yuxtapuesto**

Aa

a PREP **voy — Londres** I'm going to London; **te lo doy — ti** I'm giving it to you; **se sentó — la sombra** she sat down in the shade; **tumbarse —l sol** to lie down in the sun; **una soga —l cuello** a rope around his neck; **lo miraba — la luz de una vela** she looked at him by the light of a candle; **— dos pesetas cada uno** at two pesetas each; **— las tres y media** at three-thirty; **sentarse — la mesa** to sit down at the table; **prestar dinero —l 15%** to lend money at 15%; **en grupos de — cinco** in groups of five; **cocina — gas** gas cooker; **fotos — todo color** full-color photos; **nadie le gana — testaruda** no one touches her for stubbornness; **terminaron — puñetazos** they ended up fighting; **¡— jugar!** let's play! **¿— qué vienen?** what are they coming for? **veo — mi mamá** I see my mother

AA [**Alcohólicos Anónimos**] F AA

abacá M manila

abad -esa M abbot; F abbess

abadejo M cod

abadía F abbey

abajo ADV (dirección) down; (posición relativa) below; **mirar para —** to look down; **el piso de —** the apartment below; **véase —** see below; **— de** under, underneath; **Stefan está — del coche** Stefan is under/ underneath the car; **¡— el rey!** down with the king! **— firmante** undersigned; **echar —** to knock down; **río —** downstream; **venirse —** to go to ruin

abalanzarse[47] VI **— sobre** to lunge at, to swoop down upon

abanderado -da MF standard-bearer

abandonado ADJ abandoned; **es una persona muy abandonada** she's very unkempt

abandonar VT (a una persona, a una familia) to leave, to desert; (el hogar, un partido) to abandon; (una competencia, el poder) to give up; (una competencia, a un enamorado, el hábito de fumar) to quit; (en los naipes) to fold; (un curso) to drop out of

abandono M (descuido) neglect; (acción de abandonar, condición de abandonado) abandonment; **— de funciones** derelliction of duties

abanicar[30] VT (contra el calor) to fan; (en béisbol) to swing and miss

abanico M (accesorio) fan; (rango) array; (en béisbol) swing and a miss; **abrirse en —** to fan out

abaratar VT (bajar el precio) to lower the price of; (desprestigiar) to cheapen

abarcar[30] VT (categorías) to embrace, to encompass; (tiempo) to span

abarrotería F Méx grocery store

abarrotero -ra MF Méx grocer

abarrotes M PL Méx groceries; **tienda de —** Méx grocery store

abastecedor -ora MF supplier

abastecer[35] VT (un ejército, una ciudad) to supply; (una tienda) to stock

abastecimiento M supply

abasto M supply; **mercado de —s** farmers' market; **yo sola no doy —** I can't cope alone

abatido ADJ dejected, despondent, downcast

abatimiento M dejection, despondency

abatir VT (bajar) to lower; (derribar) to knock down; (desanimar) to depress; (matar a tiros) to shoot; **—se** to swoop down

abdicar[30] VI/VT to abdicate

abdomen M abdomen

abdominal ADJ abdominal; M sit-up

abecedario M alphabet

abedul M birch

abeja F bee; **— asesina** killer bee

abejón M bumblebee

abejorro M bumblebee

aberración F aberration

abertura F (acción) opening; (cualidad) openness

abeto M fir

abierto ADJ (no cerrado, no determinado, destapado) open; (franco) frank; **— de par en par** wide open

abierto ver abrir

abigarrado ADJ motley

abigeato M cattle rustling

abismal ADJ abysmal

abismo M abyss, chasm; **— generacional** generation gap

ablandar VT to soften

abnegación F self-denial

abobado ADJ silly

abocar[30] VI to turn onto; **—se a** to devote oneself to

abochornar VT (avergonzar) to embarrass; **—se** to become embarrassed

abocinar VT to flare

abofetear VT to slap

abogacía F legal profession; **estudiar —** to study law

abogado -da MF lawyer, attorney; **— tributarista** tax attorney, tax lawyer

abogar[40] VI **— por** to advocate, to plead for

abolengo M ancestry

abolición F abolition

abolir[73] VT to abolish

abollado ADJ dented

abolladura F dent

abollar VT to dent; **—se** to become dented

abolsarse VI to sag

abombar VT to make bulge

abominable ADJ abominable, loathsome

abominación F abomination

abominar VI to detest

abonado -da MF subscriber

abonar VT (suscribir) to subscribe; (pagar) to make a payment; (poner fertilizante) to fertilize; **—se** to subscribe; **— a una cuenta** credit an account

abono M (a una revista) subscription; (para una temporada deportiva) season ticket; (de autobús) pass; (para la tierra) fertilizer; (de dinero) payment

abordar VT (un avión, un buque) to board; (un problema) to tackle, to approach; (a una persona) to accost

aborigen ADJ aboriginal; MF native inhabitant; **— australiano** Australian aborigine

aborrascarse[30] VI to become stormy

aborrecer[35] VT to abhor, to loathe

aborrecible ADJ hateful, abhorrent

aborrecimiento M abhorrence

abortador -ora MF abortionist

abortar VI (naturalmente) to miscarry, to have a miscarriage; VI/VT (intencionadamente) to abort

abortero -ra MF abortionist

aborto M (espontáneo) miscarriage; (provocado) abortion; **— espontáneo** spontaneous abortion

abotargarse[40] VI to bloat

abotonar VT to button; **—se** to button up

abovedar VT (una iglesia) to vault, to cover with a vault; (una calle) to arch, to cover as a vault

abozalar VT to muzzle

abracadabra M abracadabra

abrasador ADJ burning

abrasar VT to burn; **—se** to be consumed

abrasión F abrasion; **— cutánea** dermabrasion

abrasivo ADJ abrasive

abrazadera F clamp

abrazar[47] VT (rodear con los brazos) to hug, to embrace; (rodear una cosa sujetando) to clasp; (una opinión) to espouse

abrazo M hug, embrace

abrevadero ADJ trough

abrevar VT (dar de beber) to water; (beber) to drink

abreviación F abbreviation

abreviar VT to abbreviate, to abridge

abreviatura F abbreviation

abridor M opener

abrigado ADJ (ropa) warm; (lugar) sheltered

abrigar[40] VT (refugiados) to shelter; (emociones) to harbor; **—se** to bundle up

abrigo M (refugio) shelter; (prenda de vestir) coat, wrap; **— impositivo** tax shelter

abril M April

abrillantar VT to make shiny

abrir[74] VI/VT (una puerta) to open; VT (un candado) to unlock; (un grifo) to turn on; **— el apetito** to whet one's appetite; **— la sesión** call a meeting to order; **— paso** to make way; M SG **abrelatas** can opener; M SG **abrebotellas** bottle opener; M SG **abrelatas** can opener; VI (el cielo) to clear up; **—se** to open up; **—se paso** to press through; **en un — y cerrar de ojos** in the twinkle of an eye

abrochar VT to fasten; **—se** to buckle [up]

abrogación F repeal

abrogar[40] VT to repeal

abrojo M bur, sticker

abrumador ADJ overwhelming, overpowering

abrumar VT to overwhelm, to weigh down; **—se** to become foggy

abrupto ADJ abrupt

absceso M abscess

absolución F acquittal

absolutamente ADV, INTERJ absolutely

absoluto ADJ absolute; **en —** absolutely not

absolver[6,74] VT to absolve, to acquit

absorbente ADJ absorbent

absorber VT to absorb

absorción F absorption

absorto ADJ absorbed, engrossed

abstemio -mia ADJ abstemious; MF teetotaler

abstención F abstention

abstenerse[58] VI to abstain; **— de** to abstain from, to refrain from, to forego

abstinencia F abstinence

abstracción F abstraction

abstracto ADJ abstract

abstraer[59] VT to abstract

abstraído ADJ lost in thought

absurdo ADJ absurd, preposterous; M absurdity

abuchear VI/VT to boo, to jeer

abucheo M boo, jeer

abuelo -la M grandfather; F grandmother; **—s** grandparents

abulia F apathy

abultado ADJ bulgy

abultar VI to bulge

abundancia F abundance, plenty

abundante ADJ abundant, plentiful

abundar VI to abound; **— en** to abound in

aburrido ADJ (sin entretenimiento) bored; (pesado) boring, tiresome

aburrimiento M boredom

aburrir VT to bore; **—se** to become bored

abusar VT **— de** to abuse; (sexualmente) to molest

abuso M abuse; **— conyugal** spousal abuse; **— de confianza** breach of trust; **— de drogas** drug abuse; **— de sustancias** substance abuse

abyecto ADJ abject

acá ADV (en este lugar) here; (hacia este lugar) over here, *lit* hither; **— y allá** here and there

acabado ADJ finished; M finish

acabar VT to finish; VI to end; **— de comer** to have just eaten; **— por** to end up by; **— con** (la corrupción) to put an end to; (las cucarachas) to get rid of; **él y yo hemos acabado** he and I are through; **se acabaron los dulces** the candy is all gone; **se nos acabaron las ideas** we ran out of ideas; **y se acabó** and that's that

academia F (corporación, escuela militar) academy; (centro privado de enseñanza) private school

académico ADJ academic

acallar VT to silence, to quiet

acalorado ADJ heated

acaloramiento M **sufrió un —** he got too hot

acalorarse VI/VT (sofocarse) to overheat; (emocionarse) to get excited

acampada F camping trip

acampante MF camper

acampar VT to camp

acanalar VT to groove

acantilado ADJ sheer, steep; M bluff, cliff

acantonarse VT to be quartered

acaparar VT (productos) to hoard; (atención) to capture; (monopolizar) *fam* to hog; **— el mercado** to corner the market

acaramelar VT to candy

acariciar VT to caress; **— una esperanza** to harbor a hope

ácaro M mite

acarrear VT (transportar) to transport; (transportar en carro) to cart; (ocasionar) to bring about

acarreo M transport

acaso ADV perhaps; **por si —** just in case

acatamiento M compliance

acatar VT to abide by, to comply with

acatarrarse VI **—se** to catch cold

acaudalado ADJ wealthy

acceder VI **— a** (un pedido) to accede to; VI (una invitación) to accept

accesibilidad F accessibility

accesible ADJ accessible, convenient

acceso M (entrada) access; (de ira) fit; **— a internet** Internet access; **— denegado** access denied; **— remoto** remote access, remote login; **de —** **prohibido** off limits

accesorio ADJ & M accessory

accidentado -da ADJ (viaje) eventful; (terreno) uneven; MF accident victim

accidental ADJ accidental

accidentarse VI to have an accident

accidente M (suceso imprevisto) accident; (del terreno) feature; (automovilístico) wreck; **— de tránsito** traffic accident; **por —** by accident

acción F (acto) action; (valor de bolsa) share of stock; **— de gracias** thanksgiving; **buenas acciones** good deeds; **acciones preferenciales** preferred stock; **acciones ordinarias** common stock

accionable ADJ actionable

accionar VT to operate

accionista MF shareholder, stockholder

acebo M holly

acechar VT (emboscar) to lie in ambush; (amenazar) to stalk

acecho M **rondar en —** to prowl; **estar al —** to lie in wait

aceitar VT to oil

aceite M oil; **— de linaza** linseed oil; **— de oliva** olive oil; **— de ricino** castor oil; **— vegetal** vegetable oil

aceitera F (recipiente) oilcan; (fábrica) oil factory

aceitoso ADJ oily

aceituna F olive

aceleración F acceleration

acelerador M accelerator

acelerar VT to accelerate, to speed up; VI to accelerate, to step on the gas; **— en vacío** to rev, to race; **—se** *Am* to get nervous

acémila F pack animal

acento M (pronunciación, signo) accent; (intensidad mayor, de voz) stress

acentuar^{26} VT (aumentar) to accentuate; (poner tilde) to accent; (reforzar la voz) to stress; **—se** to accentuate

acepción F gloss, meaning

aceptable ADJ acceptable

aceptación F acceptance

aceptar VT to accept; **— entrega** to take delivery

acequia F irrigation ditch

acera F sidewalk

acerado ADJ made of steel

acerar VT to steel

acerca PREP **— de** about, concerning

acercamiento M approach

acercar^{30} VT to bring near; **os acerco a la estación** I'll give you a ride to the station; **—se** to come near, to approach

acería F steel mill

acero M steel; **— inoxidable** stainless steel

acérrimo ADJ bitter

acertado ADJ right

acertar^1 VT to hit; VI to be right; **— con** to hit upon; **— a pasar** to happen to go by; **no —** to miss the mark

acertijo M riddle, conundrum

acervo M heritage

acetaminofén M acetaminophen

acetona F acetone

achacar^{30} VI to blame

achacoso ADJ infirm, ailing

achaparrado ADJ (planta) stunted; (persona) squat

achaque M affliction, ailment; **—s** aches and pains

achicado ADJ weak-kneed

achicar[30] VT (de tamaño) to make small; (un vestido) to take in; (agua) to bail; **—se** (acobardarse) to feel intimidated; (empequeñecerse) to get smaller

achicoria F chicory

aciago ADJ unlucky

acicalado ADJ clean-cut

acicalarse VI to dress up

acicate M incentive

acidez F (de una solución) acidity; (del vinagre) sourness; **— de estómago** heartburn

ácido M acid; **—s grasos** fatty acids; ADJ (propio del ácido) acidic; (fruta) sour, tart

acierto M (contestación) right answer; (elección) felicitous choice

aclamación F acclamation, acclaim; **por —** by acclamation

aclamar VT to acclaim, to hail

aclaración F clarification

aclarar VT (con explicaciones) to clarify; (con agua) to rinse; (la voz) to clear; VI to dawn; **aclaró después de la tormenta** it cleared up after the storm; **—se** to lighten

aclimatar VT to acclimate

acné M acne

acobardar VT to intimidate

acogedor ADJ (persona) hospitable; (cuarto) cozy

acoger[45] VT (una sugerencia) to receive; (a un refugiado) to shelter; **—se** to take refuge; **—se a la ley** to have recourse to the law

acogida F reception

acogimiento M reception

acolchar VT to pad

acollarar VT to collar

acometer VT (atacar) to attack; (emprender) to undertake

acometida F attack

acomodado ADJ well-off

acomodador -ora MF usher

acomodar VT (arreglar) to arrange; (ajustar) to adjust; (adaptar) to adapt; **—se** (ponerse cómodo) to make oneself comfortable; (adaptarse) to adapt oneself

acomodo M position; **no tengo —** I can't find a comfortable position

acompañamiento M (acción, música) accompaniment; (grupo de personas que acompaña) retinue; (comida) side dish; (tenis) follow-through

acompañante ADJ accompanying; MF (compañero) companion; (en música) accompanist

acompañar VI/VT to accompany (también en música); (escoltar) to escort; (en una carta) to enclose; **—se de** to be accompanied by; **esperemos que el tiempo acompañe** let's hope the weather cooperates; **te acompaño en el sentimiento** my thoughts are with you

acompasado ADJ (rítmico) rhythmical; (mesurado) measured

acomplejado ADJ self-conscious

acondicionar VT to prepare

acongojado ADJ grief-stricken

acongojar VT to distress; **—se** to become distressed

aconsejable ADJ advisable

aconsejar VT to advise, to counsel

acontecer[35] VI to take place

acontecimiento M event; **todo un —** quite a happening; **a esta altura de los —s** at this point in the proceedings

acopiar VT to stockpile

acopio M (acción de guardar) storing; (cosas guardadas) stockpile

acoplamiento M coupling; **— universal de cardán** universal joint

acoplar VT to couple; **—se** (piezas complementarias, partes) to couple, to join; (altavoces) to have feedback

acople M coupling, connection

acorazado ADJ armored; M battleship, warship

acorazar[47] VT to armor

acordado VI agreed-upon

acordar[5] VT to agree; VI **— en** to arrange to; **—se [de]** to remember

acorde M chord; ADJ in agreement; **en — con** in agreement with

acordeón M accordion

acordonar VT (un zapato) to lace; (un lugar) to rope off, to seal off; (una moneda) to mill

acorralar VT (meter en un corral) to corral; (arrinconar) to corner

acortamiento M shortening

acortar VT to shorten

acosar VT (perseguir) to harry; (atacar) to beset; (atormentar) to badger; (importunar sexualmente) to harass

acoso M (de presa) hunting down, pursuit; (de una persona) harassment, hounding

acostar[5] VT to put to bed; **—se** to go to bed; **—se con** to sleep with

acostumbrado ADJ (normal) accustomed; (habitual) customary; **estar — a** to be used / accustomed to

acostumbrar VT to accustom; (soler) to be accustomed to; **—se [a]** to get accustomed [to]; **acostumbraban ir al teatro** they used to go to the theater

acotación F (anotación) marginal note; (en una obra de teatro) stage directions

acotar VT (un terreno) to mark off; (un texto) to

make marginal notes on

acre ADJ acrid, pungent, sharp; M acre

acrecentamiento M growth, increase

acrecentar[1] VT to grow; **—se** to grow

acreditar VT (una cuenta) to credit; (a un profesional) to accredit; **— a una cuenta** to credit an account; **a quien pueda — ser el dueño de** to whoever can prove to be the owner of

acreedor -ora ADJ deserving; **saldo —** positive balance; MF creditor

acribillar VI (a balazos) to riddle [with]; (a pedradas) to pelt

acrílico ADJ & M acrylic

acritud F acrimony

acrobacia F (arte) acrobatics; (pirueta) stunt

acróbata MF acrobat

acrobático ADJ acrobatic

acrofobia F acrophobia

acrónimo M acronym

acta F (de nacimiento) certificate; (de una reunión) minutes; (de un congreso) proceedings

actitud F attitude, mind-set

activar VT to activate

actividad F activity

activismo M activism

activista MF activist

activo ADJ active; **en —** working; M assets; **— líquido** liquid assets; **— convertible** convertible assets

acto M (solemne, dramático) act; (acción) action; **— seguido** immediately after; **— fallido** Freudian slip; **en el —** on the spot; **hacer — de presencia** to show up

actor M actor, performer; **— de carácter** character actor

actriz F actor, actress, performer

actuación F (acción) acting; (rendimiento, desempeño) performance

actual ADJ current, present

actualidad F present time; **—es** latest news; **de — up-to-date**

actualización F (de información) update; (de ordenador) upgrade

actualizado ADJ (al día) up-to-date; (al minuto) up-to-the-minute

actualizar[47] VT to update; (programa de ordenador) to upgrade; (pantalla de ordenador) to refresh

actualmente ADV presently, currently

actuar[26] VI (comportarse) to act; (dar una representación) to perform

actuario -ria MF (judicial) clerk; (de seguros) actuary

acuarela F watercolor

acuario M aquarium

acuartelar VT to quarter

acuático ADJ aquatic

acuchillar VT (penetrar) to stab; (cortar) to slash

acuclillado ADJ squatting

acuclillarse VI to squat

acudir VI (ir) to go; (asistir) to attend; **— a** to turn to; **— al llamado** to respond to the call; **— al socorro de** to go to the rescue of; **— en masa** to flock

acueducto M aqueduct

acuerda, acuerde ver acordar

acuerdo M agreement; **— comercial** trade agreement; **— contractual** contractual agreement; **— global** package deal agreement; **estar de —** to be in agreement; **ponerse de —** to come to an agreement; **de — con** in accordance with

acumulación F (de dinero) accumulation; (de tensión) buildup

acumulador M storage battery

acumular VT (desperdicios) to accumulate; (fortuna) to amass; (deudas) to accumulate, to run up; **—se** to collect; **rabia acumulada** pent-up rage

acumulativo ADJ cumulative

acuñación F coinage, minting

acuñar VT (monedas, una expresión) to coin; (meter cuñas) to wedge

acuoso ADJ watery

acupuntor -ora MF acupuncturist

acupuntura F acupuncture

acurrucarse[30] VI to nestle, to huddle

acusación F accusation, charge

acusado -da MF accused; (en un juicio) defendant

acusador -ora MF accuser

acusar VT (culpabilizar) to accuse; (detectar) to detect; (revelar) to betray; (entre niños) to tattle, to tell; **— el golpe** to feel the blow; **— recibo** to acknowledge receipt

acuse M acknowledgment

acusetas MF SG tattletale

acusica MF tattletale

acústica F acoustics

acústico ADJ acoustic

adagio M adage

adaptabilidad F resilience, adaptability

adaptación F adaptation

adaptador M adapter

adaptar VT to adapt

adecuado ADJ appropriate

adecuar VT to adapt; **—se a** to be suitable for

adefesio M sight, hideous thing

adelantado ADJ (economía, alumno) advanced; (reloj) fast; (tren) ahead of time, ahead of schedule; **por —** in advance

adelantamiento M (de una fecha) bringing forward; (de un coche) overtaking

adelantar VT (una fecha, dinero) to advance; (la mano) to move forward; (un coche) to pass; (una noticia) to have a scoop; VI (un reloj) to gain; — **en** to make progress in; —**se** (sacar ventaja) to get ahead; (actuar antes) to go first; (innovar) to be ahead; (hablar antes de tiempo) to get ahead of oneself

adelante ADV forward; — **con los faroles** let's get started; — **de mí** in front of me; **de aquí en** — from now on; **hacia** — forward; **ir** — to go ahead; **más** — later; **sacar** — to make prosper; **seguir** — to go on; INTERJ go for it!

adelanto M (de la ciencia) advance, breakthrough; (de un coche) passing; (pago) advance; **el** — **de los relojes** setting the clocks forward

adelfa F oleander

adelgazar[47] VI to lose weight; VT to lose; (hacer perder peso) to make one lose weight; (hacer menos espeso) to thin; (hacer parecer delgado) to make one look thinner; — **cinco kilos** to lose five kilos; —**se** to get thinner

ademán M gesture; **hacer un** — **a alguien** to motion to someone

además ADV moreover, besides, in addition; — **de deberme dinero** besides / in addition to owing me money

adentrarse VI — **en** (un asunto) to go deeply into; (un lugar) to go deep into, to penetrate into; (una edad) to enter

adentro ADV inside; **ir para/hacia** — to go inside; **hablar para sus** —**s** to talk to oneself; **con lo de** — **para afuera** inside out

aderezar[47] VT (embellecer) to adorn; (condimentar) to season, to garnish

aderezo M (adorno) adornment; (de un alimento) seasoning; (de una ensalada) dressing

adeudar VT (deber) to owe; — **una cuenta** to debit an account

adeudo M (endeudamiento) indebtedness; (a una cuenta) debit

adherencia F adhesion

adherir[8] VI to adhere; —**se a** (una cosa) to stick to; (una huelga) to join; (una idea) to subscribe to

adhesión F (a una cosa) adhesion; (a una doctrina) adherence

adhesivo ADJ adhesive; M (pegamento) cement, adhesive; (calcomanía) sticker

adicción F addiction

adición F addition

adicional ADJ additional

adictivo ADJ addictive, habit-forming

adicto -ta ADJ addicted; MF addict; — **al trabajo** workaholic

adiestramiento M training

adiestrar VT to train

adinerado ADJ wealthy, well-to-do, moneyed

adiós INTERJ good-bye; **hacer** — **con la mano** to wave good-bye

adiposo ADJ fatty

aditivo M additive

adivinanza F riddle

adivinar VT to guess

adivino -na MF fortune-teller

adjetivo ADJ & M adjective

adjudicación F award

adjudicar[30] VT to award; —**se** to be awarded

adjuntar VT (incluir en una carta) to enclose; (añadir) to add, to attach, to append

adjunto ADJ (unido) attached; (incluido) enclosed; (asistente) adjunct; ADV herewith; M attachment

adminículo M gadget

administración F administration, management; — **pública** civil service; — **intermedia** middle management

administrador -ora MF administrator, manager; — **de cuentas** account manager; — **de un sitio web** webmaster

administrar VT (un medicamento) to administer; (una empresa) to administer, to manage; (justicia) to dispense; —**se** to budget

administrativo ADJ administrative

admirable ADJ admirable

admiración F admiration

admirador -ora MF admirer; (de una estrella de cine) fan

admirar VT to admire; —**se** to be amazed; —**se de** to wonder at

admisible ADJ admissible, allowable

admisión F (aceptación) admission; (reconocimiento) acknowledgment

admitir VT (dejar entrar, reconocer) to admit; (aceptar) to accept; (permitir) to allow

ADN [ácido desoxirribonucleico] M DNA

adobar VT (aderezar carne) to season; (curtir una piel) to tan; (encurtir) to pickle

adobe M adobe

adobo M sauce for seasoning

adoctrinar VT to indoctrinate

adolecer[35] VI — **de** to suffer from

adolescencia F adolescence

adolescente ADJ adolescent; MF adolescent, teenager

adonde ADV REL **esa es la casa** — **vamos** that's the house [that] we're going to, that's the house where we're going

adónde ADV INTERR & PRON where

adopción F adoption

adoptar VT to adopt

adoptivo ADJ adoptive

adoquín M cobblestone

adorable ADJ adorable

adoración F (a una persona) adoration; (a un dios) worship

adorador -ora MF worshiper

adorar VT (a una persona) to adore; (a un dios) to worship

adormecer[35] VT (dar sueño) to make drowsy;

(entumecer) to numb; —**se** (de sueño) to become drowsy; (de frío) to go numb

adormilado ADJ sleepy

adornar VT to adorn, to embellish

adorno M adornment, ornament, decoration

adquirir[4] VT (un bien) to acquire; (una característica) to take on

adquisición F (compra) acquisition; (nuevo miembro) addition; (compra de una compañía) takeover

adquisitivo ADJ purchasing

adrede ADV on purpose

adrenalina F adrenaline

aduana F (control) customs; (edificio) customshouse

aduanero -ra ADJ customs; **control —** customs control; MF customs officer

aducir[38] VT to adduce

adueñarse VI to take possession

adulación F flattery

adulador -ora ADJ flattering; MF flatterer

adular VI/VT to flatter

adulón -ona ADJ flattering; MF *fam* brown-noser

adulterar VT to adulterate

adulterio M adultery

adúltero -ra MF adulterer

adulto -ta ADJ & MF adult

adusto ADJ stern

advenedizo ADJ upstart

advenimiento M advent

adverbio M adverb

adversario -ria MF adversary, opponent

adversidad F adversity

adverso ADJ adverse

advertencia F (aviso) notice; (amonestación) warning, admonition

advertir[8] VT (avisar) to warn; (notar) to notice; (notificar) to advise, to tip off

Adviento M Advent

advierta, advierte *ver* advertir

adyacente ADJ adjacent

aéreo ADJ aerial; **correo —** airmail

aeróbico ADJ aerobic

aeróbic M aerobics

aerobio ADJ aerobic

aerodeslizador M hovercraft

aerodinámica F aerodynamics

aerodinámico ADJ aerodynamic, streamlined

aeródromo M airport

aeroespacial ADJ aerospace

aerolínea F airline

aeronáutica F aeronautics

aeronave F aircraft

aeropuerto M airport

aerosol M (suspensión) aerosol; (aparato) spray can

aerotransportado ADJ airborne

aerotransportar VT to airlift

afabilidad F affability, friendliness

afable ADJ affable, friendly

afamado ADJ famed

afán M eagerness

afanar VT *fam* to swipe; VI —**se** to work hard

afanoso ADJ hardworking

afasia F aphasia

afear VT to make ugly; —**se** to become ugly

afección F condition

afectación F affectation

afectado ADJ (dañado, lastimado) affected, stricken; (artificial) affected, unnatural

afectar VT to affect

afecto M affection, fondness; **— a** fond of

afectuoso ADJ affectionate, loving

afeitado -da ADJ clean-shaven; M shave

afeitadora F shaver

afeitar VT to shave

afelpado ADJ & M plush

afeminado ADJ effeminate

aferrado ADJ stubborn, obstinate

aferrar VT (agarrar) to grasp; (atar) to grapple; —**se** to cling

affaire M affair

Afganistán M Afghanistan

afgano -na ADJ & MF Afghan, Afghani

afianzado ADJ (garantizado) bonded; (apuntalado, amarrado) secured, firmed up

afianzar[47] VT (una pared) to secure; (un préstamo) to secure, to guarantee; (una amistad) to build up

afiche M poster

afición F (inclinación) inclination; (afecto) fondness; (hinchada) fans

aficionado -da — a fond of; MF (no profesional) amateur; (hincha) fan

aficionarse VI **— a** to become fond of

afilado ADJ sharp; M sharpening

afilador -ora MF grinder, sharpener

afilar VT to sharpen, to grind

afiliación F affiliation; **sin — política** nonpartisan

afiliarse VI **— con** to affiliate oneself with

afín ADJ kindred, related

afinación F tune-up

afinado ADJ in tune

afinador -ora MF tuner

afinar VT (una destreza) to perfect; (un plan) to fine-tune; (un piano) to tune; —**se** to become thinner

afinidad F (afecto) affinity; (parentesco) kinship

afirmación F (aseveración) assertion; (aseveración positiva) affirmation

afirmar VT (decir) to assert, to declare; (aseverar) to affirm; (sujetar) to secure; —**se** to steady oneself

afirmativa F affirmative answer

afirmativo ADJ affirmative

aflicción F affliction, woe

afligir[46] VT (dar dolor) to afflict; (entristecer) to distress

aflojar VT (una soga) to slacken, to loosen; (la vigilancia) to relax; — **el dinero** to hand over the money; VI to ease up, to slack off; —**se** to work loose, to loosen up

afluencia F influx

afluente M tributary

afluir[19] VI (río) to flow [into]; (turistas) to flock

afortunadamente ADV fortunately, luckily

afortunado ADJ fortunate, lucky

afrecho M bran

afrenta F affront

afrentar VT to offend

África F Africa

africano -na ADJ & MF African

afroamericano -na ADJ & MF African American

afrontar VT to face

afuera ADV (de un edificio) outdoors; (de un recipiente) outside; F PL **las —s** outskirts

agachar VT to lower; —**se** to crouch, to stoop

agalla F (de pez) gill; (de roble) gallnut; **tener —s** to have guts/spunk

agarrado ADJ tight-fisted

agarrar VT (sujetar) to seize, to grasp, to grab; (capturar) to catch; (adherirse) to grip; — **por sorpresa** to catch by surprise; —**le la onda a algo** to get the swing of something; —**se una neumonía** to catch a case of pneumonia; —**se** to hold on; —**se de** to latch onto; **agarré por la calle ocho** I took Eighth Street; **agarró y se fue** he up and went

agarre M (también golf) grip

agarrón M grab

agarrotarse VI (el cuerpo) to stiffen up; (un motor) to seize [up]

agasajar VT to entertain

agasajo M (acogida) welcome; (regalo) gift

agazaparse VI to crouch

agencia F agency, bureau; — **de empleo** employment agency; — **de publicidad** advertising agency; — **de viajes** travel agency; — **gubernamental** government agency

agenciar VT to wrangle

agenda F (cuaderno) daily planner; (orden del día) agenda

agente MF (representante) agent; (espía) operative; — **de policía** police officer; — **de compras** purchasing agent

ágil ADJ agile, nimble

agilidad F agility

agilizar VT to expedite

agitación F (acción de agitar, nerviosismo) agitation; (protesta) turmoil, unrest

agitado ADJ (estado) agitated; (vida) eventful, hectic; (mar) choppy; (sueño) uneasy

agitador -ora M (aparato) agitator; MF (rebelde) agitator, troublemaker

agitar VT (sacudir) to agitate, to shake up; (incitar a la protesta) to agitate; —**se** (ponerse nervioso) to get worked up; (moverse) to thrash around

aglomeración F crowd

aglomerado M particle board

aglomerarse VI to crowd together

agnóstico -ca ADJ & MF agnostic

agobiado ADJ (por los enemigos) embattled; (por el trabajo) overwhelmed

agobiante ADJ overwhelming

agobiar VT (con una carga excesiva) to weigh down; (con trabajo) to overwhelm; (con impuestos) to burden

agolparse VI to crowd together

agonía F throes of death; **ser un —s** to be a whiner

agonizante ADJ dying

agonizar[47] VI to be in the throes of death

agorafobia F agoraphobia

agorero -ra ADJ ominous; MF soothsayer

agosto M August; **hacer su —** to make hay while the sun shines

agotado ADJ (persona) worn-out, tired out; (libro) out-of-print; (mercancía) out-of-stock

agotador ADJ exhausting

agotamiento M (de una persona) exhaustion; (de un recurso) depletion

agotar VT (recurso) to exhaust, to use up, to deplete; (energía) to sap; (a una persona) to wear down; —**se** (acabarse) to be all gone; (venderse) to sell out; (secarse) to dry up; (libro) to go out of print

agraciado ADJ attractive

agraciar VT to grace

agradable ADJ (persona) agreeable, pleasant, congenial; (situación) pleasant, enjoyable

agradar VT to please

agradecer[35] VT (dar gracias) to thank; (sentir gratitud) to be grateful for; **se agradece** thank you

agradecido ADJ thankful, grateful

agradecimiento M thankfulness, appreciation; (en un libro) acknowledgment

agradezca, agradezco ver agradecer

agrado M pleasure; **de su —** to his liking

agrandamiento M enlargement

agrandar VT to enlarge

agrario ADJ agrarian

agravar VT to aggravate, to make worse; —**se** to get worse

agraviar VT to outrage

agravio M outrage

agredir[73] VT to assault

agregado -da MF (funcionario de embajada) attaché; (profesor) adjunct; M (mezcla) aggregate

agregar[40] VT to add

agresión F (violencia) aggression; (ataque) assault; — **con lesiones** assault and battery

agresividad F (actitud) aggressiveness; (propensión violenta) aggression

agresivo ADJ aggressive

agresor -ora MF aggressor, assailant

agreste ADJ (recio) rough; (silvestre) wild

agriar[28] VT to make sour; —**se** to go sour

agrícola ADJ agricultural

agricultor -ora MF agriculturist, farmer

agricultura F agriculture, farming

agridulce ADJ (sabor) sweet-and-sour; (memoria) bittersweet

agrietarse VI (cristales) to crack; (los labios) to chap

agrimensor -ora MF surveyor

agrimensura F surveying

agrio ADJ sour

agrisarse VI to gray

agropecuario ADJ agricultural

agrumarse VI to lump

agrupación F group

agrupamiento M grouping

agrupar VT (objetos, personas) to group; (documentos digitales) to queue

agua F water; — **con gas** sparkling water; — **corriente** running water; — **de colonia** cologne; — **de grifo** tap water; — **de manantial** spring water; — **dulce** fresh water; —**marina** aquamarine; — **mineral** mineral water; — **oxigenada** hydrogen peroxide; — **potable** drinking water; — **salada** salt water; —**s abajo** downstream; —**s arriba** upstream; —**s negras** sewer water; **hacer** — *fam* to take a leak; **se me hace** — **la boca** my mouth is watering

aguacate M avocado

aguacero M shower, cloudburst, downpour

aguada F watering hole

aguadero M watering hole

aguado ADJ (fruta) watery; (vino, sopa) watered-down

aguantar VT (miserias) to endure; (a una persona molesta) to bear, to stand; (un peso) to bear; (la respiración) to hold; VI (mantenerse) to stand; (durar) to last; (esperar) to wait; (no pudrirse) to keep; **aguántate** grin and bear it

aguante M (para el trabajo) endurance, stamina; (para el vino) tolerance

aguar[25] VT (añadir agua, despojar de fuerza) to water down; (estropear) to spoil; — **una fiesta** to ruin a party; —**se** to become diluted; MF SG **aguafiestas** killjoy, wet blanket

aguardar VI to wait; VT to wait for, to await

aguardentoso ADJ hoarse

aguardiente M brandy

aguarrás M turpentine

agudeza F (visual) sharpness, keenness; (del ingenio) quickness; (para los negocios) acumen; (dicho agudo) witticism

agudo ADJ (dolor, enfermedad, ángulo) acute; (vista, mente) sharp, keen; (mentón) pointed; (voz) high-pitched; (chiste) witty

agüero M portent, omen; **de mal** — portentous

aguijada F goad

aguijar VT to goad

aguijón M (de planta) spur; (de insecto) sting, stinger

aguijonear VT (a un buey) to goad, to prod; (insecto) to sting

águila F eagle; **es un** — he is sharp

aguilucho M eaglet

aguinaldo M Christmas bonus

aguja F (de coser, tejer, tocadiscos, pino, velocímetro) needle; (de reloj) hand; (riel móvil) railroad switch; (chapitel) steeple, spire; — **de croché** crochet hook; — **de punto** knitting needle; — **de zurcir** darning needle; — **hipodérmica** hypodermic needle; **como una** — **en un pajar** like a needle in a haystack

agujerear VT to pierce

agujero M (orificio) hole; (vacío legal) loophole; (déficit) shortfall; — **negro** black hole; **tapar** —**s** (reparar orificios) to plug holes; (pagar deudas) to pay debts

aguzar[47] VT to sharpen; — **el oído** to prick up one's ears

ahechaduras F PL chaff

ahí ADV there; **por** — over there, thereabouts; **de** — hence; — **te quiero ver** I want to see you in that situation

ahijado -da M godson; F goddaughter

ahínco M **trabajar con** — to work hard

ahogamiento M drowning

ahogar[40] VT (asfixiar en agua) to drown; (inundar con combustible) to flood; (asfixiar por falta de aire) to smother; (reprimir) to stifle; (asfixiar por presión al cuello) to throttle, to strangle, to choke; — **las penas bebiendo** to drown one's sorrows in drink; —**se** (en agua) to drown; (por falta de aire) to asphyxiate

ahogo M (por calor, falta de aire) suffocation; (por un esfuerzo) breathlessness; **vivir sin** —**s** to live a comfortable life

ahondar VT (hoyo) to deepen; (asunto) to dig deeper into; —**se** to become deeper

ahora ADV now; — **bien** now then; — **mismo** right now; — **sí** now we're cooking; **por** — for the present, for now; **hasta** — to date, up to now, so far

ahorcar[30] VT to hang; *fam* to string up

ahorita ADV (ahora mismo) right now; (dentro de poco) in a second

ahorrar VT (dinero) to save; (molestias) to spare

ahorrativo ADJ frugal, thrifty

ahorro M thriftiness; **—s** savings; **—s de toda la vida** life savings

ahuecar[30] VT to hollow out; **— la voz** to speak in a hollow voice

ahumado ADJ smoked; M smoking

ahumar VT to smoke

ahuyentar VT to drive away, to scare away; **—se** to get scared

airado ADJ irate

airarse VI to get angry

airbag M airbag

aire M air; (melodía) tune; (manera de ser) manner; **— acondicionado** air conditioning; **— libre** outdoors; **al — libre** outdoors; **cambiar de —s** to change surroundings; **darse —s** to posture; **en el —** up in the air; **estar en el —** to be on the air; **tener — de** to look like; **tomar —** to breathe in, to get some air

airear VT to air out

airoso ADJ graceful; **salir —** to come out smelling like a rose

aislacionismo M isolationism

aislado ADJ (persona) isolated; (lugar) secluded

aislador M insulator; ADJ insulating

aislamiento M (acción de aislarse) isolation; (cosa que aísla) insulation; (soledad) seclusion

aislante M insulator

aislar[28] VT (separar) to isolate; (envolver) to insulate; (rechazar socialmente) to ostracize

ajar VT (una planta) to wither; (las manos) to make rough; (la piel) to age

ajedrez M chess

ajeno ADJ (de otro) belonging to someone else; (extraño) alien; **— a un peligro** oblivious to a danger; **— a mi voluntad** beyond my control; **— a mi experiencia** foreign to my experience

ajetrearse VI to bustle about

ajetreo M bustle, hustle and bustle

ají M chile

ajo M garlic

ajonjolí M sesame

ajuar M (de novia) trousseau; (mobiliario) furnishings

ajustado ADJ tight, snug; **— a la ley** in accordance with the law

ajustar VT (una prenda) to adjust; (un contrato) to tweak; (una tuerca) to tighten; **— cuentas** to settle accounts; VI to fit tight; **—se a derecho** to be in accordance with the law

ajuste M (de horarios, planes) adjustment; (del cinturón) tightening; (de una máquina) fine-tuning; (de cuentas) settlement; (de una prenda) alteration; **hacer —s** to tinker with

ala F (de ave) wing; (de sombrero) brim; (en fútbol) winger; **cortarle las —s a alguien** to clip someone's wings

alabanza F praise

alabar VT to praise

alabeo M warp

alacena F pantry

alacrán M scorpion

alamar M (adorno) frog; (presilla) clasp

alambique M still

alambrada F wire fence

alambrado M (barrera) wire fence; (acción de alambrar) wiring

alambrar VT to wire

alambre M wire; **— de púas** barbed wire

alameda F poplar grove

álamo M poplar tree

alancear VT to wound with a lance, to spear

alano M mastiff

alarde M show; **hacer — de** to boast of, to show off

alardear VI **— de** to boast about

alargar[40] VT (hacer más largo) to lengthen; (un brazo, un guiso) to stretch [out]; **— la vista** to peer into the distance; **—se** to go on [longer than expected]

alargue M (fútbol) extra time

alarido M scream, howl

alarma F alarm; **— antirrobo** burglar alarm; **— contra incendios** fire alarm

alarmante ADJ alarming

alarmar VT to alarm

alba F dawn

albacea MF executor

albanés -esa ADJ & MF Albanian

Albania F Albania

albañal M sewer

albañil M mason, bricklayer

albañilería F masonry

albaricoque M apricot

albatros M albatross

alberca F (depósito) reservoir; (piscina) *Méx* swimming pool

albergar[40] VT (refugiar) to shelter; (hospedar) to lodge; (ser sede de) to house; (guardar rencor, un secreto) to harbor; **—se** (protegerse) to take shelter; (alojarse) to lodge

albergue M lodging; **dar —** (a un refugiado) to give refuge; (a un criminal) to harbor

albinismo M albinism

albino -na MF albino

albóndiga F meatball

albor M dawn

alborada F dawn

albornoz M bathrobe

alborotador -ora ADJ rowdy; MF troublemaker

alborotar VT (el pelo) to muss; (una casa) to mess up; (una turba) to rouse; (a los niños) to excite; **—se** to get excited

alboroto M hubbub, fuss

alborozado ADJ joyful

alborozar[47] VT to gladden; **—se** to rejoice

alborozo M joy

albricias F PL & INTERJ congratulations

álbum M album

alcachofa F artichoke

alcahuete -ta MF (soplón) tattletale; (mediador, encubridor) procurer

alcaide M warden

alcalde -esa MF mayor

alcaldía F (edificio) city hall; (oficio) mayoralty

álcali M alkali

alcalino ADJ alkaline

alcance M (de una persona) reach; (de los deseos) attainment; (de un misil) range; (de una ley) scope; **de corto[s] —[s]** of meager intellect; **al —** at hand, within reach; **a su —** within his reach; **al — del oído** within hearing; **dar — a** to catch up with; **de gran —** far-reaching; **de largo —** long-range

alcancía F piggybank

alcanfor M camphor

alcantarilla F (para agua sucia) sewer; (para lluvias) gully, gutter

alcantarillado M sewage system

alcanzar[47] VT (llegar, cumplir) to reach; (igualar) to catch up with; (pasar, poner en la mano) to pass; (herir a balazos) to get; **no alcanzo a verlo** I can't quite see it; **no me alcanza el dinero** I don't have enough money; **alcancé a conocer a mi abuela** I was born soon enough to meet my grandmother

alcaparra F caper

alcaucil M artichoke

alcázar M fortress

alce M (europeo, asiático) elk; (norteamericano) moose

alcoba F bedroom

alcohol M alcohol; **— etílico** ethyl alcohol; **— para fricciones** rubbing alcohol

alcohólico -ca ADJ & MF alcoholic

alcoholismo M alcoholism

alcornoque M (árbol) cork tree; (persona) blockhead

alcuza F oilcan

aldaba F (para llamar) knocker; (para cerrar) bolt

aldabón M large knocker

aldea F village, hamlet

aldeano -na MF villager; ADJ **joven aldeana** village girl

aleación F alloy

alear VT (metales) to alloy; VI (aves) to flap wings

aleatorio ADJ random

aleatorizar VT to randomize

aleccionar VT to teach a lesson

aledaños M PL vicinity

alegar[40] VT (aducir) to adduce; (pretender) to claim

alegato M (a favor de) plea; (en contra de) allegation

alegoría F allegory

alegrar VT (a una persona) to gladden; (una fiesta) to brighten up; **—se** to be glad; (por efecto del alcohol) to get tipsy

alegre ADJ (contento) joyful, cheerful, lighthearted; (ebrio) tipsy, lit

alegría F joy, merriment, cheer

alejamiento M (distanciamiento) withdrawal; (separacion de un cargo) dismissal

alejar VT (distanciar) to move away; (ahuyentar) to scare off; **—se** (físicamente) to move away; (emocionalmente) to withdraw

alelar VT to stupefy

alemán -ana ADJ & MF German; M (lengua) German

Alemania F Germany

alentador ADJ encouraging

alentar[1] VT (animar) to encourage, to cheer up; VI to breathe

alergeno/alérgeno M allergen

alergia F allergy

alérgico ADJ allergic

alergólogo -ga MF allergist

alero -ra MF (baloncesto) forward; M eaves

alerón M (de avión) aileron, flap; (de coche) spoiler

alerta ADJ & F alert

alertar VT to alert

aleta F (de pez) fin; (de ballena) fluke; (de buceador, delfín) flipper

aletargado ADJ sluggish, lethargic

aletargarse[40] VI to fall into lethargy, to become lethargic

aletazo M flap of a wing

aletear VI to flap, to flutter

aleteo M flapping, flutter

alevín M small fry

alevosía F treachery

alevoso ADJ treacherous

alfabetismo M literacy; **— digital** computer literacy

alfabetización F literacy; **— digital** computer literacy

alfabetizar[47] VI (enseñar) to teach to read and write; VT (ordenar) alphabetize

alfabeto M alphabet

alfalfa F alfalfa

alfanumérico ADJ alphanumeric

alfarería F pottery

alfarero -ra MF potter

alféizar M windowsill

alfeñique M (golosina) sugar paste; (persona) weakling

alférez MF second lieutenant; **— de fragata** ensign

alfil M bishop

alfiler M pin; **— de corbata** tie tack; **no cabe un —** it's totally full

alfiletero M pincushion

alfombra F (de pared a pared) carpet; (suelta) rug

alfombrar VT to carpet

alfombrilla F (en el suelo) mat; (para ordenador) mouse pad

alforja F saddlebag

alga F seaweed; **—s** algae

algarabía F uproar

algarrobo M locust tree

algazara F merriment

álgebra F algebra

algo PRON something; **— es —** something is better than nothing; **por — será** there must be reason; ADV somewhat, slightly

algodón M cotton; **— de azúcar** cotton candy; **se crió entre algodones** he had a protected childhood

algoritmo M algorithm

alguacil M (de policía) sheriff, marshal; (en un tribunal) bailiff

alguien PRON INDEF somebody, someone; **vino — a hablarte** someone came to talk to you; (en preguntas) anybody, anyone; **¿— lo vio?** did anyone see him?

alguno ADJ some; **—s** some, a few; **sin ruido —** without a sound; **en alguna parte** somewhere; **de alguna manera** somehow; **en algún momento** sometime; **¿lo has visto alguna vez?** have you ever seen him? **¿hay alguna forma de hacer esto?** is there any way to do this? PRON someone, something

alhaja F jewel (también persona); **—s** jewelry

alhajero M jewelry box

alharaca F fuss

alhelí M wallflower

aliado -da ADJ allied; MF ally

alianza F (con amigos, socios) alliance

aliar[28] VT to ally

alias M alias, assumed name; (uso policial) a k a

alicaído ADJ crestfallen

alicates M PL pliers

aliciente M inducement

aliento M (aire respirado) breath; (ánimo) encouragement; **cobrar —** to catch one's breath; **contener el —** to hold one's breath; **sin —** out of breath, breathless

aligerar VT to lighten; **— el paso** to quicken one's pace

alijo M cache, stash

alimentación F (comida) nourishment, food; (acción de dar de comer) feeding; **— intravenosa** intravenous feeding

alimentador M feeder; **— de hojas** paper feeder; **— de impresora** printer feeder

alimentar VT (a una persona) to feed, to nourish; (un fuego) to stoke

alimentario ADJ alimentary; **canal —**

alimentary canal

alimenticio ADJ (nutritivo) nutritious, nourishing; (relativo a los alimentos) alimentary; **industria alimenticia** food industry; **pensión alimenticia** alimony

alimento M food, nourishment

alineación F (deportes) lineup; (coche) alignment; **— a la derecha** right justification; **— a la izquierda** left justification

alinear VT (objetos) to line up; (a un deportista) to put in the lineup; **—se con** to align oneself with

aliño M condiment, seasoning

alisar VT (tela) to smooth; (pelo) to straighten

alistamiento M enlistment

alistar VT to enlist

aliviar VT (aligerar) to lighten; (mitigar) to alleviate, to relieve; (tranquilizar) to relieve; **—se** (mejorarse) to get better; (hacer sus necesidades) to relieve oneself

alivio M relief (también golf); **— de la deuda** debt relief

aljaba F quiver

aljibe M cistern

allá ADV there, over there; **más —** farther, beyond; **el más —** the hereafter; **— tú** that's your problem

allanamiento M raid; **— de morada** forcible entry

allanar VT (la tierra) to level, to smooth; (una dificultad) to iron out; (una casa) to raid; **— el camino** to smooth the way

allegado -da ADJ close to; MF relative

allegar[40] VT to gather; **—se** to arrive

allí ADV (espacial) there; (temporal) then; **por —** through there

alma F soul; **con toda el —** from the bottom of one's heart; **hasta el —** to the bone; **ni un —** not a soul; **no me cabía el — en el cuerpo** I was overjoyed; **se me fue el — al piso** my heart sank

almacén M (depósito) warehouse, storehouse, depot; (negocio) department store; **grandes almacenes** department store

almacenaje M storage

almacenamiento M storage; **— de datos** data storage; **— masivo** mass storage, bulk storage

almacenar VT to store, to stock up on; **— como** to save as

almacenista MF wholesaler

almáciga F nursery

almádena F sledgehammer

almanaque M (anuario) almanac; (calendario) calendar

almeja F clam

almendra F almond

almendro M almond tree

almiar M haystack
almíbar M syrup
almidón M starch
almidonado ADJ (persona) stiff; (camisa) starched
almidonar VT to starch
almirante M admiral
almohada F pillow; **consultarlo con la —** to sleep on it
almohadilla F (para sellos) cushion; (en las patas de los perros) pad; **— eléctrica** heating pad
almohadón M cushion
almohaza F currycomb
almohazar[47] VT to groom
almorranas F PL piles, hemorrhoids
almorzar[49] VT to lunch, to eat lunch
almuerzo M lunch
alocado ADJ wild
áloe M aloe vera
alojamiento M (residencia) lodging, accommodations; (militar) quarters; **— web** web hosting
alojar VT (a un invitado) to lodge, to accommodate; (a unos huérfanos) to house; (a las tropas) to quarter; **—se** (una bala) to lodge; (una persona) to board, to room
alondra F lark
alpaca F alpaca
alpinismo M mountain climbing
alpinista MF mountain climber, mountaineer
alpino ADJ alpine
alpiste M birdseed
alquería F farmhouse
alquilar VT to rent; **se alquila** for rent
alquiler M (pago mensual) rent; (acción de alquilar) renting; **coche de —** rental car; **dar en —** to hire out
alquitrán M tar
alquitranar VT to tar
alrededor ADV around; **— de la casa** around the house; M **—es** (de un área) surroundings; (de una ciudad) outskirts
alta F discharge; **dar de —** to discharge
altamente ADV highly
altanería F haughtiness
altanero ADJ haughty
altar M altar
alteración F alteration; **alteraciones al orden público** public disturbances
alterar VT to alter; **— el ánimo** to upset; **—se** to get upset
altercado M altercation
altercar[30] VT **— con** to quarrel with
alternador M alternator
alternancia F alternation
alternar VT to alternate; **— con** to rub elbows with
alternativa F alternative

alternativo ADJ (cambiante) alternating; (optativo) alternative
alterno ADJ alternate; **alterna y continua** AC/DC
alteza F highness
altibajos M PL ups and downs
altillo M attic
altímetro M altimeter
altiplano M high plateau
altisonante ADJ high-sounding
altitud F altitude
altivez F haughtiness
altivo ADJ haughty
alto ADJ (que está arriba) high; (que tiene altura vertical) tall; **altas finanzas** high finance; **— contraste** high contrast; **de alta calidad** high-quality; **de alta fidelidad** high-fidelity; **de — nivel** high-level; **de alta potencia** high-powered; **de — riesgo** high-risk; **de alta velocidad** high-speed; **en voz alta** aloud; **en — grado** to a great extent; **en alta mar** on the high seas; M **altavoz** loudspeaker; M **altoparlante** loudspeaker; M (altura) height; (piso) upper story; **— el fuego** cease-fire; ADV loud; **hablar —** to talk loud; **cotizarse —** to be set high; INTERJ halt!
altruismo M altruism
altura F (de persona, edificio, ola, epidemia) height; (de avión) altitude; (sobre el nivel del mar, lugar alto) elevation; **a estas —s** at this stage; **a la — de la calle ocho** at Eighth Street; **a la — de las circunstancias** equal to the circumstances
alubia F bean
alucinación F hallucination
alucinar VT (causar alucinaciones) to hallucinate; (fascinar) to fascinate; (deslumbrar) to bowl over; VI (sufrir alucinaciones) to hallucinate
alucinógeno M hallucinogen
alud M avalanche
aludir VI **— a** to allude to, to refer to
alumbrado M lighting; **— público** street lighting; ADJ lit
alumbramiento M childbirth
alumbrar VT encender, to light up; (dar a luz) to give birth to
aluminio M aluminum
alumnado M student body
alumno -na MF (de enseñanza primaria) pupil; (de enseñanza secundaria) student
alusión F allusion
aluvión M (de preguntas, pedidos) barrage; (de personas) flood
alza F appreciation; **— de precios** boost in prices
alzado ADJ elevated; MF insurgent
alzamiento M (acción de alzar) raising;

(insurrección) uprising

alzaprima F crowbar

alzar[47] VT (la mano, la voz, una casa) to raise; (a un niño) to lift up; — **la vista** to look up; —**se** to rise up in rebellion; —**se con** to make off with

amabilidad F kindness; **¿tendría la — de ... ?** would you mind ... ?

amable ADJ kind, nice

amado -da MF beloved

amaestrador -ora MF trainer

amaestramiento M training

amaestrar VT to train

amagar[40] VI/VT threaten; **amagó que iba a llover** it looked like it was going to rain; **amagó con golpearla** he made as if he was going to hit her

amago M **hacer —** to make as if

amague M (baloncesto) fake, juke

amalgamar VT to amalgamate

amamantar VT to nurse, to breast-feed

amanecer[35] VI to dawn; — **enfermo** to wake up ill; **amanecí en Londres** I woke up in London; M dawn, sunrise, daybreak

amanerado ADJ effete

amansar VT to tame

amante MF lover; — **de** fond of

amañar VT (una elección) to rig; (un documento) to tamper with

amapola F poppy

amar VT to love

amargar[40] VT to embitter

amargo ADJ bitter

amargor M bitterness

amargura F bitterness

amarillear VI/VT to yellow, to turn yellow

amarillento ADJ yellowish

amarillo -lla ADJ yellow; MF (esquirol) scab

amarra F cable, rope; —**s** moorings; **soltar —s** to cast off

amarrar VT (un barco) to moor; (una cosa) to secure, to tie down

amartillar VT (pegar con martillo) to hammer; (un arma) to cock

amasar VT (masa) to knead; (una fortuna) to amass

amateur ADJ INV & MF amateur

amatista F amethyst

Amazonas M Amazon River

Amazonia M Amazon Forest

ambages M PL **hablar sin —** to not mince words, to speak plainly

ámbar M amber

ambición F ambition

ambicionar VT to have the ambition to

ambicioso ADJ (emprendedor) ambitious; (codicioso) overambitious

ambidiestro ADJ ambidextrous

ambiental ADJ (limpieza) environmental;

(temperatura) ambient

ambiente ADJ ambient; M (condiciones biológicas) environment; (atmósfera) atmosphere, ambience, ambiance; (sector social) milieu

ambigüedad F ambiguity

ambiguo ADJ ambiguous

ámbito M (ambiente) scene; (alcance) scope; (esfera) sphere

ambivalente ADJ ambivalent

ambos ADJ & PRON both

ambulancia F ambulance

ambulante ADJ itinerant

ambulatorio ADJ ambulatory

ameba F amoeba

amedrentar VT to scare

amén INTERJ amen; **decir —** to approve without discussion; — **de** besides

amenaza F threat, menace

amenazador ADJ threatening

amenazante ADJ threatening

amenazar[47] VT to threaten; — **con** to threaten to

amenidad F (cualidad de ameno) pleasantness

amenizar[47] VI to make entertaining

ameno ADJ enjoyable, entertaining

América F America

americano -na ADJ & MF American; F sport coat

ametrallador -ora MF gunner; F machine gun

ametrallar VT to strafe, to machine-gun

amianto M asbestos

amigable ADJ friendly

amígdala F (faríngea) tonsil; (cerebral) amygdala

amigdalitis F tonsillitis

amigo -ga ADJ friendly; — **de** fond of; — **de lo ajeno** thieving; MF friend

amiguismo M cronyism

aminoácido M amino acid

aminorar VT to lessen

amistad F (relación) friendship; (amigo) friend; **trabar —** to strike up a friendship

amistoso ADJ friendly, amicable

amnesia F amnesia

amniocentesis F amniocentesis

amnistía F amnesty

amo -ma M (de esclavo, sirviente) master; (de animal) owner; F (de esclavo, de sirviente) mistress; (de animal) owner; **ama de leche** wet nurse; **ama de llaves** housekeeper; **ama de casa** homemaker

amodorrado ADJ drowsy

amodorrar VI to make drowsy; —**se** to become drowsy

amolar[5] VT to annoy

amoldar VT to mold

amonestación F admonition, warning

amonestar VT to admonish, to warn

amoníaco M ammonia

amontonamiento M pile

amontonar VT to pile up

amor M love; **— propio** self-esteem; **de mil —es** gladly; **hacerle el — a** to make love to; **por el — de Dios** for God's sake; **por — al arte** unremunerated

amoral ADJ amoral

amoratado ADJ (de golpes) black-and-blue; (de frío, por falta de oxígeno) blue

amordazar[47] VT (a una persona) to gag; (a un perro, a los críticos) to muzzle

amorfo ADJ amorphous

amorío M love affair

amoroso ADJ loving, amorous

amortajar VT to shroud

amortiguador M shock absorber

amortiguar[25] VT (un sonido) to muffle, to absorb; (un golpe) to cushion, to absorb; (un dolor) to deaden, to dull

amortización F (desvalorización periódica) depreciation; (recuperación de una inversión) recovery; (reembolso gradual) amortization, paying off

amortizar[47] VT (recupera a plazos) to amortize; (depreciar) to depreciate

amoscarse[30] VI to get peeved

amostazarse[47] VI to get peeved

amotinarse VI (en un barco) to mutiny; (en una cárcel) to riot

amparar VT (proteger) to protect; (refugiar) to shelter; **—se** to protect oneself

amparo M (protección) protection; (refugio) shelter; **al — de** under the protection of

amperio M ampere

ampicilina F ampicillin

ampliación F (de una foto) enlargement; (de una casa) extension

ampliar[28] VT (una foto) to enlarge; (una calle) to extend; (una explicación) to expand; (un volumen) to amplify; **— una imagen** to zoom in

amplificador M amplifier

amplificar[30] VT (un sonido) to amplify; (una imagen) to magnify

amplio ADJ (información, tiempo) ample; (piso) spacious, roomy; (región, resonancia, sonrisa) broad; (vestido) full; **de amplias miras** open-minded

amplitud F (de comprensión) breadth; (de onda) amplitude

ampolla F (de la epidermis) blister; (vasija) vial

ampollar VT to blister

ampuloso ADJ bombastic

amputar VT to amputate

amueblar VT to furnish

amuleto M amulet, charm

anacronismo M anachronism

ánade M duck

anadear VI to waddle

anadeo M waddle

anaerobio ADJ anaerobic

anal ADJ anal

anales M PL annals

analfabetismo M illiteracy

analfabeto -ta ADJ & MF illiterate

analgésico ADJ & M analgesic

análisis M analysis; **— costo-beneficio** cost-benefit analysis; **— de mercado** market analysis; **— de orina** urinalysis

analista MF analyst

anotación F (béisbol) run; (básquetbol) point; (fútbol americano) touchdown; (glosa) note

analítico ADJ analytical, analytic

analizador M parser

analizar[47] VT (datos) to analyze; (secuencia) to parse

analogía F analogy

analógico ADJ (relativo a la analogía) analogical; (no digital) analog

análogo ADJ analogous

ananá[s] M SG pineapple

anaquel M shelf

anaranjado ADJ & M (color) orange

anarquía F anarchy

anarquista MF anarchist

anatema M anathema

anatomía F anatomy

anatómico ADJ anatomical

anca F haunch, rump

ancho ADJ wide, broad; **a sus anchas** at his ease; **me viene** — it's too wide for me; M width, breadth; **a lo** — widthwise; **tiene un metro de** — it's one meter wide

anchoa F anchovy

anchura F width, breadth

ancianidad F old age

anciano -na ADJ elderly, aged; MF old person

ancla F anchor

anclar VI/VT to anchor

andada F **volver a las —s** to backslide

andador -ora MF walker

Andalucía F Andalusia

andaluz -za ADJ & MF Andalusian; M (dialecto) Andalusian

andamiaje M (para construcción) scaffolding; (fundamento) framework

andamio M scaffold

andanada F broadside; **una — de insultos** a barrage of insults

andante ADJ walking

andanzas F PL adventures

andar[66] VI to walk; (coche, motor, reloj) to run; (el tiempo) to pass; (un aparato) to work; **— con cuidado** to be careful; **— en coche** to travel by car, to ride in a car; **— mal** to be in bad shape, to be a mess; **— mal del corazón** to have heart trouble; **—se por las ramas / con vueltas** to beat around the bush; **no**

—se con rodeos to make no bones about it; **en eso ando** that's what I'm up to; **¡andando!** move on! **¿dónde anda a estas horas?** where is he at this hour? **¡ándale!** *Méx* (apresúrate) come on! (de acuerdo) OK; M gait

andariego ADJ fond of walking

andas F **llevar en** — *RP* to carry on one's shoulders

andén M (de tren) platform; (para peatones) sidewalk

Andes M PL Andes

andino ADJ Andean

Andorra F Andorra

andorrano -na ADJ & MF Andorran

andrajo M rag, tatter

andrajoso ADJ ragged, tattered

andrógino ADJ androgynous

anduve, anduviera, anduviese *ver* andar

anécdota F anecdote

anegar[40] VT to flood

anejo ADJ attached; M accompanying volume

anemia F anemia; **— falciforme** sickle cell anemia; **— por deficiencia de hierro** iron deficiency anemia

anémico ADJ anemic

anestesia F (acción de anestesiar) anesthesia; (sustancia) anesthetic

anestesiar VT to anesthetize

anestésico ADJ & M anesthetic

anestesiología F anesthesiology

anestesiólogo -ga MF anesthesiologist

anestesista MF anesthesiologist

aneurisma M aneurysm

anexar VT (un territorio) to annex; (con una carta) to enclose

anexión F annexation

anexo ADJ attached; M (de un edificio) annex, extension; (a una ley) rider

anfeta F *fam* speed

anfetamina F amphetamine

anfibio ADJ & M amphibian

anfiteatro M amphitheater

anfitrión -ona M host (también informático); F hostess

ángel M angel; **— de la guarda** guardian angel

angelical ADJ angelic

angélico ADJ angelic

angina F **—s** tonsillitis; **— del pecho** angina pectoris; **— laríngea** laryngeal angina

angiocardiografía F angiocardiography

angiograma M angiogram

angioplastia F angioplasty

anglosajón -ona ADJ & MF Anglo-Saxon

Angola F Angola

angolano -na, angoleño -ña, angolés -esa ADJ & MF Angolan

angostar VT to narrow, to contract

angosto ADJ narrow

angostura F (cualidad de angosto) narrowness; (desfiladero) narrows

anguila F eel; **— eléctrica** electric eel

angular ADJ angular

ángulo M (figura geométrica, enfoque) angle; (rincón, esquina) corner; **— muerto** blind spot; **— recto** right angle

anguloso ADJ angular

angustia F (desasosiego) anguish, anxiety, distress; (congoja) heartache; (desazón existencial) angst

angustiado ADJ (desasosegado) anguished, anxious; (acongojado) distraught

angustiante ADJ nerve-wracking

angustiar VT to distress; **—se** to feel distressed

angustioso ADJ distressing

anhelante ADJ longing

anhelar VT to long for, to yearn for

anhelo M longing, yearning

anidar VI to nest

anillas F PL gymnastics rings

anillo M ring; **— de boda** wedding ring; **me queda como — al dedo** it fits me like a glove

ánima F soul of the departed

animación F (viveza) animation, liveliness; (en películas) animation

animado ADJ (vivo) animate; (bullicioso) lively

animador -ora MF (de un espectáculo) host; (de un equipo) cheerleader

animal ADJ & M animal

animar VT (dar vida) to animate, to enliven; (incitar) to encourage, to urge on; (dar aliento) to cheer up; **—se** (alegrarse) to cheer up; (atreverse) to gather courage

ánimo M (espíritu) spirit; (aliento) encouragement; (humor) mood; (intención) intention; **no estoy de — para eso** I'm not in the mood for that; INTERJ hang in there!

animosidad F animosity

animoso ADJ spirited

aniñado ADJ childlike

aniquilar VT to annihilate, to wipe out

anís M anise

aniversario M anniversary

anoche ADV last night

anochecer[35] VI to get dark; **anochecimos en París** night found us in Paris; M nightfall, dusk

anomalía F anomaly

anómalo ADJ anomalous

anonadado ADJ dumbfounded

anonadar VT (aniquilar) to annihilate; (vencer) overwhelm; (desconcertar) to dumbfound; **—se** to become dumbfounded

anónimo ADJ anonymous, nameless; M anonymous letter

anorak M anorak

anorexia F anorexia

anoréxico ADJ anorexic

anormal ADJ abnormal; MF freak

anotación F (nota) annotation, notation; (en fútbol) goal

anotar VT (apuntar) to note; (marcar un tanto) to score; —**se** to sign up

anquilosarse VT (las articulaciones) to become stiff; (una institución) to become stagnant

ansia F (deseo) eagerness; (congoja) anguish

ansiar[28] VT to covet

ansiedad F anxiety

ansioso ADJ (ávido) anxious, eager; (inquieto) fretful

antagonismo M antagonism

antagonista MF antagonist

antagonizar[47] VT to antagonize

antaño ADV in the old days

antártico ADJ antarctic

Antártida F Antarctica

ante PREP before; — **este problema** in the face of this problem; — **todo** above all; M suede

anteanoche ADV night before last

anteayer ADV day before yesterday

antebrazo M forearm

antecedente ADJ & M antecedent; —**s** (profesionales) background; (criminales) record; —**s delictivos** criminal record

antecesor -ora MF (antepasado) ancestor; (predecesor) predecessor

antedatar VT to backdate

antedicho ADJ aforesaid

antelación LOC ADV **con** — beforehand

antemano LOC ADV **de** — beforehand

antena F (de radio) antenna, aerial; (de insecto) antenna, feeler

anteojera F blinder

anteojos M PL glasses, spectacles; — **de sol** sunglasses; — **bifocales** bifocals

antepasado -da MF ancestor, forebear

antepecho M sill

anteponer[56, 74] VT (poner delante, poner antes) to place before; (dar preferencia) to give priority to

anterior ADJ (en el tiempo) previous; (en el espacio) anterior, front; — **a** prior to

anterioridad F **con** — before

anteriormente ADV (antes) previously, formerly; (en la parte delantera) in front

antes ADV (previamente) before, formerly; (más temprano) sooner; **llegó** — he arrived sooner; — **de** before; — **la muerte** I'd rather die; — **bien** rather; — **de impuestos** pretax; — **del cierre** before closing; **lo** — **posible** ASAP, as soon as possible

antesala F (habitación) anteroom; (preludio) prelude; (béisbol) third base

antesalista MF third baseman

antiaborto ADJ INV antiabortion, right-to-life

antiácido ADJ & M antacid

antiaéreo ADJ antiaircraft

antialérgico ADJ antiallergic

antibacteriano ADJ antibacterial

antibalas ADJ INV bulletproof

antibalístico ADJ (misil) antiballistic; (chaqueta) bulletproof

antibiótico ADJ & M antibiotic; — **de amplio espectro** broad-spectrum antibiotic

antibloqueo ADJ INV antilock

anticipación LOC ADV **con** — in advance

anticipado LOC ADV **por** — in advance

anticipar VT (una fecha) to move up; (dinero) to advance; (el porvenir) to anticipate; —**se a los acontecimientos** to jump the gun

anticipo M advance, deposit

anticoagulante M anticoagulant

anticoncepción F contraception

anticonceptivo ADJ & M contraceptive

anticongelante M antifreeze

anticonvulsivo M anticonvulsant

anticuado ADJ antiquated, out-of-date

anticuerpo M antibody

antideportivo ADJ unsportsmanlike

antidepresivo ADJ & M antidepressant

antidiarreico M antidiarrheal

antidiurético M antidiuretic

antídoto M antidote

antieconómico ADJ wasteful

antiespasmódico M antispasmodic

antiestético ADJ unsightly

antígeno M antigen

antigualla F old piece of junk

antiguano -na ADJ & MF Antiguan

Antigua y Barbuda F Antigua and Barbuda

antigüedad F (cualidad de antiguo) antiquity; (objeto) antique; (tiempo en un cargo) seniority

antiguo ADJ (era, historia) ancient; (ropa) old; (mueble) antique; **a la antigua** in the old style; **la antigua capital** the former capital; **más** — with more seniority

antihigiénico ADJ unsanitary

antihistamínico M antihistamine

antiinflamatorio ADJ & M anti-inflammatory

Antillas F PL West Indies

antílope M antelope

antimonio M antimony

antimonopolio ADJ INV antitrust

antioxidante ADJ & M antioxidant

antiparras F PL goggles

antipatía F antipathy

antipático ADJ unfriendly, unkind

antipoliomielítico ADJ antipolio

antipsicótico M antipsychotic

antirreflejante ADJ anti-glare

antisemitismo M anti-Semitism

antiséptico ADJ & M antiseptic

antisocial ADJ antisocial

antítesis F antithesis

antitoxina F antitoxin

antitranspirante M antiperspirant

antitrust ADJ INV antitrust

antiviral M antiviral

antojadizo ADJ whimsical

antojarse VI **se le antojó comer salchicha** he took a notion to eat sausage; **esa tarea se me antoja difícil** that task seems hard to me

antojo M (deseo) whim, craving; (mancha de nacimiento) birthmark

antología F anthology, reader

antónimo M antonym

antorcha F torch

antracita F anthracite

ántrax M anthrax

antro M (bar) dive, joint; — **de perdición** den of iniquity

antropología F anthropology

antropólogo -ga MF anthropologist

anual ADJ annual, yearly

anualidad F annuity; — **variable** variable annuity

anuario ADJ annual; M yearbook

anudar VT to knot; **se le anudó la garganta** he got all choked up

anulación F (de un contrato) cancellation; (de un matrimonio) annulment

anular VT (un matrimonio) to annul; (un contrato, un evento) to cancel; (una sentencia) to overrule, to overturn; (un talón) to void; (un comando de computadora) to undo; — **una selección previa** to deselect; M ring finger

anunciador -ora MF announcer

anunciante MF advertiser

anunciar VT (información) to announce; (un producto) to advertise

anuncio M (de información) announcement; (de un producto) advertisement; — **clasificado** classified advertisement, want ad; — **publicitario** advertisement, ad; **poner un** — to place an ad

anzuelo M fishhook; **morder/picar el** — to take the bait

añadidura F addition; **por** — in addition

añadir VT to add

añejo ADJ aged, vintage

añicos M **hacerse** — to break into a thousand pieces

añil M indigo, bluing

año M year; (de la escuela) grade; (de vino) vintage; — **bisiesto** leap year; — **luz** light-year; **de cuarenta** —**s** aged forty; **del** — **hasta la fecha** year-to-date; **el** — **en curso** the current year; **el** — **pasado** last year; **en los** —**s veinte** in the 1920s; **entrado en** —**s** getting on in years; **¿cuántos** —**s tienes?** how old are you?

añojo -ja MF yearling

añoranza F longing; (del hogar) homesickness

añorar VT to long for, to be homesick for

añoso ADJ old

añublo M blight

aorta F aorta

apabullar VT (impresionar) to bowl over; (derrotar) to crush

apacentar[1] VT to graze, to pasture

apacible ADJ good-natured, laid-back

apaciguar[25] VT (pacificar) to pacify; (aplacar) to mollify, to appease; —**se** to calm down

apadrinar VT to sponsor; (en un bautismo) to act as godfather to; (en una boda) to act as best man for; (en un duelo) to second

apagado ADJ (no llamativo) flat; (no intenso) dull

apagar[40] VT (un fuego) to put out, to extinguish; (una luz) to turn off, to turn out; (motor) to turn off, to kill; (una computadora) to power down; (una vida) to kill, to snuff out; (la sed) to quench; —**se** (luz) to go out; (un color) to fade; (una voz) to trail off; (un volcán) to become extinct

apagón M blackout, outage

apalabrarse VI — **con** to make a verbal agreement with

apalancamiento M leverage

apalear VT to thrash

aparador M sideboard, buffet, cupboard

aparato M (de gimnasia artística) apparatus; (para ejercicio) machine; (de cocina) appliance; (de teléfono) telephone; (máquina, dirigencia política) machine; (boato) pomp; — **circulatorio** circulatory system; — **de televisión** television set; — **ortodóntico** braces; — **ortopédico** leg brace

aparatoso ADJ pompous

aparcamiento M (lugar para aparcar) parking lot; (acción de aparcar) parking

aparcar[30] VI/VT to park; MF SG **aparcacoches** valet

aparcero -ra MF sharecropper

aparear VT (animales) to mate; (calcetines) to match, to pair; —**se** (animales) to mate; (en un baile) to pair off

aparecer[35] VI (ponerse a la vista, publicarse) to appear; (hacer acto de presencia) to show up; **se me apareció un ángel** an angel appeared to me

aparejar VT (un cuarto, un ejército) to prepare; (problemas) to entail; (una embarcación) to rig

aparejo M (de caballo) harness; (de buque) rigging; (para pescar) tackle; —**s** equipment

aparentar VT to feign; VI to show off; **aparenta la edad que tiene** she looks her age

aparente ADJ apparent

aparezca, aparezco ver aparecer

aparición F (fantasma) apparition; (acción de aparecer) appearance

apariencia F (aspecto) appearance; (fingimiento) pretense, semblance; **las —s engañan** appearances are deceiving; **guardar las —s** to keep up appearances

apartado M section; **— postal** post office box; ADJ (recóndito) secluded; (distante) distant; **muy —** far apart

apartamento M apartment

apartamiento M separation

apartar VT (separar) sort out; **aparta las monedas de veinticinco centavos** set aside the quarters; (mover) to move away; **apartó la silla de la pared** he moved the chair away from the wall; (empujar) to push away/aside; **lo apartó de un empujón** she pushed him away; (aislar) to take aside; **lo aparté para hablarle** I took him aside to talk to him; (retirar) to take off; **apartó la cacerola del fuego** she took the pan off the fire; (alejar del cargo) to remove from office; **apartaron al ministro de su cargo** they removed the minister from his post; **apartó la vista** he looked away; **—se** to stray; **se apartaron del buen camino** they strayed from the straight and narrow; **los resultados se apartan de lo esperado** the results depart/deviate from the norm; **se apartó para que no lo atropellara el coche** he got out of the way so the car wouldn't hit him

aparte ADJ separate; ADV **bromas —** kidding aside; **dejar —** to exclude; **punto y —** new paragraph; **aside**; PREP **— de** (además de) besides; (salvo) except for

apasionado ADJ (amor, hombre) passionate; (defensa, comentario) impassioned

apasionante ADJ exciting

apasionar VT **eso me apasiona** I love that; **—se por** to be passionate about

apatía F apathy

apático ADJ apathetic

apear VT to get down; **—se** to dismount

apechugar[40] VI **— con** to put up with

apedrear VT to stone

apegado ADJ attached

apegarse[40] VI to become attached

apego M attachment

apelación F appeal

apelar VI/VT to appeal

apellidarse VI to have the surname of

apellido M surname, last name

apelotonarse VI (una almohada) to ball up; (gente) to bunch together

apenado ADJ (dolorido) grieved; (avergonzado) embarrassed

apenar VT to grieve, to pain; **—se** to be grieved

apenas ADV hardly, scarcely, barely; **— llegó,**

se desmayó no sooner had he arrived than he fainted; **— comienza la reunión** the meeting is just starting

apéndice M (órgano, parte de un libro) appendix; (añadido) appendage

apendicectomía F appendectomy

apendicitis F appendicitis

apercibir VT to warn; **—se** to notice

aperitivo M appetizer

apero M farm implement

apertura F (transparencia) openness; (oportunidad) opening; **a la —** at the opening

apesadumbrado ADJ doleful

apestar VT (hacer heder) to stink up; (causar la peste) to plague; VI to stink, to reek

apestoso ADJ (hediondo) smelly; (apestado) pestilent

apetecer[35] VI **no me apetece ir contigo** I don't feel like going with you

apetecible ADJ appetizing

apetito M appetite

apetitoso ADJ appetizing

apiadarse VI **— de** to pity, to take pity on

ápice M apex; (de la lengua) tip; **no apartarse ni un —** not to diverge a jot

apio M celery

apisonadora F steamroller

apisonar VT to pack down

aplacamiento M appeasement

aplacar[30] VT (a una persona) to appease, to mollify; (miedo) to allay; (sed, pasión) to quench; **—se** to relent

aplanadora F steamroller

aplanamiento M flattening, leveling

aplanar VT (un terreno) to level, to flatten; (con una aplanadora) to roll

aplastado ADJ flattened

aplastamiento M crushing

aplastante ADJ (derrota) crushing; (victoria) sweeping

aplastar VT (achatar) to squash, to crush; (derrotar) to plaster, to stomp; (una revolución) to squelch, to smash, to crush; **—se** to crumple

aplaudir VI/VT to applaud

aplauso[s] M SG/PL applause

aplazamiento M postponement, deferral; (de un proceso legal) continuance

aplazar[47] VT to postpone, to put off

aplicable ADJ applicable

aplicación F (acción de aplicarse) application; (de un castigo) administration; (de computadora) application, app; **— de fondo** background application

aplicado ADJ (conocimiento, ciencia) applied; (trabajador) industrious

aplicador M applicator

aplicar[30] VT to apply; **—se** to work hard, to apply oneself

aplomado ADJ (equilibrado) poised; (vertical) plumb

aplomar VT to plumb

aplomo M poise

apnea M apnea; **— obstructiva del sueño** sleep apnea

apocado ADJ timid

apocalipsis MF (desastre) apocalypse; (Biblia) Revelation

apocamiento M timidity

apocarse[30] VI to become intimidated

apodar VT to nickname

apoderado -da MF proxy, agent

apoderarse VI **— de** to take possession of, to seize

apodo M nickname

apogeo M apogee; **en su —** (una fiesta) in full swing; (un estilo) in its heyday, at its peak

apolillado ADJ (comido por las polillas) moth-eaten; (anticuado) antiquated

apología F apology

apoplejía F apoplexy

aporrear VT to club, to cudgel

aportación F contribution

aportar VT (evidencia) to provide; (dinero) to contribute

aporte M contribution

aposento M chamber

apostador -ora MF bettor

apostar[5] VI/VT (a los caballos) to bet, to wager; (a un centinela) to station, to post; **— por** (caballo) to bet on; (cambio) to commit to

apóstol M apostle

apóstrofe MF apostrophe, invocation

apóstrofo M (ortografía) apostrophe

apostura F bearing

apoyar VT (sostener) to rest; (respaldar) to support, to back; (votar por) to second; (respaldar un argumento) to buttress; **—se en** (recostarse contra) to lean on, to prop against; (basarse en) to be based on; M SG **apoyabrazos** armrest

apoyo M support

apreciable ADJ (digno de aprecio) esteemed; (perceptible) noticeable; (registrable) appreciable

apreciablemente ADV significantly

apreciación F appreciation

apreciado ADJ (amigo) dear; (tesoro) valued, prized

apreciar VT (valorar) to appreciate; (percibir) to notice; (registrar) to measure; (considerar) to take into consideration; (sentir afecto) to cherish; **—se** (un fenómeno) to be noticeable; (moneda) to appreciate

aprecio M appreciation

aprehender VT (a un delincuente) to apprehend; (contrabando) to seize; (una idea) to grasp

aprehensión F (arresto) apprehension; (incautación) seizure

apremiante ADJ pressing

apremiar VT to pressure

apremio M pressure

aprender VI/VT to learn; **— de memoria** to memorize, to learn by heart

aprendiz -za MF (de un oficio) apprentice, trainee; (de una lengua, canto) learner

aprendizaje M (de un oficio) apprenticeship; (acto de aprender) learning

aprensión F apprehension, misgivings

aprensivo ADJ apprehensive

apresar VT (aprisionar) to imprison; (incautar) to seize

aprestar VT to prepare; **—se a** to get ready to

apresurado ADJ hasty, hurried

apresurar VT to hurry, to hasten

apretado ADJ (zapato) tight; (beso) hard; (racimo) compact; (síntesis) succinct; (jornada) busy; (situación) difficult, dangerous

apretar[1] VT (un botón) to press; (un gatillo) to squeeze; (un tornillo) to tighten; (los dientes, puños) to clench; (a un bebé) to clasp; **me apretó para que le diera dinero** he pressured me to give him money; **ese profesor nos aprieta mucho** that teacher demands a lot of us; VI (zapatos) to be tight, to pinch; (sol) to be intense; (esforzarse) to try hard, to bear down; **—se** to crowd together

apretón M squeeze; **— de manos** handshake

aprieta, apriete ver apretar

aprieto M jam, fix, predicament; **en —s** in need, hard-pressed, in dire straits; **estar en un —** to be in a tight spot, to be in trouble, to be in a pickle; **poner en —s** to embarrass

aprisa ADV quickly

aprisco M (para el ganado) fold

aprisionar VT to trap

aprobación F (aceptación) approval; (adopción, promulgación) passage, adoption; (calificación) passing grade; **— de crédito** credit approval

aprobar[5] VT (una medida, una opinión) to approve of; (una ley) to pass, to approve; (un examen) to pass; (un crédito) to sign off on; VI to pass

aprontar VT to ready

apropiación F appropriation; **— indebida** embezzlement

apropiadamente ADV properly, appropriately

apropiado ADJ appropriate, suitable

apropiarse VT **— de** to appropriate

aprovechable ADJ usable

aprovechado ADJ opportunistic

aprovechamiento M use

aprovechar VT (una ocasión) to take advantage of; (el espacio) to utilize; (la enseñanza) to profit from; VI to be useful; —**se de** to take advantage of; INTERJ **¡que aproveche!** enjoy your meal!

aproximación F (acercamiento) approach; (estimado) rough estimate

aproximado ADJ approximate

aproximar VT to bring near; —**se** to approach; —**a** to approximate

aprueba, apruebe *ver* aprobar

aptitud F aptitude; —**es musicales** musical aptitude

apto ADJ apt, suitable; —**para menores** for general audiences

apuesta F bet, wager

apuesto ADJ good-looking

apuntalar VT to prop up, to shore up

apuntar VT (señalar) to point out; (dirigir sobre un blanco) to aim; (matricular) to enroll; (escribir) to write down, to note; (ayudar a un actor) to prompt; (marcar puntos) to score; VI (una flecha) to point; (canas) to sprout; —**a un blanco** to aim at a target; **me apunto para ir con vosotros** I'm game to go with you

apunte M notation; —**s** notes; **tomar —s** to take notes; **llevar el —a alguien** to pay attention to someone

apuñalar VT to stab

apurado ADJ (situación) difficult; (persona) in dire straits; (apresurado) in a hurry

apurar VT (consumir) to drink up; (apremiar) to put under pressure; —**se** *Am* to hurry

apuro M predicament, fix; (prisa) hurry; **estar en —s** to be in distress

aquejado ADJ stricken

aquejar VT to afflict, to trouble

aquel ADJ that; **aquella chica se llama María** that girl is named María; **aquellas ciudades son antiguas** those cities are old; PRON that one; —**es el mayor** that one is the oldest; **aquellos son mis hijos** those are my children; **de mis dos hijos, Juan y Pedro, este es gordo y —es flaco** of my two sons, Juan and Pedro, the latter is fat and the former is thin; **en/por —entonces** back then

aquí ADV here; **está por —** it is around here; **ven por —** come this way; **hasta —** this far; **de —a cuatro horas** four hours from now; **de —en adelante** from now on; **de —para allá** to and fro, back and forth; —**y ahora** here and now

aquietar VT to quiet; —**se** (los nervios) to calm down; (una tormenta) to subside

ara LOC ADV **en —s de** for the sake of

árabe MF (persona) Arab; M (caballo) Arabian; (lengua) Arabic; ADJ (caballo) Arabian; (costumbre, arte) Arab

Arabia Saudí, Arabia Saudita F Saudi Arabia

arácnido M arachnid

arado M plow

Aragón M Aragon

aragonés -esa ADJ Aragonese; MF (persona) Aragonese; M (dialecto) Aragonese

arancel M (impuesto) tariff; (lista de honorarios) list of fees

arancelario ADJ **acuerdo —** tariff agreement

arándano M blueberry; —**rojo** cranberry

arandela F washer

araña F (arácnido) spider; (candelabro) chandelier

arañar VT (rayar) to scratch; (herir con garras) to claw, to scratch; (raspar) to scrape, to score

arañazo M scratch

arañero M warbler

arar VI/VT to plow, to till

arbitraje M arbitration

arbitrar VT (un desacuerdo) to arbitrate; (un partido) to referee, to officiate; (un partido de béisbol) to umpire

arbitrariedad F (acción) arbitrary action; (cualidad) arbitrariness

arbitrario ADJ arbitrary

arbitrio M (libre albedrío) free will; (capricho) whim; (decisión) discretion; (deseos) wishes

árbitro -tra MF (del buen gusto) arbiter; (de conflictos) arbitrator; (de encuentros deportivos) referee

árbol M tree; (mástil) mast; —**de Navidad** Christmas tree; —**de levas** camshaft; — **genealógico** family tree

arbolado ADJ woody, wooded

arboleda F grove, clump

arbóreo ADJ arboreal

arbusto M shrub, bush

arca F ark; —**de Noé** Noah's ark; **las —s municipales** municipal coffers

arcada F arcade, archway; **tener/dar —s** to gag

arcaico ADJ archaic

arcaísmo M archaism

arcano ADJ arcane

arce M maple [tree]

arcén M shoulder of a road

archienemigo -ga MF archenemy

archipiélago M archipelago

archisabido ADJ very well-known

archivado ADJ on file

archivador M filing cabinet

archivar VT (guardar en un archivo) to file; (arrumbar) to shelve

archivo M (repositorio de documentos) archive; (fichero de ordenador) file; (acción de archivar) filing; —**comprimido** compressed file; —**cookie** cookie; — **corrupto** corrupted file; —**de datos** data file; —**de lectura/escritura** read/write file

arcilla F clay

arco M (geométrico, eléctrico) arc; (estructura

arquitectónica) arch; (arma, varilla de violín) bow; — **iris** rainbow

arder VT to burn; **la cosa está que arde** things are really getting hot; **el trigo se ardió** the wheat spoiled

ardid M scheme, artifice

ardiente ADJ (deseo) ardent; (calor, fuego, deseo) burning

ardilla F squirrel; — **de tierra** gopher; — **listada** chipmunk

ardite M **no valer un —** not to be worth a penny

ardor M (de pasión) ardor; (de fuego) heat; (por ácido) burning; — **de estómago** heartburn

arduo ADJ arduous, grueling

área F area; — **de penales** (fútbol) penalty area, box

arena F (tierra) sand; (plaza) arena; — **movediza** quicksand

arenero M sandbox

arenga F harangue

arengar[40] VT to harangue

arenisca F sandstone

arenisco ADJ sandy

arenoso ADJ sandy

arenque M herring

arete M earring

argamasa F mortar

Argelia F Algeria

argelino -na ADJ & MF Algerian

Argentina F Argentina

argentino -na ADJ Argentine, Argentinian; (como la plata) silvery; MF Argentine, Argentinian

argolla F iron ring

argón M argon

argot M slang

argucias F PL trickery

argüir[20] VT to argue

argumentar VT to argue

argumento M (razonamiento) argument; (conjunto de sucesos) plot

aridez F dryness

árido ADJ (seco) arid, dry, barren; (aburrido) dry; —**s** dry goods

ariete M (militar) battering ram; (fútbol) center forward

arisco ADJ surly

arista F (borde) edge; (de trigo) beard; **limar** —**s** to overcome difficulties

aristocracia F aristocracy

aristócrata MF aristocrat

aristocrático ADJ aristocratic

aritmética F arithmetic

aritmético ADJ arithmetical

arma F (instrumento bélico) arm, weapon; (división del ejército) branch; — **blanca** sharp weapon; — **de fuego** firearm; **a las** —**s** to arms; **de** —**s tomar** resolute; **tomar las**

—**s** to take up arms

armada F armada, fleet

armado ADJ armed; **a mano armada** at gunpoint; M assembly, putting together

armador -ora MF (naviero) shipowner; (en fútbol) playmaker; (en vóleibol) setter

armadura F (cobertura de hierro) armor; (de un edificio) framework; (de gafas) frame; (de música) key signature

armamento M armament

armar VT (proveer de armas) to arm; (abastecer una embarcación) to equip; (reforzar) to reinforce; (ensamblar) to assemble, to put together; (levantar una tienda de campaña) to pitch; — **jaleo** to whoop it up; — **relajo** to make a mess; —**se de** to arm oneself with; — **una pendencia** to pick a fight, to start a quarrel

armario M (de ropa) wardrobe, closet; (de cocina) cabinet, armoire

armatoste M unwieldy object

armazón MF framework, skeleton

Armenia F Armenia

armenio -nia ADJ & MF Armenian

armería F (depósito) armory; (tienda) gun shop

armiño M ermine

armisticio M armistice

armonía F harmony

armónico ADJ & M harmonic

armonioso ADJ harmonious

armonizar[47] VI/VT to harmonize, to blend

ARN [ácido ribonucleico] M RNA

arnés M harness

aro M (de rueda) rim; (de baloncesto) hoop; **no tocó ni —** it was an airball

aroma M (olor agradable) aroma; (del vino) bouquet

aromático ADJ aromatic

arpa F harp

arpía F shrew

arpillera F burlap

arpón M harpoon

arponear VT to harpoon

arqueado ADJ arched

arquear VT to arch

arqueología F archaeology

arqueológico ADJ archaeological

arquero -ra MF (tirador de flechas) archer; (guardametas) goalkeeper

arquetipo M archetype

arquitecto -ta MF architect

arquitectónico ADJ architectural

arquitectura F architecture

arrabal M outlying slum

arraigar[40] VT to take root

arrancar[30] VT (una planta) to uproot; (el pelo) to tear out; (un diente) to pull; (un vicio) to eradicate; (una flor) to pick; (una confesión) to extract; — **de** to wrest from; VI/VT (un vehículo) to start; **arrancó para el valle** he took off for the valley; **arrancó a sudar** he began to sweat; **sus problemas arrancan de su niñez** his problems are rooted in his childhood; **—se los cabellos** to tear one's hair [out]

arranque M (proceso de arrancar) starting; (dispositivo para arrancar) starter; (decisión, empuje) gumption; **— de ira** fit of rage

arrasar VT (destruir) to level, to raze; (derrotar) to crush; **— con** to obliterate; VI to crush

arrastrado ADJ wretched

arrastrar VT (mover por el suelo) to drag; (llevarse consigo) to sweep away; (atraer) to draw; (soportar) to bear; (pronunciar lentamente) to draw out; **— los pies** (moverse con dificultades) to shuffle; (ser renuente) to stall; VI (cortinas) to hang down to the floor; **—se** (una serpiente) to slither; (una lagartija, un insecto) to crawl; (una persona) to grovel; **— y soltar** to drag and drop, to drag and release; M SG **arrastrapiés** shuffle

array M array

arrayán M myrtle

arrear VT to drive, to herd

arrebatar VT (quitar) to snatch away, to wrest away; (quemar) to burn on the outside; **—se** to have a fit

arrebatiña F mad scramble

arrebato M fit, outburst

arreciar VI to increase in intensity

arrecife M reef

arreglar VT (poner en orden, concertar, adaptar música) to arrange; (ordenar) to tidy up; (reparar) to fix, to repair; (resolver) to settle; **— cuentas** to settle accounts; **ya te arreglo** I'll fix you; **—se** (embellecerse) to fix oneself up; (llevarse bien con) to get along with; (entablar relaciones amorosas) to start dating; (reconciliarse) to make up; (conformarse) to make do; (despejarse) to clear up; **arreglárselas** to cope, to manage

arreglo M arrangement; **con — a** in accordance with; **no tiene —** it can't be helped; **llegar a un —** to settle; **—s** alterations

arrellanarse VI to lounge, to loll

arremangado ADJ turned up, rolled up

arremangar[40] VT to roll up; **—se** to roll up one's sleeves, to knuckle down

arremeter VI to attack; **— contra** to lunge at

arremetida F thrust, lunge

arremolinarse VT (viento) to whirl around; (agua) to eddy

arrendajo M bluejay

arrendamiento M rental

arrendar VI/VT to rent, to lease; **se arrienda** for lease

arrendatario-ria MF tenant

arreo M adornment; **—s** tack, harness

arrepentido ADJ repentant, rueful

arrepentimiento M (contrición) repentance; (disgusto) regret

arrepentirse[8] VI (de los pecados) to repent; (de los errores) to regret

arrestar VT to arrest

arresto M arrest

arriar[28] VT (la bandera) to lower; (un cabo) to slacken

arriate M flower bed

arriba ADV above; **¡—! ¡**get up! **¡— las manos!** stick 'em up! **¡— Juan!** long live Juan! **de — abajo** from top to bottom; **lleno hasta —** full to the brim; **te vas para —** you are doing well; **viven —** they live upstairs

arribar VI LIT to arrive; (buque) to put into port

arribista MF social climber

arribo M LIT arrival

arriendo M leasing, rental

arriero-ra MF animal driver

arriesgado ADJ (peligroso) risky; (valiente) daring

arriesgar[40] VT to risk; **—se** to take a chance

arrimar VT (acercar) to bring near; (golpear) to strike; **—se a** (apoyarse) to lean on; (acercarse) to get near

arrinconar VT (acorralar) to corner; (poner en un rincón) to put in a corner; (abandonar) to abandon

arritmia F arrhythmia

arrobamiento M rapture

arrobarse VI to be enraptured

arrodillarse VI to kneel

arrogancia F arrogance

arrogante ADJ arrogant

arrogarse[40] VT to claim

arrojadizo ADJ for throwing

arrojar VT (lanzar) to throw, to hurl; (expulsar) to throw out; (botar) to throw away; (vomitar) to throw up, to vomit; (proyectar una luz) to shed, to throw; **— un saldo de** to show a balance of; **—se** to hurl oneself

arrojo M boldness, daring

arrollador ADJ overwhelming

arrollar VT (enrollar) to roll up; (arrastrar) to run over; (derrotar) to defeat

arropar VT (con ropa) to wrap up; (en la cama) to tuck in; **—se** to pull up the covers

arroyo M stream, creek

arroz M rice; **— integral** brown rice

arrozal M rice field

arruga F wrinkle

arrugar[40] VT to wrinkle; **— el ceño** to knit one's brow; **—se** (pasar a tener arrugas) to get wrinkles; (asustarse) to be afraid

arruinar VT (estropear) to ruin; (destruir) to destroy, to ravage; (aguar) to spoil; (dejar en la quiebra) to bankrupt, to ruin; **—se** to go to ruin

arrullar VI (una paloma) to coo; VT (a un enamorado) to whisper sweet nothings to; (a un niño) to rock to sleep, to lull to sleep

arrullo M (de la tórtola) cooing; (del agua) babbling

arrumbar VT (arrinconar) to put aside; (marginalizar) to marginalize

arsenal M (depósito) arsenal; (astillero) navy yard

arsénico M arsenic

arte M SG art; F PL arts; M (destreza) skill, ability; (actividad manual) craft; **bellas —s** fine arts; **el — por el —** art for art's sake; **malas —s** wiles; **no tener ni — ni parte en algo** to have nothing to do with something; **por — de** by means of; **por — de magia** by magic

artefacto M (aparato) contrivance, device; (bomba) bomb

arteria F artery

arterial ADJ arterial

arteriosclerosis F arteriosclerosis

artero ADJ artful, wily

artesanía F (trabajo, obra) craft; (habilidad) craftsmanship

artesano -na MF artisan; M craftsman; F craftswoman

ártico ADJ arctic

articulación F (acción de articular) articulation; (juntura) joint

articular VT (pronunciar) to articulate, to enunciate; (unir) to join

artículo M (de revista) article; (de diccionario) article, entry; **— de fondo** editorial; **— definido** definite article; **hacer el —** to give a sales pitch

artífice MF (autor) architect; M (artesano) craftsman; F craftswoman

artificial ADJ artificial

artificio M artifice

artificioso ADJ affected, contrived

artillería F artillery

artillero -ra MF (militar) gunner; (en fútbol) striker

artimaña F trick, wile

artista MF (plástica) artist; (drama, música) performer

artístico ADJ artistic

artritis F arthritis

artroscopia F arthroscopy

artroscópico ADJ arthroscopic

artrosis F degenerative joint disease

Aruba F Aruba

arveja F pea

arzobispo M archbishop

arzón M saddletree

as M ace (también atleta)

asa F handle

asado ADJ roasted; M (carne asada) roast; (carne

asada al aire libre) barbecue; (acción de asar) roasting

asador -ora M spit; MF barbecue cook

asalariado -da MF wage earner

asaltante MF mugger

asaltar VT (a una persona) to assault, to assail; (un banco) to hold up; (con preguntas) to assail; **—le a uno una idea** to be struck by an idea

asalto M (ataque) assault; (de un banco) holdup, stickup; **tomar por —** to storm

asamblea F assembly, gathering

asar VT to roast; **— a la parrilla** to grill; **— con adobo** to barbecue

asbesto M asbestos

ascendencia F ancestry

ascendente ADJ (que incrementa) ascending, rising; (que sube) upward

ascender² VT (a un empleado) to promote; (una montaña) to climb; VI to ascend; **— a** to amount to

ascendiente MF ancestor

ascenso M (acción de ascender) ascent; (en el trabajo) promotion

ascensor M elevator

asceta MF ascetic

ascético ADJ ascetic

ascienda, asciende *ver* ascender

asco M disgust, revulsion; **hacer —s a** to reject; **me da —** it makes me sick, it disgusts me; **ese hombre está hecho un —** that man is a mess; **su acné me da —** his acne is a turnoff

ascórbico ADJ ascorbic; **ácido —** ascorbic acid

ascua F ember; **estar en —s** to be on pins and needles; **tener a alguien en —s** to string someone along

aseado ADJ well-groomed

asear VT to clean up

asediar VT to besiege

asedio M siege

asegurable ADJ insurable

asegurador -ora MF underwriter

asegurar VT (una victoria) to assure; (una frontera, una cerradura) to secure; (con un contrato de seguros) to insure; **—se [de]** to make sure [of]; **te lo aseguro** I assure you

asemejarse VI **— a** to resemble

asentaderas F PL buttocks

asentamiento M (de una comunidad) settlement; (de un edificio) settling

asentar VT (datos) to enter; (una población) to establish; **—se** (posarse) to settle; (madurar) to settle down

asentimiento M assent, acquiescence

asentir⁸ VI to assent, to acquiesce; **— con la cabeza** to nod

aseo M (acción de asearse) cleaning; (cualidad de aseado) cleanliness; (cuarto de baño) bathroom; (servicio) toilet, restroom

aséptico ADJ aseptic

asequible ADJ (disponible) available; (barato, económico) affordable

aserción F assertion

aserradero M sawmill, lumber mill

aserrado ADJ serrated; M sawing

aserrar[1] VT to saw

aserrín M sawdust

aserto M assertion

asesinar VT to murder; (a una figura pública) to assassinate

asesinato M murder, killing; (de una figura pública) assassination

asesino -na ADJ murderous; MF killer, murderer; (de una figura pública) assassin; — **en serie** serial killer

asesor -ora MF consultant, advisor/adviser

asesoramiento M (profesional, legal) consulting, advising; (académico) counseling; — **de crédito** credit counseling

asesorar VT to advise

asesor -ora MF aide

asestar VT — **un golpe** to inflict/deal a blow

aseveración F assertion

aseverar VT to assert

asexual ADJ asexual

asfalto M asphalt

asfixia F suffocation, asphyxiation, asphyxia

asfixiar VT to suffocate, to smother

así ADV so, thus, like this; — — so-so; — **como** in the same way that; — **de grande** that big; — **que** so that; ¿— **que no vienes?** so you're not coming?

Asia F Asia

asiático -ca ADJ & MF Asian

asidero M hold; **eso no tiene — en la realidad** that has no basis in reality

asiduo ADJ (lector) assiduous; (cliente) steady

asiento M (lugar donde sentarse, parte de una silla, válvula) seat; (de nóminas) entry, record; **tomar** — to take a seat

asignación F (acción de asignar) assignment; (acción de dar fondos) appropriation; (lo asignado) allotment; (pago) allowance

asignar VT (una tarea) to assign; (fondos) to allot, to allocate, to earmark

asignatura F subject

asilado -da MF inmate; — **político -ca** political refugee

asilar VT (a un político) to give asylum to; (un animal) to shelter

asilo M (para los perseguidos) asylum; (para huérfanos, ancianos) home

asimétrico ADJ asymmetric, asymmetrical

asimilar VT (vitaminas, un grupo étnico) to assimilate; (información) to absorb

asimismo ADV likewise

asintomático ADJ asymptomatic

asir[50] VT to grasp, to grip; —**se a** to hold onto

asistencia F (presencia, personas presentes) attendance; (ayuda) assistance, aid; (servicio de averías) roadside assistance; (deporte) assist; — **médica** health care; — **social** (ayuda) welfare; (profesión) social work

asistente -ta ADJ assistant; MF assistant, helper; — **social** social worker

asistir VT — **a** (estar presente) to attend; (ayudar) to help, to assist

asma F asthma

asmático ADJ asthmatic

asno M ass, donkey

asociación F association; — **de propietarios** homeowners' association

asociado -da MF associate

asociar VT to associate; —**se** to join; —**se con** to fall in with

asolamiento M desolation

asolar VT to desolate, to devastate

asomar VI to show; VT to poke out, to stick out; —**se a** to look out

asombrar VT to astonish, to amaze, to astound; —**se** to be astonished

asombro M astonishment, amazement

asombroso ADJ astonishing, amazing

asomo LOC ADV **ni por** — by no means

asonancia F assonance

aspa F (de hélice) blade; (de ventilador) vane

aspartamo M aspartame

aspecto M (faceta) aspect, feature; (apariencia) looks

aspereza F roughness, harshness; **con** — sharply; **limar** —**s** to smooth over disagreements

áspero ADJ (terreno, mano) rough; (lucha) bitter; (tiempo, voz) harsh

aspiración F (ambición) aspiration, ambition; (respiración) breathing in; (succión) suction

aspiradora F vacuum cleaner

aspirante MF applicant, candidate

aspirar VT (inhalar) to breathe in, to inhale; (a un empleo) to apply for; — **a** to aspire to

aspirina F aspirin

asqueado ADJ disgusted

asquear VT to disgust

asquerosidad F nastiness; **¡estás hecho una** —! you're gross!

asqueroso ADJ nasty, disgusting, gross

asta F (de toro) horn; (de ciervo) antler; (de bandera) flagpole; (de lanza) shaft; **a media** — at half mast

asterisco M asterisk, star

asteroide M asteroid

astigmatismo M astigmatism

astilla F (de madera) chip, splinter; (de vidrio) sliver; —**s** kindling

astillar VT to chip, to splinter

astillero M shipyard

astringente ADJ & M astringent

astro M (del cielo) celestial body; (de cine) movie star

astrofísica F astrophysics

astrología F astrology

astronauta MF astronaut

astronáutica F astronautics

astronomía F astronomy

astronómico ADJ (relativo a las estrellas) astronomic(al); (muy elevado) astronomic, astronomical

astrónomo -ma MF astronomer

astucia F (listeza) cunning, guile; (treta) trick

asturiano -na ADJ & MF Asturian; (dialecto) Asturian

Asturias F SG Asturias

astuto ADJ shrewd, wily, cunning

asueto M (día libre) day off; (licencia) time off

asumir VT (una responsabilidad) to assume, to shoulder; (una mala noticia) to accept; — **un cargo** to take office

asunción F assumption; — **presidencial** presidential inauguration

asunto M (cuestión) matter; (tema de una obra) theme

asustadizo ADJ easily frightened, jumpy

asustado ADJ frightened, scared

asustar VT to frighten, to scare; —**se** to become frightened

atacante ADJ attacking; MF assailant

atacar[30] VT to attack, to assault; —**se de risa** to have a laughing fit

atado M bundle

atadura F sin —s with no strings attached

atajador M tackle

atajar VT (interrumpir) to cut off; VI (cortar camino) to take a shortcut

atajo M shortcut

atalaya F watchtower

atañer[15, 73] VI to concern, to pertain to

ataque M (de violencia, asma) attack; (de rabia, de tos) fit; (de epilepsia) seizure; (en fútbol americano) offensive series; — **cardíaco** heart attack; — **de nervios** nervous breakdown; — **relámpago** blitz

atar VT (sujetar) to tie, to bind; — **cabos** to put two and two together; —**se los zapatos** to tie one's shoes

atardecer[35] VI to get dark; M late afternoon, dusk, evening; **al** — at dusk

atareado ADJ busy

atarearse VI to busy oneself

atascadero M (lodazal) quagmire; (de tránsito) bottleneck

atascado ADJ stuck

atascar[30] VT (un tubo) to stop up; (una máquina) to jam; (el tráfico) to obstruct; —**se** (un vehículo) to get stuck; (una máquina) to get jammed

ataúd M coffin, casket

ataviar[28] VT to attire, to array; —**se** to dress up

atavío M attire, garb

ateísmo M atheism

atemorizar[47] VT to frighten

atención F attention; (médica) care; (acto de cortesía) courtesy; — **al cliente** customer care; — **médica a largo plazo** long-term care; — **prenatal** prenatal care; — **primaria** primary care; **a la** — **de** to the attention of; **llamar la** — (hacer notar) to call attention; (ser llamativo) to attract attention; (interesar) to interest; INTERJ watch out!

atender[2] VT (a un enfermo) to take care of, to look after; (una súplica) to heed; (a un cliente) to serve; (el trabajo) to attend to, to take care of; VI — **a** to pay attention to

atenerse[58] VI — **a los hechos** to bear the facts in mind, to limit oneself to the facts; — **a la ley** to abide by the law

atentado M (asesinato) assassination; (ataque fracasado) assassination attempt; (con bomba) bombing; **un** — **contra** an affront to

atentamente ADV (con atención) attentively; (despedida en cartas) yours truly / yours sincerely

atentar[1] VI — **contra la vida de alguien** to make an attempt on someone's life

atento ADJ (que presta atención) attentive; (amable) thoughtful

atenuar[26] VT (la violencia) to attenuate; (una luz) to dim; —**se** to abate

ateo -a MF atheist

aterciopelado ADJ velvety

aterido ADJ stiff with cold

aterirse[73] VI to become stiff with cold

aterrador ADJ terrifying

aterrar VT to terrify

aterrizaje M landing; — **forzoso** crash landing

aterrizar[47] VI/VT to land

aterrorizar[47] VT (intimidar) to terrorize; (dar miedo) to terrify

atesorar VT (memorias) to treasure; (dinero) to hoard

atestado ADJ crowded, crammed

atestar VT (certificar) to attest to; (llenar) to jam, to pack

atestiguar[25] VT to bear witness, to testify

atiborrar VT to stuff; —**se** to stuff one's face

atienda, atiende ver atender

atiesar VT to stiffen

atildado ADJ spruced up

atinar VT (acertar) to hit the mark; (adivinar) to guess right; **no** — **a decir palabra** not to manage to get a word out

atípico ADJ atypical

atisbar VT (mirar con disimulo) to peek at, to peep at; (vislumbrar) to catch a glimpse of; VI to peek

atisbo M glimpse, hint

atizar[47] VT (fuego) to poke, to stoke; (pasiones) to stir up, to stoke

atlántico ADJ Atlantic; M **Océano Atlántico** Atlantic Ocean

atlas M atlas

atleta MF athlete

atlético ADJ athletic

atletismo M track and field

atmósfera F atmosphere

atmosférico ADJ atmospheric

atolladero M quagmire

atolondrado ADJ scatterbrained; (muchacha) ditsy

atómico ADJ atomic

atomizador M atomizer

atomizar[47] VT to atomize

átomo M atom

atónito ADJ dumbfounded

atontado ADJ stupefied

atontar VT to stupefy

atorar VT to jam; **—se** to choke

atormentar VT to torment; **—se por** to agonize over

atornillar VT to bolt

atracadero M dock

atracar[30] VT (amarrar) to dock; (robar) to hold up, to mug; **—se** to gorge oneself

atracción F attraction

atraco M holdup, stickup

atracón M **darse un —** to gorge

atractivo ADJ attractive, fetching; M (capacidad de atraer) attractiveness, appeal; (cosa que atrae) attraction; **— sexual** sex appeal

atraer[59] VT to attract

atragantarse VI to choke

atraiga, atraigo, atrajo, atrajera, atrajese *ver* atraer

atrancar[30] VT to bolt, to bar

atrapada F catch

atrapar VT (en una trampa) to trap, to ensnare, to catch; (una pelota, el interés) to catch

atrás ADV **— de la casa** behind the house; **cuatro años —** four years back; **hacia —** backward; **para —** back/backwards; **quedarse —** to fall behind

atrasado ADJ (de tiempo) late; (en el pago) in arrears, behind; (país) backward; (un libro de biblioteca) overdue; **tengo sueño —** I'm behind in my sleep; **el reloj anda —** the clock is slow; **feliz cumpleaños —** belated happy birthday

atrasar VT (un plazo) to delay; (un objeto) to push back; (un reloj) to turn back; VI (un reloj) to run slow; **—se** to fall behind, to lag

atraso M (condición de atrasado) backwardness; (pago) back payment; (de trabajo) backlog; **con dos meses de —** two months in arrears

atravesar[1] VT (cruzar) to cross; (estar tendido) to span; (penetrar) to impale, to run through; **— un momento difícil** to go through a difficult moment; **se me atravesó un caballo** a horse crossed in front of me; **—se en la cama** to lie crossways in bed

atraviesa, atraviese *ver* atravesar

atrayendo *ver* atraer

atreverse VI to dare, to go for it; **¡atrévete!** go for it!

atrevido ADJ (audaz) bold, daring; (insolente) insolent

atrevimiento M (cualidad de atrevido) boldness, daring, audacity; (acción atrevida) daring act

atribución F attribution; **atribuciones** powers

atribuir[19] VT (imputar) to attribute, to ascribe; (conferir) to confer; VI **—se** to claim

atribular VT to distress; **—se** to be distressed

atributo M attribute

atribuya, atribuye, atribuyendo, atribuyera, atribuyese *ver* atribuir

atril M stand

atrincherar VT to entrench

atrio M atrium

atrocidad F atrocity

atrofia F atrophy

atrofiar VT to atrophy, to stunt

atronador ADJ thunderous, deafening

atronar[5] VI to make a racket

atropellar VT (a un peatón) to run over, to run down; (los derechos de alguien) to trample upon

atropello M (arrollamiento) running over; (ultraje) outrage; (abuso) trampling

atroz ADJ (modales, crimen) atrocious; (dolor) excruciating; (ofensa) grievous

atuendo M getup

atún M tuna

aturdido ADJ bewildered; **estar —** to be in a daze

aturdimiento M bewilderment

aturdir VT to bewilder, to daze

atusar VT to smooth, to fix

audacia F audacity, boldness

audaz ADJ audacious, bold

audible ADJ audible

audición F audition; **— radial** radio program

audiencia F (tribunal) court; (público) audience; (en un pleito, proceso legal) hearing

audífono M (para sordos) earphone; (para música) headphone

audio M audio; **—libro** audio book

audiología F audiology

audiovisual ADJ audiovisual; M audiovisual presentation

auditar VI/VT to audit

auditivo ADJ auditory

auditor -ora MF auditor

auditoría F (revisión) audit; (trabajo de auditor)

auditing

auditorio M (público) audience; (local) auditorium

auge M (del mercado) boom; (de una moda) heyday; (de una carrera) peak

augurar VT to foretell; **no — nada bueno** not to bode well

aula F (de clase) classroom; (de conferencia) lecture hall

aullar VI to howl

aullido M howl

aumentar VT to augment, to increase; **— los salarios** to raise pay; VI (precios) to rise, to escalate; (población) to grow; (violencia) to escalate

aumento M increase; (de expectativas) buildup; (de población) growth; (de precios) rise, upturn; (de peso) gain; **— por mérito** merit raise; **— salarial / de sueldo** pay raise

aun ADV even; **— así** even so; **— cuando** even though/if

aún ADV still

aunque CONJ though, although

aura F aura

áureo ADJ golden

aureola F halo

auricular M (de teléfono) receiver; **—es** headphones, earphones

aurora F dawn, aurora; **— boreal** aurora borealis, northern lights

auscultar VT to listen to with a stethoscope

ausencia F absence

ausentarse VT to absent oneself

ausente ADJ absent, missing

ausentismo M absenteeism

auspicios M PL auspices

austeridad F austerity

austero ADJ austere, stern

Australia F Australia

australiano -na ADJ & MF Australian

Austria F Austria

austríaco -ca ADJ & MF Austrian

autenticar[30] VT to authenticate

autenticidad F authenticity

auténtico ADJ authentic

autismo M autism

autista ADJ autistic

auto M (coche) auto; (orden judicial) writ; **— de choques** bumper car

autoadhesivo M decal; (para el parachoques) bumper sticker

autoayuda F self-help

autobiografía F autobiography

autobomba M RP fire engine

autobús M bus

autocine M drive-in movie theater

autocompasión F self-pity

autocontrol M self-control

autócrata MF autocrat

autóctono ADJ indigenous

autodestructivo ADJ self-destructive

autodeterminación F self-determination

autodisciplina F self-discipline

autoedición F desktop publishing

autoescuela F driving school

autoestima F self-esteem

autogobierno M self-government

autogol M own goal

autógrafo M autograph

autoimagen F self-image

automático ADJ automatic

automatización F automation

automatizar[47] VT (mecanizar) to automate; (hacer automáticamente) to do automatically

automóvil M automobile

automovilista MF motorist

automovilístico ADJ automotive

autonomía F autonomy; (de un vehículo) range

autonómico ADJ autonomic

autónomo ADJ (independiente) autonomous, independent; (que trabaja por su cuenta) self-employed; (que se presenta solo) stand-alone

autopista F freeway, turnpike; **— de la información** information superhighway

autopropulsado ADJ self-propelled

autopsia F autopsy

autor -ora MF author

autoridad F authority

autoritario ADJ (tiránico) authoritarian; (respetado) authoritative

autorización F authorization

autorizar[47] VT (permitir) to authorize; (dar propiedad intelectual) to license

autosatisfacción F self-satisfaction

autoservicio M (sistema de venta) self-service; (tienda) convenience store

autosuficiencia F self-reliance

autosuficiente ADJ (independiente) self-sufficient; (presumido) smug

autovía F freeway

auxiliar VT to help; ADJ auxiliary; MF assistant; **— de vuelo** flight attendant

auxilio M help

avalancha F avalanche

avalar VT to guarantee, to cosign

avaluar[26] VT to appraise

avalúo M appraisal

avance M (acción de avanzar, adelanto) advance, headway; (sinopsis de película) trailer

avanzada F scouting party

avanzado ADJ advanced

avanzar[47] VI (ir hacia adelante) to advance; (progresar) to make headway; **a medida que avanzaba la mañana** as the morning progressed; VT (un vehículo) to move forward; (una grabación) to fast-forward

avaricia F avarice

avariento ADJ avaricious, miserly

avaro ADJ miserly, avaricious

avasallar VT to subjugate

avatar M (vicisitud) vicissitude; (encarnación de un dios, personaje digital) avatar

ave F bird; **— de corral** poultry; **— de rapiña** bird of prey; **— canora** songbird; **— zancuda** wading bird

avecindarse VI to take up residence

avellana F hazelnut

avellano M hazel

avena F oats

avenencia F agreement

avenida F avenue

avenir[61] VI to reconcile; **—se a** to come around to; **—se bien** to get along

aventadora F fan, blower

aventajar VT (ser mejor) to be superior to; (sobrepasar) to get ahead of

aventón M **dar un —** *Méx* to give a lift

aventura F (suceso) adventure; (relación amorosa) fling, affair

aventurado ADJ (arriesgado) risky; (atrevido) daring

aventurar[23] VT (arriesgar) to risk; (sugerir) to venture; **—se a** to dare to

aventurero -ra ADJ adventurous; MF adventurer

avergonzado ADJ (tímido) abashed; (arrepentido) ashamed, embarrassed

avergonzar[23] VT to shame, to embarrass; **—se** to be ashamed/embarrassed

avería F (de frutas) damage, bruise; (de coche) breakdown, mechanical trouble

averiado ADJ (un coche) broken-down; (un televisor) on the blink; (un ascensor) out of service; (fruta) bruised, damaged

averiarse[28] VI (fruta) to become damaged; (un coche) to break down

averiguar[25] VT to find out, to ascertain

aversión F aversion, dislike

avestruz MF ostrich

avezado ADJ seasoned

aviación F aviation

aviador -ora MF aviator

aviar[28] VT to fix

avidez F eagerness

ávido ADJ eager, avid

avinagrado ADJ sour

avinagrar VT to sour; **—se** to become sour

avío M tidying up; **—s de pescar** fishing tackle

avión M (máquina) airplane; (ave) martin; **— comercial** airliner; **— a reacción** jet airplane; **— caza** fighter airplane

avisar VT (notificar) to advise; (alertar) to alert

aviso M notice; **— publicitario** advertisement; **estar sobre —** to be forewarned; **poner sobre —** to forewarn; **sin previo —** without warning

avispa F wasp

avispado ADJ (despierto) lively; (inteligente) smart

avisparse VI to wise up

avispero M wasp's nest; **alborotar el —** to stir up a wasp's nest

avispón M hornet

avistar VT to catch sight of

avivar VT (una llama) to fan; (una fiesta) to enliven; (un fuego, un debate) to fuel

avizorar VT to spy on

axila F underarm

ay INTERJ (de dolor) ouch; (de decepción) oh, no; (de sorpresa desagradable) oh; **¡— de mí!** poor me; **¡ay, no!** oh, no!

ayer ADV yesterday

ayuda F (asistencia) help; (después de una catástrofe) relief; **— en línea** online help

ayudante -ta MF assistant, helper, aide; **— de médico** physician's assistant

ayudantía F assistantship

ayudar VT to help, to aid

ayunar VI to fast

ayunas F PL **en —** (antes de comer) without having eaten; (despistado) clueless; **estoy en — I** am fasting

ayuno M fast, fasting

ayuntamiento M (gobierno) municipal government; (edificio) city hall

azabache M jet; ADJ jet-black, raven

azada F hoe

azadón M hoe

azafato -ta MF (en aviones) flight attendant; (en ferias) host

azafrán M saffron

azahar M orange blossom

azar M chance; **al —** by chance, at random

azaroso ADJ (arriesgado) risky; (aleatorio) random

azerbaiyano -na, azerbaijano -na ADJ & MF Azerbaijani, Azerbaijanian

Azerbaiyán F Azerbaijan

azogar[40] VT to silver

azogue M (sustancia) quicksilver, mercury; (niño inquieto) restless child; **tener — en el cuerpo** to be restless

azorar VT (alarmar) to alarm; (avergonzar) to embarrass

azotaina F flogging

azotar VT (con azote) to whip, to lash, to flog; VI/ VT (el viento) to whip, to buffet; (el sol) to beat down; (la lluvia) to sting

azote M (instrumento) whip; (golpe) lash; (aflicción) scourge; (golpe de viento) buffet

azotea F flat roof

azteca ADJ, MF Aztec

azúcar MF sugar; **— moreno -na** brown sugar

azucarar VT to sugar

azucarera F (fábrica) sugar mill; *Am* (recipiente)

sugar bowl

azucarero M sugar bowl

azucena F white lily

azufre M sulfur, sulphur

azul ADJ blue; — **acero** steel blue; — **celeste** sky blue; — **claro** light blue; — **marino** navy blue

azulado ADJ bluish

azular VT to color blue

azulear VI (tener color azul) to be blue; (ponerse azul) to become blue; VT (dar color azul) to color blue

azulejar VT to tile

azulejo M tile

azuzar[47] VT (a un perro) to sic; (a una persona) to egg on

Bb

baba F drivel, drool, slobber; (de un caracol, de agua estancada) slime; **se le cae la — por el coche nuevo** he's drooling over the new car

babear VI to drivel, to drool

babero M bib

babor M portside

babosa F slug

babosear VI/VT to slobber [on]

baboso ADJ (caracol) slimy; (persona que babea) driveling; (persona tonta) idiotic; (adulador) fawning

babuino M baboon

baca F luggage rack

bacalao M cod

bache M (pozo) pothole; (momento) bad time; (de aire) air pocket

bacheado ADJ bumpy

bachiller -ra M (graduado) high school graduate; (alumno) high school student

bachillerato M baccalaureate

bacilo M bacillus

backgammon M backgammon

bacteria F bacteria

bacteriano ADJ bacterial

bacteriología F bacteriology

badajo M bell clapper

badana F sheepskin

bagaje M baggage

bagatela F trifle

bagazo M pulp

Bahamas F PL Bahamas

bahameño -ña ADJ & MF Bahamian

bahía F (geography) bay; (computer) slot

Bahrein M Bahrain

bahreiní ADJ & MF Bahraini

bailador -ora MF folk dancer; ADJ dancing

bailar VI/VT to dance; **me bailan los pantalones** my pants are falling off; **me tocó — con la más fea** I was left holding the bag; **que me quiten lo bailado** I enjoyed it anyway

bailarín -ina MF dancer

baile M (actividad) dance; (fiesta) dance, ball; — **aeróbico** aerobic dance; — **de máscaras** masked ball; — **folklórico** folk dance; — **zapateado** clog dance

bailongo M hop

bailotear VI to dance around

baivel M bevel

baja F (de temperatura, presión) drop; (de precios) decline; (de guerra) casualty; (del ejército) discharge, dismissal; (del trabajo) leave; **dar de —** to discharge; **darse de —** to call in sick

bajada F (acción de bajar, pendiente) descent; (de un caballo) dismount; — **contra-reloj** downhill ski race

bajar VI (descender) to go down; (correr) to run down; (de un árbol) to climb down; (de un caballo) to get down; (de un ómnibus) to step off, to get off; (en calidad) to worsen; (la marea) to ebb; (una creciente) to subside; VT (las escaleras) to go down; (un avión de un tiro) to shoot down; (comida con agua) to wash down; (la cabeza) to lower; (un cargamento) to let down; (el volumen) to turn down; (focos) to dim; (la voz) to lower, to soften; (los precios) to cut; — **de categoría** to demote; — **el cursor** to scroll down; — **en picado** to dive; **—se los pantalones** to pull down one's pants

bajeza F (cualidad) baseness; (acción) vile act

bajío M shoal

bajista ADJ (bolsa) bearish; MF (músico) bassist

bajo ADJ (nubes, estante, precio, voz grave) low; (persona) short; (voz débil) soft; (río) lower; (vista, persianas) lowered; (acto) base; **baja espalda** small of the back; **de baja calidad** low-end; **de baja ley** base; **de — precio** low-cost; **de — presupuesto** low-budget; **de —s ingresos** low-income; PREP under; — **contrato** under contract; — **control** under control, in hand; — **cuerda** under-the-table; — **fianza** on bail; — **fuego** under fire; — **sospecha** under a cloud; — **tierra** underground; **poner — llave** to lock up; **por lo —** under one's breath; M (en un coro, contrabajo) bass; (de pantalón) cuff; **hacer los —s** to cuff; ADV low

bala F (de pistola) bullet; (atletismo) shot; (de cañón) ball

balada F ballad

baladí ADJ trivial

balance M (cálculo) balance; (documento)

balance sheet; (número de víctimas) toll; (movimiento) sway; **hacer un —** to take stock

balancear VT to swing; VI to sway; **—se** to sway

balanceo M (de un cuerpo) swinging, swing; (de un barco) rolling, roll

balancín M seesaw

balanza F scale; **— comercial** balance of trade; **— de pagos** balance of payments

balar VI to bleat

balasto M ballast

balazo M (disparo) shot; (herida) bullet wound

balbucear VI (un adulto) to stammer; (un bebé) to babble

balbuceo M (tartamudeo) stammer; stammering; (de bebé) babble, babbling

balcón M balcony

balde M pail, bucket; **de —** gratis; **en —** in vain

baldear VT to flush

baldío ADJ (terreno) fallow; (acción) useless

baldosa F (en una casa) floor tile; (en una calle) flagstone

balido M bleat, bleating

balística F ballistics

balístico ADJ ballistic

ballena F (animal) whale; (para corsé) whalebone

ballenato M whale calf

ballet M ballet

balneario M (de veraneo) seaside resort; (con aguas medicinales) spa

balón M ball; **baloncesto** basketball; **balonmano** handball; **— de angioplastia** angioplasty balloon; **se le fue el —** (fútbol americano) he fumbled; (fútbol) he lost the ball; M **balonvolea** volleyball

balsa F (embarcación) raft, balsa; (lago) pond

bálsamo M balsam, balm

baluarte M bulwark, stronghold

bambolear VT to sway, to swing; **—se** to sway, to swing

bamboleo M swinging, swaying

bambú M bamboo

banal ADJ banal; **una respuesta —** a pat answer

banana F banana

banano M (tree) banana tree; (fruit) banana

banca F (industria) banking; (en el juego) bank; **— electrónica** e-banking; **— en línea** online banking; **— por internet** Internet banking

bancario-ria ADJ bank, banking; MF banker

bancarrota F bankruptcy

banco M (establecimiento) bank; (asiento) bench; (de peces) school; (de arena) shoal, spit; (de suplentes) bench; **— de datos** data bank; **— de niebla** fog bank; **Banco Mundial** World Bank

banda F (de músicos) band; (cinta ancha, también de computadora) band; (cinta de vestido) sash; (de delincuentes) gang, band, ring; (dibujo) stripe; (de neumático) tread; (lindero) side, edge, border; (de un barco) side; (en deporte) sideline; **— ancha** broadband; **— de frecuencia** frequency band; **— horaria** time slot; **— magnética** magnetic strip; **— sonora** soundtrack

bandada F (de aves) flock, flight; (de peces) school

bandeja F tray; **me lo sirvieron en —** [**de plata**] they served it to me on a silver platter

bandera F flag; **jurar la —** to pledge allegiance to the flag

banderín M pennant

banderola F pennant

bandido-da MF (delincuente) bandit, outlaw; (niño terrible) rascal

bando M (decreto) edict; (partido) camp

bandolero-ra MF bandit

Bangladesh M Bangladesh

bangladeshí, bangladesí ADJ & MF Bangladeshi

banjo M banjo

banquero-ra MF banker

banqueta F (taburete) stool; (acera) *Méx* sidewalk

banquete M banquet

banquetearse VI to feast

banquillo M bench (también en fútbol)

bañar VT (a un bebé) to bathe; (una torta) to ice, to frost; **—se** (en una bañera) to take a bath; (en el mar) to swim

bañera F bathtub

bañista MF bather

baño M (acción) bath; (cuarto) bathroom, lavatory; (de torta) icing, frosting; **darse un —** (bañarse) to take a bath; (nadar) to take a swim; **— de asiento** sitz bath; **— de esponja** sponge bath; **— [de] María** double boiler; **— de remolino** whirlpool bath; **— de sangre** bloodbath

bar M bar

barahúnda F ruckus, racket

baraja F pack/deck of cards

barajada F shuffle

barajar VI/VT (naipes) to shuffle; (alternativas) to weigh

baranda F railing, guard rail

barandal M banister

barandilla F rail, railing

barata F *Méx* sale

baratear VT to sell cheap

baratija F trinket, knickknack

barato ADJ cheap

baratura F cheapness

barba F beard; **—s** whiskers; **hacer algo en las —s de alguien** to do something right under someone's nose

barbacoa F barbecue

barbadense ADJ & MF Barbadian

barbado ADJ bearded

Barbados M Barbados

barbaridad F atrocity; **una — de** a lot of; **¡qué —!** what nonsense!

barbarie F savagery

bárbaro -ra ADJ (salvaje) barbarous, barbaric; (estupendo) cool, super; MF barbarian

barbecho M fallow land

barbería F barbershop

barbero -ra MF barber

barbilla F chin

barbitúrico M barbiturate

barbudo ADJ bearded

barca F rowboat

barcaza F barge

barco M boat; **— petrolero** oil tanker

bardo M bard

bario M barium

barítono ADJ & M baritone

barlovento M windward

barniz M (para madera) varnish; (para cerámica) glaze; (de cultura) veneer

barnizar[47] VT (madera) to varnish; (cerámica) to glaze

barómetro M barometer

barón M baron

barquero -era M boatman; F boatwoman

barquillo M rolled wafer

barquinazo M **dar —s** to lurch

barra F (de hierro, arena, chocolate, en un bar) bar; (en gimnasia) crossbar; (signo ortográfico) slash; **— de estado** status bar; **— de herramientas** toolbar; **— de jabón** bar of soap; **— de menú** menu bar; **— de tareas** task bar; **— espaciadora** space bar; **— invertida** backslash

barrabasada F mischief

barraca F (de feria) stall, stand; (casucha) hovel; (depósito) shed

barracuda F barracuda

barranca M ravine

barranco M gully, ravine

barrena F (de un taladro) bit; (de un avión) tailspin; **entrar en —** to go into a tailspin

barrenar VT to drill

barredora F sweeper

barrendero -ra MF street sweeper

barrer VI/VT (pasar escoba) to sweep; (derrotar) to defeat decisively; M SG **barreminas** minesweeper

barrera F (protección) barrier; (valla) barrier, bar; **— arancelaria** tariff barrier; **— comercial** trade barrier; **— de coral** barrier reef; **— del sonido** sound barrier

barrica F vat

barricada F barricade

barrida F sweep

barrido M (acción de barrer) sweeping; (movimiento) sweep

barriga F (abdomen) belly; (panza) paunch; **rascarse la —** to do nothing

barrigón ADJ potbellied

barril M barrel, keg, drum

barrio M neighborhood, quarter; **— residencial** residential neighborhood; **—s bajos** slums

barritar VI to trumpet

barro M (lodo) mud; (arcilla) clay; (acné) pimple; **de —** earthen

barroco ADJ & M baroque

barroso ADJ muddy

barrote M bar

barruntar VT to suspect

barrunto M suspicion

bártulos M PL stuff

barullo M hubbub

basal ADJ basal

basalto M basalt

basar VT to base; **—se en** (depender de) to rely on; (fundamentar en) to be based on

basca F nausea

báscula F scale

base F (apoyo, área militar, en química, en béisbol) base; (punto de partida) basis; (de maquillaje) foundation; (de una campaña) plank; MF (baloncesto) point guard; **—s de concurso** contest rules; **— de datos** database; **— de lanzamiento** launching pad; **con — en** on the basis of; **en —a** on the basis of; **las —s** (de un partido) base, grass roots; (de un sindicato) rank and file; **salario — base** salary; **tener una — sólida** to be on a strong footing; **—s llenas** (béisbol) bases loaded; **— por bolas [intencional]** [intentional] base on balls

basic M (lenguaje de programación) BASIC

básico ADJ (fundamental) basic; (sin lujos) no-frills, bare-bones

básquet M basketball

básquetbol M basketball

bastante ADJ & PRON enough, sufficient; **tiene bastante dinero como para ser feliz** she has enough money to be happy; ADV (suficientemente) enough; **me lo has dicho bastante** you've told me that enough times; (mucho) quite a lot; **la herida me duele bastante** my injury is hurting a lot; (algo) quite, pretty; **la película estuvo bastante bien** the movie was quite good

bastar VI to be enough, to suffice; **¡basta!** enough!

bastardilla F italics

bastedad F coarseness

bastidor M (de teatro) wing; (para bordado) frame; (de coche) chassis; (de ventana) sash; **entre —es** (en teatro) offstage; (en privado) behind the scenes

bastimentos M PL provisions

basto ADJ coarse, crude; M suit in the Spanish deck of cards

bastón M cane, walking stick; **— de esquí** ski pole

basura F rubbish, garbage, trash

basural M *Am* dump

basurero -ra MF (persona) garbage collector; M (lugar) dump

bata F (para llevar en casa) robe, housecoat; (de laboratorio) lab coat; (de pacientes) hospital gown; **— de baño** bathrobe

batahola F racket, din

batalla F battle; (de un carro) wheelbase; **— naval** sea battle; **ropa de —** everyday clothing; **trabar —** to engage in battle

batallar VI to battle

batallón M battalion

batata F sweet potato

bate M baseball bat; **al —** at bat

batea F tray

bateador -ora MF batter; **— ambidiestro -ra** switch hitter; **— designado -da** designated hitter; **— emergente** pinch hitter

batear VT to bat, to hit; **— un jonrón** to hit a homerun; **— un sencillo** to hit a single

batería F (de coche, artillería, béisbol) battery; (de cocina) pots and pans; (musical) drums; **— de iones de litio** lithium-ion battery

baterista MF drummer

batiburrillo M hodgepodge

batido M shake, milk shake

batidor M whisk, beater

batidora F mixer

batintín M gong

batir VT (una alfombra) to beat; (un terreno) to comb; (mantequilla) to cream, to churn; (un récord) to break; (huevos) to beat; (crema) to whip; (alas) to flap, to beat; **— palmas** to clap, to applaud; **—se en duelo** to duel; **—se en retirada** to retreat

batuta F baton; **llevar la —** to call the shots

baudio M baud

baúl M trunk

bautismo M baptism, christening; **— de fuego** baptism of fire

bautizar[47] VT to baptize, to christen

bautizo M christening, baptism

baya F berry

bayeta F cleaning cloth

bayo ADJ bay

bayoneta F bayonet

baza F card trick; **meter — en una conversación** to participate in a conversation

bazar M bazaar

bazo M spleen

bazofia F slop

bazuca F bazooka

beagle M beagle

beato ADJ (bendito) blessed; (piadoso) beatified; (santurrón) overly pious

bebé M baby, infant

bebedero M (en un corral) drinking trough; (en el campo) watering hole; (para personas) water fountain

bebedor -ora MF drinker

beber VI/VT to drink

bebercio M *fam* booze

bebida F drink, beverage

beca F scholarship, fellowship

becario -ria MF scholar, fellow

becerro M (animal) calf; (piel) calfskin

becuadro M natural sign

befa F jeer

befar VT to jeer at

beicon M *Esp* bacon

beige ADJ & M beige

béisbol M baseball

beisbolista M baseball player

beldad F beauty

belga ADJ & MF Belgian

Bélgica F Belgium

Belice M Belize

beliceño -ña ADJ & MF Belizean

bélico ADJ warlike

belicoso ADJ (guerrero) bellicose; (peleador) feisty

beligerante ADJ & MF belligerent

bellaco M rascal, scoundrel

bellaquería F mischief

belleza F beauty

bello ADJ beautiful

bellota F acorn

bemol M (música) flat; **tener —es** to be tricky

bencina F benzine

bendecir[51] VT to bless

bendición F (parte de la misa) benediction; (acción de bendecir) blessing; (beneficio) boon, blessing

bendito ADJ (agua) holy; (alma) blessed; **— sea** may he be blessed; **dormir como un —** to sleep like a log; **es un —** he is a saint

benefactor -ora MF benefactor, patron

beneficencia F charity; **— pública** welfare

beneficiar VT to benefit; **—se de** to benefit from

beneficiario -ria MF (de una herencia, perdón, acto de bondad) beneficiary; (de un cheque) payee

beneficio M benefit (también espectáculo); **—s adicionales** perks; **—s por fallecimiento** death benefits

beneficioso ADJ beneficial

benéfico ADJ beneficent

benemérito ADJ worthy of esteem

benevolencia F benevolence

benévolo ADJ benevolent

bengala F flare

bengalés -esa ADJ & MF Bangladeshi

benigno ADJ benign

Benín M Benin

beninés -esa ADJ & MF Beninese

benjamín -ina MF youngest child

beodo ADJ drunk

berbiquí M carpenter's brace

berenjena F eggplant

bermejo ADJ reddish

bermellón M vermilion

berrear VI (animal) to bellow, to bawl; (bebé) to squall

berrido M (de animal) bellowing, bawling; (de bebé) squall, squalling

berrinche M tantrum

berro M watercress

berza F cabbage

besar VT to kiss

beso M kiss

bestia F beast

bestial ADJ bestial

best-seller M best seller

besuquear VT to kiss repeatedly; **—se** to make out

betabel M *Méx* beet

betabloqueador M beta blocker

betabloqueante M beta blocker

betún M shoe polish

Biblia F Bible

bíblico ADJ biblical

bibliografía F bibliography

biblioteca F (edificio) library; (anaquel) bookcase

bibliotecario -ria MF librarian

bicarbonato M bicarbonate; **— de sosa/soda** bicarbonate of soda

bíceps M SG bicep[s]

bicho M (insecto) bug (también en informática); (animal) *fam* critter; **— raro** odd bird; **mal —** creep; **¿qué — te ha picado?** what's gotten into you? **—s** vermin

bici F bike

bicicleta F bicycle; **— de montaña** mountain bike; **— estática** stationary bike

bicúspide ADJ bicuspid

biela F connecting rod

Bielorrusia F Belarus

bien ADV well; **—aventurado** blessed; **— arreglado** well-groomed; **— conocido** well-known; **— hecho** well-made, well-done; **— poco** very little; **agarrarse —** to hold on tight; **ahora —** now then; **apretar —** to press hard; **está —** she is fine; **más —** rather; **me doy — cuenta** I'm perfectly aware; **pues —** now; **qué —** how wonderful; **si —** although; **ya está —** that's enough; M good; **—es** property, assets; **—es**

consumibles consumable goods; **—es inmuebles** real estate; **—es muebles** personal property; **—es raíces** real estate; **—estar** well-being, welfare; **—hechor** benefactor; **persona de —** a good person; INTERJ OK!

bienio M biennium

bienvenida F welcome

bienvenido ADJ welcome

bifurcación F (en un camino) fork, forking; (en un programa de computadora) branch

bifurcarse[30] VI to fork, to branch off

bigamia F bigamy

bigote M (de hombre) mustache; (de animal) whisker

bikini M bikini

bilateral ADJ bilateral

bilingüe ADJ & MF bilingual

bilingüismo M bilingualism

bilis F bile

billar M (juego) billiards, pool; (mesa) pool table

billete M (de viaje, para espectáculos) ticket; (de banco) bill, banknote; (financiero) note; **— de ida solo** one-way ticket; **— de ida y vuelta** return ticket

billetera F billfold

billón M trillion

bimestral ADJ bimonthly

bimestre M two-month period

binario ADJ binary

bingo M bingo

binomial ADJ binomial

binomio M binomial

biodegradable ADJ biodegradable

biofeedback M biofeedback

biografía F biography

bioingeniería F bioengineering

biología F biology

biológico ADJ biological

biólogo -ga MF biologist

biombo M folding screen

biopsia F biopsy

bioquímica F biochemistry

biorritmo M biorhythm

biotecnología F biotechnology

bipartidista ADJ bipartisan

bipolar ADJ bipolar

birlar VT *fam* to pinch, to swipe

Birmania F Burma

birmano -na ADJ & MF Burmese, from Myanmar

birrete M mortarboard

bis M encore

bisabuelo -la M great-grandfather; F great-grandmother

bisagra F hinge

bisecar[30] VT to bisect

biselado ADJ beveled

biselar VT to bevel

bisemanal ADV biweekly

bisiesto ADJ año — leap year

bisnieto -ta M great-grandson; F great-granddaughter

bisonte M bison, buffalo

bistec M beefsteak

bisturí M scalpel

bisutería F costume jewelry

bit M bit

bizarría F gallantry

bizarro ADJ gallant

bizco ADJ cross-eyed

bizcocho M (pastel) sponge cake; (pastelillo) pastry

bizcochuelo M sponge cake

bizquear VI to be cross-eyed

black-jack M blackjack

blanca ADJ half note

blanco ADJ (color) white; (tez) fair; M (color) white (también clara de huevos, ojos); (de tiro) target; (de una burla) butt; — **fácil** sitting duck; **dar en el** — to hit the target; **en** — (hoja de papel, mente) blank; (sin dormir) sleepless; **en** — **y negro** in black and white

blancura F whiteness; (de tez) fairness

blancuzco ADJ whitish

blandir VT to brandish, to wield

blando ADJ (sin dureza, sin rigor) soft; (sensiblero) mushy

blandura F softness

blanqueador ADJ whitening; M bleach, whitener

blanquear VT (una pared) to whitewash; (dinero) to launder; (verduras) to blanch; —**se** to whiten

blanquecino ADJ whitish

blanqueo M whitening

blasfemar VI to blaspheme

blasfemia F blasphemy

blasón M coat of arms

blasonar VI to boast

blazer M blazer

blindado ADJ armored

blindaje M armor

blindar VT to armor

bloc M writing tablet, pad of paper

blog M blog

bloguear VI to blog

bloguero -ra MF blogger

bloque M block (también de motor, político); (edificio) building; **en** — together

bloquear VT (carretera, asalto, pase, virus digital) to block; (puerto) to blockade; (cuentas bancarias) to freeze; —**se** to choke

bloqueo M (deporte) block; (computadoras) block, blocking; (militar) blockade

blues M PL blues

bluff M bluff

blusa F blouse, top

boa F boa constrictor

boato M pomp

bobada F (tontería) foolish act; (fruslería) trifle

bobalicón -ona ADJ goofy; MF nincompoop

bobear VI to fool around, to monkey around

bobería F (cualidad) foolishness; (dicho) foolish remark; (hecho) foolish act

bobina F (de hilo) bobbin; (de alambre, de coche) coil; (de película) reel

bobinar VT to reel

bobo -ba ADJ (tonto) dumb, dimwitted, silly; (estupefacto) flabbergasted; MF dimwit, booby, fool

boca F mouth (también de río); (de un arma de fuego) muzzle; (del estómago) pit; (de una cueva) opening; —**calle** intersection; — **a** — mouth-to-mouth; — **abajo** face down; — **arriba** face up; **a** — **de jarro** at close range; **callarse la** — to shut up

bocadillo M snack; *Esp* sandwich

bocado M (de comida) bite, morsel, mouthful; (de una brida) bit

bocanada F (de líquido) mouthful; (de humo) puff; (de aire) sniff

bocazas MF SG loudmouth

boceto M sketch

bochorno M (calor) oppressive heat; (vergüenza) embarrassment

bochornoso ADJ (caluroso) sultry, oppressive, muggy; (vergonzoso) embarrassing

bocina F (de coche) horn; (megáfono) megaphone

bocinazo M honk, toot

bocio M goiter

boda F wedding; —**s de oro** golden anniversary; —**s de plata** silver anniversary

bodega F (despensa subterránea) cellar; (para vinos) wine cellar; (vinería) winery; (espacio en un barco, avión) hold; (tienda de comestibles) *Carib, Am Central* grocery store

bodeguero -ra MF (viñatero) wine producer; (almacenero) *Carib, Am Central* grocer

bofe M [de animal] lung; **echar los** —**s** to tire oneself out

bofetada F slap

boga LOC ADV **en** — in vogue, fashion

bogar[40] VI/VT to row

bogey M bogey

bohemio -mia ADJ & MF (nacionalidad) Bohemian; (estilo) bohemian

boicot M boycott

boicotear VT to boycott

boicoteo M boycott

boina F beret

bol M bowl

bola F (golf, tenis, béisbol) ball; (canica) marble; (de helado) dip; (de algodón) wad; (jugada de béisbol) ball; — **blanca** cue ball; **en** —**s** in the buff; **no dar pie con** — to be lost; **no**

dar ni — not to pay attention; **— de nudillos** knuckleball; **darle una base por —s** to walk someone; **sacar una base por —s** to walk; **— de break** break point; **— de partido** match-ball; **— de ruptura** break point

bolera F bowling alley

boleta F (de lotería) ticket; (de votación) *Méx* ballot

boletín M bulletin

boleto M ticket; **— de ida solo** one-way ticket; **— de ida y vuelta** return ticket

boliche M (juego) bowling; (bolera) bowling alley

bolígrafo M ballpoint pen; **— computadora portátil** pen computer; **— ordenador portátil** pen computer

bolita F pellet

Bolivia F Bolivia

boliviano -na ADJ & MF Bolivian

bollo M bun, roll

bolo M bowling pin; **jugar a los —s** to bowl

bolsa F (saco) bag; (cartera) purse; (órgano) sac; (marsupio) pouch; **— de valores** stock market; **— de aire** airbag; **— de estudio** scholarship; **— de miseria** pocket of poverty; **hace —s** it pooches out

bolsillo M pocket; **de —** pocket-sized

bolsista MF stockbroker

bolso M (grande) bag; (pequeño) purse

bomba F (para agua, gasolina) pump; (artefacto explosivo) bomb; (noticia, mujer) *fam* bombshell; **— atómica** atomic bomb; **— de hidrógeno** hydrogen bomb; **— de neutrones** neutron bomb; **— de tiempo** time bomb; **— fétida** stink bomb; **— incendiaria** incendiary bomb; **— inteligente** smart bomb; **lo pasamos —** we had a blast

bombacha F RP panties, underpants

bombardear VT to bombard

bombardeo M bombardment, bombing

bombardero -ra MF (tripulante) bombardier; M (avión) bomber

bombear VT to pump

bombero -ra MF firefighter

bombilla F lightbulb

bombo M (en música) bass drum; (en béisbol) fly ball; **dar —** to extol; **con —s y platillos** with great fanfare

bombón M (chocolate) bonbon; (mujer atractiva) *fam* dish

bombonería F candy store

bonachón ADJ (amable) good-natured; (inocente) naive

bonaerense ADJ from the city of Buenos Aires; MF person from Buenos Aires

bonanza F (buen tiempo) fair weather; (prosperidad) prosperity

bondad F goodness, kindness; **—es** virtues; **tenga la — de** would you please

bondadoso ADJ kind, kindly

boniato M sweet potato

bonito ADJ pretty; M tuna

bono M (título de deuda) bond; (vale) voucher

boñiga F dung

boqueada F gasp

boquear VI to gasp

boquete M opening

boquiabierto ADJ (de boca abierta) openmouthed; (asombrado) astonished

boquilla F (para cigarros) cigarette holder; (para trompeta) mouthpiece; **defender de —** to pay lip service to

bórax M borax

borbollar VI to bubble

borbollón M (burbujeo) bubbling; (alboroto) commotion; **a borbollones** bubbling over

borbotar VI to bubble, to gurgle

borboteo M bubbling, gurgling

bordado M embroidery, needlework

bordar VI/VT to embroider

borde M (de una superficie) edge, border; (de un vaso) rim, brim; (de un desastre) brink; (de una calle) *Méx* curb

bordear VT (rodear) to skirt, to go along the edge of; (adornar) to trim

bordillo M curb

bordo LOC ADV **a —** on board

bordó, bordeaux ADJ INV & M maroon

borla F (de birrete) tassel; (de algodón) powder puff

boro M boron

borra F dregs

borrachera F (estado) drunkenness; (juerga) drunken spree

borrachín -ina M drunkard

borracho -cha ADJ drunk, wasted; **no lo hago ni —** I would never do such a thing; MF drunkard, wino

borrado M erasure

borrador M (bosquejo) rough draft; (goma) eraser

borrar VT (texto escrito) to erase; (texto digital) to cut, to erase; **—se de un club** to withdraw from a club

borrasca F squall

borrego M lamb

borrico M donkey

borrón M blot, blotch, smudge; **hacer — y cuenta nueva** to start over at square one

borronear VT to smudge

borroso ADJ (imagen) blurry, blurred; (memoria) fuzzy

boscaje M thicket

Bosnia-Herzegovina F Bosnia and Herzegovina

bosnio -nia ADJ & MF Bosnian

bosque M forest, woods
bosquecillo M grove
bosquejar VT to sketch, to outline
bosquejo M sketch, outline
bosta F dung
bostezar[47] VI to yawn
bostezo M yawn
bota F (calzado) boot; (para vino) leather wine bag
botadura F launch
botánica F botany
botánico ADJ botanical
botar VT (una pelota) to bounce; (un buque) to launch; (basura) to throw out
botarate M fool
bote M (jarro) can; (embarcación) boat; (rebote) bounce; **— de basura** garbage can; **— de remos** rowboat; **— de salvamento** lifeboat; **de — en / a —** filled to overflowing; (tenis) **— pronto** half volley
botella F bottle
botero -ra M boatman; F boatwoman
botija F earthen jug
botijo M earthen jar
botín M (de guerra) booty, plunder; (de ladrón) loot, haul
botiquín M (en el baño) medicine cabinet; (de primeros auxilios) first-aid kit
botón M (de aparato, de camisa) button; (remache) stud; (de planta) bud; **botones** bellboy, page; **— de inicio** start button
bótox M botox
Botsuana F Botswana
botsuano -na MF Botswanan
botulismo M botulism
bouquet M bouquet
boutique F boutique
bóveda F (techo) arched roof, vault; **— celeste** the vault of heaven
bowling M bowling
box M (para coches de carrera) pit
boxeador -ora MF boxer, prizefighter
boxear VI/VT to box
boxeo M boxing
bóxer M boxer
boya F (en el mar) buoy; (corcho) float
boyante ADJ buoyant
boyar VI to buoy
bozal M muzzle
bozo M fuzz on the lip
bracear VI to move one's arms
bracero -ra MF migrant worker
bragas F PL underpants, panties
bragueta F fly
brainstorming M brainstorming
bramar VI (ciervo, cochino) to bellow; (león, viento) to roar
bramido M (de ciervo, cochino) bellow; (de león, viento) roar

brandy M brandy
brasa F ember
brasero M brazier
Brasil M Brazil
brasileño -ña ADJ & MF Brazilian
brasilero -ra ADJ & MF Brazilian
bravata F act of bravado
bravío ADJ wild
bravo ADJ (animal, río) wild; (terreno) rugged; (persona) brave; (barrio) tough; INTERJ bravo!
bravucón -ona ADJ bullying; MF bully
bravuconería F bullying
bravura F (de bestia) fierceness; (de persona) courage
braza F fathom
brazada F (cantidad) armful; (en natación) stroke
brazalete M bracelet
brazo M arm (también de silla); (de cornamenta) branch; (de balanza) beam; **— de mar** sound; **— derecho** right-hand man; **—s** day laborers; **con los —s abiertos** with open arms; **con los —s cruzados** with crossed arms; **ir del — to** go arm in arm; **luchar a — partido** to fight to the end
brea F pitch, tar
brecha F (en un muro) breach, gap; (entre generaciones) gap
brécol M broccoli
bregar[40] VI to struggle, to toil
breña F scrub
breve ADJ (cuento) brief, short; (bikini) scanty; **en —** shortly
brevedad F brevity, shortness; **a la —** as soon as possible
bribón -ona ADJ roguish; MF rascal, rogue, scoundrel
brida F bridle
brigada F brigade
brillante ADJ brilliant, bright; M diamond, gem
brillantez F brilliance
brillantina F glitter
brillar VI (oro) to shine; (ojos) to sparkle, to twinkle; (nieve) to glisten; **— por su ausencia** to be conspicuous by its absence
brillo M (de metal, piedras preciosas) shine, luster, sparkle; (de los ojos) twinkle; (de nieve) glistening; (del pelo, plumas) sheen; (de diamantes) sparkle; (de una pantalla) brightness; **dar —** to give luster; **sacar —** to polish
brilloso ADJ shiny
brincar[30] VI to hop, to skip
brinco M hop, skip
brindar VI (beber) to toast; (proporcionar) to provide; **— por alguien** to toast someone; **—se a hacer algo** to volunteer to do something
brindis M toast

brío M spirit

brioso ADJ spirited

brisa F breeze

británico ADJ British

brizna F blade of grass

broca F drill bit

brocado M brocade

brocal M (borde) rim; (boca de pozo) curb

brocha F paintbrush; **de — gorda** coarse

broche M (alhaja) brooch; (sujetador) clasp, clip; (para el pelo) barrette; **— de oro** grand finale

brocheta F skewer

brócoli, bróculi M broccoli

broma F (chiste) joke; (réplica) jest, wisecrack; **— pesada** practical joke; **en —** in jest; **gastar una —** to play a joke; **ni en —** no way; **no estoy para —s** I'm not in the mood for kidding

bromear VI to joke, to kid

bromista MF wag, joker

bromo M bromine

bromuro M bromide

bronca F row; **armar una —** to cause a disturbance, to raise a rumpus; **echarle la — a alguien** to bawl someone out; **tener —** to be angry

bronce M bronze

bronceado ADJ (cubierto de bronce) bronzed; (tostado) tanned; (de color bronce) bronze; M suntan

broncear VT (un objeto) to bronze; **—se** to get a tan

bronco ADJ (voz) gruff; (terreno) rough; (caballo) wild

bronquial ADJ bronchial

bronquio M bronchial tube

bronquitis F bronchitis

brotar VI (planta) to sprout; (enfermedad eruptiva) to break out; (agua) to gush, to flow, to issue

brote M (de una enfermedad) outbreak; (retoño) sprout, spear

broza F brushwood

bruces LOC ADV **de —** face down

brujería F witchcraft, devilry

brujo -ja M wizard, sorcerer; F witch

brújula F compass

bruma F mist

brumoso ADJ misty

brunch M brunch

bruneano -na ADJ & MF Bruneian

Brunéi M Brunei

bruñir[17] VT to burnish

bruscamente ADV (girar, responder) sharply; (hablar) brusquely

brusco ADJ (descortés) brusque, curt; (repentino) sudden

brusquedad F (descortesía) brusqueness; (lo repentino) suddenness

brutal ADJ brutal

brutalidad F brutality

bruto -ta ADJ (ignorante) ignorant; (maleducado, burdo) uncouth; (violento) brutish; (sin descuentos) gross; **a lo —** roughly; **en —** in the rough; **recaudar en —** to gross; MF (ignorante) blockhead; (persona violenta) brute; (mal educado) lout, brute

bucal ADJ oral

bucear VI (sumergirse) to scuba dive; (indagar) to explore

buceo M scuba diving

buche M (en las aves) crop; (bocado) mouthful

bucle M (de pelo) curl, ringlet; (en informática) loop

budín M pudding

budismo M Buddhism

budista ADJ, MF Buddhist

bueno ADJ good; **buena fe** good faith; **a la buena de Dios** haphazardly; **de buenas a primeras** out of the blue; **estar —** to be sexy; **hace buen tiempo** it is fine weather; **lo —** the good thing; **por las buenas o por las malas** by hook or by crook; **ser — con los números** to be good at figures; INTERJ OK! **—s días** good day/morning; **buenas noches** good night/evening; **buenas tardes** good afternoon

buey M ox, steer

búfalo M buffalo, bison

bufanda F scarf, muffler

bufar VI to snort; **está que bufa** he is incensed

bufete M (despacho) lawyer's office; (negocio) practice

buffet M buffet

bufido M snort

bufón -ona MF buffoon, jester

bufonear VI to clown

buhardilla F (desván) attic, garret

búho M owl

buhonero -ra MF peddler

buitre M vulture, buzzard

buje M bushing

bujía F spark plug

bulbo M bulb

bulldog M bulldog

bulevar M boulevard

Bulgaria F Bulgaria

búlgaro -ra ADJ & MF Bulgarian

bulimia F bulimia

bulla F uproar, fuss, bustle

bulldozer M bulldozer

bullicio M uproar, racket, bustle

bullicioso ADJ boisterous, rowdy

bullir[16] VI (hervir) to boil; (hacer burbujas) to bubble; (ajetrearse) to bustle; (moverse) to stir

bullón M puff

bullpen M bullpen

bulto M (paquete) bundle; (tumor) lump, growth; (silueta) shape; (saliente) bulge; **a —** approximately; **escurrir el —** to slack off
bungaló M bungalow
bungee M bungee jumping
búnker M bunker
buñuelo M fritter
buque M ship; **— de carga** freighter
burbuja F bubble
burdo ADJ coarse
burgués ADJ bourgeois
burguesía F bourgeoisie, middle class
burla F ridicule, mockery; **hacer — a alguien** to mock someone
burlar VT to mock; **—se de** to scoff at, to make fun of
burlesco ADJ burlesque
burlón ADJ mocking
burocracia F bureaucracy
burócrata MF bureaucrat
burrez F stupidity
burro M (animal) donkey, ass; (persona) dunce; ADJ dense
bursátil ADJ **mercado —** stock market
bursitis F bursitis
burundés -esa ADJ & MF Burundian
Burundi M Burundi
bus M bus; **— en serie** serial bus
busca LOC ADV **en — de** in search of
buscar[30] VT (objetos perdidos) to seek, to look for, to search for; (datos, palabras) to look up; (provocar) to provoke; (la verdad) to seek after; (minerales) to prospect for; (talento) to scout for; **— se problemas** to invite trouble; **— y reemplazar** to search and replace; **tú te lo buscaste** you asked for it; **ir a —** to fetch; M SG **buscapersonas** beeper, pager
búsqueda F search; **— del tesoro** treasure hunt; **— hacia atrás** backward search; **— por palabra clave** keyword search
busto M bust
butaca F (en la casa) armchair; (en el teatro) seat
Bután M Bhutan
butanés -esa ADJ & MF Bhutanese
butano M butane
buzo M diver
buzón M mailbox; **— de sugerencias** suggestion box
bypass M bypass operation, coronary bypass
byte M byte

Cc

cabal ADJ (completo) complete; (exacto) exact; (honrado) upright; **estar uno en sus —es** to be in one's right mind
cabalgar[40] VI to ride horseback
caballa F mackerel
caballada F herd of horses
caballejo M nag
caballeresco ADJ chivalrous
caballería F (tropas) cavalry; (equino) equine; (condición de caballero) knighthood
caballeriza F stable
caballerizo M groom
caballero M (señor) gentleman; (hidalgo) knight; **— andante** knight errant; ADJ gentlemanly
caballerosidad F chivalry
caballeroso ADJ chivalrous, gentlemanly
caballete M (soporte de madera) sawhorse; (de la nariz) bridge; (de pintor) easel; (de tejado) ridge
caballo M (animal) horse; (en ajedrez) knight; (heroína) *fam* smack; **a —** on horseback; **— de carreras** racehorse; **— de batalla** hobbyhorse; **— de fuerza** horsepower; **— de Troya** Trojan horse
cabaña F (casucha) hovel; (casa de campo) cabin, cottage; (conjunto de ganado) livestock
cabaret M cabaret
cabecear VI (mover la cabeza) to nod; (dormirse) to nod off; (un barco) to bob, to pitch; VT (balón) to head
cabeceo M (de la cabeza) nodding; (de un barco) pitching
cabecera F (de cama) headboard; (de mesa) head
cabecilla MF ringleader
cabellera F head of hair
cabello M hair; **traido por los —s** far-fetched
caber[67] VI to fit; **no cabe duda** there is no doubt; **no cabe nadie más** there is no room for anybody else; **no — uno en sí** to be puffed up with pride; **no cabe en lo posible** it is absolutely impossible; **¿en qué cabeza cabe?** who would believe that?
cabestrillo M sling
cabestro M halter
cabeza F head; **— de chorlito** scatterbrain, airhead; **— de playa** beachhead; **— de puente** bridgehead; **— de turco** scapegoat, fall guy; **— de serie** seed; **— rapada** skinhead; **a la —** at the forefront; **caerse de — to** fall head first; **echarse de — to** plunge headlong; **ir a la —** to lead the way; **por —** each; **romperse la —** to rack one's brains; **la fama se le fue a la —** fame went to his head; **sentar —** to settle down; **tiene la — cuadrada** she's a square
cabezada F nod; **dar —s** to nod off
cabezal M magnetic head
cabezazo M (golpe) head butt; (jugada de fútbol) header
cabezón ADJ (de cabeza grande) big-headed;

(testarudo) pig-headed; (con mucho alcohol) strong

cabezudo ADJ (de cabeza grande) big-headed; (testarudo) pig-headed

cabida F capacity; **dar —** to include; **tener — en** to fit in

cabina F (de pasajeros) cabin; (de piloto) cockpit; (de camión) cab; (de teléfono, control) booth

cabizbajo ADJ crestfallen, downcast

cable M cable; **— coaxial** coaxial cable; **—s del ordenador / de la computadora** media

cableado M wiring

cablevisión F cable television

cabo M (parte extrema) end; (hilo) thread; (cuerda) rope; (saliente de la costa) cape; MF (rango militar) corporal; **— suelto** loose end; **al — de** at the end of; **atar —s** to put two and two together; **de — a rabo** from beginning to end; **llevar a —** to carry out

cabotaje M coastal trade

Cabo Verde M Cape Verde

caboverdiano -na ADJ & MF Cape Verdean

cabra F goat; **— montés** mountain goat; **[loco] como una —** completely crazy

cabrá, cabría ver caber

cabrearse VI to get mad

cabrestante M winch

cabrillas F PL whitecaps

cabrio M rafter

cabrío ADJ **macho —** he-goat

cabriola F caper

cabriolar VI to cavort

cabritilla F kid [leather]

cabrito M kid [goat]

cabrón M (macho de cabra) he-goat; (cornudo) cuckold; MF (cobarde) wimp

caca F poop; **hacer —** to poop

cacahuate M _Méx_ peanut

cacahuete M _Esp_ peanut

cacao M cocoa

cacarear VI to cackle, to squawk

cacareo M cackling, squawking

cacatúa F cockatoo

cacería F hunt; **— de brujas** witch hunt

cacerola F saucepan

cacha F (de navaja) handle; (nalga) thigh, butt; **hasta la —** completely

cachalote M sperm whale

cacharro M (vasija) earthen pot; (coche viejo) clunker, jalopy

cachaza F slowness

cachazudo ADJ slow

caché M (en informática) cache; (distinción) cachet; **— de memoria** memory cache

cachear VT to body-search, to frisk

cachet M artist's fee

cachetada F slap

cachete M cheek

cachiporra F blackjack

cachivaches M PL stuff, odds and ends

cacho M hunk

cachorro M (de oso, lobo, tigre, león) cub; (de perro) puppy

cacique -ca M (de indios) chief, chieftain; MF (caudillo) political boss

cacofonía F cacophony

cacto/cactus M cactus

cada ADJ each; **— uno** each one; **— vez más** more and more; **— vez menos gente** fewer and fewer people; **— vez menos harina** less and less flour; **— vez peor** worse and worse; **doscientas pesetas — una** two hundred pesetas each/apiece

cadalso M gallows

cadáver M (para enterrar) corpse; (para disecar) cadaver

cadavérico ADJ ghastly

caddie, caddy MF caddie

cadena F (serie de piezas) chain; (de televisión) network; (cordillera) mountain range; **— alimenticia** food chain; **— de montaje** assembly line; **— perpetua** life sentence; **—s** shackles; **tirar la —** to flush

cadencia F cadence

cadera F hip

cadete M cadet

cadmio M cadmium

caducar[30] VI to lapse, to expire

caducidad F expiration

caduco ADJ (deciduo) deciduous; (decrépito) decrepit

caer[52] VI to fall; (desplomarse) to fall down; (colgar) to hang; (ir a parar) to end up; **al — la noche** at nightfall; **— en desgracia** to fall into disfavor, to fall out of favor; **— en desuso** to fall into disuse; **— en cama** to fall ill; **— en cuenta** to catch on; **— en ruina** to fall into disrepair; **—le bien/mal a uno** (una persona) to make a good/bad impression; (una comida) to agree with; **—le en suerte a uno** to fall to one's lot; **— tan bajo** to fall so low; **caiga quien caiga** let fall who may; **dejar —** to drop; **está al —** he's about to show up; **—se** (persona) to fall down; (computadora, ordenador) to crash; **se cayó el sistema** the system crashed

café M (bebida) coffee; (color) brown; (establecimiento) coffee shop, café

cafeína F caffeine

cafetal M coffee plantation

cafetera F coffeepot

cafetería F snack bar, cafeteria, diner

cafetero -ra MF coffee dealer; ADJ **industria cafetera** coffee industry

cafeto M coffee bush

caída F (acción de caer) fall, tumble, spill; (de presión arterial) drop; (de un ordenador) crash; (de una cortina) hang; (de precios) drop; — **libre** free fall; — **del sol** sunset; — **en picado** nosedive; —**s del sistema** system crashes

caído ADJ (orejas) floppy; (arco del pie) fallen; **los —s** the fallen

caiga, caigo ver caer

caimán M alligator

caja F box; — **chica** petty cash; — **de ahorros** savings bank; — **de bateo** batter's box; — **de cambios** transmission; — **de escalera** stairwell; — **de fusibles** fuse box; — **de herramientas** toolkit; — **de jubilaciones** pension fund; — **de música** music box; — **de seguridad** safe deposit box; — **de reloj** watchcase; — **fuerte** safe; — **negra** flight recorder; — **registradora** (aparato) cash register, till; (mostrador) checkout counter; — **tonta** idiot box; — **torácica** rib cage; **entrar en —** (comenzar) to get going; (establecerse) to settle down

cajero -ra MF cashier; (en un banco) teller; — **automático** ATM

cajetilla F pack [of cigarettes]

cajilla F pack [of cigarettes]

cajón M (para transportes) crate; (parte de un mueble) drawer; **eso es de —** that's a foregone conclusion

cajuela F Méx car trunk

cal F lime; **cerrar a — y canto** to close hermetically

calabacín M zucchini

calabaza F (grande y redonda) pumpkin; (pequeña y/o alargada) squash; (vaciada) gourd; **dar —s** to turn down

calabozo M dungeon

calado M draft

calamar M squid

calambre M cramp

calamidad F calamity

calamina F calamine

calandria F lark

calar VT (agujerear) to perforate; (empapar) to soak, to drench; — **a alguien** to see through someone; — **hondo** to resonate; —**se** to get drenched

calavera F skull; M libertine

calcar³⁰ VT (sobre papel) to trace; (imitar) to copy

calcetería F hosiery

calcetín M sock

calcinar VT to bake

calcio M calcium

calco M (acción de calcar) tracing; **es el — de su padre** he's the spitting image of his father

calcomanía F decal

calculador ADJ calculating

calculadora F calculator

calcular VT (computar) to calculate, to figure; (sopesar) to weigh; (prever) to reckon

cálculo M (cómputo) calculation; (aritmética) arithmetic; (integral, diferencial) calculus; — **biliar** gallstone; — **renal** kidney stone

caldear VT to warm up; — **los ánimos** to get everyone upset

caldera F (en una máquina de vapor) boiler; (recipiente con asas) kettle; (de calefacción) furnace

calderón M hold

caldo M broth, stock; — **de cultivo** culture medium

calefacción F heat, heating; — **central** central heating

calendario M calendar

caléndula F marigold

calentador M heater; — **de agua** water heater

calentamiento M warming; (en deportes) warm-up; — **global** global warming

calentar¹ VI/VT (poner caliente) to warm, to heat; —**se** (ponerse caliente, prepararse para un partido) to warm up, to heat up

calentura F fever

calesa F buggy

caletre M **no tener —** to have no brains

calibrador M caliper

calibrar VT to gauge, to calibrate

calibre M (de pistola, tubo) caliber; (de alambre) gauge; (calibrador) caliper

calicó M calico

calidad F quality; **baja —** low quality; **de —** of good quality; **de — inferior** substandard; **estoy aquí en — de representante** I'm here in my capacity as representative

cálido ADJ warm

caliente ADJ (agradable) warm; (excesivo) hot

calificación F (nota) grade, mark; (acción de asignar notas) grading; (comparación) rating; — **crediticia** credit rating; **le dieron la — de genio** they called him a genius

calificar³⁰ VT (juzgar la calidad) to rate, to adjudge; (asignar nota) to grade; —**se como** to be characterized as

calificativo ADJ qualifying; M label

caligrafía F (letra) penmanship; (arte) calligraphy

calina F haze

callado ADJ silent, quiet; **estarse —** to keep quiet

callar VT (no manifestar, no dejar decir) to quiet; VI (no hablar) to remain silent; (dejar de hablar) to go quiet; —**se la boca** to shut up, to pipe down

calle F (de ciudad) street; (golf) fairway; — **abajo** down the street; — **arriba** up the street; — **de sentido único** one-way street; **no pisar la —** to stay home

calleja F narrow street

callejear VI to walk the streets

callejero ADJ **perro —** stray dog; **caos —** chaos

in the streets

callejón M alley; — **sin salida** blind alley, dead end

callo M callus, corn

calloso ADJ callous

calma F calm; — **chicha** absolute calm; **mantener la** — (no enojarse) to keep one's temper; (no ponerse nervioso) to stay calm; **tomar las cosas con** — to take things easy

calmante ADJ & M sedative

calmar VT (nervios) to calm; (dolor) to sooth; (miedo) to allay, to quell; (sed) to quench; —**se** (una persona) to calm down; (una tormenta, la ira) to subside, to abate

calmo ADJ calm

calmoso ADJ easygoing

calor M (temperatura alta) heat; (temperatura templada) warmth; (actitud acogedora) warmth; **hace — hoy** it's hot today; **los —es** hot flashes; **tengo —** I'm hot

caloría F calorie

calumnia F calumny, slander

calumniar VT to slander, to malign

calumnioso ADJ slanderous

caluroso ADJ (día) hot; (recepción) warm

calva F bald spot

calvario M **mi vida es un** — *fam* my life is hell

calvicie F baldness

calvo ADJ bald, baldheaded; **ni tanto ni tan** — *fam* it ain't necessarily so; **quedarse** — to go bald

calza F long sock

calzada F pavement

calzado M footwear

calzador M shoehorn

calzar[47] VT (poner zapatos) to shoe; (hacer zapatos para) to make shoes for; — **a la familia** to buy shoes for the family; **calzo 42** I take size 10; —**se** to put on shoes

calzones M PL (de mujer) panties; (de hombre) shorts

calzonazos M SG henpecked man

calzoncillos M PL underpants, briefs; — **largos** long johns

cama F bed; — **de agua** waterbed; — **doble** double bed; — **elástica** trampoline; — **individual** twin bed; **guardar** — to be confined to bed; **meterse en la — con** to sleep with

camada F litter

camafeo M cameo

camaleón M chameleon

cámara F (espacio) chamber; (de neumático) inner tube; (fotográfica) camera; — **de comercio** chamber of commerce; — **de diputados** lower house; — **de gas** gas chamber; — **digital** digital camera; — **de oxígeno** oxygen tent; — **frigorífica** cold-storage locker; — **legislativa** legislature; — **hiperbárica** hyperbaric chamber; **en — lenta** in slow motion; MF (persona que maneja una cámara) camera operator

camarada MF comrade

camarero -ra M (restaurante) waiter, server; (coche cama) steward; F (restaurante) waitress, server; (coche cama) stewardess; (hotel) maid; MF (béisbol) second baseman

camarilla F clique

camarógrafo -fa M cameraman; F camerawoman

camarón M shrimp

camarote M cabin, stateroom

cambalache M (intercambio) fraudulent swap; (tienda) secondhand store

cambalachear VI/VT to swap fraudulently

cambiante ADJ (que cambia) changing; (propenso a cambiar) changeable; (temperamento) volatile

cambiar VI/VT to change; VT (una cosa por otra) to exchange, to swap, to trade; — **de marcha** to shift gears; — **de opinión/parecer** to change one's mind; — **de sitio** to move places

cambiario ADJ **sistema** — foreign exchange system

cambio M (acción de cambiar) change; (marcha) gear; (cotización) exchange rate; (de ferrocarril) railway switch; (béisbol) changeup; — **de velocidad** (en béisbol) change-up; — **de lado** (tenis) changeover; — **de divisas** foreign exchange; — **para peor** a turn for the worse; — **y fuera** over and out; **a — [de]** in return [for]; **en** — on the other hand

cambista MF money changer

Camboya F Cambodia

camboyano -na ADJ & MF Cambodian

camellear VT to push [drugs]

camello -lla MF (animal) camel; (vendedor de droga) pusher

camerino M dressing room

Camerún M Cameroon

camerunés -esa ADJ & MF Cameroonian

camilla F stretcher, litter

camillero -ra MF hospital orderly

caminante MF walker, wayfarer

caminar VI/VT to walk; (baloncesto) to travel

caminata F long walk; (por un lugar agreste) hike

camino M (carretera) road; (itinerario, dirección a seguir) way; — **de** on the way to; — **de mesa** table runner; — **de rosas** bed of roses; **abrirse** — to make way; **a medio** — halfway; **en — [a]** on the way [to]; **llevar por mal** — to lead astray; **mostrar el** — to lead the way; **ponerse en** — to set out; **señalar el** — to show the way

camión M (de cargas) truck; (para transporte de personas) *Méx* bus; — **de la basura** garbage truck; — **de mudanzas** moving van; — **de remolque** tow truck, wrecker; — **de reparto** delivery truck; — **volteador** dump truck

camionero -ra MF truck driver; *Méx* bus driver

camioneta F (furgoneta) van, minivan; (camioncito) pickup truck; (coche sin maletero) station wagon

camisa F shirt; — **de fuerza** straitjacket; **meterse en — de once varas** to get into a jam

camiseta F (exterior) T-shirt; (interior) undershirt

camisón M nightgown

camorrista ADJ rowdy

campamento M (de refugiados, exploradores) camp; (recreativo) campground

campana F bell; **tocar una —** to ring a bell

campanario M belfry, bell tower

campanilla F (campana pequeña) small bell; (flor) bluebell; (órgano en la boca) uvula

campanilleo M ringing

campánula F bellflower

campaña F campaign; — **publicitaria** advertising campaign; **hacer —** to campaign; **el ejército estaba de —** the army was on the front

campechano ADJ straightforward

campeón -ona MF champion

campeonato M championship; — **Mundial de Fútbol** Soccer World Cup

campero ADJ **hombre —** a man from the country

campesino -na MF peasant; ADJ **casa campesina** peasant house

campestre ADJ rural

camping M (lugar) campground; (actividad) camping

campiña F open country

campista MF camper

campo M (fuera de la ciudad) country, countryside; (para cultivos, deportes, ámbito del saber) field; (grupo en un conflicto) camp; — **abierto** range; MF —**corto** (béisbol) shortstop; — **de acción** field of action; — **de batalla** battlefield; — **de concentración** concentration camp; — **de golf** golf course; — **de juego** athletic field; — **de tiro** shooting range; — **libre** free rein; — **magnético** magnetic field; — **minado** minefield; — **petrolífero** oil field; — **visual** visual field; **a — traviesa** cross-country; —**santo** churchyard

campus M campus

camuflaje M camouflage

camuflar VT to camouflage

can M dog

cana F white hair; **echar una — al aire** to go out for a good time

Canadá M Canada

canadiense ADJ & MF Canadian

canal M (cauce artificial de agua) canal; (estrecho marítimo, banda de frecuencia) channel; (emisora) station; — **de parto** birth canal; — **radicular** root canal

canalé M ribbed fabric

canalizar[47] VT to channel

canalón M spout

canana F cartridge belt

canapé M (mueble) divan; (aperitivo) canape, starter

canario -ria M canary; ADJ of/from the Canary Islands; MF Canary Islander

canasta F basket (también en baloncesto)

canasto M hamper

cancelación F cancellation

cancelar VT (contrato, sello) to cancel; (deuda) to pay off; (evento) to call off

cáncer M cancer; — **de mama** breast cancer; — **de colon** colorectal cancer

cancerígeno ADJ carcinogen

canceroso -sa MF cancer patient; ADJ cancerous

cancha F (de baloncesto, tenis) court; (de fútbol) field; ¡**abran —**! gangway! **falta —** there's no room

canciller MF (de Alemania, de universidades) chancellor; (de EEUU) secretary of state

canción F song; — **de cuna** lullaby

candado M padlock

candela F (vela) candle; (fuego) fire

candelabro M candelabrum

candelero M candlestick; **en el —** in the limelight

candente ADJ red-hot

candidato -ta MF candidate

candidatura F (hecho de ser candidato) candidacy; (conjunto de candidatos) ticket

candidez F innocence

cándido ADJ naive

candil M oil lamp

candilejas F PL footlights

candor M innocence

canela F (especia) cinnamon; (árbol) cinnamon tree

canesú M yoke of a shirt

cangrejo M crab

canguro M kangaroo; MF *Esp* baby-sitter

caníbal ADJ & MF cannibal

canica F toy marble

caniche M poodle; — **enano** toy poodle

canilla F (espinilla) shin; (pantorrilla) calf; (grifo) faucet

canino ADJ canine; **tener un hambre canina** to be ravenous; M canine [tooth]

canje M exchange

canjear VT (prisioneros, libros) to exchange; (un

cupón) to redeem

cano ADJ gray-haired

canoa F canoe

canon M (regla, modelo) canon; (canción) round

canónigo M canon

canoso ADJ gray-haired

cansado ADJ (fatigado) tired, weary; (fatigoso) wearing, tiring

cansancio M weariness

cansar VT (fatigar) to tire, to tire out; (aburrir) to bore; **—se** to get tired

cantante MF singer

cantar VI/VT (hacer música) to sing; VT (anunciar) to call out; (revelar secretos) to squeal; **— a tono** to sing on key; **—le a alguien las cuarenta** to give someone a piece of one's mind; **— victoria** to declare victory; **en menos que canta un gallo** before you can say Jack Robinson; M epic poem; **eso es otro —** that's another story

cántaro M pitcher; **llover a —s** to rain cats and dogs

cantera F quarry

cantero M RP flower bed

cántico M chant

cantidad F quantity, amount; (de dinero) amount, sum; **— a pagar** amount payable; **— debida** amount due; **— pagada** amount paid; **— de gente** a lot of people

cantimplora F canteen, water bottle

cantina F (lugar donde comer) mess hall, mess, canteen; (bar) tavern

cantinela F chant

cantinero -ra MF bartender

canto M (cosa cantada) song; (piedra) pebble; **— de cisne** swan song; **— llano** chant; **— rodado** rounded pebble; **de —** on edge

cantor -ora MF singer

canturrear VI to hum

canturreo M hum, humming

caña F (planta gramínea) reed; (de azúcar) cane; (cerveza) *Esp* beer; (vaso) *Esp* beer glass; **— de pescar** fishing pole; **dale —** floor it

cañada F (barranco) ravine; (arroyo) brook

cáñamo M hemp

cañaveral M reed patch

cañería F (en la calle) piping; (en la casa) plumbing

caño M (tubo) pipe; (grifo) spout; (de arma) barrel; **de doble —** double-barreled

cañón M (arma) cannon; (pieza hueca) barrel; (cañada profunda) canyon; (de pluma, bolígrafo) shaft

cañonero M gunboat

caoba F mahogany

caos M chaos

caótico ADJ chaotic

capa F (prenda) cape, cloak; (de pintura, animal) coat; (de tierra) layer; (de hielo) sheet; **— de**

ozono ozone layer; **— freática** water table; **de — y espada** cloak and dagger

capacidad F capacity; **—es** aptitude, ability, capability; **— de almacenamiento de disco** disk capacity

capacitación F training; **— para empleados** in-service training

capacitar VT (entrenar) to train; (habilitar) to qualify

capar VT to castrate

caparazón M shell

capataz -za MF boss, overseer

capaz ADJ (habilidoso) capable, able; (apto) apt; (espacioso) spacious, roomy; (competente) competent

capear VT to ride out, to weather

capellán M chaplain

caperuza F pointed hood

capilar ADJ & M capillary

capilla F chapel; **estar en —** (castigado) to be in the doghouse; (en ascuas) to be on pins and needles

capital M (dinero) capital; (de préstamo) principal; **— de riesgo** venture capital; **— inicial** start-up funds; **el gran —** big business; F capital [city]; ADJ main

capitalino ADJ **atmósfera capitalina** capital city atmosphere

capitalismo M capitalism

capitalista MF capitalist; ADJ capitalistic

capitalización F capitalization

capitalizar[47] VT (aportar capital) to capitalize; (aprovechar) to capitalize on

capitán -ana MF captain

capitanear VT to captain

capitel M capital

capitolio M capitol

capitulación F (militar) capitulation, surrender; **capitulaciones matrimoniales** prenuptial agreement

capitular VI to capitulate

capítulo M chapter

capó M hood [of a car]

capo M mafia boss

capota F top [of a car]

capote M cloak; (de coche) *Méx* hood; **decir para su —** to say under one's breath

capricho M caprice, whim, notion

caprichoso ADJ (impredecible) capricious; (impulsivo) whimsical, fanciful; (malcriado) willful

cápsula F capsule

captación F (de agua) collection; (de clientes) attraction; (de inversiones, fondos) raising

captar VT (un concepto) to grasp; (atención, interés) to capture; (una emisión) to receive; (una indirecta) to get; **— la onda** to get the drift

captor -ora MF captor

captura F (acción de capturar) capture; (pesca capturada) catch; (fútbol americano) sack; — **de video/vídeo** video capture

capturar VT to capture; (pescado) to catch

capucha F (de cabeza) hood, cowl; (de lapicero) cap

capuchina F nasturtium

capuchino M cappuccino

capullo M (de insecto) cocoon; (de flor) bud

caqui M khaki

cara F (rostro) face; (de cubo) surface; (de papel, moneda) side; (morro) nerve; — **a** — face to face; — **o cruz** heads or tails; **dar la** — to face up to things; **de** — **al sur** facing south; **decir en la** — to tell to one's face; **de dos** —**s** two-sided; **la otra** — **de la moneda** the other side of the coin; **poner buena** — to put on a good face; **se le ve en la** — it's written all over his face; **tener** — **[dura]** to have a lot of nerve; **un ojo de la** — an arm and a leg; **volverle la** — **a** to snub

carabinero -ra MF (oficial de aduana) border patrol officer; (agente de policía) police officer; M (crustáceo) red prawn

caracol M (molusco) snail; (concha) snail shell; INTERJ **¡—es!** *fam* darn!

carácter M (temperamento, signo) character; (rasgo) characteristic; (índole) kind

característica F characteristic, feature; (en informática) feature

característico ADJ characteristic

caracterización F (descripción) characterization, description; (retrato) portrayal

caracterizar[47] VT to characterize

caramba INTERJ *fam* darn! good grief! heck!

carámbano M icicle

carambola F carom; **por** — indirectly

caramelo M (azúcar fundido) caramel; (dulce pequeño) bonbon

caramillo M reed pipe

carátula F (máscara) mask; (portada) title page

caravana F (en el desierto, convoy) caravan; (remolque) trailer

caray INTERJ *fam* shoot! darn!

carbohidrato M carbohydrate

carbón M (sustancia) coal; (pedazo) piece of coal; — **de leña** charcoal

carboncillo M charcoal drawing

carbonera F coal bin

carbono M carbon

carburador M carburetor

carburante M fuel

carca ADJ old-fashioned; MF *fam* fossil, old fogey

carcaj M quiver

carcajada F burst of laughter, guffaw

carcamal M *fam* fossil, old fogey

cárcel F jail, prison

carcelero -ra MF jailer

carcinógeno M carcinogen

carcinoma M carcinoma; — **de célula basal** basal cell carcinoma

carcomido ADJ worm-eaten

carda F card, comb

cardán M universal joint

cardar VT (lana) to card, to comb; (pelo) to rat, to tease

cardenal M (pájaro, prelado) cardinal; (moretón) bruise

cardíaco -ca ADJ cardiac; MF heart patient

cardinal ADJ cardinal

cardioangiograma M cardioangiogram

cardiograma M cardiogram

cardiología F cardiology

cardiólogo -ga MF cardiologist

cardiopulmonar ADJ cardiopulmonary

cardiovascular ADJ cardiovascular

cardo M thistle

cardumen M school of fish

carear VT to bring face to face; —**se** to meet face to face

carecer[35] VI — **de** to lack

carencia F (falta) lack; (deficiencia alimenticia) deficiency

carenciado ADJ disadvantaged

carente ADJ lacking; — **de** lacking in

carero ADJ expensive

carestía F (escasez) scarcity; (costo alto) high cost

careta F mask

carezca, carezco *ver* carecer

carga F (cosa cargada) load, freight; (de la prueba, impuesto) burden; (hipoteca) lien; (de encendedor) refill; (de explosivo, electricidad) charge; (de programas) upload; — **de municiones** round of ammunition; — **útil** payload; **volver a la** — to insist

cargado ADJ (bebida) stiff; (pausa) pregnant; (cartucho) live; — **de deudas** deep in debt; — **de espaldas** stooping

cargador M (de batería) charger; (de arma de fuego) clip, magazine

cargamento M cargo, load, shipment

cargar[40] VT (cargamentos, datos, arma, programa de ordenador) to load; (batería, a una cuenta, en baloncesto) to charge; (de obligaciones) to burden with; (a un niño) to carry; (a un estudiante) *Esp* to flunk; (molestar) to bother; — **a alguien de responsabilidades** to saddle someone with responsibilities; — **al hombro** to shoulder; — **de combustible** to fuel; — **un programa** to upload; VI to charge; — **con la culpa** to be saddled with blame; — **sobre** to charge, to attack

cargo M (función en una empresa) position; (en una factura, a una cuenta) charge; (acusación) count, charge; — **de conciencia** guilt feelings; **—s atrasados** back charges; **— de tramitación** handling charges; **a mi —** under my charge; **hacerse — de** (responsabilizarse de) to take charge of; (ser consciente de) to understand; **investir de un —** to induct into office; **los niños están a — de la maestra** the children are under the care of the teacher; **la maestra está a[l] — de los niños** the teacher is in charge of the children

cargoso ADJ fussy

carguero ADJ freight-carrying

cariado ADJ decayed

caribeño ADJ Caribbean

caricatura F (dibujo) caricature; (con texto) cartoon

caricaturista MF cartoonist

caricaturizar[47] VT to caricature

caricia F caress

caridad F charity

caries F INV cavity, tooth decay

carillón M chimes

cariño M (amor) affection, fondness; (apodo) honey; **darle —s a alguien** to send love to someone; **ella y el perro se hacen —s** she and the dog nuzzle each other; **hacer algo con —** to do something with great care; **tenerle — a alguien** to be fond of someone

cariñoso ADJ affectionate, loving

carisma M charisma

caritativo ADJ charitable

cariz M complexion; **no me gusta el — que está tomando la situación** I don't like the look of this

carmesí ADJ INV & M crimson

carmín M (carmesí) crimson; (lápiz de labios) lipstick

carnal ADJ carnal

carnaval M carnival

carne F (para comer) meat; (de animal vivo, de persona, de tomate) flesh; **— de cañón** cannon fodder; **— de cerdo** pork; **— de cordero** mutton; **— de gallina** (comida) chicken; (reacción de la piel) goose bumps; **— de res** beef; **— de venado** venison; **— y hueso** flesh and blood; **como — y uña** fam thick as thieves; **en — viva** raw; **metido en —s** overweight

carnear VT to butcher

carnero M ram

carnet/carné — de conducir driver's license; **— de identidad** ID

carnicería F (tienda) butcher's shop; (matanza) carnage, bloodbath

carnicero -ra MF butcher; ADJ (carnívoro) carnivorous; (cruel) cruel

carnívoro ADJ carnivorous

carnoso ADJ fleshy

caro ADJ expensive, high-priced, fam pricey; ADV at a high price

carona F saddle pad

carótida F carotid artery

carozo M RP pit, stone

carpa F (pez) carp; (tienda) tent

carpeta F (para documentos, también de ordenador) folder; (cartera) portfolio

carpintería F (oficio) carpentry; (taller) carpenter's shop

carpintero -ra MF carpenter

carraspear VI to clear one's throat

carraspera F scratchy throat

carrera F (conjunto de estudios) major; (trayectoria profesional) career; (competición) race; (en las medias) run; (recorrido corto) run, dash; (en fútbol americano, béisbol) run; (de pistón) stroke; **— a pie** footrace; **— de caballos** horse race; **— de relevos** relay race; **a la —** running; **hacer —** to succeed in a profession; **tomar —** to get a running start; **— impulsada** (en béisbol) run batted in; **— limpia** (en béisbol) earned run; **— sucia** (en béisbol) unearned run

carreta F wagon

carrete M (de película) reel; (de hilo) bobbin; (de alambre) spool

carretera F highway; **— de circunvalación** bypass; **— de peaje** toll road

carretero ADJ **sistema —** highway system

carretilla F (de una rueda) wheelbarrow; (de más de una rueda) dolly; **de —** by memory

carretón M large wagon

carril M (de ferrocarril) rail; (de calle) lane

carrillo M cheek, jowl; **a dos/cuatro —s** voraciously

carrillón M chimes

carrizo M reed

carro M (automóvil) car; (vehículo de dos ruedas, de golf) cart; (de máquina de escribir) roll; **— alegórico** parade float; **— blindado** armored car; **— de guerra** chariot; **poner el — delante de los bueyes** to put the cart before the horse; **subirse al —** to get on the bandwagon

carrocería F auto body

carroña F carrion

carroza F (de caballos) coach; (de desfile) parade float; (fúnebre) hearse

carruaje M carriage, coach

carta F (misiva) letter; (naipe) card; (de restaurante) menu; (constitución) charter; (mapa) chart; **— blanca** freehand; **— con anexos** cover letter; **— de agradecimiento** thank-you letter; **— de remisión** cover letter; **— de renuncia** resignation letter; **a la —** à la carte; **echarle las —s a alguien** to do a card-reading for someone; **tomar —s en la situación** to take charge of a situation

cartearse VI to correspond

cartel M poster, placard; **en —** showing; **— de la droga** drug cartel

cartelera F (de periódico) entertainment section; (publicitaria) billboard; (tablón para anuncios) bulletin board

cárter M oil pan

cartera F (para dinero) wallet, billfold; (para papeles) briefcase; (escolar) satchel; (bolsa) handbag; (de valores) portfolio

carterista MF pickpocket

cartero -ra MF letter carrier; M mailman, postman

cartílago M cartilage

cartilla F (para aprender a leer) reader; (de información) booklet; **— de racionamiento** ration book; **— de examen de vista** eye chart

cartografiar[28] VT to chart

cartón M cardboard, pasteboard; **— de cigarrillos** carton of cigarettes

cartuchera F cartridge belt

cartucho M (de pistola) cartridge, shell; (de monedas) roll; (de dinamita) stick; **— de fogueo** blank cartridge; **— de tinta / tóner** toner cartridge; **quemar el último —** to exhaust one's resources

cartulina F thin cardboard

casa F (edificio) house; (hogar) home; (negocio) business firm; **— de ancianos** old folks' home; **— de citas** cheap motel for rendezvous; **— de empeños** pawnshop; **— de la moneda** mint; **— de muñecas** dollhouse; **— de pompas fúnebres** funeral home; **— de reposo** rest home; **— de rehabilitación** halfway house; **— de subastas** auction house; **— embrujada** haunted house; **— rodante** house trailer; **— solariega** manor house; **de — en —** from house to house; **en — at** home; **entró como Perico por su —** he made himself right at home; **estás en tu —** make yourself at home; **ir a —** to go home; **la — paga** on the house; **poner una —** to set up a household; **quedarse en —** to stay home; **tirar la — por la ventana** to live it up

casaca F riding jacket

casadero ADJ marriageable

casado ADJ married

casamentero -ra MF matchmaker

casamiento M wedding, marriage ceremony

casar VT to marry off; **—se** to get married, to wed; **—se con** to get married to; **no —se con nadie** to remain independent

cascabel M (campanita) jingle bell; (de víbora) rattle; **ser un —** to be lively; **ponerle el — al gato** to stick one's neck out

cascada F cascade, waterfall

cascajo M old wreck

cascar[30] VT (quebrar) to crack; (dar bofetadas) to slap around; **—se** to crack open; M SG

cascanueces nutcracker; MF SG

cascarrabias crab, grouch; ADJ INV grouchy

cáscara F (de huevo, fruto seco) shell; (de granos, arvejas) husk; (de fruto seco) hull; (de fruta) rind; (de naranja, manzana) peel

casco M (de ciclista, militar) helmet; (de obrero) hard hat; (de barco) hull; (de naranja) shell; (uña del pie de caballería) hoof; **— urbano** built-up area

cascote M rubble

caserío M (aldea) hamlet; (casa) *Esp* farmhouse

casero -ra ADJ (doméstico) domestic; (hecho en casa) homemade; MF (cuidador) caretaker; M (propietario) landlord; F landlady

caseta F (en un mercado) booth, stall; (de guardia) guardhouse; (de perro) doghouse

casete MF cassette

casi ADV almost, nearly; **— diez mil** almost/nearly ten thousand; **— lo hago** I almost did it; **— siempre** almost always; **— nadie** hardly anyone; **— nunca** hardly ever

casilla F (en el tablero de ajedrez) square; (en una tabla) box; (en un casillero) pigeonhole, cubbyhole; **— de perro** doghouse; **sacarle a alguien de sus —s** to drive someone up the wall

casino M (club) men's club; (lugar de apuestas) casino

caso M case; **— de fuerza mayor** act of God; **— perdido** (persona incapacitada) basket case; (persona incorregible) lost cause; **en — de** in the event of; **en — de que** in case that; **el — es que** the deal is that; **en todo —** in any case, at any rate; **en último —** as a last resort; **eso no viene al —** that is beside the point; **hacer — [de]** to pay attention [to]; **hacer — omiso de** to disregard; **no hay —** there's no point; **pongamos por —** let's suppose that; **venir al —** to come to the point

caspa F dandruff

casquillo M (de bala) case; (de lámpara) socket

cassette MF cassette

casta F caste

castaña F chestnut; **— de cajú** cashew

castañetear VI to chatter; **— con los dedos** to snap one's fingers

castañeteo M (de dientes) chattering; (de dedos) snapping

castaño M (árbol) chestnut tree; (color, madera) chestnut; ADJ chestnut-colored, brown

castañuela F castanet

castellano ADJ & MF Castilian; M (lengua) Castilian

castidad F chastity

castigar[40] VT to chastise, to punish

castigo M chastisement, punishment; **¡qué —!**

what a nuisance!
Castilla F Castile
castillo M castle; **— de arena** sandcastle; **—s en el aire** *fam* pie in the sky
casting M casting
castizo ADJ traditional
casto ADJ chaste
castor M beaver
castrar VT (a un hombre, animal) to castrate; (a una mascota) to neuter, to fix; (a mascotas hembras) to spay
casual ADJ chance, accidental
casualidad F chance, coincidence; **da la — que** it so happens that; **oír por —** to overhear; **por —** by chance
casucha F shack
cata F **— de vinos** wine-tasting
catalán -ana ADJ (del catalán) Catalan; (de Cataluña) Catalonian; MF Catalan; M (lengua) Catalan
catalejo M spyglass
catalizador M catalyst
catalogar[40] VT to catalog/catalogue
catálogo M catalog, catalogue
Cataluña F Catalonia
catar VT to taste
catarata F (cascada) cataract, waterfall; (de los ojos) cataract
catarí ADJ & MF Qatari
catarro M cold
catástrofe F catastrophe
catatonia F catatonia
catecismo M catechism
cátedra F (puesto de profesor) chair, professorship; (enseñanza) teaching; (división académica) department; **sentar —** to hold forth, to pontificate
catedral F cathedral
catedrático -ca MF [full] professor
categoría F category; **de —** important; **de — mundial** world-class; **de poca —** third-rate
caterpillar M caterpillar
catéter M catheter
cateterización F catheterization
cateterizar VT to catheterize
cátodo M cathode
catolicismo M Catholicism
católico -ca ADJ Catholic; MF Catholic
catorce NUM fourteen
catre M cot
cátsup M catsup, ketchup
cauce M channel; **— de río** riverbed
cauchero -ra MF rubber gatherer; ADJ **industria cauchera** rubber industry
caucho M rubber; **— sintético** synthetic rubber
caución F security payment
caudal M (de bienes) wealth; (de agua) volume of water
caudaloso ADJ mighty

caudillo M leader
causa F (motivo) cause; (proceso) case; **— noble** worthy cause; **— perdida** lost cause; **a — de** on account of, because of; **con conocimiento de —** wittingly; **hacer — común** to work together
causante ADJ causing; MF instigator
causar VT to cause; **— problemas** to make trouble
cáustico ADJ caustic
cautela F caution
cautelar ADJ preventive
cauteloso ADJ cautious, wary
cauterizar[47] VT to cauterize
cautivar VT (capturar) to capture; (atraer) to captivate
cautiverio M captivity
cautivo -va MF captive
cauto ADJ cautious, wary
cava F (acción de cavar) digging; (sótano) cellar; (vino) cava
cavar VT to dig
caverna F cavern, cave
cavidad F cavity
cavilar VI to muse
cayado M shepherd's crook, staff
cayendo, cayera, cayese, cayeron *ver* caer
cayo M key
caza F (acción de cazar) hunt, hunting; (conjunto de animales) wild game; **— mayor** big game; **— menor** small game; **andar a la — de** to hunt for; **dar — a** to hunt down; M (avión) fighter
cazador -ora ADJ hunting; MF hunter; F Windbreaker™
cazar[47] VI/VT (buscar presas) to hunt; (matar presas) to shoot, to bag; (atrapar presas) to trap; MF SG **cazatalentos** talent scout, headhunter; M **cazatorpedero** destroyer, torpedo boat
cazo M (cacerola) pan; (cucharón) ladle, dipper
cazoleta F pipe bowl
cazuela F (recipiente) casserole; (cazo) pan
CD M CD; **— ROM** CD-ROM
cebada F barley
cebador M pump primer
cebar VT (un animal) to fatten; (bombas) to prime; (anzuelos) to bait; **—se** to vent one's anger
cebo M (para peces) bait, lure; (para animales) feed
cebolla F onion
cebollar M onion patch
cebollino M scallion
cebra F (animal) zebra; (paso) crosswalk
cecear VI to lisp
ceceo M lisp
cecina F jerky
cedazo M sieve

ceder VT (propiedad) to cede, to assign; (un sitio) to yield, to give up; VI (el frío) to diminish; (la resistencia) to give way

cedro M cedar

cédula F document; **— de identidad** identification card

céfiro M zephyr

cegar[41] VT to blind

ceguera F blindness; **— cromática** color blindness

ceja F (sobre el ojo) eyebrow; (en una encuadernación) tab; **quemarse las —s** to cram for an exam; **cejijunto** with thick eyebrows

cejar VI to back down

celada F ambush

celador -ora MF (en una escuela) school monitor; (en un barrio) security officer

celar VT to guard

celda F cell

celebración F (fiesta) celebration; (acto solemne) performance

celebrar VT (una fiesta) to celebrate; (una reunión) to hold; (un rito) to perform

célebre ADJ famous, noted

celebridad F celebrity

celeste ADJ (relativo al firmamento) celestial; (del color del cielo) azure, light blue

celestial ADJ celestial, heavenly

célibe ADJ celibate; MF unmarried person

cellisca F sleet; **caer —** to sleet

celo M (diligencia) zeal; (excitación sexual) heat; **estar en —** to be in heat; **—s** jealousy; **tener —s** to be jealous

celofán M cellophane

celosía F window lattice

celoso ADJ (que tiene celos) jealous; (diligente) zealous

célula F cell; **— adiposa** fat cell; **— estaminal embrional** stem cell

celular ADJ cellular; M mobile phone

celulitis F cellulite

celuloide M celluloid

celulosa F cellulose

cementar VT to cement

cementerio M cemetery, graveyard

cemento M cement; **— armado** reinforced concrete

cena F supper, dinner

cenagal M quagmire, swamp

cenagoso ADJ marshy, swampy

cenar VI to eat supper, to eat dinner; **vamos a — pescado** we're having fish for dinner

cencerro M cowbell

cenicero M ashtray

ceniciento ADJ ashen

cenit M zenith

cenizas F PL ashes, cinders

censar VI/VT to take a census [of]

censo M census

censor -ora MF censor; **— de cuentas** auditor

censura F (reprobación) censure; (control) censorship

censurador ADJ censuring

censurar VT (criticar) to censure; (examinar) to censor

centavo M cent

centella F sparkle; **pasar como una —** to go by in a flash

centelleante ADJ sparkling

centellear VI to sparkle, to scintillate

centelleo M sparkle

centenar M group of a hundred; **—es** hundreds

centenario M centennial; ADJ centenarian

centeno M rye

centésimo ADJ & M hundredth

centígrado ADJ centigrade

centímetro M centimeter

céntimo M cent

centinela MF sentry, sentinel

centrado ADJ (un tablón) true; (un cuadro) centered; (una persona) focused; M truing

central ADJ central; F plant; **— de teléfonos** telephone exchange; **— eléctrica** power plant; **— lechera** milk processing plant; **— nuclear** nuclear power plant

centralita F switchboard

centralizar[47] VT to centralize; **—se** to become centralized

centrar VT to center; **—se** to focus, to be focused

céntrico ADJ central

centrífugo ADJ centrifugal

centrípeto ADJ centripetal

centro M center (también de baloncesto); (de ciudad) downtown; **— comercial** shopping center; **— de gravedad** center of gravity; **— de mesa** centerpiece; MF **—campista** (fútbol) midfield player

Centroamérica F Central America

centroamericano -na M Central American

ceñido ADJ tight

ceñir[11] VT (rodear) to gird; (abrazar) to encircle; **— la corona** to be crowned; VI (estar apretado) to be tight; **—se a** (limitarse a) to limit oneself to; (arrimarse a) to get close to

ceño M **fruncir el —** to frown, to scowl

cepa F (de árbol) stump; (de viña) stock; (de bacteria) strain; **de pura —** of good stock

cepillar VT (dientes, pelo) to brush; (madera) to plane, to shave

cepillo M (para pelo, dientes) brush; (para madera) carpenter's plane; **— de dientes** toothbrush

cepo M (para cazar) trap; (para inmovilizar coches) boot

cera F wax; **— de oídos** earwax; **— para muebles** polish

cerámica F (arte) ceramics; (conjunto de

artículos) pottery, earthenware

cerámico ADJ ceramic

cerbatana F blowpipe

cerca ADV near, nearby, close; **— de** near, close to; **de —** close up; F fence

cercado M (terreno cercado) enclosure; (cerca) fence

cercanía F proximity, nearness, closeness

cercano ADJ (lugar) near, nearby; (pariente) close; **— Oriente** Near East

cercar[30] VT (rodear con una cerca) to fence, to enclose; (sitiar) to besiege

cercenar VT (cortar) to chop off; (reducir) to curtail, to encroach upon

cerciorarse VI **— [de]** to make sure [of]

cerco M (sitio) siege; (cerca) fence

cerdo -da M (animal, persona sucia) hog, pig; (carne) pork; F (puerca) sow; (de cepillo) bristle

cerdoso ADJ bristly

cereal M cereal; **—es** breakfast cereal; **cultivo — cereal** crop

cerebral ADJ cerebral

cerebro M (órgano, genio) brain; (organizador de un plan) mastermind; **lavarle el — a** to brainwash

ceremonia F ceremony

ceremonial ADJ & M ceremonial

ceremonioso ADJ ceremonious

cereza F cherry

cerezo M cherry tree

cerilla F match

cerner[2] VT to sift; **—se** (un ave) to hover; (un desastre) to loom

cernícalo M kestrel

cero M (cifra) zero; (en deportes) nothing, goose egg, zip; (en tenis) love; **— absoluto** absolute zero; **partir de —** to start from scratch; **ser un — a la izquierda** to be a nobody

cerrado ADJ (no abierto) closed; (tonto) dense; (poco comunicativo) reserved; (intransigente) closed-minded; (anguloso) sharp; M enclosure

cerrador -ora MF closer

cerradura F lock; **— de combinación** combination lock

cerrajería F locksmith's shop

cerrajero -ra MF locksmith

cerrar[1] VT (la puerta, un cajón) to close, to shut; (un trato) to close, to clinch; (un terreno) to enclose; (el gas, un grifo) to turn off; (una fábrica) to shut down, to close; **— filas** to close ranks; **— el paso** to block passage; VI to close; **—se** (una flor, una tienda) to close; (un plazo) to end; **—se el cielo** to become overcast

cerrazón F (de la mente) closed-mindedness; (del cielo) stormy skies

cerro M hill

cerrojo M bolt

certamen M contest; **— de belleza** beauty contest

certero ADJ sure

certeza F certainty

certidumbre F certainty

certificación F certification

certificado ADJ certified; M certificate; **— de nacimiento** birth certificate

certificar[30] VT (la autenticidad) to certify; (una carta) to register

cervatillo M fawn

cervecera F brewery

cervecería F bar

cerveza F beer; **— de barril** draft beer

cervical ADJ cervical

cérvix M cervix

cerviz F cervix

cesar VI to cease; **— de trabajar** to stop working; **— en un cargo** to resign from a position; **— a** to dismiss

cesárea F cesarean [section]

cese M cessation; **— el fuego** ceasefire; **— de actividades** shutdown

cesión F (de propiedad) assignment; (de derechos) waiver

césped M (ante una casa) lawn; (hierba, también para tenis) grass

cesta F basket

cestería F basketry

cesto M (cesta) basket; (para ropa) hamper

cetrino ADJ olive-colored

chabacano ADJ (modales) crude; (gustos) tacky; M *Méx* apricot

chacal M jackal

chacha F servant girl

cháchara F small talk

chacota F joke; **tomarse algo a la —** to take lightly

chacra F (establecimiento agrícola) small farm; (terreno) small plot

Chad M Chad

chadiano -na ADJ & MF Chadian

chal M shawl, wrap

chala F *Am* husk; **quitar la —** to husk

chalán M horse trader

chalé M cottage

chaleco M waistcoat, vest; **— antibalas** bulletproof vest; **— de fuerza** straitjacket; **— salvavidas** life jacket

chalupa F small canoe; *Méx* tortilla with sauce

chamaco -ca M *Méx* boy; F *Méx* girl

chamarra F sheepskin jacket

chambergo M wide-brimmed hat

chambón ADJ clumsy

champán/champaña M champagne

champiñón M mushroom

champú M shampoo

chamuscadura F scorch

chamuscar[30] VT to scorch, to singe; **—se** to get scorched, to get singed

chamusquina F scorching, singeing

chance MF chance

chancearse VI **— de** to make fun of

chancho M hog

chanchullo M *fam* monkey business

chancleta F thong, flipflop; **tirar la —** to kick up one's heels

chanclo M galosh, overshoe; **—s** rubbers

chándal M sweatsuit

chantaje M blackmail

chantajear VT to blackmail

chanza F jest

chao INTERJ bye-bye

chapa F (de metal) sheet metal; (de policía) badge; (de botella) bottle top; (de madera) veneer; **— en la puerta** shingle on the door; **hacerle — y pintura a un coche** to fix the bodywork and paint of a car

chapado ADJ **— a la antigua** old-fashioned

chapalear VI to splash

chapar VT to plate

chaparral M dry rangeland, chaparral

chaparro M scrub oak; ADJ *Méx* short

chaparrón M cloudburst

chaperón-ona MF chaperon[e]; **ir de —** to chaperon[e]

chapitel M spire, steeple

chapotear VI to splash

chapoteo M splash, splashing

chapucear VT to botch, to bungle

chapucería F (trabajo, obra) botched job; (cualidad) sloppiness

chapucero ADJ shoddy, slipshod

chapurrear VT to speak a language poorly

chapuz M dive

chapuza F botched job

chapuzar[47] VI to dive

chaqueta F jacket; **— de sport** sport jacket

charada F charades

charca F pond

charco M puddle, pool; **cruzar el —** to cross the ocean

charcutería F (tienda) delicatessen; (industria) sausage-making

charla F chat, talk

charlar VI to chat, to gab

charlatán-ana ADJ talkative; MF (parlanchín) chatterbox, windbag; (curandero) charlatan, quack

charlotear VI to chatter, to jabber

charloteo M chatter, jabber

charol M (barniz) varnish; (cuero barnizado) patent leather

charolar VT to varnish

charqui M beef jerky

charro ADJ flashy, tawdry

chárter M charter flight

chascar VT (los nudillos, un hueso) to crack; (los labios) to smack; (la lengua) to click

chascarrillo M funny anecdote

chasco M (broma) prank, practical joke; (decepción) dud; **llevarse un —** to be disappointed

chasis M frame, chassis

chasquear VT (decepcionar) to disappoint; (una cerradura, la lengua) to click; (un látigo) to crack; (los labios) to smack; (los dedos) to snap; **—se** to be disappointed

chasquido M (de látigo, madera, articulaciones) crack; (de labios) smack; (de la lengua, una cerradura) click; (de los dedos) snap

chata F bedpan

chatarra F scrap iron

chatarrería F junkyard

chatear VI to chat

chato ADJ (nariz) snub-nosed; (zapatos, pecho) flat; **— como una tabla** as flat as a pancake

chaucha F green bean

chaval-la M *Esp* boy; F *Esp* girl

chaveta F cotter pin; **perder la —** *fam* to go bonkers

che INTERJ *RP* say! hey!

checo-ca ADJ & MF Czech

chef MF chef

cheque M check; **— de viajero** traveler's check; **— de caja** bank check; **— sin fondos** bad check, worthless check

chequear VT to check

checar VT to check

chequera F checkbook

chic ADJ INV & M chic

chicha F (bebida alcohólica) *Am* corn liquor; (carne) *Esp fam* meat; **de — y nabo** two-bit; **ni — ni limonada** neither fish nor fowl

chicharra F (insecto) cicada; (timbre) buzzer

chichón M bump, lump, knot

chicle M chewing gum; **— de globo** bubblegum

chico-ca ADJ small, little; M boy; F girl; **mis —s** my kids

chicote M *Am* whip

chicotear VT *Am* to whip

chicoteo M *Am* whipping

chiflado ADJ *fam* nuts, cuckoo, loony; MF (persona loca) *fam* basket case, loon

chifladura F craziness

chiflar VI (silbar) to whistle; VT (volver loco) to drive crazy; **—se** to go crazy

chiflido M whistle

chifón M chiffon

chile M chile

Chile M Chile

chileno-na ADJ & MF Chilean

chillar VI (persona) to shriek; (puerta, ratón) to squeak; (cerdo) to squeal

chillido M (de persona) shriek; (de puerta,

ratón) squeak; (de cerdo) squeal

chillón ADJ (sonido) shrill; (color) loud, gaudy, flashy

chimenea F (salida de humo) chimney; (hogar) fireplace; (de volcán, baño, mina) vent; (de fábrica) smokestack

chimpancé M chimpanzee

china F (porcelana) china; (piedra) pebble

China F China

chinche F (insecto) bedbug; (chincheta) thumbtack; MF (persona molesta) pain

chinchilla F chinchilla

chinchorro M rowboat

chino -na ADJ Chinese; M (lengua) Chinese; MF Chinese; **vi a un chino** I saw a Chinese person; **los chinos no están de acuerdo** the Chinese don't agree; **eso es —** that's Greek to me

chip M (de ordenador, en golf) chip; (de papa/ patata) potato chip; **— de silicio** silicon chip

Chipre M Cyprus

chipriota ADJ & MF Cypriot[e]

chiquilín -ina M little boy; F little girl

chiquito ADJ tiny, wee

chiripa F stroke of good luck; **por/de —** by a fluke

chirivía F parsnip

chirona F jail

chirriante ADJ squeaky

chirriar[28] VI (puerta, freno) to squeak; (ave, freno) to screech

chirrido M (de puerta, freno) squeak; (de ave, freno) screech

chisgarabís M pipsqueak

chisguete M squirt

chisme M (rumor) gossip, piece of gossip; (objeto) *fam* gizmo, thingamajig

chismear VI to gossip

chismoso -sa ADJ gossipy; MF gossip

chispa F (partícula incandescente) spark; (ingenio) wit; **echar —s** to be furious; **pasar echando —s** to whiz by

chispeante ADJ (que echa chispas) sparkling; (ingenioso) witty

chispear VI (echar chispas) to spark; (lloviznar) to sprinkle

chisporrotear VI (fuego) to sputter; (cigarrillo) to fizzle; (carne) to sizzle

chisporroteo M (de fuego) sputter; (de carne) sizzle

chiste M (verbal) joke; (visual) cartoon; (ocurrencia) wisecrack; **— verde** dirty joke; **no le veo el —** I don't see the humor in it

chistera F top hat

chistoso ADJ funny, amusing, humorous

chivar VI/VT to snitch [on], to rat [on]

chivatar VI/VT to squeal [on], to snitch [on]

chivato -ta MF (delator) informer, snitch, stool pigeon; (chivito) kid

chivo M kid; **— expiatorio** scapegoat; **estar como un —** to be crazy as a loon

chocante ADJ shocking, jarring

chocar[30] VI (golpearse) to bump, to collide; (antagonizar) to clash; VT (sorprender) to shock; (destrozar) to wreck; **— los cinco** to shake hands

chocarrería F coarseness

chochear VI to be in one's dotage

chochera F senility, dotage

chochez F senility, dotage

chocho ADJ senile; **estar —** to be in one's dotage; **estar — con** to dote on

choclo M ear of corn

chocolate M (planta, dulce) chocolate; (bebida) cocoa, drinking chocolate

chocolatera F chocolate pot

chocolatina F chocolate bar

chófer, chofer MF chauffeur, driver

cholo -la MF (mestizo) person of mixed race; (indio) Europeanized Indian

chopo M poplar

choque M (de objetos móviles) collision, bump, crash; (eléctrico, emocional, cultural) shock; **— insulínico** insulin shock

chorizo M sausage

chorlito M plover

chorrear VI/VT (poco) to drip; (mucho) to gush

chorro M spurt, jet; **a —s** in buckets

chotearse VI **— de** to make fun of

choteo M mocking

chovinismo M chauvinism

choza F hut, shack, hovel

chubasco M squall, shower

chuchería F trinket, knickknack

chueco ADJ *Am* crooked

chuleta F (papel para copiar) cheat sheet; (golf) divot; **— de cerdo** pork chop; **— de ternera** veal cutlet

chulo -la M (dandi) dandy, dude; (bravucón) tough guy; MF working-class resident of Madrid; ADJ (fanfarrón) boastful; (bonito) cute

chupada F (de cigarro) puff; (de bebida) sip

chupar VI/VT (succionar) to suck; (fumar) to puff [on]; VT (absorber) to absorb; (vivir a costa de) to sponge off; **chúpate esa** put that in your pipe and smoke it; M SG **chupasangre** leech

chupete M pacifier

chupetín M RP lollipop, sucker

churrasco M *Am* barbecued steak

churro M fritter

chusma F rabble, riffraff

chut M hard shot

chutar VI (drogas) to shoot up; VT (un balón) to shoot; *Esp* **— la bola** to kick the ball hard

chute M narcotic fix

chuzo M watchman's pike

CIA F CIA

cianotipo M blueprint
cianuro M cyanide
cibercafé M cybercafe
ciberespacio M cyberspace
cibernética F cybernetics
ciberpunk MF cyberpunk
cicatero ADJ stingy
cicatriz F scar
cicatrizar VI (formar cicatriz) to form a scar; (curarse) to heal up
cíclico ADJ cyclical
ciclista MF bicycle rider, cyclist, biker
ciclo M cycle; **—motor** moped; **— vital** life cycle; **— de auditoría** audit cycle; **— de facturación** billing cycle; **— presupuestario** budget cycle
ciclón M cyclone
ciclotrón M cyclotron
cicuta F hemlock
ciego ADJ (no vidente) blind; (por borrachera) plastered; (por drogas) high; **quedarse —** to go blind; **a ciegas** blindly
cielo M (firmamento) sky; (paraíso) heaven; **a — abierto** under the open sky; **minería a — abierto** open pit mining; **— raso** ceiling; **¡—s!** good heavens! **estar en el séptimo —** to be in seventh heaven; **me cayó del —** it's a godsend; **poner el grito en el —** *fam* to hit the ceiling
ciempiés M centipede
cien, ciento NUM hundred; **por ciento** percent
ciénaga F swamp, mire, marsh
ciencia F (campo de investigación) science; (conocimiento) knowledge; (arte) art; **— ficción** science fiction; **—s políticas** political science; **a — cierta** with certainty; **las —s ocultas** the occult; **no tiene —** there's nothing to it
cieno M mud, mire
científico -ca ADJ scientific; MF scientist
cierra, cierre *ver* cerrar
cierre M (traba) clasp, fastener; (cremallera) zipper; (acción de cerrar) closing, closure; **— patronal** lockout; **al —** (noticias) at press time; (acciones) at the close
ciertamente ADV certainly
cierto ADJ certain; (verdadero) true; (seguro) sure; **en — sentido** in a sense; **hasta — punto** to a certain extent; **por —** by the way; INTERJ you're right!
ciervo -va M (animal) deer; (macho) stag; **— volante** stag beetle; F (hembra) doe, hind
cierzo M north wind
cifra F (numeral) digit; (número) figure; (clave) cipher, key; **— aproximada** ballpark estimate; **poner en —** to encode
cifrado M encryption; **— de datos** data encryption
cifrar VT to write in code, to encrypt; **— las**

esperanzas en to place one's hopes on; **el monto se cifra en veinte millones de pesos** the figure amounts to twenty million pesos
cigarra F cicada
cigarrera F cigar case, cigarette case
cigarrillo M cigarette
cigarro M (cigarrillo) cigarette; (puro) cigar
cigoto M zygote
cigüeña F stork
cigüeñal M crankshaft
cilíndrico ADJ cylindrical
cilindro M cylinder
cima F summit
cimarrón -ona ADJ wild; MF runaway slave
címbalo M cymbal
cimbel M decoy
cimbrar VT to sway, to vibrate
cimentar VT (una casa) to lay the foundation of; (una victoria) to secure
cimiento M foundation
cinc M zinc
cincel M chisel
cincelar VT to chisel
cincha F cinch, girth
cinchar VT to cinch, to girth
cinco NUM five
cincuenta NUM fifty
cine M cinema, movies
cineasta MF filmmaker
cinematografía F cinematography, movie-making
cinematografiar[28] VI/VT to film
cinematográfico ADJ cinematographic; **industria cinematográfica** motion-picture industry
cinestesia F kinesthesia
cingalés -esa ADJ & MF Sri Lankan
cínico -ca ADJ cynical; MF cynic
cinismo M cynicism
cinta F (de adorno) ribbon; (adhesiva) tape; (cinematográfica) film; **— aislante** electrical tape; **— de vídeo** videotape; **— magnetofónica** recording tape; **— métrica** tape measure; **— rodante** treadmill; **— transportadora** conveyor belt
cinto M belt
cintura F (de persona) waist; (de cosa) middle
cinturón M belt; **— de seguridad** safety belt
ciprés M cypress
circo M circus
circonio M zirconium
circuitería F circuitry
circuito M circuit; **— cerrado** closed circuit; **— impreso** circuit board; **— integrado** integrated circuit
circulación F (de sangre, de bienes) circulation; (de vehículos) traffic; **poner en —** to circulate

circular VI to circulate; **hay que — por la derecha** you have to drive on the right; F circular letter

circulatorio ADJ circulatory; **problemas —s** cardiovascular problems; **atasco —** traffic jam

círculo M circle; **— vicioso** vicious circle

circuncidar VT to circumcise

circundante ADJ surrounding

circundar VT to surround

circunferencia F circumference

circunlocución F circumlocution

circunscribir[74] VT to circumscribe

circunspecto ADJ circumspect

circunstancia F circumstance

circunstancial ADJ circumstantial

cirio M candle

cirro M cirrus

cirrosis F cirrhosis

ciruela F plum; **— pasa** prune

ciruelo M plum tree

cirugía F surgery; **— de corazón abierto** open-heart surgery; **— plástica/estética** plastic surgery, cosmetic surgery

cirujano -na MF surgeon

cisne M swan

cisterna F cistern

cita F (romántica) date; (con el médico) appointment; (textual) quotation, quote; **— a ciegas** blind date; **darse —** to meet

citación F citation, summons

citar VT (a un testigo) to summon; (a un autor) to cite, to quote; **—se con** (el médico) to make an appointment with; (un amigo) to make a date with

citología F (ciencia) cell biology, cytology; (toma de células vaginales) pap smear

cítrico ADJ citric; M citrus

ciudad F city

ciudadanía F citizenship

ciudadano -na MF citizen

Ciudad del Vaticano F Vatican City

ciudadela F citadel

cívico ADJ civic

civil ADJ (no criminal, no religioso) civil; (no militar) civilian

civilidad F civility

civilización F civilization

civilizador ADJ civilizing

civilizar[47] VT to civilize; **—se** to become civilized

cizalla F metal shears

cizaña F **sembrar —** to sow discord

clamar VT/VI to demand; **— por** to clamor for

clamor M clamor, outcry

clamorear VI/VT to shout

clamoreo M shouting

clamoroso ADJ clamorous

clan M clan

clandestino ADJ clandestine

claqué M tap dance

clara F egg white; **— de huevo** egg white

claraboya F skylight

clarear VI (aclararse) to become clear; (amanecer) to grow light; (desenturbiarse) to thin; VT to illuminate; **—se** to grow light

claridad F (de ideas) clarity; (de la luz) brightness, lightness

clarificar[30] VT to clarify, to clear

clarín M bugle

clarinete M clarinet

clarividente MF & ADJ clairvoyant

claro ADJ clear; (franco) straightforward; (iluminado) light, bright; **azul —** light blue; **a las claras** clearly; ADV clearly; INTERJ of course! M (espacio) gap; (en un bosque) clearing; **— de luna** moonlight

clase F (tipo) kind, sort; (grupo social, sesión docente, alumnado) class; (aula) classroom; **— alta** upper class; **— media** middle class; **— obrera** working class; **— turista** economy class; **dar —** to teach a class; **toda — de** all sorts of

clasicismo M classicism

clásico ADJ (destacado, consabido) classic; (de un período histórico) classical; M classic

clasificación F (taxonómica) classification; (deportiva) qualification; **— descendiente** descending sort

clasificado M want ad

clasificar[30] VT (ordenar) to classify; (en deportes) to qualify; **—se para** to qualify for; **—se segundo** to come in second

claustro M cloister; **— de profesores** university faculty

claustrofobia F claustrophobia

claustrofóbico ADJ claustrophobic

cláusula F clause

clausura F closing

clausurar VT (una sesión) to bring to a close, to conclude; (una tienda) to close [down]

clavadista MF diver

clavado ADV exactly; M (de clavos) nailing; (en una piscina) dive; **tirarse un —** to dive

clavar VT (perforar con un clavo) to nail, to drive a nail into; (pinchar) to stick, to poke; **—le la mirada / los ojos a alguien** to stare at someone; **— los frenos** to stomp on the brakes; **me clavaron** I got a raw deal

clave F (sistema de signos) code; (tabla de correspondencias) key; (signo musical) clef; (clavicémbalo) harpsichord; (de mapa) legend; **— de fa** bass clef; **— de seguridad** password; **— de sol** treble clef; ADJ key

clavel M carnation

clavetear VT to put pegs on

clavicémbalo M harpsichord

clavícula F collarbone, clavicle

clavija F (de guitarra) peg; (de enchufe) pin

clavo M (pieza de metal) nail; (capullo) clove; (de zapato) spike; **dar en el —** to hit the nail on the head

claxon M car horn

clearing M clearing

clemencia F clemency, mercy

clemente ADJ forgiving, merciful

cleptomanía F kleptomania

cleptómano -na MF kleptomaniac

clerecía F (funciones) ministry; (clérigos) clergy

clerical ADJ clerical

clérigo M clergyman, minister

clero M clergy

clic M click; **hacer —** to click; **hacer doble —** to double-click

cliché M (placa fotográfica) photographic plate; (expresión muy usada) cliché

cliente MF, **clienta** F (de un profesional) client; (de un negocio) customer; (de un restaurante) patron; (de un hotel) guest

clientela F clientele, customer base

clientelismo M patronage

clima M climate

climático ADJ climatic; **cambio —** climate change

climatización F air conditioning

clímax M climax

clinch M clinch

clínica F clinic

clínico ADJ clinical

clip M paper clip

cloaca F sewer

clon M clone

clonación F cloning

clonaje M cloning

clonar VT to clone

cloquear VI to cluck

cloqueo M cluck, clucking

clorhidrato M hydrochloride; **— de Ritalina** Ritalin hydrochloride

cloro M chlorine

clorofila F chlorophyll

cloroformo M chloroform

cloruro M chloride

club M club (también palo de golf); **— nocturno** nightclub

coacción F compulsion, coercion; **bajo —** under duress

coagulación F (de sangre) clotting; (por productos químicos) coagulation

coagulante M coagulant

coagular VI (con productos químicos) to coagulate; (sangre) to clot

coágulo M clot

coalición F coalition

coartada F alibi

coartar VT (una libertad) to restrict; (a una persona) to inhibit; (la creatividad) to strangle

cobalto M cobalt

cobarde ADJ cowardly; MF coward

cobardía F cowardice

cobertizo M shed

cobertor M cover

cobertura F (de nieve, aérea) cover; (de seguros, noticias, televisión) coverage; **— extendida** extended coverage

cobija F (cubierta) cover; (manta) blanket

cobijar VT to shelter; **—se** to seek shelter

cobra F cobra

cobrador -ora MF (persona) collector; M (perro) retriever

cobranza F collection

cobrar VT (impuestos) to collect; (una factura) to charge; (un cheque) to cash; (el sueldo) to earn; (víctimas) to claim; **— al entregar** to collect on delivery; **— ánimo** to take heart; **— caro** to charge a lot; **— de más** to overcharge; **— de menos** to undercharge; **— valor** to gain importance; **a —** receivable; **vas a —** you're in for it

cobre M (elemento) copper; (utensilios) copper utensils

cobrizo ADJ copper-colored

cobro M collection, charge; **— excesivo** overcharge

coca F (planta, hoja) coca; (cocaína) *fam* coke

cocaína F cocaine

cóccix M coccyx

cocear VI/VT to kick

cocer[34] VI/VT (huevos) to boil; (verduras) to cook; (cerámica) to fire; **— al vapor** to steam; **a medio —** half-cooked; **romper a —** to break into a boil; **¿qué se cuece aquí?** what's up?

coche M (automóvil, vagón) car; (autobús) coach; (vehículo tirado por caballerías) carriage; **— bomba** car bomb; **— cama** sleeper; **—comedor** dining car; **— de bebé** stroller, baby carriage; **— de bomberos** fire engine; **— de choque** bumper car; **— de golf** golf cart; **— de línea** city bus; **— deportivo** sports car; **— fúnebre** hearse; **ir en —** to go by car, to drive; **pasear en —** to go on a drive

cochera F carport

cochinada F (asquerosidad) filthy action; (maldad) dirty trick

cochinilla F woodlouse

cochino -na ADJ filthy; MF pig

cocido M stew

cociente M quotient; **— intelectual** IQ

cocina F (habitación) kitchen; (electrodoméstico) range, stove; (arte) cuisine, cookery

cocinar VI/VT to cook; (tramar) to cook up

cocinero -ra MF cook

cócker MF cocker spaniel

coco M (fruto) coconut; (cabeza) *fam* dome; (fantasma) bogeyman; **comerse el —** to get all worked up

cocodrilo M crocodile

cóctel M (bebida) cocktail, mixed drink; (fiesta) cocktail party

codazo M jab with the elbow; **dar —s** to elbow

codear VI/VT to elbow, to jab; **—se** to nudge one another; **—se con** to rub elbows with

codeína F codeine

codicia F (avaricia) greed; (deseo sexual) lust

codiciar VT (una cosa) to covet; (a una persona) to lust after

codicioso ADJ covetous, greedy

codificación F coding, encoding

codificar[30] VT (mensaje) to codify, to encrypt; (programa de computadora) to code

código M code; **— abierto** open code; **— de acceso** access code; **— de barras** bar code; **— de país** country code; **— fuente** source code; **— genético** genetic code; **— impositivo** tax code; **— postal** zip code

codo M elbow; **— a —** side by side; **— de tenista** tennis elbow; **empinar el —** to drink too much; **hablar por los —s** to talk one's head off; **hasta los —s** up to one's elbows

codorniz F quail

coeficiente M coefficient; **— de inteligencia** intelligence quotient

coerción F coercion

coetáneo ADJ contemporary

coexistencia F coexistence; **— pacífica** peaceful coexistence

cofre M coffer

coger[45] VT (a un criminal, una pelota) to catch; (con las manos) to grasp; (flores) to gather; to pick; (a un empleado) to hire; (una emisora) to receive; (cosas del suelo) to pick up; (espacio) to take up; (un pez) to land, to catch; (un camino, tren, curso) to take; **— por/de sorpresa** to catch by surprise; **— el sueño** to fall asleep; **— hacia el castillo** to turn toward the castle; **—le miedo a algo** to become scared of something; **—le el tranquillo a algo** to get into the swing of things; **—se un resfriado** to come down with a cold; **coge y le dice** he up and says

cognado ADJ & M cognate

cognitivo ADJ cognitive

cogollo M heart

cogote M neck

cohabitar VI (amigos) to live [with]; (una pareja) to cohabitate

cohecho M bribe

coheredero -ra MF joint heir

coherencia F (consecuencia) consistency; (lógica) coherence

coherente ADJ (consecuente) consistent; (lógico) coherent; (con significado) meaningful; **lo que dices no es —** you're not making any sense

cohesión F cohesion

cohesivo ADJ coherent

cohete M rocket

cohetería F rocketry

cohibición F inhibition

cohibido ADJ inhibited, self-conscious

cohibir VT to inhibit

coincidencia F coincidence

coincidir VI to coincide

coito M coitus

cojear VI to limp; **saber de qué pie cojea alguien** to know someone's weaknesses

cojera F limp

cojín M cushion

cojinete M bushing; **— de bolas** ball bearing

cojo ADJ lame, crippled

cok M coke

col F cabbage; **—es de Bruselas** Brussels sprouts

cola F (de perro, ave, avión) tail; (de vestido) train; (hilera de gente) line; (secuencia de datos o programas) queue; (pegamento) glue; **— de caballo** ponytail; **hacer —** to stand in line; **no pegar ni con —** not to go together; **traer —** to have consequences

colaboración F collaboration

colaborador -ora MF (con el gobierno) collaborator; (de periódico) contributor

colaborar VI to collaborate; (con un periódico) to contribute

colación F **sacar a —** to bring up

colacionar VT to collate

colador M (para té) strainer; (para verduras) colander

colágeno M collagen

colapso M (de puente, edificio) collapse; (de nervios) breakdown; (de mercado) crash

colar[5] VT (té) to strain; (metal líquido) to pour; VI to go through, to slip through; **esa excusa no va a —** that excuse won't wash; **—se en una fiesta** to crash a party

colateral ADJ collateral

colcha F bedspread

colchón M (para dormir) mattress; (para emergencias) cushion

colchoneta F mat

colear VI (un perro) to wag the tail; (un tema) to be pending; (un auto) to fishtail

colección F collection

coleccionar VT to collect

coleccionista MF collector

colecta F charity collection

colectividad F collective, community

colectivo M (grupo) collective; (autobús) *Am* bus

colector M (de aguas negras) sewer; (eléctrico) collector; (de coche) manifold

colega MF colleague

colegio M (escuela privada) private school; (escuela primaria) elementary school; (centro de educación secundaria) high school; (asociación profesional) association, college

colegir[14] VI to gather

cólera F rage, wrath; **montar en —** to fly into a rage; M cholera

colérico ADJ irritable, choleric

colesterol M cholesterol

coleta F pigtail

coletilla F tag

coleto M **decir para su —** to say to oneself

colgadero M hanger; ADJ hanging

colgado ADJ high and dry

colgadura F drapery; **—s** hangings

colgante ADJ hanging; M pendant

colgar[42] VT (suspender, ahorcar) to hang; (un teléfono, un abrigo) to hang up; VI (un espejo) to hang; (un andrajo) to dangle; (un asunto) to be pending; **esa falda te cuelga por atrás** that dress hangs down in the back; **—se [un ordenador]** to crash; **—se de** to get hooked on; **—se del teléfono** to tarry on the phone

colibrí M hummingbird

cólico M colic

coliflor F cauliflower

colilla F cigarette butt

colina F hill, knoll

colindante ADJ neighboring

colindar VI **— con** to border [on], to adjoin

colirio M eyedrops

coliseo M coliseum

colisión F collision

collage M collage

collar M (de perlas) necklace; (de perro) collar; **— antipulgas** flea collar

collera F horse collar

collie M collie

colmar VT (un vaso) to fill; (una demanda) to satisfy; **— de alabanzas** to lavish praise upon

colmena F beehive

colmillo M (de persona) eyetooth, cuspid; (de elefante) tusk; (de víbora) fang

colmo M **— de la locura** height of folly; **¡eso es el —!** that takes the cake; **para —** to top it all

colocación F (ubicación) placement; (puesto) position

colocar[30] VT (poner, encontrar lugar para) to place; (casar) to marry off; (invertir) to invest; **—se** (encontrar empleo) to get a job; (ubicarse) to place oneself

coloide M colloid

Colombia F Colombia

colombiano -na ADJ & MF Colombian

colon M colon

colón M (moneda) colon

colonia F (territorio, grupo de insectos) colony; (comunidad de inmigrantes) community, settlement; (vivienda) development; (perfume) cologne

colonial ADJ colonial

colonización F colonization

colonizador -ora MF colonist

colonizar[47] VT to colonize, to settle

colono -na MF (habitante de una colonia) colonist, settler; (arrendatario) tenant farmer

colonoscopia F colonoscopy

coloquial ADJ colloquial

coloquio M colloquium

color M (tono) color; (pintura) paint; (maquillaje) rouge; (de naipes) flush; **—es primarios** primary colors; **a todo —** full color; **persona de —** person of color

coloración F coloring

colorado ADJ & M red; **ponerse —** to blush

colorante ADJ & M coloring

coloreado ADJ colored; M coloring

colorear VT to color

colorete M rouge

colorido M (de un caballo) coloring; (de un comentario, paisaje) color; ADJ colorful

colosal ADJ (grande) colossal; (estupendo) wonderful

colostomía F colostomy

columbrar VT to glimpse

columna F column; **— de dirección** steering column; **— vertebral** spinal column, backbone

columnista MF columnist

columpiar VI/VT to swing

columpio M swing

colza F (planta) rape; (aceite) rapeseed oil

coma F (signo) comma; M (falta de conciencia) coma

comadre F (mujer chismosa) gossip; (partera) midwife; (parienta) godmother of one's child

comadreja F weasel

comadrona F (mujer chismosa) gossip; (partera) midwife

comandancia F command

comandante MF (rango militar) major; (militar que ejerce el mando) commander; **— en jefe** commander in chief

comandar VT to command; **— un avión** to pilot an airplane

comando M (grupo militar) commando; (orden dada al ordenador) command

comarca F district

comatoso ADJ comatose

comba F (de una pared) bulge; (de madera) warp; **saltar a la —** to jump rope

combar VI (una pared) to sag; (madera) to warp; (trayectoria de pelota) to curve

combate M combat, fight; **fuera de —** out of combat / the competition

combatiente MF combatant

combatir VI/VT to combat

combativo ADJ combative

combinación F (mezcla) combination; (billete) transfer ticket

combinar VT to combine; **—se para hacer algo** to agree to do something; **esos colores no combinan** those colors don't match

combo M combo

combustible ADJ combustible; M fuel

combustión F combustion

comedero M trough

comedia F (obra teatral) comedy; (farsa) farce; **— de situación** situation comedy, sitcom; **hacer la — de** to play the part of

comediante MF comedian

comedido ADJ moderate; *Am* obliging

comedirse[9] VI to show restraint; **— a hacer algo** *RP* to volunteer to do something

comedor M (habitación) dining room; (de empresa) cafeteria

comensal MF [fellow] diner

comentador-ora MF commentator

comentar VI/VT to comment [on], to remark [on]

comentario M (análisis) commentary; (observación) comment, remark

comentarista MF commentator

comenzar[48] VI/VT to begin, to start; **— a comer** to begin to eat; **— preguntando** to begin by asking

comer VI/VT to eat; (al mediodía) to have lunch; (en ajedrez) to take; (en el juego de damas) to jump; **dar de —** to feed; **sin —lo ni beberlo** through no fault of one's own; **—se** (corroer) to eat away; (terminar la comida) to eat up; **—se las eses** to drop one's esses; **—se las palabras** to eat one's words; **—se un semáforo en rojo** to run a red light

comercial ADJ & M commercial

comercialización F marketing, merchandising

comercializar[47] VT (volver comercial) to commercialize; (vender) to market, to merchandise

comerciante MF merchant, trader, dealer

comerciar VI to trade

comercio M commerce, trade; **— electrónico** e-business; **— exterior** foreign trade; **— minorista** retail trade; **— mayorista** wholesaler

comestible ADJ edible; M PL groceries

cometa M (cuerpo celeste) comet; F (juguete) kite

cometer VT to commit

cometido M purpose, objective

comezón F itch, itching; **tener —** to itch

cómic M comic book

comicios M PL polls

cómico-ca ADJ comic, comical; MF comedian

comida F (ocasión) meal; (alimento) food; (al mediodía) lunch; **— basura** junk food; **—**

macrobiótica health food; **— rápida** fast food

comience, comienza *ver* comenzar

comienzo M beginning; **a —s de** toward the beginning of; **al —** at first, initially; **desde un/el —** from the start

comilla F quotation mark; **entre —s** in quotes

comilón-ona MF big eater; F binge

comino M cumin; **me importa un —** *fam* I don't give a hoot; **no vale un —** *fam* it's not worth a hoot

comisaría F **— de policía** police station, precinct

comisario-ria MF (comisionado) commissioner; (jefe de policía) police chief

comisión F (acción de cometer, porcentaje ganado) commission; (comité) committee

comisionar VT to commission

comistrajo M bad food

comisura F **— de los labios** corner of the mouth

comité M committee

comitiva F retinue

como ADV (del mismo modo que) as, like; **ella pinta — yo** she paints like I do; (aproximadamente) about; **pesa — diez kilos** it weighs about ten kilos; CONJ (puesto que) since; **— no tenemos dinero** since we have no money; **— no me pagues** if you don't pay me; **era — que muy viejo** he was, like, real old; **— que te voy a permitir** as if I would let you; **— quieras** as you please; **— si** as if; **¡— si me lo fuera a creer!** a likely story!

cómo ADV INTERR & PRON (de qué manera) how; (¿perdón?) excuse me? what? **¡— brillan las estrellas!** how the stars are shining! **¡— no!** of course! **¿a — me lo vende?** what does that cost?

cómoda F chest of drawers, dresser, bureau

comodidad F (cualidad) comfort; (cosa cómoda) convenience; **—es** amenities

comodín M joker, wild card

cómodo ADJ (mueble) comfortable; (horario) convenient; (persona) lazy

Comoras F PL Comoros

compactar VT to compact

compacto ADJ compact

compadecer[35] VT to pity; **—se de** to take pity on

compadre M (amigo) pal, crony; (pariente) godfather of one's child

compañero-ra MF (camarada) companion; (de un zapato) mate; **— de clase** classmate; **— de cuarto** roommate; **— de equipo** teammate

compañía F company; **— de importación y exportación** import-export company; **— fantasma** bogus company; **— recién establecida** start-up; **en — de** in the

company of
comparable ADJ comparable
comparación F comparison
comparar VI/VT to compare; **—se con** to compare [oneself] with
comparativo ADJ comparative
comparecencia F appearance
comparecer[35] VI to appear
compartimiento M compartment
compartir VT (bienes) to share; (tiempo) to divide
compás M (instrumento de geometría) compass; (ritmo) beat; (espacio entre barras) measure, bar; (división de música) time signature; **marcar el —** to beat time
compasión F compassion
compasivo ADJ compassionate, sympathetic
compatibilidad F compatibility
compatible ADJ compatible
compatriota MF compatriot
compeler VT to compel
compendiar VT to summarize
compendio M digest, condensation
compenetración F bonding
compensación F compensation
compensar VT (un daño) to compensate; (un gasto) to offset; **compensa su falta de inteligencia con mucha disciplina** he makes up for his lack of intelligence with a lot of discipline; **te voy a — por esto** I'll make it up to you
competencia F (pugna, competición, competidores) competition; (cualidad de competente) competence
competente ADJ competent
competición F athletic competition, meet
competidor -ora ADJ competing; MF (comercial) competitor; (deportivo) athlete, participant
competir[9] VI to compete, to vie
competitividad F competitiveness
competitivo ADJ competitive
compilador M compiler
compilar VT to compile
compinche M chum, crony
compita, compite, compitiendo, compitiera, compitiese ver competir
complacencia F satisfaction
complacer[36] VT to please, to gratify; **—se [en]** to take pleasure [in]
complaciente ADJ (que complace) obliging; (que consiente) indulgent
complejidad F complexity
complejo ADJ complex; M complex; **— de inferioridad** inferiority complex
complementar VT to complement, to supplement
complementario ADJ complementary
complemento M complement; **— alimenticio** dietary supplement; **— directo** direct object; **— indirecto** indirect object; **—s** fringe benefits
completar VT (terminar) to complete; (en fútbol americano) to complete [passes]; **—se** to be completed
completo ADJ (terminado) complete; (lleno) full; **hoy tenemos el —** today we have a full house; **por —** completely
complexión F build
complicación F complication
complicado ADJ complicated
complicar[30] VT to complicate; **—le a alguien la vida** to give someone trouble
cómplice MF accomplice
complicidad F complicity
complot M plot
compondrá, compondría ver componer
componenda F (arreglo provisional) quick fix; (arreglo ilegal) shady deal
componente ADJ & M component
componer[56, 74] VT (un grupo) to compose, to make up; (imprenta) to set; (un coche descompuesto) to fix; (música) to compose; **—se de** to be composed of; **componérselas** to deal with one's problems alone
componga, compongo ver componer
comportamiento M conduct, behavior
comportarse VI/VT to conduct oneself, to behave
composición F composition
compositor -ora MF composer
compostura F (arreglo) repair; (dignidad) composure
compra F purchase; **— apalancada** LBO; **ir de —s** to go shopping; **— hostil** hostile takeover
comprador -ora MF (comercial) buyer, purchaser; (en una tienda) shopper
comprar VT to buy, to purchase; **compró su silencio** he gave her hush money
comprender VT (entender) to understand, to comprehend; (abarcar) to cover, to include
comprensible ADJ comprehensible, understandable
comprensión F (intelectual) understanding, comprehension; (emocional) sympathy, understanding
comprensivo ADJ understanding
compresa F compress
compresión F compression; **— de archivos** file compression
comprimido ADJ compressed; M tablet
comprimir VT to compress
comprobación F verification, check
comprobante M proof; **— de compra** proof of purchase
comprobar[5] VT (verificar) to verify, to check; (probar) to prove; (darse cuenta) to realize
comprometer VT (obligar) to commit; (poner

en peligro) to jeopardize, to compromise;
—se (prometer) to promise; (tomar partido)
to commit oneself; (para casarse) to get
engaged

comprometido ADJ (obligado) obligated;
(arriesgado) risky; (implicado) compromised;
(con planes de casarse) engaged; (entregado,
dedicado) committed, engaged

compromiso M (ideología, obligación,
promesa) commitment; (acuerdo)
agreement; (cita) appointment, engagement;
(de matrimonio) engagement; (solución
negociada) compromise; **no me pongas en
—** don't compromise me; **sin — de compra**
without obligation to buy

comprueba, compruebe ver comprobar

compuerta F sluice gate, floodgate

compuesto ADJ (ojos, tiempo, interés)
compound; **estar — de** to be composed of; M
compound

compuesto ver componer

compulsión F compulsion

compulsivo ADJ compulsive

compungirse[46] VI to feel sorry

computación F computing

computadora F computer; **— personal**
personal computer; **— de escritorio**
desktop computer; **— de mano** palmtop,
handheld computer; **— digital** digital
computer; **— portátil** laptop computer; **—
torre** tower model

computar VT to compute

computarizar[47] VT to computerize

cómputo M computation

comulgar[40] VI (recibir el sacramento) to take
Communion; (estar de acuerdo) to agree

común ADJ common; **en —** in common; **por lo
—** generally; **el — de las gentes** the
majority of the people

comuna F commune

comunicable ADJ communicable

comunicación F (interacción) communication;
(ponencia) presentation; **se nos cortó la —**
we got disconnected

comunicado M communiqué, report

comunicar[30] VI/VT to communicate; **—se con**
(entenderse) to communicate with; (ponerse
en contacto con) to reach; (desembocar en) to
open into

comunicativo ADJ communicative

comunidad F community; **— internauta**
Internet community; **— virtual** virtual
community

comunión F communion

comunismo M communism

comunista ADJ & MF communist

comunitario ADJ (en común) communal;
espíritu — community spirit;
presupuesto — European Union budget

con PREP with; **— lo que come, tendría que
estar obesa** given what she eats, she should
be obese; **— mucho** by far; **— que le digas
alcanza** just telling him is enough; **— tal [de]
que** provided that; **— todo** all things
considered

conato M attempt

concavidad F hollow

cóncavo ADJ concave

concebible ADJ conceivable

concebir[9] VT (engendrar) to conceive;
(entender) to conceive of

conceder VT (dar) to grant; (admitir) to concede,
to allow

concejal MF councilor

concejo M council

concentración F (densidad, atención, cantidad)
concentration; (manifestación) rally,
demonstration

concentrar VT to concentrate; **—se** (prestar
atención) to concentrate, to focus;
(manifestar) to rally

concepción F conception

concepto M (idea) concept; (artificio) conceit

conceptual ADJ conceptual

concernir[73] VT to concern

concertación F agreement

concertar[1] VT (arreglar) to arrange; (concretar)
to finalize; (planear) to concert; **—se** to agree

concesión F (admisión) concession;
(otorgamiento) grant; (permiso comercial)
franchise

concesionario M dealership

concha F shell

conchabarse VI to conspire

**conciba, concibe, concibiendo, concibiera,
concibiese** ver concebir

conciencia F (moral) conscience; (mental)
consciousness, awareness; **tomar — de** to
come to grips with; **— de marca** brand
awareness

concienzudo ADJ conscientious, thorough

concierto M (música) concert; (armonía)
harmony; (acuerdo) agreement

conciliación F conciliation

conciliar VT (personas) to conciliate; (ideas) to
reconcile; **— el sueño** to fall sleep

concilio M council

concisión F conciseness

conciso ADJ concise, brief

conciudadano -na MF fellow citizen

concluir[19] VI/VT to conclude

conclusión F conclusion

**concluya, concluye, concluyendo,
concluyera, concluyese** ver concluir

concluyente ADJ conclusive

concomitante ADJ attendant

concordancia F agreement

concordar[5] VI to agree

concordia F concord

concretamente ADV specifically; **tiene un perro, — un chihuahua** he has a dog, a chihuahua, to be precise

concretar VT (cerrar) to finalize; (especificar) to be specific about; (realizar) to realize; **—se a** to focus on

concreto ADJ concrete; **en —** specifically; M *Am* concrete

concubina F concubine

concurrencia F (reunión) gathering; (asistencia) attendance

concurrido ADJ well-attended

concurrir VI (confluir) to come together; (asistir) to attend

concursante MF contestant

concurso M (para un premio) contest; (en una licitación) call for bids; (para un puesto de trabajo) competitive examination; **— de belleza** beauty pageant

concusión F graft

concusionario -ria MF grafter

condado M county

conde M count

condecoración F decoration

condecorar VT to decorate

condena F (castigo) sentence; (crítica) condemnation; **¡qué —!** what a pain!

condenación F condemnation

condenado ADJ (perdido) damned; (sentenciado) sentenced; **está — a muerte** he's on death row

condenar VT (criticar) to condemn; (sentenciar) to sentence; **eso le condenó al fracaso** that doomed him to failure; **—se** to go to hell

condensación F condensation

condensar VI to condense

condesa F countess

condescendencia F (tolerancia) acquiescence; (superioridad) condescension

condescender[2] VI (acomodarse) to acquiesce; (dignarse) to condescend

condición F condition; **— social** social station; **a — de que** on the condition that; **condiciones** (físicas) condition; (de un contrato) terms, provisos

condicional ADJ & M conditional

condicionamiento M conditioning

condicionar VT to condition

condimentar VT to season

condimento M condiment, seasoning

condiscípulo -la MF classmate

condolencias F PL condolences; **dar las —** to offer one's condolences

condolerse[6] VI to offer one's condolences

condominio M condominium

cóndor M condor

conducción F (de electricidad) conduction; (de un difunto o prisionero) transport

conducente ADJ conducive

conducir[38] VT (a un grupo) to lead; (una orquesta, electricidad) to conduct; (un coche) to drive, to steer; **—se** to behave

conducta F (moral) conduct, behavior; (biológica) behavior; **— de alto riesgo** high-risk behavior

conducto M (de agua) conduit; (anatómico) duct; **— de aire** airway; **por — de** through

conductor -ora ADJ (de electricidad) conductive; M (de electricidad) conductor; MF (de coches) driver; (en baloncesto) point guard

conductual ADJ behavioral

conduje, condujera, condujese ver conducir

conectar VI/VT to connect

conectividad F connectivity

conector M connector; **— en serie** serial connector

conejillo M **— de Indias** guinea pig

conejo M rabbit

conexión F connection

confabulación F collusion

confección F (fabricación de ropa) dressmaking, tailoring; (calidad) workmanship; **de —** ready-made

confeccionar VT (productos) to manufacture; (ropa) to tailor, to sew

confederación F confederation

confederado -da ADJ & MF confederate

confederar VI to form a confederacy

conferencia F (discurso) lecture; (reunión) conference; **— de prensa** press conference; **dar una —** to give a lecture

conferenciante MF lecturer, speaker

conferenciar VI to confer

conferencista MF lecturer, speaker

conferir[5] VT to confer, to bestow; (un título) to confer

confesar[1] VI/VT to confess

confesión F confession

confesionario M confessional

confesor -ora MF confessor

confiabilidad F reliability

confiable ADJ reliable

confiado ADJ (seguro de sí) confident; (crédulo) trusting

confianza F confidence, trust; **en —** in confidence; **tener —** to be confident; **tener — en** to have confidence in; **tomar —s** to be overly familiar with

confianzudo ADJ overfamiliar

confiar[28] VT (un secreto) to confide; (un valor, bien) to entrust; **— en** to rely on; **confío que Dios me proteja** I trust that God will protect me

confidencia F confidence

confidencial ADJ confidential; **altamente —** top-secret

confidente MF (amigo) confidant; M (mueble) love seat

confiesa, confiese *ver* confesar

configuración F configuration

configurar VT to configure (también computadoras); **—se** to take shape

confinamiento M confinement

confinar VT to confine

confines M PL bounds, confines

confirmación F confirmation

confirmar VT to confirm

confiscación F (de una propiedad) confiscation, seizure; (de un monto) forfeiture

confiscar[30] VT to confiscate

confitar VT to candy

confite M candy

confitería F confectionery

confitura F confection

conflictivo ADJ (persona, tema) contentious; (región) volatile

conflicto M conflict

confluencia F (de calles) junction; (de ríos) confluence

conformación F creation, establishment

conformar VT to adapt; **—se** to go along; **—se con** to settle for

conforme ADJ in agreement, content; **— a** in accordance with; CONJ **— amanece** as dawn breaks

conformidad F conformity, agreement; **estar de/en — con** to be in accordance with

conformismo M conformity

confort M comfort

confortable ADJ comfortable

confortar VT to comfort

confraternidad F fraternity, fellowship

confraternizar[47] VI to fraternize

confrontación F confrontation

confrontar VT (a un enemigo) to confront; (dos listas) to compare

confundido ADJ confused, mixed-up

confundir VT to confuse, to perplex, to baffle; **—se** (personas) to become confused; (cosas) to mingle

confusión F (mental) confusion; (de cosas) clutter, disarray

confuso ADJ (que no comprende, desordenado) confused; (difícil de comprender) confusing

congelación F freezing; **— salarial** pay freeze

congelado ADJ frozen

congelador M freezer

congelar VT to freeze

congeniar VI **— con** to get along with

congénito ADJ congenital

congestión F congestion

conglomeración F conglomeration

conglomerado M conglomeration

Congo M Congo

congoja F anguish, grief

congoleño -ña ADJ & MF Congolese

congregación F (feligreses) congregation; (orden) order

congregar[40] VI to congregate

congresista MF (legislador) member of Congress; (asistente a un congreso) conference attendee, conventioneer

congreso M (cuerpo legislativo, edificio) congress; (reunión periódica) conference, convention

congresual ADJ congressional

congruencia F congruence

conífera F conifer

conjetura F conjecture, surmise

conjeturar VT to conjecture, to surmise

conjugación F conjugation

conjugar[40] VT to conjugate

conjunción F conjunction

conjuntamente ADV jointly

conjuntivitis F conjunctivitis, pinkeye

conjunto M (grupo de cosas) set; (totalidad) total, aggregate; (de ropa) outfit; **— musical** ensemble; **en —** as a whole, all told; ADJ joint

conjuración F conspiracy

conjurado -da MF conspirator

conjurar VT (conspirar) to conspire, to plot; (evitar, cancelar) to ward off

conjuro M incantation, spell

conllevar VT to entail, to involve

conmemoración F commemoration

conmemorar VT to commemorate

conmemorativo ADJ commemorative, memorial

conmigo PRON with me

conmiseración F commiseration

conmoción F commotion; **— cerebral** brain concussion, cerebral concussion

conmovedor ADJ moving, touching

conmover[6] VT to move, to touch

conmovido ADJ moved, touched

conmutador M switch

conmutar VT to commute

connatural ADJ inborn

connotación F connotation

cono M cone

conocedor -ora ADJ who know[s], aware; **muy — de la situación** well aware of the situation; MF connoisseur, expert

conocer[35] VT to know (también en sentido carnal); (reconocer) to recognize; (tratar por primera vez) to meet; **— el paño** to know the ropes; **se conoce que** it is clear that

conocido -da ADJ well-known; MF acquaintance

conocimiento M knowledge, acquaintance; **— de embarque** bill of lading; **perder el —** to lose consciousness; **poner en —** to inform; **—s** knowledge

conozca, conozco *ver* conocer

conque CONJ so

conquista F conquest

conquistador -ora MF conqueror; ADJ conquering

conquistar VT (un terreno) to conquer; (el amor de alguien) to win

consabido ADJ habitual

consagración F consecration

consagrar VT (declarar consagrado) to consecrate; (dedicar) to devote

consciente ADJ conscious; — **del problema** aware of the problem

conscribir VT to draft

consecución F attainment, achievement

consecuencia F (hecho que resulta de otro) consequence; (cualidad de consecuente) consistency; **a — de** as a result of

consecuente ADJ (que se sigue de) consequent, logical; (fiel en sus actos) consistent

consecutivo ADJ consecutive

conseguible ADJ obtainable

conseguir[12] VT (un derecho) to attain, to get; (un objetivo) to achieve; (un puesto de trabajo) to land, to get; — **hacer algo** to manage to do something

consejero -ra MF (asesor) adviser; (miembro del consejo) board member; **consejero -ra delegado -da** *Esp* CEO

consejo M (opinión) counsel, advice; (comité) council; — **de guerra** court-martial

consenso M consensus

consentimiento M consent, acquiescence

consentir[8] VT (permitir) to consent to, to acquiesce to; (mimar) to pamper, to indulge; — **en** to permit

conserje MF (limpiador) janitor; (portero) superintendent; (recepcionista) hotel clerk

conserva F canned food; **en —** canned

conservación F conservation, preservation

conservador -ora MF (en política) conservative; (de museo) curator; ADJ (de tradiciones) conservative; (de alimentos) preservative

conservadurismo M conservatism

conservante M preservative

conservar VT (guardar) to keep; (mantener) to retain; (preservar) to preserve; (ahorrar) to conserve

conservatorio M conservatory

considerable ADJ considerable

considerablemente ADV significantly

consideración F consideration; **de —** considerable; **tomar/tener en —** to take into consideration

considerado ADJ considerate, thoughtful

considerar VT to consider

consiga *ver* conseguir

consigna F (eslogan) motto, watchword; (orden) order

consignación F consignment; **a/en —** on consignment

consignar VT to consign

consignatario -ria MF consignee

consigo PRON with oneself/himself/herself/themselves

consigo, consiguiendo, consiguiera, consiguiese *ver* conseguir

consiguiente ADJ consequent; **por —** consequently

consistencia F consistency

consistente ADJ (firme) consistent; **— de** consisting of

consistir VI **— en** to consist of

consocio -cia MF fellow member

consola F console; **— de juegos** game console

consolación F consolation

consolar[8] VT to console

consolidación F consolidation

consolidar VT to consolidate

consonante ADJ & F consonant

consorcio M consortium

consorte MF consort

conspicuo ADJ conspicuous

conspiración F conspiracy, plot

conspirador -ora MF conspirator, plotter

conspirar VI to conspire, to plot

constancia F (en el amor) constancy; (en el esfuerzo) perseverance; (en el trabajo) steadiness; (prueba) documentary proof

constante ADJ & F constant; **—s vitales** vital signs

constar VI to be stated; **aquí consta que me debes cien dólares** here it states that you owe me a hundred dollars; **— de** to consist of, to be composed of; **hacer —** to mention; **me consta que** I am aware that; **que conste** let it be known

constatar VT to verify

constelación F constellation

consternación F consternation, dismay

consternar VT to dismay

constipación F constipation

constipado ADJ *Esp* (resfriado) suffering from a cold; *Am* (seco de vientre) constipated; M *Esp* head cold

constitución F constitution

constitucional ADJ constitutional

constituir[19] VT to constitute

constitutivo ADJ (constituyente) constituent; (inherente) inherent; **— de un delito** which constitutes a crime

constituya, constituye *ver* constituir

constituyente ADJ constituent

constreñimiento M constraint

constreñir[11] VT (limitar) to constrain; (apretar) to constrict, to constrain

constricción F constriction

construcción F (actividad de construir, cosa construida) construction, building;

(gramatical) construction

constructivo ADJ constructive

constructor -ora MF builder; F construction company

construir[19] VI/VT to construct, to build

construye, construyendo, construyera, construyese *ver* construir

consuelo M consolation, comfort, solace

consuetudinario ADJ (acción) habitual; (derecho) common

cónsul MF consul

consulado M consulate

consulta F (acción de consultar) consultation; (pregunta) question; (consultorio) doctor's office

consultar VT to consult; **—lo con la almohada** to sleep on it

consultivo ADJ consultative

consultor ADJ consulting

consultoría F consulting firm

consultorio M doctor's office

consumado ADJ consummate, accomplished

consumar VT to consummate

consumidor -ora MF consumer; ADJ consuming

consumir VT to consume; **—se** (agua) to boil off; (neumático) to wear out; **—se de** to be consumed by

consumismo M consumerism

consumo M consumption

consunción F consumption

contabilidad F accounting, bookkeeping

contable MF accountant, bookkeeper

contactar VI/VT to contact; **—[se] con** to get in contact/touch with

contacto M contact; **— visual** eye contact; **en — con** in touch with

contado M **al —** in cash; ADJ **—s** few

contador -ora ADJ counting; M (de dinero) counter; (de electricidad) meter; **— Geiger** Geiger counter; MF accountant; **— público -ca** CPA

contaduría F accountant's office

contagiar VT to infect

contagio M (de enfermedad) contagion; (de ordenador) infection

contagioso ADJ contagious, catching, infectious

contaminación F (del agua, de la comida) contamination; (del medio ambiente) pollution; **— sonora** noise pollution

contaminante M contaminate

contaminar VT (agua, alimentos, cultura) to contaminate; (el medio ambiente) to pollute; **—se** (agua) to become contaminated; (medio ambiente) to become polluted

contar[5] VI/VT (medir una cantidad) to count; (decir historias) to tell; **el hotel cuenta con una piscina** the hotel has a swimming pool; **cuento con mi hermano** I count on my

brother; **esto no cuenta** this doesn't count; **¿me lo vas a contar a mí?** you can say that again; **tienes que — el tiempo** you have to watch the time; M SG **cuentakilómetros** (marcador de kilómetros) odometer; (velocímetro) speedometer

contemplación F contemplation

contemplar VT (mirar, tener en cuenta) to contemplate; (consentir) to spoil; VI to contemplate

contemporáneo ADJ contemporary

contención F containment

contender[2] VI to contend

contendrá, contendría *ver* contener

contenedor M container

contenedorizar VT containerize

contener[58] VT (un líquido) to contain; (risa, lágrimas) to hold back; (entusiasmo) to restrain; (el aliento) to hold

contenga, contengo *ver* contener

contenido ADJ restrained; M content[s]

contentar VT to satisfy; **—se** to be satisfied

contento ADJ (conforme) content, contented; (feliz) happy; M contentment

conteo M count

contera F (de paraguas) tip; (de bolígrafo) cap

contestación F answer, reply

contestador M answering machine

contestar VT to answer; VI to talk back, to mouth off

contexto M context

contextura F (de un objeto) makeup; (de persona) build

contienda F (guerra) conflict; (encuentro deportivo) competition

contiene, contienes *ver* contener

contigo PRON with you

contiguo ADJ contiguous; **estar — a** to adjoin

continental ADJ continental

continente M (masa geográfica) continent; (opuesto a isla) mainland; ADJ continent

contingencia F contingency

contingente ADJ & M contingent

continuación F (de una acción) continuation; (de una película) sequel; (tenis) follow-through; **a —** after that; **a — hubo una guerra** there ensued a war

continuado ADJ continuing

continuar[26] VI/VT to continue

continuidad F continuity

continuo ADJ (ininterrumpido) continuous; (repetido) continual

contonearse VI (mujer) to swing one's hips; (hombre) to swagger

contoneo M (de mujer) swinging of the hips; (de hombre) swagger

contorno M (forma) outline, contour; (tamaño de árbol, persona) girth

contorsión F contortion

contra PREP against; M **los pro y los** — the pros and cons; **en** — against; F drawback; **llevarle la** — **a alguien** to contradict someone
contraatacar[30] VI/VT to counterattack
contraataque M (militar) counterattack; (en baloncesto) fast break
contrabajo M double bass; MF double bass player
contrabandear VI/VT to smuggle
contrabandista MF smuggler
contrabando M (actividad) smuggling; (mercancías) contraband; **hacer** — to smuggle
contracción F contraction
contrachapado M plywood
contractual ADJ contractual
contracultura F counterculture
contradecir[53,74] VT to contradict
contradicción F contradiction
contradictorio ADJ contradictory
contraejemplo M counterexample
contraer[59] VT (enfermedad) to contract; (derechos) to limit; (deudas) to incur; — **matrimonio** to get married
contraespionaje M counterespionage
contrafuerte M (de muro) buttress; (de zapato) counter
contrahecho ADJ deformed
contralor M (control) comptroller, controller; (auditor) auditor
contralto M (voz) alto; MF (persona) alto
contramandar VT to countermand
contramedida F countermeasure
contraoferta F counteroffer
contraorden F countermand
contrapartida F compensation
contrapelo LOC ADV **a** — against the grain
contrapesar VT to counterbalance
contrapeso M counterbalance
contraproducente ADJ counterproductive
contrariar[28] VT to annoy; —**se** to get annoyed
contrariedad F (fastidio) annoyance; (dificultad) snag
contrario ADJ (opuesto) opposite; (discrepante) conflicting; **al** — on the contrary; **de lo** — otherwise; **llevar la contraria** to be contrary; **por el** — on the contrary; **soy** — **al doblaje de películas** I'm against the dubbing of films; **todo lo** — just the opposite
contrarrestar VT to counteract
contrarrevolución F counterrevolution
contraseña F password, watchword
contrastar VI/VT to contrast
contraste M contrast
contrata F contract
contratación F hiring; — **externa** outsourcing
contratar VT (a un empleado) to hire; (un servicio) to contract for; —**se** to be hired; — **y despedir** hire and fire

contratiempo M mishap
contratista MF contractor, builder
contrato M contract; — **de alquiler** rental agreement; **por** — by contract
contravenir[61] VT to contravene
contraventana F shutter
contribución F (regalo, participación) contribution; (impuesto) tax; — **alternativa mínima** alternative minimum tax
contribuir[19] VT to contribute
contribuya, contribuye, contribuyendo, contribuyera, contribuyese ver contribuir
contribuyente MF taxpayer
contrincante MF opponent
contrito ADJ contrite
control M (dominio, dirección) control; (contralor médico) checkup; (vigilancia) check; (puesto) checkpoint; — **de calidad** quality control; — **de daños** damage control; — **de la natalidad** birth control; — **fronterizo** border control; — **paternal** parental control; — **remoto** remote control; **bajo** — under control
controlador -ora MF comptroller; M driver; — **de impresora** printer driver
controlar VT (restringir) to control; (vigilar) to check on
controversia F controversy
controvertido ADJ controversial
contumacia F obstinacy
contumaz ADJ stubborn
contundente ADJ (argumento) forceful; (objeto) blunt; (prueba) convincing; (victoria) resounding
contusión F bruise, contusion
contuve, contuviera, contuviese ver contener
convalecencia F convalescence
convalecer[35] VI to convalesce
convaleciente MF convalescent
convección F convection
convencer[32] VT (por lógica) to convince; (por insistencia) to persuade
convencimiento M (creencia) conviction; (acción) convincing
convención F convention
convencional ADJ conventional
convendrá, convendría, convenga, convengo ver convenir
convenido ADJ agreed-upon
conveniencia F (algo cómodo) convenience; (algo aconsejable) desirability; **a su** — at your convenience
conveniente ADJ (cómodo) convenient; (aconsejable) advisable
convenio M agreement; — **colectivo** collective bargaining; — **comercial** business agreement

convenir[61] VI (ser apropiado) to be suitable; (llegar a un acuerdo) to agree

convento M convent

convergencia F convergence

converger[45] VI to converge

conversación F conversation; **trabar — con** to engage in a conversation with

conversar VI to converse

conversión F conversion; **— de dos puntos** two-point conversion

converso-sa MF convert

convertible ADJ convertible

convertidor M converter

convertir[8] VT to convert; **—se en** to become

convexo ADJ convex

convicción F conviction

convicto-ta ADJ convicted; MF convict

convidar VT to invite; *Am* to offer

convierta, convierte *ver* convertir

convincente ADJ convincing, compelling

convine, conviniendo, conviniera, conviniese *ver* convenir

convirtiendo, convirtiera, convirtiese *ver* convertir

convite M (invitación) invitation; (banquete) banquet

convivencia F (coexistencia) coexistence; (cohabitación) cohabitation, living together

convivir VI (coexistir) to coexist; (cohabitar) to cohabitate, to live together

convocación F convocation

convocar[30] VT to convoke, to call together; (una reunión, un concurso) to convene

convocatoria F (anuncio) announcement; (llamamiento) call

convoy M convoy

convoyar VT to convoy

convulsión F convulsion

conyugal ADJ conjugal, marital

cónyuge MF spouse

coñac M cognac, brandy

cooperación F cooperation

cooperar VI to cooperate

cooperativa F cooperative, co-op

cooperativista MF member of a cooperative

cooperativo ADJ cooperative

coordenada F coordinate

coordinación F coordination

coordinado ADJ coordinate

coordinador -ora MF coordinator; ADJ coordinating

coordinar VT to coordinate

copa F (vaso) goblet, wineglass; (de árbol) top; (de sombrero) crown; (palo de la baraja) card in the suit of *copas*; (trofeo, parte de un sujetador) cup; **ir de —s** to go for a drink; **— del Mundo** World Cup

copago M copayment

copete M (de pelo) tuft; (de plumas) crest; **estar**

hasta el — to be fed up

copia F (réplica) copy; (de foto) print; **— de respaldo** backup copy; **— de respaldo automático** automatic backup copy; **— de seguridad** backup copy; **— en papel** hard copy; **— impresa** hard copy

copiadora F copy machine

copiar VT (reproducir) to copy; (en un examen) to cheat

copión -ona MF copycat

copioso ADJ copious, plentiful

copla F (canción) popular song; (estrofa) stanza

copo M (de nieve) snowflake; (de lana, algodón) wad; **—s de maíz** cornflakes

copropietario -ria MF joint owner

coprotagonista MF costar

cópula F copula

copulación F copulation

copular VI to copulate

copyright M copyright

coque M coke

coqueta F (mujer) coquette; (mueble) dressing table

coquetear VI to flirt, to dally

coquetería F flirtation

coqueto ADJ flirtatious

coraje M (valentía) courage; (enojo) anger

coral M (marino) coral; (musical) chorale

coralino ADJ coral

coraza F armor

corazón M (órgano) heart; (de manzana) core; (vocativo) honey; **con el — en la boca** (cansado) really tired; (nervioso) on edge; **de buen —** kindhearted; **de todo —** wholeheartedly; **romperle el — a alguien** to break someone's heart

corazonada F hunch

corbata F necktie, tie, cravat

corcel M charger, steed

corchea F eighth note; **— con puntillo** dotted eighth note

corchete M (en costura) hook and eye; (paréntesis recto) square bracket; (llave) brace

corcho M (para botella) cork; (para pescar) float

corcova F hump, hunchback

corcovear VI to buck

cordaje M strings

cordel M string

cordero M (animal) lamb; (piel, cuero) lambskin

cordial ADJ cordial

cordillera F mountain range

cordobés -esa ADJ from Cordoba; MF person from Cordoba

cordón M (cinta) cord; (al borde de la calle) *Am* curb; **— de apertura** ripcord; **— de zapatos** shoelace, shoestring; **— policial** police cordon; **— umbilical** umbilical cord

cordoncillo M ridge, rib

cordura F sanity

Corea F Korea; **— del Norte** North Korea; **— del Sur** South Korea

coreano -na ADJ & MF Korean

corear VI/VT to chant

coreografía F choreography

cornada F goring

cornear VT to gore

corneja F crow

córner M corner kick

corneta F cornet; MF bugler

cornisa F cornice, ledge

corno M horn; **— francés** French horn

cornudo ADJ horned; M cuckold

coro M (cantantes) choir, chorus; (música) chorus; (parte de la iglesia) loft; **cantar a —** to sing in unison

corolario M corollary

corona F crown

coronación F coronation

coronar VT to crown

coronario ADJ coronary

coronel M colonel

coronilla F crown of the head; **estar hasta la —** to be fed up

corpiño M (almilla) bodice; (sujetador) *Am* bra

corporación F guild

corporal ADJ corporal, bodily

corporativo ADJ corporate

corpulento ADJ stout, corpulent

corpus M corpus

corpúsculo M corpuscle

corral M (de granja) barnyard, farmyard; (para ganado) corral, pen

correa F (de cuero) leather strap; (de ventilador) belt; (de perro) leash

corrección F (acción de corregir) correction; (cualidad de correcto) correctness

correctamente ADV correctly, properly

correcto ADJ (apropiado) correct, proper; (acertado) right

corrector -ora MF editor; **— de pruebas** proofreader

corredizo ADJ sliding

corredor -ora ADJ running; MF (persona que corre, también en deportes) runner; (deportista automovilístico, ciclista) racer; (intermediario) broker, agent; M (pasillo) hallway, corridor

correduría F brokerage

corregir[14] VT (errores) to correct; (exámenes) to grade; **—se** (en lo moral) to mend one's ways; (en los errores) to correct oneself

correlación F correlation

correlacionar VT to correlate

correlato M correlate

correo M mail; (edificio) post office; **— aéreo** air mail; **— certificado** certified mail; **— de voz** voice mail; **— electrónico** e-mail; **— electrónico basura** junk e-mail, spam;

echar al — to mail

correoso ADJ tough

correr VI (persona, agua, calle) to run; (coche) to go fast; (una puerta) to slide; (dinero, tiempo) to pass; **— con los gastos** to take on the costs; VT (una cortina) to draw; (una carrera, un riesgo) to run; **—se** (moverse) to scoot over; (desteñir) to run, to bleed; (manchar) to smear

correría F foray

correspondencia F correspondence

corresponder VI (ser adecuado, estar en consonancia) to correspond; (pertenecer) to belong; VT (amor, favores) to reciprocate; **a mí me corresponde llamarla** it's up to me to call her, it behooves me to call her

correspondiente ADJ corresponding; MF correspondent

corresponsal MF correspondent

corretaje M broker's/agent's commission

corretear VI to run around

corrida F (acción de correr) running; (competición) race; (de banco) run; **— de toros** bullfight; **de —** without stopping

corrido ADJ (experimentado) worldly; (continuo) uninterrupted; **de —** without stopping; M ballad

corriente ADJ (que corre) running; (común) usual; (franco) frank; **el — mes** the current month; **estar al —** to be up to date; F (de agua, electricidad) current; (de dinero) flow; (de pesimismo) wave; (de aire) draft; (de computadora) streaming; **— alterna** alternating current; **— continua** direct current; **— del Golfo** Gulf Stream; **al —** in the loop; **dejarse llevar por la —** to conform; **llevarle la — a alguien** to humor someone

corrija, corrijo, corrigiendo, corrigiera, corrigiese, corrigió *ver* corregir

corrillo M group of gossips

corro M circle of people

corroborar VT to corroborate

corroer[73] VT to corrode

corromper VT (a una persona) to corrupt; (un alimento) to rot; **—se** (una persona) to become corrupt; (un alimento) to rot

corrompido ADJ corrupt

corrosión F corrosion

corrupción F corruption

corrupto ADJ corrupt

corsé M corset

cortada F shortcut

cortado ADJ (abreviado, sucinto) clipped; (tímido) shy; M (café) coffee with some milk; (desnivel) slope; (tenis) backspin, slice

cortador -ora MF (persona) cutter; F (aparato) cutter; **cortadora de césped** lawn mower

cortadura M cut

cortante ADJ (comentario, instrumento) cutting; (frío, viento) biting; (tono, instrumento) sharp

cortar VT to cut (también un texto digital); (un vestido, el uso de algo) to cut out; (a un locutor, una rama, el gas) to cut off; (un árbol) to cut down; (las uñas) to clip; (el césped) to mow; **— el paso** to block; **— por lo sano** to take drastic action; M SG **cortacésped** lawn mower; M SG **cortacircuitos** circuit breaker; M SG **cortafuego** fire line; M SG **cortafuegos** firewall; M SG **cortapapeles** paper cutter; M SG **cortaplumas** penknife; M SG **cortauñas** nail clipper; VI (el frío) to bite; (la piel) to crack; **—se** (lastimarse) to cut oneself; (intimidarse) to be intimidated; (cuajarse) to curdle, to sour; **—se el pelo** to get a haircut; **— y pegar** cut and paste

corte M (de un traje, herida) cut; (acción de cortar) cutting; (de televisión) commercial break; (estilo) style; **— de pelo** haircut; **— transversal** cross section; **— y confección** dressmaking; **eso me da —** that embarrasses me; F (real, judicial) court; (séquito) retinue; **las —s** Spanish parliament; **hacer la —** to court

cortedad F shortness

cortejar VT to court, to woo

cortejo M (séquito) entourage; (acción de cortejar) courtship

cortés ADJ courteous, polite

cortesano -na MF courtier

cortesía F courtesy, politeness

córtex M cortex

corteza F (de árbol) bark; (de pan, de la Tierra) crust; (de queso, fruta) rind; **— cerebral** cerebral cortex

corticoesteroide M corticosteriod

cortijo M country house

cortina F (de ventana) curtain; (de lluvia) sheet; **— de humo** smoke screen

cortisona F cortisone

corto ADJ (breve) short; (tonto) short on brains; (encogido) bashful; **— de vista** short-sighted; **a — plazo** in the short run, in the short term; **quedarse —** to come up short; **vestirse de —** to wear a short dress; M short [film]; M **—circuito** short circuit

cosa F thing; **como quien no quiere la —** without realizing it; **como si tal —** as cool as a cucumber; **¡cómo son las —s!** what a surprise; **decir una — por otra** to tell a lie; **esperamos — de cinco minutos** we waited about five minutes; **las —s como son** let's be honest; **las —s de la vida** that's life; **no es gran —** it's no big deal; **otra —** something else

cosecha F crop, harvest; **de su —** of his invention; **vino — 1975** wine of 1975 vintage

cosechadora F combine

cosechar VT (cultivos) to harvest; (resultados) to reap

coser VI/VT to sew

cosignatario -ria MF cosigner

cosmético ADJ & M cosmetic

cósmico ADJ cosmic

cosmología F cosmology

cosmonauta MF cosmonaut

cosmopolita ADJ cosmopolitan

cosmos M cosmos

cosmovisión F worldview

coso M doodad

cosquillas F **hacer —** to tickle; **tener —** to be ticklish

cosquillear VT to tickle

cosquilleo M tickle

cosquilloso ADJ ticklish

costa F (del mar) coast, shore; **a toda —** at all costs; **—s** costs

Costa de Marfil F Ivory Coast

costado M side; **al —** alongside; **de —** edgewise; **por los cuatro —s** from all sides

costal M sack

costanero ADJ coastal

costar⁵ VI/VT to cost; **— trabajo** to be difficult; **— un dineral** to cost a fortune; **— un ojo de la cara** to cost an arm and a leg

Costa Rica F Costa Rica

costarricense, costarriqueño -ña ADJ & MF Costa Rican

coste M cost; **— de [la] vida** cost of living; **al —** at cost

costear VT to defray costs; VI to sail along the coast

costero ADJ coastal

costilla F rib; **lo hizo a —s de su padre** he did it at his father's expense

costo M cost; **— adicional** added cost, extra cost; **— de [la] vida** cost of living; **al —** at cost; **— de mantenimiento** maintenance cost; **— de operación** operating cost

costoso ADJ costly

costra F (de pan) crust; (de herida) scab

costroso ADJ (pan) crusty; (heridas) scabby

costumbre F (hábito) habit; (tradición) custom; **de —** habitual; **tener la — de** to have the habit of; **está más cansado que de —** he's especially tired today

costura F (acción de coser) sewing; (línea de puntadas) stitching; (unión de dos piezas) seam; **alta —** high fashion, haute couture

costurero -ra M (caja) sewing box; (sastre) tailor; F seamstress

costurón M (puntada) large stitch; (cicatriz) large scar

cota F (nivel del agua) height above sea level; (estándar) benchmark

cotejar VT to check against

cotejo M comparison

cotidiano ADJ everyday

cotización F price quote, price quotation

cotizar[47] VT to quote

coto M — **de caza** game preserve; **poner** — **a** to put an end to

cotorra F (loro) parrot; (persona) chatterbox

cotorrear VI to chatter

covacha F small cave

coyote M coyote

coyuntura F (articulación) joint; (situación) juncture; **aprovechar la** — to take advantage of the situation

coz F kick; **dar coces** to kick

crack M (cocaína) crack; (deportista) ace

cráneo M cranium, skull

craso ADJ crass

cráter M crater

crayola® F crayon

creación F creation

creacionismo M creationism

creador-ora MF creator; ADJ creative

crear VI/VT to create

creatividad F creativity

creativo ADJ creative

crecer[35] VI (un niño) to grow; (masa, río) to rise; (madera, mar) to swell; (la luna) to wax

crecida F rise of a river

crecido ADJ (adulto) grown; (grande) large; (demasiado alto) overgrown

creciente ADJ (que crece) growing; (luna) crescent; M (luna) crescent; (marea) high tide; (de un río) flood

crecimiento M growth

credencial F credential

credibilidad F credibility

crédito M (solvencia, unidad de estudios) credit; (hecho de creer) credence; (fama) reputation; (préstamo) loan; — **al consumidor** consumer credit; — **rotativo** revolving credit; **dar** — **a** to believe; —**s** film credits; **vender a** — to sell on credit

credo M creed

crédulo ADJ credulous, gullible

creencia F belief

creer[18] VI/VT (tomar como cierto) to believe; (opinar) to think, to feel; —**se** to fall for; **¿quién se cree que es?** who does he think he is? **se cree artista** he fancies himself an artist; **¡ya lo creo!** I should say so!

creíble ADJ credible, believable

crema F cream (también cosmético); — **de espárragos** cream of asparagus; — **para [los] labios** lip balm, Chapstick®

cremallera F (de coche) rack; (de prenda) zipper; — **y piñón** rack and pinion

cremar VT to cremate

cremoso ADJ creamy

creosota F creosote

crepitación F crackle

crepitar VI to crackle

crepúsculo M twilight

crespo ADJ wiry, kinky

crespón M crepe

cresta F (de ola, montaña) crest; (de ave) tuft; (de gallo) comb

creyendo, creyera, creyese, creyó ver creer

creyente MF believer; ADJ believing

crezca, crezco ver crecer

cría F (acción de criar) breeding; (camada) litter; (animal joven) young

criada ver criado

criadero M — **de peces** hatchery; — **de pollos** chicken farm

criado -da MF servant; F maid

criador -ora MF breeder

crianza F (de animales) breeding; (de hijos) upbringing; (modales) manners

criar[28] VT (animales) to breed; (hijos) to bring up, to rear, to raise; **estar criando malvas** fam to be pushing up daisies; —**se** to grow up

criatura F (ser extraño) creature; (bebé) baby

criba F sieve

cribar VT to sift

crimen M (delito grave) serious crime, felony; (asesinato) murder; — **de guerra** war crime

criminal ADJ & MF criminal

criminalidad F serious crime

crin F mane

criogénico ADJ cryogenic

criollo ADJ (nacido en América) born in Spanish America; (tradicionalmente americano) traditionally Spanish American; M (lengua) creole

críquet M cricket

crisálida F chrysalis

crisantemo M chrysanthemum

crisis F crisis; — **de la edad madura** midlife crisis

crisma F crown of the head

crisol M crucible, melting pot

crisparse VI (un músculo) to contract; (los puños) to clench; (los nervios) to be on edge

cristal M (mineral, vidrio fino) crystal; (vidrio de ventana) Esp glass, pane; (lente) lens; — **labrado** cut glass

cristalería F (objetos) glassware; (establecimiento) glassware store; (fábrica) glassworks

cristalino ADJ (de cristal) crystalline; (transparente) crystal-clear; M lens of the eye

cristalizar[47] VI/VT to crystallize

cristiandad F Christendom

cristianismo M Christianity

cristiano -na ADJ & MF Christian; **hablar en** — (claramente) to speak clearly; (español) to speak Spanish

criterio M criterion

crítica F criticism; (de un libro) review

criticar[30] VT to criticize

crítico -ca ADJ critical; MF critic; (de un libro) reviewer

criticón -ona ADJ critical; MF faultfinder

Croacia F Croatia

croar VI to croak

croata ADJ & MF Croatian

crocante ADJ crisp, crunchy

croché, crochet M crochet; **hacer —** to crochet

croissant M croissant

crol M (estilo de natación) crawl, freestyle

cromado ADJ chroming

cromo M chromium, chrome

cromosoma M chromosome

crónica F (narración de eventos) chronicle; (reportaje) feature; **— policial** police report

crónico ADJ chronic

cronista MF (deportivo) reporter; (histórico) chronicler

cronología F chronology

cronológico ADJ chronological

cronometrador -ora MF timer, timekeeper

cronometraje M timing

cronometrar VT to time

cronómetro M chronometer, stopwatch

croquet M croquet

croquis M rough sketch

cross M cross-country race

cruasán M croissant

cruce M (acción, lugar) crossing; (de dos calles) crossroads, intersection; (de razas) crossbreeding; (de palabras) blend; (animal híbrido) cross; **— peatonal** crosswalk

crucero M (buque de guerra) cruiser; (viaje de placer) cruise

cruceta F crosspiece

crucial ADJ crucial

crucificar[30] VT to crucify

crucifijo M crucifix

crucigrama M crossword puzzle

crudo ADJ (comida, seda) raw; (tiempo, invierno, imágenes) harsh; (petróleo, lenguaje) crude; **agua cruda** hard water; **color —** yellowish white

cruel ADJ cruel, mean

crueldad F cruelty, meanness

cruento ADJ grisly, gruesome

crujido M (de puerta, piso) creak; (de un tallo al quebrarse) crack; (de hojas) rustle; (de un fuego) crackle

crujiente ADJ (manzana, tocino) crisp, crispy; (nueces) crunchy

crujir VI (puerta, piso) to creak; (dientes) to grate; (hojas) to rustle; (nueces) to crunch; (fuego) to crackle

cruz F (cristiana) cross; (de moneda) tails; **hacerse cruces** to dread

cruzada F crusade

cruzado M (soldado) crusader; ADJ (tenis) crosscourt; (boxeo) cross; (traje) double-breasted

cruzamiento M (de piernas, razas) crossing; (de calles) crossroads; (de razas) cross

cruzar[47] VT (la calle) to cross; (un cheque) to write across; **—le la cara a alguien** to backhand someone's face; **cruzo los dedos** I'll keep my fingers crossed; **—se con alguien** to bump into someone; **—se de brazos** to fold one's arms; **se me cruzó un ciervo** a deer crossed in front of me

cuaderno M notebook; **— de bitácora** logbook; **— de espiral** spiral notebook

cuadra F (establo) stable; (distancia) Am block

cuadrado ADJ square; **estar —** to be fat; M square; **es [un]** — he's a square; **dos al —** two squared; **elevar al —** to square

cuadrangular ADJ (geometría) quadrangular; M (béisbol) home run

cuadrar VT (estar en ángulo recto) to square; VI (corresponder) to fit; (ser conveniente) to be convenient; (ser iguales) to balance, to add up; **— con** to be in agreement with

cuadricular VT to divide into squares

cuadrilátero ADJ quadrilateral; M (en boxeo) ring; (polígono) quadrilateral

cuadrilla F (de ladrones) gang; (de obreros) crew; (baile) square dance

cuadro M (cuadrado) square; (pintura) picture; (de bicicleta) frame; (de jardín) bed; (en tela) checker; (de fútbol) team; **— clínico** symptoms; **— interior** (béisbol) infield; **— sinóptico** summary table; **a/de —s** checked

cuadrúpedo ADJ & M quadruped

cuajada F curd

cuajar VI (leche) to curdle; (queso, cemento) to set; (gelatina) to jell; (un grupo, una organización) to come about; **—se** to curdle; **la cosa no cuajó** that didn't pan out

cuajarón M clot

cual PRON REL which; **el/la —** (cosa) which; (persona) who; **lo —** which; **sea —** sea whichever it may be; ADV like; **— hoja al viento** like a leaf in the wind

cuál PRON INTERR which; **¿cuáles son los tuyos?** which ones are yours?

cualidad F quality, trait

cualitativo ADJ qualitative

cualquiera ADJ INDEF any; **de cualquier manera/forma** anyhow; **en cualquier lado** anywhere; PRON INDEF (cosa) any; (persona) anyone; **— que sea su nacionalidad** whatever his nationality may be; **— que elijas** whichever one you choose; **— podría hacer eso** anyone could do that

cuando ADV REL when; **— menos** at least; **— mucho** at most; **se rompió — lo usaba** it broke while she was using it; PREP **— la**

guerra during the war

cuándo ADV INTERR & PRON when

cuantía F (cantidad) quantity; (importancia) importance

cuántico ADJ quantum

cuantificar[30] VT to quantify

cuantioso ADJ considerable

cuantitativo ADJ quantitative

cuanto ADJ REL any; **lee — libro ve** she reads any book she sees; PRON REL **unos —s** a few; CONJ **hice — pude** I did as much as I could; ADV **— antes** as soon as possible; **— más trabajo, menos consigo** the more I work, the less I accomplish; **en —** as soon as possible; **en — a** regarding; **en — que** as

cuánto ADJ, ADV & PRON INTERR (dinero, agua) how much; (personas, libros) how many; **¿cada —?** how often? **¿— piensas quedarte?** how long do you plan to stay?

cuarenta NUM forty; **cantarle las — a alguien** to bawl someone out; **— iguales** (tenis) deuce

cuarentena F quarantine; **una — de libros** forty-odd books

cuarentón -ona MF person in his or her forties

cuaresma F Lent

cuarta F (marcha) fourth gear; (palmo) span of a hand

cuartear VT (una res) to quarter; (los labios) to chap; **—se** to chap

cuartel M barracks; **— general** headquarters; **no dar —** to give no quarter

cuartelada F military coup

cuartelazo M military coup

cuarteto M quartet

cuartilla F sheet of paper

cuarto ADJ one-fourth, quarter; M (habitación) room; (cantidad) quarter, one-fourth; **— de baño** bathroom; **— de estar** living room; **— de final** quarter finals; **— oscuro** darkroom; **¡ni que ocho —s!** no way! **tres —s** three-fourths

cuarzo M quartz

cuásar M quasar

cuate M *Méx* pal, buddy

cuatrero -ra MF cattle rustler

cuatrillizo -za MF quadruplet

cuatro NUM four; **— ojos** four-eyes; **más de —** a good number

cuba F (barril) cask, barrel; (tina) tub, vat

Cuba F Cuba

cubano -na ADJ & MF Cuban

cubeta F (recipiente rectangular) tray; (balde) pail; **— de hielo** ice tray

cúbico ADJ cubic

cubículo M cubicle

cubierta F (de libro) cover; (cosa para cubrir) covering; (neumático) tire; (de buque) deck

cubierto M place setting; **— de plata** silverware; **a —** sheltered

cubierto *ver* cubrir

cubismo M cubism

cúbito M ulna

cubo M (cuerpo geométrico, tercera potencia) cube; (balde) bucket; (de rueda) hub; (juguete) building block; **— de basura** trash can

cubrir[74] VT (con una manta) to cover; (con carteles) to plaster; (una vacante) to fill; (con pintura) to coat; (con crema batida) to smother; (de niebla) to shroud; **—se** (nublarse) to fog up; (ponerse el sombrero) to put on one's hat

cucaracha F cockroach

cuchara F (cubierto) spoon; (de excavadora) bucket; (para helado) scoop; **— sopera** soup spoon; **meter la —** to butt in

cucharada F (lo que cabe en una cuchara) spoonful; (medida) tablespoonful; (de helado) dip

cucharadita F teaspoonful

cucharear VT to spoon

cucharita F teaspoon

cucharón M (para helado) scoop, dipper; (para sopa) ladle

cuchichear VI/VT to whisper

cuchicheo M whisper

cuchilla F (cuchillo grande) large knife, cleaver; (de afeitar, de licuadora) blade; (de patín) runner

cuchillada F (golpe) stab, slash; (herida) stab wound, gash

cuchillería F (conjunto de cuchillos) cutlery; (tienda) cutlery store

cuchillo M knife; **pasar a —** to kill with a knife

cuclillas LOC ADV **en —** squatting; **sentarse en —** to squat

cuclillo M cuckoo

cuco ADJ cute

cucú INTERJ cuckoo

cucurucho M (de papel) paper cone; (para helado) ice-cream cone; (capirote) hood

cuelga, cuelgue *ver* colgar

cuello M (del cuerpo) neck; (de una prenda) collar; **— de botella** bottleneck; **— uterino** cervix; **— vuelto** turtleneck; **estoy hasta el — en deudas** I'm up to my neck in debts

cuenca F (de un río) basin; (del ojo) eye socket

cuenco M earthen bowl

cuenta F (cálculo) count, calculation; (factura) bill, check; (relación de ingresos y gastos) account; (bolita) bead; (depósito bancario) bank account; **— conjunta** joint account; **— corriente** checking account; **— de ahorros** savings account; **— de contrapartida** contra account; **— de crédito** charge account; **— de depósito en garantía** charge account; **— de gastos** expense account; **— de mercado monetario** escrow account; **— en un paraíso fiscal** offshore account; **—s por/a cobrar** accounts receivable; **—s por/a pagar** accounts payable; **— regresiva/atrás** countdown; **abrir/cerrar una —** to open/close an account; **a fin de —** when all is said and done; **ajustar —s** to settle old scores; **caí en [la] — de que** it just dawned on me that; **dar — de** to finish off; **dar —s** to give an accounting; **darse —** to realize; **en — de margen** on margin; **en resumidas —s** in short; **eso corre por mí —** that is my responsibility; **habida — de** bearing in mind; **más de la —** more than necessary; **pasar la —** to call in a favor; **tomar/tener en —** to take into account; **trabajar por — propia** to freelance; M SG **cuentagotas** eyedropper

cuenta, cuente *ver* contar

cuento M story, tale; **— chino** tall tale; **— de hadas** fairy tale; **— de nunca acabar** never-ending story; **déjese de —s** come to the point; **traer a —** to bring up; **venir a —** to be to the point

cuerda F (soga) cord, rope; (de arco) bowstring; (de guitarra) string; (de reloj) spring; **— floja** tightrope; **—s vocales** vocal cords; **bajo —** under the table; **contra las —s** on the ropes; **dar — a** to wind; **no le des —** don't get him started

cuerdo ADJ sane

cuerno M horn (también instrumento de viento); (de caracol) feeler; (de ciervo) antler; **— de la abundancia** horn of plenty; **coger el toro por los —s** to take the bull by the horns; **poner —s a** to be unfaithful to

cuero M (piel de animal) hide; (piel curtida) leather; **— cabelludo** scalp; **en —s** naked

cuerpo M body; (torso) torso; **¡— a tierra!** hit the deck! **— de bomberos** fire department; **— de policía** police force; **— de prensa** press corps; **— docente** teaching staff; **a — de rey** in great luxury; **— extraño** foreign body; **dar — a** to flesh out; **de — entero** through and through; **ganó por tres —s de ventaja** he won by three lengths; **ir de —** to have a bowel movement

cuervo M crow, raven

cuesta F slope; **— abajo** downhill; **— arriba** uphill; **a —s** piggyback

cuesta, cueste *ver* costar

cuestión F question; **en — de segundos** in a matter of seconds; **poner en —** to question; **ser — de** to be a matter of

cuestionable ADJ questionable

cuestionador ADJ questioning

cuestionar VT to question

cuestionario M questionnaire

cueva F cave

cuidado M (atención) care; (preocupación) worry; **— con el perro** beware of the dog; **— de la casa** housekeeping; **— dental** dental care; **— posparto** postnatal care; **— prenatal** prenatal care; **— terminal** end-of-life care; **al — de** under the care of; **con —** carefully; **eso me trae sin —** I don't care about that; **tener —** to be careful; **un enfermo de —** a severely ill patient; INTERJ look out!

cuidador -ora MF caregiver, caretaker

cuidadoso ADJ careful

cuidar VT to take care of, to look after; **— de** to take care of; **— la casa** to keep house; **— niños** to babysit; **—se de** to beware of

culata F (anca) haunch; (de rifle) butt; (de motor) cylinder head

culatazo M (golpe) blow with the butt of a rifle; (rebote al disparar) recoil

culebra F snake

culebrear VI to slither

culebrilla F shingles

culinario ADJ culinary

culminación F (de carrera, ceremonia) culmination, high point; (de un sueño) fulfillment

culminante ADJ climactic

culminar VI to culminate

culpa F (responsabilidad) fault, blame; (sentimiento) guilt; **echar la — a** to blame; **por — de** because of; **tener la —** to be to blame

culpabilidad F guilt

culpable ADJ guilty; MF culprit

culpar VT to blame

cultivable ADJ (planta) cultivable; (tierra) arable

cultivado ADJ (tierra) cultivated; (perlas, persona) cultured

cultivador -ora MF (persona) cultivator; F (aparato) cultivator

cultivar VT (cosecha) to grow, to raise; (la tierra) to farm; (relaciones, inteligencia) to cultivate; (microbios) to culture

cultivo M (de plantas) growing; (de la tierra) farming; (de microbios) culture; (de relaciones) cultivation; **de —** cultured

culto ADJ educated, cultured; M worship; **libertad de —** freedom of religion

cultura F culture; **— general** general knowledge

cultural ADJ cultural

culturismo M body-building

cumbre F summit

cumpleaños M SG birthday

cumplido ADJ (cortés) polite; (perfecto) perfect; M compliment; **hacer algo de —** to do something out of duty; **hacer un —** to pay a compliment

cumplimiento M (de un contrato)

performance; (de una promesa, obligación) fulfillment; (de un plazo) expiration

cumplir VT (una obligación) to fulfill, to discharge; (una promesa) to keep, to honor; (una condena) to complete, to serve; **— diez años** to turn ten; **hacer —** to enforce; VI (vencer) to expire; **— con** to meet [a goal]; **me cumple informarle que** it is my duty to inform you that

cúmulo M (grupo) host; (tipo de nube) cumulus

cuna F (que se mece) cradle; (con barandas) crib

cundir VI (extenderse) to spread; (rendir) to go a long way

cuneta F roadside ditch; **en la —** out to pasture

cuña F (pieza para hender) wedge; (bacinilla) bedpan

cuñado-da M brother-in-law; F sister-in-law

cuño M die-stamp; **de — hispano** with a Hispanic stamp

cuota F (cantidad que le corresponde a uno) quota, allotment; (cantidad que hay que pagar) dues; (mensualidad) installment; **—s del coche** car payments; **—s sindicales** union dues

cupé M coupé

cupe, cupiera, cupiese ver **caber**

cupo M (cantidad) quota; (capacidad) Am room

cupón M coupon

cúpula F dome

cura F cure, remedy; M priest

curable ADJ curable

curación F cure

curanderismo M faith healing

curandero-ra MF healer

curar VT (una enfermedad, carne) to cure; (una herida) to heal; **—se** to heal; **—se en salud** to take precautionary measures

curiosear VI to look around; (en asuntos ajenos) to pry

curiosidad F curiosity

curioso ADJ curious

Curita® F Am adhesive bandage, Band-aid®

currículo/currículum M résumé; **— vitae** CV

curro M *Esp* job

curruca F warbler

curry M curry

cursar VT (estudios) to take; (mensaje, invitación) to send

cursi ADJ (afectado) affected; (de mal gusto) tacky

cursillo M (individual) tutorial; (corto) short course

cursivo ADJ cursive; **escribir en cursiva** to write in cursive

curso M (de río, enfermedad, acontecimientos, moneda) course; (período docente) academic year; (grupo de estudiantes) class; (libro) textbook; **— legal** legal currency; **el mes en —** the current month

cursor M cursor

curtiduría F tannery

curtiembre F tannery

curtir VT (cuero) to tan; (cutis) to weather; (el carácter) to harden; **—se** (envejecerse) to get weathered; (acostumbrarse) to become accustomed to hardships

curva F curve (también béisbol); **— de campana** bell curve

curvatura F curvature

curvo ADJ curved

cúspide F summit

custodia F custody, keeping; **en —** (un monto de dinero) in escrow; (un prisionero) in custody

custodiar VT to guard

custodio-dia MF guardian

cutáneo ADJ cutaneous

cutícula F cuticle

cutis M facial skin

cuyo ADJ REL whose

cyborg M cyborg

Dd

dádiva F gift

dadivoso ADJ generous

dado ADJ given; M die; **jugar a los —s** to throw dice

dador-ora MF giver; **— de sangre** blood donor

daga F dagger

dalia F dahlia

daltónico ADJ color-blind

dama F lady; (en el juego de mesa) king; **jugar a las —s** to play checkers; **— de honor** bridesmaid

damajuana F demijohn

damasco M (fruta) apricot; (árbol) apricot tree

damisela F damsel

dandi M dandy

danés-esa ADJ Danish; MF Dane; M (lengua) Danish

danza F dance; **— del vientre** belly dance; **en —** in action

danzante MF dancer

danzar[47] VI/VT to dance

dañar VT to harm, to damage; **—se** to suffer harm

dañino ADJ harmful

daño M damage, harm; **— colateral** collateral damage; **— emergente** actual damage; **— físico** bodily harm; **—s materiales** property damage; **—s y perjuicios** damages; **hacer —** to harm

dañoso ADJ harmful

dar[62] VT (un regalo) to give; (un golpe, naipes) to

deal; (sal) to add; (una fiesta) to throw; (la hora) to strike; (un olor) to give off; (la alarma) to raise; (un paseo) to take; — **a** (un edificio) to face; (una calle) to lead to; — **a conocer** to announce; — **a entender** to intimate; — **con** to hit upon, to find; — **de alta** to discharge, to release from the hospital; — **de baja** to discharge; — **de comer** to feed; — **de sí** to perform at capacity; **esta tela da de sí** this fabric gives; — **en la pared** to hit the wall; —**le con** to scrub with; **lo misma da** it makes no difference; **¿qué más da?** what difference does it make? **dale que dale** on and on; **hoy no doy una** today I can't get anything right; **le doy cincuenta años** he must be about fifty; **me da rabia/miedo** that makes me angry/afraid; **no me da el tiempo para ir al cine** I don't have time to go to the movies; **que no le dé el sol** don't let the sun shine on it; **y dale** enough already; —**se a la bebida** to indulge in drinking; —**se por conforme** to be satisfied; —**se prisa** to hurry; **dárselas de** to boast of being; **en este lugar se dan las flores silvestres** in this location wildflowers are found

dardo M dart

dársena F dock

datar VT to date; — **de** to date from

dátil M date

dato M piece of information; —**s** data

d.C. ADV AD

de PREP — **la familia** of the family; — **Madrid** from Madrid; **habló — la guerra** he talked about the war; **el hombre — gafas** the man with glasses; **el mejor estudiante — la clase** the best student in the class; **fácil — hacer** easy to do; **más — tres** more than three; **llevar — la mano** to lead by the hand; — **regreso a España** upon returning to Spain; — **venta en farmacias** on sale in pharmacies; **ancianos — respeto** older people to be respected; — **lo más lindo** really pretty; **tonto — mí** silly me

dé *ver* dar

deambular VI to amble, to saunter; — **por** (el bosque) to wander about; (el internet) to surf

deán M dean

debacle M debacle

debajo ADV under, underneath; PREP — **de** under, below; **por — de** under

debate M debate

debatir VT to debate; —**se** to struggle

debe M debit

deber VT **deben apoyarme** they should support me; **debe de ser** it must be; **deberías sentarte** you should sit down; VT to owe; **me debes una** you owe me one; **me debo a mis alumnos** I'm devoted to my

students; M duty; —**es** homework

debidamente ADV duly

debido ADJ due; — **a** due to, owing to; **a su — tiempo** in due time

débil ADJ (sin fuerza) weak; (endeble) frail, feeble; (sonido) faint

debilidad F (falta de fuerza) weakness; (cualidad de endeble) frailty; (de un sonido) faintness

debilitamiento M weakening

debilitante ADJ debilitating

debilitar VT to weaken, to debilitate

débito M debit

debutar VI to make a debut

década F decade

decadencia F (moral) decadence, decay; (cultural, económica) decline

decadente ADJ decadent

decaer[52] VI (fuerza) to weaken; (energía) to ebb; (salud) to fail; (ánimo) to flag

decaimiento M (decadencia) decline; (debilidad) weakness

decano -na ADJ senior; MF dean

decapitar VT to behead, to decapitate

decatlón M decathlon

decena F — **s de candidatos** tens of candidates

decencia F decency

decenio M decade

decente ADJ decent; **muy —** rather good

decepción F disappointment

decepcionante ADJ disappointing

decepcionar VT to disappoint

decibelio M decibel

decidido ADJ resolute, determined; **una decidida preferencia** a decided preference

decidir VI/VT to decide; —**se** to make up one's mind; —**se a** to resolve to

deciduo ADJ deciduous

décima F tenth

decimal ADJ decimal

décimo ADJ & M tenth

decir[53, 74] VT (palabras, oraciones) to say; (una mentira, un chiste, la verdad) to tell; — **tonterías** to talk nonsense; **con —te que** suffice it to say that; **este tipo no me dice nada** this guy leaves me cold; **¡que me lo digan a mí!** you're telling me that? VI to say; **diga** hello (al contestar el teléfono); **es —** that is to say; **he dicho** I have spoken; **no es prometedor que digamos** it's hardly promising; **no me digas** you don't say; **querer —** to mean; M saying

decisión F decision; **tomar una —** to make a decision

decisivo ADJ decisive

declaración F (de amor, independencia, guerra) declaration; (de un hecho) statement; (de un testigo) deposition; — **de derechos** bill of rights; — **de impuestos / de la renta** tax return; — **de impuestos sobre la renta**

income tax return; **— jurada** affidavit; **— de la misión** mission statement; **— errónea/falsa** misstatement; **— sobre la privacidad** privacy statement

declarar VT (amor, independencia, ingresos) to declare; (un hecho) to state; **— culpable** to find guilty; **os declaro marido y mujer** I pronounce you man and wife; VI (como testigo) to testify; **—se** (un amante) to declare one's love; **—se culpable** to plead guilty; **—se en huelga** to go on strike; **—se en quiebra** to declare bankruptcy

declinar VI/VT to decline

declive M (pendiente) slope, drop; (decadencia) decline

decoración F decoration; **— de interiores** interior decorating

decorado M (de casa) decoration; (de escenario) scenery

decorar VT to decorate

decorativo ADJ decorative

decoro M decorum, propriety

decorosamente ADV decorously, properly

decoroso ADJ decorous, proper

decrépito ADJ decrepit

decrepitud F decrepitude

decretar VT to decree

decreto M (disposición ejecutiva) decree; (ley) act

dedal M thimble

dedicación F dedication

dedicar[30] VT (la vida) to dedicate, to devote; (un libro) to dedicate; **—se** to dedicate oneself; (a los estudios) to apply oneself

dedicatoria F dedication

dedo M (de la mano) finger; (del pie) toe; **— anular** ring finger; **— índice** index finger; **— mayor / del corazón** middle finger; **— meñique** little finger; **— pulgar** thumb; **chuparse el —** to be a fool; **chuparse los —s** to lick one's fingers; **cruzar los —s** to keep one's fingers crossed; **elegir a — to** appoint directly; **hacer —** to hitch a ride; **no mover un —** not to lift a finger

deducción F deduction; **— impositiva** tax deduction

deducible ADJ deductible

deducir[38] VT (concluir) to deduce, to conclude; (descontar) to deduct

defecación F bowel movement

defecar[30] VI/VT to defecate

defección F defection

defecto M defect, flaw; **por —** by default

defectuoso ADJ defective, faulty

defender[2] VT (un fuerte) to defend; (una causa) to champion; (los derechos) to stand up for, to stick up for; **se defiende en francés** he can hold his own in French

defendible ADJ defensible

defensa F defense (también deportes); MF (fútbol) defender; **— individual** man-to-man defense; **— en zonas** zone defense; **aprende — personal** he's learning self-defense; **lo dijo en — propia** he said it in self-defense

defensivo ADJ defensive; **a la defensiva** on the defensive

defensor -ora MF (en la guerra) defender; (de una causa) champion

deferencia F deference

deficiencia F deficiency

deficiente ADJ deficient

déficit M deficit, shortfall; **— presupuestario** budget deficit

defienda, defiende ver defender

definición F definition; **— por penales** penalty shoot-out

definido ADJ definite

definir VT to define

definitivamente ADV definitely; once and for all; **— voy a comprar una impresora** I am definitely going to buy a printer; **lo arreglaremos todo —** we will take care of everything once and for all

definitivo ADJ (superior) definitive; (final) final; **en definitiva** all things considered

deflación F deflation

deflector M baffle

deforestación F deforestation

deformación F deformation

deformar VT to deform; **—se** to become deformed

deforme ADJ deformed, misshapen

deformidad F deformity

defraudar VT (cometer fraude) to defraud; (decepcionar) to disappoint

defunción F death

degenerado -da ADJ & MF degenerate

degenerar VI to degenerate

degenerativo ADJ degenerative

deglución F swallowing

degollar[24] VT to slash someone's throat

degradación F degradation

degradar VT (envilecer) to degrade, to debase; (rebajar el rango) to demote; **—se** to degrade

degüello M throat-slashing; **lucha a —** fight to the death

dehesa F pasture

deidad F deity

dejada F **— de volea** drop shot, stop-volley

dejadez F slovenliness

dejado ADJ slovenly

dejar VT (abandonar, no comer, legar) to leave; (a un enamorado) to leave, to dump; (permitir) to let; (soltar) to let go; **— de** stop; **— caer** to drop; **— pasar** to pass up; **déjame en paz** leave me alone; **me dejó atónito** it left/rendered me speechless; **no**

dejes de venir don't fail to come; **te lo dejo en mil dólares** I'll sell it to you for one thousand dollars; **—se** to let oneself go; **—se crecer la barba** to grow a beard

deje M slight accent

dejo M (sabor) aftertaste; (acento) slight accent; (toque) hint; **tener un — de** to smack of

delante M apron

delante ADV in front; **— de** in front of, ahead of

delantera F (de carrera) lead; (de vestido) front; **llevar la —** to be in the lead; **tomar la —** to take the lead

delantero -ra ADJ (pata) front; MF (línea, deportista) forward; M front

delatar VT to inform against, to squeal on; **— la edad** to betray one's age

delator -ora MF accuser, informer

delegación F delegation

delegado -da MF delegate

delegar[40] VT to delegate

deleitar VT to delight; **—se en algo** to revel in something; **—se la vista con** to feast one's eyes on

deleite M delight

deletrear VT to spell; **— mal** to misspell

deleznable ADJ despicable

delfín M dolphin

delgadez F thinness

delgado ADJ thin, slender, slim

deliberación F deliberation

deliberadamente ADV deliberately

deliberado ADJ deliberate

deliberar VI/VT to deliberate

delicadeza F (tacto) gentleness; (fineza) delicacy; **con —** gently; **tuvo la — de llamar** he was kind enough to call

delicado ADJ (suave, frágil, controvertido) delicate; (enfermizo) frail; (exquisito) dainty; (quisquilloso) squeamish

delicatessen F PL delicacies

delicia F delight

delicioso ADJ delicious, delectable

delimitar VT to delimit

delincuencia F crime

delincuente ADJ & MF delinquent, criminal; **— juvenil** juvenile delinquent

delineador M eyeliner

delinear VT to delineate, to outline

delirante ADJ delirious, raving

delirar VI to be delirious, to rave

delirio M delirium; **— paranoico** paranoid delusion; **—s de grandeza** delusions of grandeur

delito M crime, offense

deltoides M SG deltoids

demacrado ADJ drawn, gaunt, haggard

demagogo -ga MF demagogue

demanda F (de mercancías) demand; (de seguros) insurance claim; (pleito) lawsuit;

por — on demand; **entablar una —** to file a lawsuit

demandado -da MF (en un pleito) defendant; (en un arbitraje) respondent

demandante MF plaintiff

demandar VT (pedir) to ask for; (poner pleito) to sue, to file a suit against

demarcar[30] VT to demarcate

demás ADJ (restante) remaining; PRON the others, the rest; **lo —** the rest; **y —** and whatnot; ADV **por lo —** moreover; **por —** useless

demasía LOC ADV **en —** excessively

demasiado ADV too; too much; **eso es — para mí** that's too much for me; **él es — alto** he's too tall; ADJ too much; too many; **— dinero** too much money; **demasiadas cosas** too many things

demencia F (locura) insanity; (senilidad) senility; (enfermedad mental) dementia

demente ADJ demented, insane, deranged

democracia F democracy

demócrata MF democrat; **Partido —** Democratic Party

democrático ADJ democratic; (del Partido —) Democrat, Democratic

democratización F democratization

demografía F demographics

demográfico ADJ demographic

demoler[6] VT to demolish, to tear down

demonio M demon; **¿qué —s haces?** what the heck are you doing? **un frío del —** bitter cold

demora F delay

demorar VT to delay; **—se** to linger

demostración F (prueba) demonstration; (de un programa digital) demo; **— de fuerza** show of force

demostrar[5] VT (mostrar) to demonstrate, to show; (comprobar) to prove, to demonstrate

demostrativo ADJ demonstrative

demudar VT to change, to alter

demuestra, demuestre ver demostrar

denegación F (de una petición) denial

dengue M dengue fever

denigrar VT to denigrate, to disparage

denodado ADJ untiring

denominación F (valor) denomination; (nombre) designation

denominador M denominator; **— común** common denominator

denominar VT to designate, to term

denostar[5] VT to revile

denotación F denotation

denotar VT to denote

densidad F density; **alta —** high density

denso ADJ (sólido) dense; (líquido) heavy

dentado ADJ (rueda) toothed; (montaña) ragged

dentadura F set of teeth; **— postiza** false teeth

dental ADJ dental

dentellada F (mordedura) bite; (señal de diente) tooth mark; **a —s** biting

dentífrico M toothpaste, dentifrice

dentista MF dentist

dentro ADV inside; (tenis) in; PREP **— de la casa** inside the house; **— de la ley** within the law; **— de quince días** (en el plazo de) within two weeks; (al cabo de) in two weeks; **por —** within

denuncia F (acusación) denunciation; (de mina, de seguro) claim

denunciar VT (un hecho negativo) to denounce; (una mina) to claim; (un delito) to report

deparar VT (tener preparado) to have in store; (proporcionar) to afford; **el destino me deparaba una sorpresa** fate had a surprise in store for me

departamento M (división) department; (piso) small apartment; (provincia) province

departir VI *lit* to commune

dependencia F (hecho de depender) dependence; (habituación) dependency; (filial) branch office

depender VI to depend; **— de** to depend on

dependiente -ta ADJ dependent; MF sales clerk, salesperson

depilación F hair removal

depilar VT to remove hair; (con cera) to wax

depilatorio ADJ & M depilatory

deplorable ADJ deplorable

deplorar VT to deplore

deponer[56, 74] VT (las armas) to lay down; (a un ministro) to depose, to remove; VI to defecate

deportar VT to deport

deporte M sport; **me gusta el —** I like sports/ athletics

deportista ADJ athletic; MF athlete

deportivo ADJ athletic; **revista deportiva** sports magazine

deposición F (de un testigo) deposition; (de un ministro) removal; (movimiento de vientre) bowel movement

depositante MF depositor

depositar VT to deposit; **—se** to settle

depositario -ria MF repository

depósito M (en el banco) deposit; (de gasolina) tank; (de agua) reservoir; (de armas) depot, dump; (de mercancías) stock room, storehouse; **— de cadáveres** morgue; **— de garantía** security deposit; **hacer un —** to make a deposit; **en —** on consignment

depravado ADJ depraved

depreciar VI to depreciate

depredador -ora MF predator

depresión F depression

depresor M depressor; **— de lengua** tongue depressor

deprimente ADJ depressing

deprimido ADJ depressed

deprimir VT to depress

deprisa ADV quickly

depuración F (de agua) purification; (de un programa) debugging

depurador M debugger

depurar VT to purify; (un programa) to debug

derby M derby

derecha F (política) right wing; (tenis) forehand; **a la —** to the right; **de —s** right-wing

derechista ADJ right-wing; MF rightist

derecho ADJ (no izquierdo) right; (recto) straight; **ponerse —** to hold oneself erect, to stand up straight; ADV straight; **volver — a casa** to go straight home; **todo —** straight ahead; M (preceptos, disciplina) law; (prerrogativa) right; **— al trabajo** right to work; **— consuetudinario** common law; **— de admisión** fee; **—s del cliente** customer rights; **— internacional** international law; **—s fees; —s aduaneros** tax on imports; **—s civiles** civil rights; **—s de autor** royalties; **—s de la mujer** women's rights; **—s de los animales** animal rights; **—s mineros** mineral rights; **estar en su —** to be entitled; **poner al —** to put on right side out; **registrar los —s** to copyright

derechura F straightness

deriva F drift; **ir a la —** to be adrift

derivación F derivation

derivado M (subproducto) by-product; (palabra) derivative

derivar VT to derive

dermabrasión F dermabrasion

dermatología F dermatology

dermatólogo -ga MF dermatologist

derogación F repeal

derogar[40] VT to repeal

derramamiento M spill, spilling; **— de sangre** bloodshed

derramar VT (un líquido) to spill; (sangre, lágrimas) to shed; **—se** to spill over, to run over

derrame M spill; **— cerebral** stroke, cerebral hemorrhage

derredor LOC ADV **en —** all around

derrengar[40] VT (dañar la espalda) to sprain one's back; (cansar) to exhaust

derretir[9] VT to melt; **—se por alguien** to be crazy about someone

derribar VT (un edificio) to demolish, to tear down; (a una persona) to knock down; (un gobierno) to topple, to overthrow; (un avión) to shoot down, to down

derrocamiento M overthrow

derrocar[30] VT (un gobierno) to overthrow, to topple; (a un dictador) to depose

derrochador -ora ADJ extravagant; MF (de dinero) spendthrift; (de recursos) squanderer

derrochar VT (dinero) to squander; (salud) to

radiate

derroche M (de recursos) waste, extravagance; (de color) profusion

derrota F defeat

derrotar VT to defeat

derrotero M course

derrubio M washout

derruido ADJ dilapidated

derrumbadero M precipice

derrumbamiento M collapse

derrumbar VT to demolish; —**se** (edificio) to collapse; (túnel, caverna) to cave in

derrumbe M (de tierra) landslide; (de un edificio) collapse

desabotonar VT to unbutton, to undo

desabrido ADJ (comida) tasteless; (persona) *Am* dull; *Esp* surly

desabrigado ADJ exposed; **no salgas tan —** put on some warm clothes before you go out

desabrochado ADJ undone, unfastened

desabrochar VT (botones) to undo; (ganchos) to unhook; (hebillas, cinturones) to unbuckle; (botones) to unbutton; —**se** to come undone

desacato M disrespect; **— al tribunal** contempt of court

desacelerar VI to decelerate

desacierto M mistake

desaconsejable ADJ inadvisable

desaconsejar VT to caution against

desacoplar VT to uncouple, to disconnect

desacostumbrado ADJ unusual

desacostumbrar VT to break of a habit; —**se** to lose a habit

desacreditar VT to discredit

desactivación F deactivation

desactivar VT (explosivo, situación) to defuse; (mecanismo) to disable; (virus) to deactivate

desacuerdo M disagreement; **estar en —** to be at odds

desafiante ADJ defiant

desafiar[28] VT (retar) to challenge, to dare; (enfrentar) to defy

desafilado ADJ dull

desafilar VT to dull; —**se** to become dull

desafinado ADJ out of tune, off-key

desafinar VT to be out of tune

desafío M (reto) challenge; (desobediencia) defiance

desafortunadamente ADV unfortunately

desafortunado ADJ unfortunate, unlucky

desafuero M (de un diputado) withdrawal of immunity; (atropello) outrage

desagradable ADJ disagreeable, unpleasant

desagradar VT to displease

desagradecido ADJ ungrateful

desagrado M displeasure

desagraviar VT to make amends, to redress

desagravio M redress

desaguadero M drainpipe

desaguar[25] VI to drain

desagüe M (acción de desaguar) drainage; (de lavabo) drain, drainpipe; (en la azotea) gutter

desaguisado M mess

desahogado ADJ (cómodo) comfortable; (espacioso) spacious

desahogar[40] VT (aliviar) to relieve; —**se** to pour out one's feelings

desahogo M relief; **vivir con —** to live an easy life

desairar VT to slight, to snub, to rebuff

desaire M slight, snub, rebuff

desajustar VT to loosen; —**se** to come loose

desalentado ADJ despondent

desalentador ADJ disheartening

desalentar[1] VT to discourage, to dishearten; —**se** to get discouraged

desaliento M discouragement, dismay

desaliñado ADJ disheveled, slovenly, unkempt

desaliño M slovenliness

desalmado ADJ heartless

desalojar VT (una piedra) to dislodge; (un tribunal) to clear; (un edificio) to evacuate; (a un inquilino) to evict; (una vivienda) to vacate

desamparado ADJ helpless, forlorn

desamparar VT to forsake

desamparo M abandonment, helplessness

desamueblado ADJ unfurnished

desangrar VT to bleed; —**se** to bleed to death

desanimado ADJ (persona) discouraged; (jornada) dull

desanimar VT to discourage

desánimo M discouragement

desaparecer[35] VI (perderse) to disappear, to vanish; (morir) to pass away

desaparezca, desaparezco *ver* desaparecer

desaparición F disappearance; (muerte) demise

desapasionado ADJ dispassionate

desapego M detachment

desapercibido ADJ unnoticed

desaprobación F disapproval

desaprobar[5] VT to disapprove of

desarmado ADJ unarmed

desarmar VT (quitar las armas) to disarm; (desmontar) to take apart

desarme M disarmament

desarraigar[40] VT to uproot

desarreglar VT to disturb, to mess up

desarreglo M (trastorno, enfermedad) disorder; (desorden) mess

desarrollador -ora MF developer

desarrollar VT (aumentar) to develop; (extender algo enrollado) to unroll; (llevar a cabo) to carry out; (aclarar) to elaborate, to flesh out; —**se** to unfold

desarrollo M development; (de una ecuación) expansion; **en —** developing

desarticulado ADJ disjointed

desaseado ADJ slovenly

desaseo M slovenliness

desasir[50] VT to let go of

desasosiego M uneasiness

desastrado ADJ (desaseado) untidy; (funesto) ill-fated

desastre M disaster

desastroso ADJ disastrous

desatado ADJ (ambición) unfettered; (zapatos) untied

desatar VT (un nudo) to untie, to loosen; (una ola de violencia) to unleash; **—se** to come untied; **—se en insultos** to let out a string of insults

desatascador M plunger

desatascar[30] VT (un inodoro) to unclog; (un objeto atrapado) to dislodge

desatención F lack of attention

desatender[2] VT (no ocuparse de algo) to neglect; (ignorar) to ignore

desatendido ADJ (descuidado) neglected; (ignorado) ignored

desatento ADJ inattentive

desatinado ADJ imprudent

desatornillar VT to unscrew

desatracar[30] VI/VT to cast off, to shove off

desavenencia F discord

desayunar VT **desayuné huevos** I had eggs for breakfast; **—se** to have breakfast; **—se [con que]** to find out [that]

desayuno M breakfast

desazón F uneasiness

desbandarse VI to disband

desbaratar VT (un plan) to disrupt; (un hechizo) to break; **—se** to break down

desbocado ADJ (caballo) runaway; (collar) loose

desbordamiento M overflow

desbordante ADJ overflowing

desbordar VI (derramar) to overflow; VT (abrumar) to overwhelm; **—se** to overflow, to spill over

desbravar VT to break

descabalgar[40] VI to dismount

descabellado ADJ harebrained

descabezar[47] VT to behead; **un sueño** to take a nap

descafeinado ADJ decaffeinated

descalabrar VT (la cabeza) to split someone's head open; (a una persona) to hurt

descalabro M disaster

descalcificación F decalcification

descalificar VT to disqualify

descalzar[47] VT to take off someone's shoes; **—se** to take off one's shoes

descalzo ADJ barefoot

descaminado ADJ **andar/ir —** to be on the wrong track

descamisado ADJ (sin camisa) shirtless; (pobre) poor

descansar VI/VT to rest; **— en paz** to rest in

peace; **—se en** to rely on

descanso M (acción de descansar) rest; (de escalera) landing; (intermisión, receso) break; (en fútbol) halftime; **en —** at ease

descapotable ADJ & M convertible

descarado ADJ shameless, impudent, brazen; **a la descarada** shamelessly

descarga F (de batería, agua, armas) discharge; (de buques) unloading; (emocional) outpouring; (de electricidad) shock; (de internet) download

descargar[40] VT (una batería, agua) to discharge; (un buque, un arma de fuego) to unload; (bomba) to drop; (un programa de computadora) to download; **—se** (una batería) to drain; (ira) to vent

descargo M **en su —** in his defense

descarnado ADJ (realidad) stark; (cara) emaciated

descaro M effrontery, impudence, nerve

descarriar[28] VT to lead astray; **—se** to go astray

descarrilarse VI to derail, to jump the track

descartar VT (un naipe) to discard; (una posibilidad) to dismiss, to discard

descarte M discard; **por —** by elimination

descascararse VI (en jirones) to peel; (en fragmentos) to chip, to flake

descendencia F (linaje) descent; (descendientes) descendants

descendente ADJ descending, downward

descender[2] VI to descend; **— de** to descend from

descendiente MF descendant

descenso M descent

descentralización F decentralization

descienda, desciende ver descender

descifrado M deciphering

descifrar VT to decipher

descodificación F decoding, decryption

descodificar[30] VT to decode, to decrypt

descolgar[42] VT (una cortina) to take down; (un teléfono) to pick up; **—se con** to come up with; **—se de** to come down from

descollar[5] VI to excel

descolorido ADJ (persona) pale; (cosa) colorless

descomponer[56, 74] VT (disgustar) to upset; (dar diarrea) to give diarrhea; (dar náuseas) to make nauseous; (separar) to break down; (cadáveres) to decompose; (un reloj) to break; **— en factores** to factor; **—se** (productos químicos) to break down; (cadáveres) to decompose; (un reloj) to break; (sentir náuseas) to be nauseous; (tener diarrea) to have diarrhea; (disgustarse) to go to pieces

descomposición F (de cadáveres) decomposition; (de productos químicos) breaking down; (diarrea) diarrhea

descomprimir VT to decompress

descompuesto ADJ (roto) broken; (caótico)

chaotic; (con diarrea) having diarrhea

descomunal ADJ enormous

desconcertado ADJ disconcerted

desconcertante ADJ disconcerting

desconcertar[1] VT to disconcert, to puzzle, to baffle; **—se** to become disconcerted

desconchar VT to chip

desconcierto M confusion

desconectado ADJ disconnected

desconectar VT to disconnect

desconexión F (acción de desconectar) disconnecting; (incomunicación) disconnect

desconfiado ADJ mistrustful, suspicious

desconfianza F mistrust

desconfiar[28] VT to distrust, to mistrust, to be wary of

descongelación F thawing

descongestionante M decongestant

descongestionar VT to decongest

desconocer[35] VT (no reconocer) to fail to recognize; (no saber) not to know; **te desconozco** you are not acting like yourself today

desconocido -da ADJ unknown; MF stranger

desconocimiento M ignorance

desconsideración F thoughtlessness

desconsiderado ADJ thoughtless, inconsiderate

desconsolado ADJ disconsolate, dejected

desconsolador ADJ disheartening

desconsolar[5] VT to dishearten; **—se** to become disheartened

desconsuelo M dejection

descontaminación F decontamination

descontaminar VT to decontaminate

descontar[5] VT (bajar el precio) to discount; (excluir) to exclude; (quitar) to dock

descontentadizo ADJ hard to please

descontentar VT to displease

descontento ADJ & M discontent

descorazonado ADJ disheartened

descortés ADJ discourteous, impolite

descortesía F discourtesy, impoliteness

descortezar[47] VT to strip the bark from

descoser VT to rip; **—se** to come unsewn

descosido ADJ unsewn; M unsewn place; **hablar como un —** to talk one's head off

descostrar VT to remove the crust from

descoyuntado ADJ dislocated, out of joint

descoyuntar VT to dislocate; **—se** to become dislocated

descrédito M discredit

descreído -da ADJ unbelieving; MF unbeliever

descreimiento M unbelief

describir[74] VT to describe

descripción F description

descriptivo ADJ descriptive

descrito ver describir

descuartizar[47] VT to quarter

descubierto ADJ (destapado) uncovered; (sin sombrero) hatless; **al —** in the open; **estar al —** to be exposed; **poner al —** to expose, to lay bare; **en —** overdrawn; M overdraft

descubierto ver descubrir

descubridor -ora MF discoverer

descubrimiento M discovery

descubrir[74] VT (hallar) to discover; (destapar) to uncover; **—se** to take off one's hat; **— el pastel** to spill the beans

descuento M discount; **— por grupo** group discount; **con —** at a discount; **los —s** extra time, injury time

descuidado ADJ (en una tarea) careless, negligent; (en el aspecto personal) slovenly

descuidar VT to neglect; **descuida, yo me ocupo de eso** don't worry, I'll take care of that; **—se** to be negligent

descuido M (falta de cuidado) neglect; (acción descuidada) oversight; **al —** offhand; **por —** by chance

desde PREP (origen) from; (tiempo) since; **— Madrid** from Madrid; **— el martes** since Tuesday; **— luego** of course; **— el principio** from the start; **— el vamos** from the get-go; **— entonces** ever since

desdecirse[53, 74] VI (contradecirse) to contradict oneself; (retractarse) to retract

desdén M disdain, scorn

desdentado ADJ toothless

desdeñar VT to disdain, to scorn

desdeñoso ADJ disdainful, scornful

desdicha F misfortune; **por —** unfortunately

desdichado ADJ wretched

desdoblamiento M division

desdoblar VT (desplegar) to unfold; (dividir) to divide

deseabilidad F desirability

deseable ADJ desirable

desear VT to desire

desecación F drying

desecar[30] VT to dry, to desiccate; **—se** to dry up, to desiccate

desechable ADJ disposable, throwaway

desechar VT (ropa vieja) to discard; (una oferta) to refuse; (una posibilidad) to dismiss

desecho M waste material; **—s** refuse, waste

desembalar VT to unpack

desembarazar[47] VT to rid of; **—se** to get rid of

desembarcadero M dock

desembarcar[30] VT (de un buque) to disembark, to go ashore; (de un avión) to deplane

desembarco M landing

desembarque M landing

desembocadura F mouth

desembocar[30] VI to flow; **— en** to flow into; **la calle Ocho desemboca en la avenida A** Eighth Street feeds into Avenue A

desembolsar VT to disburse, to pay out

desembolso M disbursement, outlay

desembragar[40] VI/VT to disengage [the clutch]

desempacar[30] VT to unpack

desempañar VT to wipe clean

desempate M (tenis) tie-break; **[partido de] desempate** playoff [game]

desempeñar VT to redeem; **— un cargo** to perform the duties of a position; **— un papel** to play a part; **—se** to get out of debt

desempeño M (de un cargo o papel) performance; (de una cosa en prenda) redemption

desempleado ADJ unemployed

desempleo M unemployment

desempolvar VT to dust off

desencadenar VT (quitar las cadenas) to unchain; (provocar, causar) to trigger, to spark

desencajado ADJ (mandíbula) dislocated; (mirada) wild; **estaba — en el funeral** he was deeply disturbed at the funeral

desencajar VT (un cajón) to unstick; (la mandíbula) to dislocate

desencantar VT (desilusionar) to disillusion; (quitar un hechizo) to remove a spell from

desencanto M disillusion

desenchufar VI/VT to unplug

desenfadado ADJ uninhibited

desenfado M lack of inhibition

desenfrenadamente ADV with wild abandon

desenfrenado ADJ (sin moderación) unbridled, wanton, rampant; (muy rápido) reckless

desenganchar VT to unhook

desengañar VT to disabuse; **—se** (de un error) to become disabused; (de una ilusión) to become disillusioned

desengaño M disillusion

desengranar VT to take out of gear

desenlace M (de un libro) ending; (de un suceso) outcome

desenmarañar VT to disentangle

desenmascarar VT to unmask, to expose

desenredar VT (el cabello) to disentangle; (una historia) to disentangle

desenrollar VT to unroll

desenroscar VT to untwist

desentenderse[2] VI to pay no attention

desentendido ADJ **hacerse el —** to pretend not to notice/know

desenterrar[1] VT (un tesoro) to unearth, to dig up; (un cadáver) to disinter

desentonado ADJ out of tune

desentonar VI (cantar mal) to sing off key; (estar fuera de lugar) to be out of place

desentrañar VT to unravel

desenvoltura F self-assurance

desenvolver[6, 74] VT (desenrollar) to unroll; (quitar la envoltura) to unwrap; **—se** to behave

desenvuelto ADJ self-assured

deseo M desire, wish; (sexual) desire; **pedir un — ** to make a wish

deseoso ADJ desirous

desequilibrado -da ADJ unbalanced; MF unbalanced person

desequilibrar VT to unbalance

desequilibrio M imbalance

deserción F desertion; **— escolar** school dropout rate

desertar VI/VT to desert; **— de** to defect from

desértico ADJ desert

desertor -ora MF (militar) deserter; (escolar) drop-out

desesperación F desperation

desesperadamente ADV desperately

desesperado ADJ desperate

desesperanza F despair, hopelessness

desesperanzado ADJ hopeless

desesperanzar[47] VT to discourage, to deprive of hope; **—se** to despair

desesperar VI to despair; VT to drive crazy

desestabilizar[47] VT to destabilize

desestimación F rejection

desestimar VT to reject

desfachatez F audacity

desfalcar[30] VT to embezzle

desfalco M embezzlement

desfallecer[35] VI (debilitarse) to grow weak; (desmayarse) to faint

desfallecimiento M (debilidad) weakness; (desmayo) faint

desfavorable ADJ unfavorable

desfibrilación F defibrillation

desfibrilador M defibrillator

desfibrilar VT to defibrillate

desfigurar VT (el rostro) to disfigure; (una estatua) to deface

desfiladero M narrow passage

desfilar VI (coches) to file by; (soldados, modelos) to parade

desfile M parade

desgana F (falta de apetito) lack of appetite; (falta de entusiasmo) lack of enthusiasm

desganado ADJ apathetic, without enthusiasm

desgarbado ADJ ungainly, gawky

desgarrado ADJ (prenda, músculo) torn; (grito) heartrending

desgarradura F tear

desgarrar VT (rasgar) to tear; (un escándalo) to dredge up; **—le el corazón a alguien** to break someone's heart; **—se** to tear, to pull

desgarro M muscle pull

desgarrón M tear

desgastar VT to wear away; **—se** to get worn away

desgaste M wear and tear

desglosar VT (una suma) to itemize; (un tema) to break down

desglose M (de una suma) itemization; (de un tema) breakdown

desgracia F (infortunio) misfortune; (infelicidad) unhappiness; **—s personales** casualties; **caer en —** to fall into disgrace/disfavor

desgraciadamente ADV unfortunately

desgraciado -da ADJ (desafortunado) unfortunate; (infeliz) unhappy; MF (persona desafortunada) unfortunate person

desgranar VT (granos) to thrash, to thresh; (guisantes) to shell

desgravable ADJ tax-deductible

desgreñado ADJ disheveled, unkempt

desgreñar VT to dishevel; **—se** to muss up one's hair

desguazar[47] VT to scrap

deshabitado ADJ (territorio) uninhabited; (casa) vacant

deshacer[54, 74] VT (una acción, comando a la computadora) to undo; (una cama) to strip; (un plato, un jarrón) to destroy; (un sólido en un líquido) to dissolve; (un nudo) to untie; **— la maleta** to unpack the suitcase; **—se de** to get rid of; **—se en elogios** to rave about

deshaga, deshago, deshará, desharía ver deshacer

desharrapado ADJ ragged

deshecho ver deshacer

deshelar VT to thaw

desheredar VT to disinherit

deshice, deshiciera, deshiciese ver deshacer

deshielo M thaw

deshierbar VT to weed

deshilachar VT to unravel, to fray

deshojado ADJ leafless

deshojar VT to strip of leaves; **—se** (un árbol) to shed leaves; (un libro) to lose pages

deshonestidad F (falta de honradez) dishonesty; (falta de recato) immodesty

deshonesto ADJ (no honrado) dishonest; (no modesto) immodest

deshonra F dishonor, disgrace

deshonrar VT to dishonor, to disgrace

deshonroso ADJ dishonorable

deshora LOC ADV **a —** at an inopportune time; **comer a —** to eat between meals

deshuesar VT (un fruto) to stone; (un animal) to bone

deshumanizar[47] VT to dehumanize

deshumidificador M dehumidifier

desidia F indolence

desierto ADJ (lugar) deserted; (premio) unawarded; M (región árida) desert; (región poco fértil y no habitada) wilderness

designación F (acción de designar, nombre) designation; (nombramiento) appointment

designar VT to designate; (a un funcionario) to appoint

designio M design

desigual ADJ (pelea) one-sided; (actuación) uneven; (números) not equal; (rango) unequal; (terreno) uneven

desigualdad F inequality; (del terreno) roughness

desilusión F disillusion, disappointment

desilusionar VT to disillusion, to disappoint; **—se** to become disillusioned/disappointed

desinencia F ending

desinfección F disinfection

desinfectante ADJ & M disinfectant

desinfectar VT to disinfect

desinfestación F disinfestation

desinflado ADJ (globo, persona) deflated; (neumático) flat; M flat tire

desinflar VT to deflate

desinformación F (falta de información) disinformation; (mala información) misinformation

desinformar VT to misinform

desinhibido ADJ uninhibited

desinstalar VT to uninstall

desintegración F disintegration; **— atómica** atomic decay

desintegrarse VI to disintegrate; (material radiactivo) to decay

desinterés M (falta de interés) lack of interest; (generosidad) unselfishness

desinteresado ADJ (apático) disinterested; (generoso) unselfish, selfless

desistir VI to desist

deslavado ADJ faded

deslavar VT (quitar color) to fade; (lavar ligeramente) to wash superficially

desleal ADJ (persona) disloyal, faithless; (competencia) unfair

desleír[10] VT to mix with a liquid

deslindar VT to mark off

desliz M slipup

deslizamiento M slide, glide

deslizar[47] VT (un patín) to slip, to slide, to glide; (una tarjeta) to swipe; **—se** (un patín) to slide, to glide; (un error) to slip by

deslucido ADJ (actuación) dull; (color) dingy

deslucir[39] VT (un espectáculo) to tarnish; (color) to make dingy

deslumbramiento M dazzle

deslumbrante ADJ dazzling

deslumbrar VT to dazzle; **—se** to be dazzled

deslustrar VT to tarnish

deslustre M tarnish

desmadejado ADJ (fatigado) exhausted; (desgarbado) ungainly

desmadejar VT to exhaust

desmán M abuse

desmantelar VT to dismantle

desmañado ADJ awkward, clumsy

desmayar VI to lose courage; **—se** to faint, to

pass out

desmayo M faint, swoon; **peleó sin —** he fought unflaggingly

desmedido ADJ excessive

desmejorar VI (empeorar el aspecto) to look worse; (debilitarse) to get worse

desmembrar VT to dismember

desmentido M denial

desmentir[8] VT to deny

desmenuzar[47] VT (pan) to crumble; (zanahorias) to mince

desmerecer[35] VI — **en valor** to not do justice; **no — de** to compare favorably with

desmesurado ADJ (esfuerzo) inordinate; (orejas) too large

desmigajar VT to crumb, to crumble

desmitificar[30] VT to debunk

desmochar VT to top, to cut the top off of

desmontar VT (limpiar un monte) to clear; (desarmar) to dismantle, to take apart; (derribar de una caballería) to throw; **—se** to dismount

desmoralizar[47] VT to demoralize; **—se** to become demoralized

desmoronar VT to crumble

desmovilizar[47] VT to demobilize

desnatar VT to skim

desnaturalizado ADJ (madre) unnatural; (aceite) denatured

desnudar VT to undress; **—se** to get undressed

desnudez F nakedness

desnudo ADJ nude, naked

desnutrición F malnutrition

desnutrido ADJ underfed, undernourished

desobedecer[35] VT to disobey

desobediencia F disobedience; **— civil** civil disobedience

desobediente ADJ disobedient

desocupación F (paro) unemployment; (abandono de vivienda) vacating

desocupado ADJ (asiento, casa) unoccupied, empty; (tiempo) idle; (que no trabaja) unemployed

desocupar VT to vacate; **—se** to become free

desodorante M deodorant

desodorizar VT to deodorize

desoír[55] VT to turn a deaf ear to

desolación F desolation

desolado ADJ desolate, bleak

desolar VT to lay waste to, to desolate; **—se** to be desolated

desollar[5] VT to skin; **— vivo** to skin alive

desorbitado ADJ (precio, reacción) out of proportion; (ojos) bulging

desorden M disorder, disarray; **— público** public disturbance; **en —** in disarray

desordenado ADJ (persona, situación) messy; (persona, estilo de vida) wild; (cuarto) untidy, disorderly; (archivo) disorganized

desordenar VT to mess up

desorganización F disorganization

desorganizado ADJ disorganized

desorientar VT (marear, hacer perder) to disorient; (confundir) to confuse; **—se** to lose one's bearings, to become disoriented

desovar VT to spawn

desoxidar VT to deoxidize

despabilado ADJ (despierto) wide-awake; (listo) on the ball

despabilar VT (cortar el pabilo) to trim the wick of; (despertar) to awaken; **—se** to wake up

despachar VT (problemas) to dispatch; (una carta) to mail; (a un cliente) to take care of; (mercancías) to ship; (a una víctima) to bump off; (un pedido) to fill; **— al público** to sell to the public; **—se a su gusto** to speak one's mind

despacho M (oficina) office; (comunicación) dispatch; (envío de cartas) mailing; (envío de mercancías) shipping

despachurrar VT to squash

despacio ADV slow, slowly

desparasitar VT to worm

desparejo ADJ uneven

desparpajo M (desenvoltura) ease; (descaro) impudence

desparramar VT to scatter; **—se** to be scattered

desparramo M (lío) commotion; (de libros) clutter

despatarrarse VT (caerse) to sprawl; (abrirse de piernas) to spread one's legs

despecho M spite; **por —** out of spite

despectivo ADJ derogatory, pejorative

despedazar[47] VT to tear to pieces

despedida F farewell; **— de soltero** bachelor party

despedir[9] VT (decir adiós) to see off; (echar de un empleo) to fire, to dismiss; (emitir un dolor) to emit, to give off; **despídeme de tus padres** say good-bye to your parents for me; **—se [de]** to take leave [of], to say good-bye [to]

despegar[40] VT (dos cosas pegadas) to detach; VI (un avión) to take off; (un cohete) to blast off; **—se** to become detached

despegue M (de avión) takeoff; (de cohete) blastoff, liftoff

despeinado ADJ unkempt

despejado ADJ (el cielo) clear, cloudless; (un camino) clear; (la frente) with one's hair pulled back; (una persona) bright

despejador M (fútbol americano) punter

despejar VT (el campo, una pelota) to clear; (en fútbol americano) to punt; VI (una duda, el cielo) to clear up; **—se** to sober up

despellejar VT to skin

despensa F pantry

despeñadero M cliff

despeñar VT to push off a precipice; **—se** to fall down a precipice

despepitar VT (una granada) to seed; (una manzana) to core; **—se por una cosa** to be crazy about something

desperdiciar VT to waste; **—se** to go to waste

desperdicio M waste; **—s** scraps

desperdigar[40] VT to scatter; **—se** to be scattered

desperezarse[47] VI to stretch

desperezo M stretch

desperfecto M damage; **— mecánico** mechanical breakdown

despertador M alarm clock

despertar[1] VT (a una persona) to awaken, to wake up; (sospecha) to arouse; (interés, deseo) to kindle; **—se** to wake up

despiadado ADJ merciless, heartless, ruthless

despida, despide, despidiendo, despidiera, despidiese ver despedir

despido M dismissal, termination; **— temporal de un empleado** layoff

despierta, despierte ver despertar

despierto ADJ (no dormido) awake; (vivaracho) alert

despilfarrador ADJ wasteful

despilfarrar VT to squander

despilfarro M waste

despistado ADJ absent-minded, out of it

despistar VT (confundir) to throw off the track; (deshacerse de) to lose; **—se** to get confused

desplantador M trowel

desplante M rude remark

desplazado -da MF displaced person

desplazamiento M (de tropas) movement; (de refugiados) displacement

desplazar[47] VT to displace; **—se** to move

desplegar[41] VT (papel plegado) to unfold; (una bandera) to unfurl; (tropas) to deploy; (interés) to display

despliegue M display

desplomarse VI (edificio, precios) to collapse; (una persona) to slump; (esperanzas) to be dashed

desplome M collapse

desplumar VT (un ave) to pluck; (a un incauto) to fleece

despoblado ADJ uninhabited; **— de árboles** treeless; M open country

despojar VT to despoil; **—se** to shed leaves

despojos M PL (de batalla) spoils; (mortales) remains

desportilladura F chip

desportillar VT to chip

desposeer VT to dispossess

déspota MF despot

despótico ADJ despotic

despotismo M despotism

despotricar[30] VI to rant

despreciable ADJ (vil) contemptible, despicable, worthless; (insignificante) negligible

despreciar VT (menospreciar) to despise, to look down on; (rechazar) to snub

desprecio M (menosprecio) contempt, disdain; (rechazo) snub

desprender VT (un cierre) to unfasten; (algo prendido) to detach; (gases) to give off; **—se de algo** to part with something; **—se la ropa** to undo one's clothes; **de lo dicho se desprende que** from what has been said it follows that

desprendimiento M (de retina) detachment; (de energía) release; (de tierra) landslide; (generosidad) generosity

despreocupado ADJ carefree

desprestigiar VT to discredit; **—se** to lose one's prestige

desprestigio M loss of prestige

desprevenido ADJ unprepared; **tomar —** to take by surprise

desproporcionado ADJ disproportionate, out of proportion

despropósito M nonsense

desprovisto ADJ **— de** lacking in

después ADV after, afterward; **— de** after; **— de todo** after all; **— de horas hábiles** after hours

despuntar VI/VT to blunt; **—se** to become blunt

desquiciar VT to unhinge; **—se** to come unhinged

desquitarse VI to get even

desquite M getting even, revenge

desregular VT to deregulate

destacable ADJ notable, noteworthy

destacado ADJ outstanding

destacamento M military detachment, military detail

destacar[30] VT (tropas) to detach; (una cualidad) to highlight, to accentuate; VI to stand out; **—se** to stand out

destajo LOC ADV **a —** by the job

destapar VT (una cacerola) to take the top off; (un plan, a un niño en cama) to uncover; **—se** (en la cama) to uncover; (desnudarse) to bare all

destartalado ADJ dilapidated

destellar VI to flash

destello M flash

destemplado ADJ (persona) feverish; (sonido) out of tune

desteñido ADJ washed-out

desteñir[11] VI/VT to fade; VI to run; **—se** to fade

desternillarse VI **— de risa** to die laughing

desterrado -da ADJ exiled, banished; MF (persona) exile

desterrar[1] VT to exile, to banish

destetar VT to wean

destierro M exile, banishment

destilación F distillation

destilar VT to distill

destilería F distillery

destinar VT (determinar el destino) to destine; (dirigir) to address; (asignar) to commit

destinatario -ria MF addressee, recipient

destino M (hado) destiny, fate, lot; (uso) use; (final de viaje) destination

destitución F dismissal

destituir[19] VT to dismiss

destornillador M screwdriver

destoxificación F detoxification

destrabar VT to untie

destreza F dexterity, skill

destripar VT to gut

destronar VT to dethrone

destrozar[47] VT (estropear) to ruin; (causar grandes daños) to destroy; (derrotar) to rout

destrozo M damage

destrucción F destruction

destructible ADJ destructible

destructivo ADJ destructive

destructor -ra F destructive; M (buque) destroyer; MF (persona) destroyer

destruir[19] VT (destrozar) to destroy, to obliterate; (estropear) to ruin

destruya, destruya, destruyendo, destruyera, destruyese ver destruir

desunir VT to divide; —**se** to come apart

desusado ADJ (no frecuente) unusual; (no usado) obsolete

desuso M disuse, obsolescence; **caer en** — to fall into disuse

desvaído ADJ faded

desvainar VT to hull, to husk

desvalido ADJ helpless

desvalijar VT (un cuarto) to ransack; (a una persona) to clean out

desvalimiento M helplessness

desván M attic

desvanecer[35] VT (un color) to fade; (un contorno) to blur; —**se** (una persona) to faint; (un color, arrugas) to fade; (un sonido) to trail off

desvanecido ADJ (una persona) fainted; (un color) faded; (un contorno) blurred

desvanecimiento M (de una persona) fainting; (de colores) fading; (de un contorno) blurring

desvariar[28] VI to rave

desvarío M raving

desvelado ADJ sleepless

desvelar VT to keep awake; —**se** to be sleepless

desvelo M (falta de sueño) sleeplessness; —**s** (esfuerzos) efforts

desvencijado ADJ dilapidated, rickety; **estoy** — I'm all beat up

desventaja F disadvantage; **estar en** — to be at a disadvantage

desventura F misfortune

desventurado ADJ unfortunate

desvergonzado ADJ shameless

desvergüenza F shamelessness

desvestir[9] VT to undress; —**se** to get undressed, to undress

desviación F (de una norma) deviation, divergence; (en ruta) detour; (de fondos) diversion; (de la columna vertebral) curvature; — **estándar** standard deviation

desviar[28] VT (la vista) to avert; (fondos, tráfico) to divert; (un golpe) to ward off; (una conversación) to steer; (un tren) to sidetrack; —**se de** (un camino) to stray from; (una norma) to deviate from

desvío M (camino secundario) side road; (desviación) detour

desvirtuar[26] VT to distort; —**se** to become distorted

desvivirse VI — **por hacer algo** to bend over backward to do something; — **por alguien** to go out of one's way for someone

detallado ADJ detailed

detallar VT to detail, to go into detail about

detalle M (pormenor) detail; (venta al por menor) retail; (lista) list; **¡qué** —! how thoughtful! **con/al/en** — in detail

detallista ADJ (cuidadoso) meticulous; (considerado) thoughtful; M (comercio) retail; MF retailer

detección F detection

detectar VT to detect

detective M detective; — **privado** private eye

detector M detector; — **de incendios** smoke detector; — **de mentiras** lie detector; — **de metales** metal detector

detención F (arresto) detention, arrest; (de un vehículo) stop; — **domiciliaria** house arrest; — **ilegal** false arrest

detendrá, detendría ver detener

detener[58] VT (arrestar) to detain, to arrest; (parar) to stop; —**se** to stop; —**se en** to linger on; —**se a pensar** to stop to think

detenga, detengo ver detener

detenidamente ADV closely

detenido ADJ thorough

detenimiento LOC ADV **con** — with care

detergente ADJ & M detergent

deteriorado ADJ in disrepair

deteriorar VT to deteriorate

deterioro M deterioration, disrepair

determinación F determination; — **del grupo sanguíneo** blood typing

determinado ADJ (cierto) certain; **es lo que suponen determinadas personas** that is what certain people suppose; (específico) definite, specific; **pidió una cantidad determinada** he asked for a specific amount

determinante ADJ determining; M determiner

determinar VT to determine

detestable ADJ detestable

detestar VT to detest

detiene, detienes ver detener

detonación F detonation; **hacer detonaciones** to backfire

detonar VI/VT to detonate

detrás ADV behind; **— de** (en el espacio) behind; (en el tiempo) after; **por —** behind

detritus M INV debris

detuve, detuviera, detuviese ver detener

deuce M deuce

deuda F debt; **— incobrable** bad debt

deudor-ora ADJ & MF debtor; **— hipotecario** mortgagor

devaluación F devaluation

devanar VT to spool; **—se los sesos** to rack one's brain

devaneo M (pasatiempo) idle pursuit; (amorío) fling

devastador ADJ devastating

devastar VT to devastate

devengar[40] VT to earn

devoción F devotion

devolución F (de un producto) return; (de poder político) devolution

devolver[6, 74] VT (dar al dueño) to return; (enviar por correo) to send back; **— al remitente** to return to sender; **— la llamada** to call back; VI (vomitar) to throw up

devorar VT to devour

devoto ADJ (pío) devout; (que muestra devoción) devoted

devuelto, devuelva, devuelve ver devolver

dextrosa F dextrose

di ver dar, decir

día M day; **— a —** day-to-day; **— tras —** day after day; **al —** up-to-date; **al otro —** on the next day; **de — en —** by day; **de todos los —s** everyday; **el — de mañana** in the future; **hoy —** nowadays; **no veo el —** I can't wait; **ponerse al —** to catch up; **por —** by the day; **todo el —** all day; **todos los —s** every day; **un — sí y otro no** every other day; **vivir al —** to live from hand to mouth

diabetes F SG diabetes

diablo M devil; **pobre —** poor devil; **¿por qué —s dices eso?** *fam* why the heck are you saying that?

diablura F devilry, mischief

diabólico ADJ (ritual) diabolic, devilish; (perverso) diabolical

diácono M deacon

diacrítico ADJ & M diacritic

diafragma M diaphragm

diagnosis F diagnosis

diagnosticar[30] VT to diagnose

diagnóstico ADJ diagnostic; M diagnosis

diagonal ADJ & F diagonal

diagrama M diagram; **— de flujo** flow chart; **— de pastel** pie chart

dial M dial

dialéctica F dialectic

dialéctico ADJ dialectic

dialecto M dialect

dialectología F dialectology

diálisis F dialysis

dialogar[40] VI to dialogue, to hold talks

diálogo M dialogue, conversation; **fue un — de sordos** they talked past each other

diamante M diamond; **— en bruto** diamond in the rough

diámetro M diameter

diana F bull's-eye

diapasón M tuning fork

diapositiva F slide

diario ADJ daily; M (periódico) newspaper; (de sucesos personales) journal, diary; (de navegación) log; **a —** every day; **de —** everyday; **llevar un —** to keep a diary

diarrea F diarrhea

diastólico ADJ diastolic

diatriba F diatribe

dibujante MF illustrator

dibujar VT to draw; **—se** to appear, to loom

dibujo M (arte de dibujar, cosa dibujada) drawing; (diseño) design; **— al carbón** charcoal drawing; **—s animados** animated cartoon

dicción F diction

diccionario M dictionary

dice, dicen ver decir

dicha F happiness

dicharachero ADJ witty

dicho ADJ aforementioned; M saying

dicho ver decir

dichoso ADJ happy; **todo el — día** the whole blessed day

diciembre M December

diciendo ver decir

dicotomía F dichotomy

dictado M (ejercicio) dictation; (orden) dictate; **escribir al —** to take dictation

dictador-ora MF dictator

dictadura F dictatorship

dictamen M (opinión) report; (judicial) ruling

dictaminar VI (dar una opinión) to report; (fallar) to rule

dictar VT to dictate; **— clase** to teach class; **— sentencia** to rule

diecinueve NUM nineteen

dieciocho NUM eighteen

dieciséis NUM sixteen

diecisiete NUM seventeen

diente M (de persona, sierra) tooth; (de víbora) fang; (de rueda dentada) cog; (de tenedor) prong; **— de león** dandelion; **— de leche** baby tooth; **—s postizos** false teeth; **entre**

—s under one's breath; tener buen — to have a good appetite

diera, diese ver dar

diesel M diesel

diestra F right hand

diestro -tra ADJ (habilidoso) skillful, deft; (no zurdo) right-handed; MF right-handed person; **a diestra y siniestra** on all sides

dieta F (ingesta) diet; (dinero para gastos) per diem; **estar a —** to be on a diet

dietético ADJ dietary

dietista MF dietitian

diez NUM ten

diezmar VT to decimate

diezmo M tithe; **pagar el —** to tithe

difamación F (oral) slander; (escrita) libel

difamar VT to defame, to malign; (oralmente) to slander; (por escrito) to libel

difamatorio ADJ slanderous

diferencia F difference; **a — de** unlike; **hacer —s entre** to treat differently; **partir la —** to split the difference

diferenciación F differentiation, distinction

diferencial ADJ & M (distancia, pieza de coche) differential; F (matemática) differential

diferenciar VT to differentiate; **—se de** to differ from

diferente ADJ different

diferir[8] VT (aplazar) to defer; VI (ser diferente) to differ

difícil ADJ difficult, hard

difícilmente ADV (apenas) hardly; (con dificultad) with difficulty

dificultad F difficulty

dificultar VT to make difficult

dificultoso ADJ difficult

difteria F diphtheria

difundir VT (luz) to diffuse; (noticias) to broadcast

difunto -ta ADJ & MF deceased

difusión F (de luz) diffusion; (de noticias) broadcasting

difuso ADJ diffuse

diga ver decir

digerible ADJ digestible

digerir[8] VT to digest

digestible ADJ digestible

digestión F digestion

digestivo ADJ digestive

digesto M digest

digital ADJ digital

digitalizar[47] VT to digitalize, to digitize

digitar VI/VT to type

dígito M digit

dignarse VI to deign

dignatario -ria MF dignitary

dignidad F dignity

digno ADJ (respetable) worthy; (orgulloso) dignified; **— de confianza** trustworthy; **—**

de elogio praiseworthy

digo ver decir

digresión F digression

dije M charm

dije, dijera, dijese ver decir

dilación F delay; **sin —** without delay

dilatación F (de un metal, parte dilatada) expansion; (del ojo) dilation

dilatar VT (pupilas, capilares) to dilate; (metal, músculo) to expand; (tiempo, plazo) to defer; (prolongar) to prolong; **—se en un asunto** to dwell on a subject

dilema M dilemma

diletante MF dilettante

diligencia F (laboriosidad) diligence, industry; (vehículo) stagecoach; (tarea) errand; **— debida** due diligence

diligente ADJ diligent, industrious

dilucidar VT to elucidate

diluido ADJ dilute

diluir[19] VT (una solución) to dilute; (pintura, sopa) to thin

diluvio M deluge

dimensión F dimension

dimes M PL **— y diretes** gossip; **andar en — y diretes** to quibble

diminutivo ADJ & M diminutive

diminuto ADJ (tamaño) diminutive; (cantidad) minute

dimisión F resignation

dimitir VI to resign

Dinamarca F Denmark

dinámica F dynamics

dinámico ADJ dynamic

dinamismo M vigor

dinamita F dynamite

dinamitar VT to dynamite

dínamo M dynamo

dinastía F dynasty

dineral M fortune

dinero M money; **— contante y sonante** ready cash, hard cash; **— de plástico** plastic, credit card; **— sucio** dirty money

dinosaurio M dinosaur

diodo M diode; **— electroluminiscente** light-emitting diode

Dios M God; **dios** god; **— dirá** we'll see; **— los cría y ellos se juntan** birds of a feather flock together; **— mediante** God willing; **¡— mío!** my God! **— te lo pague** may God reward you; **— y su madre** everybody and their dog; **a la buena de —** any old way; **como — manda** as it should be; **¡por —!** oh, my! **que — te oiga** I hope you're right

diosa F goddess

diploma M diploma

diplomacia F diplomacy

diplomático -ca ADJ diplomatic; MF diplomat

diptongo M diphthong

diputación F council

diputado-da MF representative

dique M (presa) dike; (al lado de un río) levee; — **seco** dry dock

dirá ver decir

dirección F (sentido, rumbo) direction; (domicilio) address; (administración) management; (administración de una escuela) principal's office; (mecanismo, acción de conducir) steering; — **asistida** power steering; — **de correo electrónico** e-mail address

directiva F (orden) directive; (norma) guidelines; (junta de directores) board of directors

directrices F PL guidelines

directivo-va ADJ leadership; MF officer

directo ADJ (sin desviaciones, intermediarios) direct; (derecho) straight; **en** — live

director-ora MF (de una empresa) director, manager; (de una escuela) principal; (de orquesta) conductor; — **de correos** postmaster; — **general** CEO; — **técnico** coach

directorio M (índice) directory; (junta directiva) board of directors; — **[de] raíz** root directory; — **padre** parent directory

diría ver decir

dirigente MF leader; — **sindical** union leader

dirigible M dirigible

dirigir[46] VT (una obra teatral) to direct; (una empresa) to manage; (una orquesta) to conduct; (a un turista) to guide; (un saludo, una carta, una pregunta, una crítica) to address; —**se a** (hablar con) to address; (ir a) to go to; (tratar de) to be aimed at

discapacidad F disability

discapacitado ADJ disabled

discar[30] VI/VT Am to dial

discernimiento M discernment, insight

discernir[3] VT to discern

disciplina F discipline

disciplinar VT to discipline

discípulo-la MF disciple

disco M (cartílago, objeto plano y circular) disk; (fonográfico) record; — **compacto** compact disc; — **comprimido** compressed disk; — **de iniciación** boot disk; — **duro** hard disk; — **duro interno** internal hard disk; — **volador** Frisbee®; **es un** — **rayado** he's a broken record

díscolo ADJ unruly

disconforme ADJ dissatisfied

discontinuo ADJ discontinuous

discordancia F discord

discordia F discord

discoteca F (lugar donde bailar) discotheque; (colección de discos) record collection

discreción F discretion; **a** — at one's own discretion

discrepancia F discrepancy

discrepar VI to disagree; — **de** to take issue with

discreto ADJ (prudente) discreet; (separado) discrete; **un partido** — a sorry game

discriminación F discrimination; — **por edad** age discrimination; — **positiva** affirmative action; — **sexual** sexual discrimination

discriminar VI to discriminate; — **a** to discriminate against

disculpa F (excusa) excuse; (perdón) apology

disculpable ADJ excusable

disculpar VT (excusar) to excuse; (perdonar) to forgive, to pardon; —**se** to apologize

discurrir VI (transcurrir) to pass; (exponer) to discourse

discursear VI to make speeches

discurso M (enunciado) discourse; (disertacíon pública) speech, address; — **de apertura** keynote address

discusión F (charla) discussion; (riña) argument

discutible ADJ debatable, questionable

discutir VT (hablar sobre) to discuss; (oponerse a) to dispute; VI (reñir) to argue

disecar[30] VT (cortar) to dissect; (preparar para conservar) to stuff

diseminación F dissemination

diseminar VT to disseminate

disensión F dissension, dissent

disenso M dissent

disentería F dysentery

disentir[8] VI to dissent, to disagree

diseñador-ora MF designer

diseñar VT to design

diseño M design; — **de interiores** interior design; — **de página** page layout; — **gráfico** graphic design

disertación F lecture

disertar VI to lecture

disfraz M (para ocultarse) disguise; (de carnaval) costume

disfrazar[47] VT to disguise

disfrutar VI/VT to enjoy; — **de** to enjoy

disfrute M enjoyment

disfunción F dysfunction

disgustado ADJ (molesto) upset; (enojado) angry

disgustar VT to upset; —**se** (molestarse) to get upset; (enfadarse) to get angry

disgusto M (desagrado) unpleasantness; (discusión) quarrel; **a** — (con desgana) against one's will; (con incomodidad) uncomfortably; (en disconformidad) in conflict; **esa niña no da más que** —**s** that girl keeps us upset all the time

disidente ADJ & MF dissident

disimulado ADJ **hacerse el** — to pretend not to notice

disimular VI (fingir) to dissemble; (ocultar) to

conceal

disimulo M (fingimiento) dissimulation; (ocultamiento) concealment

disipación F dissipation

disipar VT (niebla, calor) to dissipate; (dudas) to dispel; (miedo) to allay; (dinero) to squander; **—se** to dissipate; (miedo, dudas) to allay, to lift

dislexia F dyslexia

dislocación F dislocation

dislocar[30] VT to dislocate; **—se** to get dislocated

disminución F (acción de disminuir) decrease, lessening; (desprecio) belittling; (de ventas) dip, decrease

disminuir[19] VT (menguar) to diminish, to decrease, to lessen; (despreciar) to belittle

disminuya, disminuye, disminuyendo, disminuyera, disminuyese ver disminuir

disolución F dissolution

disoluto ADJ dissolute, loose

disolvente M solvent; **— de pintura** paint thinner

disolver[6, 74] VT (sal) to dissolve; (reunión) to break up

disonancia F discord

dispar ADJ disparate

disparar VT (un arma de fuego) to shoot, to fire; (una cámara) to click; (la inflación) to trigger; VI (en fútbol) to shoot; **—le a alguien** to shoot at someone; **—se** (aumentar) to take off; (salir) to shoot out

disparatado ADJ absurd

disparatar VI to talk nonsense

disparate M absurdity, nonsense; **decir —s** to talk nonsense; **un — de plata** a ton of money

disparo M (acción de disparar) shooting; (tiro, herida) shot, gunshot; (tiro de fútbol) shot at goal

dispensa F dispensation

dispensación F dispensation

dispensar VT to dispense; **— de** to exempt from

dispensario M dispensary

dispersar VT to disperse

dispersión F dispersal

disperso ADJ (diseminado) dispersed, scattered; (distraído) absent-minded, distracted; (no concentrado) disperse

display M display

displicencia F flippancy

displicente ADJ (comportamiento) flippant; (actitud) cavalier

dispon, dispondrá, dispondría ver disponer

disponer[56, 74] VT (colocar) to arrange; (preparar) to prepare, to dispose; (mandar) to order; **— de** to have; **—se** to set about; **—se para** to get ready for

disponga, dispongo ver disponer

disponibilidad F availability

disponible ADJ (asiento, taxi) available; (dinero)

on hand; (inventario) in stock

disposición F (voluntad) disposition; (colocación) arrangement; (de ánimo) mood; **a — de** at the disposal of

dispositivo M device; **— analógico** analog device; **— de almacenamiento** storage device; **— de salida** output device; **— intrauterino** intrauterine device

dispuesto ADJ ready; **bien —** willing; **no estar — a** to be unwilling to

dispuesto, dispuse, dispusiera, dispusiese ver disponer

disputa F (controversia) dispute; (riña) argument

disputar VI/VT to dispute; **—se el poder** to vie/challenge/contend for power; **—se la posición** to jockey for position

disquete M floppy disk; **— de iniciación** bootable diskette

disquetera F disk drive

distancia F distance; **a —** at arm's length; **guardar —s** to keep at a distance; **¿a qué — está?** how far away is it?

distanciarse VT to distance oneself

distante ADJ distant

distar VI **dista mucho de** it's a far cry from; **dista diez kilómetros de** it's ten kilometers from

distender[2] VT (aflojar) to relax; (dilatar) to expand

distensión F distension; **— muscular** muscle strain

distinción F distinction

distinguido ADJ distinguished

distinguir[44] VT to distinguish

distintivo ADJ distinctive, distinguishing; M distinguishing characteristic

distinto ADJ (diferente) different; (claro) distinct

distorsión F distortion

distorsionar VT to distort

distracción F distraction

distraer[59] VT (la atención) to distract; (fondos, mano de obra) to divert; **—se** (divertirse) to entertain oneself; (dispersarse) to become distracted, *fam* to space out

distraído ADJ distracted, absent-minded; **hacerse el —** to play dumb

distribución F distribution

distribuidor -ora MF (persona) distributor; M (pieza de un motor) distributor

distribuir[19] VT to distribute

distrito M district

Distrito de Columbia M District of Columbia

distrofia F dystrophy; **— muscular** muscular dystrophy

disturbio M disturbance, trouble

disuadir VT (mediante palabras) to dissuade; (mediante acciones) to deter

DIU [dispositivo intrauterino] M IUD

diurético ADJ & M diuretic

diurno ADJ (actividad) daytime; (animal) diurnal

divagación F rambling

divagar[40] VI to ramble on, to digress

diván M divan; (de psiquiatra) couch

divergencia F divergence

divergir[46] VI to diverge

diversidad F diversity

diversión F (pasatiempo) amusement, entertainment, fun; (hecho de distraer la atención) diversion

diverso ADJ diverse; **—s** various

diverticulitis F diverticulitis

divertido ADJ amusing, entertaining

divertir[8] VT to amuse, to entertain; **—se** to have a good time, to have fun

dividendo M dividend

dividir VT to divide; (un territorio) to partition

divierta, divierte ver divertir

divieso M boil

divinidad F divinity

divino ADJ divine; **estuvo —** it was heavenly; **lo pasé —** I had a wonderful time

divirtiendo, divirtiera, divirtiese, divirtió ver divertir

divisa F (señal) emblem; (moneda) currency; (moneda extranjera) foreign currency

divisar VT to make out, to catch sight of

división F division; (de un territorio) partition

divisorio ADJ dividing

divorciar VT to divorce; **—se** to get divorced

divorcio M divorce

divulgación F dissemination; **— financiera** financial disclosure

divulgar[40] VT (un secreto) to divulge; (información) to disseminate

dobladillo M hem; **hacer —s** to hem

doblado ADJ (hipócrita) hypocritical; M (de tela, papel) folding; (de tubos) bending

doblaje M dubbing

doblar VT (una sábana) to fold; (el capital) to double; (una esquina) to turn; (la voz de un actor) to dub; VI (un coche) to turn; (una campana) to knell; **—se** to bend over

doble ADJ double (también en tenis); **— agente** double agent; **— falta** double fault; **— indemnización** double indemnity; **— matanza** double play; **— pulsación** double click; **— personalidad** split personality; **— visión** double vision; **de — caño** double-barreled; **de — filo** double-edged; **de — sentido** two-way; MF (persona muy parecida, actor sustituto) double; M (repique) knell; **—s** doubles; **—s mixtos** mixed doubles; **el —** double

doblegar[40] VT to break

doblete M double

doblez M fold; F deceitfulness

doce NUM twelve

docena F dozen; **— del fraile** baker's dozen

docente ADJ teaching

dócil ADJ (persona, animal) docile, pliant; (pelo) manageable

docto ADJ learned

doctor -ora MF doctor; **— en medicina** MD

doctorado M doctorate

doctrina F doctrine

documentación F documentation (también para computadoras)

documental ADJ & M documentary

documentar VT to document

documento M document; **— de instrucciones previas** living will; **— voluntad anticipada** living will

dogma M dogma

dogmático ADJ dogmatic

dogo M pug

dólar M dollar

dolencia F ailment

doler[6] VI to ache, to hurt; **me duele el brazo** my arm aches, my arm is sore; **—se de** (compadecerse) to feel sorry for; (arrepentirse) to regret

doliente ADJ aching; MF mourner

dolor M (físico) pain, ache; (espiritual) sorrow, pain; **— de barriga** bellyache; **— de cabeza** headache; **— de espalda** backache; **— de muela** toothache; **— de oídos** earache; **— de garganta** sore throat; **—es del crecimiento** growing pains; **— de garganta** sore throat; **—es de parto** labor pains

dolorido ADJ aching, sore

doloroso ADJ painful

doma F (de caballos) breaking; (de leones) taming

domado ADJ (caballo) broken; (león) tamed

domador -ora MF (de perros) trainer; (de leones) lion tamer

domar VT (caballos, personas) to break; (leones) to tame

domesticar[30] VT to domesticate, to tame

doméstico -ca ADJ domestic; MF servant

domiciliarse VI to take up residence; **¿dónde se domicilia usted?** where do you reside?

domicilio M (casa) dwelling; (dirección) address

dominación F domination

dominador ADJ (predominante) dominant; (tiránico) domineering, overbearing

dominante ADJ (predominante) dominant; (tiránico) domineering, overbearing

dominar VT (tener bajo su autoridad, ser más alto) to dominate; (reprimir) to control, to rein in; (tener sometido a su voluntad) to domineer

domingo M Sunday; **— de Ramos** Palm Sunday; **— de Pascua** Easter Sunday

Dominica F Dominica

dominicano -na ADJ & MF Dominican [de la República Dominicana]

dominio M (sobre una tierra, derecho de usar una cosa) dominion; (de sí mismo) control; (de una lengua) mastery, command; (hecho de dominar) domination; (ámbito, campo) domain; — **público** public domain

dominiqués -esa ADJ & MF Dominican [de Dominica]

dominó M (pieza) domino; (juego) dominoes

domo M dome

don M (gracia) gift; (título, jefe mafioso) don; **un — nadie** a nobody

dona F *Méx* doughnut, donut

donación F donation

donador -ora MF donor

donaire M grace

donante MF donor; — **universal** universal donor

donar MF to donate

doncella F *lit* maiden

donde ADV REL where; **de** — whence, from which; **ir — el herrero** to go to the blacksmith's shop; — **no** otherwise; **—quiera** wherever; **donde no comas, no te dejo salir a jugar** if you don't eat, I won't let you go out to play

dónde ADV INTERR where

donoso ADJ graceful

donut M *Esp* doughnut, donut

doña F doña

dopamina F dopamine

dopar VT to dope

dorado ADJ (cubierto de oro) gilt; (de color oro) golden; M dolphin fish

dorar VT to gild; — **la píldora** to sweeten the pill

dormido ADJ asleep

dormir[7] VI/VT to sleep; — **a** to put to bed; — **a un paciente** to anesthetize a patient; — **la mona** to sleep it off; — **la siesta** to take a nap; **se me ha dormido el brazo** my arm has fallen asleep; —**se** to fall asleep

dormitar VI to doze, to snooze

dormitorio M bedroom

dorso M back, reverse

dos NUM two; — **puntos** colon; — **veces** twice; **cada — por tres** constantly; **en un — por tres** in a jiffy; **los —** both of them

DOS M DOS

doscientos NUM two hundred

dosel M canopy

dosificar[30] VT to dose

dosis F (de medicamento) dose; (de droga) hit

dotación F (de fondos) endowment; (de personal) complement

dotar VT to endow

dote F dowry; —**s** talents

doy *ver* dar

draga F dredge

dragado M dredging

dragar[40] VT (para limpiar) to dredge; (para buscar objetos) to drag; M SG **dragaminas** minesweeper

dragón M (animal fantástico) dragon; (planta) snapdragon

drama M drama

dramático ADJ dramatic

dramatizar[47] VT to dramatize

dramaturgo -ga MF playwright, dramatist

drapear VI to drape

drástico ADJ drastic

drenaje M drainage

drenar VI/VT to drain

dribbling M dribble, dribbling

driblar VI/VT to dribble

drible M dribble

dril M drill

drive M drive

drive-in M drive-in

driver M driver

droga F drug; — **anticancerosa** anticancer drug; —**s de diseño** designer drugs; **tomar** —**s** to do drugs; MF **drogadicto -ta** drug addict

drogar[40] VT to drug

drogata MF junkie

drogota MF junkie

droguería F (tienda) drugstore; (industria) drug industry

droguero -ra MF druggist

dropar VI to drop

ducado M dukedom

ducha F shower

ducharse VI to shower

ducho ADJ skillful

dúctil ADJ (metal) ductile; (persona) flexible, supple

duda F doubt; **en —** in doubt; **fuera de —** beyond doubt; **no cabe —** there's no doubt; **poner en —** to cast doubt on; **sin —** without a doubt, undoubtedly; **sin lugar a —s** without doubt; **tengo una —** I have a question

dudar VT (no creer) to doubt; (vacilar) to hesitate; — **de** to have doubts about

dudoso ADJ doubtful; **de dudosa honestidad** of dubious honesty

duela F stave

duela, duele *ver* doler

duelo M (combate) duel; (luto) mourning; (pena) grief; (dolientes) mourners; **estar de —** to be in mourning

duende M (gnomo) goblin, gremlin; (gracia) charm

dueño -ña MF owner; **me sentí — de la situación** I felt like I was in control of the situation; M landlord; F landlady

duerma, duerme *ver* **dormir**

dueto M duet

dulce ADJ (sabor, personalidad) sweet; (clima) pleasant; (agua) fresh; **—amargo** bittersweet; M (cosa dulce) sweet; (mermelada) preserves, conserve

dulcería F confectionery

dulcificar[30] VT to sweeten

dulzón ADJ unpleasantly sweet

dulzor M sweetness

dulzura F sweetness

duna F dune

dúo M duet; **decir a —** to say in unison

duodeno M duodenum

dúplex M duplex

duplicado ADJ & M duplicate; **por —** in duplicate

duplicar[30] VT to duplicate

duplicidad F duplicity

duque M duke

duquesa F duchess

durabilidad F durability

duración F duration; (de una película, vocal) length; **— de la vida** lifespan

duradero ADJ (ropa) durable, serviceable; (pilas) long-lasting

durante PREP during; **— el mandato de los Demócratas** under the Democrats; **— muchos años** for/over many years

durar VI/VT to last

duraznero M peach tree

durazno M (fruto) peach; (árbol) peach tree

dureza F (de metal) hardness; (del clima, de la expresión, de una tempestad) severity; (del invierno) harshness; (de un boxeador) toughness; (del cuero) stiffness

durmamos, durmiendo *ver* **dormir**

durmiente ADJ sleeping; M railroad tie, sleeper

durmiera, durmiese *ver* **dormir**

duro ADJ (metal, golpe, droga, agua) hard; (clima, tormenta) severe; (invierno, expresión, sonido) harsh; (soldado) tough; (grifo) stuck; (viento) strong; (autoridad) inflexible; (pan) stale; (cuero) stiff; **— de corazón** hard-hearted; **— de entendederas** slow on the uptake; **a duras penas** barely; M five-peseta coin; **no tengo un —** I'm flat broke

DVD M DVD

Ee

e CONJ and

ebanista MF cabinetmaker

ébano M ebony

ebrio ADJ drunk, inebriated

ebullición F boiling

eccema M eczema

echar VT (una pelota, redes) to throw, to cast; (yemas, hojas) to sprout; (a un empleado) to fire; (humo, olor) to give off; (un líquido) to pour; (a un borracho) to throw out; **— abajo** to knock down; **— a la basura** to throw away; **— al mar** to put to sea; **— al correo** to mail; **— anclas** to drop anchor; **— a pique** to sink; **— carnes** to get fat; **— de menos** to miss; **— de ver** to notice; **— mano de** to seize upon; **— la culpa** to blame; **— por la borda** to jettison; **— raíces** to take root; **— sangre** to bleed; **— suertes** to draw lots; **— una carta** to mail a letter; **— una siesta** to take a nap; **— un vistazo a** to glance at, to take a look at; **te echo una carrera** I'll race you; **—le el muerto a alguien** to pass the buck to someone; **—se** to lie down; **—se a** to start to; **—se a correr** to bolt; **—se a perder** to spoil; **—se a reír** to burst out laughing; **—se a un lado** to dodge; **—se atrás** to back down/off; **—se para atrás** to lean back

ecléctico ADJ eclectic

eclesiástico ADJ & M ecclesiastic

eclipsar VT (ocultar) to eclipse; (superar) to eclipse, to outshine, to overshadow; **—se** to fade

eclipse M eclipse; **— de sol** solar eclipse; **— de luna** lunar eclipse

eco M echo; **hacer —** to echo; **hacerse — de** to repeat

ecocardiograma M echocardiogram

ecología F (medio ambiente) environment; (ciencia) ecology

ecológico ADJ (ambiental) environmental, ecological; (bueno para la naturaleza) eco-friendly

ecologista ADJ environmental; MF environmentalist

economato M commissary

economía F (actividades de producción) economy; (ciencia) economics; (familiar) finances; **— doméstica** home economics; **—s savings; hacer —s** to be thrifty

económico ADJ (relativo a la economía) economic; (frugal) frugal, thrifty; (barato) economical

economista MF economist

economizar[47] VT to economize, to save

ecosistema M ecosystem

ecuación F equation

ecuador M equator

Ecuador M Ecuador

ecualizar[47] VT to equalize

ecuatoriano -na ADJ & MF Ecuadorian

ecuménico ADJ ecumenical

edad F age; — **avanzada** ripe old age; — **de merecer** marriageable age; — **de Piedra** Stone Age; — **del consentimiento sexual** age of consent; — **Media** Middle Ages; — **mental** mental age

edición F (ejemplar) edition; (acción de editar) publication; — **de sobremesa** desktop publishing

edicto M edict

edificación F building

edificar[30] VT (construir) to build; (infundir sentimientos morales) to edify, to uplift

edificio M building

editar VT to edit, to publish

editor-ora ADJ publishing; MF editor

editorial ADJ publishing; F publishing house; M editorial

editorializar[47] VI to editorialize

edredón M comforter

educación F (escolar) education; (social) breeding; — **a distancia** distance learning; — **cívica** civics; — **especial** special education; — **en línea** e-learning; — **física** physical education; — **para adultos** continuing education; — **superior** higher education

educado ADJ (cortés) well-bred; (instruido) educated

educador-ora MF educator

educar[30] VT (desarrollar conocimientos) to educate; (entrenar) to train

educativo ADJ educational

edulcorante M sweetener

EEUU [Estados Unidos] M SG/PL USA

efectivamente ADV actually; **más de los que — encuentran** more than they actually find; INTERJ exactly

efectividad F effectiveness; **tener —** to be valid, to become valid

efectivo ADJ (eficaz) effective; (real) actual; **hacer —** (un cheque) to cash; (una deuda) to pay off; (una amenaza) to make good on; M cash; **en —** in cash; **—s** troops

efecto M (resultado) effect, result; (letra comercial) bill of exchange; (rotación) English, spin; **en —** in fact; **llevar a —** to carry out; **surtir —** to work; — **invernadero** greenhouse effect; **—s especiales** special effects; **—s personales** personal effects; **perder —** to wear off; **rebotar con —** to glance off; **a estos —s** to this effect; **para los —s** to all intents and purposes; **por — de** as a consequence of

efectuar[26] VT to effect; **—se** to be carried out

eficacia F efficacy, effectiveness; — **de una ley** force of law

eficaz ADJ effective

eficiencia F efficiency

eficiente ADJ efficient

efigie F effigy; **quemar en —** to burn in effigy

efímero ADJ ephemeral, fleeting

efusivo ADJ effusive

egipcio -cia ADJ & MF Egyptian

Egipto M Egypt

égloga F pastoral

ego M ego

egocéntrico ADJ egocentric, self-centered

egoísmo M selfishness

egoísta ADJ selfish; MF selfish person

egotismo M egotism

egresado -da MF graduate

eje M (de la Tierra) axis; (de un vehículo) axle; — **del pistón** piston rod; **eso me parte por el —** that messes up my plans

ejecución F (de un condenado) execution; (de un plan, una orden) carrying out, execution; (de una tarea) performance; (de una propiedad) foreclosure

ejecutable ADJ executable

ejecutar VT (a un condenado) to execute; (un plan, una orden) to carry out; (una tarea, música) to perform; (una propiedad) to foreclose on

ejecutivo -va ADJ & MF executive; — **de empresa** corporate officer

ejemplar ADJ exemplary, model; M (libro) copy; (individuo) specimen

ejemplario M handout

ejemplificar[30] VT to exemplify

ejemplo M (cosa típica) example; (modelo) model; **a — de** on the example of; **dar —** to set an example; **por —** for example

ejercer[32] VT (una profesión) to practice; (influencia, fuerza) to exert; (poder) to wield

ejercicio M exercise; (de una profesión) practice; **hacer —** to exercise; — **contable** accounting period; — **físico** physical exercise; **—s de Kegel** Kegel exercises; **en —** active

ejercitar VT (la vista, los músculos) to exercise; (a soldados) to drill; (a alumnos) to train; **—se** to train

ejército M army; **el —** the military

ejido M common

ejote M *Méx* green bean

el ART DEF M the; — **de la derecha** the one on the right; — **que** the one that; — **que sepa** whoever knows

él PRON PERS M SG (como sujeto) he; — **dijo** he said; (como objeto) him; **para —** for him; **le di el libro a —** I gave the book to him; **estamos hablando de —** we're talking about him; **el libro de —** his book

elaboración F (de miel, comida) making; (de un método) development; (de un informe) drafting

elaborado ADJ elaborate

elaborar VT (un método) to elaborate, to

develop; (comida) to make; (un informe) to draft

elasticidad F elasticity

elástico ADJ (sustancia) elastic; (cuerpo) supple; (horario) flexible; M elastic

elección F (votación) election; (selección) choice, selection; **no tuve** — I had no choice

electo ADJ elect

elector-ora ADJ electoral; MF elector

electoral ADJ electoral

electricidad F electricity; — **estática** static electricity

electricista MF electrician

eléctrico ADJ (aparato) electric; (instalación, corriente) electrical

electrificar[30] VT to electrify

electrizado ADJ electrified

electrizante ADJ electrifying

electrizar[47] VT (suministrar electricidad) to electrify; (emocionar) to galvanize, to electrify

electrocardiograma M electrocardiogram

electrocutar VT to electrocute

electrodo M electrode

electrodoméstico M electrical appliance

electroencefalograma M electroencephalogram

electroimán M electromagnet

electrólisis F electrolysis

electromagnético ADJ electromagnetic

electrón M electron

electrónica F electronics

electrónico ADJ electronic

elefante M elephant

elegancia F elegance

elegante ADJ (armonioso) elegant; (bien vestido) stylish, classy

elegibilidad F eligibility

elegible ADJ eligible

elegir[14] VT (seleccionar) to choose, to select; (votar) to elect

elemental ADJ (sencillo) elementary; (básico) elemental

elemento M element

elenco M cast

elevación F elevation; **tirar por** — to throw high in the air

elevado ADJ (pensamiento, estilo) elevated; (fiebre, montaña) high; (precios) high; M (béisbol) fly ball

elevador M elevator

elevar VT (en una jerarquía) to elevate; (precios, voz, objeto) to raise; (el espíritu) to uplift; — **la vista** to look up; — **al cuadrado** to square; — **al cubo** to cube; —**se a** to go up to, to rise to; **el rascacielos se eleva sobre la ciudad** the skyscraper towers over the city

elfo M elf

eliminación F elimination

eliminar VT to eliminate

eliminatoria F (atletismo, natación) heat; —**s** (fútbol) playoffs

elíptico ADJ elliptical

elite/élite F elite

elitista ADJ & MF elitist

ella PRON PERS F SG (como sujeto) she; — **dijo** she said; (como objeto) her; **para** — for her; **le di el libro a** — I gave the book to her; **el libro de** — her book

ellas PRON PERS F PL (como sujeto) they; — **dijeron** they said; (como objeto) them; **para** — for them; **les di el libro a** — I gave them the book; **el libro de** — their book

ello PRON NEUTRO it; — **es que** the fact is that

ellos PRON PERS M PL (como sujeto) they; — **dijeron** they said; (como objeto) them; **para** — for them; **les di el libro a** — I gave them the book; **el libro de** — their book

elocuencia F eloquence

elocuente ADJ eloquent; **las estadísticas son** —**s** the statistics speak for themselves

elogiar VT to praise

elogio M praise

elote M *Méx* corn on the cob

elucidación F elucidation

elucidar VT to elucidate

eludir VT to elude, to avoid, to dodge

emanación F emanation, flow

emanar VI/VT to emanate

emancipación F emancipation

emancipar VT to emancipate; —**se** to become free

emascular VT to emasculate

embadurnar VT to daub

embajada F embassy

embajador-ora MF ambassador

embalador-ora MF packer

embalaje M packing, packaging

embalar VT to pack; VI to accelerate

embaldosar VT to tile

embalsamar VT (a un muerto) to embalm; (un animal) to stuff

embalse M reservoir

embanderar VT to adorn with flags

embarazada ADJ pregnant

embarazar[47] VT (impedir) to hamper; (fecundar) to make pregnant; —**se** to get pregnant

embarazo M (obstáculo) impediment; (estado de embarazada) pregnancy

embarazoso ADJ embarrassing, awkward

embarcación F boat, embarkation, craft

embarcadero M wharf, pier

embarcar[30] VT (pasajeros) to embark; (mercancías) to load; —**se** to embark, to go aboard; —**se en** to embark upon

embargar[40] VT to seize; **estar embargado de emoción** to be overcome with emotion

embargo M embargo; **— judicial** seizure; **imponer un —** to embargo; **sin —** nevertheless, however

embarque M (de mercancías) loading; (de pasajeros) embarkation

embarrado ADJ smeared with mud

embarrar VT to smear with mud, to muddy

embate M lashing

embaucador M confidence man

embaucar[30] VT to dupe

embeber VT to soak up; **—se** to be absorbed

embelesar VT to enrapture

embeleso M rapture

embellecer[35] VI/VT to beautify

embestida F charge

embestir[7] VI/VT to charge

embetunar VT to polish

emblanquecer[35] VI/VT to whiten

emblema M emblem

embobar VT to amaze; **—se** to be amazed

embolia F embolism; **— cerebral** cerebral embolism

émbolo M piston, plunger

embolsar VT (dinero) to pocket; (una compra) to bag

emborrachar VT (a una persona) to intoxicate; (el carburador) to flood; **—se** to get drunk

emborronar VT (manchar) to blot; (hacer impreciso) to blur

emboscada F ambush; **tender una —** to lie in ambush

emboscar[30] VT to ambush; **—se** to lie in ambush

embotamiento M (efecto de embotar) dullness, bluntness; (acción de embotar) dulling

embotar VT to dull

embotelladora F bottling plant

embotellamiento M (de cerveza) bottling; (de tráfico) traffic jam, bottleneck

embotellar VT (cerveza) to bottle; (tráfico) to bottle up

embozar[47] VT to conceal

embragar[40] VI to engage the clutch

embrague M clutch

embriagado ADJ drunken

embriagar[40] VT to intoxicate; **—se** to become intoxicated

embriaguez F intoxication, drunkenness

embridar VT to bridle

embrión M embryo

embrionario ADJ embryonic

embriónico ADJ embryonic

embrollar VT (involucrar) to embroil; (confundir) to muddle

embrollo M muddle

embromar VT to kid

embrujar VT to bewitch

embrujo M spell

embrutecer[35] VT to stupefy

embudo M funnel

embuste M lie

embustero -ra MF liar, trickster

embutido M sausage

embutir VT to cram, to jam

emergencia F emergency

emergente ADJ emergent, emerging

emerger[45] VI (surgir) to emerge; (salir del agua) to surface

emigración F (de personas) emigration; (de animales) migration

emigrante ADJ & MF emigrant

emigrar VI (personas) to emigrate; (animales) to migrate

eminencia F eminence; **— gris** gray eminence

eminente ADJ eminent

emisario -ria MF emissary; M outlet

emisión F (de acciones, billetes) issue; (de un olor) discharge; (de programas) broadcast; (de gas) emission

emisor ADJ emitting; M transmitter

emisora F radio/television station

emitir VT (un olor, vapor) to emit; (juicios) to pronounce; (dinero, acciones) to issue; VI/VT (programas) to broadcast; **—se** to be on the air; **el programa se emite en horas de la mañana** the program airs in the morning

emoción F emotion; **¡qué —!** what a thrill!

emocional ADJ emotional

emocionante ADJ (conmovedor) touching; (apasionante) exciting

emocionar VT (apasionar) to excite; (conmover) to move, to touch; **—se** (estar ilusionado) to be excited; (estar conmovido) to be touched

emoticón M emoticon

emoticono M emoticon

emotivo ADJ emotional

empacador -ora MF packer

empacar[30] VT (regalos, mercancías) to pack; (algodón) to bale

empachar VI to cause indigestion; **—se** to suffer indigestion; **—se de** to get sick on, to stuff oneself with

empacho M (indigestión) indigestion; (cohibición) inhibition; **no tener — en** to have no qualms about

empalagar[40] VI/VT to cloy

empalagoso ADJ cloying, saccharine

empalar VT to impale

empalizada F stockade, palisade

empalmar VT to splice; **— con** to join

empalme M (de caminos) junction; (de cuerdas) splice; **— genético** gene splicing

empanada F turnover, pie

empanar VT to bread

empañado ADJ (vidrio) misty, foggy; (metal, reputación) tarnished

empañar VT (vidrio) to fog up; (metal, reputación) to tarnish

empapado ADJ soggy, sopping wet

empapamiento M soaking

empapar VT (mojar) to soak, to drench; (recoger con algo) to soak up; **—se** (mojarse) to get soaked; (enterarse) to find out all about

empapelado M wallpapering

empapelar VT to paper, to wallpaper; **— las calles** to plaster the streets

empaque M (acción de empacar) packing; (envoltorio) packaging

empaquetadura F gasket

empaquetar VT to pack, to package; **—se** to get dolled up

emparedado M sandwich

emparejar VT (una carga, un partido) to even up; VI/VT (los enamorados) to pair up; (calcetines, zapatos) to match up

emparentado ADJ akin, related

emparentar VT to relate by marriage; **—se** to become related by marriage

empastar VT to fill

empaste M filling

empatar VI to tie; **— una marca** to tie a record

empate M tie, draw

empatía F empathy

empecinado ADJ stubborn

empedernido ADJ (criminal) hardened; (mujeriego) incorrigible; (solterón) confirmed

empedernirse[73] VI to become hardened

empedrado M (acción) paving with stones; (cosa) cobblestone pavement; ADJ paved with stones

empedrar[1] VT to pave with stones

empeine M (del pie) instep; (del vientre) groin

empellón M shove; **a empellones** with shoves, shoving

empeñar VT to pawn; **— la palabra** to pledge; **—se** (endeudarse) to go into debt; (obstinarse) to insist; (esforzarse) to apply oneself; **—se en** to engage in

empeño M (prenda) pawn; (insistencia) insistence; (deseo) desire; (esfuerzo) exertion; **poner — en** to strive for

empeorar VT to make worse, to aggravate; VI to worsen; **—se** to get worse

empequeñecer[35] VT to make smaller; VI to get smaller

emperador -triz M emperor; F empress

emperifollarse VI to deck oneself out, to doll oneself up

empezar[48] VI/VT to begin, to start; **— a** to start to; **— de cero** to start from scratch; **para —** for starters; **no tengo ni para — con él** I can't touch him; **— por** to begin with; **empezamos mal** we got off to a bad start; **un paquete sin —** an unopened box; **por algo se empieza** you have to start somewhere

empinado ADJ steep

empinar VT to raise; **— el codo** to drink; **—se** (una persona) to stand on tiptoes; (un caballo) to rear; (una torre) to tower

empírico ADJ empirical

empizarrar VT to cover with slate

emplastar VT to plaster

emplasto M plaster

emplazamiento M (colocación) placement; (lugar) location

empleado -da MF employee; **— temporal** temp

emplear VT (usar) to employ, to use; (dar trabajo) to employ; **—se en** to be employed in

empleo M (ocupación) employment, work; (puesto de trabajo) job; (utilización) use

emplumado ADJ feathery

emplumar VT (adornar) to adorn with feathers; (pegar plumas en el cuerpo) to tar and feather; VI (echar plumas) to grow feathers

empobrecer[35] VI/VT to impoverish

empollar VT (huevos) to hatch, to brood; VI/VT (para un examen) to cram

empollón -ona MF *fam* egghead, overachiever

empolvar VT to cover with dust; **—se** (con cosméticos) to powder oneself; (con polvo) to get dirty

emponzoñar VT to poison

empotrado ADJ built-in

emprendedor ADJ enterprising

emprender VT (una tarea) to undertake; (un viaje) to embark on; **—la con alguien** to attack someone

empresa F (cosa que se emprende) undertaking; (compañía) company, enterprise; **libre —** free enterprise; **— privada** private enterprise; **— pública** public company; **— tiburón** raider

empresarial ADJ **—es** business administration studies; **grupo —** business group

empresario -ria MF entrepreneur

empréstito M loan

empujar VT (mover) to push; (mover con violencia) to shove; (apresurar) to hurry

empuje M (ánimo) drive; (fuerza de propulsión) thrust; (fuerza hacia arriba) lift

empujón M shove, push; **dar empujones** to jostle

empuñadura F (espada) hilt; (cuchillo) handle; (palo de golf, raqueta) grip

empuñar VT to grasp

emular VT to emulate

en PREP in; **— Asturias** in Asturias; (sobre una superficie) on, upon; **— la mesa** on the table; **sentarse — el suelo** to sit down on the floor; **me lo vendió — mil pesetas** she sold it to me for a thousand pesetas; **— la parada del autobús** at the bus stop; **— la noche** at night; **ir — tren** to go by train

enaguas F PL petticoat

enajenación M (locura) insanity; (transferencia) transfer

enajenar VT (trasladar) to transfer; (alienar) to alienate; **—se** to become alienated

enaltecer[35] VT to extol

enamorado -da ADJ in love; MF lover

enamoramiento M crush

enamorar VT to make fall in love; **—se [de]** to fall in love [with]

enanismo M dwarfism

enano -na MF (personaje imaginario, persona deforme) dwarf; (persona pequeña bien proporcionada) midget

enarbolar VT (una bandera) to raise on high; (un garrote) to brandish

enardecer[35] VT to inflame; **—se** to become inflamed

enardecimiento M inflaming

encabezado M header

encabezamiento M heading

encabezar[47] VT (una carta, una obra, un gobierno) to head; (un desfile) to lead

encabritarse VI (un caballo) to rear [up]; (una persona) to get furious

encadenar VT (poner en cadenas) to chain; (unir) to link

encajar VI/VT (colocar) to fit; VI (un gol) to allow; **el policía me encajó una multa** the policeman stuck me with a fine; **tu historia no encaja** your story doesn't hold water

encaje M (tejido) lace; (reserva bancaria) reserve; (acción de encajar) fitting together

encajonar VT (meter en una caja) to box; (apretar) to squeeze in

encallar VI to run aground, to strand; (una ballena) to beach; VT to ground

encamarse VI **— con** to go to bed with, to sleep with

encaminar VT to direct; **—se hacia** to head for

encanecer[35] VI to go gray; VT to cause to go gray

encanijado ADJ sickly

encanijarse VI to become sickly

encantado ADJ (contento) delighted; (hechizado) enchanted; **— de conocerla** pleased to meet you

encantador -ora ADJ charming, delightful; MF charmer

encantamiento M enchantment

encantar VT to enchant; **eso me encanta** I love that

encanto M (encantamiento) enchantment; (atractivo) charm; **un — de persona** a delightful person; **como por —** as if by magic

encapotado ADJ overcast

encapotarse VI to become overcast

encapricharse VI **— con/de/por** to become infatuated with

encapuchar VT (a una persona) to hood; (un

bolígrafo) to put the top on

encaramar VT to raise; **—se** to climb up on; **—se al primer puesto** to rise to first place

encarar VT to face; **me encaró el fusil** he pointed the rifle at me; **—se con** to face

encarcelamiento M imprisonment

encarcelar VT to imprison, to jail, to incarcerate

encarecer[35] VI (subir de precio) to increase in price; VT (rogar) to beg

encarecidamente ADV earnestly

encargado -da ADJ on order; MF person in charge; **— de curso** lecturer

encargar[40] VT (responsabilizar) to put in charge; (pedir) to order; (mandar) to commission, to order; **— a alguien una tarea** to charge someone with a task; **—se de** to take care of

encargo M (pedido) order; (tarea) assignment, charge, errand; **construido por/de —** custom-built; **hecho por —** made to order

encariñarse VI **— de** to become fond of

encarnación F incarnation

encarnado ADJ (color) red; (uña) ingrown

encarnar VT (un ideal) to embody; (a un personaje) to play; **se me encarnó una uña** one of my nails got ingrown

encarnizado ADJ fierce

encarnizarse[47] VI **— con alguien** to attack someone viciously

encarte M insert

encasillar VT to pigeonhole

encauzamiento M channeling

encauzar[47] VT to channel

encefalitis F encephalitis; **— espongiforme bovina** mad cow disease

encendedor M cigarette lighter

encender[2] VT (un cigarro, fuego) to light; (un fósforo) to strike; (una luz, radio) to switch on, to turn on; (una computadora) to power on, to power up; (pasión) to arouse; VI **—se** (una persona, sexualmente) to become aroused; (una lámpara) to turn on

encendido ADJ (rojo) bright; (excitado) aroused; M ignition

encerado M (pizarrón) blackboard; (acción de encerar) waxing; (capa de cera) wax coating; ADJ waxed

encerar VT to wax, to polish

encerrar[1] VT (palabras entre paréntesis) to enclose; (una oveja) to pen; (a una persona) to lock up; (un contenido) to contain; (un peligro) to involve; **—se** (aislarse) to isolate oneself; (obstinarse) to become fixated

encestar VI to make a basket

enchapar VT (metal) to plate; (madera) to veneer

enchilada F enchilada

enchufar VT (un aparato eléctrico) to plug in; (a un protegido) to fix up; **— un tubo con otro** to fit one pipe into another

enchufe M (entrada eléctrica) socket, plug-in, electrical outlet; (situación ventajosa) connection

encías F PL gums

enciclopedia F encyclopedia

encienda, enciende ver encender

encierra, encierre ver encerrar

encierro M (confinamiento) confinement; (lugar) enclosure

encima ADV (arriba) on top; (además) in addition; **— de** on top of, atop; **por — de** above; **sacarse de —** to get rid of; **orinarse — to** urinate on oneself; **ya tenía el coche — the** car was already on top of me; **no lleves tanto dinero —** don't carry so much money on you; **se nos vienen — los exámenes** the exams are upon us; **mi madre siempre me está —** my mother is always on me; **lo leí por —** I scanned it

encimera F counter

encina F oak

encinta ADJ pregnant

enclaustrar VT to cloister

enclavarse VI to be located

enclave M enclave

enclenque ADJ (endeble) sickly; (desvencijado) rickety

encoger[45] VI/VT to shrink; **—se** (una prenda) to shrink; (una persona) to be intimidated; **—se de hombros** to shrug one's shoulders

encogido ADJ (tímido) shy; M (encogimiento) shrinkage, shrinking

encogimiento M (acción de encoger) shrinkage, shrinking; **— de hombros** shrug

encolar VT to glue

encolerizar[47] VT to incense; **—se** to become incensed, to lose one's temper

encomendar[1] VT to entrust; **—se** to commend oneself

encomienda F (encargo) assignment, task; (colonial) encomienda [colonial land grant]

enconar VT to inflame; VI **—se** (discusión) to become inflamed; (herida) to fester

encono M animosity

encontrado ADJ contrary, opposing

encontrar[5] VT (hallar) to find; (verse con) to meet; **— a** to run into; **—se** (estar ubicado) to be located; (hallarse) to feel; **—se con** (verse por acuerdo) to meet with; (verse, por coincidencia) to run into; (enterarse) to find out; **vas a encontrarte la casa en obras** you'll find the house under construction

encontronazo M collision

encordado M strings

encordar[5] VT to string

encorvado ADJ stoop-shouldered

encorvamiento M slouch, stoop

encorvar VT to stoop; **—se** to bend over

encostrarse VI to scab

encrespar VT (el pelo) to curl; (el mar) to make choppy; **—se** (el pelo) to get curly; (el mar) to get choppy

encrucijada F crossroads

encuadernación F (oficio) bookbinding; (producto) binding

encuadernar VT to bind

encuadrar VT to frame; **la poesía de esta época se encuadra en tres tendencias** the poetry of this period can be classified into three tendencies

encubierto ADJ covert

encubrimiento ADJ (de un delincuente) concealment; (de un escándalo) cover-up

encubrir[74] VT (un secreto) to conceal; (un escándalo) to cover up, to hush up

encuentra, encuentre ver encontrar

encuentro M (casual) encounter; (planeado) meeting; (partido) game; (de atletismo) meet; **salir al —** (ir a encontrar) to go out to meet; (contradecir) to counter

encuerar VT to strip

encuesta F survey, poll

encuestado-da MF respondent

encuestar VI/VT to survey, to poll

encumbrado ADJ elevated, lofty

encumbramiento M elevation

encumbrar VT to elevate

encurtido M pickle

encurtir VT to pickle

ende LOC ADV **por —** hence

endeble ADJ (persona) feeble; (material, argumento) flimsy; (mesa) rickety

endémico ADJ endemic

endemoniado ADJ (poseído por el diablo) possessed by the devil; (niño) devilish; (pregunta) tough

enderezar[47] VT to straighten; **enderézate** stand up straight; **la niña se enderezó con los años** the girl straightened out after a few years

endeudamiento M indebtedness

endeudarse VI to get into debt

endiablado ADJ devilish

endocrino ADJ endocrine

endocrinología F endocrinology

endodermo M endoderm

endomingado ADJ dressed in one's Sunday best

endorfina F endorphin

endosante MF endorser

endosar VT to endorse

endoso M endorsement

endrogar VT to drug

endulzante M sweetener

endulzar[47] VT to sweeten; **se endulzó el tiempo** the weather became milder

endurecer[35] VT to harden, to stiffen; VI **—se** (músculos) to get hard; (pegamento) to set

endurecimiento M hardening

enebro M juniper

eneldo M dill

enema MF enema

enemigo -ga ADJ & MF enemy; **buques —s** enemy ships; **ser — de algo** to dislike something

enemistad F enmity

enemistar VT to cause enmity between; **—se con** to become an enemy of

energético ADJ **política energética** energy policy

energía F energy; **— eólica** wind power; **— hidráulica** water power; **— nuclear** nuclear energy; **— solar** solar energy; **— térmica** thermal energy

enérgicamente ADV strongly

enérgico ADJ (persona) energetic; (protesta, medida, tono) forceful

enero M January

enervar VT (debilitar) to enervate; (irritar) to irritate

enfadado ADJ angry

enfadar VT to anger; *fam* to piss off; VI **—se** to get angry

enfado M anger

enfadoso ADJ annoying

enfardar VT to bale

énfasis M emphasis

enfático ADJ emphatic

enfatizar[47] VT to emphasize

enfermar VT to sicken; VI to become sick; **—se** to become ill

enfermedad F (malestar) sickness, illness; (cardiovascular, de Parkinson) disease; (social) ill; **— contagiosa** contagious disease; **— coronaria** heart disease; **— de altura** altitude sickness; **— de Alzheimer** Alzheimer's disease; **— de las vacas locas** mad cow disease; **— del legionario** legionnaire's disease; **— de Lou Gehrig** Lou Gehrig's disease; **— de Lyme** Lyme disease; **— de Parkinson** Parkinson's disease; **— degenerativa articular** degenerative joint disease; **— mental** mental illness; **— parasitaria** parasitic disease; **— por radiación** radiation sickness

enfermería F infirmary

enfermero -ra M male nurse; F nurse

enfermizo ADJ (persona) sickly, infirm; (obsesión, aspecto) unhealthy; (imaginación) sick

enfermo -ma ADJ sick, ill; **me tiene — que vengan tarde** I'm sick of them coming late; MF patient; **— del corazón** heart patient

enfisema M emphysema

enflaquecer[35] VI to get thin

enfocar[30] VT (los ojos) to focus; (un faro) to point; (una cámara) to train; (un tema) to approach

enfoque M (método) approach; (acción de enfocar) focusing

enfrentamiento M clash, confrontation

enfrentar VT (enemigos) to confront; (una dificultad) to face, to tackle; **— a dos personas** to pit two people against each other; **—se con** to clash with

enfrente ADV opposite; **— de** in front of, opposite

enfriamiento M (del aire) cooling; (de una persona) chill; (de la economía, las relaciones) cooling off

enfriar[28] VT to cool, to chill; VI **—se** to cool off

enfundar VT to sheathe

enfurecer[35] VT to infuriate, to enrage; VI **—se** to become enraged, to rage

enfurruñado ADJ sulky

enfurruñarse VI to sulk

engalanar VT (una mesa) to decorate; (a una muchacha) to dress up; **—se** to dress up

enganchar VT (bueyes) to hitch; (una red) to snag; (un teléfono) to hook up; (a los televidentes, a un adicto) to hook; VI **—se** to get hooked

enganche M (del gas, teléfono) connection, hookup; (de drogas) addictiveness; (de vagones) coupling; (de caballos) team; (primer pago) *Méx* down payment

enganchón M snag

engañador ADJ deceiving

engañar VT (mentir) to deceive; (ser infiel) to cheat on; **— el hambre** to ward off hunger; **—se** to deceive oneself

engaño M deceit, deception

engañoso ADJ (una persona) deceitful; (un hecho) misleading

engastar VT to set

engaste M setting

engatusar VT to coax, to cajole

engendrar VT (emociones) to engender; (hijos) to father

englobar VT to encompass

engomar VT to glue

engordar VI to get fat, to put on weight; VT to make fat, to fatten; **esta semana he engordado dos kilos** I gained two kilos this week

engorroso ADJ irksome

engoznar VT to hinge

engranado ADJ meshed, interlocking; **estar —** to be in gear

engranaje M gears, gearing; **el — del partido** the party apparatus

engranar VT (meter una marcha) to put in gear, to throw into gear; (encajar) to mesh; **— la marcha atrás** to put [the car] in reverse

engrandecer[35] VT (a una persona) to aggrandize; (un palacio) to make more grandiose

engrapar VT to staple, to cramp

engrasar VT (untar) to grease; (manchar) to make greasy; (sobornar) to grease someone's palm; **—se** to get greasy

engrase M grease job

engreído ADJ conceited

engreírse[10] VI to become conceited

engrillar VT to shackle

engrosar VT (una manifestación) to swell; (un volumen) to grow; (una persona) to get fat

engrudo M paste

engullir[16] VT to gobble

enhebrar VT (un hilo) to thread; (cuentas) to string; **— idioteces** to string together a bunch of idiocies

enhorabuena F congratulation; INTERJ congratulations

enigma M (misterio) enigma, conundrum; (adivinanza) riddle; (problema) puzzle

enjabonar VT (poner jabón) to soap, to lather; (adular) to flatter

enjaezar[47] VT to harness

enjalbegar[40] VT to whitewash

enjambre M swarm

enjaular VT (un animal) to cage; (a una persona) to jail

enjuagar[40] VT (la ropa) to rinse; (ropa) to rinse out; (platos) to rinse off

enjuague M (limpieza) rinse, rinsing; (trama) scheme; **— bucal** mouthwash

enjugar[40] VT (la frente) to wipe; (lágrimas) to wipe away

enjuiciar VT to prosecute, to try

enjuto ADJ dry; (delgado) thin

enlace M (de trenes, web) link; (químico) bond; (boda) marriage; (persona) liaison; **— muerto** dead link

enladrillado M brick pavement

enladrillar VT to brick, to pave with bricks

enlatar VT to can

enlazar[47] VT (unir) to link (también en la web); (sujetar con lazo) to rope, to lasso; VI to connect; **—se** to connect

enlodar VT to muddy; **—se** to get muddy

enloquecedor ADJ maddening

enloquecer[35] VT to drive crazy; VI to go crazy; **—se** to go crazy

enlosado M flagstone pavement

enlosar VT to pave with flagstones

enmantecar[30] VT to butter

enmarañar VT (pelo) to entangle; (problema) to complicate

enmarcar[30] VT (un cuadro) to frame; **se enmarca dentro de** it takes place in the context of

enmascarar VT to mask

enmendar[1] VT (una ley) to amend; (un texto) to revise; **— la situación** to mend matters; **no me enmiendes la plana** don't correct me;

VI **—se** to mend one's ways

enmienda F (de una ley) amendment; (de un texto) revision

enmohecer[35] VT to mold; **—se** to get moldy, to mold

enmudecer[35] VT to silence; VI to go silent

ennegrecer[35] VI/VT to blacken

ennoblecer[35] VT to ennoble

enojadizo ADJ hotheaded

enojado ADJ angry, mad

enojar VT to anger; **—se** to get angry

enojo M anger

enojoso ADJ bothersome

enorgullecer[35] VT to fill with pride; **—se de** to take pride in

enorme ADJ enormous

enormemente ADV vastly

enramada F bower

enrarecido ADJ thin, rare

enrarecimiento M rarity, thinness

enredadera F creeper

enredar VT (enmarañar) to entangle; (complicar) to complicate; (involucrar) to mix up; VI to cause trouble; **—se** to get tangled up; **—se con** to become involved with

enredijo M tangle, snarl

enredo M (enredijo) snarl; (lío) mess; (amancebamiento) affair

enredoso ADJ complicated

enrejado M (de metal) grating, grate; (de varillas) lattice

enrejar VT to install a grate on

enrevesado ADJ involved

enriquecer[35] VT to enrich; **—se** to become rich

enriquecimiento M enrichment

enrojecer[35] VI/VT to redden

enrollar VT (manga, alfombra) to roll up; (hilo, cuerda, cinta) to wind up; **—se con** to become involved with

enronquecer[35] VT to make hoarse; VI to become hoarse

enroscar[30] VT (soga) to coil, to roll up; (tuerca) to screw in; (tapa) to screw on; **—se** (vid) to twine; (serpiente) to coil up

ensacar[30] VT to sack

ensalada F salad

ensalzar[47] VT to extol

ensanchar VT to widen; **—se** (una calle) to widen; (una falda) to flare

ensanche M (de una calle) widening; (de una ciudad) expansion

ensangrentado ADJ gory, bloody

ensangrentar VT to smear blood on; **—se** to get covered with blood

ensartar VT (cuentas) to string; (aguja) to thread; (con un pincho) to pierce; (historias) to rattle off

ensayar VT (probar) to try out; (intentar) to try; (analizar un metal) to assay; (practicar una obra teatral) to rehearse

ensayo M (intento) trial, attempt; (de teatro) rehearsal; (obra literaria) essay; (nuclear) testing; (de un metal) assay; — **clínico** clinical trial; — **general** dress rehearsal; **por — y error** by trial and error

enseguida ADV at once, immediately

ensenada F cove

enseña F ensign, flag

enseñanza F teaching, education; —**s** teachings

enseñar VT (mostrar) to show; (instruir) to teach; — **a** to teach how to

enseres M PL household utensils

ensillar VT to saddle, to saddle up

ensimismarse VI to lose oneself in thought

ensoberbecer[35] VT to make haughty; —**se** to become haughty

ensombrecer[35] VT (oscurecer) to make shadowy; (entristecer) to sadden

ensoñación F dream

ensordecedor ADJ deafening

ensordecer[35] VT to deafen

ensortijar VT to curl

ensuciar VT to dirty, to sully; —**se** (mancharse) to get dirty; (defecar) to soil oneself

ensueño M reverie, dream

entablar VT (relaciones) to establish; (un conflicto) to start; (una conversación) to strike up; (una demanda) to file; (una pelea) to pick

entablillar VT to splint

entallar VT to take in

entarimar VT to floor with planks

ente M (ser) entity; (excéntrico) weirdo; (agencia) agency

enteco ADJ sickly

entender[2] VT (comprender) to understand; (oír) to hear; — **de** to know about; —**se con** (comunicar) to communicate with; (llevarse bien) to get along with; **dar a** — to intimate; **yo me entiendo** I know what I'm doing; **se entiende** of course

entendido -da ADJ (comprendido) understood; (experto) expert; **tengo — que** I understand that; **caridad mal entendida** misguided charity; MF expert

entendimiento M understanding

enterado ADJ informed; **darse por —** to acknowledge; **estar — de** to be privy to

enterar VT to inform; —**se [de]** to find out [about]; **recién me entero** I just found out; **para que te enteres** just so you know

entereza F fortitude

enternecedor ADJ touching

enternecer[35] VT to touch; —**se** to be touched

entero ADJ (completo) entire, whole; (número) whole; **se mantuvo — durante el funeral** he held himself together during the funeral; M integer, whole number

enterramiento M (de un cable) burying; (de un difunto) burial

enterrar[1] VT (cable, muerto) to bury; (balón) to dunk

entibiar VT to make lukewarm; —**se** to become lukewarm

entidad F entity; **de —** significant; — **bancaria** banking institution

entienda, entiende ver entender

entierro M burial, funeral

entintar VT to stain with ink

entoldar VT to cover with an awning

entomología F entomology

entonación F intonation

entonar VT to sing; VI to sing in tune; — **con** to go well with; —**se** to get tipsy

entonces ADV then; **desde —** ever since; **hasta — until then; el — presidente** the then president; CONJ (así que) so

entornado ADJ half-open

entornar VT (una puerta) to leave ajar; (los ojos) to close partially

entorno M (lo que rodea) surroundings; (medio ambiente, informático) environment; — **de trabajo** work environment

entorpecer[35] VT (los sentidos) to dull; (el paso) to hinder; —**se** to become sluggish

entorpecimiento M (de los sentidos) dullness; (del paso) hindrance

entrada F (sitio por donde se entra, de un actor) entrance; (acción de entrar, artículo de diccionario) entry; (asistentes a un espectáculo) gate; (oportunidad para actuar) opening; (billete, derecho, precio de entrar) admission; (llegada) arrival; (primer plato) appetizer; (pago inicial) down payment; (tiempo en béisbol) inning; —**s** cash receipts; — **de coches** driveway; — **de datos** data input; — **por partida doble** double entry; **de —** from the start

entramado M lattice

entrante ADJ (alcalde) incoming; (año) next; M recess

entrañable ADJ (amistad) close; (persona) endearing

entrañas F PL (intestinos) entrails, fam guts; (sentimientos) heart, core; — **de la tierra** bowels of the earth; **de mis —** of my own flesh and blood

entrar VI (ir hacia adentro) to go in; (comenzar el día de trabajo) to come in; (caber) to fit; **dejar —** to let in; **hacer — en razón** to bring to reason; — **a medicina** to go into medicine; — **en calor** to warm up; — **en coma** to go into a coma; — **en/a un cuarto** to enter a room; — **en materia** to get to the meat of a matter; — **en vigencia/vigor** to go into effect; **me entró miedo** I became afraid; **me entró sueño** I got sleepy; **no sé**

cómo —le a esa chica I don't know how to approach that girl; **la física no me entra** I can't learn physics; **no entra entre mis favoritos** it is not included among my favorites; **la semana que entra** next week; **este vestido no me entra** this dress doesn't fit me; **seis entra dos veces en doce** six goes into twelve two times; **hazle —** show him in; VT (datos) to enter, to input

entre PREP (dos) between; (muchos) among; **— vaso y vaso** between glasses; **— dientes** under one's breath

entreabierto ADJ ajar, half-open

entreabrir[74] VT (puerta) to crack open; (los ojos) to half-open

entreacto M intermission

entrecano ADJ graying

entrecejo M space between the eyebrows

entrecortado ADJ (voz) faltering; (respiración) irregular

entrecortarse VI to falter

entrecruzar[47] VT to interlace; **—se** to cross

entredicho LOC ADV **en —** in doubt

entrega F (de un paquete) delivery; (de un manuscrito) submission; (al vicio) surrender; (de una novela) installment; (de revista) issue; **a la —** on delivery; **por —s** serial; **— a domicilio** home delivery; **— de premios** presentation of awards; **— el mismo día** same-day delivery; **— gratuita** free delivery; **— inicial** down payment

entregar[40] VT (un paquete) to deliver; (a un rehén, prisionero) to hand over; (a un delincuente) to turn in; (a una hija en matrimonio) to give; (premios) to hand out, to present; (tarea escolar) to hand in; (el coche) to trade in; **—se [a]** (la policía) to surrender [to]; (a una misión) to dedicate oneself to

entrelazar[47] VT to intertwine

entremés M (obra de teatro) interlude; (comida) hors d'oeuvre

entremeter VT to insert; **—se en** (meterse) to get mixed up in; (inmiscuirse) to meddle in

entremetido -da ADJ meddlesome, nosy; MF meddler, busybody

entremezclar VT to intermingle

entrenador -ora MF trainer, coach; **— en jefe** head coach

entrenamiento M training

entrenar VI/VT to train

entrepierna F (del cuerpo) crotch; (de pantalón) inseam

entrepiso M mezzanine

entresacar[30] VT (seleccionar) to cull; (adelgazar) to thin

entresuelo M (de hotel) mezzanine; (de cine) balcony

entretanto ADV meanwhile

entretejer VT (el pelo, una tela) to weave; (una historia) to weave together

entretener[58] VT (hacer atrasar) to delay; (distraer) to distract; (divertir) to entertain; **—se** (divertirse) to amuse oneself; (detenerse) to delay

entretenido ADJ entertaining

entretenimiento M entertainment, amusement

entrever[72, 74] VT (apenas) to catch a glimpse of; (a lo lejos) to make out

entreverar VT to mix, to intersperse; **—se** to meddle

entrevía F gauge

entrevista F interview; **— de salida** exit interview

entrevistar VT to interview; **—se con** to have an interview with

entristecer[35] VT to sadden; **—se** to become sad

entrometerse VI to meddle, to interfere

entrometido -da ADJ meddlesome, nosy; MF meddler, busybody

entronque M (ferroviario) junction; (parentesco) relationship

entropía F entropy

entumecido ADJ (dedo, diente) numb; (músculo) stiff

entumecimiento M (de los dedos, dientes) numbness; (de los músculos) stiffness

enturbiar VT (el agua) to muddy; (una decisión) to muddle; (el juicio, la alegría) to cloud; **—se** (agua) to get muddy; (alegría) to be marred

entusiasmado ADJ enthusiastic, excited

entusiasmar VT to excite; **—se** to be excited

entusiasmo M enthusiasm, excitement

entusiasta MF enthusiast; ADJ enthusiastic

enumerar VT to enumerate

enunciado M utterance

enunciar VT (palabras) to enunciate; (una teoría) to articulate, to enunciate

envainar VT to sheathe

envalentonar VT to embolden, to make bold; **—se** to become bold

envanecer[35] VT to make vain; **—se** to become vain

envarado ADJ stiff, staid

envaramiento M stiffness

envasar VT to package; **— al vacío** to vacuum-pack

envase M packaging

envejecer[35] VT to make old; **ese maquillaje te envejece** that makeup makes you look older; VI to grow old, to age

envejecimiento M aging

envenenamiento M poisoning

envenenar VT to poison

envergadura F (de un avión) wingspan; (de un ave) wingspread; (de un evento, proyecto) importance

envés M SG back

enviado -da MF (político) envoy; (periodístico) correspondent

enviar[28] VT to send; **— por fax** to fax

enviciar VT to corrupt; **—se con** to get hooked on

envidia F envy

envidiable ADJ enviable

envidiar VT to envy

envidioso ADJ envious, jealous

envilecer[35] VT to debase

envío M (acción) shipping; (mercancía) shipment; (manuscrito) submission; **— de anotación** touchdown pass; **— rápido** express delivery

envite M bet

envoltorio M (cosa envuelta) bundle; (envoltura) wrapper

envoltura F wrapping, wrapper; **— de plástico transparente** shrinkwrap

envolver[6, 74] VT (involucrar) to involve; (cubrir) to wrap; (atrapar) to entangle; (rodear) to surround; **—se** to become involved

envuelto, envuelva, envuelve ver envolver

enyesar VT (enlucir con yeso) to plaster; (escayolar) to put in a cast

enzima MF enzyme

épica F epic

epicentro M epicenter

épico ADJ epic

epidemia F epidemic

epidémico ADJ epidemic

epidermis F epidermis

epifanía F epiphany

epiglotis F epiglottis

epilepsia F epilepsy

epiléptico ADJ epileptic

epílogo M epilogue

episódico ADJ episodic

episodio M episode

epitafio M epitaph

epítome M epitome

época F (momento) time, period; (período histórico) age; (temporada) season; (período geológico) epoch

epopeya F epic poem

equidad F equity

equidistante ADJ equidistant

equilibrado ADJ balanced; M balancing

equilibrar VT to balance; **— un presupuesto** to balance a budget

equilibrio M equilibrium, balance; **perder el —** to lose one's balance; **hacer —s** to do a balancing act

equino ADJ & M equine

equinoccio M equinox

equipaje M baggage, luggage

equipamiento M equipment

equipar VT to equip, to outfit

equiparar VT to equate

equipo M (materiales) equipment; (grupo) team; **— de vida** life-support system; **— deportivo** sweatsuit; **— de esquí** ski gear

equitación F (arte) horsemanship; (actividad) riding

equitativo ADJ equitable

equivalente ADJ equivalent

equivaler[60] VI to be equivalent; **lo que equivale a decir** which amounts to saying

equivocación F mistake

equivocado ADJ mistaken, wrong; **estar —** to be wrong/mistaken

equivocar[30] VT to mistake; **—se** to be mistaken, to make a mistake, to miscalculate; **—se sala** to choose the wrong room; **si no me equivoco** unless I'm mistaken; **me equivoqué de baño** I went into the wrong bathroom

equívoco ADJ (ambiguo) equivocal; (moralmente dudoso) questionable; M misunderstanding

era F (período) era, age; (lugar donde se trilla) threshing floor; (parcela) plot

era, eras ver ser

erario M treasury

erecto ADJ erect; (postura) upright

eres ver ser

ergonomía F ergonomics

ergonómico ADJ ergonomic

erguido ADJ erect, upright

erguir[13] VT to lift, to raise; **—se** to rise

erial M uncultivated land

erigir[46] VT (construir) to erect; (fundar) to found; **—se en** to set oneself up as

Eritrea F Eritrea

eritreo -a ADJ & MF Eritrean

erizado ADJ bristly; **— de** bristling with

erizar[47] VT to set on end; **—se** to bristle

erizo M hedgehog; **— de mar** sea urchin; **ser un —** to be a grouch

ermitaño -ña MF (persona) hermit; M (cangrejo) hermit crab

erógeno ADJ erogenous

erosión F erosion

erradicación F eradication

erradicar[30] VT to eradicate, to root out

errado ADJ erroneous, in error

errante ADJ wandering

errar[21] VT to miss; **— el cálculo** to miscalculate; VI (estar equivocado) to be mistaken; (vagar) to roam, to rove, to wander

errata F misprint, typographical error

errático ADJ erratic

erróneo ADJ erroneous

error M error, mistake; **— de hecho** factual error; **— de imprenta** misprint; **— no forzado** unforced error; **— tipográfico** typo

eructar VI to belch, to burp

eructo M belch, burp

erudición F erudition, learning, scholarship

erudito -ta ADJ (persona) erudite; (obra) scholarly, learned; MF scholar

erupción F eruption; **hacer —** to erupt

es *ver* ser

esbelto ADJ slender

esbozar[47] VT to outline; **— una sonrisa** to give a hint of a smile

esbozo M sketch, outline; **— de una sonrisa** hint of a smile

escabechar VT to pickle

escabroso ADJ (agreste) rugged; (espinoso) thorny; (sórdido) lurid, sordid

escabullirse[16] VI (ladrones) to slip away, to steal away; (lagartijas) to scurry away/off; **— de** to wriggle out of

escafandra F (para el agua) scuba gear; (para el espacio) spacesuit

escala F (escalera, escalafón) ladder; (serie de grados, notas, serie ascendente) scale; (parada) stopover; **— de sueldos** salary range, wage scale; **hacer — en** to stop over at; **— salarial** wage scale, pay scale; **a — nacional** nationwide; **a/de gran —** large-scale; **sin —s** nonstop

escalada F (de una montaña) climb; (de violencia) escalation

escalador -ora MF climber

escalar VT (subir) to scale, to climb; (cambiar de tamaño) scale

escaldadura F scald

escaldar VT (la piel) to scald; (las verduras) to blanch; **—se** to get scalded

escalera F (en un edificio) stairs, staircase; (portátil) ladder; (de naipes) straight; **— mecánica** escalator; **— de caracol** spiral/winding staircase; **— de color** straight flush; **— de incendios** fire escape; **— real** royal flush

escalfar VT to poach

escalinata F grand staircase

escalofriante ADJ chilling, hair-raising

escalofrío M chill; **—s** the shivers

escalón M (peldaño) step, stair; (de escalera de mano, de escalafón) rung; (terraza) rung; (formación militar) echelon

escalonar VT (distribuir) to stagger; (aterrazar) to terrace

escalope M scallop

escama F (de animal) scale; (de piel, corteza) flake

escamar VT to scale

escamoso ADJ (animal) scaly; (piel) flaky

escamotear VT (esconder) to palm; (robar) to snatch; (eludir) to shirk

escampar VI to clear up

escandalizar[47] VT (chocar) to scandalize; (causar escándalo) to cause a scandal; **—se** to be shocked

escándalo M (suceso vergonzoso) scandal; (riña) uproar

escandaloso ADJ (chocante) scandalous, shocking; (ruidoso) raucous

escandir VT *lit* to scan

escaneado M scanning

escanear VT to scan

escáner M scanner; **— color** color scanner

escaño M seat in parliament

escapada F (escape) escape

escapar VI (de un lugar, una situación) to escape; (de alguien, de una responsabilidad) to run away; **—se** (persona) to escape; (gas) to leak; **se me escapó una sonrisa** I inadvertently smiled; **Matilde se me está escapando de las manos** Matilde is getting out of hand

escaparate M shop window

escapatoria F (de un lugar) escape, way out; (legal) loophole

escape M (fantasía, escapatoria) escape; (de coche) exhaust; (de gas, agua) leak

escápula F scapula

escarabajo M beetle

escaramuza F skirmish

escaramuzar[47] VI to skirmish

escarbar VI/VT to dig, to scratch; **— en los archivos** to dig around in the files; **—se los dientes** to pick one's teeth

escarcha F frost

escarchar VI to frost

escardar VT to weed

escarlata ADJ INV & M (color) scarlet; F (enfermedad) scarlet fever

escarlatina F scarlet fever

escarmentar[1] VI to learn one's lesson; VT to teach a lesson

escarmiento M lesson; **que te sirva de —** let that be a lesson to you

escarnecer[35] VT to deride

escarnio M derision

escarpa F steep slope

escarpado ADJ steep, precipitous; M steep slope

escasear VI to be scarce

escasez F (falta) shortage; (carestía) scarcity, want

escaso ADJ sparse, scarce; **una docena escasa** a scant dozen; **— de** short on; **— de personal** short-handed

escatimar VT to skimp on; **no — gastos** to spare no expense

escena F (fragmento de una obra de teatro, episodio) scene; (escenario) stage; **montar una —** to make a scene; **en —** on stage; **poner en —** to stage; **entrar en —** to go on stage

escenario M stage

escénico ADJ **pánico —** stage fright

escenificación F staging

escepticismo M skepticism

escéptico -ca ADJ skeptical; MF skeptic

escisión F split

esclarecer[35] VT to elucidate

esclavitud F slavery

esclavizar[47] VT to enslave

esclavo -va MF slave

esclerosis F sclerosis; **— múltiple** multiple sclerosis

esclusa F (de un canal) lock; (de una presa) floodgate, sluice gate

escoba F broom

escobilla F whisk broom

escocer[34] VI to sting

escocés -esa ADJ Scottish; **[cuadros] escoceses** plaid; MF Scot; M (whisky) Scotch; (lengua) Scots

Escocia F Scotland

escoger[45] VT to choose

escolar MF pupil; ADJ **año —** school year

escoliosis F scoliosis

escollo M (arrecife) reef; (obstáculo) obstacle

escolta F (policial) escort; MF (persona) escort; (baloncesto) shooting guard

escoltar VT to escort

escombros M PL rubble, debris

esconder VT to hide; VI **—se** to hide

escondidas LOC ADV **a —** on the sly; **entrar a — to** sneak in; **meter algo a —** to sneak something in; **jugar a las —** to play hide and seek

escondite M (en un juego) hiding place; (de ladrón) hideout; (de cazador) blind; **jugar al — to** play hide and seek

escondrijo M hiding place

escopeta F shotgun

escoplo M chisel

escora F listing

escorar VI to list

escorbuto M scurvy

escoria F (de metales) slag; (de la sociedad) scum, dregs

escorpión M scorpion

escotado ADJ low-cut

escote M (parte del vestido) neckline; (parte del cuerpo) cleavage; **pagar a —** to go Dutch

escotilla F hatch

escozor M smarting sensation; **— vaginal** vaginal itching

escribiente MF clerk

escribir[74] VI/VT to write; **¿cómo se escribe?** how do you spell it? **— a máquina** to type

escrito ADJ written; **— a máquina** typewritten; **no —** unwritten; **por —** in writing; M document

escrito *ver* escribir

escritor -ora MF writer, author

escritorio M (mueble) desk; (oficina) office

escritura F (acción de escribir) writing; (certificado de propiedad) deed; **— de traspaso** conveyance; **— de venta** bill of sale

escrúpulo M scruple, qualm; **sin —s** unscrupulous

escrupuloso ADJ scrupulous

escrutar VT (a una persona) to scrutinize; (el horizonte) to scan; (votos) to count

escrutinio M (examen) scrutiny; (recuento) vote count

escuadra F (de buques, soldados) squadron; (instrumento) square

escuadrilla F (de aviones) flight of aircraft; (de buques) squadron

escuadrón M squadron; **— de la muerte** death squad

escualidez F (delgadez) skinniness; (suciedad) squalor

escuálido ADJ (sucio) squalid; (delgado) thin

escuchar VT to listen to; (oír) to hear; VI to listen; **— a hurtadillas** to eavesdrop

escudar VT to shield

escudo M (arma defensiva) shield; (moneda de Portugal) escudo; **— de armas** coat of arms

escudriñar VT (a una persona) to scrutinize, to peer at; (el horizonte) to scan

escuela F school; **— industrial** trade school; **— normal** school of education; **— pública** public school; **— primaria** elementary school; **— secundaria** secondary school; **tener —** to have good technique

escueto ADJ (explicación) succinct; (verdad) simple

esculpir VI/VT to sculpture, to sculpt

escultor -ora MF sculptor

escultura F sculpture

escupir VI/VT to spit

escupitajo M spit

escurridizo ADJ (acera) slippery; (ladrón) elusive, slippery

escurrir VI/VT (platos, verduras) to drain; (ropa) to wring out; **—se** to slink away

ese ADJ DEM that, those; **esa chica se llama Matilde** that girl is called Matilde; **esas ciudades son antiguas** those cities are old; PRON that one, those; **ese es el mayor** that one is the oldest; **esos son mis hijos** those are my children

esencia F essence

esencial ADJ essential; **lo —** the gist, the bottom line, the name of the game

esfera F (cuerpo sólido) sphere; (espacio, ámbito) realm, sphere; (de reloj) face, dial; **— de influencia** sphere of influence

esférico ADJ spherical; M soccer ball

esfínter M sphincter

esforzado ADJ valiant

esforzarse[49] VI to try hard, to exert oneself; **—**

esfuerzo M effort

esfumar VT to tone down; **—se** to vanish, to fizzle out

esgrima F fencing; **practicar —** to fence

esgrimir VT (armas) to brandish, to wield; (argumentos) to employ

eslabón M chain link; **— perdido** missing link

eslabonar VT to link

eslavo-va ADJ Slavic; MF Slav

eslogan M slogan

eslovaco ADJ & MF Slovakian; M (lengua) Slovakian

Eslovaquia F Slovakia

Eslovenia F Slovenia

esloveno-na ADJ & MF Slovene; M (lengua) Slovene

esmaltar VT to enamel

esmalte M enamel; **— de uñas** nail polish

esmeradamente ADV carefully

esmerado ADJ careful, painstaking

esmeralda F emerald

esmerarse VI to take pains

esmerilado ADJ frosted; M frosting

esmerilar VT to frost

esmero M care

esmirriado ADJ scrawny

esmoquin M tuxedo

esnifar VT to snort

esnob M snob

esnórquel M snorkel

eso PRON DEM that; **— es verdad** that's true; **— sí** granted; **a — de las tres** at about three o'clock; **de —, nada** no way! yeah, right! **en — llega y me dice** at that moment he arrives and says to me; **y — que le dije que viniese temprano** even when I told him to come early

esófago M esophagus

esotérico ADJ esoteric

espaciado M pitch, spacing; **— de palabras** word spacing

espacial ADJ spatial; **nave —** spaceship

espaciar VT to space; **—se** to space out

espacio M (capacidad) space, room; (superficie) expanse; (separación entre líneas) space, spacing; (en un formulario) blank space; (porción de tiempo) span; **— aéreo** aerospace; **— entre caracteres** letterspacing; **— exterior** outer space; **— noticioso** newscast; **a doble —** double-spaced; **a un —** single-spaced; **por — de una semana** for a week

espacioso ADJ spacious, roomy

espada F sword; **—s** (palo de naipes) swords; **— de doble filo** double-edged sword; **estar entre la — y la pared** to be between a rock and a hard place

espalda F back; **a —s de alguien** behind

someone's back; **caerse de —s** to fall on one's back; **nadar [de] —** to do the backstroke; **tener las —s anchas** to take a lot of abuse; **volver las —s** to turn one's back

espaldar M chair back

espantadizo ADJ easily scared

espantado ADJ frightened

espantajo M scarecrow

espantar VT to frighten, to scare; (ahuyentar) to frighten away, to scare away; **—se** to get scared; M SG **espantapájaros** scarecrow

espanto M fright, dread; **estás hecho un —** you look a sight; **estoy curado de —** nothing surprises me anymore

espantoso ADJ frightful, dreadful

España F Spain

español-ola ADJ Spanish; MF Spaniard; M (lengua) Spanish

esparadrapo M surgical tape

esparcimiento M (recreo) relaxation; (reparto) spreading

esparcir[33] VT to scatter, to spread; **—se** to amuse oneself

espárrago M asparagus

espasmo M spasm, jerk

espasmódico ADJ spasmodic, jerky

espástico ADJ spastic

espátula F spatula

especia F spice

especial ADJ & M special; **en —** in particular, especially

especialidad F specialty, specialization

especialista MF specialist

especialización F specialization

especializar[47] VT to specialize; **—se en** to specialize in, to major in

especialmente ADV (de forma particular) specially; **esto lo hice — para ti** I made this specially for you; (en especial) especially; **este tipo es — bueno** this kind is especially good

especie F (clase) kind; (categoría biológica) species; **—s en peligro de extinción** endangered species; **pagar en —** to pay in kind; **una — de** a kind of

especiero M spice rack

especificar[30] VT to specify

específico ADJ & M specific

espécimen M specimen

espectacular ADJ spectacular

espectáculo M (escándalo) spectacle; (actuación pública) show; (vista) sight; **dar el —** to make a spectacle of oneself

espectador-ora MF (de un espectáculo) spectator; (de un suceso) onlooker

espectro M (fantasma) specter; (de la luz, de un antibiótico) spectrum

especulación F speculation

especulador-ora MF speculator

especular VT to speculate; ADJ mirror; **imagen — mirror** image

especulativo ADJ speculative

espejismo M (en el desierto) mirage; (ilusión) illusion

espejo M mirror; **— de cuerpo entero** full-length mirror; **— retrovisor** rearview mirror

espeluznante ADJ hair-raising

espeluznar VT to terrify; **—se** to be terrified

espera F (acción de esperar) wait; (aplazamiento) extension; **estar en — de** to be waiting for

esperanza F hope; **— de vida** life expectancy; **con una — de voto del 12,5%** expected to get 12.5% of the vote

esperanzado ADJ hopeful

esperanzador ADJ hopeful

esperanzar[47] VT to give hope to

esperar VT (tener esperanza) to hope; (estar embarazada, anticipar) to expect; (aguardar) to wait for; VI to wait; **como era de —** not surprisingly; **era de —** it was to be expected; **espera sentado** don't hold your breath; **estoy esperando un milagro** I'm hoping for a miracle; **todavía espera confirmación** it still awaits confirmation

esperma MF sperm

espermicida M spermicide

esperpento M fright, grotesque person or thing

espesar VT to thicken

espeso ADJ (pelo, sopa, niebla) thick; (cejas) bushy

espesor M thickness

espesura F (espesor) thickness; (lugar poblado de matorrales) thicket

espetar VT (decir bruscamente) to blurt out; (pinchar) to skewer

espeto, espetón M spit

espía MF spy

espiar[28] VT to spy; VT to spy on

espichar VI *fam* to croak, to bite the dust

espiga F spike

espigar[40] VT to glean; VI to grow spikes; **—se** to grow tall

espina F (de planta) thorn; (de pez) fish bone; **— dorsal** spinal column; **me quedé con la —** I was left wondering

espinaca F spinach

espinal ADJ spinal

espinazo M spine, backbone

espinilla F (en la pierna) shin; (de animal) shank; (acné, comedón) blackhead

espino M thorny shrub

espinoso ADJ thorny

espionaje M espionage

espiración F expiration

espiral ADJ & F spiral

espirar VI/VT to exhale, to breathe out, to expire

espíritu M (ánima, fantasma, intención de una

ley) spirit; (alma) soul; **— fuerte** free spirit; **— deportivo** sportsmanship; **— emprendedor** can-do attitude, entrepreneurship; **— Santo** Holy Spirit

espiritual ADJ & M spiritual

espiritualidad F spirituality

espita F spigot

espléndido ADJ (estupendo) splendid; (dispendioso) lavish

esplendor M splendor

esplendoroso ADJ magnificent

espliego M lavender

espolear VT to spur

espoleta F bomb fuse

espolón M (de gallo, planta, estímulo) spur; (de buque) ram

espolvorear VT to dust, to sprinkle

esponja F (animal, utensilio) sponge; (borracho) souse

esponjado ADJ spongy

esponjar VT to make spongy; **—se** to become spongy

esponjoso ADJ spongy

esponsales M PL betrothal

espontaneidad F spontaneity

espontáneo ADJ spontaneous

espora F spore

esposar VT to handcuff

esposo -sa M husband; F wife; **esposas** handcuffs

espuela F spur

espulgar[40] VT to delouse

espuma F (de cerveza) froth; (de jabón) suds, lather; (de la boca) foam; (de colchón) foam rubber; (de mar) foam, spray; **echar — por la boca** to foam at the mouth; **hacer —** to make suds

espumar VT (quitar la espuma) to skim; (formar espuma) to foam

espumarajo M foam; **echar —s por la boca** to foam at the mouth

espumillón M tinsel

espumoso ADJ foamy

esputo M sputum

esquela F note; **— mortuoria** death notice

esquelético ADJ skeletal

esqueleto M (huesos) skeleton; (armazón) framework; **mover el —** (bailar) to dance; (moverse) to move

esquema M outline; **romperle los —s a alguien** (planes) to ruin one's plans; (conceptos) to shatter one's preconceptions

esquí M (tabla) ski; (deporte) skiing; **— acuático** (tabla) water ski; (deporte) waterskiing; **hacer — acuático** to water-ski

esquiar[28] VI to ski

esquila F (cencerro) cowbell; (acción de esquilar) shearing

esquilador -ora MF sheep shearer

esquilar VT to shear, to clip

esquileo M shearing

esquimal ADJ & MF Eskimo; M (lengua) Eskimo

esquina F corner; **en cada —** everywhere

esquinero ADJ **mesa esquinera** corner table; M cornerback

esquirol M strikebreaker

esquivar VT (a una persona) to avoid; (un golpe) to dodge

esquivo ADV (tímido) shy, coy; (huraño) aloof; (reservado) elusive; (indirecto) evasive

esquizofrenia F schizophrenia

estabilidad F stability

estabilización F stabilization

estabilizar[47] VT to stabilize

estable ADJ (mesa) stable; (precio) firm; (huésped) long-term

establecer[35] VT to establish; (averiguar) to ascertain; **— una cita** to set up an appointment; **—se** to settle

establecimiento M establishment

establezca, establezco ver establecer

establishment M establishment

establo M stable

estaca F (con punta) stake; (gruesa) club

estacada F stockade; **dejar en la —** to leave in the lurch

estacar[30] VT (atar) to stake; (delimitar) to stake off

estación F (de tren, autobús, radio) station; (del año) season; **— bípeda** bipedal stance; **— de bomberos** fire station; **— de esquí** ski resort; **— de servicio** gas/filling station; **— de trabajo** workstation; **— espacial** space station

estacional ADJ seasonal

estacionamiento M (acción) parking; (lugar) parking lot

estacionar VT (tropas) to station; (un vehículo) to park; **—se** (un coche) to park; (precios) to level off

estacionario ADJ stationary

estadía F stay

estadio M (recinto deportivo) stadium; (fase) stage

estadista M statesman; F stateswoman

estadística F (ciencia) statistics; **—s** (datos numéricos) statistics

estado M (situación, unidad política) state; **— civil** marital status; **— de cuenta** bank statement; **— de alarma** state of emergency; **— de ánimo** state of mind; **— de excepción** martial law; **— de guerra** state of war; **— de sitio** state of siege; **— mayor** chiefs of staff; **— policíaco** police state; **de — sólido** solid state; **en — interesante** expecting; **en — vegetativo** in a vegetative state, brain-dead

Estados Unidos M PL/SG United States

estadounidense ADJ & MF American

estafa F swindle, scam, racket

estafador -ora MF swindler, racketeer

estafar VT to swindle

estalactita F stalactite

estalagmita F stalagmite

estallar VI (una bomba) to explode; (un globo) to burst; (una guerra) to break out; (una persona) to snap; **— de risa** to burst out laughing; **— en una carcajada** to burst out laughing; **hacer —** to set off

estallido M (explosión) explosion; (ruido) bang, report

estampa F (de revista) illustration; (imagen) image; (apariencia) appearance; **de buena —** good-looking; **la viva — de la madre** the spitting image of her mother; **la viva — de la desolación** the very picture of desolation

estampado ADJ printed; M (tela) print; (acción) printing

estampar VT (en tela, papel) to print; (con un molde, en metal) to stamp; **— le un beso a alguien** to plant a kiss on someone

estampida F stampede

estampido M bang

estampilla F stamp

estampillar VT to stamp

estancado ADJ stagnant

estancamiento M stagnation (también económico)

estancar[30] VT to stem; to dam; to block; **—se** to stagnate

estancia F (estadía) stay; (habitación) hall; (hacienda) RP cattle ranch

estanco ADJ waterproof; M government store

estándar ADJ & M standard

estandarización F standardization

estandarizar[47] VT to standardize

estandarte M standard, banner

estanque M pond

estante M (tabla) shelf; (mueble) bookcase

estantería F (mueble) bookcase; (de biblioteca) stack

estañar VT to tin-plate

estaño M tin

estar[63] VI to be; **— a tres kilómetros de aquí** to be three kilometers from here; **— bien** to be all right; **— mal/enfermo del corazón** to have heart trouble; **— de más** to be unnecessary; **— para** to be about to; **— por** (a favor de) to be in favor of; (a punto de) to be about to; **— trabajando duro** to be working hard; **¿a cuántos estamos?** what day of the month is it? **ahí está** that's it; **¿está Alice?** is Alice there? **están muy buenos tus zapatos nuevos** your new shoes are nice; **estate tranquilo** don't worry; **no —** to be out; **cuarto de —** living room

estatal ADJ **compañía —** state-run company

estático ADJ static

estatua F statue

estatura F (importancia) stature; (altura física) height

estatutario ADJ statutory

estatuto M (ley) statute; (de una sociedad) bylaw; — **de quiebras** bankruptcy law

este ADJ DEM this, these; **esta chica se llama Hilary** this girl is called Hilary; **estas ciudades son antiguas** these cities are old; PRON DEM this one, these; — **es el mayor** this one is the oldest; **estos son mis hijos** these are my children; M & ADJ east; **hacia el** — eastward

estela F (de una embarcación) wake; (de humo, polvo) trail; **dejar una** — to leave a trail

estelar ADJ stellar

estenotipista MF court reporter

estentóreo ADJ booming

estepa F steppe

estera F mat

estercolar VT to fertilize with manure

estercolero M dunghill

estéreo ADJ & M stereo; **en** — in stereo

estereotipo M stereotype

estéril ADJ (gasa, esfuerzo) sterile; (mujer) barren

esterilidad F sterility

esterilizar[47] VT to sterilize

esternón M sternum, breastbone

esteroide M steroid; — **anabólico** anabolic steroid

estertor M death rattle

estética F aesthetics

estético ADJ aesthetic

estetoscopio M stethoscope

estibador M stevedore, longshoreman

estibar VT to stow

estiércol M manure

estigma M stigma

estigmatizar[47] VT to stigmatize

estilarse VI to be in style; **eso no se estila aquí** that's not done here

estilística F stylistics

estilístico ADJ stylistic

estilo M (literario, estético, caligráfico) style; (de natación) stroke; — **de vida** lifestyle; — **espalda** backstroke; — **indirecto** reported speech; — **libre** freestyle; — **mariposa** butterfly stroke; — **pecho** breaststroke; — **perrito** dog paddle; **cosas por el** — things like that

estima F esteem, regard

estimación F (cálculo) estimate; (estima) estimation

estimado ADJ esteemed; — **Sr.** Dear Sir

estimar VT (apreciar) to esteem; (determinar el valor) to estimate; (opinar) to think

estimulación F stimulation

estimulante ADJ stimulating; M stimulant

estimular VT (despertar, excitar) to stimulate; (alentar) to encourage

estímulo M stimulus

estío M lit summer

estipendio M stipend

estipulación F stipulation

estipular VT to stipulate

estirado ADJ stuck-up

estirar VT (alargar) to stretch; — **el cuello** to crane one's neck; — **la pata** fam to kick the bucket; (crecer) to grow; —**se** to stretch

estirón M growth spurt; **pegar un** — to have a growth spurt

estirpe F lineage

estival ADJ **vacaciones** —**es** summer vacation

esto PRON DEM this; — **es** that is to say; **a todo** — meanwhile; **en** — at this point

estocada F thrust; **lanzar una** — to thrust

estofa F type; **de baja** — low-class

estofado M stew

estofar VT to stew

estoico -ca ADJ & MF stoic

estolón M runner

estómago M stomach

Estonia F Estonia

estonio -nia ADJ & MF Estonian; M (lengua) Estonian

estopa F tow

estorbar VT (obstaculizar) to hinder, to impede; (molestar) to be a nuisance

estorbo M (obstáculo) hindrance, impediment; (molestia) nuisance

estornino M starling

estornudar VI to sneeze

estornudo M sneeze

estoy ver estar

estrado M bench

estrafalario ADJ bizarre, outlandish

estragar[40] VT (físicamente) to devastate; (moralmente) to corrupt

estrago M havoc; **hacer** —**s** to wreak havoc

estrangular VT to strangle

estratagema F stratagem

estrategia F strategy; (de negocios, deportes) game plan; — **de salida** exit strategy

estratégico ADJ strategic

estrato M stratum, layer; — **social** social class

estratosfera F stratosphere

estrechamente ADV closely

estrechamiento M constriction

estrechar VT (angostar) to narrow; (abrazar) to embrace; **la estrechó en sus brazos** he held her in his arms; —**se** to get narrower; —**se la mano** to shake hands

estrechez F (cualidad de estrecho) narrowness; (acción de estrechar) narrowing; (aprietos) dire straits

estrecho ADJ narrow; **la falda le quedaba estrecha** the skirt was too tight for her; M strait

estrella F star; — **binaria** binary star; — **de cine** movie star; — **de mar** starfish; — **fugaz** shooting star, falling star; **ver las —s** to see stars

estrellado ADJ (como una estrella) starlike; (cubierto de estrellas) starry

estrellar VT (aplastar) to smash; (romper) to crack; —**se** (avión) to crash; (intento) to fail; —**se contra** to smash into

estremecer[35] VT to make shudder; **el terremoto estremeció París** the earthquake rocked Paris; —**se** to shudder

estremecimiento M shudder

estrenar VT (un vestido) to wear for the first time; (una película, obra de teatro) to debut; (una bicicleta) to try out for the first time; (un título) to use for the first time; —**se** to debut

estreno M (de una película) premiere; (de un objeto) first use; (de una actividad) debut

estreñido ADJ (constipado) constipated; (antipático) uptight

estreñimiento M constipation

estreñir[11] VT to constipate; —**se** to become constipated

estrépito M racket, clatter; **causar** — to clatter

estrepitoso ADJ noisy

estrés M stress

estresante ADJ stressful, high-pressure

estresar VT to stress [out]

estría F (en la piel) stretch mark; (en una columna) flute; (en mármol) striation

estriado ADJ (piel) covered with stretch marks; (columna) fluted; (piedra) streaked

estriar[28] VT to flute; —**se** to get stretch marks

estribación F spur

estribar VI — **en** (apoyarse en) to lean on; (radicar en) to lie in

estribillo M refrain

estribo M (de silla, oído) stirrup; (de coche) running board; **perder los —s** to fly off the handle

estribor M starboard

estricnina F strychnine

estricto ADJ strict

estridente ADJ strident

estrofa F verse, stanza

estrógeno M estrogen

estropajo M scrubber; **tengo la boca que es un** — my mouth is as dry as a bone

estropajoso ADJ sinewy

estropear VT to ruin

estructura F structure

estructuración F structuring

estructural ADJ structural

estructurar VT to structure

estruendo M din, racket

estruendoso ADJ thunderous

estrujamiento M (para romper) crushing; (para sacar jugo) squeezing

estrujar VT (aplastar) to crush; (apretar) to squeeze

estrujón M squeeze

estuario M estuary

estucar[30] VT to stucco

estuche M (para joyas) jewelry box; (para pastillas) pill box; (para lentes) glasses case

estuco M stucco

estudiantado M student body

estudiante MF student

estudiantil ADJ **vida** — student life

estudiar VI/VT to study

estudio M (acción de estudiar, investigación, habitación) study; (taller de artista) studio; (apartamento pequeño) studio apartment; **en** — under study; — **del impacto ambiental** environmental impact study

estudioso -sa ADJ studious; MF scholar

estufa F (para calentar) heater, stove; (para cocinar) stove

estupefaciente ADJ & M narcotic

estupefacto ADJ stunned, speechless

estupendo ADJ stupendous, terrific; **me la pasé — en la casa de Hilary** I had a great time at Hilary's house

estupidez F stupidity; **estupideces** nonsense

estúpido ADJ stupid

estupor M stupor

estupro M statutory rape

estuve, estuviera, estuviese *ver* estar

etanol M ethanol

etapa F stage; **por —s** by stages

etcétera CONJ et cetera, and so forth

éter M ether

eternidad F eternity

eternizarse[47] VI to drag on

eterno ADJ eternal, everlasting

ética F ethics

ético ADJ ethical

etimología F etymology

etíope ADJ & MF Ethiopian

Etiopía F Ethiopía

etiqueta F (de comportamiento) etiquette; (en una lata, botella) label; (en una prenda) tag; — **adhesiva** sticker; — **de identificación** name tag; — **de precio** price tag; **nos trataron con** — they treated us very formally; **vestirse de** — to dress formally

etiquetar VT (latas, botellas, personas) to label; (prendas) to tag

etnicidad F ethnicity

étnico ADJ ethnic

etnografía F ethnography

etnología F ethnology

eucalipto M eucalyptus

eufemismo M euphemism

euforia F euphoria

eunuco M eunuch

euro M euro

Europa F Europe

europeo -a ADJ & MF European

euskera M Basque [language]

eutanasia F euthanasia

evacuación F (de un lugar) evacuation; (del vientre) bowel movement; (de agua) drainage

evacuar VT (un lugar, a una persona) to evacuate; (el vientre) to void; (agua) to drain; VI to defecate

evadir VT to evade; **—se** to escape

evaluación F evaluation; **— del rendimiento** performance review

evaluar[26] VT (analizar) to evaluate, to assess; (tasar) to estimate; (calificar) to test

evangélico ADJ evangelical

evangelio M gospel

evaporación F evaporation

evaporar VT to evaporate; **—se** to vanish

evasión F (fiscal) evasion; (de prisioneros, de la realidad) escape; **— de capitales** capital flight; **— de impuestos** tax evasion

evasiva F **salirse con —s** to beat around the bush

evasivo ADJ evasive

evasor -ora MF evader

evento M event

eventual ADJ (posible) possible; (temporal) temporary

evidencia F evidence; **dejar/poner en — a alguien** to show someone up; **quedar/ ponerse en —** to become apparent

evidenciar VT to make evident; **—se** to become evident

evidente ADJ evident, obvious

evidentemente ADV & INTERJ obviously

evitar VT (eludir) to avoid; (ahorrar) to spare

evocación F evocation

evocar[30] VT (una memoria) to evoke; (a los espíritus) to conjure up

evolución F evolution

evolucionar VI to evolve

evolutivo ADJ evolutionary

ex MF *fam* ex

exacerbar VT (intensificar) to exacerbate; (irritar) to aggravate

exactamente ADV & INTERJ exactly, precisely; **llegaron — a las tres** they arrived exactly at three

exactitud F accuracy, precision

exacto ADJ exact, precise, accurate; INTERJ exactly

exageración F exaggeration

exagerado -a ADJ exaggerated; **Jorge es un —** Jorge always exaggerates

exagerar VI/VT to exaggerate

exaltación F (elogio) praise; (excitación) excitement

exaltar VT to exalt; **—se** to get excited

examen M (inspección) examination; (prueba) examination, test, exam; **— de ingreso** entrance examination; **— dérmico de alergias** scratch test; **— final** final examination; **— físico** physical examination; **— médico** medical exam, checkup; **dar un —** to take a test; **poner un —** to give a test

examinar VT (inspeccionar) to examine; (someter a un examen) to test

exasperar VT to exasperate, to aggravate

excavación F (geológica) excavation; (arqueológica) dig

excavador -ora MF (persona) excavator; F (aparato) excavator, earthmover

excavar VT to excavate, to dig

excedente ADJ & M surplus

exceder VT (sobrepasar) to exceed; (superar) to surpass; **— de** to go beyond

excelencia F excellence; **por —** par excellence

excelente ADJ excellent, great

excentricidad F eccentricity

excéntrico ADJ eccentric

excepción F exception; **a — de** with the exception of

excepcional ADJ exceptional

excepto ADV & PREP except

exceptuar[26] VT to except

excesivo ADJ excessive

exceso M excess; **— de costos** overrun; **— de equipaje** excess baggage; **beber en —** to drink to excess; **comer en —** to overeat

excitación F (de músculos) excitement; (sexual) arousal

excitante ADJ stimulating

excitar VT (un nervio) to excite; (impulso sexual) to arouse; **—se** (sexualmente) to get aroused; (átomos) to be excited

exclamación F exclamation

exclamar VT to exclaim

excluir[19] VT to exclude

exclusión F exclusion

exclusivo ADJ exclusive

excomulgar[40] VT to excommunicate

excrecencia F excrescence

excreción F excretion

excremento M excrement

excretar VT to excrete

excursión F excursion, outing

excusa F excuse

excusable ADJ excusable

excusado M *Méx* toilet

excusar VT to excuse

exención F exemption

exento ADJ exempt; **— de impuestos** tax-exempt

exequias F PL funeral rites

exfoliación F exfoliation

exhalar VI/VT (aire) to exhale, to breathe out; (un olor) to give off; **— un suspiro** to sigh

exhaustivo ADJ exhaustive, thorough
exhausto ADJ exhausted
exhibición F (manifestación) exhibition; (despliegue) display
exhibicionismo M exhibitionism
exhibir VT (fotos) to exhibit; (mercancías) to display; (el carnet de identidad) to show; **—se** to show off; **le gusta exhibirse en traje de baño** she likes to show off in her bathing suit; **esa película ya no se exhibe** that movie is not showing anymore
exhortar VT to exhort, to urge
exhumación F exhumation
exigencia F demand
exigente ADJ demanding, exacting
exigir[46] VT to demand; **exigen a alguien que sepa inglés** they require someone who knows English
exiguo ADJ meager; **exigua mayoría** scant majority
exiliado -da MF exile
exiliar VT to exile
exilio M exile
eximido ADJ exempt; **— por la cláusula del abuelo** grandfathered
eximio ADJ illustrious
eximir VT (de impuestos) to exempt; (de sospecha) to clear; (de una responsabilidad) to excuse
existencia F existence; **complicarle la — a alguien** to cause someone trouble; **la lucha por la —** the fight for survival; **—s** stock on hand; **en —** in stock, on hand
existencial ADJ existential
existente ADJ extant, existing
existir VI to exist
éxito M success; (musical) hit; **— de taquilla** blockbuster; **tener —** to be successful; **tiene — con las mujeres** he's popular with women
exitoso ADJ successful
éxodo M exodus
exonerar VT to exonerate
exorbitante ADJ exorbitant
exorcisar VT to exorcise
exorcismo M exorcism
exótico ADJ exotic
expandir VT (dilatar) to expand, to spread; (propagar) to disseminate; **—se** to expand, to spread
expansión F (crecimiento) expansion; (diversión) relaxation
expansivo ADJ (que crece) expansive; (efusivo) effusive
expatriado -da MF expatriate
expatriar VT to expatriate, to exile
expectación F anticipation
expectativa F (esperanza) expectation; (posibilidad) prospect; **estar a la — de algo**

to be on pins and needles; **— de vida** life expectancy
expectorante M expectorant
expectorar VI/VT to expectorate, to cough up
expedición F (viaje) expedition; (de documentos) issuing; (de mercancías) delivery
expedicionario -ria ADJ expeditionary; MF member of an expedition
expedidor -ora ADJ shipping; MF shipper
expediente M (administrativo) file, dossier; (policial, académico, médico) record
expedir[9] VT (enviar) to dispatch; (emitir) to issue
expeler VT to expel
expendedor -ora MF vendor; **— automático** vending machine
experiencia F experience
experimentación F experimentation
experimentado ADJ experienced
experimental ADJ experimental
experimentar VI (hacer experimentos) to experiment; VT (sufrir, tener experiencia) to experience
experimento M experiment
experto -ta ADJ & MF expert; **— en computación** wizard, *fam* techie
expiación F atonement
expiar[28] VT to atone for
expirar VI to expire
explanada F (terreno junto al mar) esplanade; (terreno nivelado) leveled area
explayarse VI to become extended; **— sobre** to enlarge upon
explicable ADJ explainable, explicable
explicación F explanation
explicar[30] VT to explain; **—se** to make oneself clear; **no me explico por qué** I can't figure out why
explicativo ADJ explanatory
explícito ADJ explicit
exploración F exploration
explorador -ora ADJ exploring; MF (expedicionario) explorer; (militar) scout
explorar VI/VT to explore; (con fines diagnósticos) to scan; (con fines militares) to scout
exploratorio ADJ exploratory
explosión F explosion; **hacer —** to explode
explosivo ADJ & M explosive
explotación F exploitation
explotar VT (sacar provecho) to exploit; (hacer explosión) to explode
expondrá, expondría *ver* exponer
exponente M exponent
exponer[56, 74] VT (al sol, al peligro) to expose; (al público) to exhibit, to display; (explicar) to state, to set forth; **—se al peligro** to expose oneself to danger

exponga, expongo ver **exponer**

exportación F (acción) exportation, export; (cosa) export

exportador -ora ADJ exporting; MF exporter

exportar VI/VT to export

exposición F (feria) exposition; (de arte) exhibition; (explicación) explanation; (al sol, a una influencia, al peligro) exposure

expresar VT to express

expresión F expression; **valga la —** so to speak

expresividad F expressiveness

expresivo ADJ expressive

expreso ADJ (explícito) express; (rápido) fast; M express train; **café —** espresso

exprimidor M juicer

exprimir VT (naranjas) to squeeze; (zumo) to squeeze out

expropiar VT to expropriate

expuesto ADJ exposed; **lo —** what has been said

expuesto ver **exponer**

expulsar VT to expel; (de un bar) to throw out; (de un partido) to eject

expulsión F expulsion

expuse, expusiera, expusiese ver **exponer**

exquisito -ta ADJ (arte) exquisite; (comida) delicious

extasiado ADJ rapt

extasiarse[28] VI to be enraptured

éxtasis M ecstasy (también droga)

extender[2] VT (el brazo, radio de acción, gratitud) to extend; (un tapete, una masa, un idioma) to spread; (un cheque) to draw up; **—se** to extend; **la fiesta se extendió hasta las 3** the party lasted until 3 o'clock

extendido ADJ (brazos) outstretched; (costumbre) widespread

extensión F (del antebrazo, de significado, telefónica) extension; (de terreno) expanse; (de un texto) length; (eléctrica) extension cord; **por —** by extension; **tener mucha —** to be widespread

extensivo ADJ extensive; **hacer —** to extend

extenso ADJ (calendario, plan, grupo) extensive; (narración, programa de radio) extended

extenuado ADJ exhausted

exterior ADJ (de fuera) exterior, outer; (mundo) outside; (política) foreign; M (parte de afuera) exterior, outside; (aspecto) outward appearance; (fútbol americano) end; **en —es** on location

exteriorizar[47] VT to externalize

exterminación F extermination

exterminar VT to exterminate

exterminio M extermination

externo ADJ external

extienda, extiende ver **extender**

extinción F extinction

extinguidor M fire extinguisher

extinguir[44] VT (un fuego) to extinguish, to put

out; (una especie) to make extinct, to wipe out; **—se** (animal, volcán) to go extinct

extinto ADJ extinct

extintor M fire extinguisher

extirpación F removal

extirpar VT to remove

extorsión F extortion

extorsionar VT to extort money from

extorsionista MF racketeer

extra ADJ extra; **horas —s** overtime; MF (actor) extra; M (cosa accesoria) extra; F (pago extraordinario) bonus

extrabursátil ADJ over-the-counter

extracción F extraction

extracto M (resumen) abstract; (de café) extract

extradición F extradition

extraditar VT to extradite

extraer[59] VT (esencia) to extract; (minerales) to mine; (un diente) to pull

extraiga, extraigo, extraje, extrajera, extrajese ver **extraer**

extrajudicial ADJ out-of-court

extramarital ADJ extramarital

extranjero -ra ADJ foreign; MF foreigner; **en el — abroad**

extrañar VT (sorprender) to surprise; (echar de menos) to miss; **no es de — que** it's no wonder that; **no me extraña** it doesn't surprise me; **—se** to be surprised

extrañeza F surprise

extraño -ña ADJ (persona, costumbre) strange; (partícula) foreign; MF stranger

extraoficial ADJ unofficial

extraordinario ADJ extraordinary

extrapolar VI/VT to extrapolate

extrasensorial ADJ extrasensory

extraterrestre ADJ & M alien, extraterrestrial

extravagancia F (cualidad de extravagante) extravagance; (comportamiento extravagante) outrageous behavior

extravagante ADJ flamboyant, outrageous

extraviar[28] VT (perder) to misplace; (confundir) to lead astray; **—se** to lose one's way, to get lost

extravío M loss

extrayendo ver **extraer**

extremadamente ADV extremely

extremado ADJ extreme

extremar VT to maximize

extremidad F extremity

extremo ADJ (máximo, mínimo, extraordinario) extreme; (más lejano) farthest; **con — cuidado** with utmost care; M (punto más alejado) extreme; (de una región) end; **llegar al — de** to go so far as to; **— Oriente** Far East; **extrema izquierda** far left; **F extrema unción** last rites

extrovertido -da ADJ extroverted; MF extrovert

exuberante ADJ (vegetación, jóvenes)

exuberant; (mujer) voluptuous

exudar VI/VT to exude

exultante ADJ exhilarated, exultant

exultar VI to exult

eyacular VI/VT to ejaculate

eyectar VT to eject

Ff

fábrica F factory, plant; (de acero, textiles) mill

fabricación F manufacture, manufacturing

fabricante MF manufacturer; (de coches) maker

fabricar[30] VT (producir) to manufacture, to make; (construir) to build; (inventar) to concoct, to fabricate

fabril ADJ manufacturing

fábula F (relato) fable; (mentira) falsehood

fabuloso ADJ (imaginario) imaginary; (magnífico) awesome, fabulous

facción F faction; **facciones** facial features

faceta F facet

facha F **estaba hecho una —** he was a sight

fachada F facade

facial ADJ facial

fácil ADJ (sencillo) easy; (promiscuo) easy, loose; **— de entender** self-explanatory; **— de usar** user-friendly

facilidad F ease; (habilidad) facility, knack

facilitar VT (hacer más fácil) to facilitate; (proporcionar) to furnish

facsímil M fax

factible ADJ feasible

fáctico ADJ factual

factor M factor; **—es de riesgo** risk factors

factoría F trading post

factura F bill, invoice; **— detallada** itemized invoice

facturable ADJ billable

facturación F billing

facturar VT (importe) to invoice; (equipaje) to check

facultad F (habilidad) faculty; (autoridad) authority; (división de una universidad) college; **— de odontología** dental school

facundia F gift of gab

faena F (trabajo corporal) chore; (labor) task; (molestia) nuisance

fagot M bassoon

fairway M fairway

faisán M pheasant

faja F (cinta) sash; (prenda interior) girdle; (de tierra) ribbon, strip

fajar VT (ceñir) to gird; (envolver) to wrap up; (golpear) to thrash

fajo M (de dinero) wad; (de papel, paja) sheaf

falacia F fallacy

falaz ADJ fallacious

falda F (prenda de vestir) skirt (también mujeres); (de una montaña) slope

faldón M (de una camisa) tail, shirttail; (de un saco) coattail

falible ADJ fallible

falla F (en un argumento) flaw; (en un motor) miss; (de una máquina) failure; (geológica) fault; **las Fallas** Valencian holiday

fallar VI (no funcionar) to fail; (un motor) to miss; VI/VT (un juez) to find, to rule

fallecer[35] VI to pass away, to decease

fallecimiento M passing, decease

fallo M (de un programa) bug, glitch; (de la memoria) lapse; (de un juez) ruling, finding

falsear VT to falsify

falsedad F (dicho falso) falsehood; (condición de falso) falseness

falsificación F (de dinero) counterfeit; (de un documento) forgery

falsificar[30] VT (documento) to falsify, to fake; (dinero) to counterfeit; (una firma) to forge; (libros de contabilidad) to cook

falso ADJ (dato) false, untrue; (sentimientos) fake, phony; (dinero) counterfeit; (promesa) hollow; (amigo) faithless, two-faced; (excusa) made-up; **falsa alarma** false alarm; **jurar en —** to perjure oneself; **paso en —** a false step; **salida en —** false start

falta F (defecto) fault; (carencia) lack, want; (ausencia) absence, miss; (jugada ilícita) foul; (de ortografía) mistake; **— de aire** shortness of breath, breathlessness; **— de pago** default; **— de respeto** disrespect; **— personal** (baloncesto) personal foul; **— de pie** foot fault; **a — de** for want of, in the absence of; **cometer —** to commit a foul; **hacer —** to be necessary; **me haces —** I miss you; **sin —** without fail

faltar VI (ausentarse) to be absent; (no haber) to be lacking; **— a la palabra** to break a promise; **— a la verdad** to misstate oneself; **—le el respeto a** to disrespect; **— poco para las cinco** to be almost five o'clock; **me falta tiempo** I don't have enough time; **¡no faltaba más!** (con indignación) that's the last straw! (no hay de qué) don't mention it! (no te molestes) I wouldn't hear of it

falto ADJ lacking; **— de esperanza** devoid of hope

fama F (condición de conocido) fame; (reputación) reputation; **de — mundial** world-famous

famélico ADJ ravenous

familia F family; **— nuclear** nuclear family; **en — in** the family; **jefe de —** head of household; **la señora de Juan tuvo —** John's wife had a baby

familiar ADJ (muy conocido) familiar; (de familia) familial; **tamaño —** family-size; **coche —** family car; **vida —** family life; MF relative; **—es** next of kin

familiaridad F familiarity

familiarizar[47] VT to familiarize, to acquaint; **—se** to acquaint oneself, to become familiar with

famoso ADJ famous

fanático -ca ADJ fanatic; MF fanatic, zealot; (de deportes) freak

fanatismo M fanaticism

fanega F bushel

fanfarria F fanfare

fanfarrón -ona MF braggart, show-off; ADJ blustering

fanfarronear VI to bluster

fanfarronería F bluster, swagger

fango M mire

fangoso ADJ miry

fantasear VI to fantasize

fantasía F (imaginación) imagination; (imagen) fantasy; **de —** fake, artificial

fantasioso ADJ (niño) imaginative; (idea) fanciful

fantasma M ghost, phantom

fantasmagórico ADJ ghostly

fantástico ADJ fantastic

farándula F show business

fardo M (paquete) bundle; (de heno, algodón) bale

farfolla F husk

farfulla F jabber

farfullar VI to jabber

faringe F pharynx

faríngeo ADJ pharyngeal

farmacéutico -ca ADJ pharmaceutical; MF pharmacist, druggist

farmacia F pharmacy, drugstore

fármaco M medicine, pharmaceutical

farmacología F pharmacology

faro M (torre) lighthouse; (luz de alerta) beacon; (luz del coche) light; **— delantero** headlight

farol M (portátil) lantern; (del alumbrado público) street lamp, streetlight; (con pie de hierro) lamppost; (jactancia, envite) bluff; **darse —** to show off, to put on airs

farra F spree; **ir de —** to go on a spree

farsa F (engaño) sham, hoax; (obra teatral, imitación ridícula) farce, mockery

farsante MF fraud, fake

fascículo M installment

fascinación F fascination

fascinante ADJ fascinating, riveting

fascinar VI/VT to fascinate

fascismo M fascism

fascista ADJ & MF fascist

fase F phase

fastidiado ADJ irked

fastidiar VT to irk

fastidio M annoyance

fastidioso ADJ annoying, wearisome

fatal ADJ (mortal) fatal; (terrible) terrible; **mujer —** femme fatale; ADV very badly; **me fue — en el examen** I did very poorly on the exam

fatalidad F (desgracia) misfortune; (destino) destiny

fatídico ADJ ill-fated

fatiga F fatigue, exhaustion; **— ocular** eye strain; **—s** hardships

fatigado ADJ tired, weary

fatigar[40] VT to tire out

fatigoso ADJ (cansado) tiring; (aburrido) tiresome

fauces F PL jaws

faul M foul

fauna F fauna

favor M favor; **a —de** in favor of; **por —** please

favorable ADJ favorable

favorecer[35] VT to favor

favorezca, favorezco ver favorecer

favoritismo M favoritism

favorito -ta ADJ favorite; MF favorite; (en una elección) front-runner; (de la maestra) pet

fax M fax

faxear VT to fax

faz F face

FBI M FBI

fe F faith; **— de bautismo** baptismal certificate; **— de erratas** list of errors; **— de nacimiento** birth certificate; **buena —** good faith; **de buena —** in good faith; **dar — de** to vouch for

fealdad F ugliness

febrero M February

febril ADJ (con fiebre) feverish; (actividad) feverish, hectic

fecal ADJ fecal

fecha F date; **— de vencimiento** date due, due date

fechado ADJ dated

fechar VT to date

fechoría F misdeed

fecundación F fertilization

fecundar VT (un huevo) to fertilize; (una hembra) to impregnate

fecundo ADJ fertile

federación F federation

federal ADJ federal

felicidad F happiness; **¡—es!** congratulations

felicitación F congratulation; **¡felicitaciones!** congratulations!

felicitar VT to congratulate

feligrés -esa MF parishioner; **feligreses** congregation

felino ADJ feline; M cat

feliz ADJ happy

felizmente ADV happily
felpa F plush
felpudo M doormat
femenino ADJ (como una mujer, relativo al género gramatical) feminine; (de la mujer) female
feminidad F femininity
feminismo F feminism
feminista MF feminist
fémur M femur
fenómeno M phenomenon
feo ADJ (cara) ugly, homely; (dentadura) bad; (accidente) nasty
féretro M coffin
feria F (mercado) market; (exposición) fair; (espectáculo) carnival; (celebración) holiday
feriante MF trader at fairs, stallholder
fermentación F fermentation
fermentar VT (leche) to ferment; (cerveza) to brew
fermento M ferment
ferocidad F ferocity
feroz ADJ ferocious, fierce
férreo ADJ (puente) iron; (disciplina) harsh
ferretería F (tienda) hardware store; (artículos) hardware
ferrocarril M railroad, railway
ferroviario -ria ADJ railroad; MF railroad employee
ferry M ferryboat
fértil ADJ fertile
fertilidad F fertility
fertilización F fertilization
fertilizante M fertilizer
fertilizar[47] VT to fertilize
ferviente ADJ fervent
fervor M fervor, zeal
fervoroso ADJ zealous
festejar VT to celebrate
festejo M celebration
festín M feast; **darse un —** to treat oneself
festival M festival
festividad F festivity
festivo ADJ festive, celebratory; **día —** holiday
festón M scallop
festonear VT to scallop
fetal ADJ fetal
fetiche M fetish
fétido ADJ foul-smelling
feto M fetus
feudal ADJ feudal
feudo M manor
fiabilidad F reliability
fiable ADJ reliable
fiador -ora MF guarantor, voucher; (prestamista) backer; (de un preso) bondsman
fiambre M (carne) cold cut; (cadáver) *fam* stiff
fianza F (de un préstamo) security, guaranty; (de un preso) bail

fiar[28] VT (garantizar) to vouch for; **—se de** to trust
fiasco M fiasco
fibra F fiber; **— de vidrio** fiberglass; **— óptica** optical fiber
fibrosis F fibrosis; **— cística** cystic fibrosis
fibroso ADJ fibrous
ficción F fiction
ficha F (de teléfono) token; (de dominó) domino; (de damas) checker; (en poker, ruleta) chip; (tarjeta) index card; MF (delincuente) delinquent, criminal
fichar VT to open a file on; VI to punch in
fichero M (de computadora) file; (archivador) filing cabinet; **— de datos** data file
ficticio ADJ (no real) fictitious; (novelesco) fictional
fidedigno ADJ trustworthy
fideicomisario -ria MF trustee
fideicomiso M trusteeship
fidelidad F (de un amante) fidelity, faithfulness; (de una traducción) closeness; (a la bandera) allegiance
fideo M noodle
fiduciario -ria ADJ & MF fiduciary
fiebre F fever; **— aftosa** foot-and-mouth disease; **— amarilla** yellow fever; **— de candilejas** stage fright; **— del oro** gold rush; **— reumática** rheumatic fever; **— tifoidea** typhoid fever; **tener —** to run a fever
fiel ADJ (leal) faithful; (exacto) true, accurate; M pointer on a scale; **los —es** the congregation
fieltro M (tela) felt; (sombrero) felt hat
fiera F beast; **ponerse hecho una —** to go berserk
fiereza F ferocity
fiero ADJ (salvaje) fierce; (muy grande) huge
fiesta F (festejo) party; (día feriado) holiday; **aguar una —** to ruin a party
fiestero -ra ADJ fond of parties; MF merrymaker, party animal
figura F figure
figurado ADJ figurative
figurar VI (aparecer) to appear, to figure; (lucirse) to show off; **—se** to imagine; **¡figúrate!** imagine!
figurativo ADJ figurative
figurín M fashion plate
figurón M dummy
fijación F fixing; **— de precios** pricing
fijador M hairspray
fijar VT (un cartel) to fix, to fasten; (una fecha) to set; (precios) to peg; **—se en** (notar) to notice; (prestar atención) to pay attention to, to focus on
fijo ADJ (sujeto, incambiado) fixed; (inmóvil) fixed, stationary; (firme) firm; (definitivo) definite; (permanente) permanent

fila F (uno detrás del otro) row, file; (hombro a hombro) rank; (de espera) line; (de documentos) queue; **— india** single file; **cerrar —s** to close ranks; **romper —s** to break ranks

filamento M filament

filantropía F philanthropy

filarmónica F philharmonic

filarmónico ADJ philharmonic

fildear VT to field

fildeo M fielding

filete M (de carne) fillet; (de un plato) rim

filetear VT to fillet

filiación F (membresía) affiliation; (datos personales) personal information; (lazo de parentesco) filiation; **— política** political affiliation

filial ADJ filial; F affiliate, subsidiary

filibusterismo M filibustering

filigrana F filigree

Filipinas F Philippines

filipino -na ADJ & MF Filipino, Filipina

filme M film, movie

filmación F filming, shooting

filmar VT to film, to shoot

filo M (de una navaja) cutting edge; (biológico) phylum; **de doble —** two-edged; **al — de las dos** at around two o'clock

filón M seam, vein, pocket

filoso ADJ sharp

filosofía F philosophy

filosófico ADJ philosophical

filósofo -fa MF philosopher

filtración F (purificación) filtration; (pérdida) leak; (percolación) seepage

filtrar VT (purificar) to filter; (perder) to leak; (clasificar) to screen; **—se** (gotear) to leak through; (percolarse) to seep

filtro M filter; **— de aire** air filter; **— amor** love potion

fin M (conclusión, objetivo) end; **— de año** New Year's Eve; **el — del mundo** (lugar apartado) boondocks; **— de semana** weekend; **— de siglo** turn of the century; **al —** at last; **al — y al cabo** at any rate; **a — de que** so that; **a — de mes** toward the end of the month; **de — de año** year-end; **en —** in conclusion; **poner — a** to put an end to; **por —** at last, finally; **sin —** (ilimitado) myriad; (continuo) endless

finado ADJ late

final ADJ final, last; F (deportiva) final; M (de una historia) ending; (de un terreno) end; (de una carrera) finish; (de una filmación) wrap

finalidad F objective, purpose

finalista MF finalist

finalización F completion

finalizar[47] VT to finish; **— una sesión** lo log off/out

finalmente ADV at last, finally

financiación F (para una compra) financing; (para un proyecto) funding

financiamiento M (para una compra) financing; (para un proyecto científico) funding; **— por el propietario** owner financing

financiar VT (una compra) to finance; (un proyecto) to underwrite, *fam* to bankroll

financiero -ra ADJ financial; MF financier

finanza F finance; **—s** finances

finca F (inmueble) property; (granja) farm, country estate

finés -esa MF Finn; M (lengua) Finnish; ADJ Finnish

fineza F (atención) courtesy; (suavidad) smoothness

fingir[46] VI/VT (sorpresa) to feign; (un ataque al corazón) to fake; **fingió que la quería** he pretended to love her

finiquito M settlement

finito ADJ finite

finlandés -esa MF Finn; M (lengua) Finnish; ADJ Finnish

Finlandia F Finland

fino ADJ (vino, arena, pelo, metal) fine; (sentidos) keen, sharp; (medias) sheer; (hielo, alambre, voz) thin; (modales) smooth, refined

finta F fake, juke

firma F (compañía) firm; (rúbrica) signature; **— consultora** consulting firm

firmamento M sky

firmante MF signer

firmar VI/VT (documento, carta) to sign; (contrato) to enter

firme ADJ (estructura) firm; (control) tight; (colores) fast; (amarras) secure; (mano) steady, sure; (resistencia) stiff; (apoyo, resistencia) strong, staunch, steadfast; **mantenerse —** to stand one's ground; **¡—s!** attention!

firmemente ADV firmly

firmeza F (de una estructura) firmness; (de la mano) steadiness; (de la resistencia) stiffness; (del apoyo) strength; **con —** firmly

fiscal ADJ fiscal; MF public prosecutor, district attorney

fiscalía F prosecution

fiscalización F (de comportamiento) supervision; (de gastos) oversight

fiscalizar[47] VT (comportamiento) to supervise; (gastos) to oversee

fisgar[40] VI to snoop

fisgón -ona ADJ snooping; MF snoop

fisgonear VI to snoop

físico -ca ADJ physical; MF (persona) physicist; M (cuerpo) physique; F physics

fisiología F physiology

fisiológico ADJ physiological

fisioterapia F physical therapy
fisonomía F features
fístula F fistula
fisura F fissure
fiyano ADJ Fijian
Fiyi M Fiji
flácido, fláccido ADJ (sin firmeza) limp, flaccid; (gordo) flabby
flaco ADJ thin, skinny; **su lado** — his weakness
flacura F thinness
flagrante ADJ gross; **en** — **delito** in the act
flamante ADJ brand-new
flamear VI (llamear) to flame; (ondear) to flap
flamenco-ca ADJ Flemish; MF Flemish person; M (lengua) Flemish; (ave) flamingo; (baile) flamenco
flamígero ADJ flaming
flan M caramel custard
flanco M (de un animal, ejército) flank; (de un neumático) sidewall
flanquear VT to flank
flaquear VI (intención) to waver; (salud) to wane
flaqueza F weakness
flash M (noticias, visión, memoria digital) flash; (lámpara) flashbulb, flash
flashback M flashback
flatulencia F flatulence
flauta F flute; — **dulce** recorder
flautín M piccolo
flecha F arrow
flechar VT to wound with an arrow
flechazo M (herida) wound from an arrow; (enamoramiento) love at first sight
fleco M (de una alfombra) fringe; (de pelo) bangs
flema F phlegm
flequillo M bangs
fletamento M charter
fletar VT to charter
flete M (contratación) charter; (envío) transport; (precio de transporte) freight
flexibilidad F (ductilidad) flexibility; (libertad) latitude
flexible ADJ (material) flexible; (cuerpo humano) limber, supple; (opinión) pliant, pliable
flojear VT to slacken
flojedad F laxity, looseness; (debilidad) weakness
flojera F (debilidad) weakness; (pereza) laziness
flojo ADJ (suelto) loose, slack; (holgazán) lazy; (inferior) crummy; (débil) weak; (sin fundamento) flimsy
floppy M floppy disk
flor F flower, blossom, bloom; (cumplido) compliment; — **de la edad** prime of life; — **de Pascua** poinsettia; — **y nata** the cream of the crop; **a** — **de** flush with; **en** — in bloom
flora F flora (también bacteriana); — **intestinal** intestinal flora

floración F blooming, blossoming
floral ADJ flowery
floreado ADJ flowery
florear VT (adornar con flores) to decorate with flowers; (adornar) to adorn
florecer[35] VI (echar flores) to flower, to bloom; (prosperar) to flourish, to thrive
floreciente ADJ (próspero) flourishing, prosperous; (florecido) blooming
florecimiento M flourishing
floreo M flourish
florería F florist's shop
florero M flower vase
florete M fencing foil
florido ADJ flowery
florista MF florist
floritura F flourish
flota F fleet
flotador M (para nadar) float; (de un avión) pontoon; ADJ floating
flotante ADJ floating, buoyant
flotar VI (estar suspendido, variar en valor) to float; (moverse en la superficie) to drift; (ir por el aire) to waft
flote M flotation; **a** — afloat; **poner a** — to set afloat
fluctuación F fluctuation; (amplitud de variación) range
fluctuar[26] VI to fluctuate
fluidez F (cualidad de fluido) fluency; (cualidad de diluido) thinness
fluido ADJ (que fluye) fluid, flowing; (no vacilante) fluent; M fluid
fluir[19] VI to flow
flujo M (de agua) flow; (vaginal) discharge; (de datos) streaming; — **continuo de datos de audio** audio streaming; — **continuo de datos de vídeo** video streaming; — **de caja** cash flow; — **de trabajo** work flow
flúor M (elemento gaseoso) fluorine; (sal) fluoride
fluorescente ADJ fluorescent
fluoruro M fluoride
fluvial ADJ **transporte** — river transportation
fluyente ADJ flowing
FMI [Fondo Monetario Internacional] M IMF
fobia F phobia
foca F seal
foco M (punto central) focus; (bombilla) bulb; (lámpara potente) spotlight
fofo ADJ mushy
fogata F (fuego abierto) bonfire; (en un campamento) campfire
fogonazo M flash
fogoso ADJ fiery, spirited
folclor, folclore M folklore
folclórico/folklórico ADJ folkloric; **cuento** — folktale

foliculitis F folliculitis
folículo M follicle
folio M folio
foliolo M leaflet
follaje M foliage
folleto M pamphlet, brochure
follón M (confusión) mess; (alboroto) ruckus
fomentar VT (estudio) to promote; (amistad) to foster; (discordia) to foment; (apoyo) to drum up
fomento M encouragement
fonda F inn
fondear VI to anchor
fondillos M PL seat of pants
fondista MF (posadero) innkeeper; (corredor) long-distance runner
fondo M (parte más profunda) bottom; (parte posterior) rear; (del mar) bed; (de un cuadro, foto) background; (de dinero) fund; (de una biblioteca) holdings; (de un jardín) backyard; **— común** pool; **— de contingencia** contingency fund; **— especulativo** hedge fund; **— físico** endurance; **— musical** background music; **— mutuo** mutual fund; **—s** funds; **—s administrados** managed funds; **— sin comisión de entrada** no-load fund; **a —** in depth; **carrera de —** long-distance race; **de cuatro en —** four abreast; **de —** (exhaustivo) in depth; (subyacente) underlying; **sin —** bottomless; **tocar —** to hit rock bottom
fonética F phonetics
fonético ADJ phonetic
fonógrafo M phonograph
fonología F phonology
fontanería F plumbing
fontanero -ra MF plumber
footing M jogging
forajido -da MF outlaw
foráneo ADJ foreign; **influencia foránea** outside influence
forastero -ra MF stranger, outsider
forcejear VI to struggle
forcejeo M struggle
fórceps M PL forceps
forense ADJ forensic; MF forensic scientist
forestal ADJ forest; **división —** forestry division
forja F (fogón) forge; (acción de forjar) forging; (taller) blacksmith's shop
forjado ADJ wrought
forjar VT (metales, un acuerdo) to forge; (un acuerdo) to hammer out; (un documento) to frame
forma F (figura) form, shape; (manera) manner; **— de pago** mode of payment; **— de pensar** mind-set; **ponerse en —** to get in shape; **no hay —** no way; **dar —a** to shape
formación F formation

formal ADJ (que atañe a la forma) formal, serious; (fiable) reliable
formaldehído M formaldehyde
formalidad F (convencionalidad) formality; (fiabilidad) reliability
formalismo M formality
formalizar[47] VT to make official; **—se** to settle down
formar VT (crear) to form; (reunir tropas) to muster; (entrenar) to train; **—se** (montañas) to form; (estudiantes) to be educated
formatear VT to format
formateo M formatting
formativo ADJ formative
formato M format; **— de archivo/fichero** file format; **— de texto enriquecido** rich text format
formidable ADJ formidable
formón M wood chisel
fórmula F formula
formulación F (acción de formular) formulation; (fórmula) formula; (redacción) wording
formular VT to formulate; (un plan, una pregunta) to frame; (un documento) to word
formulario M form
fornicar[30] VI to fornicate
fornido ADJ stout, sturdy
foro M forum; (de un escenario) back
forrado ADJ (con un forro) lined; (bien provisto) flush
forraje M forage, fodder
forrajear VI to forage
forrar VT (un saco) to line; **—se** to line one's pockets
forro M lining; (de un libro) jacket
fortalecer[35] VT to fortify, to strengthen
fortalecimiento M strengthening
fortaleza F (construcción) fortress, fort; (fuerza) fortitude
fortificación F fortification
fortificar[30] VT to fortify
fortuito ADJ fortuitous, accidental
fortuna F fortune; **por —** fortunately; **probar — ** to try one's luck; **hacer —** to become rich
forúnculo M boil
forzar[49] VT to force, to coerce; **— la entrada** to break into
forzoso ADJ (por la fuerza) forcible; (inevitable) necessary; (aterrizaje) forced
fosa F (sepultura) grave; (de la nariz) cavity; (en el fondo del mar) trench
fosfato M phosphate
fósforo M (sustancia) phosphorus; (cerilla) match
fósil ADJ & M fossil
foso M (de un castillo) moat; (de un taller, teatro) pit
foto F snapshot, photo

fotocopia F photocopy
fotocopiadora F photocopier
fotocopiar VI/VT to photocopy
fotoeléctrico ADJ photoelectric
fotogénico ADJ photogenic
fotografía F (foto) photograph; (arte) photography; — **digital** digital photography
fotografiar[28] VT to photograph
fotógrafo -fa MF photographer
fotón M photon
fotosíntesis F photosynthesis
foul M foul
frac M tails
fracasar VI (un proyecto) to fail; (de una película) to bomb; (una embarcación) to break up
fracaso M (de un proyecto) failure; (de una película) flop, bomb
fracción F fraction
fractura F fracture, break; — **fina** hairline fracture
fracturar VT to fracture, to break; **se fracturó la cadera** she broke her hip
fragancia F fragrance
fragante ADJ fragrant; **en** — in the act
fragata F frigate
frágil ADJ (delicado) delicate; (quebradizo) fragile, brittle; (una paz) tenuous
fragilidad F (condición de quebradizo) brittleness, delicacy; (debilidad) frailty
fragmentación F fragmentation
fragmento M fragment; (de metal, piedra) scrap; (de una conversación) snatch; (de un texto) extract, excerpt
fragoso ADJ rugged
fragua F (fogón) forge; (taller) blacksmith's shop
fraguar[25] VT to forge; (una trama) to hatch; VI (cemento, yeso) to set
fraile M friar
frambuesa F raspberry
frambueso M raspberry bush
francamente ADV —, **me horroriza** frankly, to be honest, it horrifies me; **lo pasaban — bien** they were doing pretty well; —, **es ridículo** it is simply ridiculous
francés -esa ADJ French; M (lengua) French; (hombre) Frenchman; F (mujer) Frenchwoman
Francia F France
franco ADJ (sincero) frank, candid; (exento) free; **una franca mayoría** a clear majority; **un tratado —-americano** a Franco-American treaty
francotirador -ora MF sniper
franela F flannel
franja F ribbon
franquear VT (una frontera) to cross; (una carta) to frank; **—se** to be frank
franqueo M postage

franqueza F (personal) frankness; (institucional) openness
franquicia F (concesión) franchise; (exención) exemption
frasco M (recipiente de vidrio) flask; (de medicina, perfume) bottle; (de mermelada) jar
frase F phrase
frasear VI/VT to phrase
fraternal ADJ fraternal, brotherly
fraternidad F fraternity
fraternizar[47] VI fraternize
fraterno ADJ fraternal
fraude M fraud
fraudulento ADJ fraudulent
frazada F blanket
frecuencia F frequency; **con** — frequently
frecuentar VT to frequent; (una tienda) to patronize
frecuente ADJ frequent
fregadero M sink
fregado M scrubbing
fregar[41] VT to scour, to scrub
fregona F (persona) scrubwoman, drudge; (utensilio) mop
freír[10, 74] VI/VT to fry
frenar VT (un coche) to brake; (la inmigración) to restrain; (los impulsos) to bridle; VI to brake, to apply the brakes
frenesí M frenzy; (de actividad) flurry
frenético ADJ frantic
freno M (de coche) brake; (de caballo) bit; (contra el contrabando) curb
frente F forehead; **el sudor de la** — the sweat of one's brow; M (parte delantera, zona de combate, zona meteorológica) front; (de un edificio) face; — **a** (ante) in the face of; (al otro lado) facing; — **a** — face to face; **de** — head-on; **en** — **de** in front of; **hacer** — to face; **pasar al** — to come to the fore
fresa F (fruta) strawberry; (herramienta) mill
fresadora F milling machine
fresar VT to mill
fresco ADJ (reciente, descansado, insolente) fresh; (frío) cool, brisk; (poco abrigado) light; (no cocinado) raw; (pintura) wet; M (frío) coolness; (pintura) fresco
frescor M (de verduras) freshness; (del aire) coolness
frescura F (de verduras, de carácter) freshness; (del tiempo) coolness; (comentario) impudent remark
fresno M ash tree
friabilidad F looseness
frialdad F coldness, coolness
fricción F friction, rubbing
friccionar VT to rub
friega F rubbing, massage
frigorífico M (electrodoméstico) refrigerator;

(cámara) refrigeration chamber
frijol M bean
frío ADJ (de temperatura, de temperamento) cold; (helado) frigid; M cold; **tener —** to be cold
friolento ADJ sensitive to cold
friolera F **la — de $50,000** a trifling $50,000
fritada F dish of fried food
frito ADJ fried; M dish of fried food
fritura F (acción de freír) frying; (comida frita) dish of fried food
frivolidad F frivolity
frívolo ADJ frivolous
fronda F foliage
frondoso ADJ leafy
frontal ADJ (ataque) frontal; (colisión) head-on
frontera F frontier, border
fronterizo ADJ frontier
frontón M (juego) jai alai; (pista) jai alai court
frotación F rubbing
frotar VI/VT to rub
frote M rub
frotis M smear
fructífero ADJ fruitful
fructificar[30] VI to bear fruit
fructosa F fructose
frugal ADJ frugal
frunce M (volante) ruffle; (defecto) pucker
fruncir[33] VT to gather; **— el ceño** to frown, to knit one's brow; **— los labios** to purse one's lips
fruslería F trifle
frustración F frustration
frustrar VT (los planes) to frustrate, to thwart, to foil; (las esperanzas) to shatter, to dash; **—se** to fail, to miscarry
fruta F fruit
frutero -era MF fruit vendor; M fruit dish
fruto M fruit; **—s del mar** seafood
fue ver ser, ir
fuego M fire; (para un cigarro) light; **— antiaéreo** antiartillery fire; **—s artificiales** fireworks; **abrir el —** to begin to fire; **alto el —** cease-fire; **bajo —** under fire; **arma de —** firearm; **entre dos —s** between a rock and a hard place; **hacer —** to fire; **prender/poner/pegar — a** to set fire to
fuelle M bellows
fuel-oil M fuel oil
fuente F (surtidor) fountain; (manantial, referencia) spring; (caracteres de imprenta) font; **de buena —** from the horse's mouth
fuera ADV (en el exterior) outside; (tenis) out; **— de** outside of; **— de borda** outboard; **— de combate** out of commission; **— de juego** (fútbol) offside; **— de límites** (golf) out of bounds; **— de línea** offline; **— de serie** one of a kind; **— de servicio** out of service;

INTERJ out!
fuera, fuéramos ver ser, ir
fuero M (jurisdicción) jurisdiction; (privilegio) privilege, charter
fuerte ADJ (hombre, bebida) strong; (ruido) loud; (cuero) tough; (personalidad) forceful; (estantería) sturdy; (plato) hearty; M (castillo) fort; (talento especial) strong point; ADV (tirar) strongly; (respirar) heavily; (gritar) loud; **soplar —** to bluster; **pisar —** to stomp; **atar —** to tie tight
fuerza F (de una máquina) force; (de una persona, animal) strength; **— aérea** air force; **— bruta** brute force; **— de la naturaleza** force of nature; **— de tarea** task force; **— de voluntad** willpower; **—s armadas** armed forces; **a — de** by dint of; **con —** strongly; **hacer —** to press on; **por la —** by force; **sacar — de flaqueza** to pull oneself together
fuerza, fuerce ver forzar
fuese, fuésemos ver ser, ir
fuga F (escape) escape, flight; (de la cárcel) jailbreak; (de gas) leak; (de capitales) drain, flight
fugarse[40] VI to flee, to escape; **— con el dinero** to abscond with the money
fugaz ADJ fleeting
fugitivo -va ADJ fugitive; MF fugitive
fui, fuimos ver ser, ir
fulano -na MF so-and-so; **—, zutano y mengano** Tom, Dick, and Harry
fulgor M radiance
fulgurar VI to flash
full M full house
fullero -ra MF (tramposo) cheat; (en naipes) card sharp
fulminante M cap; ADJ devastating
fulminar VT to strike with lightning; to thunder; **lo fulminó con la mirada** she gave him a withering look
fumadero M crackhouse
fumador -ora MF smoker
fumar VI/VT to smoke; **—se mucho dinero** to blow a lot of money
fumigar[40] VT to fumigate, to fog
función F (uso) function; (representación) performance; (cargo) office; **— de búsqueda** search function
funcional ADJ functional; **una casa —** a practical/livable house
funcionamiento M operation, working
funcionar VI to function, to work; (motor) to run
funcionario -ria MF government employee, official; **— de préstamos** loan officer
funda F (de un mueble) cover; (de una almohada) pillowcase, slip; (de navaja) sheath
fundación F foundation

fundador -ora MF founder

fundamental ADJ (básico) fundamental; (importante) crucial

fundamentalmente ADV fundamentally, mainly

fundamentar VT to base, to support; —**se en/ sobre** to be based on, to be supported by

fundamento M foundation, basis; —**s** fundamentals

fundar VT (un instituto) to found, to establish; (un argumento) to base

fundición F (fábrica) foundry; (acción de fundirse) fusing

fundido ADJ molten; M (en cinematografía) fade-in/fade-out

fundidor -ora MF foundry worker

fundir VT (combinar) to fuse; (derretir) to melt; (moldear) to mold; —**se** (combinarse) to fuse; (romperse una bombilla) to burn out

fúnebre ADJ (relativo a funerales) funeral; (lúgubre) funereal

funeral ADJ & M funeral

funerario -ria ADJ funeral; F funeral parlor; MF funeral director

funesto ADJ ill-fated, unlucky

fungible ADJ fungible

fungicida M fungicide

funicular M cable car

funky ADJ funky

furgón M (vagón) boxcar; (camioneta de policía) police van; — **blindado** armored vehicle; — **de cola** caboose

furia F fury

furibundo ADJ furious, livid

furioso ADJ (persona) furious; (tempestad) fierce

furor M fury; **hacer —** to be all the rage

furtivo ADJ furtive, stealthy

fuselaje M fuselage

fusible M electric fuse

fusil M rifle

fusilamiento M execution by firing squad

fusilar VT to execute with firearms

fusión F (de hielo) melting; (nuclear) fusion; (empresarial) merger; (de documentos digitales) merge; **fusiones y adquisiciones** mergers and acquisitions

fusionar VT (metales) to fuse; (compañías, documentos digitales) to merge

fusta F crop

fustigar[40] VT (golpear) to lash, to whip; (criticar) to lash out at

fútbol M soccer; — **americano** football

futbolista MF soccer player

fútil ADJ futile, trivial

futilidad F triviality

futuro ADJ future; M future; —**s** futures

Gg

gabán M overcoat

gabardina F trench coat

gabinete M (ministerial) cabinet; (administrativo) office

Gabón M Gabon/Gabun

gabonés -esa ADJ & MF Gabonese

gacela F gazelle

gaceta F gazette

gacetilla F short news item

gachas F PL — **de avena** oatmeal

gacho ADJ (orejas) drooping; (cabeza) bowed; (ojos) lowered

gafar VT to jinx

gafas F PL glasses

gafe M jinx

gaffe M gaffe, faux pas

gag M gag

gaita F bagpipe

gaje M —**s del oficio** occupational hazards

gajo M (de planta) branch; (de naranja) section

gala F (cena) banquet; —**s** finery; **hacer — de** to boast of, to flaunt; **vestirse de —** to dress up

galán M (pretendiente) gallant, suitor; (en cine) leading man

galante ADJ gallant

galantear VT to court

galanteo M courting

galantería F (caballerosidad) gallantry; (cumplido) compliment

galardón M award

galaxia F galaxy

galera F galley (también prueba de imprenta); *RP* top hat

galerada F galley proof

galería F (salón) gallery; (pasillo) corridor; (tiendas) mall, gallery; (de coro) loft; (subterráneo) tunnel; —**s** *Esp* department store

Gales M Wales

galés -esa ADJ & MF Welsh

galgo M greyhound

Galicia F Galicia

gallardete M pennant

gallardía F (elegancia) elegance; (valentía) bravery

gallardo ADJ (elegante) elegant; (valiente) brave

gallego -ga ADJ Galician; M (lengua) Galician; MF Galician

gallera F cockpit

galleta F (salada) cracker; (dulce) cookie

gallina F (pollo) chicken; (hembra adulta) hen; MF coward; — **ciega** blind man's bluff; **la — de los huevos de oro** the goose that laid the golden egg

gallinero M (de gallinas) chicken coop; (de teatro) gallery; **alborotar el —** to raise a ruckus

gallito ADJ cocksure, cocky; M braggart

gallo M cock, rooster; (de la voz) break; **tener —s en la garganta** to have a frog in one's throat; **en menos que canta un —** before you can say Jack Robinson

galón M (de líquido) gallon; (de tela) stripe

galopar VI/VT to gallop

galope M gallop; **al —** at a gallop

galvanizar[47] VT to galvanize

gama F gamut, range

gamba F large shrimp

gamberro -rra MF (rebelde, pandillero) punk, hoodlum; *Esp* (en fútbol) hooligan

Gambia F Gambia

gambiano -na ADJ & MF Gambian

gamo M buck

gamuza F (animal) chamois (también piel); (piel de venado) buckskin, deerskin; (piel de vaca) suede

gana F urge; **con —s** with a vengeance; **de buena —** willingly; **tener —s de** to feel like; **tengo —s [de ir al baño]** I have to go [to the bathroom]; **no me da la —** I just don't feel like it

ganadería F (cría) cattle breeding; (ganado) livestock

ganadero -ra M cattleman; F cattlewoman; ADJ **industria ganadera** cattle industry

ganado M livestock; **— ovino** sheep; **— porcino** swine; **— vacuno** cattle

ganador -ora MF winner; ADJ winning

ganancia F profit, gain, return; **—s** (recaudación de un evento) proceeds; (de un juego) winnings; (de un negocio) earnings; **—s pre-impositivas** before-tax earnings

ganapán M (obrero) menial worker; (trabajo) bread and butter

ganar VI/VT (una guerra, la lotería) to win; (kilos, eficacia) to gain; VT (un sueldo) to earn; (tiempo, espacio) to save; (tierra) to reclaim; **dejarse — por algo** to give in to something; **nos ganaron el partido** they beat us; **—se la vida** to make a living

ganchillo M crochet

gancho M hook (también en boxeo, baloncesto); (rama) snag; (para sujetar) clip; (atractivo) lure; **echar a uno el —** to hook someone; **tener —** to be attractive

gandul -la MF loafer

ganga F bargain, steal

gangoso ADJ twangy

gangrena F gangrene

gangrenarse VI to gangrene

gángster M gangster

ganguear VI to twang

ganso M (animal) goose; (macho) gander; (tonto) *fam* ding-a-ling

ganzúa F picklock

gañido M yelp

gañir[17] VI to yelp

garabatear VI/VT to scribble

garabato M scribble; **hacer —s** to scribble

garaje M garage

garante MF voucher

garantía F (de producto) guarantee, warranty; (de promesa) security, guaranty; (de un derecho) guarantee; (comercial) backing; **— de devolución de dinero** money-back guarantee; **— de préstamo** loan guarantee

garantizar[47] VT (producto) to guarantee, to warranty; (promesa) to warrant

garañón M stud, horse

garbanzo M chickpea

garbo M grace

garboso ADJ graceful

garfio M hook

garganta F (faringe) throat; (cuello) neck; (valle estrecho) gorge

gárgara F gargle; **hacer —s** to gargle

gargarismo M gargle

garita F sentry box

garito M gambling house

garra F (de ave) claw; (de león) paw with claws; **caer en las —s de alguien** to fall into someone's clutches

garrafa F decanter

garrapata F tick

garrapatear VI/VT to scribble

garrapiñar VT to candy

garrocha F pole

garrote M club

garrucha F pulley

gárrulo ADJ garrulous

garza F heron

gas M gas; **—es** (de motor) fumes; (de intestino) gas; **— ionizado** plasma; **— lacrimógeno** tear gas; **— mostaza** mustard gas; **— natural** natural gas; **— nervioso** nerve gas; **a todo —** at full speed

gasa F (tela) gauze; (para heridas) dressing

gaseosa F soda, soft drink

gaseoso ADJ gaseous

gasoducto M pipeline

gasolina F gasoline, gas

gasolinera F gas station

gastado ADJ (neumático) smooth; (ropa) worn-out, shabby

gastador -ora ADJ extravagant, wasteful; MF spendthrift

gastar VT (dinero, tiempo) to spend; (energía) to expend; (neumáticos, ropa) to wear out, to use up; **— una broma** to play a trick; **—se** to wear out

gasto M (desembolso) expense, expenditure;

(desgaste) wear; **—s de desplazamiento**
travel costs; **—s del hogar** household
expenses; **—s de subsistencia** living
expenses; **—s de viaje** travel expenses; **—s
menores** incidentals
gástrico ADJ gastric
gastritis F gastritis
gastroenteritis F gastroenteritis
gastrointestinal ADJ gastrointestinal
gastronomía F gastronomy
gatas LOC ADV **a —** on all fours
gatear VI to creep, to crawl
gatillo M (de arma de fuego) trigger; (de
dentista) forceps
gatito M kitten
gato M (felino) cat; (aparato para levantar) jack;
— montés wildcat, mountain lion; **aquí
hay — encerrado** I smell a rat; **a gatas** on
all fours; **dar — por liebre** to sell someone a
pig in a poke
gaucho M gaucho
gaveta F small drawer
gavilán M hawk
gavilla F (de maíz) sheaf; (de maleantes) gang
gaviota F seagull
gayola F *fam* big house
gazmoñería F prudery
gazmoño -ña MF prude; ADJ prudish
gaznate M gullet
gazpacho M *Esp* gazpacho
geco M gecko
géiser M geyser
gel M gel
gelatina F gelatin
gélido ADJ frigid
gema F gem, jewel
gemelo -la ADJ & MF identical twin; **—s**
(mellizos) identical twins; (binoculares)
binoculars, opera glasses; (botón) studs
gemido M (de dolor) moan, groan; (de queja)
whine
gemir[9] VI (gruñir) to moan, to groan;
(lloriquear) to whine
gen, gene M gene; **— recesivo** recessive gene
genealogía F genealogy
generación F generation
generador M generator
general ADJ & MF general; **por lo —** generally
generalidad F generality
generalización F (de un concepto)
generalization; (de una moda) spreading
generalizar[47] VI/VT to generalize; **—se** to
become widespread
generalmente ADV generally, usually
generar VT generate
genérico ADJ generic
género M (clase) kind; (gramatical) gender;
(tela) material; (literario) genre; (biológico)
genus; **— humano** human race; **—s** dry

goods
generosidad F generosity
generoso ADJ generous
genética F genetics
genético ADJ genetic
genial ADJ brilliant
genio MF (persona inteligente) genius; M
(inteligencia) genius, brilliance;
(temperamento) temperament, nature; (mal
humor) temper; **de mal —** mean; **de buen
—** good-natured
geniudo ADJ quick-tempered
genocidio M genocide
genoma M genome
gente F people; **— de campo** country folk; **—
de color** persons of color; **— en obra** men at
work; **— joven** young people; **— menuda**
small fry; **buena —** good person
gentil ADJ (cortés) gracious; (no judío) gentile;
MF gentile
gentileza F graciousness
gentío M crowd
gentuza F rabble, riffraff
genuino ADJ genuine
geocéntrico ADJ geocentric
geoestacionario ADJ geostationary
geofísica F geophysics
geografía F geography
geográfico ADJ geographical
geología F geology
geológico ADJ geological
geometría F geometry
geométrico ADJ geometric
geopolítico ADJ geopolitical
Georgia F Georgia
georgiano -na ADJ & MF Georgian
geotérmico ADJ geothermal
geranio M geranium
gerencia F management
gerente MF manager
geriatría F geriatrics
geriátrico ADJ geriatric
germánico ADJ Germanic
germen M germ
germinar VI to germinate, to sprout
gerundio M gerund, present participle
gestación F gestation
gesticular VI (con ademanes) to gesture; (con
movimientos exagerados) to gesticulate
gestión F (acción) step, measure; (dirección
empresarial, digital) management;
(administración política) administration;
—es negotiations; **— de datos** data
management; **hacer gestiones para** to take
steps to
gestionar VT (negociar) to negotiate;
(administrar) to administer, to manage
gesto M (con la cara) face; (con las manos)
gesture; **hacerle —s a alguien** to make

faces at someone
gestor -ora MF agent
Ghana F Ghana
ghanés -esa ADJ & MF Ghanaian
giba F hump, hunch
gibón M gibbon
Gibraltar M Gibraltar
gibraltareño -ña ADJ & MF Gibraltarian
giga F jig
gigabyte M gigabyte
gigahercio M gigahertz
gigante ADJ giant, gigantic; MF giant
gigantesco ADJ gigantic
gimnasia F gymnastics
gimnasio M gymnasium, gym
gimotear VI to whimper
gimoteo M whimper
ginebra F gin
ginecología F gynecology
ginecólogo -ga MF gynecologist
gingivitis F gingivitis
gira F tour
girar VI/VT (una llave, un volante, un coche, a la derecha) to turn; VI (un trompo, un disco) to revolve, to spin, to whirl; VT (dinero) to wire
girasol M sunflower
giratorio ADJ rotary, revolving
giro M (movimiento circular) rotation, spin; (cambio de dirección) turn; (expresión) turn of phrase; (monetario) draft, remittance; — **de cheques sin fondos** check kiting; — **postal** money order
giroscopio M gyroscope
gitano -na ADJ & MF gypsy
glacial ADJ glacial, bitter
glaciar M glacier
gladiador M gladiator
glamoroso ADJ glamorous
glamour M glamour
glándula F gland; —**s sudoríparas** sweat glands
glandular ADJ glandular
glaseado M (de torta) glaze; ADJ (papel) glossy
glasear VT to glaze
glaucoma M glaucoma
glicerina F glycerin
global ADJ (mundial) global; (de conjunto) blanket, overall
globalización F globalization
globo M (esfera) globe; (de árbol de Navidad) ball; (lleno de gas) balloon; (en tenis) lob; — **ocular** eyeball; — **terráqueo** globe
globulina F globulin
glóbulo M globule; — **rojo** red cell; — **blanco** white cell
gloria F glory
glorieta F (pérgola) arbor; (rotonda) traffic circle
glorificar[30] VT to glorify

glorioso M glorious
glosa F gloss
glosar VT to gloss
glosario M glossary
glotal ADJ glottal
glótico ADJ glottal
glotis F glottis
glotón -ona ADJ gluttonous; MF glutton
glotonería F gluttony
glucosa F glucose
gluglutear VI to gobble
gluten M gluten
gobernabilidad F governability
gobernación F (acción de gobernar) governing; (entidad gubernamental) government
gobernador -ora ADJ governing; MF governor
gobernante ADJ governing; MF ruler
gobernar[1] VI/VT to govern, to rule; (un buque) to steer
gobierno M government
goce M enjoyment
gofre M waffle
gol M goal; — **de campo** (fútbol americano) field goal; — **del empate** (fútbol) equalizer; — **en contra** (fútbol) own goal
goleador -ora MF (artillero) shooter; (máximo anotador) top scorer
goleta F schooner
golf M golf
golfo -fa M (mar) gulf; (sinvergüenza) rascal
gollería F delicacy
golondrina F swallow
golosina F sweet, goody, tidbit
goloso ADJ sweet-toothed
golpazo M bang, whack
golpe M (físico) blow, knock, whack; (emocional) blow; (estafa) sting; (robo) holdup; (golf) stroke; (de viento) buffet; (con el codo) jab; (con los nudillos) rap; — **bajo** low blow; — **cortado** (tenis) backspin, slice; — **cruzado** (tenis) crosscourt shot; — **de aproximación** (golf) approach shot; — **de calor** heat stroke; — **de derecha** (tenis) forehand; — **de estado** coup; — **de gracia** coup de grâce; — **de penalidad** (golf) penalty stroke; — **de sol** sunstroke; **de** — suddenly; **de un** — all at once
golpear VI/VT (pegar) to strike, to hit; (llamar) to knock, to rap; (dar una paliza) to beat, to batter; (patear) to kick; (codear) to jab
golpecito M tap
golpetear VI (dedos) to tap; (lluvia) to patter; (motor) to knock; (algo suelto) to rattle
golpeteo M (con los dedos) tap; (de lluvia) patter; (de un motor) knock; (de algo suelto) rattle
goma F (chicle) gum; (caucho) rubber; (neumático) tire; (en béisbol) home; — **de borrar** eraser; — **de mascar** chewing gum;

— elástica rubber band; **—espuma** foam
gomero M rubber tree
gomoso ADJ slimy
gónada F gonad
góndola F gondola
gong M gong
gonorrea F gonorrhea
gordinflón ADJ *pey* fatso
gordito ADJ chubby
gordo ADJ fat; **se armó la gorda** all hell broke loose; **hacer la vista gorda** to turn a blind eye
gordura F (cualidad) fatness; (sebo) fat
gorgojo M weevil
gorila M (primate) gorilla; (portero) bouncer; (guardaespaldas) bodyguard
gorjear VI (ave) to warble, to chirp, to twitter; (niño) to gurgle
gorjeo M (de ave) warble, twitter, chirp; (de niño) gurgle
gorra F cap; **de —** at someone else's expense; **vivir de —** to sponge
gorrino M piglet
gorrión M sparrow
gorro M cap
gorrón M sponge, sponger
gorronear VI/VT to mooch, to freeload
gospel M gospel
gota F (de líquido) drop; (de sudor) bead; (enfermedad) gout; **— a —** drop by drop; **—s oftálmicas** eyedrops; **ser dos —s de agua** to be like two peas in a pod; **sudar la — gorda** (transpirar) to sweat profusely; (trabajar) to work hard
gotear VI (caer gota a gota) to drip; (rápidamente) to dribble, to trickle; (salirse) to leak; (llover) to sprinkle
goteo M drip (también intravenoso); (rápido) dribble, trickle
gotera F leak
gotero M dropper
gótico ADJ Gothic; M (lengua) Gothic
gourmet ADJ & MF gourmet
gozar[47] VT to enjoy; **— de** to enjoy
gozne M hinge
gozo M pleasure, enjoyment
gozoso ADJ enjoyable
grabación F recording
grabado M (en piedra) engraving; (con ácido) etching
grabador -ora MF (persona) engraver; F (aparato) tape recorder; (empresa) recording company
grabar VI/VT (en piedra) to engrave; (con ácido) to etch; (en cinta magnetográfica) to record, to tape; (en computadora) to write; **— en la memoria** to etch/imprint on one's memory
gracejo M wit
gracia F (garbo, desenvoltura) grace,

gracefulness; (humor) humor; (monería) antic; (favor) favor; (indulto) pardon; **¡—s!** thanks! thank you! **—s a Dios** thank God; **caer en —** to please; **dar —s** to say the blessing; **dar las —s** to thank; **hacer —** to amuse; **tener —** to be funny
grácil ADJ supple, graceful
gracioso ADJ (chistoso) amusing, funny; (gentil) gracious
grada F step, bleachers
gradación F gradation
graderías F PL bleachers
grado M (de temperatura, de parentesco, de un ángulo, de universidad) degree; (militar) rank; (de alcohol) proof; **de buen —** willingly; **en alto —** to a great extent; **en mayor o menor —** to some extent; **quemadura de primer —** first-degree burn
graduación F (de una escuela) graduation, commencement; (militar) military rank; (de alcohol) proof; (de un lente óptico) correction
graduado -da MF graduate
gradual ADJ gradual
graduar[26] VT (ajustar) to adjust; (regular) to calibrate; **—se** to graduate, to get a degree
graffiti M graffiti
grafiar[28] VT to graph
gráfica F (arte) graphics; (representación) graph, chart; **— de pastel** pie graph
graficar[30] VT to chart
gráfico -ca ADJ graphic; **acento —** written accent; M (representación) graph, chart; MF (empleado) printer
grafito M graphite
grama F lawn
gramática F grammar
gramatical ADJ grammatical
gramo M gram
grana ADJ & F scarlet
granada F (fruta) pomegranate; (proyectil) grenade; **— de mano** hand grenade
Granada F Grenada
granadino -na ADJ & MF Grenadian
granado M pomegranate tree; ADJ notable
granate M garnet
Gran Bretaña F Great Britain
grande ADJ (de tamaño) large, big; (de importancia) great; **un gran poeta** a great poet; **divertirse en —** to have a whale of a time; **a —s alturas** at high altitudes; **de gran alcance** far-reaching; **de/a gran escala** large-scale; **en gran parte** in large measure, largely; **gran almacén** department store
grandeza F greatness; **delirios de —** delusions of grandeur
grandiosidad F grandeur
grandioso ADJ grandiose, grand

granero M (edificio) granary, grain barn; (recipiente) bin, crib; **el — de América** the breadbasket of America

granito M granite

granizada F hailstorm

granizar[47] VI to hail

granizo M hail

granja F farm

granjearse VI to win for oneself

granjero -ra MF farmer

grano M (de una foto, arena, semilla) grain; (cereal) cereal, grain; (barrito) pimple; **— de café** coffee bean; **ir al —** to come to the point

granuja MF ragamuffin

granular VT to granulate; **—se** to become granulated

granuloso ADJ granular

grapa F (para sujetar madera) clamp; (para sujetar papel) staple

grapadora F stapler

grasa F (aceite) grease; (animal) fat

grasiento ADJ greasy

graso ADJ (cutis) oily; (leche) fatty; (pelo) greasy

grasoso ADJ greasy

gratificación F bonus

gratificar[30] VT to gratify

gratis ADJ INV & ADV free

gratitud F gratitude, thankfulness

grato ADJ pleasant

gratuito ADJ (gratis) free; (arbitrario) wanton, gratuitous

grava F gravel

gravamen M (impuesto) tax, assessment; (carga sobre una propiedad) lien, encumbrance

gravar VT (con un impuesto) to tax, to assess; (con una carga) to encumber

grave ADJ (enfermedad, decisión) grave, serious; (sonido) low, deep; (injuria) grievous; (personalidad) earnest

gravedad F (fuerza de atracción) gravity; (de una situación) seriousness; (de una tormenta) severity; (de la voz) depth; (de una personalidad) earnestness

gravemente ADV (herido) seriously; (enfermo) seriously, gravely

gravitación F gravitation

gravitatorio ADJ gravitational

gravoso ADJ burdensome

graznar VI (cuervo) to caw, to croak; (pato) to quack; (ganso) to honk

graznido M (de cuervo) caw, croak; (de pato) quack; (de ganso) honk

Grecia F Greece

greda F clay

green M green

gregario ADJ gregarious

gremial ADJ **acuerdo —** union agreement

gremio M (conjunto de personas) trade; (asociación histórica) guild; (sindicato) trade union

greña F mop of hair

grey F flock, fold

griego -ga ADJ & MF Greek

grieta F crevice, crack

grifo M faucet, spigot, tap

grillete M fetter, shackle

grillo M (insecto) cricket; **—s** (grilletes) shackles

grima F uneasiness; **dar —** (disgustar) to be upsetting; (asquear) to be disgusting

gringo -ga ADJ & MF *pey* American

gripe, gripa F flu, influenza; **— asiática** Asiatic flu

gris ADJ & M gray

grisáceo ADJ grayish

gritar VI/VT (vociferar) to shout, to yell; (chillar) to scream

gritería F shouting

grito M (voz alta) shout, cry; (chillido) scream; **el último —** the last word; **estar en un —** to be in agony; **pedir a —s** to clamor for; **poner el — en el cielo** to hit the ceiling

grosella F currant

grosellero M currant

grosería F (cualidad) rudeness; (hecho, dicho) profanity, something rude

grosero ADJ (descortés) rude, ill-mannered, boorish; (vulgar) vulgar, profane; (sin arte) coarse, unrefined

grosor M thickness

grotesco ADJ grotesque

grúa F (máquina) crane; (guinche, remolcadora) wrecker, tow truck

grueso -sa ADJ (persona) thick-set, heavy; (tabla) thick; (palabra, arena) coarse; M (grosor) thickness; (mayoría) majority; F gross

grulla F crane

grumo M lump

grumoso ADJ lumpy

gruñido M (de perro) growl, snarl; (de cerdo) grunt; (humano) grumble

gruñir[17] VI (el cerdo) to grunt; (el perro) to growl, to snarl; (el ser humano) to grumble

gruñón -ona ADJ grumpy; MF grumpy person

grupa F rump; **volver —s** to turn around

grupo M group; **— de apoyo** support group; **— de presión** lobby; **— étnico** ethnicity; **— paritario** peer group; **— sanguíneo** blood type; **— de usuarios** user group

gruta F grotto, cavern

guacal M crate

guacamole M *Méx* guacamole

guacho M (cría de ave) chick; *Am* (animal huérfano) orphan

guadaña F scythe

guagua F (fruslería) trifle; *Carib* bus; *Chile* baby; LOC ADV **de —** for nothing, free

guaje -ja MF urchin

guano M guano, bird dung

guantada F slap

guante M glove (también en deporte); **arrojar el — to** challenge; **echarle el — a alguien** to capture someone; **te queda como un —** it fits you like a glove

guantelete M gauntlet

guantera F glove compartment

guapetón -ona MF *fam* fox

guapo ADJ (hombre) good-looking, handsome; (mujer) good-looking, pretty; (valiente) brave; **¡hola —!** hey, good-looking!

guarapo M cane syrup

guarda MF (guardián) guard; F (almacenamiento) storage

guardabarros M (fútbol) goalkeeper

guardar VT (almacenar) to keep, to store; (observar) to observe; (datos) to save; (proteger) to guard; **— como** to save as; **— rencor** to hold a grudge; **— un secreto** to keep a secret; **—se de** to guard against; M SG **guardabarros** fender; M SG **guardacostas** Coast Guard cutter; MF SG **guardaespaldas** bodyguard; M SG **guardafangos** fender; M SG **guardapelo** locket; M SG **guardarropa** (armario, ropa) wardrobe; (en un local) cloakroom; MF SG **guardabosque[s]** forest ranger, forester; MF SG **guardafrenos** brake operator; MF SG **guardaagujas** switch operator; MF SG **guardameta** goalie

guardería F nursery, day-care center

guardia MF (vigilante) guard; (en baloncesto) point guard; **— civil** civil guard; F (vigilancia) guard; **bajar la —** to let down one's guard; **de —** (militar) on duty, on watch; (médico) on call; **en —** en garde; **hacer/montar —** to stand guard

guardián -ana MF guardian, keeper

guarecerse[35] VT to take shelter

guarida F den, lair

guarismo M cipher

guarnecer[35] VT (un plato) to garnish; (un vestido) to trim; (una fortaleza) to man, to garrison

guarnición F (de tropas) garrison; (de comida) trimmings; **guarniciones** harness

guarro ADJ filthy; M pig

guasa LOC ADV **de/a —** in jest, as a joke

guasón -ona MF joker

guata F padding

Guatemala F Guatemala

guatemalteco -ca ADJ & MF Guatemalan

guau INTERJ woof

guay ADJ *Esp* cool, great

guayaba F guava

guayabera F tropical pleated shirt

gubernamental ADJ governmental

gubernativo ADJ governmental

gubia F gouge

guedeja F shock of hair

guepardo M cheetah

guerra F war, warfare; **dar —** to aggravate; **en pie de —** at war; **— fría** cold war

guerrear VI to war

guerrero -ra MF warrior; **operación guerrera** war operation; **espíritu —** warrior spirit

guerrilla F guerrilla army

guerrillero -ra MF guerrilla

gueto M ghetto

guía MF (persona) guide, leader; F (cosa o animal) guide; **— para padres** parenting guide; **— telefónica** telephone directory

guiar[28] VT to guide, to lead; **—se por** to follow

guijarro M pebble

guinche M *Am* (grúa) winch; (remolque) tow truck

guinda F cherry

guindilla F *Esp* small hot pepper

Guinea F Guinea

guineano -na ADJ & MF Guinean

guingán M gingham

guiñada F wink

guiñapo M rag

guiñar VI/VT to wink

guiño M wink

guion M (ortografía) hyphen; (libreto) script, screenplay

guionista MF screenwriter

guirnalda F garland; (de Navidad) tinsel

guisa F **a — de** by way of

guisado M stew, hash

guisante M pea

guisar VI/VT (cocer) to cook; (en olla) to stew

guiso M stew, casserole

guitarra F guitar

gula F gluttony

gusano M worm; **— de seda** silkworm

gustar VT (agradar) to be pleasing to; **ella me gusta** I like her; **le gustan los perros** he likes dogs; **no me gustan las fiestas** I dislike parties; **te guste o no te guste** whether you like it or not; **cuando gustes** whenever you want; **— de** (preferir) to be fond of; (saborear) to taste

gusto M (sentido, sabor, sentido estético) taste; (agrado) pleasure; (preferencia personal) like; **a —** at ease; **a mi —** to my liking; **dar —** to be a pleasure; **darle el — a alguien** to humor someone; **darse el — to** indulge oneself; **de mal —** in bad taste; **el — es mío** the pleasure is mine; **estar a —** to be comfortable; **mucho —** nice to meet you; **por —** for fun; **tener el — de** to have the pleasure of; **tomarle el — a una cosa** to become fond of something

gustoso ADJ (que gusta de) fond of; (agradable) pleasant; ADV willingly

Guyana F Guyana
guyanés -esa ADJ & MF Guyanese

Hh

ha, has ver haber
haba F (frijol) bean; (frijol verde) lima bean
habano M cigar
haber[68] V AUX to have; **— comido cuatro veces en un día** to have eaten four times in a day; **habérselas con** (un problema) to grapple with; (una persona) to have it out with; **ha de llegar mañana** he is to arrive tomorrow; **hay** there is, there are; **hay viento** it is windy; **hubo un problema** there was a problem; **había gente** there were people; **hay que** it is necessary to; **no hay de qué** don't mention it; **no hay forma** no way; **no hay problema** no problem; **¿qué hay?** what's up? **todo lo habido y por haber** everything possible; M (hacienda) assets; (columna en una cuenta) credit; **—es** earnings
habichuela F bean; **— verde** string bean
hábil ADJ adept, able; **día —** workday
habilidad F ability, skill
habilidoso ADJ deft, skillful
habilitar VT (equipar) to outfit; (autorizar) to authorize
habitación F (vivienda) dwelling; (cuarto) room
habitante MF (de un país, región) inhabitant; (de un barrio) resident
habitar VT to inhabit
hábitat M habitat
hábito M habit (también vestimenta religiosa); **—s de compra** buying habits
habitual ADJ habitual, usual
habituar[26] VT to accustom; **—se** to get used to
habla F (lenguaje) speech; (variedad local) dialect; **— infantil** baby talk; **al —** in communication with; **quedarse sin —** to be left speechless
hablador ADJ talkative
habladurías F idle talk, gossip
hablante ADJ speaking; **castellano—** Castilian-speaking; MF speaker; **castellano—** Castilian speaker
hablar VI/VT to talk; **— de política** to talk about politics; **— hasta por los codos** to talk one's head off; **— no cuesta nada** talk is cheap; **— por teléfono** to talk on the phone; **— solo / para sí** to talk to oneself; to speak; **— francés** to speak French; **— sin rodeos** to speak one's mind; **— por señas** to use sign language; **hablando mal y pronto** pardon my French; **no —se** not to be on speaking terms; **no me hagas —** don't get me started on it; **hablando en serio, ¿qué es lo que quieres?** seriously, what do you want?
hablilla F malicious tale
habrá, habría ver haber
hacedor -ora MF maker
hacendado -da MF landowner
hacendoso ADJ industrious, diligent
hacer[54, 74] VT (crear) to do, to make; (causar) to make; (resolver) to do; (decir) to go; **la vaca hace 'mu'** the cow goes moo; **— clic** to click; **— economías** to scrimp; **— frío/calor/viento** to be cold/hot/windy; **— una oferta** make an offer; **— un pastel** to make a cake; **— un crucigrama** to do a crossword puzzle; **— un gol** to score a goal; **me hizo llorar** he made me cry; **hace mucho tiempo** a long time ago; **hace poco** a short while ago; **hizo como si estuvieras presente** he acted as if you were here; **a lo hecho, pecho** you've got to face the music; **la hiciste buena** you've really screwed up; **¿qué le vamos a hacer?** that's life; **¿qué se hizo de Juan?** whatever became of Juan? **haz el trabajo** do the work; **hecho a pedido** built to order; **—se rico** to become rich; **—se el tonto** to play the fool; **—se el listo** to pull a stunt; **—se pasar por el jefe** to pose as the boss; **—se a un lado** to step aside; **—se amigo de** to befriend; **—se a la oscuridad** to get used to the dark; **—se cargo** to take over; **—se [del] rogar** to play hard to get
hacha F (grande) ax[e]; (pequeña) hatchet
hachís M hashish
hacia PREP (en dirección a) toward; (aproximadamente) about; **— abajo** downward; **— adelante** forward; **— adentro** inward; **— afuera** outward; **— arriba** upward; **— atrás** backward; **— el este** eastward; **— la izquierda** to the left; **dar —** to face
hacienda F (bienes) estate; (establecimiento agropecuario) ranch; (impositiva) Internal Revenue Service
hacina F shock
hacinar VT (liar) to shock; (atestar) to crowd in
hada F fairy
hado M fate
haga, hago ver hacer
Haití M Haiti
haitiano -na ADJ & MF Haitian
halagar[40] VT to flatter, to compliment
halago M flattery, compliment
halagüeño ADJ (palabras) flattering; (perspectiva) promising
halcón M falcon
hálito M breath
halitosis F halitosis

hallar VI to find; **—se** to be; **—se en un aprieto** to be in a pickle; **—se mal de salud** to be in a bad way

hallazgo M finding; **ese documento fue un sensacional** that document was a real find

halo M halo

halógeno ADJ & M halogen

halterofilia F weight training, weightlifting

hamaca F hammock

hambre F (deseo de comer) hunger; (hambruna) famine; **tener —** to be hungry; **pasar —** to go hungry; **morirse de —** to starve

hambrear VI/VT to starve

hambriento ADJ (con hambre) hungry; (famélico) famished, starving

hambruna F famine

hamburguesa F hamburger

hampa F underworld

hámster M hamster

hándicap M handicap

handicapar VT to handicap

hangar M hangar

hará, haría ver hacer

haragán -ana ADJ indolent; MF loafer

haraganear VI to loaf

haraganería F laziness

harapiento ADJ ragged, tattered

harapo M rag, tatter

hardware M hardware

harén M harem

harina F (fina) flour; (gruesa) meal; **— de avena** oat flour; **— de maíz** cornmeal; **es — de otro costal** that's another kettle of fish

hartar VT to satiate; **—se** (de comida) to have one's fill; (de aburrimiento) to get fed up

hartazgo M surfeit, excess

harto ADJ (satisfecho) full; **estar —** to be fed up; **ese asunto me tiene —** I'm sick and tired of the whole business

hasta PREP (temporal) till, until; (espacial) [up] to; **— ahora** to date / so far; **— cierto punto** to a certain extent; **— luego** good-bye, see you later; **— pronto** see you later; **caminó — la esquina** he walked to the corner; **lo llenó — el borde** he filled it up to brim; **estar — la coronilla** to be fed up; ADV even; **— mi madre lo notó** even my mother noticed it; **— que** until

hastiado ADJ jaded

hastial M gable

hastiar[28] VT to cloy, to tire; **—se** to grow weary of

hastío M tedium

hato M (envoltorio) bundle; (rebaño) herd

hay ver haber

haya F beech

haya, hayamos ver haber

hayuco M beechnut

haz[1] M (de leña) bundle; (de luz) beam; (de flechas) sheaf

haz[2] ver hacer

hazaña F deed, exploit, feat

hazmerreír M laughingstock

he VT IMPERSONAL **he aquí la lista** here's the list

he, hemos ver haber

hebilla F buckle

hebra F (de hilo) thread; (vegetal) fiber

hebreo -a ADJ & MF Hebrew

heces F PL (de vino, café) dregs; (excremento) feces

hechicería F enchantment

hechicero -ra ADJ bewitching; M sorcerer; F sorceress

hechizar[47] VT (embrujar) to bewitch, to enchant; (fascinar) to enthrall

hechizo M charm, spell

hecho M fact; **los —s de la noche del 17** the events of the night of the 17th; **de —** in fact

hecho ver hacer

hechura F cut

hectárea F hectare

heder[2] VI to stink, to reek

hediondez F stench

hediondo ADJ stinking, smelly

hedonismo M hedonism

hedor M stink, stench

hegemonía F hegemony

helada F (frente frío) freeze; (escarcha) frost

heladera F refrigerator

heladería F ice-cream parlor

helado ADJ (muy frío) frozen, freezing; (con hielo) icy; M ice cream

helar[1] VI/VT to freeze

helecho M fern

hélice F (espiral) helix; (de avión) propeller; (de barco) screw, propeller

helicóptero M helicopter

helio M helium

hematoma M hematoma

hembra F (de animal) female; (de venado) doe; (de ballena, foca) cow; (de ave) hen

hemisferio M hemisphere (también cerebral)

hemofilia F hemophilia

hemoglobina F hemoglobin

hemorragia F hemorrhage; **— cerebral** cerebral hemorrhage; **— vaginal** vaginal bleeding

hemorroide F hemorrhoid

henchir[9] VT to swell

hender[2] VI/VT to cleave, to split

hendido ADJ cleft, split

hendidura F (quebradura) crack; (geológica) fissure

henil M hayloft

heno M hay; **fiebre de —** hay fever

hepatitis F hepatitis

heraldo M herald

herbicida M weedkiller, herbicide
herbívoro ADJ herbivorous; M herbivore
herboso ADJ grassy
heredad F homestead
heredar VI/VT (recibir) to inherit; (dar) to bequeath
heredero -ra M heir; F heiress; **—s y cesionarios** heirs and assigns
hereditario ADJ hereditary
hereje MF heretic
herejía F heresy
herencia F (económica) inheritance; (cultural) heritage; (genética) heredity
herida F (lastimadura) injury; (abierta) wound; **— de bala** gunshot wound; **— perforada** puncture wound; **respirar por la —** to reopen an old wound
herido ADJ (lastimado) injured; (con herida abierta) wounded
herir[8] VI/VT (lastimar) to injure; (con herida abierta) to wound; (sentimientos) to hurt
hermafrodita MF hermaphrodite
hermanastro -tra M stepbrother; F stepsister
hermandad F (de hombres) brotherhood; (de mujeres) sisterhood
hermanito -ta M little brother; F little sister
hermano -na MF sibling; M brother (también religioso); **— mayor** older brother; **— menor** younger brother; F sister (también religiosa); **— mayor** older sister; **— menor** younger sister
herméticamente ADV tight, tightly
hermético ADJ hermetic, airtight; (a prueba de agua) watertight; (que no revela secretos) secretive
hermosear VT to beautify
hermoso ADJ beautiful, lovely
hermosura F beauty
hernia F hernia
héroe M hero
heroico ADJ heroic
heroína F (droga) heroin; (personaje) heroine
heroísmo M heroism
herpes M (erupción) herpes; (en la boca) cold sore; **— febril** fever blister
herradura F horseshoe
herraje M ironwork
herramienta F tool
herrar[1] VT (un caballo) to shoe; (una vaca) to brand
herrería F blacksmith's shop
herrero -ra MF blacksmith
herrumbre F rust
hervidero M swarm
hervidor M kettle
hervir[8] VI/VT to boil; **— a fuego lento** to simmer; **— de** to be swarming with; **me hervía la sangre** I was seething
hervor M boiling; **levantar el —** to come to a boil

heterodoxo ADJ unorthodox
heterogéneo ADJ heterogeneous
heterosexual ADJ heterosexual; *fam* straight
hexágono M hexagon
hiato M hiatus
hibernar VI to hibernate
hibridación F hybridization
híbrido ADJ & M hybrid
hice, hiciera *ver* hacer
hidalgo M nobleman
hidalguía F (nobleza) nobility; (generosidad) generosity
hidrato M hydrate
hidráulico ADJ hydraulic
hidroavión M hydroplane, seaplane
hidrocarburo M hydrocarbon
hidroeléctrico ADJ hydroelectric
hidrofobia F hydrophobia
hidrógeno M hydrogen
hiedra F ivy
hiel F gall
hielo M ice; **— seco** dry ice; **romper el —** to break the ice
hiena F hyena
hierba F (pasto) grass; (especia) herb; (marihuana) *fam* weed; **—buena** mint; **mala — weed; y otras —s** and so on
hierro M iron (también de golf); **— corrugado** corrugated iron; **— forjado** wrought iron; **— fundido** cast iron; **—s** handcuffs
hígado M liver; **malos —s** ill will
higiene F hygiene
higiénico ADJ hygienic
higienista MF hygienist
higo M fig; **me importa un —** I couldn't care less
higuera F fig tree
hijastro -tra M stepson; F stepdaughter
hijo -ja M son; **— de su madre** *fam* son of a gun; **John Smith —** John Smith Jr.; **sin —s** childless; F daughter
hilachas F loose threads
hilado M spinning
hilandería F (fábrica) spinning mill; (técnica) spinning
hilandero -ra MF spinner
hilar VI/VT to spin; **— fino** to split hairs
hilaridad F mirth
hilera F row, line
hilo M (para coser) thread; (para tejer, hilar) yarn; (alambre) filament; **— de agua** trickle; **— de pensamiento** train of thought; **— de perlas** string of pearls; **— de voz** thin voice; **— dental** floss; **al —** in a row; **mover —s** to pull strings; **seguir el — de** to keep track of; **pender de un —** to be hanging by a thread; **perder el —** to lose track
hilván M basting

hilvanar VT to baste, to tack

himen M hymen

himno M (religioso) hymn; (patriótico) anthem

hincapié M emphasis; **hacer —** to emphasize

hincar[30] VT — **los dientes en** to sink one's teeth into; **—se** to kneel

hincha MF (aficionado) supporter; F (antipatía) *Esp* grudge

hinchado ADJ (inflamado) swollen, bloated; (exagerado) inflated

hinchar VT (un río) to swell; (un globo) to blow up; **— por el equipo de Uruguay** to pull for the Uruguayan team; **—se** (cuerpo) to swell; (pulmones) to inflate; (mejillas) to bulge; (de orgullo) to puff up; (el pan) to rise

hinchazón F swelling

hindi M Hindi

hindú ADJ & MF Hindu

hinojos LOC ADV **de —** on one's knees

hipar VI hiccup

hiperactivo ADJ hyperactive, overactive

hiperdocumento M hyperdocument

hiperenlace M hyperlink

hipermedia M hypermedia

hipermercado M superstore

hipermétrope ADJ farsighted

hipersensible ADJ (a la luz) hypersensitive; (a la crítica) touchy

hipertensión F hypertension, high blood pressure

hiperventilar VI to hyperventilate

hipervínculo M hyperlink

hipnosis F hypnosis

hipnoterapia F hypnotherapy

hipnotizar VI/VT to hypnotize, to mesmerize

hipo M (espasmo) hiccup; (sollozo) sob; **tengo —** I have the hiccups

hipoalérgico ADJ hypoallergenic

hipocondríaco -ca, hipocondriaco -ca ADJ & MF hypochondriac

hipocresía F hypocrisy

hipócrita ADJ hypocritical, two-faced; MF hypocrite

hipódromo M racetrack

hipogloso M halibut

hipoglucemia F hypoglycemia

hipopótamo M hippopotamus

hipoteca F mortgage; **— con tasa de interés ajustable** adjustable-rate mortgage; **— de tasa fija** fixed-rate mortgage

hipotecar[30] VT to mortgage

hipotecario ADJ **banco —** mortgage bank

hipótesis F hypothesis

hipotiroidismo M hypothyroidism

hiriente ADJ (comentario) catty, hurtful

hirviente ADJ boiling

hisopo M swab

hispánico -ca ADJ Hispanic

hispano -na ADJ Hispanic, Spanish-speaking; MF (por su lengua) Spanish-speaking person; (por su etnia) Hispanic

Hispanoamérica F Spanish America

hispanoamericano ADJ Spanish-American

histamina F histamine

histerectomía F hysterectomy

histérico ADJ hysterical

historia F (el pasado, estudio del pasado) history; (relato) story; **— clínica** case history, medical history; **dejarse de —s** to stop fooling around; **esa es otra —** that's another story; **la — se repite** history repeats itself; **pasar a la —** to be a thing of the past

historiador -ora MF historian

historial M record; **— de crédito** credit history

histórico ADJ (de importancia histórica) historic; (pertinente a la historia) historical

historietas F PL funnies

histrionismo M histrionics

hito N landmark, milestone; **de — en —** fixedly; **marcar un —** to be a milestone

hobby M hobby

hocicar[30] VI/VT (un cerdo) to root; (un caballo) to nose

hocico M snout, muzzle

hockey M hockey

hogaño ADV *lit* nowadays

hogar M (lumbre) hearth, fireplace; (casa, asilo) home

hogareño ADJ domestic; **persona hogareña** homebody

hoguera F bonfire, campfire

hoja F (de planta) leaf; (de mesa plegable) flap; (de papel) sheet; (de libro) page; (de navaja) blade; **— clínica** medical chart; **— de afeitar** razor blade; **— de depósito** deposit slip; **— de ejercicios** worksheet; **— de metal** foil; **echar —s** to leaf; **— de servicio** record; F **—lata** tin plate

hojaldre M puff pastry

hojarasca F fallen leaves

hojear VT to page through, to flip through, to browse

hojuela F flake; **—s de maíz** cornflakes

hola INTERJ hello, hi

Holanda F Holland

holandés -esa ADJ Dutch; M (hombre) Dutchman; (lengua) Dutch; F Dutchwoman

holding M holding company

holgado ADJ (vida) comfortable; (pantalón) loose-fitting, baggy; (cuarto) roomy

holganza F (haraganería) idleness; (diversión) leisure

holgar[42] VI to loaf; **huelga decir** it is needless to say

holgazán -ana ADJ lazy, idle; MF idler, loafer, slouch

holgazanear VI to idle, to loaf

holgazanería F laziness

holgura F (de movimiento) ease; (financiera) comfort; (de la ropa) looseness

holístico ADJ holistic

hollejo M skin

hollín M soot, smut

holocausto M holocaust

hombre M man; — **anuncio** sandwich man; — **de bien** man of good will; — **de familia** family man; — **de las cavernas** caveman; — **de la calle** man on the street; — **de negocios** businessman; — **del saco** bogeyman; — **de paja** straw man; — **lobo** werewolf; — **orquesta** one-man band; — **rana** frogman; **es bien** — he's a real he-man; INTERJ come on!

hombrera F shoulder pad

hombro M shoulder; **encogerse de —s** to shrug; **cargar al** — to shoulder; **en/a —s** piggyback; **poner el** — to lend a hand

hombruno ADJ mannish

home M home

homenaje M homage, tribute

homeopatía F homeopathy

homeopático ADJ homeopathic

homicida MF murderer

homicidio M homicide, murder; — **culposo/involuntario** manslaughter; — **sin premeditación** manslaughter

homofobia F homophobia

homofóbico ADJ homophobic

homogeneizar[47] VT to homogenize

homogéneo ADJ homogeneous

homólogo -ga MF counterpart

homóplato M shoulder blade

homosexual ADJ homosexual; *fam* gay

honda F sling, slingshot

hondo ADJ deep; M hollow

hondonada F hollow, dell

hondura F depth; **meterse en —s** to get in over one's head

Honduras F Honduras

hondureño -ña ADJ & MF Honduran

honestidad F (castidad) chastity, modesty; (honradez) honesty

honesto ADJ (casto) chaste, modest; (honrado) honest, straightforward

hongo M (seta) mushroom; (moho) fungus; **aburrirse como un** — to be bored stiff

honor M honor; **con —es** with honors; **tener el** — **de** to have the honor of; **hacerle los —es a** to be appreciative of

honorable ADJ honorable

honorario ADJ honorary; M PL fee

honra F honor

honradez F honesty

honrado ADJ honest

honrar VT (respetar) to honor; (dignificar) to do credit to

honroso ADJ honorable

hora F hour; — **de dormir** bedtime; — **oficial** standard time; — **punta** rush hour; —**s extra[s]** overtime; **a esta** — at this time; **¿a qué** —? at what time? **a todas** —**s** at all hours; **a última** — at the last minute; **decir la** — to tell time; **en** — on time; **es** — **de** it is time to; **es** — **de que me vaya** it's time for me to go; **kilómetros por** — kilometers per hour; **no ver la** — **de** to be dying to; **por** — by the hour; **¿qué** — **es?** what time is it? **ya era** — it was about time

horadar VT to bore

horario M (agenda) schedule, timetable; (manecilla del reloj) hour hand; — **de trabajo** work schedule

horca F (cadalso) gallows; (tridente) pitchfork; — **de ajos** string of garlic

horcajadas LOC ADV **a** — astraddle, astride

horda F horde

horizontal ADJ horizontal

horizonte M (del cielo) horizon; (de una ciudad) skyline

horma F (de zapato) shoe last; (de queso) wheel

hormiga F ant; — **blanca** termite

hormigón M concrete

hormigonera F cement mixer

hormiguear VI (moverse en grandes cantidades) to swarm; (dar sensación de hormigueo) to tingle

hormigueo M tingle

hormiguero M anthill

hormona F hormone; — **del crecimiento** growth hormone

hornada F batch

horneado M baking

hornear VI/VT to bake

hornilla F burner

horno M (industrial) furnace; (doméstico) oven; (para cerámica) kiln; — **de microondas** microwave oven; **alto** — blast furnace; **el** — **no está para bollos** it's not a good time; **recién salido del** — brand-new

horóscopo M horoscope

horquilla F (para el pelo) hairpin; (horca) pitchfork

horrendo ADJ (asesinato) horrific, ghastly; (vestido) hideous, ghastly

horrible ADJ horrible

horripilante ADJ gruesome, hair-raising

horror M (miedo, repulsión) horror; (monstruosidad) abomination; (espectáculo) sight; **tenerle** — **a** to be scared of

horrorizar[47] VT to horrify, to shock, to appall

horroroso ADJ appalling, awful

hortaliza F vegetable; —**s** produce

hortera ADJ tacky, uncool, cheesy

horticultura F horticulture

hosco ADJ sullen, surly

hospedaje M lodging

hospedar VT to lodge, to accommodate; **—se** to lodge, to room

hospicio M (para peregrinos) hospice; (para huérfanos) orphanage

hospital M hospital

hospitalario ADJ hospitable

hospitalidad F hospitality

hostal M hostel

hostería F inn, hostelry

hostia F (oblea) host, wafer; (golpe) whack

hostigamiento M harassment

hostigar[40] VT to harass, to harry

hostil ADJ hostile

hostilidad F hostility

hotel M hotel

hotelero -ra MF hotel keeper

hoy ADV today; **— [en] día** nowadays; **de — en adelante** from now on; **— por —** at present

hoya F river basin

hoyo M hole (también de golf); (muy profundo) pit; **— en uno** (golf) hole in one

hoyuelo M dimple

hoz F sickle

hozar[47] VI to root

HTML M HTML

hube, hubiera, hubo ver haber

hucha F piggy bank

hueco ADJ (vacío) hollow; (vanidoso) vain, affected; **palabras huecas** empty words; M (entre los dientes) gap; (cavidad) hollow; (de ascensor) shaft

huelga MF strike, work stoppage; **— de hambre** hunger strike; **declararse en —** to strike; **en — on** strike

huelguista MF striker

huella F (rastro) trace, trail; (de pie) footprint, track; (de rueda) track; **— dactilar/digital** fingerprint; **seguir las —s de alguien** to follow in someone's footsteps

huérfano -na ADJ & MF orphan

huerta F (de verduras) large vegetable garden; (de árboles frutales) large orchard; **la — valenciana** the farming region of Valencia

huerto M (de verduras) vegetable garden; (de árboles frutales) orchard

hueso M (de animal) bone; (de fruta) stone, pit; **calado hasta los —s** soaked to the bone; **la sin —** the tongue; **no dejarle un — sano a alguien** to break someone's bones; **un — duro de roer** a hard pill to swallow

huésped MF (invitado) guest; (anfitrión) host (también de parásitos)

hueste F host

huesudo ADJ bony

hueva F spawn

huevo M egg; **— de Pascua** Easter egg; **— duro** hard-boiled egg; **— estrellado/frito** fried egg; **— pasado por agua** soft-boiled egg; **—s revueltos** scrambled eggs; **ir pisando**

—s to walk on eggshells

huida F flight

huir[19] VI to flee, to fly

hule M oilcloth

hulla F soft coal; **— blanca** hydroelectric power

humanidad F (cualidad y condición) humanity; (conjunto de los seres humanos) humankind; **—es** humanities

humanismo M humanism

humanitario ADJ (organización, ayuda) humanitarian; (generoso) humane

humano ADJ (del hombre) human; (generoso) humane; M human

humareda F cloud of smoke

humeante ADJ (hoguera) smoking; (sopa) steaming

humear VI (echar humo) to give off smoke; (echar vapor) to give off steam

humedad F (del aire) humidity; (de un paño) dampness; (en la tierra) moisture; (en una pared) moisture stain

humedal M wetland

humedecer[35] VT (sello, ojo) to moisten; (paño) to dampen; **se le humedecieron los ojos** his eyes grew teary

húmedo ADJ (trapo) damp; (aire) humid; (tierra) moist; (tiempo) wet, soggy

humero M flue, funnel

humidificar[30] VT to humidify

humildad F (actitud) humility; (condición) lowliness

humilde ADJ (actitud) humble; (condición) low, lowly, mean

humillación F humiliation

humillar VT (insultar) to humiliate; (disminuir) to humble; **—se** to grovel

humo M (de combustión) smoke; (de gases tóxicos) fume; (de agua) vapor, steam; **—s** conceitedness; **bajarle los —s a alguien** to cut someone down to size; **echar —** to put out smoke; **estar que echa —** to be fuming; **hacerse —** to vanish into thin air

humor M (actitud risueña) humor; (estado de ánimo) mood

humorada F witty remark

humorismo M (humor) humor; (profesión) comedy

humorista MF comedian

humorístico ADJ humorous

humoso ADJ smoky

hundimiento M (acción de hundirse) sinking; (hoyo) sinkhole

hundir VT (hacer naufragar) to sink, to scuttle; (arruinar) to destroy; (enterrar) to bury; **—se** (barco) to sink; (empresa, edificio, precios) to collapse; (tierra) to subside; (sol) to go down

húngaro -ra MF Hungarian

Hungría F Hungary

huracán M hurricane

huraño ADJ sullen, unsociable

hurgar[40] VI (en una bolsa) to rummage; (en la basura) to scavenge; **—se las narices** to pick one's nose

hurón M ferret

huronear VI to ferret out

hurra INTERJ hurrah

hurtadillas LOC ADV **a —** stealthily

hurtar VT to steal, to swipe; **— el cuerpo** to dodge; **—se** to hide

hurto M (robo) theft, larceny; (robo en tiendas) shoplifting; **— con escalo** break-in

husky M (perro) husky

husmear VT (un pedazo de carne) to sniff at; (a un delincuente) to smell out; (peligro) to smell; (en los asuntos ajenos) to nose around, to poke around

husmeo M sniff

huso M spindle; **— horario** time zone

huy INTERJ (de sorpresa) wow; (de pena) oh

huya, huye, huyendo, huyera, huyese *ver* huir

Ii

iba, ibas *ver* ir

ibérico ADJ Iberian

iberoamericano -na ADJ Ibero-American

ibuprofeno M ibuprofen

iceberg M iceberg

ictericia F jaundice

ictérico ADJ jaundiced

ID [investigación y desarrollo] F R&D

ida F outward journey; **—s y venidas** comings and goings

idea F (reflexión) idea, thought; (intuición) inkling

ideal ADJ & M ideal

idealismo M idealism

idealista ADJ idealistic; MF idealist

idear VT (un método) to devise, to think out, to plan; (un plan) to conceive; (una solución) to engineer; (un complot) to hatch

ídem PRON & ADV ditto

idéntico ADJ identical

identidad F identity

identificación F identification

identificar[30] VT to identify

ideología F ideology

ideológico ADJ ideological

idilio M idyll

idioma M language

idiosincrasia F idiosyncrasy

idiota ADJ idiotic, lamebrained; MF *fam* idiot

idiotez F idiocy

ido[1] ADJ out of it

ido[2] *ver* ir

idolatrar VT to idolize

idolatría F idolatry

ídolo M idol

idóneo ADJ (calificado) expert; (ideal) ideal

iglesia F church

iglú M igloo

ignición F ignition

ignifugar[40] VT to fireproof

ignorancia F ignorance

ignorante ADJ ignorant, uneducated; MF ignoramus

ignorar VT (no saber) to be unaware of; (hacer caso omiso de) to ignore, to disregard; (despreciar) to shrug off, to discount

igual ADJ (idéntico) equal; (semejante) same, alike; (derecho) even; **me da —** it's all the same to me; **al — que** just like; M equal sign

igualar VT (alisar) to level; (ser igual a) to equal; (hacer iguales) to equalize; (compararse con) to match

igualdad F equality

igualmente ADV (de manera igual) equally; **quedaron — sorprendidos** they were similarly surprised; **¡que te vaya bien! —** I hope things go well for you! likewise

ijada F loin

ijar M loin

ilegal ADJ illegal, unlawful, lawless

ilegítimo ADJ illegitimate

ileso ADJ unharmed, unhurt

ilícito ADJ illicit

ilimitado ADJ (crédito) unlimited; (energía) boundless; (horizonte) limitless

iluminación F (luz) illumination, lighting; (moral, académica) enlightenment

iluminado ADJ lit

iluminar VT (con luz) to illuminate, to brighten; (con conocimiento) to enlighten; **—se** to light up

ilusión F (idea o imagen falsa) illusion; (deseo) dream, fond hope; (entusiasmo) thrill; **— óptica** optical illusion; **me da —** I'm looking forward to

ilusionado ADJ excited

iluso ADJ naive

ilusorio ADJ illusory

ilustración F illustration; **la —** the Enlightenment

ilustrador -ora MF illustrator

ilustrar VT (dibujar) illustrate; (educar) to enlighten

ilustre ADJ illustrious

imagen F (representación, reputación) image; (foto, televisión) picture; (unidad de película fotográfica) frame; **— especular** mirror image; **la — del tacto** the soul of tact; **— por resonancia magnética** magnetic resonance imaging; **imágenes por**

ultrasonido ultrasound imaging
imaginable ADJ conceivable
imaginación F imagination
imaginar VT (crear una imagen mental) to imagine, to picture; (idear) to dream up
imaginario ADJ imaginary
imaginativo ADJ imaginative
imán M magnet
imantar VT to magnetize
imbatible ADJ unbeatable
imbécil ADJ idiotic
imbuir[19] VT to imbue
imitación F imitation
imitador -ora MF (copión) imitator; (mímico) mimic; **un — de Elvis** an Elvis impersonator
imitar VT (copiar) to imitate; (hacer mímica) to mimic; (representar a un personaje) to impersonate
impaciencia F impatience
impaciente ADJ impatient; *fam* antsy
impactar VI/VT to impact
impacto M impact
impagado ADJ unpaid
impala M impala
impar ADJ odd, uneven
imparcial ADJ (sin prejuicios) impartial, unbiased, neutral; (justo) evenhanded; (apartidario) nonpartisan
imparcialidad F impartiality
impartir VT to impart
impasible ADJ impassive
impasse M impasse
impávido ADJ undaunted
impeachment M impeachment
impecable ADJ (perfecto) flawless; (limpio) spick and span
impedimento M (obstáculo) impediment, hindrance; (incapacidad) handicap
impedir[9] VT to impede, to prevent, to hinder; (acceso) to bar
impeler VT (empujar) to impel; (inducir) to drive
impenetrable ADJ impenetrable
impensable ADJ unthinkable
imperante ADJ prevailing
imperar VI to prevail
imperativo ADJ & M imperative
imperceptible ADJ imperceptible
imperdible ADJ that shouldn't be missed; **una película —** a must-see movie; M safety pin
imperecedero ADJ undying
imperfecto ADJ & M imperfect
imperial ADJ imperial
imperialismo M imperialism
impericia F lack of skill
imperio M (organización política) empire; (gobierno) rule; **— industrial** manufacturing empire
imperioso ADJ (mandón) imperious; (necesario) imperative

impermeabilizar[47] VT to waterproof
impermeable ADJ (al agua) waterproof; (a la crítica) impervious; M raincoat, slicker
impersonal ADJ impersonal
impertinencia F (actitud) impertinence, impudence; (réplica) backtalk
impertinente ADJ impertinent, impudent
impétigo M impetigo
ímpetu M impetus
impetuoso ADJ impetuous, brash
impida, impide, impidiendo, impidiera, impidiese *ver* impedir
impío ADJ godless
implacable ADJ implacable, relentless
implantación F (de un diente) implantation; (de una costumbre, sistema) establishment, introduction
implantar VT to implant
implante M implant; **— dental** dental implant
implementación F implementation
implementar VT to implement
implemento M implement
implicación F (lógica) implication; (en un delito) involvement
implicar[30] VT (involucrar) to implicate, to involve; (conllevar) to entail
implícitamente ADV implicitly, by implication
implícito ADJ implicit
implorar VI/VT to implore
impondrá, impondría *ver* imponer
imponente ADJ (impresionante) imposing; (espantoso) forbidding
imponer[56, 74] VT to impose, to force upon; (gravar) to assess; **—se** to get one's way
imponible ADJ taxable
impopular ADJ unpopular
importación F import
importancia F importance
importante ADJ (persona) important; (cantidad) substantial; (tema, asunto) weighty; (suceso, ocasión) momentous
importar VI (ser importante) to matter; **me importa un comino** I don't give a hoot; **no importa** it makes no difference; VT (introducir productos) to import
importe M amount
importunar VT to besiege
importuno ADJ inopportune
imposibilidad F impossibility
imposibilitar VT to make impossible
imposible ADJ impossible
imposición F (de ideas) imposition; (de impuestos) assessment
impositivo ADJ **sistema —** tax system
impostor -ora MF impostor, fraud
impotencia F impotence
impotente ADJ (sin poder) powerless; (sin libido) impotent

impreciso ADJ inaccurate
impredecible ADJ unpredictable
impregnar VT to impregnate
impremeditado ADJ unpremeditated
imprenta F (arte, oficio) printing; (máquina) press, printing press
imprescindible ADJ indispensable
impresión F (efecto en el ánimo) impression; (acción de imprimir) printing; (huella) imprint
impresionante ADJ (logro) impressive, imposing; (edificio) grand, imposing; (panorama) breathtaking
impresionar VT to impress; **—se** to be overwhelmed; **para —** for show
impreso M printed matter
impresor -ora MF (persona) printer; F (aparato) printer; **impresora de burbuja** bubble-jet printer; **impresora de inyección de tinta** ink-jet printer; **impresora en serie** serial printer; **impresora gráfica** plotter; **impresora láser** laser printer; **impresora local** local printer
imprevisible ADJ unpredictable
imprevisto ADJ unforeseen; M unforeseen event
imprimir[74] VI/VT (producir un impreso) to print; (marcar con presión) to imprint
improbable ADJ improbable, unlikely
improductivo ADJ unproductive
impromptu M impromptu
impropio ADJ (inadecuado) unbecoming; (atípico) atypical
improvisación F improvisation, role-playing
improvisado ADJ impromptu
improvisando ADV ad lib
improvisar VI/VT to improvise
improviso LOC ADV **de —** all of a sudden
imprudencia F (actitud) recklessness; (acción) reckless act
imprudente ADJ unwise, ill-advised
impublicable ADJ unprintable
impúdico ADJ immodest
impuesto M tax, duty; **—a la herencia** inheritance tax; **—s atrasados** back taxes; **— de tasa única** flat tax; **— de sucesión** inheritance tax; **—s taxation; — sobre ingresos** income tax; **— sobre las donaciones** gift tax; **— sobre las ventas** sales tax; **— sobre rentas** income tax
impuesto ver imponer
impugnar VT to contest, to dispute
impulsar VT (empujar) to propel, to drive; (estimular) to boost
impulsivo ADJ impulsive
impulso M (estímulo) boost; (deseo espontáneo) impulse, urge
impune ADJ unpunished
impunidad F impunity

impureza F impurity
impuro ADJ (sustancia) impure; (pensamiento) impure, unclean
impuse, impusiera, impusiese ver imponer
inacabado ADJ unfinished
inaccesible ADJ inaccessible
inaceptable ADJ (inadmisible) unacceptable; (insuficiente) inadequate
inacostumbrado ADJ unwonted
inactividad F inactivity
inactivo ADJ inactive
inadaptado -da ADJ maladjusted; MF misfit
inadecuado ADJ unsuitable
inadmisible ADJ (comportamiento) unacceptable; (pruebas) inadmissible
inadvertido ADJ unnoticed, unobserved
inagotable ADJ (recursos) inexhaustible; (optimismo) unfailing
inaguantable ADJ unbearable
inalámbrico ADJ cordless, wireless
inalterable ADJ unalterable, unchangeable
inalterado ADJ unchanged
inamovible ADJ immovable
inanición F starvation
inanimado ADJ inanimate
inapetencia F lack of appetite
inapreciable ADJ (invalorable) invaluable; (muy pequeño) too small to be seen
inapropiado ADJ unsuitable
inasequible ADJ inaccessible
inaudible ADJ inaudible
inaudito ADJ (historia, situación) unheard-of, unprecedented; (sufrimiento) untold
inauguración F (de un gobierno) inauguration; (de un monumento) dedication
inaugurar VT (un gobierno) to inaugurate; (un monumento) to dedicate
inca ADJ & MF Inca
incalculable ADJ untold
incandescencia F glow
incandescente ADJ incandescent, glowing
incansable ADJ untiring, tireless
incapacidad F inability
incapacitar VT to disable, to incapacitate
incapaz ADJ incapable
incautación F seizure
incauto ADJ unwary
incendiar VT to set fire to; VI/VT to burn; **—se** to catch fire, to burn down
incendiario -ria ADJ incendiary; MF arsonist
incendio M fire, blaze, conflagration; **— doloso** arson; **— forestal** forest fire
incentivo M incentive, inducement
incertidumbre F uncertainty, suspense
incesante ADJ incessant, ceaseless
incesto M incest
incestuoso ADJ incestuous
incidencia F incidence
incidental ADJ incidental

incidente M incident

incidir VI — **en un asunto** to affect/influence a situation

incienso M incense

incierto ADJ uncertain

incinerar VT to incinerate

incipiente ADJ incipient

incisión F incision

incisivo ADJ incisive; M incisor

incitar VT to incite, to whip up

incivilizado ADJ uncivilized

inclemencia F **las —s del tiempo** foul weather

inclemente ADJ inclement, foul

inclinación F (tendencia) inclination, bent, disposition; (acción de inclinar) tilting; (posición inclinada) tilt; (de un techo) slant; (del terreno) slope; (de opinión) bias

inclinar VT (ladear) to tilt; (bajar) to hang; — **la cabeza** to hang one's head; —**se** (doblarse en la cintura) to bend over; (tener tendencia a) to tend; (hacer una reverencia) to bow

incluido ADJ included; **con todo —** all-inclusive

incluir[19] VT (incorporar) to include; (abarcar) to include, to comprise; **incluyéndote a ti, somos cuatro** including you, there are four of us

inclusión F inclusion; **con — de** including

inclusive ADV even

inclusivo ADJ inclusive

incluso ADV even

incluya, incluye, incluyendo, incluyera, incluyese *ver* incluir

incobrable ADJ noncollectible, uncollectable

incógnita F unknown [quantity]

incógnito LOC ADV **de —** incognito

incoherente ADJ incoherent

incoloro ADJ colorless

incomestible ADJ inedible

incomformista ADJ & MF nonconformist

incomible ADJ inedible

incomodar VT to inconvenience

incomodidad F uneasiness

incómodo ADJ (silla) uncomfortable; (situación) awkward, inconvenient; (baúl) cumbersome; (silencio) uneasy; (que siente molestia) ill at ease

incomparable ADJ incomparable, peerless

incompatible ADJ incompatible

incompetente ADJ incompetent

incompleto ADJ incomplete

incomprensible ADJ incomprehensible

incomunicación F disconnect, miscommunication

inconcebible ADJ inconceivable

inconcluso ADJ unfinished

incondicional ADJ unconditional, unqualified

inconexo ADJ disconnected

inconformista MF nonconformist

inconfundible ADJ unmistakable

inconsciente ADJ (sin sentido) unconscious, senseless; (ignorante) unaware, oblivious

inconsecuencia F inconsistency

inconsecuente ADJ inconsistent

inconsolable ADJ heartbroken

inconstancia F inconstancy

inconstante ADJ inconstant, changeable

inconstitucional ADJ unconstitutional

incontable ADJ countless

incontenible ADJ uncontrollable

incontinente ADJ incontinent

incontrolable ADJ uncontrollable

incontrovertible ADJ incontrovertible

inconveniencia F inconvenience

inconveniente ADJ improper; M inconvenience, downside

incorporación F (inclusión) inclusion; (asimilación) incorporation

incorporado ADJ built-in

incorporar VT (incluir) to include; (asimilar) to incorporate; (agregar) to build into; —**se** (erguirse) to sit up

incorrectamente ADV incorrectly, wrongly

incorrecto ADJ incorrect, wrong

incorregible ADJ incorrigible

incredulidad F disbelief

incrédulo ADJ incredulous

increíble ADJ (inverosímil) incredible, unbelievable; (extraordinario) amazing

incrementar VT to augment

incremento M increment, increase

incriminar VT to incriminate

incrustación F inlay

incrustado ADJ (en piedra) embedded; (joyas) inlaid

incrustar VT (piedra) to embed; (oro) to inlay; —**se en** to become embedded in

incubadora F incubator

incuestionable ADJ unquestionable

inculcar[30] VT to inculcate, to instill

inculto ADJ (sin modales) uncultured, unrefined; (sin instrucción) uneducated

incumbencia F **no es de tu —** it's none of your business

incumplimiento M (de contrato) breach; (de deberes) nonperformance; (de deudas) default; (de metas) failure to accomplish; (de promesas) failure to keep

incumplir VT (contratos) to breach; (deberes) to fail to perform; (deudas) to default on; (metas) to fail to accomplish; (promesas) to renege on, to fail to keep

incurable ADJ incurable

incurrir VI — **en** (una deuda, un gasto) to incur; (un error) to fall into

incursión F raid, foray

incursionar VI to foray

indagación F investigation, probe

indagar[40] VI/VT to investigate, to inquire into
indebido ADJ improper
indecencia F indecency
indecente ADJ indecent
indecible ADJ unspeakable
indecisión F indecision
indeciso ADJ (que no ha decidido) undecided; (que suele vacilar) wishy-washy
indecoroso ADJ improper
indefendible ADJ indefensible
indefenso ADJ defenseless
indefinible F indefinable
indefinido ADJ (plazo) indefinite; (silueta) undefined
indeleble ADJ indelible
indelicado ADJ indelicate
indemnización F (resarcimiento) indemnity; (de guerra) reparation; (de un pleito) recovery; — **por despido** severance pay
indemnizar[47] VT to indemnify
independencia F independence; (de un individuo) self-reliance
independiente ADJ independent
indescriptible ADJ indescribable
indeseable ADJ undesirable, unwelcome
indestructible ADJ indestructible
indeterminado ADJ indeterminate, undetermined
indexación F indexing
indexar VT to index
India F India
indicación F (señal) indication; (instrucción) instruction; **indicaciones** directions
indicador M pointer, indicator; — **clave** key indicator; —**es anticipados** leading indicators
indicar[30] VT (señalar) to indicate, to point out; (registrar) to read, to register; (mostrar) to show
indicativo ADJ & M indicative
índice M (lista alfabética) index; (tabla de materias) table of contents; (dedo) index finger; — **de confianza del consumidor** consumer confidence index; — **de mortalidad** mortality rate; — **de precios al consumidor** consumer price index
indicio M clue, sign
Indico M **Océano** — Indian Ocean
indiferencia F indifference; (frialdad) coolness
indiferente ADJ (apático) indifferent, unconcerned; (frío) cool; (sin entusiasmo) lukewarm; (no conmovido) unmoved; **esa chica me es** — I don't care about that girl
indígena ADJ indigenous; MF native
indigente ADJ destitute, indigent
indigestión F indigestion
indignación F indignation
indignado ADJ indignant
indignar VT to make indignant; —**se** to become

indignant
indigno ADJ unworthy
índigo M indigo
indio -dia ADJ & MF Indian
indirecta F hint
indirecto ADJ (estilo, consecuencia) indirect; (ruta) roundabout
indisciplinado ADJ unruly
indiscreción F indiscretion
indiscreto ADJ indiscreet
indiscutible ADJ unquestionable
indispensable ADJ indispensable
indisponer[56, 74] VT to indispose; —**se** to become indisposed
indispuesto ADJ (disgustado) upset; (enfermo) indisposed
indistinto ADJ indistinct, vague
individual ADJ (derechos) individual; (habitación) single; —**es** singles
individualidad F individuality
individualismo M individualism
individualista ADJ & MF individualist
individuo ADJ & M individual
indivisible ADJ indivisible
indiviso ADJ undivided
indocumentado -da ADJ (carta) undocumented; (persona) without identity papers; MF illegal immigrant
índole F type
indolencia F indolence
indolente ADJ indolent
indoloro ADJ painless
indomable ADJ indomitable
indomado ADJ unbroken
Indonesia F Indonesia
indonesio -sia ADJ & MF Indonesian
inducción F induction
inducir[38] VT to induce, to prompt
indudable ADJ undeniable; unquestionable
indudablemente ADV undoubtedly
indulgencia F indulgence
indulgente ADJ indulgent, lenient
indultar VT to pardon
indulto M pardon
indumentaria F apparel
industria F industry, trade; — **petrolera** oil industry
industrial ADJ industrial; MF industrialist
industrialización F industrialization
industrioso ADJ industrious
inédito ADJ unpublished
inefable ADJ ineffable
ineficaz ADJ ineffective, ineffectual
ineficiente ADJ inefficient
inelegible ADJ ineligible
ineludible ADJ inescapable, unavoidable
inempleable ADJ unemployable
inepto ADJ inept
inequívoco ADJ unequivocal

inercia F inertia

inerte ADJ inert

inescrutable ADJ inscrutable

inesperado ADJ unexpected

inestabilidad F instability

inestable ADJ (personalidad, estructura) unstable; (andar) unsteady

inestimable ADJ inestimable, invaluable

inevitable ADJ (conclusión) inevitable; (accidente) unavoidable

inexacto ADJ inaccurate

inexcusable ADJ inexcusable

inexistente ADJ nonexistent

inexorable ADJ inexorable

inexperto ADJ (trabajador) inexperienced, unskilled; (ojo) untrained

inexplicable ADJ inexplicable

inexpresivo ADJ inexpressive, wooden

infalible ADJ (a toda prueba) infallible, foolproof; (confiable) unfailing

infame ADJ infamous

infamia F infamy

infancia F childhood

infante -ta MF (hijo -ja del rey) infante -ta; M (soldado) infantryman

infantería F infantry; — **de marina** marine corps

infantil ADJ (como niño) childlike; (aniñado) childish, infantile

infarto M infarction, heart attack; — **cardíaco** heart attack; — **cerebral** stroke, cerebral infarction; — **del miocardio** myocardial infarction

infección F infection; — **del tracto urinario** urinary tract infection; — **respiratoria alta** upper respiratory infection

infeccioso ADJ infectious

infectar VT to infect; —**se** to become infected

infecto ADJ foul, repugnant

infelicidad F misery

infeliz ADJ unhappy, wretched, miserable; MF poor wretch

inferencia F inference

inferior ADJ (en calidad) inferior, subpar; (en posición) lower

inferioridad F inferiority

inferir[8] VT to infer

infernal ADJ (calor) infernal; (ruido) unholy

infertilidad F infertility

infestación F infestation

infestar VT to infest

infiel ADJ unfaithful, faithless, untrue

infierno M (bíblico) hell; (lugar caliente) inferno; **en el quinto** — in the middle of nowhere

infinidad F infinity; **una** — **de** a large number of

infinitivo ADJ & M infinitive

infinito ADJ infinite; M infinity

inflación F inflation; — **básica** core inflation

inflado ADJ bloated; M pumping up

inflamable ADJ flammable

inflamación F inflammation

inflamar VT to inflame; —**se** to become inflamed

inflar VT (neumáticos) to inflate, to pump up; (globos) to blow up; (precios) to balloon

inflexible ADJ (rígido) inflexible; (testarudo) unbending, adamant

infligir[46] VT to inflict

influencia F influence, pull, clout; (sobre las masas) sway

influir[19] VI — **en/sobre** to influence; (las masas) to sway

influjo M influence

influya, influye, influyendo, influyera, influyese ver influir

influyente ADJ influential

infomercial M infomercial

información F information; (periodística) story

informal ADJ (no formal) informal, casual; (poco fiable) unreliable

informante MF (para un estudio) informant; (de la policía) informer

informar VT (enterar) to inform, to appraise; (un militar) to debrief; (un periodista) to report; (un abogado) to advise; —**se** to become informed

informática F computer science, information technology

informático -ca ADJ computing; MF computer specialist

informativo ADJ informative; M (televisión, radio) news program

informatizar[47] VT to computerize

informe M (de noticias) report; (militar) debriefing; — **de crédito** credit report; —**s de guía** information; ADJ shapeless

infortunio M misfortune

infracción F (de reglamentos) infraction, infringement; (de contrato) breach; (de tránsito) violation; (en deportes) penalty

infractor -ora MF lawbreaker

infraestructura F infrastructure

infrarrojo ADJ & M infrared

infrascrito -ta MF undersigned

infravalorado ADJ underrated, undervalued

infringir[46] VT to infringe, to breach, to violate

infructuoso ADJ fruitless, unsuccessful

ínfulas F PL airs; **darse** — to put on airs

infundado ADJ groundless, unfounded

infundir VT to infuse, to imbue

infusionar VT to steep

ingeniar VT to contrive; **ingeniárselas para** to contrive to

ingeniería F engineering; — **genética** genetic engineering; — **química** chemical engineering

ingeniero -ra MF engineer; — **civil** civil engineer; — **electricista** electrical engineer; — **en computación** computer engineer; — **informático** computer engineer

ingenio M (mental) ingenuity, cleverness; (verbal) wit; (artefacto) artifact; — **de azúcar** (refinería) sugar refinery, sugar mill; (plantación) sugar plantation

ingeniosidad F ingenuity

ingenioso ADJ ingenious, resourceful

ingenuidad F ingenuousness, naiveté

ingenuo -nua ADJ (inocente) naive, ingenuous; (crédulo) gullible; MF dupe

ingerir VI/VT to ingest

ingestión F ingestion

ingle F groin

inglés -esa ADJ English; M Englishman; (lengua) English; F Englishwoman

ingobernable ADJ unruly

ingratitud F ingratitude

ingrato -ta ADJ thankless, ungrateful; MF ingrate

ingrávido ADJ weightless

ingrediente M ingredient; **ese libro tiene todos los —s de un éxito** that book has all the makings of a best seller

ingresar VT (datos) to input; (dinero en una cuenta) to deposit; VI (a un hospital) to be admitted; (a un sistema) to log in

ingreso M (permiso para entrar) entrance, entry; (depósito bancario) deposit; (renta) income; **—s** (de una firma) earnings; (del estado) revenue; — **bruto** gross income; — **neto ajustado** adjusted net income; **—s discrecionales** discretionary income; **—s disponibles** disposable income

inhábil ADJ unskilled

inhabilidad F inability

inhabilitar VT to disqualify

inhalación F inhalation; — **de humo** smoke inhalation

inhalar VI/VT to breathe in, to inhale

inherente ADJ inherent

inhibición F inhibition

inhibidor ADJ inhibiting; M inhibitor

inhibir VT to inhibit

inhospitalario ADJ inhospitable

inhóspito ADJ inhospitable

inhumano ADJ inhuman

iniciación M initiation, induction

inicial ADJ initial; (pago) up-front; F (letra) initial; (béisbol) first base

inicialista MF first baseman

inicializar[47] VT to initialize

inicialmente ADV initially

iniciar VT (conversaciones) to initiate; (en un grupo) to induct; (software) to launch; (computadora) to boot up; (negociaciones) to enter

iniciativa F initiative

inicio M beginning, start

inimitable ADJ inimitable

ininflamable ADJ fireproof

ininteligible ADJ unintelligible

ininterrumpido ADJ unbroken, uninterrupted

injerencia F interference

injertar VT to graft

injerto M graft; — **óseo** bone graft

injugable ADJ unplayable

injuria F (insulto) insult, verbal abuse; (daño) damage

injuriar VT to insult, to abuse verbally

injurioso ADJ insulting, injurious, verbally abusive

injustamente ADV unjustly, unfairly, wrongly

injusticia F (desigualdad) injustice; (acto injusto) wrong; (error judicial) miscarriage of justice

injustificable ADJ unjustifiable

injustificado ADJ uncalled-for, unwarranted

injusto ADJ unjust, unfair

inmaculado ADJ immaculate, spotless

inmaduro ADJ immature

inmanejable ADJ unmanageable

inmaterial ADJ immaterial

inmediaciones F PL vicinity

inmediato ADJ immediate, instant; **de —** at once

inmensidad F immensity, vastness

inmenso ADJ immense, vast

inmerso ADJ (en agua) submerged; (en el trabajo) absorbed; (en un tema, una situación) immersed

inmerecido ADJ unearned

inmigración F immigration

inmigrante ADJ & MF immigrant

inmigrar VI to immigrate

inminente ADJ imminent, impending

inmiscuir[19] VI to mix; **-se** to meddle

inmodestia F immodesty

inmodesto ADJ immodest

inmoral ADJ immoral

inmoralidad F immorality

inmortal ADJ & MF immortal

inmortalidad F immortality

inmóvil ADJ motionless, immobile

inmovilizar[47] VT (impedir los movimientos) to immobilize; (contra el suelo) to pin

inmueble M building

inmune ADJ immune

inmunidad F immunity

inmunodeficiencia F immunodeficiency

inmutable ADJ unchangeable, immutable

innato ADJ innate, inborn

innecesario ADJ unnecessary, needless

innegable ADJ undeniable

innoble ADJ ignoble

innocuo ADJ innocuous, harmless

innovación F innovation

innovador-ora ADJ innovating, innovative; MF innovator

innovar VI to innovate; VT to modernize

innumerable ADJ innumerable, countless

inocencia F innocence

inocente ADJ innocent, guiltless; MF dupe

inocuo ADJ innocuous, harmless

inodoro ADJ odorless; M toilet, commode

inofensivo ADJ inoffensive, harmless

inolvidable ADJ unforgettable

inoperable ADJ inoperable

inoportuno ADJ inopportune, untimely

inorgánico ADJ inorganic

inoxidable ADJ rustproof

inquietante ADJ distressing, worrisome

inquietar VT to worry

inquieto ADJ (movedizo) restless; (preocupado) uneasy

inquietud F (intranquilidad) restlessness; (preocupación) alarm, concern

inquilino-na MF (de un apartamento) tenant, renter; (de una pensión) lodger

inquina F spite

inquirir[4] VI/VT to inquire

inquisición F inquisition

inquisitivo ADJ inquisitive

insaciable ADJ insatiable

insalubre ADJ unhealthy, unsanitary

insatisfactorio ADJ unsatisfactory

insatisfecho ADJ dissatisfied, unhappy

inscribir[74] VT (grabar) to inscribe; (matricular) to register, to enroll; —se to register, to enroll

inscripción F (grabado) inscription; (matriculación) registration, enrollment

insecticida M insecticide

insectívoro ADJ insectivorous

insecto M insect

inseguridad F insecurity; **la — urbana** the lack of safety in cities / the city

inseguro ADJ (personalidad) insecure; (vehículo) unsafe; (andar) unsteady; (computadora) vulnerable to hacking

inseminación F insemination

insensato-ta ADJ foolish; MF fool

insensibilizar[47] VT to desensitize

insensible ADJ (cruel) insensitive, callous; (imperturbable) unfeeling, thick-skinned; (entumecido) numb

inseparable ADJ inseparable

inserción F insertion

insertar VT to insert

inservible ADJ useless

insidioso ADJ insidious

insigne ADJ famous

insignia F insignia, badge

insignificante ADJ insignificant, unimportant

insincero ADJ insincere

insinuación F (sugerencia) insinuation; (comentario sexual) innuendo

insinuante ADJ suggestive

insinuar[26] VT to insinuate, to suggest; —se to insinuate oneself

insípido ADJ insipid, flavorless

insistencia F (machaconería, testarudez) insistence; (perseverancia) persistence

insistente ADJ (testarudo, repetitivo) insistent; (perseverante) persistent

insistir VI/VT (repetir) to insist; (perseverar) to persist; **— en** to insist on; **— sobre** to harp on

insolación F (por sol) sunstroke; (por calor) heatstroke

insolencia F (falta de respeto) insolence; (comentario) smart remark

insolente ADJ insolent, sassy

insólito ADJ (situación) unusual; (accidente) freak, freakish

insoluble ADJ insoluble

insolvente ADJ insolvent

insomne ADJ wakeful, unable to sleep

insomnio M insomnia

insoportable ADJ (persona, conducta) unbearable, impossible; (dolor) excruciating, unbearable

insospechado ADJ unsuspected

insostenible ADJ untenable

inspección F (revisación) inspection; (encuesta) canvass

inspeccionar VT to inspect, to survey

inspector-ora MF inspector

inspiración F (idea) inspiration; (inhalación) inhalation

inspirar VI/VT to inspire; VI to inhale, to breathe in

instalación F (de programas, fontanería) installation; (de aparatos electrónicos) setup; **instalaciones** fixtures

instalar VT (programas, fontanería) to install; (aparatos electrónicos) to set up; —se to take up residence

instancia LOC ADV **a —s de** at the request of

instantánea F snapshot

instantáneo ADJ instantaneous

instante M instant; **al —** right away

instar VT to enjoin

instauración F establishment

instigador-ra MF instigator

instigar[40] VT to instigate, to abet

instintivo ADJ instinctive

instinto M instinct; **— suicida** death wish

institución F institution; **— benéfica** charity

institucional ADJ institutional

instituir[19] VT to institute

instituto M (institución, agencia) institute; (escuela secundaria) high school

institutriz F governess

instrucción F instruction, schooling

instructivo ADJ instructive

instructor -ora MF instructor

instruir[19] VT to instruct, to school

instrumental ADJ instrumental

instrumentar VT (un plan) to implement; (música) to do the instrumentation for

instrumento M instrument; — **de cuerda** string instrument; — **de metal** brass instrument; — **de percusión** percussion instrument; — **de viento** wind instrument; —**s quirúrgicos** surgical instruments

insubordinado ADJ insubordinate

insuficiencia F (incapacidad) insufficiency; (falla de los órganos) failure; — **cardíaca congestiva** congestive heart failure; — **coronaria** coronary failure; — **renal** kidney failure, renal failure; — **respiratoria** respiratory failure

insuficiente ADJ insufficient, inadequate

insufrible ADJ insufferable

insulina F insulin

insulso ADJ bland

insultar VT to insult

insulto M insult, put-down

insuperable ADJ (resultado) insuperable; (obstáculo) insurmountable

insurgente ADJ & MF insurgent

insurrección F insurrection

insurrecto -ta ADJ rebellious; MF rebel

intachable ADJ blameless

intacto ADJ intact, unbroken

intangible ADJ intangible

integración F (de razas) integration; (de elementos) incorporation

integral ADJ (parte) integral; ADJ (harina) whole-grain

integrante F integral

integrar VT (crear) to form; (ser miembro de) to be a member of

integridad F integrity

íntegro ADJ (objeto) whole; (texto) unabridged; (comportamiento) upright

intelecto M intellect

intelectual ADJ & MF intellectual

inteligencia F intelligence (también militar); (persona) mind; — **artificial** artificial intelligence

inteligente ADJ intelligent, bright, smart

inteligible ADJ intelligible

intemperie LOC ADV **a la** — exposed to the weather

intención F intention, intent

intencional ADJ intentional

intendente MF (civil) administrator; (militar) quartermaster general

intensidad F intensity

intensificar[30] VT to intensify; —**se** (frío) to intensify; (violencia) to escalate

intensivo ADJ intensive

intenso ADJ (actividad) intense; (debate) fierce; (calor) severe

intentar VI/VT to try; VT to attempt

intento M (tentativa) try, attempt; (propósito) intention

interacción F interaction

interactivo ADJ interactive

interactuar[26] VI to interact

intercalación F insertion

intercalar VT to insert

intercambiador M interchange

intercambiar VI/VT to exchange

intercambio M exchange

interceder VI to intercede

interceptación F interception (también en fútbol americano)

interceptar VT intercept (también en fútbol americano)

intercesión F intercession

intercesor -ora MF advocate

interés M (intelectual, financiero) interest; (preocupación) concern; (participación comercial) stake; — **compuesto** compound interest; — **mutuo** mutual interest; **intereses ocultos** hidden agenda

interesado ADJ (atento) interested; (preocupado) concerned; (egoísta) self-serving

interesante ADJ interesting

interesar VT to interest; —**se por** to become interested in

interestatal ADJ interstate

interestelar ADJ interstellar

interface MF interface

interfaz MF interface; — **digital de instrumentos musicales** musical instrument digital interface

interferencia F (en los negocios ajenos) interference; (en una transmisión) interference, static; — **externa** outside interference

interferir[8] VT to jam; VI to interfere

interferón M interferon

ínterin M interim; **en el** — meanwhile

interino ADJ acting, interim

interior ADJ (habitación) inside; (mundo, vida) inner; (zona geográfica) inland; (mercado, comercio) domestic; M (parte) inside part, interior; **el** — **de la caja** the inside of the box; (de un país) the country, the provinces; **una ciudad del** — a provincial town

interiorizar[47] VT to internalize

interjección F interjection

interlineal ADJ interlinear

interlock M interlock

interlocutor -ora MF interlocutor

interludio M interlude

intermediario -ria M middleman; MF (mensajero) go-between; ADJ intermediary

intermediarista MF second baseman

intermedio -a ADJ intermediate; M intermission; **por — de** through; F (béisbol) second base

interminable ADJ interminable, unending, endless

intermitente ADJ intermittent; M turn signal

internación F inpatient care

internacional ADJ international

internado -da M (escuela) boarding school; (práctica) internship; MF (alumno) boarding student; (en un hospital) patient

internalizar[47] VT to internalize

internar VT (en una cárcel) to intern; (en un hospital) to admit, to hospitalize; (en un hospital psiquiátrico) to commit

internauta MF Internet user

internet M Internet, web; **— inalámbrico** wireless Internet; **— móvil** mobile Internet

internista MF internist

interno -na ADJ (correo) internal; (mercado) domestic; MF (persona que vive internada) inmate; (residente médico) intern

interpersonal ADJ interpersonal

interponer[56, 74] VT to interpose; **—se** to intervene

interpretación F (de un texto) interpretation; (artística) performance, rendition

interpretar VT (ideas) to interpret; (música) to perform; (intenciones) to construe

intérprete MF (traductor, explicador) interpreter; (músico) artist, performer

interracial ADJ interracial

interrelacionado ADJ interrelated

interrogación F interrogation

interrogador -ora MF questioner; ADJ questioning

interrogar[40] VI/VT (la policía) to interrogate; (con intensidad) to grill; (a un testigo) to question, to cross-examine

interrogativo ADJ interrogative

interrogatorio M interrogation, questioning

interrumpir VI/VT (cortar) to interrupt; VT (servicios) to cut off; (producción de un modelo) to discontinue; (en una conversación) to intrude, to cut in; (software) to abort

interrupción F interruption; (en una conversación) intrusion; (de producción) stoppage; (software) abort

interruptor M switch

intersección F intersection

intersticio M interstice

intervalo M (período) interval; (en el teatro) intermission, interlude

intervención F intervention; **— de teléfono** wiretap

intervendrá, intervendría, intervenga, intervengo ver intervenir

intervenir[61] VI to intervene; **— un teléfono** to wiretap

interventor -ora ADJ controlling, intervening; MF (en las elecciones) observer; (en lo fiscal) auditor

intervine, interviniendo, interviniera, interviniese ver intervenir

intervíu F interview

intestino ADJ & M intestine; **— delgado** small intestine; **— grueso** large intestine; **—s** bowels

intimar VI to become friendly

intimidad F intimacy

intimidar VT (una persona) to intimidate; (una tarea) to daunt

íntimo ADJ intimate, close

intitular VT to entitle; **—se** to be entitled

intolerable ADJ intolerable

intolerancia F intolerance, bigotry; **— a la lactosa** lactose intolerance

intolerante MF intolerant, narrow-minded

intoxicación F intoxication, poisoning; **— con plomo** lead poisoning; **— por alimentos** food poisoning

intoxicar[30] VT to poison, to intoxicate

intransigente ADJ intransigent, uncompromising

intransitivo ADJ intransitive

intravenoso ADJ IV [intravenous]

intrepidez F fearlessness

intrépido ADJ (sin miedo) intrepid, fearless; (aventurero) adventurous

intriga F intrigue

intrigante MF schemer; ADJ scheming

intrigar[40] VI/VT to intrigue, to scheme

intrincado ADJ intricate

intrínseco ADJ intrinsic

introducción F introduction

introducir[38] VT (incorporar) to introduce; (colocar) to put in, to insert

introduzca, introduzco ver introducir

introspección F introspection

introvertido -da ADJ introverted; MF introvert

intrusión F intrusion

intrusivo ADJ intrusive

intruso -sa ADJ intruding; MF intruder

intubación F intubation

intuición F intuition

intuir[19] VT to sense

intuitivo ADJ intuitive

inundación F flood

inundar VI/VT (de agua, de pedidos) to inundate, to flood; (de regalos) to shower

inusitado ADJ unusual

inútil ADJ (medida) useless, pointless; (esfuerzo) futile; (persona) worthless, good-for-nothing

inutilidad F uselessness; (de un esfuerzo) futility

inutilizar[47] VT to render useless, to put out of

commission

invadir VI/VT to invade

invalidar VT to render invalid

inválido -da ADJ (discapacitado) invalid; (nulo) void; MF invalid

invalorable ADJ priceless, invaluable

invariable ADJ invariable

invasión F invasion

invasivo ADJ invasive

invasor -ora MF invader; ADJ invading

invencible ADJ invincible

invención F invention (también mentira); (mental) construct

inventar VT (un dispositivo) to invent; (una historia) to fabricate, to make up

inventariar[28] VT to inventory

inventario M inventory

inventiva F ingenuity

inventivo ADJ inventive

invento M invention

inventor -ora MF inventor

invernadero M greenhouse, hothouse; **efecto — greenhouse** effect

invernal ADJ wintry

invernar[1] VI to winter

inverosímil ADJ unlikely, farfetched

inversión F (trasposición) inversion; (financiera) investment

inversionista MF investor

inverso ADJ inverse, reverse; **a la inversa** the other way around

inversor -ora MF investor

invertir[6] VT (dar vuelta) to invert, to reverse; VI/VT (dinero) to invest

investidura F inauguration, investment

investigación F (policial) investigation, inquiry; (científica) research

investigador -ora MF investigator; (científico) researcher

investigar[40] VI/VT (policía) to investigate, to look into; (científico) to research

investir[9] VI/VT to invest; **— de un cargo** to induct into office

invicto ADJ unbeaten

invierno M winter

invierta, invierte, invirtiendo, invirtiera, invirtiese, invirtió *ver* invertir

invisible ADJ (no visible) invisible; (oculto) unseen

invitación F invitation

invitado -da MF guest

invitar VI/VT to invite

invocación F invocation

invocar[30] VT (razones, argumentos) to invoke; (espíritus) to conjure

involucrar VT (implicar) to implicate; (consistir de) to involve

involuntario ADJ (automático) involuntary; (accidental) inadvertent

inyección F (en medicina) injection, shot; (en coches) fuel injection

inyectado ADJ **— de sangre** bloodshot

inyectar VT to inject

ion, ión M ion

ionizar[47] VT to ionize

ir[64] VI to go; **— a caballo** to ride horseback; **— a pie** to walk; **— [a] por** to fetch; **— aprendiendo** to learn gradually; **— corriendo** to run; **— de mal en peor** to go from bad to worse; **— en coche** to drive/ride in a car; **— tirando** to scrape along; **no me va ni me viene** it's all the same to me; **¿cómo te va?** how are you? **los platos no van aquí** the plates don't belong here; **¡vaya!** well now! **¡vaya a saber uno!** go figure! **¡vamos!** let's go! come on! **¡vaya hombre!** what a man! **¡ve a freír espárragos!** take a hike! **va por dos años que me casé** it's going on two years since I got married; **voy a comer** I'm going to eat; **va y se come un hongo venenoso** she goes and eats a poisonous mushroom; **en lo que va del año** since the beginning of the year; **ya van siete veces que me lo dice** that makes seven times that she's told me; **voy a ir de rojo** I'm going dressed in red; **para que no vayas a creer** lest you should think; **no vayas a caerte** don't fall; **¡qué va!** no way! **—se** to go away, to leave; **—se a la quiebra** to go broke; **—se a las manos** to come to blows; **—se a pique** to founder; **—se de vacaciones** to take a vacation

ira F ire, wrath

Irak M Iraq

Irán M Iran

iraní ADJ & MF Iranian

iraquí ADJ & MF Iraqi

irascible ADJ irascible, quick-tempered

iridiscente ADJ iridescent

iris M iris

Irlanda F Ireland

irlandés -esa MF Irish; ADJ Irish

IRM [imagen por resonancia magnética] F MRI

ironía F irony

irónico ADJ ironic, wry

irracional ADJ irrational, unreasonable

irradiar VT to radiate, to irradiate

irreal ADJ unreal

irreconocible ADJ unrecognizable

irrecuperable ADJ irretrievable

irreflexivo ADJ thoughtless

irrefutable ADJ irrefutable

irregular ADJ (situación) irregular; (borde, filo) ragged; (pulso) unsteady; (superficie) rough, uneven; (comportamiento) erratic, haphazard

irregularidad F irregularity

irremediable ADJ hopeless
irremplazable ADJ irreplaceable
irreparable ADJ irreparable
irreprochable ADJ irreproachable, flawless
irresistible ADJ irresistible
irrespetuoso ADJ disrespectful
irresponsabilidad F irresponsibility
irresponsable ADJ irresponsible
irreverente ADJ irreverent
irreversible ADJ irreversible
irrevocable ADJ irrevocable
irrigación F irrigation
irrigar[40] VI/VT to irrigate
irritable ADJ irritable
irritación F irritation
irritante ADJ (molesto) irritating, grating;
  (agresivo) abrasive
irritar VI/VT to irritate, to aggravate
irrumpir VI to burst into
isla F island, isle; **—s Fiyi** Fiji Islands; **—s**
  Malvinas Falkland Islands; **—s Marshall**
  Marshall Islands; **—s Salomón** Solomon
  Islands; **—s Vírgenes** Virgin Islands
islam, Islam M Islam
islámico ADJ Islamic
islamismo M Islam
islandés -esa MF Icelander; ADJ Icelandic
Islandia F Iceland
isleño -ña MF islander
isobara F isobar
isométrico ADJ isometric
isótopo M isotope
Israel M Israel
israelí ADJ & MF Israeli
istmo M isthmus
Italia F Italy
italiano -na ADJ & MF Italian
itálico ADJ italic; F **itálica** italics
ítem M item
itinerante ADJ itinerant
itinerario M itinerary
IVA [impuesto al valor añadido/agregado]
  M sales tax, VAT
izar[47] VT to hoist, to raise
izquierda F left (también política); (mano) left
  hand; **a la —** to the left
izquierdista ADJ & MF leftist
izquierdo ADJ left

Jj

jab M jab
jabalí M [wild] boar
jabalina F javelin
jabón M soap

jabonera F soap dish
jabonoso ADJ soapy
jaca F nag
jacinto M hyacinth
jactancia F boastfulness
jactancioso ADJ boastful, blustering
jactarse VI to boast, to brag
jacuzzi M Jacuzzi™, hot tub
jade M jade
jadear VI to pant, to gasp
jadeo M panting, gasping
jaez M harness
jaguar M jaguar
jalar VI/VT to pull, to tug
jalea F jelly
jaleo M (lío) mess; (barahúnda) ruckus
jam M jam session
Jamaica F Jamaica
jamaicano -na ADJ & MF Jamaican
jamaiquino -na ADJ & MF Jamaican
jamás ADV never
jamelgo M hack
jamón M ham
Japón M Japan
japonés -esa ADJ & MF Japanese
jaque M check; **— mate** checkmate; **tener a**
  uno en — fam to have someone by the short
  hairs
jaqueca F migraine
jarabe M syrup; **— de ipecacuana** ipecac syrup
jarana F revelry; **ir de —** to paint the town red
jarcia F rigging
jardín M (de flores) garden; (de césped) yard;
  (béisbol) outfield; **— de niños** kindergarten;
  — infantil nursery
jardinero -ra MF (de oficio) gardener; (en
  béisbol) outfielder
jarra F (cántaro) jug, pitcher; (taza) mug; **en —s**
  akimbo
jarro M pitcher, jug
jarrón M vase
jaspe M (piedra silícea) jasper; (mármol) veined
  marble
jaula F cage, coop
jauría F pack
jazmín M jasmine
jazz M jazz
jeans M PL jeans
jefatura F headquarters
jefe MF, **jefa** F (laboral) boss; (militar)
  commander; (departamental) chair, head;
  (policial) chief; **— del estado mayor** chief
  of staff; **— de departamento** department
  head
jején M gnat
jengibre M ginger
jerarquía F hierarchy
jerez M sherry
jerga F jargon, slang

jerigonza F (sinsentido) gibberish, gobbledygook; (juego lingüístico) pig Latin

jeringa F syringe

jeringar[40] VT to annoy

jeroglífico ADJ & M hieroglyphic

jersey M sweater

jesuita ADJ & M Jesuit

Jesús INTERJ God bless you! gesundheit!

jeta F (hocico) snout; (cara) mug

jet-set M jet set

jilguero M goldfinch

jinete M rider

jinetear VI to ride horseback

jingle M jingle

jirafa F giraffe

jobar INTERJ holy cow! holy Moses! holy mackerel!

jóckey M jockey

jocoso ADJ jocular

jofaina F basin

jogging M jogging

jolgorio M rumpus

jonrón M home run

Jordania F Jordan

jordano -na ADJ & MF Jordanian

jornada F (día laboral) workday; (coloquio) colloquium

jornal M daily wage

jornalero -ra MF day laborer

joroba F hump

jorobado -da ADJ & MF hunchback

jorobar VT (molestar) to hassle; (estropear) to gum up

jota F jay; **no saber ni —** to know zilch

joven ADJ young; MF young person

jovial ADJ jolly

joya F jewel; (persona apreciada) gem; **—s** jewelry

joyería F jewelry store, jeweler's

joyero -ra MF jeweler

joystick M joystick

juanete M bunion

jubilación F (retiro) retirement; (pagos) pension; **— anticipada** early retirement

jubilado ADJ retired; MF retiree

jubilar VT to pension, to retire; **—se** to retire

jubileo M jubilee

júbilo M glee

jubiloso ADJ jubilant, joyous

judaísmo M Judaism

judicial ADJ judicial

judío -ía ADJ Jewish; MF Jew; F bean; **judía blanca** navy bean; **judía pinta** pinto bean; **judía verde** green bean

juego M (actividad recreativa) play; (deporte) game; (conjunto de piezas) set; (muebles) suite; **— de apuestas** gambling; **— de damas** checkers; **— ofimático** office suite; **— de palabras** pun, play on words; **—s**

Olímpicos Olympic Games; **estar en —** to be at stake; **hacer —** to match

juerga F binge; **irse de —** to go on a binge, to party

juerguista MF merrymaker

jueves M Thursday

juez MF, **jueza** F (en un tribunal) judge; (en deportes) referee; **— de paz** justice of the peace; **— de línea** linesman; **— de silla** judge, umpire

jugada F play, move; **— de tres puntos** three-point play

jugador -ora MF (deportista) player; (apostador) gambler

jugar[43] VI to play; (apostar) to gamble; **— a la baraja / a los naipes** to play cards; **— con fuego** to play with fire; **— en casa** to play a home game; **— limpio** to play fair; **—se** to risk

jugarreta F bad turn

jugo M juice

jugoso ADJ juicy

juguete M plaything, toy

juguetear VI to toy with, to fiddle with

juguetón -ona ADJ playful

juicio M (criterio) judgment; (proceso) trial; **— por quiebra** bankruptcy proceedings; **perder el —** to lose one's mind; **a mi —** in my estimation

juicioso ADJ sensible, judicious

juke-box M jukebox

julio M July

jumbo ADJ jumbo; M jumbo jet

jumper M jumper

junco M (planta) rush, reed; (barco chino) junk

jungla F jungle

junio M June

junta F (reunión) meeting; (concejo) council; (juntura) joint; (pieza de motor) gasket; **— directiva** board of directors

juntar VT (tubos) to attach; (flores) to gather, to pick; (ganado) to round up, to wrangle; **— polvo** to gather dust; **— valor** to muster courage; **—se** (acumularse) to gather; (asociarse) to band together; (reunirse) to come together

junto ADJ together; LOC ADV **— a** next to; **— con** together with

juntura F (lugar) juncture; (articulación) joint

jurado -da MF (individuo) juror; M (grupo) jury

juramentar VI/VT to swear in; **—se** to be sworn in

juramento M oath; **— hipocrático** Hippocratic oath

jurar VI/VT to swear, to vow; **— en falso** to perjure oneself; **— la bandera** to pledge allegiance to the flag

jurídico ADJ legal

jurisdicción F jurisdiction

jurisprudencia F (doctrina) jurisprudence; (derecho) law

justa F joust, tilt

justamente ADV (exactamente) precisely; (con justicia) fairly

justicia F justice

justificación F justification

justificar[30] VT to justify

justo ADJ (ecuánime) just; (equitativo) equitable; (pío) righteous, upright; ADV exactly, right; **— después de** right after; **— en ese momento** exactly at that moment

juvenil ADJ (inmaduro) juvenile; (de apariencia joven) youthful

juventud F youth

juzgado M court

juzgar[40] VI/VT to judge, to pass judgment [on]; **— mal** to misjudge

Kk

kaki M khaki

kart M go-cart

kayak M kayak

Kazajstán M Kazakhstan

kazako -ka ADJ & MF Kazak[h]

Kenia F Kenya

keniata ADJ & MF Kenyan

kermés F bazaar

keroseno M kerosene

ketchup M catsup, ketchup

kg *ver* kilogramo

kilo M kilo

kilobyte M kilobyte

kilogramo M kilogram

kilometraje M mileage

kilómetro M kilometer

kilovatio M kilowatt; F **—-hora** kilowatt-hour

Kirguistán M Kyrgyzstan

Kiribati M Kiribati

kosher ADJ kosher

Kuwait M Kuwait

kuwaití ADJ & MF Kuwaiti

Ll

la ART DEF F the; **— del sombrero verde** the one with the green hat, that one with the green hat; PRON PERS it, her; PRON REL **— que** she who, the one that

laberinto M labyrinth, maze

labia F gift of gab

labial ADJ labial

labihendido N harelipped

labio M lip; **—s agrietados** chapped lips; **— leporino** cleft lip, harelip; **con — leporino** harelipped

labor F (trabajo) labor; (tarea) task; (manualidad) handiwork

laboral ADJ work-related; **legislación —** labor legislation

laboratorio M laboratory

laborioso ADJ (trabajoso) laborious; (trabajador) hardworking

laborterapia F occupational therapy

labrado ADJ carved

labrador -ora MF (persona) farmhand; M (perro) labrador

labranza F plowing

labrar VT to till; **—se una carrera** to carve out a career

laca F lacquer

lacar[30] VT to lacquer

lacayo M lackey, flunky

laciar VT *RP* to straighten

lacio ADJ straight

lacónico ADJ (persona) laconic; (comentario) terse

lacra F (física) scar; (moral) blight

lacre M sealing wax

lacrimógeno ADJ tear-producing

lactancia F lactation; **— materna** breast-feeding

lactar VT to nurse

lácteo ADJ (como la leche) milky; (hecho de leche) dairy

lactosa F lactose

LAD [lipoproteína de alta densidad] F HDL

ladeado ADJ (torcido) awry, askew; (asimétrico) lopsided

ladear VT (una superficie) to tilt; (la cabeza) to cock; (un avión) to bank; (ignorar) to snub, to ignore; **—se** to tilt, to lean

ladeo M tilt

ladera F hillside

ladilla F crab louse

ladillo M sidebar

ladino ADJ artful

lado M side; **— a —** side by side; **al —** nearby; **¡a un —!** gangway! **de —** sideways; **hacerse a un —** to move over

ladrar VI (perro) to bark; VI/VT (persona) to snap [at]

ladrido M bark, barking

ladrillo M brick

ladrón -ona MF (de casas) burglar; (con violencia) robber; (con astucia) thief; (de tiendas) shoplifter

lagartija F (animal) lizard; (ejercicio) push-up

lagarto M alligator; **— varano** monitor lizard

lago M lake

lágrima F tear, teardrop

lagrimear VI to weep

laguna F (de agua) lagoon; (de la memoria, conocimiento) gap; (legal) loophole

laico -ca MF layperson; ADJ lay

laja F slab

lamentable ADJ (desafortunado) lamentable, regrettable; (ruinoso) woeful

lamentablemente ADV unfortunately

lamentación F lamentation

lamentar VT (una acción) to lament, to regret; (una muerte) to grieve; —**se** to lament, to wail

lamento M lament, lamentation

lamer VT (pasar la lengua) to lick; (rozar) to lap

lamida F lick

lámina F (de vidrio, metal) sheet; (de metal) plate; (grabado) print

laminar VT to laminate

lámpara F lamp

lamparilla F night-light

lampiño ADJ (sin pelo) hairless; (sin barba) beardless

lana F wool; — **de acero** steel wool

lanar ADJ wool-bearing

lance M incident

lancear VT to lance, to spear

lanceta F lancet, lance

lancha F launch, boat; — **a motor** motorboat

langosta F (crustáceo) lobster; (insecto) locust

langostino M prawn

languidecer[35] VI to languish, to wilt

languidez F languor

lánguido ADJ languid, listless

lanilla F flannel

lanolina F lanolin

lanudo ADJ wooly, shaggy

lanza F lance, spear; **romper una — por alguien** to stick one's neck out for someone

lanzadera F shuttle

lanzador -ora MF (beisbol) pitcher

lanzamiento M (de un cohete, producto) launch; (de suministros) drop; (de una roca grande) heave; (de una pelota, en béisbol) pitch; (en tenis) toss

lanzar[47] VT (un cohete) to launch; (un producto) to launch, to roll out; (una pelota) to throw; (una bala) to fire; (algo pesado) to heave; (lodo) to sling; VI/VT (vomitar) to puke; —**se** to launch forth/out; — **un tiro libre** to shoot a free throw; M SG —**llamas** flamethrower

lanzazo M thrust with a lance

Laos M Laos

laosiano -na ADJ & MF Laotian

lápida F (piedra) stone tablet; (de sepultura) gravestone, tombstone

lapidar VT to stone

lapidario ADJ & M lapidary

lápiz M pencil; — **de color** crayon; — **de labios** lipstick

lapso M lapse, span

lapsus M lapse, slip of the tongue

laptop M laptop

laquear VT to lacquer

largar[40] VT (soltar) to cough up; —**se** fam to scram, to buzz off, to shove off

largo ADJ (camino, cuento) long; (discurso) lengthy; **de — alcance** long-range; **¡— de aquí!** scram! M —**metraje** feature film; **a la larga** in the long run; **a lo —** lengthwise; M length

larguero M crossbar

largueza F generosity

larguirucho ADJ lanky

largura F length

laringe F larynx

laringitis F laryngitis

larva F larva

láser M laser

lástima F pity; **¡qué —!** what a shame!

lastimadura F hurt

lastimar VT (herir) to hurt; (insultar) to hurt one's feelings; —**se** to get hurt

lastimoso ADJ pitiful

lastrar VT to ballast

lastre M ballast

lata F (envase) tin can, can; (con tapa) canister; (pesadez) bore; **dar la —** to be a nuisance

latente ADJ latent, dormant

lateral ADJ lateral, side

látex M latex

latido M (individual) beat, throb; (colectivo) beating; (del corazón) heartbeat

latifundio M large estate

latigazo M (golpe) lash; (chasquido) crack of a whip

látigo M whip

latín M Latin

latino -na ADJ (relativo a los hispanos) Latino; (relativo a la lengua latina) Latin; M Latino; F Latina

Latinoamérica F Latin America

latinoamericano ADJ Latin American

latir VI to beat, to throb

latitud F latitude (también flexibilidad)

latón M brass

latrocinio M larceny

laudable ADJ laudable

laurel M laurel; **dormirse sobre los —es** to rest on one's laurels

lava F lava

lavable ADJ washable

lavabo M (retrete) lavatory, toilet; (recipiente) sink

lavadero M laundry; — **automático** Laundromat™

lavado M wash, washing; — **de cerebro**

brainwashing; **— de dinero** money
laundering; **— en seco** dry cleaning
lavadora F washing machine
lavanda F lavender
lavandera F washerwoman
lavandería F laundry
lavar VI/VT to wash; (ropa) to launder; **—se** to
wash up; **—se las manos** to wash one's
hands; M SG **lavaplatos/lavavajillas**
dishwasher
lavativa F enema
lavatorio M washroom
laxante M laxative
laxitud F laxity
laxo ADJ lax
lazada F bowknot
lazar[47] VT to lasso
lazarillo M (persona) guide for the blind; (perro)
guide dog
lazo M (soga) lasso, rope; (vuelta) loop; (nudo
corredizo) noose; (relación) tie, bond
LBD [lipoproteína de baja densidad] F LDL
le PRON PERS **— dije** I told you/him/her; **— vi**
Esp I saw him/you; **se — murió el perro**
his/her dog died on him/her
leal ADJ loyal, trusty
lealtad F loyalty, allegiance; **— de marca** brand
loyalty
lección F lesson, assignment; **darle una — a
alguien** to teach someone a lesson
lechada F whitewash
leche F (de vaca) milk; **— desnatada** skim milk;
— en polvo powdered milk; **— entera**
whole milk; **— homogeneizada**
homogenized milk; **— malteada** malted
milk; **mala —** nasty disposition; **ir a toda —**
to barrel along; **ese tío es la —** that guy's a
case; **es un mala —** *fam* he's a nasty creep
lechería F dairy
lechero -ra ADJ dairy; M milkman; F milkmaid
lecho M bed (también de río)
lechón M suckling pig
lechoso ADJ milky
lechuga F lettuce
lechuza F screech owl, barn owl
lector -ora MF reader; **— de código de barras**
bar code reader; M **— de tarjetas** card reader
lectura F (acción) reading; (material) reading
matter
leer[18] VI/VT to read
legación F legation
legado M legacy, bequest
legajo M file
legal ADJ legal, lawful
legalidad F (conjunto de normas) law; (cualidad
de legal) legality
legalización F (de un documento)
authentication; (de una actividad)
legalization; **— de una validación**

testamentaria probate
legalizar[47] VT to legalize
legar[40] VT to will, to bequeath
legendario ADJ legendary
leggings M PL leggings
legible ADJ (descifrable) legible; (fácil de leer)
readable
legión F legion
legionario M legionnaire
legionelosis F legionnaire's disease
legislación F legislation
legislador -ora MF legislator, lawmaker
legislar VI/VT to legislate
legislativo ADJ legislative
legislatura F legislature
legitimidad F legitimacy
legítimo ADJ legitimate, lawful, rightful
lego -ga MF layperson; ADJ lay
legua F league
legumbre F legume
leído ADJ well-read
lejanía F distance
lejano ADJ (distancia) distant, faraway;
(parentesco) remote
lejía F (producto de limpieza) bleach; (de sosa)
lye
lejos ADV far away, far; **a lo —** in the distance; **—
de** far from; **desde —** from afar
lelo ADJ silly
lema M (frase típica) motto; (propaganda
política) slogan
lencería F lingerie
lengua F (órgano) tongue; (idioma) language; **—
materna** mother tongue
lenguado M sole
lenguaje M language (también en informática);
— compilador compiler language; **—
corporal** body language; **— [de] máquina**
machine language; **— de programación**
programming language; **— de signos** sign
language; **— ensamblador** assembly
language
lenguaraz ADJ gossipy
lengüeta F (de un instrumento de viento) reed;
(de un zapato) tongue
lengüetazo M lick
lentamente ADV slowly
lente MF lens; **— filtrador** filter lens; **—s**
eyeglasses; **—s de contacto** contact lenses;
—s negros/oscuros sunglasses, shades
lenteja F lentil
lentitud F slowness
lento ADJ (despacioso) slow; (tonto) dull;
(letárgico) sluggish; ADV slowly
leña F firewood
leñador -ora MF woodcutter, lumberjack
leñera F woodshed
leño M log
leñoso ADJ woody

león M lion; — **marino** sea lion
León M Leon
leona F lioness
leonés ADJ Leonese
leopardo M leopard
lepra F leprosy
lerdo ADJ slow
lesbiano -na ADJ lesbian; F lesbian
lesión F injury, lesion; — **ocular** eye injury
lesionar VT to injure; —**se** to get injured
Lesotho M Lesotho
letal ADJ lethal
letárgico ADJ lethargic
letargo M lethargy
letón -ona ADJ & MF Latvian
Letonia F Latvia
letra F (del alfabeto) letter; (caligrafía)
handwriting; (de una canción) lyrics, words;
— **bastardilla/cursiva** italics; — **chica**
fine print; — **de cambio** bill of exchange; —
de imprenta block letter; — **manuscrita**
longhand; **sin** —**s** uneducated
letrado ADJ learned, literate
letrero M sign
letrina F latrine
leucemia F leukemia
leudar VI to rise; VT to leaven
leva F (de tropas) levy; (de motor) cam
levadura F leaven, yeast
levantamiento M (revuelta) uprising;
(suspensión) suspension; — **de pesas**
weight-lifting
levantar VT (la mano) to raise; (una caja) to lift;
(un interruptor) to switch; (del piso) to pick
up; (perdices) to flush; (a un dormido) to
wake up, to rouse; (un edificio) to put up; —
el campamento to break camp; — **falso**
testimonio to bear false witness; — **la**
mesa to clear the table; — **la sesión** to
adjourn the meeting; — **vuelo** to take flight;
—**se** (de la cama) to get up, to rise, to arise;
(de una silla) to stand up, to get up; (un
edificio) to go up
levar VT — **anclas** to weigh anchor
leve ADJ (brisa) light; (resfrío) mild; (problema)
slight
levedad F (de una brisa) lightness; (de un resfrío)
mildness
levemente ADV lightly
léxico M lexicon, dictionary; ADJ lexical
lexicografía F lexicography
ley F law, statute; — **de prescripción** statute of
limitations; — **de [los] rendimientos**
decrecientes law of diminishing returns; —
marcial martial law; **de buena** — of good
quality
leyenda F (mitología) legend; (texto que
acompaña una figura) caption
leyendo, leyera, leyese, leyeron *ver* leer

liar[28] VT (paquetes) to bundle; (cigarros) to roll;
—**se** to get involved
libanés -esa ADJ & MF Lebanese
Líbano M Lebanon
libelo M libel
libélula F dragonfly
liberación F (de un país ocupado) liberation; (de
pecados) deliverance; (de presos) release
liberal ADJ & MF liberal
liberalidad F liberality
liberalismo M liberalism
liberalización F liberalization
liberar VT (de un deber) to relieve; (a un pueblo)
to liberate; (del sufrimiento) to deliver; (a un
preso) to free, to release
Liberia F Liberia
liberiano -na ADJ & MF Liberian
líbero M sweeper
libertad F liberty, freedom; — **condicional**
parole; — **de expresión** free speech; **poner**
en — to set free; **poner en** — **bajo fianza** to
let out on bail; **poner en** — **condicional** to
parole
libertador -ora MF liberator
libertar VT to liberate
libertinaje M licentiousness
libertino -na MF libertine
Libia F Libya
libidinoso ADJ libidinous
libido F libido
libio -bia ADJ & MF Libyan
libra F pound (también moneda)
librar VT (a un preso) to free, to set free; (de una
obligación) to release; (un cheque) to write;
(una letra de cambio) to draft; (una guerra) to
wage; —**se de** to get rid of
libre ADJ (persona) free; (asiento) vacant;
(camino) clear; (traducción) loose; (de una
obligación) exempt; — **albedrío** free will; —
cambio/comercio free trade; — **de cargos**
toll-free; — **de gravámenes** free and clear;
— **de intereses** interest-free; — **de**
impuestos duty-free, tax-free; — **de virus**
virus-free; — **pensador** freethinker
librería F bookstore
librero -ra MF bookseller
libresco ADJ bookish
libreta F small notebook; — **de direcciones**
address book
libreto M libretto
libro M book; — **de bolsa** pocket book; — **de**
cocina cookbook; — **de texto** textbook; —
electrónico e-book; — **en rústica**
paperback; — **mayor** ledger
licencia F (carnet de conducir, libertad poética)
license; (permiso) leave; (permiso para
ausentarse) leave of absence; — **de sitio** site
license; — **por maternidad** maternity leave
licenciado -da MF college graduate

licenciar VT to discharge; —**se** to graduate from college

licenciatura F bachelor's degree

licencioso ADJ licentious

liceo M high school

licitación F bid

lícito ADJ lawful, permissible

licor M liqueur, cordial

licuadora F blender

líder MF leader

liderar VT to head up

liderar VT to lead

liderazgo M (de una organización, condición de líder) leadership; (en una competencia) lead

lidiar VI/VT to contend, to grapple

liebre F hare; **levantar la** — to let the cat out of the bag

Liechtenstein M Liechtenstein

liechtensteiniano -na MF Liechtensteiner

lienzo M canvas

liftado M top spin

lifting M face-lift

liga F (alianza, grupo deportivo) league; (cinta elástica) garter; — **mayor** major league

ligado M slur

ligadura F ligature

ligamento M ligament

ligar[40] VT (atar) to bind; (conectar notas) to slur; VI (conquistar sexualmente) to score; —**se** to bind; —**se las trompas** to have one's tubes tied

ligeramente ADV lightly

ligereza F (de peso) lightness; (de temperamento) levity

ligero ADJ (poco pesado) light; (rápido) swift; (pequeño) slight; **a la ligera** lightly

liguero M garter belt

lija F sandpaper

lijar VI/VT to sandpaper, to sand

lila ADJ & MF lilac

lima F (fruta) lime; (árbol) lime tree; — **de uñas** nail file

limar VI/VT to file

limero M lime tree

limitación F (restricción) limitation; (defecto) shortcoming

limitar VT (restringir) to limit; (gastos) to curb; —**se a** to limit oneself to

límite M (restricción) limit; (de una región) boundary; (de la paciencia) bounds; — **de edad** age limit; — **de tiempo** time limit; — **de velocidad** speed limit

limítrofe ADJ bordering

limo M slime

limón M lemon

limonada F lemonade

limonero M lemon tree

limosna F alms, handout

limpiador M cleanser

limpiar VI/VT to clean; VT (una superficie) to wipe; (la piel) to cleanse; (un camino, una pantalla de computadora, la reputación) to clear; (animales) to dress; (zapatos) to shine; (un derrame) to mop up, to wipe up; (dejar sin dinero) to clean out; M SG

limpiaparabrisas windshield wiper; M SG

limpiavidrios squeegee

límpido ADJ limpid

limpieza F (pulcritud) cleanliness, neatness; (operación militar) mop-up; — **étnica** ethnic cleansing

limpio ADJ (casa) clean, neat; (piel, conciencia) clear; (juego) fair; (sin dinero) broke; **pasar en** — to make a clean copy

limusina F limousine

linaje M lineage, ancestry

linaza F linseed

lince M (animal) lynx; (persona astuta) sly fox; **con ojos de** — sharp-eyed

linchar VT to lynch

lindante ADJ neighboring

lindar VI to border, to adjoin

linde MF boundary

lindero ADJ adjoining; M boundary

lindo ADJ pretty; **un día** — a nice day; **de lo** — a lot

línea F (raya, cola) line; (en béisbol) line drive; — **aérea** airline; — **de banda** (fútbol) sideline; — **de conducta** course of action; — **de crédito** credit line; — **de fondo** baseline; — **de golpeo** line of scrimmage; — **de meta** goal line; — **de montaje** assembly line; — **ofensiva** offensive line; **batear una** — to line out; **en** — online

lineal ADJ linear

linfa F lymph

linfocito M lymphocyte

linfoma M lymphoma

lingüista MF linguist

lingüística F linguistics

lingüístico ADJ linguistic

linimento M liniment

lino M (tela) linen; (fibra) flax

linóleo M linoleum

linterna F (a pilas, de bolsillo) flashlight; (de un faro) lantern

lío M (bulto) bundle; (enredo, molestia) mess, hassle; (amorío) affair, fling; **armar un** — to raise a ruckus; **meterse en un** — to get oneself into a mess

liofilizar VI/VT to freeze-dry

liposucción F liposuction

liquidación F (ajuste de cuentas, de bienes) settlement, liquidation; (rebaja) sale, clearance sale; (pago completo) payment in full

liquidar VT (bienes, mercancías) to liquidate, to sell off; (una cuenta, herencia) to settle; (a una persona) *fam* to waste, to off, to whack

liquidez F liquidity

líquido ADJ & M liquid; **— amniótico** amniotic fluid

lira F (moneda) lira

lírica F lyric poetry

lírico ADJ lyric, lyrical

lirio M iris, lily; **— de los valles** lily of the valley

lirismo M lyricism

lisiado ADJ (descapacitado) handicapped; (lesionado) injured

lisiar VT to handicap

liso ADJ (neumático) bald; (camino) even, smooth; (terreno) flat; (pelo) straight; **azul — solid** blue

lisonja F flattery

lisonjear VI/VT to flatter

lisonjero -ra MF flatterer; ADJ flattering

lista F (de palabras) list; (de miembros) roster; (de alumnos) roll; (banda) stripe; (de precios) schedule, list; **— de control** checklist; **— de correo** mailing list; **— de espera** waiting list; **— negra** blacklist; **pasar —** to call the roll

listado ADJ striped; M listing, printout

listo ADJ (preparado) ready, set; (inteligente) clever, smart; **hacerse el —** to pull a stunt

listón M (tabla) board; (en salto de altura) crossbar

lisura F smoothness

litera F (cama en el tren, barco) berth; (cama superpuesta) bunk bed

literal ADJ literal

literario ADJ literary

literato -ta MF writer

literatura F literature

litigante MF litigant

litigio M (pleito) lawsuit; (acción de litigar) litigation

litio M lithium

litoral ADJ seaside; M seaboard, seacoast

litro M liter

Lituania F Lithuania

lituano -na ADJ & MF Lithuanian

liviano ADJ (leve) light; (promiscuo) promiscuous

lívido ADJ livid

living M living room

llaga F sore

llama F (fuego) flame; (animal) llama

llamada F (de teléfono, a la acción) call; (grito) hail; (nota al pie) footnote; **— de cobro revertido / por cobrar** collect call

llamado M (acción de convocar) call; (petición) appeal

llamador M knocker

llamamiento M (conversación) call; (exhortación) appeal; **hacer un —** to appeal

llamar VT (un nombre, una huelga, por teléfono) to call; (a la puerta) to knock; (gritar) to hail; **— la atención** to call attention; **me llamo Juan** my name is Juan

llamarada F blaze, flare

llamativo ADJ (impactante) striking, bold; (chabacano) gaudy, flashy

llameante ADJ flaming

llamear VI to flare, to flame

llana F trowel

llano ADJ (sencillo) plain; (liso) flat, smooth, level; (de poca profundidad) shallow; M plain

llanta F (reborde metálico) rim; (neumático) tire

llanto M crying, weeping

llanura F plain, prairie

llave F (para puertas) key; (de armas de fuego) lock; (en lucha libre) lock, hold; (grifo) faucet, tap; (interruptor) light switch; (de gas) cock; **— de tuercas** wrench; **— inglesa** pipe wrench; **— maestra** master key

llavero M key ring

llegada F arrival

llegar[40] VI (arribar) to arrive, to get there/here; (alcanzar) to reach; **— a las manos** to come to blows; **— a ser** to become; **— a un acuerdo** to strike a deal; **— a un arreglo** to cut a deal; **— tarde** to be late

llenar VT (un recipiente) to fill; (un formulario) to fill out; **— el tanque** to tank up, to gas up; **—se** to fill up; **—se de** to get filled with; **—se de oro** to make a killing

lleno ADJ full; **— de** full of; **de —** totally; M **un — completo** a full house

llevadero ADJ bearable

llevar VT (transportar) to carry, to take; (transportar en coche) to drive; (tener puesto) to wear; (contener) to hold; (inducir) to lead, to drive; **— a cabo** to carry out; **— la cuenta** to keep score; **— la ventaja** to have an advantage; **— los libros** to keep the books; **— un mes aquí** to have been here one month; **le llevo dos años a mi hermano** I'm two years older than my brother; **llevo las de perder** the odds are against me; **—se** to carry away, to take away; **—se bien con** to get along with

llorar VI (con ruido) to cry, to bawl; (con lágrimas) to weep; VT (una pérdida) to lament; (una muerte) to mourn

lloriquear VI to whimper

lloriqueo M whimper

llorón -ona ADJ weeping; MF crybaby, whiner

lloroso ADJ tearful, weeping

llovedizo ADJ **agua llovediza** rainwater

llover[6] VI/VT to rain; **— a cántaros** to rain cats and dogs; **llueva o truene** rain or shine

llovizna F drizzle

lloviznar VI to drizzle, to mist

lluvia F (precipitación) rain; (de preguntas,

críticas) barrage; (de protestas, flechas, piedras) volley; (de golpes, chispas) shower; **— ácida** acid rain; **— de ideas** brainstorming; **— torrencial** driving rain

lluvioso ADJ rainy

lo PRON PERS **— bueno** the good thing; **— de la protesta** the matter of the protest; **— que quiero** what I want; **sé — bueno que eres** I know how good you are; **yo — vi** I saw it/him/you

loable ADJ laudable, praiseworthy

loar VT to laud

lobato M wolf cub

lobbista, lobista MF lobbyist

lobby M lobby

lobezno M wolf cub

lobo M wolf

lobotomía F lobotomy

lóbrego ADJ gloomy

lóbulo M lobe

local ADJ local; M premises

localidad F (pueblo) town, locality; (en un teatro) seat

localización F location

localizar[47] VT (encontrar) to locate; (limitar) to localize

loción F lotion

loco -ca ADJ insane, mad, crazy; **— de remate** stark raving mad; MF lunatic, insane person; M madman

locomotora F locomotive, train engine

locuaz ADJ garrulous, loquacious

locura F madness, insanity

locutor -ora MF radio announcer

lodazal M quagmire

lodo M mud

lodoso ADJ muddy

logaritmo M logarithm

logia F lodge

lógica F logic

lógicamente ADV logically

lógico ADJ (razonado) logical; (bien fundado) sound

logística F logistics

lograr VT to achieve, to accomplish; **logré convencerle** I managed to / succeeded in convincing him

logro M (lo conseguido) accomplishment, achievement; (hazaña) feat

loma F knoll

lombriz F (de tierra) earthworm; (de estómago) tapeworm

lomo M (de animal) back ridge; (corte de carne) loin

lona F canvas

longaniza F cured sausage

longevidad F longevity

longevo ADJ long-lived

longitud F (distancia angular) longitude; (largo) length; **— de onda** wavelength

lonja F (mercado) commodity exchange; (tajada) slice of meat

loquería F fam booby hatch, funny farm

loquero -ra MF (psiquiatra) fam shrink; M (manicomio) fam funny farm

lord M lord

loro M parrot

losa F (lápida) slab; (baldosa) flagstone

lote M lot

lotería F lottery

loza F (basta) crockery; (fina) china

lozanía F freshness, bloom

lozano ADJ fresh, blooming

LSD MF LSD

lubina F bass

lubricante ADJ & M lubricant

lubricar[30] VI/VT to lubricate

lucero M morning star; **— del alba** morning star

lucha F (pugna, contienda) struggle; (pelea) fight; **— libre** wrestling

luchador -ora MF fighter; (en lucha libre) wrestler

luchar VI/VT (contra un enemigo) to fight; (con un problema) to struggle; (en lucha libre) to wrestle; **— por** to strive for

lucidez F lucidity

lúcido ADJ lucid, clear-headed

luciérnaga F firefly, glowworm

lucio M pike

lucir[39] VI (mostrarse) to look; (favorecer, sentar bien) to look good on, to suit; VT (llevar) to model, to sport; (alardear de) to flaunt; **—se** (sobresalir) to excel; (ostentar) to show off

lucrativo ADJ lucrative, profitable

lucro M **sin fines de —** not for profit

luctuoso ADJ sad, mournful, dismal

luego ADV afterward, then, next; **— de** after; **desde —** of course; **hasta —** so long

lugar M place; **— común** platitude; **— de nacimiento** birthplace, place of birth; **— de trabajo** workplace; **dar — a** to give rise to; **no hay —** there's no room; **en — de** instead of

lúgubre ADJ mournful, gloomy

lujo M luxury; **darse un —** to indulge oneself; **con — de detalles** in great detail

lujoso ADJ (ropa) luxurious; (hotel) plush

lujuria F lust

lujurioso ADJ lustful

lumbago M lumbago

lumbar ADJ lumbar

lumbre F (fuego) fire; (luz) light

luminosidad F brilliance, luminosity

luminoso ADJ luminous

luna F (satélite) moon; (espejo) large mirror; **— de miel** honeymoon; **estar en la —** to be distracted; **— llena** full moon

lunar ADJ lunar; M (en la piel) mole; (en una tela) polka dot
lunático -ca ADJ & MF lunatic
lunes M Monday
lupa F magnifying glass
lúpulo M hops
lupus M lupus
lustrar VT to shine, to polish
lustre M luster, shine
lustroso ADJ (revista) glossy; (pelo) shiny, sleek
luto M mourning
luxación F dislocation
Luxemburgo M Luxembourg
luxemburgués -esa MF Luxembourger; ADJ Luxembourgian
luz F light (también aparato); (del sol) sunshine; (abertura) aperture; — **trasera** taillight; — **verde** green light; **dar a** — to give birth; **sacar a** — to disclose

Mm

macabro ADJ grim
macanudo ADJ cool
Macao M Macao
macarrones M PL macaroni
Macedonia F Macedonia
macedonio -nia ADJ & MF Macedonian
maceta F flower pot
machacar[30] VT (aplastar) to pound, to crush; (insistir) to harp on; (en baloncesto) to dunk
machacón ADJ persistent
machetazo M hack with a machete
machete M machete
machismo M [male] chauvinism
macho M (animal masculino) male; (mulo) he-mule; (varón) man; (hombre muy varonil) he-man; — **cabrío** he-goat; — **y hembra** hook and eye; ADJ (masculino) male; (fuerte) strong; INTERJ man!
machote ADJ butch
machucar[30] VT to bruise
macilento ADJ pale
macizo ADJ massive; M plateau
Madagascar M Madagascar
madeja F skein
madera F wood (también en golf); (árboles maderables) timber; (para construcción) lumber; — **contrachapada** plywood; — **flotante** driftwood; — **noble** hardwood; —**s** woodwinds; **tocar** — to knock on wood
maderaje M woodwork
madero M trunk
madrastra F stepmother
madre F mother; — **de alquiler** surrogate

mother; — **patria** mother country; —**perla** mother-of-pearl; — **política** mother-in-law; —**selva** honeysuckle; **ciento y la** — everybody and their dog
madriguera F burrow, hole
madrileño -ña ADJ & MF [person] from Madrid
madrina F godmother
madrugada F early morning hours; **a las dos de la** — at two in the morning
madrugador -ra ADJ & MF early bird
madrugar VI to get up early; — **con gripe** to wake up with a cold
maduración F (animales, personas) maturation, maturing; (frutos) ripening; (vino) aging
madurar VI to mature, to grow up
madurez F (de persona) maturity; (de fruta) ripeness
maduro ADJ (persona) mature; (fruta) ripe
maestría F master's degree; — **en administración de empresas** master of business administration
maestro -tra MF (docente) [school]teacher; (artesano) master; (director) maestro
mafia F mafia
mafioso -sa MF mafioso
magia F magic
mágico ADJ magic, magical
magisterio M (actividad) teaching; (conjunto de los maestros) teachers; (profesión) teaching profession
magistrado -da MF magistrate
magistral ADJ masterful, masterly
magma M magma
magnánimo ADJ magnanimous
magnate MF magnate, tycoon
magnesia F magnesia
magnesio M magnesium
magnético ADJ magnetic
magnetismo M magnetism
magnetizar[47] VT to magnetize
magnificar[30] VT to magnify
magnificencia F magnificence
magnífico ADJ (palacio) magnificent; (día) glorious
magnitud F magnitude
magno ADJ great
magnolia F magnolia
magnolio M magnolia tree
mago M magician, wizard
magro ADJ lean
magulladura F bruise, contusion
magullar VI/VT (machucar) to bruise; (mutilar) to mangle
mahonesa F mayonnaise
maicena® F cornstarch
maíz M corn, maize
maizal M cornfield
majadería F stupidity

majadero ADJ stupid

majar VT to pound

majestad F majesty

majestuoso ADJ majestic, stately

majo ADJ (atractivo) good-looking; (agradable) charming

mal M (maldad) evil; (enfermedad) malady, affliction; (daño) harm; — **de altura** altitude sickness; — **de ojo** evil eye; ADV wrong, badly; — **aconsejado** misguided; — **adquirido** ill-gotten; — **hablado** foulmouthed; **hablar** — **de alguien** to speak ill of someone; **hacer** — to do wrong; **lo hice mal** I did it badly

malabarista MF juggler

malandanza F misfortune

malaria F malaria

Malasia F Malaysia

malasio -sia ADJ & MF Malaysian

Malawi M Malawi

malawiano -na ADJ & MF Malawian

malbaratar VT to undersell

malcontento ADJ discontented

malcriado ADJ spoiled

malcriar VT to spoil

maldad F evil, wickedness

maldecir[51] VI/VT to curse

maldición F curse

maldito ADJ accursed

Maldivas F PL Maldives

maldivo -va ADJ & MF Maldivian

maleable ADJ malleable

maleante MF gangster, hoodlum

malear VT to corrupt

maleducado ADJ ill-mannered, ill-bred

maleficio M evil spell

maléfico ADJ evil

malentendido M misunderstanding

malestar M (de estómago) upset; (físico) discomfort; (espiritual) malaise; (social) unrest

maleta F suitcase, bag; **hacer la** — to pack one's suitcase

maletero M car trunk

maletín M briefcase

malévolo ADJ (persona) malevolent; (comentario) snide

maleza F (en el monte) underbrush, scrub; (en un jardín) weeds

malformación F malformation

malgache ADJ & MF Madagascan

malgastar VI/VT to waste, to throw away

malgasto M waste

malhechor -ora MF evildoer, criminal

malhumorado ADJ grumpy, ill-humored

Mali, Malí M Mali

malí ADJ & MF Malian

malicia F malice

malicioso ADJ malicious, spiteful

malignidad F malignancy

maligno ADJ (persona) vicious, evil; (tumor) malignant

malinterpretar VI/VT to misunderstand

malla F (de armadura) mail; (de metal) mesh

malo ADJ bad; (calidad, letra) poor; (enfermo) ill; **mal estado** disrepair; **mal humor** bad mood; **mala fama** ill repute; **mala fe** bad faith; **mala hierba** weed; **mala pasada** bad turn; **mala racha** slump; **mala suerte** bad luck

malograr VT to spoil, to ruin; —**se** to fail, to miscarry

malpagar[40] VI/VT to underpay

malparto M miscarriage

malsano ADJ unhealthy, unwholesome

malta F malt

Malta F Malta

maltés -esa ADJ & MF Maltese

maltratar VT to mistreat, to abuse

maltrato M mistreatment, abuse

maltrecho ADJ battered

malvado ADJ wicked, evil

malvavisco M marshmallow

malversación F misuse, misappropriation

malversar VT to misuse, to embezzle

mamá F mama, mamma, mom

mamado ADJ drunk

mamar VI (un bebé) to suckle, to nurse; VI/VT to suck

mamario ADJ mammary

mamarracho M sight

mami F mommy

mamífero ADJ mammalian, mammal; M mammal

mamografía F mammography

mampara F partition

mamut M mammoth

manada F (de ballenas) pod; (de vacas) herd; (de lobos) pack

manantial M (naciente) spring; (fuente inagotable) wellspring

manar VI to stream out

mancha F (marca) stain, spot; (de tinta) blot; (cosa borrosa) blur; (aceitosa) smear, smudge; (menoscabo) tinge; (en la piel) blemish

manchado ADJ spotted

manchar VI/VT (ensuciar) to spot; (menoscabar) to stain, to blemish

manchón M large spot

mancilla F blemish

mancillar VT to defile, to sully

manco ADJ one-armed

mancuerna F dumbbell

mandado M errand

mandamás M *fam* big enchilada, big kahuna

mandamiento M commandment

mandante MF principal

mandar VI/VT (dar órdenes) to command, to

order; (enviar) to send; — **buscar a** to send
for; — **decir** to send word; **¿quién manda?**
who's in charge? —**se hacer un traje** to
have a suit made; **¿mande?** (hola) hello;
(perdón) excuse me? what?

mandarina F tangerine

mandatario -ria MF (mediante contrato) agent;
(abogado) attorney; (de estado) head of state

mandato M (orden) command, order; (cargo
político) term, mandate

mandíbula F (quijada) jaw; (hueso) jawbone

mandil M apron

mandioca F manioc

mando M (de un estado) rule; (de un aparato)
control; — **a distancia** remote control

mandolina F mandolin

mandón -ona ADJ bossy, domineering; MF
bossy person, control freak

mandonear VI/VT to domineer, to boss around

manea F hobble

manear VT to hobble

manecilla F clock hand

manejable ADJ manageable

manejar VT (un vehículo) to drive, to steer; (un
negocio) to run, to manage; (una máquina) to
operate

manejo M (de un negocio) running,
management; (de asuntos) handling; (de una
máquina) operation

manera F manner, way; **a — de** like; **de alguna
—** somehow; **de cualquier —** anyway; **de
ninguna —** on no account; **de — que** so that

manga F (de una camisa) sleeve; (de una nave)
beam; (de agua) hose; (tenis) set; — **de
viento** windsock; **en —s de camisa** in
shirtsleeves; **ser de — ancha** to be
broad-minded; **sacar algo de la —** to pull
something out of a hat

manganeso M manganese

mangle M mangrove

mango M (agarradera) handle, grip; (fruta,
árbol) mango

mangosta F mongoose

manguera F hose

manguito M muff

maní M peanut

manía F (moda, estado patológico) mania;
(hábito) bad habit; (tic) tic

maníaco -ca ADJ maniacal; MF maniac

maníaco-depresivo ADJ manic-depressive

maniatar VT to tie the hands; (manear) to
hobble

maniático ADJ (que tiene manías) crotchety;
(melindroso) fastidious

manicomio M *pey* insane asylum

manicura F manicure

manicurar VT to manicure

manido ADJ hackneyed

manifestación F (muestra) manifestation;
(protesta) demonstration

manifestante MF demonstrator

manifestar[1] VI/VT to manifest, to show;
(expresar) to air; (protestar en público) to
demonstrate; (declarar) to state

manifiesta, manifieste *ver* manifestar

manifiesto ADJ & M manifest; **poner de —** to
underscore; M (dogma) manifesto; — **de
vuelo** manifest

manija F handle

maniobra F (militar) maneuver; (para llamar la
atención) stunt; — **de Heimlich** Heimlich
maneuver

maniobrar VI/VT to maneuver

manipulación F (de la opinión pública)
manipulation; (de alimentos) handling

manipular VT (influir) to manipulate; (tocar
con las manos) to handle

maniquí M (muñeco) mannequin; MF (modelo)
model

manivela F crank

manjar M delicacy

mano F hand (también de naipes); (de pintura)
coat; (fútbol) handball; — **de obra** workforce; —**s a la obra** let's get to
work; —**s de mantequilla** butterfingers; **a
—** (presente) at hand; (con la mano) by hand;
a — armada at gunpoint; **dar una —** to lend
a hand; **dar una — de pintura** to put on a
coat of paint; **darle una — a alguien** to
lend someone a hand; **darse la —** (saludo) to
shake hands; (señal de afecto) to hold hands;
de primera — firsthand; **de segunda —**
secondhand; **estar a — con alguien** to be
even with someone; **hecho a —** handmade;
poner las —s en el fuego por alguien to
go out on a limb for someone; **quedar a —** to
break even; **se le fue la —** he got carried
away; **ser — to lead** [in a card game]; **tener
buena — con/para algo** to have a knack for
something; **tomarse de la —** to hold hands

manojo M (de monedas) handful; (de llaves)
bunch

manómetro M pressure gauge

manopla F (guante) mitten; (en béisbol) glove

manosear VT to feel, to finger

manoseo M feel, grope

manotazo M swat; **tirarle un — a alguien** to
take a swipe at someone

manotear VI to swat at

mansalva LOC ADV **a —** at will

mansedumbre F gentleness, meekness

mansión F mansion

manso ADJ (humilde) meek; (domesticado)
tame; (apacible) gentle

manta F (gruesa) blanket, cover; (liviana) throw

manteca F lard, shortening; *RP* butter; — **de
cacao** cocoa butter

mantecoso ADJ rich, buttery

mantel M tablecloth

mantendrá, mantendría *ver* mantener

mantener[58] VT (conservar, sostener) to maintain; (dejar prolongadamente) to keep; (alimentar, costear a alguien) to provide for; (apoyar a lo largo del tiempo) to sustain; **— a flote** to buoy up; **— el orden público** to keep the peace; **— en secreto** to keep under wraps; **— en suspenso** to keep in suspense; **— la calma** to remain calm; **—se** (quedarse) to remain; (ganarse la vida) to support oneself; **—se al corriente** to keep abreast; **—se al tanto** to stay informed; **—se en contacto** to keep in touch; **—se firme** to stand pat, to stick to one's guns

mantenga, mantengo *ver* mantener

mantenimiento M maintenance, upkeep

mantequera F (platillo) butter dish; (aparato para hacer mantequilla) churn

mantequilla F butter; **— de maní** peanut butter

mantiene, mantienes *ver* mantener

mantilla F mantilla

manto M mantle (también geológico); (de juez) robe

mantón M shawl

mantra M mantra

mantuve, mantuviera, mantuviese *ver* mantener

manual ADJ & M manual

manubrio M handlebar

manufactura F manufacture

manufacturar VT to manufacture

manufacturero -ra ADJ manufacturing; MF manufacturer

manuscrito ADJ written by hand; M manuscript

manutención F maintenance

manzana F (fruta) apple; (de ciudad) block; **— de la discordia** bone of contention

manzanar M apple orchard

manzano M apple tree

maña F (destreza) skill, knack; (artimaña) cunning

mañana F (división del día) morning; (futuro) tomorrow; ADV tomorrow; **— por la —** tomorrow morning

mañanero -ra MF early bird

mañoso ADJ tricky

mapa M map; **— de memoria** memory map; **— en relieve** relief map

mapache M raccoon

maple M maple

maqueta F mock-up

maquillaje M makeup

maquillar[se] VI/VT to put on makeup

máquina F (aparato) machine; (motor) engine; **— de búsqueda** search engine; **— de coser** sewing machine; **— de escribir** typewriter; **— de lavar** washing machine; **— de vapor** steam engine; **— expendedora** vending machine; **— fotográfica** camera

maquinación F scheming, plotting

maquinador -ora MF schemer

maquinal ADJ automatic

maquinar VI/VT to plot, to scheme

maquinaria F (aparato) machinery, apparatus; (del gobierno) machine

maquinilla F clipper; **— de afeitar** razor

maquinista M (de locomotora) locomotive engineer; (obrero) machinist

mar MF sea; **— de fondo** undercurrent; **llover a mares** to rain cats and dogs; **en alta —** on the high seas; **un — de cosas** a lot of things; **hacerse a la —** to put to sea

maraca F maraca

maraña F (de hilos) tangle, snarl; (de pelo) mat

marañón M cashew

maratón M marathon

maravilla F (portento) wonder, marvel; (flor) marigold; **a las mil —s** wonderfully

maravillar VT to amaze; **—se** to be amazed, to marvel

maravilloso ADJ marvelous, wonderful

marca F (récord) record; (de ganado) brand; (de producto) brand, brand name, label; (de coche) make; **— comercial** name brand; **— de nacimiento** birthmark; **— de fábrica** trademark; **— genérica** generic brand; **— registrada** registered trademark; **de —** name-brand

marcadamente ADV sharply

marcado ADJ (acento) thick; (contraste) sharp, stark; (descenso) steep; (parecido) strong

marcador M (lapicero) marker; (en deporte) scoreboard; **— de libros** bookmark; **— genético** genetic marker; **¿cómo va el —?** what's the score?

marcar[30] VT (una respuesta) to mark; (ganado) to brand; (el ritmo) to beat; (la hora) to say; (un tanto) to score; (medida) to read, to show; (un número telefónico) to dial; **— para seleccionar** to highlight; **— un gol** to score a goal

marcha F (caminata, pieza musical) march; (partida) leaving; (progreso) course; (modo de andar) gait; (cambio en un coche) gear; (animación) nightlife; **— atrás** reverse; **ponerse en —** to get going; **puesta en —** beginning; **sobre la —** as you go

marchante MF (vendedor) art dealer; (cliente) customer

marchar VI (soldado) to march; (máquina, vehículo) to run; **—se** to go away

marchista MF walker

marchitar VT to wither; **—se** to wither, to shrivel up

marchito ADJ withered, shriveled up

marcial ADJ martial

marco M (de un cuadro, de una puerta, de referencia) frame; (moneda) mark

marea F tide; **— baja** low tide; **— alta** high tide

mareado ADJ (en un barco) seasick; (en un coche) carsick; (de alegría) giddy; (con vértigo) dizzy, lightheaded

marear VT (dar vértigo) to make dizzy; (en un barco) to make seasick; **—se** (tener vértigo) to get dizzy; (en un barco) to get seasick

marejada F tidal wave

maremoto M tidal wave

mareo M (en un barco) seasickness; (en un vehículo) motion sickness; (vértigo) dizziness

marfil M ivory

marfileño -ña ADJ & MF Ivorian

margarina F margarine

margarita F daisy; **echar —s a los cerdos** to cast pearls before swine

margen M (de un papel) margin; (de la sociedad) fringe; MF (de un río) bank; **— de error** margin of error; **— de ganancia** profit margin, markup; **— de seguridad** margin of safety; **al —** on the outside

marginación F (de un grupo) marginalization; (de un individuo) isolation; **hay cierta — entre entre los colegas** there is a certain distance among the colleagues; **la — de ciertos grupos minoritarios** the marginalization of certain minorities

marginado -da ADJ & MF outcast

marginal ADJ marginal

marginar VT to marginalize

mariachi M mariachi

marido M husband

mariguana, marihuana F marijuana; *fam* pot

marimba F marimba

marina F navy; **— mercante** merchant marine

marinar VT to marinate

marinero -ra ADJ (buque) seaworthy; (nación) seafaring; MF sailor

marino -na ADJ marine; MF sailor; (oficial) naval officer

marioneta F marionette

mariposa F (insecto) butterfly (también en natación); (tuerca) wing nut; **— nocturna** moth

mariquita F ladybug

mariscal M marshal; **— de campo** (militar) field marshal; (fútbol americano) quarterback

mariscos M PL shellfish

marítimo ADJ maritime

marketing M marketing

marmita F pot

mármol M marble

marmóreo ADJ marble

marmota F groundhog

maroma F rope

marqués M marquis

marquesa F marquise

marrano M hog

marrón ADJ brown

marroquí ADJ & MF Moroccan

Marruecos M Morocco

marshalés -esa ADJ & MF Marshallese

marsopa F porpoise

martes M Tuesday

martillar VI/VT to hammer

martillo M hammer (también hueso del oído, pieza de revólver); (de juez) gavel; **— neumático** jackhammer

martinete M (martillo grande) pile driver; (pieza de piano) piano hammer

martini M martini

mártir MF martyr

martirio M martyrdom

martirizar[47] VT to martyr, to torment

marxismo M Marxism

marzo M March

mas CONJ but

más ADJ more; PREP plus; ADV more; (más tiempo) longer; **— allá de** beyond; **— bien** rather; **— de tres** more than three; **— o menos** more or less; **— que nada** primarily; **— que nunca** more than ever; **— que tú** more than you; **a lo —** at best; **a — tardar** at the latest; **de —** extra; **el — allá** the hereafter; **es de lo — simpático** he's really nice; **es —** furthermore; **está de —** it is superfluous; **otro —** yet another; **por — que** no matter how much; **y — todavía** and then some

masa F mass; (de agua) body; (de harina) batter; (para amasar) dough; **en —** en masse, in large numbers; **las —s** the masses; **— de hojaldre** puff pastry

masacrar VT to massacre, to slaughter

masacre M massacre

masaje M massage

masajear VT to massage

masajista M masseur; F masseuse

mascar[30] VI/VT (chicle) to chew; (con ruido) to crunch

máscara F mask; **— de gas** gas mask

mascarada F masquerade

mascota F (animal doméstico) pet; (emblema de un equipo) mascot

masculino ADJ (como un hombre, género gramatical) masculine; (del hombre) male

mascullar VI/VT to mumble

masilla F putty

masivo ADJ massive

masón M mason

masonería F masonry

masoquismo M masochism

mastectomía F mastectomy

máster M master; **— en administración de empresas** master of business administration

masticar[30] VT to chew

mástil M (en un barco) mast; (para una bandera) flagpole, flagstaff

mastín M mastiff

masturbarse VI to masturbate

mata F bush; — **de pelo** head of hair

matadero M slaughterhouse

matador ADJ horrendous; M bullfighter

matanza F slaughter, killing

matar VT to kill; (animales) to butcher, to slaughter; — **a tiros** to gun down; — **de hambre** to starve; VT **matasellar** to cancel a stamp; M SG **matamoscas** flyswatter; M SG **matasellos** postmark; M SG **matasanos** quack [doctor]

mate M (en ajedrez) checkmate; (planta, bebida) mate; ADJ (pintura) flat; **hacer un —** (baloncesto) to dunk the ball

matemática, matemáticas F mathematics

matemático -ca ADJ mathematical; (exacto) precise; MF mathematician

materia F (sustancia) matter; (tema de estudio) school subject; (tema) topic; — **extraña** extraneous matter; — **fecal** fecal matter; — **gris** gray matter; — **prima** raw material

material ADJ (necesidades) material; (autor) real; M material

materialismo M materialism

maternal ADJ (instinto) maternal; (amor) motherly

maternidad F (relacionado con el nacimiento) maternity; (estado de ser madre) motherhood

materno ADJ maternal

matiné M matinee

matiz M (de un color) tint, shade, hue; (de ironía) tinge; (de sentido) nuance

matizar[47] VT (mezclar colores) to blend, to tinge; (moderar) to qualify

matón -ona MF (persona que intimida a los pequeños) bully; (pandillero, peleador) thug

matorral M (mata) thicket; (región) bush

matraz M flask

matriarca F matriarch

matrícula F (alumnado) enrollment, matriculation; (de un coche) registration; (placa) license plate; (costo de la universidad) tuition fees

matriculación F matriculation

matricular VT to matriculate, to enroll

matrilineal ADJ matrilineal

matrimonial ADJ marital

matrimonio M (estado civil) matrimony, marriage; (pareja) married couple

matriz F (en matemáticas) matrix; (bidimensional) array; (útero) womb; (plantilla) stencil; **casa —** main office

matrona ADJ frumpy, matronly; F matron

matutino ADJ of the morning

maullar VI to mew

maullido M mew

mauriciano -na ADJ & MF Mauritian

Mauricio M Mauritius

Mauritania F Mauritania

mauritano -na MF Mauritanian

maxilar M jawbone

máxima F maxim

maximizar VT to maximize

máximo ADJ & M maximum; (autoridad) ultimate; (cuidado) utmost; — **histórico** all-time high

maya ADJ & MF Maya, Mayan

mayo M (mes) May; (palo) maypole

mayonesa F mayonnaise

mayor ADJ (de tamaño) greater, larger; (de edad) older, elder; (rango, clave) major; **al por —** wholesale; **dedo —** middle finger; **el — número de votos** the most votes; M (adulto) adult

mayoral M boss

mayordomo M butler

mayoreo M wholesale

mayoría F majority; — **de edad** legal age, majority; **en su —** largely

mayorista MF wholesale dealer

mayoritario ADJ majority

mayúsculo -la ADJ (letra) capital; (problema) major; F capital letter

mazmorra F dungeon

mazo M mallet

mazorca F (con maíz) ear of corn; (sin maíz) corncob

me PRON PERS **él — vio** he saw me; **él — habló** he talked to me; **se — murió el perro** my dog died on me

mecánico -ca ADJ mechanical; MF mechanic; F mechanics

mecanismo M mechanism; — **de seguridad** safety device

mecanografía F typewriting

mecanografiar[28] VI/VT to type

mecanógrafo -fa MF typist

mecedora F rocking chair, rocker

mecenas MF SG/PL patron, sponsor

mecenazgo M patronage

mecer[32] VI/VT (cuna) to rock; (columpio) to swing

mecha F (de una vela) wick; (de explosivos) fuse; (de pelo) lock; —**s** (en el pelo) highlights

mechar VT (rellenar con tocino) to lard; (robar) to shoplift

mechero -ra MF shoplifter; M burner; — **Bunsen** Bunsen burner

mechón M lock, strand

medalla F medal

médano M dune

media F (hasta el muslo) stocking; (hasta la cintura) pantyhose; (calcetín) sock; (promedio) mean; M PL (medios de comunicación) media

mediación F mediation
mediador -ora MF mediator
mediados LOC ADV **a — de mayo** in mid-May
mediana F median
mediano ADJ (intermedio en tamaño) medium; (intermedio en calidad) average; **de tamaño — middle-sized; de mediana edad** middle-aged
medianoche F midnight
mediante PREP by means of
mediar VI (en un asunto) to mediate, to intervene; (tiempo) to intervene; **mediaba febrero** it was mid-February
medible ADJ measurable
medicación F medication
medicamento M medicine, drug
medicar VT to medicate; **—se** to self-medicate
medicina F medicine; **— defensiva** defensive medicine; **— familiar** family practice
medición F (de una cantidad) measurement; (de un terreno) survey
médico -ca MF doctor, physician; **— forense** coroner, medical examiner; **— general** general practitioner; **— tratante** attending physician; ADJ medical
medida F (dimensión) measure; (acto de medir) measurement; **— cautelar** restraining order; **— para áridos** dry measure; **a — que** as; **en la — en que** to the extent that; **hacer a la —** to make to measure; **hecho a la —** made-to-measure; **tomar —s** to take measures; **tomarle las —s a alguien** to measure someone
medidor M gauge, meter
medieval ADJ medieval
medio ADJ (la mitad) half; **— pastel** half a cake; (promedio) average; **el ciudadano —** the average man; **—día** (hora) noon, midday; (hora de comer) lunch hour, noon hour; (punto cardinal) south; (territorio) the south; **— hermano** half-brother; **a media asta** at half-mast; **a — camino** halfway; **clase media** middle class; **el americano —** the average American; **media hora** half an hour; **mi media naranja** my better half; **temperatura media** mean temperature; **— tiempo** (fútbol) halftime; **de — tiempo** part-time; **media volea** (tenis) half-volley; **hacer una cosa a medias** to do something halfway; **ir a medias** to go halves; M (centro) middle; (ambiente) medium; **—s** means, resources; **— ambiente** environment; **—s de comunicación** media; **— de transporte** means of transport; **en [el] — de** in the middle of; **en — de la calle** in the middle of the street; **meterse de por —** to intervene; **por — de** by means of; **por todos los —s** by all possible means; ADV half; **a — derretir** half-melted

medioambiental ADJ environmental
mediocre ADJ mediocre; (actuación) lackluster
mediocridad F mediocrity
medir[9] VI/VT to measure; VT (consecuencias) to gauge; (terreno) to survey; **— a pasos** to step off; **—se** to be moderate
meditación F meditation
meditar VI to meditate, to ponder
mediterráneo ADJ Mediterranean
médium MF medium, psychic
medroso ADJ fearful
médula F marrow, pith; **— espinal** spinal cord; **— ósea** bone marrow
medusa F jellyfish, man-of-war
megabyte M megabyte
megáfono M megaphone
megahercio, megahertz M megahertz
megalomanía F megalomania
mejilla F cheek
mejor ADJ better; **el — the** best; **en el — de los casos** at best; **te deseo lo —** I wish you the best; ADV better; **a lo —** maybe; **tanto —** so much the better
mejora F improvement
mejoramiento M improvement
mejorar VT to improve, to improve upon; (software, aparato) to upgrade; (las posibilidades de uno) to better; VI (ventas) to pick up; **—se** to get better/well
mejoría F improvement
melancolía F melancholy, gloom
melancólico ADJ melancholy, gloomy
melanoma M melanoma
melaza F molasses
melena F mane
melindre M affectation
melindroso ADJ affected, finicky
mella F notch; **hacer —** to make a dent
mellar VT to notch
mellizo -za ADJ & MF twin
melocotón M peach
melocotonero M peach tree
melodía F melody
melódico ADJ (agradable al oído) melodious; (relativo a la melodía) melodic
melodioso ADJ melodious
melodrama M melodrama
melómano -na ADJ music-loving; MF music lover
melón M melon, cantaloupe
membrana F (en un órgano) membrane; (en las patas de los patos) web
membrete M letterhead
membrillo M (fruta) quince; (árbol) quince tree
membrudo ADJ stout
memorable ADJ memorable
memorándum M memorandum
memoria F (facultad de recordar, recuerdo) memory; (obra autobiográfica) memoir;

(actas) proceedings; — **de acceso directo** random access memory [RAM]; — **de caché** cache memory; — **de ROM** read-only memory; — **de sólo lectura** read-only memory [ROM]; — **expandida** expanded memory; — **intermedia** buffer; — **residente** internal memory; **de** — by heart; **hacer** — to try to remember/recollect

memorial M memorial

memorizar[47] VI/VT to memorize

mención F mention

mencionar VT to mention

mendigar[40] VI to beg

mendigo-ga MF beggar

mendrugo M large crumb

menear VT (las caderas) to wiggle, to wriggle, to shake; (la cola) to wag

meneo M (de las caderas) wiggle; (de la cola) wag

menesteroso ADJ needy, destitute

mengua F diminution, waning

menguante ADJ waning

menguar[25] VI (luna) to wane; (energía) to flag; (provisiones) to dwindle

meningitis F meningitis

menjurje M concoction

menopausia F menopause

menor ADJ (de tamaño) smaller; (de cantidad) lesser, smaller; (de edad) younger; (de importancia, en música) minor; **el** — (de tamaño) the smallest; (de cantidad) the least, the smallest; (de edad) the youngest; MF — **de edad** minor; **al por** — retail

menos ADV (no contables) less; (contables) fewer; — **de** less than, fewer than; — **de lo que se esperaba** less than expected, fewer than expected; — **mal** just as well; **a** — **que** unless; **al** — at least; **dar de** — to shortchange; **echar de** — to miss; **lo** — the least; **no es para** — there is good reason; **por lo** — at least; **signo de** — minus sign; **venir a** — to decline; **el que trabaja** — the one who works the least; **no puede** — **que hacerlo** he cannot help doing it; **tienes** — **que yo** you have less than I; **trabaja** — **que yo** she works less than I; PREP (salvo) except, but; **las cinco** — **cuarto** quarter to five; ADJ & PRON less, least; — **agua** less water; — **problemas** fewer problems; M minus

menoscabar VT to impair, to undermine

menoscabo M impairment

menospreciar VI/VT (despreciar) to despise; VT (burlarse de) to belittle, to demean

menosprecio M contempt

mensaje M message; — **de error** error message; — **de texto** text message

mensajería F carrier; — **instantánea** instant messaging

mensajero-ra MF messenger, courier

menstruación F menstruation

menstruar VI to menstruate

mensual ADJ monthly

mensualidad F (recibida) monthly allowance; (pagada) monthly installment

mensuario ADJ monthly

mensurable ADJ measurable

menta F mint, peppermint; — **verde** spearmint

mental ADJ mental

mentalidad F mentality

mente F mind

mentecato-ta ADJ foolish, simple; MF simpleton

mentir[8] VI to lie

mentira F lie, falsehood

mentirilla F fib, white lie

mentiroso-sa ADJ lying; MF liar

mentón M chin

mentor-ora MF mentor

menú M menu (también de computadoras); — **abatible** pull-down menu; — **del día** daily special; — **de inicio** start menu; — **emergente** pop-up menu

menudeo LOC ADV **al** — retail

menudo ADJ (pequeño) small; (insignificante) insignificant; **a** — often, frequently; **dinero** — small change; — **perro** that's some dog; M (entrañas) entrails

meñique ADJ & M little finger, *fam* pinkie; **dedo** — little finger

meollo M (médula) marrow; (parte sustancial de un asunto) marrow, pith, core; (seso) brain

mequetrefe M runt, pipsqueak

mercachifle M peddler, huckster

mercadear VT to market

mercadeo M merchandising; — **de nicho** niche marketing

mercader M merchant

mercadería F merchandise

mercado M market, marketplace; — **alcista** bull market; — **bajista** bear market; — **de divisas** currency exchange; — **de prueba** test market; — **de pulgas** flea market; — **de valores** stock market; — **extrabursátil** aftermarket; — **libre** free market; — **negro** black market; — **secundario** aftermarket

mercadotecnia F marketing

mercancía F merchandise, goods

mercante ADJ merchant

mercantil ADJ mercantile

merced LOC ADV — **a** thanks to; **a [la]** — **de** at the mercy of

mercenario-ria ADJ & MF mercenary

mercería F notions store

mercurio M mercury, quicksilver

merecedor ADJ deserving

merecer[35] VT to deserve, to merit

merecido M deserved punishment, due

merendar[1] VI to have a snack

merendero M picnic area

merezca, merezco *ver* merecer

meridiano ADJ & M meridian

meridional ADJ southern; MF southerner

merienda F afternoon snack

mérito M merit

meritorio ADJ meritorious, worthy

merluza F hake

merma F decrease

mermar VI/VT to decrease, to dwindle

mermelada F (de fresa, pera) jam; (de cítricos) marmalade

mero ADJ mere; **la mera idea** the very idea; M grouper

merodear VI to loiter

mes M month

mesa F (mueble) table; (consejo) board; (formación geológica) mesa; **— de noche** nightstand; **levantar la —** to clear the table; **poner la —** to set the table

mesada F monthly allowance

mesero -ra M waiter; F waitress

meseta F plateau

mesón M inn, lodge

mesonero -ra MF innkeeper

mestizo -za ADJ (perros) mongrel; MF (mezcla de europeo e india) mestizo; (perro de raza mezclada) mongrel

mesura F moderation

mesurado ADJ (persona, opinión) moderate; (respuesta) measured

meta F (objetivo) goal; (en una carrera) finish line

metabólico ADJ metabolic

metabolismo M metabolism

metafísica F metaphysics

metafísico ADJ metaphysical

metáfora F metaphor

metafórico ADJ metaphorical

metal M metal; **— precioso** precious metal

metálico ADJ metallic; M cash

metalurgia F metallurgy

metamorfosis F metamorphosis

metano M methane

metástasis F metastasis

metastatizar VI to metastasize

meteorito M meteorite

meteoro M meteor

meteorología F meteorology

meteorológico ADJ meteorological; **parte —** weather report

meteorólogo -ga M weatherman; F weatherwoman

meter VT (en una bolsa) to put [into], to stick [into]; (un lío) to force [into]; (invertir) to invest; **— el estómago** to suck in one's stomach; **— la pata** to make a mistake; **— miedo** to scare; **— ruido** to make noise; **— un gol** to score a goal; **—se** to meddle; **—se a bailar** to begin to dance; **—se con** to mess

with; **—se en camisa de once varas** to get oneself into a fix

metódico ADJ methodical

método M method

metodología F methodology

metralleta F portable machine gun

métrico ADJ metric

metro M (medida, ritmo poético) meter; (cinta de medir) measuring tape; (tren subterráneo) subway, metro

metrónomo M metronome

metrópoli F metropolis

metropolitano ADJ metropolitan; M subway

mexicano -na ADJ & MF Mexican

México M Mexico

mezcla F (de ingredientes) mixture, mix; (en albañilería) mortar; (de café, especias) blend

mezclador -ora MF (persona) mixer; F (aparato) mixer

mezclar VT (ingredientes) to mix, to blend; (naipes) to shuffle; (números) to scramble; **—se** (combinarse) to mix; (tener trato con) to mingle; (entrometerse) to meddle

mezcolanza F hodgepodge

mezquindad F (crueldad) meanness; (tacañería) stinginess

mezquino ADJ (cruel) mean, mean-spirited, petty; (insignificante) small, petty; (tacaño) tight, stingy

mezquita F mosque

mi ADJ POS my

mí PRON PERS me; **es para —** it's for me; **me vio a —** he saw me; **me la dio a —** he gave it to me

miau M meow

mico M long-tailed monkey

micra F micron

micro M (autobús) bus; (micrófono) microphone

microbio M microbe, germ

microbiología F microbiology

microcirugía F microsurgery

microcomputadora F microcomputer

microeconomía F microeconomics

microficha F microfiche

microfilm M microfilm

micrófono M microphone

Micronesia F Micronesia

micronesio -sia ADJ & MF Micronesian

microonda F microwave; M SG **—s** microwave oven

microordenador M microcomputer

microorganismo M microorganism

microprocesador M microprocessor

microscópico ADJ microscopic

microscopio M microscope; **— electrónico** electron microscope

mida, mide, midiendo, midiera, midiese *ver* medir

miedo M fear; **— al escenario** stage fright;

tener — to be afraid

miedoso ADJ fearful

miel F honey

miembro M (integrante) member; (extremidad) limb

mienta, miente ver mentir

mientras CONJ (durante) while, as; (siempre y cuando) as long as; — **que** while; — **tanto** meanwhile; ADV in the meantime

miércoles M Wednesday

mies F grain; —**es** fields of grain

miga F crumb; **hacer buenas** —**s** to get along well

migaja F crumb

migración F migration

migrante ADJ migrant

migraña F migraine

migrar VI to migrate

migratorio ADJ migratory

mil NUM thousand; — **millones** billion; **llegamos a las** — **y quinientas** we got there very late

milagro M miracle, wonder

milagroso ADJ miraculous

milano M kite

milenio M millennium

milicia F militia

miligramo M milligram

mililitro M milliliter

milímetro M millimeter

militancia F (actitud) militance; (actitud) militancy

militante ADJ & MF militant

militar ADJ military; MF soldier; VI to militate

milla F mile

millaje M mileage

millar M thousand

millón M million

millonario-ria MF millionaire

millonésimo ADJ & M millionth

mimar VT to pamper, to spoil, to coddle

mimbre M wicker

mímico ADJ mimic; F mimicry

mimo M (trato cariñoso) caressing, cuddling; MF (actor) mime

mimoso ADJ cuddly

mina F (yacimiento) mine; (explosivo) [land] mine; (de un lápiz) lead; (fuente) storehouse

minado M mining

minar VT (sembrar minas) to mine; (socavar) to undermine; VI (cavar) to burrow

mineral M mineral; (de oro) ore; ADJ mineral

minería F mining

minero-ra MF miner; ADJ mining

mingitorio M urinal

miniatura F miniature

mini-break M (tenis) mini-break

minicomputadora F minicomputer

minifalda F miniskirt

minifundio M subsistence farm

minimizar[47] VT (gastos) to minimize; (a una persona) to belittle; VI (un incidente) to play down

mínimo ADJ (cantidad) least; (tamaño) smallest; M minimum; **como** — at least; **en lo más** — at all

minino M kitty

miniordenador M minicomputer

ministerial ADJ cabinet, ministerial

ministerio M (religioso) ministry; (gubernamental) ministry, department

ministro-tra MF minister, secretary; — **de justicia** attorney general

minoría F minority

minoridad F minority

minorista MF retailer

minoritario ADJ minority

mintiendo, mintiera, mintiese, mintió ver mentir

minucioso ADJ (detalle) minute; (trabajo) thorough; (persona) fastidious

minúsculo ADJ (tamaño) small, minuscule; (cantidad) negligible; **letra minúscula** lowercase letter

minusvalía F disability

minusválido-da ADJ disabled; MF disabled person

minutas F (honorarios) lawyers' fees; (actas) minutes

minutero M minute hand

minuto M minute

mío ADJ & PRON mine; **este libro es** — this book is mine; **un amigo** — a friend of mine

miope ADJ shortsighted, nearsighted

miopía F nearsightedness, myopia

mira F (dispositivo de arma) gun sight; (intención) intention; **con** —**s a** with a view to

mirada F gaze, look; — **asesina** dirty look; — **de soslayo** side glance; — **fija** stare

mirador M vantage point, overlook

miramiento M consideration

mirar VI/VT to look [at]; (un partido, televisión) to watch; — **de soslayo** to look askance [at]; — **fijamente** to stare [at]; ¡**mira [tú]**! you don't say!

miríada F myriad

mirilla F peephole

mirlo M blackbird

mirón M (curioso) onlooker; (erótico) voyeur

mirto M myrtle

misa F mass

misantropía F misanthropy

misántropo-pa MF misanthrope

misceláneo ADJ miscellaneous

miserable ADJ (vil, pobre) wretched, unhappy; (insignificante) paltry; (tacaño) miserly

miseria F (desgracia) misery; (pobreza) poverty,

squalor; (cantidad despreciable) trifle

misericordia F mercy

misericordioso ADJ merciful, gracious

mísero ADJ miserable

misil M missile; **— balístico** ballistic missile; **— crucero** cruise missile

misión F mission (también religiosa)

misionero -ra MF missionary

mismo ADJ same; **ese — día** that very day; **se nombró a sí —** he named himself; **lo —** the same thing; **me da lo —** it's all the same to me; **yo —** I myself

misoginia F misogyny

misterio M mystery

misterioso ADJ mysterious

místico -ca ADJ mystical; MF mystic

mitad F half; **por la —** in half; **en la — de** in the middle of; **a — de[l] camino** midway

mítico ADJ mythic, mythical

mitigar[40] VT to mitigate

mitin M political meeting

mito M myth

mitocondria F mitochondria

mitología F mythology

mitológico ADJ mythological

mixto ADJ mixed; **escuela mixta** coed school

mobiliario M furniture

mocasín M (zapatilla, culebra) moccasin; (zapato sin cordones) loafer

mochar VT to chop off

mochila F backpack, knapsack

moción F motion

moco M (interno) mucus

moda F fashion; **de —** fashionable, in style; **ponerse de —** to catch on

modales M PL manners

modalidad F form, variant; **ganó oro en la — de espalda** she won gold in the backstroke; **la — italiana es más conocida** the Italian form is better known

Moldavia F Moldova

modelar VI/VT to model

modelo ADJ & MF model

módem M modem

moderación F moderation, restraint

moderado -da ADJ (posición política) moderate; (invierno) mild; (precio) reasonable; (respuesta) measured; (clima) temperate; MF moderate

moderar VT (restringir) to moderate, to restrain; (presidir) to moderate

modernidad F (actualidad) modern age; (actualidad) modern world

modernismo M (cualidad de moderno) modernity, modernness; (tendencia artística) modernism

modernización F modernization

moderno ADJ modern

modestia F modesty

modesto ADJ modest

módico ADJ moderate, reasonable

modificación F modification

modificar[30] VT to modify

modismo M idiom

modista MF dressmaker

modo M (manera) mode, manner, way; (categoría gramatical) mood; (de computadora/ordenador) mode; **— a prueba de fallos/errores** safe mode; **— de ahorro** power-save mode; **— de dormir** sleep mode; **— de entrega** mode of delivery; **— de reescritura** overwrite mode; **a — de** by way of; **del mismo —** in like manner, similarly; **de ningún —** by no means; **de — que** so that; **de otro —** otherwise; **de ningún —** not at all; **de todos —s** anyway; **en cierto —** in a way; **ni —** no dice; **no hay —** no way

modorra F drowsiness

modulación F modulation

modular VT to modulate

módulo M (componente) module; (unidad) unit

mofa F jeer, ridicule

mofarse VI **— de** to make fun of, to scoff at

mofeta F skunk

moflete M fat cheek, jowl

mohair M mohair

mohín M grimace

moho M mold, mildew

mohoso ADJ moldy

mojado -da ADJ wet

mojadura F wetting

mojar VT (humedecer) to wet; (sumergir) to dip; **—se** to get wet

mojigatería F prudery

mojigato -ta ADJ prudish; MF prude

mojo M dip

mojón M landmark

molar ADJ molar

moldavo -va ADJ & MF Moldovan

molde M (norma) mold, cast; (tortera) cake pan; (patrón) pattern; (de imprenta) die; **letras de — block** letters

moldeado M molding

moldear VT to mold, to cast

moldura F molding

mole F mass

molécula F molecule

molecular ADJ molecular

moler[6] VI/VT to mill, to grind; **— a palos** to beat thoroughly

molestar VT to bother, to pester; **no te molestes** don't bother

molestia F bother, nuisance; **no te tomes la —** don't go to the trouble

molesto ADJ (que molesta) bothersome, irksome; (que está molesto) uneasy, uncomfortable

molibdeno M molybdenum

molienda F grinding
molinero -ra MF miller
molinete M (puerta) turnstile; (juguete) pinwheel
molinillo M mill, grinder
molino M mill; **— de viento** windmill
mollete M muffin
molusco M mollusk
momentáneo ADJ momentary
momento M (tiempo) moment; (impulso) momentum; **al —** immediately; **a cada —** continually; **en todo —** all the time; **no veo el —** I can't wait
momia F mummy
Mónaco M Monaco
monada F (acción graciosa) antic; (persona atractiva) *fam* peach
monarca MF monarch
monarquía F monarchy
monárquico -ca MF monarchist; ADJ monarchical
monasterio M monastery
mondar VT to pare; **—se los dientes** to pick one's teeth; M SG **mondadientes** toothpick
moneda F (dinero metálico) coin; (divisa) currency; **— corriente** common currency; **— de curso legal** legal tender; **— falsa** counterfeit money
monegasco -ca ADJ & MF Monegasque
monería F antic
monetario ADJ monetary
mongol -la ADJ & MF Mongolian
Mongolia F Mongolia
mongoloide ADJ mongoloid
monigote M puppet
monitor -ora M (aparato) monitor; **— [a] color** color monitor; MF (persona) monitor
monitorear VT to monitor
monitoreo M monitoring
monitorización F monitoring; **— fetal** fetal monitoring
monja F nun
monje M monk
mono -na MF (simio) monkey; **— araña** spider monkey; M (mimo) mimic; (prenda de trabajo) overalls, coverall; (síndrome de abstinencia) withdrawal symptoms; **dormir la mona** to sleep it off; ADJ cute
monogamia F monogamy
monokini M topless swimsuit
monólogo M monologue, monolog
mononucleosis F mononucleosis
monopatín M (tabla) skateboard; (con manillar) scooter; (de nieve) snowboard
monopolio M monopoly
monopolizar[47] VT (un producto) to monopolize; (un mercado) to corner
monotonía F monotony
monótono ADJ monotonous

monseñor M monsignor
monserga F nonsense
monstruo M (ser imaginario, persona perversa) monster; (persona grotesca) freak; ADJ INV monstrous
monstruosidad F monstrosity
monstruoso ADJ monstrous
monta F mount; **de poca —** of little value
montaje M (de un aparato) assembly, set up; (de una película) editing
montante M (total) total; (ventana de puerta) transom; (columna) upright
montaña F mountain; **— rusa** roller coaster
montañés -esa ADJ mountain; MF mountain dweller
montañismo M mountaineering
montañoso ADJ mountainous
montar VT (ir a caballo, en bicicleta) to ride; (un aparato) to assemble; (una película) to edit; (subirse al caballo) to mount, to get on; **— en cólera** to fly into a rage; **— una escena** to make a scene; **—se a caballo** to mount a horse
montaraz ADJ coarse
monte M (montaña) mount; (zona agreste) wilderness; **— de piedad** pawnshop
montés ADJ (salvaje) wild; (de la montaña) of the mountains
montículo M mound; (béisbol) pitcher's mound
monto M amount; **— debido** amount due; **— pagado** amount paid
montón M (pila) pile, heap; (de papel) stack; (de nieve) drift; (de flores) basketful; (de gente) bunch; **a montones** in abundance; **del —** run-of-the-mill
montura F (animal) mount; (silla) saddle; (armazón de gafas) frame, rim
monumental ADJ monumental
monumento M monument
moño M (de pelo) bun; (adorno) bow
mopa F mop
moquearse VI to become snotty
moquillo M distemper
MOR [movimentos oculares rápidos] M PL REM
mora F (fruta) blackberry, mulberry; (tardanza) delay, delinquency; **en —** in default, past due
morada F dwelling, abode
morado ADJ purple; **ojo —** black eye
morador -ora MF dweller
moral ADJ moral; F (principios éticos) morals; (estado de ánimo) morale; M mulberry tree
moraleja F moral
moralidad F morality
moralista MF moralist
moralizar[47] VI/VT to moralize
morar VI to dwell, to abide
mórbido ADJ morbid
morbilidad F (predisposición a la enfermadad)

morbidity

morbosidad F (que produce enfermedad) morbidity

morboso ADJ (mórbido) morbid; (atractivo) sexy

morcilla F blood sausage

mordacidad F sharpness

mordaz ADJ (comentario) cutting, sharp; (persona) sharp-tongued

mordaza F (de la boca) gag; (de un torno) vise jaw

mordedor ADJ biting, snappy

mordedura F bite

morder[6] VI/VT to bite; **—se la lengua** to bite one's tongue

mordida F (mordisco) bite; (soborno) bribe, kickback

mordiscar[30] VI/VT to nibble; to nip

mordisco M nibble, nip

mordisquear VI/VT to nip; to nibble

mordisqueo M nibble

moreno ADJ (piel) dark, dark-skinned, swarthy; (pelo) dark, brunette

moretón M bruise

morfina F morphine

morgue F morgue

moribundo ADJ dying, moribund

morir[7, 74] VI (persona, animal) to die; (calle) to end; **—se de envidia** to eat one's heart out; **—se de hambre** to starve; **—se de miedo** to die of fear; **—se de risa** to die laughing; **—se por algo** to crave something; **—se por alguien** to be crazy about someone

morisco ADJ Moorish

moro -ra ADJ Moorish; MF Moor; **—s y cristianos** (personas) Moors and Christians; (plato) beans and rice; **no hay —s en la costa** the coast is clear

morocho ADJ dark-haired, brunet, brunette

moroso ADJ delinquent, deadbeat

morrear VI to make out

morriña F homesickness

morro M (monte) knoll; (caradura) gall, nerve; (de un avión) nose; (de animal) snout

morrón M bell pepper

morsa F walrus

mortaja F shroud

mortal ADJ mortal, deadly; MF mortal

mortalidad F mortality

mortandad F death toll

mortecino ADJ fading

mortero M mortar

mortífero ADJ deadly

mortificación F mortification, chagrin

mortificar[30] VT to mortify, to chagrin

mortuorio ADJ mortuary; **casa mortuaria** funeral home

mosaico M mosaic

mosca F (insecto) fly; (dinero) dough; **—**

muerta hypocrite; **no se oía volar una —** you could have heard a pin drop

mosquear VT (crear desconfianza) to cause distrust; (hacer enfadar) to enrage; **—se** (desconfiar) to distrust; (enfadarse) to become enraged

mosquitero M (pantalla de ventana) window screen; (red) mosquito net

mosquito M mosquito

mostacho M mustache, moustache

mostaza F mustard

mostrador M counter

mostrar[5] VT to show; **—se reticente** to appear reticent

mostrenco ADJ stray

mota F speck, speckle

mote M nickname

moteado ADJ speckled, spotted

motear VT to speck, to speckle

motejar VI **— de** to brand as

motel M motel

motín M (en un barco) mutiny; (de prisioneros) riot

motivación F motivation

motivar VT (impulsar) to motivate; (causar) to cause

motivo M (causa) motive, reason; (figura repetida) motif, theme; **con — de** on the occasion of

moto F bike, motorcycle

motocicleta F motorcycle

motociclista MF biker, motorcyclist

motor ADJ of motion; M motor, engine; **— de reacción** jet engine; **— de búsqueda** search engine; **— de combustión interna** internal combustion engine; **— fuera de borda** outboard engine

motriz ADJ **fuerza —** motive power

movedizo ADJ restless

mover[6] VT to move; **— palancas** to pull strings; **—se** to move, to budge

movible ADJ movable

movido ADJ (vida, fiesta) eventful; (foto) blurred; **— por gas** powered by gas

móvil M (motivo) motive; (teléfono) mobile telephone; (adorno, juguete) mobile; ADJ (que se mueve) mobile; (que puede ser movido) movable; **un blanco —** a moving target

movilidad F mobility

movilización F mobilization

movilizar[47] VI/VT to mobilize

movimiento M (cambio de posición) movement, motion; (organización, pieza de reloj) movement; (comercial) traffic; **—s oculares rápidos** REM [rapid eye movements]; **los rojos tienen poco —** the red ones don't sell well; **un cuerpo en —** a moving body

Mozambique M Mozambique

mozambiqueño -ña ADJ & MF Mozambican

mozárabe ADJ Mozarabic

mozo -za ADJ young; **en mis años —s** in my youth; M (joven) young man; (sirviente) servant; F (joven) young woman; (sirvienta) servant; **— de cordel** porter; **buen —** handsome man

mucama F chambermaid

muchacho -cha M boy, youngster; F (chica) girl; (de servicio) maid

muchedumbre F crowd, throng

mucho ADJ a lot of; (cosas contables) many; (cosas incontables, en oraciones interrogativas y/o negativas) much; **¿tienes — tiempo?** do you have much time? **no tenemos — tiempo** we don't have much time; **tenemos —s problemas** we have many problems; ADV much; (demasiado) too much; **hace — que no lo veo** I haven't seen him for a long time; **ni con —** not by a long shot; **ni — menos** not by any means; **por — que** no matter how much; PRON a lot, many; (en preguntas y oraciones negativas) much; **¿había —s?** were there many?

mucoso ADJ mucous

muda F (de ropa, voz) change; (de plumas, piel de serpiente) molt

mudable ADJ fickle

mudanza F move

mudar VT (condiciones, clima) to change; (el pelo) to shed; (la piel, plumas) to molt; **—se [de casa]** to move [house]; **—se de ropa** to change clothes

mudez F dumbness, muteness

mudo -da ADJ (incapaz de hablar) mute, dumb; (por emoción) speechless; (película) silent; MF mute

mueble M piece of furniture; **—s** furniture

mueblería F (tienda) furniture store; (fábrica) furniture factory

mueca F grimace; **hacer —s** to grimace

muela F (diente) molar tooth; (piedra) grindstone; **— del juicio** wisdom tooth; **— impactada** impacted molar

muelle M (para embarcaciones) wharf, pier; (resorte) spring; **— en espiral** coil; **— real** mainspring

muera, muere ver morir

muérdago M mistletoe

muerte F death; **— cerebral** brain death; **— súbita** (fútbol) sudden death; (tenis) tie-break; **dar —** to kill; **sus clases son la —** his classes are unbearable; **de mala —** disreputable

muerto ADJ dead, lifeless; **— de cansancio** dead tired; **— de hambre** famished; **estoy — de sed** I'm parched; **echarle el — a uno** to pass the buck; **ni — not** in a million years

muerto ver morir

muesca F notch, indentation

muestra F (ejemplo) sample (también en computadoras); (señal) sign, token; **— de orina** urine specimen; **dar —s de impaciencia** to show impatience

muestra, muestre ver mostrar

muestrear VT to sample (también para computadoras)

muestreo M sampling

mueva, mueve ver mover

mugido M moo, lowing

mugir[46] VI to moo, to low

mugre F dirt, grime, crud

mugriento ADJ grimy, dirty

mujer F (género) woman; (esposa) wife; **— de negocios** businesswoman; **— de la vida** prostitute

mujeriego ADJ womanizing; M womanizer, *fam* player

mula ver mulo

mulato -ta ADJ & MF mulatto

muleta F crutch

muletilla F cliché

mullido ADJ fluffy

mullir[16] VT to fluff

mulo -la MF mule (también en el tráfico de drogas)

multa F fine, penalty; (de tránsito) ticket

multar VT to fine; (en tránsito) to ticket

multianual ADJ multiyear

multicultural ADJ multicultural

multilateral ADJ multilateral

multimedia M & ADJ INV multimedia

multipantalla ADJ multiscreen

múltiple ADJ multiple

multiplicación F multiplication

multiplicar[30] VI/VT to multiply; **—se** to breed

multiplicidad F multiplicity

múltiplo M multiple

multitarea F multitasking

multitud F multitude, throng

mundano ADJ mundane, worldly

mundial ADJ global, worldwide; **la guerra —** the world war

mundo M world; **todo el —** everybody; **tener — to** be worldly; **el tercer —** the third world; **el — al revés** the world upside-down

munición F ammunition, munition

municipal ADJ municipal; **servicios —es** city services

municipalidad F municipality

municipio M municipality; (ayuntamiento) city hall

muñeca F (juguete) doll; (articulación del brazo) wrist; **— de trapo** ragdoll

muñeco M (juguete) boy doll; (de ventrílocuo) dummy; **— de nieve** snowman

muñón M stump

mural ADJ & M mural
muralla F wall
murciélago M bat
muriendo, muriera, muriese *ver* morir
murmullo M (voz baja) murmur; (ruido de agua) babble
murmuración F gossip
murmurar VI/VT (voz) to murmur; VI (agua) to babble
muro M wall; **— de contención** retaining wall
murria F the blues; **tener —** to have the blues
musa F muse
musaraña F shrew
muscular ADJ muscular
músculo M muscle
musculoso ADJ muscular
muselina F muslin
museo M museum
musgo M moss
musgoso ADJ mossy
música F music; **— de cámara** chamber music; **— folclórica** folk music; **— incidental** incidental music
musical ADJ & M musical
músico -ca ADJ musical; MF musician
musitar VI to mutter
muslo M thigh
mustio ADJ (triste) sad, humble; (marchito) limp; (deslucido) faded
musulmán -ana ADJ & MF Muslim, Moslem
mutación F mutation
mutante ADJ & MF mutant
mutilar VT to mutilate, to mangle; (a un ser vivo) to maim, to mutilate; (una estatua) to deface
mutuo ADJ mutual
muy ADV very; **estás — grande para eso** you're too big for that
Myanmar M Myanmar

Nn

nabo M turnip
nácar M mother-of-pearl
nacarado ADJ pearly
nacer[35] VI (un bebé) to be born; (una calle) to begin; **— de** (río) to spring from; **— de nuevo** to have a new lease on life
naciente ADJ (tendencia) incipient; (sol) rising; M (de río) origin
nacimiento M (alumbramiento) birth; (pesebre) nativity scene; (naciente) origin [of a river]; **— del pelo** hairline
nación F nation
nacional ADJ & MF national

nacionalidad F nationality
nacionalismo M nationalism
nacionalista ADJ & MF nationalist
nacionalizar[47] VT to nationalize
nada PRON nothing; *fam* squat, zilch; **— del otro mundo** nothing special; **— en absoluto** nothing at all; **como si —** as if nothing had happened; **de —** you are welcome, don't mention it; **no es por —, pero** I hope you don't mind my saying this, but; **no sirve para —** it's useless; **no tener — que ver con** to have nothing to do with; **no tengo — de dinero** I don't have any money; **para —** in the least; **quedar en la —** to fall through; **salir de la —** to come out of nowhere; ADV not at all; **no me gusta [para] —** I don't like it at all; (tenis) **quince a —** forty love; F (existencial) nothingness
nadador -ora MF swimmer
nadar VI/VT to swim; **— en la abundancia** to be in the lap of luxury
nadería F trifle, nothing
nadie PRON nobody; **— más** no one else; **no vi a — en el parque** I didn't see anyone in the park; **un don —** a nobody
nafta F gasoline
nailon M nylon
naipe M playing card
nalgada F smack on the bottom
nalgas F PL buttocks
Namibia F Namibia
namibio -bia ADJ & MF Namibian
nana F (canción de cuna) lullaby; (lastimadura) boo-boo; (niñera) babysitter
nanosegundo M nanosecond
nanotecnología F nanotechnology
napalm M napalm
napias F PL *fam* snout
naranja F (fruta) orange; ADJ INV & M (color) orange; **— de ombligo** navel orange; **mi media —** my better half
naranjal M orange grove
naranjo M orange tree
narcisismo M narcissism
narciso M narcissus, daffodil
narcolepsia F narcolepsy
narcótico ADJ & M narcotic
narcotizar[47] VT to drug
narcotraficante MF drug trafficker
narcotráfico M drug trafficking
nariz F nose; **— chata** pug nose; **sonarse la —** to blow one's nose; F PL **narices** nostrils; **se dio de narices contra la ventana** he bumped his nose on the window; **estoy hasta las narices** I've had it up to here
narración F narration
narrador -ora MF narrator
narrar VT to narrate, to recount
narrativa F narrative

narrativo ADJ narrative

NASA F NASA

nasal ADJ nasal

nata F skin of boiled milk; *Esp* cream

natación F swimming

natal ADJ (relativo al nacimiento) natal; (suelo) native; **mi ciudad —** my hometown

natalidad F birth rate

natilla[s] F SG/PL custard

nativo-va ADJ & MF native

nato ADJ **es un músico —** he's a born musician

natural ADJ (no artificial) natural; (nacido en un lugar) native; (nacido fuera del matrimonio) illegitimate; (sin afectación) unaffected; M nature; **al —** unprocessed

naturaleza F nature; **— muerta** still life

naturalidad F naturalness

naturalista MF naturalist

naturalización F naturalization

naturalizar[47] VT to naturalize; **-se** to become naturalized

naturalmente ADV (de forma natural) naturally; (desde luego) of course

naufragar[40] VI (un barco) to shipwreck; (una empresa) to fail

naufragio M shipwreck

náufrago-ga MF shipwrecked person

Nauru M Nauru

nauruano-na ADJ & MF Nauruan

náusea F nausea; **—s** morning sickness; **dar —s** to nauseate; **hasta la —** ad nauseam; **tener —s** to be nauseated, to be sick to one's stomach

nauseabundo ADJ nauseating

nauseoso ADJ (que siente náuseas) nauseous, queasy; (que provoca náuseas) nauseating

náutica F navigation

náutico ADJ nautical

navaja F (de explorador) jackknife, pocketknife; (de barbero) razor

navajazo M (golpe) stab with a jackknife; (herida) stab wound

naval ADJ naval

navarro ADJ & MF Navarrese

nave F (embarcación) vessel; (parte de una catedral) nave; **— espacial** spaceship

navegable ADJ navigable

navegación F (de mar, río) navigation; (deportiva) boating; (en internet) surfing, browsing

navegador M browser; **— web** web browser

navegante MF navigator; ADJ navigating

navegar[40] VI/VT (buque) to navigate; (barco a vela) to sail; (en internet) to browse, to surf

Navidad F Christmas

navideño ADJ **fiesta navideña** Christmas party

navío M ship

nazi MF Nazi

neblina F mist

neblinoso ADJ misty

nebulosidad F cloudiness

nebuloso ADJ (poco claro) nebulous; (que tiene niebla) foggy

necesario ADJ necessary

neceser M toiletry bag

necesidad F (urgencia, sensación de falta) need; (cosa necesaria) necessity; **hacer sus —es** to relieve oneself; **de primera —** indispensable; **por —** out of necessity

necesitado ADJ needy

necesitar VT to need

necio-cia ADJ asinine, foolish

necrología F necrology

necrosis F necrosis

néctar M nectar

nectarina F nectarine

nefasto ADJ unholy

nefritis F nephritis

negación F (partícula gramatical) negation; (rechazo) denial

negar[41] VT (decir que no es verdad) to deny; (no consentir) to refuse; (no reconocer) to disavow; **-se [a]** to refuse [to]

negativa F (rechazo verbal) denial; (falta de cooperación) refusal

negativo ADJ negative; **signo —** minus sign; M [photographic] negative

negligencia F (falta de atención) negligence, neglect; (médica) malpractice

negligente ADJ negligent, neglectful

negociación F negotiation; **— laboral** collective bargaining

negociador-ora MF negotiator; ADJ negotiating

negociante MF businessperson

negociar VI/VT (acordar) to negotiate; (comerciar) to trade

negocio M (tienda, actividad comercial) business; (transacción) business deal, business transaction; **— de ventas por correo** mail-order business; **— principal** core business; **hombre de —s** businessman; **mujer de —s** businesswoman; **hacer —** to make a profit

negrear VI to appear black; VT to blacken

negrilla F boldface

negritas F PL boldface type

negro-ra ADJ black (también café sin leche); (futuro) bleak; **pasarlas negras** to undergo hardships; F (nota) quarter-note; MF (persona) person of color, black person

negrura F blackness

negruzco ADJ blackish

némesis F nemesis

nene-na M baby boy; F baby girl

nenúfar M water lily

neologismo M neologism

neón M neon

neonatal ADJ neonatal

neozelandés -esa MF New Zealander

Nepal M Nepal

nepalés -esa ADJ & MF Nepali

nepalí ADJ & MF Nepalese

nepotismo M nepotism

nervado ADJ veined

nervio M nerve; — **pellizcado** pinched nerve; — **pinzado** pinched nerve; **perder los —s** to lose one's cool; **tener los —s de punta** to be on edge

nerviosismo M nervousness

nervioso ADJ (relativo a los nervios) nervous; (inquieto) nervous, jumpy

nervudo ADJ sinewy, wiry

neto ADJ (mejoría) distinct; (ganancia) net

neumático M tire; ADJ pneumatic

neural ADJ neural

neuralgia F neuralgia

neurastenia F neurasthenia

neurocirugía F neurosurgery

neurocirujano -na MF neurosurgeon

neurólogo -ga MF neurologist

neurona F neuron, nerve cell

neurosis F neurosis

neurótico -ca ADJ & MF neurotic

neurotransmisor M neurotransmitter

neutral ADJ neutral

neutralidad F neutrality

neutralizar⁴⁷ VT to neutralize

neutro ADJ neutral; (género) neuter

neutrón M neutron

nevada F snowfall

nevado ADJ snowy

nevar¹ VI to snow

nevera F icebox, refrigerator

nevisca F snow flurry

ni CONJ & ADV — **con mucho** not by a long shot; — **hablar** forget it; — **habló conmigo** he didn't even talk to me; — **idea** [it] beats me; — **modo** no way; — **que esto fuera un hotel** it's not like this is a hotel; — **siquiera** not even; — **soñar** fat chance; — **trabaja —estudia** he neither works nor studies; — **una palabra** not a word; **no tiene amigos —enemigos** he has no friends nor enemies; **no es rico — mucho menos** he's not even close to being rich

Nicaragua F Nicaragua

nicaragüense ADJ & MF Nicaraguan

nicho M niche, recess

nicotina F nicotine

nidada F (huevos) nest of eggs; (crías) hatch, brood

nido M nest

niebla F fog

niega, niegue ver negar

nieto -ta M grandson; F granddaughter; —**s** grandchildren

nieve F snow (también droga en polvo)

Níger M Niger

Nigeria F Nigeria

nigeriano -na ADJ & MF Nigerian

nigerino -na ADJ & MF Nigerien

nigua F chigger

nihilismo M nihilism

nilón M nylon

nimio ADJ insignificant

ninguno ADJ & PRON **no tengo** — I have none / I don't have any; **ningún amigo mío** no friend of mine; **no tengo ningún libro** I don't have any books; — **de los dos** neither one; **de ningún modo** in no way

niñera F (ocasional) babysitter; (permanente) nanny

niñería F childish act

niñez F (infancia) childhood; (de niño) boyhood; (de niña) girlhood

niño -ña M child, kid, boy; F child, kid, girl; **niña del ojo** pupil [of the eye]; ADJ childish

níquel M nickel

niquelado ADJ nickel-plated

níspero M loquat

nitidez F sharpness

nítido ADJ sharp

nitrato M nitrate

nitrógeno M nitrogen

nitroglicerina F nitroglycerine

nivel M level (también herramienta); (grado jerárquico) echelon; — **de cobertura** coverage level; — **de mar** sea level; — **de vida** standard of living; **a —** straight; **a — de** level with

nivelar VT (emparejar) to level; (aplanar) to grade

níveo ADJ snowy

no ADV no; — **quiero** I don't want to; — **acreditado** unlicensed; — **afiliado** unaffiliated; — **ajustado** unadjusted; — **autorizado** unauthorized; — **comercial** noncommercial; — **confirmado** unconfirmed; — **conforme** nonconforming; — **declarado** undeclared; — **disponible** unavailable; — **divulgado** undisclosed; — **esencial** nonessential; — **especificado** unspecified; — **ético** unethical; — **gubernamental** nongovernmental; — **negociable** nonnegotiable; — **reembolsable** nonrefundable; — **relacionado** unrelated; — **residente** nonresident; — **restringido** unrestricted; — **solicitado** unsolicited; — **tributable** nontaxable; — **bien llegaron** no sooner had they arrived; — **sólo** not only; — **sea que** lest; **a — ser que** unless

noble ADJ noble; M nobleman; F noblewoman

nobleza F nobility

nocaut M knockout

noche F (período sin luz) night; (horas de la noche) nighttime; **—buena** Christmas Eve; **—vieja** New Year's Eve; **— y día** day and night; **de —** at night; **de la — a la mañana** overnight; **esta —** tonight; **por la —** at night

noción F notion; **no tener ni —** to have no clue

nocivo ADJ harmful, noxious

nocturno ADJ (que actúa de noche) nocturnal; (que sucede todas las noches) nightly

nodo M node

nodriza F wet nurse

nódulo M node

nogal M walnut tree

nómada MF nomad

ningunear VT to dismiss

nomás ADV *Am* **aquí —** close by; **así —** just like that; **entre —** come right in

nombramiento M (civil) appointment; (militar) commission

nombrar VT (a un funcionario) to name, to appoint; (a un oficial militar) to commission

nombre M name; **— completo** full name; **— de acceso** login name; **— de pila** first name; **— de soltera** maiden name; **— del usuario** username; **en — de** on behalf of; **eso no tiene —** that's unheard of; **hacerse un —** to make a name for oneself

nomenclatura F nomenclature

nomeolvides M SG forget-me-not

nómina F payroll

nominación F nomination

nominal ADJ nominal

nominar VT to nominate

non ADJ odd; M odd number

nopal M prickly pear

noquear VT to knock out

norcoreano -na ADJ & MF North Korean

nordeste ADJ & M northeast

nórdico ADJ Nordic

noreste ADJ & M northeast

norma F norm, standard; **—s industriales** industry standards

normal ADJ (estándar, común) normal, standard; F (escuela) teacher's college; (línea) perpendicular line

normalidad F normalcy, normality; **con toda —** normally; **todo volvió a la —** everything returned to normal

normalizar[47] VT to normalize

normalmente ADV normally, usually

normativa F norm

noroeste ADJ & M northwest

norte ADJ & M north

norteamericano -na ADJ & MF (de América del Norte) North American; (de EEUU) American

norteño -ña ADJ northern; MF northerner

Noruega F Norway

noruego -ga ADJ & MF Norwegian; M (lengua) Norwegian

nos PRON us; **él — vio** he saw us; **— dio el libro** he gave us the book, he gave the book to us

nosotros -as PRON we; **para —** for us

nostalgia F nostalgia

nostálgico ADJ nostalgic

nota F (musical) note; (anotación) annotation; (calificación) grade, mark; **— al pie de página** footnote; **de —** of note; **exagerar la —** to overdo something

notable ADJ notable, noteworthy, remarkable

notablemente ADV (destacadamente) notably; (visiblemente) noticeably

notación F notation

notar VT (percibir) to note, to notice; (señalar) to note

notariar VT to notarize

notario -ria MF notary

noticia F piece of news; **—s** news; **tener —s de alguien** to hear from someone

noticiario M newscast, news bulletin

noticiero M newscast

notificación F (informe) notification; (policial) summons; **— de despido** pink slip

notificar[30] VT to notify

notorio ADJ (conocido públicamente) well-known; (evidente) obvious

novato -ta MF (profesional) novice; (policía, atleta) rookie

novecientos NUM nine hundred

novedad F novelty; **—es** news; **sin —** all's well

novedoso ADJ novel

novela F novel; **— policial** detective novel

novelesco ADJ fictional

novelista MF novelist

noveno ADJ ninth

noventa NUM ninety

noviazgo M engagement

novicio -cia MF novice

noviembre M November

novillo -lla M steer; **hacer —s** to play hooky; F heifer

novio -via M (comprometido) fiancé; (no formal) boyfriend; (de boda) bridegroom; F (comprometida) fiancée; (no formal) girlfriend; (de boda) bride

novocaína F novocaine

nubarrón M thunderhead

nube F (atmosférica) cloud; (de humo) billow; **poner por las —s** to praise to the skies; **está en las —s** his head is in the clouds; **los precios están por las —s** prices have gone through the roof

nublado ADJ (cielo) cloudy, overcast; (los ojos, de emoción) misty; (los ojos, por falta de sueño) bleary

nublar VT to blur; **—se** (el cielo) to become overcast; (los ojos) to cloud over

nubosidad F (de un concepto) nebulousness;

(del cielo) cloudiness
nuboso ADJ cloudy
nuca F nape
nuclear ADJ nuclear
núcleo M (de célula, átomo) nucleus; (de reactor) core; (de sistema operativo) kernel
nudillo M knuckle
nudismo M nudism
nudista ADJ & MF nudist
nudo M knot (también en la madera, medida de velocidad); (de una obra teatral) turning point; (en el pelo) tangle; (en plantas) node; (en la garganta) lump; **— corredizo** slipknot; **— de rizo** square knot
nudoso ADJ knotty, gnarled
nuera F daughter-in-law
nuestro ADJ POS our; **— hijo** our son; PRON ours; **esto es —** this is ours
nuevamente ADV again
nueve NUM nine
nuevo ADJ new; **de —** again; **¿qué hay de —?** what's new?
nuez F walnut; **— de Adán** Adam's apple; **— moscada** nutmeg
nulidad F (legal) nullity; (persona) nonentity
nulo ADJ null and void, invalid
numeral ADJ & M numeral
numerar VT to number
numérico ADJ numerical
número M (dígito) number; (en un espectáculo) act; (de una revista) issue; (cifra) figure; **— de serie** serial number
numeroso ADJ numerous
nunca ADV never, not ever; **no viene —** he never comes, he doesn't ever come; **más que —** more than ever; **casi —** hardly ever; **peor que —** worse than ever
nupcial ADJ nuptial, bridal
nupcias F PL nuptials
nutria F otter
nutrición F nutrition
nutrido ADJ **el congreso tuvo una nutrida concurrencia** the conference was well attended
nutriente M nutrient
nutrir VT to nourish
nutritivo ADJ nutritious, nourishing

Ññ

ñandú M rhea
ñato ADJ *Am* pug-nosed
ñoño ADJ bland
ñu M gnu

Oo

o CONJ or; **— se casa — lo mato** either he gets married or I'll kill him; **— sea** that is
oasis M oasis
obedecer[35] VI/VT to obey; **esto obedece a que** this is due to the fact that
obedezca, obedezco *ver* obedecer
obediencia F obedience
obediente ADJ obedient
obertura F musical overture
obesidad F obesity
obeso ADJ obese
obispo M bishop
obituario M obituary
objeción F objection
objetable ADJ objectionable
objetar VI/VT to object, to take exception [to]
objetividad F objectivity
objetivo ADJ objective; M (lente) objective; (meta) aim, objective
objeto M object
oblea F wafer
oblicuo ADJ (inclinado) oblique; (sesgado) biased
obligación F (deber) obligation, duty; (deuda) obligation; (título financiero) bond
obligado ADJ (forzado) forced; (obligatorio) compulsory, obligatory; **me vi — a comprar otro coche** I was forced / had to buy another car
obligar[40] VT to force, to compel, to oblige; **—se [a]** to obligate oneself [to]
obligatorio ADJ obligatory, compulsory
oboe M oboe
obra F (artística, literaria, de construcción) work; (lugar de construcción) construction site; **— maestra** masterpiece; **en —s** under construction
obrar VI to act; **obra en nuestro poder** we acknowledge receipt of
obrero -ra MF worker; ADJ working
obscenidad F obscenity; **—es** filth
obsceno ADJ obscene
obscuridad *ver* oscuridad
obsequiar VT to present, to give; **me obsequió perfume** he gave me perfume
obsequio M gift
obsequioso ADJ obsequious
observación F (mirada) observation; (comentario) remark
observador -ora MF observer; ADJ observant
observancia F observance
observar VI/VT (mirar) to observe; (hacer un comentario) to remark, to observe
observatorio M observatory

obsesión F obsession
obsesionado ADJ obsessed
obsesionar VT to obsess; **—se con** to obsess over, to be obsessed with
obsesivo-compulsivo ADJ obsessive-compulsive
obstaculizar VT to impede
obstáculo M (impedimento) obstacle, hindrance, impediment; (en carreras) hurdle
obstante LOC PREP **no — tu oposición** notwithstanding your opposition; LOC ADV **no —, voy a ir** nevertheless, I am going to go
obstar VT to preclude
obstetra MF obstetrician
obstetricia F obstetrics
obstinación F obstinacy
obstinado ADJ obstinate, bullheaded
obstinarse VI to be obstinate
obstrucción F (de justicia, de un caño) obstruction, blockage; (del intestino) obstruction, occlusion; **— intestinal** intestinal obstruction
obstruir[19] VT (un movimiento, procedimiento) to obstruct, to block; (un aparato) to jam; VI **—se** to get jammed
obtención F acquisition
obtendrá, obtendría ver obtener
obtener[58] VT (bienes) to obtain, to get; (permiso) to secure; (con dificultad) to procure
obtenga, obtengo, obtiene, obtienes ver obtener
obturador M (de una cámara fotográfica) shutter; (de un coche) choke
obtuve, obtuviera, obtuviese ver obtener
obviamente ADV obviously
obviar VT to obviate, to circumvent
obvio ADJ obvious
ocasión F (vez, instancia) occasion; (oportunidad) opportunity; (ganga) bargain; **de —** reduced
ocasional ADJ occasional
ocasionar VT to occasion, to cause
ocaso M sunset, twilight
occidental ADJ occidental, western; MF westerner
occidente M west
oceánico ADJ oceanic
océano M ocean
oceanografía F oceanography
ocelote M ocelot
ochenta NUM eighty
ocho NUM eight
ochocientos NUM eight hundred
ocio M (diversión) leisure; (inacción) idleness
ociosidad F idleness
ocioso ADJ (inactivo) idle; (no usado) unused
oclusión F occlusion
octágono M octagon

octano M octane
octava F octave
octavilla F tract
octavo ADJ & M eighth
octeto M byte
octógono M octagon
octubre M October
ocular M eyepiece; ADJ **infección —** eye infection
oculista MF oculist, eye doctor
ocultar VT to conceal; (información) to withhold
ocultismo M the occult
oculto ADJ (invisible) unseen; (sobrenatural) occult; (escondido) hidden, under wraps
ocupación F (trabajo) occupation; (capacidad) occupancy
ocupado ADJ (persona, teléfono) busy; (asiento, aseo) occupied
ocupante MF occupant
ocupar VT (usar) to occupy; (contratar) to employ; **—se de** to take care of, to address
ocurrencia F witticism, quip
ocurrente ADJ witty
ocurrir VI to occur
oda F ode
odiar VI/VT to hate
odio M hatred, hate
odioso ADJ (tarea) odious; (persona) hateful, obnoxious
odontología F dentistry
odre M wineskin
OEA [Organización de Estados Americanos] F OAS
oeste ADJ & M west
ofender VI/VT to offend; **—se** to get offended, to take offense
ofensa F offense
ofensiva F (militar) offensive; (deportiva) offense; (fútbol americano) offensive series
ofensivo ADJ offensive, obnoxious
oferta F (oportunidad) offer; (rebaja) special offer; **— de apertura** opening bid; **en —** on sale; **— de prueba** trial offer; **— pública inicial** initial public offering
offset M offset
oficial -la ADJ official; MF (militar) officer; (obrero calificado) skilled worker; **— general** high-ranking officer
oficialismo M party in power
oficialista ADJ in power
oficiar VI to officiate; **— de** to serve as
oficina F (despacho) office; (dependencia gubernamental) bureau; **— central** home office, headquarters; **— en el hogar** home office
oficinista MF office worker
oficio M (actividad laboral) trade, craft; (comunicación oficial) official communication; **tiene mucho —** he knows

his stuff; **buenos —s** good offices

oficioso ADJ (entrometido) officious; (no oficial) unofficial, off-the-record

ofrecer[35] VT (un regalo) to offer; (en una subasta) to bid; (una cena) to give; **— resistencia** to put up resistance; **¿qué se le ofrece a usted?** how can I help you?

ofrecimiento M (acción de ofrecer) offering; (oferta) offer

ofrenda F offering

oftalmólogo -ga MF ophthalmologist

ofuscar[30] VT to bewilder

ogro M ogre

ohmio M ohm

oído M (facultad) hearing; (órgano) inner ear; (musical) ear; **— medio** middle ear; **al —** confidentially; **de —** by ear

oiga, oigo ver oír

oír[55] VI/VT (percibir) to hear; (atender) to listen; **— decir que** to hear that; **— hablar de** to hear about; **— misa** to attend mass; **¡oye!** listen! hey!

ojal M buttonhole

ojalá INTERJ **— estuviera aquí** I wish he were here; **— que venga** I hope that he comes

ojeada F glimpse

ojear VT to glimpse

ojera F dark circle under the eye

ojeriza F animosity

ojeroso ADJ with dark circles under the eyes

ojiva F (arco) pointed arch; (explosivo) warhead

ojo M (órgano, centro de huracán, instinto, yema de patata) eye; **¡—!** careful! look out! **a — de buen cubero** as a rule of thumb; **a —s vistas** clearly; **me costó un — de la cara** it cost me an arm and a leg; **¿no tienes —s en la cara?** are you blind? **dichosos los —s que te ven** you're a sight for sore eyes; **— de buey** porthole; **— de la cerradura** keyhole; **— de lince** eagle-eye; **— morado** black eye; **— por —** an eye for an eye

ola F wave; (de un olor) waft; (de protesta) storm

oleada F wave, surge

oleaje M swell, surge

óleo M oil painting

oleoducto M oil pipeline

oleoso ADJ oily

oler[22] VI/VT to smell (también sospechar); **— a** to smell of

olfatear VI/VT to scent, to sniff

olfateo M sniff, sniffing

olfato M (facultad) sense of smell; (instinto) nose

olfatorio ADJ olfactory

olimpíada F Olympiad; **—s** Olympic Games

olímpico ADJ Olympian

oliva F olive

olivar M olive grove

olivo M olive tree

olla F pot; **— de grillos** snake pit; **— podrida**

stew of mixed vegetables and meat

olmo M elm

olor M smell, odor

oloroso ADJ odorous

olvidadizo ADJ forgetful

olvidar VI/VT to forget; **—se [de]** to forget; **se me olvidó algo** I forgot something

olvido M oblivion; **caer en el —** to be forgotten; **echar al —** to cast into oblivion; **tus —s** your forgetfulness

Omán M Oman

omaní ADJ & MF Omani

ombligo M navel

OMC [Organización Mundial del Comercio] F WTO

omisión F omission; **por —** by default

omiso ADJ **hacer caso — [de]** to ignore

omitir VT (eliminar) to omit, to leave out; (no notar) to overlook

ómnibus M bus

omnipotente ADJ omnipotent

omnisciencia F omniscience

omnisciente ADJ omniscient

omnívoro ADJ omnivorous

omóplato M scapula

OMS [Organización Mundial de la Salud] F WHO

once NUM eleven

oncología F oncology

onda F wave; **— corta** shortwave; **— expansiva** shock wave; **— sonora** sound wave; **agarrarle la — a algo** to get in the swing of things; **captar la —** to get the drift

ondeado ADJ wavy

ondeante ADJ flying

ondear VI to wave

ondulación F ripple, ruffle, roll

ondulado ADJ (pelo) wavy; (paisaje) rolling

ondulante ADJ undulating

ondular VI to undulate; VI/VT to wave

ónix M onyx

omnipotencia F omnipotence

onomatopeya F onomatopoeia

ONU [Organización de las Naciones Unidas] F UN

onza F ounce

opacar[30] VT (oscurecer) to dull; (eclipsar) to overshadow

opaco ADJ (no transparente) opaque; (no brillante) dull

ópalo M opal

opción F option; **opciones** stock options; **— de venta** put option

opcional ADJ optional

OPEP [Organización de Países Exportadores de Petróleo] F OPEC

ópera F (composición) opera; (teatro) opera house

operable ADJ operable

operación F operation

operador -ora M (en matemáticas) operator; MF (de teléfono) operator

operar VI/VT (usar maquinaria) to operate; VT (intervenir quirúrgicamente) to operate on; (llevar a cabo) to carry out; VI (hacer cuentas) to do mathematical operations

operario -ria MF operator, operative

operativo ADJ (que funciona) operative; (vigente) in effect; M *Am* — **policial** police operation

opiáceo M opiate

opinar VI/VT to hold an opinion, to think

opinión F opinion, view, feeling; **cambiar de** — to change one's mind

opio M opium

oponente MF (en un debate) opponent; (en una película) costar

oponer[56, 74] VT to oppose; —**se** to conflict; —**se a** to oppose, to be against

oponga, opongo *ver* oponer

oporto M port wine

oportunidad F (chance) opportunity, chance; (pretexto) opening; (fútbol americano) down

oportunista ADJ & MF opportunistic

oportuno ADJ (conveniente) opportune, timely; (adecuado) appropriate

oposición F opposition; **oposiciones** competitive examinations

opositor -ora MF opponent

opresión F oppression

opresivo ADJ oppressive

opresor -ora MF oppressor

oprimir VT (al pueblo) to oppress; (un botón) to press; (un enlace digital) to click

optar VI to choose; — **por** to choose

optativo ADJ optional

óptico -ca ADJ optical; MF optician; F optics

optimismo M optimism

optimista ADJ optimistic; MF optimist

optimizar VT to optimize

óptimo ADJ optimal

optometría F optometry

optometrista MF optometrist

opuesto ADJ opposite, contrary; **se mostró — al casamiento** he was against the marriage; **dos fuerzas opuestas** two opposing forces; **lo** — the opposite; **dirección opuesta** the opposite/reverse direction

opulencia F opulence

opulento ADJ (decoración) opulent; (sociedad) affluent

opuse, opusiera, opusiese *ver* oponer

oración F (frase) sentence; (plegaria) prayer

oráculo M oracle

orador -ora MF orator, speaker

oral ADJ oral

orangután M orangutan

orar VI/VT to pray

oratoria F oratory

oratorio M oratory

órbita F (de los cuerpos celestes) orbit; (de los ojos) eye socket

orbitador M orbiter

orbital ADJ orbital

orbitar VI/VT to orbit

orca F killer whale

orden M (limpieza, secuencia) order; — **ascendente** ascending order; — **de clasificación** sort order; — **del día** order of the day; **perturbar el — público** to disturb the peace; **sin — ni concierto** haphazard; F (mando) command, order; (grupo religioso) order; — **de cateo** warrant; — **de compra** purchase order; — **judicial** court order; **a sus órdenes** at your service

ordenación F (arreglo) ordering, organization; (de un cura) ordination; (informatización) computerization

ordenado ADJ orderly, neat

ordenador M *Esp* computer; — **de mano** palmtop; — **de sobremesa** desktop computer; — **digital** digital computer; — **portátil** laptop computer; — **torre** tower computer

ordenamiento M (arreglo) ordering, putting in order; (conjunto de leyes) legal code; — **territorial** land use

ordenanza F ordinance; MF orderly

ordenar VT (arreglar) to sort, to put in order; (mandar) to order, to command; (conferir órdenes religiosos) to ordain; —**se** to become ordained

ordeñar VT to milk

ordeño M milking

ordinal ADJ ordinal

ordinariez F vulgarity

ordinario ADJ (corriente) ordinary; (vulgar) vulgar

orear VT to air out

orégano M oregano

oreja F [outer] ear; (de un martillo) claw; (en un utensilio) flap; **aguzar la** — to prick up one's ears; **sonreír de — a** — to smile from ear to ear; **estar hasta las —s en algo** to be up to one's neck in something

orejera F earmuff

orfanato M orphanage

orfebre MF (con oro) goldsmith; (con plata) silversmith

orgánico ADJ organic

organigrama M organizational chart, flow chart

organismo M organism

organista MF organist

organización F organization

organizado ADJ organized

organizador -ora MF organizer

organizar[47] VT (una reunión, evento) to organize; (un ataque) to stage; (una fiesta) to give, to throw

organizativo ADJ organizational, organizing

órgano M organ

orgía F orgy

orgullo M pride; **es mi —** she's my pride and joy

orgulloso ADJ proud

orientación F (vocacional, psicológica) orientation, guidance; (de velas) trim; (de estudios) track; (de un objeto) lie; (del terreno) lay; **— horizontal** landscape; **— vertical** portrait

orientado ADJ oriented; **— al cliente** customer-oriented

oriental ADJ oriental, eastern; MF oriental

orientar VT to orient; **—se** to get one's bearings

oriente M Orient, east

orificio M orifice

origen M origin; (de un problema, conflicto) source; (antecedentes familiares) birth

original ADJ original; M (de una pintura) original; (de una cinta magnética) master

originalidad F originality

originar VT to originate, to give rise to; **—se** to originate, to arise

originario ADJ (original) original; **— de** (cierto origen) coming from, native of

orilla F (de un lago, mar) shore, bank; (de una cama) edge; (de una prenda) hem

orillar VT (una calle) to border; (una prenda) to hem

orín M rust; M PL **orines** urine

orina F urine

orinal M chamber pot

orinar VI/VT to urinate

oriundo ADJ **ser — de** (persona) to hail from; (cosa) to originate in

orla F (de un uniforme) trimming; (de una alfombra) fringe

orlar VT to fringe

orlón™ M Orlon™

ornamentación F ornamentation

ornamental ADJ ornamental

ornamentar VT to ornament, to embellish

ornamento M ornament

ornar VT to adorn

ornitología F ornithology

oro M gold; **— blanco** white gold; **— en lingotes** gold bullion; **— negro** black gold; **— puro** solid gold; **prometer el — y el moro** to promise the moon

orondo ADJ self-satisfied

oropel M tinsel

oropéndola F oriole

orquesta F orchestra

orquestar VT to orchestrate

orquídea F orchid

ortiga F nettle

ortodoncia F orthodontics

ortodoxo ADJ orthodox

ortografía F orthography, spelling

oruga F caterpillar

orujo M rape

orzuelo M sty

osadía F boldness, daring

osado ADJ bold, daring

osamenta F skeleton

osar VI/VT to dare

oscilación F oscillation

oscilar VI to oscillate, to seesaw; **— entre** to range between

oscurecer VI (ponerse oscuro) to get dark; VT (poner oscuro) to darken; (volver poco inteligible, ocultar) to obscure; **—se** to get darker

oscuridad F (lugar sin luz) dark, darkness; (condición de oscuro) darkness; (falta de claridad conceptual, anonimato) obscurity

oscuro ADJ (sin luz) dark; (turbio) murky; (poco claro, poco conocido) obscure; **lentes —s** dark glasses; **gris —** dark gray; **a oscuras** in the dark

óseo ADJ bony

osezno M bear cub

osificarse VI to ossify

ósmosis F osmosis

oso -sa M bear; F she-bear; **— blanco/polar** polar bear; **— hormiguero** anteater

ostentación F ostentation, show, display; **hacer — de** to flaunt

ostentar VI/VT to display, to show off, to flaunt

ostentoso ADJ ostentatious, showy

osteoartritis F osteoarthritis

osteoporosis F osteoporosis

ostión M large oyster

ostra F oyster

OTAN [Organización del Tratado del Atlántico Norte] F NATO

otero M hillock

otitis F otitis; **— externa** swimmer's ear

otoñal ADJ autumnal

otoño M autumn, fall

otorgamiento M grant

otorgar[40] VT (permiso) to grant, to concede; (premio) to award

otro ADJ (uno adicional) another; (uno diferente) other; **otra vez** again; **otra cosa** something else; **— más** another one; **al — día** the next day; **de — modo** otherwise; **en otra parte** somewhere else; **la otra cara de la moneda** the flip side; **por otra parte** on the other hand; PRON (uno más) another one; (una persona diferente) someone else; (una cosa diferente) something else

out ADV & M out; **— forzado** force out

ovación F ovation, acclaim

oval ADJ oval

ovalado ADJ oval
óvalo M oval
ovárico ADJ ovarian
ovario M ovary
oveja F (ovino) sheep; (hembra) ewe
ovejero M sheepdog
overoles M PL overalls
ovillar VT to ball; **—se** to curl up into a ball
ovillo M ball of yarn; **hacerse un —** to curl up
OVNI [objeto volador no identificado] M UFO
ovoide N egg-shaped
ovulación F ovulation
ovular VI to ovulate
óvulo M egg
oxidación F oxidation, rusting
oxidado ADJ oxidized, rusty
oxidar VI/VT to oxidize, to rust
óxido M (compuesto químico) oxide; (herrumbre) rust
oxígeno M oxygen
oye, oyendo, oyera, oyese ver oír
oyente MF (que oye) listener, hearer; (alumno no oficial) auditor
ozono M ozone

Pp

pabellón M (puesto de feria) pavilion; (parte de un edificio) wing; (bandera) flag; (sección de hospital) ward; **— de la oreja** outer ear
pabilo M wick
paca F bale
pacana F (fruto) pecan; (árbol) pecan tree
pacer[35] VI to pasture, to graze; VT to crop, to graze
paciencia F patience; **con —** patiently; **tener —** to be patient
paciente ADJ & MF patient; **— ambulatorio -ria** outpatient; **— externo -na** outpatient; **— de alto riesgo** high-risk patient
pacificación F pacification
pacificar[30] VT to pacify
pacífico ADJ peaceful; M **Océano Pacífico** Pacific Ocean
pacifismo M pacifism
pactar VT (hacer un pacto) to make a pact / an agreement; (decidir de común acuerdo) to agree; VI **— con el diablo** to sell one's soul to the devil
pacto M pact, covenant
paddock M (de caballos) paddock; (de coches) pit
padecer[35] VI/VT to suffer; **— de cáncer** to suffer from cancer
padecimiento M suffering

padezca, padezco ver padecer
padrastro M (marido de la madre) stepfather; (uñero) hangnail
padre M father; **—s** parents, folks; **— de familia** male head of the household; **—nuestro** the Lord's Prayer; **John Smith, — John Smith Sr.; ser —** to become a father; ADJ **un lío —** a real mess
padrino M (de bautizo) godfather; (de boda) best man; (en un duelo) second
paella F paella
paga F (salario) pay; (para un niño) allowance; **— de tiempo y medio** time-and-a-half pay; **— por mérito** merit pay
pagadero ADJ payable, due
pagado ADJ paid; **— de sí mismo** self-satisfied
pagador -ora MF payer
paganismo M paganism
pagano -na ADJ & MF pagan
pagar[40] VT (cuentas, deudas) to pay; (préstamo) to pay off; (mercancías) to pay for; **—se de** to be proud of; **— el pato** to be left holding the bag; **pagan justos por pecadores** the just pay for the sins of others; **— a plazos** to pay in installments; **— al contado** to pay cash; **— con la misma moneda** to pay in kind; **— en especie** to pay in kind
pagaré M promissory note
página F page; **— de estilo** stylesheet; **— web** web page
paginar VT to paginate
pago M payment; **— en efectivo** cash payment; ADJ paid
paila F large pan
país M country; **— de origen** country of origin; **— en desarrollo** developing country; **— exportador de petróleo** oil-exporting country
paisaje M landscape, scenery
paisajismo M landscape architecture
paisano -na M countryman; F countrywoman
paja F straw (también para beber de un vaso); **a humo de —s** thoughtlessly; **por un quítame allá esas —s** for a trifle
pajar M hayloft
pájaro M bird; **— carpintero** woodpecker; **— pinto** cautious person; **un — francés** a French guy
paje M page
pajizo ADJ straw-colored
pajonal M Am grassland
pala F (para cavar) shovel; (para recoger basura) dustpan; (de hélice, remo) blade; (de zapato) upper; (para remar, de ping-pong) paddle; **— mecánica** power shovel; **lo tuvimos que recoger con —** he was exhausted
palabra F (unidad léxica) word; (facultad) speech; **— clave** key word; **—s mayores** a big deal; **cuatro —s** a few words; **cumplir**

con la — to keep one's word; **dejar con la — en la boca** to cut someone off in midsentence; **en pocas —s** in a nutshell; **faltar a la —** to break a promise; **la última —** the final say; **ni una —** not a word; **no dijo —** he didn't breathe a word; **un hombre de —** a man of his word; **tener la —** to have the floor; **tomar la —** to take the floor; **traducción — por —** word-for-word translation; **tragarse/comerse las propias —s** to eat one's words

palabrerío M verbiage

palabrero ADJ long-winded

palabrota F curse word, four-letter word; **—s** profanity

palacio M palace

paladar M palate; **— hendido** cleft palate; **— óseo** hard palate

paladear VT to relish

paladín M champion, crusader

palanca F (para levantar algo) lever; (para abrir algo) crowbar; (fuerza) leverage; **— de cambios** gearshift lever; **— de juegos** joystick; **— del regulador** throttle lever; **hacer —** to use leverage

palangana F basin

Paláu M Palau

palco M box

palenque M fence

paleontología F paleontology

Palestina F Palestine

palestino -na MF Palestinian; ADJ Palestinian

paleta F (de pintor) palette; (de albañil) trowel; (de ping-pong, para mezclar, batir) paddle; (hélice) blade; (de caramelo) lollipop, sucker; (de helado) Popsicle™

paletilla F shoulder

paleto -ta MF hayseed, hick

paliar VT to alleviate

paliativo M palliative

palidecer[35] VI to turn pale

palidez F pallor, paleness

pálido ADJ pallid, pale

palillo M (de dientes) toothpick; (de tambor) drumstick; (para comida china) chopstick; **tocar todos los —s** to try everything

palique M chitchat

paliza F beating, whipping; **dar una —** to beat, to whip

palma F (árbol) palm [tree]; (hoja) palm leaf; (de la mano) palm [of the hand]; **batir —s** to clap; **llevarse la —** to take the prize; **conocer como la — de la mano** to know like the back of one's hand

palmada F (en la espalda) slap; (aplauso) clap; (en el trasero) spank; **dar una —** (en la espalda) to slap; (en el trasero) to spank

palmear VT to slap on the back

palmera F palm tree

palmípedo M web-footed bird

palmo M span; **— a —** inch by inch

palmotear VT to slap on the back

palo M (de madera) stick; (de barco) mast; (de naipes) suit; (fútbol) goalpost; **—s** (fútbol americano) goalposts; **— de golf** golf club; **— de escoba** broomstick; **dar —s** to hit with a stick; **de tal — tal astilla** a chip off the old block

paloma F dove, pigeon

palomar M pigeon loft

palomilla F wing nut

palomita F (béisbol) fly ball; **—s** popcorn; **hacer —** to pop corn

palote M rolling pin

palpable ADJ palpable

palpar VT to feel

palpitación F palpitation

palpitante ADJ palpitating; **una cuestión —** a burning question

palpitar VI to palpitate

palta F Am avocado

paludismo M malaria

pampa F Am prairie

pamplinas F PL baloney, hogwash

pan M bread; (pieza) loaf of bread; **— comido** piece of cake, cinch; **— de cada día** everyday occurrence; **— rallado/molido** bread crumbs; **al —, — y al vino, vino** to call a spade a spade; **contigo, — y cebolla** love is all we need; **ganarse el —** to make a living

pana F corduroy

panacea F panacea, magic bullet

panadería F bakery

panadero -ra MF baker

panal M honeycomb

Panamá M Panama

panameño -ña ADJ & MF Panamanian

panamericano ADJ Pan-American

panceta F RP bacon

páncreas M SG pancreas

panda M panda bear

pandearse VT to buckle, to sag

pandemia F pandemic

pandémico M pandemic

pandeo M sag

pandereta F tambourine

pandilla F gang, band

panecillo M roll

panegírico M eulogy

panel M panel; **— de control** control panel

panera F breadbasket

panfleto M pamphlet

pánico ADJ & M panic

panoja F ear of corn

panorama M (paisaje) panorama; (horizonte) outlook

panorámico ADJ panoramic

panqueque M pancake

pantaletas F PL panties

pantalla F (de lámpara) lampshade; (para películas) screen; (de monitor) screen, display; (para actividades ilícitas) cover, front; **la — grande** the silver screen; **— dividida** split screen; **— táctil** touchscreen, touch-sensitive display

pantalón M pants, trousers; **— corto** shorts; **pantalones** pants, trousers; **llevar bien puestos los pantalones** to be master in one's own home

pantano M swamp, marsh

pantanoso ADJ swampy, marshy

panteón M vault

pantera F panther

pantomima F mime, pantomime

pantorrilla F calf

pantufla F slipper

panty M pantyhose

panza F paunch, belly

panzudo ADJ potbellied

pañal M diaper; **estar en —es** to be in its infancy

paño M (de tela) cloth; (de lana) woolen cloth; (para limpiar) rag; **— higiénico** sanitary napkin; **— mortuorio** pall; **— de manos** towel; **— de cocina** dishcloth; **— de mesa** tablecloth; **ella es mi — de lágrimas** I always cry on her shoulder; **—s menores** underwear

pañuelo M (de nariz) handkerchief; (de cuello) scarf

papa M pope; F *Am* potato; **no saber ni —** not to know a thing; **—s fritas** French fries

papá M papa, dad

papacito M (padre) daddy; (hombre apuesto) hunk

papada F double chin

papado M papacy

papagayo M parrot

papaíto M daddy

papal ADJ papal

papar VT to eat; MF SG **papamoscas** (pájaro) flycatcher; (tonto) half-wit; MF SG **papanatas** twerp

paparruchas F PL baloney, bull

papaya F papaya

papel M (para escribir) paper; (dramático) role, part; **— aluminio** aluminum foil; **— carbón** carbon paper; **— cuadriculado** graph paper; **— de cartas** stationery; **— de estaño** tinfoil; **— de estraza** brown paper; **— de lija** sandpaper; **— de seda** tissue paper; **— encerado** wax paper; **— higiénico** toilet paper; **— moneda** paper money; **— tisú** tissue paper; **desempeñar un —** to play a role; **en el —** on paper; **hacer buen —** to cut a good figure

papeleo M paperwork

papelera F (fábrica) paper factory; (cubo) wastepaper basket

papelería F stationery store

papeleta F (para escribir) slip of paper; (para votar) ballot

paperas F PL mumps

papito M daddy

páprika F paprika

papú ADJ & MF Papua New Guinean

paquete M (envuelto) package; (atado) bundle; (programas de ordenador) package; **— de programas de productividad** office suite; **— turístico** package tour

Paquistán M Pakistan

paquistano -na ADJ & MF Pakistani

par ADJ even; M (de cosas idénticas) pair; (de cosas diferentes) couple; (título nobiliario) peer; (en golf) par; **a la —** at par; **sin —** peerless; **de — en —** wide-open

para PREP in order to, for; **lo hice — ganar dinero** I did it in order to earn money; **demasiado — mí** too much for me; **trabajo — mi padre** I work for my father; **— ser perro es inteligente** for a dog he's smart; **— mi sorpresa** to my surprise; **voy — Madrid** I'm going to Madrid; **— las dos** by two o'clock; **— atrás** backwards; **— empezar** for starters; **— llevar** to go; **¿— qué?** what for? **— que** so that, so as to; **— siempre** forever; **— su información** FYI [for your information]; **habla — sí** he talks to himself; **— mis adentros** to myself; **— morirse de risa** hilarious; **no es — tanto** it's no big deal; **sin qué ni — qué** without rhyme or reason

parabién M congratulations; **dar el —** to congratulate

parada F (acción de parar) stop; (de perro de caza) point; (de taxis) stand; (militar) parade; (relevo de guardia) changing of the guard; (de balón) parry; (en fútbol americano) tackle

paradero M whereabouts

paradigma M paradigm

parado ADJ (inmóvil) stationary; (sin trabajo) unemployed, idle; **salir bien —** to come out on top

paradoja F paradox

paradójico ADJ paradoxical

parafernalia F paraphernalia

parafina F paraffin

parafrasear VI/VT to paraphrase

paráfrasis F paraphrase

paraguas M SG umbrella

Paraguay M Paraguay

paraguayo -ya ADJ & MF Paraguayan

paraíso M paradise

paraje M spot

paralelo -la ADJ & M parallel; F parallel line; **hacer —s** to draw parallels; **barras**

paralelas parallel bars

parálisis F (inmovilidad física, espiritual) paralysis; (condición médica) paralysis, palsy; — **cerebral** cerebral palsy

paralítico -ca ADJ & MF paralytic

paralización F (de tránsito) gridlock; (del cuerpo) paralysis

paralizar[47] VT (movimiento) to paralyze; (negociaciones) to stall; —**se** to gridlock

paramédico -ca ADJ & MF paramedic

parámetro M parameter

paramilitar ADJ & MF paramilitary

páramo M cold highland, moor

parangón M comparison; **sin** — incomparable

parangonar VT to compare

paraninfo M auditorium

paranoia F paranoia

paranoico -ca ADJ & MF paranoid

paranormal ADJ paranormal

parapléjico -ca MF paraplegic

parapsicología F parapsychology

parar VI/VT (detener) to stop; (motor) to stall; VT (un pase de pelota) to block; (un golpe) to parry; — **de hacer algo** to stop doing something; **y para de contar** and that's it; — **en seco** to stop short; **ir a** — to end up; **habló sin** — he talked nonstop; —**se** (detenerse) to stop; (erguirse) Am to stand up; —**se a pensar** to stop to think; M SG **parabrisas** windshield; M SG **paracaídas** parachute; M SG **paracaídas dorado** golden parachute; M **paracaidismo** parachuting; M SG **parachoques** bumper; M SG **pararrayos** lightning rod; M **parasol** parasol; MF **paracaidista** parachutist

parasítico ADJ parasitic

parásito M parasite

parcela F parcel, plot

parcelación F subdivision

parcelar VT to parcel [out]

parche M (para remendar, informático) patch; (de tambor) drumhead; (médico) Band-aid®; — **de ojo** eye patch

parcial ADJ partial

pardillo M linnet

pardo ADJ (color) gray-brown; (mulato) mulatto

pareado M couplet

parear VT to match

parecer[35] VI to seem; — **que** to seem like, to look like; **¿qué te parece?** what do you think? —**se a** to resemble, to look like; M (opinión) opinion; (aspecto) appearance; **al** — apparently; **a mi** — to my mind / way of thinking; **del mismo** — like-minded

parecido ADJ alike, similar; **bien** — good-looking; M similarity, resemblance

pared F wall; **poner a alguien contra la** — to corner; **subirse por las** —**es** to be furious; **de** — **a** — wall-to-wall; **reloj de** — wall clock

paredón M execution wall

pareja F (de personas) couple; (de cosas) [matching] pair; (compañero) partner

parejo ADJ (hermanos) alike; (carrera) even; (dientes) straight; **correr [al]** — to go hand in hand

parental ADJ parental

parentela F kin

parentesco M kinship, relation

paréntesis M parenthesis

parezca, parezco ver parecer

pargo M red snapper

paria MF pariah, outcast

paridad F parity

pariente MF, **parienta** F relative, relation; — **consanguíneo** blood relative

parir VI/VT to give birth [to]

parlamentar VI to parley

parlamentario -ria ADJ parliamentary; MF member of parliament

parlamento M (en una obra de teatro) speech; (negociación) parley; (cuerpo legislativo) parliament

parlanchín ADJ talkative; MF chatterbox

parlotear VI to chatter, to rattle on

parloteo M chatter

paro M (huelga breve) stoppage; (falta de trabajo) unemployment; (ave) tit; — **cardiaco** cardiac arrest; — **laboral** work stoppage

parodia F parody

parodiar VT to parody

parpadear VI (un ojo, pantalla) to blink; (una vela) to flicker; (una estrella) to twinkle

parpadeo M (del ojo) blink; (de una vela) flicker; (de una estrella) twinkle; (de una pantalla) blinking

párpado M eyelid

parque M park; — **automotor** fleet of cars; — **de atracciones** amusement park; — **zoológico** zoo

parra F grapevine

párrafo M paragraph; **echar un** — **con** to have a chat with

parral M grape arbor

parranda F binge, spree; **andar de** — to go out partying

parrandear VI to revel

parrandero -ra MF party animal

parrilla F (sobre el fuego) grill; (en el horno) broiler; (de calles) grid; (de coche) grille

parrillada F barbecue dish

párroco M parish priest

parroquia F (distrito) parish; (iglesia) parish church

parroquial ADJ parochial

parroquiano -na MF (de iglesia) parishioner; (de tienda) regular

parte F (sección) part; (lugar) place; (papel en

una obra teatral) lines; (persona legal) party;
— **integrante** built-in part; — **interesada**
interested party; —**s pudendas** private
parts, *fam* privates; **a otra** — somewhere
else; **a —s iguales** fifty-fifty; **de un tiempo
a esta** — for some time; **de — de** on behalf
of; **de — a** — completely; **echar a mala** — to
take amiss; **en** — partly; **en gran** — in large
measure; **en otra** — elsewhere; **en/por
todas** —s everywhere; **formar — de** to be
part of; **ir por** —**s** to proceed by steps; **la
mayor — de** most of; **la — del león** the
lion's share; **no está en ninguna** — it's
nowhere to be found; **no va a ninguna** —
it's going nowhere; **por otra** — on the other
hand; **tomar — en** to take part in; M report;
dar — to report; **dar — de enfermo** to call
in sick; **dar — de un crimen** to report a
crime

partera F midwife

partición F (of a country) partition; (of a cell)
division

participación F (en un proyecto) participation,
involvement; (en un negocio) interest; — **de
nacimiento** birth announcement

participante MF (en un grupo) participant; (en
una carrera) entrant; (en un concurso)
contestant

participar VI to participate; VT to announce; —
de/en to participate in, to share in

partícipe MF participant

participio M participle

partícula F particle

particular ADJ (específico) particular; (poco
usual) peculiar; (privado) private; **en** — in
particular; **clases** —**es** private lessons; M
(detalle) particular; (asunto) matter; MF
private citizen

partida F (fondos) appropriation; (grupo de
personas) party; (cantidad de mercancía)
parcel, lot; (de ajedrez) game; (acción de
partir) departure; — **de nacimiento** birth
record; **jugar una mala** — to play a mean
trick; **por — doble** double-entry

partidario -ria MF (de una medida) supporter,
advocate; (de un partido político) partisan

partidista ADJ & MF partisan

partido M (grupo político) party; (de golf)
round; (de tenis, fútbol) game, match; **es un
buen** — he's a good match; **sacar — de** to
take advantage of; **tomar** — to take sides;
¿cómo va el —? what's the score? ADJ split,
cleft

partir VT (dividir) to divide; (repartir) to share;
(quebrar) to break; **eso me parte por el eje**
that screws me up; **que te parta un rayo** go
jump in the lake; VI (salir) to depart, to leave;
a — **de entonces** since then; **a** — **del lunes**
starting Monday; —**se de risa** to die of
laughter

partisano -na MF partisan

partitura F musical score

parto M childbirth, delivery; — **prematuro**
premature birth; **estar en trabajo de** — to
be in labor

parvulario M kindergarten, nursery

párvulo -la MF nursery school child

pasa F raisin

pasable ADJ passable

pasada F (acción de pasar) passing; (con una
máquina) pass; **una mala** — a mean trick; **de**
— by the way

pasadizo M secret passage

pasado M past; ADJ (anterior) past; (demasiado
maduro) overripe; — **mañana** day after
tomorrow; **el año** — last year; **el — mes de
septiembre** last September

pasador M (de un cierre) pin; (de la puerta) latch

pasaje M (sitio por donde se pasa, fragmento de
texto) passage; (billete) ticket; (precio de un
viaje) fare; (conjunto de los pasajeros)
passengers

pasajero -ra ADJ fleeting, transitory; MF (en un
coche, tren) passenger; (en un taxi) fare

pasante M (tenis) passing shot; MF (compañía)
intern

pasaporte M passport

pasar VI (no querer jugar, ir de un lado a otro,
seguir su proceso, transcurrir) to pass;
(ocurrir) to happen; — **a ser** to become; — **de
moda** to go out of style; — **hambre** to go
hungry; — **por** to pass by; — **por alto** to pass
over; — **una tarjeta por un lector** to swipe
a card; —**le por la cabeza a alguien** to
occur to someone; **pasan de los 80 años**
they're over 80 years old; **te pasaste de la
casa** you missed the house; —**se** to spoil;
—**se de la raya** to cross the line; —**se de sol**
to get too much sun; —**se de listo** to
outsmart oneself; **se me pasó ir a buscarte**
I totally forgot to pick you up; **me la paso
bien** I have a good time; VT (la sal, una
prueba, la plancha, una pelota) to pass; (un
sofocón) to endure; (una tarde) to spend; —
las de Caín to go through hell; — **en
limpio** to make a new copy; — **por alto** to
overlook; — **los 50 kmh** to exceed 50 kmh;
— **revista** to pass in review; **nos pasó un
Volvo** a Volvo passed us; **no lo paso** I can't
stand him; M **tienen un buen** — they have a
comfortable life; M **pasamano** (de barco)
guard rail, gangway; (de escalera) banister,
railing; M **pasatiempo** pastime

pasarela F (en un barco) gangplank; (en un
desfile de modas) runway

Pascua F (fiesta cristiana) Easter; (fiesta judía)
Passover; — **Florida / de Resurrección**
Easter Sunday; — **de Navidad** Christmas

pase M (deporte) pass; — **cruzado** cross; — **de anotación** touchdown pass; — **de cabeza** header; — **pantalla** screen pass

pasear VI (a pie) to take a walk; (en bici, a caballo) to go on a ride; (en coche) to go for a drive, to go on a ride; —**se** to parade, to take a walk; —**se a caballo** to go horseback riding; VT (un perro) to walk a dog

paseo M (a pie) walk, stroll; (a caballo, en bicicleta) ride; (en coche) drive, ride; (calle donde se pasea) mall; (recreativo) outing; **irse a** — to go jump in a lake; **dar un** — (a pie) to take a walk; **a** — step by step; (en coche) to go on a drive

pasillo M (de un teatro) aisle; (de un edificio) hallway, corridor; (para vuelo aéreo) corridor; — **de dobles** alley

pasión F passion

pasivo ADJ passive; **voz pasiva** passive voice; M (en un negocio) liabilities; (de una cuenta) debit side

pasmado ADJ astounded

pasmar VT to astound, to stun; —**se** to be astounded, to be stunned

pasmo M astonishment

pasmoso ADJ astonishing, stunning

paso M (acción de pasar, lugar donde pasar) pass; (de pie, de danza, distancia, de un proceso) step; (velocidad) pace; (de caballerías) walk; (de tornillo) pitch; (de coche) wheelbase; — **elevado** overpass; — **a nivel** grade crossing; — **de tortuga** snail's pace; — **a** — step by step; **dar** — (dejar pasar) to let pass; (dejar actuar) to make possible; **dar** —**s** to take steps; **hacer** —**s** to travel; **de** — by the way, in passing; **estar de** — to be passing through; **marcar el** — to set the pace; **al** — **que** while; **salir del** — to get out of a difficulty; **dicho sea de** — incidentally; **a cada** — at every turn; — **del tiempo** passage of time; **abrir** — **para** to make way for; **abrirse** — to plow through, to press through; ADJ dried

pasta F (de almidón) paste; (de harina) dough; (de fideos) pasta; (de libro) hard cover, binding; (dinero) *fam* dough; **de buena** — of good disposition; — **dentífrica/dental** toothpaste

pastar VI/VT to pasture, to graze

pastel M (torta) cake; (tarta) pie; (pintura, cuadro) pastel; — **de cumpleaños** birthday cake; — **de limón** lemon pie; — **de carne** meat pie; **descubrir el** — to spill the beans; ADJ pastel

pastelería F (establecimiento) pastry shop; (conjunto de pasteles) pastry

pastelero -ra M pastry cook

pasterizar, pasteurizar[9] VT to pasteurize

pastilla F (de medicina) tablet, pill; (para la tos) drop; (de jabón) bar

pastizal M grassland

pasto M (terreno) pasture, grassland; (hierba) grass; **ser** — **de** to be a victim of

pastor -ora MF (de ovejas) shepherd; (sacerdote protestante) pastor, minister; M — **alemán** German shepherd

pastoral ADJ pastoral; F pastoral letter

pastoril ADJ pastoral

pastoso ADJ pasty

pastura F feed

pat M putt

pata F (de animal, mueble) foot, leg; (de pollo) drumstick; (de un enchufe) pin; — **palmada** webfoot; — **de gallo** crow's feet; **en cuatro** —**s** on all fours; **a [la]** — **coja** skipping on one leg; **estirar la** — *fam* to kick the bucket; **mala** — bad luck; **metedura de** — faux pas; **meter la** — to slip up; —**s arriba** upside down; ADJ **patihendido** cloven-hoofed; **patitieso** dumbfounded; **patizambo** (hacia adentro) knock-kneed; (hacia afuera) bow-legged

patada F kick (también en deportes); **libros a** —**s** tons of books; **en dos** —**s** in a jiffy; **dar** —**s** to kick; **echar a** —**s** to kick out; — **lateral** (fútbol americano) onside kick

patalear VI (en el aire) to kick; (en el suelo) to stamp

pataleo M (en el aire) kick; (en el suelo) stamp

pataleta F fit; **tener una** — to throw a fit

patán M boor

patata F *Esp* potato; —**s fritas** French fries; — **caliente** hot potato

pateador M kicker

patear VT (algo, a alguien) to kick; (el suelo) to stamp; VI to tramp around; VI/VT (en golf) to putt; VI to kick; — **al arco** to shoot at goal

patentar VT to patent

patente ADJ & F patent; **se hizo** — **su ignorancia** he betrayed his ignorance; — **en trámite** patent pending

paternal ADJ (del padre) paternal; (como un padre) fatherly

paternidad F paternity, fatherhood; **prueba de** — paternity test

paterno ADJ paternal

patético ADJ moving

patetismo M pathos

patíbulo M gallows scaffold, gallows

patilla F (de gafas) arm; —**s** (de pelo) sideburns

patín M (tabla) skate; (de trineo) runner; — **de ruedas** roller skate; — **de cuchilla / de hielo** ice skate

patinaje M skating

patinar VI (una persona) to skate; (un coche sobre hielo) to skid; (un embrague) to slip; (en un examen) to blank out

patinazo M (de embrague) slip; (de coche) skid

patio M (de casa) patio, courtyard; (de escuela)

playground

pato M (ave) duck; (macho) drake; **pagar el —** to take the rap

patochada F blunder

patógeno M pathogen

patología F pathology

patológico ADJ pathological

patoso ADJ clumsy

patotero -ra MF *Am* hooligan

patraña F tall tale

patria F fatherland, homeland

patriarca M patriarch

patriarcal ADJ patriarchal

patrimonial ADJ inherited, patrimonial

patrimonio M patrimony; **— cultural** cultural heritage; **— neto** net worth; **— personal** personal assets

patriota MF patriot

patriótico ADJ patriotic

patriotismo M patriotism

patrocinador -ora MF sponsor

patrocinar VT to sponsor

patrocinio M sponsorship; **— empresarial** corporate backing

patrón -ona MF (protector) patron; (jefe) employer; (de navío) skipper; M (dueño de pensión) landlord; (de costura) pattern; (punto de referencia) yardstick, standard; (de planta) stock; (de un parásito) host; **— de oro** gold standard; F (dueña de pensión) landlady

patronal ADJ management; **asociación —** employers' association; F management

patronato M board of trustees

patrono -na MF patron

patrulla F (grupo de policías o soldados) patrol, squad; (coche) squad car

patrullar VI/VT to patrol

patrullero -ra M patrol car, squad car; MF patrol officer

pausa F (musical) pause, rest; **trabajar con —** to work slowly; **hacer —** to pause

pauta F guideline

pavimentar VT to pave

pavimento M pavement

pavo M turkey; **— real** peacock; ADJ silly

pavón M peacock

pavonearse VI to strut, to swagger

pavoneo M strut, swagger

pavor M dread

pavoroso ADJ frightful

payasada F clownish act or remark; **—s** antics, horseplay

payasear VI to clown around, to horse around

payaso M (de circo) clown; (persona poco seria) buffoon; **hacer el —** to clown around

paz F peace; **estamos en —** we are even; **[que] en — descanse** may she rest in peace; **hacer las paces** to make up; **dejar en —** to leave alone

PC M PC

peaje M (tasa) toll; (cabina donde se paga) tollbooth

peatón -ona MF pedestrian

peca F freckle

pecado M sin; **— mortal** mortal sin

pecador -ora MF sinner; ADJ sinful

pecaminoso ADJ sinful

pecar[30] VI to sin; **— contra** to transgress against; **— de bueno** to be too good; **— de generoso** to be generous to a fault; **— de oscuro** to be exceedingly unclear

pecera F (pequeña) fish tank, fishbowl; (grande) aquarium

pechera F (de camisa) front; (de delantal) bib

pecho M (parte del cuerpo) chest; (mama) breast; **dar el —** to nurse; **nadar —** to do the breaststroke; **tomar a —[s]** to take to heart; **sacar —** to puff out one's chest

pechuga F breast

pechugona ADJ buxom

pecio M flotsam and jetsam

pecoso ADJ freckled

pectoral ADJ & M pectoral

peculado M embezzlement

peculiar ADJ peculiar

peculiaridad F peculiarity

pedagogía F pedagogy, education

pedagógico ADJ pedagogical, teaching

pedagogo -ga MF pedagogue

pedal M pedal

pedalear VI/VT to pedal

pedante ADJ pedantic; MF pedant

pedazo M piece; **— de idiota** absolute idiot; **él es un — de pan** he's a saint; **hacer —s** to tear to pieces; **caerse a —s** to fall to pieces; **— por —** piece by piece

pederasta M pederast, pedophile

pedófilo -la MF pedophile

pederastia F pederasty

pedernal M flint

pedestal M pedestal

pedestre ADJ pedestrian

pediatra MF pediatrician

pediatría F pediatrics

pedido M (comercial) order; (petición) request; **hacer un —** to place an order; **— fijo** standing order; **— pendiente** back order; **— urgente** rush order

pedigrí M pedigree

pedigüeño -ña MF mooch, moocher; ADJ **no seas —** stop mooching

pedir[9] VT (requerir) to ask for, to request; (exigir) to demand; (encargar) to order, to requisition; **— prestado** to borrow; **— socorro** to cry for help; **— un deseo** to make a wish; **— que** to ask/pray that; **— la mano de una mujer** to ask a woman's hand in marriage; **— por alguien**

to ask to speak to someone

pedofilia F pedophilia

pedrada F **dar una —** to hit with a stone; **matar a —s** to stone to death

pedregal M rocky ground

pedregoso ADJ stony

pedrería F precious stones

pedrusco M boulder

pedúnculo M stem

pega F snag

pegadizo ADJ catchy

pegado ADJ (adherido) stuck; (contiguo) adjoining, contiguous; **quedarse —** to get an electric shock; **— al televisor** glued to the television

pegajoso ADJ sticky, tacky

pegamento M glue

pegar[40] VT (con el puño) to hit, to strike; (algo con pegamento) to stick, to glue; (botones) to sew on; **— con** to match; **— contra** to touch; **— un cuadrangular** to hit a homerun; **— un grito** to yell; **— un sencillo** to hit a single; **— un susto** to give a scare; **— un salto** to jump; **—le a la bola** to hit the ball; **—le un tiro a alguien** to shoot someone; **—se** (adherir) to stick together, to cling; (contagiarse) to be contagious; **—se a** to latch onto; **no — un ojo** not to sleep a wink

pegote M glob

pegotear VT to gum up

peinado M (estilo) coiffure, hairdo; (acción) combing

peinador -ora MF hairdresser

peinar VT to comb (también registrar); (en una peluquería) to style; **— a contrapelo** to rub the wrong way

peine M comb

pelada F bald spot

pelado ADJ (sin pelo) hairless; (pobre) poor; (sin cáscara) peeled; (sin árboles) treeless; (sin plumas) plucked; (sin dinero) broke

pelador M peeler

pelaje M coat, fur

pelar VT (el pelo) to cut the hair of; (las plumas) to pluck the feathers from; (frutas, verduras, huevo) to peel; (a un jugador) to fleece; **duro de —** hard to deal with; **el agua está que pela** the water is really hot; **—se** to peel; M SG **pelagatos** nobody

peldaño M step, stair

pelea F (de palabra) fight, quarrel; (de obra) fight, scrape; (de boxeo) fight; **— a puñetazos** fistfight; **— de perros** dogfight

pelear VI (con palabras) to fight, to quarrel; (con obras) to fight, to scuffle; **—se con alguien** to have a fight with someone

pelechar VI (perder la piel) to shed; (mejorar) to get better

pelele M (persona sin carácter) wimp; (muñeca) straw doll

peletería F (tienda) fur store; (comercio) fur trade

pelícano M pelican

película F film (también membrana); (obra cinematográfica) motion picture, film, movie; **de —** extraordinary; **dar una —** to show a film; **— muda** silent film

peligrar VI to be in danger

peligro M danger, peril; **ese muchacho es un —** that boy is dangerous; **en —** in danger; **poner en —** to imperil/endanger/jeopardize

peligroso ADJ dangerous, perilous

pellejo M (piel de animal) hide, pelt; (odre) wineskin; **salvar el —** to save one's skin; **ser todo —** to be skin and bones; **jugarse el —** to risk one's life

pellizcar[30] VT to pinch

pellizco M pinching

pelma MF jerk

pelo M (de persona) hair; (de animal) fur; (de alfombra) pile; **con —s y señales** with every possible detail; **de medio —** low-class; **eso me viene al —** that suits me perfectly; **montar en —** to ride bareback; **ni un —** not at all; **no tener —s en la lengua** not to mince words; **se le ponen los —s de punta** his hair stands on end; **se salvó por un —** he was saved by the skin of his teeth; **tomarle el — a alguien** to tease someone, to pull someone's leg; **traído de los —s** far-fetched; ADJ **pelirrojo** redheaded

pelón ADJ bald

pelota F (objeto) ball; (juego) ballgame; **— vasca** jai-alai; **pasar la —** (dar el balón) to pass the ball; (dar la responsabilidad) to pass the buck

pelotear VI to rally

peloteo M rally

pelotera F brawl

pelotero -ra MF (jugador de béisbol) baseball player; (juego para niños) ball pit

pelotón M (pelota grande) large ball; (de tierra seca) clod; (de ciclistas) pack; (de soldados) platoon; (de fusilamiento) firing squad

peltre M pewter

peluca F wig

peludo ADJ (persona) hairy; (animal) furry; (perro) shaggy

peluquería F (para hombres) barbershop; (para mujeres) salon

peluquero -ra MF (de hombres) barber; (de mujeres) hairdresser

peluquín M toupee

pelusa F (de tela, ropa) lint, fluff; (de melocotón, de la piel) fuzz; (de plantas) hair; (de polvo) dust bunny

pelvis F pelvis

pena F (castigo) penalty; (tristeza) sorrow; (vergüenza) embarrassment; **— de muerte**

death penalty, capital punishment; **—s**
hardships; **a duras —s** with great difficulty;
me da — it grieves me; **hecho una —**
looking like a mess; **¡qué —!** what a shame!
sería una — perder it would be a shame to
lose; **so — de** on pain of; **valer la —** to be
worthwhile

penacho M (de plumas) tuft, crest; (de humo)
plume

penal ADJ penal; M penitentiary

penalidad F (penuria) hardship; (castigo)
penalty

penalizar⁴⁷ VT to penalize

penalti, penalty M penalty kick

penar VI to suffer; VT to punish

penco M plug, nag

pendencia F wrangle, fight

pendenciero ADJ quarrelsome

pender VI to hang, to dangle

pendiente F slope, incline; M *Esp* earring; ADJ
(aretes) dangling; (negocio) pending,
unfinished; (pago) outstanding; **quedo — de
tu llamada** I look forward to your call

pendón M banner

péndulo M pendulum

pene M penis

penetración F penetration

penetrante ADJ (mirada, sonido) penetrating,
piercing; (frío) biting; (comentario) cutting;
(inteligencia) keen

penetrar VT (pasar al interior) to penetrate, to
pierce; (comprender) to comprehend

penicilina F penicillin

península F peninsula

peninsular ADJ peninsular

penitencia F (religiosa) penance; (castigo)
detention; **¡estás en —!** you're grounded!

penitenciaría F penitentiary

penitente ADJ & MF penitent

penoso ADJ (triste) painful, grievous; (difícil)
trying; (que da vergüenza) embarrassing

pensador-ora MF thinker; ADJ reflective

pensamiento M (facultad, acción, efecto)
thought; (flor) pansy

pensante ADJ thinking

pensar¹ VI/VT to think; **— en** to think about/
over; **— hacer algo** to intend to do
something; **eso da que —** that seems
questionable; **no lo pienses dos veces**
don't think twice

pensativo ADJ pensive, thoughtful

pensión F (asignación periódica) pension,
allowance; (comidas) board; (hostal)
boardinghouse; **— completa** room and
board; **tener en —** to have as a boarder

pensionado M boarding school

pensionar VT to pension

pensionista MF (que vive en una pensión)
boarder; (que cobra una pensión) pensioner

pentágono M pentagon

pentagrama M musical staff

penthouse M penthouse

penúltimo ADJ next to the last, penultimate

penumbra F semi-darkness, dimness

penuria F (escasez) shortage; (pobreza) poverty

peña F boulder; **— folclórica** folklore club

peñasco M crag

peñascoso ADJ craggy

peñón M crag

peón -ona MF (obrero) unskilled laborer,
farmhand; **— caminero** road worker; M (en
ajedrez) pawn; (en damas) piece

peonada F gang of laborers

peonaje M gang of laborers

peonza F toy top

peor ADJ worse, worst; **este libro es —** this
book is worse; **el — libro** the worst book;
ADV worse; **trabaja —** he works worse; **—
que** worse than; **— que nunca** worse than
ever; **en el — de los casos** if worst comes to
worst; **lo —** the worst [thing]; **tanto —** so
much the worse

pepa F **es un viva la —** it's bedlam

pepino M cucumber

pepita F (simiente) seed; (tumor de gallina) pip;
(masa de oro) nugget

pequeñez F (cualidad de pequeño) smallness;
(cosa insignificante) trifle

pequeño -ña ADJ (de poco tamaño) small, little;
(de corta edad) young; (de poca importancia)
trivial

pera F pear; **pedirle —s al olmo** to ask the
impossible

peral M pear tree

perca F perch; **— americana** black bass

percal M percale

percance M accident, mishap

percatarse VI (darse cuenta) to realize; (notar)
to notice

percebe M barnacle

percepción F perception

perceptible ADJ perceptible, noticeable

perceptivo ADJ perceptive

percha F (para el armario) clothes hanger; (palo
para colgar cosas) peg; (palo para aves) perch;
(perchero) coat rack

perchero M coat rack

percibir VT (experimentar) to perceive, to sense;
(recibir) to collect

percudir VT to make grimy; **—se** to get grimy

percusión F percussion

percutor M firing pin

perdedor -ora MF loser

perder² VT (dejar de tener algo, extraviar) to
lose, to mislay; (echar a perder) to misplace)
to spoil, to ruin; (ser derrotado) to lose; (no
aprovechar) to waste; (no llegar a tiempo, no
disfrutar) to miss; **— el conocimiento** to

lose consciousness; **— el tiempo** to waste time; **— los estribos** to fly off the handle; **— hojas** to shed leaves; **— pie** to lose one's footing; **— terreno** to lose ground; **echarse a —** to spoil; **el vaso pierde agua** the glass leaks water; **llevo las de —** the odds are against me; **—se** (extraviarse) to lose one's way, to get lost; (apartarse del buen camino) to go astray, to stray; **se han perdido las llaves** the keys have gotten lost; **—se de vista** to disappear; **—[se] una oportunidad** to pass up / miss an opportunity; **— el balón** (fútbol americano) to fumble; (fútbol) to lose the ball

perdición F perdition, damnation

pérdida F (acción de perder, cosa perdida) loss; (de dinero dado en prenda) forfeiture; **entrar en —** to nosedive; **— de tiempo** waste of time; **— de balón** (fútbol americano) fumble, turnover; (fútbol) loss of ball possession; **—s cubiertas** covered losses; **—s totales** total loss

perdido -da ADJ (extraviado) lost, missing; (aislado) isolated; (promiscuo) promiscuous; **un borracho —** an utter drunkard; **estar — por alguien** to be crazy about someone; M degenerate

perdigón M (pollo de perdiz) young partridge; (bolita de plomo) birdshot, buckshot

perdiz F partridge

perdón M (privado) forgiveness; (oficial) pardon; **con — de los presentes** present company excepted; **no tener —** to be unforgivable; INTERJ excuse me

perdonar VT (en privado) to forgive; (oficialmente) to pardon

perdurable ADJ lasting

perdurar VI to last

perecedero ADJ perishable

perecer[35] VI to perish

peregrinación F pilgrimage

peregrinar VI to go on a pilgrimage

peregrino -na MF pilgrim; ADJ far-fetched

perejil M parsley

perenne ADJ perennial

pereza F laziness, idleness, sloth

perezoso ADJ lazy, idle; M (animal) sloth

perfección F perfection; **a la —** to perfection, perfectly

perfeccionamiento M perfecting

perfeccionar VT to perfect

perfeccionista MF perfectionist

perfectamente ADV perfectly; **tú hablas español —** you speak Spanish quite well

perfecto ADJ perfect, flawless; **es un — tarado** he's an utter idiot; **es un — desconocido** he's a complete stranger

perfil M profile; **de —** from the side

perfilar VT to outline; **—se** (marcarse) to be

outlined; (definirse) to become clear

perforación F (de una superficie) perforation; (de un pozo) drilling; (de la piel) piercing

perforar VT (agujerear) to perforate; (buscar petróleo) to drill

perfumar VT to perfume, to scent

perfume M perfume, scent

perfumería F perfumery

pergamino M parchment

pérgola F arbor

pericia F expertness, know-how

perico M (loro) parakeet; (cocaína) *fam* snow

periferia F periphery, fringe

periférico ADJ & M peripheral

perilla F (adorno, remate) knob; (pelo de barbilla) goatee; **me viene de —s** it's exactly what I need

perímetro M perimeter

periódico M newspaper; **— mensual** monthly periodical; ADJ periodic

periodismo M journalism

periodista MF journalist

periodístico ADJ journalistic

período M period (también menstruación); (de materia radiactiva) half-life; **— de prueba** (para un trabajo) probationary period; (para una mercancía) trial period; **— glaciar** ice age

peripecia F vicissitude

peripuesto ADJ dressed up, dolled up, decked out

periquito M parakeet

periscopio M periscope

perista MF fence

perito -ta ADJ expert, practiced; MF technician

peritonitis F peritonitis

perjudicar[30] VT to harm

perjudicial ADJ harmful, detrimental

perjuicio M harm

perjurar VT to swear; VI to commit perjury; **—se** to commit perjury

perjurio M perjury

perla F (de nácar) pearl; (persona) gem; (de sudor) bead; (de sabiduría) nugget; (frase inoportuna) blooper; **me viene de —s** it suits me perfectly

perlado ADJ pearly

permanecer[35] VI to remain, to stay

permanencia F (carácter de permanente) permanence; (acción de permanecer) stay

permanente ADJ permanent

permanezca, permanezco *ver* permanecer

permeable ADJ permeable

permear VT to permeate

permisible ADJ permissible

permisivo ADJ permissive

permiso M (para ir al baño) permission; (para faltar al servicio militar) furlough; (para faltar al trabajo) leave; (para casarse, conducir) license, permit; — **de trabajo** work permit; **con** — excuse me

permitir VT (dar permiso) to permit, to allow; (posibilitar) to enable; —**se** (una libertad) to take the liberty of; (un lujo) to allow oneself; **¿me permite?** may I?

permuta F exchange

permutación F permutation

permutar VT to exchange

pernetas LOC ADV **en** — barelegged

pernicioso ADJ pernicious

pernicorto ADJ short-legged

perno M bolt, pin

pero CONJ but; ADV **muy** — **muy lindo** very, very pretty; M objection; **no hay** — **que valga** there are no buts about it

perogrullada F platitude

perorar VI to hold forth

perorata F lecture

peróxido M peroxide

perpendicular ADJ perpendicular

perpetrar VT to perpetrate

perpetuar[26] VT to perpetuate

perpetuo ADJ perpetual

perplejidad F perplexity, bewilderment

perplejo ADJ perplexed, bewildered; VT **dejar** — to perplex

perrera F (lugar donde guardar perros) pound; (rabieta) tantrum

perrero -ra MF dogcatcher; ADJ dog-loving

perro M dog; — **caliente** hot dog; — **callejero** stray dog; — **cobrador** retriever; — **de caza** hunting dog; — **de lanas** poodle; — **esquimal** husky; — **faldero** lapdog; — **guía** guide dog; — **guardián** watchdog, guard dog; — **pastor** sheepdog; — **policía** police dog; ADJ miserable; **en la perra vida** never

perruno ADJ canine

persa ADJ & MF Persian; M (lengua) Persian

persecución F (religiosa) persecution; (policial) pursuit, chase

perseguidor -ora MF (que sigue) pursuer; (que acosa) persecutor

perseguir[12] VT (seguir para alcanzar) to pursue, to chase; (seguir para encontrar) to track down; (acosar) to hound; (tratar de destruir) to persecute

perseverancia F perseverance

perseverar VI to persevere

Persia F Persia

persiana F blind, shade

persiga, persigo, persigue, persiguiendo, persiguiera, persiguiese *ver* perseguir

persistencia F persistence

persistente ADJ persistent

persistir VI to persist

persona E person; — **influyente** player; — **legal** legal entity; **en** — in person; — **mayor**

adult

personaje M (persona importante) personage; (de obra literaria) character; **es todo un** — he's quite a character

personal ADJ personal; M personnel, staff

personalidad F personality

personalmente ADV personally

personificar[30] VT to personify, to embody

perspectiva F (punto de vista, distancia, técnica de dibujo) perspective; (panorama) view, vista; (posibilidad) prospect; **tener en** — to have planned

perspicacia F insight, sharpness

perspicaz ADJ perspicacious, perceptive

persuadir VT to persuade

persuasión F persuasion

persuasivo ADJ persuasive

pertenecer[35] VI to belong

perteneciente ADJ belonging

pertenencias F PL belongings

pertenezca, pertenezco *ver* pertenecer

pértiga F pole

pertinente ADJ pertinent, relevant

pertrechos M PL military supplies

perturbación F disturbance

perturbar VT to perturb, to disturb

Perú M Peru

peruano -na ADJ & MF Peruvian

perversidad F (distorsión) perversity; (maldad) wickedness

perversión F perversion

perverso ADJ (distorsionante) perverse; (malvado) wicked

pervertido -da MF pervert

pervertir[8] VT (enviar) to pervert; (distorsionar) to distort; —**se** to become perverted

pesa F (para pesar) weight; (para hacer ejercicio) dumbbell; —**s y medidas** weights and measures

pesadez F (cualidad de pesado) heaviness; (tedio) tiresomeness; (persona pesada) tiresome person

pesadilla F nightmare

pesado -da ADJ (que pesa mucho, difícil de digerir) heavy; (aburrido) tiresome; (robusto) heavy-set; (tardo) slow; MF bore, pest

pesadumbre F grief, sorrow

pésame M condolence, expression of sympathy

pesar VT (apenar) to sadden; (medir el peso de) to weigh; (recaer sobre) to weight down; VI (tener peso, importancia) to weigh; M grief, sorrow; LOC ADV **a** — **de** in spite of

pesaroso ADJ (triste) sad; (arrepentido) repentant

pesca F (acción de pescar) fishing; (lo pescado) catch; **ir de** — to go fishing

pescadería F fish market

pescado M fish

pescador -ora MF fisherman

pescar[30] VI/VT (capturar peces) to fish; (sacar del agua, coger, comprender, sorprender, pillar) to catch; (obtener) to land, to nail

pescozón M blow to the back of the head

pescuezo M neck

pesebre M (para pienso) manger, crib; (belén) nativity scene

peseta F peseta

pesimismo M pessimism

pesimista MF pessimist

pésimo ADJ dismal, wretched

peso M (fuerza, importancia) weight; (cosa opresiva) burden; (cosa pesada) load; **vender al —** to sell by weight; **levantar en —** to lift off the ground

pesquería F fishery

pesquero ADJ fishing; M fishing boat

pesquisa F inquiry

pestaña F (del ojo) eyelash; (en costura) fringe; (de papel, texto) tab; **quemarse las —s** to burn the midnight oil

pestañear VI to blink; **sin —** unflinchingly

pestañeo M blink

peste F (enfermedad) plague; (persona molesta) pest; (hedor) stench; **— bubónica** bubonic plague; **— negra** black death; **hablar —s de alguien** to speak badly of someone

pestilencia F pestilence

pestillo M deadbolt, latch

petaca F (para tabaco) tobacco pouch; (para whisky) flask

pétalo M petal

petardear VI to backfire

petardeo M backfire

petate M bundle; **liar el —** to pack up and go

petición F petition, request

peticionar VT to petition

petirrojo M robin

pétreo ADJ stony

petróleo M petroleum, oil; **— crudo** crude oil

petrolero -ra ADJ oil, petroleum; **plataforma —** oil rig; M oil tanker; F oil company

petrolífero ADJ (que contiene petróleo) oil-bearing; (que produce petróleo) oil-producing; (relativo al petróleo) oil

petulancia F smugness

petulante ADJ smug

petunia F petunia

peyorativo ADJ pejorative

peyote M peyote

pez M fish; **— dorado** goldfish; **— espada** swordfish; **— gordo** fam fat cat, big shot; **— vela** sailfish; **— volador** flying fish; **como — en el agua** perfectly at ease; F pitch

pezón M nipple

pezuña F hoof

phishing M phishing

piadoso ADJ pious, saintly

piafar VI to stamp

pianista MF pianist, piano player

piano M piano; **— de cola** grand piano; **— vertical** upright piano

pianola F player piano

piar[28] VI to peep, to chirp

pica F (lanza) pike; (palo de baraja) spade

picada F (de insecto) bite; (de avión) nosedive; **caer en —** to dive

picadillo M meat [and vegetable] hash

picado ADJ (mar) rough, choppy; (carne) chopped; (de viruela) poked; M (de avión) nosedive; **caer en —** to dive

picador M picador; ADJ stinging

picadora F grinder; **— de carne** meat grinder

picadura F (de serpiente) bite; (de insecto) sting, bite

picante ADJ (especia) spicy, hot; (queso) sharp; (obsceno) risqué; M (especia fuerte) strong seasoning; (cualidad) spiciness

picar[30] VI/VT (un pez) to bite; (un ave) to peck; (comer en pequeñas cantidades) to nibble; VT (tomates) to chop up; (carne) to mince; (una vaca) to goad, to poke; (la curiosidad) to pique; (con espuelas) to spur; VI (una comida picante) to sting; (el sol) to burn; (la piel) to itch, to smart; (un avión) to dive; **— alto** to aim high; **—se** to spoil; **se pica el mar** the sea is getting rough; **se me picó un diente** I got a cavity; M SG **picapleitos** pey shyster; M **picaporte** latch

picardía F mischief

picaresco ADJ picaresque

pícaro -ra MF rogue, rascal; ADJ roguish, mischievous

picazón F (en la piel) itch; (en la garganta) tickle; **provoca —** it causes itching

picea F spruce

pichi M jumper

pichón M (paloma) pigeon; (cría de ave) chick

picnic M picnic

pico M (de ave) beak, bill; (de montaña) peak; (herramienta) pick; (de tetera) spout; **cuarenta y —** forty-odd; **cerrar el —** to shut one's mouth; **tener el — de oro** to be very eloquent

pícolo M piccolo

picotazo M peck

picotear VI/VT (aves) to peck; (personas) to nibble

pictórico ADJ pictorial

pida, pide, pidiendo, pidiera, pidiese ver pedir

pídola F leapfrog

pie M (del cuerpo, de calcetín, de cama, medida) foot; (de foto) caption; (de copa) stem; (de lámpara) stand; (de página) bottom; (para un actor) cue; (de árbol) trunk; (de mueble) leg; **— de atleta** athlete's foot; **— de autor**

byline; **— de imprenta** printer's mark; **— zambo** clubfoot; **a —** on foot; **un soldado de a —** a footsoldier; **— de banco** silly remark; **a — juntillas** firmly; **al — de la letra** to the letter; **caer de —** to have good luck; **con un — en el estribo** with one foot out of the door; **dar —** (a una crítica) to give rise to; (a un actor) to cue; **de/en —** standing; **en — de guerra** (enojado) on the warpath; (belicoso) on a war footing; **estar de —** to be standing; **estar en — de igualdad con** to be on a par with; **esto no tiene ni —s ni cabeza** I can't make heads or tails of this; **ir a — to walk; perder —** to lose one's footing; **ponerse de —** to stand up

piedad F (cualidad de pío) piety; (misericordia) mercy; **tener —** to show mercy

piedra F stone; **— angular** cornerstone, keystone; **— caliza** limestone; **— de afilar** whetstone; **— de toque** touchstone; **— pómez** pumice; **— preciosa** gemstone; **ser — de escándalo** to be an object of scandal

piel F (humana) skin; (animal) hide, pelt; (para confección) fur; **— de gallina** goosebumps; **— de naranja** cellulite

piensa, piense ver pensar

pienso M feed; **ni por —** no way

pierda, pierde ver perder

pierna F leg; **— de ternera** leg of lamb; **dormir a — suelta** to sleep like a log

pieza F (de artillería, de tela, de música, de teatro) piece; (habitación) room; **— de repuesto** replacement part; **de una —** astonished; **menuda —** a piece of work

pífano M fife

pifia F goof, miscue

pifiar VT to goof up, to miscue

pigmento M pigment

pigmeo -a MF pygmy

pijama M pajamas

pila F (recipiente) basin; (bautismal) baptismal font; (cúmulo) pile, heap, stack; (generador) battery; **— atómica** atomic reactor

pilar M pillar

píldora F pill; **—s para dormir** sleeping pills

pillaje M pillage, plunder

pillar VT (saquear) to pillage, to plunder; (atrapar, coger) to catch; (en un juego infantil) to tag

pillo -lla ADJ (travieso) naughty; (taimado) sly; MF (adulto) scoundrel; (niño) scamp

pilluelo -la MF urchin

pilón M (fuente) large basin; (soporte) pylon

pilotar, pilotear VT to pilot, to fly

pilote M pile, stilt

piloto MF (conductor) pilot; (llama pequeña de gas) pilot light; **— automático** autopilot; **— de pruebas** test pilot

pimentar VT to pepper

pimentero M pepper shaker

pimentón M paprika

pimienta F pepper; **— blanca** white pepper; **— de cayena** red pepper; **— negra** black pepper

pimiento M pepper, bell pepper; **— verde** green pepper

pimpollo M (de rosa) rosebud; (de vid) shoot

PIN M PIN

pináculo M pinnacle

pinar M pine grove

pincel M artist's brush

pincelada F stroke; **dar las últimas —s** to put on the final touches

pinchadura F flat tire

pinchar VT (perforar) to prick, to puncture; (apuñalar) to poke; (inyectar) to inject; (intervenir un teléfono) to wiretap; (provocar) to needle; VI to have a flat; **ni corta ni pincha** he doesn't count; M SG **pinchadiscos** disk jockey, DJ

pinchazo M (acción de pinchar) puncture, prick; (neumático) flat tire; (puñalada) stab; (de teléfono) wiretap

pincho M (palo afilado) spike; (de rotisería) spit

pingajo M (harapo) tatter; (harapiento) person dressed in rags

ping-pong M ping-pong

pingüe ADJ abundant

pingüino M penguin

pino M (árbol) pine; (ejercicio) handstand; **en el quinto —** in the boondocks

pinta F (mancha) dot; (aspecto) looks; (medida de líquidos) pint

pintada F grafitti

pintado ADJ (animales, plantas) colorful; **ese traje te queda —** you look great in that suit

pintar VT (colorear) to paint; (describir) to depict; **este marcador no pinta** this marker won't write; **no — nada** to count for nothing; **las cosas no pintaban bien** things did not look well; **—se** to put on makeup

pintarrajear VT to daub, to smear with paint; **—se** to put on too much makeup

pinto ADJ paint, dapple[d]

pintor -ora MF painter; **— de brocha gorda** house painter

pintoresco ADJ picturesque, colorful

pintorrear VT to smear with paint

pintura F (acción de pintar, obra) painting; (sustancia) paint; **— al óleo** oil painting; **— en aerosol** spray paint; **— fresca** wet paint

pinza F (de cangrejo) claw; (de médico) clamp; (de vestido) dart; (instrumento) clothespin; **—s** tweezers

piña F (fruto del pino) pinecone; (ananás) pineapple; (bomba) hand grenade

piñata F piñata

piñón M (semilla del pino) pine nut; (rueda del engranaje) pinion; (de bicicleta) sprocket

pío ADJ pious; INTERJ peep; **ni —** not a word

piojo M louse; **como —s en costura** like sardines

piojoso ADJ lousy

pionero -ra MF pioneer

pipa F (para fumar) pipe; (semilla) sunflower seed; **pasarlo —** to have a great time

pipí M pee; **hacer —** *fam* to pee

pipiolo -la MF novice

pique M (rivalidad) rivalry; (desavenencia) falling-out; **echar a —** to sink; **irse a —** to capsize

piquete M picket (también de huelga)

piquetear M to picket

piragua F dugout canoe

pirámide F pyramid

pirata MF pirate; **— informático -ca** hacker

piratear VT to pirate

piratería F piracy

piromanía F pyromania

pirómano -na MF pyromaniac

piropo M compliment

pirotecnia F pyrotechnics

pirulí M sucker, lollipop

pisada F (paso) footstep; (huella) footprint; **seguir las —s de** to follow in the footsteps of

pisar VT (oprimir con el pie) to step on, to tread on; (apisonar) to mash; **jamás pisó una plaza de toros** he never set foot in a bullring; **ir pisando huevos** to walk on eggshells; VI to step on; **— fuerte** to throw one's weight around; M SG **pisapapeles** paperweight

piscifactoría F fishery, fish farm

piscina F swimming pool

piso M (suelo) floor; (planta) story; (vivienda) apartment; **de — a techo** from the ground up

pisotear VT to tramp on, to trample, to stomp on

pisotón M stamp; **dar un —** to stamp, to step on

pista F (rastro) track, scent; (noticia) clue; (de aterrizaje) runway; (de circo) arena, ring; (de patinaje) skating ring; (de tenis) court; (de baile) floor; (de carreras) track, racetrack; **seguir la —** to track; **— para bicicletas** bike lane

pistola F (revólver) pistol; (para pintura) gun

pistolera F holster

pistolero MF gunner; M gunman; F gun woman

pistón M (válvula) piston; (explosivo) cap

pitada F drag, puff

pitar VI to toot, to whistle; VI/VT (rechiflar) to boo

pitazo M honk

pitido M (silbido) whistle, toot; (en deportes) whistle

pitillo M cigarette

pito M whistle; **entre —s y flautas** when all is said and done; **¿qué —s toca?** what's his role here?

pitón M (serpiente) python; (punta de cuerno) tip of a bull's horn

pituitario ADJ pituitary

pivot MF *Am* (baloncesto) center

pivotar VI to pivot

pivote M pivot; **— central** kingpin

píxel M pixel

pizarra F (roca) slate; (pizarrón) blackboard, chalkboard

pizarrón M blackboard, chalkboard

pizca F (de sal) pinch, dash; (de evidencia) shred; (de verdad) grain; (de suciedad) speck; **no entiendo ni —** I don't understand a bit/jot

pizza F pizza

placa F (fotográfica) plate; (de policía) badge; (condecoración, sarro) plaque; (de coche) license plate; (de computadora/ordenador) board, card; **— lógica** logic board; **— madre** motherboard

placaje M tackle

placar[30] VI/VT to tackle

placebo M placebo

placenta F placenta, afterbirth

placentero ADJ pleasant

placer[36] M pleasure, enjoyment; VT *lit* to please

plácido ADJ placid

plaf INTERJ plop

plaga F (enfermedad) plague; (persona, insecto) pest

plagar[40] VT to infest; **—se de** to become infested with

plagio M plagiarism

plan M plan; **— de estudios** curriculum; **— de juego** game plan; **— de salud administrado** managed care; **se vistió en — de vampiresa** she was dressed to kill

plana F newspaper page; **— mayor** top brass; **enmendar la — a uno** to correct a person's mistakes

plancha F (electrodoméstico) iron; (lámina) metal plate; (parrilla) griddle; **hacer la —** to float; **tirarse una —** to fall flat on one's face

planchado M ironing

planchar VT to iron, to press; **me dejó planchado** it left me speechless

plancton M plankton

planeador M glider

planeamiento M planning

planear VI/VT to plan; VI (volar) to glide, to plane; VT (madera) to plane

planeo M gliding

planeta M planet

planetario M planetarium

planificación F organization, planning; **—**

familiar family planning; **— para contingencias** contingency planning

planificador M planner, scheduler; **— de rutas** trip planner

planificar[30] VI/VT to plan

planilla F (de sueldos) payroll; (digital) worksheet; *Am* **— de cálculo** spreadsheet

plano ADJ flat, even; M (superficie) plane; (de un edificio) plan; (de calles) map; **— inclinado** inclined plane; **caer de —** to fall flat; **de —** flatly; **primer —** foreground

planta F (vegetal) plant; (del pie) sole; **— baja** ground floor

plantación F plantation

plantar VT (una planta, cruz) to plant; (a un novio) to dump; (a un colega) to make wait; **—se** to stand firm, to refuse to move; **— una bofetada a alguien** to give someone a slap; **dejar plantado** to stand up

planteamiento M (enfoque) approach; (exposición) presentation; **es un — poco provechoso** it is not a very beneficial approach

plantear VT (presentar) to present; **me planteó sus planes** she explained her plans to me; (provocar) to give rise to; **eso plantea un problema** that gives rise to a problem; **—se** to occur to; **¿te has planteado lo que pasa si te quedas sin trabajo?** have you thought about what will happen if you become unemployed?

plantel M (personal) staff; (almáciga) nursery

plantilla F (pieza suelta) insole; (patrón para calcar) pattern, stencil; (digital) template

plantío M grove

plasma M plasma (también de pantalla)

plasmar VT (captar) to capture; (dar forma plástica o sensible) to mold, to shape; **—se** to materialize

plasta ADJ tiresome; F (cosa informe) lump; (persona) bore

plástico ADJ & M plastic

plata F (metal, color, objeto de plata) silver; *Am* (dinero) money; **hablar en —** to speak in plain language

plataforma F platform (también política y digital); **— de lanzamiento** launching pad; **— petrolífera** oil rig; **— continental** continental shelf

platanar M banana grove

plátano M (fruta) banana; (para cocinar) plantain; (bananero) banana tree; (árbol ornamental) plane tree

platea F main floor of a theater

plateado ADJ & M (color) silver; M (acción de platear) silver-plating

platear VT to silver-plate

platero -ra MF silversmith

plática F chat

platicar[30] VI to chat

platija F flounder

platillo M (plato pequeño) saucer; (instrumento musical) cymbal; **— volador** flying saucer

platino M platinum

plato M (recipiente) plate; (comida) dish; (béisbol) home plate; **— fuerte** main dish/course; **— hondo** bowl; **— sopero** soup dish

plausible ADJ plausible

playa F beach

playboy M playboy

plaza F (espacio amplio) plaza, public square; (puesto de trabajo) job; **de cuatro —s** four-seater; **— de toros** bullring; **— mayor** main square

plazo M term; **a corto —** short-term; **a largo —** long-term, long-range; **a — fijo** fixed-term; **a —s** on credit; **cumplir un —** to meet a deadline

plazoleta F court

plazuela F court

pleamar M high tide

plebe F rabble

plebeyo -ya ADJ & MF plebeian

plegable ADJ folding

plegadera F paper folder

plegadizo ADJ folding

plegar[41] VT to fold; **—se [a]** (ceder) to yield [to]; (unirse) to join

pleitesía F compliance

pleito M (pelea) dispute; (demanda judicial) litigation, lawsuit; **poner —** to sue

plenamente ADV fully

plenario ADJ & M plenary

plenitud F **— de la vida** prime of life

pleno ADJ complete; **en — día** in broad daylight; **en — invierno** in the dead of winter; **en — rostro** right on the face; **en — verano** in midsummer; **en plena vista** in plain sight; M full session

pliego M leaflet

pliegue M (en papel) fold; (en tela) pleat

plomada F plumb

plomería F plumbing

plomero -ra MF plumber

plomizo ADJ leaden

plomo M (metal, color) lead; (pesa) lead weight; (perdigón) shot; **a —** plumb; **caer a —** to fall vertically; **sin —** unleaded; ADJ INV tiresome

pluma F (de ave) feather, quill; (para escribir) pen; **— fuente** fountain pen

plumaje M plumage

plumero M dust mop, duster

plumífero ADJ feathery

plumón M down

plural ADJ & M plural

pluralidad F plurality

pluriempleo M moonlighting

pluscuamperfecto ADJ & N pluperfect

plutonio M plutonium

pluvial ADJ **aguas —es** rainwater

pluviómetro M rain gauge

PNB [producto nacional bruto] M GNP

población F (conjunto de personas) population; (acción de poblar) settlement; (pueblo) town

poblado M hamlet

poblador -ora MF settler

poblar[5] VT (habitar) to populate; (colonizar) to settle; **—se de** to become covered with

pobre ADJ poor; MF **los —s** the poor

pobrecito -ta MF poor thing

pobreza F (miseria) poverty; (escasez) scarcity

pocilga F pigsty, pigpen

pocillo M cup

poción F potion

poco ADJ (no mucho) little; **poca paciencia** little patience; **al — rato** after a little while; (no muchos) few; **—s pasajeros** few passengers; **al — tiempo** shortly; **a los —s meses** after a few months; **de pocas luces** stupid; **en pocas palabras** in a nutshell; ADV little; **trabaja —** he works little; **— caritativo** not very charitable; **— conocido** little known; **— a —** little by little; **— más o menos** about; **hace —** a short while ago; **por — me caigo** I almost fell; **tener en —** to hold in low esteem; PRON **a little, a bit; un — a little bit, a little while; como —** at least; **unos —s** a few

poda F trim

podadera F pruning hook

podar VT to prune, to trim

poder[69] VI to be able to; **no puedo llegar antes de las cinco** I can't get there before five; **¿puedo sentarme?** may I be seated? **puede que venga** she may come; **a más no —** to the utmost; **no puedo más** I can't go on; **nadie puede con ella** nobody can deal with her; **no puede menos que venir** he can't help but come; **no puede menos que hacerlo** he cannot help doing it; M (fuerza) power; (escrito que da autoridad) proxy, power of attorney; **— ejecutivo** executive branch; **— judicial** judiciary branch; **— legislativo** legislative branch; **por —** by proxy

poderío M power, might

poderoso ADJ powerful, mighty

podiatra MF podiatrist

podiatría F podiatry

podio M podium

podólogo -ga MF podiatrist

podrá, podría ver poder

podredumbre F rot

podrido ADJ rotten

podrir ver pudrir

poema M poem

poesía F (género lírico) poetry; (poema) poem

poeta MF, **poetisa** F poet

poética F poetics

poético ADJ poetic

polaco -ca ADJ Polish; M (lengua) Polish; MF Pole

polaina F legging

polar ADJ polar

polaridad F polarity

polarización F polarization

polca F polka

polea F pulley

polémica F polemic, controversy

polémico ADJ polemic

polen M pollen

poli MF cop; F fam cops

policía F (en conjunto) police; (mujer) policewoman; M policeman; MF police officer

policíaco ADJ police

policial ADJ police; **parte —** police report

poliéster M polyester

poliestireno M Styrofoam™

poligamia F polygamy

polígota ADJ & MF polyglot

polígrafo M polygraph

poliinsaturado ADJ polyunsaturated

polilla F moth

polímero M polymer

polinizar[47] VT to pollinate

polio F polio

pólipo M polyp

política F (actividad relativa al gobierno) politics; (conjunto de orientaciones) policy; **— exterior** foreign policy

político -ca ADJ (relativo a la política) political; (diplomático) politic; MF politician

poliuretano M polyurethane

póliza F policy; **— de seguros** insurance policy

polizón -ona MF stowaway

polizonte M pey cop

polla F pullet

pollada F brood

pollera F (mujer) woman who raises and sells chickens; (falda) Am skirt

pollo M (cría de ave) young chicken; (carne) chicken

polo M (punto geográfico) pole; (juego) polo; **— acuático** water polo; **— de atención** focus of attention; **— Norte** North Pole

Polonia F Poland

poltrona F easy chair

polvareda F cloud of dust; **levantar una —** (causar escándalo) to raise a ruckus; (causar una nube de polvo) to kick up the dust

polvera F compact

polvo M (suciedad) dust; (partículas) powder; **— de hornear** baking powder; **juntar —** to gather dust; **limpio de — y paja** net

pólvora F gunpowder

polvoriento ADJ dusty

polvorín M (almacén de pólvora) magazine; (situación explosiva) powder keg

pomada F salve

pomelo M grapefruit

pómez F pumice

pomo M doorknob

pompa F (boato) pomp; (burbuja) soap bubble; **—s fúnebres** funeral ceremony

pomposo ADJ pompous

pómulo M cheekbone

pon *ver* poner

ponchado M (béisbol) strikeout

ponchar VT (un neumático) to puncture; **— a alguien** (en béisbol) to strike someone out; **—se** (un neumático) to become punctured; (en béisbol) to strike out

ponche M (bebida) punch; (en béisbol) strikeout

ponchera F punch bowl

poncho M poncho

ponderación F (acción de ponderar) pondering; (valor relativo) weighting

ponderar VT (considerar) to ponder, to consider; (exagerar) to exaggerate; (ajustar valores) to weight

pondrá, pondría *ver* poner

ponencia F presentation

poner[56, 74] VT to put, to place; (la mesa, un reloj) to set; (huevos) to lay; (azúcar) to add; (un examen) to give; (el televisor) to turn on; (un pleito) to file; **— a alguien a hacer algo** to assign someone to do something; **— en claro** to clarify; **— en limpio** to recopy, to make a clean copy; **— nombre a un niño** to name a child; **— sangre** to give a transfusion; **cada uno pone mil pesetas** each person contributes a thousand pesetas; **pongamos que** let us suppose that; **¿qué pone ahí?** what does it say there? **—se** (volverse) to become; (el sol) to set; (ropa) to put on; **—se a** to begin to; **—se al corriente** to become informed; **—se de acuerdo** to come to an agreement; **—se de pie** to stand up; **—se por delante en el marcador** (deporte) to take the lead

póney M pony

ponga, pongo *ver* poner

poniente M (oeste) west; (viento del oeste) west wind

pontón M pontoon

ponzoña F poison

ponzoñoso ADJ poisonous

pool M pool

popa F poop, stern

populacho M mob

popular ADJ (conocido y citado) popular; (del pueblo) folk

popularidad F popularity

populoso ADJ populous

popurrí M (de perfume) potpourri; (musical) medley

poquito *ver* poco

por PREP **— barco** by boat; **— casualidad** by chance; **— Dios** by God; **— etapas** by stages; **— las buenas o — las malas** by hook or by crook; **— litro** by the liter; **¿— qué?** why? for what reason? **multiplicar —** to multiply by; **lo agarró — la garganta** he grabbed him by the throat; **mi amor —** ella my love for her; **— poco tiempo** for a short time; **— primera vez** for the first time; **— vía de argumento** for the sake of argument; **— ejemplo** for instance; **— el momento** for the time being; **hazlo — mí** do it for my sake; **trabaja — mí** work on my behalf; **no me gustan — su olor** I don't like them because of their smell; **lo supe — él** I found out through him; **pasé — Londres** I passed through London; **un viaje — la costa** a trip along the coast; **— lo que cuentas** from what you're telling me; **— adelantado** in advance; **— escrito** in writing; **— la mañana** in the morning; **— lo general** in general; **— rachas** in spurts; **está — Badajoz** it's near Badajoz; **— fin** at last; **— el mes de marzo** around the month of March; **— ciento** percent; **— consiguiente** consequently; **— escrito** in writing; **— poco se muere** he almost died; **está — hacer** it is yet to be done; **él está — hacerlo** (a favor de) he is in favor of doing it; (a punto de) he is about to do it; **recibir — esposa** to take as a wife; **tener —** to consider, to think of as

porcelana F porcelain, china

porcentaje M percentage; **— de bateo** (béisbol) batting average

porche M porch, stoop

porcino ADJ ganado — swine; M pig

porción F (parte) portion, share; (de alimento) helping

pordiosear VT to panhandle

pordiosero -ra MF panhandler

porfía F obstinacy

porfiado ADJ willful

porfiar[28] VT to insist

pormenor M detail

pormenorizar[47] VT to detail, to go into detail about

porno M porn

pornografía F pornography

pornográfico ADJ pornographic

poro M pore

poroso ADJ porous

poroto M *Am* bean

porque CONJ because

porqué M reason; **el — de su tristeza** the reason for his sadness

porquería F (suciedad) filth; (acción despreciable) dirty trick; (cosa de mala calidad) crud; (comida de mala calidad) junk food

porra F club, cudgel

porrista MF cheerleader

portada F (de un libro) title page; (de una revista) front cover

portador -ora MF (de enfermedad) carrier; (de cheque) bearer; **— del féretro** pallbearer

portal M portal, doorway; **— de videos/vídeos** video portal

portar VT to carry; **—se** to behave; **—se mal** to misbehave; M SG **portaaviones** aircraft carrier; M SG **portaequipajes** luggage bin; M **portaestandarte** standard-bearer; M **portafolio** briefcase; M SG **portalámparas** socket; M SG **portaligas** garter belt; M SG **portamonedas** coin purse; M **portaobjeto** slide; M SG **portapapeles** clipboard; MF **portavoz** spokesperson

portátil ADJ portable

portazo M slam; **dar un —** to slam the door

porte M (envío) freight; (por correo) postage; (aspecto) bearing, carriage; (capacidad de carga) capacity; (tamaño) size; **— de armas** the carrying of arms; **enviar — pagado** to send prepaid

portear VT to carry

portentoso ADJ portentous

porteño -ña MF (de Buenos Aires) person from Buenos Aires; (de un puerto) person from a port city; ADJ (de Buenos Aires) from Buenos Aires; (de un puerto) from a port city

portería F (de un edificio) entrance area; (en fútbol) goal

portero -ra MF (de un edificio) doorkeeper, superintendent; (en fútbol) goalkeeper; M **— automático** intercom

portón M gate

portuario ADJ harbor, port; **trabajador —** dockworker

Portugal M Portugal

portugués -esa ADJ & MF Portuguese; M (lengua) Portuguese

porvenir M future

pos LOC PREP **en — de** after

posada F inn, lodge

posaderas F PL. *fam* rear end

posadero -ra MF innkeeper

posar VT (la mano, los ojos) to rest; VI (en el suelo) to sit down; (como modelo) to pose; **—se** (partículas) to settle; (mariposa) to alight; (pájaro) to perch

posdata F postscript

pose F pose

poseedor -ora MF possessor

poseer[18] VT to possess

poseído ADJ possessed

posesión F possession

posesivo ADJ & M possessive

poseyendo, poseyera, poseyese, poseyó *ver* poseer

posfechar VT to postdate

posguerra F postwar period

posibilidad F possibility

posibilitar VT (hacer posible) to make possible; (permitir) to allow, to permit

posible ADJ possible; **hacer lo —** to do one's best; **es —** it's possible

posición F (ubicación) position; (opinión) stance; (rango) standing; **— de negociación** bargaining position; **— fetal** fetal position

posicionamiento M (acción de posicionar, también de productos) placement, positioning; (actitud política) position, stance

posicionarse VI to position oneself

positivo ADJ & M positive

poso M (de vino) dregs; (de café) grounds

posparto M postpartum

posponer[56, 74] VT (aplazar) to postpone, to defer, to put off; (relegar) to put after

posta F (relevo) relay; (perdigón) buckshot

postal ADJ postal; F postcard

poste M (palo) post; (en fútbol) upright, goalpost

póster M poster

postergar[40] VT (para un ascenso) to pass over; (posponer) to postpone

posteridad F posterity; **eso quedará para la —** that will remain for all eternity

posterior ADJ (espacial) back, rear; (anatómico) posterior; (temporal) later; **nuestro divorcio fue — a la compra del negocio** our divorce came after we purchased the business

posterioridad LOC ADV **con —** later, subsequently

posteriormente ADV (atrás) in the back; (después) afterward[s]; **vocal pronunciada —** vowel pronounced in the back [of the mouth]

postigo M shutter

postizo ADJ false; **familia postiza** adoptive family; M hairpiece

postnasal ADJ postnasal

postrado ADJ prostrate, prone

postrar VT to prostrate

postre M dessert; **a la —** at last

postulado M postulate

postulante MF candidate

postular VT to postulate

póstumo ADJ posthumous

postura F posture (también opinión)

potable ADJ drinkable, potable

potasio M potassium

pote M (cilíndrico) jar; (panzudo) jug

potear VI/VT to putt

potencia F (sexual) potency; (de una fuerza, nación) power; **es un asesino en —** he's a potential murderer; **— naval** sea power; **de**

alta — high-powered; **segunda** — the second power

potencial ADJ & M potential

potenciar VT (a una persona) to empower; (proyectos, relaciones) to promote, to support

potentado -da MF potentate

potente ADJ potent, powerful

potranco -ca M colt; F filly

potrero M pasture; *Am* cattle ranch, stock farm

potro M (caballo) colt; (en gimnasia) vaulting horse; — **de tormento** rack

pozo M (de agua, petróleo) well; (hoyo profundo) pit; (minero) mine shaft; **sacar del** — to rescue; — **negro** sink; — **sin fondo** bottomless pit; — **séptico** septic tank

práctica F (repetición, costumbre) practice; (destreza) skill; **en la** — in practice; **poner en** — to put into practice; — **comercial desleal** deceptive practice

prácticamente ADV (casi) practically, virtually; (de forma práctica) practically; (en la práctica) in practice

practicante ADJ practicing; MF (que practica) practitioner; (asistente de médico) physician's assistant

practicar[30] VI/VT (una habilidad) to practice; (un agujero) to make

práctico ADJ (sencillo) practical; (adiestrado) skillful; M — **de puerto** harbor pilot

pradera F prairie, grassland

prado M meadow, pasture

pragmático ADJ pragmatic

preadolescente ADJ & MF preteen, preadolescent

preámbulo M preamble

preaprobado ADJ preapproved

precalentamiento M warmup

precanceroso ADJ precancerous

precario ADJ precarious, *fam* touch-and-go

precaución F precaution

precaverse VT to take precautions

precavido ADJ cautious

precedencia F precedence

precedente ADJ preceding; M precedent; **sin** — unprecedented; **sentar** — to set a precedent

preceder VI/VT to precede

precepto M precept

preciado ADJ (estimado) prized; (valioso) valuable

preciarse VI — **de** to be proud of

precintar VT to seal

precinto M seal

precio M price; **poner** — **a** to put a price on; **no tener** — to be priceless; — **de compra** purchase price; — **de lista** list price; — **de mercado** market price; — **de referencia** bench price; — **justo en el mercado** fair market price; — **sugerido** suggested retail

price; — **sugerido por el fabricante** manufacturer's suggested retail price; — **vigente** going price

preciosista ADJ precious

precioso ADJ (metal, piedra, objeto de gran valor) precious; (muy bonito) beautiful, adorable

precipicio M precipice, cliff

precipitación F precipitation (también atolondramiento)

precipitado ADJ precipitate, hasty, rash; M precipitate

precipitar VI to precipitate; VT to hurl; —**se** (apresurarse) to be hasty; (arrojarse) to plunge, to plummet; (depositarse) to precipitate; (adelantarse) to come to a head

precisamente ADV precisely, exactly, just; — **de eso te quería hablar** that is just what I wanted to talk to you about; (de hecho) as a matter of fact; —, **se alojó en este hotel** as a matter of fact he stayed in this hotel

precisar VT (determinar) to determine precisely; (necesitar) to need

precisión F precision, accuracy; **precisiones** clarifications

preciso ADJ precise, accurate; **es** — **que vengas** you must come; **en este** — **instante** at this very moment

precoz ADJ (niño) precocious; (diagnóstico) early

precursor -ora MF precursor, forerunner

predecesor -ora MF predecessor

predecir[53, 74] VT to predict, to foretell

predestinar VT to predestine

predeterminado ADJ predetermined

predicación F preaching

predicado ADJ & M predicate

predicador -ora MF preacher

predicar[30] VI/VT to preach

predicción F prediction

predilección F predilection

predilecto ADJ favorite, pet

predio M piece of land

predisponer[56, 74] VT to predispose

predisposición F predisposition

predominante ADJ predominant, prevailing

predominar VI to predominate

predominio M predominance

preeclampsia F preeclampsia

preeminente ADJ foremost

preempacado ADJ prepacked

preescolar ADJ nursery; MF nursery school child

preestablecido ADJ preset

preestreno M preview

preexistente ADJ preexisting

prefacio M preface

preferencia F preference; (en el tráfico) right of way; **de** — predominantly

preferente ADJ (tratamiento) preferential;

(acciones) preferred

preferible ADJ preferable

preferido ADJ preferred, favorite

preferir[8] VT to prefer

prefiera, prefiere *ver* preferir

prefijar VT to prefix

prefijo M prefix

prefiriendo, prefiriera, prefiriese *ver* preferir

pregonar VT (noticias) to make public; (mercancías) to hawk

pregrabado ADJ prerecorded

pregunta F question; **hacer una —** to ask a question; **—s frecuentes** frequently asked questions

preguntar VI/VT to ask, to inquire; **— por** (pedir información) to inquire about; (pedir para hablar) to ask for; **—se** to wonder

preguntón ADJ inquisitive

prehistórico ADJ prehistoric

prejuicio M prejudice, bias

prejuzgar[40] VT to prejudge

preliminar ADJ & M preliminary

preludiar VT to prelude

preludio M prelude

prematrimonial ADJ premarital

prematuro ADJ (bebé) premature; (muerte) untimely

premeditado ADJ premeditated

premenstrual ADJ premenstrual

premiar VT to reward; **las obras premiadas** the award-winning works

première M premiere

premio M (galardón) prize, award; (de la moneda) appreciation; **Juan Pérez, — nacional de poesía** Juan Pérez, winner of the national poetry award; **— gordo** jackpot

premisa F premise

premonición F premonition

prenatal ADJ prenatal

prenda F (fianza) pawn, pledge; (de vestir) article of clothing, garment; **dejar en —** to pawn; **en — de** as a token of

prendar VT to charm; **—se de** to fall in love with

prendedor M brooch, pin

prender VT (agarrar) to grab; (sujetar) to clasp; (enganchar) to fasten; (detener) to arrest; (arraigar) to take root; (encender) to turn on, to switch on; **— fuego** to set on fire; **la vacuna no prendió** the vaccination didn't take

prensa F press; **tener mala —** to have bad press

prensar VT to press

prensil ADJ prehensile

prenupcial ADJ prenuptial

preñada ADJ pregnant

preñar VT to impregnate

preñez F pregnancy

preocupación F worry, concern

preocupado ADJ worried, concerned, anxious

preocupante ADJ worrisome

preocupar VT to worry, to concern; **—se de** to worry about; **—se por** to be concerned about

preocupón -ona MF worrywart

preparación F preparation

preparado ADJ ready; M preparation

preparar VT to prepare; **—se** to get ready, to brace oneself; **— el cuerpo de un difunto** to embalm a body

preparativo ADJ preparatory; M preparation

preparatorio ADJ preparatory; **escuela preparatoria** preparatory school

preponderancia F preponderance

preponderante ADJ preponderant

preponderar VI to predominate

preposición F preposition

prepucio M foreskin

prerrequisito M prerequisite

prerrogativa F prerogative

presa F (animal de caza) prey, quarry; (dique) dam

presagiar VT to forebode

presagio M omen, sign

présbita, présbite ADV & MF farsighted

prescindible ADJ dispensable

prescindir VI **— de** to dispense with, to do without

prescribir[74] VT to prescribe

prescripción F prescription

presencia F presence; **— de ánimo** presence of mind

presenciar VT to witness

presentable ADJ presentable

presentación F (de un tema) presentation; (de una persona) introduction

presentador -ora MF (de programa de televisión) host; (de noticiero) anchor

presentar VT (una idea) to present; (a una persona) to introduce; (la declaración de impuestos, una demanda) to file; (un informe) to submit; (documentos) to produce; (una queja) to lodge; (una renuncia) to tender; **—se** (aparecer) to appear; (hacerse conocer) to introduce oneself

presente ADJ present; M (tiempo) present; (regalo) present, gift; **al —** at the present time; **tener —** to bear in mind; **en el — [contrato]** herein; **por la — [carta]** hereby

presentimiento M presentiment, foreboding, hunch

presentir[8] VT to have a presentiment of

preservación F (protección) preservation; (ahorro) conservation

preservar VT (proteger) to preserve; (ahorrar) to conserve

presidencia F presidency

presidencial ADJ presidential

presidente MF, **presidenta** F (de un país) president; (de una reunión, junta) chair
presidiario -ria MF prisoner
presidio M prison
presidir VI to preside; VT to preside over
presilla F loop
presión F pressure; — **atmosférica** atmospheric pressure; — **arterial** blood pressure; — **arterial alta** high blood pressure, hypertension; — **de aire** air pressure
presionar VT (un botón) to press; (al gobierno) to lobby
preso -sa MF prisoner, inmate
prestación F provision; **prestaciones** benefits
prestador -ora MF lender
prestamista MF (de dinero) lender; (en un montepío) pawnbroker
préstamo M loan; — **convencional** conventional loan; — **garantizado** guaranteed loan
prestar VT to loan, to lend; — **ayuda** to give help; — **atención** to pay attention; — **juramento** to take an oath; — **servicio** to render service
prestatario -ria MF borrower
prestidigitación F sleight of hand
prestigio M prestige
prestigioso ADJ prestigious
presumido ADJ conceited, presumptuous
presumir VT (suponer) to presume; VI (ostentar) to show off; — **de valiente** to boast of one's valor
presunción F presumption
presuntamente ADV allegedly
presunto ADJ (dueño, autor de una obra) presumed; (autor de un crimen) alleged; — **heredero** heir apparent
presuntuoso ADJ presumptuous
presuponer[56, 74] VT to presuppose
presupuestación F budgeting
presupuestario ADJ budget, budgetary
presupuesto M (de gastos e ingresos) budget; (de costos) estimate; — **equilibrado** balanced budget
presuroso ADJ hasty
pretencioso ADJ pretentious
pretender VI (sostener) to claim, to purport; — **ser** to claim to be; — **al trono** to pretend to the throne; VT (intentar) to attempt
pretendiente MF, **pretendienta** F (al trono) pretender; (a un puesto) aspirant; M (de una mujer) suitor, admirer
pretensión F pretension
pretérito ADJ past; M past tense; — **perfecto** present perfect
pretexto M pretext, pretense; **so — de** under pretense of
pretil M railing

pretina F waistband
prevalecer[35] VI to prevail
prevaleciente ADJ prevalent
prevé, prevea, preveía ver prever
prevención F (protección) prevention; (recelo) caution
prevenido ADJ forewarned
prevenir[61] VT (precaver) to prevent; (prever) to foresee; (advertir) to warn; — **contra** to protect oneself against
preventivo ADJ preventive, precautionary
prever[72, 74] VT to foresee, to anticipate
previamente ADV previously
previo ADJ previous, prior; — **examen de salud** after undergoing a health examination
previsible ADJ foreseeable
previsión F foresight, anticipation
previsto ver prever
previsualización F previewing
prieto ADJ swarthy
prima F (cuota de seguro) premium; (recargo) surcharge; (pago extraordinario) bonus
primario ADJ primary
primate M primate
primavera F spring
primaveral ADJ springlike
primero ADJ & ADV first; **primer ministro** prime minister; **primer piso** second floor; **primer plano** foreground; **primera base** (posición) first base; (jugador) first baseman; **primera enseñanza** primary education; **primera persona** first person; **primer tiempo** first half; —**s auxilios** first aid; a **primera vista** at first sight; **de primer grado** first degree; **de primera** top-notch; **de primera mano** firsthand; **por primera vez** for the first time; — **del mes** first of the month; **Juan llegó** — Juan arrived first; F (marcha) first gear; (clase en un avión) first class
primicia F (fruto primero) first fruit; (noticia) scoop
primitivo ADJ primitive
primo -ma MF (hijo de tío) cousin; (persona incauta) sucker, dupe; — **hermano** first cousin; — **segundo** second cousin; ADJ prime
primogénito -ta ADJ & MF firstborn
primogenitura F birthright
primor M (esmero) care; (cosa fina) lovely thing
primordial ADJ primordial
primoroso ADJ exquisite
princesa F princess
principal ADJ principal, main; **la causa — de muerte** the leading cause of death; **el dormitorio** — the master bedroom
principalmente ADV mainly, principally
príncipe M prince
principesco ADJ princely

principiante MF beginner; ADJ beginning

principiar VT to commence

principio M (fundamento, regla de conducta) principle, tenet; (hecho de empezar, tiempo, lugar) beginning, start; **a — s de** toward the beginning of; **— activo** active ingredient; **al —** at the beginning, at first; **de — a fin** from beginning to end; **desde el —** from the beginning; **en —** in principle

pringar[40] VT (ensuciar) to get greasy; (mojar) to dip

pringoso ADJ greasy

pringue MF grease

prioridad F (autoridad, preferencia) priority, precedence; (en el tráfico) right of way

prioritario ADJ having priority, most important

prisa F haste, hurry; **a toda —** at full speed; **correr —** to be urgent; **darse —** to hurry; **las — s comienzan a la una** the rush starts at one; **tener —** to be in a hurry; **sin —** leisurely

prisión F prison; **— perpetua** life in prison

prisionero -ra MF prisoner; **— de guerra** prisoner of war

prisma M prism

prismáticos M PL binoculars

privacidad F privacy

privación F privation; **pasar privaciones** to suffer want

privado ADJ private; **en —** in private

privar VT to deprive; **—se de** to deprive oneself of

privativo ADJ exclusive

privatización F privatization

privatizar[47] VT to privatize

privilegiado ADJ privileged

privilegiar VT to favor, to give a privilege to

privilegio M privilege

pro M advantage; **en — de** in favor of; **en — y en contra** for and against

proa F prow, bow

proaborto ADJ INV pro-choice

probabilidad F (chance) likelihood; (en estadística) probability; **tienes pocas — es de ganar** you have little chance of winning; **¿qué — es tiene?** what are her odds?

probable ADJ probable, likely; **lo más — es que haya venido** in all likelihood he came

probador M dressing room

probar[5] VT (alimento, bebida) to taste, to try, to sample; (una hipótesis) to prove; (una guitarra) to try out; (un coche) to test-drive; **—se un vestido** to try on a dress; **— fortuna** to try one's luck; **prueba a venir más temprano** try to come earlier; **no — bocado** not to eat a bite

probatorio ADJ probationary

probeta F test tube

problema M problem; **él sólo da —s** he's

nothing but trouble

problemático -ca ADJ problematic; F problems

procedencia F origin

procedente ADJ **— de** from

proceder VI to proceed; **— de** to come from; **— a** to proceed to; **— contra** to take action against

procedimiento M procedure; **—s** proceedings

procesable ADJ actionable

procesado -da MF accused; M processing

procesador ADJ processing; M processor; **— de textos** word processor

procesamiento M prosecution; **— de datos** data processing; **— de textos** word processing

procesar VT to prosecute, to try

procesión F procession; **la — va por dentro** he doesn't let it show

proceso M (etapas) process; (juicio) trial, legal proceedings

proclama F proclamation

proclamación F proclamation

proclamar VT to proclaim; **—se campeón** to be proclaimed winner

proclive ADJ prone

procrear VI/VT to procreate

proctología F proctology

procurador -ora MF attorney

procurar VT (intentar) to endeavor; (obtener) to procure, to obtain

prodigar[40] VT to lavish; **—se** to be lavish

prodigio M prodigy

prodigioso ADJ prodigious

pródigo -ga ADJ (derrochador) prodigal; (muy generoso) lavish; MF spendthrift

producción F (acción de producir) production; (cantidad producida) production, yield; **— masiva** mass production

producir[38] VT (efectos, mercancías, películas) to produce; (fruta, resultados) to yield, to bear; **—se** to happen

productividad F productivity

productivo ADJ (rendidor) productive; (exitoso) successful

producto M product; **— interno bruto** gross national product

productor -ora MF producer; ADJ **un país — de petróleo** an oil-producing country

produje, produjera, produjese ver producir

pro-elección ADJ INV pro-choice

proeza F exploit

profanación F desecration

profanar VT to profane, to desecrate

profano ADJ profane

profecía F prophecy

proferir[8] VT to utter

profesar VT to profess

profesión F profession

profesional ADJ & MF professional; **— de la**

salud health care provider
profesionista MF *Méx* professional
profesor -ora MF (universitario) professor; (de
    enseñanza secundaria) teacher; (de tenis)
    instructor
profesorado M faculty
profeta MF prophet
profético ADJ prophetic
profetizar[47] VI/VT to prophesy
prófugo -ga ADJ & MF fugitive
profundidad F (del mar, de comprensión, de un
    armario) depth; (sabiduría) profundity
profundizar[47] VT to deepen; VI to go into
    deeply
profundo ADJ (idea, comentario, razonamiento)
    profound; (mar, pozo, armario, voz) deep
profuso ADJ profuse
progesterona F progesterone
programa M (de boxeo) card; (de televisión)
    show, program; (de un curso) syllabus; (de un
    congreso) program; **— antivirus** antivirus
    program, antivirus software; **— de
    protección contra virus** virus protection
    software; **— de instalación** setup program,
    install program; **— instalador** setup
    program, install program; **— para
    recuperar datos borrados** undelete
    utility; **—s almacenados en circuitos
    integrados** firmware
programable ADJ programmable
programación F programming
programador -ora MF programmer
programar VT (una computadora) to program;
    (un evento) to schedule
progresar VT to progress, to advance
progresión F progression
progresista ADJ & MF progressive
progresivo -va ADJ & MF progressive
progreso M progress
prohibición F prohibition, ban
prohibido ADJ forbidden; **prohibida la
    entrada** no admittance; **— el paso** no
    trespassing
prohibir[29] VT to prohibit, to ban; **se prohíbe
    fumar** no smoking
prohijar VT to adopt
prójimo -ma MF fellow human
prole F offspring
proletariado M proletariat
proletario -ria ADJ & MF proletarian
proliferación F proliferation, spread
prolífico ADJ prolific
prolijo ADJ (verboso) wordy; (esmerado) overly
    careful
prologar[40] VT to preface
prólogo M prologue, foreword, preface
prolongación F prolongation
prolongado ADJ extended

prolongar[40] VT to prolong; **—se** to wear on
promediar VT to average
promedio M average, mean; **de/en —** on
    average; **— de carreras limpias
    permitidas** earned run average
promesa F promise; **romper una —** to break a
    promise; **una joven —** a promising young
    player
prometedor ADJ promising
prometer VT to promise; VI to show promise
prometido -da ADJ engaged; M fiancé; F fiancée
prominente ADJ prominent
promiscuo ADJ promiscuous
promisorio ADJ promissory; **un futuro —** a
    promising future
promoción F (oferta comercial) promotion;
    (conjunto de personas) class
promocional ADJ promotional
promocionar VT to promote, to publicize
promontorio M promontory
promotor -ora MF (de un producto) promoter;
    (de bienes inmuebles) developer
promover[6] VT (ideas, producto, a un alumno) to
    promote; (la paz, una causa) to foster, to
    further
promulgación F enactment
promulgar[40] VT to promulgate, to enact
pronombre M pronoun
pronominal ADJ pronominal
pronosticar[30] VT to forecast
pronóstico M (del tiempo, de la economía)
    forecast; (de una enfermedad) prognosis
prontitud F promptness, dispatch
pronto ADJ (rápido) quick; (listo) ready; ADV
    soon, promptly; **de —** suddenly; **¡hasta —!**
    see you soon! **tan — como** as soon as
pronunciación F pronunciation
pronunciado ADJ pronounced
pronunciamiento M declaration,
    pronouncement
pronunciar VT (un sonido, una sentencia) to
    pronounce; (un discurso) to make, to deliver;
    —se (acusarse) to be pronounced;
    (expresarse) to declare one's opinion
propagación F propagation, spread
propaganda F (de ideas) propaganda; (de
    mercancías) advertising, publicity; **hacer —**
    to advertise
propagar[40] VT to propagate
propalar VT to spread
propano M propane
propasarse VI to go too far
propensión F propensity
propenso ADJ prone
propiciar VT to favor
propicio ADJ propitious, auspicious
propiedad F (cualidad, pertenencia, finca)
    property; (derecho de dueño) ownership;
    (corrección) precision; **— mayoritaria**

majority ownership; — **privada** private property; —**es** estate; —**es colindantes** adjoining properties

propietario -ria M (de una tienda) proprietor, owner; (de un apartamento) landlord; F (de una tienda) owner; (de un apartamento) landlady; — **ausente** absentee landlord

propina F tip, gratuity; **dar [una]** — to tip

propinar VT — **una paliza** to give a beating

propio ADJ (correcto) proper; **el significado** — the proper meaning; (típico) like; **no es — de él quejarse así** it's not like him to complain like that; (conveniente) appropriate; **una expresión propia** an appropriate expression; (que le pertenece) own; **su hijo** his own son; **un hijo** — a son of his own; **por tu** — bien for your own good; (mismo) same; **al** — **tiempo** at the same time

propondrá, propondría ver proponer

proponente MF proponent

proponer[56, 74] VT to propose; —**se** to set out to

proponga, propongo ver proponer

proporción F proportion, ratio; **proporciones** dimensions

proporcional ADJ proportional, proportionate

proporcionar VT (ajustar a proporción) to proportion; (brindar) to furnish, to provide

proposición F (lógica) proposition; (de matrimonio) proposal; **proposiciones deshonestas** indecent proposals

propósito M purpose, intent; **a** — (adecuado) apropos; (voluntariamente) on purpose, intentionally, deliberately; (además) by the way, incidentally; **a** — **de** apropos of

propuesta F proposal

propuesto ver proponer

propugnar VT to urge

propulsar VT to propel

propulsión F propulsion; — **a chorro** jet propulsion

propulsor -ora ADJ propelling; MF promoter

propuse, propusiera, propusiese ver proponer

prorratear VT to prorate

prórroga F (plazo) extension of time; (de un préstamo) renewal; (fútbol americano) overtime; (fútbol) extra time

prorrogar[40] VT (un pago) to put off, to defer; (un plazo) to extend; (un préstamo) to renew

prorrumpir VI to burst; — **en llanto** to burst into tears; — **en carcajadas** to burst out laughing

prosa F prose

prosaico ADJ prosaic

proscribir[74] VT to banish, to disenfranchise

proscripción F banishment

proseguir[12] VI to proceed

prosódico ADJ prosodic

prospectar VT to prospect

prospector -ora MF prospector

prosperar VI to prosper, to flourish, to thrive

prosperidad F prosperity

próspero ADJ prosperous

próstata F prostate [gland]

prostitución F prostitution

prostituir[19] VT to prostitute

prostituto -ta MF prostitute

protagonista MF protagonist

protagonizar[47] VT to star in

protección F protection; — **al consumidor** consumer protection; — **contra copias** copy protection; — **contra grabación** write protection; — **contra lectura** read protect; — **por contraseña** password protection

proteccionista ADJ & MF protectionist

protector -ora ADJ protective; MF protector; — **de pantalla** screen saver; — **de tensión** surge protector; — **sobrecargas de voltaje** surge protector; — **solar** sunblock

protectorado M protectorate

proteger[45] VT (a alguien vulnerable) to protect; (a un artista) to sponsor; — **contra grabación** to write-protect

protegido -da MF protégé[e]; — **por contraseña** password protected

proteína F protein

prótesis F prosthesis; — **de cadera** hip prosthesis

protesta F protest

protestante MF Protestant

protestar VI/VT to protest

protocolo M protocol

protón M proton

protoplasma M protoplasm

prototipo M prototype

protozoario M protozoan

protuberancia F protuberance, bulge, bump

protuberante ADJ bulging

provecho M (beneficio) benefit; (eructo) burp; **¡buen—!** bon appétit! **sacar — [de]** to benefit [from], to profit [from]

provechoso ADJ beneficial, advantageous

proveedor -ora MF (de un servicio) provider; (de un producto) supplier, vendor; — **de acceso** access provider; — **de acceso a internet** Internet access provider

proveer[18, 74] VT to provide; — **de** to provide with; —**se de** to provide oneself with

provenga, provengo ver provenir

proveniente ADJ — **de** coming from

provenir[61] VI to arise; — **de** to stem from

proverbio M proverb

providencia F providence

providencial ADJ providential

provincia F province

provincial ADJ provincial

provinciano -na ADJ & MF provincial

provine, proviniendo, proviniera,

proviniese, provino *ver* **provenir**
provisión F provision, supply, store
provisional ADJ temporary, provisional
provisorio ADJ temporary
provocación F provocation
provocar[30] VT (ira) to provoke; (sexualmente) to excite; (un incendio) to start; (una respuesta) to elicit
provocativo ADJ provocative
proximidad F proximity, nearness; **en las —es** in the vicinity
próximo ADJ (posterior) next; (cercano) near, nearby; **el lunes — pasado** last Monday; **de próxima aparición** forthcoming
proyección F projection
proyectar VT (un plan) to project; (una película) to screen; (una sombra) to cast; **—se** to overhang, to jut
proyectil M projectile
proyecto M (idea) project; (arquitectónico) plan; **— de ley** bill
proyector M (para películas) projector; (en el teatro) spotlight
prudencia F prudence
prudente ADJ prudent
prueba F (de imprenta, argumento irrefutable) proof; (argumento parcial) evidence; (intento, dificultad) trial, test; (examen) test, examination; (de ropa) fitting; **— beta** beta test; **— de detección** screening test; **— de doble incógnita** double-blind test; **— de embarazo** pregnancy test; **— de esfuerzo** stress test; **— de esfuerzo máximo** exercise electrocardiogram; **— de fuego** trial by fire; **— de ingresos** means test; **— de paternidad** paternity test; **— de Rorschach** Rorschach test; **a —** on approval; **a — de fallos** foolproof; **a — de incendio** fireproof; **poner a —** to put to the test
prueba, pruebe *ver* **probar**
psicoanálisis M psychoanalysis
psicodélico ADJ & M psychedelic
psicología F psychology
psicológico ADJ psychological
psicólogo -ga MF psychologist
psicópata MF psychopath
psicosis F psychosis
psicosomático ADJ psychosomatic
psicoterapia F psychotherapy
psicótico ADJ psychotic
psiquiatra MF psychiatrist
psiquiatría F psychiatry
psíquico ADJ psychic
psoriasis F psoriasis
púa F (con punta aguda) spike; (de alambre) barb; (de guitarra) pick; (de erizo) quill; (de tridente) prong
puaf, puaj INTERJ yuck, ugh
pubertad F puberty

publicación F publication
publicar[30] VT to publish; (revelar) to divulge
publicidad F publicity, advertising; **— de cebo y anzuelo** bait-and-switch advertising; **— engañosa** false advertising; **— exterior** outdoor advertising; **hacer —** to advertise
publicitario -ria MF advertising agent; ADJ publicity
público ADJ public; M (testigo) public; (en un espectáculo) audience; **en —** in public
publirreportaje M infomercial
puchero M (vasija) pot; (guiso) stew; (gesto) pout; **hacer —s** to pout
puck M puck
pude, pudiendo, pudiera, pudiese *ver* **poder**
pudiente ADJ wealthy
pudín M pudding
pudor M (sexual) modesty; (emocional) reserve
pudrir[74] VI to rot
pueblerino ADJ provincial
pueblo M (población) town; (nación) people, folk
pueda, puede *ver* **poder**
puente M bridge (también dental, de gafas, de nariz); (fin de semana) long weekend; **— aéreo** (regular) shuttle; (de emergencia) airlift; **— cardiopulmonar** cardiopulmonary bypass, coronary bypass; **— colgante** suspension bridge; **— levadizo** drawbridge
puénting M bungee jumping
pueril ADJ childish
puerta F (de casa) door; (de aeropuerto, de ciudad) gate; (entrada) entrance; **— de acceso** gateway; **vender de — en —** to sell door to door; **dar a alguien con la — en las narices** to slam the door in someone's face; **llamar a la —** to knock on the door; **— trasera** back door; **a — cerrada** behind closed doors
puerto M port (también en informática); **— de acceso** gateway; **— de entrada** port of entry; **— de ratón** mouse port; **— paralelo** parallel port; **— serie/serial** serial port; **— USB** USB port; **llegar a buen —** to bring to a satisfactory conclusion
puertorriqueño -ña ADJ & MF Puerto Rican
pues CONJ (puesto que) since, for; ADV (entonces) then; **— bien** well then, now
puesta F **— al día** update; **— del sol** sunset, setting of the sun; **— en marcha** (de un proyecto) setting in motion; (de un coche) starting; **— en libertad** freeing
puestero -ra MF vendor, seller
puesto ADJ **bien —** (casa) well-appointed; (persona) well made-up; **llevar —** to have on; M (posición) place; (de venta) booth, stand; (de trabajo) post, position; **— de socorros** first-aid station; **quedarse con lo —** to be

left with only the clothes on one's back; CONJ — **que** since

puesto *ver* poner

pugilato M boxing

pugilista MF boxer, prizefighter

pugna F struggle; **estar en — con** to be in conflict with

pugnaz ADJ feisty

puja F (del viento) push; (en una subasta) bid

pujanza F vigor

pujar VI (para dar a luz) to push; (en una subasta) to bid; — **por** to strive to

pujo M contraction

pulcritud F neatness

pulcro ADJ neat

pulga F flea; **tener malas —s** to be ill-tempered

pulgada F inch

pulgar M thumb

pulido ADJ polished; M polishing

pulimento M (de modales) refinement; (de metales) buffing; (polvo para pulir) scouring powder

pulir VT (metal, un discurso) to polish; (madera) to sand

pulla F taunt, dig

pulmón M lung; — **de acero** iron lung

pulmonar ADJ pulmonary; **capacidad —** lung capacity

pulmonía F pneumonia

pulpa F pulp

púlpito M pulpit

pulpo M octopus

pulque M *Méx* pulque

pulquería F *Méx* pulque bar

pulsación F (de corazón) pulse; (de ratón de computadora) click; (de tecla) keystroke

pulsar VT (una tecla) to press; (cuerdas de guitarra) to pluck; (la opinión pública) to gauge; — **y arrastrar** to click and drag

púlsar M pulsar

pulsera F (alhaja) bracelet; (de reloj) watchband; **reloj de —** wristwatch

pulso M (pulsación) pulse; (firmeza de mano) steadiness; **echar un —** to arm-wrestle; **tomar el —** to take the pulse; **a —** with great effort

pulular VI to swarm, to teem with

pulverizar[47] VT to pulverize

puma F mountain lion, cougar, puma

puna F cold, arid tableland of the Andes

punitivo ADJ punitive

punk ADJ & M punk

punkero -ra MF punk

punta F (de cuchillo) point; (de la lengua, de un lápiz) tip; (de calcetín) toe; — **de lanza** spearhead; **una — de** a bunch of; **a — de cuchillo** at knifepoint; — **de flecha** arrowhead; **de —** on end; **iba caminando**

de —s he was tiptoeing; **sacar — a un lápiz** to sharpen a pencil; **en la — de la lengua** on the tip of the tongue; **me pone los nervios de —** it makes me nervous; M —**pié** kick; ADJ **puntiagudo** sharp, pointed

puntada F stitch, prick

puntal M (de un edificio) prop; (de la economía) mainstay

puntear VT (una guitarra) to pluck; (un mapa) to make dots on; (una lista) to check off

puntería F aim; **tener buena —** to be a good shot

puntero M pointer

puntilla F point lace; **de —s** on tiptoe

punto M (puntuación) period; (de cinturón) notch; (marca, signo) point, dot; (anotación, tema, lugar) point; (puntada) stitch; — **álgido** fever pitch; — **culminante** (de una carrera) peak; (de una historia) climax; (de negociaciones) critical stage; — **de apoyo** foothold; — **de condensación** dewpoint; — **de congelación** freezing point; — **de ebullición** boiling point; — **de juego** game point; — **de manga** set point; — **de origen** point of origin; — **de partida** point of departure; — **de partido** match-point; — **de referencia** point of reference, benchmark; — **de vista** viewpoint, point of view; — **extra** (fútbol americano) point after touchdown; — **muerto** (en un negocio) stalemate, deadlock; (en un coche) neutral; — **y coma** semicolon; **al —** at once; **a —** ready; **a — de** on the point/verge of; **cogerle el —** to figure out; **dos —s** colon; **el — medio** the halfway mark; **en —** on the dot; **hacer —** to knit; **hasta cierto —** to a certain extent; **poner los —s sobre las íes** to dot one's i's and cross one's t's

puntuación F punctuation

puntual ADJ (en hora) punctual, prompt; (específico) specific

puntualidad F punctuality

puntualizar[47] VT to point out

puntuar[26] VT to punctuate

punzada F (de dolor) stab; (de remordimiento, hambre) pang, twinge

punzante ADJ sharp, piercing

punzar[47] VT to prick

punzón M (en papel) hole punch; (en cuero) awl

puñado M handful; **a —s** by the handful

puñal M dagger

puñalada F stab; **coser a —s** to stab to death

puñetazo M punch, slug; **dar un —** to punch; **dar un — en la mesa** to bang on the table

puño M (mano cerrada) fist; (en una manga) cuff; (de espada) handle; **arreglarlo con los —s** to duke it out; **de mi — y letra** by my own hand

pupa F *Esp* boo-boo

pupila F pupil

pupilo -la MF ward

pupitre M school desk

puré M purée; **— de patatas/papas** mashed potatoes; **hacer —** to smash

pureza F purity

purga F (política) purge; (medicinal) purgative

purgación F atonement

purgante ADJ & M purgative, laxative

purgar⁴⁰ VT (el vientre, a un rival) to purge; (frenos) to bleed; (pecados) to atone for

purgatorio M purgatory

purificar³⁰ VT to purify

purista ADJ & MF purist

puritano ADJ puritanical

puro ADJ pure; **lo hizo de — bueno** he did it out of sheer kindness; **a pura fuerza** by sheer force; **la pura verdad** the plain truth; **son puras mentiras** that's a lot of bull; **de purasangre** thoroughbred; M cigar

púrpura ADJ & M purple

pus M pus

puse, pusiera, pusiese *ver* poner

putrefacto ADJ putrid, decayed

putter M putter

Qq

Qatar M Qatar

quásar M quasar

que PRON REL that; (con antecedente no humano) which; (con antecedente humano) who, whom; **el/la —** the one that; **lo — tú dices** what you say; **vino la suegra, lo — complicó la visita** the mother-in-law came, which complicated the visit; CONJ that; **no creo — haya tiempo** I don't think [that] there's time; **estoy — me muero** I feel like I'm about to die; **Carlos es más alto — Luis** Carlos is taller than Luis; **más/menos —** more/less than; **déjalo aquí — lo voy a necesitar después** leave it here because I will need it later; **por mucho — no** matter how much; **a — gana** I bet he'll win; **— yo sepa** as far as I know

qué ADJ INTERR & PRON what, which; **¿— libro vas a usar?** what/which book are you going to use? **¿— dices?** what are you saying? **no sé — dijo** I don't know what he said; **¡— bonito!** how beautiful! **¡— de gente!** what a lot of people! **¿y eso —?** so what! **no hay de —** don't mention it; **¿— sé yo?** what do I know? **¿— tal?** how are you? **¡— más da!** what's the difference! **¡— va!** *fam* oh yeah? yeah right! **¡a mí —!** so what!

quebrada F (valle) ravine; (arroyo) creek

quebradizo ADJ breakable, brittle

quebrado ADJ (roto) broken; (rajado) cracked; (sin dinero) broke; M fraction

quebrantar VT (una casa, la salud) to weaken; (la ley) to violate

quebranto M weakening

quebrar¹ VT (romper) to break; (rajar) to crack; VI (irse a la bancarrota) to go bankrupt, to go under, to fail; **—se** to break [up]; **se quebró la muñeca** he broke his wrist; **—se uno la cabeza** to rack one's brain

queda F **toque de —** curfew

quedar VI (permanecer) to remain; (no haberse terminado) to be left; **queda leche en el vaso** there's milk in the glass; (estar ubicado) to be located; **la iglesia queda en la esquina** the church is located on the corner; (sentar bien la ropa) to suit; **— bien** to come out well; **— en** to agree to; **—se** to remain, to stay; **—se con una cosa** (comprar) to take/buy something; (llevarse) to take something

quehacer M chore, errand

queja F (protesta) complaint; (oficial) grievance

quejarse VI (protestar) to complain; (protestar ruidosamente) to gripe, to squawk; (protestar incesantemente) to whine

quejica ADJ whiny; MF nag, whiner

quejido M (de tono grave) moan, groan; (de tono agudo) squawk

quejoso ADJ whiny

quema F burning

quemado -da MF burn victim

quemador M burner

quemadura F (lugar quemado) burn; (sensación) burning; (enfermedad de plantas) blight

quemar VT to burn (también cedés); **—se** (un edificio) to burn up/down; (al sol) to sunburn

quemazón F burning sensation

quepa, quepamos *ver* caber

querella F lawsuit

querellante MF plaintiff

querellarse VI to file suit

querer⁷⁰ VI/VT (desear) to want; (amar) to love; **como quieras** as you please; **cuando quieras** whenever you want; **no quiso hacerlo** he refused to do it; **quiere llover** it is about to rain; **sin —** unwillingly; **— decir** to mean; **lo quiero mucho** I want it badly

querido -da ADJ beloved, dear; MF (enamorado) sweetheart; (como tratamiento) dear, darling

queroseno M kerosene

querrá, querría *ver* querer

quesería F dairy, cheese factory

queso M cheese; **— crema / de untar** cream cheese; **— suizo** swiss cheese

quiche M quiche

quicio M hinge; **sacar a uno de —** to drive someone up the wall

quiebra F bankruptcy (también moral); (de un mercado) crash; (de un comercio) failure; **— bancaria** bank failure

quiebra, quiebre *ver* quebrar

quiebre M break

quien PRON REL who, whom; **Juan, — recién cumplió cuarenta años** Juan, who just turned forty; **— hizo eso** whoever did that; **a — corresponda** to whom it may concern; **—quiera** whoever; **de —** whose; **con —** with whom

quién PRON INTERR & PRON who; **¿— es?** who is it? **no sé — entró** I don't know who came in; **¿a — se lo diste?** who did you give it to? to whom did you give it?

quiera, quiere *ver* querer

quieto ADJ still

quietud F stillness

quijada F jaw

quilate M carat

quilla F keel

química F chemistry

químico -ca ADJ chemical; MF chemist

quimioterapia F chemotherapy

quince NUM fifteen (también en tenis)

quincena F (de cosas) group of fifteen; (de días) two-week period

quincenal ADV biweekly

quincha F thatch

quinchar VT to thatch

quinesiología F kinesiology

quingombó M okra

quinientos NUM five hundred

quinina F quinine

quinqué M oil lamp

quinta F (casa) villa; (reclutamiento) draft

quinto ADJ, ADV, & M fifth

quiosco M kiosk, newsstand

quiquiriquí INTERJ cock-a-doodle-doo

quirófano M surgery, operating room

quiropráctico -ca ADJ chiropractic; MF chiropractor; F chiropractic

quirúrgico ADJ surgical

quise, quisiera, quisiese *ver* querer

quisquilloso ADJ particular, fussy

quiste M cyst

quitar VT (una mancha) to remove; (una prenda de vestir) to take off; (despojar de) to take away; M SG **quitaesmalte** nail polish remover; M SG **quitanieves** snowplow; M SG **quitamanchas** spot remover; VI **—se** to take off; **—se a alguien de encima** to get rid of someone; **quítate de ahí** move over

quite M **salir al — de** to go to the rescue of

quizá, quizás ADV perhaps, maybe

Rr

rabadilla F (coxis) tailbone; (de un ave) rump

rábano M radish; **me importa un —** I couldn't care less

rabia F (enfermedad) rabies; (enojo) rage; **me tiene —** he hates me; **dar —** to anger

rabiar VI to rage, to fume; **guapa a —** drop-dead beautiful

rabieta F tantrum

rabino -na MF rabbi

rabioso ADJ (hidrofóbico, apasionado) rabid, mad; (enojado) mad, furious

rabo M (cola) tail; (cabo) stem; **mirar con el — del ojo** to look out of the corner of one's eye; **con el — entre las piernas** with his tail between his legs

rabón ADJ bobtail

racha F (de suerte) streak; (de viento) gust

racial ADJ racial

racimo M (de plátanos, personas) bunch; (de uvas) cluster

raciocinio M reasoning

ración F (de guerra) ration, allowance; (de comida) portion

racional ADJ rational (también número)

racionalizado ADJ (justificado) rationalized; (reestructurado) streamlined

racionalizar[47] VT (una acción) to rationalize; (un negocio) to streamline

racionamiento M rationing

racionar VT to ration

racismo M racism

racista ADJ & MF racist

radar M radar

radiación F radiation

radiactivo ADJ radioactive

radiador M radiator

radial ADJ radial

radiante ADJ radiant

radiar VT (calor) to radiate; (por radio) to broadcast

radical ADJ (extremo) radical; (células) root; M (en química) radical; (en gramática) root

radicalismo M radicalism

radicar[30] VI to be located; **— en** to lie in; **—se** to take up residence

radio M (hueso, segmento de un círculo) radius; (elemento radiactivo) radium; F (aparato, difusión) radio; (emisora) radio station; **— de acción** sphere of influence

radiodifusión F broadcasting

radiodifusora F radio station

radioescucha MF radio listener

radiofónico ADJ radio

radiografía F x-ray

radiografiar[28] VT (hacer rayos x) to x-ray; (examinar con cuidado) to examine carefully

radiología F radiology

radiólogo -ga MF radiologist

radiotelescopio M radio telescope

radioterapia F radiation therapy

radiotransmisor M radio transmitter

radón M radon

raer[52] VI/VT to scrape [off]; (un artículo de ropa) to wear out

ráfaga F (de viento) gust, blast; (de luz) flash; (de ametralladora) burst

raído ADJ threadbare

raigón M stump

raíz F root; — **cuadrada** square root; **a — de** due to; **arrancar de** — to uproot; **cortar de** — to nip in the bud; **echar raíces** to take root

raja F (de melón) slice; (de falda) slit; (de leña) stick

rajadura F (en piedra, metal) crack; (en tela) rent, rip

rajar VT (una piedra) to crack; (un tronco) to split; **—se** (partir) to split open; (acobardarse) to chicken out, to blink; ADV **a rajatabla** strictly

ralea F ilk

ralear VI to thin out

ralentización F (de la economía) slump; (de un motor) idle

rallador M grater

rallar VT to grate, to shred

ralo ADJ sparse, thin

RAM M RAM

rama F branch, limb; (delgada) twig; **andarse por las —s** to beat around the bush; **algodón en** — raw cotton

ramaje M foliage

ramal M (de soga) strand; (de vía férrea) branch, spur

ramificarse[30] VI to divide into branches, to branch off

ramillete M bouquet, bunch, spray

ramo M (de flores) bouquet; (de una ciencia) branch; (de una actividad) line; — **de olivo** olive branch

rampa F ramp

ramplón ADJ vulgar

rana F frog

ranchero -ra MF rancher; **música ranchera** Mexican country music

rancho M (comida para soldados) mess; (comida mala) swill; (finca) ranch; (choza) hut; **hacer — aparte** to keep to oneself

rancio ADJ rancid; **de — abolengo** of ancient lineage

rango M (militar) rank; (categoría) standing

ranilla F frog [of a hoof]

ránking M (tenis) ranking

ranura F (corte) groove; (para insertar monedas, cartas) slot; — **para accesorios** accessory slot, expansion slot

rapar VT (pelo) to shave off; (cabeza) to shave

rapaz ADJ (animal) predatory; (destructivo) rapacious

rape M **cortar al** — to crop

rapé M snuff

rapear VI to rap

rápidamente ADV (con mucha velocidad) fast; (en poco tiempo) quickly

rapidez F (de un coche) speed; (de un movimiento) rapidity, quickness

rápido ADJ (con mucha velocidad) fast; (en poco tiempo) quick; M **—s** rapids; ADV (con mucha velocidad) fast; (en poco tiempo) quickly

rapiña F pillage

raptar VT to kidnap, to abduct

rapto M (secuestro) abduction, kidnapping; (arrebato) fit

raqueta F racket (también de tenis)

raquítico ADJ feeble, sickly

raramente ADV seldom, rarely

rareza F (escasez) rarity; (cosa rara) oddity; (cualidad de extraño) strangeness

raro ADJ (infrecuente) rare; (extraño) strange, funny; **rara vez** seldom, rarely; **sentirse —** to feel funny; **gas —** rare gas; **tierra rara** rare earth

ras LOC ADV **a — de la tierra** low to the ground

rascar[30] VT to scratch; M SG **rascacielos** skyscraper

rasgado ADJ **ojos —s** slit eyes

rasgadura F tear, rip

rasgar[40] VT to tear, to rip

rasgo M (propiedad) trait, feature; **a grandes —s** in broad strokes

rasgón M tear

rasguñar VT to scratch

rasguño M scratch

raso ADJ (superficie) smooth; (cucharada) level; **al** — in the open air; M satin

raspado M scrape

raspador M scraper

raspadura F scrape

raspar VT to scrape

raspón M scrape

rastra F harrow; **a —s** dragging, pulling

rastrear VT (a un animal) to trail, to track, to trace; (un terreno) to search

rastreo M sweep, search

rastrero ADJ (planta) creeping; (persona) contemptible

rastrillar VT to rake

rastrillo M rake

rastro M (huella) track, trail; (olor) scent; (mercado) flea market; **ni —s** no trace

rastrojo M stubble

rasurado M shave
rasurador -ora MF razor
rasurar VT to shave
rata F rat
ratear VT to pilfer
ratería F petty larceny, pilferage
ratero -ra MF pickpocket
ratificación F ratification
ratificar[30] VT to ratify
rato M while; **—s perdidos** leisure hours; **a cada —** frequently; **a —s** from time to time; **pasar el —** to kill time; **pasar un buen —** (divertirse) to have a pleasant time; (permanecer) to spend a long time; **un largo —** a great while
ratón M mouse (también de computadora); **— almizclero** muskrat; **— en serie** serial mouse
ratonera F mousetrap
raudal LOC ADV **a —es** in great quantities
raudo ADJ swift
raya F (línea) line; (linde) boundary; (lista) stripe; (en el pelo) part; (en un pantalón) crease; (de ortografía) dash; (en un zapato) scuff; (pez marino) stingray; **tener a —** to hold in check; **pasarse de la —** to be out of line, to cross the line
rayado ADJ (papel) lined; (vestido) striped; **hablaba como disco —** he talked like a broken record
rayar VT (papel) to rule, to make lines on; (disco, espejo) to scratch; (zapatos) to scuff; **— el alba** to dawn; **— en** to border on
rayo M (de luz) ray, beam, streak; (de relámpago) flash of lightning; (de rueda) spoke; (de esperanza) ray, flicker; **— láser** laser beam; **—s infrarrojos** infrared rays; **—s X** x-rays
rayón M rayon
raza F (de personas) race; (de animal) breed
razón F (facultad) reason; (proporción) ratio; **— social** company name; **a — de** at the rate of; **¡con —!** no wonder! **entrar en —** to listen to reason; **te doy la —** I admit you're right; **perder la —** to lose one's mind; **tener —** to be right
razonable ADJ reasonable
razonamiento M reasoning
razonar VI (pensar) to reason; (arguir) to argue
reabastecer[35] VT to replenish
reabrir[74] VT to reopen
reacción F reaction; **— en cadena** chain reaction; **— nuclear** nuclear reaction
reaccionar VI to react
reaccionario ADJ & MF reactionary
reacio ADJ averse, reluctant
reacondicionar VT to rebuild
reactivo M reagent
reactor M reactor; **— nuclear** nuclear reactor
readaptación F readjustment

readaptar VT to readjust
reafirmar VT to reaffirm; **—se** to reassert
reagrupar VT to regroup
reajustar VT to readjust
reajuste M readjustment
real ADJ (verdadero) real, actual; (del rey) royal; M fairground
realce M **dar —** to enhance
realeza F royalty
realidad F reality, actuality; **en —** really, actually; **en — no es abogado** he's not really a lawyer; **— virtual** virtual reality
realismo M realism
realista ADJ (auténtico) realistic; (partidario del rey) royalist; MF (no idealista) realist; (partidario del rey) royalist
realización F (de un sueño) realization, fulfillment; (de una tarea) completion; (de una película) production
realizador -ora MF (director) director; (productor) producer
realizar[47] VT (un sueño) to realize, to fulfill; (película) to produce
realmente ADV really
realzar[47] VT (mejorar) to enhance; (destacar) to accentuate; (intensificar) to heighten
reanimación F resuscitation; **— cardiopulmonar** cardiopulmonary resuscitation
reanimar VT (devolver fuerzas) to revive; (dar ánimos) to rally
reanudación F renewal; **— del juego** (fútbol) restart of play
reanudar VT (una amistad) to renew; (una reunión) to resume; (un partido del fútbol) to restart
reaparecer[35] VI to reappear
reasumir VT to resume
reata F lariat, lasso
reavivar VT to revive
rebaja F markdown, price cut; **con —** at a discount, on sale; **de —s** cut-rate
rebajado N on sale, reduced
rebajar VT (precios) to cut, to lower, to slash; (una bebida) to water down; (una crítica) to tone down; VI/VT (los cambios) to downshift; **—se** to lower oneself; **—se a** to stoop to
rebanada F slice
rebanar VT to slice
rebaño M flock, fold
rebasar VT (un coche) to overtake; (un límite) to exceed
rebatir VT to refute
rebato M alarm
rebelarse VI to rebel, to revolt
rebelde ADJ (niño) rebellious; (pelo) unruly; MF rebel
rebeldía F rebelliousness, defiance; (no comparecencia) default

rebelión F rebellion

rebenque M whip

rebobinar VT to rewind

reborde M edge

rebosante ADJ (de líquido) brimming, overflowing; (de salud) flush, glowing; **— de alegría** overjoyed

rebosar VI (líquido) to overflow, to brim over; (de alegría) to bubble over; (de salud) to glow

rebotar VI/VT (en baloncesto) to rebound, to bounce; (chocar) to bounce; (cambiar de dirección una bala) to ricochet; (cambiar de dirección una pelota) to carom

rebote M (en baloncesto) rebound, bounce; (de bala) ricochet

rebotear VI (en baloncesto) to rebound

rebozar⁴⁷ VT to cover with batter; **—se** to muffle up

rebozo M shawl; **sin —** frankly

rebullir¹⁶ VI to stir

rebuscado ADJ (estilo) overly elaborate; (persona) affected

rebuscar³⁰ VT (espigar) to glean; VI **— en** (la memoria) to search through; (un cajón) to rummage in

rebuznar VI to bray

rebuzno M bray, braying

recabar VT to raise

recado M (mensaje) message; (quehacer) errand; **— de escribir** writing materials

recaer⁵² VI to relapse; **— sobre** to fall to

recaída F relapse

recalar VI to make a stop at

recalcar³⁰ VT to accentuate

recalcitrante ADJ obstinate

recalentar¹ VT (volver a calentar) to warm over; (calentar en exceso) to overheat

recamar VT to embroider

recámara F (de un arma de fuego) chamber; Méx (dormitorio) bedroom

recapitular VI/VT to recapitulate, to sum up

recargado ADJ busy

recargar⁴⁰ VT to overload, to burden

recargo M (emocional) burden; (de precio) surcharge, premium; **— por mora** late fee

recatado ADJ (cauteloso) cautious; (modesto) modest

recato M (cautela) caution; (modestia) modesty

recaudación F collection, levy; **— de fondos** fundraising

recaudador -ora MF tax collector

recaudar VT (impuestos) to collect, to levy; (fondos) to raise; **— en bruto** to gross; **— fondos** to raise funds; **lo recaudado** proceeds

recaudo M **estar a buen —** to be in a safe place

rección F government

recelar VT to suspect; **— de** to be suspicious of

recelo M misgivings

receloso ADJ mistrustful

recepción F reception

receptáculo M receptacle, holder

receptor M receiver (también en fútbol americano); (en béisbol) catcher; **— abierto** wide receiver; **— cerrado** tight end

recesión F recession

receta F (de cocina) recipe; (de médico) prescription

recetar VT to prescribe

rechazar⁴⁷ VT (una propuesta, un plan) to reject; (un ataque) to repel, to repulse; (una invitación) to decline, to turn down, to refuse; (una acusación) to deny; (a un amante) to spurn, to reject

rechazo M (de un amante) rejection; (de un ataque) repulse; (de una oferta) refusal; (de una acusación) denial

rechifla F whistling, booing

rechiflar VT to whistle, to boo

rechinamiento M (de una puerta) creaking, squeaking; (de los dientes) grinding

rechinante ADJ squeaky

rechinar VI (una puerta) to squeak, to creak; VI/VT (los dientes) to grind; **eso me rechina** that grates on my nerves

rechoncho ADJ plump, chubby, roly-poly

recibidor -ora MF receiver; M reception room

recibimiento M reception

recibir VT (premio) to receive, to get; (visitas) to receive, to welcome; (una noticia trágica) to take; **— noticias de** to hear from; **—se** to graduate; **—se de médico** to graduate from medical school

recibo M receipt; **de —** acceptable; **al — de** upon receipt of; **acusar —** to acknowledge receipt; **acuse de —** acknowledgment of receipt

reciclaje M recycling

reciclar VI/VT to recycle

recidiva F relapse

recién ADV recently; **— casado** newlywed; **— comprado** brand-new; **— llegado** newly arrived; **— nacido** newborn; **— me entero** it's news to me

reciente ADJ recent

recinto M enclosure

recio ADJ strong, rugged

recipiente M container

recíproco ADJ reciprocal

recitación F recitation

recital M recital

recitar VT to recite, to speak

reclamación F (protesta) protest; (demanda) claim

reclamante MF claimant

reclamar VT (protestar) to protest; (demandar) to claim; VI (aves) to call

reclamo M (reclamación) claim; (queja) complaint; (voz de animal) call, cry;

(dispositivo) bird call; (señuelo) decoy

reclinar VT to lean; —**se** to recline

recluir[19] VT to confine; —**se** to be a recluse

recluso -sa MF (preso) inmate; (ermitaño) recluse

recluta F recruitment; MF (voluntario) recruit; (forzoso) conscript

reclutamiento M (voluntario) recruitment; (forzoso) conscription

reclutar VT (voluntariamente) to recruit; (por la fuerza) to draft, to conscript

recobrar VI to recover, to recuperate; VT to recover, to regain

recodo M bend, turn

recoger[45] VT (el cabello) to gather; (un cuarto) to tidy up; (citas en un texto) to collect; (la mesa) to clear; (polvo) to sweep up; (a un desamparado) to shelter; (los frutos del campo) to glean; —**se** (retirarse) to retire, to withdraw; (acumularse) to gather

recogida F (del cabello) gathering; (de un cuarto) tidying up; (de la mesa) clearing; (de un desamparado) sheltering

recogido ADJ (apartado) secluded; (tranquilo) peaceful, quiet

recogimiento M (aislamiento) seclusion; (meditación) meditation

recolección F (de frutos, datos) collecting, gathering; (de carga) pickup; (cosecha) harvest

recolectar VT to gather, to forage

recomendable ADJ advisable

recomendación F recommendation

recomendar[1] VT to recommend

recomienda, recomiende ver recomendar

recompensa F recompense, reward

recompensar VT to recompense, to reward

reconcentrar VI to concentrate intensely; —**se** to concentrate, to become absorbed in thought

reconciliación F reconciliation

reconciliar VT to reconcile

recóndito ADJ remote

reconfortante ADJ heartwarming, comforting

reconfortar VT to comfort

reconocer[35] VT (identificar) to recognize; (admitir) to admit, to acknowledge; (explorar) to reconnoiter

reconocible ADJ recognizable

reconocimiento M (identificación) recognition; (admisión, agradecimiento) acknowledgment; (exploración) scouting; — **de habla** speech recognition; — **de voz** voice recognition; **visual** visual recognition; **hacer un** — to reconnoiter

reconozca, reconozco ver reconocer

reconsiderar VT to reconsider

reconstrucción F reconstruction

reconstruir[19] VT to reconstruct, to rebuild

reconstruya, reconstruye, reconstruyendo, reconstruyera, reconstruyese ver reconstruir

recopilación F collection, compilation

recopilar VT to compile

récord M record

recordar[5] VT (acordarse) to remember, to recollect, to recall; (hacer acordar) to remind

recordatorio M reminder

recorrer VT (andar una distancia) to cover; (examinar) to go over, to look over

recorrido M (ruta) run, route; (distancia) distance

recortado ADJ jagged

recortar VT (pelo, hilos, presupuesto) to trim; (uñas, periódicos) to clip; (una película) to shorten; —**se** to be outlined

recorte M (de pelos, hilos) trimming; (de uñas, periódicos) clipping; (de sueldo, de gastos) cut; (de recursos) cutback; (sobrante) trimming; — **salarial** pay cut

recostar[5] VT (sobre) to lay; (contra) to lean; —**se** to recline

recoveco M (en un camino) turn; (rincón) cranny

recreación F recreation

recrear VT to entertain; —**se** to amuse oneself

recreativo ADJ recreational; **actividades recreativas** leisure activities; **sala recreativa** game room

recreo M (recreación) recreation, relaxation; (tiempo de descanso) recess; (lugar de juego) playground

recriminar VT to recriminate

recrudecer[35] VI to flare up

recrudecimiento M flareup

recta F (de una pista) straight; (en béisbol) fastball; — **final** final stretch

rectangular ADJ rectangular

rectángulo M rectangle

rectificar[30] VT to rectify

rectitud F uprightness, righteousness

recto ADJ (no curvo) straight; (honrado) upright, righteous; (estricto) strict; **todo** — straight ahead; M rectum

rector -ora MF university president, chancellor

recua F herd

recubrir[74] VT to cover; — **con pintura** to coat with paint

recuento M account; — **sanguíneo** blood count

recuerda, recuerde ver recordar

recuerdo M (acción de recordar, cosa recordada) memory, recollection; (objeto que hace recordar) souvenir, token; —**s** regards; **dale** —**s a tu hermana** say hi to your sister

recular VI (retroceder) to move backward; (retroceder en un coche) to back up; (retroceder ante un desafío) to back down

recuperación F (salarial, de salud) recovery; (de datos, documentos guardados) retrieval; (de objetos, datos, documentos perdidos) recovery

recuperar VT (una cosa perdida) to recover; (datos, documentos guardados) to retrieve; (tiempo perdido) to make up for; (dinero perdido) to recoup; **—se** to recuperate

recurrente ADJ MF (que reclama) complainant; ADJ (repetitivo) recurring, recurrent

recurrir VT to appeal; **— a** to resort to, to have recourse to

recurso M (acción de recurrir) recourse; (reclamación) appeal; **—s** resources; **—s humanos** HR [human resources]; **—s naturales** natural resources

recusar VT (a una persona) to reject; (a un juez) to challenge

red F (para pescar, de tenis) net; (malla tejida) mesh; (de conexiones, para computadora) network; (para engañar) snare; (internet) World Wide Web, Internet; **— [de área] local** local area network

redacción F (ensayo) composition; (acción de redactar) drafting; (en un periódico) editorial department

redactar VT (un ensayo) to draft; (trabajo escolar) to compose

redactor-ora MF editor

redada F (de peces) catch, haul; (policial) raid

redar VT to throw a net

redecilla F hairnet

redención F redemption

redil M sheepfold, sheep pen; **volver al —** to come back into the fold

redimir VT (a un pecador) to redeem; (a un esclavo) to set free

rédito M (de ahorros) interest; (de acciones) yield

redituar[26] VT to yield

redoblar VT (esfuerzos) to double; VI/VT (un tambor) to roll

redoble M drumroll

redoma F flask

redonda F whole note; **a la —** all around

redondear VT (una figura) to make round; (una cifra) to round up

redondel M ring

redondez F roundness

redondo ADJ round; **en —** all around; **caer — to** collapse; **salir —** to turn out perfect

reducción F reduction, cutback; **— de sueldo** cut in salary; **hacer — de personal** to cut back on personnel

reducidor-ora MF *Am* fence

reducir[38] VT (una cantidad) to reduce; (un hueso) to set; (actividades) to curtail, to cut down on; (costos) to cut; (personal) to downsize, to cut back on; **—se a** to boil down to

reduje, redujera, redujese *ver* reducir

redundante ADJ redundant

reduzca, reduzco *ver* reducir

reedificar[30] VT to rebuild

reelección F reelection

reelegir[14] VT reelect

reembolsar VT to reimburse, to refund

reembolso M reimbursement, refund

reemplazable ADJ replaceable

reemplazar[47] VT to replace

reemplazo M replacement, substitute

reencarnación F reincarnation

reescribir[74] VT to rewrite

reestructuración F restructuring

reexpedir[9] VT to forward

referencia F reference

referéndum M referendum

referente LOC ADV **— a** relative to

referir[8] VT (narrar) to narrate; **—se a** to refer to

refiera, refiere *ver* referir

refinación F refinement

refinado ADJ refined, genteel

refinamiento M refinement

refinanciar VI/VT to refinance

refinar VT to refine

refinería F refinery

refiriendo, refiriera, refiriese *ver* referir

reflector M (en una bicicleta) reflector; (en deportes) floodlight; (militar, policial) searchlight

reflejar VT (luz) to reflect; (imagen) to mirror; **—se** to be reflected

reflejo M (luz) reflection; (movimiento) reflex; **—s** frosting; ADJ reflex

reflexión F reflection

reflexionar VI to reflect; **— sobre** to think over

reflexivo ADJ (gramatical) reflexive; (pensativo) thoughtful

reflujo M (de agua) ebb; (gástrico) reflux

reforma F (política) reform; (religiosa) reformation

reformador-ora MF reformer

reformar VT (un gobierno, a un delincuente) to reform; (ropa) to make alterations in; **—se** to mend one's ways

reformatorio M reformatory

reformista MF reformer

reforzado ADJ reinforced; M reinforcement

reforzar[49] VT (una construcción) to reinforce; (las defensas) to beef up; (un argumento) to bolster, to buttress

refracción F refraction

refractario ADJ refractory

refrán M proverb, saying

refrenar VT (un caballo) to rein in; (emociones) to restrain, to check

refrendar VT (una sentencia) to uphold; (un documento) to countersign, to endorse

refrendario-ria MF endorser

refrendo M endorsement

refrescante ADJ refreshing

refrescar[30] VT to refresh (también pantalla de computadora); (el tiempo) to get cool; **—se** to cool off

refresco M (bebida) soft drink; (comida ligera) refreshment

refriega F fray, scuffle

refrigeración F refrigeration

refrigerador ADJ refrigerating; M refrigerator

refrigerante ADJ cooling; M coolant

refrigerar VT to cool, to refrigerate

refrigerio M refreshment

refrito ADJ (comida) refried; M (obra) rerun

refuerzo M (acción de reforzar) reinforcement; (de tela) backing; (de una vacuna) booster

refugiado -da MF refugee

refugiar VT to shelter; **—se** to take shelter

refugio M refuge, shelter; **— antiaéreo** bomb shelter; **— fiscal** tax shelter

refulgente ADJ resplendent

refundir VT to recast

refunfuñar VI to grumble, to mutter

refunfuño M grumbling, muttering

refunfuñón -ona ADJ grouchy, grumpy; MF grouch

refutar VT to refute

regadera F watering can

regadío M (tierra irrigada) irrigated land; (riego) irrigation

regalar VT (dar como presente) to give as a gift; (vender barato, donar) to give away; (agasajar) to regale

regaliz M licorice

regalo M (presente) present, gift; (para los sentidos) treat, delight

regañar VI (un perro) to snarl; VT (a un niño) to scold, to go off on; (constantemente) to nag; LOC ADV **a regañadientes** reluctantly

regaño M scolding, reprimand

regañón -ona ADJ nagging, scolding; MF scold

regar[41] VT (campos) to irrigate; (flores) to water

regate M dribble

regatear VI (precios) to haggle, to bargain; (fútbol) to dribble

regateo M bargaining

regazo M lap

regeneración F regeneration; **— audible** audible feedback

regente MF, **regenta** F regent; F regent's wife; ADJ ruling

reggae M reggae

régimen M (gobierno) regime; (dieta) diet; **— de vida** lifestyle

regimiento M regiment

regio ADJ (propio del rey) regal; (excelente) swell

región F region

regional ADJ regional

regir[14] VT to govern (también en sintaxis); VI to be in force; **—se por** to be guided by

registrador -ora MF (empleado) recorder, registrar; M **— de vuelo** flight recorder

registrar VT (examinar) to search; (dejar constancia) to record, to register; (inscribir) to log; **— al desnudo** to strip-search

registro M (de la voz, lingüístico) register; (de nacimientos) record, register; (del equipaje) search; (de un órgano) stop; (en la computadora) log; **— al desnudo** strip search

regla F (norma) rule; (utensilio para medir) ruler; (menstruación) period; **en —** in order; **por — general** as a general rule

reglamentación F (acción de reglamentar) regulation; (conjunto de reglas) regulations

reglamento M regulations; **—s y disposiciones administrativas** rules and regulations

regocijar VT to gladden; **—se** to rejoice

regocijo M joy, rejoicing

regodearse VI (en la desgracia propia) to wallow; (en la desgracia ajena) to gloat

regodeo M (en la desgracia propia) wallowing; (en la desgracia ajena) gloating

regordete ADJ plump

regresar VI to return

regreso M return; **estar de —** to be back

reguero M trail; **correr como un — de pólvora** to spread like wildfire

regulación F (acción de regular) regulation; (de una máquina) adjustment

regulador M regulator, governor, throttle; **— de voltaje** dimmer

regular VT (reglamentar) to regulate; (ajustar una máquina) to adjust; ADJ regular; **una paliza** quite a beating; ADV so-so

regularidad F regularity

regularizar[47] VT (reglamentar) to regulate; (formalizar) to formalize; **—se** to become regular

regurgitar VI/VT to regurgitate

rehabilitación F rehabilitation

rehabilitador ADJ remedial

rehabilitar VT to rehabilitate

rehacer[54, 74] VT to remake; **—se** to recover

rehén MF hostage

rehuir[19] VT (a una persona) to shun; (responsabilidades) to shirk

rehusar[26] VT to refuse; **—se a** to refuse to

reimpresión F reprint

reina F queen

reinado M reign

reinante ADJ (política, opinión) prevailing; (monarca) ruling

reinar VI to reign

reincidencia F (episodio) relapse; (cualidad) recidivism

reincidir VI to relapse

reiniciar VT to reboot, to reset

reino M (territorio de un rey) kingdom, realm; (período de reinado) reign; (división biológica) kingdom; (ámbito) realm

reinserción F reinsertion; **— laboral** reemployment

reinstaurar VT to reinstate

reintegrar VT to rebate; **—se a** to return to

reintegro M rebate

reinvertir VI/VT to reinvest, to roll over

reír[10] VI to laugh; **—se de** to laugh at

reiterar VT to reiterate

reivindicación F (demanda) demand; (rehabilitación) vindication; (responsabilidad) responsibility; **la — del atentado** the responsibility for the act

reivindicar[30] VT (vengar) to vindicate; (responsabilizarse) to take responsibility, to claim

reja F (enrejado) grate, grating; (pieza de arado) plowshare; **entre —s** behind bars

rejilla F (para equipaje) luggage rack; (de coche) grille

rejuvenecer[35] VT to rejuvenate; VI to become rejuvenated

relación F (conocido) relation, connection; (trato) relationship, involvement; (relato) account, report; (lista) list; **relaciones** (conocidos) connections; (trato) dealings; **relaciones públicas** public relations; **con — a** in relation to

relacionado ADJ related, germane

relacionar VT to relate, to connect; **—se con** to relate to

relajación F relaxation

relajamiento M relaxation

relajante ADJ (actividad) relaxing; (droga) sedative; M **— muscular** muscle relaxant

relajar VT to relax; **—se** (abandonarse moralmente) to become lax; (tranquilizarse) to chill [out], to relax

relajo M (aflojamiento) relaxation; (desorden) mess

relamerse VI to lick one's lips

relámpago M lightning

relampaguear VI (el cielo) to lightning; (los ojos, cosa reluciente) to flash

relampagueo M flash of lightning

relatar VT to relate, to recount

relatividad F relativity

relativo ADJ relative; **— a** relative to

relato M (informe) account; (cuento) story, tale

relé M relay

relegar[40] VT to relegate

relevancia F importance

relevante ADJ important

relevar VT (a un trabajador, guardia) to relieve

relevista MF (atletismo) relay runner; (béisbol) reliever; **— de cierre** (béisbol) closer

relevo M (soldado) relief; **carrera de —s** relay race

relicario M reliquary, locket

relieve M relief; **de —** (mapa) relief; (persona) prominent; **poner de —** to emphasize; **letras en —** raised letters

religión F religion

religioso-sa ADJ religious; M monk; F nun

relinchar VI to neigh

relincho M neigh

reliquia F relic

rellenado M filling

rellenar VT (un vaso) to refill, to replenish; (un tanque de gasolina) to fill, to fill up; (un formulario) to fill out; (un hueco) to fill in; (una almohada) to stuff

relleno ADJ (un pimiento) stuffed; (la cara) full, round; (la figura, el cuerpo) plump; M (de comida) stuffing, dressing; (de un colchón) padding

reloj M (de pared) clock; (de muñeca, bolsillo) watch; (de horno) timer; **— de pulsera** wristwatch; **— de sol** sundial; **— despertador** alarm clock; **contra —** against the clock; **como un —** regularly, like clockwork

relojería F (tienda) watch shop; (actividad) clock-making

relojero-ra MF watchmaker

reluciente ADJ shining

relucir[39] VI to shine; **sacar a —** to bring up

relumbrar VI to glare

relumbre M glare

REM M REM

remachar VT (una victoria, un clavo) to clinch; (un remache) to rivet

remache M (acción de remachar) riveting; (clavo) clinching; (tachuela, clavija) rivet

remanente M remainder

remar VI/VT to row, to paddle

remarcado VT mark-up

rematador-ora MF auctioneer

rematar VT (acabar) to finish; (matar) to finish off; (perfeccionar) to give the finishing touches to; (subastar) to auction; VI (patear un balón) to take a shot

remate M (de una obra) finishing touch; (tiro) shot; (subasta) auction; (tenis) smash; **— de un chiste** punch line; **loco de —** stark raving mad

remedador-ora MF mimic

remedar VT to mimic, to ape, to mock

remediar VT to remedy

remedio M remedy, cure; **sin —** unavoidable; **no tiene —** it can't be helped; **no tengo más —** I can't help it; **el — es peor que la enfermedad** the remedy is worse than the disease

remedo M mockery

remendar[1] VT (ropa) to mend, to patch; (calcetines) to darn; (zapatos) to repair

remendón -ona MF cobbler

remero -ra MF rower

remesa F (de mercancías) shipment; (de dinero) remittance

remiendo M (de ropa) patch; (de zapatos) repair

remilgado ADJ fussy, prim

remilgo M fussiness, primness

reminiscencia F reminiscence

remisión F remission

remitente MF sender

remitir VT (enviar) to remit; (dirigir a otra parte de un texto) to refer; **—se** (ceder) to yield; **a las pruebas me remito** the evidence speaks for itself

remo M (pala) oar, paddle; (deporte) rowing

remodelación F (de una casa) remodeling; (de una ciudad) redevelopment, renewal; (de una organización) reorganization

remodelar VI/VT to remodel

remojar VT to soak

remojo M soaking; **poner en —** to soak

remojón M soaking

remolacha F beet

remolcador M tugboat

remolcar[30] VT to tow

remolino M (de viento) whirlwind; (de agua) whirlpool, eddy; (de pelo) cowlick; (juguete) pinwheel; **— de gente** throng, crowd

remolón -ona ADJ dallying; MF dallier

remolonear VI to dally

remolque M (acción de remolcar) tow; (vehículo remolcado) towed vehicle; (vehículo que remolca) tow truck; (caravana de camión) trailer; **llevar a —** to tow

remontada F (deporte) comeback

remontar VT (una cometa) to fly; (una pendiente, un río) to go up; **—se** to rise; **el globo se remonta** the balloon goes up; **el coche se remonta a los años 20** the car dates from the '20s; **para comprenderlo, debemos remontarnos a su juventud** in order to understand him, we must go back to his youth

remorder[6] VT to gnaw at

remordimiento M remorse

remoto ADJ remote, distant; **no tiene la más remota idea** he doesn't have the slightest idea

remover[6] VT (un cargo, un obstáculo) to remove; (un asunto problemático) to stir up

remuneración F remuneration, compensation

remunerar VT remunerate, compensate

remunerado ADJ gainful

renacentista ADJ Renaissance

renacer[35] VI to be reborn

renacimiento M (resurgimiento) revival; (período histórico) Renaissance

renacuajo M (cría de rana) tadpole; (hombre esmirriado) shrimp

renal ADJ renal

rencilla F quarrel

rencor M rancor; **guardar —** to bear a grudge

rencoroso ADJ resentful

rendición F surrender

rendido ADJ exhausted

rendija F crack

rendimiento M (lo rendido) yield, output; (productividad) performance; **— previo** past performance

rendir[9] VT (someter) to subdue; (producir) to yield; (fatigar) to fatigue; **— homenaje** to pay homage; **— cuentas a** to answer to; VI (obtener buenos resultados) to perform well; **—se** (darse por vencido) to surrender, to give in; (fatigarse) to become fatigued

renegado -da MF renegade

renegar[41] VT (negar) to deny insistently; (repudiar) to renounce; **— de** to gripe about

renegociar VI/VT to renegotiate

renglón M line; **a — seguido** immediately following

rengo ADJ lame

renguear VI to limp

renguera F limp

reno M reindeer

renombrado ADJ renowned

renombre M renown; **de —** of note

renovable ADJ renewable

renovación F renewal; **— urbana** urban renewal

renovador -ora ADJ (artista) innovating; (baño) refreshing; MF innovator

renovar[5] VT (un edificio) to renovate; (ataques, temores) to renew

renquear VT to limp

renta F (de una persona) income; (de un gobierno) revenue; (alquiler) rent; **— anual** annuity; **—s internas** internal revenue; **vivir de la —** to live on the interest

rentabilidad F profitability; **cuentas y depósitos de alta —** high-return accounts and deposits

rentable ADJ (negocio, inversión) profitable; (idea) viable

renuencia F reluctance

renuente ADJ reluctant, loath; **ser — a** to be loath to

renueva, renueve *ver* renovar

renuevo M sprout

renuncia F (dimisión) resignation; (a un derecho) waiver; (a una herencia) renunciation

renunciar VI **— a** (un cargo) to resign; (la ciudadanía) to renounce; (un derecho) to relinquish, to waive

reñido ADJ contested

reñir[11] VI (discutir) to quarrel, to bicker, to argue; (pelear) to fight, to scuffle; (rezongar) to scold

reo -a MF defendant, accused

reojo M **mirar de —** to look out of the corner of one's eye

reorganización F reorganization

reorganizar[47] VT to reorganize, to regroup

repaginar VT to repaginate

repantigarse[40] VI to lounge

reparación F (compensación) reparation, redress; (arreglo) repair

reparador -ra ADJ refreshing; M serviceman; F service woman

reparar VT (arreglar) to repair; (compensar) to redress; **— en** to notice

reparo M **no tener —s en** to have no qualms about; **sin —s** freely; **hacer —s** to object

repartición F distribution

repartir VT (tierras, un botín) to distribute; (volantes) to hand out; (periódicos) to deliver; (naipes) to deal; (días libres) to space out

reparto M (de tierras) distribution; (de periódicos) delivery; (de naipes) dealing; (ruta de entrega) route; (lista de actores) cast; **— proporcional** apportionment

repasar VT (una lección) to review, to go over again; (en la memoria) to retrace; (leer por encima) to skim

repaso M review

repelente ADJ repellent

repeler VT to repel, to repulse

repente M **de —** suddenly

repentinamente ADV suddenly

repentino ADJ sudden

repercusión F repercussion

repercutir VI to have repercussions

repertorio M repertoire

repetición F (reiteración) repetition; (en tenis) let

repetido ADJ repeated; **repetidas veces** repeatedly

repetir[9] VI/VT (reiterar) to repeat; VI (eructar) to belch; (tomar una segunda ración) to have seconds; **— como loro** to parrot; **—se** to recur

repicar[30] VI/VT to ring

repique M ringing, ring

repiquetear VI/VT to ring

repiqueteo M ringing

repisa F shelf

repita, repitiendo, repitiera, repitiese, repito ver repetir

replegar[41] VT to fold; **—se** to retreat

repleto ADJ replete

réplica F (contestación) reply, comeback; (copia) replica; (temblor secundario) aftershock

replicación F replication

replicar[30] VI/VT (responder) to reply, to rejoin;

(reproducirse) to replicate

repliegue M (pliegue marcado) crease; (retirada) retreat

repollo M cabbage

reponer[56, 74] VT (reemplazar) to replace; (restituir) to restore; (replicar) to reply; (una obra de teatro) to revive; (una película) to show again; **—se** to recover one's health

reportaje M feature story

reportar VT (beneficios) to yield; VI (en una organización) to answer to; **—se enfermo** to call in sick

reportero -ra MF reporter

reposado ADJ quiet, calm

reposar VI to repose, to rest; **dejar —** to let steep; M SG **reposacabezas** headrest; M SG **reposapiés** footrest

reposición F (reemplazo) replacement; (de una obra de teatro) revival

reposo M (descanso) repose, rest; (sosiego) calm

repostería F (establecimiento) pastry shop; (actividad) baking

repostero -ra MF pastry cook

reprender VT to reprimand, to scold, to rebuke

reprensión F rebuke

represa F (dique) dam; (reservorio de agua) reservoir

represalia F reprisal

represar VT to dam

representación F (interpretación) representation; (delegación) delegation; (de un papel) portrayal; (de una obra de teatro) performance

representante MF (legislativo) representative; (comercial) agent

representar VT (una imagen) to represent, to depict; (una obra de teatro) to perform; (un personaje) to portray; **tiene treinta años, pero no los representa** he's thirty years old, but he doesn't look it; **tu presencia representa mucho para mí** your presence means a lot to me

representativo ADJ representative

represión F (psicológica) repression; (política) repression, suppression, crackdown

represivo ADJ repressive

reprimenda F reprimand, rebuke

reprimido ADJ repressed, pent-up

reprimir VT (impulsos) to repress; (una tendencia) to check; (enemigos políticos) to suppress, to crack down on; (una rebelión) to quell

reprobación F reproof

reprobar[5] VT to reprove; VI/VT (no aprobar un examen) to flunk, to fail

reprochar VT to reproach, to rebuke

reproche M reproach, rebuke

reproducción F reproduction

reproducir[38] VI/VT to reproduce; **—se** to

reproduce, to breed

reproductor -ora ADJ breeding; **aparato —** VCR; MF breeding animal

reproduje, reprodujera, reprodujese, reproduzca, reproduzco ver reproducir

reptar VI to crawl

reptil M reptile

república F republic

republicano -na ADJ & MF republican; (del Partido Republicano) Republican

repudiar VT (a la sociedad) to repudiate; (a un hijo) to disown; (una herencia) to renounce

repuesto M spare part; **de —** spare

repugnancia F repugnance, disgust, revulsion

repugnante ADJ repugnant, disgusting, loathsome

repugnar VI to be repugnant; VT to disgust, to cloy

repulir VT to polish up

repulsa F rebuff, repulse

repulsar VT to repulse

repulsivo ADJ repulsive, creepy

repuntar VI to rally

reputación F reputation

reputado ADJ reputable

requemar VT to burn

requerimiento M request

requerir[8] VT to require

requesón M cottage cheese

requiebros M PL advances

requisa F requisition

requisar VT (interceptar, incautar) to commandeer, to requisition; (registrar) to search

requisito M requirement, requisite

res F animal; **— lanar** sheep; **— vacuna** cow

resabio M (dejillo) aftertaste; (vicio) bad habit

resaca F (de mar) undertow; (malestar físico) hangover

resaltar VI (sobresalir) to stand out; (poner de relieve) to highlight

resarcir[33] VT to compensate for

resbaladizo ADJ slippery, slick

resbalar VI (deslizar) to slip; (ser/estar resbaladizo) to be slippery; **—se** to slip

resbalón M slip; **darse un —** to slip

resbaloso ADJ (que resbala) slippery; *Méx fam* (inmoral) sleazy

rescatar VT (a un secuestrado) to ransom; (a una persona en peligro) to rescue

rescate M (para un secuestrado) ransom; (de una persona en peligro) rescue

rescindir VT to rescind

rescoldo M embers

resecar[30] VT to dry; **—se** to dry out

reseco ADJ dried-up, parched

resentido ADJ resentful

resentimiento M resentment, grudge; **guardar —** to hold a grudge, to have hard feelings

resentirse[8] VI to hurt, to suffer; **— de** to resent

reseña F book review

reseñar VT to review

reserva F (de provisiones, de oro, de jugadores, del ejército) reserve; (de localidades, de hotel, de indios) reservation; (de animales) preserve; **sin —s** without reservations; **tener —s** to have reservations

reservación F *Am* reservation

reservado ADJ (distante) aloof; (discreto) reserved

reservar VT to reserve; **me reservo mi opinión** I'll spare you my opinion

resfriado M common cold; **estoy —** I've got a cold

resfriarse VI to catch cold

resfrío M cold, head cold

resguardar VT to shelter; **—se de** to seek shelter from

resguardo M (abrigo) shelter; (comprobante) deposit slip

residencia F residence

residencial ADJ (para vivir) residential; (en las afueras) suburban

residente ADJ & MF resident

residir VI to reside

residuo M residue

resignación F resignation

resignarse VI to resign oneself

resina F resin

resistencia F (fuerza opuesta) resistance; (de la calefacción) element; (aguante) endurance, stamina

resistente ADJ resistant, tough

resistir VT (una tentación) to resist; (un ataque) to withstand; **—se a un arresto** to resist arrest; VI to resist, to hold [up]

resollar[5] VI (por enfermedad) to wheeze; (después de un esfuerzo) to pant; (por alivio) to sigh

resolución F (acción de resolver) resolution; (ánimo) determination, resolve; **— óptica** optical resolution

resolver[6, 74] VT (decidir) to decide; (solucionar) to solve; **—se a** to resolve to

resonancia F resonance

resonar[5] VI (sonidos) to resound, to boom; (una polémica) to resonate

resoplar VI (con enfado) to huff and puff; (un caballo) to snort

resoplido M (con enojo) puff; (de caballo) snort

resorte M spring

respaldar VT to back, to stand behind

respaldo M (parte de una silla) back; (apoyo) support, backing; **— automático** automatic backup; **— de archivos** backup; **— global** global backup

respectivo ADJ respective

respecto LOC ADV — **a/de** with respect to, concerning; **a ese** — on that score; **con** — **a** with regard to, regarding, vis-à-vis

respetable ADJ respectable

respetar VT to respect

respeto M respect, regard; **con todo** — with all due respect; **faltar el/al** — to slight, to disregard

respetuoso ADJ respectful

respingado M upturned

respingar[40] VI (dar respingos) to buck; (asustarse) to shy away

respingo M (salto) buck; (susto) start

respiración F respiration, breathing; — **boca a boca** mouth-to-mouth resuscitation

respirar VI/VT (inhalar y exhalar) to breathe; (sentir alivio) to breathe easy; **dejar** — to give a breather

respiratorio ADJ respiratory

respiro M (acto de respirar) breathing; (descanso) respite; **dame un** — I need a break

resplandecer[35] VI (brillar) to glare; (de felicidad) to glow

resplandeciente ADJ resplendent, radiant

resplandor M brilliance, radiance

responder VI (reaccionar) to respond; VT (contestar) to answer; (corresponder) to correspond

respondón ADJ saucy

responsabilidad F (obligación de aceptar consecuencias) responsibility; (obligación de informar) accountability

responsabilizar VT to hold liable, to hold responsible

responsable ADJ (que debe aceptar las consecuencias) responsible; (obligado legalmente) liable; (que tiene que informar) accountable

respuesta F response, answer

resquebrajadura F crack

resquebrajar VI to crack

resquicio M (rendija) crack; (laguna legal) loophole

resta F subtraction

restablecer[35] VT (un servicio) to reestablish; (una costumbre) to revive; —**se** to recover

restador -ora MF receiver

restante ADJ remaining

restañar VT to stanch/staunch

restar VT (sustraer) to subtract; (quitar) to take away from; (quedar) to remain; — **importancia a** to make light of

restauración F restoration

restaurante M restaurant

restaurar VT (el gobierno) to restore; (muebles) to refurbish

restitución F restitution

restituir[19] VT to pay back, to give back

resto M (lo demás) rest; (sobrante) remainder; (tenis) return of service; —**s** (de un edificio) remains; (de una comida) leftovers; **echar el** — to go all out

restorán M restaurant

restregar[41] VT to scrub, to scour

restricción F restriction

restringir[46] VT to restrict, to constrain

resucitación F resuscitation, revival

resucitar VT to resuscitate, to revive

resuello M (por enfermedad) wheeze; (por fatiga) panting

resuelto ADJ (de carácter decidido) resolute, strong-willed; (de actitud decidida) resolved

resuelto, resuelva, resuelve ver resolver

resulta LOC ADV **de** —**s** as a result

resultado M (de una operación matemática) result; (de un suceso) outcome; (de un partido) score; — **final** (fútbol) final score; —**s científicos** findings, —**s electorales** returns; **como** — as a result; **dar buen** — to pan out; **dar por** — to result in

resultante ADJ resulting, consequent

resultar VI to result; — **de** to result from; **resulta que** it turns out that; **resultó ser un idiota** he turned out to be an idiot, he proved to be an idiot

resumen M summary, abstract; **en** — in sum, in brief

resumir VT to summarize, to sum up; —**se a** to be condensed to, to boil down to

resurgimiento M revival

resurgir[46] VI to arise again

resurrección F resurrection

retablo M altarpiece

retaguardia F rear guard

retal M remnant

retama F broom

retar VT to challenge

retardar VI/VT to retard

retardo M lag

retazo M remnant

retén M (aparato) retainer; (de vigilancia) checkpoint

retención F retention; — **de líquido** fluid retention; — **impositiva** tax withholding

retendrá, retendría ver retener

retener[58] VT (una pelota, la atención) to hold; (salarios, fondos) to garnish, to withhold

retenga, retengo ver retener

retina F retina

retintín M (en los oídos) ringing; (de cascabeles) jingle

retirada F (de tropas) retreat, withdrawal; (de un diplomático, producto) recall

retirar VT (apartar) to move away; (dinero) to withdraw; (algo dicho) to take back, withdraw; (un producto) to recall; —**se** (para dormir, de un empleo, de la carrera militar) to retire; (un ejército) to retreat, to pull back

retiro M (refugio) retreat; (jubilación) retirement; (de fondos) withdrawal; **— de deuda** debt retirement

reto M challenge

retocar[30] VT to retouch, to touch up

retomar VT to take up again

retoñar VI to sprout

retoño M sprout, shoot, bud

retoque M retouching

retorcer[34] VT (una toalla mojada) to wring out; (la muñeca) to wrench, to twist; **—se** (de dolor) to writhe; (de inquietud) to squirm

retorcido ADJ (persona) devious; (rama) gnarled

retorcimiento M (de dolor) writhing; (de inquietud) squirming

retórica F rhetoric

retornar VT to return

retorno M (de un viajero) return (también en un teclado); (de una costumbre, moda) revival; **— de línea automático** word wrap

retozar[47] VI (en juegos infantiles) to frolic, to romp; (en juegos eróticos) to cavort

retozo M frolic, romp

retractarse VI to take back one's words

retraer[59] VT (las garras) to retract; **—se** to withdraw

retraído ADJ shy

retraimiento M shyness

retrasado ADJ (falto de desarrollo) backward; (deficiente mental) retarded

retrasar VT (atrasar) to delay; (un reloj) to set back; **—se** to fall behind

retraso M delay, lag

retratar VT (describir) to portray; (pintar un retrato) to paint a portrait

retrato M (pintura) portrait; (descripción) portrayal

retreta F retreat

retrete M lavatory

retribución F (acción de retribuir) remuneration; (pago) salary

retro ADJ retro

retroactivo ADJ retroactive

retroalimentación F feedback

retroceder VI (recular) to step back; (por miedo) to recoil, to shrink back; (en un coche) to back up; (al mecanografiar) to backspace; (dar marcha atrás) to backtrack; (tropas) to retreat, to fall back; (una inundación) to recede

retroceso M (pérdida) step back; (de un arma de fuego) recoil; (económico) recession; (en un teclado) backspace

retrogradismo M backwardness

retrógrado ADJ backward

retroiluminación F backlighting

retroiluminado ADJ backlit

retroproyector M overhead projector

retrovirus M retrovirus

retrucar[30] VT to counter

retruécano M play on words

retumbar VI to rumble, to roll

retumbo M rumble

retuve, retuviera, retuviese *ver* retener

reubicar[30] VT to relocate

reuma M rheumatism

reumatismo M rheumatism

reumatoide ADJ rheumatoid

reunificación F reunification

reunión F (de negocios) meeting; (informal) get-together; (de ex-alumnos) reunion

reunir[27] VT (juntar) to gather; (convocar) to reunite, to bring together; (coleccionar) to collect; (juntar coraje) to muster; (juntar dinero) to raise; **—se** (formal) to meet; (informal) to get together; (un gentío) to gather

revancha F (venganza) revenge; (en deportes) return game

revelación F revelation

revelado M film development

revelador ADJ revealing

revelar VT (un secreto) to reveal; (película) to develop; (un escándalo) to expose; (información) to disclose; **—se** to show oneself

revendedor -ora MF (de mercadería) middleman; (de entradas) scalper

revender VT (vender de nuevo) to resell; (entradas) to scalp

reventar[1] VI/VT (estallar) to burst, to bust; (morir) to die; (fastidiar) to annoy

reventón M (acción de reventar) bursting; (de un neumático) blowout

reverberar VI to reverberate

reverdecer[35] VI (ponerse verde de nuevo) to become green again; (renovarse) to gain new strength

reverencia F (adoración) reverence; (gesto) bow

reverenciar VT to revere

reverendo -da ADJ & MF reverend

reverente ADJ reverent

reverso M reverse

revertir[8] VI to revert; **— en beneficio de** to be of benefit to

revés M (lado opuesto) reverse; (en tenis) backhand; (contratiempo) setback, downturn; **al —** (con lo de adelante hacia atrás) backwards; (con lo de arriba hacia abajo) upside down; (con lo de adentro hacia afuera) inside out; **dar vuelta al —** to turn inside out

revestimiento M overlay; (de piso) flooring; (de pared exterior) siding; (de pared interior) paneling

revestir[9] VT (un camino) to surface; (una pared) to cover; (conllevar) to be marked by

revisar VT (examinar) to review, to go over; (un

coche) to service

revisión F (de un libro) review; (de una película vieja) revival; (médica, mecánica) checkup

revisor -ora MF (en un tren, autobús) conductor; (de un texto) proofreader

revista F (inspección) inspection; (de tropas) muster; (publicación) magazine, journal, periodical; (espectáculo) revival; **— de historietas** comic book; **— electrónica** e-zine; **pasar —** to pass in review

revistar VT to inspect

revitalizar VT to revitalize

revivir VI/VT to revive

revocación F (de un derecho, de un fallo) revocation; (de una ley) repeal

revocar[30] VT (un fallo) to reverse; (una ley) to repeal; (una pared) to plaster

revolcar[31] VT (derribar) to knock over; **—se** (cerdos) to wallow; (niños) to roll around

revolear VT to roll

revolotear VI to flutter, to flit

revoltijo M (de cosas) jumble; (de pelo) muss

revoltoso -sa ADJ unruly, disorderly; MF troublemaker

revolución F (cambio radical) revolution; (giro) revolution, turn; **revoluciones por minuto** revolutions per minute

revolucionario -ria ADJ revolutionary, earthshaking; MF revolutionary

revolver[6, 74] VT (remover) to stir up; (registrar) to rummage in; (desordenar) to mess up; (huevos) to scramble; (ensalada) to toss; **eso me revuelve el estómago** that makes my stomach turn; **—se en la cama** to toss and turn in bed

revólver M revolver, pistol

revuelo M stir, commotion

revuelta F revolt

revuelto ADJ (el mar) rough; (el ánimo) restless; (el pelo) disheveled; **huevos —s** scrambled eggs

rey M king; **los —es Magos** the Wise Men

reyerta F melee, squabble

rezagarse[40] VI to straggle behind, to lag behind

rezar[47] VI/VT (a Dios) to pray; (un letrero) to say

rezo M prayer

rezongar[40] VI/VT (murmurar) to grumble; (quejarse) to gripe

rezongón -ona ADJ grumpy; MF grouch

rezumar VT to ooze

ría, ríe ver reír

riachuelo M brook

riada F flash flood

ribazo M steep bank

ribera F shore, bank; (de río) riverbank

ribereño ADJ on the bank

ribete M (de uniforme) trimming; (de alfombra) binding; (de ropa) piping; (de mosaico) border; **tener —s de** to have hints of

ribetear VT (un uniforme) to trim; (una alfombra) to bind; (un diseño) to border

ricacho ADJ very rich

rico ADJ (persona) rich, wealthy, affluent; (suelo) rich; (adorno) exquisite; (manjar) delicious; (niño) cute

ridiculizar[47] VT to ridicule, to deride

ridículo ADJ (sin sentido) ridiculous; (absurdo, risible) ludicrous; **hacer el —** to act the fool; **poner en —** to ridicule; **ponerse en —** to make a spectacle of oneself

riego M irrigation

riel M rail

rienda F rein; **dar — suelta** to give a free hand

riendo, riera, rieron, riese ver reír

riesgo M risk; **— ocupacional** occupational hazard/risk; **en —** at risk; **correr un —** to run a risk

rifa F raffle

rifar VT to raffle

rifirrafe M free-for-all

rifle M rifle

rigidez F rigidity

rígido ADJ rigid

rigor M (exactitud) rigor; (dureza) harshness; **en — in reality; de —** indispensable

riguroso ADJ (estricto) rigorous; (duro) harsh

rima F rhyme

rimar VI/VT to rhyme

rimbombante ADJ grandiose

rímel M mascara

rin M rim

rincón M (ángulo) corner; (lugar retirado) nook, alcove

rinconera F (estantería) corner cupboard; (mesa) corner table

rinda, rinde, rindiendo, rindiera, rindiese ver rendir

ring M boxing ring

ringlera F row

rinoceronte M rhinoceros

rinoplastia F rhinoplasty, *fam* nose job

rinovirus M rhinovirus

riña F (discusión) quarrel; (pelea) scrap, fight, spat

riñón M (órgano) kidney; (región lumbar) lower back

río M river; **— abajo** downstream

rió ver reír

ripio M rubble

riqueza F wealth; **—s** riches

risa F (carcajada) laugh; (acción, sonido de reír) laughter; **reventar/desternillarse de —** to burst with laughter; **morirse de —** to die laughing; **¡qué —!** what a joke!

risco M crag, bluff

risible ADJ laughable

risita F (burlona) snicker; (ahogada) chuckle

risotada F guffaw, gale of laughter

ristra F string

risueño ADJ (sonriente) smiling; (alegre) cheerful

rítmico ADJ rhythmical

ritmo M rhythm; **— cardíaco** heart rate; **— de vida** pace of life

rito M rite

ritual ADJ & M ritual

rival ADJ & MF rival

rivalidad F rivalry; **— entre hermanos** sibling rivalry

rivalizar[47] VI to rival; **— con** to compete with

rizado ADJ curly; M curling

rizar[47] VT (pelo) to curl, to crimp; (agua) to ripple

rizo M (en el pelo) curl, ringlet; (en el agua) ripple, ruffle; (pirueta de avión) loop

robar VT (a una persona) to rob; (un objeto, dinero) to steal; **—se una base** to steal a base

roble M oak tree

robledal M oak grove

robo M (violento) robbery; (furtivo) theft; **— a mano armada** armed robbery, holdup; **— con allanamiento** burglary; **— de base** base steal; **— de identidad** identity theft

robot M robot

robótica F robotics

robusto ADJ (fuerte) robust; (grueso) stout, stocky; (sólido) sturdy

roca F rock

roce M (de una bala) graze; (de dos superficies) rub, rubbing; (con la ley, la policía) brush

rociada F (acción de rociar) sprinkling, spraying; (de insultos) volley

rociar[28] VI/VT (con agua) to spray, to sprinkle; (con jugo, aliño) to baste

rocín M nag

rocío M (del alba) dew; (en aerosol) spray, mist

rock M rock

rocoso ADJ rocky

rodada F (superficial) track; (profunda) rut

rodadura F rolling

rodaja F flat round slice

rodaje M (de un coche) running; (de una película) shoot

rodante ADJ rolling

rodar[5] VI (girar) to roll; (caer) to tumble down; (vagar) to roam; (filmar) to shoot

rodear VT (cercar) to surround; (cubrir) to wrap around; (evitar) to go around

rodeo M (desvío) detour; (modo de expresarse) circumlocution; (espectáculo) rodeo

rodilla F knee; **de —s** on one's knees; **hincarse de —s** to kneel down

rodillo M (para pintar) roller; (para cocinar) rolling pin; (para caminos) road roller

rododendro M rhododendron

roedor M rodent

roer[73] VI/VT to gnaw

rogar[42] VT to pray, to beg, to beseech; **hacerse [del] —** to play hard to get; **se ruega no molestar** please do not disturb

rojez F redness

rojizo ADJ reddish

rojo ADJ & M red; **al — vivo** red-hot

rol M role

roletazo M ground ball; **lo sacaron con un —** he grounded out

rollizo ADJ plump; M log

rollo M (de papel, de película, de grasa) roll; (de árbol) log; (de cuerda) reel; (de tela) bolt; (discurso aburrido) long story; (mentira) lie; (lío) mess, hassle; (relación amorosa) affair; (manuscrito) scroll; (de alambre) coil; **dar el — to hassle**

ROM M ROM

romance ADJ Romance; M (lengua románica) Romance language; (español) Spanish language; (relación amorosa) romance; (composición métrica) ballad; **en buen — in** plain language

románico ADJ (arte) Romanesque; (lengua) Romance

romano -na ADJ & MF Roman

romanticismo M (corriente literaria) romanticism; (sentimentalismo) romance

romántico -ca ADJ & MF romantic

rombo M diamond

romería F pilgrimage

romero -ra MF (persona) pilgrim; M rosemary

romo ADJ (sin punta) blunt; (sin filo) dull

romper[74] VI/VT (un jarrón) to break; VT (relaciones) to sever; **— a** to start to; **— con** to break up with; **— el alba** to dawn; **— filas** to break ranks; **— un contrato** to break a contract; **rompió las aguas / la fuente** her water broke; **de rompe y rasga** coarse; M SG **rompecabezas** jigsaw puzzle; M SG **rompehuelgas** strikebreaker; M SG **rompeolas** breakwater

rompible ADJ breakable

rompientes M PL surf

rompimiento M (con el pasado) break; (de una promesa) breach

rompope M *Méx* eggnog

ron M rum

roncar[30] VI to snore

roncha F (de sarampión) spot; (de mosquito) bite

ronco ADJ hoarse, raspy

ronda F (de policía) patrol, beat; (de niños) circle; (de bebidas, de negociaciones, de golf) round

rondar VT (patrullar) to patrol; (acercarse) to hang around; (cantar serenatas) to serenade; **rondaba los cuarenta** she was around forty years old

ronquera F hoarseness

ronquido M snore

ronronear VI to purr

ronroneo M purr

ronzal M halter

roña F (enfermedad de plantas) scab; (sarna) mange; MF (tacaño) skinflint

roñoso ADJ (planta) scabby; (animal) mangy; (persona) stingy

ropa F clothing, clothes; — **blanca** linens; — **vieja** stew made from leftover meat

ropaje M apparel

ropería F checkroom

ropero M (armario) wardrobe; (cuarto) closet

roque M castle

rorro M baby

rosa F (flor) rose; (marca) blemish; — **de los vientos** mariner's compass; ADJ INV (rosado) rose-colored, pink

rosado ADJ (saludable) rosy; (de color de rosa) rose-colored, pink; M rosé wine

rosal M rosebush

rosario M rosary

rosbif M roast beef

rosca F (de tornillo) screw; (pan) ring-shaped roll; **pasarse de** — to go off the deep end

roséola F roseola

rostro M (cara) face; (morro) nerve

rotación F rotation

rotar VI/VT to rotate

rotativo ADJ (movimiento) rotary; (cultivos) rotating; M newspaper

rotatorio ADJ rotary

roto ADJ (averiado) broken; (cansado) exhausted; (ropa, voz) ragged

roto ver romper

rotor M rotor

rótula F kneecap

rotular VT to label

rótulo M (título) title; (etiqueta) label

rotundo ADJ resounding; **una negativa rotunda** a categorical denial

rotura F (de un aparato) break; (de un órgano, tubo) rupture; — **de servicio** (tenis) service break

roturar VT to plow

round M (en boxeo) round

rozadura F chafing

rozamiento M friction

rozar[47] VT (herir levemente) to graze; (arañar) to scrape; (irritar) to rub, to chafe; (limpiar un terreno) to clear; —**se con alguien** to have dealings with someone; **rozaba en los cuarenta** she was almost forty years old

Ruanda F Rwanda

ruandés -esa ADJ & MF Rwandan

rubéola/rubeola F rubella

rubí M (piedra preciosa) ruby; (en un reloj) jewel

rubicundo ADJ (permanente) ruddy; (temporal) flush

rubio -a ADJ & MF blond

rubor M (de la piel) blush, flush; (de las mejillas) bloom, glow

ruborizarse[47] VI to blush

rúbrica F (trazo) flourish; (título) title

rucio ADJ gray

rudeza F rudeness, coarseness

rudo ADJ rude, coarse; — **golpe** hard blow

rueca F spinning wheel

rueda F (de coche) wheel; (de personas) circle; (rodaja) slice; — **de prensa** news conference; **ir sobre** —**s** to be smooth sailing

ruedo M (de un circo) ring; (de vestido) hem

ruego M (plegaria) prayer; (petición) plea, entreaty

rufián M (matón) ruffian

rugby M rugby

rugido M roar

rugir[46] VI (animal) to roar; (estómago) to growl

rugoso ADJ rough

ruibarbo M rhubarb

ruido M noise; — **de fondo** background noise; **mucho** — **y pocas nueces** much ado about nothing

ruidoso ADJ noisy, loud

ruin ADJ (persona, cosa) vile; (animal) puny

ruina F (destrucción) destruction; (edificio derruido, estado de pobreza) ruin; (persona) wreck; (perjuicio) downfall; **en** —**s** in ruins

ruindad F (actitud) vileness; (acto) vile act

ruinoso ADJ ruinous

ruiseñor M nightingale

rulero M RP roller, curler

ruleta F roulette

rulo M roller, curler

Rumania F Romania, Rumania

rumano -na ADJ & MF Romanian, Rumanian

rumba F rumba

rumbear VI (dirigirse a) to head in a certain direction; (bailar) to dance the rumba

rumbo M course, route; — **a** toward

rumiar VI (meditar, comer el rumen) to ruminate; (reflexionar) to ruminate, to mull over, to brood over

rumor M rumor

runrún M (rumor) rumor; (sonido sordo) humming

ruptura F (de relaciones) break; (de órganos internos) rupture

rural ADJ rural

Rusia F Russia

ruso -sa ADJ & MF (persona) Russian; M (lengua) Russian

rústico ADJ (rural) rustic, rural; (tosco) coarse; **en rústica** paperback

ruta F (itinerario) route; (carretera) highway; (en informática) path

rutina F routine

Ss

sábado M Saturday
sábalo M shad
sábana F bed sheet
sabana F savannah
sabañón M chilblain
saber[71] VI/VT to know; (tener sabor) to taste; —
  nadar to know how to swim; **supo la
  verdad** he found out the truth; **las
  vacaciones me han sabido a poco** my
  vacation was too short; **a ciencia cierta**
  to know for sure; **— de biología** to know all
  about biology; **a —** namely; **hacer —** to let
  know; **para que sepas** for your
  information; **sabérselas todas** to know the
  ropes; **vaya a —** who knows? **no sabe un
  comino** he doesn't know squat; **— a** to taste
  like; **sabe bien** it tastes good; M knowledge,
  learning; **a mi leal — y entender** as far as I
  know; M SG **sabelotodo** know-it-all
sabiduría F wisdom
sabiendas LOC ADV **a —** knowingly
sabiondo -da ADJ & MF wise guy; know-it-all
sabio -bia ADJ wise, sage; MF (estudioso)
  scholar; (sabedor) sage, wise person
sable M saber
sabor M taste, flavor
saborear VT to savor, to relish
sabotaje M sabotage
sabotear VT to sabotage
sabrá, sabría ver saber
sabroso ADJ (comida) savory, tasty; (cuento)
  juicy
sabueso M (perro) bloodhound; (detective)
  sleuth
sacador -ora MF (en deportes) server
sacar[30] VT (cosas de la maleta, a pasear) to take
  out; (manchas, dinero del banco) to get out;
  (los zapatos) to take off; (malas notas, carnet
  de conducir) to get; (una copia) to make; (una
  foto) to take; (una conclusión) to draw; (la
  lengua, la cabeza por la ventana) to stick out;
  (una pelota de tenis) to serve; (una asignatura
  escolar) *Esp* to pass; **— ampollas** to blister;
  — brillo to polish up; **— provecho [de]** to
  benefit [from]; **— a bailar** to ask to dance; **—
  a colación** to broach; **— a luz** to divulge; **—
  de un apuro** to bail out; **me saca de quicio**
  he gets my goat, he gets on my nerves; **— el
  cuerpo** to dodge; **— el mejor partido de** to
  make the best of; **—le el jugo a algo** to make
  the most of; **— en limpio** to deduce; **—se el
  sombrero** *Am* to take off one's hat;
  ¡sáquese de allí! *Am* get out of there! **—

punta to sharpen; **— a alguien** (béisbol) to
  get someone out; M SG **sacabocados** punch;
  M SG **sacacorchos** corkscrew; M SG
  sacamuelas quack dentist; M SG
  sacapuntas pencil sharpener
sacarina F saccharine
sacarosa F sucrose
sacerdocio M priesthood
sacerdote M priest
saciar VT to satiate; **—se** to be satiated
saco M (bolsa) sack; (chaqueta) blazer, sport coat;
  (aparato de boxeo) punching bag; (parte de
  órgano interno) sac; **— de dormir** sleeping
  bag; **— de noche** overnight bag; **echar en —
  roto** to waste one's effort
sacramento M sacrament
sacrificar[30] VT (en un rito religioso) to sacrifice;
  (una mascota) to put to sleep
sacrificio M sacrifice (también en béisbol)
sacrilegio M sacrilege
sacrílego ADJ sacrilegious
sacristán M sexton
sacro M sacrum
sacudida F (sacudón) shake, jolt; (de terremoto)
  tremor; (de la cabeza) toss; (eléctrica) shock
sacudir VT (sarandear) to shake; (las alfombras)
  to beat; (el polvo) to dust; **ir sacudiéndose**
  to rattle along, to jolt along; **—se de alguien**
  to get rid of someone
sádico ADJ sadistic
sadismo M sadism
saeta F arrow
safari M safari
sagaz ADJ shrewd, astute
sagrado ADJ sacred, holy; **Sagradas
  Escrituras** Holy Scripture
sahumar VT to perfume with incense
sahumerio M burning of incense
sainete M one-act farce; **esa familia es un —**
  that family is a complete mess
sal F (mineral) salt; (gracia) wit; **— de Epsom**
  Epsom salt; **— gorda** cooking salt; **—
  yodada** iodized salt; **— de mesa** table salt;
  dar — to spice up; **— y pimienta**
  (condimentos) salt and pepper; (gracia) life,
  spark
sal ver salir
sala F (de estar) parlor, living room; (grande)
  hall, large room; **— de justicia** courtroom;
  — de clase classroom; **— de chat** chat
  room; **— de cuidados intensivos** intensive
  care unit; **— de espera** waiting room; **— de
  directorio** boardroom; **— de lectura**
  reading room; **— de operaciones** operating
  room; **— de recuperación** recovery room
salado ADJ (con sal) salty, savory; (gracioso)
  witty; *Am* (caro) expensive; M (acción) salting
salamandra F salamander
salar VT to salt; **—se** to become salty

salarial ADJ salary, wage

salario M pay, wages; — **base** base pay; — **bruto** gross pay; — **de subsistencia** living wage; — **mínimo** minimum wage

salchicha F sausage

saldar VT to settle

saldo M (resultado final) balance; (venta especial) sale; —**s** (restos) remnants; — **pendiente** balance due

saldrá, saldría ver salir

salegar⁴⁰ VT to give salt to; M salt lick

salero M (dispensador) salt cellar, salt shaker; (gracia) charm

saleroso ADJ charming

salga, salgo ver salir

salida F (partida) departure; (puerta) exit, way out; (comienzo de una carrera) start; (militar) sally; (eléctrica, de computadora) output; (de una crisis) way out; **este artículo tiene mucha** — this article sells well; **dar la** — to start a race; — **del sol** sunrise; — **de emergencia** emergency exit; — **en falso** false start

saliente ADJ (roca) salient, projecting; (gobierno) outgoing; M salient, projection, overhang

salina F salt mine

salino ADJ saline

salir⁵⁷ VI (del interior al exterior, para divertirse) to go out; (de un país) to depart, to leave; (del trabajo) to quit; (de un programa de computadora) to exit, to quit; (manchas de tinta) to come out; (un anillo del dedo) to come off; (el sol) to rise; (una publicación) to appear; (flores) to sprout; — **a bolsa** to go public; **trabajando no se puede** — **de pobre** you can't work your way out of poverty; **salió a su madre** she takes after her mother; — **a la luz** to surface; — **adelante** to overcome difficulties; — **bien** to turn out well; — **con** to date; — **ganando** to come out ahead; — **mal** to go wrong; **¿a cuánto sale?** how much is it? **no me sale ser amable con él** I can't bring myself to be nice to him; — **se** (gotear) to leak; (rebosar) to overflow; (proyectarse) to stick out

salitre F saltpeter

saliva F saliva

salmón M salmon

salmonela F salmonella

salmuera F brine

salobre ADJ salty

salomonense ADJ & MF Solomon Islander

salón M (de estar) living room, parlor; (de conferencias) hall; — **de belleza** beauty salon; — **de clase** classroom; — **de exposición y ventas** showroom; — **de exhibición** exhibition hall; — **de té** tearoom

salpicadero M dashboard

salpicadura F spatter, splash, splatter

salpicar³⁰ VI/VT (humedecer) to sprinkle, to spatter, to splash; (adornar) to punctuate; (dispersar) to intersperse

salpicón M meat salad

salpimentar¹ VT to salt and pepper

salsa F (blanca) sauce; (picante) salsa; **en su** — in her element; — **tártara** tartar sauce; — **de soya** soy sauce; — **de tomate** ketchup

saltar VI/VT (brincar) to jump, to leap; (una cerca) to jump over, to vault; (un renglón) to skip; (una ley) to ignore; VI (los fusibles) to trip; — **a la vista** to be obvious; — **sobre** to pounce on; **se le saltaron los ojos** his eyes bugged out; **se le saltó un botón** one of his buttons popped off; **se me saltaron las lágrimas** it brought tears to my eyes; M SG **saltamontes** grasshopper

salteador-ora MF bandit

saltear VT to stir-fry

salto M jump, leap; — **alto** high jump; — **con esquí** ski jump; — **con pértiga** pole vault; — **de agua** waterfall; — **de cama** dressing gown; — **de línea** return; — **de línea forzado** hard return; — **de línea suave** soft return; — **de longitud** broad jump; — **de página** page break; — **de página forzado** forced page break, hard page break; — **de página suave/automático** soft page break; — **del ángel** swan dive; — **mortal** somersault; — **triple** triple jump; **a** — **de mata** from hand to mouth; **dar un** — (saltar) to jump; (el corazón) to skip a beat

saltón ADJ (que salta) jumping; (que resalta) bulging; M grasshopper

salubridad F sanitation

salud F health; — **mental** mental health; — **pública** public health; **curarse en** — to take precautions; INTERJ cheers!

saludable ADJ healthy, healthful

saludar VT (decir hola) to greet; (dar la bienvenida) to salute, to hail; (en el ejército) to salute; (hacer un gesto amistoso con la mano) to wave

saludo M (hola) greeting, salutation; (gesto) wave; (militar) salute; **retirar el** — **a alguien** to stop speaking to someone; —**s** best wishes, regards

salva F salvo

salvación F salvation

salvado M (harina) bran; (béisbol) save

salvador-ora MF savior; ADJ saving

salvadoreño-ña ADJ & MF Salvador[i]an

salvaguarda F safeguard

salvaguardar VT to safeguard

salvajada F (acción) savage act; (comentario) savage remark

salvaje ADJ (feroz) savage; (no domesticado)

wild; MF savage

salvajismo M savagery

salvamento M (de gente) rescue; (de bienes, propiedades) salvage; (béisbol) save

salvar VT (la vida, el alma) to save; (de un peligro) to rescue; (propiedad) to salvage; (un obstáculo) to clear; (un camino difícil) to negotiate; — **el pellejo** to save one's skin; **el puente salva el río** the bridge spans the river; —**se** to pull through; —**se por poco** to have a narrow escape; **sálvese quien pueda** every man for himself; M SG **salvapantallas** screen saver; M SG **salvavidas** (aparato) life preserver, life jacket; MF (persona) lifeguard

salvia F sage

salvo ADJ safe; **a —** safe; M —**conducto** safe-conduct; PREP save, except; — **en caso de desastre** barring a disaster

Samoa F Samoa

samoano-na ADJ & MF Samoan

sanar VI/VT to heal; M **sanalotodo** cure-all

sanatorio M (para convalecientes) sanatorium; (para enfermos) hospital

sanción F sanction

sancionar VT to sanction

sandalia F sandal

sandez F (acción) stupidity, foolishness; (dicho) foolish remark

sandía F watermelon

saneamiento M sanitation

sanear VT to drain

sangrar VI/VT to bleed; VT (un árbol) to tap; (un párrafo) to indent

sangre F blood; — **fría** coolness under pressure; **a — fría** in cold blood; **hacerse mala —** to get upset; **eso lo llevo en la —** that's in my blood; **de — caliente** warm-blooded; — **azul** blue blood; **sudar —** to sweat bullets; **de pura —** thoroughbred; **chupar la — a alguien** to be a parasite on someone

sangría F (bebida) wine punch; (acción de sangrar) bleeding; (espacio tipográfico) indentation; (pérdida) drain

sangriento ADJ (manchado de sangre, que provoca pérdida de sangre) bloody; (sanguinario) bloodthirsty

sanguijuela F leech

sanguinario ADJ bloody, vicious

sanguíneo ADJ blood; **grupo —** blood group

sanidad F public health

sanitario-ria ADJ sanitary; M —**s** bathroom fittings; MF public health worker

sanmarinense ADJ & MF San Marinese

sanmarinés-esa ADJ & MF San Marinese

sano ADJ (persona) healthy; (juicio) sound; (dieta) healthful; (vaso) unbroken; — **y salvo** safe and sound; **en su — juicio** of sound mind

sánscrito M Sanskrit

sanseacabó INTERJ **te quedas y —** you're staying and that's that

santalucense ADJ & MF St. Lucian

santiamén LOC ADV **en un —** in a jiffy, lickety-split

santidad F sanctity, holiness

santificar[30] VT to sanctify

santiguarse[25] VI to cross oneself

santo-ta ADJ saintly, holy; **esperar todo el — día** to wait the whole blessed day; MF saint; **día del —** saint's day; **quedarse para vestir —s** to be a spinster; **¿a — de qué?** for what reason? **¡por todos los —s!** my goodness!

santotomense ADJ & MF São Tomean

santuario M sanctuary

santurrón-ona ADJ & MF goody-goody

saña F fury

sañudo ADJ furious

sapo M toad (también hombre feo); **echar —s y culebras** to swear, to curse; **sentirse como un — de otro pozo** to feel like a fish out of water

saque M (tenis) service, serve; — **de inicio** (fútbol) kickoff; — **de banda** throw-in; — **de esquina** corner kick; — **de meta** goal kick; — **de puerta** goal kick; — **inicial** kick-off; — **ganador** ace; — **y volea** (tenis) serve and volley

saquear VT to sack, to plunder, to pillage

saqueo M sacking, plundering, pillaging

sarampión M measles; — **alemán** rubella

sarape M *Méx* serape

sarcasmo M sarcasm

sarcástico ADJ sarcastic

sarcófago M sarcophagus

sarcoma M sarcoma

sardina F sardine

sardo-da ADJ & MF Sardinian

sardónico ADJ sardonic

sargento-ta MF sergeant; F battle-ax[e]

sarmentoso ADJ gnarled

sarmiento M vine

sarna F mange

sarnoso ADJ mangy

sarpullido M rash

sarro M tartar, plaque

sarta F string; **una — de mentiras** a pack of lies; **una — de idiotas** a bunch of idiots

sartén F frying pan, skillet

sastre-tra MF tailor

sastrería F tailor shop

satánico ADJ satanic

satélite M satellite; — **artificial** man-made satellite

satén M satin

sátira F satire

satírico ADJ satirical

satirizar[47] VT to satirize

satisfacción F satisfaction
satisfacer[54, 74] VT (un deseo) to satisfy; (una deuda) to pay; **—se** to be satisfied
satisfactorio ADJ (aceptable) satisfactory; (exitoso) successful
satisfaga, satisfago, satisfará, satisfaría *ver* satisfacer
satisfecho ADJ contented, satisfied
satisfecho, satisfice, satisficiera, satisficiese *ver* satisfacer
saturar VT (una solución) to saturate; (un mercado) to glut; (líneas de teléfono) to overload
sauce M willow; **— llorón** weeping willow
saudí, saudita ADJ & MF Saudi Arabian
savia F sap
saxofón M saxophone
sazón F season; **a la —** at that time; **en —** ripe
sazonar VT (condimentar) to season, to flavor; (madurar) to ripen
scooter M scooter
scout MF scout
se PRON PERS **— coronó a sí mismo** he crowned himself; **— lavó la cara** he washed his face; **— besaron** they kissed each other; **— habla español** Spanish is spoken; **— lo puede combatir** it can be fought
sé *ver* saber
sea, seas *ver* ser
sebo M tallow, fat
seborrea F seborrhea
secador M hair dryer
secadora F clothes dryer
secante ADJ drying
secar[30] VT (la ropa) to dry; (las manos) to dry off; **—se** (planta) to dry up; (río) to run dry; (madera) to season
sección F (militar) platoon; (de un almacén) department; (un texto) section
seccionar VT to section
seco ADJ (ropa) dry; (río) dried-up; (planta) withered; (respuesta) curt, brief; **en —** on dry land; **parar en —** to stop short; **quedar —** to fall dead; **estar —** to be broke; **lavar en —** to dry-clean; **a secas** plain
secreción F secretion
secretar VT to secrete
secretaría F secretariat
secretariado M (profesión) secretarial profession; (secretaría) secretariat; (conjunto de secretarias) secretarial pool
secretario -ria MF secretary; **— general** secretary general
secretear VI to whisper
secreto ADJ (oculto) secret; (policía) undercover; M (cosa oculta) secret; (condición de oculto) secrecy; **— a voces** open secret; **en —** in secret; **— bancario** account holder confidentiality

secta F sect
sector M sector
sectorial ADJ sectorial
secuaz M henchman
secuela F consequence; **—s** aftermath
secuencia F (de acontecimientos) sequence; (de datos) string
secuenciar VT to sequence
secuestrador -ora MF kidnapper
secuestrar VT (a una persona) to kidnap, to abduct; (una propiedad) to seize; (un avión) to hijack
secuestro M (de una persona) kidnapping; (de propiedad) seizure; (de un avión) hijacking
secular ADJ secular
secundar VT (apoyar) to second; (imitar) to imitate; (seguir) to follow suit
secundaria F secondary school
secundario ADJ secondary
sed F thirst; **tener —** to be thirsty
seda F silk; **como una — (suave)** soft as silk; (afable) sweet-tempered
sedación F sedation
sedán M sedan
sedante ADJ & M sedative
sedar VT to sedate
sedativo ADJ & M sedative
sede F (gubernamental) seat; (religiosa) see; **— central** headquarters
sedentario ADJ sedentary
sedería F (conjunto de artículos de seda) silk goods; (tienda de sedas) silk shop
sedero -ra MF (que vende) silk dealer; (que fabrica) silk weaver; ADJ **industria sedera** silk industry
sedición F sedition
sediento ADJ thirsty; **estar — de** to thirst for
sedimento M sediment
sedoso ADJ silken, silky
seducción F seduction
seducir[38] VT (corromper) to seduce; (atraer) to entice; (persuadir con argucias) to lure
seductivo ADJ alluring
seductor -ora ADJ alluring; M seducer; F seductress
sefardí ADJ Sephardic; MF Sephardi; M (variedad del español) Sephardi
sefardita ADJ & MF Sephardi
segador -ora MF (persona) mower, reaper; F (máquina) mower, reaper
segar[41] VT (hierba) to mow; (mies) to reap
seglar ADJ secular; M layman; F laywoman
segmento M segment
segregar[40] VT (separar) to segregate; (producir secreciones) to secrete
seguido ADJ in a row; **dos horas seguidas** two hours in a row; ADV straight through; **trabajaron —** they worked continuously
seguidor -ora MF follower

seguimiento M (persecución) pursuit; (atención continuada) follow-up

seguir[12] VT (camino, instrucciones) to follow; (estudios) to pursue; (progreso de un avión) to track; **sigue trabajando** he keeps on working, he continues to work; **sigue allí** he is still there; **de lo anterior se sigue que** from the preceding it follows that; **— los pasos de** to follow in the footsteps of; **—le la corriente a alguien** to play along with someone; **— el tren** to keep up; **— el hilo de** to keep track of; **— la pista de** to trail

según PREP according to; **— se mire** depending on how you see it; **— pasa el tiempo** as time goes by; **— tus instrucciones** per your instructions; CONJ as; **— se informa** reportedly; **lo haré — me digas** I will do it as you tell me to

segundero M second hand

segundo -da ADJ & ADV second; MF second in command; **— tiempo** (fútbol) second half; **— servicio** (tenis) second serve; **segunda base** (posición en béisbol) second base; M (jugador) second baseman; **segunda hipoteca** second mortgage; **segunda intención** ulterior motive; **de segunda mano** secondhand, preowned; **de segunda** second-rate

segundón -ona MF (hijo) second-born child; (persona mediocre) also-ran

seguramente ADV certainly, surely; **lenta pero —** slowly but surely

seguridad F (contra el delito) security; (contra accidentes) safety; **— en sí mismo** self-confidence; **— social** social security

seguro ADJ (a prueba de delincuentes) secure; (que no ofrece o siente duda) sure, certain; (libre de peligro) safe; (firme) stable; **es — que** it is certain that; **su — servidor** yours truly; **— de sí mismo** self-assured; M (contrato contra riesgos) insurance; (dispositivo) safety device, restraint; **— contra accidentes** accident insurance; **— contra daños a terceros** liability insurance; **— contra incendios** fire insurance; **— contra inundaciones** flood insurance; **— contra todo riesgo** comprehensive insurance; **— de discapacidad** disability insurance; **— de vida** life insurance; **— de vida a término** term life insurance; **— de vida permanente** whole life insurance; **— médico** health insurance; **en —** in safety; **sobre —** without risk

seis NUM six

selección F selection, choice; **— de texto** highlighting; **— natural** natural selection; **— nacional** national team

seleccionado M **— nacional** national team

seleccionar VT to select, to choose

selectivo ADJ selective

selecto ADJ select, choice

sellar VT (poner sello) to stamp; (precintar) to seal

sello M (de correo) stamp; (de documento oficial) seal; (instrumento) seal, stamp; (de discos) label; **— de goma** rubber stamp; **— fiscal** revenue stamp

selva F (templada o fría) forest; (tropical) jungle; **— virgen** virgin forest

semáforo M traffic light

semana F week; **entre —** during the week

semanal ADJ weekly

semanario M weekly publication

semántica F semantics

semblante M countenance

semblanza F biographical sketch

sembrado M sown ground

sembradora F planting machine

sembrar[1] VT (plantar) to sow, to plant; (esparcir) to scatter; (minas) to lay; (pánico, alegría) to spread

semejante ADJ similar, like; **— afirmación** such a statement; **un tipo —** such a guy; M fellow human being

semejanza F resemblance, similarity; **a — de** in the manner of

semejar VT to resemble

semental ADJ stud; M stud, stallion

semestral ADJ biannual

semestre M semester

semianual ADJ biannual

semicírculo M semicircle

semiconductor M semiconductor

semifinal ADJ & F semifinal

semilla F seed

semillero M seedbed; **— de vicios** hotbed of vice

seminario M (religioso) seminary; (universitario) seminar

semítico ADJ Semitic

senado M senate

senador -ora MF senator

sencillez F simplicity; **con —** simply

sencillo ADJ (no complicado, humilde) simple; (fácil) easy, simple; (sin adornos) plain; (no afectado) straightforward; M (béisbol) single

senda F (construida) path, pathway; (natural) track, trail

sendero M (construido) path, pathway; (natural) track, trail

sendos ADJ **tenían — sombreros** each one had a hat

Senegal M Senegal

senegalés -esa ADJ & MF Senegalese

senil ADJ senile

senilidad F senility

seno M (pecho) breast; (hueco) sinus; (útero)

womb; (en matemática) sine; **— de la familia** bosom of the family

sensación F (física) sensation; (mental) feeling, impression; **tengo la — de que** I have the feeling that; **fue la — de la fiesta** she was the life of the party

sensacional ADJ sensational

sensatez F common sense

sensato ADJ sensible, level-headed

sensibilidad F (modo de pensar) sensibility; (percepción) sensitiveness

sensibilizar⁴⁷ VT to sensitize

sensible ADJ (que siente) sensitive; (notable) perceptible; **tengo el brazo muy — por el accidente** my arm is very tender because of the accident; **Juana es muy — en estas ocasiones** Juana is very emotional on these occasions

sensiblería F sentimentality

sensiblero ADJ sentimental, mushy

sensitivo ADJ sensitive

sensor M sensor

sensorial ADJ sensory

sensual ADJ (carnal) sensual; (de los sentidos) sensuous

sensualidad F sensuality

sentada F (acto de sentarse) sitting; (protesta) sit-in; **de una —** at one sitting

sentado ADJ **dar por —** to take for granted

sentar¹ VT to seat; **— bien** to agree with; **me sentó muy mal lo que dijo** what he said did not sit well with me; **este peinado te sienta** this hairdo becomes you; **no te sienta ese traje** that suit does not fit you; **— precedente** to set a precedent; **—se** to sit down

sentencia F (dicho) maxim; (fallo) ruling; (condena) sentence; (indemnización) award

sentenciar VT (condenar) to sentence; (fallar) to rule

sentido ADJ heartfelt; M (facultad) sense; (significado) meaning; (dirección) way; **— común** common sense; **— de la vista** sense of sight; **— del gusto** sense of taste; **— del humor** sense of humor; **— del oído** sense of hearing; **— del olfato** sense of smell; **— del tacto** sense of touch; **aguzar el —** to prick up one's ears; **de un solo —** one-way; **de dos —s** two-way; **dejar sin —** to render unconscious; **en cierto —** in a sense; **perder el —** to faint; **quedar —** to have one's feelings hurt; **sin —** meaningless; **tener —** to make sense

sentimental ADJ sentimental

sentimentalismo M sentimentality

sentimiento M feeling, sentiment

sentir⁸ VT (percibir) to feel; (oír) to hear; (lamentar) to regret; **—se** to feel; **—se capaz de** to feel up to; **—se de los pies** to have pains in the feet

seña F (gesto) sign; (rasgo) trait; (marca) mark; **—s** name and address; **por más —s** as an additional proof; **—s de vida** life signs; **hablar por —s** to use sign language; **hacer —s** to signal

señal F (de tráfico, de violencia, de vida, de la cruz) sign; (de violencia) mark; (de radio) signal; (pago anticipado) deposit; **en — de** in token of

señalar VT (marcar, señalar) to mark; (mostrar, mencionar) to point out; (fijar) to fix; **—se** to distinguish oneself

señor M (título) Mr.; (forma de tratamiento) sir; (dueño) lit master, lord; **el Señor** the Lord; **un gran —** a great man

señora F (dama) lady; (forma de tratamiento) madam, ma'am; (título) Mrs., Ms.; (esposa) wife

señorear VI to dominate

señoría F lordship; **su —** Your Honor

señorial ADJ lordly

señorío M (dominio) dominion; (dignidad) lordship

señorita F miss; **toda una —** quite a young lady

señorito M (joven) master; (dandi) dandy

señuelo M decoy, lure

sepa, sepamos ver **saber**

separación F separation

separado ADJ (apartado) separate; (estado civil) separated; **por —** separately

separar VT (apartar) to separate; (clasificar) to sort out; (despedir de un cargo) to remove; **—se** to separate, to part company

separata F offprint, reprint

septentrional ADJ northern

septicemia F blood poisoning

septiembre, setiembre M September

séptimo ADJ & M seventh

sepulcro M tomb

sepultar VT to bury, to inter

sepultura F (acción) burial; (lugar) grave, tomb; **dar —** to bury

sepulturero -ra MF gravedigger

sequedad F dryness

sequía F drought

séquito M retinue, entourage

ser⁶⁵ VI to be; **— de Valencia** to be from Valencia; **— de madera** to be made of wood; **a no — que** unless; **así es** that's right; **érase una vez** once upon a time; **es decir** that is to say; **es de esperar** it is to be expected; **es más** what's more; **la boda es hoy** the wedding takes place today; **son las nueve** it is nine o'clock; **somos cuatro** there are four of us; V AUX to be; **fue elegido presidente** he was elected president; M (entidad viviente) being; (esencia) essence; (existencia) existence; **un — humano** a human being

serbio -bia ADJ Serbian; MF (persona) Serb, Serbian; M (lengua) Serbian

serenar VI to quiet; **—se** (el alma) to become serene, to calm down; (el tiempo) to clear up

serenata F serenade; **dar —** to serenade

serenidad F serenity, peace of mind

sereno ADJ (mar, alma) serene; (cielo) clear; **al — in** the night air; M night watchman

serie F series; **— de instrucciones** (en un programa de computadora) macro; **en —** serial; **— ofensiva** offensive series

seriedad F seriousness, earnestness

serio ADJ (problema) serious; (persona) earnest, serious; **en —** seriously

sermón M (prédica) sermon; (reprimenda) lecture

sermonear VI/VT (predicar) to preach; (reprender) to lecture

serpentear VI to wind, to meander

serpiente F snake

serrado ADJ serrated

serranía F mountainous region

serrano -na M mountain man; F mountain woman; ADJ **zona serrana** mountain region

serrín M sawdust

serrucho M handsaw

servicial ADJ helpful

servicio M (también en tenis) service; (sirvientes) servants; (para un comensal) place setting; (aseo) restroom, facilities; **— a la habitación** room service; **— de ayuda al usuario** helpdesk; **— de contestador** answering service; **— de entrega** delivery service; **— directo** ace; **— militar** military service; **a su —** at your service; **de — pesado** heavy-duty; **estar en —** to be in commission; **poner en —** to commission, to put into service

servidor -ora MF (persona) servant; **un —** yours truly; **su seguro —** yours truly; M (ordenador) server; **— remoto** remote server

servidumbre F servitude

servil ADJ (personalidad) servile; (trabajo) menial

servilleta F napkin

servir[9] VI to serve; **— de** to serve as; **— para** to be used for; **para — le** at your service; **no — para nada** to be of no use; **¿en qué le puedo —?** how can I help you? **—se de** to make use of; **sírvase usted hacerlo** please do it

sésamo M sesame; **¡ábrete —!** open sesame!

sesenta NUM sixty

sesgado ADJ biased

sesgar[40] VT (una tela) to cut on the bias; (una opinión) to slant; (las estadísticas) to skew

sesgo M (en la tela) bias; (de los ojos, de orientación) slant; **al —** obliquely

sesión F (reunión, período) session; (de fotografía) sitting; (de una película) showing; **— de ejercicio** workout

seso M brain; **de poco —** foolish; **devanarse los —s** to rack one's brain

sestear VI to take a nap

sesudo ADJ (persona) brainy; (explicación) intelligent; (testarudo) *Méx* stubborn

set M set

seta F mushroom

setenta NUM seventy

seto M hedge

sétter M setter

seudónimo M pseudonym, pen name

severidad F severity, harshness

severo ADJ severe, stern, harsh

sevillano -na ADJ & MF Sevillian; F PL Sevillian dances

sexar VT to sex

sexismo M sexism

sexista MF sexist

sexo M (género) sex; **el bello —** the fair sex

sexto ADV, ADJ & M sixth

sexual ADJ sexual

sexualidad F sexuality

sexy ADJ sexy

Seychelles F PL Seychelles

SFA [Sistema de frenos antibloqueo] M ABS

shock M shock

short, shorts M shorts

si CONJ if; **yo voy — tú vas** I'm going if you're going; **no sé — viene o no** I don't know whether she's coming or not; **¡— ya te lo dije!** but I already told you! **— bien** although; **por — acaso** just in case; **— Dios quiere** God willing; **— no me equivoco** unless I'm mistaken

sí ADV yes; *fam* yeah; **¿—?** really? **— que fui** I did go; **creo que —** I think so; M consent; **me dio el —** she said yes; PRON himself, herself, itself, oneself, themselves; **de por —** in itself; **estar sobre —** to be on the alert; **volver en — to** come to; **pagado de —** self-satisfied; **estar fuera de —** to be beside oneself; **hablar para —** to talk to oneself; **dio todo de —** she gave her all; **cada cual para —** every man for himself

sicario M hitman

sicomoro M sycamore

SIDA [síndrome de inmunodeficiencia adquirida] M AIDS

siderurgia F steel industry

sidra F cider

siega F (de la hierba) mowing; (de las mieses) reaping

siembra F (acción de sembrar) sowing; (época) sowing time

siempre ADV always; **— nos has apoyado** you've always been very supportive of us; **desde —** since forever; **para/por —** forever;

por — jamás forevermore; **— que** (en cualquier momento) whenever; (con tal que) provided that; **— y cuando** provided that; **como —** as usual; **hoy no eres el mismo de —** you're not yourself today

sien F temple

sienta, siente *ver* sentar, sentir

sierpe F *lit* serpent

sierra F (herramienta) saw; (cordillera) small mountain range; **— de cadena** chainsaw

siesta F siesta, afternoon nap; **dormir la —** to take an afternoon nap

siete NUM seven

sífilis F syphilis

sifón M (para líquidos) siphon; (tubo) trap

siga, sigamos *ver* seguir

sigilo M stealth

sigla F acronym

siglo M century

signatario -ria MF signer

significación F (sentido) meaning; (importancia) significance

significado M meaning, sense

significar[30] VT to mean, to signify

significativo ADJ significant, meaningful

signo M sign; **— de admiración** exclamation point; **— de igual** equal sign; **— de interrogación** question mark; **— de más** plus sign; **— de menos** minus sign; **— de multiplicación** multiplication sign; **—s vitales** vital signs

sigo, siguiendo *ver* seguir

siguiente ADJ following; **al día —** the next day

siguiera, siguiese *ver* seguir

sílaba F syllable

silbar VI (soplar aire) to whistle; (rechiflar) to hiss

silbato M whistle (también en fútbol)

silbido M whistle

silenciador M (de arma) silencer; (de coche) muffler

silenciar VT to silence

silencio M silence, quiet; **guardar —** to keep quiet

silenciosamente ADV quietly

silencioso ADJ silent, quiet

silicio M silicon

silla F chair; (de montar) saddle; **— de ruedas** wheelchair; **— eléctrica** electric chair; **— plegadiza** folding chair

sillín M saddle, seat

sillón M (mueble) armchair

silo M silo

silogismo M syllogism

silueta F silhouette

siluro M catfish

silvestre ADJ wild

silvicultura F forestry

sima F chasm

simbiosis F symbiosis

simbólico ADJ symbolic

simbolismo M symbolism

simbolizar[47] VT to symbolize

símbolo M symbol; **— de status** status symbol; **— sexual** sex symbol

simetría F symmetry

simétrico ADJ symmetrical

simiente F seed

símil M simile

similar ADJ similar

similitud F resemblance, similarity

simio M ape

simpatía F friendliness; **no le tengo mucha —** I don't like him much

simpático ADJ (amistoso) nice, friendly, congenial; (sistema nervioso) sympathetic

simpatizante ADJ supporting, sympathizing; MF supporter, sympathizer

simpatizar[47] VI (con alguien) to like; (con una idea) to be sympathetic toward

simple ADJ (no complicado) simple; (mero) mere; (tonto) simpleminded

simplemente ADV simply, merely

simpleza F (sencillez) simplicity; (estupidez) stupidity

simplicidad F simplicity

simplificar[30] VT to simplify

simplista ADJ (intepretación) simplistic; (explicación) glib, simplistic

simplón -ona ADJ simpleminded; MF simpleton

simposio M symposium

simulación F simulation

simulacro M **— de batalla** mock battle; **— de incendio** fire drill

simulador -ora MF simulator; M **— de vuelo** flight simulator

simular VT to simulate, to feign

simultanear VI perform simultaneously

simultáneo ADJ simultaneous

sin PREP without; **— aliento** out of breath; **— amueblar** unfurnished; **— azúcar** sugar-free; **— comentarios** no comment; **— compromiso** without obligation; **— condiciones** unconditionally, with no strings attached; **— culpa** no-fault; **— declarar** unreported; **— derecho** nonvoting; **— duda** without doubt, undoubtedly; **— embargo** nevertheless; **— escrúpulos** unscrupulous; **— excepciones** across the board; **— falta** without fail; **— garantía** unsecured; **— intereses** interest-free; **— lujos** no-frills; **— marcar** unmarked; **— peligro** safely; **— percances** safely; **— problemas** trouble-free; **— receta** over-the-counter; **— restricciones** open-ended; **— riesgo** risk-free; **— seguro médico** uninsured; **— sentido** meaningless

sinagoga F synagogue

sincerarse VI to clear the air, to come clean
sinceridad F sincerity
sincero ADJ (personalidad) sincere; (opinión) candid; (agradecimiento) heartfelt, wholehearted
sincrónico ADJ (proceso) synchronous; (enfoque lingüístico) synchronic
sincronización F timing
sincronizar[47] VT to synchronize
sindical ADJ (relativo al síndico) trustee; (relativo al sindicato) union; **dirigente —** union leader
sindicar[30] VT to unionize, to syndicate
sindicato M (de trabajadores) syndicate, trade union, labor union; (de bancos) syndicate
síndico -ca MF receiver, trustee
síndrome M syndrome; **— de abstinencia** withdrawal symptoms; **— de choque tóxico** toxic shock syndrome; **— de Down** Down's syndrome; **— de muerte infantil súbita** crib death, sudden infant death syndrome
sinergia F synergy
sinfín M **un — de cosas** a lot of things
sinfonía F symphony
Singapur M Singapore
singapurense ADJ & MF Singaporean
singular ADJ (número) singular; (excepcional) unique
siniestro ADJ sinister; M disaster
sinnúmero M myriad
sino CONJ but; **no vino — que llamó** she didn't come but instead called; **no tengo dos — tres** I have not two but three; **no es — madera** it's only wood
sinónimo ADJ synonymous; M synonym
sinopsis F synopsis
sinrazón F injustice
sinsabor M trouble
sinsonte M mockingbird
sintamos ver sentir
sintaxis F syntax
síntesis F synthesis; **— de habla** speech synthesis; **— de habla** voice synthesis
sintético ADJ (producto) synthetic; (fibras) man-made
sintetizador M synthesizer
sintetizar[47] VT to synthesize
sintiendo, sintiera, sintiese ver sentir
síntoma M symptom
sintonía F tuning; **en —** on the same wavelength
sintonizador M tuner
sintonizar[47] VT (una emisora) to tune in; (un sintonizador) to fine-tune; **los dos sintonizan bien** the two are on the same wavelength
sinuoso ADJ (camino) sinuous, winding; (comportamiento) devious
sinusitis F sinusitis

sinvergüenza MF creep
siquiera ADV at least; **dame — unos días** give me a few days at least; **ni —** not even
sirena F (ninfa, bocina) siren; (mitad mujer, mitad pez) mermaid
Siria F Syria
sirio -ria ADJ & MF Syrian
sirve, sirviendo, sirviera, sirviese ver servir
sirviente MF, **sirvienta** F servant
sisar VT to pilfer, to swipe
sisear VI to hiss
siseo M hiss, hissing
sísmico ADJ seismic
sistema M system; **— binario** binary system; **— de asistencia de salud** health care system; **— de cifrado** encryption system; **— de reconocimiento óptico de caracteres** optical character recognition; **— experto** expert system; **— inmune** immune system; **— mundial de posicionamiento** global positioning system; **— nervioso central** central nervous system; **— operativo** operating system; **— solar** solar system
sistemático ADJ systematic
sistematizar[47] VI/VT to systematize
sistémico ADJ systemic
sistólico ADJ systolic
sitial M **— de honor** seat of honor
sitiar VT to besiege
sitio M (espacio vacío) room; (ubicación) place, site; (asedio) siege; **no hay —** there's no room; **esto no está en su —** this is out of place; **— web** website; **poner — a** to lay siege to; **poner a alguien en su —** to put someone in his place
sito ADJ situated
situación F (circunstancia) situation; (legal, financiera, social) status
situado ADJ situated; **estar —** to be located
situar[26] VT to locate, to place; **—se** to be located
sketch M sketch, skit
slalom M slalom
smog M smog
smoking M dinner jacket
so PREP **— pena de** under penalty of; **— pretexto de** under the pretext of; INTERJ whoa; ADV **— tonto** you stupid idiot!
sobaco M armpit
sobar VT (la masa) to knead; (a una persona) to fondle; (un traje) to wear out
soberanía F sovereignty
soberano -na ADJ & MF sovereign
soberbia F pride, haughtiness
soberbio ADJ (orgulloso) proud, haughty; (magnífico) magnificent
sobornar VT to bribe
soborno M (acción) bribery; (mordida) bribe, *fam* payola
sobra F surplus; **—s** leftovers, leavings; **de —**

sabes you know full well; **está de —** it is superfluous; **las piezas de —** spare parts

sobrado ADJ more than enough

sobrante ADJ leftover, remaining; surplus

sobrar VI (dinero, libros) to be left over, to remain; (personas) to be in the way

sobre PREP (encima de) above, over; (en contacto con) on, upon; (acerca de) about; **un préstamo — su coche** a loan on his car; **— todo** above all, especially; **— las 9:30** at about 9:30; **marchar — Madrid** to march toward Madrid; M (para cartas) envelope; (de sopa) packet; **— manila** manila envelope; **irse al —** to hit the sack

sobreactuar[26] VI to ham it up

sobrealimentador M supercharger

sobrecalificado ADJ overqualified

sobrecarga F overload; **— de voltaje** power surge; **— sensorial** sensory overload

sobrecargar[40] VT to overload

sobrecogedor ADJ awesome

sobrecoger[45] VI/VT to awe; **—se** to be in awe; **—se de pánico** to be panic-stricken

sobrecogimiento M awe

sobrecompensar VI to overcompensate

sobrecorrección F overcorrection

sobredosis F overdose

sobreendeudado N debt-ridden

sobreentenderse[2] VI to be understood

sobreentendido ADJ understood; M assumption

sobreestimar VT to overestimate

sobreexcitado ADJ overexcited, wired

sobreexcitar VT to overexcite

sobreextendido ADJ overextended

sobregirar VT to overdraw

sobregiro M overdraft

sobrehumano ADJ superhuman

sobrellevar VT to bear, to endure

sobremanera ADV beyond measure

sobremesa F after-dinner conversation

sobrenadar VI to float

sobrenatural ADJ supernatural

sobrenombre M nickname

sobrepasar VT to exceed

sobrepeso M overweight

sobreponerse[56, 74] VT to superimpose; VI **— a** (valer más que) to outweigh; (recuperarse) to get over

sobreproteger[45] VT to overprotect, to smother

sobrepujar VT to surpass

sobresaliente ADJ outstanding; MF understudy

sobresalir[57] VI (ser notable) to stand out; (estar en un plano más saliente) to project, to jut out; (ser excelente) to excel

sobresaltar VT to startle, frighten; **—se** to be startled, to start

sobresalto M start, scare

sobrestante M foreman

sobresueldo M extra pay

sobretasa F surtax

sobretodo M overcoat

sobrevenir[61] VI to happen unexpectedly

sobrevivencia F survival

sobreviviente MF survivor; ADJ surviving

sobrevivir VI/VT to survive

sobriedad F sobriety

sobrino -na M nephew; F niece; **— nieto** great-nephew; **sobrina nieta** great-niece

sobrio ADJ sober

socarrar VT to singe

socarrón ADJ sarcastic

socarronería F sarcasm

socavar VT (excavar por debajo) to dig under; (debilitar) to undermine, to undercut

socavón M sinkhole; shaft, tunnel

sociable ADJ sociable, gregarious

social ADJ social

socialismo M socialism

socialista ADJ & MF socialist

socializar[47] VT to socialize

sociedad F (grupo humano) society; (firma) company, partnership; **— anónima** corporation; **— de consumo** consumer society; **alta —** high society

socio -cia MF (de una firma) partner; (de un club) member; **— minoritario** minority partner; **— principal** senior partner; **— comercial** trading partner

socioeconómico ADJ socioeconomic

sociología F sociology

sociópata MF sociopath

socorrer VT to help

socorro INTERJ & M help; **acudir al — de** to go to the rescue of; **pedir —** to cry out for help

soda F soda

sodio M sodium

sodomía F sodomy

soez ADJ vulgar

sofá M sofa, couch; **—-cama** sleeper, sofa bed

sofisma M fallacy

sofisticado ADJ sophisticated

sofocante ADJ suffocating, oppressive

sofocar[30] VI/VT (ahogar) to suffocate; (una rebelión) to quash, to quell, to suppress; (un incendio) to put out

sofoco M suffocation

softball M softball

software M software; **— de fuente abierta** open source software

soga F rope; **estar con la — al cuello** to have a rope around one's neck

sois ver **ser**

soja F (planta) soy; (semilla) soybean

sojuzgar[40] VT to subjugate, to subdue

sol M sun; **de — a —** from sunrise to sunset; **hace —** it is sunny; **tomar el —** to sunbathe; **ella es un —** she's a gem; **arrimarse al —**

que más calienta to know which side one's bread is buttered on
solamente ADV only, solely
solana F sunny place
solapa F lapel
solapado ADJ underhanded
solar M (terreno) lot; (casa ancestral) manor; ADJ solar
solaz M *lit* recreation
soldado -da MF soldier; **— raso** private; **— de línea** regular soldier
soldador M soldering iron
soldadura F (acción de adherir con estaño) soldering; (resultado) solder; (acción de adherir sin estaño) welding; (resultado) weld; **— autógena** arc welding
soldar[5] VI/VT (con estaño) to solder; (sin estaño) to weld; **—se** to mend
soleado ADJ sunny
solear VT to put in the sun; **—se** to sun oneself
soledad F solitude, loneliness
solemne ADJ solemn; **— disparate** downright foolishness
solemnidad F solemnity
solenoide M solenoid
soler[6, 73] VI **suelo levantarme a las siete** I usually get up at seven; **solía acostarme tarde** I used to go to bed late; **no suele importarle** he usually doesn't mind
solferino ADJ reddish-purple
solicitante MF applicant
solicitar VT (permiso) to request; (un puesto, una beca) to apply for
solícito ADJ solicitous
solicitud F (para beca, puesto) application; (de información, permiso) request; **— de préstamo** loan application; **a — de** at the request of
solidaridad F solidarity
solidario ADJ supportive, sympathetic
solidez F solidity
solidificar[30] VT to solidify
sólido ADJ (materia) solid; (mueble) sturdy; (argumento) strong; M solid
solista MF soloist
solitario -ria ADJ solitary; MF (persona) recluse; M (juego de cartas, brillante) solitaire; F tapeworm
sollozar[47] VI to sob
sollozo M sob
solo ADJ (desamparado) lonely, lonesome; (no acompañado) alone; **tengo un — coche** I have only one car; **a solas** alone; **habla solo** he talks to himself; **ni una sola palabra** not a single word; ADV just, only; **— quiero saber** I just/only want to know; M solo
solomillo M sirloin
solsticio M solstice
soltar[5] VT (a un prisionero) to let go, to release;

(el vientre) to loosen; (una carcajada) to let out; (bombas) to drop; (un disparate) to say; **— amarras** to cast off; **— el hervor** to come to a boil; **— tacos** to swear; **—se** to loosen up; **—se el pelo** to kick up one's heels
soltero -ra ADJ single, unmarried; M bachelor; F unmarried woman
solterón -ona M old bachelor; F *pey* spinster
soltura F ease; **hablar con —** to speak fluently
soluble ADJ soluble
solución F solution; **— salina** saline solution
solucionar VT to solve
solventar VT to settle
solvente ADJ & M solvent
somalí ADJ & MF Somalian
Somalia F Somalia
sombra F (de una figura) shadow; (protección del sol) shade; (para ojos) eye shadow; **hacer —** to overshadow; **dar —** to shade; **no fiarse ni de su propia —** to be scared of one's own shadow; **a la —** in the shade; **sin — de duda** without a shadow of a doubt
sombreado ADJ (protegido del sol) shady; (oscuro) shadowy
sombrear VT to shade
sombrerería F millinery
sombrerero -ra MF milliner
sombrero M hat; **— de copa** top hat; **— hongo** derby
sombrilla F parasol
sombrío ADJ (oscuro) dark; (triste) somber, gloomy
somero ADJ (agua) shallow; (discusión) superficial
someter VT (proponer algo) to submit; (poner bajo dominio) to subject; **—se a** to undergo
sometimiento M (propuesta) submission; (dominio) subjection
somnífero M sleeping pill
somnolencia F drowsiness, sleepiness
somnoliento ADJ drowsy
somos *ver* ser
son M sound; LOC ADV **al — de** to the sound of; **venimos en — de paz** we come in peace
son *ver* ser
sonaja F rattle
sonajero M rattle
sonámbulo -la MF sleepwalker
sonar[5] VI (hacer un sonido) to sound; (mencionarse) to be mentioned; (ser familiar) to sound familiar; **— a** to sound like; VT (bocina) to sound; (tambor) to beat; (campana, timbre) to ring; **—se la nariz / los mocos** to blow one's nose; **suena que** it is rumored that; M sonar
sonda F (de médico) catheter; (cohete) probe; **— de alimentación** feeding tube; **tirar una — to** sound
sondear VT (medir la oportunidad) to sound, to

fathom; (investigar la opinión) to sound out
sondeo M survey
soneto M sonnet
sonido M sound
sonoridad F (de la voz) sonority; (de un instrumento) tone; (de un sonido lingüístico) voicing
sonoro ADJ sonorous
sonreír[10] VI to smile
sonriente ADJ smiling
sonrisa F smile
sonrojarse VI to blush
sonrojo M blush, flush
sonrosado ADJ rosy
sonsacar[30] VT to extract
soñador -ora MF dreamer
soñar[5] VI/VT to dream; — **con** to dream of; — **despierto** to daydream; — **que** to dream that; **ni** — *fam* fat chance
soñoliento ADJ sleepy
sopa F (líquido) soup; (pan mojado) sop; **estar hecho una** — to be sopping wet; — **crema** cream soup
sopapo M smack
sopera F soup tureen
sopesar VT to weigh
sopetón LOC ADV **de** — all of a sudden
soplador -ora MF blower
soplar VI/VT (el viento) to blow; (la sopa) to blow on; (en un examen) to whisper the answers
soplete M blowtorch
soplo M breath, puff; **en un** — in a jiffy; — **cardíaco** heart murmur
soplón -ona MF informer, snitch, stool pigeon
sopor M lethargy
soportar VT (un peso) to support, to bear; (una molestia, a una persona) to stand, to bear; (un programa de computadora) to support
soporte M (de un peso, de un programa) support; (de una bicicleta) kickstand; — **técnico** technical support
soprano M (voz) soprano; F (cantante) soprano
sorber VI/VT to sip; —**se los mocos** to sniffle
sorbete M sherbet
sorbo M sip; **de un** — in one gulp
sordera F deafness
sórdido ADJ sordid, tawdry, sleazy
sordina F mute
sordo -da ADJ (persona) deaf; (dolor) dull; (sonido) dull, muffled; **hacer oídos** —**s** to turn a deaf ear; MF deaf person; **hacerse el** — to pretend not to hear
sordomudo -da ADJ deaf and dumb; MF deaf-mute
sorna F irony
sorprendente ADJ surprising, startling
sorprendentemente ADV surprisingly
sorprender VT to surprise; —**se** to be surprised
sorpresa F surprise; — **de cumpleaños** party

favor; **para mí** — to my surprise; **pillar por** — to catch by surprise
sortear VT (elegir al azar) to draw lots, to raffle; (esquivar) to dodge
sorteo M drawing, raffle
sortija F (anillo) ring; (de pelo) ringlet
sortilegio M spell, charm
SOS M SOS
sosa F soda
sosegado ADJ composed, sedate
sosegar[41] VT to calm, to quiet; —**se** to quiet down, to compose oneself
sosiego M quiet, calm
soslayo LOC ADV **de** — oblique, slanting; **mirar de** — to look out of the corner of one's eye
soso ADJ (comida) tasteless, insipid; (persona) dull
sospecha F suspicion
sospechar VT to suspect
sospechoso -sa ADJ suspicious; MF suspect
sostén M (apoyo, sustento) support, prop; (persona que sostiene) supporter, provider; (prenda) brassiere; — **de la familia** breadwinner
sostendrá, sostendría *ver* sostener
sostener[58] VT (una nota musical) to hold, to sustain; (una familia) to support; (un peso) to support, to hold; (una opinión) to claim, to uphold
sostenga, sostengo *ver* sostener
sostenible ADJ sustainable
sostenido ADJ sustained; M sharp
sostiene, sostienes, sostuve, sostuviera, sostuviese *ver* sostener
sota F jack, knave
sótano M cellar, basement
soto M thicket
soy *ver* ser
soya F (semilla) soybean; (planta) soy
squash M squash
Sr. M Mr.
Sra. F (casada) Mrs.; (sin indicación de estado civil) Ms.
S.R.C. [se ruega contestar] LOC RSVP
status M status
stop M stop sign
su ADJ POS (de él) his; (de ella) her; (de usted, ustedes) your; (de ellos, ellas) their
suave ADJ (pelo, piel) soft; (tiempo, droga) mild; (brisa, persona, animal) gentle; (coñac) smooth; **hablan** — they speak gently
suavemente ADV lightly, gently
suavidad F (de pelo, piel) softness; (de coñac) smoothness; (de tiempo, droga) mildness; (de brisa, persona, animal) gentleness
suavizante M fabric softener
suavizar[47] VT to soften
suazi ADJ & MF Swazi
Suazilandia F Swaziland

subalterno -na ADJ & MF subordinate

subarrendar VI/VT to sublet

subasta F auction

subastador -ora MF auctioneer

subastar VT to sell at auction, to auction

subcomité M subcommittee

subconsciente ADJ subconscious

subcontratar VT to subcontract, to contract out, to farm out

subdesarrollado ADJ underdeveloped

súbdito -ta MF subject

subdividir VT subdivide

subdivisión F subdivision

subempleado ADJ underemployed

subestimar VT to underestimate

subgerente MF assistant manager

subida F (de precios, de río) rise; (de montaña) climb; (de drogas) high; (cuesta) slope; **—s y bajadas** ups and downs

subido ADJ (color) bright; **— de tono** risqué

subíndice M subscript

subir VI (los precios) to rise, to go up; (la marea) to surge; (a un tren) to board; (a un autobús, coche) to get into; VT (algo del sótano) to bring up; (una montaña) to climb; (precios) to raise; **— a la red** to upload; **—se** to ride up; **el vino se me sube a la cabeza** wine goes to my head; M **subibaja** seesaw

súbitamente ADV suddenly

súbito ADJ sudden

subjetividad F subjectivity

subjetivo ADJ subjective

subjuntivo ADJ & M subjunctive

sublevación F revolt

sublevar VT (instigar) to incite to rebellion; (indignar) to infuriate; **—se** to revolt

sublime ADJ sublime

submarino ADJ underwater; M submarine

suboficial M noncommissioned officer

subordinado -da ADJ & MF subordinate

subordinar VT to subordinate

subproducto M by-product

subproletariado M underclass

subrayado ADJ underlined; M underscore, underlining

subrayar VT (con una línea) to underline, to underscore; (enfatizar) to emphasize, to underscore

subrepticio ADJ surreptitious

subrutina F subroutine

subsanar VT (una deficiencia) to remedy; (un error) to correct

subsecretario -ia MF undersecretary; **— de justicia** solicitor general

subsidiar VT to subsidize

subsidiario ADJ subsidiary

subsidio M subsidy

subsiguiente ADJ subsequent

subsistencia F survival

subsistir VI to subsist, to survive

subteniente MF second lieutenant

subterfugio M subterfuge

subterráneo ADJ subterranean, underground; M subway

subtítulo M (de un capítulo, película) subtitle; (pie de foto) caption

subtotal M subtotal

suburbano -na ADJ of shantytowns; MF shantytown resident

suburbio M shantytown

subvaluar[26] VT to underestimate

subvención F subsidy

subvencionar VT to subsidize

subversivo ADJ subversive

subyacente ADJ underlying

subyacer[37] VI to underlie

subyugar[40] VT (dominar) to subjugate; (hechizar) to charm

succión F suction

sucedáneo -a ADJ & MF substitute

suceder VI to happen, to occur; **— al trono** to succeed to the throne; VT to succeed

sucesión F (herencia, secuencia) succession; (heredero) descendant

sucesivo ADJ successive; **en lo —** in the future

suceso M (evento) event, occurrence; (incidente) incident

sucesor -ora MF successor

suciedad F (porquería) dirt, filth; (cualidad de sucio) filthiness

sucinto ADJ concise

sucio ADJ (baño, ropa) dirty, filthy; (trabajo, chiste) dirty; (conciencia) guilty; **blanco —** off-white; **este traje es —** this suit gets dirty easily

sucumbir VI to succumb

sucursal F branch, subsidiary

sudadera F sweatshirt

sudado ADJ sweaty

Sudáfrica F South Africa

sudafricano -na ADJ & MF South African

Sudamérica F South America

sudamericano -na ADJ & MF South American

Sudán M Sudan

sudanés -esa ADJ & MF Sudanese

sudar VT to sweat; **— la gota gorda** to sweat blood

sudeste ADJ southeast, southeastern; M southeast

sudoeste ADJ southwest, southwestern; M southwest

sudor M sweat

sudoración F sweating

sudoroso ADJ sweaty

Suecia F Sweden

sueco -ca ADJ Swedish; M (lengua) Swedish; MF Swede; **hacerse el —** to pretend not to understand

suegro -a M father-in-law; F mother-in-law

suela F (de zapato) sole; (pez) flounder

suela, suele ver **soler**

sueldo M salary

suelo M (tierra) soil, ground; (piso) floor; **arrastrar por el —** to drag; **por los —s** at rock-bottom

suelta, suelte ver **soltar**

suelto ADJ (no atado) loose, unattached; (flojo) loose; (libre) free; M loose change

suena, suene ver **sonar**

sueña, sueñe ver **soñar**

sueño M (acto de dormir) sleep; (acto de soñar) dream; (ganas de dormir) sleepiness; **en —s** dreaming; **conciliar el —** to get to sleep; **tener —** to be sleepy; **ni en —[s]** never; **perder el —** to lose sleep; **— profundo** sound sleep; **estar en el séptimo —** to be deeply asleep

suero M serum; **— de leche** buttermilk; **— fisiológico** saline solution

suerte F (destino) fate; (fortuna) luck; (clase) kind; **de —** in luck; **dejar a su —** to leave to his own devices; **echar —s** to cast lots; **mala — (desgracia)** bad luck; (lo siento) too bad; **tener —** to be lucky; **tentar a la —** to court danger; **tocarle algo en — a alguien** to be one's lot

suertudo -da ADJ lucky; MF lucky devil

suéter M sweater

suficiencia F adequacy; **¡tiene una —!** she's so arrogant!

suficiente ADJ (adecuado) sufficient, adequate; (arrogante) smug; M (calificación mínima) lowest passing grade; PRON enough; **ser —** to be enough; **tiempo más que —** ample time

sufijo M suffix

sufragar[40] VT to defray; **— los gastos** to meet the expenses

sufragio M suffrage

sufrido ADJ (madre) long-suffering; (tela) durable

sufrimiento M suffering

sufrir VI/VT (pasar apremios) to suffer; VT (soportar) to stand; (una lesión) to sustain; (un cambio) to undergo; (una pena) to grieve; **— de** to suffer from; **— de los pies** to have foot pains

sugerencia F suggestion

sugerir[8] VT to suggest

sugestión F suggestion

sugiere, sugirió, sugiriendo, sugiriera, sugiriese ver **sugerir**

suicida MF suicide [victim]

suicidarse VI to commit suicide

suicidio M suicide

suite F suite

Suiza F Switzerland

suizo -za ADJ & MF Swiss; M sweet roll

sujeción LOC ADV **con —** a subject to

sujetar VT (fijar) to attach; (unir) to hold; (someter) to subdue, to hold down; **—se** to hold on; M SG **sujetalibros** bookend; M SG **sujetapapeles** paper clip

sujeto ADJ held by; **—** a subject to; M (de oración, de experimento) subject; (individuo) individual

sulfato M sulfate

sulfurarse VI to hit the roof

sulfúrico ADJ sulfuric

sulfuro M sulfide

suma F (resultado aritmético) sum; (operación aritmética) addition; (cantidad) amount, sum; **en —** in sum

sumadora F adding machine

sumamente ADV extremely

sumar VT to add, to add up; **—se a** to join

sumario M brief; ADJ summary

sumergible ADJ waterproof

sumergir[46] VT to submerge, to dip; **—se** to dive; **—se en** to immerse oneself in

sumidero M (socavón) sinkhole; (desagüe) drain

suministrar VT to furnish, to supply with

suministro M provision, supply; **— de energía** power supply; **—s** supplies, provisions

sumir VT to immerse

sumisión F submission

sumiso ADJ submissive

súmmum M ultimate, acme; **el — de la moda** the cat's meow

sumo ADJ utmost, paramount; **a lo —** at the most

suntuoso ADJ sumptuous, luxurious

supe, supiera, supiese ver **saber**

súper ADJ & ADV super; F (gasolina) high-octane gasoline; M (supermercado) supermarket

superabundancia F overabundance, glut

superación F (de expectativas) surpassing; (de límites) exceeding; (de un récord) breaking; (de una dificultad) overcoming

superar VT (las expectativas) to surpass; (un límite) to exceed; (una dificultad) to overcome, to surmount; (una prueba) to pass; (a un rival) to outdo; **—se** to improve oneself

superávit M surplus

supercomputadora F supercomputer

superdirecta F overdrive

superdotado ADJ gifted

superego M superego

superestrella F superstar

superficial ADJ (conocimiento, herida, persona) superficial; (persona) shallow

superficialidad F shallowness

superficie F (parte exterior) surface; (de una figura geométrica) area

superfluo ADJ superfluous

superíndice M superscript

superintendente MF superintendent
superior ADJ (mejor) superior; (más alto) higher; (más grande, intenso) greater; MF superior
superioridad F superiority
superlativo ADJ & M superlative
supermercado M supermarket
superordenador M supercomputer
superponer[56, 74] VT to superimpose
superpotencia F superpower
superproducción F overproduction
supersónico ADJ supersonic
superstición F superstition
supersticioso ADJ superstitious
supervisar VT to supervise
supervisión F supervision
supervisor -ora MF supervisor
supervivencia F survival; **la — del más apto** the survival of the fittest
superviviente ADJ surviving; MF survivor
superyó M superego
supino ADJ supine
suplantar VT to supplant
suplementar VT to supplement
suplementario ADJ supplemental
suplemento M supplement
suplente ADJ & MF substitute
súplica F entreaty, plea
suplicar[30] VT to plead, to beseech
suplicio M ordeal
suplir VT (sustituir) to substitute for; (compensar) to make up for
supondrá, supondría *ver* suponer
suponer[56, 74] VT (dar por sentado) to suppose, to presume, to surmise; (implicar) to involve; **es de — que ya esté preparado** presumably he's already prepared
suponga, supongo *ver* suponer
suposición F supposition, surmise
supositorio M suppository
supremacía F supremacy
supremo ADJ supreme
supresión F (de una idea) suppression; (de una palabra) deletion
suprimir VT (una idea) to suppress; (la esclavitud) to abolish; (una palabra) to delete
supuestamente ADV supposedly, allegedly
supuesto ADJ (hipotético) supposed; (alegado) alleged, ostensible; **dar por —** to assume; **por —** of course; M supposition, assumption
supuesto *ver* suponer
supuración F discharge
supurante ADJ festering, running
supurar VI to fester, to discharge
supuse, supusiera, supusiese *ver* suponer
sur ADJ & M south; **hacia el —** southward; **rumbo al —** southward
surcar[30] VT to plow
surco M (en la tierra) furrow; (en un camino) rut;

(en un disco) groove; (en el rostro) wrinkle
surcoreano -na ADJ & MF South Korean
sureño -ña ADJ southern; MF southerner
sureste ADJ southeast, southeastern; M southeast
surfear VI/VT to surf (también en el internet)
surfing M surfing; **hacer —** to surf
surgimiento M rise
surgir[46] VI (situación) to arise; (manantial) to rise; (problema) to emerge, to crop up
Surinam M Surinam, Suriname
surinamés -esa ADJ & MF Surinamer
surmenage M burnout
suroeste ADJ southwest, southwestern; M southwest
surrealismo M surrealism
surrealista ADJ surreal, surrealistic; MF surrealist
surtido M stock, assortment; ADJ assorted
surtidor M (bomba) pump; (chorro, pieza de carburador) jet
surtir VT to provide; **— efecto** to produce the desired effect; **— un pedido** to fill an order
susceptible ADJ susceptible
suscitar VT to stir up
suscribir[74] VT (una opinión) to subscribe to, to endorse; (un seguro) to underwrite; **—se a** to subscribe to
suscripción F subscription
suscriptor -ora MF (de un revista) subscriber; (en el mercado de acciones) underwriter
susodicho ADJ above-mentioned
suspender VT (colgar) to suspend, to hang; (interrumpir) to suspend, to stop; (cancelar) to cancel; (castigar) to suspend; VI/VT (no aprobar) to fail, to flunk
suspense M suspense
suspensión F suspension
suspenso ADJ hanging; **quedarse —** to freeze; M (en un examen) failure; (en una película) suspense; **en —** in suspense
suspensorio M jock [strap]
suspicaz ADJ suspicious
suspirar VT to sigh; **— por** to yearn for
suspiro M sigh
sustancia F substance; **— peligrosa** hazardous substance
sustancial ADJ substantial
sustancioso ADJ substantial
sustantivo M noun; ADJ substantive
sustentable ADJ sustainable
sustentar VT to sustain
sustento M (alimento) sustenance; (apoyo) support; **ganarse el —** to earn a living
sustitución F substitution; **— protésica de la cadera** hip replacement
sustituible ADJ replaceable
sustituir[19] VI/VT to substitute for, to replace; **Juan sustituyó a María** John substituted

for Mary; **sustituí la leche por agua** I replaced the milk with water

sustituto -ta MF substitute

sustituya, sustituye, sustituyendo, sustituyera, sustituyese *ver* sustituir

susto M scare, fright

sustracción F subtraction

sustraer[59] VT to take away; **—se a** to avoid

susurrar VI/VT (una persona, el viento) to whisper; (agua) to murmur, to ripple; (hojas) to rustle

susurro M (de una persona, del viento) whisper; (del agua) murmur; (de las hojas) rustle

sutil ADJ subtle

sutileza F (delicadeza) subtlety; (fineza excesiva) nicety, quibble

sutilizar[47] VT to quibble over

sutura F suture

suyo ADJ & PRON POS (de él) his; (de ella) her; (de usted, de ustedes) your; (de ellos, de ellas) their; PRON (de él) his; (de ella) hers; (de usted, de ustedes) yours; (de ellos, de ellas) theirs; **salirse con la suya** to get one's own way; **hacer de las suyas** to be up to one's tricks; **los —s** his/her/your/their family

swing M swing

Tt

tabaco M tobacco

tábano M horsefly

tabaquismo M smoking

taberna F tavern, saloon

tabernero -ra MF bartender

tabicar[30] VT to partition

tabique M partition

tabla F (madera) board, plank; (teatro) stage; (pliegue) pleat; (gráfica) table, chart; **— de surf** surfboard; **— de planchar** ironing board; **—s** (escenario) stage; **—s de la ley** the tables of the law; **—s de multiplicar** multiplication tables; **— periódica** periodic table; **— de contenidos** table of contents; **— de cortar** cutting board; **hacer —s** to tie

tablado M stage

tablero M (para juegos de mesa) board; (de instrumentos) panel, instrument panel; (de coche) dashboard; (pizarra) blackboard; (para noticias) bulletin board; **— de mando** control panel

tableta F (de aspirina) tablet; (de chocolate) bar

tablilla F (de arcilla) tablet; (de cama) slat; (para fracturas) splint

tabloide M tabloid

tablón M plank

tabú M taboo

tabulador M tab

tabular VT (en una tabla, planilla) to tabulate, to chart; (en la computadora) to tab

taburete M stool, footstool

TAC [tomografía axial computarizada] F CAT scan

tacañería F stinginess, tightness

tacaño -ña ADJ stingy, miserly; MF miser, penny-pincher

tacha F (mancha visible) blemish; (al honor) blot

tachado M strikethrough

tachar VT (borrar) to cross out, to delete; (acusar) to accuse of

tachón M crossing out

tachonar VT to stud

tachuela F tack, thumbtack

tácito ADJ tacit

taciturno ADJ taciturn

taco M (de artillería) wad; (palo de billar) billiard cue; (comida ligera) snack; (palabrota) swear word; (comida) *Méx* taco; **—s** (en el zapato) cleats; **soltar —s** *Esp* to swear

tacómetro M tachometer

tacón M heel

taconear VI to click one's heels

taconeo M clicking

táctica F tactic

táctil ADJ tactile

tacto M (acción de tocar) touch; (sentido) sense of touch; (diplomacia) tact; **con mucho —** gently

TAE [tasa anual equivalente] F APR

tahúr -ura MF gambler

tailandés -esa ADJ & MF Thai, Thailander

Tailandia F Thailand

taimado ADJ sly, devious

Taiwán M Taiwan

taiwanés -esa ADJ & MF Taiwanese

tajada F (de pan, jamón) slice; (de carne) slab; **sacar —** to take one's cut

tajante ADJ (inequívoco) unequivocal; (cortante) sharp

tajar VT to slice

tajear VI/VT to slash

tajo M (corte) slash, hack; (cañón) gorge; (separación) gap

tal ADJ such; **— cual** just so; **— vez** perhaps; **un — García** a certain García; **a — grado** to such an extent; **de — palo — astilla** a chip off the old block; **en — caso** in such a case; CONJ **— como** like, just as; **con — [de] que** provided that; ADV **¿qué —?** how is it going? PRON **y — and so on**; **como si —** as if nothing had happened

taladrar VT to bore, to drill

taladro M drill

talante M temperament

talar VT (un árbol) to chop down; (un bosque) to

lumber

talco M talcum

talento M talent

talentoso ADJ talented, gifted

talismán M charm

talla F (altura) height; (moral, intelectual) stature; (de ropa) size; (de madera) carving

tallado M carving

tallar VT (piedra) to carve; (madera) to whittle, to carve; (naipes) to deal

tallarín M noodle

talle M (cintura) waist, waistline; **tiene buen —** she has a good figure; **corto de —** short-waisted

taller M (para trabajo manual, enseñanza artística, congresos) workshop; (de artista plástico) studio; (de mecánico) garage, shop

tallo M stalk, stem

talón M (de pie, calcetín) heel; (de cheque) stub; **— de Aquiles** Achilles' heel; **girar sobre los talones** to turn on one's heels; **pisarle los talones a alguien** to be hot on someone's heels

talonario M checkbook

talonear VI to walk briskly

tamal M tamale

tamaño M size; **de — mediano** medium-sized; **de — natural** life-sized; **ADJ** such a big, so big a; **tamaña injusticia** such a big injustice

tambalearse VI (un borracho) to stagger; (un boxeador) to reel; (un viejo) to dodder; (un objeto) to wobble

tambaleo M stagger

también ADV also, too, as well; **este — me gusta** I like this one too, I like this one as well, I also like this one

tambor M (instrumento musical, pieza de máquina) drum; (músico) drummer; (cilindro) cylinder; **a — batiente** with fanfare

tamborilear VI to drum, to tap

tamborilero -ra MF drummer

tamiz M sieve

tamizar[47] VT to sift

tampoco CONJ either; **no lo hizo —** he did not do it either; **ni yo —** me either/neither

tampón M tampon

tan ADV **es — rica** she is so rich; **— alto como Juan** as tall as Juan; **— pronto como** as soon as; **es — idiota** he's such an idiot; **vecinos — simpáticos** such nice neighbors

tanda F (de personas) group; (de galletas) batch; (de ejercicios) set

tándem M tandem

tanga F thong

tangente ADJ & F tangent; **salirse por la —** (irse de tema) to go off on a tangent; (evadir) to beat around the bush

tangerina F tangerine

tangible ADJ tangible

tango M tango

tanque M tank

tantán M African drum

tantear VT (calcular) to estimate roughly; (averiguar) to sound out, to feel out; (apuntar) to score; (palpar) to grope

tanteo M (cálculo) estimate; (número de tantos) score; **al —** approximately

tanto ADJ, PRON, & ADV **lloró — que se le enrojecieron los ojos** he cried so much his eyes got red; **yo tengo — como tú** I have as much as you do; **me quiere —** he loves me so; **no te quiero —** I don't love you that much; **a cada —s pasos** every so many steps; **cuarenta y —s** forty-odd; **a — el kilo** at so much per kilo; **el — por ciento** at such and such a percentage; **estar al —** to be in the know; **no es para —** it's not such a big deal; **— da** it's all the same; **— como** as much as; **— en la ciudad como en el campo** both in the city and in the country; **entre/mientras — meanwhile; **mantenerse al —** to stay informed; **otros —s** just so many more; **por lo —** therefore; **a las tantas** until late at night; M (en los deportes) point

Tanzania F Tanzania

tanzano -na ADJ & MF Tanzanian

tañer[15] VT *lit* (una guitarra) to play; VI (una campana) to ring, to toll

tañido M (de guitarra) twang; (de campanas) toll

tapa F (de botella) cap; (de libro) cover; (de coche) hood; (de olla, bote) lid, top; *Esp* (comida) bar snack

tapadera F (de recipiente) lid; (de un fraude) cover

tapado ADJ stuffy

tapar VT (una olla) to cover; (una salida) to block; (un caño) to plug up, to stop up; (encubrir) to cover up for; M SG **tapacubos** hubcap; M SG **tapajuntas** flashing; M SG **taparrabos** loincloth

tapete M runner

tapia F garden wall

tapiar VT to board up

tapicería F (para paredes) tapestry; (para muebles) upholstery; (tienda de textiles de decoración) tapestry shop; (arte) tapestry making; (tienda de textiles para muebles) upholstery shop

tapioca F tapioca

tapir M tapir

tapiz M (para pared) tapestry, wall hanging; (para muebles) upholstery

tapizar[47] VT to upholster

tapón M (de botella) stopper; (de lavabo) plug; (de corcho) cork; (en baloncesto) block; **— de oído** earplug; **tapones** (en el zapato de fútbol) cleats

taponar VT (baloncesto) to block
taponazo M pop of a cork
taquigrafía F shorthand
taquígrafo -fa MF stenographer
taquilla F ticket office, box office
tarambana MF knucklehead
tarántula F tarantula
tararear VI/VT to hum
tarareo M hum, humming
tarascada F (mordedura) snap, bite; (réplica) rude answer
tardanza F lateness
tardar VI to take time; **¿cuánto tarda el trámite de divorcio?** how long does it take to get divorced? **—se** to take a long time; **tu padre se tarda** your father is taking a long time; **a más —** at the latest
tarde F (después del almuerzo) afternoon; (hacia el anochecer) evening; **buenas —s** good afternoon; ADV late; **ya es —** it is late; **o temprano** sooner or later; **más —** later on; **llegar —** to be late
tardío ADJ late
tardo ADJ lit slow
tarea F (trabajo) task, chore; (escolar) homework
tarifa F (impuesto) tariff; (lista de precios) list of prices; (de transporte) fare; (precio estipulado) rate
tarima F platform
tarjeta F card (también dispositivo de computadora); **— amarilla** yellow card; **— bancaria** bank card; **— comercial** business card; **— de circuito integrado** smart card; **— de sonido** sound card; **— gráfica** graphics card; **— inteligente** smart card; **— postal** postcard; **— de cobro automático / — de débito** debit card; **— de crédito** credit card; **— de Navidad** Christmas card; **— roja** red card; **marcar —** to punch in
tarro M jar
tarta F tart, pie
tartajear VI to stutter
tartamudear VI to stutter, to stammer
tartamudeo M stammer, stutter
tartamudez F stuttering
tartamudo -da MF stutterer, stammerer; ADJ stuttering, stammering
tártaro M tartar
tartera F round baking pan
tarugo M (trozo de madera) piece of wood; (tonto) blockhead
tasa F (índice) rate; (impuesto) tax; **— de desempleo** unemployment rate; **— de interés** interest rate; **— de mortalidad** death rate; **— de natalidad** birth rate; **— de ocupación** occupancy rate; **— de paro** unemployment rate; **— prima** prime rate
tasación F valuation, appraisal
tasajo M jerky

tasar VT to appraise, to assess
tatarabuelo -la M great-great-grandfather; F great-great-grandmother
tataranieto -ta M great-great-grandson; F great-great-granddaughter
tatuaje M tattoo
tatuar[26] VT to tattoo
tauromaquia F bullfighting
taxi M taxi, taxicab
taxidermia F taxidermy
taxista MF taxi driver, cab driver
taxonomía F taxonomy
Tayikistán M Tajikistan
tayiko -ka ADJ & MF Tajik
taza F (de té, café) cup; (del inodoro) bowl
tazón M (para beber) mug; (para comer) bowl
té M (bebida) tea; (fiesta) tea party
te PRON PERS you; **yo — amo** I love you; **— digo mañana** I'll tell you tomorrow; **no — mires en el espejo** don't look at yourself in the mirror
teatral ADJ theatrical
teatro M theater; **— de títeres** puppet show; **no hagas —** don't make such a production
techado M (techo) roof; (acción de techar) roofing
techar VT to roof
techo M (exterior) roof; (interior) ceiling; **— de cristal** glass ceiling
techumbre F roof
tecla F key; **— de alt** alt key; **— de alternativa gráfica** alt gr key; **— de borrado** delete key; **— de cambio** shift key; **— de comando** command key; **— de control** control key; **— de escape** escape key; **— de fin** end key; **— de función** function key; **— de mayúsculas** shift key; **— de ordenación** sort key; **— de reinicio** reset key; **— de retorno** return key; **— de retroceso** backspace key, return key; **— de tabulación** tab key; **— fin** end key; **dar uno en la —** to hit the nail on the head
teclado M keyboard; **— numérico** keypad
teclear VT (pulsar las teclas) to key in, to type; (hacer ruido) to click
tecleo M keying in, clicking
técnica F (método) technique; (tecnología) technology
técnico -ca ADJ technical; MF (en mecánica) technician; (de fútbol) coach
tecnología F technology; **— de punta** cutting-edge technology
tecnológico ADJ technological
tectónica F tectonics
tedio M boredom
tedioso ADJ tedious
tee M tee
teja F (de cerámica) tile; (de madera u otros materiales) shingle

tejado M roof

tejar M tile factory; VT to cover with tiles

tejedor -ora MF weaver

tejer VI/VT (cesta, tela) to weave; (suéter) to knit; M **tejemaneje** (fraude) hanky-panky; (actividad) goings-on

tejido M (tela) textile, fabric; (de células) tissue; (acción de hilar) weaving; (acción y efecto de tejer) knitting

tejo M disk

tejón M badger

tela F (paño) cloth, fabric; (lienzo para pintar) canvas; (de araña) web; (dinero) money; — **adhesiva** adhesive tape; — **de cebolla** onion skin; **en —** hardbound; **poner en — de juicio** to call into question

telar M loom

telaraña F cobweb, spider's web

tele F TV

telebobo -ba MF couch potato

telecomunicación F telecommunication

teleconferencia F teleconference

teledifusión F telecast

teledirección F remote guidance

teleférico M cable car

telefonazo M buzz, ring

telefonear VI/VT to telephone, to phone

telefónico ADJ **llamada telefónica** telephone call

telefonista MF telephone operator

teléfono M (aparato) telephone, phone; (número) telephone number

telegrafiar[28] VI/VT to telegraph, to wire

telegráfico ADJ telegraphic

telégrafo M telegraph

telegrama M telegram

telemarketing M telemarketing

telemercadeo M telemarketing

telémetro M range finder

telenovela F soap opera

teleobjetivo M zoom lens

telepatía F telepathy

telescopio M telescope

telespectador -ora MF viewer

telesquí M ski lift

teletipo M Teletype™

teletrabajo M telecommuting

televidente MF television viewer

televisar VT to televise

televisión F television; — **de alta definición** high-definition television

televisivo ADJ (apto para la televisión) televisable; (relativo a la televisión) television

televisor M television set; — **a/en color** color television

telón M theater curtain; — **de acero** iron curtain

tema M (de una obra literaria, musical) theme; (de conversación) topic, subject; (de un CD) song, track

temario M agenda

temático ADJ thematic

temblar[1] VI (la mano, la tierra) to tremble; (la voz) to shake, to quaver; (de frío) to shiver; (de miedo) to shudder; (la luz) to flicker

temblequear VI to dodder

temblón ADJ trembling

temblor M (acción de temblar) trembling; (de tierra) tremor; (de una llama) flicker; (de la voz) quaver; (de frío) shiver; (de miedo) shudder; — **de tierra** earthquake

tembloroso ADJ (mano) shaky; (llama) flickering; (voz) quavering; (de miedo) shuddering; (de frío) shivering

temer VI/VT to fear, to be afraid [of]; — **por** to fear for; **mucho me temo que** I fear that

temerario ADJ rash, reckless

temeridad F temerity, recklessness

temeroso ADJ fearful

temible ADJ dreadful, dread

temor M fear

témpano M (bloque de hielo) block of ice; (persona fría) cold fish

temperamento M temperament, disposition

temperancia F temperance

temperatura F temperature

tempestad F tempest, storm; **una — en un vaso de agua** a tempest in a teapot

tempestuoso ADJ tempestuous, stormy

templado ADJ (clima) moderate, temperate; (ánimo) serene; (actitud) moderate

templanza F temperance

templar VT (moderar, dar fuerza) to temper; (calentar) to warm up; (una guitarra) to tune

temple M (dureza) temper; (coraje) mettle; **de mal —** in a bad mood

templo M temple

temporada F season (también de fútbol); — **baja** off-season; — **de caza** hunting season

temporal ADJ (relativo al tiempo) temporal; (secular) worldly; (no permanente) temporary; M storm; **capear el —** to weather the storm

tempranero -ra ADJ early rising; MF early riser

temprano ADJ & ADV early

tenacidad F tenacity

tenaz ADJ tenacious

tenazas F PL (de cangrejo) pincers; (de mecánico) pliers; (de dentista) forceps; (para hielo) tongs

tendedero M clothesline

tendencia F tendency; (orientación) orientation; (de la moda) trend; **de — mayoritaria** mainstream; — **a la baja** downturn; — **al alza** upturn, upward trend

tender[2] VT (un mantel) to spread out; (la ropa) to hang out; (la mano) to extend; (un cable) to lay; (una trampa) to set; VI — **a** to tend to;

—se to stretch out

tendero -ra MF (de una tienda) storekeeper; (de una tienda de comestibles) grocer

tendido M (de cables) laying; (de ropa mojada) hanging out; (conjunto de cables) cables

tendinitis F tendonitis

tendón M tendon, sinew; **— de Aquiles** Achilles' tendon

tendrá, tendría *ver* tener

tenebroso ADJ (oscuro) dark; (sombrío) gloomy

tenedor -ora M table fork; MF holder, payee; **— de libros** bookkeeper

teneduría F **— de libros** bookkeeping

tener[58] VT to have; **tiene el pelo castaño** she has brown hair, her hair is brown; **— en cuenta** to bear in mind; **— en mucho** to esteem highly; **— por** to consider; **— que** to have to; **— ganas** to feel like; **tengo escrita la carta** I have the letter written; **— éxito** to be successful; **— miedo** to be afraid; **— sueño** to be sleepy; **— frío** to be cold; **— hambre** to be hungry; **tiene cinco años** she is five years old; **—se** to stand straight; **no — más remedio** to have no other choice; **— que ver con** to have to do with

tenería F tannery

tenga, tengo *ver* tener

tenia F tapeworm

teniente MF lieutenant

tenis M (juego) tennis; M PL (zapatos) sneakers, tennis shoes

tenista MF tennis player

tenor M (voz, estilo) tenor; (tono) tone, tenor; ADJ **saxofón —** tenor saxophone

tensión F tension

tenso ADJ (nervioso) tense; (extendido) taut

tentación F temptation

tentáculo M tentacle

tentador ADJ tempting

tentar[1] VT to tempt; **— a la suerte** to court danger; **— por todos los medios** to try everything

tentativa F attempt, try

tentativo ADJ tentative

tentempié M snack

tenue ADJ (tela) delicate; (luz) tenuous, dim, faint; (sonido) feeble

tenuidad F faintness, softness

teñir[11] VT (de color) to dye; (de emoción) to tinge

teología F theology

teológico ADJ theological

teólogo -ga MF theologian

teoría F theory; **en —** in theory

teórico ADJ theoretical

tepe M sod

tequila M tequila

terabyte M terabyte

terapeuta MF therapist

terapéutico ADJ therapeutic

terapia F (médica) therapy; (psicológica, marital) counseling; **— de electroshock** shock therapy; **— electroconvulsiva** shock therapy; **— hormonal** hormone therapy; **— ocupacional** occupational therapy

tercero ADJ third; **tercera base** third base; **tercera persona** third person; **tercera edad** old age; **tercer mundo** third world; M (en un contrato) third party; (en béisbol) third baseman

terciar VI/VT to arbitrate

tercio M third

terciopelo M velvet

terco ADJ obstinate, stubborn

tergiversación F distortion, misrepresentation

tergiversar VT (palabras) to distort; (datos) to skew

termal ADJ thermal

térmico ADJ heat, thermal

terminación F (de un proyecto) termination, completion; (de una palabra, cuento) ending; (de un piso) finish

terminal ADJ terminal; MF (de aeropuerto, de omnibus) terminal; M (de computadora, eléctrica) terminal

terminante ADJ (negativa) flat; (prohibición) absolute

terminar VI/VT (completar) to finish, to conclude; VI (tener como final) to end; **— por** to end up; **no termino de entender** I still can't understand; **terminó con las ratas** he got rid of the rats; **sin —** unfinished

término M (final) end; (período de tiempo) period; (límite) boundary; (palabra) term; **— medio** medium; **a —** (trabajo) with a deadline; (embarazo) full-term; **en primer —** first of all; **en —s generales** in general terms; **en último —** as a last resort; **estar en buenos —s** to be on good terms; **por — medio** on average; **poner —** to end

terminología F terminology

termita F termite

termo M thermos

termodinámico ADJ thermodynamic

termómetro M thermometer

termonuclear ADJ thermonuclear

termostato M thermostat

ternero -ra MF (animal) calf; F (carne) veal

terneza F tenderness

terno M three-piece suit

ternura F tenderness

terquedad F obstinacy, stubbornness

terraplén M embankment

terrateniente MF landholder

terraza F (terreno) terrace; (de casa) veranda; (delante de un bar) deck; (azotea) flat roof

terremoto M earthquake

terrenal ADJ earthly

terreno M (campo) piece of land, tract of land;

(lote) lot; (formación geológica) terrain; (campo científico) field; — **de juego parejo** level playing field; **ganarle — a alguien** to gain on someone; **perder —** to lose ground; **tantear el —** to put out feelers; **todo —** with four-wheel drive

terrestre ADJ terrestrial, earthly

terrible ADJ terrible, awful

terrier M terrier

territorio M territory

terrón M (de tierra) clod; (de azúcar) lump

terror M terror, dread

terrorismo M terrorism

terrorista ADJ & MF terrorist

terso ADJ (liso) smooth; (pulido) polished

tersura F smoothness

tertulia F social gathering

tesis F thesis; — **doctoral** dissertation

tesón M determination

tesonero ADJ determined

tesorería F treasury

tesorero -ra MF treasurer

tesoro M (riqueza) treasure; (tesorería) treasury

test M test

testaferro M straw man

testamentaria F (gestiones) execution; (bienes) estate

testamento M testament, will

testarudez F stubbornness

testarudo ADJ stubborn, headstrong

testículo M testicle

testificar[30] VI to testify

testigo MF witness; — **de cargo** witness for the prosecution; — **ocular** eyewitness; M proof

testimoniar VI to give testimony

testimonio M testimony, proof, evidence; **levantar falso —** to bear false witness; **en — de su amor** as a testament to his love

testosterona F testosterone

teta F teat

tétanos M SG tetanus, lockjaw

tetera F teapot, teakettle

tetilla F nipple

tetina F nipple

tetraciclina F tetracycline

tetraplégico -ca ADJ & MF quadriplegic

tétrico ADJ gloomy

teutónico ADJ Teutonic

textear VT to text

textil ADJ & M textile

texto M (algo escrito) text; (libro escolar) textbook; — **listo para cámara** camera-ready copy

textual ADJ verbatim

textura F texture

tez F complexion

ti PRON PERS you; **para —** for you; **te lo doy a —** I give it to you

tía F (pariente) aunt; *fam* (mujer) woman, chick;

— **abuela** great-aunt

tibieza F (poco fervor, afecto) lukewarmness; (calor) warmth

tibio ADJ (ni caliente ni frío) tepid, lukewarm; (templado) warm

tiburón M shark

tic M twitch, tic

tictac M **hacer —** to tick

tiempo M (cronológico) time; (climático) weather; (gramatical) tense; (de un partido de cuatro tiempos) quarter; (de un partido de dos tiempos) half; — **compartido** timeshare; — **completo** full-time; — **de descuento** extra time; — **extra** overtime; — **libre** leisure hours, free time; — **parcial** part-time; — **pretérito** past tense; — **real** real time; — **suplementario** (fútbol americano) overtime; (fútbol) extra time; — **y medio** time and a half; **a —** on time; **al mismo —** at the same time; **antes de —** ahead of time; **a su —** in due course; **a un —** at the same time; **con —** in advance; **de medio —** half-time; **en aquel —** back then; **en mis —s** in my day; **hace buen —** the weather is nice; **hace mucho —** a long time ago; **mal —** rough weather; **motor de dos —s** two-stroke motor; **perder el —** to goof off, to waste time; **tener — de sobra** to have time to spare; **todo el —** all the time; **tomar el —** to clock

tienda F (de venta) store; (de campaña) tent; — **minorista** retail store; — **virtual** online store

tienda, tiende *ver* tender

tiene, tienes *ver* tener

tientas LOC ADV **a —** blindly; **andar a —** to feel one's way

tiento M care; **coger el —** to get the hang of something

tierno ADJ (fácil de cortar) tender; (joven) young; (cariñoso) affectionate

tierra F (planeta) earth; (superficie) land; (país) country; (suelo) soil; — **adentro** inland; —**s altas** highlands; —**s bajas** lowlands; — **batida** clay; — **de cultivo** farmland; — **de nadie** no-man's-land; — **firme** mainland; —**s raras** rare earths; **bajo —** underground; **caer a —** to fall to the ground; **dar en — con alguien** to overthrow someone; **echar por —** to knock down; **por —** overland

tieso ADJ stiff; **quedarse —** *fam* to kick the bucket

tiesto M flowerpot

tiesura F stiffness

tifoideo -a ADJ & F typhoid

tifón M typhoon

tifus M (causado por salmonella) typhoid fever; (causado por rickettsia) typhus

tigre M tiger

tijera[s] F SG/PL (instrumento para cortar) scissors; (patada de fútbol) scissor kick

tijereta F scissor kick

tijeretada F snip

tijeretazo M snip

tijeretear VT to snip

tildar VT to brand

tilde F (en la ñ) tilde; (en las vocales) accent [mark]

tilín M *fam* ding-a-ling

timador M confidence man

timbrar VT to stamp

timbrazo M ring

timbre M (aparato) buzzer, doorbell; (cualidad de la voz) timbre; (sello) stamp; (impuesto) stamp tax; (insignia heráldica) crest

timidez F timidity, shyness

tímido ADJ timid, shy, bashful

timo M confidence game, scam; **— en pirámide** Ponzi scheme

timón M helm, rudder

timonear VT to steer

timonel M pilot

timorato ADJ timorous, faint-hearted

tímpano M eardrum

tina F (bañera) tub; (de tintorero) vat

tinaja F large earthen jar

tinglado M (armazón) shed; (plataforma) platform

tinieblas F PL darkness; **en —** in the dark

tinitus M tinnitus

tino M (buen juicio) good judgment; (puntería) marksmanship

tinta F ink; **medias —s** wishy-washiness

tinte M (sustancia) dye, stain; (matiz) tint

tintero M inkwell; **eso se me quedó en el —** I never got to that

tintín M clink

tintinear VI to tinkle, to clink

tintineo M tinkle, tinkling

tinto ADJ red

tintorería F dry cleaner

tintorero -ra MF dry cleaner

tintura F (en medicina) tincture; (tinte) dye, tint

tiñoso ADJ scabby

tío -a M (hermano de la madre o el padre) uncle; **— abuelo** great-uncle; (tipo) guy; F (hermana de la madre o el padre) aunt; (tipa) woman, gal

tiovivo M merry-go-round

tipear, tipiar VI/VT to type

típico ADJ typical

tiple M treble

tipo -pa M (especie, imprenta) type; (tío) *fam* guy, dude; *Am* rate of interest; **— de cambio** rate of exchange; **— de interés** interest rate; **— de letra** typeface, font; **— de letra por omisión** base font; **un buen —** (hombre guapo) a good-looking fellow; (buena persona) a regular guy; **tiene buen —** he's good looking; F (tía) *pey* woman, broad

tipografía F printing

tipología F typology

tira F (de papel, tocino, tela) strip; (de cuero, zapato) strap; **— cómica** comic strip

tirada F (de una pelota) throw; (de una publicación) issue, print run; (distancia) stretch; **de una —** all at once

tirador -ora MF (persona que dispara) shooter; M (tirachinas) slingshot; (pomo de la puerta) knob

tiranía F tyranny

tiránico ADJ tyrannical

tirano -na ADJ tyrannical; MF tyrant

tirante ADJ (cable) taut; (relaciones) strained; M (de caballería) trace; (de vestido) strap; (apoyo) brace, strut; **—s** suspenders

tirantez F tension, strain

tirar VT (pelota) to throw, to toss, to pitch; (derechos, dinero) to throw away; (una bala) to shoot; (una moneda) to flip, to toss; (dados) to cast; (una cuerda) to tug, to tug; VI/VT (en baloncesto) to shoot; VI **— a puerta** to shoot at goal; **—se** (echarse) to lie down; (en fútbol) to fake a foul; **— al suelo** to throw down; **— a** to tend toward; **— abajo** to knock over; **— de** to tug at; **— la cadena** to flush; **— la casa por la ventana** to live it up; **— la chancleta** to kick up one's heels; **—se solo** to go it alone; **tirárselas de** to pretend to be; **no me tira la política** I'm not attracted to politics; **el coche tira a un lado** the car pulls to one side; **ir tirando** to get along; **trabajar con él es un constante tira y afloja** working with him is a roller-coaster; M **tirabuzón** (sacacorchos) corkscrew; (espiral) coil; M SG **tirachinas** slingshot

tiritar VI (de frío) to shiver; (de miedo) to shudder

tiro M (lanzamiento) throw; (disparo) shot; (deporte) shooting; (de cocaína) hit; (de dados) roll; (de caballos) team; (de chimenea) draft; (fútbol) shot; **— al arco** archery; **— al blanco** target practice; **— de esquina** corner kick; **— de penalidad** penalty kick; **— en suspensión** jump shot; **— libre** (baloncesto) free throw; (fútbol) free kick; **errar el —** to miss the mark; **matar a —s** to gun down; **ni a —s** absolutely not; **pegarle un — a alguien** to shoot someone; **me salió el — por la culata** the plan backfired on me

tiroides ADJ & M thyroid

tirón M (tironeo) jerk, tug, pull; (atracción fuerte, lesión de un músculo) pull; **de un —** all at once; **un — de orejas** a slap on the wrist

tironear VI/VT to jerk, to tug at

tirotear VI to shoot; **—se** to exchange shots

tiroteo M (tiros) shooting, gunfire; (entre bandos) shootout

tirria F dislike; **tenerle — a una persona** to have a strong dislike for someone

tisana F herbal tea

tísico ADJ consumptive

tisis F consumption

titánico ADJ titanic

titanio M titanium

títere M (marioneta) puppet; (persona) puppet, dupe; **—s** puppet show; **no dejar — con cabeza** to leave no one standing

titilación F flicker

titilar VI to flicker, to twinkle

titileo M twinkle

titubear VI (vacilar) to hesitate, to waver; (oscilar) to totter, to dodder

titubeo M hesitation

titular VT to entitle; **—se** to graduate; ADJ permanent; M (de periódico) headline; MF (de cargo) incumbent

titularidad F tenure

título M (de una obra, persona, liga) title; (derecho) claim, legal right; (universitario) degree, diploma; **— de propiedad** title deed; **—s de crédito** credits; **a — de** by way of

tiza F chalk

tiznado ADJ sooty

tiznar VT to smear with soot

tizne M soot

tizón M (leña) burning log; (parásito) smut

TNT M TNT

toalla F towel; **tirar la —** to throw in the towel

toallero M towel rack

tobillo M ankle

tobogán M slide

tocado M headdress; ADJ touched

tocador M (mueble) dressing table, vanity table; (habitación) *lit* boudoir

tocante a PREP concerning

tocar[30] VT (con los dedos) to touch; (un instrumento musical) to play; (una campana) to ring; (un timbre) to buzz; (a la puerta) to knock; (la bocina) to honk, to blast; (una alarma) to sound; (mencionar) to touch upon; **— en** to stop over in; **—le a uno** to be one's turn; **— fondo** to hit bottom; **— la pelota** (béisbol) bunt; M SG **tocadiscos** record player

tocayo -ya MF namesake

tocino M bacon

tocón M stump

todavía ADV still, as yet, yet; **— está aquí** she's still here; **¿— no has comido?** have you not eaten yet? **— no ha llegado** she still has not arrived, as yet she has not arrived; **me dio — más** she gave me even more

todo ADJ all; (cada uno) every, each; **— hombre** every man; **—s los días** every day; **a — correr** at top speed; **a toda costa** at all costs; **a toda marcha** in high gear; **a toda vela** under full sail; **a toda velocidad** at full speed; **a — volumen** at full blast; **de — corazón** wholeheartedly; **de —s modos** still, anyway, all the same; **del — entirely**; **en — caso** in any case, at any rate, in any event; **es — un personaje** he's quite a character; **por — lados** everywhere; **— el día** all day; **— el tiempo** all the time; **— el mundo** everyone; **todas las noches** nightly; **toda la noche** all through the night; **toda clase de** all sorts of; **en/por todas partes** everywhere, far and wide; **con toda el alma** from the bottom of one's heart; **con toda sinceridad** in all earnestness; PRON **de una vez por todas** once and for all; **— se vale** anything goes; **—s juntos** all together; ADV **— derecho** straight ahead; **— lo contrario** quite the opposite; **— recto** straight ahead; **— sucio** all dirty; **— o nada** all or nothing; **ante —** first of all; **así y — in** spite of that; **con — in** spite of that; **del — completely; sobre — especially; M whole; —poderoso** almighty; **el — es más que la suma de las partes** the whole is more than the sum of its parts

toga F (de catedrático) gown; (de juez) robe

Togo M Togo

togolés -esa ADJ & MF Togolese

toldería F Indian village

toldo M awning, canopy

tolerancia F tolerance

tolerante ADJ tolerant, broad-minded

tolerar VT to tolerate; **no lo puedo — I** can't stand it

tolete M oarlock

toma F (de una ciudad) taking; (cinematográfica) take; (de juramento) administration; (de teléfono) jack; **— de agua** faucet; **— de corriente** electric outlet; **— de poder** takeover; **— y daca** give-and-take

tomar VT (una pastilla) to take; (un juramento) to administer; (un vestido) to take in; (a un empleado) to hire; (una bebida) to drink; **— a pecho** to take to heart; **— asiento** to take a seat; **— desprevenido** to take by surprise; **— el sol** to sunbathe; **—lo a mal** to take the wrong way; **— el pelo a** to make fun of, to kid, to pull someone's leg; **— medidas** to take action; **— posesión** to take possession; **— una decisión** to make a decision; **—le las medidas a alguien** to measure someone for clothes; **—se de la mano** to hold hands; **—se la molestia** to bother to

tomate M tomato

tomillo M thyme

tomo M volume

tomografía F scan; — **axial computarizada** CAT scan; — **cerebral** brain scan

ton LOC ADV **sin — ni son** for no reason

tonada F tune

tonel M (barril) barrel; (persona) *pey* fatso

tonelada F ton

tóner M toner

Tonga F Tonga

tongano -na ADJ & MF Tongan

tongo M setup

tonicidad F tone; — **muscular** muscle tone

tónico -ca ADJ & M tonic; F (tono) tone; (agua) tonic [water]

tono M (al hablar) tone; (musical) pitch; (intervalo musical) step; — **de ocupado** busy signal; — **menor** minor key; — **muscular** muscle tone; **a** — on key; **bajar el** — to lower the volume; **darse** — to put on airs; **de buen** — in good taste; **fuera de** — out of place; **subido de** — risqué

tontear VI to fool around

tontería F (cualidad de tonto) stupidity; (hecho o dicho tonto) foolishness, nonsense

tonto -ta ADJ (ingenuo) foolish; (de poca inteligencia) stupid, dumb; **a tontas y a locas** haphazardly; MF (persona ingenua) fool; (persona de poca inteligencia) *fam* dummy, blockhead, dimwit; — **de capirote** dunce; **hacer[se] el** — to play the fool

topacio M topaz

topar VT to butt; —**se con** to bump into

tope M (de precios) ceiling, cap; (de tren) bumper; (de puerta) doorstop; **a** — a lot; **hasta el** — to the maximum; **estar hasta el** — to be completely full

topetazo M butt

tópico M (lugar común) cliché; (tema) topic; ADJ topical

topless ADJ topless

topo M mole (también espía)

toque M (con la mano) touch; (de campana) ringing; (de tambor) beat; (de trompeta) blare; (de pintura) dab; — **de queda** curfew; — **de pelota** (béisbol) bunt; **dar los últimos** —**s** to put the finishing touches; **dar** —**s** to dab; **un** — **femenino** a woman's touch

toquetear VI/VT to finger

toqueteo M feel

tórax M thorax

torbellino M whirlwind

torcedura F twist, sprain, strain

torcer[34] VT (el cuello) to twist; (una articulación) to sprain, to strain; (tergiversar) to distort; —**le el pescuezo a alguien** to wring someone's neck; VI (un río) to bend

torcido ADJ crooked, bent

tordo M thrush

torear VT (lidiar) to fight a bull; (provocar) to provoke

torero -ra MF bullfighter

tormenta F storm; — **de arena** sandstorm; — **eléctrica** electrical storm

tormento M torment

tormentoso ADJ stormy

tornadizo ADJ changeable

tornado M tornado, twister

tornar VI (regresar) to return; VT (cambiar) to turn; — **a hacer algo** to do something again

tornasolado ADJ iridescent

tornear VT to turn on a lathe

torneo M tournament

tornillo M screw; — **de banco** vise; **faltarle a uno un** — to have a screw loose

torniquete M (eje giratorio) turnstile; (contra hemorragia) tourniquet

torno M (para levantar cosas pesadas) hoist, winch; (para cerámica) lathe, pottery wheel; **en** — [a] around

toro M bull; **coger/agarrar el** — **por los cuernos** to take the bull by the horns

toronja F grapefruit

torpe ADJ (poco habilidoso) clumsy, awkward; (lento) slow, sluggish

torpedear VT to torpedo

torpedero -ra MF (en béisbol) shortstop; M (barco) torpedo boat; (avión) torpedo plane

torpedo M torpedo

torpeza F (falta de habilidad) clumsiness; (lentitud) slowness, sluggishness

torpor M torpor

torrar VT to roast

torre F (de castillo) tower; (de buque de guerra) turret; (en ajedrez) castle; — **de control** control tower; — **de marfil** ivory tower; — **de perforación** oil derrick; — **de vigilancia** watchtower

torrencial ADJ torrential

torrente M torrent; — **de lágrimas** flood of tears; — **sanguíneo** bloodstream

torreón M large tower

torreta F turret

tórrido ADJ torrid

torsión F torsion

torso M torso

torta F (postre) cake; (bofetada) slap

tortícolis F kink

tortilla F (de huevo) omelet; (de harina) *Méx* tortilla; **se dio vuelta la** — the tables have turned

tórtola F turtledove

tortuga F tortoise, turtle; — **marina** sea turtle; **a paso de** — at a snail's pace

tortuoso ADJ (camino) tortuous; (carácter) devious

tortura F torture

torturante ADJ torturous

torturar VT to torture

torvo ADJ fierce

tos F cough; — **ferina** whooping cough

tosco ADJ coarse, crude

toser VI to cough

tosquedad F coarseness, crudeness

tostada F toast

tostado ADJ (pan) toasted; (café) roasted; M (acción de tostar pan) toasting; (color, bronceado) tan; (acción de tostar café) roasting

tostador -ora MF toaster

tostar[5] VT (pan) to toast; (piel) to tan; (café) to roast

total ADJ & M total; **en** — all together; —, **a mí no me importa** anyway, I don't care

totalidad F **la** — **del dinero** all the money; **en su** — as a whole

totalitario ADJ totalitarian

totalmente ADV totally, perfectly

tour M tour

tóxico ADJ toxic

toxina F toxin

traba F (estorbo) hindrance; (de caballo) hobble

trabajador -ora ADJ (esforzado) hardworking; (proletario) working; MF worker

trabajar VI/VT to work; — **un taxi** to drive a taxi; VI (una tienda) to be open; — **duro** to work hard; — **horas extras** to work overtime

trabajo M (actividad) work; (acción de trabajar) working; (empleo) job; (informe académico) paper; — **manual** manual labor; **da mucho** — it's a lot of work; **sin** — unemployed

trabajoso ADJ laborious

trabar VT (una puerta) to jam; (un caballo) to hobble; (a un boxeador) to clinch; (una salsa) to thicken; (negociaciones) to impede; — **amistad con alguien** to strike up a friendship with someone; — **batalla** to join battle; — **conversación** to strike up a conversation; M SG **trabalenguas** tongue twister

tracción F traction

tractocamión M tractor-trailer

tractor M tractor

tradición F tradition

tradicional ADJ traditional

traducción F translation

traducir[38] VI/VT to translate

traductor -ora MF translator

traduje, tradujera, tradujese, traduzca, traduzco ver traducir

traer[59] VT (venir con) to bring; (llevar puesto) to have on; (contener) to feature; — **a colación** to bring up; — **a mal a alguien** to mistreat someone; **este niño se las trae** this child is something else; **¿qué te traes entre manos?** what are you up to? —**se secretos**

to have secrets

tráfago M bustle

traficante MF dealer

traficar[30] VI to traffic, to trade

tráfico M traffic

tragar[40] VI/VT (ingerir) to swallow; (comer) fam to stuff one's face; (consumir gasolina) to guzzle; (aguantar) to stand; (hacer desaparecer) to engulf; —**se algo** to swallow [accidentally]; **no me lo trago** I don't buy that; M **tragaluz** skylight; M/F SG **tragamonedas/tragaperras** slot machine

tragedia F tragedy

trágico ADJ tragic

trago M (lo tragado) swallow; (bebida alcohólica) shot, slug; **a** —**s** (beber) in sips; (poco a poco) little by little; **echar/tomar un** — to take a drink; **pasar un mal** — to suffer a difficulty

traición F (política) treason; (personal) betrayal; (acto desleal) treachery; **a** — by treachery

traicionar VT to double-cross

traicionero ADJ treacherous

traidor -ora ADJ treacherous; MF (político) traitor; (personal) betrayer

traiga, traigo ver traer

trailer M trailer

traílla F leash

traje M (conjunto) suit; (de fiesta) gown; — **de baño** swimsuit

traje, trajera, trajese ver traer

trajeado ADJ **bien** — well-dressed

trajín M hustle and bustle

trajinar VI to rush around

trama F (argumento) plot; (intriga) scheme; (conjunto de hilos) woof

tramador -ora MF plotter

tramar VT (con hilos) to weave; (intrigar) to plot, to scheme

tramitación F processing

tramitar VT to take steps to obtain

trámite M procedure, paperwork

tramo M (de carretera) stretch; (de puente) span; (de hielo) patch; (de escalera) flight

tramoyista MF stagehand

trampa F (de caza) trap, snare; (engaño) trick; — **de arena** (golf) sand trap; **hacer** — to cheat, to trick; **tender una** — to set a trap

trampear VI to cheat

trampilla F trapdoor

trampolín M (de piscina) springboard; (de circo) trampoline

tramposo -sa ADJ deceitful; MF cheat

tranca F crossbar

trance M (momento difícil) pass, difficult moment; (estado mental) trance; **el último** — the last moment of life; **a todo** — at any cost

tranco M stride; **a** —**s** hurriedly; **en dos** —**s** in a jiffy

tranquera F wooden fence

tranquilidad F tranquillity, calm, quiet

tranquilizante M tranquilizer

tranquilizar[47] VT to quiet, to calm down; **—se** to calm down, to wind down

tranquilo ADJ (silencioso) quiet, peaceful; (apacible) calm, cool; (despreocupado) calm, at ease; (no excitable) sedate, laid-back; (sin olas) smooth, tranquil

transacción F transaction; **— comercial** business transaction; **transacciones** trading; **transacciones a precio de mercado** arm's-length transactions

transar VI to compromise

transatlántico ADJ transatlantic; M transatlantic liner

transbordar VI to transfer

transbordo M transfer

transcribir[74] VT to transcribe

transcripción F transcript

transcultural ADJ cross-cultural

transcurrir VI to elapse

transcurso M passing, passage; **en el — de un año** in the course of a year

transeúnte MF passerby, transient

transferencia F transfer; **— electrónica** wire transfer

transferible ADJ transferable

transferir[8] VT to transfer (también en computadora)

transformación F transformation

transformador M transformer

transformar VT to transform

transfusión F transfusion; **dar una — de sangre** to give a transfusion

transgénico ADV genetically modified

transgredir[73] VT to transgress

transgresión F transgression

transgresor-ora MF lawbreaker

transición F transition

transigir[46] VI to compromise

transistor M transistor

transitable ADJ passable

transitar VI/VT to travel

transitivo ADJ transitive

tránsito M (acción de viajar) transit, passage; (tráfico) traffic; **de/en —** in transit

transitorio ADJ transitory

transmisible ADJ communicable

transmisión F transmission; **— automática** automatic transmission; **— por la web** webcast

transmisor M transmitter; ADJ transmitting

transmitir VI/VT (enviar) to transmit; (una enfermedad) to communicate; (por radio o televisión) to broadcast; **— por la web** to webcast

transnacional ADJ transnational

transparencia F (visual) transparency; (institucional) openness

transparente ADJ transparent

transpiración F perspiration, sweating

transpirar VI/VT to transpire, to perspire

transportación F transportation, transport

transportar VT (mercancías, gente) to transport; (mercancías) to ship, to haul

transporte M (acción) transport, transportation; (vehículo de transporte) transport [vessel]; **— de locura** fit of madness; **— público** mass transit

transportista MF teamster, trucker

transversal ADJ transverse; F transversal

transverso ADJ transverse

tranvía M (transporte urbano) streetcar, trolley; (tren de cercanías) local train

trapacería F racket

trapacero -ra MF racketeer

trapeador M mop

trapear VI/VT *Am* to mop

trapecio M trapeze

trapezoide ADJ & M trapezoid

trapiche M sugar mill

trapisonda F trick

trapo M rag; **—s** *fam* duds; **a todo —** at full speed; **tratar a alguien como un —** to treat someone like dirt; **—s sucios** dirty laundry

tráquea F trachea, windpipe

traqueotomía F tracheotomy

traquetear VI (hacer sonido) to rattle, to clatter; (llevar a todos lados) to drag from place to place

traqueteo M rattle, clatter

tras PREP (temporal) after; (espacial) after, behind, in back of; **correr —** to run after; **día — día** day after day; **una vez — otra** time after time

trascendencia F (concepto filosófico) transcendence; (importancia) importance

trascendental ADJ (que sobrepasa la realidad) transcendental; (importante) important

trascendente ADJ (que sobrepasa la realidad) transcendental; (importante) important

trascender VT (sobrepasar) to transcend; VI (surgir) to emerge; (extender) to extend

trasegar[41] VT (vino) to pour from one container to another; (objetos) to move around; (papeles) to shuffle

trasero ADJ (punto, asiento) rear, back; (pata) hind; M (de persona) *fam* rear, rear end, bottom

traslación F transfer

trasladar VT (a un empleado) to transfer; (una reunión) to postpone; **—se** to travel

traslado M transfer

traslapo M overlap

trasnochar VI to stay up late

traspapelar VT to mislay, to misplace; **—se** to become mislaid

traspasar VT (pasar por) to transfix; (ir más allá de) to go beyond; (pasar un límite) to transgress, to cross over; (una propiedad) to transfer

traspaso M transfer

traspié M stumble, slip; **dar un —** to stumble

trasplantar VT to transplant

trasplante M transplant

trasponer[56, 74] VT to transpose

trasquilar VT (una oveja) to shear; (a una persona) to fleece

trastabillar VI to stumble

trastazo M bump

traste M (de guitarra) fret, stop; (trasero) buttocks; **dar al — con** to destroy; **irse al —** to go down the drain

trasto M piece of junk; **—s** stuff

trastocar[30] VT to disrupt

trastornar VT (alterar psíquicamente) to disturb; (alterar el funcionamiento) to disrupt; **—se** to go crazy

trastorno M (molestia) trouble; (patología) disorder; **— bipolar** bipolar disorder; **— de Asperger** Asperger's syndrome; **— de déficit de atención** attention deficit disorder; **— de la alimentación** eating disorder; **— de la personalidad** personality disorder; **— de personalidad múltiple** multiple personality disorder; **— del sueño** sleep disorder

trasudar VI/VT to perspire

trata F trade; **— de blancas** white slave trade

tratable ADJ (curable) treatable; (amistoso) approachable

tratado M (acuerdo) treaty; (libro) treatise

tratamiento M (acción de tratar) treatment; (fórmula de cortesía) form of address; **— de canal** root canal; **— de convalecencia** aftercare; **— de residuos** waste treatment; **— de textos** *Esp* word processing; **— postoperatorio** aftercare

tratante MF dealer, trader

tratar VT (una enfermedad, a un paciente, un asunto) to treat; VI (intentar) to try; **— como** to treat like; **— con** to have dealings with; **— de** to try to, to attempt; **— sobre** to be about; **lo trató de imbécil** she called him an idiot; **—le a uno de** to address someone as; **— en** to deal in; **—se con** to have to do with; **—se de** to be a question of, to be about

trato M (acuerdo) treatment; (acción de tratar) dealings; (convenio) deal; (comercio) trade; (modales) manners; **¡— hecho!** it's a deal! **tener buen —** to have good manners; **cerrar un —** to strike a bargain

trauma M trauma

traumático ADJ traumatic

traumatismo M trauma

través LOC ADV **a/al — de** through, across; **a —**

de las declaraciones throughout the declarations; **de —** across; **mirar de —** to look askance [at]

travesaño M crossbar (también en fútbol)

travesía F crossing, sea voyage, passage

travesura F mischief, prank; **—s** naughtiness; **hacer —s** to play pranks

traviesa F railway tie

travieso ADJ mischievous, naughty

trayecto M course, route

trayectoria F (de proyectil) trajectory, path; (profesional) career, track record

trayendo *ver* traer

traza F (huella) trace; (aspecto) appearance; **tiene —s de no acabar nunca** it looks as if it will never end

trazado M (de ciudad) layout; (de edificio) blueprint; (de un plan) outline

trazador M **— gráfico** plotter

trazar[47] VT (un dibujo) to trace, to sketch; (un plan) to outline; (un edificio) to blueprint; **— el curso** to plot a course

trazo M stroke

trébol M clover

trece NUM thirteen

trecho M stretch; **a —s** at intervals; **de — en —** at intervals

tregua F (de guerra) truce; (descanso) lull, respite

treinta NUM thirty (también en tenis)

treintañero -ra MF thirtysomething

tremendo ADJ (extraordinario) tremendous; (terrible) terrible

trementina F turpentine

tremolar VI (bandera) to flutter; (voz) to trill

trémolo M quaver

trémulo ADJ tremulous, trembling

tren M train; **— de aterrizaje** landing gear; **— de carga / de mercancías** freight train; **— de cercanías** local train; **— de vida** lifestyle; **— expreso** express train; **a todo —** at top speed; **perder el —** to miss the boat; **seguir el —** to keep up

trenza F braid

trenzar[47] VT to braid

trepador -ora ADJ (planta) climbing; (ciclista) climber; MF social climber; F climbing plant

trepar VI to climb

trepidar VI to tremble

tres NUM three

trescientos NUM three hundred

treta F trick, wile

triaje M triage

triangular ADJ triangular

triángulo M triangle; **— recto** right triangle

tribu F tribe

tribulación F tribulation

tribuna F (de orador) rostrum; (para el público) grandstand

tribunal M (sala del juez) court, courtroom; (cuerpo de jueces) panel of judges

tributable ADJ taxable

tributar VT to pay tribute with; VI to pay taxes

tributario ADJ & M tributary

tributo M (pago obligatorio) tribute; (impuesto) tax

triceps M triceps

triciclo M tricycle

tridimensional ADJ three-dimensional

trifulca F fight

trigo M wheat

trigueño ADJ (tez) swarthy; (pelo) dark-blond

trillado ADJ trite

trilladora F threshing machine

trillar VT to thresh

trillizo -za ADJ & MF triplet

trilogía F trilogy

trimestral ADJ quarterly

trimestre M quarter

trinar VI to trill; **está que trina** she is furious

trinchante M carving knife

trinchar VT to carve

trinche M pitchfork

trinchera F (fosa) trench; (gabardina) trench coat

trinchero M carving table

trineo M sleigh, sled

trinitense ADJ & MF Trinidadian

trino M trill

trinquete M ratchet

trío M trio

tripas F PL guts; **hacer de — corazón** to pluck up one's courage

triple ADJ triple; M (también en béisbol) triple; (baloncesto) three-point basket

triplicar[30] VT to triple, to treble

trípode M tripod

triptongo M triphthong

tripulación F crew

tripulante MF crew member

tripular VT to man

triquiñuela F caper

triquitraque M firecracker

triscar[30] VI to frisk

triste ADJ sad, sorrowful

tristeza F sadness, sorrow

tristón ADJ glum

tritón M newt

trituradora F (para desechos) garbage disposal unit; (para papel) paper shredder

triturar VI/VT (documentos) to shred; (granos) to grind

triunfador -ora MF winner; ADJ triumphant

triunfal ADJ triumphal

triunfante ADJ triumphant

triunfar VT to triumph

triunfo M triumph

trivial ADJ trivial, commonplace, trite

trizas F PL **hacer —** to tear into shreds

trocar[31] VT (transformar) to change into; (cambiar una cosa por otra) to exchange

trocear VT to divide into pieces

trocha F trail

trofeo M trophy

troje M granary

trola F whopper

trole M trolley

trolebús M trolley bus

tromba F waterspout; **salir en —** to storm out

trombón M trombone

trombosis F thrombosis; **— coronaria** coronary thrombosis

trompa F (de elefante) trunk; (instrumento musical) horn; **— de Eustaquio** eustachian tube; **— de Falopio** fallopian tube

trompada F blow with the fist

trompeta F trumpet

trompetazo M trumpet blast

trompetear VI to trumpet

trompo M spinning top

tronada F thunderstorm

tronar[5] VI to thunder

tronchar VT to chop off

tronco M (de árbol) trunk, log; (del cuerpo) trunk, torso; **— del encéfalo** brain stem; **dormir como un —** to sleep like a log

tronera F (de buque) gun port; (de mesa de billar) pocket

trono M throne (también wáter)

tropa F (en el ejército) troop; (oficiales) rank and file; **—s de asalto** storm troops; **—s de choque** shock troops

tropel LOC ADV **en —** in droves

tropezar[48] VI to stumble, to trip; **—[se] con alguien** to run into someone; **— con algo** to come across something

tropezón M stumble, trip; **salir a tropezones** to stumble out; **darse un —** to stumble

tropical ADJ tropical

trópico M tropic

tropiezo M stumble

troquel M die

trotar VI to trot, to jog

trote M trot; **al —** at a trot; **no estoy para estos —s** I'm too old for this

troza F log

trozar[47] VT to cut up

trozo M (de roca, madera, torta) piece; (de un texto) section; (de carbón) lump; (de carne) slab

trucha F trout

truco M clever trick

truculento ADJ gruesome

trueno M thunder

trueque M (intercambio) exchange; (transacción sin dinero) bartering

truhán -ana MF scoundrel

truja F cigarette
trust M trust
tu ADJ POS your
tú PRON PERS you
tuba F tuba
tuberculosis F tuberculosis
tubería F (tubo) pipe; (conjunto de tubos) piping
tubo M (cilindro hueco) tube; (de agua, órgano) pipe; (digestivo) tract; **— de ensayo** test tube; **— de escape** tailpipe; **— digestivo** gastrointestinal tract
tubular ADJ tubular
tuerca F nut
tuerto ADJ one-eyed
tuétano M marrow; **hasta los —s** through and through
tufillo M whiff
tufo M (humo) fumes; (hedor) stench
tugurio M hovel; **—s** slums
tulipán M tulip
tullido -da ADJ crippled; MF *pey* cripple
tullir VT to cripple; **—se** to become crippled
tumba F (panteón) tomb; (sepultura) grave; **soy una —** my lips are sealed
tumbar VT to knock down, to flatten; **—se** to lie down, to stretch out
tumbo M tumble, somersault; **dar —s** (persona) to stagger; (coche) to bump along
tumor M tumor; **— cerebral** brain tumor; **— maligno** malignancy
tumorectomía F lumpectomy
tumulto M (alboroto) tumult, uproar; (muchedumbre) mob
tumultuoso ADJ tumultuous
tuna F (fruta) prickly pear; *Esp* (grupo de cantantes) minstrel group
tunante -ta MF scamp
tunda F thrashing
túnel M tunnel
tunesino -na ADJ & MF Tunisian
Túnez M Tunisia
tungsteno M tungsten
túnica F tunic; **— de laboratorio** lab gown
tupido ADJ dense, compact
tupir VT (hacer tupido) to compact; (cubrir) to cover; **—se** to stuff oneself
turba F (muchedumbre) mob; (carbón fósil) peat
turbación F confusion
turbamulta F throng
turbante M turban
turbar VT to disturb; **—se** to become disturbed
turbina F turbine
turbio ADJ (pasado, secreto) dark; (agua, materia) murky
turbocompresor M turbocharger
turborreactor M turbojet
turbulencia F turbulence
turbulento ADJ turbulent
turco -ca ADJ Turkish; MF Turk; M (lengua) Turkish
turcomano -na ADJ & MF Turkmen
turismo M (actividad) tourism; (conjunto de turistas) tourists; **hacer —** to go sightseeing
turista MF tourist
turístico ADJ (relativo al turismo) tourist; **atracción turística** tourist attraction; **clase turística** coach class
Turkmenistán M Turkmenistan
turnarse VI to take turns
turno M (vuelta) turn; (de trabajo) shift; (en béisbol) at bat
turquesa F turquoise
Turquía F Turkey
turrón M nougat
tutear VT to address as "tú"
tutela F guardianship
tutelar VT to have charge of
tutor -ora MF (de un menor) guardian; M (de planta) prop
tutorial M tutorial
Tuvalu M Tuvalu
tuvaluano -na ADJ & MF Tuvaluan
tuve, tuviera, tuviese *ver* tener
tuyo ADJ & PRON POS your, yours; **el amigo —** your friend; **esto es —** this is yours
tweed M tweed

Uu

u CONJ or
ubicación F location
ubicar[30] VT (situar) to locate; (identificar) to place; **—se** to be located
ubicuo ADJ ubiquitous
ubre F udder
UCP [unidad central de proceso] F CPU
Ucrania F Ukraine
ucraniano -na ADJ & MF Ukrainian
UE [Unión Europea] F EU
ufanarse VI to glory [in], to be proud [of]
ufano ADJ proud
Uganda F Uganda
ugandés -esa ADJ & MF Ugandan
ujier M bailiff
úlcera F (lesión superficial) sore; (en el estómago) ulcer; (en la boca) canker, canker sore
ulcerar VI to ulcerate
ulceroso ADJ ulcerous
ulterior ADJ ulterior
últimamente ADV of late
ultimar VT to finalize
ultimátum M ultimatum
último ADJ (palabra, capítulo) last, final;

(destino) ultimate; (más reciente) latest; **estar en las últimas** to be on one's last legs; **la última palabra** the last word; **en los —s tiempos** lately; **en última instancia** ultimately; **a última hora** at the last moment; **por** — finally

ultrajante ADJ outrageous

ultrajar VT to outrage

ultraje M outrage, indignity

ultraligero M ultralight

ultramar LOC ADV **de** — overseas

ultramoderno ADJ ultramodern

ultrasonido M ultrasound

ultratumba LOC ADV **de** — from beyond the grave

ultravioleta ADJ & M ultraviolet

ulular VI (viento) to howl; (búho) to hoot

ululato M (viento) howling; (búho) hooting

umbral M threshold, doorstep; — **de rentabilidad** breakeven point

umbrío ADJ shady

un, uno, una ART INDEF a, an; **un hombre** a man; **un actor** an actor; **una mujer** a woman; **una manzana** an apple; NUM one; **de a** — one at a time; **es la una** it is one o'clock; PRON one; **uno por uno** one by one; **—s** some; **unos cuantos** some; **uno tiene que cuidarse** you've got to take care of yourself; **yo tengo uno** I have one; **uno tras otro** one after the other; **uno más** (tenis) let; **uno al lado del otro** side by side; **los unos a los otros / el uno al otro** one another / each other

unánime ADJ unanimous

unanimidad F unanimity

uncir [33] VT (a un buey) to yoke; (a un carro) to hitch

ungüento M ointment, salve

único ADJ (solo) only; **una única vez** a single time; (extraordinario) unique; **eres** — you're one of a kind

unidad F (indivisibilidad) unity; (ejemplar) unit; (fracción militar) unit, outfit; (de computadora) drive; — **central de proceso/procesamiento** central processing unit; — **de cuidado coronario** coronary care unit; — **de cuidados intensivos** intensive care unit; — **de disco duro** hard disk drive; — **de disquete** diskette drive; — **monetaria** currency unit

unido ADJ united; **una familia unida** a close-knit family

unificar [30] VT to unify

uniformar VT (estandarizar) to standardize; (dar uniformes) to furnish with uniforms

uniforme ADJ & M uniform

uniformidad F uniformity

unilateral ADJ unilateral

unión F (acción de unir, cosas unidas) union;

(lugar en que se unen dos cosas) junction; (indivisibilidad) unity

unir VT (una nación) to unite; (dos construcciones) to join; (cinta magnética, genes) to splice; (caños) to couple; VI/VT (con lazos) to bind

unisex ADJ INV unisex

unísono ADJ unison; **al** — in unison

unitario ADJ (partidario de la unidad) unitarian; (que tiene unidad) unitary

universal ADJ universal

universidad F (de enseñanza e investigación) university; (de enseñanza) college

universitario -ria ADJ university; (relativo a los deportes) collegiate; MF college student

universo M universe

untar VT (la piel con crema) to oil; (el pan con mantequilla) to spread on; (la cara con pintura) to smear; —**le la mano a alguien** to grease someone's palm

untuoso ADJ (graso) oily; (zalamero) slick, unctuous

uña F (de dedo) fingernail; (de gato) claw; — **encarnada** hangnail; **como** — **y carne** thick as thieves; **con** —**s y dientes** tooth and nail

uñero M hangnail

uranio M uranium

urbanidad F refinement, polish

urbanismo M (modo de vida) urbanism; (planificación) city planning

urbanización F development

urbanizar [47] VT to build up

urbano ADJ (relativo a la ciudad) urban; (refinado) suave; **autobús** — city bus

urbe F metropolis

urdimbre F warp

urdir VT (una tela) to weave; (una historia) to concoct; (un plan) to devise, to work out

uretra F urethra

urgencia F (prisa) urgency; (crisis médica) emergency; **con** — urgently; —**s** emergency room

urgente ADJ urgent, pressing

urgir [46] VT to urge; VI to be urgent

úrico ADJ uric

urinario ADJ urinary; M urinal

URL M URL

urna F (para cenizas) urn; (electoral) ballot box; **acudir a las** —**s** to go to the polls

urólogo -ga MF urologist

urraca F (ave) magpie; (persona acaparadora) packrat

urticaria F hives

Uruguay M Uruguay

uruguayo -ya ADJ & MF Uruguayan

usado ADJ (utilizado) used; (desgastado) worn

usar VT (emplear) to use; (ponerse) to wear; —**se** to be in use; **sin** — unused

USB M USB

uso M (empleo) use; (costumbre) usage, custom; **al — de la época** according to the custom of the time

usted PRON PERS you; **—es** you, you all, y'all

usual ADJ usual

usuario -ria MF (de un servicio) user; (en una biblioteca) borrower

usufructo M enjoyment

usufructuar[26] VT to enjoy the use of

usura F usury

usurero -ra MF usurer, loan shark

usurpar VT to encroach upon, to usurp

utensilio M utensil

uterino ADJ uterine

útero M uterus, womb

útil ADJ useful, helpful; M PL **—es** utensils

utilidad F usefulness, utility

utilitario ADJ utilitarian

utilización F use, utilization

utilizar[47] VT (emplear) to utilize; (explotar) to use

utopía F utopia

uva F grape

úvula F uvula

uvular ADJ uvular

Uzbekistán M Uzbekistan

uzbeko -ka ADJ & MF Uzbek

Vv

va, vamos *ver* ir

vaca F cow; **— marina** sea cow

vacación F vacation; **de vacaciones** on vacation

vacante ADJ vacant; F vacancy, opening

vaciar[28] VT (una botella) to empty; (una naranja) to hollow out; (una estatua) to cast; (una computadora) to dump

vacilación F hesitation

vacilante ADJ (dudoso) vacillating, hesitating; (tembloroso) shaky

vacilar VI to vacillate, to hesitate, to waver; **— [con]** *fam* to make fun [of]

vacío ADJ (envase) empty; (casa) vacant; (comentarios) idle; (expresión) blank; M (condición) emptiness; (lugar) void; (espacio sin aire) vacuum; **envasado al —** vacuum-packed; **hacer el —** to give the cold shoulder

vacuna F (inoculación) vaccine; (enfermedad) cowpox

vacunación F vaccination

vacunar VI/VT to vaccinate

vacuno ADJ bovine

vadear VT to ford

vado M ford, crossing

vagabundear VI to wander idly

vagabundo -da ADJ vagabond, vagrant; MF (pordiosero) tramp, bum; (trabajador errante) drifter, transient; (en la playa) beachcomber

vagancia F vagrancy

vagar[40] VI to wander, to roam

vagina F vagina

vaginal ADJ vaginal

vaginitis F vaginitis

vago -ga ADJ (idea) vague; (silueta) shadowy; (impresión) faint, vague; (persona) lazy; MF vagrant, tramp

vagón M railway car; **— restaurante** dining car

vaguedad F faintness

vahído M dizzy spell

vaho M steam

vaina F (de una espada) sheath; (de legumbres) pod, shell; (molestia) nuisance; (cosa mal recordada) thing

vainilla F vanilla

vaivén M swaying, swinging; **vaivenes** ups and downs

vajilla F tableware, dishes; **— de barro** earthenware; **— de porcelana** chinaware

vale M voucher; INTERJ oh well, OK

valedero ADJ valid

valenciano -na ADJ & MF Valencian

valentía F courage, valor, bravery

valentón -ona ADJ cocky; MF cocky person

valer[60] VT (tener un determinado valor) to be worth; VI (ser válido) to be valid; (estar permitido) to be allowed; (ser de utilidad) to be useful; **— la pena** to be worthwhile; **— más que** to outweigh; **—se de** to avail oneself of; **—se por sí mismo** to be self-sufficient; **¿cuánto vale?** how much is it? **hacer — los derechos** to assert one's rights; **hacerse —** to stand up for oneself; **le valió una paliza** that earned him a beating; **más vale solo que mal acompañado** better alone than in poor company; **no hay pero que valga** no buts about it; **más vale tarde que nunca** better late than never; **no vale ni un comino** it's not worth a hoot; **no vale** that's not fair; **¡vale!** OK! **¡válgame Dios!** gracious! **todo vale** anything goes

valeroso ADJ valorous, brave

valga, valgo *ver* valer

valía F worth

validez F validity

válido ADJ (entrada, cupón) valid; (cheque) good; (argumento) solid

valiente ADJ valiant, brave, courageous

valija F (para viajes) valise, suitcase; (para el correo) pouch

valioso ADJ valuable

valla F (en un jardín) fence; (en carreras) hurdle

vallar VT to fence

valle M valley, vale

valor M (precio) value, worth; (valentía) valor, mettle; **— contable** book value; **—es** securities; **—es en cartera** holdings; **— nominal** face value, par value; **—es respaldados por hipoteca** mortgage-backed securities; **armarse de —** to muster up one's courage

valoración F valuation

valorar VT (apreciar) to value; (determinar el valor) to appraise; (aumentar el valor) to make more valuable

valorizar[47] VT to make more valuable; **—se** to become more valuable

vals M waltz

valsar VI to waltz

valuación F valuation, appraisal

valuar[26] VT to appraise

valva F valve

válvula F valve; **— reguladora de aceleración** throttle

vampiresa F vamp

vampiro M vampire

vanagloria F boastfulness

vanagloriarse VI to boast

vanaglorioso ADJ boastful

vándalo -la MF vandal

vanguardia F vanguard; **a la —** at the forefront

vanidad F vanity, conceit

vanidoso ADJ vain

vano ADJ vain; **en —** in vain

Vanuatu M Vanuatu

vanuatuense ADJ & MF Vanuatuan

vapor M (de agua) vapor, steam; (buque) steamship; **—es** fumes; **cocer al —** to steam; **echar —** to give off steam

vapulear VT to thrash

vapuleo M thrashing

vaquería F cowshed

vaqueriza F cowshed

vaquero -ra M cowboy; **—s** blue jeans; F cowgirl; ADJ **botas vaqueras** cowboy boots

vaqueta F cowhide

vaquilla F heifer

vara F (rama) stick; (palo) rod

varadero M dry dock

varar VT to beach, to strand; VI to run aground

varear VT to whip with a stick

variable ADJ variable, changeable; F variable

variación F variation

variado ADJ varied

variante F variant

variar[28] VI/VT to vary

varicela F chicken pox

várices, varices F PL varicose veins

varicoso ADJ varicose

variedad F variety, assortment

varilla F (palo delgado) small rod; (para azotar) switch; (de paraguas) rib

vario ADJ varied; **—s** various, several

variopinto ADJ variegated

varita F wand

varón M male [person]

varonil ADJ (masculino) manly; (hombruno) mannish

vasco -ca ADJ & MF Basque; M (lengua) Basque

vascuence ADJ Basque; M (lengua) Basque

vascular ADJ vascular

vasectomía F vasectomy

vaselina F Vaseline™

vasija F vessel

vaso M (de vidrio) glass; (de papel, plástico) cup; (corto y grueso) tumbler; (sanguíneo) vessel; **— de precipitado** beaker

vástago M (de planta) shoot, sprout; (de persona) offspring; (de motor) rod

vasto ADJ vast

vataje M wattage

vaticinar VT to foretell

vaticinio M prediction

vatio M watt

vaya, vayamos, ve ver ir

vea, veamos ver ver

vecindad F (cercanía) vicinity; (barrio) neighborhood

vecindario M neighborhood

vecino -na MF (cercano, contiguo) neighbor; (residente de una zona) resident; ADJ neighboring

vector M vector

vedar VT to prohibit

vega F fertile plain

vegan ADJ & MF vegan

vegetación F vegetation

vegetal ADJ vegetable; M vegetable, plant

vegetar VI to vegetate

vegetariano -na ADJ & MF vegetarian

vehemencia F vehemence

vehemente ADJ vehement

vehículo M vehicle

veía, veíamos ver ver

veinte NUM twenty

veintena F (aproximadamente) group of [about] twenty; (exactamente) score

veinticinco NUM twenty-five

veintiuno NUM twenty-one; M (juego de naipes) blackjack

vejancón -ona M codger; F old woman

vejar VT to humiliate

vejestorio -ria M codger; F old woman

vejete M codger

vejez F old age

vejiga F (órgano) bladder; (ampolla) blister

vela F (período de vigilancia) vigil, watch; (de cera) candle; (de un navío) sail; **a toda —** under full sail; **en —** without sleep; **hacerse**

a la — to set sail

velada F (noche) evening; (fiesta) evening party

velador M nightstand

velar VI (no dormir) to keep vigil, to stay awake; (cubrir con velo) to veil; (exponer a la luz una película fotográfica) to expose; **— por** to look after

velatorio M wake

veleidoso ADJ fickle

velero M sailboat; ADJ swift-sailing

veleta F weathervane; MF fickle person

vello M (del cuerpo) body hair; (de frutas) fuzz

vellón M fleece

velloso ADJ fuzzy

velludo ADJ hairy

velo M veil; **— del paladar** soft palate

velocidad F velocity, speed; **— de transferencia** transfer rate; **a toda —** at full speed

velocímetro M speedometer

velorio M wake

veloz ADJ swift, fast

ven ver venir

vena F (vaso sanguíneo, veta) vein; (estado de ánimo) mood; (de locura) streak; **estar en —** to be in the mood, to be inspired

venado M (animal) deer; (macho) stag; (carne) venison

vencedor-ora ADJ winning; MF winner, victor

vencer[32] VT (a un enemigo) to conquer, to vanquish; (a un equipo) to defeat, to beat; (obstáculos) to overcome; (en valor, inteligencia) to surpass; VI **—se** (un plazo) to expire; (un colchón) to cave in

vencido ADJ (derrotado) defeated; (a pagar) due, overdue, past due; **darse por —** to give up, to surrender

vencimiento M (de una deuda) maturity; (de un contrato) expiration

venda F (para una herida) bandage; (sobre los ojos) blindfold

vendaje M bandage; **— quirúrgico** surgical dressing

vendar VT (una herida) to bandage; (los ojos) to blindfold

vendaval M gale

vendedor-ora MF vendor, seller, salesperson; **— mayorista** wholesaler

vender VI/VT (comercializar) to sell; (traicionar) to betray; **—se a** to go over to; **se vende** for sale

vendetta F vendetta

vendible ADJ marketable

vendimia F vintage

vendrá, vendría ver venir

veneciana F venetian blind

veneno M (sustancia dañina) poison; (ponzoña de víbora) venom

venenoso ADJ (planta) poisonous; (víbora) venomous

venerable ADJ venerable

veneración F veneration, reverence

venerar VT (a una persona) to venerate, to revere; (a Dios) to worship

venezolano -na ADJ & MF Venezuelan

Venezuela F Venezuela

venga, vengamos ver venir

vengador-ora ADJ avenging; MF avenger

venganza F vengeance, revenge, payback

vengar[40] VT to avenge; **—se de** to retaliate for, to avenge, to take revenge

vengativo ADJ vindictive, vengeful

venida F coming

venidero ADJ forthcoming

venir[61] VI to come; **— a colación** to come up [in conversation]; **— al caso / a cuento** to be relevant; **— bien** to be convenient; **—le a uno bien** to be suitable to someone; **—se abajo** to collapse; **¿a qué viene eso?** what is the point of that? **el año que viene** next year; **lo mejor está por —** the best is yet to come; **no me vengas con excusas** no excuses; **venga lo que venga** come what may

venta F sale; **— al por mayor** wholesale; **— al por menor** retail; **— de liquidación** fire sale; **en —** for sale; **poner a la —** to put up for sale

ventaja F (también en tenis) advantage; (en una carrera) head start; **— al resto** ad out; **— al saque** ad in; **— al servicio** ad in

ventajoso ADJ advantageous

ventana F window (también digital); **tirar por la —** to throw out the window

ventanal M large window

ventanilla F [de coche, avión] window; (de la nariz) nostril

ventarrón M gale, high wind

ventear VI to sniff the wind

ventilación F (aireado) ventilation; (hueco para el aire) vent

ventilado ADJ airy

ventilador M (abertura) ventilator; (aparato) electrical fan

ventilar VT to ventilate, to air out; (una cuestión) to air

ventisca F blizzard

ventisquero M (lugar ventoso) place prone to blizzards; (lugar nevado) snowfield

ventolera F gust of wind; **darle a uno la — de** to take a notion to

ventosear VI to break wind

ventoso ADJ windy, breezy

ventrículo M ventricle

venturoso ADJ fortunate; **futuro —** bright future

veo ver ver

ver[72, 74] VI/VT (un paisaje) to see; (televisión,

espectáculos) to watch; (un programa de computadora) to view; **a —** let's see; **eso aún está por —se** that is still to be seen; **no lo puedo —** I can't stand him; **no veo la hora de terminar** I'm dying / I can't wait to finish; **no tener nada que — con** not to have anything to do with; **te veo preocupado** you look worried; **a mi modo de —** in my opinion; **—se obligado a** to be obliged to; **vérselas con algo** to confront something; **vérselas negras** to have a hard time

vera LOC ADV **a la —** beside

veracidad F truthfulness

veranear VI to spend the summer

veraneo M summer vacation

veraniego ADJ summer

verano M summer

veras LOC ADV **de —** really; **¿de —?** oh really? oh yeah?

veraz ADJ truthful

verbal ADJ verbal

verbena F carnival

verbo M verb

verborrágico ADJ long-winded

verboso ADJ verbose, wordy

verdad F truth; **¿—?** really? **— a medias** half-truth; **de —** indeed; **una pistola de —** a real pistol; **faltar a la —** to fib

verdaderamente ADV really, truly

verdadero ADJ true, real

verde ADJ green (también inmaduro, sin experiencia, ecologista); (chiste) off-color; **— oliva** olive-green; **ponerse —** to stuff oneself; M green; **poner — a alguien** to run someone down

verdear VI/VT to turn green

verdín M scum

verdor M greenness

verdoso ADJ greenish

verdugo M executioner, hangman

verdugón M welt

verdulero -ra MF vegetable vendor

verdura F (hortaliza) vegetable; (verdor) *lit* verdure; **—s** produce

vereda F (en el campo) path; (para peatones) *Am* sidewalk; **entrar en —** to toe the line

veredicto M verdict

verga F yard

vergonzoso ADJ (que da vergüenza) shameful, disgraceful; (que siente vergüenza) sheepish, bashful

vergüenza F (humillación) shame; (incomodidad) embarrassment; (escándalo) disgrace; **tener —** to be ashamed; **tener — ajena** to cringe; **es una —** it's a shame; **me dan — mis dientes** I'm embarrassed about my teeth; **me da — decírtelo** I'm embarrassed to tell you

vericueto M twists and turns

verídico ADJ truthful, true

verificación F verification, cross-check

verificar[30] VT to verify, to check; **—se** to take place

verja F grate

vermú M vermouth

vernáculo ADJ & M vernacular

verruga F wart

versado ADJ versed

versalillas F PL small caps

versalitas F PL small caps

versar VI **— sobre** to deal [with], to treat

versátil ADJ versatile

versión F (de un texto) version; (traducción) translation; (de una canción) rendition; **beta** beta version; **— impresa** printout; **— original** original [of a film]

verso M line [of poetry]; **— libre** free verse; **— suelto/blanco** blank verse

versus PREP versus

vértebra F vertebra

vertebrado ADJ & M vertebrate

vertebral ADJ spinal

vertedero M dump, landfill

verter[2] VT (echar líquido) to pour; (vaciar) to pour out; (derramar) to spill; **— en** to empty into; **—se** to spill

vertical ADJ (en ángulo recto) vertical; (erguido) upright; (empinado) sheer

vertido M (acción) dumping; (lo vertido) waste; **— de petróleo** oil spill

vertiente F (pendiente) slope; (cuenca) watershed; ADJ flowing

vertiginoso ADJ dizzy, giddy

vértigo M (falta de equilibrio) vertigo; (frenesí) hectic pace

vertigoso ADJ dizzy, giddy

vesícula F gall bladder

vestíbulo M (de un edificio) vestibule, lobby; (de una casa) hallway

vestido M dress; **— de noche** evening gown; **— de novia** bridal dress

vestidura F attire

vestigio M vestige, trace, remnant

vestimenta F attire, dress; (estrafalaria) getup

vestir[9] VT to dress, to clothe; **—se** to get dressed; **—se de gala** to dress up

vestuario M (ropa) wardrobe; (en el teatro) costumes; (lugar para vestirse) changing room

veta F (de minerales) vein, seam; (de madera) grain; (de humor) strain

vetar VT to veto

veteado ADJ veined

veterano -na ADJ & MF veteran

veterinario -ria MF veterinarian; ADJ veterinary; F veterinary medicine

veto M veto

vetusto ADJ ancient

vez F time; **a la —** at the same time; **a su —** in turn; **a veces** sometimes; **cada — más** more and more; **cada — que** whenever; **de — en cuando** from time to time; **de una —** (por entero) all at once; (por fin) one and for all; **de una — por todas** once and for all; **en — de** instead of, in lieu of; **por primera —** for the first time; **otra —** again; **una — [que]** once; **una — tras otra** over and over; **una y otra —** over and over again; **raras veces** seldom; **hacer las veces de** to take the place of

vía F (camino) road; (de ferrocarril) track; (medio de acceso) avenue; **— de transmisión local** local bus; **— Láctea** Milky Way; **— navegable** waterway; **— respiratoria** airway; **—s urinarias** urinary tract; **por — de** by means of; **en —s de** in the process of; PREP via

viabilidad F viability

viable ADJ viable

viaducto M tunnel

viajante MF traveler; **— de comercio** ; M traveling salesman; F saleswoman

viajar VI (por tierra, aire) to travel, to journey; (por mar) to voyage; (con drogas) to trip

viaje M (por tierra, aire) trip, journey; (por mar) voyage; (en coche, caballo) ride; (por efecto de las drogas) trip; **— de ida y vuelta** round trip; **buen —** have a nice trip; **de —** out of town

viajero-ra MF traveler

viandante MF passerby

viático M (de viaje) per diem; (religioso) last rites

víbora F viper; **— de cascabel** rattlesnake

vibración F (de una cuerda) vibration; (de la lengua) trill

vibrador M vibrator

vibrante ADJ vibrating

vibrar VI/VT to vibrate

vicegobernador-ora MF lieutenant governor

vicepresidente MF, **vicepresidenta** F vice president

vicerrector-ora MF provost

viceversa ADV vice versa

viciado ADJ (aire) stale; (costumbre) stuffy; (corrupto) foul

viciar VT (estropear) to foul; (corromper) to corrupt

vicio M (mala costumbre) vice, bad habit; **de —** unjustifiably; **quitarse el — de** to wean oneself of

vicioso ADJ (persona) dissolute; (gasto) unjustifiable; (gramática) faulty

vicisitud F vicissitude

víctima F (de un crimen) victim; (en un accidente) casualty, victim

victimizar[47] VT to victimize

victoria F victory

victorioso ADJ victorious

vid F vine, grapevine

vida F life; **— media** half-life; **— mía** sweetheart; **— nocturna** nightlife; **— sentimental** love life; **así es la —** that's life; **de toda la —** lifelong; **de — o muerte** life-and-death; **en la — voy a hacer eso** I would never do that; **esto es —** this is the life; **ganarse la —** to earn a living; **sin —** lifeless

vidente MF seer; ADJ seeing

vídeo, video M (aparato) VCR; (técnica) video; (cinta) videocassette

videocámara F camcorder

videocasete F videocassette

videoclip M videoclip

videoconferencia F videoconference

videoconsola F video console

videojuego M video game

vidriado M glaze; ADJ glazed

vidriar VT to glaze

vidriera F show window

vidriero-ra MF glazier, glassmaker

vidrio M (sustancia) glass; (en una ventana) pane; **pagar los —s rotos** to be left holding the bag

vidrioso ADJ glassy

vieira F scallop

viejo-ja ADJ old; (chiste) stale; M (anciano) old man; (padre) father; **— amigo** longtime friend; **— verde** dirty old man; **los —s** the old folks; F (anciana) old woman; (madre) mother

viento M wind; **hace —** it is windy; **a los cuatro —s** in all directions

vientre M (abdomen) abdomen; (barriga) belly; (útero) womb

viernes M Friday

Vietnam M Vietnam

vietnamita ADJ & MF INV Vietnamese

viga F (de madera) beam, rafter; (de metal) girder

vigencia F **entrar en —** to go into effect; **estar en —** to be in force

vigente ADJ effective, in force

vigésimo NUM twentieth

vigía F lookout, reef; MF lookout

vigilancia F (cuidado) vigilance; (en una tienda) surveillance

vigilante ADJ vigilant; M watchman; F watchwoman

vigilar VI/VT to keep watch [over]; VT to keep an eye on; (policía) to stake out

vigilia F vigil, watch

vigor M vigor; **en —** in force; **entrar en —** to become effective

vigorizar[47] VT to invigorate

vigoroso ADJ vigorous

VIH [virus de inmunodeficiencia humana] M HIV

vil ADJ vile, base, low

vileza F villainy, baseness

vilipendiar VT to revile

villa F (aldea) village; (casa) country house

villancico M Christmas carol

villanía F villainy

villano -na ADJ villainous; MF villain

vilo LOC ADV **en —** (en el aire) suspended; (en ascuas) in suspense

vinagre M vinegar

vinculación F connection

vincular VT to link (también para páginas web); **—se** to link up

vínculo M link, tie; (en la web) link

vindicar[30] VT to vindicate

vine, viniendo, viniera, viniese ver venir

vinilo M vinyl

vino M wine; **— blanco** white wine; **— espumoso** sparkling wine; **— rosado** rosé wine; **— tinto** red wine

viña F vineyard

viñatero -ra MF winegrower

viñedo M vineyard

viola F viola

violación F (de la ley) violation, infringement; (sexual) rape

violado ADJ & M violet

violar VT (una ley) to violate, to break; (una mujer) to rape, to ravish; (una promesa) to breach; (una cerradura) to pick; (derechos) to infringe upon; (mandamientos) to trespass against

violencia F violence; **— doméstica** domestic violence

violentar VT (a una persona) to manhandle; (una casa) to break into; **—se** to get mortified

violento ADJ (deporte, tratamiento) violent, rough; (marido) abusive; (entrada) forcible; (ataque) vicious

violeta ADJ & M violet

violín M (para música clásica) violin; (para música folclórica) fiddle

violinista MF violinist

violonchelo M cello

VIP M VIP

virada F veer

viraje M swerve

viral ADJ viral

virar VI/VT (vehículo) to swerve, to veer; VI (barco) to tack

virgen ADJ & MF virgin; ADJ (cassette) blank; (selva) undisturbed

virginal ADJ virginal

viril ADJ virile, manly

virilidad F virility, manliness

virología F virology

virreinato M viceroyalty

virrey M viceroy

virtual ADJ virtual

virtud F (moral) virtue; (práctica) asset

virtuosismo M virtuosity

virtuoso -sa ADJ (moral) virtuous; ADJ & MF (artístico) virtuoso

viruela F smallpox

virulento ADJ virulent

virus M virus (también de computadoras); **— de inmunodeficiencia humana** human immunodeficiency virus

viruta F wood shaving

visa F visa

visado M visa

visar VT to endorse

visceral ADJ visceral

viscoso ADJ viscous

visera F visor

visibilidad F visibility

visible ADJ visible

visigodo -da ADJ Visigothic; MF Visigoth

visillo M window shade

visión F (capacidad de ver, lo visto) vision; (persona fea) sight; **— en túnel** tunnel vision

visionario -ria ADJ & M visionary

visita F (acción de visitar) visit; (persona) visitor, caller; (a un edificio) tour; (en una página web) hit; **— de médico** house call

visitación F visitation

visitador -ora MF visitor, caller; (inspector) inspector; (vendedor de medicamentos) pharmaceutical sales representative

visitante MF caller, visitor; ADJ visiting (también en fútbol)

visitar VT (a un amigo, país) to visit; (a un paciente) to make a house call

vislumbrar VT to make out

viso M slip

visón M mink

víspera LOC ADV **en —s de** on the eve of

vista F (panorama) view, vista; (visión) eyesight; **a la —** in sight; **— cansada** eye strain; **a primera —** at first sight; **a simple —** with the naked eye; **bajar la —** to lower one's eyes; **conocer de —** to know by sight; **con —s a** with a view to; **en — de** considering; **hacer la —gorda** to look the other way; **¡hasta la —!** good-bye; **perder de —** to lose sight of; **tener a la —** to have before one's eyes; **tener — a** to look out on

vistazo M glance, glimpse, look; **dar/echar un — a** to glance over

visto ADJ **bien —** well thought of; **mal —** looked down upon; **— que** whereas; M **— bueno** approval; **dar el —bueno** to approve

visto ver ver

vistoso ADJ showy

visual ADJ visual

visualizador M display

visualizar[47] VT (en la imaginación) to visualize; (en pantalla) to display

vital ADJ vital; **fuerzas —es** life force

vitalicio ADJ life, for life; M lifetime pension

vitalidad F vitality

vitamina F vitamin

viticultor -ora MF winegrower

vítor M cheer

vitorear VI/VT to cheer

vitral M stained-glass window

vitrina F (ventana) shop window; (armario) showcase

vituperación F vituperation

vituperar VT to revile

vituperio M vituperation

viudo -da M widower; F widow; **viuda negra** black widow spider

vivacidad F vivacity

vivaracho ADJ vivacious

vivaz ADJ vivacious, lively

víveres M PL provisions

vivero M nursery

viveza F (vivacidad) liveliness; (inteligencia) cleverness

vívido ADJ vivid

vivienda F (casa) dwelling; (alojamiento) housing; **— unifamiliar** single-family home

viviente ADJ living

vivir VI/VT to live; **vive una vida normal** he leads a normal life; **vivieron felices y comieron perdices** they lived happily ever after; **¡viva!** hurrah! **¡viva el rey!** long live the king!

vivisección F vivisection

vivo ADJ (viviente) alive, living; (ágil) lively; (vistoso, intenso) vivid; (listo) clever; **en —** before a live audience; **en — y en directo** live; **de viva voz** by word of mouth

vocablo M word

vocabulario M vocabulary

vocación F (profesional) vocation, calling; (religioso) call

vocal ADJ (de la voz) vocal; (no consonántico) vowel; F vowel; MF member

vocálico ADJ vocalic

vocear VI/VT (gritar) to cry out; (anunciar) to page

vocerío M clamor

vocero -ra MF spokesperson

vociferante ADJ vociferous

vociferar VI to clamor

vodevil M vaudeville

vodka M vodka

volado ADJ (drogado) high; (escrito arriba) superscript

volador ADJ flying

volante ADJ flying; M (en un vestido) ruffle, frill; (en un coche) steering wheel; (en un motor) flywheel; (folleto) leaflet, handbill

volar[5] VI/VT to fly; **— por su cuenta** to fly solo; **ir volando** to hurry; VT (un puente) to blow up; VI (hojas) to blow; **—se** (hacer explosión) to blow up; (enojarse) to lose one's temper; (irse volando) to fly away

volátil ADJ volatile

volcada F **hacer una —** (baloncesto) to dunk the ball

volcán M volcano

volcánico ADJ volcanic

volcar[31] VT (voltear) to tip over, to knock over; (derramar) to spill; (vaciar) to empty; VI to roll over; **—se** (un coche) to tip over, to overturn; (en baloncesto) to dunk

volea F (en vóleibol) volley; (en béisbol) fly ball; (en tenis) volley

volear VI/VT to volley

voleibol, vóleibol M volleyball

volición F volition

volqueta F *Am* dump truck

volquete M dump truck

voltaje M voltage

voltear VT (una lámpara) to knock over, to turn over; (la cara) to turn away

voltereta F somersault, tumble; **dar una —** to somersault; **dar —s** to tumble

voltio M volt

voluble ADJ (malhumorado) moody; (mercado de valores) volatile

volumen M volume

voluminoso ADJ voluminous, bulky

voluntad F will; **a —** at will; **buena —** good will, willingness; **mala —** ill will; **por su propia —** of his own volition

voluntario -ria ADJ voluntary; MF volunteer

voluntarioso ADJ (bien dispuesto) willing; (testarudo) willful

voluptuoso ADJ voluptuous

voluta F scroll; **—s de humo** spirals of smoke

volver[6, 74] VI (regresar al punto de partida) to return, to come back; (ir de nuevo) to return, to go back, to go again; **— a comer** to eat again; **— del revés** to turn inside out; **— en sí** to regain consciousness; **—se** (regresar) to go back; (ponerse) to become; **—se contra** to turn against; **—se atrás** to turn back; **—se hacia** to go toward; **—se loco** to go crazy; VT (la cara) to turn away; (la página) to turn; **— las espaldas** to turn one's back

vomitar VI/VT to vomit, to throw up

vómito M vomit

voraz ADJ voracious, ravenous

vórtice M vortex

vos PRON *fam RP, Am Central* you

vosotros -as PRON PERS *Esp* you, you guys; (sur de EEUU) you all, y'all

votación F voting

votante MF voter

votar VI (emitir el voto) to vote; VT (elegir) to vote for; (aprobar) to vote into law; — **a/por** to vote for; — **a favor** to vote in favor; — **en contra** to vote against; — **es un deber importante** voting is an important duty

voto M (opinión) vote; (promesa) vow; — **de confianza** vote of confidence

voy ver ir

voz F (sonido, aptitud, voto) voice; (en un diccionario) headword; **a — en cuello** at the top of one's lungs; **alzar la —** to raise one's voice; **correr la —** to be rumored; **en — alta** aloud; **en — baja** quietly, softly; **a voces** shouting; **dar voces** to shout

vozarrón M loud voice

vudú M voodoo

vuela, vuele ver volar

vuelco M **dar un —** to overturn, to turn over; **todo daría un —** everything would change radically; **me dio un — el corazón** my heart skipped a beat

vuelo M (en avión) flight; (de una falda) flare; **al — en** on the fly; **de alto —** prestigious; **levantar/alzar el —** to fly away

vuelta F (movimiento circular) turn; (regreso, devolución) return; (carrera ciclista) tour; (en una pista) lap; (curva) twist; (de un collar) loop; (en deportes) round; (dinero) change; — **de tuerca** unforeseen event; **a la — de la esquina** around the corner; **a — de correo** by return mail; **dar —** to turn upside down; **dar — al revés** to turn inside out; **dar — a una página / una llave** to turn a page / a key; **dar —s** to spin; **dar —s en la cama** to toss and turn; **dar — a algo** to turn something upside down; **dar la —** to turn around; **dar una —** to take a walk, to take a spin; **darse —** to roll over; **estar de — (**de regreso) to be back; (desencantado) to be jaded; **me da —s la cabeza** my head is spinning; **no tiene —s de hoja** there are no two ways about it

vuelto M *Am* change

vuelto, vuelva, vuelve ver volver

vuestro ADJ POS *Esp* — **hermano** your brother; **un amigo —** a friend of yours; PRON **el —** yours

vulgar ADJ (común) ordinary; (tosco) vulgar

vulgaridad F vulgarity

vulgo M common people

vulnerable ADJ vulnerable

Ww

wafle M waffle

waflera F waffle iron

wáter M toilet

web F web, Internet, World Wide Web

whisky M whisk[e]y; — **escocés** scotch

wifi [fidelidad inalámbrica] F Wi-Fi™

windsurf M windsurfing

wok M wok

Xx

xenofobia F xenophobia

xilofón, xilófono M xylophone

Yy

y CONJ and

ya ADV (desde antes) already; (ahora) now; (pronto) soon; ¡—! enough! — **era hora** it was about time; ¡— **lo creo!** I should say so! — **no** no longer; — **que** since; — **sea que** whether; — **te arreglo** I'll fix you; — **verás** mark my words; — **voy** I am coming

yacer[37] VI to lie

yacimiento M (de minerales) deposit; (de petróleo) field

yanqui ADJ & MF *pey* American

yapa F freebie

yarda F yard (también en fútbol americano)

yate M yacht

yegua F mare

yelmo M helmet

yema F (de huevo) egg yolk; (de una planta) bud, shoot; — **de huevo** egg yolk; — **del dedo** fingertip

Yemen M Yemen

yemení ADJ & MF Yemeni

yen M yen

yendo ver ir

yerba ver hierba

yermo ADJ (estéril) barren; (desolado) bleak, stark

yerno M son-in-law

yesca F tinder

yeso M (mineral) gypsum; (en construcción, medicina) plaster [of Paris]; (escayola) cast

Yibuti M Djibouti

yibutiano-na ADJ & MF Djiboutian

yo PRON PERS I; M (ego) ego

yodo M iodine

yoduro M iodide

yoga M yoga

yogur M yogurt

yo-yo M yo-yo
yuan M yuan
yuca F (ornamental) yucca; (comestible) manioc
yudo M judo
yugo M yoke
Yugoslavia F Yugoslavia
yugoslavo -va ADJ & MF Yugoslavian
yugular ADJ & F jugular
yunque M anvil
yunta F yoke
yuppie MF yuppie
yuxtaponer[56, 74] VT juxtapose

Zz

zacate M grass (también en tenis)
zafar VT to release; —**se** (soltarse) to slip off; (no cumplir) to cop out; —**se de un aprieto** to squirm out of a difficulty
zafio ADJ boorish
zafiro M sapphire
zafra F [sugar] harvest
zaga LOC ADV **a la —** behind; F **ir a la —** to be behind; **quedar a la —** to fall behind
zaguán M vestibule, hall
zaino ADJ chestnut-colored
zalamería F (tacto) smoothness; (lisonja) flattery
zalamero -ra MF flatterer; ADJ (empalagoso) smooth, unctuous; (lisonjero) flattering
Zambia F Zambia
zambiano -na ADJ & MF Zambian
zambo ADJ knock-kneed
zambullida F dive, plunge
zambullir[16] VT to plunge, to dip; —**se** to dive, to plunge
zanahoria F carrot
zanca F leg of a wading bird
zancada F stride; **dar —s** to stride
zancadilla F intentional tripping; **hacer una —** to trip
zanco M stilt
zancudo ADJ long-legged, lanky; M *Am* mosquito
zángano M drone (también holgazán)
zangolotear VI/VT to jiggle
zangoloteo M jiggle
zanja F ditch, trench
zanjar VT to settle
zapapico M pickax[e]
zapata F brake shoe
zapatear VI to tap the feet in dancing
zapateo M tapping with the feet in dance
zapatería F shoe store
zapatero -ra MF (fabricante) shoemaker;

(vendedor) shoe dealer; (remendón) cobbler
zapatilla F (pantufla) slipper; (de vestir) pump; —**s** sneakers
zapato M shoe; —**s con tacos** (fútbol americano) cleats; —**s con tapones** (fútbol) cleats; —**s del mismo par** matching shoes
zar M czar
zarandear VT to jiggle; —**se** to flop around
zarandeo M jiggle
zarcillo M (arete) earring; (de planta) tendril
zarigüeya F opossum
zarpa F claw
zarpar VI to sail, to set sail
zarpazo M blow with a claw; **dar —s** to claw
zarza F bramble, briar
zarzamora F blackberry
zepelín M blimp, zeppelin
zigoto M zygote
zigzag M zigzag
zigzaguear VI to zigzag, to weave one's way
Zimbabue M Zimbabwe
zimbabuo -bua ADJ & MF Zimbabwean
zirconio M zirconium
zócalo M baseboard; *Méx* main square
zodíaco M zodiac
zombi M zombie
zona F (área) zone; (culebrilla) shingles; — **de anotación/ensayo** (fútbol americano) end zone; — **de calentamiento** (béisbol) bullpen; — **de strike** (béisbol) strike zone; — **gris** gray area; — **tampón** buffer zone
zonificación F zoning
zonzo ADJ silly, foolish
zoo M zoo
zoología F zoology
zoológico ADJ zoological; M zoo
zoom M (de cámara fotográfica) zoom lens; (de computadora) zoom
zopenco -ca MF dolt, numbskull
zorrillo M skunk
zorro -a MF (animal) fox; F (hembra) vixen; ADJ (astuto) foxy, cunning
zorzal M thrush
zozobra F anxiety, worry
zozobrar VI to founder
zueco M clog
zumbar VI (hacer sonidos los insectos) to buzz, to drone, to hum; (hacer ruido las máquinas) to whir, to whiz; (tintinear los oídos) to ring; (dar golpe) to sock
zumbido M (sonido de insectos) buzz, drone, hum; (sonido de máquina) whir, whiz; (sonido en los oídos) ring
zumo M fruit juice
zurcido M (remiendo) darn; (acción de remendar) darning
zurcir[33] VT to darn
zurdo -da ADJ left-handed, southpaw; MF *fam* southpaw

zuro M corncob

zurra F whipping

zurrar VT to whip, to thrash

zutano -na M so-and-so, what's-his-name; F so-and-so, what's-her-name

Inglés–Español · English–Spanish

Lista de abreviaturas / List of Abbreviations

adj	adjetivo	adjective
adv	adverbio, adverbial	adverb, adverbial
Am	América	America
art	artículo	article
Carib	Caribe	Caribbean
conj	conjunción	conjunction
def	definido	definite
dem	demostrativo	demonstrative
f	femenino	feminine
fam	familiar	familiar
indef	indefinido	indefinite
interj	interjección	interjection
interr	interrogativo	interrogative
inv	invariable	invariable
lit	literario	literary
loc	locución	locution
m	masculino	masculine
Mex	México	Mexico
n	sustantivo	noun
num	numeral	numeral
pej, pey	peyorativo	pejorative
pl	plural	plural
poss	posesivo	possessive
prep	preposición, preposicional	preposition, prepositional
pron	pronombre	pronoun
rel	relativo	relative
RP	Río de la Plata	River Plate
sg	singular	singular
Sp	España, español	Spain, Spanish
v aux	verbo auxiliar	auxiliary verb
vi	verbo intransitivo	intransitive verb
vt	verbo transitivo	transitive verb
vulg	vulgar	vulgar

Pronunciación inglesa

I. VOCALES

Símbolo fonético	Ortografía inglesa	Explicación
[i]	see, pea	como la *i* en hilo
[ɪ]	bit	el sonido más aproximado es la *i* en *virtud*, pero la [ɪ] inglesa es más abierta, tirando a *e*
[e]	late, they	equivale aproximadamente a *ei*
[ɛ]	set	semejante a la *e* de *perro*, pero más abierta
[ɝ]	work, bird	como la *u* de *cud* (ver abajo) pero articulada simultáneamente con una *r*
[æ]	sat	sonido intermedio entre *e* y *a*
[ɑ]	hot	como la vocal de *pan*
[ɔ]	saw, laud	sonido intermedio entre *a* y *o*
[o]	low, mode	equivale aproximadamente a *ou*
[ʊ]	book, pull	como la *u* de *turrón*, pero más abierta
[u]	June, moon	como la *u* de *uno*
[ʌ]	cud	una *e* muy relajada
[ə]	adept	una *e* muy relajada y átona
[ɚ]	teacher	una *e* átona relajada articulada simultáneamente con una *r*

II. DIPTONGOS

Símbolo fonético	Ortografía inglesa	Explicación
[aɪ]	pie, aisle	como *ai* en *aire*
[aʊ]	now, foul	como *au* en *causa*
[ɔɪ]	boy	como *oy* en *hoy*
[ju]	use	como *iu* en *ciudad*

III. CONSONANTES

Símbolo fonético	Ortografía inglesa	Explicación
[b]	bat	semejante a la *b* española
[d]	day	semejante a la *d* española, pero articulada en los alvéolos y con más tensión
[f]	fun, photo	como la *f* española

[g]	go	como la *g* de *goma*, pero con más tensión
[h]	hat	muy suave como la *j* de los dialectos caribeños del español
[j]	year	como la *i* del diptongo de *hielo*
[k]	cat, kill	como la *c* de *carro*, pero seguida de aspiración en posición inicial de sílaba (sobre todo tónica)
[l]	let	como la *l* de *lado*
[ɫ]	ball	como la *l* final catalana
[m]	much	como la *m* española
[n]	no	como la *n* española
[p]	pea	como la *p* española, pero seguida de aspiración en posición inicial de sílaba (sobre todo tónica)
[r]	red	no tiene equivalente en español; se pronuncia con la punta de la lengua enrollada hacia arriba, sin tocar el paladar
[s]	sea	como la *s* hispanoamericana (no la castellana)
[t]	tea	como la *t* española pero articulada en los alvéolos y seguida de aspiración en posición inicial de sílaba (sobre todo tónica)
[v]	very	se articula con los dientes incisivos superiores colocados en el labio inferior
[w]	weed	equivale a la *u* del diptongo de *fui*
[z]	zero, rose	como la *s* de *mismo* cuando se sonoriza, pero aun más sonora
[ɒ]	latter, ladder	como la *r* de *para*
[θ]	thin	como la *z* del español castellano en *zagal*
[ð]	this	como la *d* de *cada*
[ʃ]	sheet, machine, notation	una *s* muy palatal como en francés *chapeau* o italiano *lasciare*
[ʒ]	measure, beige	como la *ll* argentina en *valle*, cuando es sonora
[tʃ]	church	como la *ch* de *charla*
[ʤ]	judge	como la *y* de *inyectar*
[ṇ]	eaten, button	representa la *n* silábica, articulada sin la vocal anterior
[ŋ]	ring	como la *n* española en *mango* y *banco*
[ḷ]	rental	representa la *l* silábica, articulada como la *l* final catalana
[hw]	where	combinación de los sonidos [h] y [w] arriba descritos

Notas sobre gramática inglesa

El sustantivo

Género. En la gramática inglesa el género solo desempeña un papel importante en el sistema pronominal, p. ej. **he runs** 'él corre', **she runs** 'ella corre', **I see him** 'lo veo', **I see her** 'la veo'. En los sustantivos que designan a personas, se emplean varios métodos para distinguir entre los sexos, v. gr. el agregado de un sufijo, como en **actor** 'actor', **actress** 'actriz', el agregado de una palabra, como en **baby boy** 'niño', **baby girl** 'niña', **she-bear** 'osa', **male nurse** 'enfermero', o el uso de palabras completamente distintas, como en **uncle** 'tío', **aunt** 'tía'.

Número. Generalmente se forma el plural añadiendo **-s** al singular: **paper, papers** 'papel, papeles', **book, books** 'libro, libros', **chief, chiefs** 'jefe, jefes'.

Los sustantivos que terminan en **-ss, -x, -sh, -z** y **-o** añaden **-es** para formar el plural: **kiss, kisses** 'beso, besos', **box, boxes** 'caja, cajas', **dish, dishes** 'plato, platos', **buzz, buzzes** 'zumbido, zumbidos', **hero, heroes** 'héroe, héroes' (excepción: **piano, pianos**). Esto vale también para **-ch** cuando se pronuncia [č], como en **arch, arches** 'arco, arcos', pero no cuando se pronuncia [k], como en **monarch, monarchs** 'monarca, monarcas'.

Los sustantivos que terminan en **-fe**, y ciertos sustantivos que terminan en **-f**, cambian estas letras en **v** y añaden **-es** en el plural: **leaf, leaves** 'hoja, hojas', **life, lives** 'vida, vidas', **wife, wives** 'esposa, esposas', **knife, knives** 'cuchillo, cuchillos' (pero **reef, reefs** 'arrecife, arrecifes').

Para formar el plural de los sustantivos terminados en **-y** precedida de consonante se cambia la **-y** en **-ies**: **fly, flies** 'mosca, moscas', **family, families** 'familia, familias'. En cambio, los sustantivos terminados en **-y** precedida de vocal forman el plural añadiendo **-s** al singular: **day, days** 'día, días'.

Ciertos sustantivos forman el plural de una manera irregular: **man, men** 'hombre, hombres', **woman, women** 'mujer, mujeres', **mouse, mice** 'ratón, ratones', **louse, lice** 'piojo, piojos', **goose, geese** 'ganso, gansos', **tooth, teeth** 'diente, dientes', **foot, feet** 'pie, pies', **ox, oxen** 'buey, bueyes'.

Ciertos sustantivos que terminan en **-is** forman el plural cambiando la **i** de la terminación en **e**: **axis, axes** 'eje, ejes', **crisis, crises** 'crisis' (sg., pl.).

El adjetivo

El adjetivo inglés es invariable en cuanto a género y número. Normalmente se coloca delante del sustantivo: **an interesting woman** 'una mujer interesante', **a large man** 'un hombre grande', **beautiful birds** 'aves hermosas'.

Los comparativos y superlativos. Aunque no hay una regla general, por lo común los adjetivos monosílabos, los adjetivos acentuados en la última sílaba y algunos bisílabos comunes forman el comparativo de aumento y el superlativo añadiendo **-er** y **-est** (como **tall**). Los demás adjetivos van precedidos de **more** (para el comparativo) y **most** (para el superlativo) (como **careful**). Nótese que (1) si la palabra termina en **-e** muda, se añaden **-r** y **-st** en vez de **-er** y **-est** (ver **wise**), (2) los adjetivos terminados en **-y** cambian esta letra en **i** (ver **happy**), (3) los adjetivos terminados en consonante (menos **r**) precedida de vocal doblan la consonante (ver **fat**):

Positivo	Comparativo	Superlativo
tall alto	**taller** más alto	**the tallest** el más alto
careful cuidadoso	**more careful** más cuidadoso	**the most careful** el más cuidadoso
wise sabio	**wiser** más sabio	**the wisest** el más sabio
happy feliz	**happier** más feliz	**the happiest** el más feliz
fat gordo	**fatter** más gordo	**the fattest** el más gordo

Los adjetivos siguientes forman el comparativo y el superlativo de una manera irregular:

good	better	best
bad, ill	worse	worst
much	more	most

El adverbio

Muchos adverbios se forman añadiendo **-ly** al adjetivo: **courteous** 'cortés', **courteously** 'cortésmente', **bold** 'atrevido', **boldly** 'atrevidamente'. Existen las irregularidades ortográficas siguientes en la formación de los adverbios que terminan en **-ly:** (1) los adjetivos terminados en **-ble** cambian la **-e** en **-y: possible, possibly**, (2) los terminados en **-ic** añaden **-ally: poetic, poetically**, (3) los terminados en **-ll** añaden solo **-y: full, fully**, (4) los terminados en **-ue** pierden la **-e** final: **true, truly**, (5) los terminados en **-y** cambian la **-y** en **i: happy, happily**.

La mayor parte de los adverbios forman el comparativo y el superlativo con los adverbios **more** 'más' y **most** 'el/la más'. Asimismo los adverbios monosílabos añaden **-er** y **-est:**

Positivo	Comparativo	Superlativo
boldly	more boldly	most boldly
generously	more generously	most generously
soon	sooner	soonest
early	earlier	earliest
late	later	latest
fast	faster	fastest

Los adverbios siguientes forman el comparativo y el superlativo de una manera irregular:

well	better	best
badly	worse	worst
little	less	least
far	farther, further	farthest, furthest

Sufijos comunes del inglés

-dom a partir de bases nominales, forma sustantivos con los sentidos de dominio, jurisdicción, estado, condición: **kingdom** 'reino' (**king** 'rey'), **martyrdom** 'martirio' (**martyr** 'mártir'), **freedom** 'libertad' (**free** 'libre')

-ee a partir de verbos, forma sustantivos indicando a la persona que recibe una acción: **addressee** 'destinatario' (**to address** 'dirigir'), **employee** 'empleado' (**to employ** 'emplear').

-eer a partir de bases diversas, forma sustantivos que denotan oficio u ocupación: **auctioneer** 'subastador' (**to auction** 'subastar'), **puppeteer** 'titiritero' (**puppet** 'títere')

-en *a.* forma adjetivos que denotan la sustancia de que está hecha una cosa: **golden** 'dorado' (**gold** 'oro'), **wooden** 'de madera' (**wood** 'madera')
    b. forma verbos a partir de adjetivos: **to whiten** 'blanquear' (**white** 'blanco'), **to darken** 'oscurecer' (**dark** 'oscuro')

-er *a.* forma sustantivos a partir de verbos para indicar agente: **player** 'jugador' (**to play** 'jugar'), **speaker** 'hablante' (**to speak** 'hablar'), **baker** 'panadero' (**to bake** 'hornear')
    b. forma sustantivos a partir de sustantivos para denominar al residente de un lugar: **New Yorker** 'neoyorquino' (**New York** 'Nueva York'), **islander** 'isleño' (**island** 'isla')

-ess se usa para formar el género femenino de ciertos sustantivos: **princess** 'princesa' (**prince** 'príncipe'), **countess** 'condesa' (**count** 'conde')

-fold indica el número de veces que se repite algo: **twofold** 'dos veces' (**two** 'dos'), **hundredfold** 'cien veces' (**hundred** 'cien')

-ful *a.* forma adjetivos a partir de sustantivos para indicar la presencia de una cualidad: **hopeful** 'esperanzado' (**hope** 'esperanza'), **careful** 'cuidadoso' (**care** 'cuidado'), **willful** 'voluntarioso' (**will** 'voluntad')
    b. forma adjetivos a partir de verbos para indicar tendencia: **forgetful** 'olvidadizo' (**to forget** 'olvidar')

c. forma sustantivos a partir de sustantivos indicando la capacidad: **handful** 'puñado' (**hand** 'mano'), **spoonful** 'cucharada' (**spoon** 'cuchara')

-hood   forma abstractos a partir de sustantivos concretos: **motherhood** 'maternidad' (**mother** 'madre'), **childhood** 'niñez' (**child** 'niño'), **likelihood** 'probabilidad' (**likely** 'probable')

-ing   a.   forma adjetivos a partir de verbos: **running water** 'agua corriente' (**to run** 'correr'), **drinking water** 'agua potable' (**to drink** 'beber'), **waiting room** 'sala de espera' (**to wait** 'esperar'), **washing machine** 'máquina lavadora' (**to wash** 'lavar')

      b.   se usa para formar sustantivos que expresan la acción de un verbo: **understanding** 'entendimiento' (**to understand** 'entender'), **supplying** 'abastecimiento' (**to supply** 'abastecer')

      c.   se usa para formar sustantivos que denominan una cosa que desempeña una acción: **clothing** 'ropa' (**to clothe** 'vestir'), **covering** 'cobertura' (**to cover** 'cubrir')

-ish   forma adjetivos a partir de sustantivos indicando semejanza o atenuación: **boyish** 'como un niño' (**boy** 'niño'), **womanish** 'como mujer, mujeril' (**woman** 'mujer'), **whitish** 'blancuzco' (**white** 'blanco')

-less   se agrega a sustantivos para indicar falta de algo: **childless** 'sin hijos' (**child** 'hijo'), **penniless** 'sin dinero' (**penny** 'centavo'), **endless** 'interminable, sin fin' (**end** 'fin')

-like   se añade a sustantivos para indicar semejanza: **lifelike** 'que parece vivo' (**life** 'vida'), **childlike** 'infantil' (**child** 'niño'), **tigerlike** 'como un tigre' (**tiger** 'tigre')

-ly   a.   se añade a adjetivos para formar adverbios: **slowly** 'lentamente' (**slow** 'lento'), **happily** 'felizmente' (**feliz** 'happy')

      b.   deriva adjetivos a partir de sustantivos indicando una cualidad: **motherly** 'maternal' (**mother** 'madre'), **gentlemanly** 'caballeroso' (**gentleman** 'caballero'), **friendly** 'amistoso' (**friend** 'amigo')

      c.   deriva adjetivos o adverbios de tiempo a partir de sustantivos: **daily** 'diario', 'diariamente' (**day** 'día'), **weekly** 'semanal', 'semanalmente' (**week** 'semana')

-ness   forma nombres de cualidades a partir de adjetivos: **goodness** 'bondad' (**good** 'bueno'), **darkness** 'oscuridad' (**dark** 'oscuro'), **foolishness** 'tontería' (**fool** 'tonto')

-ship	se emplea para derivar sustantivos a partir de sustantivos y verbos para denotar

    a.   cualidades abstractas: **friendship** 'amistad' (**friend** 'amigo')

    b.   arte o destreza: **horsemanship** 'equitación' (**horseman** 'jinete')

    c.   dignidad, oficio, cargo o título: **professorship** 'cátedra' (**professor** 'catedrático'), **lordship** 'señoría' (**lord** 'señor')

    d.   la duración de una acción: **courtship** 'cortejo' (**to court** 'cortejar')

-some	se añade a verbos para formar adjetivos que expresan tendencia excesiva: **tiresome** 'aburrido' (**to tire** 'aburrir'), **quarrelsome** 'pendenciero' (**to quarrel** 'discutir')
-th	es el sufijo que forma números ordinales a partir de los cardinales: **fifth** 'quinto' (**five** 'cinco'), **tenth** 'décimo' (**ten** 'diez')
-ward	se añade a sustantivos y adverbios para indicar movimiento hacia un lugar: **homeward** 'hacia casa' (**home** 'casa'), **downward** 'hacia abajo' (**down** 'abajo')
-wise, **-ways**	se añaden a sustantivos para indicar dirección o posición: **edgewise** 'de lado' (**edge** 'borde'), **lengthwise** 'a lo largo' (**length** 'largo'), **sideways** 'de lado' (**side** 'lado')

-y

    a.   es un sufijo diminutivo: **doggy** 'perrito' (**dog** 'perro'), **Johnny** 'Juanito' (**John** 'Juan')

    b.   se añade a sustantivos para formar adjetivos que indican abundancia: **rocky** 'rocoso' (**rock** 'roca'), **rainy** 'lluvioso' (**rain** 'lluvia'), **hairy** 'peludo' (**hair** 'pelo'), **angry** 'enojado' (**anger** 'enojo')

    c.   se añade a sustantivos para formar adjetivos que expresan semejanza: **rosy** 'rosado' (**rose** 'rosa')

Verbos irregulares de la lengua inglesa

Se denominan verbos irregulares los que no forman el pretérito o el participio pasivo con la adición de **-d** o **-ed** al presente. Obsérvese que en ciertos verbos (aquí señalados con asterisco) coexiste la forma regular al lado de la irregular. Las formas poco usadas aparecen entre paréntesis.

Presente	Pretérito	Participio pasivo
*abide	(abode)	abided
am, is, are	was, were	been
arise	arose	arisen
*awake	awoke	awoken

Presente	*Pretérito*	*Participio pasivo*
bear	bore	borne
beat	beat	beaten
become	became	become
befall	befell	befallen
beget	begat	begotten
begin	began	begun
behold	beheld	beheld
bend	bent	bent
*beseech	(besought)	(besought)
beset	beset	beset
bet	bet	bet
bid 'ofrecer'	bid	bid
bid 'mandar'	bade	bidden
bind	bound	bound
bite	bit	bitten, bit
bleed	bled	bled
blow	blew	blown
break	broke	broken
breed	bred	bred
bring	brought	brought
build	built	built
*burn	burnt	burnt
burst	burst	burst
buy	bought	bought
cast	cast	cast
catch	caught	caught
choose	chose	chosen
cling	clung	clung
*clothe	(clad)	(clad)
come	came	come
cost	cost	cost
creep	crept	crept
cut	cut	cut
deal	dealt	dealt
dig	dug	dug
*dive	dove	dived
do	did	done
draw	drew	drawn
*dream	dreamt	dreamt
drink	drank	drunk
drive	drove	driven
*dwell	dwelt	dwelt
eat	ate	eaten
fall	fell	fallen

Presente	Pretérito	Participio pasivo
feed	fed	fed
feel	felt	felt
fight	fought	fought
find	found	found
*fit	fit	fit
flee	fled	fled
fling	flung	flung
fly	flew	flown
forbear	(forbore)	(forborne)
forbid	forbade	forbidden
foresee	foresaw	foreseen
foretell	foretold	foretold
forget	forgot	forgotten
forgive	forgave	forgiven
forsake	forsook	forsaken
freeze	froze	frozen
get	got	got, gotten
give	gave	given
go	went	gone
grind	ground	ground
grow	grew	grown
hang[1]	hung	hung
have, has	had	had
hear	heard	heard
*hew	hewed	hewn
hide	hid	hidden, hid
hit	hit	hit
hold	held	held
hurt	hurt	hurt
keep	kept	kept
*kneel	knelt	knelt
*knit	knit	knit
know	knew	known
lay	laid	laid
lead	led	led
*lean	(leant)	(leant)
*leap	leapt	leapt
*learn	(learnt)	(learnt)
leave	left	left
lend	lent	lent
let	let	let

1. Es regular cuando significa 'ahorcar'.

Presente	Pretérito	Participio pasivo
lie[2]	lay	lain
*light	lit	lit
lose	lost	lost
make	made	made
mean	meant	meant
meet	met	met
mistake	mistook	mistaken
*mow	mowed	mown
pay	paid	paid
*plead	pled	pled
put	put	put
quit	quit	quit
read [rid]	read [rɛd]	read [rɛd]
rend	rent	rent
*rid	rid	rid
ride	rode	ridden
ring	rang	rung
rise	rose	risen
run	ran	run
*saw	sawed	sawn
say	said	said
see	saw	seen
seek	sought	sought
sell	sold	sold
send	sent	sent
set	set	set
*sew	sewed	sewn
shake	shook	shaken
*shave	shaved	shaven
*shear	sheared	shorn
shed	shed	shed
shine[3]	shone	shone
shoe	shod	shod
shoot	shot	shot
*show	showed	shown
shrink	shrank (shrunk)	shrunk (shrunken)
shut	shut	shut
sing	sang	sung
sink	sank	sunk
sit	sat	sat
slay	slew	slain

2. Es regular cuando significa 'mentir'.
3. Suele ser regular cuando es transitivo, en el sentido 'pulir, dar brillo'.

Presente	Pretérito	Participio pasivo
sleep	slept	slept
slide	slid	slid
sling	slung	slung
slink	slunk	slunk
slit	slit	slit
*smell	(smelt)	(smelt)
smite	smote	smitten
*sow	sowed	sown
speak	spoke	spoken
*speed	sped	sped
*spell	(spelt)	(spelt)
spend	spent	spent
*spill	(spilt)	(spilt)
spin	spun	spun
spit	spat, spit	spat, spit
split	split	split
*spoil	(spoilt)	(spoilt)
spread	spread	spread
spring	sprang, sprung	sprung
stand	stood	stood
*stave	(stove)	(stove)
steal	stole	stolen
stick	stuck	stuck
sting	stung	stung
stink	stank	stunk
*strew	strewed	strewn
stride	strode	stridden
strike	struck	struck, stricken
string	strung	strung
*strive	strove	striven
swear	swore	sworn
*sweat	sweat	sweat
sweep	swept	swept
*swell	swelled	swollen
swim	swam	swum
swing	swung	swung
take	took	taken
teach	taught	taught
tear	tore	torn
tell	told	told
think	thought	thought
throw	threw	thrown
thrust	thrust	thrust
tread	trod	trodden

Presente	*Pretérito*	*Participio pasivo*
understand	understood	understood
undertake	undertook	undertaken
undo	undid	undone
uphold	upheld	upheld
upset	upset	upset
*wake	woke	woken
wear	wore	worn
weave	wove	woven
*wed	wed	wed
weep	wept	wept
*wet	wet	wet
win	won	won
wind	wound	wound
withdraw	withdrew	withdrawn
withhold	withheld	withheld
withstand	withstood	withstood
wring	wrung	wrung
write	wrote	written

Aa

a [ə, e] INDEF ART un *m*, una *f*; **what — fool!** ¡qué tonto! **such — fool** tan tonto; **I'm — teacher / Catholic** soy maestro / católico

AA [Alcoholics Anonymous] [éé] N AA *f*

aback [əbǽk] ADV **to be taken —** estar desconcertado

abandon [əbǽndən] VT abandonar; N **with wild —** desenfrenadamente

abandonment [əbǽndənmənt] N abandono *m*, desamparo *m*

abashed [əbǽʃt] ADJ humillado, avergonzado

abate [əbét] VI/VT (trend, payments) disminuir, mitigar[se]; (storm) calmarse, atenuarse

abbey [ǽbi] N abadía *f*

abbot [ǽbət] N abad *m*

abbreviate [əbríviet] VT abreviar

abbreviation [əbriviéʃən] N (act of abbreviating) abreviación *f*; (short form) abreviatura *f*

abdicate [ǽbdıket] VI/VT abdicar

abdomen [ǽbdəmən] N abdomen *m*, vientre *m*

abdominal [æbdámənł] ADJ abdominal; **— distension** distensión abdominal *f*

abduct [æbdʌ́kt] VT secuestrar, raptar

abduction [æbdʌ́kʃən] N secuestro *m*, rapto *m*

aberration [æbəréʃən] N anomalía *f*, aberración *f*

abet [əbét] VT instigar

abeyance [əbéəns] ADV LOC **in —** pendiente, en suspenso

abhor [əbhɔ́r] VT aborrecer

abhorrence [əbhɔ́rəns] N aborrecimiento *m*

abhorrent [əbhɔ́rənt] ADJ aborrecible

abide [əbáıd] VT (tolerate) soportar; VI (dwell) morar, permanecer; **to — by** acatar, atenerse a

ability [əbílıdı] N (skill) habilidad *f*; (aptitude) capacidad *f*

abject [ǽbdʒékt] ADJ abyecto; **in — poverty** en extrema miseria

ablaze [əbléz] ADV en llamas

able [ébəł] ADJ hábil, capaz; **to be — to** (be capable of) poder; (have an acquired skill) saber

abnegate [ǽbnıget] VT renunciar

abnormal [æbnɔ́rmət] ADJ anormal

aboard [əbɔ́rd] ADV a bordo; **all —!** (train) ¡viajeros al tren! (ship) ¡pasajeros a bordo! **to go —** embarcarse, abordar

abode [əbód] N morada *f*

abode [əbód] *see* abide

abolish [əbálıʃ] VT abolir, suprimir

abolition [æbəlíʃən] N abolición *f*

abominable [əbámənəbəł] ADJ abominable

abomination [əbɑmənéʃən] N (action, thing) abominación *f*; (condition, vice) horror *m*

aboriginal [æbərídʒənəł] ADJ aborigen

aborigine [æbərídʒəni] N aborigen *mf*; **Australian —** aborigen australiano -na *mf*

abort [əbɔ́rt] VT (fetus) abortar; VI/VT (mission) suspender; (software) interrumpir; N (software) interrupción *f*

abortion [əbɔ́rʃən] N aborto *m*

abortionist [əbɔ́rʃənıst] N abortador -ora *mf*, abortero -ra *mf*

abortive [əbɔ́rDıv] ADJ frustrado

abound [əbáund] VI abundar; **to — with** abundar en

about [əbáut] PREP (concerning) acerca de, tocante a; (near, surrounding) alrededor de, por; **to be — one's business** atender a su negocio; ADV más o menos, alrededor de; **at — ten o'clock** a eso de las diez, sobre las diez; **to be — to do something** estar por / para hacer algo, estar a punto de hacer algo; **I'm all — transparency** insisto en la transparencia

above [əbʌ́v] PREP **you could see the towers — the buildings** se veían las torres sobre los edificios; **everyone — five years of age** todos los de más de cinco años; **he's — me in the company** es mi superior en la compañía; **to be — suspicion** estar libre de toda sospecha; **I thought you were — such things** no pensaba que te rebajarías a eso; ADV **the apartment —** el apartamento de arriba; **books of fifty pages and —** libros de cincuenta páginas y más; **the remark quoted —** la observación anteriormente citada; **— all** sobre todo; **—-mentioned** susodicho, ya mencionado

abrasion [əbréʒən] N abrasión *f*

abrasive [əbrésıv] ADJ (material) abrasivo; (person, tone) irritante

abreast [əbrést] ADV al lado; **to keep —** mantenerse al corriente; **four —** de cuatro en fondo

abridge [əbrídʒ] VT abreviar

abroad [əbrɔ́d] ADV en el extranjero; **to go —** ir al extranjero

abrupt [əbrʌ́pt] ADJ abrupto

ABS [antilock braking system] [ébiés] N SFA *m*

abscess [ǽbsɛs] N absceso *m*

abscond [æbskánd] VI fugarse

absence [ǽbsəns] N (nonpresence) ausencia *f*; (lack) falta *f*; **in the — of** a falta de

absent [ǽbsənt] ADJ ausente; **—-minded** distraído, despistado; **to be — from school** faltar a la escuela

absentee [æbsəntí] N ausente *mf*; **— landlord** propietario -ria ausente *mf*

absenteeism [æbsəntízəm] N ausentismo *m*

absolute [ǽbsəlút] ADJ (ruler, certainty)

absoluto; (prohibition) terminante

absolutely [æbsəlútli] ADV absolutamente; — **not** en absoluto; INTERJ —! ¡sí, señor! ¡claro!

absolve [æbzálv] VT absolver

absorb [əbzɔ́rb] VT (liquid) absorber; (shock) amortiguar; (people, information) asimilar; **he is —ed in his work** está absorto en su trabajo

absorption [əbzɔ́rpʃən] N absorción f

abstain [æbstén] VI abstenerse; — **from** abstenerse de

abstention [æbsténʃən] N abstención f

abstinence [æbstənəns] N abstinencia f

abstract [æbstrækt] ADJ abstracto; N (summary) resumen m, extracto m; **in the —** en abstracto

abstraction [æbstrækʃən] N abstracción f

absurd [əbsə́d] ADJ absurdo, disparatado

absurdity [əbsə́DIDi] N (quality) absurdo m; (action) disparate m

abundance [əbándəns] N abundancia f

abundant [əbándənt] ADJ abundante

abuse¹ [əbjús] N (of privileges) abuso m; (of authority) abuso m, desmán m; (physical) maltrato m; (verbal) injuria f

abuse² [əbjúz] VT (privileges) abusar de; (physically) maltratar; (verbally) injuriar

abusive [əbjúsɪv] ADJ (physically) violento; (verbally) injurioso

abysmal [əbízməl] ADJ abismal; — **results** resultados desastrosos m pl

abyss [əbís] N abismo m

A/C [**air conditioning**] [ésí] N aire acondicionado m

academic [ækədémɪk] ADJ (university) académico; (school) escolar; N profesor -ora universitario -ria mf

academy [əkǽdəmi] N academia f

accede [æksíd] VI acceder; **to —** acceder a

accelerate [ækséləret] VI/VT acelerar

acceleration [ækseləréʃən] N aceleración f

accelerator [ækséləreDə] N acelerador m

accent¹ [æksɛnt] N (pronunciation) acento m; (written) tilde f, acento escrito/ortográfico m

accent² [æksént] VT (syllable) acentuar

accentuate [æksént∫uet] VT (differences, facts, syllables) acentuar, recalcar; (beauty) realzar

accept [æksépt] VT aceptar

acceptable [ækséptəbəl] ADJ aceptable

acceptance [ækséptəns] N (action) aceptación f; (approval) aprobación f

access [ǽksɛs] N acceso m; — **code** código de acceso m; — **provider** proveedor -ora de acceso mf; — **denied** acceso denegado m; VT acceder a

accessibility [æksɛsəbílIDi] N accesibilidad f

accessible [æksésəbəl] ADJ accesible

accessory [æksésəri] ADJ accesorio; N (to clothes, to gadgets) accesorio m; (to a crime)

cómplice mf; — **slot** ranura para accesorios f

accident [ǽksɪDənt] N accidente m; (mishap) percance m; — **insurance** seguro contra accidentes m; **by —** por casualidad

accidental [æksɪdéntl] ADJ (injury) accidental; (discovery, meeting) casual, fortuito

acclaim [əklém] VT aclamar; N aclamación f, ovación f

acclamation [ækləméʃən] N aclamación f

acclimate [ǽkləmet] VI/VT (to physical conditions) aclimatar[se]; (to an ambience) acostumbrar[se]

accolade [ǽkəled] N elogio m

accommodate [əkámədet] VT (adjust) tener en cuenta; (lodge) hospedar, alojar; (contain) tener capacidad para; VI **to — oneself** adaptarse

accommodation [əkamədéʃən] N (adjustment) acomodación f, adaptación f; —**s** (lodging) alojamiento m; (facilities) comodidades f pl

accompaniment [əkámpənimənt] N acompañamiento m

accompanist [əkámpənɪst] N acompañante mf

accompany [əkámpəni] VI/VT acompañar

accomplice [əkámplɪs] N cómplice mf

accomplish [əkámplɪʃ] VT (objective) lograr; (mission) completar

accomplished [əkámplɪʃt] ADJ (actor, athlete) consumado; (musician) talentoso

accomplishment [əkámplɪʃmənt] N (achievement) logro m; (skill) habilidad f; (completion) realización f

accord [əkɔ́rd] N acuerdo m, convenio m; **of one's own —** voluntariamente; VT otorgar, conceder

accordance [əkɔ́rdns] ADV LOC **in — with** de acuerdo con, de conformidad con

according to [əkɔ́rDɪŋ] ADV LOC según

accordingly [əkɔ́rDɪŋli] ADV (therefore) por consiguiente; (correspondingly) como corresponde

accordion [əkɔ́rDiən] N acordeón m

accost [əkɔ́st] VT abordar

account [əkáunt] N (bill) cuenta f; (story) relato m, relación f; — **manager** administrador -ora de cuentas mf; —**s payable** cuentas por/a pagar f pl; —**s receivable** cuentas por/a cobrar f pl; **to open [close] an —** abrir [cerrar] una cuenta; **on — of** a causa de, debido a; **on my —** por mí; **on one's own —** por cuenta propia; **on no —** de ninguna manera; **of no —** de ningún valor; **to take into —** tener en cuenta; VI **to — for** dar cuenta de; **how do you — for that?** ¿cómo se explica eso?

accountability [əkauntəbílIDi] N responsabilidad f

accountable [əkáuntəbəl] ADJ responsable

accountant [əkáuntnt] N Am contador -ra mf; Sp

contable *mf*

accounting [əkáʊntɪŋ] N contabilidad *f*; **— firm** empresa de contadores públicos *f*; **— period** ejercicio contable *m*

accredit [əkrédɪt] VT acreditar

acculturate [əkʌ́ltʃərət] VI/VT aculturar[se]

accumulate [əkjúmjəlet] VI/VT acumular[se]

accumulation [əkjumjəléʃən] N acumulación *f*

accuracy [ǽkjəəsi] N (of measure, instrument) precisión *f*, exactitud *f*; (of a translation) fidelidad *f*

accurate [ǽkjəɪt] ADJ (measure, instrument) preciso, exacto; (translation) fiel

accursed [əkə́sɪd] ADJ maldito

accusation [ækjuzéʃən] N acusación *f*

accuse [əkjúz] VT acusar

accused [əkjúzd] ADJ acusado; N acusado -da *mf*, reo -a *mf*, procesado -da *mf*

accuser [əkjúzə] N acusador -ra *mf*

accustom [əkástəm] VT acostumbrar, habituar; **to — oneself** acostumbrarse, habituarse; **to be —ed to** tener la costumbre de, estar acostumbrado a

AC/DC [alternating current / direct current] [ésidísi] ADJ alterna y continua

ace [es] N (cards, athlete, aviator) as *m*; (tennis) saque ganador *m*, servicio directo *m*; VT (a test) sacarse la máxima nota en

acetaminophen [əsɛDəmínəfən] N acetaminofén *m*

acetone [ǽsəton] N acetona *f*

ache [ek] N dolor *m*; **—s and pains** achaques *m pl*; VT doler; **my stomach —s** me duele el estómago

achieve [ətʃív] VT (a goal) conseguir, lograr; (a level) alcanzar

achievement [ətʃívmənt] N (attainment) consecución *f*; (success) logro *m*, realización *f*

Achilles tendon [əkíliz téndən] N tendón de Aquiles *m*

aching [ékɪŋ] ADJ doliente, dolorido

achy [éki] ADJ dolorido

acid [ǽsɪd] ADJ ácido; N ácido *m*; (hallucinogen) LSD *m*; **— rain** lluvia ácida *f*; **— test** prueba de fuego *f*

acidic [əsídɪk] ADJ ácido

acidity [əsídɪDi] N acidez *f*

acknowledge [æknálɪdʒ] VT (merits) reconocer; (faults) admitir, reconocer; (help) agradecer; **to — receipt** acusar recibo

acknowledgment [æknálɪdʒmənt] N (of merits) reconocimiento *m*; (of merits, faults) reconocimiento *m*, admisión *f*; (gratefulness) agradecimiento *m*; **— of receipt** acuse de recibo *m*

acme [ǽkmi] N súmmum *m*

acne [ǽkni] N acné *m*

acorn [ékɔrn] N bellota *f*

acoustics [əkústɪks] N acústica *f*

acquaint [əkwént] VT informar, familiarizar; **to — oneself with** informarse de, familiarizarse con; **to be —ed with** (a person, city, country) conocer; (a piece of news) estar enterado de

acquaintance [əkwéntn̩s] N (with facts) conocimiento *m*; (a person) conocido -a *mf*

acquiesce [ækwiés] VT asentir, condescender; (unwillingly) consentir

acquiescence [ækwiésəns] N asentimiento *m*, consentimiento *m*, condescendencia *f*

acquire [əkwáɪr] VT (knowledge, skill, purchase) adquirir; (fortune, information) obtener; (disease) contraer

acquisition [ækwəzíʃən] N (knowledge, skill, purchase) adquisición *f*; (fortune, information) obtención *f*

acquisitive [əkwízɪDɪv] ADJ codicioso

acquit [əkwít] VT absolver

acquittal [əkwídl̩] N absolución *f*

acre [ékə] N acre [0.405 hectáres] *m*

acrid [ǽkrɪd] ADJ acre

acrimony [ǽkrəmoni] N acritud *f*

acrobat [ǽkrəbæt] N acróbata *mf*

acrobatic [ækrəbǽDɪk] ADJ acrobático; N **—s** acrobacia *f*

acronym [ǽkrənɪm] N acrónimo *m*, sigla *f*

acrophobia [ækrəfóbiə] N acrofobia *f*

across [əkrɔ́s] PREP **to lay one stick — the other** poner dos palos cruzados; **there's a bridge — that river** hay un puente sobre ese río; **he came — his old love letters** encontró sus viejas cartas de amor; **the library is — the street** la biblioteca está al otro lado de la calle; **— the board** de manera uniforme, sin excepciones; ADV **cut the boards — corta los tablones a lo ancho; **five hundred miles —** de quinientas millas de ancho; **the meaning doesn't come —** el significado no se entiende

acrylic [əkrílɪk] ADJ N acrílico *m*

act [ækt] N (deed, part of play) acto *m*; (part of show) número *m*; (law) ley *f*, decreto *m*; **— of God** caso de fuerza mayor *m*; VI (behave) actuar, comportarse; (take measures) obrar; (play a part, chemical process) actuar; (represent) representar; (function) funcionar; **to — up** (child) portarse mal; (car) funcionar mal; **to — out** (event) representar; (feelings) exteriorizar

acting [ǽktɪŋ] N actuación *f*; (in a drama) representación *f*; ADJ (interim) interino; (substitute) suplente

action [ǽkʃən] N (practical measure, plot of a play) acción *f*; (deed) acto *m*; (functioning) funcionamiento *m*; **to take —** tomar medidas

actionable [ǽkʃənəbəl] ADJ accionable, procesable

activate [ǽktɪvet] VT activar

active [ǽktɪv] ADJ activo

activism [ǽktɪvɪzəm] N activismo *m*

activist [ǽktɪvɪst] N activista *mf*

activity [ǽktɪvɪɾi] N actividad *f*

actor [ǽktə·] N actor *m*

actress [ǽktrɪs] N actriz *f*

actual [ǽktʃuəl] ADJ verdadero, real

actually [ǽktʃuəli] ADV en realidad, efectivamente

actuary [ǽktʃueri] N actuario -ria *mf*

acuity [əkjúɪɾi] N agudeza *f*

acumen [ǽkjəmən] N perspicacia *f*, agudeza *f*

acupuncture [ǽkjupʌŋktʃə·] N acupuntura *f*

acupuncturist [ǽkjupʌŋktʃə·ɪst] N acupuntor -ora *mf*

acute [əkjút] ADJ (pain, illness) agudo; (observation) perspicaz, penetrante

AD [édí] ADV d.C.

ad [ǽd] N anuncio publicitario *m*; — **in** (tennis) ventaja al saque *f*, ventaja al servicio *f*; — **out** (tennis) ventaja al resto *f*; — **lib** ADJ improvisado; ADV improvisando; **to** — **lib** VI improvisar

adamant [ǽdəmənt] ADJ inflexible, firme

Adam's apple [ǽdəmz ǽpəl] N nuez de Adán *f*

adapt [ədǽpt] VT adaptar; VI **to** — **to** adaptar[se] a, acomodar[se] a

adaptation [ǽdəptéʃən] N adaptación *f*

adapter [ədǽptə·] N adaptador *m*

add [ǽd] VT añadir, agregar; (find sum) sumar; —**ed cost** costo adicional *m*; **to** — **to** aumentar; **to** — **up** (find sum) sumar; (make sense) cuadrar; N —**-on** accesorio *m*

addict [ǽdɪkt] N adicto -ta *mf*

addicted [ədíktɪd] ADJ adicto

addiction [ədíkʃən] N adicción *f*

addition [ədíʃən] N (of numbers) suma *f*; (to a collection, staff) adición *f*, adquisición *f*; (to a building) anexo *m*; **in** — **[to]** además [de]

additional [ədíʃənəl] ADJ adicional

additive [ǽdɪɾɪv] N aditivo *m*

address¹ [ədrés] N (street) dirección *f*, domicilio *m*; (speech) discurso *m*; — **book** libreta de direcciones *f*; **form of** — tratamiento *m*

address² [ədrés] VT (write the address) dirigir; (speak to) dirigirse a; (deal with) ocuparse de

addressee [ædrɛsí] N destinatario -ria *mf*

adduce [ədús] VT aducir

adept [ədépt] ADJ hábil

adequacy [ǽdɪkwəsi] N suficiencia *f*

adequate [ǽdɪkwɪt] ADJ (sufficient) suficiente; (acceptable) aceptable

adhere [ædhír] VI adherirse; **to** — **to** adherirse a

adherence [ædhírəns] N adhesión *f*

adhesion [ædhíʒən] N (thing or tissue that adheres) adherencia *f*; (act of sticking together) adhesión *f*

adhesive [ædhísɪv] ADJ adhesivo; — **tape** cinta adhesiva *f*

adjacent [ədʒésənt] ADJ adyacente

adjective [ǽdʒɪktɪv] ADJ & N adjetivo *m*

adjoin [ədʒɔ́in] VT lindar con, colindar con; —**ing** colindante; VI estar contiguo a

adjourn [ədʒ৯·n] VT **to** — **the meeting** levantar la sesión; **meeting** —**ed** se levanta la sesión

adjournment [ədʒ৯·nmənt] N levantamiento de la sesión *m*

adjudge [ədʒʌ́dʒ] VT (declare) declarar; (deem) calificar

adjudicate [ədʒúdɪket] VI arbitrar; VT declarar

adjunct [ǽdʒʌŋkt] ADJ adjunto; N agregado -da *mf*

adjust [ədʒʌ́st] VT (fix) ajustar, graduar; (adapt a machine) regular; —**ed net income** ingreso neto ajustado *m*; VI ajustarse, adaptarse

adjustable [ədʒʌ́stəbəl] ADJ ajustable; —**-rate mortgage** hipoteca con tasa de interés ajustable *f*

adjustment [ədʒʌ́stmənt] N ajuste *m*; (to a machine) regulación *f*

administer [ædmínɪstə·] VT (a business) administrar, gestionar; (a punishment) aplicar; (an oath) tomar[le]

administration [ædmínɪstréʃən] N administración *f*; (period in power) gestión *f*; (of punishment) aplicación *f*; (of an oath) toma *f*

administrative [ædmínɪstreɾɪv] ADJ administrativo

administrator [ædmínɪstreɾə·] N administrador -ra *mf*; (civil) intendente *mf*

admirable [ǽdmərəbəl] ADJ admirable

admiral [ǽdmərəl] N almirante *m*

admiration [ædməréʃən] N admiración *f*

admire [ædmáɪr] VT admirar

admirer [ædmáɪrə·] N admirador -ora *mf*; (suitor) pretendiente *mf*

admissible [ædmísəbəl] ADJ admisible

admission [ædmíʃən] N (acceptance) admisión *f*; (access, ticket price) entrada *f*; (confession) confesión *f*

admit [ædmít] VT (allow entry) admitir; (to a hospital) internar; (acknowledge) reconocer, admitir

admittance [ædmítns] N entrada *f*; **no** — prohibida la entrada

admonish [ædmánɪʃ] VT amonestar

admonition [ædmənɪʃən] N (warning) advertencia *f*; (reproof) amonestación *f*

adobe [ədóbi] N (mud) adobe *m*; (house) casa de adobe *f*

adolescence [ædlésəns] N adolescencia *f*

adolescent [ædlésənt] ADJ & N adolescente *mf*

adopt [ədápt] VT (child, custom) adoptar; (suggestion) aprobar

adoption [ədápʃən] N (of a child, custom) adopción *f*; (of a suggestion) aprobación *f*

adoptive [ədáptɪv] ADJ adoptivo

adorable [ədɔ́rəbəl] ADJ adorable, precioso
adoration [ӕpəréʃən] N adoración *f*
adore [ədɔ́r] VT adorar; **I — playing tennis** me encanta jugar al tenis
adorn [ədɔ́rn] VT adornar, ornar
adornment [ədɔ́rnmənt] N adorno *m*
adrenal [ədrín] ADJ suprarrenal
adrenaline [ədrénəlɪn] N adrenalina *f*
adrift [ədríft] ADJ & ADV a la deriva
adult [ədʌ́lt] ADJ & N adulto -ta *mf*
adulterate [ədʌ́ltəret] VT adulterar
adulterer [ədʌ́ltərə·] N adúltero -ra *mf*
adultery [ədʌ́ltəri] N adulterio *m*
advance [ӕdvӕns] VI (move forward) avanzar; (make progress) avanzar, progresar; (bring forward) adelantar; VT (promote) promover; (propose) proponer; (pay beforehand) adelantar, anticipar; N (movement) avance *m*; (progress) adelanto *m*; (loan) adelanto *m*, anticipo *m*; **—s** (sexual) requiebros *m pl*; **in —** por adelantado, con anticipación
advanced [ӕdvӕnst] ADJ (idea, stage) avanzado; (country) adelantado
advancement [ӕdvӕnsmənt] N (movement) avance *m*; (rank) ascenso *m*; (knowledge) progreso *m*
advantage [ӕdvӕntɪdʒ] N ventaja *f* (also tennis); **it would be to your —** te convendría; **to take — of** aprovecharse de
advantageous [ӕdvӕntédʒəs] ADJ ventajoso, provechoso
advent [ӕdvent] N advenimiento *m*
adventure [ӕdvéntʃə·] N aventura *f*
adventurer [ӕdvéntʃərə·] N aventurero -ra *mf*
adventuresome [ӕdvéntʃə·səm] ADJ atrevido, osado
adventurous [ӕdvéntʃəəs] ADJ (seeking adventure) aventurero, intrépido; (daring) atrevido, audaz
adverb [ӕdvə·b] N adverbio *m*
adversary [ӕdvə·sɛri] N adversario -ria *mf*
adverse [ӕdvə́s] ADJ adverso
adversity [ӕdvə́sɪdi] N adversidad *f*
advertise [ӕdvə·taɪz] VT anunciar, hacer publicidad/propaganda para; VI hacer propaganda/publicidad; **to — for a cook** poner un anuncio buscando cocinero
advertisement [ӕdvə·táɪzmənt] N anuncio publicitario *m*, aviso *m*
advertiser [ӕdvə·taɪzə·] N anunciante *mf*
advertising [ӕdvə·taɪzɪŋ] N publicidad *f*; — **agency** agencia de publicidad *f*; — **campaign** campaña publicitaria *f*; — **agent** agente publicitario -ria *mf*
advice [ӕdváɪs] N consejo *m*; (expert) asesoramiento *m*
advisable [ӕdváɪzəbəl] ADJ aconsejable, recomendable
advise [ӕdváɪz] VI/VT (counsel) aconsejar,

advertir; VT (inform) avisar, informar; (expertly) asesorar
adviser, advisor [ӕdváɪzə·] N consejero -ra *mf*, asesor -ora *mf*
advocacy [ӕdvəkəsi] N defensa *f*
advocate[1] [ӕdvəkɪt] N (promoter) partidario -ria *mf*; (defender) defensor -ora *mf*, intercesor -ora *mf*; (lawyer) abogado -da *mf*
advocate[2] [ӕdvəket] VT abogar por, defender
aerial [ériəl] ADJ aéreo; N antena *f*
aerobic [eróbɪk] ADJ (exercise) aeróbico; (air-breathing) aerobio; N **—s** aeróbic *m*
aerodynamic [erodaɪnӕmɪk] ADJ aerodinámico; N **—s** aerodinámica *f*
aeronautics [ɛrənɔ́dɪks] N aeronáutica *f*
aerosol [ɛ́rəsɑl] N aerosol *m*
aerospace [érospes] N espacio aéreo *m*; ADJ aeroespacial
aesthetic [ɛsθédɪk] ADJ estético; N **—s** estética *f*
affable [ӕfəbəl] ADJ afable
affair [əfér] N (social) acontecimiento social *m*; (business) asunto *m*, negocio *m*; (love) aventura amorosa *f*, affaire *m*
affect [əfɛ́kt] VT (have effect on) afectar; (move) conmover; (feign) fingir
affectation [ӕfɛktéʃən] N afectación *f*, melindre *m*
affected [əfɛ́ktɪd] ADJ (moved) afectado, conmovido; (feigned) fingido, artificioso, melindroso
affection [əfɛ́kʃən] N afecto *m*, cariño *m*
affectionate [əfɛ́kʃənɪt] ADJ afectuoso, cariñoso
affidavit [ӕfɪdévɪt] N declaración jurada *f*
affiliate[1] [əfíliet] VT afiliar; VI afiliarse, asociarse
affiliate[2] [əfíliɪt] N filial *f*
affiliation [əfɪliéʃən] N (relation) afiliación *f*; (membership) filiación *f*; **political —** filiación política *f*
affinity [əfínɪDi] N afinidad *f*
affirm [əfə́m] VT afirmar
affirmation [ӕfə·méʃən] N afirmación *f*
affirmative [əfə́məDɪv] ADJ afirmativo; — **action** discriminación positiva *f*; N **reply in the —** dar una respuesta afirmativa
affix[1] [əfíks] VT fijar; **to — one's signature** poner su firma, firmar
affix[2] [ӕfíks] N afijo *m*
afflict [əflíkt] VT aquejar; **to be —ed with** padecer de, sufrir de
affliction [əflíkʃən] N (misery) aflicción *f*; (ailment) achaque *m*, mal *m*
affluent [ӕfluənt] ADJ (society) opulento; (person) rico
afford [əfɔ́rd] VT **I cannot — a car** no me alcanza el dinero para un coche; **he cannot — to waste time** no puede darse el lujo de perder tiempo; **I cannot — the risk** no me puedo permitir ese riesgo; **we will — you every opportunity** se te darán todas las

oportunidades

affordable [əfɔ́rdəbəl] ADJ asequible

affront [əfrʌ́nt] N afrenta *f*

Afghan, Afghani [ǽfgæn/æfgǽni] ADJ & N afgano -na *mf*

Afghanistan [æfgǽnɪstæn] N Afganistán *m*

afire [əfáɪr] ADJ & ADV en llamas

afloat [əflót] ADJ & ADV flotando, a flote

afraid [əfréd] ADJ asustado; **to be — [of]** temer, tener miedo [a]

afresh [əfréʃ] ADV de nuevo, desde el principio

Africa [ǽfrɪkə] N África *f*

African [ǽfrɪkən] ADJ & N africano -na *mf*

African American [ǽfrɪkənəmérɪkən] ADJ & N afroamericano -na *mf*

after [ǽftɚ] PREP (temporal) después de, tras; (spatial) detrás de; **— all** después de todo; ADV después; CONJ después [de] que

afterbirth [ǽftɚbɚθ] N placenta *f*

aftercare [ǽftɚkɛr] N (post-illness) tratamiento de convalecencia *m*; (postoperative) tratamiento post-operatorio *m*

after-hours [ǽftɚ áʊrz] ADV después de horas hábiles

afterlife [ǽftɚlaɪf] N el más allá *m*

aftermarket [ǽftɚmɑrkɪt] ADJ de mercado secundario; N (for merchandise) mercado secundario *m*; (for stocks) mercado extrabursátil *m*

aftermath [ǽftɚmæθ] N secuelas *f pl*

afternoon [æftɚnún] N tarde *f*; INTERJ **good —!** ¡buenas tardes!

aftershave [ǽftɚʃev] N loción para después del afeitado *f*

aftershock [ǽftɚʃɑk] N réplica *f*

aftertaste [ǽftɚtest] N (in the mouth) dejo *m*; (bad memory) resabio *m*

aftertax profit [ǽftɚtækspráfɪt] N ganancia neta *f*

afterthought [ǽftɚθɔt] N **it was just an —** se nos ocurrió después

afterward, afterwards [ǽftɚwɚd[z]] ADV después, posteriormente

again [əgén] ADV otra vez, de nuevo; **— and —** repetidas veces; **to fall —** volver a caerse

against [əgénst] PREP contra; **— the grain** a contrapelo; **— all odds** a pesar de todo

age [edʒ] N (of a person) edad *f*; (era) era *f*, época *f*; **— of consent** edad de consentimiento sexual *f*; **— discrimination** discriminación por edad *f*; **— limit** límite de edad *m*; **old —** vejez *f*; **of —** mayor de edad; **to come of —** llegar a la mayoría de edad; **under —** menor de edad; VI/VT envejecer

aged¹ [edʒd] ADJ (wine) añejo; **— forty** de cuarenta años

aged² [édʒɪd] ADJ anciano

ageless [édʒlɪs] ADJ (everlasting) eterno; (not showing age) siempre joven; (classic) clásico

agency [édʒənsi] N agencia *f*; **through the — of** por mediación de

agenda [ədʒéndə] N orden del día *m*, agenda *f*

agent [édʒənt] N agente *mf*; (commercial) representante *mf*, gestor -ora *mf*; (legal) apoderado -da *mf*

aggrandize [əgrǽndaɪz] VT engrandecer

aggravate [ǽgrəvet] VT (worsen) exacerbar, agravar; (annoy) irritar, exasperar, exacerbar

aggregate [ǽgrɪgɪt] N conjunto *m*; (rock) agregado *m*; ADJ total, global

aggression [əgréʃən] N (attack) agresión *f*; (propensity to violence) agresividad *f*

aggressive [əgrésɪv] ADJ (violent) agresivo; (dynamic) emprendedor

aggressiveness [əgrésɪvnɪs] N agresividad *f*

aggressor [əgrésɚ] N agresor -ra *mf*

aghast [əgǽst] ADJ horrorizado

agile [ǽdʒəl] ADJ ágil

agility [ədʒílɪdi] N agilidad *f*

aging [édʒɪŋ] N (of a person) envejecimiento *m*; (of wine) maduración *f*

agitate [ǽdʒɪtet] VT (shake) agitar; (perturb) turbar; (campaign) alborotar

agitation [ædʒɪtéʃən] N agitación *f*

agitator [ǽdʒɪtedɚ] N agitador -ra *mf*

agnostic [ægnástɪk] ADJ & N agnóstico -ca *mf*

ago [əgó] ADV **many years —** hace muchos años; **long —** hace mucho tiempo

agog [əgág] ADJ planchado, boquiabierto

agonize [ǽgənaɪz] VI sufrir angustiosamente; **to — over** atormentarse por

agony [ǽgəni] N (pain) dolor *m*, tormento *m*; (anguish) angustia *f*

agoraphobia [ægɚəfóbiə] N agorafobia *f*

agrarian [əgrériən] ADJ agrario

agree [əgrí] VI (be in agreement) estar de acuerdo; (in grammar, mathematics) concordar; (color, food) sentarle bien; **to — upon** acordar, convenir, pactar; **they —d to meet the next day** quedaron en reunirse al día siguiente, acordaron reunirse al día siguiente; **the two sides —d to a truce** los dos bandos pactaron una tregua

agreeable [əgríəbəl] ADJ (nice) agradable; (willing) conforme

agreement [əgrímənt] N (concord, document) acuerdo *m*, concertación *f*, convenio *m*; (grammatical) concordancia *f*; **to be in —** estar de acuerdo; **to come to an —** ponerse de acuerdo, pactar

agricultural [ægrɪkʌ́tʃɚəl] ADJ (related to crops) agrícola; (related to crops and cattle) agropecuario

agriculture [ǽgrɪkʌtʃɚ] N agricultura *f*

aground [əgráʊnd] ADV **to run —** encallar, varar

ahead [əhéd] ADV delante; **— of time** adelantado, con antelación; **to go —** ir

adelante, adelantarse; **to get —** prosperar;
our team is — nuestro equipo va primero;
the years — los años venideros

aid [ed] N (help) asistencia *f*; (assistant) ayudante
mf; VT ayudar; **to — and abet** instigar

aide [ed] N (high-ranking) asesor -ora *mf*;
(low-ranking) ayudante *mf*

**AIDS [acquired immune deficiency
syndrome]** [edz] N SIDA *m*

ail [el] VI/VT **what —s you?** ¿qué tienes? ¿qué te
aflige? **he's —ing** está enfermo

aileron [élərɑn] N alerón *m*

ailing [élɪŋ] ADJ (person) achacoso, enfermizo;
(economy) debilitado

ailment [élmənt] N achaque *m*, dolencia *f*

aim [em] N (with a weapon) puntería *f*;
(objective) objetivo *m*; VT (a weapon) apuntar;
(a question, blow) dirigir; **to — to please**
tratar de agradar

aimless [émlɪs] ADJ (purposeless) sin propósito;
(directionless) sin rumbo

air [er] N aire *m*; **—bag** airbag *m*, bolsa de aire *f*;
—brake freno neumático *m*; **to —
condition** poner aire condicionado; **—
conditioner** acondicionador de aire *m*; **—
conditioning** aire acondicionado *m*,
climatización *f*; **—craft** aeronave *f*; **—craft
carrier** portaaviones *m sg*; **—field**
aeródromo *m*; **— force** fuerza aérea *f*;
—head cabeza de chorlito *mf*; **—lift** puente
aéreo *m*; **—line** línea aérea *f*, aerolínea *f*; **—
mail** correo aéreo *m*; **—plane** avión *m*; **—
piracy** piratería aérea *f*; **—port** aeropuerto
m; **—power** fuerza aérea *f*; **— pressure**
presión de aire *f*; **— raid** ataque aéreo *m*; **—
rifle** escopeta de aire comprimido *f*; **—ship**
dirigible *m*; **— strike** bombardeo aéreo *m*;
—strip pista de aterrizaje *f*; **—-to-**
aire-aire; **— traffic control** control del
tráfico aéreo *m*; **—way** conducto de aire *m*,
vía respiratoria *f*; **up in the —** en el aire,
incierto; **in the open —** al aire libre; **to be
on the —** estar en el aire, emitirse; **to put on
—s** presumir, darse ínfulas; **to vanish into
thin —** evaporarse; VT (an opinion)
manifestar; **to —lift** aerotransportar; **to —
out** orear, ventilar; ADJ aéreo; **—borne**
(troops) aerotransportado; (particles)
transportado por el aire; **— conditioned** con
aire acondicionado, climatizado; **—tight**
hermético

aisle [aɪl] N pasillo *m*; (of a church) nave lateral *f*

ajar [əʤár] ADJ entornado, entreabierto

aka [ékéé] ADV (also called) también conocido
como; (in police usage) alias

akin [əkín] ADJ (related) emparentado; (similar)
semejante

à la mode [ɑlɑmód] ADV con helado

alarm [əlárm] N (warning) alarma *f*; (worry)

inquietud *f*; **— clock** despertador *m*; **to
sound an —** tocar a rebato; VT (worry)
alarmar; (frighten) asustar

alarming [əlármɪŋ] ADJ alarmante

Albania [ælbéniə] N Albania *f*

Albanian [ælbéniən] ADJ & N albanés -esa *mf*

albatross [ǽlbətrɑs] N albatros *m*

albinism [ǽlbɪnɪzəm] N albinismo *m*

albino [ælbáɪno] N albino -na *mf*

album [ǽlbəm] N álbum *m*

alcohol [ǽlkəhɔl] N alcohol *m*

alcoholic [ælkəhɔ́lɪk] ADJ & N alcohólico -ca *mf*

alcoholism [ǽlkəhɔlɪzəm] N alcoholismo *m*

alcove [ǽlkov] N rincón *m*

ale [el] N cerveza inglesa *f*

alert [əlɚ́t] ADJ (vigilant) alerta; (awake)
despierto; **to be —** (on guard) estar alerta;
(lively) ser despierto; N alerta *f*; VT alertar,
avisar

alfalfa [ælfǽlfə] N alfalfa *f*

algae [ǽlʤi] N algas *f pl*

algebra [ǽlʤəbrə] N álgebra *f*

Algeria [ælʤíriə] N Argelia *f*

Algerian [ælʤíriən] ADJ & N argelino -na *mf*

algorithm [ǽlɡərɪðəm] N algoritmo *m*

alias [éliəs] N alias *m sg*

alibi [ǽləbaɪ] N coartada *f*

alien [éliən] N (visitor from space) extraterrestre
mf; (foreigner) extranjero -ra *mf*; ADJ ajeno

alienate [élianet] VT (people) alienar, alejar;
(property) enajenar

alight [əláɪt] VI (rider) apearse; (bird, insect)
posarse

align [əláɪn] VI/VT alinear[se]

alignment [əláɪnmənt] N alineación *f*

alike [əláɪk] ADJ parecido, igual; **to be —**
parecerse, ser iguales; ADV del mismo modo

alimentary [æliméntəri] ADJ alimenticio; **—
canal** canal alimentario *m*

alimony [ǽləmoni] N pensión alimenticia *f*

alive [əláɪv] ADJ (living) vivo; **— with** lleno de;
**the symphony came — under his
direction** la sinfonía cobró vida bajo su
dirección

alkali [ǽlkəlaɪ] N álcali *m*

alkaline [ǽlkəlɪn] ADJ alcalino

all [ɔl] ADJ todo; **— the time** todo el tiempo; N
todo *m*; **to give one's —** dar todo de sí; PRON
todo; **is that —?** ¿eso es todo? — **or nothing**
todo o nada; ADV completamente, todo; **— at
once** (uninterrupted) de una vez; (sudden) de
repente; **—-inclusive** con todo incluido; **—-
time high** máximo histórico *m*; **— told** en
conjunto; **he's — dirty** está todo sucio; **it is
— over** se acabó; **not at —** de ninguna
manera; **nothing at —** nada en absoluto;
once [and] for — de una vez por todas;
she's — right está bien; INTERJ **— right**
bueno

allay [əlé] VT (fear, doubt) calmar, disipar; (anger) aplacar

allegation [ælɪɡéʃən] N acusación f

allege [əléʤ] VT (state) afirmar; (claim) alegar

alleged [əléʤd] ADJ (event) supuesto; (perpetrator) presunto

allegedly [əléʤɪdli] ADV supuestamente, presuntamente

allegiance [əliʤəns] N lealtad f, fidelidad f; **to pledge — to the flag** jurar la bandera

allegory [æligɔri] N alegoría f

allergen [ælərʤɪn] N alergeno/alérgeno m

allergic [əlɚʤɪk] ADJ alérgico

allergist [ælɚʤɪst] N alergólogo -ga mf

allergy [ælɚʤi] N alergia f

alleviate [əlíviet] VT (suffering) aliviar; (hunger) paliar

alley [æli] N callejón m; (tennis) pasillo de dobles m; **right up her —** ideal para ella

alliance [əláɪəns] N alianza f

allied [əláɪd, ǽlaɪd] ADJ aliado

alligator [æligeɾə] N caimán m; Am lagarto m

alliterate [əlíɾəret] VI hacer aliteración

allocate [æləket] VT asignar

allot [əlát] VT asignar

allotment [əlátmənt] N asignación f, cuota f

allow [əláu] VI/VT (permit) permitir; (make possible) posibilitar; (admit) admitir; **to — for** tener en cuenta

allowable [əláuəbəl] ADJ admisible, permisible

allowance [əláuəns] N (regular payment) asignación f, pensión f; (monthly payment) mensualidad f; (for a child) paga f, mesada f; (payment for a particular purpose) pago m; (food) ración f; **to make — for** tener en cuenta

alloy¹ [ælɔɪ] N aleación f

alloy² [əlɔɪ] VT alear

allude [əlúd] VI aludir; **to — to** aludir a

allure [əlúr] VI/VT seducir, atraer; N atractivo m

alluring [əlúrɪŋ] ADJ seductivo, atractivo

allusion [əlúʒən] N alusión f

ally¹ [ǽlaɪ] N aliado -da f

ally² [əláɪ] VT **to — oneself with** aliarse con

almanac [ɔ́lmənæk] N almanaque m

almighty [ɔlmáɪti] ADJ todopoderoso

almond [ɔ́mənd] N almendra f; **— tree** almendro m

almost [ɔ́lmost] ADV casi; **I — fell down** por poco me caigo

alms [ɔmz] N limosna f

aloe vera [æloviɾə] N áloe m

alone [əlón] ADJ solo; **— among his contemporaries** único entre sus contemporáneos; ADV solo, solamente; **she — knew that** solo ella sabía eso; **all — a** solas; **to leave —** no tocar, dejar en paz

along [əlɔ́ŋ] PREP **he was walking — the street** andaba por la calle; **all — the coast a** lo largo de toda la costa; **— with** junto con; **all —** desde el principio; **to carry — with oneself** llevar consigo; **to go — with** acceder a, conformarse con; **to get — with** llevarse bien con

alongside [əlɔ́ŋsáɪd] PREP al lado de; **— the boat** al lado del bote; ADV al lado, al costado; **the dog ran —** el perro corría al costado

aloof [əlúf] ADJ reservado, esquivo; ADV apartado

aloud [əláud] ADV en voz alta

alphabet [ǽlfəbet] N alfabeto m, abecedario m

alphanumeric [ǽlfənumérɪk] ADJ alfanumérico

alpine [ǽlpaɪn] ADJ alpino

already [ɔlrédi] ADV ya

also [ɔ́lso] ADV también, además; **—ran** (horse, candidate) caballo/candidato vencido m

alt [ælt] see alternate¹

altar [ɔ́ltə] N altar m; **—piece** retablo m

alter [ɔ́ltə] VI/VT (change) alterar; (neuter) capar, castrar

alteration [ɔ̀ltəréʃən] N (change) alteración f, cambio m; **—s** arreglos m pl, reformas f pl

altercation [ɔ̀ltəkéʃən] N altercado m

alternate¹ [ɔ́ltənɪt] ADJ alternativo, alterno; **— route** ruta alternativa f; **— spelling** ortografía alterna f; **he visits us on — Mondays** nos visita un lunes sí y otro no; **alt key** tecla de alt f; **alt gr key** tecla de alternativa gráfica f; N suplente mf

alternate² [ɔ́ltənet] VI/VT alternar

alternation [ɔ̀ltənéʃən] N alternancia f

alternative [ɔ̀ltɚnədɪv] ADJ alternativo; **— minimum tax** contribución alternativa mínima f; N alternativa f

alternator [ɔ́ltəneɾə] N alternador m

although [ɔlðó] CONJ aunque, si bien

altimeter [æltímɪdə] N altímetro m

altitude [ǽltɪtud] N altura f, altitud f; **— sickness** mal de altura m

alto [ǽlto] N contralto mf; ADJ alto

altogether [ɔ̀ltəɡéðə] ADV (completely) completamente; (all included) en total

altruism [ǽltruɪzəm] N altruismo m

aluminum [əlúmənəm] N aluminio m; **— foil** papel de aluminio m

always [ɔ́lwez] ADV siempre

Alzheimer's disease [ɔ́ltshaɪmɚz dɪzɪz] N enfermedad de Alzheimer f

a.m. [éém] ADV de la mañana

am [æm] see be

amalgamate [əmǽlɡəmet] VI/VT (metals) amalgamar[se]; (companies) fusionar[se]

amass [əmǽs] VT acumular, amasar

amateur [ǽmətʃɚ] ADJ amateur; N amateur mf; aficionado -da mf

amaze [əméz] VT maravillar, asombrar

amazement [əmézmənt] N asombro m

amazing [əmézɪŋ] ADJ asombroso, increíble

Amazon [ǽməzɑn] N (region) Amazonia *f*; (river) Amazonas *m sg*

ambassador [æmbǽsədə-] N embajador -ora *mf*

amber [ǽmbə-] N ámbar *m*; ADJ (quality) ambarino; (material) de ámbar; (color) [de] color ámbar

ambidextrous [æmbɪdékstrəs] ADJ ambidiestro

ambience, ambiance [ǽmbɪəns] N ambiente *m*

ambient [ǽmbiənt] ADJ ambiental; — **temperature** temperatura ambiente *f*

ambiguity [æmbɪgjúɪɒi] N ambigüedad *f*

ambiguous [æmbígjuəs] ADJ ambiguo

ambition [æmbíʃən] N ambición *f*, aspiración *f*

ambitious [æmbíʃəs] ADJ ambicioso

ambivalent [æmbívələnt] ADJ ambivalente

amble [ǽmbəl] VI deambular

ambulance [ǽmbjələns] N ambulancia *f*

ambulatory [ǽmbjələtɔri] ADJ ambulatorio

ambush [ǽmbʊʃ] N emboscada *f*, celada *f*; **to lie in** — tender una emboscada; VT emboscar

ameliorate [əmíliəret] VI/VT mejorar

amen [ámén] INTERJ amén

amenable [əménəbəl] ADJ bien dispuesto

amend [əménd] VT enmendar; **to make —s [for]** compensar [por]

amendment [əméndmənt] N enmienda *f*

amenities [əménɪɒiz] N PL comodidades *f pl*

America [əmérɪkə] N América *f*

American [əmérɪkən] ADJ & N (continental) americano -na *mf*; (USA) americano -na *mf*, norteamericano -na *mf*, estadounidense *mf*

amethyst [ǽməθɪst] N amatista *f*

amiable [émiəbəl] ADJ amable

amicable [ǽmɪkəbəl] ADJ amistoso, amigable

amid [əmíd] PREP en medio de, entre

amino acid [əmínoǽsɪd] N aminoácido *m*

amiss [əmís] ADV **something is** — algo anda mal

ammonia [əmónjə] N amoníaco *m*

ammunition [æmjəníʃən] N munición *f*

amnesia [æmníʒə] N amnesia *f*

amnesty [ǽmnɪsti] N amnistía *f*

amniocentesis [æmniosɪntísɪs] N amniocentesis *f*

amniotic [æmniáɒɪk] ADJ amniótico; — **fluid** líquido amniótico *m*

amoeba [əmíbə] N ameba *f*

among [əmʌ́ŋ] PREP entre

amoral [emɔ́rəl] ADJ amoral

amorous [ǽmərəs] ADJ (sexually aroused) excitado; (in love) enamorado

amorphous [əmɔ́rfəs] ADJ amorfo

amortization [æmə-Dɪzéʃən] N amortización *f*

amortize [ǽmə-taɪz] VT amortizar

amount [əmáʊnt] N (of a substance) cantidad *f*; (of money) suma *f*, importe *m*; — **due** cantidad debida *f*, monto debido *m*; — **paid** cantidad pagada *f*, monto pagado *m*; — **payable** cantidad a pagar *f*; VI (add up to)

ascender [a]; **that —s to stealing** eso equivale a robar

ampere [ǽmpɪr] N amperio *m*

amphetamine [æmfÉɒəmin] N anfetamina *f*

amphibian [æmfíbiən] N anfibio *m*

amphibious [æmfíbiəs] ADJ anfibio

amphitheater [ǽmfəθiəɒə-] N anfiteatro *m*

ampicillin [æmpɪsílɪn] N ampicilina *f*

ample [ǽmpəl] ADJ (in quantity) suficiente; (in size) amplio

amplifier [ǽmpləfaɪə-] N amplificador *m*

amplify [ǽmpləfaɪ] VT (an explanation) ampliar; (a sound) amplificar

amplitude [ǽmplɪtud] N amplitud *f*

amputate [ǽmpjətet] VT amputar

amuck, amok [əmʌ́k] ADV **to run** — (kill people) perpetrar un ataque homicida; (go crazy) volverse loco

amulet [ǽmjəlɪt] N amuleto *m*

amuse [əmjúz] VT (make laugh) divertir; (help pass time) entretener; **to — oneself** divertirse, entretenerse

amusement [əmjúzmənt] N diversión *f*, entretenimiento *m*

amusing [əmjúzɪŋ] ADJ (entertaining) divertido; (funny) gracioso, chistoso

amygdala [əmígdələ] N amígdala *f*

an [ən, æn] INDEF ART un *m*, una *f*

anabolic [ænəbɑ́lɪk] ADJ anabólico; — **steroid** esteroide anabólico *m*

anachronism [ənǽkrənɪzəm] N anacronismo *m*

anaerobic [ænəróbɪk] ADJ anaerobio

anal [énl] ADJ anal; (neurotic) rígido, neurótico

analgesic [ænʤízɪk] N & ADJ analgésico *m*

analogical [ænəlɑ́ʤɪkəl] ADJ analógico

analogous [ənǽləgəs] ADJ análogo

analogue, analog [ǽnəlɔg] ADJ analógico; — **device** dispositivo analógico *m*

analogy [ənǽləʤi] N analogía *f*

analysis [ənǽlɪsɪs] N análisis *m*

analyst [ǽnəlɪst] N analista *mf*

analytic, analytical [ænəlíɒɪk[əl]] ADJ (approach) analítico; (person) analítico, analista

analyze [ǽnəlaɪz] VT analizar

anarchist [ǽnə-kɪst] N anarquista *mf*

anarchy [ǽnə-ki] N anarquía *f*

anathema [ənǽθəmə] N anatema *m*

anatomical [ænətɑ́mɪkəl] ADJ anatómico

anatomy [ənǽɒəmi] N anatomía *f*

ancestor [ǽnsɛstə-] N antepasado -da *mf*, ascendiente *mf*

ancestral [ænsɛ́strəl] ADJ ancestral, de los antepasados; — **home** casa solariega *f*

ancestry [ǽnsɛstri] N linaje *m*, ascendencia *f*, abolengo *m*

anchor [ǽŋkə-] N ancla *f*; — **man** presentador *m*; — **woman** presentadora *f*; **to drop** — anclar, echar anclas; VT (a boat) anclar; (an

argument) basar; VI echar anclas, fondear
anchovy [ǽntʃovi] N anchoa *f*
ancient [énʃənt] ADJ antiguo; *pej* vetusto
and [ænd] CONJ y; (before i, hi) e; **— so forth**
etcétera, y así sucesivamente
Andalusia [ændəlúʒə] N Andalucía *f*
Andalusian [ændəlúʒən] ADJ & N andaluz -za *mf*
Andes [ǽndiz] N Andes *m pl*
Andorra [ændɔ́rə] N Andorra *f*
Andorran [ændɔ́rən] ADJ & N andorrano -na *mf*
androgynous [ændrádʒənəs] ADJ andrógino
anecdote [ǽnɪkdot] N anécdota *f*
anemia [əními̯ə] N anemia *f*
anemic [ənímɪk] ADJ anémico
anesthesia [ænɪsθíʒə] N anestesia *f*
anesthesiologist [ænəsθiziálədʒɪst] N
anestesiólogo -ga *mf*, anestesista *mf*
anesthesiology [ænɪsθiziá[ə]dʒi] N
anestesiología *f*
anesthetic [ænɪsθɛ́DIK] ADJ anestésico; N
(substance) anestesia *f*
anesthetize [ənɛ́sθətaɪz] VT anestesiar
aneurysm [ǽnjərɪzəm] N aneurisma *m*
anew [ənú] ADV de nuevo, otra vez
angel [éndʒəɫ] N ángel *m*
angelic [ændʒɛ́lɪk] ADJ angélico, angelical
anger [ǽŋɡ] N enojo *m*, enfado *m*; VT enojar,
enfadar
angina pectoris [ændʒáɪnəpɛ́ktəɹɪs] N angina de
pecho *f*
angiocardiography [ændʒiokɑrdiáɡrəfi] N
angiocardiografía *f*
angiogram [ǽndʒiogræm] N angiograma *m*
angioplasty [ǽndʒiəplæsti] N angioplastia *f*; **—
balloon** balón de angioplastia *m*
angle [ǽŋɡəɫ] N (geometrical) ángulo *m*; (point
of view) punto de vista *m*, perspectiva *f*; VI
pescar
Anglo-Saxon [ǽŋɡlosǽksən] ADJ & N
anglosajón -ona *mf*
Angola [æŋɡólə] N Angola *f*
Angolan [æŋɡólən] ADJ & N angolano -na *mf*,
angoleño -ña *mf*
angry [ǽŋɡri] ADJ enojado, enfadado
angst [áŋkst] N angustia *f*
anguish [ǽŋɡwɪʃ] N angustia *f*, ansia *f*, congoja *f*
angular [ǽŋɡjələ] ADJ angular; (face) anguloso
animal [ǽnəməɫ] ADJ & N animal *m*; **— rights**
derechos de los animales *m pl*
animate[1] [ǽnəmɪt] ADJ animado
animate[2] [ǽnəmet] VT (enliven) animar;
(encourage) alentar; **—d cartoon** dibujo
animado *m*
animation [ænəméʃən] N animación *f*
animosity [ænəmásɪDi] N animosidad *f*, ojeriza
f, encono *f*
anise [ǽnɪs] N anís *m*
ankle [ǽŋkəɫ] N tobillo *m*
annals [ǽnɫz] N anales *m pl*

annex[1] [ǽnɛks] N anexo *m*
annex[2] [ənɛ́ks] VT anexar
annexation [ænɛkséʃən] N anexión *f*
annihilate [ənáɪəlet] VT aniquilar
anniversary [ænəvɚ́səri] N aniversario *m*
annotate [ǽnətet] VT anotar
annotation [ænətéʃən] N (action, result)
anotación *f*; (result) nota *f*
announce [ənáʊns] VT (make known) anunciar,
dar a conocer; (declare) anunciar
announcement [ənáʊnsmənt] N (of an
engagement, birth, candidacy) anuncio *m*; (of
a conference or competition) convocatoria *f*
announcer [ənáʊnsɚ] N anunciador -ra *mf*; (on
radio) locutor -ora *mf*
annoy [ənɔ́ɪ] VI/VT fastidiar, contrariar
annoyance [ənɔ́ɪəns] N fastidio *m*,
contrariedad *f*
annual [ǽnjuəɫ] ADJ anual; N (book) anuario *m*;
(plant) planta anual *f*
annuity [ənjúɪDi] N anualidad *f*, renta anual *f*
annul [ənʌ́ɫ] VT anular
annulment [ənʌ́ɫmənt] N anulación *f*
anomalous [ənáməɫəs] ADJ anómalo
anomaly [ənáməli] N anomalía *f*
anonymous [ənánəməs] ADJ anónimo
anorak [ǽnəræk] N anorak *m*
anorexia [ænərɛ́ksiə] N anorexia *f*
anorexic [ænərɛ́ksɪk] ADJ anoréxico
another [ənʌ́ðɚ] ADJ otro; **— day** otro día; PRON
otro; **I want —** quiero otro; **one —** el uno al
otro, los unos a los otros
answer [ǽnsɚ] N (to a question) respuesta *f*,
contestación *f*; (to a problem) solución *f*; VI
contestar, responder; **to — for** ser
responsable de/por; VT contestar
answering [ǽnsəɹɪŋ] ADJ **— machine**
contestador automático *m*; **— service**
servicio telefónico contratado *m*, servicio de
contestador *m*
ant [ænt] N hormiga *f*; **—eater** oso hormiguero
m; **—hill** hormiguero *m*
antacid [æntǽsɪd] N & ADJ antiácido *m*
antagonism [æntǽɡənɪzəm] N antagonismo *m*
antagonist [æntǽɡənɪst] N antagonista *mf*
antagonize [æntǽɡənaɪz] VT antagonizar
antarctic [æntárktɪk] ADJ antártico
Antarctica [æntárktɪkə] N Antártida *f*
antecedent [æntəsídənt] ADJ & N antecedente *m*
antelope [ǽntəlop] N antílope *m*
antenna [ænténə] N antena *f*
anterior [æntíriə] ADJ anterior
anthem [ǽnθəm] N himno *m*
anthology [ænθáɫədʒi] N antología *f*
anthracite [ǽnθrəsaɪt] N antracita *f*
anthrax [ǽnθræks] N ántrax *m*
anthropologist [ænθrəpáɫədʒɪst] N
antropólogo -ga *mf*
anthropology [ænθrəpáɫədʒi] N antropología *f*

anthropomorphize [ænθrəpəmɔ́rfaɪz] VI/VT antropomorfizar

antiabortion [æntiəbɔ́rʃən] ADJ antiaborto *inv*

antiaircraft [æntiérkræft] ADJ antiaéreo

antiallergic [æntiəl̩ɝ́dʒɪk] ADJ antialérgico

antibacterial [æntibæktíriəl] ADJ antibacteriano

antiballistic [æntibəlístɪk] ADJ antibalístico

antibiotic [æntibaɪádɪk] N & ADJ antibiótico *m*

antibody [æntibadi] N anticuerpo *m*

anticancer [æntikǽnsə] ADJ anticanceroso *f*

anticipate [æntísəpet] VI/VT (foresee) prever; (jump the gun) anticiparse [a]

anticipation [æntisəpéʃən] N previsión *f*; **with great —** con gran expectación

anticlimactic [æntikləmǽktɪk] ADJ decepcionante

anticoagulant [æntikoǽgjələnt] ADJ & N anticoagulante *m*

anticonvulsant [æntikənvʌ́lsənt] ADJ & N anticonvulsivo *m*

antics [æntɪks] N payasadas *f pl*, monerías *f pl*, monadas *f pl*

antidepressant [æntidiprésənt] ADJ & N antidepresivo *m*

antidiarrheal [æntidaɪərɪəl] ADJ & N antidiarreico *m*

antidiuretic [æntidaɪərɛ́dɪk] ADJ & N antidiurético *m*

antidote [æntidot] N antídoto *m*

antifreeze [æntifriz] N anticongelante *m*

antigen [æntidʒən] N antígeno *m*

anti-glare [æntiglér] ADJ antireflejante

Antigua and Barbuda [æntígəændbɑrbúdə] N Antigua y Barbuda *f*

Antiguan [æntígən] ADJ & N antiguano -ana *mf*

antihistamine [æntihístəmin] N & ADJ antihistamínico *m*

anti-inflammatory [æntiɪnflǽmətɔri] ADJ & N antiinflamatorio *m*

antilock [æntilak] ADJ antibloqueo; **— brakes** frenos antibloqueo *mpl*

antimony [æntəmoni] N antimonio *m*

antioxidant [æntiáksɪdənt] N antioxidante *m*

antipathy [æntípəθi] N antipatía *f*

antiperspirant [æntipɝ́spəənt] N antitranspirante *m*

antipsychotic [æntisaɪkádɪk] ADJ & N antipsicótico *m*

antiquated [æntɪkwedɪd] ADJ (custom) anticuado; (word) desusado

antique [æntík] ADJ antiguo; N antigüedad *f*

antiquity [æntíkwɪdi] N antigüedad *f*

anti-Semitism [æntisémɪtɪzəm] N antisemitismo *m*

antiseptic [æntiséptɪk] ADJ & N antiséptico *m*

antisocial [æntisóʃəl] ADJ antisocial

antispasmodic [æntispæzmádɪk] ADJ & N antiespasmódico *m*

antithesis [æntíθəsɪs] N antítesis *f*

antitoxin [æntitáksɪn] N antitoxina *f*

antitrust [æntitrást] ADJ antimonopolio, antitrust

antiviral [æntivaírəl] ADJ & N antiviral *m*

antivirus [æntivaɪrəs] ADJ antivirus

antler [æntlə-] N asta *f*, cuerno *m*

antonym [æntənɪm] N antónimo *m*

antsy [æntsi] ADJ (impatient) impaciente; (anxious) ansioso

anvil [ǽnvəl] N yunque *m*

anxiety [æŋzáɪɪdi] N ansiedad *f*, angustia *f*

anxious [æŋkʃəs] ADJ (worried) ansioso, preocupado; (desirous) ansioso, deseoso

any [éni] ADJ & PRON cualquier[a], cualesquier[a], alguno; **— woman** cualquier mujer, una mujer cualquiera; **— houses** unas casas cualesquiera; *lit* cualesquiera casas; **in — case** en todo caso; **do you have — money?** ¿tienes dinero? **I don't have —** no tengo; **do you like — of these?** ¿te gusta alguno de estos?

anybody [énibadi] PRON alguien, cualquiera; **— could do that** cualquiera podría hacer eso; **is — here?** ¿hay alguien aquí? **he does not know —** no conoce a nadie

anyhow [énihaʊ] ADV de todos modos, en todo caso

anymore [énimór] ADV **he doesn't work —** ya no trabaja, no trabaja más

anyone [éniwʌn] PRON alguien, cualquiera; **— could do that** cualquiera podría hacer eso; **is — here?** ¿hay alguien aquí? **he does not know —** no conoce a nadie

anyplace [éniples] ADV en cualquier parte/lugar; **you can buy it —** se puede comprar en cualquier lugar; **he's not going —** no va a ninguna parte

anything [éniθɪŋ] PRON cualquier cosa, algo; **— is fine** cualquier cosa me viene bien; **— you wish** todo lo que quieras; **do you have — for a cough?** ¿tienes algo para la tos? **I don't know —** no sé nada

anytime [énitaɪm] ADV en cualquier momento

anyway [éniwe] ADV de todos modos, de cualquier manera, en todo caso

anywhere [énihwɛr] ADV en cualquier parte/lugar; **you can buy it —** se puede comprar en cualquier lugar; **he's not going —** no va a ninguna parte

aorta [eɔ́rdə] N aorta *f*

apart [əpárt] ADV **they are three miles —** están a tres millas de distancia; **they kept him — from the group** lo apartaron del grupo; **each factor viewed —** cada factor visto por separado; **to take —** desarmar, desmontar; **to tear —** despedazar, hacer pedazos; **to tell —** distinguir

apartment [əpártmənt] N apartamento *m*; *Sp*

piso *m*

apathetic [æpəθÉDIK] ADJ apático

apathy [ǽpəθi] N apatía *f*, abulia *f*

ape [ep] N simio *m*; VT remedar

aperture [ǽpətʃə] N abertura *f*; (of a pipe) luz *f*

apex [épeks] N (of tongue) ápice *m*; (of a mountain) cumbre *f*

aphasia [əféʒə] N afasia *f*

apiece [əpís] ADV cada uno

apnea [ǽpniə] N apnea *f*

apocalypse [əpákəlɪps] N apocalipsis *mf*

apogee [ǽpədʒi] N apogeo *m*

apologetic [əpáladʒéDIK] ADJ lleno de disculpas

apologize [əpáladʒaɪz] VI disculparse

apology [əpáladʒi] N (expression of regret) disculpa[s] *f* [*pl*]; (justification) apología *f*

apoplexy [ǽpəpleksi] N apoplejía *f*

apostle [əpásəl] N apóstol *m*

apostrophe [əpástrəfi] N (punctuation) apóstrofo *m*; (invocation) apóstrofe *m*

app [æp] N (computer software) aplicación *f*

appall [əpɔ́l] VT horrorizar

appalling [əpɔ́lɪŋ] ADJ horroroso

apparatus [æpərǽDəs] N (single) aparato *m*; (group) maquinaria *f*

apparel [əpǽrəl] N indumentaria *f*, ropa *f*; (fine) ropaje *m*

apparent [əpǽrənt] ADJ (visible) visible; (clear) obvio, evidente; (seeming) aparente

apparition [æpəríʃən] N aparición *f*, fantasma *m*

appeal [əpíl] N (legal) apelación *f*, recurso *m*; (request) llamamiento *m*, llamado *m*; (attraction) atractivo *m*; VT apelar, recurrir [contra]; VI **to — to** atraer

appear [əpír] VI (show up) aparecer[se]; (seem) parecer, aparentar; (be published) salir; (come before a judge) comparecer

appearance [əpírəns] N (looks) apariencia *f*, traza *f*, estampa *f*; (act of appearing) aparición *f*; (coming before a judge) comparecencia *f*

appease [əpíz] VT aplacar, apaciguar

appeasement [əpízmənt] N aplacamiento *m*, apaciguamiento *m*

appellate [əpélit] N **— court** tribunal de apelaciones *m*

append [əpénd] VT adjuntar

appendage [əpéndɪdʒ] N apéndice *m*

appendectomy [æpɪndéktəmi] N apendicectomía *f*

appendicitis [əpendəsáɪDɪs] N apendicitis *f*

appendix [əpéndɪks] N apéndice *m*

appetite [ǽpɪtaɪt] N apetito *m*

appetizer [ǽpɪtaɪzə] N aperitivo *m*

appetizing [ǽpɪtaɪzɪŋ] ADJ apetecible, apetitoso

applaud [əplɔ́d] VI/VT aplaudir

applause [əplɔ́z] N aplauso[s] *m* [*pl*]

apple [ǽpəl] N manzana *f*; **— grove** manzanar *m*; **— of my eye** niña de mis ojos *f*; **—sauce** compota de manzana *f*; **— tree** manzano *m*;

Adam's — nuez de Adán *f*

appliance [əpláɪəns] N aparato *m*; (electric) aparato electrodoméstico *m*, electrodoméstico *m*

applicable [ǽplɪkabəl] ADJ aplicable

applicant [ǽplɪkənt] N aspirante *mf*, solicitante *mf*

application [æplɪkéʃən] N (act of applying, computer software) aplicación *f*; (form) solicitud *f*, formulario *f*

applicator [ǽplɪkeDə] N aplicador *m*

apply [əpláɪ] VT aplicar; **to — for** solicitar, pedir; **are you —ing for the scholarship?** ¿te presentas para la beca? ¿estás solicitando la beca? **to — oneself** aplicarse, dedicarse

appoint [əpɔ́ɪnt] VT (designate) nombrar, designar; (furnish) amueblar, equipar; **a well —ed house** una casa bien amueblada

appointee [əpɔɪntí] N persona nombrada *f*

appointment [əpɔ́ɪntmənt] N (designation) nombramiento *m*, designación *f*; (engagement) cita *f*; **doctor's —** cita/hora con el médico *f*; **—s** mobiliario *m sg*, accesorios *m pl*

apportion [əpɔ́rʃən] VT repartir proporcionalmente

apportionment [əpɔ́rʃənmənt] N reparto proporcional *m*

appraisal [əpréz əl] N (of a property) tasación *f*, valuación *f*; (of a situation) evaluación *f*

appraise [əpréz] VT (a property) avaluar, valorar, tasar; (a situation) evaluar

appreciable [əpríʃəbəl] ADJ apreciable

appreciate [əpríʃiet] VT (value) apreciar, estimar; (recognize) reconocer, percibir; (thank) agradecer; **to — in value** apreciarse

appreciation [əpríʃiéʃən] N (esteem) aprecio *m*; (thanks) agradecimiento *m*; (monetary value) apreciación *f*, alza *f*

apprehend [æprɪhénd] VT (arrest) aprehender; (understand) comprender

apprehension [æprɪhénʃən] N (arrest) aprehensión *f*; (worry) aprensión *f*

apprehensive [æprɪhénsɪv] ADJ aprensivo

apprentice [əpréntɪs] N aprendiz -iza *mf*; VT poner de aprendiz

apprenticeship [əpréntɪsʃɪp] N aprendizaje *m*

apprise [əpráɪz] VT informar

approach [əprótʃ] N (act of approaching) aproximación *f*; (method) enfoque *m*, acercamiento *m*; (means of access) acceso *m*, entrada *f*; **— shot** golpe de aproximación *m*; VI (go nearer) acercarse, aproximarse; (in golf) aprochar; VT (a problem) abordar, enfocar; **to — someone about a problem** plantearle a alguien un problema

approachable [əprótʃəbəl] ADJ tratable

approbation [æprəbéʃən] N aprobación *f*

appropriate[1] [əprópr+t] ADJ apropiado,

adecuado

appropriate² [əpróupriet] VT apropiarse; (funds) asignar

appropriation [əproupriéʃən] N (act of seizing) apropiación f; (assignment of funds) asignación f; (assigned funds) partida f

approval [əprúvəl] N aprobación f; **on —** a prueba

approve [əprúv] VI/VT aprobar

approximate¹ [əpráksəmɪt] ADJ aproximado

approximate² [əpráksəmet] VT aproximarse a

approximately [əpráksəmɪtli] ADV aproximadamente

APR [annual percentage rate] [épiár] N TAE f

apricot [æprɪkat] N albaricoque m; Am damasco m; Mex chabacano m

April [éprəl] N abril m

apron [éprən] N (for a cook) delantal m; (for a workman) mandil m

apropos [æprəpóu] ADV a propósito; ADJ oportuno, pertinente; **— of** a propósito de

apt [æpt] ADJ (prone, able) capaz; (suited) pertinente; **is he — to be at home?** ¿estará en casa?

aptitude [æptɪtud] N aptitud f, capacidad f

aquamarine [ɑkwəmərín] N aguamarina f

aquarium [əkwériəm] N (tank) acuario m, pecera f; (building) acuario m

aquatic [əkwátɪk] ADJ acuático

aqueduct [ækwɪdʌkt] N acueducto m

Arab [ǽrəb] ADJ & N árabe mf

Arabic [ǽrəbɪk] ADJ árabe, arábigo; N (language) árabe m

arable [ǽrəbəl] ADJ cultivable

Aragonese [ærəgəníz] ADJ & N aragonés -esa mf

arbiter [árbɪDə] N árbitro -ra mf

arbitrariness [árbɪtrerɪnɪs] N arbitrariedad f

arbitrary [árbɪtreri] ADJ arbitrario; **— action** arbitrariedad f

arbitrate [árbɪtret] VI/VT (mediate) arbitrar [en]; terciar [en]; (submit to mediation) someter al arbitraje

arbitration [arbɪtréʃən] N arbitraje m

arbitrator [árbɪtreDə] N árbitro -tra mf

arbor [árbə] N pérgola f, glorieta f

arboreal [arbóriəl] ADJ arbóreo

arc [ark] N arco m

arcade [arkéd] N (series of arcs) arcada f; (shops) galería f; (video game center) sala de juegos electrónicos f

arcane [arkén] ADJ arcano

arch [artʃ] N arco m; (curved roof) bóveda f; **—way** arcada f; VI/VT arquear[se]

archaeological [arkiəládʒɪkəl] ADJ arqueológico

archaeology, archeology [arkiálədʒi] N arqueología f

archaic [arkéɪk] ADJ arcaico

archaism [árkeɪzəm] N arcaísmo m

archbishop [artʃbíʃəp] N arzobispo m

archenemy [ártʃénəmi] N archienemigo -ga mf

archer [ártʃə] N arquero -ra mf

archery [ártʃəri] N tiro al arco m

archetype [árkɪtaɪp] N arquetipo m

archipelago [arkəpéləgo] N archipiélago m

architect [árkɪtekt] N arquitecto -ta mf; (creator) artífice mf

architectural [arkɪtéktʃəl] ADJ arquitectónico

architecture [árkɪtektʃə] N arquitectura f

archive [árkaɪv] N archivo m

arctic [árktɪk] ADJ ártico

ardent [árdnt] ADJ ardiente

ardor [árdə] N ardor m, fervor m

arduous [árdʒuəs] ADJ arduo

are [ar] see be

area [ériə] N (space) área f; (region) zona f; (of a geometric figure) superficie f, área f

arena [ərínə] N (for sports) estadio m; (in a circus) pista f

Argentina [ardʒəntínə] N Argentina f

Argentinian [ardʒəntíniən] ADJ & N argentino -na mf

argon [árgan] N argón m

argue [árgju] VT (reason) argüir, argumentar; VI (bicker) discutir, reñir

argument [árgjəmənt] N (reason) argumento m; (altercation) disputa f, discusión f

arid [ǽrɪd] ADJ árido

arise [əráɪz] VI (get up) levantarse; (appear) surgir; (result) provenir, resultar

arisen [ərízən] see arise

aristocracy [ærɪstákrəsi] N aristocracia f

aristocrat [ərístəkræt] N aristócrata mf

aristocratic [ərɪstəkrǽDɪk] ADJ aristocrático

arithmetic¹ [əríθmətɪk] N aritmética f

arithmetic² [ærɪθmédɪk] ADJ aritmético

ark [ark] N arca f; **Noah's —** arca de Noé f

arm [arm] N brazo m; **—chair** sillón m, butaca f; **—pit** sobaco m, axila f; **—rest** (in a car) apoyabrazos m sg; (on a sofa) brazo m; **— in —** del brazo; **at —'s length** a distancia; **—'s-length transactions** transacciones a precio de mercado f pl; **with open —s** con los brazos abiertos; **—s** armas f pl; VT armar; **—ed forces** fuerzas armadas f pl; **—ed robbery** robo a mano armada m

armada [armádə] N armada f, flota f

armament [árməmənt] N armamento m

Armenia [armíniə] N Armenia f

Armenian [armíniən] ADJ & N armenio -nia mf

armful [ármfʊl] N brazada f

armistice [ármɪstɪs] N armisticio m

armoire [armwár] N armario m

armor [ármə] N (of a knight) armadura f; (on a vehicle) blindaje m; (on insects) coraza f; VT (a car) blindar; (a tank) acorazar

armored [ármə-d] ADJ (van) blindado; (tank) acorazado

armory [árməri] N armería f

army [ármi] N ejército m; (multitude) muchedumbre f

aroma [ərómə] N aroma m

aromatic [ærəmǽDɪk] ADJ aromático

arose [əróz] see arise

around [əráund] ADV **there were books all —** había libros por todos lados; **there is a supermarket — here** hay un supermercado por aquí; **it was the only farm for miles —** era la única granja en millas a la redonda; **the tree is forty centimeters —** el árbol tiene cuarenta centímetros de circunferencia; **I'll show you —** te enseño el lugar; **the wheels turned —** las ruedas giraban; **turn —** date la vuelta; **she finally came —** al final la convencimos; **he hasn't been —** no ha estado por aquí; **— five o'clock** a eso de las cinco; PREP **a ribbon — her wrist** una cinta alrededor de su muñeca; **tie a string — your finger** átate un hilo al dedo; **stay — the house** quédate cerca de la casa; **we drove — the block** dimos vuelta a la manzana; **he wandered — the park** deambuló por el parque; **the church — the corner** la iglesia a la vuelta de la esquina; **a town with mountains — it** un pueblo rodeado de montañas; **motion — its axis** movimiento en torno a su eje; **—-the-clock** veinticuatro horas al día; **we walked — town** dimos una vuelta por el pueblo

arouse [əráuz] VI despertar; VT (suspicion) despertar; (sexual response) excitar

arraign [ərén] VT hacer comparecer ante un juez

arrange [əréndʒ] VT arreglar

arrangement [əréndʒmənt] N (array) arreglo m; (placement) disposición f; (agreement) acuerdo m; **to make —s [for]** hacer arreglos [para]

array [əré] N (arrangement) abanico m, selección f; (placement of troops) orden m, formación f; (attire) gala f; (in software) vector m; VT (troops) formar; (attire) ataviar

arrears [ərírz] ADV LOC **in —** atrasado; N atrasos m pl

arrest [ərést] N arresto m, detención f; VI/VT arrestar, detener

arrhythmia [əríðmiə] N arritmia f

arrival [əráɪvəl] N llegada f; lit arribo m; **the new —s** los recién llegados

arrive [əráɪv] VI llegar; lit arribar

arrogance [ǽrəgəns] N arrogancia f

arrogant [ǽrəgənt] ADJ arrogante

arrow [ǽro] N flecha f; lit saeta f; **—head** punta de flecha f

arsenal [ársənl] N arsenal m

arsenic [ársənɪk] N arsénico m

arson [ársən] N incendio doloso m

art [ɑrt] N arte m [sg] f [pl]; (works) obras f pl; (skill) destreza f; **fine —s** bellas artes f pl; **master of —s** maestría en humanidades f; **— deco** art déco m

arterial [ɑrtíriəl] ADJ arterial

arteriosclerosis [ɑrtirisklərósɪs] N arteriosclerosis f

artery [árDəri] N arteria f

artful [ártfəl] ADJ (aesthetic) artístico; (deceitful) artero, astuto

arthritis [ɑrθráɪDɪs] N artritis f

arthroscopic [ɑrθrəskápɪk] ADJ artroscópico

arthroscopy [ɑrθrəskápi] N artroscopia f

artichoke [árDɪtʃok] N alcachofa f

article [árDɪkəl] N artículo m; **— of clothing** prenda de vestir f

articulate[1] [ɑrtíkjəlɪt] ADJ (clear) claro; (eloquent) elocuente; **he's very —** se expresa muy bien

articulate[2] [ɑrtíkjəlet] VI/VT (pronounce, join) articular; (express) enunciar

articulation [ɑrtɪkjəléʃən] N articulación f

artifact [árDəfækt] N artefacto m, ingenio m

artifice [árDəfɪs] N artificio m

artificial [ɑrDəfíʃəl] ADJ artificial; (affected) afectado; **— insemination** inseminación artificial f; **— intelligence** inteligencia artificial f

artillery [ɑrtíləri] N artillería f

artisan [árDɪzən] N artesano -na mf, artífice mf

artist [árDɪst] N (painter, sculptor) artista mf; (performer) intérprete mf

artistic [ɑrtístɪk] ADJ artístico

Aruba [ərúbə] N Aruba f

as [æz] CONJ **— for me** en lo que a mí respecta; **— if** como si; **— is** en la condición en que está; **— it were** por decirlo así; **— of** a partir de; **— per** según; **— the illness worsened** a medida que empeoraba la enfermedad; **— yet** hasta ahora, todavía; **the same —** lo mismo que; **it broke — I was using it** se rompió cuando lo usaba; **she knitted — we talked** tejía mientras conversábamos; **he played — never before** jugó como nunca; PREP **— a child, I always felt loved** de niño, siempre me sentí querido; **— a teacher, I must be tough** como maestro, tengo que ser estricto; ADV **tan, tanto**; **— large —** tan grande como; **— long — you wish** todo el tiempo que quieras; **— much —** tanto como; **— well** también; **it's not — important** no es tan importante

ASAP [as soon as possible] [ésæp] ADV lo antes posible

asbestos [æzbéstəs] N asbesto m, amianto m

ascend [əsénd] VI ascender; **—ing order** orden ascendente m

ascent [əsént] N ascenso m

ascertain [æsərtén] VT averiguar, establecer

ascetic [əsédɪk] ADJ ascético; N asceta *mf*

ascorbic [əskórbɪk] ADJ ascórbico

ascribe [əskráɪb] VT atribuir, imputar

aseptic [əséptɪk] ADJ aséptico

asexual [esékʃuəl] ADJ asexual

ash [æʃ] N (residue, remains) ceniza *f*; (species of tree) fresno *m*; **—tray** cenicero *m*; **— Wednesday** miércoles de ceniza *m*

ashamed [əʃémd] ADJ avergonzado; **to be —** tener vergüenza, avergonzarse

ashen [éʃən] ADJ ceniciento

ashore [əʃór] ADV (movement) a tierra; (location) en tierra; **to go —** desembarcar

Asia [éʒə] N Asia *f*

Asian [éʒən] ADJ & N asiático -ca *mf*

Asiatic [eʒiædɪk] ADJ **— flu** gripe asiática *f*

aside [əsáɪd] ADV **all kidding —** bromas aparte; **his father took him —** su padre lo llamó aparte; **he threw his coat —** tiró su saco a un lado; PREP **— from** aparte de, además de; N (theater) aparte *m*

asinine [ǽsɪnaɪn] ADJ necio

ask [æsk] VT (inquire) preguntar; (request) pedir; **to — a question** hacer una pregunta; **to — about** preguntar por; **to — for** pedir; **to — for someone** pedir para hablar con alguien; **to — a woman's hand in marriage** pedir la mano de una mujer; **to — out** invitar a salir; **what's your —ing price?** ¿cuánto pides? **you —ed for it** te lo has buscado

askance [əskǽns] ADV **to look —** (obliquely) mirar de soslayo/través/reojo; (suspiciously) mirar con recelo

askew [əskjú] ADJ ladeado, torcido

asleep [əslíp] ADJ dormido; **to fall —** dormirse; **my arm is —** se me ha dormido/entumecido el brazo

asparagus [əspǽrəgəs] N espárrago *m*

aspartame [ǽspətem] N aspartamo *m*

aspect [ǽspekt] N aspecto *m*

aspen [ǽspɪn] N álamo temblón *m*

Asperger's disorder [ǽspə-gə-zdɪsórdə-] N trastorno de Asperger *m*

asphalt [ǽsfɔlt] N asfalto *m*

asphyxia [æsfíksiə] N asfixia *f*

aspiration [æspəréʃən] N aspiración *f*

aspire [əspáɪr] VI aspirar

aspirin [ǽsprɪn] N aspirina *f*

ass [æs] N asno *m*, burro *m*, borrico *m*

assail [əsél] VT (physically) asaltar, atacar; (verbally) atacar

assailant [əsélənt] N atacante *mf*, agresor -ora *mf*

assassin [əsǽsɪn] N asesino -na *mf*

assassinate [əsǽsənet] VT asesinar

assassination [əsæsənéʃən] N asesinato *m*

assault [əsɔ́lt] N asalto *m*, agresión *f*; **— rifle** rifle de asalto *m*; **— and battery** agresión con lesiones *f*; VT asaltar, agredir; (sexually) violar

assay¹ [æsé] VT (situation) examinar, analizar; (metal) ensayar

assay² [ǽse] N ensayo *m*

assemble [əsémbəl] VI/VT (call together) reunir[se], congregar[se]; VT (put together) armar, montar

assembly [əsémbli] N (meeting) asamblea *f*, reunión *f*; (putting together) montaje *m*, armado *m*; **— language** lenguaje ensamblador *m*; **— line** cadena de producción *f*, línea de montaje *f*

assent [əsént] N asentimiento *m*; VI asentir

assert [əsə́t] VT (declare) aseverar, afirmar; **to — one's rights** hacer valer los derechos de uno; **to — oneself** obrar con firmeza

assertion [əsə́ʃən] N (declaration) aseveración *f*, afirmación *f*, aserto *m*; **an — of ownership** una afirmación de los derechos de propiedad

assess [əsés] VT (evaluate for tax purposes) tasar; (impose tax) gravar, imponer; (measure performance) evaluar

assessment [əsésmənt] N (estimate) avalúo *m*, tasación *f*; (tax) imposición *f*, gravamen *m*; (testing) evaluación *f*

asset [ǽset] N (useful thing) ventaja *f*; (useful quality) virtud *f*; **—s** activo *m*, bienes *m pl*; (on balance sheet) haber *m*, activo *m*; **personal —s** bienes muebles *m pl*; **real —s** bienes inmuebles *m pl*

assiduous [əsídʒuəs] ADJ (constant) asiduo; (industrious) diligente

assign [əsáɪn] VT (allot) asignar; (appoint, designate) designar; (transfer property) ceder

assignment [əsáɪnmənt] N (act of assigning) asignación *f*; (task) encargo *m*, encomienda *f*; (mission) misión *f*; (transfer of property) cesión [de bienes] *f*; (homework) tarea *f*; (lesson) lección *f*

assimilate [əsíməlet] VI/VT asimilar[se]

assist [əsíst] VI/VT ayudar, asistir; N (in sports) asistencia *f*

assistance [əsístəns] N ayuda *f*, asistencia *f*

assistant [əsístənt] N ayudante *mf*, asistente -ta *mf*; ADJ auxiliar; **— manager** subgerente *mf*

assistantship [əsístəntʃɪp] N ayudantía *f*

associate¹ [əsóʃiɪt] ADJ asociado; N (acquaintance) compañero -ra *mf*; (co-worker) colega *mf*; (employee) empleado -da *mf*

associate² [əsóʃiet] VI/VT asociar[se]; **to be —d with** asociarse con

association [əsosiéʃən] N asociación *f*

assonance [ǽsənəns] N asonancia *f*

assorted [əsɔ́rdɪd] ADJ variado, surtido

assortment [əsɔ́rtmənt] N (act of assorting) clasificación *f*; (selection of wares) surtido *m*; (selection of tools, etc.) colección *f*

assume [əsúm] VT (responsibility, role) asumir;

(right) arrogarse; (suppose) dar por sentado, suponer; **—d name** alias *m*

assumption [əsámpʃən] N (premise) suposición *f*, supuesto *m*; (unstated belief) sobreentendido *m*; (seizure) toma *f*; (acceptance of duties) asunción *f*

assurance [əʃúrəns] N (promise) promesa *f*, palabra *f*; (reassurance) palabras de apoyo *f pl*; (certainty) certeza *f*; (confidence) confianza *f*

assure [əʃúr] VT (give confidence) asegurar; (encourage) infundir confianza

assuredly [əʃúridli] ADV seguramente, sin duda

asterisk [ǽstərɪsk] N asterisco *m*

asteroid [ǽstərɔɪd] N asteroide *m*

asthma [ǽzmə] N asma *f*

asthmatic [æzmǽDɪk] ADJ asmático

astigmatism [əstígmətɪzəm] N astigmatismo *m*

astonish [əstánɪʃ] VT asombrar, pasmar

astonishing [əstánɪʃɪŋ] ADJ asombroso, pasmoso

astonishment [əstánɪʃmənt] M asombro *m*, pasmo *m*

astound [əstáund] VT pasmar, asombrar

astraddle [əstrǽdl̩] ADV a horcajadas

astray [əstré] ADV **to go —** perderse, extraviarse; **to lead —** (seduce) llevar por mal camino, seducir; (perplex) confundir

astride [əstráɪd] ADV a horcajadas

astringent [əstríndʒənt] ADJ & N astringente *m*

astrology [əstrálədʒɪ] N astrología *f*

astronaut [ǽstrənɔt] M astronauta *mf*

astronautics [æstrənɔ́Dɪks] N astronáutica *f*

astronomer [əstránəmə] N astrónomo -ma *mf*

astronomic [æstrənámɪk] ADJ astronómico

astronomical [æstrənámɪkəl] ADJ astronómico

astronomy [əstránəmi] N astronomía *f*

astrophysics [æstrofíziks] N astrofísica *f*

Asturian [əstúriən] ADJ & N asturiano -na *mf*

Asturias [əstúriəs] N Asturias *f sg*

astute [əstút] ADJ astuto, sagaz

asylum [əsáɪləm] N asilo *m*

asymmetric, asymmetrical [esɪmétrɪk[əl]] ADJ; asimétrico

asymptomatic [esɪmptəmǽDɪk] ADJ asintomático

at [æt] PREP **— the end of the story** al final de la historia; **— five o'clock** a las cinco; **— high altitude** a grandes alturas; **— last** por fin, al fin; **— once** enseguida; **— the table** a/ en la mesa; **— five dollars a kilo** a cinco dólares el kilo; **— Easter** en Pascua; **— home** en casa; **— war** en guerra; **wait — the door** espera en la puerta; **he is — peace with himself** está en paz consigo mismo; **the children are — play** los niños están jugando; **look — that** mira eso; **amazed —** pasmado por; **he laughed — me** se rió de mí

ate [et] *see* eat

atheism [éθiɪzəm] N ateísmo *m*

atheist [éθiɪst] N ateo -a *mf*

athlete [ǽθlit] N deportista *mf*; (track and field) atleta *mf*; **—'s foot** pie de atleta *m*

athletic [æθléDɪk] ADJ deportivo; (concerning track and field; well-built) atlético

athletics [æθléDɪks] N deporte *m*; (track and field) atletismo *m*

Atlantic [ætlǽntɪk] ADJ atlántico; **— Ocean** Océano Atlántico *m*

atlas [ǽtləs] N atlas *m*

ATM [automatic teller machine] [étiém] N cajero automático *m*

atmosphere [ǽtməsfɪr] N (air) atmósfera *f*; (mood) ambiente *m*

atmospheric [ætməsfírɪk] ADJ atmosférico

atom [ǽDəm] N átomo *m*; **— bomb** bomba atómica *f*

atomic [ətámɪk] ADJ atómico; **— age** era atómica *f*; **— energy** energía atómica *f*; **— number** número atómico *m*; **— weight** peso atómico *m*

atomize [ǽDəmaɪz] VT atomizar

atomizer [ǽDəmaɪzə] N atomizador *m*

atone [ətón] VI **to — for** expiar, purgar

atonement [əttónmənt] N expiación *f*, purgación *f*

atop [ətáp] PREP encima de

atrium [étriəm] N (of office building, hotel) vestíbulo *m*, patio central *m*; (of church) atrio *m*

atrocious [ətróʃəs] ADJ atroz

atrocity [ətrásɪDi] N atrocidad *f*, barbaridad *f*

atrophy [ǽtrəfi] N atrofia *f*; VI/VT atrofiar[se]

attach [ətǽtʃ] VI/VT (pipe, cable) unir[se], juntar; (paper) sujetar; (wages) retener; (significance) atribuir; (an electronic file) adjuntar; **to be —ed to someone** estar apegado a alguien

attaché [ætəʃé] N agregado -da *mf*

attachment [ətǽtʃmənt] N (act of attaching) unión *f*; (pipe, cable) conexión *f*; (of wages) retención *f*; (significance) atribución *f*; (to an e-mail) adjunto *m*; (affection) apego *m*, cariño *m*; (accessory) accesorio *m*

attack [ətǽk] N ataque *m*, acometida *f*; VI/VT atacar, acometer

attain [ətén] VT (rank) alcanzar; (ambition) lograr *m*, realizar *f*; VI (age) llegar a

attainment [əténmənt] N (rank) alcance *m*; (ambition) logro *m*, realización *f*

attempt [ətémpt] N tentativa *f*, intento *m*; (murder) atentado *m*; VT tratar [de], intentar

attend [əténd] VT (meeting) asistir a, acudir a; VI **to — to** (a sick person) atender, cuidar; (a speaker) prestar atención; **—ing physician** médico -ca tratante *mf*

attendance [əténdəns] N asistencia *f*

attendant [əténdənt] N (at a gas station) encargado -da *mf*; (servant) sirviente -ta *mf*; ADJ concomitante

attention [əténʃən] N atención *f*; (courtesy) atenciones *f pl*; — **deficit disorder** trastorno de déficit de atención *m*; **to pay** — prestar atención; **to pay** — **to** atender a; **to call** — llamar la atención; INTERJ —! ¡firmes!

attentive [əténtɪv] ADJ (focused) atento; (courteous) cortés

attenuate [əténjuet] VT atenuar

attest [ətést] VT (bear witness to) atestiguar; (manifest) demostrar; VI certificar, dar fe, atestar

attic [ǽdɪk] N desván *m*, altillo *m*

attire [ətáɪr] N atavío *m*, vestidura *f*; VT ataviar

attitude [ǽdɪtud] N (mental) actitud *f*; (physical) postura *f*; (insolence) insolencia *f*, descaro *m*

attorney [ətə́ni] N abogado -da *mf*, mandatario -ria *mf*; — **General** Ministro -tra de Justicia *mf*

attract [ətrǽkt] VT atraer; **to** — **attention** llamar la atención

attraction [ətrǽkʃən] N (act, power) atracción *f*; (charm) atractivo *m*; (of customers) captación *f*

attractive [ətrǽktɪv] ADJ atractivo; (beautiful) atractivo, agraciado

attractiveness [ətrǽktɪvnɪs] N atractivo *m*

attribute[1] [ǽtrəbjut] N atributo *m*

attribute[2] [ətrɪ́bjut] VT atribuir

attribution [ætrəbjúʃən] N atribución *f*

attrition [ətríʃən] N (wearing out) desgaste *m*; (casualties) bajas *f pl*; **war of** — guerra de agotamiento *f*

atypical [etípɪkəł] ADJ atípico

auburn [ɔ́bən] N & ADJ castaño rojizo *m*

auction [ɔ́kʃən] N subasta *f*, remate *m*; — **house** casa de subastas *f*; VI/VT subastar, rematar

auctioneer [ɔkʃəníɚ] N subastador -ra *mf*, rematador -ra *mf*

audacious [ɔdéʃəs] ADJ audaz, atrevido

audacity [ɔdǽsɪdi] N audacia *f*, desfachatez *f*, atrevimiento *m*

audible [ɔ́dəbəł] ADJ audible; — **feedback** regeneración audible *f*

audience [ɔ́diəns] N público *m*, auditorio *m*; (TV, radio) audiencia *f*

audio [ɔ́dio] ADJ de audio; — **book** audiolibro *m*; — **frequency** audiofrecuencia *f*; —**visual** audiovisual; —**visuals** audiovisuales *m pl*; — audio *m*

audiology [ɔdiálədʒi] N audiología *f*

audit [ɔ́dɪt] VI/VT (class) asistir de oyente; (accounts) auditar; N auditoría *f*; — **cycle** ciclo de auditoría *m*

auditing [ɔ́dɪtɪŋ] N auditoría *f*

audition [ɔdíʃən] N audición *f*; VI dar una audición [para]

auditor [ɔ́dɪdɚ] N (of accounts) auditor -ora *mf*, contralor -ora *mf*; (of a class) oyente *mf*

auditorium [ɔdɪtɔ́riəm] N auditorio *m*, paraninfo *m*

auditory [ɔ́dɪtɔri] ADJ auditivo

augment [ɔgmént] VT incrementar, aumentar

August [ɔ́gəst] N agosto *m*

aunt [ænt] N tía *f*

aura [ɔ́rə] N aura *f*

aurora [ərɔ́rə] N aurora *f*; — **borealis** aurora boreal *f*

auspices [ɔ́spɪsɪz] N auspicios *m pl*

auspicious [ɔspíʃəs] ADJ propicio

austere [ɔstír] ADJ austero

austerity [ɔstérɪdi] N austeridad *f*

Australia [ɔstréljə] N Australia *f*

Australian [ɔstréljən] ADJ & N australiano -na *mf*

Austria [ɔ́striə] N Austria *f*

Austrian [ɔ́striən] ADJ & N austríaco -ca *mf*

authentic [ɔθéntɪk] ADJ auténtico

authenticate [ɔθéntɪket] VT autenticar

authentication [ɔθentɪkéʃən] N legalización *f*

authenticity [ɔθentísɪdi] N autenticidad *f*

author [ɔ́θɚ] N (professional) escritor -ra *mf*; (creator) autor -ora *mf*

authoritarian [əθɔrɪtériən] ADJ autoritario

authoritative [əθɔ́rɪtedɪv] ADJ (official) autorizado; (dictatorial) autoritario

authority [əθɔ́rɪdi] N autoridad *f*; (permission) autorización *f*; **to have on good** — saber de buena fuente; **it's not within your** — no está dentro de tus facultades

authorization [ɔθərɪzéʃən] N autorización *f*

authorize [ɔ́θəraɪz] VT autorizar, habilitar

autism [ɔ́tɪzəm] N autismo *m*

autistic [ɔtístɪk] ADJ autista

auto [ɔ́do] *see* automobile, automatic

autobiography [ɔdobaɪágrəfi] N autobiografía *f*

autocrat [ɔ́dəkræt] N autócrata *mf*

autograph [ɔ́dəgræf] N autógrafo *m*

autoimmune [ɔdoɪmjún] ADJ autoinmune

automated [ɔ́dəmedɪd] ADJ automatizado

automatic [ɔdəmǽdɪk] ADJ automático; (response) maquinal; — **backup** (copy) copia de respaldo automático *f*; (process) respaldo automático *m*; — **pilot** piloto automático *m*; — **transmission** transmisión automática *f*

automation [ɔdəméʃən] N automatización *f*

automobile [ɔdəməbił] N automóvil *m*

automotive [ɔdəmódɪv] ADJ (sport) automovilístico; (industry) automotor, automotriz

autonomic [ɔdənámɪk] ADJ autonómico

autonomous [ətánəməs] ADJ autónomo

autonomy [ətánəmi] N autonomía *f*

autopilot [ɔ́dopaɪlət] N piloto automático *m*

autopsy [ɔ́tapsi] N autopsia *f*

autumn [ɔ́dəm] N otoño *m*

autumnal [ɔtámnəł] ADJ otoñal

auxiliary [ɔgzíləri] ADJ & N auxiliar *mf*

avail [əvéł] VI/VT servir; **to** — **oneself of**

aprovecharse de; N utilidad f; **of no** — de ninguna utilidad; **to no** — en vano

availability [əvelǝbíliDi] N (of a person, taxicab, funds) disponibilidad f; (of merchandise) existencias f pl

available [əvélǝbǝl] ADJ disponible, asequible

avalanche [ǽvǝlæntʃ] N avalancha f, alud m

avarice [ǽvǝrɪs] N avaricia f

avaricious [ævǝríʃǝs] ADJ avaro, avariento

avatar [ǽvǝtǝr] N avatar m

avenge [əvéndʒ] VT vengar

avenger [əvéndʒǝ] N vengador -ra mf

avenue [ǽvǝnu] N avenida f; (means of access) vía f

aver [əvɚ] VT afirmar

average [ǽvrɪdʒ] N promedio m; **on** — de promedio; ADJ medio, mediano; **just** — (person) del montón; (thing) nada del otro mundo; VT promediar; **he** — **s 20 miles an hour** hace un promedio de 20 millas por hora

averse [əvɚ́s] ADJ reacio; **he's not** — **to a glass of wine** no se opone a una copa de vino

aversion [əvɚ́ʒǝn] N aversión f

avert [əvɚ́t] VT (eyes) desviar, apartar; (danger) evitar

aviation [evié∫ǝn] N aviación f

aviator [évieDɚ] N aviador -ra mf

avid [ǽvɪd] ADJ ávido

avocado [ævǝkáDo] N aguacate m; Am palta f

avocation [ævǝké∫ǝn] N pasatiempo m

avoid [əvɔ́ɪd] VI/VT (stay away from) evitar; (dodge) esquivar

avow [əváu] VT confesar

avowal [əváuǝl] N confesión f

avuncular [əvʌ́ŋkjǝlǝ] ADJ propio de un tío; — **attitude** actitud paternal y amistosa

await [əwét] VT aguardar

awake [əwék] ADJ despierto; VI/VT despertar[se]

awaken [əwékǝn] VI/VT despertar[se]

award [əwɔ́rd] N premio m, galardón m; (judicial) adjudicación f; VT otorgar, adjudicar

aware [əwér] ADJ consciente, enterado; **I'm** — **of that** eso me consta

awareness [əwérnɪs] N conciencia f

away [əwé] ADV **far** — lejos; — **from his family** lejos de su familia; **she looked** — apartó la vista; **she's** — no está; **he's been painting** — **all day** se ha pasado todo el día pintando; **right** — ahora mismo, ahorita; **ten miles** — a diez millas de distancia; **to give** — regalar; **to go** — irse; **to take** — quitar; **to blow** — (destroy) [hacer] volar; (astonish) dejar atónito

awe [ɔ] N sobrecogimiento m; **to be in** — sobrecogerse; VT sobrecoger

awesome [ɔ́sǝm] ADJ (awe-inspiring) sobrecogedor; (impressive) fabuloso

awestruck [ɔ́strʌk] ADJ pasmado

awful [ɔ́fǝl] ADJ terrible, horroroso; ADV espantoso

awhile [əhwáɪl] ADV un rato

awkward [ɔ́kwǝd] ADJ (clumsy) torpe, desmañado; (embarrassing) embarazoso; (unwieldy) incómodo

awl [ɔl] N punzón m

awning [ɔ́nɪŋ] N toldo m

awoke [əwók] see wake

awoken [əwókn] see wake

awry [ərái] ADJ (clothes) mal puesto; (hat) ladeado; **my plans went** — mis planes fracasaron rotundamente

ax, axe [æks] N hacha f; VT eliminar

axis [ǽksɪs] N eje m

axle [ǽksǝl] N eje m

Azerbaijan [æzǝbaɪdʒán] N Azerbaiyán m

Azerbaijani, Azerbaijanian [æzǝbaɪdʒáni[ǝn]] ADJ & N azerbaijano -na mf, azerbaiyano -na mf

Aztec [ǽztek] ADJ & N azteca mf

azure [ǽʒǝ] ADJ [azul] celeste; N azul celeste m

Bb

babble [bǽbǝl] N (baby talk) balbuceo m; (chatter) parloteo m; (murmur) murmullo m; VI (to talk like a baby) balbucear; (to chatter) parlotear; (to murmur) murmurar

baboon [bæbún] N babuino m

baby [bébi] N bebé mf; **who's the** — **in your family?** ¿quién es el menor/benjamín en tu familia? — **blue** celeste m; — **boomer** persona nacida entre 1946 y 1965 f; — **carriage** cochecito de bebé m; — **food** comida para bebés f; — **girl** nena f; — **sister** hermanita f; — **sitter** niñera f; — **talk** habla infantil f; — **tooth** diente de leche m; **to** — **sit** cuidar niños; **she had a** — dio a luz; VT mimar

baccalaureate [bækǝlɔ́riǝt] N bachillerato m

bachelor [bǽt∫ǝlǝ] N soltero m; —**'s degree** licenciatura f; — **of Arts** (degree) licenciatura en filosofía y letras f; (person) licenciado -da en filosofía y letras mf

bacillus [bǝsíləs] N bacilo m

back [bæk] N (human body part) espalda f; (animal body part) lomo m; (opposite side) dorso m; (of chair) respaldo m, espaldar m; —**ache** dolor de espalda m; —**bone** columna vertebral f, espinazo m; —**pack** mochila f; **behind one's** — a espaldas de uno; **he has no** —**bone** no tiene carácter; **in** — **of** detrás de, tras; **in the** — **of the house** atrás de la casa; **to fall on one's** — caer de espaldas; **to**

turn one's — volver las espaldas; ADJ — **charges** cargos atrasados *m pl*; — **door** puerta trasera *f*; — **issues** números atrasados *m pl*; — **order** pedido pendiente *m*; — **taxes** impuestos atrasados *m pl*; **on the** — **burner** en suspenso; — **-and-forth movement** movimiento de vaivén *m*; VT respaldar, apoyar; VI dar marcha atrás; **to** — **down** echarse [para] atrás, recular; **to** — **up** (in a car) dar marcha atrás; (a file) hacer una copia de seguridad de; ADV (look) atrás / para atrás; (fall) de espaldas; **to** — **off** echarse atrás; — **and forth** de aquí para allá; **he ran** — **to the house** volvió corriendo a la casa; **he's** — **from work** está de vuelta del trabajo

backbite [bǽkbaɪt] VI/VT difamar

back date [bǽk det] VT antedatar

backer [bǽkɚ] N (financial) fiador -ra *mf*; (political) partidario -ria *mf*

backfire [bǽkfaɪr] VI (automobile) petardear, hacer detonaciones; (plan) ser contraproducente; N petardeo *m*

backgammon [bǽkgæmən] N backgammon *m*

background [bǽkgraʊnd] N (of a picture) fondo *m*; (experience) antecedentes *m pl*; (software) — **application** aplicación de fondo *f*; — **noise** ruido de fondo *m*; **I have a** — **in computers** tengo conocimientos de informática; **I know what goes on in the** — sé lo que pasa entre bastidores; **a humble** — orígenes humildes *m pl*

backhand [bǽkhænd] N revés *m*

backing [bǽkɪŋ] N (support) respaldo *m*, apoyo *m*; (guarantee) garantía *f*; (fabric) refuerzo *m*

backlash [bǽklæʃ] N reacción violenta *f*

backlighting [bǽklaɪtɪŋ] N retroiluminación *f*

backlit [bǽklɪt] ADJ retroiluminado

backlog [bǽklɑg] N atraso *m*

backpack [bǽkpɑg] N mochila *f*; VI viajar con mochila

backseat [bǽksit] N asiento trasero *m*

backslash [bǽkslæʃ] N barra invertida *f*

backslide [bǽkslaɪd] VI volver a las andadas, reincidir

backspace [bǽkspes] N (action) retroceso *m*; (key) tecla de retroceso *f*; VI apretar la tecla de retroceso

backspin [bǽkspɪn] N efecto *m*, cortado *m*

backstage [bǽksteʤ] ADV entre bastidores

backtrack [bǽktræk] VI retroceder, dar marcha atrás

backup [bǽkʌp] N (support) respaldo *m*; (copy) copia de seguridad *f*

backward [bǽkwəd] ADV hacia atrás, para atrás; — **search** búsqueda hacia atrás *f*; **to go** — recular; ADJ (underdeveloped) atrasado; (reactionary) retrógrado

backwardness [bǽkwədnɪs] N (underdevelopment) atraso *m*; (conservatism)

retrogradismo *m*; (timidity) timidez *f*

backyard [bǽkjárd] N patio trasero *m*

bacon [békən] N tocino *m*, Sp beicon *m*

bacteria [bæktíriə] N bacteria[s] *f* [*pl*]

bacterial [bæktíriəl] ADJ bacteriano

bacteriology [bæktiriáləʤi] N bacteriología *f*

bad [bæd] ADJ malo; (man) perverso; (teeth) feo; (drug) dañoso; (flood) grave; (fruit) podrido; — **blood** enemistad *f*; — **check** sin fondos *m*; — **debt** deuda incobrable *f*; — **faith** mala fe *f*; **to go from** — **to worse** ir de mal en peor; **he has a** — **heart** está enfermo del corazón; **to look** — tener mal aspecto; *fam* quedar mal; ADV mal; **not** — no está nada mal; **too** — ¡qué pena! VT **to** —**mouth** difamar [a]

bade [bed] *see* bid

badge [bæʤ] N insignia *f*, chapa *f*

badger [bǽʤɚ] N tejón *m*; VT acosar

badly [bǽdli] ADV (do) mal; (want) mucho; (hurt) gravemente

baffle [bǽfəl] VT (confuse) confundir; (frustrate) desconcertar; N deflector *m*

bag [bæg] N bolsa *f*, bolso *m*; (suitcase) maleta *f*; (under eyes) ojera *f*; — **lady** vagabunda *f*; — **pipe** gaita *f*; VT (groceries) empacar, embolsar; (prey) cazar

baggage [bǽgɪʤ] N (suitcases) equipaje *m*; (impediments) bagaje *m*; — **car** vagón de equipajes *m*; — **check** contraseña de equipajes *f*; — **claim** recogida de equipaje *f*; — **tag** etiqueta *f*; — **inspection** revisión de equipaje *f*

baggy [bǽgi] ADJ flojo, holgado

Bahamas [bəháməz] N Bahamas *f pl*

Bahamian [bəhémiən] ADJ & N bahameño -ña *mf*

Bahrain [barén] N Bahréin *m*

Bahraini [baréni] ADJ & N bahreiní *mf*

bail [bel] N fianza *f*; — **out** rescate financiero *m*; **to let out on** — poner en libertad bajo fianza; VT pagar la fianza; **to** — **someone out** pagarle la fianza a alguien; **to** — **someone out of a predicament** sacar a alguien de un apuro; **to** — **out water** achicar, vaciar; VI **to** — **out** (of a plane) tirarse con paracaídas de un avión; (of a situation) abandonar

bailiff [bélɪf] N ujier *mf*

bait [bet] N cebo *m*; VT (prepare hook) cebar; (attract customers) seducir; (harass) acosar; — **and switch advertising** publicidad de cebo y anzuelo *f*

bake [bek] VI/VT (in an oven) hornear; (in the sun) calcinar, abrasar; **I'm baking in this heat** me estoy asando, me muero de calor

baker [békɚ] N panadero -ra *mf*; —**'s dozen** la docena del fraile *f*

bakery [békəri] N panadería *f*

baking [békɪŋ] N (act of baking) horneado m; (activity) repostería f; — **powder** polvo de hornear m; — **soda** bicarbonato de sodio m

balance [bǽləns] N (instrument) balanza f; (equilibrium) equilibrio m; (debit, credit) saldo m, balance m; — **due** saldo pendiente m; — **sheet** balance m; — **of payments** balanza de pagos f; — **of trade** balanza comercial f; **to lose one's** — perder el equilibrio; VT equilibrar, hacer equilibrio con; **to** — **the risks with the benefits** sopesar los riesgos y los beneficios; VI (accounts) cuadrar; —**ed budget** presupuesto equilibrado m; **to** — **a budget** equilibrar un presupuesto

balanced [bǽlənst] ADJ equilibrado

balancing [bǽlənsɪŋ] N equilibrado m

balcony [bǽɫkəni] N balcón m; (in a theater) palco m, entresuelo m

bald [bɔɫd] ADJ (person) calvo, pelón; (mountain) pelón; (tire) liso; — **eagle** águila americana de cabeza blanca f; —**headed** calvo; — **spot** calva f; **he went** — se quedó calvo

baldness [bɔ́ɫdnɪs] N calvicie f

bale [beɫ] N paca f, fardo m; VT empacar, enfardar

balk [bɔk] VI oponerse, rehusarse a

ball [bɔɫ] N (tennis, baseball, golf) pelota f, bola f; (baseball, opposite of strike) bola f; (basketball, football, soccer) balón m; (billiards) bola f; (of string, thread) ovillo m; (cannon) bala [de cañón] f; (dance) baile m; — **and chain** grillete m; — **bearing** cojinete de bolas m; — **game** juego de pelota m; (baseball) partido de béisbol m; —**park estimate** cifra aproximada f; VT ovillar

ballad [bǽləd] N balada f; (historical) romance m

ballast [bǽləst] N lastre m; (railroad) balasto m; VT lastrar

ballerina [bælərínə] N bailarina de ballet f

ballet [bælé] N ballet m

ballistic [bəlístɪk] ADJ balístico; — **missile** misil balístico m; N —**s** balística f

balloon [bəlún] N globo m; — **mortgage** hipoteca con pago final mayor f; VI (travel in a balloon) pasear en globo; VI/VT (grow) inflar[se]

ballot [bǽlət] N (system of voting) votación f; (paper) papeleta f; Mex boleta f; — **box** urna f

balm [bam] N bálsamo m

balmy [bámi] ADJ templado

baloney [bəlóni] N pamplinas f pl, paparruchas f pl

balsa [bɔ́ɫsə] N (wood) madera balsa f; (raft) balsa f

balsam [bɔ́ɫsəm] N (resin) bálsamo m; (tree) especie de abeto m

bamboo [bæmbú] N bambú m

ban [bæn] N prohibición f; (church) excomunión f; VT prohibir

banal [bénl] ADJ banal

banana [bənǽnə] N plátano m, banana f; — **grove** platanar m; — **split** banana split m; — **tree** plátano m, banano m

band [bænd] N (group) banda f, pandilla f; (group of musicians) banda f, conjunto m; (cloth) banda f; (ribbon) cinta f; (leather) tira f; **to join the** —**wagon** subirse al carro/tren; —**width** amplitud de banda f; VI/VT **to** — **together** unirse, juntarse

bandage [bǽndɪdʒ] N venda f, vendaje m; VT vendar

Band-aid® [bǽnded] N Curita® f, parche m

bandit [bǽndɪt] N bandido -da mf, bandolero -ra mf, salteador -ora mf

bang [bæŋ] N (blow) golpe m, golpazo m; (sound) estampido m, estallido m; —**s** fleco m, flequillo m; **I get a** — **out of seeing my grandkids** me emociona ver a mis nietos; VI/VT (hit) golpear; (make noise) hacer estrépito

Bangladesh [bæŋglədéʃ] N Bangladesh m

Bangladeshi [bæŋglədéʃi] ADJ & N bangladeshí mf, bangladesí mf, bengalés -esa

banish [bǽnɪʃ] VT desterrar

banishment [bǽnɪʃmənt] N destierro m, proscripción f

banister [bǽnɪstɚ] N barandal m, pasamano[s] m, balaustrada f

banjo [bǽndʒo] N banjo m

bank [bæŋk] N (financial institution) banco m; (in gambling) banca f; (of a body of water) orilla f, ribera f, margen m; (slope) escarpa f; — **card** tarjeta bancaria f; — **account** cuenta bancaria f; — **check** cheque de caja m; — **failure** quiebra bancaria f; —**note** billete m; — **statement** estado de cuenta m; — **vault** cámara f; ADJ bancario, de banco; VT (money) depositar en un banco; VI (snow, sand) amontonar; (airplane) ladear; **to** — **on** contar con; **to** —**roll** financiar

banker [bǽŋkɚ] N (bank owner) banquero -ra mf; (bank employee) bancario -ria mf

banking [bǽŋkɪŋ] N (activity) actividad bancaria f; (industry) banca f; ADJ bancario, de banco

bankrupt [bǽŋkrəpt] ADJ en bancarrota, en quiebra; VT arruinar, quebrar

bankruptcy [bǽŋkrəptsi] N bancarrota f, quiebra f; — **law** estatuto de quiebras m; — **proceedings** juicio por quiebra m; **to go into** — declararse en quiebra

banner [bǽnɚ] N estandarte m, pendón m; ADJ sobresaliente

banquet [bǽŋkwɪt] N banquete m, gala f

baptism [bǽptɪzəm] N (sacrament) bautismo m; (action) bautizo m

baptize [bǽptaɪz] VT bautizar

bar [bɑr] N (of iron, sand, soap, of a tavern) barra f; (of chocolate) barra f, tableta f; (vertical rod) barrote *m*; (obstacle) barrera *f*, obstáculo *m*; (in music) compás *m*; (saloon) bar *m*; **—bell** barra para pesas *f*; **—code** código de barras *m*; **—code reader** lector de código de barras *m*; **— graph** gráfica de barras *f*; **—keeper/tender** tabernero -ra *mf*, cantinero -ra *mf*; **—room** bar *m*; **—room brawl** pelea de borrachos *f*; **behind —s** tras las rejas; **to be admitted to the —** recibirse de abogado; VT (door, exit) atrancar; (access) impedir; (from membership) excluir; **— none** sin excepción; **—ring a disaster** salvo en caso de desastre

barb [barb] N púa *f*; **—ed wire** alambre de púas *m*; *Sp* alambre de espino *m*

Barbadian [barbéDiən] ADJ & N barbadense *mf*

Barbados [barbéDOS] N Barbados *m*

barbarian [barbériən] ADJ & N bárbaro -ra *mf*

barbaric [barbǽrɪk] ADJ bárbaro

barbarous [bárbəəs] ADJ bárbaro

barbecue [bárbɪkju] N (meat dish) barbacoa *f*, asado *m*, parrillada *f*; **— sauce** adobo de barbacoa *m*; VI/VT asar con adobo

barber [bárbə] N peluquero *m*, barbero *m*; **—shop** peluquería *f*, barbería *f*

barbiturate [barbítʃə‑ɪt] N barbitúrico *m*

bard [bard] N bardo *m*

bare [ber] ADJ (legs, walls) desnudo; (pantry) vacío; **—back** a pelo; **—-bones** básico; **—faced** descarado; **—foot** descalzo; **the — necessities** lo imprescindible; **—headed** con la cabeza descubierta; **—legged** con las piernas desnudas; **— majority** escasa mayoría *f*; **to lay —** poner al descubierto; **with his — hands** con las propias manos

barely [bérli] ADV apenas

bargain [bárgɪn] N (agreement) trato *m*; (inexpensive purchase) ganga *f*, ocasión *f*; **— basement** sección de ofertas *f*; **into the —** por añadidura; **to strike a —** cerrar un trato; VI (haggle) regatear; (expect) contar con

bargaining [bárgənɪŋ] N (haggling) regateo *m*; (negotiation) negociación *f*; **—ing position** posición de negociación *f*

barge [bardʒ] N barcaza *f*; VI **to — into a room** irrumpir en un cuarto

baritone [bérɪton] N & ADJ barítono *m*

barium [bériəm] N bario *m*

bark [bark] N (of a dog) ladrido *m*; (on a tree) corteza *f*; VI/VT ladrar

barley [bárli] N cebada *f*

barn [barn] N (for animals) establo *m*; (for grain) granero *m*; **— owl** lechuza *f*; **—yard** corral *m*

barnacle [bárnəkəl] N percebe *m*

barometer [bərámɪDə] N barómetro *m*

baron [bærən] N barón *m*

baroque [bərók] ADJ & N barroco *m*

barracks [bǽrəks] N cuartel *m*

barracuda [bærəkúDə] N barracuda *f*

barrage [bəráʒ] N (of artillery fire) barrera de fuego *f*; (of questions) lluvia *f*, aluvión *m*

barrel [bǽrəl] N barril *m*, tonel *m*; (gun) cañón *m*, caño *m*; **he's a — of laughs** es un payaso; **he is scraping the bottom of the —** está desesperado; VI **to — along** ir disparado

barren [bǽrən] ADJ (land) árido, yermo; (female) estéril

barrette [bərét] N broche *m*

barricade [bǽrɪkéd] N barricada *f*; VT cerrar con barricadas; VI atrincherarse

barrier [bǽriə] N barrera *f*; **— reef** barrera de coral *f*

barrio [bário] N barrio hispano *m*

barter [bárdə] VI hacer trueque; VT trocar; N trueque *m*

bartering [bárdə‑ɪŋ] N trueque *m*

basal cell carcinoma [bésəlsɛlkarsɪnómə] N carcinoma de célula basal *m*

basalt [bésɔlt] N basalto *m*

base [bes] N base *f*; **—ball** béisbol *m*; **—ball player** beisbolista *m*, pelotero -ra *mf*; **—board** zócalo *m*; ADJ bajo, vil; (metal) de baja ley; **— font** tipo de letra por omisión *m*; **—line** línea de fondo *f*; **— on balls** base por bolas *f*; **— pay** salario base *m*; **—s loaded** bases llenas *f pl*; **— steal** robo de base *m*; VI/VT basar, fundamentar; **to be —d on** fundamentarse en; **the general is —d in Berlin** el general está estacionado en Berlín

baseless [béslɪs] ADJ sin fundamento

basement [bésmənt] N sótano *m*

baseness [bésnɪs] N bajeza *f*, vileza *f*

bash [bæʃ] VT golpear; N (party) fiesta *f*

bashful [bǽʃfəl] ADJ tímido, vergonzoso

bashfulness [bǽʃfəlnɪs] N timidez *f*

basic [bésɪk] ADJ básico

basin [bésɪn] N (bowl) palangana *f*, jofaina *f*; (of a fountain) pilón *m*; (geographical formation) cuenca *f*; (pond) estanque *m*

basis [bésɪs] N fundamento *m*, base *f*; **on the — of** en base a, con base en; **on a regular —** regularmente

bask [bæsk] VI (in the sun) asolearse; (in praise) deleitarse

basket [bǽskɪt] N canasta *f*, cesta *f*, cesto *m*; (in basketball) canasta *f*; **—ball** (game) baloncesto *m*, básquetbol *m*, básquet *m*; (ball) balón de baloncesto *m*; **— case** (crazy person) chiflado -da *mf*; (helpless person) caso perdido *m*; **to make a —** (in basketball) encestar

basketful [bǽskɪtfəl] N (contents of a basket) canasto *m*; (large amount) montón *m*

basketry [bǽskɪtri] N cestería *f*

Basque [bæsk] ADJ & N (person) vasco -ca *mf*; (language) vascuence *m*, vasco *m*, euskera *m*

bass[1] [bes] N (voice, bass guitar) bajo *m*; (double bass) contrabajo *m*; **— clef** clave de fa *f*; **—**

drum bombo *m*; **— horn** tuba *f*

bass² [bæs] (marine fish) lubina *f*; (freshwater fish) perca *f*

bassist [bésɪst] N bajista *mf*

bassoon [bæsún] N fagot *m*

bastard [bǽstəd] N & ADJ bastardo -da *mf*

baste [best] VT (fabric) hilvanar; (meat) rociar

bat [bæt] N (baseball, cricket) bate *m*; (animal) murciélago *m*; VT golpear; **he is at —** está al bate; **it was his first at—** fue su primer turno; VI (baseball) batear; **not to — an eye** no pestañear

batch [bætʃ] N (of cookies) hornada *f*; (of cement, files) tanda *f*; (of data) colección *f*

bath [bæθ] N baño *m*; **—robe** bata [de baño] *f*; Sp albornoz *m*; **—room** (in a house) baño *m*, cuarto de baño *m*; (public) Sp aseo *m*; Am servicio *m*, baño *m*; **—tub** bañera *f*

bathe [beð] VI/VT bañar[se]; **bathing suit** traje de baño *m*

bather [béðə] N bañista *mf*

baton [bətón] N batuta *f*

battalion [bətǽljən] N batallón *m*

batter [bǽðə] N (in baking) pasta *f*, masa *f*; (in baseball) bateador -ora *mf*; **—'s box** caja de bateo *f*; VT golpear

battery [bǽɾəri] N (of car, artillery, in baseball) batería *f*; (of electronic devices) pila *f*; (of tests) serie *f*; (assault) asalto *m*

batting [bǽɾɪŋ] N bateo *m*; **— average** porcentaje de bateo *m*

battle [bǽdl] N batalla *f*; **—ax[e]** (weapon) hacha de guerra *f*; (woman) *pej* sargenta *f*; **— cry** grito de guerra *m*; **—field** campo de batalla *m*; **—ship** acorazado *m*; VI batallar; **to — cancer** luchar contra el cáncer

bawl [bɔl] VI berrear; **to — somebody out** echarle la bronca a uno

bay [be] N (body of water) bahía *f*; (howl) aullido *m*; **— leaf** hoja de laurel *f*; **— window** ventana saliente *f*; **to hold at —** tener a raya; ADJ bayo; VI aullar

bayonet [beanét] N bayoneta *f*

bazaar [bəzár] N (market place) bazar *m*; (benefit) kermés *f*

bazooka [bəzúkə] N bazuca *f*

be [bi] VI ser, estar; **I am from Uruguay** soy de Uruguay; **there were four of us** éramos cuatro; **he is a doctor** es médico; **it's her** es ella; **sugar is sweet** el azúcar es dulce; **London is in England** Londres está en Inglaterra; **this water is cold** esta agua está fría; **the windows were open** las ventanas estaban abiertas; **there is a problem** hay un problema; **to — cold/warm/hungry/ right / in a hurry** tener frío/calor/hambre/ razón/prisa; **to be cold/hot/windy** hacer frío/calor/viento

beach [bitʃ] N playa *f*; **—comber** vagabundo -da

mf; **—head** cabeza de playa *f*; VT varar, encallar

beacon [bíkən] N faro *m*

bead [bid] N (of glass) cuenta *f*; (of sweat) gota *f*, perla *f*; **to get a — on somebody** apuntarle a alguien; VT (string) enhebrar/ensartar cuentas; (decorate) adornar con cuentas

beagle [bígəl] N beagle *m*

beak [bik] N pico *m*

beaker [bíkə] N vaso de precipitados *m*

beam [bim] N (of light) rayo *m*, haz *m*; (of a building) viga *f*; (of a ship) manga *f*; (of a scale) brazo *m*; **broad in the —** ancho de caderas; VI/VT (light, radio) emitir; (smile) estar radiante

bean [bin] N judía *f*, habichuela *f*; Sp alubia *f*; Am frijol *m*, Am poroto *m*; **Lima —** haba *f*; **—stalk** tallo de habas / frijol *m*; **Jack and the —stalk** Juanito y las habichuelas; **I don't know —s about that** no sé ni papa / ni jota de eso

bear [ber] N oso *m*; **— hug** abrazo fuerte *m*; **— market** mercado bajista *m*; VT (hold up, tolerate) soportar, aguantar; (suffer) sobrellevar; (have a child) dar a luz; (produce young) parir; (produce fruit) producir; **to — down** (mash) apretar; (push) pujar; **to — a grudge** guardar rencor; **to — in mind** tener en cuenta; **to — oneself with dignity** portarse con dignidad; **to — out** confirmar; **to — testimony** dar testimonio; **to — interest** devengar interés; **to — gifts** traer regalos; **to — a resemblance** parecerse; **to — the cost of something** asumir el costo de algo; **it doesn't — repeating** no merece repetirse

bearable [bérəbəl] ADJ llevadero, soportable

beard [bird] N (on a man) barba *f*; (of wheat) aristas *f pl*

bearded [bírdɪd] ADJ barbado, barbudo

bearer [bérə] N portador -ora *mf*

bearing [bérɪŋ] N porte *m*; **to lose one's —s** perder el rumbo, desorientarse; **it has no — on our situation** no tiene relación con nuestra situación

bearish [bérɪʃ] ADJ (of bears) osuno; (of stock market) bajista

beast [bist] N bestia *f*

beat [bit] VT (wings, eggs) batir; (a person) golpear; (drum) tocar; (an opponent) vencer; (tempo) marcar; VI (heart) latir; (drum) sonar; **to — around the bush** andarse por las ramas; **to — off** rechazar; **to — up** dar una paliza; **—s me!** ¡ni idea! N (blow) golpe *m*; (drum) toque *m*; (heart) latido *m*; (tempo) compás *m*; (policeman's territory) ronda *f*; ADJ cansado

beaten [bítn] ADJ (mixed) batido; (defeated) vencido; **— path** camino trillado *m*

beaten [bítn] *see* beat

beater [bíɾəˈ] N batidor *m*

beating [bíɾɪŋ] N (whipping) paliza *f*; (pulsation) latido *m*

beau [bo] N pretendiente *m*

beautiful [bjúɾəfəɫ] ADJ hermoso; — **people** jet set *m*

beautify [bjúɾəfaɪ] VT embellecer, hermosear

beauty [bjúɾi] N belleza *f*, hermosura *f*; (woman) beldad *f*; — **contest/pageant** concurso/certamen de belleza *m*; — **parlor** salón de belleza *m*

beaver [bívəˈ] N castor *m*

became [bikém] *see* become

because [bɪkɔ́z] CONJ porque; — **of** por, a causa de, debido a

beckon [békən] VT llamar por señas

become [bikʌ́m] VT (turn into) convertirse en; **the water became ice** el agua se convirtió en hielo; **he became a doctor** llegó a ser médico; (suit) sentar bien; **that suit —s you** ese traje te luce bien; VI (change emotional or physical condition) ponerse; **she became ill** se puso enferma; (undergo a drastic change) volverse; **he became crazy** se volvió loco; **to — angry** enojarse; **to — frightened** asustarse; **to — old** envejecer; **what has — of him?** ¿qué ha sido de él?

becoming [bikʌ́mɪŋ] ADJ (appropriate) propio; **that dress is — to you** te sienta bien ese vestido

bed [bɛd] N (furniture) cama *f*; *lit* lecho *m*; (of a river) cauce *m*; (of the sea) fondo *m*; (in a garden) cuadro *m*; —**bug** chinche *mf*; —**clothes** ropa de cama *f*; —**pan** cuña *f*, chata *f*; —**ridden** postrado en cama; —**rest** reposo *m*; —**rock** lecho de roca *m*; —**room** alcoba *f*, dormitorio *m*; *Mex* recámara *f*; **at the —side** al lado de la cama; —**side table** mesita de noche *f*; —**side manner** manera de tratar a los pacientes *f*; —**sore** llaga *f*; —**spread** colcha *f*; —**spring** resorte del colchón *m*; —**time** hora de dormir *f*; —**wetting** enuresis nocturna *f*; **to go to —** acostarse; **to put to —** acostar

bedding [bédɪŋ] N ropa de cama *f*

bee [bi] N (insect) abeja *f*; (social gathering) tertulia *f*; **to have a — in one's bonnet** tener una idea metida en la cabeza; —**hive** colmena *f*; — **sting** picadura de abeja *f*

beech [bitʃ] N haya *f*; —**nut** hayuco *m*

beef [bif] N (meat) carne de vaca/res *f*; (complaint) queja *f*; —**jerky** cecina *f*; —**steak** bistec *m*; VI quejarse; **to — up** reforzar

been [bɪn] *see* be

beep [bip] N pitazo *m*; VI/VT (alarm) sonar; (horn) tocar

beeper [bípəˈ] N buscapersonas *m sg*

beer [bir] N cerveza *f*

beet [bit] N remolacha *f*

beetle [bídɫ] N escarabajo *m*

befall [bɪfɔ́ɫ] VT acontecerle a

befallen [bɪfɔ́lən] *see* befall

befell [bɪfɛ́ɫ] *see* befall

befit [bɪfɪ́t] VT convenir

before [bɪfɔ́r] ADV (temporal) antes, con anterioridad; (spatial) delante; PREP (temporal) antes de; (spatial) delante de; *lit* ante; CONJ antes [de] que, antes de; — **beginning** antes de que comiences, antes de comenzar; —**-tax earnings** ganancias pre-impositivas *f pl*

beforehand [bɪfɔ́rhænd] ADV de antemano, con anterioridad

befriend [bɪfrɛ́nd] VT hacerse amigo de

beg [bɛɡ] VI (ask for alms) mendigar, pedir limosna; VI/VT (implore) rogar; **to — for mercy** pedir misericordia; **she —ged me to do it** me rogó que lo hiciera; **to — the question** dar por sentado lo mismo que se arguye

began [bɪɡǽn] *see* begin

begat [bɪɡǽt] *see* beget

beget [bɪɡɛ́t] VT engendrar

beggar [béɡəˈ] N mendigo -ga *mf*

begin [bɪɡín] VI/VT comenzar, empezar; **the ten dollars won't — to cover the expense** los diez dólares ni siquiera cubren los gastos

beginner [bɪɡínəˈ] N principiante *mf*

beginning [bɪɡínɪŋ] N principio *m*; (temporal only) comienzo *m*; — **with** comenzando con/por; **at the —** al/por el principio

begotten [bɪɡátn] *see* beget

begrudge [bɪɡrʌ́dʒ] VT aceptar de mala gana

begun [bɪɡán] *see* begin

behalf [bɪhǽf] PREP LOC **on — of** (in place of) por, en nombre de, de parte de; (in favor of) a favor de

behave [bɪhév] VI portarse, comportarse; — **yourself!** ¡pórtate bien!

behavior [bɪhévjəˈ] N comportamiento *m*, conducta *f*

behavioral [bɪhévjərəɫ] ADJ conductual, relativo a la conducta / al comportamiento

behead [bɪhɛ́d] VT decapitar, descabezar

beheld [bɪhɛ́ɫd] *see* behold

behind [bɪháɪnd] ADV detrás; (in payments, schedule) atrasado; **he fell — his competitors** quedó a la zaga de sus competidores; **an hour —** una hora de retraso; **from —** desde atrás; **to fall —** atrasarse; **to leave something —** dejar atrás algo; PREP detrás de, tras; **we're all — you** todos te apoyamos; **who's — this evil plot?** ¿quién está detrás de este plan macabro? — **one's back** a espaldas de uno; N trasero *m*

behold [bɪhóɫd] VT contemplar; — **the future**

king! ¡he aquí el futuro rey!

behoove [bɪhúv] VI **it behooves [one]** le corresponde [a uno]

beige [beʒ] ADJ & N beige m

being [bíɪŋ] N ser m; **for the time —** por ahora

Belarus [belərús] N Bielorrusia f

belated [bɪléɪdɪd] ADJ atrasado, tardío

belch [bɛltʃ] VI eructar, repetir; N eructo m

belfry [bélfri] N campanario m

Belgian [béldʒən] ADJ & N belga mf

Belgium [béldʒəm] N Bélgica f

belief [bɪlíf] N creencia f; (strong opinion) convicción f

believable [bɪlívəbəł] ADJ creíble

believe [bɪlív] VI/VT creer

believer [bɪlívə] N creyente mf; (proponent) partidario -ria mf

belittle [bɪlídł] VT (a person) menospreciar, disminuir; (a situation) minimizar

Belize [bəlíz] N Belice m

Belizean [bəlíziən] ADJ & N beliceño -ña mf

bell [bɛł] N campana f; (small) campanilla f; **—boy/hop** botones m sg; **— curve** curva de campana f; **—flower** campanilla f, campánula f; **— jar** campana de cristal f; **— pepper** pimiento m, morrón m; **— tower** campanario m; **with all the —s and whistles** con todos los accesorios

bellicose [bélɪkos] ADJ belicoso

belligerent [bəlídʒəənt] ADJ & N beligerante mf

bellow [bélo] VI/VT bramar, berrear; N bramido m; **—s** fuelle m

belly [béli] N barriga f, vientre m, panza f; **—ache** dolor de barriga m; **— button** ombligo m; **— dance** danza del vientre f; **— laugh** carcajada f

belong [bɪlóŋ] VI (ownership) pertenecer; **this car —s to me** este coche me pertenece; (correspondence) corresponder; **this key —s to this door** esta llave corresponde a esta puerta; (placement) ir; **this —s on the shelf** esto va en el estante

belongings [bɪlóŋɪŋz] N pertenencias f pl

beloved [bɪlávɪd] ADJ querido; N amado -da mf

below [bɪló] ADV abajo; **five — [zero]** cinco bajo cero; PREP bajo, debajo de, abajo de

belt [bɛłt] N (for the waist) cinturón m, cinto m; (for a machine) correa f; (region) zona f; **— line** cintura f; VT pegar; **to — out a song** cantar una canción a voz en cuello

bemoan [bɪmón] VT lamentarse de, quejarse de

bench [bɛntʃ] N banco m; (without a back) banqueta f; (in sports) banco m, banquillo m; (in court) estrado m; **—mark** (upper limit) cota f; (parameter) punto de referencia m; **— price** precio de referencia m; **opinion of the —** opinión del tribunal f

bend [bɛnd] VI/VT (make curved) doblar[se]; (force) someter; **to — over** inclinarse; **to — over backward** desvivirse; **to — the rules** hacer una excepción; N (road) curva f, recodo m; **—s** enfermedad de los buzos f

bending [bɛndɪŋ] N doblado m

beneath [bɪníθ] ADV abajo; PREP debajo de, bajo; (in rank) inferior a; **— contempt** totalmente despreciable; **that's — me** no es digno de mí

benediction [bɛnɪdíkʃən] N bendición f

benefactor [bénəfæktɚ] N benefactor -ora mf; lit bienhechor -ora mf

beneficent [bənéfɪsənt] ADJ benéfico

beneficial [bɛnəfíʃəł] ADJ beneficioso

beneficiary [bɛnəfíʃieri] N beneficiario -ria mf

benefit [bénəfɪt] N beneficio m, provecho m; **— performance** función de beneficencia f; VI/VT beneficiar[se], sacar provecho

benevolence [bənévələns] N benevolencia f

benevolent [bənévələnt] ADJ benévolo

benign [bɪnáɪn] ADJ benigno

Benin [benín] N Benín m

Beninese [beníníz] ADJ & N beninés -esa mf

bent [bɛnt] N inclinación f; **to be — on** estar resuelto a

bent [bɛnt] see bend

benzine [bénzin] N bencina f

bequeath [bɪkwíð] VT legar, heredar

bequest [bɪkwést] N legado m

berate [bɪrét] VT reprender

bereaved [bɪrívd] ADJ de luto

beret [bəré] N boina f

berry [béri] N baya f

berserk [bə-rzɚk] ADJ fuera de sí; **he went —** se puso hecho una fiera, se enfureció

berth [bɚθ] N litera f; **to give a wide — to** mantener una distancia prudencial de

beseech [bɪsítʃ] VT suplicar, rogar

beset [bɪsét] VT (attack) acosar; (surround) rodear

beside [bɪsáɪd] PREP al lado de; **sit down — me** siéntate a mi lado; **to be — oneself** estar fuera de sí; **that is — the point** eso no viene al caso; ADV al lado

besides [bɪsáɪdz] ADV además; **they have a table but not much —** tienen una mesa pero poca cosa más; PREP además de, aparte de

besiege [bɪsídʒ] VT (lay siege) sitiar, cercar; (importune) importunar, asediar

best [bɛst] ADJ mejor; **—-case scenario** la mejor situación; **— man** padrino de boda m; **— seller** bestseller m; **she's the —** ella es la mejor; ADV mejor; **at —** a lo más, en el mejor de los casos; N **the — is still to come** lo mejor está por venir; **to do one's —** hacer lo mejor posible; **to get the — of** a person ganarle a una persona; **to make the — of** sacar el mejor partido de; VT vencer

bestial [béstʃəl] ADJ bestial

bestow [bɪstó] VT conferir; **to — gifts upon** dar regalos a

bet [bɛt] N apuesta f; VI/VT apostar; **to — on** apostar por

beta [bépə] N — **blocker** betabloqueador m, betabloqueante m; — **test** prueba beta f; — **version** versión beta f

betray [bɪtré] VT (a person) traicionar; (a secret) revelar; (a feeling) traslucir, delatar; **to — one's ignorance** hacer patente su ignorancia

betrayal [bɪtréəl] N traición f

betrayer [bɪtréə] N traidor -ra mf

betrothal [bɪtróðəl] N esponsales f pl

better [bépə] ADJ mejor; — **half** media naranja f; **the — part of a year** la mayor parte de un año; ADV mejor; **he lives — than a mile away** vive a más de una milla; **so much the — tanto mejor**; —-**off** en mejor posición económica; **to be — off** estar mejor así; **to change for the —** cambiar para bien; **to get — mejorar[se]**, aliviarse; VT mejorar; **to — oneself** mejorarse, mejorar de situación; N **the — of the two** el/la mejor de los dos

better, bettor [bépə] N apostador -ra mf

between [bɪtwín] PREP entre; ADV en medio

bevel [bévəl] N bisel m; VT biselar

beverage [bévrɪdʒ] N bebida f

bevy [bévi] N (of birds, people) bandada f; (of deer) manada f

beware [bɪwér] VI cuidarse [de]; — **of the dog** cuidado con el perro

bewilder [bɪwíldə] VT dejar perplejo, aturdir; **to be —ed** estar perplejo

bewilderment [bɪwíldəmənt] N perplejidad f, aturdimiento m

bewitch [bɪwítʃ] VT hechizar, embrujar

beyond [bɪjánd] ADV más allá; PREP más allá de; — **my reach** fuera de mi alcance; N **the great —** el más allá

Bhutan [butǽn] N Bután m

Bhutanese [butníz] ADJ & N butanés -esa mf

biannual [baɪǽnjuəl] ADJ bianual, semestral, semianual

bias [báɪəs] N (prejudice) prejuicio m; (in fabric) sesgo m; ADJ sesgado, oblicuo; VT predisponer; —**ed** parcial

bib [bɪb] N babero m; (of an apron) pechera f

Bible [báɪbəl] N Biblia f

biblical [bíblɪkəl] ADJ bíblico

bibliography [bɪbliágrəfi] N bibliografía f

bicarbonate [baɪkárbənɪt] N bicarbonato m

bicep, biceps [báɪsɛp[s]] N bíceps m sg

bicker [bíkə] VI reñir

bicuspid [baɪkáspɪd] ADJ bicúspide

bicycle [báɪsɪkəl] N bicicleta f; VI andar en bicicleta

bid [bɪd] N (in an auction, contest) licitación f,

---

puja f; (in card games) apuesta f; (attempt) tentativa f; VI/VT (offer) pujar; (command) mandar; (invite) rogar; (enter a bid in cards) apostar; **to — good-bye** despedirse; **to — up** pujar el precio

bidden [bídn] see bid

bidding [bídɪŋ] N (in auction) puja f; **at someone's —** por orden de alguien; **to do someone's —** cumplir con los deseos de alguien

bide [baɪd] VI/VT **to — one's time** esperar una oportunidad

biennium [baɪéniəm] N bienio m

bifurcate [báɪfə·ket] VI/VT bifurcar[se]

big [bɪg] ADJ grande; — **Bang Theory** Teoría del Big Bang f; — **brother** hermano mayor m; — **bucks** mucha plata f; — **business** el gran capital m; — **deal** asunto importante m; — **deal!** ¡no es para tanto! — **Dipper** Osa Mayor f; — **enchilada** fam mandamás m, fam pez gordo m; —-**headed** cabezón, cabezudo; —-**hearted** magnánimo; — **house** fam gayola f; — **kahuna** fam mandamás m, fam pez gordo m; — **name** personalidad prominente f; — **picture** panorama general m; — **shot** fam pez gordo m; — **sister** hermana mayor f; —-**ticket** caro; —**wig** fam pez gordo m; — **with child** embarazada; **jazz was — in the 1920s** el jazz era popular en los años veinte; **she's a — deal** es una persona importante; ADV **she wants to go —time** se muere por ir; **to talk —** jactarse, fanfarronear; Am lucirse; **to go over —** tener éxito; **to be — on** ser entusiasta de

bigamy [bígəmi] N bigamia f

bigot [bígət] N intolerante m

bigotry [bígətri] N intolerancia f

bike [baɪk] N (bicycle) bici f; (motorcycle) moto f

biker [báɪkə] N (bicyclist) ciclista mf; (motorcyclist) motociclista mf

bikini [bɪkíni] N bikini m

bilateral [baɪlǽpə·əl] ADJ bilateral

bile [baɪl] N (secretion) bilis f; (ill temper) mal genio m; — **duct** conducto biliar m

bilingual [baɪlíŋgwəl] ADJ & N bilingüe mf

bilingualism [baɪlíŋgwəlɪzəm] N bilingüismo m

bill [bɪl] N (statement) factura f; (in a restaurant) cuenta f; (poster) cartel m; (bank note) billete m; (for movies, theater) programa m; (of a bird) pico m; (legislative) proyecto de ley m; —**board** cartelera f; —**fold** cartera f; billetera f; — **of exchange** letra de cambio f; — **of lading** conocimiento de embarque m; — **of rights** declaración de derechos f; — **of sale** escritura de venta f; VT cobrar, mandar la factura a

billable [bíləbəl] ADJ facturable

billiards [bíljə·dz] N billar m

billing [bílıŋ] N (theater) orden de importancia en espectáculos m; (business) facturación f; — **cycle** ciclo de facturación m

billion [bíljən] NUM mil millones m pl

billow [bílo] N (of smoke) nube f; (of water) ola f; VI ondular, hacer olas

bimonthly [baimánθli] ADV bimestral

bin [bın] N (for clothes, food) cajón m, recipiente m; (on an airplane) portaequipajes m sg; (for coal) carbonera f; (for grain) granero m

binary [báineri] ADJ binario; — **star** estrella binaria f

bind [baind] VI/VT (unite) unir; (connect) ligar; (tie) atar; (put a cover on a book) encuadernar; (press tightly) apretar; (oblige by contract) obligar

binding [báindıŋ] N (of a book) encuadernación f; (on a rug) ribete m; ADJ obligatorio

binge [bınʤ] N (alcoholic) juerga f, parranda f; (food) comilona f; VI (on alcohol) emborracharse; (on food) atiborrarse

bingo [bíŋgo] N bingo m

binoculars [bənákjələ˞z] N gemelos m pl, prismáticos m pl

binomial [bainómiəl] N binomio m; ADJ binomial

biochemistry [baiokémistri] N bioquímica f

biodegradable [baiodigrédəbəl] ADJ biodegradable

bioengineering [baioenʤəníriŋ] N bioingeniería f

biofeedback [baiofídbæk] N biofeedback m, retroalimentación biológica f

biography [baiágrəfi] N biografía f

biological [baiəláʤikəl] ADJ biológico

biologist [baiáləʤist] N biólogo -ga mf

biology [baiáləʤi] N biología f

biopsy [báiɑpsi] N biopsia f

biorhythm [báioriðəm] N biorritmo m

biotechnology [baioteknáləʤi] N biotecnología f

bipartisan [baipártizən] ADJ bipartidista

bipolar [baipólə˞] ADJ bipolar; — **disorder** trastorno bipolar m

birch [bə˞ʧ] N abedul m

bird [bə˞d] N ave f; (small) pájaro m; — **of prey** ave de rapiña f; — **seed** alpiste m; **odd** — persona peculiar f

birth [bə˞θ] N (act of being born) nacimiento m; (act of giving birth) parto m; (lineage) linaje m; (origin) origen m; — **certificate** certificado de nacimiento m, fe/acta de nacimiento f; — **control** (policy) control de la natalidad m; (devices) anticonceptivos m pl; —**day** cumpleaños m sg; **in his / her** —**day suit** como Dios lo/la trajo al mundo; —**mark** antojo m, marca de nacimiento f; —**place** lugar de nacimiento m; —**rate** natalidad f, tasa de natalidad f;

—**right** derechos de nacimiento m pl; (of oldest child) primogenitura f; **to give** — dar a luz, parir, alumbrar; **by** — de nacimiento

biscuit [bískıt] N panecillo m

bisect [báisekt] VT bisecar

bishop [bíʃəp] N obispo m; (in chess) alfil m

bison [báisən] N bisonte m, búfalo m

bit [bıt] N (small piece) pedacito m, trocito m; (some) poquito m; (of a bridle) bocado m, freno m; (of a drill) broca f, barrena f; (computer) bit m; **I don't care a** — no me importa en absoluto

bit [bıt] see bite

bitch [bıʧ] N perra f

bite [bait] VI/VT morder; (be duped) dejarse engañar; (insect, fish, snake) picar; **to** — **off** arrancar de un mordisco; N (act, wound) mordedura f, dentellada f; (morsel, small meal) bocado m, bocadito m; (of an insect) picadura f, roncha f

bitten [bítn] see bite

bitter [bídə˞] ADJ (taste) amargo; (cold) glacial; (enemy) acérrimo; (person) resentido; —**sweet** dulceamargo, agridulce; **to fight to the** — **end** luchar hasta morir; N —**s** cerveza amarga f

bitterness [bídə˞nıs] N (taste) amargor m; (feelings) amargura f; (anger) rencor m, resentimiento m

biweekly [baiwíkli] ADV (every two weeks) quincenal; (twice a week) bisemanal

bizarre [bizár] ADJ (event) extraño; (appearance) estrafalario

blab [blæb] VI parlotear; VT descubrir el pastel

black [blæk] ADJ (color, ethnicity) negro; (night) oscuro; —**-and-blue** lleno de moretones, amoratado; N negro -a mf; — **bean** frijol negro m; —**berry** zarzamora f, mora f; —**bird** mirlo m; —**board** pizarrón m, pizarra f; — **death** peste negra f; — **eye** ojo amoratado/morado m; —**head** espinilla f; — **hole** agujero negro m; —**jack** (weapon) cachiporra f; (card game) black-jack m, veintiuno m; —**list** lista negra f; — **magic** magia negra f; —**mail** chantaje m; — **mark** mancha f; — **market** mercado negro m; —**out** apagón m; — **pepper** pimienta negra f; — **pudding** morcilla f; — **sheep** oveja negra f; —**smith** herrero m; —**smith's shop** herrería f, forja f; —**top** asfalto m; — **widow spider** viuda negra f; **to put down in** —**and white** poner por escrito; VI **to** — **out** (faint) desmayarse, perder el conocimiento; VT **to** —**mail** chantajear

blacken [blækən] VT ennegrecer, negrear; VI (sky) oscurecerse

blackness [blækni̇s] N negrura f

bladder [blǽdə˞] N vejiga f

blade [bled] N (of a knife) hoja f; (of grass) brizna

f; (of an oar) pala *f*, paleta *f*; (of a propeller) aspa *f*

blame [blem] VT culpar, echar la culpa a, achacar la culpa a; **to be to** — tener la culpa; N (responsibility) culpa *f*; (reproof) reproche *m*

blameless [blémlɪs] ADJ intachable

blanch [blæntʃ] VI palidecer; VT (whiten) blanquear; (scald) escalar

bland [blænd] ADJ insulso

blank [blæŋk] ADJ (not written on) en blanco; (not recorded on) virgen; (unadorned, expressionless) vacío; (confused) desconcertado; — **cartridge** cartucho de fogueo *m*; — **check** cheque en blanco *m*; — **verse** verso blanco *m*; N (place to be filled in on a form) espacio [en blanco] *m*; (gap) vacío *m*; VI **to** — **out** quedarse en blanco

blanket [blǽŋkɪt] N manta *f*, frazada *f*; Am cobija *f*; ADJ global; VT cubrir

blare [blɛr] VI hacer un ruido estruendoso; N estruendo *m*; (of a trumpet) toque *m*

blaspheme [blæsfím] VI/VT blasfemar [contra]

blasphemy [blǽsfəmi] N blasfemia *f*

blast [blæst] N (of wind) ráfaga *f*; (of criticism) lluvia *f*; (of a trumpet) trompetazo *m*; (explosive charge) carga *f*; (explosion) explosión *f*; — **furnace** alto horno *m*; —**off** despegue *m*; **we had a** — lo pasamos bomba; **at full** — a todo volumen; VI/VT (blow a horn) pitar, tocar; (shatter) volar; (criticize) criticar duramente; (blow hard) azotar; **to** — **off** despegar

blatant [blétnt] ADJ descarado

blaze [blez] N (flame) llamarada *f*; (fire) incendio *m*; (glow) resplandor *m*; (mark) señal *f*; — **of anger** arranque de ira *m*; VI (burn) arder; (shine) resplandecer; **to** — **a trail** marcar una senda

blazer [blézɚ] N blazer *m*, saco *m*

bleach [blitʃ] VI/VT (intentional) blanquear[se]; (accidental) desteñir[se]; N blanqueador *m*; Sp lejía *f*

bleachers [blítʃɚz] N gradas *f pl*

bleak [blik] ADJ (terrain) yermo, desolado; (winter) crudo; (wind) helado; (future) negro

bleary [blíri] ADJ nublado

bleat [blit] N balido *m*; VI balar

bled [blɛd] *see* bleed

bleed [blid] VI (lose blood) sangrar; (run, as in colors) correrse, desteñir[se]; **my heart** —**s for the poor** los pobres me dan lástima; VT (let blood) desangrar; (extort) extorsionar; (clean brakes) purgar

blemish [blémɪʃ] N mancha *f*, tacha *f*; VT manchar

blend [blɛnd] VI/VT (tea, paint) mezclar, entremezclar; (sea and sky) fundirse; (voices) armonizar; N mezcla *f*

blender [bléndɚ] N licuadora *f*

bless [blɛs] VT bendecir; INTERJ — **you!** ¡salud! ¡Jesús!

blessed[1] [blésɪd] ADJ (beatified) beato; (happy) bienaventurado, feliz; — **event** feliz acontecimiento *m*; **the whole** — **day** todo el santo día; **not a** — **drop of rain** ni una bendita gota de agua

blessed[2] [blɛst] ADJ — **with** dotado de

blessing [blésɪŋ] N bendición *f*; **to say the** — dar gracias

blew [blu] *see* blow

blight [blaɪt] N (plant disease) quemadura *f*, añublo *m*; (scourge) lacra *f*; VT (cause to wither) marchitar; (ruin) arruinar

blimp [blɪmp] N zepelín *m*

blind [blaɪnd] ADJ ciego; — **alley** callejón sin salida *m*; — **date** cita a ciegas *f*; —**fold** venda para los ojos *f*; **to** —**fold** vendar los ojos a; — **man's bluff** juego de la gallina ciega *m*; — **spot** ángulo muerto *m*; **to fly** — volar a ciegas; **to go** — quedarse ciego; N (shade) persiana *f*; (hunter's hiding place) escondite *m*; VT (make blind) cegar; (darken) oscurecer

blinder [bláɪndɚ] N anteojera *f*

blindly [bláɪndli] ADV a ciegas

blindness [bláɪndnɪs] N ceguera *f*

blink [blɪŋk] VI/VT (move eyelids) pestañear, parpadear; (go on and off, as of a light) parpadear; (ignore) pasar por alto; (flee a challenge) rajarse; N parpadeo *m*, pestañeo *m*; **on the** — averiado

blinker [blíŋkɚ] N intermitente *m*

blinking [blíŋkɪŋ] N parpadeo *m*

blip [blɪp] N (on radar) punto *m*; (moment) bache *m*

bliss [blɪs] N dicha *f*, felicidad absoluta *f*

blister [blístɚ] N ampolla *f*; (small) vejiga *f*; VT sacar ampollas; VI ampollarse

blitz [blɪts] N ataque relámpago *m*

blizzard [blízɚd] N ventisca *f*

bloat [blot] VI hinchar[se], abotagar[se]

bloated [blódɪd] ADJ hinchado, inflado

blob [blɑb] N pedazo de algo sin forma *m*

block [blɑk] N (piece of stone, cement) bloque *m*; (piece of wood) trozo de madera *m*; (toy) cubo *m*; (in sports) bloqueo *m*; (in basketball) tapón *m*; (length from one street to the next) cuadra *f*; (square block) manzana *f*; (obstacle) obstáculo *m*; (group of tickets) sección *f*; —**buster** éxito de taquilla *m*; —**head** tarugo -ga *mf*, alcornoque *m*; VT (obstruct, also in sports) bloquear, tapar; (in basketball) taponar; (stop a pass) parar; **to** — **out** (an essay) esbozar, bosquejar; (the sun) ocultar

blockade [blɑkéd] N bloqueo *m*; VT bloquear

blockage [blákɪdʒ] N obstrucción *f*

blocking [blákɪŋ] N bloqueo *m*

blog [blɑg] N blog *m*; VI bloguear; —**ging** blogueo *m*

blogger [blágɚ] N bloguero -ra *mf*

blond [bland] ADJ & N rubio -a *mf*

blood [blʌd] N sangre *f*; **—bank** banco de sangre *m*; **—bath** carnicería *f*, baño de sangre *m*; **— count** recuento sanguíneo *m*; **— group** grupo sanguíneo *m*; **—hound** sabueso *m*; **— plasma** plasma sanguíneo *m*; **— poisoning** septicemia *f*; **— pressure** presión arterial *f*; **— relative** pariente consanguíneo *mf*; **—shed** derramamiento de sangre *m*; **—shot** inyectado de sangre; **—thirsty** sanguinario, sangriento; **— type** grupo sanguíneo *m*; **— vessel** vaso sanguíneo *m*; **in cold — a** sangre fría

bloody [blʌ́di] ADJ (violent) sangriento; (smeared) ensangrentado

bloom [blum] N (flower) flor *f*; (flowering) floración *f*; (youthfulness) lozanía *f*; (flush) rubor *m*; **in — en** flor; VI florecer

blooming [blúmɪŋ] ADJ (flowering) floreciente; (thriving) lozano

blooper [blúpɚ] N perla *f*

blossom [blásəm] N (flower) flor *f*; VI florecer

blot [blat] N (on paper) mancha *f*, borrón *m*; (on honor) tacha *f*; VI/VT manchar[se], emborronar[se]; **to — out** (obscure) borrar, tachar

blotch [blatʃ] VT borronear, manchar, cubrir con manchas; N mancha *f*, borrón *m*

blouse [blaʊs] N blusa *f*

blow [blo] VI (wind) soplar; (leaf) volar; (siren) sonar; (horse) resoplar; VT (play a horn) sonar; **to — a fuse** quemar un fusible; **to — away** (amaze) dejar atónito; (carry away on the wind) llevarse el viento; **to — down** tirar abajo; **to —-dry** secar con secador; **to — off** (ignore) ignorar; **to — one's nose** sonarse las narices / la nariz; **to — on the soup** soplar la sopa; **to — one's brains out** levantarse la tapa de los sesos; **to — out** reventar[se]; **to — over** (knock down) derribar; (dissipate) disiparse; **to — up** (a balloon) inflar, hinchar; (a bridge) volar; **this party —s** esta fiesta es pésima; N (stroke, shock) golpe *m*; (wind) tempestad *f*; (breath) soplo *m*; **—-out** (tire failure) reventón *m*; (party) fiestón *m*; **—pipe** cerbatana *f*; **—torch** soplete *m*; **—up** (fight) pelea *f*, riña *f*; (photo) ampliación *f*; **to come to —s** irse a las manos

blower [blóɚ] N (artisan) soplador *m*; (machine) aventadora *f*

blown [blon] *see* blow

blue [blu] ADJ azul; (sad) triste, melancólico; (from cold) amoratado; N azul *m*; **—bell** campanilla *f*; **—berry** arándano *m*; **—bird** pájaro azul *m*; **—blood** sangre azul *f*; **— book** lista de precios de mercado *f*; **—-chip** de primera línea; **—-collar** de clase obrera; **—jay** arrendajo *m*; **— jeans** vaqueros *m pl*;

—print (of a building) cianotipo *m*; (of a project) plan *m*, trazado *m*; **—-ribbon** distinguido; **— whale** ballena azul *f*; **— light** [azul] celeste *m*; **the —s** (sadness) melancolía *f*, murria *f*; (genre of music) blues *m pl*; VI ponerse azul, azulear; VT azular, teñir de azul; **to —print** trazar

bluff [blʌf] N (cliff) acantilado *m*, risco *m*; (false boast) bluff *m*; (in poker) farol *m*; VT hacer un bluff; **to call a —** poner en evidencia

bluffer [blʌ́fɚ] N bluff *m*

bluing [blúɪŋ] N añil *m*

bluish [blúɪʃ] ADJ azulado

blunder [blʌ́ndɚ] N disparate *m*, patochada *f*; VI meter la pata; **to — upon/into** tropezar con

blunt [blʌnt] ADJ (not sharp) romo; (rounded) contundente; (frank) directo, franco; VT despuntar

blur [blɚ] VT (to obscure) emborronar, desvanecer; (to make vision blurry) nublar; VI empañarse, nublarse; N [indistinct sight] mancha *f*; **it's a — in my mind** sólo tengo un recuerdo vago de eso

blurred [blɚd] ADJ borroso

blurry [blɚ́i] ADJ borroso

blurt [blɚt] VT **to — [out]** espetar

blush [blʌʃ] VI sonrojarse, ponerse colorado, ruborizarse; N (act of blushing) sonrojo *m*; (effect of blushing) rubor *m*; **at first — a** primera vista

bluster [blʌ́stɚ] VI (blow hard) soplar fuerte, rugir; (boast) fanfarronear; N (sound of wind) ventarrón *m*; (attitude) fanfarronería *f*

blustering [blʌ́stɚɪŋ] ADJ fanfarrón, jactancioso; **— wind** ventarrón *m*

BM [bowel movement] [bíém] N defecación *f*

boa constrictor [bóəkənstríktɚ] N boa *f*

boar [bɔr] N jabalí *m*

board [bɔrd] N (wood) tabla *f*, listón *m*; (for a game) tablero *m*; (meals) pensión *f*; (for bulletins) cartelera *f*; **— of directors** junta directiva *f*; **—ing school** pensionado *m*, internado *m*; **—inghouse** pensión *f*; **— of trustees** patronato *m*; **—room** sala de directorio *f*; **on — a** bordo; **to go by the —** irse por la borda; VI (lodge) alojarse; **to — up** tapiar, cerrar con tablas; VT (boat, plane, train) abordar; (provide lodging) alojar

boarder [bɔ́rdɚ] N pensionista *mf*

boast [bost] N alarde *m*; VI jactarse, vanagloriarse, blasonar; VT (the town —s two new schools** el pueblo ostenta dos escuelas nuevas

boastful [bóstfəl] ADJ jactancioso, vanaglorioso

boastfulness [bóstfəlnɪs] N jactancia *f*, vanagloria *f*

boat [bot] N (any water vessel) embarcación *f*; (open and small) bote *m*, lancha *f*; (closed, larger) barco *m*; **—house** cobertizo para botes *m*; **—man** barquero *m*, botero *m*

boating [bódɪŋ] N navegación *f*; **to go —** navegar

bob [bab] N (horsetail) cola cortada *f*; (of the head) sacudida *f*; (haircut) melena corta *f*; (of a pendulum) pesa *f*, plomada *f*; **—tail** rabón *m*; VI sacudirse; (a ship) cabecear; VT **to — one's hair** cortarse el pelo en melena

bobbin [bábɪn] N carrete *m*, bobina *f*

bobcat [bábkæt] N lince rojo *m*

bode [bod] VI **that doesn't — well** eso no augura nada bueno

bodice [bádɪs] N corpiño *m*

bodily [bádl̩i] ADJ corporal; **— harm** daño físico *m*

body [bádi] N (of a person, animal, wine, fabric) cuerpo *m*; (torso) tronco *m*; (corpse) cuerpo *m*, cadáver *m*; (of a text, army, etc.) parte principal *f*; (of water) masa *f*; (of a car) carrocería *f*; (of an airplane) fuselaje *m*; **— armor** armadura corporal *f*, armadura de cuerpo *f*; **— bag** bolsa para cadáveres *f*; **— building** culturismo *m*; **— count** número de muertos *m*; **—guard** guardaespaldas *m sg*; **— language** lenguaje corporal *m*; **— temperature** temperatura *f*; **— shop** taller de carrocería *m*; VT **to —search** cachear

bog [bag] N pantano *m*; VI hundir[se]; **to get —ged down** atascarse

bogey [bógi] N (golf) bogey *m*

bogeyman [búgimæn] N coco *m*; RP cuco *m*

bogus [bógəs] ADJ falso, fraudulento; **— company** compañía fantasma *f*

Bohemian [bohímiən] ADJ & N bohemio -a *mf*

boil [bɔɪl] VI/VT (water) hervir; (eggs) cocer; (ocean) bullir; (angry person) echar chispas; **to — down to** reducirse a; **to — over** derramarse; N (inflammation) forúnculo *m*, divieso *m*; (act of boiling) hervor *m*; **—ing point** punto de ebullición *m*; **to come to a — soltar/romper el hervor**

boiler [bɔ́ɪlə] N caldera *f*

boisterous [bɔ́ɪstə‑əs] ADJ bullicioso

bold [bold] ADJ (not fearful) atrevido, osado; (unconventional) audaz; (visually striking) llamativo; **—faced** descarado; **—face type** negrita *f*, negrilla *f*

boldness [bóldnɪs] N (courage) atrevimiento *m*, osadía *f*; (unconventional attitude) audacia *f*

Bolivia [bəlíviə] N Bolivia *f*

Bolivian [bəlíviən] ADJ & N boliviano -na *mf*

bolster [bólstə] N cojín cilíndrico *m*; VT reforzar; **to — someone's courage** alentar a alguien

bolt [bolt] N (door lock) pestillo *m*, cerrojo *m*; (crossbar) aldaba *f*; (pin) perno *m*, tornillo grande *m*; (of cloth) rollo *m*; **it came as a — from the blue** cayó como bomba; VT (fasten) atornillar; (lock door) cerrar con

tranca, atrancar; (devour) engullir; (break with) romper con; VI echarse a correr

bomb [bam] N bomba *f*; **—shell** bomba *f*; **— shelter** refugio antiaéreo *m*; VT (attack with bombs) bombardear; VI (fail) fracasar

bombard [bambárd] VT bombardear

bombardier [bambədír] N bombardero -ra *mf*

bombardment [bambárdmənt] N bombardeo *m*

bombastic [bambǽstɪk] ADJ grandilocuente, ampuloso

bomber [bámə‑] N bombardero *m*, avión de bombardeo *m*

bombing [bámɪŋ] N (from airplanes) bombardeo *m*; (terrorist) atentado *m*

bona fide [bónəfaɪd] ADJ genuino; **— offer** oferta seria *f*

bonbon [bánban] N caramelo *m*; (chocolate) bombón *m*

bond [band] N (tie) lazo *m*; (fetter) cadenas *f pl*; (financial instrument) bono *m*, obligación *f*; (adhesion) adherencia *f*; (chemical) enlace *m*; VI/VT (stick to) adherirse; (connect) establecer vínculos

bondage [bándɪdʒ] N servidumbre *f*, esclavitud *f*

bonded [bándɪd] ADJ afianzado

bonding [bándɪŋ] N (mother-child) lazos afectivos *m pl*; (male) compenetración *f*

bondsman [bándzmən] N fiador *m*

bone [bon] N hueso *m*; (of fish) espina *f*; **— china** porcelana fina *f*; **— graft** injerto óseo *m*; **—head** estúpido -da *mf*; **— marrow** médula ósea *f*; **—yard** cementerio *m*; **— of contention** manzana de la discordia *f*; **to make no — s about it** no andarse con rodeos; VT deshuesar; (fish) quitar las espinas; **to — up on something** estudiar algo

bonfire [bánfaɪr] N hoguera *f*, fogata *f*

bonnet [bánɪt] N gorro *m*

bonus [bónəs] N (extra salary) gratificación *f*, prima *f*; (at Christmas) aguinaldo *m*

bony [bóni] ADJ (with large bones) huesudo; (made of bones) óseo

boo [bu] VI/VT abuchear, rechiflar; INTERJ ¡bu! N rechifla *f*, abucheo *m*

boo-boo [búbu] N (minor injury) lastimadura *f*; Sp *fam* pupa *f*; Am *fam* nana *f*; **to make a —** meter la pata

booby [búbi] N (fool) bobo -a *mf*; (bird) bobo *m*; **— hatch** *fam* loquería *f*; **— prize** premio al peor competidor *m*; **— trap** trampa explosiva *f*

booger [búgə‑] N moco [seco] *m*

book [bʊk] N libro *m*; **—binding** encuadernación *f*; **—case** estante *m*, estantería *f*, biblioteca *f*; **—end** sujetalibros *m sg*; **—keeper** tenedor -ra de libros *mf*; Sp contable *mf*; **—keeping** teneduría de libros *f*, contabilidad *f*; **—mark** marcador de libros *m*; **—mobile** biblioteca móvil *f*; **— review** reseña *f*; **—seller** librero -ra *mf*; **—shelf** estante *m*; **—store** librería *f*; **— value** valor contable *m*; **by the —** siguiendo las reglas; **on the —s** registrado en los libros; **to keep —s** llevar los libros; VT (reserve) reservar; (hire) contratar; (record charges against) fichar

bookish [búkɪʃ] ADJ (person) estudioso; (allusion) libresco

booklet [búklɪt] N cartilla *f*

boom [bum] VI (resound) resonar; (prosper) prosperar; N (noise) explosión *f*; (increase) auge *m*

boon [bun] N (blessing) bendición *f*; (favor) favor *m*

boondocks [búndɑks] ADV LOC **[out] in the —** *fam* en los quintos infiernos, en el quinto pino

boondoggle [búndɑgəl] N despilfarro *m*

boor [bur] N patán -ana *mf*

boorish [búrɪʃ] ADJ grosero, zafio

boost [bust] VT (to shove) empujar [desde abajo o detrás]; (to promote) estimular, impulsar; N (shove) empujón [desde abajo] *m*; (aid) estímulo *m*, impulso *m*; **— in prices** alza de precios *f*

booster [bústɚ] N (person) animador -ra *mf*; (rocket) acelerador *m*; (electronic device) amplificador *m*; (vaccination) refuerzo *m*

boot [but] N (shoe) bota *f*; (trunk of a car) cajuela *f*; (clamp for cars) cepo *m*; **—black** limpiabotas *m sg*; **—disk** disco de iniciación *m*; **—legger** contrabandista de licores *m*; **—able diskette** disquete de iniciación *f*; **to give the —** poner de patitas en la calle; **to — [out]** echar a patadas; **to — up** (a computer) iniciar

booth [buθ] N (telephone) cabina *f*; (sales) puesto *m*; (ticket) taquilla *f*

booty [búdi] N (loot) botín *m*; (buttocks) trasero *m*

booze [buz] N *fam* bebercio *m*, bebida alcohólica *f*

borax [bɔ́ræks] N bórax *m*

border [bɔ́rdɚ] N (line between countries) frontera *f*; (edge, brink) borde *m*; (bed of flowers) ariete *m*; (design) ribete *m*; **— control** control fronterizo *m*; **— patrol officer** carabinero -ra *mf*; ADJ **—line** (on a border) fronterizo; (not up to standards) dudoso; VI/VT (make a design) ribetear; **to — on** colindar con; **it —s on madness** raya en la locura

bordering [bɔ́rdɚɪŋ] ADJ limítrofe

bore [bɔr] N (hole) agujero *m*; (of a gun, cylinder) calibre *m*; (uninteresting person) aburrido -da *mf*, pesado -da *mf*; (uninteresting thing) lata *f*; VT (make a hole) taladrar, horadar; (fail to interest) aburrir

bore [bɔr] *see* bear

bored [bɔrd] ADJ aburrido; **I'm —** estoy aburrido

boredom [bɔ́rdəm] N aburrimiento *m*, tedio *m*

boric acid [bɔ́rɪk ǽsɪd] N ácido bórico *m*

boring [bɔ́rɪŋ] ADJ aburrido; **he's —** es aburrido

born [bɔrn] ADJ nacido; **he's a — dancer** es un bailarín nato; **she's a — liar** es una mentirosa de nacimiento; **to be —** nacer

borne [bɔrn] *see* bear

boron [bɔ́rɑn] N boro *m*

borrow [bɔ́ro] VT pedir prestado; **I —ed money from Fred** le pedí dinero prestado a Fred; **may I — your car?** ¿me prestas tu coche? **I —ed these books from the library** saqué estos libros de la biblioteca

borrower [bɔ́roɚ] N (of money) prestatario -ria *mf*; (of library books) usuario -ria *mf*

Bosnia and Herzegovina [bázniənhɚtsəgəvínə] N Bosnia-Herzegovina *f*

Bosnian [bázniən] ADJ & N bosnio -nia *mf*

bosom [búzəm] N pecho *m*, seno *m*; **in the — of the family** en el seno de la familia; **— buddy** amigo íntimo *m*

boss [bɔs] N jefe -fa *mf*; (on a plantation) mayoral *m*, capataz *m*; (political) dirigente *m*; (mafia) capo *m*; VT **to — around** mandonear

bossy [bɔ́si] ADJ mandón

botanical [bətǽnɪkəl] ADJ botánico

botany [bátṇi] N botánica *f*

botch [bátʃ] VT chapucear, estropear; N chapucería *f*, chapuza *f*

both [boθ] ADJ & PRON ambos, los dos

bother [báðɚ] VT molestar, fastidiar; VI molestarse, tomarse la molestia; N molestia *f*

bothersome [báðɚsəm] ADJ (activity) molesto, enojoso; (person) enfadoso, molesto

botox [bótaks] N bótox *m*

Botswana [batswánə] N Botsuana *f*

bottle [bádḷ] N botella *f*; (for medicine, perfume) frasco *m*; **—neck** atascadero *m*, embotellamiento *m*; **— top** chapa de botella *f*; VT embotellar; **to — up** atascar, embotellar

bottom [bádəm] N (of a hole) fondo *m*; (of a pile, page, bed) pie *m*; (lower part) base *f*, parte de abajo *f*; (buttocks) trasero *m*; **to be at the — of the class** ser el último de la clase; **to hit — tocar fondo; who is at the — of all this?** ¿quién está detrás de todo esto? ADJ de abajo; **— line** (business) balance final *m*; (essential element) lo esencial; VI **to — out** tocar fondo

bottomless [bádəmlɪs] ADJ sin fondo; **— supply** recursos ilimitados *m pl*; **— accusation** acusación infundada *f*; **he's a — pit** es un barril sin fondo

botulism [bátʃəlɪzəm] N botulismo *m*

boudoir [búdwar] N tocador *m*

bough [baʊ] N rama *f*

bought [bɔt] *see* buy

bouillon [búljɑn] N caldo *m*

boulder [bóldɚ] N peña f, pedrusco m

boulevard [búləvɑrd] N bulevar m

bounce [baʊns] N (of a ball) bote m, rebote m; (vitality) vitalidad f; VT echar, botar; **to — a check** rebotar un cheque; VI rebotar; **to — back** recuperarse

bouncer [baʊnsɚ] N gorila m

bound [baʊnd] N (jump) salto m; **—s** límite m, confín m; ADJ (tied up) atado; (confined) confinado; (obliged) obligado; (as a book) encuadernado; **to be — for** ir rumbo a; **to be — up in one's work** estar absorto en su trabajo; **it is — to happen** es seguro que pasará; **I am — to do it** estoy resuelto a hacerlo; VI (jump) saltar; (be contiguous) lindar

bound [baʊnd] *see* bind

boundary [báʊndri] N (of a country, city) límite m, término m; (of a property) linde m f, lindero m

boundless [báʊndlɪs] ADJ ilimitado, sin límites

bountiful [báʊntəfəl] ADJ abundante

bounty [báʊnti] N (abundance) abundancia f; (reward) recompensa f

bouquet [bukéɪ] N (of flowers, large) ramo m; (of flowers, small) ramillete m; (of wine) aroma m, bouquet m

bourgeois [burʒwá] ADJ & N burgués -sa m f

bourgeoisie [burʒwazí] N burguesía f

bout [baʊt] N (sports) encuentro m; **a — of flu** una gripe

boutique [butík] N boutique f

bovine [bóvaɪn] ADJ vacuno

bow[1] [baʊ] N (gesture) reverencia f; (prow) proa f; VI (bend at the waist) hacer una reverencia; (yield) someterse; **to — out** retirarse; VT inclinar

bow[2] [bo] N (for arrows, violin) arco m; (curve) curva f; (decoration) moño m; **—knot** lazada f; **—-string** cuerda de arco f; ADJ **—-legged** patizambo; VI/VT (bend) arquear[se]; (play a violin with a bow) tocar con arco

bowel [báʊəl] N **—s** intestinos m pl; **—s of the earth** entrañas de la tierra f pl; **— movement** evacuación del vientre f

bower [báʊɚ] N enramada f

bowl [bol] N (container) bol m, tazón m; (dish) plato hondo m; (depression) cuenco m; (of a toilet) taza f; (of a pipe) cazoleta f; VT **to — over** apabullar, deslumbrar

bowling [bólɪŋ] N boliche m, bowling m; **let's go —** vamos al boliche; **— alley** boliche m, bolera f

box [baks] N (container) caja f; (for jewelry) estuche m; (in the theater) palco de teatro m; (for the jury) tribuna f; (on a page) cuadro m; (in soccer) área de penales f; **— car** vagón de carga m; **— office** taquilla f; **— seat** asiento de palco m; VT (put in a box) meter en una caja; (hit)

abofetear; (engage in sport) boxear

boxer [báksɚ] N (fighter) boxeador -ra m f, pugilista m f; (breed of dog) bóxer m; **— shorts** calzoncillo[s] m

boxing [báksɪŋ] N boxeo m, pugilato m; **— glove** guante de boxeo m; **— ring** ring m, cuadrilátero m

boy [bɔɪ] N (baby) niño m; (young man) muchacho m, chico m; **— scout** boy scout m; **—friend** novio m

boycott [bóɪkɑt] VT boicotear; N boicoteo m, boicot m

boyhood [bóɪhʊd] N niñez f, juventud f

boyish [bóɪʃ] ADJ de muchacho

brace [bres] N (in construction) tirante m; (pair) par m; (printed character) corchete m; (of a carpenter) berbiquí m; **—s** (for teeth) aparato ortodóntico m; (for a leg) aparato ortopédico m; VT (against a shock) agarrarse; (support) asegurar

bracelet [bréslɪt] N brazalete m, pulsera f

bracket [brǽkɪt] N (support) soporte m, sostén m; (typographic sign) paréntesis recto m, corchete m; (division) banda f; VT (fix with brackets) fijar con soportes; (write in brackets) colocar entre paréntesis rectos; (associate) agrupar

brag [bræg] VI jactarse [de], hacer alarde [de]

braggart [brǽgɚt] ADJ & N fanfarrón -na m f

braid [bred] N trenza f; VT trenzar

brain [bren] N cerebro m; (food) seso m; **she blew out his —s** le levantó la tapa de los sesos; **he's short on —s** es corto de inteligencia; **he is the —s in this operation** él es el cerebro en esta operación; **to rack one's —s** devanarse los sesos, romperse la cabeza; **— death** muerte cerebral f; **— drain** fuga de cerebros f; **— scan** tomografía cerebral f; **— trust** grupo de expertos m; **— stem** tronco del encéfalo m; **—storming** lluvia de ideas f; **— tumor** tumor cerebral m; VT **to — someone** romperle la crisma a alguien; **to —wash** lavarle el cerebro a; ADJ **—-dead** clínicamente muerto, en estado vegetativo

brainy [bréni] ADJ sesudo

brake [brek] N freno m; **— drum** tambor del freno m; **— fluid** líquido para frenos m; **—man** guardafrenos m sg; **— shoe** zapata f; **to apply the —s** frenar; VI/VT frenar

bramble [brǽmbəl] N zarza f

bran [bræn] N salvado m; (for birds) afrecho m

branch [bræntʃ] N (of a plant, of a family) rama f; (of a train track) ramal m; (of antlers) brazo m; (of a science) ramo m; (of a business) sucursal f; (of the armed forces) arma f; (in a computer program) bifurcación f; (of a river) tributario m; VI/VT ramificar[se]

brand [brænd] N (make, mark) marca f; (of

humor, etc.) tipo m; (mark of disgrace) estigma m; — **awareness** conciencia de marca f; — **loyalty** lealtad de marca f; — **name** marca f; ADJ —**-new** flamante, recién comprado; VT (burn) herrar, marcar; (stigmatize) estigmatizar; **to — as** tildar de, tachar de

brandish [brǽndɪʃ] VT blandir, esgrimir

brandy [brǽndi] N (fine) brandy m; (cheap) aguardiente m

brash [bræʃ] ADJ (impudent) descarado; (impetuous) impetuoso

brass [bræs] N (metal) latón m; (attitude) descaro m; (high-ranking officers) la plana mayor; — **instrument** instrumento de metal m; **to get down to — tacks** ir al grano; ADJ de latón

brassiere [brəzír] N sostén m

brat [bræt] N mocoso -sa mf

bravado [brəvádo] N alarde m

brave [brev] ADJ valiente, gallardo; N guerrero indio m; VT desafiar

bravery [brévəri] N valentía f, gallardía f

brawl [brɔl] N reyerta f, riña f, pelotera f; VI reñir

bray [bre] N rebuzno m; VI rebuznar

brazen [brézən] ADJ (impudent) descarado; (made of brass) de latón

brazier [bréʒɚ] N brasero m

Brazil [brəzɪl] N Brasil m

Brazilian [brəzɪljən] ADJ & N brasileño -ña mf, brasilero -ra mf

breach [britʃ] N (opening) brecha f; (infraction) infracción f; (severance) ruptura f; — **of contract** incumplimiento de contrato m; — **of faith** abuso de confianza m; VT (make an opening) abrir una brecha en; (violate a law) violar, infringir

bread [brɛd] N pan m; —**basket** panera f; — **box** panera f; —**winner** sostén de la familia m; ADJ —**-and-butter** básico; VT empanar

breadth [brɛdθ] N anchura f, ancho m; (size) extensión f; (perspective) amplitud f

break [brek] VI (fracture) romperse; (pause) parar; VT (a record) batir; (a code) descifrar; (a law) violar; (news) dar, divulgar; (a bone) fracturar; (a horse) domar, desbravar; (a habit) quitar[se]; (a contract, promise) romper; (one's spirit) quebrar, doblegar; (one's heart) desgarrar; (cause to go bankrupt) arruinar; **to — a ten-dollar bill** conseguir cambio para un billete de diez dólares; **to — away** escaparse; **to — down** (a person) descomponerse; (a car) averiarse; (resistance) vencer; (continuity) interrumpir; **to — even** quedar a mano; **to — into** violentar; **to — loose** liberarse; **to — out** (war) estallar; (one's face) brotarse; (from prison) escaparse; **to — up** (into pieces) quebrarse; (a relationship) romper con; N (weather) cambio

m; (from work) descanso m; (with tradition) quiebre m, rompimiento m; (of a bone) fractura f; (from prison) fuga f; (opportunity) oportunidad f; —**in** hurto con escalo m; —**down** (analysis) análisis m; (automotive) avería f; (nervous) colapso m; —**down of charges** desglose de cargos m; —**even point** umbral de rentabilidad m; — **point** (in tennis) bola de break f, bola de ruptura f; —**through** adelanto m; (military) penetración f; —**water** rompeolas m sg; **lucky —** golpe de suerte m

breakable [brékəbəl] ADJ quebradizo, rompible

breaker [brékɚ] N rompiente f

breakfast [brɛkfəst] N desayuno m; VI desayunar

breast [brɛst] N (of a woman) seno m, pecho m; (of a bird) pechuga f; —**bone** esternón m; — **cancer** cáncer de mama m; —**-feeding** lactancia materna f; —**stroke** (estilo de natación) pecho m; VI/VT **to —-feed** amamantar, dar de mamar

breath [brɛθ] N aliento m; *lit* hálito m; (current of air) soplo m; **in the same —** al mismo tiempo; **out of —** sin aliento; **to catch one's —** recobrar el aliento; **to hold one's —** aguantar la respiración; **to take a —** inhalar; **to take a deep —** respirar hondo; **under one's —** entre dientes, por lo bajo; ADJ —**taking** impresionante

breathe [brið] VI/VT respirar; **to — in** inspirar, aspirar; **to — into** infundir; **to — out** exhalar, espirar; **he did not — a word** no dijo palabra

breathing [bríðɪŋ] N respiración f

breathless [brɛθlɪs] ADJ sin aliento

breathlessness [brɛθlɪsnɪs] N falta de aire f

bred [brɛd] *see* breed

breed [brid] VT (mate) criar; (bring up) educar; (give rise to) engendrar; VI reproducirse, multiplicarse; N (species) raza f; (type) clase f

breeder [brídɚ] N (person who breeds) criador -ora mf; (animal used for breeding) [animal] reproductor m

breeding [brídɪŋ] N (of animals) cría f; (of people) educación f, modales m pl

breeze [briz] N brisa f

breezy [brízi] ADJ (windy) ventoso; (jaunty) ameno

brevity [brévɪDi] N brevedad f

brew [bru] VT (coffee) hacer; (mischief) fomentar, tramar; (beer) fabricar; VI (storm) armarse una tormenta; **let the tea —** deja reposar el té; N (mixture) mezcla f; (beer) cerveza f

brewery [brúəri] N cervecera f, fábrica de cerveza f

briar [bráɪɚ] N zarza f

bribe [braɪb] N soborno m, cohecho m; *Mex* mordida f; VT sobornar

bribery [bráibəri] N soborno m

brick [brik] N ladrillo m; **—bat** (piece of brick) pedazo de ladrillo m; (insult) insulto m; **—layer** albañil m; **—laying** albañilería f; VT (adorn with bricks) revestir de ladrillo; (pave with bricks) enladrillar

bridal [bráidl] ADJ nupcial; **— dress** vestido de novia m

bride [braid] N novia f; **—groom** novio m; **—smaid** dama de honor f

bridge [bridʒ] N puente m; (of the nose) caballete m; (card game) bridge m; VT (a river) tender un puente sobre; (a gap) llenar, salvar

bridle [bráidl] N (harness) brida f; (restraint) freno m; VT (put on a bridle) poner una brida; (restrain) frenar; VI (be insulted) ofenderse

brief [brif] ADJ (short) breve, escueto; (concise) conciso, escueto; (curt) seco; N sumario m, resumen m; (report) expediente m; **—case** portafolio[s] m sg, maletín m; **—s** calzoncillos m pl; **in —** en suma; VT informar

briefing [brífiŋ] N reunión para dar instrucciones f

brigade [brigéd] N brigada f

bright [brait] ADJ (shining) brillante; (full of light) iluminado; (smart) inteligente; (promising) venturoso, prometedor; (radiant) radiante; (colorful) subido

brighten [bráitn] VT (a room) iluminar; VI **to — up** (person) animar[se]; (sky) despejarse

brightness [bráitnɪs] N (light) claridad f; (cheerfulness) viveza f; (intelligence) inteligencia f

brilliance [bríljəns] N (of hair, of a historical period) brillantez f; (of intellect) genio m

brilliant [bríljənt] ADJ (shining) brillante; (intelligent) genial; (splendid) espléndido; N brillante m, diamante m

brim [brim] N borde m; (of a hat) ala f; **to fill to the —** llenar hasta el borde; **to be filled to the —** estar de bote en bote; VI **to — over** rebosar; **to be —ming with** estar rebosante de

brine [brain] N salmuera f

bring [briŋ] VT traer; (cause) ocasionar, causar; **to — about** producir, ocasionar; **to — down** (kill) bajar; (depress) deprimir; **to — forth** (give birth) dar a luz; (produce) producir; **to — to a stop** parar; **to — a session to a close** clausurar una sesión; **to — together** reunir, juntar; **to — oneself to do something** poder hacer algo; **to — a good price** redituar una buena ganancia; **to — up** (raise children) criar, educar; (mention) mencionar

brink [briŋk] N borde m; **on the — of** al borde de

brisk [brisk] ADJ (walk) rápido; (weather) fresco; (trading) activo

bristle [brisəl] N cerda f; VI erizar[se]; **to — with** estar erizado de

bristly [brísli] ADJ (with bristles) erizado, cerdoso; (irascible) irascible

Britain [brítn̩] N Gran Bretaña f

British [brítɪʃ] ADJ británico

brittle [brídl] ADJ quebradizo, frágil

brittleness [brídl̩nɪs] N fragilidad f

broach [brotʃ] VT sacar a colación

broad [brod] ADJ (wide) ancho; (vast) vasto; (ample) amplio; **—band** banda ancha f; **—cast** emisión f; (on TV) transmisión por televisión f; **—cast station** emisora f; **— hint** insinuación clara f; **— jump** salto de longitud m; **—minded** tolerante; **—side** andanada f; **— spectrum antibiotic** antibiótico de amplio espectro m; **in — daylight** en pleno día; N pej tipa f; VT **to —cast** (communicate electronically) transmitir, emitir, radiar

broadcasting [bródkæstɪŋ] N (radio) radiodifusión f; (TV) transmisión por televisión f

brocade [brokéd] N brocado m

broccoli [brákəli] N brócoli m, brécol m

brochure [broʃúr] N folleto m

broil [brɔil] VI/VT asar[se] [a la parrilla]

broiler [brɔílə] N (oven) parrilla f; (chicken) pollo [para asar] m

broke [brok] ADJ **to be —** estar limpio, estar pelado; **to go —** irse a la quiebra

broke [brok] see break

broken [brókən] ADJ (fragmented) roto, quebrado; (tamed) domado; (not functioning) descompuesto; (not continuous) interrumpido; **—down** averiado, descompuesto; **— English** inglés chapurrado/chapurreado m; **—hearted** deshecho, con el corazón destrozado

broken [brókən] see break

broker [brókə] N (intermediary) agente mf; (stock salesperson) corredor -ora de bolsa mf

brokerage [brókə-ɪdʒ] N correduría f

bromide [brómaid] N bromuro m

bromine [brómin] N bromo m

bronchial [bráŋkiəl] ADJ bronquial; **— tube** bronquio m

bronchitis [braŋkáidɪs] N bronquitis f

bronco [bráŋko] N caballo no domado m

bronze [branz] N bronce m; VT broncear

brooch [brutʃ] N broche m, prendedor m

brood [brud] N pollada f, nidada f; VI/VT empollar; **to — over** rumiar

brook [bruk] N riachuelo m, cañada f; VT tolerar

broom [brum] N (tool) escoba f; (plant) retama f; **—stick** palo de escoba m

broth [brɔθ] N caldo m

brothel [bráθəl] N burdel m

brother [bráðə] N hermano m; **—-in-law**

cuñado *m*; **oh —!** ¡caray!

brotherhood [bráðə-hʊd] N hermandad *f*

brotherly [bráðə-li] ADJ fraternal

brought [brɔt] *see* bring

brow [braʊ] N (eyebrow) ceja *f*; (ridge of eye) arco superciliar *m*; (forehead) frente *f*

brown [braʊn] ADJ (skin) moreno; (eyes, shoes, clothes) café, marrón; (hair) castaño; (dun) pardo; (tanned) bronceado; **— bear** oso pardo *m*; **— rice** arroz integral *m*; **— sugar** azúcar moreno -na *mf*; VI/VT (food) dorar[se]; N (color) café *m*, castaño *m*, moreno *m*, pardo *m*

brownie [bráʊni] N bizcocho de chocolate *m*; **— points** méritos *m pl*

browse [braʊz] VT (a book) hojear; VI (grass) pacer, pastar; (Internet) navegar

browser [bráʊzə-] N navegador *m*

browsing [bráʊzɪŋ] N navegación *f*

bruise [bruz] N (on skin) moretón *m*, cardenal *m*, contusión *f*; (on fruit) magulladura *f*, cardenal *m*; VI/VT magullar[se], machucar[se]

brunch [brʌntʃ] N brunch *m*, desayuno tardío *m*

Brunei [brunái] N Brunéi *m*

Bruneian [brunáiən] ADJ & N bruneano -na *mf*

brunette, brunet [brunét] ADJ & N moreno -na *mf*, morocho -cha *mf*; *Cuba* trigueño -ña *mf*

brunt [brʌnt] N impacto *m*

brush [brʌʃ] N (for teeth, clothes) cepillo *m*; (for paint, shaving) brocha *f*; (artist's) pincel *m*; (vegetation) maleza *f*; (contact) roce *m*; **—-off** despedida brusca *f*; **—-wood** (dead) broza *f*; (live) maleza *f*; VT (clean with a brush) cepillar; (touch lightly) rozar; **to — aside** echar a un lado; **to — up on** repasar; **to — off** (clean) quitar con cepillo; (reject) despedir bruscamente a alguien

brusque [brʌsk] ADJ brusco

Brussels sprouts [brásəɫspraʊts] N coles de Bruselas *f pl*, repollitos de Bruselas *m pl*

brutal [brúdɫ] ADJ brutal

brutality [brutǽlɪdi] N brutalidad *f*

brute [brut] N (animal) bestia *f*; (person) bruto -ta *mf*; ADJ bruto

bubble [bábəɫ] N burbuja *f*; (in soap) pompa *f*; (in boiling water) borbollón *m*; (illusion) encanto *m*; **— bath** baño de burbujas *m*; **—gum** chicle de globo *m*; **—-jet printer** impresora de burbuja *f*; VI (make bubbles) borbotar, borbollar; (boil) bullir, hervir; **to — over with joy** rebosar de alegría

bubonic plague [bubánɪkplég] N plaga bubónica *f*

buck [bʌk] N (deer) gamo *m*; (male of other animals) macho *m*; (leap of horse) respingo *m*; **— private** soldado raso *m*; **—shot** posta *f*, perdigón *m*; **—skin** gamuza *f*; **—wheat** trigo sarraceno *m*; **to pass the —** echarle el muerto a uno; ADJ **—-toothed** de dientes salidos; VI (horse) respingar, corcovear; **to — a trend** oponerse; **to — up** cobrar ánimo

bucket [bákɪt] N cubo *m*, balde *m*; (of a loader) cuchara *f*; **— seat** asiento delantero individual *m*

buckle [bákəɫ] N (clasp) hebilla *f*; (kink in a board) torcedura *f*; VT (to clasp) abrocharse; (to bend) torcerse, pandearse; **to — down** esforzarse; **to — up** abrocharse

bud [bʌd] N botón *m*, retoño *m*; VI (make buds) echar retoños

Buddhism [búdɪzəm] N budismo *m*

Buddhist [búdɪst] ADJ & N budista *mf*

buddy [bádi] N camarada *mf*

budge [bʌdʒ] VI moverse

budget [bádʒɪt] N presupuesto *m*; VT (money) presupuestar; (time, personal resources) administrar; **— cycle** ciclo presupuestario *m*; **— deficit** déficit presupuestario *m*

budgetary [bádʒɪteri] ADJ presupuestario

budgeting [bádʒɪdɪŋ] N presupuestación *f*

buff [bʌf] N (leather) gamuza *f*; (tan color) color beige *m*; (wheel for polishing) pulidor *m*; (devotee) aficionado *m*; **in the —** en cueros; ADJ (beige) de color beige; (muscular) musculoso; VT pulir

buffalo [báfəlo] N bisonte *m*, búfalo *m*; **— wings** alitas *f pl*

buffer [báfə-] N (in a computer) memoria intermedia *f*; (shock absorber) amortiguador *m*; (polishing device) pulidor -ra *mf*; **— zone** zona tampón *f*

buffet[1] [báfɪt] N (blow) golpe *m*, puñetazo *m*; (shock) azote *m*; VT (hit) golpear; (hit repeatedly) azotar

buffet[2] [bəfé] N (cabinet) aparador *m*; (meal) buffet *m*

buffoon [bəfún] N payaso -a *mf*, bufón -ona *mf*

bug [bʌg] N bicho *m*; (disease-causing) microbio *m*, virus *m*; (for eavesdropping) micrófono oculto *m*; (in a computer program) fallo *m*, bicho *m*; VT (bother) molestar; (install microphones) colocar micrófonos ocultos; **his eyes —ged out** se le saltaron los ojos

buggy [bági] N (cart) calesa *f*; (baby carriage) cochecillo *m*

bugle [bjúgəɫ] N clarín *m*; VI tocar el clarín

build [bɪɫd] VT (construct) construir, edificar; (manufacture) fabricar; **to — into** incorporar; **to — up** (make stronger) fortalecer; (accumulate) acumular; (enhance) desarrollar; (urbanize) urbanizar; N **—-up** (of military forces) concentración *f*; (of substance) acumulación *f*; (of anticipation) aumento *m*; N (of human body) complexión *f*

builder [bíɫdə-] N contratista *mf*, constructor -ora *mf*

building [bíɫdɪŋ] N (thing built) edificio *m*; (act of building) construcción *f*, edificación *f*;

(unit in a housing complex) bloque *m*; —
block (solid mass) bloque [de construcción]
m; (toy) cubo *m*; (essential element) elemento
fundamental *m*

built [bɪlt] ADJ —-**in** (furniture appliance)
empotrado; (feature) incorporado; —-**in
part** parte integrante *f*; —-**to-order** hecho a
pedido; —-**up** urbanizado

built [bɪlt] *see* build

bulb [bʌlb] N (plant) bulbo *m*; (light) bombilla *f*;
Am foco *m*

bulbous [bʌ́lbəs] ADJ bulboso

Bulgaria [bʌlgériə] N Bulgaria *f*

Bulgarian [bʌlgériən] ADJ & N búlgaro -ra *mf*

bulge [bʌldʒ] N bulto *m*, protuberancia *f*; VI
abultar, hincharse

bulgy [bʌ́ldʒi] ADJ abultado

bulimia [bjulímiə] N bulimia *f*

bulk [bʌlk] N (mass) cantidad *f*, volumen *m*;
(greater part) mayor parte *f*; — **storage**
almacenamiento masivo *m*; **in** — a granel; VI
to — **up** echar músculos

bulky [bʌ́lki] ADJ voluminoso

bull [bʊl] N toro *m*; —**dog** buldog *m*; —**dozer**
bulldozer *m*; —**fight** corrida de toros *f*;
—**fighter** torero *m*; —**fighting**
tauromaquia *f*, —**frog** rana grande *f*; —
market mercado alcista *m*; —**pen** (baseball)
zona de calentamiento *f*; —**'s eye** diana *f*; **to
hit the —'s-eye** dar en el blanco; ADJ
—**headed** terco, obstinado

bullet [bʊ́lɪt] N bala *f*; —**proof** antibalas *inv*,
antibalístico

bulletin [bʊ́lɪtn] N boletín *m*; — **board** tablero
m, cartelera *f*

bullion [bʊ́ljən] N oro en lingotes *m*

bully [bʊ́li] N matón -ona *mf*, bravucón -ona *mf*;
VT intimidar

bulwark [bʊ́lwək] N baluarte *m*

bum [bʌm] N (lazy person) holgazán -ana *mf*;
(hobo) vagabundo -da *mf*; (sports fan)
fanático -ca *mf*; ADJ falso; VI **to** — **around**
holgazanear; VT **to** — **something from
someone** gorronearle algo a alguien

bumblebee [bʌ́mbəlbi] N abejorro *m*, abejón *m*

bump [bʌmp] VT chocar; **to** — **along** ir dando
tumbos; **to** — **off** despachar; **to** — **into**
toparse con; N (blow) choque *m*, trastazo *m*;
(lump) protuberancia *f*; (lump on a person)
chichón *m*

bumper [bʌ́mpə] N parachoques *m sg*, tope *m*;
— **car** coche de choque *m*, autito chocador *m*;
— **crop** cosecha abundante *f*; —-**to**—
traffic caravana de autos *f*; —**sticker**
autoadhesivo *m*

bumpy [bʌ́mpi] ADJ bacheado, lleno de baches

bun [bʌn] N (bread) bollo *m*; (in hair) moño *m*

bunch [bʌntʃ] N (of things) manojo *m*; (of
people) montón *m*, grupo *m*; (of grapes,

bananas) racimo *m*; (of flowers) ramillete *m*;
VI/VT juntar[se], agrupar[se]

bundle [bʌ́ndl] N (of things) paquete *m*, fardo *m*,
envoltorio *m*; (of clothes) lío *m*, atado *m*; (of
belongings) hato *m*, petate *m*; (of firewood)
haz *m*; VT (tie together) liar, atar; **to** — **up**
abrigarse; **to** — **off** despachar

bungalow [bʌ́ŋgəlo] N bungaló *m*

bungee jumping [bʌ́ndʒidʒʌ́mpɪŋ] N bungee *m*,
puénting *m*

bungle [bʌ́ŋgəl] VT estropear; VI chapucear

bunion [bʌ́njən] N juanete *m*

bunk [bʌŋk] N (place to sleep) litera *f*; (nonsense)
tonterías *f pl*; — **bed** litera *f*; VI dormir en una
litera

bunker [bʌ́ŋkə] N búnker *m*

bunny [bʌ́ni] N conejito *m*

bunt [bʌnt] N (baseball) toque de pelota *m*; VT
tocar la pelota

buoy [búi] N boya *f*; VI boyar; **to** — **up** mantener
a flote, animar

buoyant [bɔ́iənt] ADJ (floating) boyante,
flotante; (optimistic) optimista

burden [bɝ́dn] N (load) carga *f*; (responsibility)
peso *m*; — **of proof** peso de la prueba *m*; VT
(heavily) recargar; (oppressively) agobiar

burdensome [bɝ́dnsəm] ADJ agobiante, gravoso

bureau [bjúro] N (government department)
oficina *f*, agencia *f*; (chest of drawers)
cómoda *f*

bureaucracy [bjurákrəsi] N burocracia *f*

bureaucrat [bjúrəkræt] N burócrata *mf*

burglar [bɝ́glə] N ladrón -ona *mf*; — **alarm**
alarma antirrobo *f*; — **proof** a prueba de
robos

burglary [bɝ́gləri] N robo con allanamiento *m*

burial [bériəl] N entierro *m*, enterramiento *m*; —
ground enterramiento *m*; — **place** lugar de
sepultura *m*

Burkina Faso [bəkínəfáso] N Burkina Faso *m*

burlap [bɝ́læp] N arpillera *f*

burlesque [bəlésk] ADJ burlesco; N espectáculo
de variedades *m*

burly [bɝ́li] ADJ corpulento

Burma [bɝ́mə] N Birmania *f*

Burmese [bəmíz] ADJ & N birmano -na *mf*

burn [bɝn] VI/VT quemar[se], abrasar[se]; (a
house) incendiar[se]; (a CD) quemar; (food)
quemar[se], requemar[se]; **he got —ed in
the transaction** lo estafaron en el negocio;
the bulb is still —ing la bombilla sigue
prendida; **the iodine —ed his skin** el yodo
le quemó la piel; VI (with heat, passion) arder,
abrasar; **my skin —s** me arde la piel; **he's
—ing with desire** arde en deseos; **to** —
down incendiarse; **to** — **off** (fog) disiparse;
to — **out** (bulb) fundirse; (worker) agotarse;
to — **up** quemarse completamente; N
quemadura *f*; —**out** surmenage *m*

burner [bɜ́nə] N (person or thing that burns something) quemador -ra *mf*; (on stove) hornilla *f*; **Bunsen** — mechero Bunsen *m*

burning [bɜ́nɪŋ] ADJ (desire) ardiente, abrasador; (question) urgente; N (caused by acid) ardor *m*; (caused by fire) quemadura *f*

burnish [bɜ́nɪʃ] VT bruñir

burnt [bɜrnt] *see* burn

burp [bɜp] N eructo *m*; VI eructar, repetir

burr, bur [bɜ] N abrojo *m*

burrow [bɜ́o] N madriguera *f*; VI (dig) hacer madrigueras; (live) vivir en una madriguera

bursitis [bɜsáɪDɪs] N bursitis *f*

burst [bɜst] VI reventar[se]; **to — into a room** irrumpir en un cuarto; **to — into tears** romper en llanto; **to — out** salir disparado; **to — with laughter** estallar/reventar de risa; N (of activity) explosión *f*; (of laughter) carcajada *f*; (of machine-gun fire) ráfaga *f*; (of speed) aceleración *f*

Burundi [burúndi] N Burundi *m*

Burundian [burúndiən] ADJ & N burundés -esa *mf*

bury [béri] VT (body, treasure) enterrar; (body) sepultar; **to be buried in thought** estar absorto/meditabundo

bus [bʌs] N autobús *m*, ómnibus *m*; *Mex* camión *m*; *RP* colectivo *m*; *Chile* micro *m*; *Cuba* guagua *f*; (in a computer) bus *m*; VT transportar en autobús

bush [bʊʃ] N (plant) arbusto *m*, mata *f*; (region) matorral *m*; **to beat around the —** andarse por las ramas

bushed [bʊʃt] ADJ fatigado

bushel [bʊ́ʃəl] N fanega *f*

bushing [bʊ́ʃɪŋ] N buje *m*, cojinete *m*

bushy [bʊ́ʃi] ADJ (whiskers) espeso; (plants) poblado de arbustos

business [bíznɪs] N (trade, store) negocio *m*; (occupation) ocupación *f*; (commercial activity) comercio *m*; **— acumen** buen sentido para los negocios *m*; **— agreement** convenio comercial *m*; **— card** tarjeta comercial *f*; **— day** día hábil *m*; **— group** grupo empresarial *m*; **— hours** horas hábiles *f pl*, horario de atención al público *m*; **— is booming** el negocio florece; **—like** (efficient) eficiente; (cold) impersonal; **—man** hombre de negocios *m*, negociante *m*; **— suit** traje *m*; **— transaction** negocio *m*, transacción comercial *f*; **—woman** mujer de negocios *f*, negociante *f*; **I'm tired of the whole —** este asunto me tiene harto; **I mean —** hablo en serio; **to do — with** comerciar con; **he has no — doing it** no tiene derecho a hacerlo; **it's none of your —** no es asunto tuyo; **mind your own —** no te metas en lo que no te importa

bust [bʌst] N (statue, body part) busto *m*; VI/VT

(burst, hit, break) reventar; (force into bankruptcy) hacer quebrar; (lower in rank) degradar

bustle [bʌ́səl] N (noise) bullicio *m*; (movement) ajetreo *m*, tráfago *m*; VI (move busily) ajetrear[se]; (be crowded) bullir

busy [bízi] ADJ ocupado, atareado; (overdecorated) recargado; **—body** entrometido -da *mf*; **—signal** señal de ocupado *f*; VI **to — oneself** ocuparse

but [bʌt] CONJ (on the contrary) pero; (excepting) sino; PREP menos; **any day —** today cualquier día menos hoy; **he's nothing — trouble** sólo da problemas; ADV **— for you** si no fuera por ti

butane [bjútén] N butano *m*

butch [bʊtʃ] ADJ machote

butcher [bʊ́tʃə] N carnicero -ra *mf*; **—'s shop** carnicería *f*; VT (cattle) matar; (people) masacrar; (performance) estropear

butchery [bʊ́tʃəri] N carnicería *f*

butler [bʌ́tlə] N mayordomo *m*

butt [bʌt] N; (of a rifle) culata *f*; (of a cigarette) colilla *f*; (blow with head) topetazo *m*, cabezada *f*, cabezazo *m*; **the — of ridicule** el blanco de las burlas; VT embestir, topar; **to — in** entrometerse; **to — into a conversation** meter baza; *Am* meter la cuchara

butter [bʌ́Də] N mantequilla *f*; **— cup** botón de oro *m*; **— dish** mantequera *f*; **—fingers** manos de mantequilla *mf sg*; **—milk** suero de leche *m*; **— scotch** dulce de azúcar y mantequilla *m*; VT (bread) untar con mantequilla; (a cake*pan*) enmantecar

butterfly [bʌ́Dəflaɪ] N mariposa *f*; **— stroke** estilo mariposa *m*

buttery [bʌ́Dəi] ADJ mantecoso

buttocks [bʌ́Dəks] N nalgas *f pl*, asentaderas *f pl*, cachas *f pl*

button [bʌ́tn] N botón *m*; **—hole** ojal *m*; VI/VT abotonar[se]; VT **to —hole** hacer ojales; VT **to —hole someone** detener a alguien

buttress [bʌ́trɪs] N apoyo *m*, sostén *m*; (of a building) contrafuerte *m*; VT apoyar, reforzar

buy [baɪ] VT comprar; **to — on credit** comprar a crédito; **to — in installments** comprar a plazos; **to — off** sobornar; **to — out** comprar la parte de; **to — up** acaparar; **I don't — that** no me lo trago; N (purchase) compra *f*; (bargain) ganga *f*

buyer [báɪə] N comprador -ra *mf*

buying [báɪɪŋ] N **— frenzy** frenesí de compras *m*; **— habits** hábitos de compras *m pl*

buzz [bʌz] N zumbido *m*; (feeling of intoxication) borrachera *f*; (phone call) telefonazo *m*; **—word** palabra de moda *f*; **— saw** sierra circular *f*; VI (insect, ears) zumbar; (group) murmurar; VT hacer zumbar; **to — the bell** tocar el timbre; **to give someone a —**

pegarle/echarle un telefonazo a alguien; **to — off** largarse

buzzard [bázɑd] N buitre m

buzzer [bázɚ] N timbre m, chicharra f

by [baɪ] PREP por; **— and —** a la larga; **— chance** por casualidad; **— dint of** a fuerza de; **— far** con mucho; **— night** de noche; **— the way** a propósito; **— the liter** por litro; **— this time tomorrow** mañana a esta hora; **— two o'clock** para las dos; **we drove — the church** pasamos por la iglesia; **a 4 — 3 room** un cuarto de 4 por 3; **multiply 2 — 2** multiplica 2 por 2; **we live — the church** vivimos al lado de la iglesia; **she had a son — him** tuvo un hijo con él; **piece — piece** pedazo a/por pedazo; ADV **the factory is close —** la fábrica está cerca; **the bus drove —** pasó el autobús

bye-bye [báɪbáɪ] INTERJ ¡adiós! ¡chaucito!

bygones [báɪɡɔnz] N **let — be —** lo pasado pisado

bylaw [báɪlɔ] N estatuto m

by-line [báɪlaɪn] N pie de autor m

bypass [báɪpæs] VT evitar; N desvío m; **— operation** bypass m

by-product [báɪprɑdɐkt] N subproducto m; (chemical) derivado m

bystander [báɪstændɚ] N persona presente f

byte [baɪt] N byte m, octeto m

Cc

cab [kæb] N (of a truck) cabina f; (taxi) taxi m; **— driver** taxista mf

cabaret [kæbɑré] N cabaret m

cabbage [kébɪdʒ] N col f, repollo m, berza f

cabin [kébɪn] N (hut) cabaña f; (in an airplane) cabina f; (in a ship) camarote m

cabinet [kébnɪt] N (for dishes) armario m; (for medicines) botiquín m; (for display) vitrina f; (of ministers) gabinete m; **—level appointment** nombramiento ministerial m; **—maker** ebanista mf

cable [kébəl] N cable m; (on ships) amarra f; (telegram) telegrama m; **— car** funicular m, teleférico m; **— television** televisión por cable f, cablevisión f; VI/VT telegrafiar

caboose [kabús] N furgón de cola m

cache [kæʃ] N (of weapons) alijo m; (in a computer) caché m; **— memory** memoria de caché f

cachet [kæʃé] N caché m

cackle [kékəl] VI (hen) cacarear; (people) parlotear; N (hen) cacareo m; (people) parloteo m

cacophony [kəkáfəni] N cacofonía f

cactus [kéktəs] N cacto m, cactus m

cad [kæd] N pej canalla mf

cadaver [kadévɚ] N cadáver m

caddie [kédi] N caddy m, caddie m

cadence [kédns] N cadencia f

cadet [kədét] N cadete mf

cadmium [kédmiəm] N cadmio m

café [kæfé] N (coffee only) café m; (coffee and food) cafetería f

cafeteria [kæfɪtɪriə] N cafetería f

caffeine [kæfín] N cafeína f

cage [kedʒ] N jaula f; VT enjaular

cahoots [kahúts] ADV LOC **in —** arreglados

cajole [kədʒól] VI/VT engatusar, persuadir con halagos

cake [kek] N pastel m, torta f; (sponge) bizcocho m; (soap) pastilla f; **a piece of —** pan comido; **to take the —** ser el colmo; VI/VT apelmazar[se]

calamine [kéləmaɪn] N calamina f

calamity [kəlémɪti] N calamidad f

calcium [kélsiəm] N calcio m

calculate [kélkjəlet] VI/VT calcular; **his actions were —d to fool us** con sus acciones trataba de engañarnos

calculating [kélkjəletɪŋ] ADJ calculador

calculation [kælkjəléʃən] N cálculo m

calculator [kélkjəledɚ] N calculadora f

calculus [kélkjələs] N cálculo m

calendar [kéləndɚ] N calendario m; **— year** año civil m

calf [kæf] N (of leg) pantorrilla f, canilla f; (animal) ternero -ra mf, becerro -rra mf; **— skin** piel de becerro f

caliber [kéləbɚ] N calibre m

calibrate [kéləbret] VT calibrar, graduar

calico [kéliko] N calicó m

caliper [kéləpɚ] N (on brakes) calibrador m; (for measuring) calibre m

call [kɔl] VT (summon, by telephone, a name, a strike) llamar; (cry out) gritar; (a meeting) convocar; **she —ed me a liar** me llamó mentiroso; **— me back** llámame tú, devuélveme la llamada; VI/VT (birds) reclamar; **to — roll** pasar lista; VI (call out) gritar; **to — a meeting to order** abrir la sesión; **to — at a port** hacer escala en un puerto; **to — for** pedir; **to — off** cancelar; **to — on** (visit) visitar; (depend on) acudir a; **to — together** convocar; **to — up** llamar por teléfono; N (by telephone) llamada f; (summons) llamamiento m, llamado m; (to the ministry) vocación f; (for conference papers) convocatoria f; (device for calling birds) reclamo m; **to be on —** estar de guardia; **there's no — for panic** no hay motivo de alarma; **it's your —** tú decides; **within —** al alcance de la voz

caller [kɔ́lə] N visita *f*, visitante *mf*; (by telephone) persona que llama *f*; — **ID** identificador de llamadas *m*

calligraphy [kəlígrəfi] N caligrafía *f*

calling [kɔ́lɪŋ] N vocación *f*

callous [kǽləs] ADJ (having calluses) calloso; (insensitive) insensible

callus [kǽləs] N callo *m*

calm [kɑm] ADJ tranquilo, reposado, calmo; N calma *f*, tranquilidad *f*, sosiego *m*; VT calmar, tranquilizar, sosegar; **to — down** calmar[se]

calmness [kámnɪs] N calma *f*, tranquilidad *f*

calorie [kǽləri] N caloría *f*

calumny [kǽləmni] N calumnia *f*

cam [kæm] N leva *f*

Cambodia [kæmbóðiə] N Camboya *f*

Cambodian [kæmbóðiən] ADJ & N camboyano -na *mf*

camcorder [kǽmkɔrdə] N videocámara *f*

came [kem] *see* come

camel [kǽməl] N camello *m*

cameo [kǽmio] N camafeo *m*; — **appearance** actuación especial *f*

camera [kǽmrə] N cámara *f*, cámara fotográfica *f*; —**man** cámara *m*, camarógrafo *m*; —-**ready copy** texto listo para cámara *f*; —**woman** cámara *f*, camarógrafa *f*

Cameroon [kæmərún] N Camerún *m*

Cameroonian [kæmərúniən] ADJ & N camerunés -esa *mf*

camouflage [kǽməflɑʒ] N camuflaje *m*; VT camuflar

camp [kæmp] N (campsite) campamento *m*; (faction) bando *m*; —**fire** fogata *f*, hoguera *f*; —**ground** campamento *m*, cámping *m*; —**site** campamento *m*; VI/VT acampar

campaign [kæmpén] N campaña *f*; VI hacer campaña

camper [kǽmpə] N acampante *mf*, campista *mf*

camphor [kǽmfə] N alcanfor *m*

camping [kǽmpɪŋ] N cámping *m*, acampada *f*; **let's go** — vamos de camping / de acampada

campus [kǽmpəs] N campus *m*

can [kæn] N lata *f*, bote *m*; — **of worms** caja de Pandora *f*; — **opener** abrelatas *m sg*; VT enlatar; V AUX — **you come tomorrow?** ¿puedes venir mañana? — **you see me?** ¿me ves? I — **ride a bicycle** sé andar en bicicleta; **a** —-**do attitude** un espíritu emprendedor

Canada [kǽnəðə] N Canadá *m*

Canadian [kənéðiən] ADJ & N canadiense *mf*

canal [kənǽl] N canal *m*

canary [kənéri] N canario *m*; **Canary Islands** Islas Canarias *f pl*

Canary Islands [kənériáilənz] N Islas Canarias *f pl*

cancel [kǽnsəl] VT cancelar; (a stamp) matasellar; (an order) anular

cancellation [kænsəléʃən] N (of a flight, performance) cancelación *f*; (of an order) anulación *f*

cancer [kǽnsə] N cáncer *m*; — **patient** canceroso -sa *mf*; ADJ —-**causing** cancerígeno

cancerous [kǽnsəəs] ADJ canceroso

candelabrum, candelabra [kændəlábrəm -brə] N candelabro *m*

candid [kǽndɪd] ADJ franco, sincero

candidacy [kǽndɪðəsi] N candidatura *f*

candidate [kǽndɪdɪt] N (for office) candidato -ta *mf*; (for a job) aspirante *mf*, postulante *mf*

candle [kǽndl] N vela *f*, candela *f*; (on the altar) cirio *m*; —**stick** candelero *m*

candor [kǽndə] N franqueza *f*

candy [kǽndi] N dulce *m*, caramelo *m*, confite *m*; (with chocolate) bombón *m*; — **store** bombonería *f*; VT confitar, acaramelar; (nuts) garapiñar; VI (syrup) cristalizarse

cane [ken] N (sugar) caña *f*; (walking) bastón *m*; — **chair** silla de mimbre *f*

canine [kénaɪn] ADJ canino, perruno; N (dog) can *m*, perro *m*; (tooth) canino *m*

canister [kǽnɪstə] N lata *f*

canker [kǽŋkə] N úlcera *f*

cannery [kǽnəri] N fábrica de conservas *f*

cannibal [kǽnəbəl] N caníbal *m*

cannon [kǽnən] N cañón *m*; — **fodder** carne de cañón *f*

canny [kǽni] ADJ sagaz, astuto

canoe [kənú] N canoa *f*

canon [kǽnən] N (rule, melody, body of works) canon *m*; (priest) canónigo *m*

canopy [kǽnəpi] N (of a bed) dosel *m*; (of a building) toldo *m*

cantaloupe [kǽntlop] N melón *m*

canteen [kæntín] N (snack bar) cantina *f*; (container) cantimplora *f*

canvas [kǽnvəs] N (fabric) lona *f*; (for painting) lienzo *m*

canvass [kǽnvəs] VI/VT (poll) encuestar; (solicit votes) solicitar votos en; (solicit sales) buscar pedidos comerciales en; N solicitud *f*

canyon [kǽnjən] N cañón *m*

cap [kæp] N (head covering without visor) gorro *m*; (head covering with visor) gorra *f*; (of a bottle) tapa *f*; (of a pen) capucha *f*, contera *f*; (limit) tope *m*; (for capgun) fulminante *m*, pistón *m*; VT (to cover, put a cap on) tapar; (to complete) rematar; (to limit) limitar

capability [kepəbílɪti] N capacidad *f*

capable [képəbəl] ADJ capaz

capacious [kəpéʃəs] ADJ amplio

capacity [kəpǽsɪti] N capacidad *f*

cape [kep] N (clothing) capa *f*; (promontory) cabo *m*

caper [képə] N (skipping) cabriola *f*; (prank) treta *f*, triquiñuela *f*; (crime) delito *m*; (food) alcaparra *f*; VI retozar

Cape Verde [kepvɜ́d] N Cabo Verde *m*
Cape Verdean [kepvɜ́dian] ADJ & N caboverdiano -na *mf*
capillary [kǽpəleri] N & ADJ [vaso] capilar *m*
capital [kǽpɪdl̩] N (city) capital *f*; (wealth) capital *m*; (of a column) capitel *m*; (letter) mayúscula *f*; **to make — of** sacar partido de, aprovecharse de; ADJ (city) capital; (financial) de capital; **— gains** ganancias en bienes de capital *f pl*; **— investment** inversión de capital *f*; **— punishment** pena de muerte *f*
capitalism [kǽpɪdlɪzəm] N capitalismo *m*
capitalist [kǽpɪdlɪst] N capitalista *mf*
capitalistic [kǽpɪdlístɪk] ADJ capitalista
capitalization [kǽpɪdlɪzéʃən] N capitalización *f*
capitalize [kǽpɪdlaɪz] VT (finance) capitalizar; (write) escribir con mayúscula; **to — on** sacar provecho de
capitol [kǽpɪdl̩] N capitolio *m*
capitulate [kəpítʃəlet] VI capitular
cappuccino [kæpətʃíno] N capuchino *m*
caprice [kəprís] N capricho *m*
capricious [kəpríʃəs] ADJ caprichoso
capsize [kǽpsaɪz] VI/VT volcar[se]
capsule [kǽpsəl̩] N cápsula *f*
captain [kǽptɪn] N capitán *m*; VT capitanear
caption [kǽpʃən] N (with illustration) pie *m*; (subtitle) subtítulo *m*
captivate [kǽptəvet] VT cautivar
captive [kǽptɪv] ADJ & N cautivo -va *mf*; **— animals** animales en cautiverio *m pl*
captivity [kæptívɪdi] N cautiverio *m*
captor [kǽptɚ] N captor -ra *mf*
capture [kǽptʃɚ] VT (apprehend, record data) capturar; (give expression to) plasmar; (attract) cautivar; (conquer) tomar; N captura *f*
car [kɑr] N (automobile) coche *m*, automóvil *m*; *Am* carro *m*, auto *m*; (railroad) vagón *m*, coche *m*; (elevator) cabina *f*; *Am* elevador *m*; **— bomb** coche bomba *m*; **—fare** pasaje *m*; **—jacking** secuestro de vehículo *m*; **—load** carga de un coche *f*; **—port** cochera *f*; **— wash** túnel de lavado *m*; ADJ **—sick** mareado; **to get — sick** marearse en el coche
caramel [kǽrəməl̩] N caramelo *m*
carat [kǽrət] N quilate *m*
caravan [kǽrəvæn] N caravana *f*
carbohydrate [karbəháɪdret] N carbohidrato *m*, hidrato de carbono *m*
carbon [kárbən] N carbono *m*; **— copy** copia en papel carbón *f*; **— dioxide** dióxido de carbono *m*; **— monoxide** monóxido de carbono *m*; **— paper** papel carbón *m*
carburetor [kárbəreɾɚ] N carburador *m*
carcass [kárkəs] N (of an animal) cuerpo muerto *m*; (of a ship) casco *m*
carcinogen [karsínədʒən] N cancerígeno *m*, carcinógeno *m*

carcinoma [karsənómə] N carcinoma *m*
card [kard] N (piece of stiff paper) tarjeta *f*; (for games) naipe *m*, carta *f*; (for boxing events) programa *m*; (for textiles) carda *f*; (witty person) gracioso -sa *mf*; (in a computer) tarjeta *f*, placa *f*; **—board** (thick) cartón *m*; (thin) cartulina *f*; **— reader** lector de tarjetas *m*; **— sharp** fullero -ra *mf*; **pack of —s** baraja *f*; **to play —s** jugar a la baraja, jugar a los naipes; **he's holding all the —s** tiene todas las ventajas; VT (comb) cardar; (ask for identification) pedir identificación
cardiac [kárdiæk] ADJ cardiaco, cardíaco
cardinal [kárdnəl̩] ADJ (number, main) cardinal; (colored red) rojo, bermellón; N (bishop, bird) cardenal *m*
cardioangiogram [karDioǽndʒiəgræm] N cardioangiograma *m*
cardiogram [kárDiogræm] N cardiograma *m*
cardiologist [karDiáləʤɪst] N cardiólogo -ga *m*
cardiology [karDiáləʤi] N cardiología *f*
cardiopulmonary [karDiopúlmənəri] ADJ cardiopulmonar; **— bypass** puente cardiopulmonar *m*
cardiovascular [karDiováskjələ-] ADJ cardiovascular
care [kɛr] N (worry) preocupación *f*; (attention) cuidado *m*, atención *f*, tiento *m*; (extreme attention) esmero *m*, primor *m*; **—giver** cuidador -ra de enfermos *mf*; **—taker** (of a house) casero -ra *mf*; **to be under the — of** estar al cuidado de; **to take — of** cuidar de, atender; ADJ **—free** despreocupado; VI (be concerned) importarle a uno; **to — about** interesarle a uno, importarle a uno; **to — for** (look after) cuidar de; (love) tenerle cariño a; **to — to** tener ganas de; **I couldn't — less** me importa un rábano; **what does he —?** ¿a él qué le importa? **would you — for a drink?** ¿te puedo ofrecer algo?
careen [kərín] VI ladearse a toda velocidad
career [kərír] N carrera *f*, trayectoria *f*
careful [kɛrfəl̩] ADJ (cautious) cuidadoso, cauteloso; (painstaking) esmerado; **to be — tener cuidado**
carefully [kɛrfəli] ADV (safely) con cuidado; (painstakingly) esmeradamente
carefulness [kɛrfəlnɪs] N cuidado *m*
careless [kɛrlɪs] ADJ descuidado
caress [kərɛ́s] N caricia *f*; VT acariciar
cargo [kárgo] N cargamento *m*
Caribbean [kærəbíən] N Caribe *m*; ADJ caribeño
caricature [kǽrɪkətʃɚ] N caricatura *f*; VT caricaturizar
caries [kɛ́riz] N caries *f*
carnage [kárnɪʤ] N carnicería *f*
carnal [kárnl̩] ADJ carnal
carnation [karnéʃən] N (flower) clavel *m*; (color) rosado *m*

carnival [kárnəvəl] N carnaval *m*; (traveling) feria *f*

carnivorous [karnívə‑əs] ADJ carnívoro, carnicero

carol [kærəl] N villancico *m*; VI cantar villancicos

carom [kærəm] N carambola *f*; VI rebotar

carotid artery [kərápɪdárɖəri] N [arteria] carótida *f*

carouse [kəráuz] VI andar de parranda

carp [karp] N carpa *f*; VI (complain) quejarse

carpenter [kárpəntə‑] N carpintero ‑ra *mf*

carpentry [kárpəntri] N carpintería *f*

carpet [kárpɪt] N alfombra *f*; **—bagger** político ‑ca oportunista *mf*; VT alfombrar

carriage [kærɪdʒ] N (wheeled vehicle) carruaje *m*, coche *m*; (posture) porte *m*

carrier [kæriə‑] N (one who carries) portador ‑ra *mf*; (postal worker) cartero ‑ra *mf*; (transport company) mensajería *f*

carrion [kæriən] N carroña *f*

carrot [kærət] N zanahoria *f*

carry [kæri] VT llevar; **do you — Italian wine?** ¿venden vino italiano? **the bill carried** se aprobó el proyecto de ley; **you — yourself well** te comportas bien; **he can't — a tune** no puede seguir una tonada; **this suitcase will — a lot** esta maleta es espaciosa; **to — away** llevarse; **he got carried away** se le fue la mano; **to — on** continuar; **to — out** (complete) llevar a cabo, ejecutar; (take out) sacar; N **‑on** maleta de mano *f*

cart [kart] N (also golf) carro *m*; VT acarrear

cartilage [kárdlɪdʒ] N cartílago *m*

carton [kártn] N caja de cartón *f*

cartoon [kartún] N (drawing) caricatura *f*; (strip) tira cómica *f*; (film) dibujo animado *m*

cartoonist [kartúnɪst] N caricaturista *mf*

cartridge [kártrɪdʒ] N cartucho *m*; **— belt** cartuchera *f*, canana *f*

carve [karv] VI/VT (a piece of wood) tallar; (a turkey) trinchar; **to — out a career** labrarse una carrera

carving [kárvɪŋ] N (action) tallado *m*; (figure) talla *f*; **— knife** trinchante *m*

cascade [kæskéd] N cascada *f*

case [kes] N caso *m*; (box) caja *f*; (of a pillow) funda *f*; **— history** historia clínica *f*; **in — [that]** en caso de [que]; **in — it rains** por si llueve; **in any —** en todo caso; **just in —** por si acaso; **get off my —!** ¡déjame en paz! **—‑ sensitive** sensible a la diferencia entre mayúsculas y minúsculas

cash [kæʃ] N efectivo *m*; **— advance** anticipo en efectivo *m*; **— and carry** al contado y sin entrega a domicilio; **— flow** corriente en efectivo *f*; **— on delivery** entrega contra reembolso *f*; **— payment** pago en efectivo *m*; **— register** caja registradora *f*; **to pay —** pagar al contado; VT cobrar

cashew [kǽʃu] N marañón *m*, castaña de cajú *f*, *Sp* anacardo *m*

cashier [kæʃír] N cajero ‑ra *mf*; **—'s check** cheque de caja *m*

casino [kəsíno] N casino *m*

cask [kæsk] N tonel grande *m*

casket [kǽskɪt] N ataúd *m*

casserole [kǽsəroʊl] N (container) cazuela *f*; (food) guiso *m*

cassette [kəsét] N cassette *mf*, casete *mf*

cast [kæst] VT (throw) tirar, echar; (form an object) moldear, vaciar; (give out dramatic roles) repartir papeles; **to — a ballot** votar; **to — about** buscar; **to — a glance** echar un vistazo; **to — aside** desechar; **to — doubt** poner en duda; **to — light on** aclarar; **to — lots** echar suertes; **to — off** (a ship) soltar amarras; (something rejected) deshacerse de; **to — out** exiliar; **to be — down** estar abatido; N (form) molde *m*; (in theater) reparto *m*, elenco *m*; (for broken bones) yeso; **to put in a —** enyesar; **— iron** hierro fundido *m*

castanet [kæstənét] N castañuela *f*

caste [kæst] N casta *f*

castigate [kǽstɪget] VT (criticize) criticar, reprender; (punish) castigar

Castile [kæstíl] N Castilla *f*

Castilian [kæstíljən] N & ADJ castellano ‑na *mf*; **— speaker** castellanohablante *mf*; ADJ **— speaking** castellanohablante

casting [kæstɪŋ] N (throwing) tiro *m*; (piece of metal) pieza fundida *f*; (selection of actors) cásting *m*

castle [kǽsəl] N castillo *m*; (chess piece) torre *f*, roque *m*

castor oil [kæstə‑ɔɪl] N aceite de ricino *m*

castrate [kǽstret] VT castrar; (animals) capar

casual [kǽʒuəl] ADJ (informal) informal; (offhand) al pasar

casualty [kǽʒuəlti] N (of war) baja *f*; (in an accident) víctima *f*

cat [kæt] N (domestic) gato ‑ta *mf*; (others) felino *m*; **—'s meow** súmmum *m*; **—fish** siluro *m*

Catalan [kǽdlæn] ADJ & N catalán ‑ana *mf*; (language) catalán *m*

catalog, catalogue [kǽdlɔg] N catálogo *m*; VT catalogar

Catalonia [kædlóniə] N Cataluña *f*

Catalonian [kædlóniən] ADJ catalán

catalyst [kǽdlɪst] N catalizador *m*

cataract [kǽdərækt] N catarata *f*

catastrophe [kətǽstrəfi] N catástrofe *f*

catatonia [kædətóniə] N catatonia *f*

catch [kætʃ] VT (a criminal, ball) atrapar; *Sp, Cuba* coger; (a fish) pescar, capturar; (someone in an act) pillar; (a bus) agarrar; (what someone said) comprender, agarrar; **to — a glimpse of** vislumbrar; **to — cold**

resfriarse; **to — fire** prenderse fuego; **to — on** (understand) caer en cuenta; (become popular) ponerse de moda; **to — oneself** contenerse; **to — one's eye** llamarle a uno la atención; **to — sight of** avistar; **to — unawares** sorprender; **to — up** (with a person) alcanzar; (on work) ponerse al día, actualizarse; VI (get entangled) enredarse; (snap into place) agarrar; N (act of catching prey, quantity caught) captura f, redada f, pesca f; (prey) presa f; (device) pestillo m; (act of catching a ball) atrapada f; **—phrase** eslogan m; **— twenty-two** paradoja f; **he is a good** — es un buen partido; **to play** — jugar a la pelota; **what's the** —? ¿cuál es la treta?

catcher [kǽtʃə] N (baseball) receptor -ora mf

catching [kǽtʃɪŋ] ADJ contagioso

catchy [kǽtʃi] ADJ pegadizo

catechism [kǽdɪkɪzəm] N catecismo m

category [kǽdɪɡɔri] N categoría f

cater [kéɪdə] VI/VT abastecer de alimentos [banquetes, fiestas, etc.]; **to — to** atender a

caterpillar [kǽdəpɪlə] N (insect) oruga f; (tractor) tractor oruga m, caterpillar m

cathedral [kəθídɹəl] N catedral f

catheter [kǽθɪDə] N catéter m, sonda f

catheterization [kæθəDə-ɪzéʃən] N cateterización f

catheterize [kǽθəDə-aɪz] VT cateterizar

cathode [kǽθod] N cátodo m; **— rays** rayos catódicos m pl

Catholic [kǽθlɪk] N & ADJ católico -ca mf

Catholicism [kəθálɪsɪzəm] N catolicismo m

CAT [computerized axial tomography] **scan** [kǽtskæn] N TAC f

catsup [kǽtʃəp] N cátsup m, ketchup m, salsa de tomate f

cattle [kǽdl] N ganado (vacuno) m; **—breeding** ganadería f; **—man** ganadero m; **— rustler** cuatrero m; **— rustling** abigeato m

catty [kǽDi] ADJ malicioso

caught [kɔt] see catch

cauliflower [kɔ́lɪflaʊə] N coliflor f

cause [kɔz] N causa f, causante f; **— for celebration** motivo de celebración m; **the democratic** — la causa democrática f; **without** — sin motivo; VT (make happen) causar, ocasionar; (motivate) motivar; **to — to flee** hacer huir; **the heat —d her to faint** el calor la hizo desmayar

caustic [kɔ́stɪk] ADJ cáustico

cauterize [kɔ́Dəɹaɪz] VT cauterizar

caution [kɔ́ʃən] N (prudence) cautela f, recato m; (warning) advertencia f; —! ¡cuidado! ¡atención! VT advertir; **to — against** desaconsejar

cautious [kɔ́ʃəs] ADJ cauto, cauteloso, precavido

cava [kávə] N (wine) cava f

cavalier [kævəlír] N caballero m, galán m; ADJ (disdainful) desdeñoso; (overly casual) displicente

cavalry [kǽvəlɹi] N caballería f

cave [kev] N cueva f, caverna f; **—man** hombre de las cavernas m; VI **to — in** (yield) ceder; (collapse) derrumbarse, desplomarse

cavern [kǽvə-n] N caverna f, gruta f

cavity [kǽvɪDi] N cavidad f; (in a tooth) caries f; (nasal) fosa f

cavort [kəvɔ́rt] VI cabriolar, retozar

caw [kɔ] N graznido m; VI graznar

CD [compact disc] [sidí] N CD m, disco compacto m; **— player** reproductor de discos compactos m; **—-ROM** CD-ROM m

cease [sis] VI cesar; VT interrumpir; N **—fire** alto el fuego m; Am cese el fuego m

ceaseless [síslɪs] ADJ incesante

cedar [sídə-] N cedro m

cede [sid] VT ceder

ceiling [sílɪŋ] N techo m, cielo raso m; (cap) tope m; (sky) altura máxima f

celebrate [séləbret] VI/VT celebrar, festejar

celebrated [séləbreDɪd] ADJ célebre

celebration [seləbréʃən] N (action) celebración f, festejo m; (festivities) fiesta f

celebratory [seləbratori] ADJ festivo

celebrity [səlébrɪDi] N celebridad f

celery [séləri] N apio m

celestial [səléstʃəl] ADJ celeste; (heavenly) celestial; **— body** astro m

celibate [sélɪbɪt] ADJ célibe

cell [sɛl] N (room) celda f; (structural) célula f; **— biology** citología f

cellar [sélə-] N sótano m; (for wine) bodega f, cava f

cello [tʃélo] N violonchelo m

cellophane [séləfen] N celofán m

cellular [séljələ-] ADJ celular; **— phone** celular m; Sp móvil m

cellulite [séljəlaɪt] N celulitis f

celluloid [séljələɪd] N celuloide m

cellulose [séljələs] N celulosa f

cement [sɪmént] N cemento m; (glue) adhesivo m; **— mixer** hormigonera f; VI/VT cementar

cemetery [sémɪteri] N cementerio m

censor [sénsə] N censor -ora mf; VT censurar

censorship [sénsə-ʃɪp] N censura f

censure [sénʃə] N censura f; VT censurar

census [sénsəs] N censo m; **to take a —** censar

cent [sɛnt] N centavo m, céntimo m

centennial [sénténiəl] ADJ & N centenario m

center [séntə-] N centro m; (in basketball) centro m, Am pivot m; **— forward** (soccer) ariete mf; **— of gravity** centro de gravedad m; VI/VT centrar(se)

centigrade [séntɪɡred] ADJ centígrado

centimeter [séntəmidə-] N centímetro m

centipede [séntəpid] N ciempiés m

central [séntrəl] ADJ central; (downtown) céntrico; N central de teléfonos f; **— heating** calefacción central f; **— nervous system** sistema nervioso central m; **— processing unit** unidad central de proceso/procesamiento f

Central [séntrəl] ADJ **— African Republic** República Centroafricana f; **— America** Centroamérica f; **— American** centroamericano

centralize [séntrəlaɪz] VI/VT centralizar[se]; **to be/become —d** centralizarse

centrifugal [sɛntrífəgəl] ADJ centrífugo

centripetal [sɛntrípɪdl] ADJ centrípeto

century [séntʃəri] N siglo m

CEO [chief executive officer] [síío] N Am director -ora general mf, Sp consejero -ra, delegado -da mf

ceramic [sərǽmɪk] ADJ cerámico; N **—s** cerámica f

cereal [síriəl] N (breakfast food) cereal m; (the grain itself) grano m; ADJ cereal

cerebral [səríbrəl] ADJ cerebral; **— concussion** conmoción cerebral f; **— cortex** corteza cerebral f; **— embolism** embolia cerebral f; **— hemorrhage** hemorragia cerebral f; **— palsy** parálisis cerebral f

ceremonial [sɛrəmóniəl] ADJ & N ceremonial m

ceremonious [sɛrəmóniəs] ADJ ceremonioso

ceremony [sɛrəmoni] N ceremonia f

certain [sɝtn] ADJ seguro; **— people** determinadas personas f pl; **— rules are inviolable** ciertas/determinadas reglas son inviolables; **death and taxes are —** lo único seguro son los impuestos y la muerte; **he's — to come** seguro que viene; **it is — that it rained** seguro que llovió

certainly [sɝtnli] ADV seguramente, sin duda; **she — gets her way** no cabe duda de que se sale con la suya; INTERJ ¡cómo no!

certainty [sɝtnti] N certeza f, certidumbre f

certificate [sətífɪkɪt] N certificado m; **— of baptism** fe de bautismo f; **— of deposit** certificado de depósito

certification [sɝdəfɪkéʃən] N certificación f

certify [sɝdəfaɪ] VT certificar; **certified check** cheque certificado m; **certified mail** correo certificado m; **certified public accountant** contador -ora público -ca mf

cervical [sɝvɪkəl] ADJ cervical

cervix [sɝvɪks] N (neck) cerviz f; (uterine) cérvix m, cuello uterino m

cesarean section [sɪzɛriənsɛkʃən] N cesárea f

cessation [sɛséʃən] N cese m

cesspool [sɛspul] N pozo séptico m, fosa séptica f

Chad [tʃæd] N Chad m

Chadian [tʃǽdiən] ADJ & N chadiano -na mf

chafe [tʃef] VI/VT rozar[se]; N rozadura f

chaff [tʃæf] N ahechaduras f pl

chagrin [ʃəgrín] N mortificación f; VT mortificar

chain [tʃen] N cadena f; **— reaction** reacción en cadena f; **— saw** sierra f; **— smoker** persona que fuma como una chimenea f; **— store** tienda de cadena f; VI/VT encadenar[se]

chair [tʃɛr] N silla f; (academic) cátedra f; (of a meeting) presidente -ta mf; (of a department) jefe -fa mf; **—man** presidente m, director m, jefe m; **—manship** dirección f; **—person** presidente -ta mf, jefe -fa mf; **—woman** presidenta f, jefa f

chalk [tʃɔk] N (substance) caliza f; (piece) tiza f; **—board** pizarrón m, pizarra f, tablero m; VT marcar con tiza; **to — up** (attribute) atribuir; (score) marcar

chalky [tʃɔki] ADJ de/con/como tiza

challenge [tʃǽlɪndʒ] N desafío m, reto m; (of a jury) recusación f; VT (defy) desafiar, retar; (take exception) cuestionar, disputar; (recuse) recusar; **to be vertically —d** ser muy bajito

chamber [tʃémbɚ] N (legislative) cámara f; (in a palace) aposento m; (of a cannon) recámara f; **—maid** camarera f, mucama f; **— music** música de cámara f; **— of commerce** cámara de comercio f; **— pot** orinal m; **—s** (of a judge) despacho m

chameleon [kəmíljən] N camaleón m

chamois [ʃǽmi] N gamuza f

champagne [ʃæmpén] N champán m, champaña mf

champion [tʃǽmpiən] N campeón -ona mf; (of a cause) defensor -ora mf, paladín m; VT defender

championship [tʃǽmpiənʃɪp] N campeonato m

chance [tʃæns] N (opportunity) oportunidad f; (probability) probabilidad f; (unpredictable element) casualidad f, azar m; **by —** por casualidad; **game of —** juego de azar m; **to take a —** correr riesgo, arriesgarse; ADJ casual; VI arriesgarse; **we —d to meet him at the bar** nos encontramos con él en el bar por casualidad

chancellor [tʃǽnsələ] N (chief minister) canciller m; (of a university) rector -ora de universidad mf

chandelier [ʃændəlír] N araña de luces f

change [tʃendʒ] VT cambiar; **to — clothes** cambiarse de ropa; **to — into** transformar[se] en; **to — trains** cambiar de tren; N cambio m; (money returned) vuelta f; Am vuelto m; (fresh clothes) muda de ropa f; **— of heart** cambio de opinión m; **— over** (tennis) cambio de lado m; **—-up** (baseball) cambio m, cambio de velocidad m

changeable [tʃéndʒəbəl] ADJ (variable) cambiante, variable; (fickle) inconstante, tornadizo; **— silk** seda tornasolada f

channel [tʃǽnl] N canal m; (bed of stream) cauce m; VT canalizar, encauzar

chant [tʃænt] N (plain song) canto llano *m*;
(hymn) cántico *m*; (repeated slogan) cantinela
f; VI/VT (sing) cantar; (repeat a slogan) corear

chaos [kéas] N caos *m*

chaotic [keáDɪk] ADJ caótico

chap [tʃæp] VI/VT cuartear[se], agrietar[se];
—**ped lips** labios agrietados *m pl*; —**stick®**
crema para los labios *f*; N (fellow) tipo *m*

chaparral [ʃæpərǽl] N chaparral *m*

chapel [tʃǽpəl] N capilla *f*

chaperon, chaperone [ʃǽpəron] N chaperón
-ona *f*; VI ir de chaperón -ona

chaplain [tʃǽplɪn] N capellán *m*

chapter [tʃǽptə] N capítulo *m*

char [tʃɑr] VI/VT (reduce to ashes) carbonizar[se];
(scorch) chamuscar[se]

character [kǽrɪktə] N carácter *m*; (of a novel)
personaje *m*; — **actor** actor de carácter *m*;
Chinese —**s** caracteres chinos *m pl*; **he's
quite a** — es todo un personaje; **that's out
of** — **for him** eso no es característico de él

characteristic [kǽrɪktərɪ́stɪk] ADJ
característico; N característica *f*; (genetic)
carácter *m*

characterization [kǽrɪktəɪzéʃən] N
caracterización *f*

characterize [kǽrɪktəraɪz] VT (describe)
caracterizar; (attribute) calificar

charade [ʃəréd] N farsa *f*; —**s** charada *f*

charcoal [tʃɑ́rkol] N carbón de leña *m*; —
drawing dibujo al carbón *m*

charge [tʃɑrdʒ] VT (demand money) cobrar;
(load) cargar; (buy on credit) cargar a cuenta;
(attack) embestir; (in basketball) cargar; **to** —
off a loss restar una pérdida; **to** —
someone with a task encargarle a alguien
una tarea; **to** — **with murder** acusar de
homicidio; N (mission) misión *f*, encargo *m*;
(accusation) cargo *m*, acusación *f*; (charge in
account) cargo *m*, débito *m*; (explosives,
electricity) carga *f*; (attack) embestida *f*; —
account cuenta de crédito *f*; — **card** tarjeta
de crédito *f*; **there will be a** — **for delivery**
se cobra entrega a domicilio; **to be in** — **of**
estar a cargo de; **under my** — a mi cargo

charger [tʃɑ́rdʒə] N (for a battery) cargador *m*;
(horse) corcel *m*

chariot [tʃǽriət] N carro de guerra *m*

charisma [kərɪ́zmə] N carisma *m*

charitable [tʃǽrɪDəbəl] ADJ caritativo

charity [tʃǽrɪDi] N (virtue, aid to the poor)
caridad *f*; (institution) institución benéfica *f*,
institución de beneficencia *f*; **to give to** —
dar dinero a las instituciones benéficas; **to
live on** — vivir de la caridad

charlatan [ʃɑ́rlətən] N charlatán -ana *mf*

charm [tʃɑrm] N (attractiveness) encanto *m*,
saleroso *m*; (trinket) dije *m*; (spell) sortilegio
m, hechizo *m*; (amulet) talismán *m*, amuleto

m; VT (delight) encantar; (influence)
hechizar, subyugar

charming [tʃɑ́rmɪŋ] ADJ encantador, saleroso;
Sp majo

chart [tʃɑrt] N (table) tabla *f*; (graph) gráfica *f*;
(marine map) carta *f*; (of musical hits) lista de
éxitos *f*; VT (in a table) tabular; (in a graph)
graficar; (a region) cartografiar; **to** — **a
course** trazar una ruta

charter [tʃɑ́rtə] N (of a city) fuero *m*; (of an
organization) estatuto *m*; (document granting
rights) constitución *f*, carta *f*; (hire) flete *m*; —
flight [vuelo] chárter *m*; — **member** socio
-cia fundador -ora *mf*; VT (a corporation)
aprobar los estatutos; (a flight) fletar

chase [tʃes] VT (hunt) cazar; (follow rapidly)
perseguir; **to** — **after** correr tras; **to** — **away**
ahuyentar; N caza *f*, persecución *f*

chasm [kǽzəm] N sima *f*

chassis [tʃǽsi] N chasis *m*, bastidor *m*

chaste [tʃest] ADJ casto, honesto

chastise [tʃǽstaɪz] VT (punish) castigar;
(criticize) criticar

chastisement [tʃǽstáɪzmənt] N (punishment)
castigo *m*; (criticism) crítica *f*

chastity [tʃǽstɪDi] N castidad *f*, honestidad *f*

chat [tʃæt] N charla *f*; *Mex* plática *f*; — **room** sala
de chat *f*; VI charlar; *Mex* platicar; VI chatear

chattel [tʃǽdl] N (movable property) bien
mueble *m*; (slave) esclavo -va *mf*

chatter [tʃǽDə] VI (jabber) cotorrear, parlotear;
VT (click rapidly) castañetear; N (of speech)
cotorreo *m*, parloteo *m*; (of teeth) castañeteo
m; —**box** charlatán -ana *mf*, cotorra *f*

chauffeur [ʃofə] N chófer *m*

chauvinism [ʃóvənɪzəm] N (nationalist)
chovinismo *m*; (sexist) machismo *m*

cheap [tʃip] ADJ (economical) barato; (stingy)
avaro; **life is** — **there** la vida no vale nada
allí; **talk is** — hablar no cuesta nada; **to feel**
— sentirse despreciable; N — **shot** golpe bajo
m; —**skate** tacaño -ña *mf*

cheapen [tʃípən] VI/VT (lower in price)
abaratar[se]; VT (lower in esteem)
desvalorizar

cheapness [tʃípnɪs] N (low price) baratura *f*;
(stinginess) avaricia *f*

cheat [tʃit] N tramposo -sa *mf*, fullero -ra *mf*; VT
engañar; **to** — **at cards** hacer trampa en/a las
cartas, trampear; **to** — **on a test** copiar; **to** —
on one's spouse engañar a la pareja de uno

check [tʃɛk] VT (stop) refrenar; (restrain)
reprimir; (leave luggage) facturar; (leave a
coat) dejar; (verify) comprobar, verificar; *Am*
chequear; *Mex* checar; (in chess) dar jaque; **to**
— **against** cotejar con; **to** — **into a hotel**
registrarse; **to** — **into something** averiguar
algo; **to** — **off** puntear; **to** — **out a book**
sacar [prestado] un libro; **to** — **up on**

controlar; **that —s out** lo hemos comprobado; N (bank) cheque m; (means of restraint) control m; (ticket) ficha f; (mark) marca f; (in a restaurant) cuenta f; (in fabric) cuadro m; (checked fabric) tela a cuadros f; (examination) comprobación f; (in chess) jaque m; **—book** chequera f, talonario m; **—ing account** cuenta corriente f; **— kiting** giro de cheques sin fondos m; **—list** lista de control f; **—mate** jaque mate m; **—out counter** caja f; **—point** control m, retén m; **—room** guardarropa m; **— stub** talón m; **—up** examen físico m

checker [tʃɛkɚ] N (on a fabric) cuadro m; (on a checkerboard) casilla f; (game piece) ficha f; (cashier) cajero -ra mf; (person who checks) verificador -ora mf; **—board** tablero m; **—ed cloth** tela a cuadros f; **—ed past** pasado oscuro m; **—s** juego de damas m; VT cuadricular

cheek [tʃik] N (on face) mejilla f; Am cachete m; (impudence) descaro m; (of buttocks) nalga f; **—bone** pómulo m

cheer [tʃir] N (shout) viva m, vítor m; (applause) aplausos m pl; (encouragement) ánimo m; (joy) alegría f; **—leader** animador -ora mf; Am porrista mf; INTERJ **—s!** ¡salud! VI/VT vitorear; **to — on** dar ánimo; **to — up** animar[se]

cheerful [tʃirfəl] ADJ (person) risueño, alegre; (room) alegre

cheerfulness [tʃirfəlnɪs] N alegría f

cheerless [tʃirlɪs] ADJ triste, sombrío

cheese [tʃiz] N queso m; **—burger** hamburguesa con queso f; **—cake** tarta de queso f

cheesy [tʃizi] ADJ (of cheese) de queso; (cheap) barato; (uncool) Sp hortera

cheetah [tʃiɾə] N guepardo m

chef [ʃɛf] N chef m

chemical [kɛmɪkəl] ADJ químico; **— engineering** ingeniería química f; **— warfare** guerra química f; N producto químico m

chemist [kɛmɪst] N químico -ca f

chemistry [kɛmɪstri] N química f

chemotheraphy [kimoθɛɹəpi] N quimioterapia f

cherish [tʃɛrɪʃ] VT apreciar; **I — the memory of him** tengo muy buenos recuerdos de él

cherry [tʃɛri] N cereza f; **— tree** cerezo m

chess [tʃɛs] N ajedrez m; **—board** tablero de ajedrez m

chest [tʃɛst] N (body part) pecho m; (box) arca f; **— of drawers** cómoda f

chestnut [tʃɛsnʌt] N castaña f; **— tree** castaño m; ADJ castaño; (horse) zaino

chew [tʃu] VT (food) masticar; (nonfood) mascar; **—ing gum** goma de mascar f; Am chicle m; **to — a hole** hacer un agujero a mordiscones; **to — out** reprender; **to — over** meditar

sobre; **to — up** romper a mordiscones; N mascada f, bocado m

chewy [tʃui] ADJ correoso

chic [ʃik] ADJ & N chic m

chick [tʃɪk] N (young chicken) pollito m; (young bird) pichón m; (young woman) fam chavala f, tía f; **—pea** garbanzo m

chicken [tʃɪkɪn] N gallina f; (flesh) pollo m; **— coop** gallinero m; **—hearted** cobarde; **— pox** varicela f

chicory [tʃɪkəri] N achicoria f

chide [tʃaɪd] VT regañar

chief [tʃif] N jefe m; (of a tribe) cacique m; **— of staff** (military) jefe del estado mayor m; (of a division) secretario -ria general mf; ADJ principal; **— justice** presidente de la Suprema Corte de los Estados Unidos m

chieftain [tʃiftən] N cacique m

chiffon [ʃɪfɑn] N chifón m

chigger [tʃɪgɚ] N nigua f

chilblain [tʃɪlblen] N sabañón m

child [tʃaɪld] N (young person) niño -ña mf; (offspring) hijo -ja mf; **—birth** parto m, alumbramiento m; **—like** infantil, aniñado; **—proof** a prueba de niños; **—'s play** cosa de niños f; **to be with —** estar embarazada; ADJ **of —bearing age** en edad de procrear

childhood [tʃaɪldhud] N niñez f, infancia f

childish [tʃaɪldɪʃ] ADJ infantil, pueril

childless [tʃaɪldlɪs] ADJ sin hijos

Chile [tʃɪli] N Chile m

Chilean [tʃɪliən] ADJ & N chileno -na mf

chili, chile [tʃɪli] N (pepper) chile m, ají m; (meat dish) chile con carne m

chill [tʃɪl] N (coldness) frío m; (fear, cold with shivering) escalofrío m; **it had a —ing effect on the group** le cayó al grupo como un baldazo de agua fría; VI/VT enfriar[se]; **to — out** tranquilizarse, relajarse

chilly [tʃɪli] ADJ frío

chime [tʃaɪm] N (sound) repique m; (instrument) carillón m, carrillón m; VI repicar; VT tañer; **to — in** intervenir [en una conversación]

chimney [tʃɪmni] N chimenea f

chimpanzee [tʃɪmpænzi] N chimpancé m

chin [tʃɪn] N barbilla f, mentón m

china [tʃaɪnə] N (material) porcelana f, china f; (dishes) vajilla de porcelana f, china f; **—ware** vajilla de porcelana f

China [tʃaɪnə] N China f

Chinese [tʃaɪniz] ADJ chino; N (inhabitant of China) chino -na mf; (language) chino m

chink [tʃɪŋk] N grieta f

chip [tʃɪp] N (of wood) astilla f; (in glass) desportilladura f; (in gambling) ficha f; (in computers) chip m; **he's a — off the old block** de tal palo, tal astilla; **he has a — on his shoulder** guarda resentimientos; VI/VT (wood) astillar[se]; (glass, plaster)

desportillarse, desconchar[se]; (paint)
descascarar[se]; (in golf) chipear; **to — in**
contribuir; **to — a tooth** romperse un diente
chipmunk [tʃípmʌŋk] N ardilla listada f
chiropractic [kaɪrəpræktɪk] ADJ quiropráctico;
N quiropráctica f
chiropractor [káɪrəpræktɚ] N quiropráctico -ca
mf
chirp [tʃɚp] N pío m, gorjeo m; VI/VT piar,
gorjear
chisel [tʃízəl] N escoplo m; (for stone) cincel m;
(for wood) formón m; VT cincelar; (swindle)
estafar
chiseler [tʃízlɚ] N estafador -ra mf
chit-chat [tʃíttʃæt] N palique m; VI charlar
chivalrous [ʃívəlrəs] ADJ (of knights)
caballeresco; (courteous to women)
caballeroso
chivalry [ʃívəlri] N caballerosidad f
chloride [klɔ́raɪd] N cloruro m
chlorine [klɔ́rin] N cloro m
chloroform [klɔ́rəfɔrm] N cloroformo m
chlorophyl, chlorophyll [klɔ́rəfɪl] N clorofila f
chocolate [tʃɔ́klɪt] N chocolate m; (bar)
chocolatina f; **— pot** chocolatera f
choice [tʃɔɪs] N (act of selecting, thing selected)
selección f; (alternative) opción f; **to have no
other —** no tener más remedio; ADJ selecto
choir [kwaɪr] N coro m
choke [tʃok] VI/VT (suffocate) ahogar[se];
(strangle) estrangular[se]; (on food)
atragantarse, atorarse; (obstruct) tapar[se]; VI
(in sports) bloquearse; **I'm all —d up** estoy
muy conmovido; **to — back/down**
contener; N (act of choking on something)
atragantamiento m; (act of choking someone)
estrangulación f; (device in cars) obturador m;
(in sports) bloqueo m
cholera [kɑ́lərə] N cólera m
choleric [kɑ́lərɪk] ADJ colérico
cholesterol [kəléstərɔl] N colesterol m
choose [tʃuz] VI/VT elegir, seleccionar, escoger;
to — optar por
choosy [tʃúzi] ADJ quisquilloso
chop [tʃɑp] VI/VT cortar; **to — down** talar; **to —
off** mochar, tronchar; **to — up** picar; N (act
of chopping) golpe m; (cut of meat) chuleta f;
—s morro m; **—stick** palillo m
choppy [tʃɑ́pi] ADJ picado, agitado
choral [kɔ́rəl] ADJ coral
chord [kɔrd] N (mathematical) cuerda f;
(musical) acorde m; **it struck a — with me**
me conmovió
chore [tʃɔr] N tarea f, faena f, quehacer m; **it's
such a —** es un trabajo horrible
choreography [kɔriágrəfi] N coreografía f
chorus [kɔ́rəs] N coro m
chose [tʃoz] see choose
chosen [tʃózən] ADJ **my — profession** la

profesión de mi preferencia; **the — one** el
elegido, la elegida
chosen [tʃózən] see choose
christen [krísən] VT bautizar
Christendom [krísəndəm] N cristianismo m
christening [krísənɪŋ] N bautizo m, bautismo m
Christian [kríʃən] ADJ & N cristiano -na mf; **—
name** nombre de pila m
Christianity [krɪstʃiǽnɪDi] N cristianismo m
Christmas [krísməs] N Navidad f, Pascua de
Navidad f; **— card** tarjeta de Navidad f; **—
Eve** Nochebuena f; **— gift** regalo de Navidad
m; **— tree** árbol de Navidad m; ADJ navideño
chrome [krom] N cromo m; ADJ cromado
chromium [krómiəm] N cromo m
chromosome [króməsom] N cromosoma m
chronic [kránɪk] ADJ crónico
chronicle [kránɪkəl] N crónica f; VT registrar
chronicler [kránɪklɚ] N cronista mf
chronological [krɑnəládʒɪkəl] ADJ cronológico
chronology [krɑnálədʒi] N cronología f
chronometer [krɑnámɪDɚ] N cronómetro m
chrysalis [krísəlɪs] N crisálida f
chrysanthemum [krɪsǽnθəməm] N
crisantemo m
chubby [tʃʌ́bi] ADJ rechoncho, gordito
chuck [tʃʌk] N (cut of meat) paletilla f; VT (to
throw) lanzar; (to discard) tirar, botar
chuckle [tʃʌ́kəl] N risita f; VI reírse levemente
chum [tʃʌm] N compinche mf
chunk [tʃʌŋk] N trozo m, pedazo m; **a — of cash**
un montón de plata
church [tʃɚtʃ] N iglesia f; **—man** clérigo m
churn [tʃɚn] N mantequera f; VI/VT (make
butter) batir; (agitate) agitar, revolver
CIA [Central Intelligence Agency] [síáíé] N
CIA f
cicada [sɪkéDə] N chicharra f
cider [sáɪDɚ] N (alcoholic) sidra f;
(non-alcoholic) Am jugo de manzana m; Sp
zumo de manzana m
cigar [sɪgár] N puro m, habano m; **— store**
tabaquería f; **close, but no —** bien, pero te
quedaste corto
cigarette [sɪgərét] N cigarrillo m; Sp pitillo m;
Am cigarro m; **— case** cigarrera f; Sp pitillera
f; **— holder** boquilla f; **— lighter**
encendedor m
cinch [sɪntʃ] N (for a saddle) cincha f; (something
easy) pan comido m; (favorite) favorito -ta mf;
VT cinchar
cinder [síndɚ] N ceniza f, rescoldo m
cinema [sínəmə] N cine m
cinematography [sɪnəmətágrəfi] N
cinematografía f
cinnamon [sínəmən] N canela f; **— tree** canelo f
cipher [sáɪfɚ] N cifra f, guarismo m; VI/VT
cifrar[se]
circle [sɚ́kəl] N círculo m; (literary) ámbito m,

círculo m; VT (draw a circle) encerrar en un círculo; VI (go around) dar una vuelta

circuit [sɜ́kɪt] N circuito m; — **board** circuito impreso m; — **breaker** cortacircuitos m sg

circuitry [sɜ́kɪtri] N circuitería f

circular [sɜ́kjələ] ADJ circular; — **saw** sierra circular f; N circular f

circulate [sɜ́kjəlet] VI circular; VT (distribute) poner en circulación

circulation [sɜkjəléʃən] N circulación f

circulatory [sɜ́kjələtɔri] ADJ circulatorio; — **system** aparato circulatorio m

circumcise [sɜ́kəmsaɪz] VT circuncidar

circumference [səkʌ́mfəns] N circunferencia f

circumlocution [sɜkəmlokjúʃən] N circunlocución f, rodeo m

circumscribe [sɜkəmskráɪb] VT circunscribir

circumspect [sɜ́kəmspekt] ADJ circunspecto

circumstance [sɜ́kəmstæns] N circunstancia f; —**s** condiciones financieras f pl

circumstantial [sɜkəmstǽnʃəl] ADJ circunstancial; — **evidence** pruebas circunstanciales f pl

circumvent [sɜkəmvént] VT evitar, obviar

circus [sɜ́kəs] N circo m

cirrhosis [sɪrósɪs] N cirrosis f

cirrus [sírəs] N cirro m

cistern [sístən] N cisterna f, aljibe m

citadel [sídədel] N ciudadela f

citation [saɪtéʃən] N (summons) citación f; (quote, quotation) cita f; (commendation for bravery) mención f

cite [saɪt] VT (quote, summon) citar; (comment on) mencionar

citizen [sídɪzən] N (of a nation) ciudadano -na mf; (of a city or region) habitante mf

citizenship [sídɪzənʃɪp] N ciudadanía f

citrus [sítrəs] ADJ & N cítrico m

city [sídi] N ciudad f; — **council** concejo m; — **hall** ayuntamiento m, alcaldía f; — **planning** urbanismo m; ADJ municipal, urbano

civic [sívɪk] ADJ cívico; N —**s** educación cívica f

civil [sívəl] ADJ (civilian) civil; (polite) cortés; — **disobedience** desobediencia civil f; — **engineer** ingeniero -ra civil mf; — **rights** derechos civiles m pl; — **service** administración pública f; — **war** guerra civil f

civilian [sɪvíljən] ADJ & N civil mf

civility [sɪvílɪdi] N civilidad f, cortesía f

civilization [sɪvəlɪzéʃən] N civilización f

civilize [sívəlaɪz] VT civilizar

clad [klæd] ADJ vestido

claim [klem] VT (demand) reclamar, reivindicar; (assert) sostener, pretender; **to — to be** pretender ser; **to — responsibility** atribuirse la responsabilidad; **to — a mine** denunciar una mina; N (demand) reclamación f, reclamo m; (assertion)

afirmación f; (right) derecho m, título m; (on insurance) demanda f, denuncia f

claimant [klémənt] N demandante mf, reclamante mf; (to the throne) pretendiente mf

clairvoyant [klervɔ́iənt] ADJ & N clarividente mf

clam [klæm] N almeja f; VI **to — up** callarse

clamber [klǽmbə] VI/VT (climb with effort) trepar con dificultad; (climb on all fours) subir gateando

clammy [klǽmi] ADJ frío y húmedo

clamor [klǽmə] N clamor m, vocerío m; VI clamar, vociferar

clamorous [klǽmərəs] ADJ clamoroso

clamp [klæmp] N (support) grapa f; (vice) tornillo m; (wrap-around) abrazadera f; (medical) pinza f; VT sujetar; **to — down on** reprimir

clan [klæn] N clan m

clandestine [klændéstɪn] ADJ clandestino

clang [klæŋ] VI sonar; N sonido metálico m

clap [klæp] N (tap) palmada f; (blow) golpe seco m; — **of thunder** trueno m; VT (on the back) palmear; (in approval) aplaudir; (a book) cerrar de golpe

clapper [klǽpə] N badajo m

clarification [klærəfɪkéʃən] N aclaración f

clarify [klǽrəfaɪ] VT aclarar, clarificar

clarinet [klærənét] N clarinete m

clarity [klǽrɪdi] N claridad f

clash [klæʃ] N (noise) estruendo metálico m; (collision) choque m; (conflict) conflicto m, enfrentamiento m; VI/VT (collide) chocar; (oppose, fight) enfrentarse a; (not go with) no combinar, no pegar

clasp [klæsp] N (fastener) broche m, cierre m; (grip) apretón m; VT (fasten) abrochar; (grip) apretar; (embrace) abrazar, prender

class [klæs] N clase f; (graduation class) promoción f, graduación f; **in a — by itself** único; —**mate** compañero -ra de clase mf, condiscípulo -la mf; —**room** salón de clase m, aula f; — **struggle** lucha de clases f; VI/VT clasificar[se]

classic [klǽsɪk] ADJ & N clásico -ca mf

classical [klǽsɪkəl] ADJ clásico

classicism [klǽsɪsɪzəm] N clasicismo m

classification [klæsəfɪkéʃən] N clasificación f

classify [klǽsəfaɪ] VT clasificar; **classified ad** anuncio clasificado m

classy [klǽsi] ADJ elegante

clatter [klǽdə] N (noise) estrépito m; (movement) traqueteo m; VI (make noise) causar estrépito; (move) traquetear

clause [klɔz] N cláusula f

claustrophobia [klɔstrəfóbiə] N claustrofobia f

claustrophobic [klɔstrəfóbɪk] ADJ claustrofóbico

clavicle [klǽvɪkəl] N clavícula f

claw [klɔ] N (of a bear) garra f, zarpa f; (of a cat) uña f; (of a crab) pinza f; (of a hammer) orejas f pl; (of a document) acicalado; VI/VT arañar; **they —ed their way through** se abrieron paso con las uñas

clay [kle] N arcilla f; (for ceramics) greda f; (in tennis) tierra batida f

clean [klin] ADJ limpio; (free from impurities, not ornate) puro; (honorable) decente; **—-cut** (person) acicalado; (concept) bien definido; **— joke** broma inocente f; **—-shaven** afeitado; **he has a — record** no tiene antecedentes; **you'd better come —** deberías confesar; VI/VT limpiar; **he —ed me out** me limpió, me desvalijó; **to — up** (a room) limpiar, asear; (a document) pasar en limpio; (get rich) forrarse; N **—up** limpieza f

cleaner [klínə] N limpiador -ra mf; **—s** tintorería f

cleanliness [klénlinis] N limpieza f; (personal) aseo m

cleanse [klenz] VT limpiar

cleanser [klénzə] N limpiador m

clear [klir] ADJ claro; (skin, conscience) limpio; (sky) despejado; (path) libre; **—-cut** (clearly defined) bien definido; (obvious) claro; **—-headed** lúcido; **— profit** ganancia neta f; **to keep — of someone** evitar a alguien; **to pass — through** pasar de lado a lado; **to be in the —** estar libre de culpa; VT (the mind, confusion, voice) aclarar[se]; (a road, one's reputation, computer screen) limpiar; (of criminal charges) absolver; (of suspicion) eximir; (liquid) clarificar; (a legislative bill, plan) aprobar, obtener autorización para; (land for farming) desmontar; (a hurdle) salvar; (a net gain) sacar; **to — the air** sincerarse; **to — the table** levantar la mesa; **to — up** (a mystery) aclarar[se]; (the sky) despejar[se]

clearance [klírəns] N (space) espacio libre m; (vertical) margen de altura m; (permission) autorización f; **— sale** liquidación f

clearing [klírɪŋ] N (terrain) claro m; (of checks) compensación f; **— house** banco de compensación m

cleats [klits] N (projection) tacos m pl, tapones m pl; (shoes) zapatos con tacos m pl

cleavage [klívidʒ] N (cut) hendidura f; (in dress) escote m

cleave [kliv] VT hender[se]; **to — to** adherirse a

cleaver [klívə] N cuchilla f

clef [klɛf] N clave f

cleft [klɛft] N hendidura f; ADJ hendido, partido; **— lip** labio leporino m; **— palate** paladar hendido m

clemency [klémənsi] N clemencia f

clench [klɛntʃ] VT agarrar, asir; (teeth, fist) apretar

clergy [klɝdʒi] N clero m, clerecía f; **—man**

clérigo m, pastor m; **—woman** pastora f

clerical [klérɪkəl] ADJ (of the clergy) clerical, eclesiástico; (of office personnel) de oficina; **— error** error de copia m; **— work** trabajo de escritorio m

clerk [klɝk] N (sales) dependiente -ta mf; (office) empleado -da de oficina mf; (court) escribiente mf, actuario -ria mf; VI trabajar como actuario -ria

clever [klévə] ADJ (ingenious) ingenioso; (smart) listo, vivo; (dexterous) habilidoso

cleverness [klévənis] N (ingenuity) ingenio m; (intelligence) inteligencia f, viveza f; (dexterity) habilidad f

cliché [kliʃé] N cliché m, muletilla f; Sp tópico m

click [klɪk] N (sound) clic m, chasquido m; (sound of heels) taconeo m; (on a computer) clic m, pulsación f; VI chascar; (on a computer) hacer clic, oprimir, pulsar; (heels) taconear; VT chascar, chasquear; **— and drag** pulsar y arrastrar

clickable image [klíkəbəlímɪdʒ] N imagen en donde se puede pulsar f

client [kláiənt] N (of professional or store) cliente -ta mf; (of social service) beneficiario -ria mf

clientele [klaiəntél] N clientela f

cliff [klɪf] N precipicio m, despeñadero m; (by the sea) acantilado m

climate [kláimɪt] N clima m

climatic [klaimǽdɪk] ADJ climático

climax [kláimæks] N clímax m, punto culminante m; VI culminar, alcanzar el clímax

climb [klaim] N (ascent) subida f; (in alpinism) escalada f; VI/VT (ascend) subir; (ascend with effort) trepar[se] [a], encaramar[se] [a]; VT (a mountain, wall) escalar; **to — down** bajar

climber [kláimə] N (in alpinism) escalador -ora mf; (plant) trepadora f

clinch [klɪntʃ] VT (resolve) rematar; (hammer down) remachar; (hug, in boxing) trabar; (secure) sujetar; (finalize) cerrar; N (nail) remache m; (embrace) abrazo m; (in boxing) clinch m

cling [klɪŋ] VI (to stick to) pegarse; (to hold onto) aferrarse

clinic [klínɪk] N clínica f; (workshop) taller m

clinical [klínɪkəl] ADJ clínico; **— trial** ensayo clínico m

clink [klɪŋk] N tintín m; VI tintinear

clip [klɪp] VT (cut) cortar; (trim) recortar; (shear) esquilar; (shorten) acortar; (hit) tocar; (fasten) abrochar; (attach paper) sujetar con un clip; N (fastener) gancho m; (for paper) clip m; (of cartridge) cargador m; (brooch) broche m; **—board** portapapeles m sg

clipper [klípə] N (shearer) esquilador -ra mf; **—s** (scissors) tijeras f pl; (hair trimmer) maquinilla f

clipping [klípɪŋ] N recorte m

clique [klɪk] N (political) camarilla f; (in school) pandilla f

cloak [klok] N capa f; (military) capote m; **—room** guardarropa m; VT (put a cloak on) vestirse con una capa; (hide) encubrir

clock [klak] N reloj m; **—-making** relojería f; **—radio** reloj m; **—work** maquinaria de reloj f; **like —work** con precisión, sin falta; VT **you swim and I'll — you** tú nadas y yo te tomo el tiempo; **the police —ed him at 90 mph** la policía lo pescó haciendo noventa millas por hora

clockwise [klákwaɪz] ADV en el sentido de las manecillas de reloj

clod [klad] N (piece of dirt) terrón m, pelotón m; (dolt) tonto -ta mf, necio -cia mf

clog [klag] VI/VT obstruir[se], tapar[se]; N (shoe) zueco m; **— dance** baile zapateado m

cloister [klɔ́ɪstə] N claustro m; (monastery) monasterio m; VT enclaustrar

clone [klon] N clon m; VT clonar

cloning [klónɪŋ] N clonaje m, clonación f

close¹ [kloz] VI/VT cerrar[se]; VT (a hole) tapar; **— an account** cerrar una cuenta; **to — a meeting** levantar una sesión; **to — down a store** clausurar una tienda; **to — in upon** (oppress) oprimir; (approach) cercar a uno; **— out** liquidar; N fin m; (act of closing) cierre m; **at the —** al cierre

close² [klos] ADJ (near) cercano; (dense) tupido; (intimate) íntimo, entrañable; **— attention** mucha atención f; **— by** cercano, Am aquí nomás; **—-fought** reñido; **—-knit** muy unido; **— translation** traducción fiel f; **at — range** de cerca; **that was a — call** nos salvamos por poco; N **—-up** primer plano m; ADV cerca

closed [klozd] ADJ cerrado; **— circuit** circuito cerrado m; **—-minded** cerrado; **—-mindedness** cerrazón f

closely [klósli] ADV (examine) de cerca; (resemble) mucho; (study) detenidamente; (work) estrechamente

closeness [klósnɪs] N (of location) cercanía f; (of friendship) intimidad f; (correctness) fidelidad f

closer [klózə] N (baseball) relevista de cierre mf, cerrador -ora mf

closet [klázɪt] N ropero m, armario m; VI enclaustrarse; ADJ a escondidas

closure [klóʒə] N (conclusion) cierre m; (sense of completeness) clausura f

clot [klat] VI/VT coagular[se]; N coágulo m, cuajarón m

cloth [klɔθ] N tela f, tejido m; (wool) paño m; ADJ de tela; **— bound** encuadernado en tela; **man of the —** clérigo m

clothe [kloð] VT vestir; N **—s** ropa f; **—sline** tendedero m; **—spin** pinza f

clothier [klóðjə] N comerciante en ropa o paño mf

clothing [klóðɪŋ] N ropa f

clotting [klátɪŋ] N coagulación f

cloud [klaud] N nube f; **—burst** chaparrón m, aguacero m; VT nublar, anublar; (make indistinct, place under suspicion) enturbiar; **to — up** nublarse, anublarse; **to be on — nine** estar en el séptimo cielo; **under a —** bajo sospecha

cloudiness [kláudɪnɪs] N nebulosidad f, nubosidad f

cloudless [kláudlɪs] ADJ despejado

cloudy [kláudi] ADJ nublado; Sp nuboso; (gloomy) sombrío

clout [klaut] N influencia f

clove [klov] N clavo m; **— of garlic** diente de ajo m

cloven [klóvən] ADJ hendido; **—-hoofed** patihendido

clover [klóvə] N trébol m; **—leaf** trébol m; **to be in —** vivir en el lujo

clown [klaun] N payaso m; VI payasear, bufonear

cloy [klɔɪ] VI/VT (to satiate) hastiar; (to be too sweet for) repugnar

club [klʌb] N (society, nightclub) club m; (stick) porra f, garrote m; (suit of cards) basto m; **—foot** pie zambo m; **—house** casa de club f; VT aporrear

cluck [klʌk] VI cloquear; N cloqueo m

clue [klu] N pista f, indicio m; **to have no —** no tener ni noción

clueless [klúlɪs] ADJ (absent-minded) despistado; (uninformed) en ayunas

clump [klʌmp] N (of bushes) matorral m; (of trees) arboleda f; VI/VT apiñar[se]

clumsiness [klʌ́mzinɪs] N torpeza f

clumsy [klʌ́mzi] ADJ torpe, desmañado, chambón; Sp patoso

clung [klʌŋ] see cling

clunker [klʌ́ŋkə] N cacharro m

cluster [klʌ́stə] N grupo m; (of grapes) racimo m; VI/VT agrupar[se], arracimar[se]

clutch [klʌtʃ] N (in a car) embrague m; **— pedal** pedal del embrague m; **to step on the —** pisar el embrague; **—es** garras f pl; VT (seize) asir; (hold) apretar

clutter [klʌ́də] N desparramo m, desorden m, confusión f; VT **books —ed her desk** tenía libros desparramados por todo el escritorio

coach [kotʃ] N (carriage) coche m, carruaje m, carroza f; (bus) autobús m; (in sports) entrenador -ra mf; (in soccer) técnico -ca mf, director -ora técnico -ca mf; (in air travel) clase turista f; (tutor) profesor -ra particular mf; **—man** cochero m; VI/VT entrenar

coagulant [koǽgjələnt] ADJ & N coagulante m

coagulate [koǽgjəlet] VI/VT coagular[se]

coagulation [koægjəléʃən] N coagulación f

coal [koł] N carbón m; — **bin** carbonera f; — **tar** alquitrán m

coalition [koəlíʃən] N coalición f

coarse [kɔrs] ADJ (fabric) burdo, basto; (sand) grueso; (manners, language) grosero, tosco, rudo

coarseness [kɔ́rsnɪs] N (fabric) bastedad f; (language, manners) tosquedad f, rudeza f; (of a joke) chocarrería f

coast [kost] N costa f; — **Guard** Guardia Costera f; —**line** costa f; ADJ & ADV —**to**— de costa a costa; VI (on a sled) deslizar[se]; (in a car, on a bike) tirarse por una bajada; **he —ed through medical school** la Facultad de Medicina le resultó muy fácil

coastal [kóstl] ADJ costero

coat [kot] N abrigo m; (of paint) capa f, mano f; (on animals) pelaje m; — **of arms** escudo m de armas m, blasón m; — **rack** percha f, perchero m; —**tail** faldón m; VT cubrir; (with paint) recubrir, dar una mano a; (with grease) engrasar; (with soap) enjabonar; (with sugar) bañar

coax [koks] VT persuadir con halagos, engatusar

coaxial cable [koǽksiəłkébəł] N cable coaxial m

cob [kab] N mazorca f, panoja f; —**web** telaraña f

cobalt [kóbɔłt] N cobalto m

cobbler [kɑ́blə-] N (person who repairs shoes) zapatero -ra mf, remendón -ona mf; (dessert) budín de bizcocho y fruta m

cobblestone [kɑ́bəłston] N adoquín m

cobra [kóbrə] N cobra f

cocaine [kokén] N cocaína f

coccyx [kɑ́ksɪks] N cóccix m

cock [kak] N (rooster) gallo m; (male bird) macho de ave de corral m; (faucet) llave f; (gun part) martillo m; —**fight** riña de gallos f; —**pit** (for cockfights) gallera f; (in an airplane) cabina f; —**scomb** cresta de gallo f; ADJ —**sure** gallito; VT (a gun) amartillar; (one's head) ladear

cock-a-doodle-doo [kákədúdl̩dú] INTERJ quiquiriquí

cockatoo [kákətu] N cacatúa f

cocker spaniel [kákə-spǽnjəł] N cócker m

cockroach [kákrotʃ] N cucaracha f

cocktail [kákteł] N cóctel m; — **party** cóctel m

cocky [káki] ADJ gallito, valentón

cocoa [kóko] N (powder) cacao m; (drink) chocolate m

coconut [kókənʌt] N coco m

cocoon [kəkún] N capullo m

cod [kad] N Sp abadejo m; Am bacalao m; —**liver oil** aceite de hígado de bacalao m

coddle [kádl̩] VT mimar

code [kod] N código m; — **switching** alternancia de códigos f; VT codificar

codeine [kódin] N codeína f

codger [kádʒə-] N vejete m, vejancón m

codify [kádəfaɪ] VT codificar

coding [kódɪŋ] N codificación f

coed [kóed] ADJ mixto; N alumna universitaria f

coefficient [koəfíʃənt] N coeficiente m

coerce [koɚ́s] VT forzar, obligar

coercion [koɚ́ʒən] N coacción f

coexist [koɪgzíst] VI coexistir, convivir

coexistence [koɪgzístəns] N coexistencia f, convivencia f

coffee [kɔ́fi] N café m; (with a little milk) cortado m; — **bean** grano de café m; — **break** descanso para tomar el café m; — **bush** cafeto m; — **maker** máquina de café f, cafetera f; —**pot** cafetera f; — **shop** (for coffee) café m; (for coffee and light meals) cafetería f; — **table** mesa baja f

coffer [kɔ́fə-] N cofre m

coffin [kɔ́fɪn] N ataúd m, féretro m

cog [kag] N diente m; —**wheel** rueda dentada f

cogent [kódʒənt] ADJ convincente

cognac [kónjæk] N coñac m

cognate [kágnet] ADJ & N cognado m

cognitive [kágnɪdɪv] ADJ cognitivo

cohabitate [kohǽbɪtet] VI cohabitar, convivir

cohabitation [kohæbɪtéʃən] N cohabitación f, convivencia f

coherent [kohírənt] ADJ coherente; (sticking together) cohesivo

cohesion [kohíʒən] N cohesión f

coiffure [kwafjúr] N peinado m

coil [kɔɪl] VI/VT arrollar[se], enrollar[se]; (snake) enroscar[se]; N (roll) rollo m; (spiral) tirabuzón m; (electric) bobina f; — **spring** muelle en espiral m

coin [kɔɪn] N moneda f; ADJ —**operated** de monedas; VT acuñar (also words)

coinage [kɔ́ɪnɪdʒ] N acuñación f (also of words)

coincide [koɪnsáɪd] VI coincidir

coincidence [koínsɪdəns] N coincidencia f, casualidad f

coitus [kóɪdəs] N coito m

coke [kok] N (coal) cok m, coque m; (cocaine) fam coca f

cola [kólə] N gaseosa f

colander [káləndə-] N colador m

cold [kołd] ADJ frío; — **cream** cold cream m; — **cuts** fiambres m pl; — **fish** fam témpano m; — **snap** ola de frío f; — **sore** herpes m sg; — **war** guerra fría f; **to be** — tener frío; **to be out** — quedar seco; **it is — today** hace frío hoy; **he gave me the — shoulder** me hizo el vacío; **he quit — turkey** dejó de un día para otro; **he got — feet** se acobardó; N frío m; (illness) resfrío m, resfriado m, catarro m; **to catch a —** resfriarse

coldness [kóldnɪs] N frialdad f

colic [kálɪk] N cólico m

colicky [kálɪki] ADJ que sufre de cólico

coliseum [kalɪsíəm] N coliseo *m*

collaborate [kəlǽbəret] VI colaborar

collaboration [kəlæbəréʃən] N colaboración *f*

collaborator [kəlǽbəreD&] N colaborador -ora *mf*

collage [kəláʒ] N collage *m*

collagen [kálədʒən] N colágeno *m*

collapse [kəlǽps] VI (fold into sections) plegarse; (cave in) hundirse, derrumbarse; (fail) fracasar; (faint) desmayarse; (empty of air, decline in value) colapsar[se]; N (falling in) derrumbe *m*, derrumbamiento *m*, desplome *m*; (breakdown) colapso *m*

collar [kál&] N (for restraining dogs, necklace) collar *m*; (of a shirt) cuello *m*; —**bone** clavícula *f*; VT acollarar; (grab by the neck) agarrar por el cuello; **I was —ed by the boss** el jefe me agarró de charla

collate [kólet] VT (put in order) colacionar; (compare) cotejar

collateral [kəlǽD&əl] ADJ (on the side) colateral; (auxiliary) subsidiario; N garantía subsidiaria *f*; —**damage** daño colateral *m*

colleague [kálig] N colega *mf*

collect [kəlékt] VT (gather) recoger; (build a collection) coleccionar; (receive taxes) recaudar; VI/VT (receive payment) cobrar, percibir; (assemble) reunir[se]; (accumulate) acumular[se]; **to — oneself** calmarse; N —**call** llamada de cobro revertido *f*, llamada por/a cobrar *f*; —**on delivery** pago contra reembolso *m*

collection [kəlékʃən] N (set of collectibles, clothes) colección *f*; (for charity) colecta *f*; (of taxes) recaudación *f*, cobranza *f*, cobro *m*; (of data, fruit) recolección *f*; (of texts) recopilación *f*; (of water) captación *f*

collective [kəléktɪv] ADJ colectivo; —**bargaining** convenio colectivo *m*; N colectivo *m*, colectividad *f*

collector [kəléktɚ] N (of taxes) recaudador -ora *mf*; (of collectibles) coleccionista *mf*; (of other things) colector -ora *mf*

college [kálɪdʒ] N (institution) universidad *f*; (university division) facultad *f*; (association) colegio *m*; **let's give it the old — try** esforcémonos al máximo

collegial [kəlídʒəl] ADJ cooperador

collegiate [kəlídʒɪt] ADJ universitario

collide [kəláɪd] VI/VT chocar

collie [káli] N collie *m*

collision [kəlíʒən] N colisión *f*, choque *m*

colloid [kálɔɪd] N coloide *m*

colloquial [kəlókwiəl] ADJ coloquial; —**expression** frase familiar *f*

colloquium [kəlókwiəm] N coloquio *m*, jornada *f*

collusion [kəlúʒən] N confabulación *f*

cologne [kəlón] N colonia *f*

Colombia [kəlámbiə] N Colombia *f*

Colombian [kəlámbiən] ADJ & N colombiano -na *mf*

colon[1] [kólən] N (punctuation) dos puntos *m pl*; (bowels) colon *m*

colon[2] [kəlón] (currency of El Salvador and Costa Rica) colón *m*

colonel [kɝnl̩] N coronel *m*

colonial [kəlóniəl] ADJ colonial

colonist [kálənɪst] N (settler) colono *m*; (colonizer) colonizador -ra *mf*

colonization [kalənɪzéʃən] N colonización *f*

colonize [kálənaɪz] VT colonizar

colonoscopy [kolənáskəpi] N colonoscopia *f*

colony [káləni] N colonia *f*

color [kál&] N color *m*; (colorfulness) colorido *m*; —**blindness** ceguera cromática *f*; —**monitor** monitor [a] color *m*; —**scanner** escáner color *m*; **the —s** la bandera; **he showed his true —s** se mostró tal cual era; **persons of —** gente de color *f*; **a — TV** un televisor en/a color; ADJ —**blind** daltónico; —**fast** de colores firmes; VT (give color) colorear; (make colorful) dar colorido; (influence) influir; (blush) ruborizarse

colorectal cancer [kolərékt[kǽnsɚ] N cáncer de colon *m*

colored [kál&d] ADJ coloreado; (biased) sesgado

colorful [kál&fəl] ADJ (full of color) colorido; (animals, plants) pintado; (eccentric) pintoresco

coloring [kál&ɪŋ] N (tone) colorido *m*; (action) coloración *f*; (substance) colorante *m*

colorless [kál&lɪs] ADJ (without color) incoloro; (bleached) descolorido

colossal [kəlásəl] ADJ colosal

colostomy [kəlástəmi] N colostomía *f*

colt [kolt] N potro *m*

column [káləm] N columna *f*

columnist [káləmnɪst] N columnista *mf*

coma [kómə] N coma *m*

comatose [kómətos] ADJ comatoso

comb [kom] N (for hair) peine *m*; (of a rooster) cresta *f*; (for wool) carda *f*; (for horses) almohaza *f*; (of honey) panal *m*; VT (hair) peinar; (wool) cardar; (search an area) peinar, batir; **to — one's hair** peinarse

combat[1] [kámbæt] N combate *m*

combat[2] [kəmbǽt] VI/VT combatir

combatant [kəmbǽtn̩t] ADJ & N combatiente *mf*

combative [kəmbǽDɪv] ADJ combativo

combination [kambənéʃən] N combinación *f*; —**lock** cerradura de combinación *f*

combine[1] [kəmbáɪn] VI/VT combinar[se]

combine[2] [kámbaɪn] N cosechadora *f*

combo [kámbo] N combo *m*

combustible [kəmbástəbəl] ADJ & N combustible *m*

combustion [kəmbástʃən] N combustión *f*

come [kʌm] vi venir; **an idea came to me** se me ocurrió una idea; **Christmas is coming** llega la Navidad; **milk —s from cows** la leche se saca de las vacas; **no harm will — to you** no te va a pasar nada; **the dress —s to her knees** el vestido le llega a las rodillas; **to — about** suceder; **to — across** (find) encontrar; (make an impression) parecer; **to — along** (accompany) acompañar; (appear) surgir; **how's your paper coming along?** ¿cómo va tu trabajo? **to — again** volver, volver a venir; **to — back** volver; **to make a —back** resurgir; (in sports) recuperarse; **to — down with a cold** cogerse un resfriado; **to — downstairs** bajar; **to — from** ser de; **to — in** entrar; **to — out** salir; **to — over** venir para acá; **to — to** volver en sí; **to — together** (meet) juntarse, unirse; (reach agreement) ponerse de acuerdo; **to — up** subir; **your name came up** tu nombre vino a colación; **to — up short** quedarse corto; N **—back** (reply) réplica f; (in sports) remontada f, recuperación f

comedian [kəmídiən] N cómico -ca mf, comediante m

comedy [kámədi] N (genre) comedia f; (profession) humorismo m

comet [kámɪt] N cometa m

comfort [kámfət] vt reconfortar; N (feeling of ease) comodidad f, confort m, holgura f; (solace) consuelo m

comfortable [kámfəɹɅəbəl] adj cómodo, confortable; **— life** vida holgada/ desahogada f

comforter [kámfəɹɅɘ] N edredón m

comic [kámɪk] adj cómico, chistoso, gracioso; **— book** revista de historietas f, cómic m; **—s** tiras cómicas f pl, historietas f pl; **— strip** tira cómica f

comical [kámɪkəl] adj cómico, gracioso

coming [kámɪŋ] N venida f; **— of Christ** advenimiento de Cristo m; **— from** proveniente de, originario de; **—s and goings** idas y venidas f pl; adj que viene, próximo

comma [kámə] N coma f

command [kəmǽnd] vt (order) mandar; (have authority over) comandar; **to — respect** inspirar respeto, imponerse; N (order) mandato m, orden f; (post) comandancia f; (dominance) dominio m; (on a computer) comando m; **— key** tecla de comando f; **he has a good — of English** domina bien el inglés; **to be in — of** estar al mando de; **to be under the — of** estar al mando de; **at your — a** sus órdenes

commandeer [kaməndír] vt apoderarse de; (for the military) requisar

commander [kəmǽndə] N (leader) jefe -fa mf; (army officer) comandante mf; (navy officer) capitán -ana de fragata mf; **— in chief** comandante en jefe mf

commandment [kəmǽndmənt] N mandamiento m

commemorate [kəméməɹet] vt conmemorar

commemoration [kəmeməɹéʃən] N conmemoración f

commence [kəméns] vi/vt comenzar, principiar

commencement [kəménsmənt] N (beginning) comienzo m; (graduation) graduación f, colación f

commend [kəménd] vt (praise) alabar; (entrust) encomendar

commendation [kamandéʃən] N (praise) alabanza f; (mention) mención de honor f

commensurate [kəménsəɹɪt] adj proporcional, acorde

comment [káment] N comentario m; **no —** sin comentarios; vi/vt comentar

commentary [kámənteri] N comentario m

commentator [kámənteɾɘ] N (person who comments) comentador -ra mf; (talking head) comentarista mf

commerce [káməs] N comercio m

commercial [kəmə́ʃəl] adj comercial; N (on radio or television) anuncio m

commercialize [kəmə́ʃəlaɪz] vt comercializar

commiserate [kəmízəɹet] vi/vt compadecerse de

commiseration [kəmɪzəɹéʃən] N conmiseración f

commissary [káməseri] N economato m

commission [kəmíʃən] N (act, committee, payment) comisión f; (of a broker) corretaje m; (charge) encargo m; (mission) misión f; (title) nombramiento m; **to be in —** estar en servicio; **to be out of —** estar fuera de servicio; **to put out of —** (object) inutilizar; (person) retirar de servicio; vt (authorize) comisionar; (order) encargar; (appoint) nombrar; (get ready) poner en servicio; **—ed officer** oficial m

commissioner [kəmíʃənɘ] N comisario -ria mf

commit [kəmít] vt (perpetrate) cometer; (entrust) encargar; (direct) destinar; **to — an error** cometer un error; **to — a foul** cometer/hacer falta; **to — oneself to** comprometerse a/con; **to — to an asylum** internar; **to — to memory** aprender de memoria

commitment [kəmítmənt] N compromiso m

committed [kəmíɾɪd] adj (to a cause) comprometido

committee [kəmíɾi] N comité m, comisión f

commode [kəmód] N wáter m, inodoro m

commodity [kəmáɾɪɾi] N (product) mercancía f, artículo m, producto m; (raw material) materia prima *f*

common [kámən] ADJ (shared, frequent) común; (general) general; (vulgar) ordinario; (unremarkable) simple; — **cold** resfriado *m*; — **denominator** denominador común *m*; — **law** derecho consuetudinario *m*; — **sense** sentido común *m*, sensatez *f*; — **soldier** soldado raso *m*; — **stock** acciones ordinarias *f pl*; —**wealth** (state) estado *m*; (republic) república *f*; ADJ —**place** trivial; N —**s** (land) ejido *m*

commotion [kəmóʃən] N conmoción *f*, revuelo *m*

communal [kəmjúnl] ADJ comunitario

commune[1] [kəmjún] VI (communicate) comunicarse, departir; (take communion) comulgar

commune[2] [kámjun] N comuna *f*

communicable [kəmjúnɪkəbəl] ADJ comunicable; (disease) transmisible

communicate [kəmjúnɪket] VI/VT comunicar[se]; (disease) transmitir[se]

communication [kəmjunɪkéʃən] N comunicación *f*

communicative [kəmjúnɪkədɪv] ADJ comunicativo

communion [kəmjúnjən] N comunión *f*

communiqué [kəmjunɪké] N comunicado *m*

communism [kámjənɪzəm] N comunismo *m*

communist [kámjənɪst] N & ADJ comunista *mf*

community [kəmjúnɪdi] N comunidad *f*, colectividad *f*; — **spirit** espíritu comunitario *m*

commute [kəmjút] VT (reduce a sentence) conmutar; VI viajar diariamente al trabajo

commuter [kəmjúdə-] N persona que viaja diariamente al trabajo *f*

Comoros [káməroz] N Comoras *f pl*

compact[1] [kámpækt, kəmpækt] ADJ compacto; (dense) tupido, apretado; (concise) conciso; (make denser) tupir

compact[2] [kámpækt] N (agreement) pacto *m*; (case for powder) polvera *f*; — **disk** disco compacto *m*; VT compactar

compactness [kəmpæktnɪs] N densidad *f*; (conciseness) concisión *f*

companion [kəmpænjən] N (comrade, partner) compañero -ra *mf*; (caregiver) acompañante *mf*

companionship [kəmpænjənʃɪp] N compañía *f*

company [kámpəni] N compañía *f*; **to keep** — **with** codearse con, frecuentar

comparable [kámpəəbəl] ADJ comparable

comparative [kəmpæəədɪv] ADJ comparativo

compare [kəmpér] VI/VT comparar[se]; **beyond** — incomparable, sin parangón

comparison [kəmpæəɪsən] N comparación *f*; **in** — **with** comparado con

compartment [kəmpártmənt] N compartimiento *m*

compass [kámpəs] N (for drawing) compás *m*; (for directions) brújula *f*

compassion [kəmpæʃən] N compasión *f*

compassionate [kəmpæʃənɪt] ADJ compasivo

compatibility [kəmpædəbílɪdi] N compatibilidad *f*

compatible [kəmpædəbəl] ADJ compatible (also of computers)

compatriot [kəmpétriət] N compatriota *mf*

compel [kəmpél] VT (force) obligar; (demand) exigir

compelling [kəmpélɪŋ] ADJ (argument) convincente; (story) emocionante

compensate [kámpənset] VT (make up for) compensar, resarcir; (pay) remunerar

compensation [kampənséʃən] N (making up for) compensación *f*; (remuneration) remuneración *f*

compete [kəmpít] VI/VT competir

competence [kámpɪdəns] N competencia *f*

competent [kámpɪdənt] ADJ competente

competition [kampɪtíʃən] N competencia *f*; (sports match) competición *f*, contienda *f*

competitive [kəmpédɪdɪv] ADJ competitivo; — **examination** *Sp* oposición *f*; *Am* concurso *m*; — **sports** deportes de competición *m pl*

competitiveness [kəmpédɪtɪvnɪs] N competitividad *f*

competitor [kəmpédɪdə-] N (business) competidor -ora *mf*; (sports) atleta *mf*

compilation [kampɪléʃən] N recopilación *f*

compile [kəmpáɪl] VT recopilar, compilar

compiler [kəmpáɪlə] N compilador *m*; — **language** lenguaje compilador *m*

complacency [kəmplésənsi] N confianza infundada *f*

complacent [kəmplésənt] ADJ confiado

complain [kəmplén] VI quejarse

complainant [kəmplénənt] ADJ & N recurrente *mf*

complaint [kəmplént] N queja *f*; (official) reclamo *m*; (civil charge) demanda *f*; (ailment) dolencia *f*

complement[1] [kámpləmənt] N complemento *m*; (of staff) dotación *f*

complement[2] [kámpləmɛnt] VT complementar

complementary [kampləméntri] ADJ complementario

complete [kəmplít] ADJ completo, pleno; **a** — **stranger** un perfecto desconocido; VT completar; **to** — **a pass** completar un pase

completion [kəmplíʃən] N finalización *f*, terminación *f*; **she brought the project to** — completó el proyecto

complex[1] [kámplɛks] ADJ complejo

complex[2] [kámplɛks] N complejo *m*

complexion [kəmplékʃən] N (skin) cutis *m*; (color) tez *f*; (perspective) cariz *m*

complexity [kəmpléksɪDi] N complejidad f
compliance [kəmpláɪəns] N (obedience) conformidad f, acatamiento m; (polite reverence) pleitesía f; **in — with** en conformidad con
complicate [kámplɪket] VT complicar
complicated [kámplɪkeɪDɪd] ADJ complicado
complication [kamplɪkéʃən] N complicación f
complicity [kəmplísɪDi] N complicidad f
compliment [kámpləmənt] N cumplido, halago m; (on looks) piropo m; (from a suitor) galantería f; **to pay someone a —** hacerle un cumplido a alguien; **to send one's —s** enviar saludos; VI/VT elogiar, halagar
comply [kəmplái] VI obedecer; **to — with** cumplir con, acatar
component [kəmpónənt] ADJ & N componente m
compose [kəmpóz] VI/VT componer; **to — oneself** sosegarse
composed [kəmpózd] ADJ sosegado; **to be — of** estar compuesto de, componerse de, constar de
composer [kəmpózə-] N compositor -ra mf
composite [kəmpázɪt] ADJ compuesto; N amalgama f
composition [kampəzíʃən] N (make-up, musical piece) composición f; (aggregate material) compuesto m; (school essay) composición f, redacción f
composure [kəmpóʒə-] N compostura f
compound¹ [kámpaʊnd] ADJ & N compuesto m; **— fracture** fractura expuesta f; **— interest** interés compuesto m
compound² [kámpaʊnd] VT (combine) combinar; (worsen) empeorar
comprehend [kamprɪhénd] VT comprender
comprehensible [kamprɪhénsəbəl] ADJ comprensible
comprehension [kamprɪhénʃən] N comprensión f
comprehensive [kamprɪhénsɪv] ADJ exhaustivo; **— insurance** seguro contra todo riesgo m
compress¹ [kəmprés] VT comprimir; **—ed disk** disco comprimido m; **—ed file** archivo comprimido m
compress² [kámprɛs] N compresa f
compression [kəmpréʃən] N compresión f
comprise [kəmpráɪz] VT comprender, incluir; **to be —d of** comprender, incluir
compromise [kámprəmaɪz] N (arrangement) arreglo por concesiones mutuas m, compromiso m; (intermediate thing) cruce m, término medio m; VI/VT (make agreement) transigir; Am transar; (jeopardize) comprometer
comptroller [kəntrólə-] N controlador -ra mf; Am contralor -ora mf
compulsion [kəmpʌ́lʃən] N (impulse)

compulsión f, coacción f; (coercion) coerción f
compulsive [kəmpʌ́lsɪv] ADJ compulsivo
compulsory [kəmpʌ́lsəri] ADJ obligatorio, obligado
computation [kampjutéʃən] N cómputo m, cálculo m
compute [kəmpjút] VI/VT computar, calcular
computer [kəmpjúDə-] N Am computadora f; Sp ordenador m; **— engineer** ingeniero -ra en computación mf, ingeniero -ra informático -ca mf; **— graphics** gráficos por computadora/ordenador m pl; **— literacy** (process) alfabetización digital f; (result) alfabetismo digital m; **— science** informática f; **— virus** virus de computadora/ordenador m
computerization [kəmpjuDərɪzéʃən] N Sp ordenación f, Am computarización f
computerize [kəmpjúDəraɪz] VI/VT informatizar, computarizar
computing [kəmpjúDɪŋ] N informática f; ADJ informático
comrade [kámræd] N camarada mf
concave [kánkev] ADJ cóncavo
conceal [kənsíl] VT encubrir, ocultar, disimular
concealment [kənsílmənt] N encubrimiento m, disimulo m
concede [kənsíd] VI/VT (recognize) conceder, reconocer; (allow) conceder
conceit [kənsít] N (vanity) vanidad f; (literary device) concepto m
conceited [kənsíDɪd] ADJ engreído, presumido
conceivable [kənsívəbəl] ADJ imaginable, concebible
conceive [kənsív] VI/VT concebir; (a plan) concebir, idear
concentrate [kánsəntret] VI/VT concentrar[se]
concentration [kansəntréʃən] N concentración f; **— camp** campo de concentración m
concept [kánsept] N concepto m
conception [kənsépʃən] N concepción f
conceptual [kənséptʃuəl] ADJ conceptual
concern [kənsə́n] VT (be of interest) concernir, atañer; (worry) preocupar; **to — oneself with** ocuparse de; **to whom it may —** a quien corresponda; N (interest) interés m; (matter) asunto m; (worry) preocupación f; (company) compañía f; **to be of no —** no tener consecuencia
concerned [kənsə́nd] ADJ (involved) involucrado; (anxious) preocupado; **as far as I am —** en lo que a mí respecta; **to be — about** preocuparse por
concerning [kənsə́nɪŋ] PREP tocante a, respecto a
concert¹ [kánsət] N concierto m
concert² [kənsə́t] VT concertar
concession [kənséʃən] N concesión f
conciliate [kənsíliet] VI/VT (make compatible)

conciliar; (appease) aplacar

conciliation [kənsɪliéʃən] N conciliación *f*

concise [kənsáɪs] ADJ conciso, sucinto

conciseness [kənsáɪsnɪs] N concisión *f*

conclude [kənklúd] VI/VT concluir

conclusion [kənklúʒən] N conclusión *f*

conclusive [kənklúsɪv] ADJ concluyente

concoct [kankákt] VT (contrive) fabricar, urdir; (prepare by cooking) preparar

concoction [kankákʃən] N mejunje *m*

concord [kánkɔrd] N (peace) concordia *f*; (agreement) convenio *m*, acuerdo *m*

concrete[1] [kankrít] ADJ concreto

concrete[2] [kánkrit] N hormigón *m*; (made of concrete) de hormigón

concubine [kánkjəbaɪn] N concubina *f*

concur [kənkɚ] VI estar de acuerdo

concussion [kankáʃən] N (brain injury) conmoción cerebral *f*; (shock) concusión *f*

condemn [kəndém] VT condenar; (acquire public ownership) expropiar; (declare unsafe) declarar ruinoso

condemnation [kandɛmnéʃən] N condenación *f*, condena *f*

condensation [kandɛnséʃən] N condensación *f*; (of a book) compendio *m*

condense [kəndéns] VI/VT condensar[se]

condescend [kandəsénd] VI condescender a

condescension [kandəsénʃən] N condescendencia *f*

condiment [kándəmənt] N condimento *m*, aliño *m*

condition [kəndíʃən] N condición *f*; **he's got a heart —** sufre del corazón, tiene una afección cardíaca; **he's in good physical —** está en buen estado físico; **the patient is in critical —** el paciente está en estado crítico; **on — that** a condición de que; VT (restrict on a condition, establish a conditioned response) condicionar; (accustom oneself) acostumbrarse

conditional [kəndíʃən] ADJ & N condicional *m*

conditioning [kəndíʃənɪŋ] N condicionamiento *m*

condolences [kəndólənsɪz] N pésame *m*, condolencias *f*; **to express one's —** dar las condolencias

condominium [kandəmíniəm] N condominio *m*

condone [kəndón] VT tolerar

conducive [kəndúsɪv] ADJ conducente

conduct[1] [kándəkt] N conducta *f*, comportamiento *m*

conduct[2] [kəndákt] VI/VT (behave) conducirse, comportarse; (carry out) llevar a cabo; (direct, lead) dirigir; (serve as channel for) conducir

conduction [kəndákʃən] N conducción *f*

conductor [kəndáktɚ] N (substance that conducts) conductor *m*; (of an orchestra) director -ora *mf*; (of a train) revisor -ora *mf*

conduit [kánduɪt] N conducto *m*

cone [kon] N cono *m*; (container) cucurucho *m*

confection [kənfékʃən] N (of clothes) confección *f*; (of candy) confitura *f*

confectionery [kənfékʃəneri] N confitería *f*; (shop) dulcería *f*; (candies) dulces *m pl*

confederacy [kənfédəɚsi] N confederación *f*

confederate[1] [kənfédəɚɪt] ADJ & N confederado -da *mf*

confederate[2] [kənfédəret] VI/VT confederar[se]

confederation [kənfédəɚéʃən] N confederación *f*

confer [kənfɚ] VT (grant) conferir, atribuir; (consult) consultar; (negotiate) conferenciar

conference [kánfəɚns] N (consultation) consulta *f*; (professional meeting) congreso *m*; (legislative) asamblea general *f*; (sports league) liga *f*; **— call** llamada en conferencia *f*

confess [kənfés] VI/VT confesar[se]

confession [kənféʃən] N confesión *f*

confessional [kənféʃən] N confesionario *m*

confessor [kənfésɚ] N confesor *m*

confidant [kánfɪdant] N confidente *mf*

confide [kənfáɪd] VI/VT (entrust) confiar; VI (tell secrets to) hacer confidencias a

confidence [kánfɪdəns] N confianza *f*; (certainty) seguridad *f*; (secret communication) confidencia *f*; **— game** timo *m*; **— man** timador *m*, embaucador *m*; **in —** en confianza

confident [kánfɪdənt] ADJ seguro; **he's a — person** tiene mucha confianza

confidential [kanfɪdénʃəl] ADJ confidencial; (secretary, etc.) de confianza

configuration [kənfɪgjəɚéʃən] N configuración *f* (also for computers)

configure [kənfígjɚ] VT configurar

confine[1] [kənfáɪn] VT confinar, recluir; **to — oneself to** limitarse a

confine[2] [kánfaɪn] N confin *m*

confinement [kənfáɪnmənt] N confinamiento *m*

confirm [kənfɚm] VT confirmar

confirmation [kanfɚméʃən] N confirmación *f*

confiscate [kánfɪsket] VT confiscar

confiscation [kanfɪskéʃən] N confiscación *f*

conflagration [kanfləgréʃən] N incendio *m*

conflict[1] [kánflɪkt] N conflicto *m*, contienda *f*; **— of interest** conflicto de intereses *m*

conflict[2] [kənflíkt] VI oponerse

confluence [kánfluəns] N confluencia *f*

conform [kənfɔrm] VI/VT conformar[se]

conformity [kənfɔrmɪɾi] N (agreement) conformidad *f*; (passive acquiescence) conformismo *m*

confound [kanfáʊnd] VT (bewilder) desconcertar; (confuse) confundir; **— it!** *fam* ¡caramba!

confront [kənfránt] VT (set face to face, fight)

confrontar; (face up to) enfrentarse a

confrontation [kʌnfrəntéʃən] N confrontación f, enfrentamiento m

confuse [kənfjúz] VT confundir

confused [kənfjúzd] ADJ (person) confundido; (situation) confuso; **to become —** confundirse

confusing [kənfjúzɪŋ] ADJ confuso

confusion [kənfjúʒən] N confusión f

congeal [kəndʒíl] VI/VT cuajar[se]

congenial [kəndʒínjəl] ADJ agradable, simpático

congenital [kəndʒénɪdl] ADJ congénito

congestion [kəndʒéstʃən] N congestión f

congestive heart failure [kəndʒestɪv hárt feljə] ADJ insuficiencia cardíaca congestiva f

conglomeration [kənglaməréʃən] N (unit) conglomeración f; (mass) conglomerado m

Congo [káŋgo] N Congo m

Congolese [kaŋgəlíz] ADJ & N congoleño -ña mf

congratulate [kəngrǽtʃəlet] VT felicitar

congratulation [kəngrætʃəléʃən] N felicitación f, parabién m; **—s!** ¡enhorabuena! ¡albricias!

congregate [káŋgriget] VI/VT congregar[se]

congregation [kaŋgrɪgéʃən] N (worshipers) fieles m pl, feligreses m pl; (act of congregating, committee of cardinals) congregación f

congress [káŋgrɪs] N (professional) congreso m; (political) asamblea legislativa f; (US) congreso m; **—man** (US) congresista m; **—woman** (US) congresista f

congressional [kəngréʃənl] ADJ congresual

congruence [kəngrúəns] N congruencia f

conifer [kánəfə] N conífera f

conjecture [kəndʒéktʃə] N conjetura f; VI/VT conjeturar

conjugal [kándʒəgəl] ADJ conyugal

conjugate [kándʒəget] VI/VT conjugar[se]

conjugation [kandʒəgéʃən] N conjugación f

conjunction [kəndʒáŋkʃən] N conjunción f

conjunctivitis [kəndʒʌŋktəváɪdɪs] N conjuntivitis f

conjure [kándʒə] VT invocar; **to — up** evocar; VI hacer hechizos

connect [kənékt] VI/VT conectar[se], enlazar[se]; (buildings, callers) comunicar[se]; (concepts) relacionar[se]; (pipes) acoplar[se]; **—ing rod** biela f

connection [kənékʃən] N (act of connecting) conexión f, vinculación f; (of telephone) comunicación f, enganche m; (of concepts) relación f; (of pipes) acople m; (affinity) afinidad f; (supplier) contacto m; **—s** contactos m pl, enchufe m

connectivity [kanɛktívɪdi] N conectividad f

connive [kənáɪv] VI conspirar

connoisseur [kanəsúr] N conocedor -ora f

connotation [kanətéʃən] N connotación f

conquer [káŋkə] VT (win) conquistar;

(overcome) vencer

conqueror [káŋkərə] N conquistador -ora mf; (one who overcomes) vencedor -ora mf

conquest [káŋkwest] N conquista f

conscience [kánʃəns] N conciencia f

conscientious [kanʃiéntʃəs] ADJ concienzudo

conscious [kánʃəs] ADJ consciente

consciousness [kánʃəsnɪs] N conciencia f; **to lose —** perder el conocimiento

conscript¹ [kənskrípt] VT reclutar

conscript² [kánskrɪpt] N recluta mf

conscription [kənskrípʃən] N reclutamiento m

consecrate [kánsɪkret] VT consagrar

consecration [kansɪkréʃən] N consagración f

consecutive [kənsékjədɪv] ADJ consecutivo

consensus [kənsénsəs] N consenso m

consent [kənsént] N consentimiento m; VI consentir

consequence [kánsɪkwɛns] N consecuencia f; (negative) secuela f

consequent [kánsɪkwənt] ADJ consiguiente, resultante; N (in mathematics) consecuente m; (in logic) consiguiente m

consequently [kánsɪkwəntli] ADV por consiguiente, en consecuencia

conservation [kansə-véʃən] N conservación f, preservación f

conservatism [kənsə́-vətɪzəm] N conservadurismo m

conservative [kənsə́-vədɪv] ADJ & N conservador -ora mf

conservatory [kənsə́-vətɔri] N conservatorio m

conserve¹ [kənsə́v] VT conservar, preservar

conserve² [kánsə-v] N confitura m

consider [kənsídə] VT considerar

considerable [kənsídə-əbəl] ADJ considerable

considerate [kənsídə-ɪt] ADJ considerado

consideration [kənsɪdə-réʃən] N consideración f; (respect) miramiento m; (payment) remuneración f

considering [kənsídə-ɪŋ] PREP en vista de, teniendo en cuenta; **she cooks well, —** para ser ella, cocina bien

consign [kənsáɪn] VT consignar

consignee [kansaɪní] N consignatario -ria mf

consignment [kənsáɪnmənt] N consignación f; **on —** a/en consignación

consist [kənsíst] VI consistir [en]

consistency [kənsístənsi] N (adherence to principles) coherencia f, consecuencia f; (density) consistencia f

consistent [kənsístənt] ADJ (adherent to principles) consecuente, coherente; (cohering) consistente

consolation [kansəléʃən] N consuelo m, consolación f

console¹ [kənsól] VT consolar

console² [kánsoł] N consola f

consolidate [kənsálɪdet] VI/VT consolidar[se]

consolidation [kənsɑlɪdéʃən] N consolidación f

consonant [kánsənənt] N consonante f; ADJ consonante, conforme

consort¹ [kənsɔ́rt] VI **to — with** asociarse con

consort² [kánsɔrt] N consorte mf

consortium [kənsɔ́rʃiəm] N consorcio m

conspicuous [kənspíkjuəs] ADJ evidente

conspiracy [kənspírəsi] N conspiración f, conjura f

conspirator [kənspírədə·] N conspirador -ora mf, conjurado -da mf

conspire [kənspáir] VI conspirar, conjurar

constable [kánstəbəl] N oficial de policía mf; (keeper of fortress) condestable m

constancy [kánstənsi] N constancia f

constant [kánstənt] ADJ & N constante f

constellation [kanstəléʃən] N constelación f

consternation [kanstə·néʃən] N consternación f

constipate [kánstəpet] VT estreñir

constipated [kánstəpeɪɾɪd] ADJ estreñido

constipation [kanstəpéʃən] N estreñimiento m

constituent [kənstítʃuənt] ADJ componente, constitutivo; N (component) componente m; (voter) votante mf; (part of a sentence) constituyente m

constitute [kánstɪtut] VT constituir

constitution [kanstɪtúʃən] N constitución f

constitutional [kanstɪtúʃənl] ADJ constitucional; N caminata f

constrain [kənstrén] VT constreñir, restringir

constraint [kənstrént] N constreñimiento m

constrict [kənstríkt] VT constreñir

constriction [kənstríkʃən] N (action) constricción f; (place) estrechamiento m

construct¹ [kənstrákt] VT construir

construct² [kánstrakt] N invención f

construction [kənstrákʃən] N construcción f; **— company** constructora f

constructive [kənstráktɪv] ADJ constructivo

construe [kənstrú] VT interpretar

consul [kánsəl] N cónsul mf

consulate [kánsəlɪt] N consulado m

consult [kənsʌ́lt] VI/VT consultar; VI (serve as a consultant) asesorar

consultant [kənsʌ́ltənt] N asesor -ora mf

consultation [kansəltéʃən] N consulta f

consultative [kənsʌ́ltəɾɪv] ADJ consultivo

consulting [kənsʌ́ltɪŋ] N asesoramiento m, consultoría f; ADJ consultor; **— firm** firma consultora f

consumable [kənsúməbəl] ADJ **— goods** bienes consumibles m pl

consume [kənsúm] VI/VT consumir

consumer [kənsúmə·] N consumidor -ora mf; **— confidence index** índice de confianza del consumidor m; **— credit** crédito al consumidor m; **— protection** protección al consumidor f

consumerism [kənsúmərɪzəm] N

consumismo m

consuming [kənsúmɪŋ] ADJ (need) imperioso; (drive) abrasador

consummate¹ [kánsəmet] VT consumar

consummate² [kánsəmɪt] ADJ consumado

consumption [kənsʌ́mpʃən] N (using up) consumo m; (wasting of the body) consunción f; (tuberculosis) tisis f

consumptive [kənsʌ́mptɪv] ADJ tísico

contact [kántækt] N contacto m; **— lens** lente de contacto mf; VI/VT (touch) tocar; (communicate with) contactar

contagion [kəntédʒən] N (spread) contagio m; (disease spread) enfermedad contagiosa f

contagious [kəntédʒəs] ADJ contagioso

contain [kəntén] VI/VT contener

container [kənténə·] N recipiente m; (on a ship) contenedor m; **—ship** buque portacontenedores m

containerize [kənténəraɪz] VT contenedorizar

containment [kənténmənt] N contención f

contaminate [kəntǽmənet] VT contaminar

contamination [kəntæmənéʃən] N contaminación f

contemplate [kántəmplet] VT (observe) contemplar; (consider) considerar

contemplation [kantəmpléʃən] N (observation) contemplación f; (consideration) consideración f

contemporary [kəntémpəreri] ADJ contemporáneo

contempt [kəntémpt] N desprecio m, menosprecio m; **— of court** desacato al tribunal m

contemptible [kəntémptəbəl] ADJ despreciable, rastrero

contemptuous [kəntémptʃuəs] ADJ desdeñoso

contend [kənténd] VI (struggle) contender, lidiar; (argue) disputar; VT afirmar

content¹ [kəntént] ADJ (happy) contento; (resigned) conforme; N **to one's heart's —** a discreción

content², contents [kántent[s]] N contenido m

contented [kənténtɪd] ADJ contento, satisfecho

contention [kənténʃən] N (opinion) opinión f; **in —** (disputed) en discusión; (still eligible) con posibilidades

contentious [kənténʃəs] ADJ conflictivo

contentment [kənténtmənt] N contento m

contest¹ [kántest] N (competition) concurso m, certamen m; (struggle) contienda f

contest² [kəntést] VT (compete) contender; (dispute) disputar; (challenge) impugnar

contestant [kəntéstənt] N concursante mf, participante m

context [kántekst] N contexto m

contiguous [kəntígjuəs] ADJ contiguo, pegado

continent [kántənənt] N (landmass) continente m; ADJ (sexually abstinent) continente; (of bodily functions) capaz de controlar los esfínteres

continental [kɑntɲɛ́ntl̩] ADJ continental

contingency [kəntíndʒənsi] N contingencia f; **— fund** fondo de contingencia m; **— planning** planificación para contingencias f

contingent [kəntíndʒənt] ADJ & N contingente m

continual [kəntínjuəl] ADJ continuo

continuance [kəntínjuəns] N continuación f; (delay) aplazamiento m

continuation [kəntɪnjuéʃən] N continuación f

continue [kəntínju] VI/VT continuar

continuing [kəntínjuɪŋ] ADJ continuado; **— education** educación para adultos f

continuity [kɑntɪnúɪdi] N continuidad f

continuous [kəntínjuəs] ADJ (uninterrupted in time) continuo; (uninterrupted in space) ininterrumpido

contortion [kəntɔ́rʃən] N contorsión f

contour [kɑ́ntur] N contorno m

contra account [kɑ́ntrə əkáunt] N cuenta de contrapartida f

contraband [kɑ́ntrəbænd] N contrabando m

contraception [kɑntrəsɛ́pʃən] N anticoncepción f

contraceptive [kɑntrəsɛ́ptɪv] ADJ & N anticonceptivo m

contract¹ [kɑ́ntrækt] N contrato m; **— killer** asesino -na a sueldo mf; **by —** por contrato

contract² [kɑ́ntrǽkt] VI/VT contraer[se]; (assign by contract) contratar; **to — out** subcontratar

contraction [kəntrǽkʃən] N contracción f; (in childbirth) contracción f, pujo m

contractor [kɑ́ntræktə] N contratista mf

contractual agreement [kɑntrǽktʃuələgrímənt] N acuerdo contractual m

contradict [kɑntrədíkt] VI/VT contradecir

contradiction [kɑntrədíkʃən] N contradicción f

contradictory [kɑntrədíktəri] ADJ contradictorio

contraption [kəntrǽpʃən] N chisme m, coso m

contrary [kɑ́ntreri] ADJ contrario, opuesto; (obstinate) testarudo; N lo contrario; **on the — al** contrario

contrast¹ [kɑ́ntræst] N contraste m

contrast² [kəntrǽst] VI/VT contrastar

contravene [kɑntrəvín] VT contravenir

contribute [kəntríbjut] VI contribuir; (to a newspaper) colaborar; VT contribuir con, aportar

contribution [kɑntrəbjúʃən] N (donation, article) contribución f; (scientific) aporte m, aportación f

contributor [kəntríbjətə] N colaborador -ra mf

contrite [kəntráɪt] ADJ contrito

contrivance [kəntráɪvəns] N artefacto m

contrive [kəntráɪv] VI/VT ingeniar; **he —d to get their money** se las ingenió para sacarles el dinero

contrived [kəntráɪvd] ADJ artificioso

control [kəntról] VI/VT controlar; N control m; (of a machine) mando m; **who's in —?** ¿quién manda? **under —** bajo control; **— freak** mandón -ona mf; **— key** tecla de control/ mando f; **— panel** panel de control m; **— tower** torre de control f

controller [kəntrólə] N (comptroller) controlador -ora mf; Am contralor m; (device) regulador m

controversial [kɑntrəvə́ʃəl] ADJ controvertido

controversy [kɑ́ntrəvə·si] N controversia f, polémica f

contusion [kəntúʒən] N contusión f, magulladura f

conundrum [kənándrəm] N (riddle) adivinanza f, acertijo m; (mystery) enigma m

convalesce [kɑnvəlɛ́s] VI convalecer

convalescence [kɑnvəlɛ́səns] N convalecencia f

convalescent [kɑnvəlɛ́sənt] ADJ & N convaleciente mf

convection [kənvɛ́kʃən] N convección f

convene [kənvín] VT convocar; VI reunirse

convenience [kənvínjəns] N (practicality) conveniencia f; (appliance) comodidad f; **— store** autoservicio m; **at your —** cuando le venga bien

convenient [kənvínjənt] ADJ conveniente, oportuno; (at hand) accesible

convent [kɑ́nvent] N convento m

convention [kənvɛ́nʃən] N (political assembly) convención f; (professional assembly) congreso m; (pact) convenio m; (international agreement, acceptable usage) convención f

conventional [kənvɛ́nʃənl̩] ADJ (not original) convencional; (traditional) clásico; **— loan** préstamo convencional m

conventioneer [kənvenʃənír] N congresista mf

converge [kənvə́dʒ] VI converger

convergence [kənvə́dʒəns] N convergencia f

conversant [kənvə́sənt] ADJ **— with** versado en

conversation [kɑnvəséʃən] N conversación f; **— piece** tema de conversación m

converse [kənvə́s] VI conversar

conversion [kənvə́ʒən] N conversión f

convert¹ [kənvə́t] VI/VT convertir[se]

convert² [kɑ́nvət] N converso -sa mf

converter [kənvə́tə] N convertidor m

convertible [kənvə́təbl̩] ADJ convertible; (car) descapotable; **— assets** activo convertible m; N (car) descapotable m

convex [kɑ́nveks] ADJ convexo

convey [kənvé] VT (carry) llevar; (transfer) transferir; (transmit) transmitir; (communicate) comunicar

conveyance [kənvéəns] N (vehicle) vehículo m; (transfer of property) transferencia f; (document) escritura de traspaso f

conveyer, conveyor [kənvéə·] N transmisor

362

-ora *mf*; — **belt** cinta transportadora *f*

convict[1] [kánvɪkt] N convicto -ta *mf*

convict[2] [kənvíkt] VI/VT declarar culpable

conviction [kənvíkʃən] N (belief) convicción *f*, convencimiento *m*; (act of convicting) declaración de culpabilidad *f*; (on one's record) condena *f*

convince [kənvíns] VT convencer

convincing [kənvínsɪŋ] ADJ convincente, contundente

convocation [kanvəkéʃən] N (act) convocación *f*; (group of people) asamblea *f*

convoke [kənvók] VT convocar

convoluted [kánvəlúɒɪd] ADJ retorcido

convoy [kánvɔɪ] N convoy *m*; VT convoyar

convulse [kənváls] VI/VT convulsionar[se]

convulsion [kənválʃən] N convulsión *f*

coo [ku] VI arrullar; N arrullo *m*

cook [kuk] N cocinero -ra *mf*; —**book** libro de cocina *m*; VT cocinar, guisar; **to — the books** falsificar los libros de contabilidad; **to — up a plan** urdir un plan; **her —ing is outstanding** cocina muy bien; **now we're —ing!** ahora sí

cookery [kúkari] N cocina *f*

cookie [kúki] N (sweet food) galletita dulce *f*; (computer record) archivo cookie *m*

cool [kuł] ADJ (not hot) fresco; (indifferent) frío, indiferente; (calm) tranquilo; (good) excelente; *Carib* chévere; *RP* macanudo; *Sp* guay; **that's not —** eso no se hace; **—ing-off period** tregua *f*; N (cold) fresco *m*; (composure) tranquilidad *f*; VT (make cooler) enfriar; (air condition) refrigerar; **to — off** (get cold) enfriarse; (get cooler) refrescar[se]; (calm down) calmarse

coolant [kúlənt] N refrigerante *m*

cooler [kúlə] N (room) cámara frigorífica *f*; (container) nevera portátil *f*

coolness [kúłnɪs] N (cold weather) fresco *m*, frescor *m*; (indifference) frialdad *f*, indiferencia *f*

coon [kun] N (raccoon) mapache *m*; **a —'s age** una eternidad

co-op [kóap] N cooperativa *f*

coop [kup] N jaula *f*; (for chickens) gallinero *m*; VT enjaular; **to — up** encerrar

cooperate [koápəret] VI cooperar

cooperation [koapəréʃən] N cooperación *f*

cooperative [koápə-əɒɪv] ADJ (helpful) cooperativo; (relative to a cooperative) cooperativista; N cooperativa *f*

coordinate[1] [koórdnɪt] ADJ coordinado; N coordenada *f*; —**s** (clothes) conjunto *m*

coordinate[2] [koórdnet] VI/VT coordinar

coordinating [koórdnedɪŋ] ADJ coordinador

coordination [koórdnéʃən] N coordinación *f*

coordinator [koórdnedə-] N coordinador -ora *mf*

cop [kap] N *fam* poli *mf*, polizonte *m*; VI **to — out**

zafarse

copayment [kópemənt] N copago *m*

cope [kop] VI **to — with** arreglárselas con; **I cannot — with this** no puedo con esto

copious [kópiəs] ADJ copioso

copper [kápə-] N cobre *m*; (cop) *fam* poli *mf*; ADJ de cobre

copulate [kápjəlet] VI copular

copulation [kapjəléʃən] N copulación *f*

copy [kápi] N (reproduction) copia *f*; (specimen, example) ejemplar *m*; (news story) texto *m*; —**cat** copión -ona *mf*; — **machine** copiadora *f*; — **protection** protección contra copias *f*; —**right** copyright *m*, derechos de autor *m pl*; **this material is —righted** reservados todos los derechos; VT copiar; **to —right** registrar los derechos

coquette [kokét] N coqueta *f*

coral [kórał] N coral *m*; ADJ (related to coral) coralino; (made of coral) de coral; — **reef** arrecife de coral *m*

cord [kɔrd] N (thread) cuerda *f*; (for shoes) cordón *m*; (firewood measure) medida de leña *f*; —**s** pantalones de pana *m pl*

cordial [kórdʒəł] ADJ cordial; N licor *m*

cordless [kórdlɪs] ADJ inalámbrico

corduroy [kórdərɔɪ] N pana *f*; —**s** pantalones de pana *m pl*

core [kor] N (of fruit) corazón *m*; (of a problem) meollo *m*; (of a magnet, reactor) núcleo *m*; — **business** negocio principal *m*; — **inflation** inflación básica *f*; VT despepitar

cork [kɔrk] N (woody material) corcho *m*; (stopper, buoy) tapón *m*; —**screw** sacacorchos *m sg*, tirabuzón *m*; — **tree** alcornoque *m*; VT tapar con un corcho

corn [kɔrn] N (plant) maíz *m*; (painful growth) callo *m*; —**bread** pan de maíz *m*; —**cob** mazorca *f*; *Sp* zuro *m*; — **on the cob** choclo *m*; *Mex* elote *m*; —**ed beef** corned beef *m*; —**field** maizal *m*; *Mex* milpa *f*; —**flakes** copos de maíz *m pl*; —**meal** harina de maíz *f*; —**starch** Maicena™ *f*

corner [kórnə-] N (angle) ángulo *m*; (of a space) rincón *m*; (of two streets) esquina *f*; —**back** (football) esquinero *m*; — **kick** (soccer) saque/tiro de esquina *m*, córner *m*; —**stone** piedra angular *f*; — **table** mesa rinconera *f*; VT (trap) arrinconar, acorralar; (monopolize) monopolizar; VI doblar, *Sp* girar; — **the market** acaparar el mercado

cornered [kórnə-d] ADJ (animal) acorralado; (person) arrinconado

cornet [kornét] N corneta *f*

cornice [kórnɪs] N cornisa *f*

corny [kórni] ADJ sensiblero; (joke) viejo

corollary [kórəleri] N corolario *m*

coronary [kórəneri] ADJ coronario; — **bypass** puente cardiopulmonar *m*; — **care unit**

unidad de cuidado coronario *f*; **— failure** insuficiencia coronaria *f*; **— thrombosis** trombosis coronaria *f*

coronation [kɔrənéʃən] N coronación *f*

coroner [kɔ́rənə] N médico -ca forense *mf*

corporal [kɔ́rpəəl] ADJ corporal; N (rank) cabo *m*

corporate [kɔ́rpəɪt] ADJ corporativo; **— backing** patrocinio empresarial *m*; **— officers** ejecutivos -vas de empresa *mf pl*

corporation [kɔrpəréʃən] N sociedad anónima *f*

corps [kor] N cuerpo *m*

corpse [kɔrps] N cadáver *m*

corpulent [kɔ́rpjələnt] ADJ corpulento

corpus [kɔ́rpəs] N corpus *m*

corpuscle [kɔ́rpʌsəl] N corpúsculo *m*; (of blood) glóbulo *m*

corral [kəráɫ] N corral *m*; VT acorralar

correct [kərɛ́kt] VT corregir; ADJ correcto; **that is** — es cierto

correction [kərɛ́kʃən] N corrección *f*; (for glasses) graduación *f*

correctness [kərɛ́ktnɪs] N corrección *f*

corrector [kərɛ́ktə] N corrector -ora *mf*

correlate[1] [kɔ́rəlet] VI/VT correlacionar

correlate[2] [kɔ́rəlɪt] N correlato *m*

correlation [kɔrəléʃən] N correlación *f*

correspond [kɔrɪspánd] VI (be in agreement) corresponder, responder; (exchange letters) cartearse, escribirse

correspondence [kɔrɪspándəns] N correspondencia *f*

correspondent [kɔrɪspándənt] ADJ correspondiente; N (writer of letters) correspondiente *mf*; (news gatherer) corresponsal *mf*, enviado -da *mf*

corresponding [kɔrɪspándɪŋ] ADJ correspondiente; (secretary) encargado de la correspondencia

corridor [kɔ́rɪdɔr] N corredor *m*, pasillo *m*

corroborate [kərábəret] VT corroborar

corrode [kəród] VI/VT corroer[se]

corrosion [kəróʒən] N corrosión *f*

corrupt [kərápt] ADJ (dishonest) corrupto; (rotten) corrompido; **to become —** corromperse; VT corromper, viciar; **—ed file** archivo corrupto *m*

corruption [kərápʃən] N corrupción *f*

corset [kɔ́rsɪt] N corsé *m*

cortex [kɔ́rtɛks] N córtex *m*, corteza cerebral *f*

corticosteriod [kɔrdɪkostérɔɪd] N corticoesteroide *m*

cortisone [kɔ́rdɪzon] N cortisona *f*

cosigner [kósaɪnə] N cosignatario -ria *mf*

cosmetic [kazmÉdɪk] ADJ & N cosmético *m*; **— surgery** cirugía estética *f*

cosmic [kázmɪk] ADJ cósmico

cosmology [kazmáləʤi] N cosmología *f*

cosmonaut [kázmənɔt] N cosmonauta *mf*

cosmopolitan [kazməpálɪtṇ] ADJ cosmopolita

cosmos [kázmos] N cosmos *m*

cost [kɔst] N costo *m*; Sp coste *m*; **—s** (in court) costas *f pl*; **at —** al coste/costo; **at all —s** a toda costa; **— of living** costo/coste de vida *m*; **to sell at —** vender al costo / al coste; VT costar; **how much does this —?** ¿cuánto vale/cuesta esto? ADJ **—-benefit analysis** análisis costo-beneficio *m*; **— effective** económico

costar [kóstar] N coprotagonista *mf*, oponente *mf*

Costa Rica [kóstárɪka] N Costa Rica *f*

Costa Rican [kóstárɪkən] ADJ & N costarricense *mf*, costarriqueño -ña *mf*

costly [kóstli] ADJ costoso, caro

costume [kástum] N (style of clothing) vestimenta *f*; (in the theater) vestuario *m*; (disguise) disfraz *m*; **— jewelry** bisutería *f*

cot [kat] N catre *m*

cottage [kádɪʤ] N (small house) casita *f*; (vacation house) cabaña *f*, chalé *m*; **— cheese** requesón *m*

cotter pin [kádə-pɪn] N chaveta *f*

cotton [katṇ] N algodón *m*; **— candy** algodón de azúcar *m*; **— gin** desmontadora de algodón *f*; **—seed** semilla de algodón *f*; **—wood** álamo [de Virginia] *m*

couch [kautʃ] N sofá *m*; (psychiatrist's) diván *m*; **— potato** telebobo -ba *mf*; VT expresar

cougar [kúgə] N puma *f*

cough [kɔf] VI toser; **to — up** (spit) expectorar; (hand over) soltar, largar; N tos *f*; **— drop** pastilla para la tos *f*; **— syrup** jarabe para la tos *m*

could [kʊd] V AUX I **— do it if I wanted** podría hacerlo si quisiera, **— you arrive early?** ¿podrías llegar temprano? **— I leave early?** ¿puedo salir temprano? **you — be right** quizá tengas razón

council [káunsəl] N (religious) concilio *m*; (advisory) consejo *m*, junta *f*; (provincial) diputación *f*; (municipal) concejo *m*; **—man** concejal *m*; **—woman** concejal *f*, concejala *f*

councilor [káunsələ] N concejal *mf*

counsel [káunsəl] N (advice) consejo *m*; (lawyer) abogado -da *mf*; VI/VT (give advice) aconsejar

counseling [káunsəlɪŋ] N (academic) asesoramiento *m*, orientación *f*; (psychological, marriage) terapia *f*

counselor [káunsələ] N consejero -ra *mf*; (lawyer) abogado -da *mf*

count [kaunt] VI/VT contar; **to — in** incluir; **to — on** contar con; **to — oneself lucky** considerarse dichoso; **to — out** excluir; N (reckoning) cuenta *f*; (charge) cargo *m*; (noble) conde *m*; (in baseball) conteo *m*; **—down** cuenta regresiva *f*

countenance [káuntṇəns] N (expression) semblante *m*; (face) cara *f*; VT (tolerate) tolerar; (approve) aprobar

counter [káʊntɚ] N (in a kitchen) *Sp* encimera f; *Am* mostrador m; (in a store) mostrador m; (in a bar) barra f; (in board games) tablero m; (counting device) contador m; **over the —** sin receta; ADJ contrario, opuesto; ADV **— to** contra; **to run — to** ser contrario a; VT (an argument) retrucar (a blow), devolver; VI/VT (reply) replicar

counteract [kaʊntɚækt] VT contrarrestar

counterattack [káʊntɚətæk] N contraataque m; VI/VT contraatacar

counterbalance[1] [kaʊntɚbǽləns] VI/VT contrapesar

counterbalance[2] [káʊntɚbæləns] N contrapeso m

counterclockwise [kaʊntɚklɑ́kwaɪz] ADV en el sentido opuesto al de las manecillas del reloj

counterculture [káʊntɚkʌltʃɚ] N contracultura f

counterespionage [kaʊntɚéspiənɑʒ] N contraespionaje m

counterexample [káʊntɚɪgzæmpəl] N contraejemplo m

counterfeit [káʊntɚfɪt] N falsificación f; ADJ falso; **— money** moneda falsa f; VT falsificar

countermand[1] [kaʊntɚmǽnd] VT contramandar

countermand[2] [káʊntɚmænd] N contraorden f

countermeasure [káʊntɚmɛʒɚ] N contramedida f

counteroffer [káʊntɚɔfɚ] N contraoferta f

counterpart [káʊntɚpart] N homólogo -ga mf

counterproductive [kaʊntɚprədáktɪv] ADJ contraproducente

counterrevolution [kaʊntɚrɛvəlúʃən] N contrarrevolución f

countersign [káʊntɚsaɪn] N contraseña f; VT refrendar

countess [káʊntɪs] N condesa f

countless [káʊntlɪs] ADJ incontables, innumerables

country [kántri] N (nation) país m; (territory) territorio m; (homeland) patria f; (rural area) campo m; ADJ (of the countryside) rural; (uncouth) rústico; **— club** club campestre m; **— code** código de país m; **—man** compatriota m; **— music** música country f; **— of origin** país de origen m; **—side** (rural area) campo m; (scenery) paisaje m; **—woman** compatriota f

county [káʊnti] N condado m; **— fair** feria [de ganado] f; **— seat** capital de condado f

coup [ku] N (success) golpe maestro m; (putsch) golpe de estado m; **— d'état** golpe de estado m

coupe [kup] N cupé m

couple [kápəl] N (of times, of forces, of people) par m; (romantic) pareja f; VI/VT (pair up)

formar parejas; VT (connect) acoplar; VI (copulate) copular

couplet [káplɪt] N pareado m

coupling [káplɪŋ] N (mechanical action) acoplamiento m, enganche m; (device) acople m, enganche m; (mating) cópula f

coupon [kjúpɑn] N cupón m

courage [kɚɪdʒ] N valentía f, valor m, coraje m

courageous [kɚédʒəs] ADJ valiente

courier [kúriɚ] N mensajero -ra mf

course [kɔrs] N (of a river, of study, of a disease) curso m; (of a road, route) trayecto m; (of a ship, plane) derrotero m; (progression of time) marcha f; (dish) plato m; **— of action** línea de conducta f, proceder m; **in the — of a year** en el transcurso de un año; **in due —** a la larga; INTERJ **of —** claro, por supuesto, naturalmente; VI correr, fluir

court [kɔrt] N (courtyard) patio m; (atrium) patio interior m; (in sports) cancha f, pista f; (in a city) plazuela f, plazoleta f; (lower tribunal) juzgado m; (higher tribunal) tribunal m; (session) audiencia f; (royal residence, retinue) corte f; **—-martial** consejo de guerra m; **— of law** tribunal de justicia m; **— order** orden judicial f; **— reporter** estenotipista mf; **— room** tribunal m; **—yard** patio m; **to settle out of —** llegar a un arreglo extrajudicial; **to pay — to** cortejar; VT cortejar, galantear; **to — danger** tentar a la suerte; **to —-martial** someter a consejo de guerra; VI estar de novios

courteous [kɚ́diəs] ADJ cortés

courtesy [kɚ́DIsi] N (attitude) cortesía f; (act) fineza f, atención f

courtier [kɔ́rdiɚ] N (member of the court) cortesano -na mf; (sycophant) adulador -ora mf

courtship [kɔ́rtʃɪp] N cortejo m

cousin [kázən] N primo -ma mf; **first —** primo -ma hermano -na mf

cove [kov] N ensenada f

covenant [kávənənt] N pacto m; (religious) alianza f

cover [kávɚ] VI/VT cubrir, recubrir; (with lid, screen) tapar; (replace) sustituir; (include, deal with) comprender; (traverse) recorrer; (sing) hacer una versión; **—ed losses** pérdidas cubiertas f pl; **to — up** (wrap up) tapar bien; (hide) ocultar; N (lid) tapa f; (book) cubierta f, tapa f; (blanket) manta f; (for appliances, furniture) funda f; (front for activity) tapadera f, pantalla f; (shelter) resguardo m, abrigo m; **—all** mono m; **— charge** entrada f; **— girl** modelo de portada f; **— letter** carta con anexos f, carta de remisión f; **—-up** encubrimiento m; **to send under separate —** enviar por separado; **to take —** resguardarse; **under —** de incógnito;

under — of dark bajo el manto de la noche

coverage [kávɚɪʤ] N cobertura *f*; **— level** nivel de cobertura *m*

covert [kovɚ́t] ADJ encubierto

covet [kávɪt] VT (desire wrongly) codiciar; (want) ansiar

covetous [kávɪdəs] ADJ codicioso

cow [kau] N (bovine female) vaca *f*; (female of other animals) hembra *f*; **—bell** cencerro *m*, esquila *f*; **—boy** vaquero *m*; **—hide** cuero de vaca *m*, vaqueta *f*; **—lick** remolino *m*; **—pox** vacuna *f*; **—shed** vaquería *f*, vaqueriza *f*; **to have a —** tener una pataleta; VT intimidar

coward [káuɚd] N cobarde *mf*

cowardice [káuɚdɪs] N cobardía *f*

cowardly [káuɚdli] ADJ cobarde

cower [káuɚ] VI achicarse

cowl [kaul] N capucha *f*

coy [kɔɪ] ADJ (coquettish) remilgado; (evasive) esquivo

coyote [kaɪódi, káɪot] N coyote *m*

cozy [kózi] ADJ (warm) acogedor; (beneficial) conveniente; VI **to — up to** adular

CPA [certified public accountant] [sípíé] N contador -ora público -ca con licencia *mf*

CPI [consumer price index] [sípíáɪ] N índice de precios al consumidor *m*

CPR [cardiopulmonary resuscitation] [sípíár] N reanimación cardiopulmonar *f*

CPU [central processing unit] [sípíjú] N UCP *f*

crab [kræb] N cangrejo *m*; (mechanism) carro corredizo *m*; (grouch) cascarrabias *mf sg*; **—apple** manzana silvestre *f*; **—s** (parasites) ladillas *f pl*; VI (fish) pescar cangrejos; (complain) quejarse

crack [kræk] VI (single fissure) rajarse; (multiple fissures) resquebrajarse, agrietarse; (psychological breakdown) sufrir un ataque de nervios; (of voice) quebrarse; VT (knuckles) hacer un chasquido con, chascar, chasquear; (nuts) cascar; (jokes) contar; (a prisoner) quebrar; (a case) resolver; (a code) descifrar; (a door) entreabrir; **to — down on** reprimir; **that — s me up** eso me hace desternillar de risa; N (fissure) rajadura *f*, grieta *f*, resquebrajadura *f*; (sound) chasquido *m*; (joke) pulla *f*, chanza *f*; **—cocaine** crack *m*; **—down** represión *f*; **—house** fumadero *m*; **—pot** excéntrico -ca *mf*; **at the — of dawn** al romper el alba; **I'd like a — at the championship** me gustaría poder participar en el campeonato

cracked [krækt] ADJ rajado, quebrado; (crazy) chiflado; **it's not all it's — up to be** no es para tanto

cracker [krǽkɚ] N galleta *f*

crackle [krǽkəl] N (of paper) crujido *m*; (of fire) crepitación *f*; VI crujir, crepitar

cradle [krédl̩] N cuna *f*

craft [kræft] N (skill) destreza *f*; (cunning) astucia *f*; (occupation) arte *m*, oficio *m*; (boat) embarcación *f*; **—sman** artesano *m*; **—swoman** artesana *f*; VT fabricar

crafty [krǽfti] ADJ astuto, taimado

crag [kræg] N risco *m*, peñasco *m*, peñón *m*

craggy [krǽgi] ADJ peñascoso

cram [kræm] VT (pack in) embutir; VI (study intensely) memorizar; Sp empollar; **the bar was —med with people** el bar estaba atestado

cramp [kræmp] N (spasm) calambre *m*; (staple) grapa *f*; VI/VT (to suffer a spasm) acalambrar[se]; VT (to staple) engrapar; **you're —ing my style** me estorbas

cranberry [krǽnberi] N arándano rojo *m*

crane [kren] N (bird) grulla *f*; (machine) grúa *f*; VT **to — one's neck** estirar el cuello

cranium [kréniəm] N cráneo *m*

crank [kræŋk] N (mechanism) manivela *f*; (grouch) cascarrabias *mf sg*; (overzealous advocate) fanático -ca *mf*; **—case** cárter superior del aceite *m*; **—shaft** cigüeñal *m*; VI/VT arrancar con manivela

cranky [krǽŋki] ADJ (irritable) irritable; (eccentric) excéntrico

cranny [krǽni] N (crevice) rendija *f*; (corner) recoveco *m*

crash [kræʃ] VI (collide) estrellarse; (market) quebrar; (stay overnight with someone) quedarse a dormir; (hang up, as with a computer) bloquearse, caerse; (sleep) dormir; VT **to — a party** colarse en una fiesta; N (noise) estallido *m*; (collision) choque *m*; (financial collapse) quiebra *f*, colapso *m*; (computer failure) bloqueo *m*, caída *f*; **—landing** aterrizaje forzoso *m*

crass [kræs] ADJ craso

crate [kret] N cajón *m*, guacal *m*; VT poner en cajones

crater [krédɚ] N cráter *m*

cravat [krəvǽt] N corbata *f*

crave [krev] VT anhelar; **I — chocolate** me muero por un chocolate

craving [krévɪŋ] N antojo *m*

crawl [krɔl] VI (on hands and knees) gatear; (on the belly) arrastrarse, reptar; (proceed slowly) avanzar a paso de tortuga; **to be —ing with** hormiguear de; N (swimming stroke) crol *m*; **traffic is going at a —** el tráfico va a paso de tortuga

crayon [kréan] N lápiz de color *m*, Crayola™ *f*

craze [krez] N (fad) moda pasajera *f*; VI/VT enloquecer[se]

craziness [krézɪnɪs] N locura *f*, chifladura *f*

crazy [krézi] ADJ & N loco -ca *mf*; **I'm — about you** estoy loco por ti; **that's —!** ¡qué locura! **to go —** volverse loco, enloquecerse

creak [krik] N (of wooden floor) crujido *m*; (of a

hinge) rechinamiento m; VI (a wooden floor) crujir; (a hinge) rechinar

cream [krim] N (milk product) crema f; Sp nata f; (medicament) crema f; — **cheese** queso de untar m, queso crema m; — **of tomato soup** sopa crema de tomate f; **the — of the crop** la flor y nata; VT (decream) desnatar; (butter, sugar) batir; (vegetables) preparar con salsa blanca; (defeat) aplastar

creamy [krími] ADJ cremoso

crease [kris] N (in trousers) raya f, repliegue m; (wrinkle) arruga f; VT (trousers) planchar la raya; (wrinkle) arrugar

create [kriét] VI/VT crear

creation [kriéʃən] N creación f

creationism [kriéʃənɪzəm] N creacionismo m

creative [kriéDɪv] ADJ creativo

creativity [kriætívɪDi] N creatividad f

creator [kriéDɚ] N creador -ra mf

creature [krítʃɚ] N (being) ser m; (animal) animal m; **a — of your imagination** un producto de tu imaginación

credence [krídns] N crédito m

credentials [krɪdéntʃəlz] N credenciales f pl

credibility [krɛdɪbílɪDi] N credibilidad f

credible [krɛdəbəl] ADJ creíble

credit [krɛdɪt] N crédito m; (commendation) reconocimiento m; — **approval** aprobación de crédito f; — **card** tarjeta de crédito f; — **counseling** asesoramiento de crédito m; — **line** línea de crédito f; — **history** historial de crédito m; — **rating** calificación crediticia f; — **report** informe de crédito m; **—s** créditos m pl; — **underwriters** aseguradores de crédito m pl; — **union** banco cooperativo m; **on —** a crédito; **to give — to** (believe) dar crédito; (ascribe) acreditar; ADJ **—worthy** solvente; VT (believe) creer; (enter as credit) acreditar; (attribute) atribuir; — **an account** abonar/acreditar a una cuenta

creditor [krɛdɪDɚ] N acreedor -ora mf

credulous [krɛdʒələs] ADJ crédulo

creed [krid] N credo m

creek [krik] N arroyo m, quebrada f

creep [krip] VI (crawl on belly) arrastrarse; (crawl on all fours) gatear; (grow upward) trepar; (go slowly) andar a paso de tortuga; **to — up on** acercarse furtivamente a; N (obnoxious person) pej persona repulsiva f, sinvergüenza mf; **that gives me the —s** eso me da asco; Sp eso me da grima

creeper [krípɚ] N enredadera f, planta trepadora f

creepy [krípi] ADJ repulsivo

cremate [krímet] VT cremar

Creole [kriól] ADJ & N criollo -lla mf

creosote [kríəsot] N creosota f

crepe [krep] N (fabric) crespón m; (band of fabric) crespón negro m

crept [krɛpt] see creep

crescent [krɛsənt] N media luna f; ADJ creciente

crest [krɛst] N (of a wave, rooster) cresta f; (of feathers) penacho m, copete m; (of mountain) cima f, cumbre f; (of heraldic arms) timbre m; **—fallen** alicaído, cabizbajo; VI **the river —ed at two meters above flood level** el río creció hasta dos metros por encima de lo normal

crevice [krɛvɪs] N grieta f

crew [kru] N (for ships, etc.) tripulación f; (of workers) cuadrilla f; — **member** tripulante mf

crib [krɪb] N (bed) cuna f; (manger) pesebre m; (bin for grain) granero m; (cheat notes) hoja para copiar f; — **death** síndrome de muerte súbita infantil m; VI copiar

cricket [krɪkɪt] N (insect) grillo m; (game) críquet m

crime [kraɪm] N (illegal act) delito m; (act of violence against people) crimen m; (criminal activity) delincuencia f, criminalidad f

criminal [krɪmənəl] ADJ & N delincuente mf, malhechor -ora mf; (perpetrator of violent crimes) criminal mf; — **record** antecedentes delictivos m pl

crimp [krɪmp] VT rizar; N rizo m

crimson [krɪmzən] ADJ & N carmesí m, carmín m

cringe [krɪndʒ] VI **it makes me —** me da vergüenza ajena

cripple [krɪpəl] N offensive tullido -da mf; (in the legs) pey cojo -ja mf; (in the arms) offensive manco -ca mf; VT tullir

crisis [kráɪsɪs] N crisis f

crisp [krɪsp] ADJ (apple, bacon) crocante, crujiente; (weather) fresco y despejado; (hair) crespo; VI/VT volver crujiente

crispy [krɪspi] ADJ crocante, crujiente

criterion [kraɪtírian] N criterio m

critic [krɪDɪk] N crítico -ca mf

critical [krɪDɪkəl] ADJ crítico; — **stage** punto culminante m

criticism [krɪDɪsɪzəm] N crítica f

criticize [krɪDɪsaɪz] VT criticar

croak [krok] VI (make the sound of a frog) croar; (make the sound of a crow) graznar; (die) fam espichar; N (sound made by frogs) canto de rana m; (sound made by crows) graznido m

Croatia [kroéʃə] N Croacia f

Croatian [kroéʃən] ADJ & N croata mf

crochet [kroʃé] N ganchillo m, croché m, crochet m; — **hook** aguja de croché f; VI hacer ganchillo, hacer croché

crock [krak] N (pot) vasija f; (lies) pamplinas f pl

crockery [krákɚi] N loza f

crocodile [krákədaɪl] N cocodrilo m

croissant [krəsánt] N cruasán m, croissant m

crony [króni] N compinche mf, compadre m, comadre f

cronyism [krónɪtzəm] N amiguismo *m*

crook [krʊk] N (criminal) delincuente *mf*; (curve) curva *f*; (hook) gancho *m*; (staff) cayado *m*

crooked [krúkɪd] ADJ (bent) torcido; *Am* chueco; (dishonest) deshonesto

crop [krɑp] N (harvest) cosecha *f*; (group of contemporaries) promoción *f*; (of a bird) buche *m*; (horse whip) fusta *f*; **— rotation** rotación de cultivos *f*; VT (graze) pastar, pacer; (trim) recortar; **to — up** surgir

croquet [kroké] N cróquet *m*

cross [krɔs] N (symbol) cruz *f*; (street intersection) cruce *m*; (soccer) pase cruzado *m*; (act of mixing) cruzamiento *m*; (in boxing) cruzado *m*; **—bar** (soccer) travesaño *m*, larguero *m*; (in gymnastics) barra *f*; (in high jump) listón *m*; (of a door) tranca *f*; **—-check** verificación *f*; **—court shot** golpe cruzado *m*; **—-fertilization** fecundación cruzada *f*; **—piece** cruceta *f*; **—-reference** referencia cruzada *f*; **—road** encrucijada *f*; **— section** corte transversal *m*; **—walk** cruce peatonal *m*, cebra *f*; **—word puzzle** crucigrama *m*; **to bear one's —** cargar la cruz; VI/VT (intersect, form a cross, breed, meet) cruzar[se]; (make sign of the cross) santiguarse; **to —-check** verificar; VT (betray) traicionar; (move to other side) cruzar; **to — examine** interrogar; **to — out** tachar; **to — over** (change allegiance) cambiar de bando; (go to the other side) traspasar; **to —-reference** hacer una referencia cruzada; **you've —ed the line** te pasaste de la raya; ADJ (transverse) transversal; (angry) enojado; **—-country** a campo traviesa; **—-cultural** transcultural; **—-eyed** bizco; **to be —-eyed** bizquear

crossing [krɔ́sɪŋ] N (street or railroad intersection, pedestrian path) cruce *m*; (hybridization, act of mixing) cruzamiento *m*; (of ocean) travesía *f*; (of a border) paso *m*; (of a river) vado *m*

crotch [krɑtʃ] N entrepierna *f*

crotchety [krátʃɪdi] ADJ cascarrabias *inv*

crouch [kraʊtʃ] VI (stoop) agacharse; (prepare to spring) agazaparse

croup [krup] N tos *f*, croup *m*

crow [kro] N (bird) cuervo *m*; (sound of rooster) canto del gallo *m*; **—bar** alzaprima *f*; **—'s-foot** pata de gallo *f*; **to eat —** comerse sus propias palabras; VI cantar; (gloat, brag) jactarse

crowd [kraʊd] N (group of people) muchedumbre *f*, gentío *m*, aglomeración *f*; (at a performance) público *m*; (clique) pandilla *f*; VI (push forward) agolparse; VI/VT (gather in large numbers) apiñar[se], amontonar[se], aglomerar[se]; (gather in a confined space) hacinar[se]

crowded [kráʊdɪd] ADJ **it is — in here** hay demasiada gente aquí; **the restaurant is —** el restaurante está lleno

crown [kraʊn] N corona *f*; (of head) coronilla *f*, crisma *f*; (of a hat) copa *f*; **— jewels** joyas de la corona *f pl*; VT coronar; (hit on head) dar un coscorrón

crucial [krúʃəl] ADJ (element) fundamental; (moment) crucial

crucible [krúsəbəl] N crisol *m*

crucifix [krúsəfɪks] N crucifijo *m*

crucify [krúsəfaɪ] VT crucificar

crud [krʌd] N (filth) mugre *f*; (worthless thing, sickness, despicable person) *fam* porquería *f*

crude [krud] ADJ (vulgar, unpolished) basto, tosco; **— oil** petróleo crudo *m*

cruel [krúəl] ADJ cruel

cruelty [krúəlti] N crueldad *f*

cruise [kruz] VI (take a cruise) tomar un crucero; (patrol) patrullar; **— control** control de crucero *m*; **cruising speed** velocidad de crucero *f*; N crucero *m*; **— missile** misil crucero *m*

cruiser [krúzə] N crucero *m*

crumb [krʌm] N (small) miga *f*, migaja *f*; (large) mendrugo *m*; VT (break into crumbs) desmigajar; (remove crumbs) sacar las migas

crumble [krámbəl] VI/VT (bread) desmigajar[se]; (clods of dirt) desmenuzar[se]; (house) desmoronar[se]

crummy [krámi] ADJ (place) *fam* de mala muerte; (object) *fam* de porquería; (show) flojo

crumple [krámpəl] VI/VT (crush) arrugar[se]; VI (collapse) aplastarse

crunch [krʌntʃ] VI/VT (eat noisily) mascar; N (sound) crujido *m*; (shortage) crisis *f*; **—es** abdominales *m pl*

crunchy [krántʃi] ADJ crocante, crujiente

crusade [kruséd] N cruzada *f*; VI (engage in a campaign) hacer una campaña

crusader [krúséDə] N cruzado -da *mf*; **a — for human rights** un paladín de los derechos humanos

crush [krʌʃ] VI/VT aplastar, machacar; (stone) demoler; N (act of crushing) aplastamiento *m*; (crowd) tumulto *m*; (infatuation) enamoramiento *m*; **—ing victory** victoria contundente *f*

crust [krʌst] N (of bread, earth) corteza *f*; (of bread) costra *f*; (of pie) tapa *f*

crusty [krásti] ADJ (with a crust) costroso; (grouchy) irascible

crutch [krʌtʃ] N muleta *f*

cry [kraɪ] N (shout) grito *m*; (weeping) llanto *m*; (call of a bird) reclamo *m*; **—baby** llorón -ona *mf*; **a far — from** muy distante de, muy lejos de; VI (shout) gritar; (weep) llorar; **to — over spilt milk** hacer como la lechera; **to — for**

attention reclamar atención; **to — for help** pedir socorro; **to — out** vocear

cryogenic [kraɪəʤénɪk] ADJ criogénico

crystal [krístl] N cristal m; **— ball** bola de cristal f; **— clear** cristalino

crystalline [krístlɪn] ADJ cristalino

crystallize [krístlaɪz] VI/VT cristalizar[se]

cub [kʌb] N (lion) cachorro m; (bear) osezno m; (whale) ballenato m; (wolf) lobato m, lobezno m; **— reporter** reportero -ra novato -ta mf

Cuba [kjúbə] N Cuba f

Cuban [kjúbən] ADJ & N cubano -na mf

cubbyhole [kʌ́bihol] N casilla f

cube [kjúb] N cubo m; **— root** raíz cúbica f; VT (cut) cortar en cubos; (raise to the third power) elevar al cubo

cubic [kjúbɪk] ADJ cúbico

cubicle [kjúbɪkəl] N cubículo m

cubism [kjúbɪzəm] N cubismo m

cuckold [kʌ́kəld] N cornudo m, cabrón m; VT poner los cuernos a

cuckoo [kúku] N cuclillo m, cuco m; **— clock** reloj de cucú m; ADJ & N chiflado -da mf; INTERJ cucú

cucumber [kjúkʌmbə] N pepino m

cud [kʌd] N **to chew the —** rumiar

cuddle [kʌ́dl] VI/VT hacer[se] mimos; N mimo m

cuddly [kʌ́dli] ADJ mimoso

cudgel [kʌ́ʤəl] N porra f; VT aporrear

cue [kju] N (in theater) pie m; (psychological stimulus) estímulo m; **— ball** bola blanca f; **— stick** taco de billar m; VT dar pie, dar la señal

cuff [kʌf] N (of sleeve, glove) puño m; (of pants) bajo m; (blow) bofetada f; **hand—s** esposas f pl; VT (in making pants) hacer los bajos; (put on handcuffs) esposar; (hit) abofetear

cuisine [kwizín] N cocina f

cul-de-sac [kʌ́ldəsæk] N callejón sin salida m

culinary [kjúlənɛri, kálənɛri] ADJ culinario

cull [kʌl] VT (choose) seleccionar, entresacar; (collect) recoger

culminate [kʌ́lmənet] VI/VT culminar

culmination [kʌlmənéʃən] N culminación f

culprit [kʌ́lprɪt] N culpable mf

cult [kʌlt] N (sect) secta religiosa f; (worship) culto m

cultivable [kʌ́ltəvəbəl] ADJ cultivable

cultivate [kʌ́ltəvet] VT cultivar

cultivated [kʌ́ltəvedɪd] ADJ (land) cultivado; (plant) de cultivo; (person) culto

cultivation [kʌltəvéʃən] N (tillage) cultivo m; (education) cultura f

cultivator [kʌ́ltəvedə] N (person) cultivador -ora mf; (implement) cultivadora f

cultural [kʌ́ltʃəəl] ADJ cultural

culture [kʌ́ltʃə] N cultura f; (microorganisms) cultivo m; **— shock** choque cultural m; VT (microorganisms) cultivar

cultured [kʌ́ltʃəd] ADJ (person) culto; (pearl) cultivado, de cultivo

cumbersome [kʌ́mbəsəm] ADJ (bulky) voluminoso; (unwieldy) incómodo

cumulative [kjúmjələdɪv] ADJ acumulativo

cumulus [kjúmjələs] N cúmulo m

cunning [kʌ́nɪŋ] ADJ (sly) astuto, zorro; N astucia f, maña f

cup [kʌp] N (with handle) taza f, pocillo m; (without handle) vaso m; (measure) taza f; (trophy, brassiere part) copa f; **—board** armario m, aparador m

cur [kɚ] N (dog) perro m; (villain) pej villano -na mf

curable [kjúrəbəl] ADJ curable

curator [kjúredə] N conservador -ora mf

curb [kɚb] N (of a street) Sp bordillo m; Mex borde m; RP cordón m; (of a well) brocal m; (restraint) freno m, restricción f; VT (emotions) refrenar; (spending) limitar

curd [kɚd] N cuajada f; VI/VT cuajar[se], coagular[se]

curdle [kɚdl] VI/VT cuajar[se], coagular[se]; **my blood —d** se me heló la sangre

cure [kjur] N (healing, preserving meat) cura f, curación f; (method) tratamiento m; VI/VT curar[se]; **—all** sanalotodo m

curfew [kɚfju] N toque de queda m, queda f

curio [kjúrio] N curiosidad f

curiosity [kjuriásɪdi] N curiosidad f

curious [kjúrias] ADJ curioso

curl [kɚl] VI/VT (form ringlets) rizar[se], ensortijar[se]; (coil) enroscar[se]; (smoke) alzarse en espirales; **to — up** ovillar[se]; N (of hair) rizo m, bucle m; (of smoke) espiral f

curler [kɚlə] N Sp rulo m; Mex tubo m; RP rulero m

curly [kɚli] ADJ rizado

currant [kɚənt] N (fruit) grosella f; (tree) grosellero m

currency [kɚənsi] N (money) moneda f, divisa f; (acceptance) aceptación f; **— exchange** mercado de divisas m; **— unit** unidad monetaria f

current [kɚənt] ADJ (commonly used) corriente; (prevalent) actual; **the — issue of a magazine** el último número de una revista; **— year** año en curso m; N (of river, electricity, air) corriente f

currently [kɚəntli] ADV actualmente

curriculum [kəríkjələm] N plan de estudios m, currículo m

curry [kɚri] N curry m

curse [kɚs] N (ill wish) maldición f; (swear word) palabrota f; VI/VT (wish ill) maldecir; (swear) decir palabrotas

cursive [kɚsɪv] ADJ cursivo; N cursiva f

cursor [kɚsə] N cursor m

curt [kɚt] ADJ (abrupt) seco, brusco; (brief) breve

curtail [kətél] VT restringir, cercenar

curtain [kɜ́rtṇ] N cortina f; (theater) telón m; VT ponerle cortinas a

curvature [kɜ́rvətʃʊr] N curvatura f; (of the spine) desviación f

curve [kɜrv] N (also in baseball) curva f; **he threw me a —** me agarró desprevenido; VI/VT encorvar[se]; (road) torcer[se], desviar[se]

curved [kɜrvd] ADJ curvo

cushion [kúʃən] N (pad) almohadilla f; (emergency resources, pad of air) colchón m; (pillow) almohadón m; (decorative pillow) cojín m; VT (put pads) poner almohadones; (soften a blow) amortiguar

cuspid [kʌ́spɪd] N colmillo m

cuss [kʌs] VI decir palabrotas; N **—word** f palabrota f; **strange old —** fam bicho raro m

custard [kʌ́stəd] N flan m, natilla[s] f sg or pl

custodian [kʌstóʊdiən] N (caretaker) cuidador -ora mf; (guardian) custodio -dia mf

custody [kʌ́stədi] N custodia f; **to take into —** detener

custom [kʌ́stəm] N costumbre f, uso m; **—s** (government department) aduana f; (taxes) derechos de aduana m pl; **—[s]house** aduana f; ADJ **—-built** construido por encargo; **—-made** hecho a medida

customary [kʌ́stəmɛri] ADJ acostumbrado

customer [kʌ́stəmər] N cliente -ta mf; **— base** clientela f; **— care** atención al cliente f; **— rights** derechos del cliente m pl; ADJ **—-oriented** orientado al cliente

customize [kʌ́stəmaɪz] VT adaptar por encargo

cut [kʌt] VI/VT cortar; (shorten) acortar; (harvest) talar; (lower) rebajar; **—!** ¡corte[n]! **to — a deal** llegar a un arreglo; **to — across** (take a shortcut) cortar por; (transcend) trascender; **to — and paste** cortar y pegar; **to — back** reducir; **to — class** faltar a clase; **to — costs** reducir costos; **to — down on** reducir; **to — in** (interrupt) interrumpir; (in traffic) atravesarse; **to — prices** bajar los precios; **may I — in?** ¿me permite? **to — off** (interrupt) interrumpir; (intercept) interceptar; **to — out** omitir; **to be — out for** estar hecho para; **to — up** (divide) trozar; (misbehave) portarse mal; N corte m; (in salary) recorte m, reducción f; (of prices) rebaja f; (of a suit) hechura f, corte m; (insult) desaire f; **—back** recorte m; **— glass** cristal labrado m; **—off date** fecha límite f; ADJ **—-and-dried** predeterminado; **—-rate** de rebajas; **—throat** despiadado

cutaneous [kjuténiəs] ADJ cutáneo

cute [kjut] ADJ mono, rico; **to act —** ser afectado, ser melindroso

cuticle [kjúDɪkəl] N cutícula f

cutlery [kʌ́tləri] N (knives, knife store) cuchillería f; (eating utensils) cubiertos m pl

cutlet [kʌ́tlɪt] N filete m

cutter [kʌ́Dər] N (person) cortador -ora mf; (device) cortadora f; (sleigh) trineo m; **Coast Guard —** guardacostas m sg

cutting [kʌ́Dɪŋ] ADJ (sharp) cortante; (cold) penetrante; (sarcastic) mordaz, sarcástico; **—board** tabla de cortar f; **— edge** filo m; **—-edge technology** tecnología de punta f; N (action) cortado m

CV [curriculum vitae] [siví] N currículo m, currículum vitae m

cyanide [sáɪənaɪd] N cianuro m

cybercafe [saɪbə·kafé] N cibercafé m

cybernetics [saɪbə·nɛ́Dɪks] N cibernética f

cyberpunk [sáɪbə·pʌŋk] N ciberpunk m

cyberspace [sáɪbə·spes] N ciberespacio m

cyborg [sáɪbɔrg] N cyborg m

cycle [sáɪkəl] N ciclo m

cyclical [síklɪkəl] ADJ cíclico

cyclone [sáɪklon] N ciclón m

cyclotron [sáɪklətrɑn] N ciclotrón m

cylinder [sílɪndə·] N cilindro m; (of a gun) tambor m; **— head** culata f

cylindrical [silíndrɪkəl] ADJ cilíndrico

cymbal [símbəl] N címbalo m, platillo m

cynic [sínɪk] N cínico -ca mf

cynical [sínɪkəl] ADJ cínico

cynicism [sínɪsɪzəm] N cinismo m

cypress [sáɪprɪs] N ciprés m

Cypriot, Cypriote [sípriət] ADJ & N chipriota mf

Cyprus [sáɪprəs] N Chipre m

cyst [sɪst] N quiste m

cystic [sístɪk] ADJ cístico; **— fibrosis** fibrosis cística f

cytology [saɪtáləʤi] N citología f

czar [zɑr] N zar m

Czech [tʃɛk] ADJ & N checo -ca mf; **— Republic** República Checa f

Dd

dab [dæb] VT (pat) dar toques; (apply) aplicar con golpecitos; N toque m

dabble [dǽbəl] VI (splash) chapotear; (be interested superficially) ser aficionado a

dachshund [dáksənd] N perro salchicha m

dad [dæd] N papá m

daddy [dǽdi] N papaíto m, papito m, papacito m

daffodil [dǽfədɪl] N narciso m

dagger [dǽgə·] N daga f, puñal m

dahlia [dǽljə] N dalia f

daily [déli] ADJ diario; **— planner** agenda f; **— wage** jornal m, salario m; N (newspaper) diario m

dainty [dénti] ADJ (delicate) delicado, exquisito; (finicky) remilgado

dairy [déri] N (milk) lechería f; (cheese) quesería

f; ADJ (industry) lechero; (product) lácteo; N producto lácteo *m*

daisy [dézi] N margarita *f*; **to be pushing up daisies** *fam* estar criando malvas

dale [del] N valle *m*

dally [dǽli] VI (flirt) coquetear; (risk danger) jugar con fuego; (waste time) remolonear

dam [dæm] N presa *f*, represa *f*; VT represar

damage [dǽmɪʤ] N daño *m*, destrozo *m*; **—control** control de daños *m*; **—s** daños y perjuicios *m pl*; **to pay —s** indemnizar *m*; VI/VT dañar[se]

damaging [dǽmɪʤɪŋ] ADJ perjudicial

dame [dem] N (noblewoman) dama *f*; (woman) *pej* tipa *f*

damn [dæm] VT condenar

damnation [dæmnéʃən] N condenación *f*, perdición *f*

damned [dæmd] ADJ condenado

damp [dæmp] ADJ húmedo; N humedad *f*; VT (wet) humedecer; (deaden) amortiguar; (extinguish) apagar

dampen [dǽmpən] VT (wet) humedecer; (deaden) amortiguar; (depress) deprimir

dampness [dǽmpnɪs] N humedad *f*

damsel [dǽmzəl] N damisela *f*

dance [dæns] N (act of dancing, party, activity) baile *m*; (artistic activity, animal courtship movements) danza *f*; **—music** música bailable *f*; VI/VT (at a party) bailar; (in ballet, of animals) danzar; **she—d her way to stardom** llegó al estrellato bailando

dancer [dǽnsɚ] N bailarín -ina *mf*, danzante *mf*

dancercise [dǽnsɚsaɪz] N baile aeróbico *m*

dandelion [dǽndlaɪən] N diente de león *m*

dandruff [dǽndrəf] N caspa *f*

dandy [dǽndi] N dandi *m*, señorito *m*; ADJ estupendo

Dane [den] N danés -esa *mf*

danger [déndʒɚ] N peligro *m*

dangerous [déndʒɚəs] ADJ peligroso

dangle [dǽŋgəl] VI/VT (hang) colgar; (sway) bambolear[se]; **her legs were dangling off the bench** sus piernas pendían del banco

Danish [dénɪʃ] ADJ danés; N bollo dulce *m*

dare [der] VI/VT (be brave) atreverse [a], osar; (challenge) desafiar; **how — you?** ¿cómo te atreves? N desafío *m*; **—devil** temerario -ria *mf*

daring [dérɪŋ] N atrevimiento *m*, osadía *f*; ADJ atrevido, osado, arriesgado

dark [dɑrk] ADJ (in color) oscuro; (of hair) moreno, morocho, trigueño; (gloomy) sombrío, tenebroso; (evil, ignorant) oscuro; (shameful) turbio; **— Ages** [Alta] Edad Media *f*; **—room** cuarto oscuro *m*; **—-skinned** moreno; N oscuridad *f*; **after —** después de que oscurece

darken [dárkən] VI/VT oscurecer

darkness [dárknɪs] N (complete) oscuridad *f*, tinieblas *f pl*; (partial) penumbra *f*

darling [dárlɪŋ] ADJ & N amado -da *mf*, querido -da *mf*; **my —** vida mía, amor mío

darn [dɑrn] VT zurcir, remendar; **—ing needle** aguja de zurcir *f*; N zurcido *m*; **it is not worth a —** no vale un comino; INTERJ ¡caramba! ¡caracoles!

dart [dɑrt] N (missile) dardo *m*; (tuck) pinza *f*; (swift movement) movimiento rápido *m*; **—board** diana *f*; **to play —s** jugar a los dardos; VI disparar; **to — out** salir disparado

dash [dæʃ] VI/VT (of waves, porcelain) estrellar[se]; VT (plans) frustrar; VI (hopes) desplomarse; **to — by** pasar corriendo; **to — off/out** salir disparado; **to — off a letter** escribir de prisa una carta; N (line) raya *f*; (run) corrida *f*; (race) carrera *f*; (small amount) pizca *f*; (splash) salpicadura *f*; **the one-hundred-meter —** la carrera de los cien metros llanos/planos; **—board** tablero *m*, salpicadero *m*

data [détə, dǽtə] N datos *m pl*; **—base** base de datos *f*; **—bank** banco de datos *m*; **— encryption** cifrado de datos *m*; **— file** archivo de datos *m*; **— input** entrada de datos *f*; **— management** gestión de datos *f*; **— processing** procesamiento de datos *m*, fichero de datos *m*; **— recovery** recuperación de datos *f*; **— storage** almacenamiento de datos *m*

date [det] N (time) fecha *f*; (appointment) cita *f*; (person) acompañante *mf*; (fruit) dátil *m*; **— due** fecha de vencimiento *f*; **out of —** anticuado; **to —** hasta ahora; **up to —** al día; VI (be dated) estar fechado; (go out socially) salir; VT (write the date) fechar; (show to be old-fashioned) delatar la edad; (go out socially) salir con; **to — from** datar de, remontarse a

dated [dédɪd] ADJ (having a date) fechado; (old-fashioned) anticuado

daub [dɔb] VT (smear) embarrar, embadurnar; (apply unskillfully) pintarrajear

daughter [dɔ́dɚ] N hija *f*; **—-in-law** nuera *f*

daunt [dɔnt] VT (intimidate) intimidar; (dishearten) desanimar

dauntless [dɔ́ntlɪs] ADJ intrépido

davenport [dǽvənpɔrt] N sofá grande *m*

dawn [dɔn] N alba *f*, amanecer *m*, aurora *f*; **the — of civilization** los albores de la civilización; VI amanecer, aclarar; **it just —ed on me that** caí en [la] cuenta de que

day [de] N día *m*; **— after tomorrow** pasado mañana *m*; **— before yesterday** anteayer *m*; **—break** amanecer *m*; **at —break** al amanecer; **—care** guardería *f*; **—dream** fantasía *f*; **— laborer** jornalero -ra *mf*;

—light luz del día f; **—light saving time** adelanto de la hora en verano m; **—time** día m; **—time activity** actividad diurna f; **—-to-** día a día; **by —** de día; **by the —** por día; **eight-hour —** jornada de ocho horas f; **in my —** en mis tiempos; **in the old —s** antaño; **make my —** dame el gusto; **New Year's —** Año Nuevo m; ADJ diurno; VI **to —dream** soñar despierto

daze [dez] VT aturdir; N **to be in a —** estar aturdido

dazzle [dǽzəl] VI/VT deslumbrar

deacidify [diəsídɪfaɪ] VT neutralizar la acidez

deacon [díkən] N diácono m

deactivate [diǽktɪvet] VI/VT desactivar

deactivation [diæktɪvéʃən] N desactivación f

dead [dɛd] ADJ muerto; **he's a — duck** está muerto; **—-end job** puesto sin perspectivas m; **— sure** completamente seguro; **— tired** muerto de cansancio; N **— air** aire viciado m; **—beat** moroso -sa mf; **—bolt** pestillo m; **— end** callejón sin salida m; **— letter** letra muerta f; **—line** fecha límite f; **— link** enlace muerto m; **—lock** punto muerto m; **—pan** de palo; **— ringer** fiel retrato m; **—wood** (person) persona inútil f; (thing) cosa inútil f; **the —** los muertos; **in the — of the night** en el silencio de la noche; **in the — of winter** en pleno invierno; VI **to —lock** trancarse

deaden [dédn] VT amortiguar

deadly [dédli] ADJ (enemy) mortal; (poison) letal; (weapon) mortífero; ADV mortalmente; **— dull** sumamente aburrido

deaf [dɛf] ADJ sordo; **—-mute** ADJ & N sordomudo -da mf

deafen [défən] VT (make deaf) ensordecer; (deaden) amortiguar

deafening [défənɪŋ] ADJ ensordecedor, atronador

deafness [défnɪs] N sordera f

deal [diɫ] VT (cards) dar, repartir; (drugs) vender; (a blow) dar, asestar; **to — in** comerciar en; **biology —s with the study of life** la biología se ocupa del estudio de la vida; **I have to — with all kinds of people** tengo que vérmelas con todo tipo de gente; N (business transaction) trato m, negocio m; (shady transaction) componenda f; (act of dealing cards) reparto m; **a great — of** una gran cantidad de; **it's a —** ¡trato hecho! **I got a raw —** me clavaron

dealer [dílə] N (in cars, antiques) comerciante mf; (in drugs, arms) traficante mf; (of cards) el/la que reparte mf

dealership [díləʃɪp] N concesionario m

dealings [díliŋz] N trato m, relaciones f pl; (business) negocios m pl

dealt [dɛɫt] see deal

dean [din] N (of university, professional group) decano -na mf; (in church) deán m

dear [dir] ADJ (beloved) querido; (expensive) caro; (cherished) apreciado; **— Sir/Madam** Estimado señor / Estimada señora; **my —est wish** mi deseo más ferviente; N **he's such a —!** ¡es un amor! **my —** querido mío m / querida mía f; ADV caro; **that cost me —** eso me costó caro; **— me!** ¡Dios mío! **oh — !** ¡Dios mío!

dearth [dɝθ] N escasez f

death [dɛθ] N muerte f; **—bed** lecho de muerte m; **— benefits** beneficios por fallecimiento m; **— certificate** partida de defunción f; **— penalty** pena de muerte f; **— rate** tasa de mortalidad f; **— row** pabellón de los condenados a muerte m; **he's on — row** está condenado a muerte; **— squad** escuadrón de la muerte m; **— toll** mortandad f; **—trap** trampa mortal f; **— wish** instinto suicida m; **to put to —** ejecutar; **we have discussed this to —** hemos discutido esto hasta el hartazgo; **I'm sick to — of this job** estoy harto de este trabajo

debacle [dɪbákəl] N debacle f

debase [dɪbés] VT degradar, envilecer

debatable [dɪbébəbəl] ADJ discutible

debate [dɪbét] N debate m; VI/VT (discuss) debatir, discutir; (weigh a decision) considerar

debilitate [dɪbílɪtet] VT debilitar

debilitating [dɪbílɪtepɪŋ] ADJ debilitante

debit [débɪt] N débito m, adeudo m; (column in an account) debe m; (total sum owed) pasivo m; **— card** tarjeta de débito f; VT adeudar; **to — an account** adeudar una cuenta

debriefing [dɪbrifɪŋ] N informe m

debris [dəbrí] N (ruins) escombros m pl; (detritus) detritus m [pl]

debt [det] N deuda f; **— relief** alivio de la deuda m; **bad —** cuenta incobrable f; **to get into —** endeudarse; ADJ **—-ridden** sobreendeudado

debtor [détə] N deudor -ora mf

debug [dibág] VT depurar

debugger [dibágə] N depurador m

debugging [dibágɪŋ] N depuración f

debunk [dibáŋk] VT (ideas, beliefs) desacreditar; (myths) desmitificar

debut [debjú] N (of a play or film) estreno m; (in society) presentación en sociedad f; **to make a —** (an actor) debutar; (in society) presentarse en sociedad; VI/VT (a film) estrenar[se]; (a product) lanzar[se] al mercado

decade [déked] N década f, decenio m

decadence [dékədəns] N decadencia f

decadent [dékədənt] ADJ decadente

decaffeinated [dɪkǽfɪnepɪd] ADJ descafeinado

decal [díkæl] N calcomanía f, autoadhesivo m

decalcification [dɪkælsɪfɪkéʃən] N

descalcificación f

decanter [dikǽntə] N garrafa f

decapitate [dikǽpitet] VT decapitar

decathlon [dikǽθlɑn] N decatlón m

decay [dikéʔ] VI/VT (biological matter) descomponer[se]; (teeth) cariar[se]; VI (health) deteriorarse; (radioactive matter) desintegrarse; N (moral) decadencia f; (biological) descomposición f; (nuclear) desintegración f; (tooth) caries f

decayed [dikéd] ADJ (flesh) putrefacto; (tooth) cariado

decease [disís] N muerte f, fallecimiento m; VI morir, fallecer

deceased [disíst] ADJ & N difunto -ta mf

deceit [disít] N engaño m, trampa f

deceitful [disítfəl] ADJ tramposo, engañoso

deceive [disív] VI/VT engañar

decelerate [disǽləret] VI desacelerar

December [disémbə] N diciembre m

decency [dísənsi] N decencia f

decent [dísənt] ADJ decente

decentralization [disentrəlizéʃən] N descentralización f

deception [disépʃən] N engaño m

deceptive [diséptɪv] ADJ engañoso; — **practice** práctica comercial desleal f

decibel [désəbəl] N decibelio m

decide [disáɪd] VT (make a decision) decidir; (award victory) fallar; **what —d you to come?** ¿qué te motivó a venir?

decided [disáɪdɪd] ADJ (resolute) decidido; (clear) claro

deciduous [disídʒuəs] ADJ deciduo, caduco; — **tooth** diente de la primera dentición m

decimal [désəməl] ADJ decimal

decimate [désəmet] VT diezmar

decipher [disáɪfə] VT descifrar

decision [disíʒən] N decisión f; (in court) fallo m

decisive [disáɪsɪv] ADJ decisivo

deck [dɛk] N (of a boat) cubierta f; (of a house) terraza f; (of playing cards) baraja f; **hit the —!** ¡cuerpo a tierra! VT (knock down) tumbar; (decorate) decorar; **to — oneself out** emperifollarse

declaration [dekləréʃən] N declaración f, pronunciamiento m

declare [diklér] VI/VT declarar, afirmar

decline [dikláɪn] N (deterioration) decadencia f; (slope) declive m; (reduction in prices) baja f; VI/VT declinar; (an offer) rechazar; **to — to do something** negarse a hacer algo

decode [dikód] VT descodificar

decompose [dikəmpóz] VT/VI descomponer[se]

decompress [dikəmprés] VT descomprimir

decongest [dikəndʒést] VT descongestionar

decongestant [dikəndʒéstənt] N descongestionante m

decontaminate [dikəntǽminet] VT

descontaminar

decontamination [dikəntæminéʃən] N descontaminación f

decorate [dékəret] VT decorar; (award medals) condecorar

decoration [dekəréʃən] N (embellishment) adorno m; (interior decorating) decoración f; (medal of honor) condecoración f

decorative [dékəɔDɪv] ADJ decorativo

decorous [dékəəs] ADJ decoroso

decorum [dikórəm] N decoro m

decoy [díkɔɪ] N (artifact) señuelo m, reclamo m; (live animal or person) cimbel m; VT atraer con señuelo/cimbel

decrease[1] [díkris] N disminución f, merma f

decrease[2] [dikrís] VI/VT disminuir, mermar

decree [dikrí] N decreto m; VI/VT decretar

decrepit [dikrépit] ADJ decrépito

decrepitude [dikrépitud] N decrepitud f

decry [dikráɪ] VT condenar

decrypt [dikrípt] VT descifrar

decryption [dikrípʃən] N descifrado m, descodificación f

dedicate [déDɪket] VI/VT dedicar[se]; VT (a highway) inaugurar

dedication [deDɪkéʃən] N (act of dedicating) dedicación f; (in a book) dedicatoria f; (of a highway, etc.) inauguración f

deduce [didús] VT deducir

deduct [didʌkt] VT deducir

deductible [didʌktəbəl] ADJ deducible, desgravable; N deducible m

deduction [didʌkʃən] N deducción f

deed [did] N (action) acción f; (exploit) hazaña f; (certificate of ownership) escritura f

deem [dim] VT considerar

deep [dip] ADJ (extending down) hondo, profundo; (dark) oscuro; (of a voice) grave; — **in debt** cargado de deudas; — **in thought** absorto; —-**sea** de altura; **he's got — pockets** es un ricachón; **he went off the — end with his hobby** se le fue la mano con el pasatiempo; **she went — into the woods** se adentró en el bosque; **ten meters —** de diez metros de profundidad; **— freeze** congelador m; **the —** el piélago, el abismo; ADV **to dive —** bucear en las profundidades; VT **deep-six** hacer desaparecer

deepen [dípən] VI/VT ahondar, profundizar

deer [dir] N ciervo m, venado m; —**skin** gamuza f

deface [dɪfés] VT (disfigure) desfigurar; (smear with paint) pintarrajear; (mutilate) mutilar

defame [dɪfém] VT difamar

default [dɪfɔ́lt] N (negligence) negligencia f; (failure to pay) incumplimiento m; (failure to appear in court) rebeldía f; (computer setting) opción por defecto f; **in —** en mora; **by —** por defecto, por omisión; (in sports) por abandono de los contrincantes; VI (on a loan) incumplir, no pagar; (in a sports match) no comparecer

defeat [dɪfít] vт vencer, derrotar; N derrota f

defecate [défɪket] vi defecar, evacuar

defect[1] [dífekt] N defecto m

defect[2] [dɪfékt] vi desertar

defection [dɪfékʃən] N defección f

defective [dɪféktɪv] ADJ defectuoso

defend [dɪfénd] vi/vт defender

defendant [dɪféndənt] N (criminal) acusado -da mf, reo -a mf; (civil) demandado -da mf

defender [dɪféndə·] N defensor -ora mf; (sports) defensa mf

defense [dɪféns] N defensa f

defenseless [dɪfénslɪs] ADJ indefenso

defensible [dɪfénsəbəl] ADJ defendible

defensive [dɪfénsɪv] ADJ defensivo; — **medicine** medicina defensiva f; N **on the —** a la defensiva

defer [dɪfə́·] vт (a meeting) diferir, posponer; (a payment) prorrogar; (an appointment) dilatar; (from military service) eximir; **to — to another's opinion** remitirse a la opinión de otro

deference [défə·əns] N deferencia f

deferral [dɪfə́·əl] N aplazamiento m

defiance [dɪfáɪəns] N (challenge) desafío m; (resistance to authority) rebeldía f; **in —** of en abierta oposición a

defiant [dɪfáɪənt] ADJ desafiante

defibrillate [dɪfíbrəlet] vт desfibrilar

defibrillation [dɪfíbrɪléʃən] N desfibrilación f

defibrillator [dɪfíbrɪledə·] N desfibrilador m

deficiency [dɪfíʃənsi] N deficiencia f

deficient [dɪfíʃənt] ADJ deficiente

deficit [défɪsɪt] N déficit m; — **spending** gastos deficitarios m pl

defile [dɪfáɪl] vт (violate) mancillar; (desecrate) profanar; (to make dirty) ensuciar

define [dɪfáɪn] vi/vт definir

defining [dɪfáɪnɪŋ] ADJ decisivo

definite [défənɪt] ADJ (clearly defined) definido, determinado; (certain) seguro; **she was — in her demands** ella fue terminante es sus exigencias; **— article** artículo definido m

definitely [défənɪtli] ADV sin duda, definitivamente

definition [defəníʃən] N definición f

definitive [dɪfíníDɪv] ADJ (final) definitivo; (authoritative) de mayor autoridad

deflate [dɪflét] vт desinflar[se]

deflation [dɪfléʃən] N deflación f

deflect [dɪflékt] vi/vт desviar[se]

deforestation [dɪfɔrɪstéʃən] N deforestación f

deform [dɪfɔrm] vi/vт deformar[se]

deformed [dɪfɔrmd] ADJ deforme

deformity [dɪfɔrmɪDi] N (body part) deformidad f; (act or result of deforming) deformación f

defraud [dɪfrɔd] vт defraudar

defray [dɪfré] vт sufragar, costear

defrost [dɪfrɔ́st] vi/vт descongelar[se]

deft [dɛft] ADJ diestro, habilidoso

defunct [dɪfʌ́ŋkt] ADJ caduco; **the Whig party is now —** el partido de los whigs se disolvió

defuse [difjúz] vт (bomb) desactivar; (situation) distender

defy [dɪfáɪ] vт (challenge) desafiar; (resist) resistir

degenerate[1] [dɪdʒénəɪt] ADJ & N degenerado -da mf

degenerate[2] [dɪdʒénəret] vi degenerar[se]

degenerative [dɪdʒénəɪətɪv] ADJ degenerativo; **— joint disease** artrosis f, enfermedad degenerativa articular f

degradation [dɛgrədéʃən] N degradación f

degrade [dɪgréd] vi/vт degradar[se]

degree [dɪgrí] N (stage) grado m; (academic) título m; **by —s** gradualmente; **to a —** hasta cierto punto; **to get a —** graduarse

dehumanize [dihjúmənaɪz] vi/vт deshumanizar

dehumidifier [dihjumíDɪfaɪə·] N deshumidificador m

dehydrate [dihádret] vi/vт deshidratar[se]

deign [den] vi dignarse

deity [díiDi] N deidad f

déjà vu [deʒavú] N deja vu m

dejected [dɪdʒéktɪd] ADJ abatido, desconsolado

dejection [dɪdʒékʃən] N abatimiento m, desconsuelo m

delay [dɪlé] N demora f, retraso m; vт demorar, retrasar; vi demorar, retrasarse

delectable [dɪléktəbəl] ADJ delicioso; N delicia f

delegate[1] [déligɪt] N delegado -da mf

delegate[2] [déliget] vт delegar

delegation [deligéʃən] N delegación f, representación f

delete [dɪlít] vт (omit) suprimir; (cross out) tachar; **— key** tecla de borrado f

deleterious [delɪtíriəs] ADJ nocivo

deletion [dɪlíʃən] N supresión f

deliberate[1] [dɪlíbə·ɪt] ADJ (intentional) deliberado; (careful) cuidadoso

deliberate[2] [dɪlíbə·et] vi/vт deliberar

deliberately [dɪlíbə·ɪtli] ADV a propósito, deliberadamente

deliberation [dɪlíbə·éʃən] N deliberación f

delicacy [délɪkəsi] N (fineness, precision, sensitivity) delicadeza f; (food) manjar m, delicatessen f pl, golleria f; (breakability) fragilidad f

delicate [délɪkɪt] ADJ delicado, tenue; (breakable) frágil; (acute) fino

delicatessen [delɪkətésən] N (store) tienda de fiambres f, charcutería f; RP rotisería f; (foods) delicatessen f pl

delicious [dɪlíʃəs] ADJ delicioso, rico

delight [dɪláɪt] N (pleasure) deleite m, regalo m;

(source of pleasure) delicia *f*; VT/VT deleitar[se]

delighted [dɪláɪɪd] ADJ encantado; **to be — to** alegrarse de; **I'm — to meet you** me alegro de conocerla; **I'd be — to dance with you** me encantaría bailar contigo

delightful [dɪláɪtfəl] ADJ encantador

delimit [dɪlímɪt] VT delimitar

delineate [dɪlíniet] VT delinear

delinquent [dɪlíŋkwənt] ADJ & N (debtor) moroso -sa *mf*; (wrongdoer) delincuente *mf*; (juvenile) delincuente juvenil *mf*

delirious [dɪlíriəs] ADJ (hysterical) delirante; (happy) contentísimo; **to be —** delirar

delirium [dɪlíriəm] N delirio *m*

deliver [dɪlívɚ] VT (hand over) entregar; (hand out) repartir; (liberate) liberar; (pronounce a speech) pronunciar; (administer a blow) dar; (have a baby) dar a luz; (assist a birth) atender en un parto; **to — the goods** cumplir con lo prometido

deliverance [dɪlívɚəns] N liberación *f*

delivery [dɪlívəri] N (handing out) entrega *f*, expedición *f*; (things to be delivered) pedido *m*; (birth) parto *m*; (speaking) ejecución *f*, expresión oral *f*; **on —** a la entrega; **— service** servicio de entrega *m*; **— truck** camión de reparto *m*; **to take —** aceptar entrega

dell [dɛl] N hondonada *f*

deltoids [délt3ɪdz] N deltoides *m sg*

delude [dɪlúd] VT engañar

deluge [déljudʒ] N diluvio *m*; VT abrumar

delusion [dɪlúʒən] N (act of deluding, state of being deluded) engaño *m*; **—s of grandeur** delirios de grandeza *m pl*

deluxe [dɪláks] ADJ de lujo

demagogue, demagog [déməgag] N demagogo -ga *mf*

demand [dɪmǽnd] VT (ask for) exigir; (require) requerir, exigir; N exigencia *f*, reivindicación *f*; **on —** por demanda

demanding [dɪmǽndɪŋ] ADJ exigente

demarcate [dɪmárket] VT demarcar

demean [dɪmín] VT menospreciar

demeanor [dɪmínɚ] N conducta *f*, comportamiento *m*

demented [dɪméntɪd] ADJ demente

dementia [dɪménʃə] N demencia *f*

demijohn [démidʒan] N damajuana *f*

demise [dɪmáɪz] N fallecimiento *m*, desaparición *f*

demo [démo] N demostración *f*

demobilize [dimóbəlaɪz] VT desmovilizar

democracy [dɪmákrəsi] N democracia *f*

democrat [déməkræt] N demócrata *mf*

democratic [deməkrǽdɪk] ADJ democrático

democratization [dɪmakrədɪzéʃən] N democratización *f*

demographics [deməgrǽfɪks] N demografía *f*

demolish [dɪmálɪʃ] VT demoler, derrumbar

demon [dímən] N demonio *m*

demonstrate [démənstret] VT (prove) demostrar; (show a product) hacer una demostración; VI manifestar

demonstration [demənstréʃən] N (proof, exhibition) demostración *f*; (protest) manifestación *f*, concentración *f*

demonstrative [dɪmánstrəɪv] ADJ demostrativo

demonstrator [démənstredɚ] N manifestante *mf*

demoralize [dɪmɔ́rəlaɪz] VT desmoralizar

demote [dɪmót] VT degradar, bajar de categoría

den [dɛn] N (of an animal) guarida *f*; (room in a house) cuarto de estar *m*; (cave) cueva *f*; **— of iniquity** antro de perdición *m*

dengue fever [déŋgi fívɚ] N dengue *m*

denial [dɪnáɪəl] N (assertion that an allegation is false) desmentido *m*; (refusal to approve) denegación *f*, negativa *f*; (refusal to recognize) negación *f*; **he is in —** no lo quiere aceptar

denigrate [dénɪgret] VT denigrar

denim [dénɪm] N tela de vaquero *f*

Denmark [dénmark] N Dinamarca *f*

denomination [dɪnɑmənéʃən] N (name, monetary value) denominación *f*; (sect) secta religiosa *f*

denominator [dɪnámɪnedɚ] N denominador *m*

denotation [dinotéʃən] N denotación *f*

denote [dɪnót] VT denotar

denounce [dɪnáʊns] VT denunciar

dense [dɛns] ADJ (compacted) denso, tupido, cerrado; (stupid) *fam* burro, duro de entenderas

density [dénsɪɪ] N densidad *f*

dent [dɛnt] N abolladura *f*; **to make a — in a task** hacer mella en una tarea; VI/VT abollar[se]

dental [déntl] ADJ dental; **— care** cuidado dental *m*; **— floss** hilo dental *m*; **— hygienist** higienista dental *mf*; **— implant** implante dental *m*; **— plaque** placa dental *f*; **— school** facultad de odontología *f*

dentifrice [déntəfrɪs] N dentífrico *m*, pasta dental *f*

dentist [déntɪst] N dentista *mf*

dentistry [déntɪstri] N odontología *f*

dentures [déntʃɚz] N dientes postizos *m pl*

denunciation [dɪnʌnsiéʃən] N denuncia *f*, acusación *f*

deny [dɪnáɪ] VT (state that something is false) negar, desmentir; (refuse to approve) rechazar; **to — oneself** abstenerse

deodorant [dióDəənt] N desodorante *m*

deodorize [dióDəraɪz] VT desodorizar

deoxidize [diáksɪdaɪz] VT desoxidar

depart [dɪpárt] VI (leave) salir, partir; (deviate)

desviarse, apartarse; (die) fallecer, dejar de existir

departed [dɪpárDɪd] ADJ & N difunto -ta *mf*

department [dɪpártmənt] N (of company, school, country) departamento *m*; (of government) ministerio *m*; (of a store) sección *f*; (of knowledge, expertise) especialidad *f*; **— head** jefe -fa de departamento *mf*; **— store** gran almacén *m*

departure [dɪpártʃə] N (scheduled) salida *f*; (not scheduled) partida *f*; (deviation) desviación *f*

depend [dɪpénd] VI depender; **to — on** (rely on) contar con; (be conditioned by) depender de; **—ing on the number of guests** dependiendo de la cantidad de invitados

dependable [dɪpéndəbəl] ADJ confiable, fiable

dependence [dɪpéndəns] N dependencia *f*

dependency [dɪpéndənsi] N dependencia *f*

dependent [dɪpéndənt] ADJ dependiente; **success is — on perseverance** el éxito depende de la perseverancia; N familiar a cargo *mf*

depict [dɪpíkt] VT (verbally) describir; (visually) representar

depilate [dépəlet] VT depilar[se]

depilatory [dɪpílətɔri] ADJ & N depilatorio *m*

deplane [diplén] VI desembarcar

deplete [dɪplít] VT agotar

depletion [dɪplíʃən] N agotamiento *m*

deplorable [dɪplɔ́rəbəl] ADJ deplorable

deplore [dɪplɔ́r] VT deplorar

deploy [dɪplɔ́ɪ] VT desplegar

deport [dɪpɔ́rt] VT deportar; VI comportarse

deportment [dɪpɔ́rtmənt] N comportamiento *m*, conducta *f*

depose [dɪpóz] VT (overthrow) deponer, derrocar; (testify) declarar; (take testimony) tomar declaración

deposit [dɪpázɪt] VT (add to an account) depositar; *Sp* ingresar; (place) colocar; N (amount added to an account) depósito *m*; *Sp* ingreso *m*; (of a mineral) yacimiento *m*; (earnest money) señal *f*, anticipo *m*; **— slip** hoja de depósito *f*

deposition [depəzíʃən] N (removal from office) deposición *f*; (testimony) declaración *f*

depositor [dɪpázɪDə] N depositante *mf*

depot [dípo] N (of trains) estación *f*; (of buses) terminal *mf*; (for storage) almacén *m*, depósito *m*; (for military training) cuartel *m*

depraved [dɪprévd] ADJ depravado

deprecate [déprɪket] VT despreciar

depreciate [dɪpríʃiet] VT (currency) depreciar[se]; (goods) desvalorizar[se], amortizar[se]

depreciation [dɪpriʃiéʃən] N (of currency) depreciación *f*; (of goods) amortización *f*

depress [dɪprés] VT deprimir

depressed [dɪprést] ADJ deprimido

depressing [dɪprésɪŋ] ADJ deprimente

depression [dɪpréʃən] N depresión *f*

deprive [dɪpráɪv] VT privar

depth [dɛpθ] N (of hole, feeling) profundidad *f*, hondura *f*; (of the voice) gravedad *f*; **in the —s** en las profundidades; **in —** a fondo; **what is the — of that bookshelf?** ¿cuánto miden estos estantes de fondo? **he has sunk to such —s** ha caído muy bajo; **in the — of the night** bien entrada la noche; **in the — of winter** en lo más crudo del invierno

deputation [depjətéʃən] N delegación *f*

deputy [dépjəti] N (elected official) diputado -da *mf*; (substitute) suplente *mf*

derail [dɪrél] VI/VT descarrilar[se]

deranged [dɪréndʒd] ADJ trastornado, demente

derby [dɚbi] N (hat) sombrero hongo *m*; (race) derby *m*

deregulate [dɪrégjəlet] VT desregular

derelict [dérəlɪkt] ADJ (deserted) abandonado; (negligent) negligente; N (ship) buque abandonado *m*; (person) vagabundo -da *mf*

dereliction [derəlíkʃən] N **— of duties** abandono de funciones *m*

deride [dɪráɪd] VT escarnecer, ridiculizar

derision [dɪríʒən] N escarnio *m*

derivation [derəvéʃən] N derivación *f*

derivative [dɪrívəDɪv] ADJ & N derivado *m*

derive [dɪráɪv] VI/VT derivar[se]; **to — pleasure from** disfrutar de

dermabrasion [dɚ́məbreʒən] N abrasión cutánea *f*, dermabrasión *f*

dermatologist [dɚmətáləʤɪst] N dermatólogo -ga *mf*

dermatology [dɚmətáləʤi] N dermatología *f*

derogatory [dɪrágətɔri] ADJ despectivo

derrick [dérɪk] N torre de perforación *f*

descend [dɪsénd] VI/VT descender; **—ing sort** clasificación descendiente *f*; **to — upon** caer sobre

descendant [dɪséndənt] ADJ & N descendiente *mf*

descent [dɪsént] N (act of descending, decline) descenso *m*; (slope) bajada *f*; (lineage) descendencia *f*

describe [dɪskráɪb] VT describir

description [dɪskrípʃən] N descripción *f*, caracterización *f*; **of all —s** de todas clases

descriptive [dɪskríptɪv] ADJ descriptivo

desecrate [désɪkret] VT profanar

desecration [desɪkréʃən] N profanación *f*

desegregate [diségrɪget] VI/VT eliminar la segregación racial

deselect [disilékt] VT anular [una selección previa]

desensitize [disénsɪtaɪz] VT insensibilizar

desert[1] [dézɚt] ADJ (barren, empty) desierto; (of the desert) desértico; N desierto *m*

desert[2] [dɪzɚ́t] VI/VT (a person, place)

abandonar; (military service) desertar

deserter [dɪzɜ́ːdə] N desertor -ora *mf*

desertion [dɪzɜ́ːʃən] N (of a person or place) abandono *m*; (from the military) deserción *f*

deserve [dɪzɜ́ːv] VT merecer

deserving [dɪzɜ́ːvɪŋ] ADJ merecedor

desiccate [dɛ́sɪket] VI/VT desecar[se]

design [dɪzáɪn] VI/VT (prepare a sketch of) diseñar, trazar; (plan) planear, idear; N (model, pattern) diseño *m*; (sketch) esbozo *m*; **he has —s on her** le ha echado el ojo

designate [dɛ́zɪgnet] VT designar, denominar; **—d hitter** bateador -ora designado -da *mf*

designation [dɛzɪgnéʃən] N denominación *f*, designación *f*

designer [dɪzáɪnə] N diseñador -ora *mf*; **— drugs** drogas de diseño *f pl*

desirability [dɪzaɪrəbílɪDi] N deseabilidad *f*, conveniencia *f*

desirable [dɪzáɪrəbəl] ADJ deseable

desire [dɪzáɪr] VT desear; **I — your cooperation** requiero tu cooperación; N deseo *m*

desirous [dɪzáɪrəs] ADJ deseoso

desist [dɪsíst] VI desistir

desk [dɛsk] N escritorio *m*; (school) pupitre *m*; **—top computer** *Am* computadora de escritorio *f*, *Sp* ordenador de sobremesa *m*; **—top publishing** edición de sobremesa *f*, autoedición *f*

desolate¹ [dɛ́səlɪt] ADJ (barren) desolado

desolate² [dɛ́səlet] VT desolar, asolar

desolation [dɛsəléʃən] N desolación *f*, asolamiento *m*

despair [dɪspɛ́r] N desesperanza *f*; VI desesperarse, perder la esperanza

despairing [dɪspɛ́rɪŋ] ADJ de desesperación

desperate [dɛ́spərɪt] ADJ desesperado

desperately [dɛ́spərɪtli] ADV desesperadamente; **— ill** gravemente enfermo; **he's — looking for funds** está desesperado buscando financiación

desperation [dɛspəréʃən] N desesperación *f*

despicable [dɪspíkəbəl] ADJ despreciable, deleznable

despise [dɪspáɪz] VT despreciar, menospreciar

despite [dɪspáɪt] N despecho *m*; PREP a pesar de

despoil [dɪspɔ́ɪl] VT despojar

despondency [dɪspándənsi] N abatimiento *m*, desaliento *m*

despondent [dɪspándənt] ADJ abatido, desalentado

despot [dɛ́spət] N déspota *mf*

despotic [dɪspádɪk] ADJ despótico

despotism [dɛ́spətɪzəm] N despotismo *m*

dessert [dɪzɜ́ːt] N postre *m*

destabilize [distébəlaɪz] VT desestabilizar

destination [dɛstənéʃən] N destino *m*

destine [dɛ́stɪn] VT destinar; **she's —d for**

greatness promete grandes cosas

destiny [dɛ́stəni] N destino *m*

destitute [dɛ́stɪtut] ADJ menesteroso, indigente; **— of** falto de, desprovisto de

destroy [dɪstrɔ́ɪ] VT (demolish) destruir, deshacer; (kill an animal) sacrificar; (ruin a reputation) arruinar

destroyer [dɪstrɔ́ɪə] N (person who destroys) destructor -ora *mf*; (ship) destructor *m*

destructible [dɪstráktəbəl] ADJ destructible

destruction [dɪstrákʃən] N (act of demolishing) destrucción *f*; (act of killing) matanza *f*; (act of ruining a reputation) ruina *f*

destructive [dɪstráktɪv] ADJ destructivo, destructor

detach [dɪtǽtʃ] VT separar, desprender; (troops) destacar

detachment [dɪtǽtʃmənt] N (physical) separación *f*; (emotional) desapego *m*; (of troops) destacamento *m*; (of the retina) desprendimiento *m*

detail¹ [dítel] N detalle *m*, pormenor *m*; (military) destacamento *m*; **to go into —** detallar, pormenorizar

detail² [dítel] VT detallar, pormenorizar; (assign duties) destacar

detain [dɪtén] VT detener

detect [dɪtɛ́kt] VT detectar

detection [dɪtɛ́kʃən] N detección *f*

detective [dɪtɛ́ktɪv] N detective *mf*; **— novel** novela policial *f*

detector [dɪtɛ́ktə] N detector *m*

detention [dɪtɛ́nʃən] N (in jail) detención *f*; (in school) castigo *m*

deter [dɪtɜ́ː] VT (dissuade) disuadir; (prevent) prevenir

detergent [dɪtɜ́ːdʒənt] N detergente *m*

deteriorate [dɪtíriəret] VI deteriorar[se]

deterioration [dɪtiriəréʃən] N deterioro *m*

determination [dɪtɜːmənéʃən] N (act of determining) determinación *f*; (resolution) resolución *f*; (persistence) tesón *m*, perseverancia *f*

determine [dɪtɜ́ːmɪn] VT determinar; **to — to do something** decidirse a hacer algo

determined [dɪtɜ́ːmɪnd] ADJ (resolute) decidido, resuelto; (persistent) tesonero

determiner [dɪtɜ́ːrmɪnə] N (grammatical) determinante *m*

determining [dɪtɜ́ːrmɪnɪŋ] ADJ determinante

detest [dɪtɛ́st] VT detestar, abominar de

detestable [dɪtɛ́stəbəl] ADJ detestable

dethrone [diθrón] VT destronar

detonate [dɛ́tnet] VI/VT detonar

detonation [dɛtnéʃən] N detonación *f*

detour [dítur] N desvío *m*; VI/VT desviar[se]

detoxification [ditaksəfɪkéʃən] N destoxificación *f*

detract [dɪtrǽkt] VT distraer; VI **to — from**

disminuir

detrimental [dɛtrəméntl] ADJ perjudicial

deuce [dus] N (in tennis) deuce *m*, cuarenta iguales

devaluation [divæljuéʃən] N devaluación *f*

devastate [dévəstet] VT devastar, asolar

devastating [dévəsteDɪŋ] ADJ devastador

develop [dɪvéləp] VI/VT (mature, elaborate) desarrollar[se]; (build houses on) construir, edificar; (treat film) revelar; **she—ed an allergy** le vino una alergia; **—ing country** país en desarrollo *m*

developer [dɪvéləpə] N (of computer programs) desarrollador -ora *mf*; (of real estate) promotor -ora *mf*; **a late —** persona de maduración tardía *f*

development [dɪvéləpmənt] N (evolution) desarrollo *m*; (buildings) urbanización *f*, colonia *f*; (of a photograph) revelado *m*

developmental [dɪveləpméntl] ADJ relativo al desarrollo

deviate [díviet] VI/VT desviar[se]

deviation [diviéʃən] N desviación *f*

device [dɪváɪs] N (gadget) dispositivo *m*; (literary convention) recurso *m*; (emblem) divisa *f*; **they left me to my own—s** me dejaron que me las arreglara sola

devil [dévəl] N diablo *m*; **lucky—!** ¡suertudo! **what the—are you saying?** ¿qué diablos dices? **—'s advocate** abogado del diablo *m*

devilish [dévəlɪʃ] ADJ (evil) diabólico; (extreme) endiablado, endemoniado

deviltry [dévəltri] N (mischief) diablura *f*; (witchcraft) brujería *f*

devious [díviəs] ADJ (roundabout) sinuoso, tortuoso; (crafty) taimado, retorcido

devise [dɪváɪz] VT idear, urdir

devoid [dɪvɔ́ɪd] ADJ **—of** falto de, desprovisto de

devolution [dɛvəlúʃən] N devolución *f*

devote [dɪvót] VT dedicar; (consecrate) consagrar

devoted [dɪvóDɪd] ADJ (friend) leal; (parent) dedicado; (worshiper) devoto

devotion [dɪvóʃən] N devoción *f*

devour [dɪváur] VT devorar

devout [dɪváut] ADJ devoto

dew [du] N rocío *m*; **—drop** gota de rocío *f*; **—point** punto de condensación *m*

dexterity [dɛkstérɪDi] N destreza *f*

dextrose [dékstros] N dextrosa *f*

diabetes [daɪəbíDiz] N diabetes *f*

diabolic [daɪəbálɪk] ADJ diabólico

diacritic [daɪəkríDɪk] ADJ & N diacrítico *m*

diagnose [daɪəgnós] VT diagnosticar

diagnosis [daɪəgnósɪs] N diagnóstico *m*, diagnosis *f*

diagnostic [daɪəgnástɪk] ADJ diagnóstico

diagonal [daɪǽgənl] ADJ & N diagonal *f*

diagram [dáɪəgræm] N diagrama *m*

dial [dáɪəl] N (of a watch, clock) esfera *f*; (of

radio) dial *m*; **—tone** *Sp* señal de marcar *f*; *Am* tono de discar *m*; VI/VT (a telephone number) *Sp* marcar; *Am* discar

dialect [dáɪəlɛkt] N dialecto *m*

dialectic [daɪəlɛ́ktɪk] ADJ dialéctico; N dialéctica *f*

dialectology [daɪəlɛktáləʤi] N dialectología *f*

dialogue, dialog [dáɪəlɑg] N diálogo *m*; VI dialogar

dialysis [daɪǽlɪsɪs] N diálisis *f*

diameter [daɪǽmɪDə] N diámetro *m*

diamond [dáɪəmənd] N (stone) diamante *m*; (shape) rombo *m*

diaper [dáɪpə] N pañal *m*; VT poner pañales

diaphragm [dáɪəfræm] N diafragma *m*

diarrhea [daɪəríə] N diarrea *f*

diary [dáɪəri] N diario *m*

diastolic [daɪəstálɪk] ADJ diastólico

diatribe [dáɪətraɪb] N diatriba *f*

dice [daɪs] N PL dados *m pl*; VT cortar en cubos; **no—!** (impossibility) no hay forma, *Am* ¡ni modo! (refusal) de ninguna manera

dichotomy [daɪkátəmi] N dicotomía *f*

dicker [díkə] VI regatear

dictate [díktet] VI/VT dictar; N dictado *m*, precepto *m*

dictation [dɪktéʃən] N dictado *m*; **to take—** escribir al dictado

dictator [díkteDə] N dictador -ora *mf*

dictatorship [dɪktéDəʃɪp] N dictadura *f*

diction [díkʃən] N dicción *f*

dictionary [díkʃəneri] N diccionario *m*

did [dɪd] *see* do

didactic [daɪdǽktɪk] ADJ didáctico

die [daɪ] VI morir[se]; **to—down/away** disminuir; **to—off** irse muriendo; **to—out** morirse, extinguirse; **my car—d** se me murió el coche; N (game piece) dado *m*; (press) molde *m*; (stamp) cuño *m*, troquel *m*; **—hard** intransigente *mf*

diesel [dízəl] N diesel *m*; **—engine** motor diesel *m*

diet [dáɪɪt] N (food) dieta *f*; (controlled intake of food) dieta *f*, régimen *m*; **to be/go on a—** estar a dieta/régimen; **to put on a—** poner a dieta; VI estar a dieta, hacer dieta

dietary [dáɪɪteri] ADJ dietético

dietitian [daɪɪtíʃən] N dietista *mf*

differ [dífə] VI diferir; **to—with** disentir, no estar de acuerdo con; **to—from** ser diferente de

difference [dífəəns] N diferencia *f*; **it makes no—** no importa, da igual

different [dífəənt] ADJ diferente, distinto

differential [dɪfərénʃəl] ADJ & N (difference, car part) diferencial *m*; **—equation** diferencial *f*

differentiate [dɪfərénʃiet] VI/VT diferenciar[se], distinguir[se]

differentiation [dɪfərɛnʃiéʃən] N diferenciación *f*

differently [dífəəntli] ADV de manera

diferente; **they act** — no se comportan igual

difficult [dífikəlt] ADJ difícil

difficulty [dífikʌlti] N dificultad f; **with** — con dificultad, difícilmente

diffident [dífidənt] ADJ tímido

diffuse¹ [dıfjúz] VI/VT difundir

diffuse² [dıfjús] ADJ difuso

diffusion [dıfjúʒən] N difusión f

dig [dıg] VI/VT cavar; (by machine) excavar; (superficially) escarbar; **to — in the files** escarbar en los archivos; **to — under** socavar; **to — up** desenterrar; **he dug his heels into the ground** clavó los talones en el suelo; **I — your new shoes** están muy buenos tus zapatos nuevos; N (archaeological site) excavación f; (sarcastic remark) pulla f; **a — in the ribs** un codazo

digest¹ [dıdʒést] VI/VT digerir

digest² [dáıdʒest] N (summary) compendio m; (legal) digesto m

digestible [dıdʒéstəbəl] ADJ digerible, digestible

digestion [dıdʒéstʃən] N digestión f

digestive [dıdʒéstıv] ADJ digestivo

digit [dídʒıt] N dígito m

digital [dídʒıtl] ADJ digital; **— camera** cámara digital f; **— computer** Am computadora digital f, Sp ordenador digital m; **— photography** fotografía digital f

digitalize [dídʒıdlaız] VT digitalizar

digitize [dídʒıtaız] VT digitalizar

dignified [dígnəfaıd] ADJ digno

dignitary [dígnıteri] N dignatario -ria mf

dignity [dígnıDi] N dignidad f

digress [dıgrés] VI divagar

digression [dıgréʃən] N digresión f

dike [daık] N dique m

dilapidated [dılæpıdeıDıd] ADJ (machine) destartalado; (furniture) desvencijado; (house) derruido, venido abajo

dilate [dáılet] VI/VT dilatar[se]

dilation [daıléʃən] N dilatación f

dilemma [dılémə] N dilema m

dilettante [dílıtant] N diletante mf

diligence [dílədʒəns] N diligencia f

diligent [dílədʒənt] ADJ diligente, hacendoso

dill [dıl] N eneldo m; **— pickle** pepinillo en vinagre con eneldo m

dilute [dılút] VI/VT diluir[se]; ADJ diluido

dim [dım] ADJ (light) tenue; (outline) difuso; (room) oscuro, en penumbras; (person) fam de pocas luces; **—wit** fam tonto, bobo; VI/VT (make less bright) atenuar; VT (switch to low beam) bajar

dime [daım] N moneda de diez centavos f; **unskilled workers are a — a dozen** sobran los obreros no cualificados

dimension [dıménʃən] N dimensión f

diminish [dımínıʃ] VI/VT disminuir, menguar; **the law of —ing returns** la ley de los rendimientos decrecientes

diminution [dımənúʃən] N disminución f, mengua f

diminutive [dımínjətıv] ADJ diminuto; N diminutivo m

dimmer [dímə] N regulador de voltaje m

dimness [dímnıs] N oscuridad f, penumbra f

dimple [dímpəl] N hoyuelo m; VT formar hoyuelos

din [dın] N estruendo m, estrépito m

dine [daın] VI cenar; **to — out** cenar afuera

diner [dáınə] N (restaurant) cafetería f; (on a train) coche comedor m; (person) comensal mf

ding-a-ling [díŋəlıŋ] N (silly person) ganso -sa mf; (eccentric person) excéntrico -ca mf; (sound) tilín m

dingy [díndʒi] ADJ deslucido

dining [dáınıŋ] ADJ **— car** coche comedor m; **— room** comedor m

dinner [dínə] N (main meal) comida f; (at midday) almuerzo m; (in the evening) cena f; **— jacket** smoking m; **—time** hora de la comida f

dinosaur [dáınəsɔr] N dinosaurio m

dint [dınt] ADV LOC **by — of** a fuerza de

dip [dıp] VT (make wet) mojar; (scoop) sacar; (immerse) sumergir; (immerse in insecticide) bañar; (immerse in sauce, coffee) pringar, mojar; VI (sun) hundirse; (stocks) bajar; (road) hacer una bajada; (airplane) descender súbitamente; N (act of wetting) mojada f; (portion of ice-cream) bola f, cucharada f; (sauce) mojo m; (reduction in sales) disminución f; (low place in a road) declive m; (low place in the land) hondonada f; (swim) baño m; (airplane maneuver) descenso rápido m; (irritating person) pej pesado -da mf

diphtheria [dıpθíriə] N difteria f

diphthong [dípθɔŋ] N diptongo m

diploma [dıplómə] N diploma m

diplomacy [dıplóməsi] N diplomacia f

diplomat [dípləmæt] N diplomático -ca mf

diplomatic [dıpləmǽDık] ADJ diplomático

dipper [dípə] N cucharón m, cazo m

dire [daır] ADJ terrible, espantoso; **— need** necesidad f acuciante f; **— predictions** predicciones funestas f pl; **— situation** situación extrema f

direct [dırékt] ADJ directo; **— current** corriente continua f; **— object** complemento directo m; **— quotation** cita textual f; ADV directo, directamente; VI/VT dirigir; **he —ed me to leave** me mandó irme

direction [dırékʃən] N dirección f; **—s** indicaciones f pl; **I'm thinking in that —** me inclino por eso

directive [dıréktıv] ADJ N directiva f

director [dıréktə] N (theater, movies) director

-ra *mf*; (film, TV) realizador -ora *mf*

directory [dɪréktəri] N directorio *m*

dirigible [dərídʒəbəl] ADJ & N dirigible *m*

dirt [dɝt] N (filth) suciedad *f*; (foul substance) mugre *f*; (earth) tierra *f*; **—bag** *offensive* porquería *f*; **I've got some — on him** le conozco los trapos sucios; ADJ **— cheap** baratísimo; **—-poor** pobrísimo

dirty [dɝdi] ADJ sucio, mugriento; **— joke** chiste verde *m*; **— look** mirada asesina *f*; **— money** dinero sucio *m*; **— shame** pena horrible *f*; **— trick** trampa *f*; **— word** palabrota *f*; *Sp* taco *m*; **— work** trabajo sucio *m*; VI/VT ensuciar; ADV **to talk —** decir cosas obscenas

disability [dɪsəbílɪɾi] N (incapacity) discapacidad *f*, minusvalía *f*; **— insurance** seguro de discapacidad *m*

disable [dɪsébəl] VT (person) incapacitar; (device) desactivar

disabled [dɪsébəld] ADJ discapacitado, minusválido

disabuse [dɪsəbjúz] VT desengañar

disadvantage [dɪsɪdvǽntɪdʒ] N desventaja *f*; **to be at a —** estar en desventaja

disadvantaged [dɪsɪdvǽntɪdʒd] ADJ carenciado

disagree [dɪsəgrí] VI (differ in opinion) disentir, no estar de acuerdo; (differ) diferir; **pizza —s with me** no me cae bien la pizza

disagreeable [dɪsəgríəbəl] ADJ desagradable

disagreement [dɪsəgrímənt] N (lack of agreement, argument) desacuerdo *m*; (discrepancy) discrepancia *f*

disallow [dɪsəláu] VT desaprobar; (in sports) anular

disappear [dɪsəpír] VI desaparecer

disappearance [dɪsəpírəns] N desaparición *f*

disappoint [dɪsəpɔ́ɪnt] VI/VT decepcionar, desilusionar; **to be —ed** estar desilusionado

disappointing [dɪsəpɔ́ɪntɪŋ] ADJ decepcionante

disappointment [dɪsəpɔ́ɪntmənt] N decepción *f*, desilusión *f*

disapproval [dɪsəprúvəl] N desaprobación *f*

disapprove [dɪsəprúv] VI/VT desaprobar

disarm [dɪsárm] VI/VT desarmar[se]

disarmament [dɪsárməmənt] N desarme *m*

disarray [dɪsəré] VT desordenar; N confusión *f*, desorden *m*; **in —** en desorden

disaster [dɪzǽstɚ] N desastre *m*

disastrous [dɪzǽstrəs] ADJ desastroso

disavow [dɪsəváu] VT negar

disband [dɪsbǽnd] VT disolver; VI desbandarse

disbelief [dɪsbɪlíf] N incredulidad *f*

disbelieve [dɪsbɪlív] VI/VT descreer

disburse [dɪsbɝs] VT desembolsar

disbursement [dɪsbɝsmənt] N desembolso *m*

discard¹ [dɪskárd] VT (a card) descartar; (garbage) desechar

discard² [dískard] N (card) descarte *m*; (garbage) desecho *m*

discern [dɪsɝn] VT (distinguish mentally) discernir; (perceive) percibir

discernment [dɪsɝnmənt] N discernimiento *m*

discharge¹ [dɪstʃárdʒ] VI/VT (battery, load, firearm) descargar[se]; (obligation) cumplir; (prisoner) poner en libertad, soltar; (odor) despedir; (soldier) dar de baja; (patient) dar de alta; (a debt) pagar; (pus) supurar

discharge² [dístʃardʒ] N (of a battery, load, firearm) descarga *f*; (of an obligation) cumplimiento *m*; (of a prisoner) puesta en libertad *f*; (of an odor) emisión *f*; (of a soldier) baja *f*; (of a patient) alta *f*; (of a debt) pago *m*; (of oil) pérdida *f*; (of pus) supuración *f*; (uterine, vaginal) flujo *m*; (from a job) despido *m*

disciple [dɪsáɪpəl] N discípulo -la *mf*

discipline [dísəplɪn] N disciplina *f*; VT disciplinar

disclaimer [dɪsklémɚ] N descargo de responsabilidad *m*

disclose [dɪsklóz] VT revelar

disco [dísko] N discoteca *f*

discolor [dɪskálɚ] VI/VT decolorar[se]

discomfort [dɪskámfɚt] N malestar *m*

disconcert [dɪskənsɝt] VT desconcertar

disconnect [dɪskənékt] VI/VT desconectar; N desconexión *f*

disconnected [dɪskənéktɪd] ADJ (broken) desconectado; (incoherent) inconexo

disconsolate [dɪskánsəlɪt] ADJ desconsolado

discontent [dɪskəntént] N descontento *m*

discontinue [dɪskəntínju] VT suspender, interrumpir

discontinuous [dɪskəntínjuəs] ADJ discontinuo

discord [dískɔrd] N (lack of concord) discordia *f*, desavenencia *f*; (dissonance) disonancia *f*, discordancia *f*

discotheque [dískotek] N discoteca *f*

discount [dískaunt] VT (deduct from a charge, take into account in advance) descontar; (sell at a reduced price) rebajar; (disregard) ignorar; N descuento *m*; **at a —** con descuento, con rebaja

discourage [dɪskɝɪdʒ] VT desanimar, desalentar; **to — from** disuadir de

discouragement [dɪskɝɪdʒmənt] N desánimo *m*, desaliento *m*

discourse¹ [dískɔrs] N (conversation, talk) discurso *m*; (treatise) disertación *f*

discourse² [dískɔrs] VI (talk) discurrir; (treat a subject) disertar

discourteous [dɪskɝɾiəs] ADJ descortés

discourtesy [dɪskɝɾɪsi] N descortesía *f*

discover [dɪskávɚ] VT descubrir

discoverer [dɪskávɚɚ] N descubridor -ora *mf*

discovery [dɪskávɚri] N descubrimiento *m*

discredit [dɪskrédɪt] VT (injure the reputation of) desacreditar; (give no credence to) no creer; N descrédito *m*

discreet [dɪskrít] ADJ discreto

discrepancy [dɪskrépənsi] N discrepancia *f*

discrete [dɪskrít] ADJ (separate) separado; (en matemáticas) discreto

discretion [dɪskréʃən] N discreción *f*; **at your own —** a discreción; **at the judge's —** al arbitrio del juez

discretionary [dɪskréʃəneri] ADJ discrecional; **— income** ingresos discrecionales *m pl*

discriminate [dɪskrímənet] VI/VT distinguir; **to — against** discriminar a

discrimination [dɪskrɪmɪnéʃən] N discriminación *f*

discuss [dɪskás] VT discutir

discussion [dɪskáʃən] N discusión *f*

disdain [dɪsdén] N desdén *m*, desprecio *m*; VT (treat with contempt) desdeñar; (think unworthy of a response) no dignarse a

disdainful [dɪsdénfəl] ADJ desdeñoso

disease [dɪzíz] N enfermedad *f*

diseased [dɪzízd] ADJ enfermo

disembark [dɪsɪmbárk] VI/VT desembarcar

disenfranchise [dɪsɪnfræntʃaɪz] VT (politician) proscribir; (minorities) privar de derechos, desheredar

disengage [dɪsɪngédʒ] VI/VT (a clutch) soltar[se]; (from a situation) distanciar[se]

disentangle [dɪsɪntǽŋgəl] VI/VT desenredar[se], desenmarañar[se]

disfavor [dɪsfévɚ] VT mirar con malos ojos; N **to fall into —** (a person) caer en desgracia; (a fashion) caer en desuso

disfigure [dɪsfígjɚ] VT desfigurar

disgrace [dɪsgrés] N (dishonor) deshonra *f*; (shame) vergüenza *f*; **to fall into —** caer en desgracia; VT deshonrar

disgraceful [dɪsgrésfəl] ADJ vergonzoso

disgruntled [dɪsgrántəld] ADJ descontento, resentido

disguise [dɪsgáɪz] VT disfrazar[se]; N disfraz *m*

disgust [dɪsgást] VT (repel) asquear, repugnar; (displease) disgustar; N asco *m*, repugnancia *f*

disgusted [dɪsgástɪd] ADJ asqueado, repugnado

disgusting [dɪsgástɪŋ] ADJ asqueroso, repugnante

dish [dɪʃ] N (plate, food, quantity) plato *m*; (serving container) fuente *f*; (attractive person) *fam* bombón *m*; **—es** vajilla *f*; **—cloth/towel** paño de cocina *m*, repasador *m*; **—washer** lavaplatos *m sg*, lavavajillas *m sg*; **—water** agua de fregar *f*; VI/VT (serve food) servir; **to — out** repartir

dishearten [dɪshártn] VT desanimar, descorazonar, desalentar

disheartening [dɪshártnɪŋ] ADJ descorazonador, desalentador

dishevel [dɪʃévəl] VT desgreñar

disheveled [dɪʃévəld] ADJ (hair) desgreñado,

revuelto; (clothes) desaliñado

dishonest [dɪsánɪst] ADJ deshonesto

dishonesty [dɪsánɪsti] N deshonestidad *f*

dishonor [dɪsánɚ] N deshonra *f*; VT deshonrar; (a check) no pagar

dishonorable [dɪsánɚəbəl] ADJ deshonroso

disillusion [dɪsɪlúʒən] N desilusión *f*, desencanto *m*; VT desilusionar, desencantar

disinfect [dɪsɪnfékt] VT desinfectar

disinfectant [dɪsɪnféktənt] N desinfectante *m*

disinfection [dɪsɪnfékʃən] N desinfección *f*

disinfestation [dɪsɪnfestéʃən] N desinfestación *f*

disinformation [dɪsɪnfɚméʃən] N desinformación *f*

disinherit [dɪsɪnhérɪt] VT desheredar

disintegrate [dɪsíntɪgret] VI/VT desintegrar[se]

disintegration [dɪsɪntɪgréʃən] N desintegración *f*

disinterested [dɪsíntrɪstɪd] ADJ desinteresado

disjointed [dɪsdʒɔ́ɪntɪd] ADJ desarticulado

disk, disc [dɪsk] N disco *m*; (game piece) tejo *m*; (in a computer) disco *m*, disquete *m*; **— brake** freno de disco *m*; **— capacity** capacidad de almacenamiento de disco *f*; **— drive** disquetera *f*; **— jockey** pinchadiscos *mf sg*

diskette [dɪskét] N disquete *m*; **— drive** unidad de disquete *f*

dislike [dɪsláɪk] N aversión *f*, tirria *f*; VT **I — parties** no me gustan las fiestas

dislocate [dɪslóket] VT dislocar, descoyuntar

dislocation [dɪslokéʃən] N dislocación *f*, luxación *f*

dislodge [dɪsládʒ] VT (force out) desatascar; (displace) desprender

disloyal [dɪslɔ́ɪəl] ADJ desleal

dismal [dízməl] ADJ pésimo; **a — failure** un fracaso rotundo

dismantle [dɪsmǽntl] VT (a factory) desmantelar; (a car, watch) desmontar

dismay [dɪsmé] VT (disappoint) consternar; (daunt) desalentar; (alarm) alarmar; N (disappointment) consternación *f*; (loss of courage) desaliento *m*; (alarm) alarma *f*

dismember [dɪsmémbɚ] VT desmembrar

dismiss [dɪsmís] VT (fire a private employee) despedir; (fire a public employee) destituir, cesar; (reject a possibility) desechar, descartar; (discharge from military service) dar de baja; (reject a claim) desestimar; (ignore a person) ningunear; **class —ed!** ¡pueden retirarse!

dismissal [dɪsmísəl] N (firing) destitución *f*, despido *m*; (of a possibility) rechazo *m*; (from military service) baja *f*; (of a claim) desestimación *f*; (of a person) ninguneo *m*

dismount [dɪsmáʊnt] VI (get off a horse) desmontarse, apearse; (take apart) desarmar; N bajada *f*

disobedience [dɪsəbídɪəns] N desobediencia *f*

disobedient [dɪsəbíDiənt] ADJ desobediente

disobey [dɪsəbé] VI/VT desobedecer

disorder [dɪsɔ́rDə-] N (confusion) desorden *m*; (public disturbance) desorden público *m*; (illness) trastorno *m*, desarreglo *m*

disorderly [dɪsɔ́rDə-li] ADJ (untidy) desordenado; (unruly) revoltoso; — **conduct** alteración del orden público *f*

disorganization [dɪsɔrgənɪzéʃən] N desorganización *f*

disorganized [dɪsɔ́rgənaɪzd] ADJ desorganizado

disown [dɪsón] VT repudiar

disparage [dɪspǽrɪdʒ] VT denigrar

disparate [díspə-ɪt] ADJ dispar

dispassionate [dɪspǽʃənɪt] ADJ desapasionado

dispatch [dɪspǽtʃ] VT despachar; N (sending off) envío *m*; (putting to death) ejecución *f*; (news story, official communication) despacho *m*; (promptness) prontitud *f*

dispel [dɪspɛ́l] VT disipar

dispensable [dɪspɛ́nsəbəl] ADJ prescindible

dispensary [dɪspɛ́nsəri] N dispensario *m*

dispensation [dɪspɛnséʃən] N (relaxation of law) dispensa *f*; (act of handing out) dispensación *f*

dispense [dɪspɛ́ns] VT (goods) dispensar; (justice) administrar; **to — from an obligation** eximir de una obligación; **to — with** prescindir de

dispersal [dɪspə́-səl] N dispersión *f*

disperse [dɪspə́-s] VI/VT dispersar[se]; ADJ disperso

dispersed [dɪspə́-st] ADJ disperso

displace [dɪsplés] VT (evict) desalojar; (take up space, remove from office) desplazar; **—d person** (domestic) desplazado -da *mf*; (foreign) expatriado -da *mf*

displacement [dɪsplésmənt] N (of refugees, of a ship) desplazamiento *m*; (of an engine) cilindrada *f*

display [dɪsplé] VT (exhibit) exhibir, exponer; (unfold) desplegar; (flaunt) ostentar; (show on a computer screen) visualizar; N (of wares, etc.) exhibición *f*, despliegue *m*; (advertisement) cartel *m*; (flaunting) ostentación *f*; (computer screen) pantalla *f*, visualizador *m*, display *m*

displease [dɪsplíz] VT contrariar, desagradar, descontentar; VI molestar

displeasure [dɪsplɛ́ʒə-] N disgusto *m*, desagrado *m*

disposable [dɪspózəbəl] ADJ — **income** ingresos disponibles *m pl*

disposal [dɪspózəl] N (arrangement) disposición *f*; (elimination) eliminación *f*

dispose [dɪspóz] VT (give inclination) predisponer; (set in order, make ready) disponer; **to — of** descartar, eliminar

disposition [dɪspəzíʃən] N (attitude) temperamento *m*; (inclination) inclinación *f*, tendencia *f*; (arrangement, disposal) disposición *f*

dispossess [dɪspəzɛ́s] VT desposeer

disproportionate [dɪsprəpɔ́rʃənɪt] ADJ desproporcionado

disprove [dɪsprúv] VT refutar

dispute [dɪspjút] N disputa *f*; VT discutir, impugnar

disqualify [dɪskwálɪfaɪ] VT (deprive of rights) inhabilitar; (exclude from a sport event) descalificar

disregard [dɪsrɪgárd] VT hacer caso omiso de, ignorar; N (neglect) descuido *m*; (disrespect) falta de respeto *f*

disrepair [dɪsrɪpɛ́r] N mal estado *m*; **in —** deteriorado

disreputable [dɪsrɛ́pjəDəbəl] ADJ (of bad reputation) de mala reputación; (shabby) de mala muerte

disrespect [dɪsrɪspɛ́kt] N desacato *m*, falta de respeto *f*; VT faltar el respeto

disrespectful [dɪsrɪspɛ́ktfəl] ADJ irrespetuoso

disrobe [dɪsrób] VI/VT desvestir[se]

disrupt [dɪsrʌ́pt] VT (cause disorder) trastornar, trastocar; (interrupt) interrumpir

dissatisfied [dɪssǽtɪsfaɪd] ADJ insatisfecho, disconforme

dissatisfy [dɪssǽDɪsfaɪ] VT no satisfacer

dissect [daɪsɛ́kt] VT (cut apart) disecar; (analyze argument) analizar minuciosamente

dissemble [dɪsɛ́mbəl] VI/VT (hide) disimular; (feign) fingir

disseminate [dɪsɛ́mənet] VT (spread out) diseminar, propagar; (publicize) divulgar

dissemination [dɪsɛmənéʃən] N (spreading out) diseminación *f*; (publicizing) divulgación *f*

dissension [dɪsɛ́nʃən] N disensión *f*, disenso *m*

dissent [dɪsɛ́nt] VI disentir; N disenso *m*

dissertation [dɪsə-téʃən] N (formal discourse) disertación *f*; (doctoral treatise) tesis de doctorado *f*

dissident [dísɪDənt] N disidente *mf*

dissimilar [dɪssímələ-] ADJ diferente

dissimulation [dɪsɪmjəléʃən] N disimulo *m*

dissipate [dísəpet] VI/VT disipar[se]

dissipation [dɪsəpéʃən] N disipación *f*

dissolute [dísəlut] ADJ disoluto, vicioso

dissolution [dɪsəlúʃən] N disolución *f*

dissolve [dɪzálv] VI/VT disolver[se]

dissuade [dɪswéd] VT disuadir

distance [dístəns] N distancia *f*, recorrido *m*; **— learning** educación a distancia *f*; **in the —** a lo lejos, en la lejanía; VT distanciarse de, distanciar

distant [dístənt] ADJ (far away, aloof) distante; (remote) lejano, remoto; **to be — from** distar de

distaste [dɪstést] N aversión *f*

distasteful [dɪstéstfəl] ADJ desagradable

distemper [dɪstémpə] N moquillo m

distend [dɪsténd] VI/VT distender[se]

distill [dɪstɪ́l] VI/VT destilar[se]

distillation [dɪstəléʃən] N destilación f

distillery [dɪstɪ́ləri] N destilería f

distinct [dɪstɪ́ŋkt] ADJ (different) distinto; (clear) bien delineado, neto

distinction [dɪstɪ́ŋkʃən] N (honor) distinción f; (differentiation) distinción f, diferenciación f; **he passed with —** aprobó con sobresaliente

distinctive [dɪstɪ́ŋktɪv] ADJ distintivo

distinguish [dɪstɪ́ŋgwɪʃ] VI/VT distinguir

distinguished [dɪstɪ́ŋgwɪʃt] ADJ distinguido

distinguishing [dɪstɪ́ŋgwɪʃɪŋ] ADJ distintivo

distort [dɪstɔ́rt] VT (an object) deformar; (reports, sound) distorsionar

distortion [dɪstɔ́rʃən] N (object) deformación f; (image, sound) distorsión f; (of a statement) tergiversación f

distract [dɪstrǽkt] VT distraer, entretener

distracted [dɪstrǽktɪd] ADJ distraído, disperso

distraction [dɪstrǽkʃən] N distracción f; **to drive to —** volver loco

distraught [dɪstrɔ́t] ADJ angustiado

distress [dɪstrés] N (anxiety) angustia f; (pain) dolor m, congoja f; **to be in —** (a person) estar en apuros; (a ship, plane) estar en peligro; VT (cause anxiety) angustiar, atribular; (cause pain) acongojar, afligir

distressing [dɪstrésɪŋ] ADJ inquietante

distribute [dɪstrɪ́bjut] VT distribuir, repartir

distribution [dɪstrəbjúʃən] N distribución f, reparto m

distributor [dɪstrɪ́bjədə] N distribuidor m

district [dɪ́strɪkt] N distrito m, comarca f; **— attorney** fiscal de distrito mf

District of Columbia [dɪ́strɪktəvkəlʌ́mbiə] N Distrito de Columbia m

distrust [dɪstrʌ́st] N desconfianza f; VT desconfiar de

distrustful [dɪstrʌ́stfəl] ADJ desconfiado

disturb [dɪstɨ́b] VI/VT (interrupt, interfere, perplex) perturbar; (trouble) turbar, perturbar, trastornar; (mess up) desarreglar; **do not —** se ruega no molestar

disturbance [dɪstɨ́bəns] N disturbio m; (weather) perturbación f

disuse [dɪsjús] N desuso m; **to fall into —** caer en desuso

ditch [dɪtʃ] N (trench) zanja f; (roadside) cuneta f; (for irrigation) acequia f; VT (make ditches) abrir zanjas; (get rid of) deshacerse de; (crash-land an airplane on water) hacer un amarizaje

dither [dɪ́ðə] VI (hesitate) titubear; N **it threw her into a —** se puso muy nerviosa

ditsy [dɪ́tsi] ADJ atolondrado, cabeza de chorlito

ditto [dɪ́do] PRON & ADV ídem

diuretic [daɪəréDɪk] ADJ & N diurético m

diurnal [daɪɨ́n̩l] ADJ diurno

divan [dɪvǽn] N diván m, canapé m

dive [daɪv] VI (into water) zambullirse, chapuzar, Am tirarse un clavado; (into an activity) zambullirse; (with scuba equipment) bucear; (airplane) bajar en picado -da; (submarine) sumergirse; N (of a person) zambullida f, chapuz m; (of an airplane) picado -da mf; (cheap bar) antro m

diver [dáɪvə] N saltador -ora mf; (high-dive) clavadista mf; (scuba) buzo mf

diverge [dɪvɨ́dʒ] VI (branch off, differ in opinion) divergir; VI/VT (deviate) desviar

divergence [dɪvɨ́dʒəns] N (separation, difference in opinion) divergencia f; (deviation) desviación f

diverse [dɪvɨ́s] ADJ (of various kinds) diverso; (different) diferente

diversify [dɪvɨ́səfaɪ] VI/VT diversificar[se]

diversion [dɪvɨ́ʒən] N (entertainment) entretenimiento m; (distraction) distracción f; (military) diversión f; (turning aside) desvío m, desviación f

diversity [dɪvɨ́sɪDi] N diversidad f

divert [dɪvɨ́t] VI/VT (turn aside) desviar, distraer; (distract) entretener

diverticulitis [dɪvə tɪkjəláɪDɪs] N diverticulitis f

divest [dɪvést] VT (strip) despojar; (get rid of) deshacerse de

divide [dɪváɪd] VI/VT dividir[se]; (classify) clasificar[se]; N línea divisoria f

dividend [dɪ́vɪdɛnd] N dividendo m

divine [dɪváɪn] ADJ divino; VI/VT adivinar

divinity [dɪvɪ́nɪDi] N (godhead, state or quality of being divine) divinidad f; (theology) teología f

division [dɪvɪ́ʒən] N división f

divorce [dɪvɔ́rs] N divorcio m; VI/VT divorciar[se]

divot [dɪ́vət] N (golf) chuleta f

divulge [dɪvʌ́ldʒ] VT divulgar, publicar

dizziness [dɪ́zinɪs] N mareo m

dizzy [dɪ́zi] ADJ (person) mareado; (height) vertigoso; (speed) vertiginoso; **— spell** vahido m

DJ [**disc jockey**] [díʤe] N pinchadiscos mf sg

Djibouti [ʤɪbúti] N Yibuti m

Djiboutian [ʤɪbúʔiən] ADJ & N yibutiano -na mf

DNA [**deoxyribonucleic acid**] [diéné] N ADN m

do [du] VI/VT hacer; **to — away with** eliminar; **to — one's hair** arreglarse el pelo; **to — the dishes** lavar los platos; **to — drugs** tomar drogas; **to — in** matar; **to — time** cumplir una condena; **to — well** prosperar; **to — without** prescindir de; **we were —ing 100 kph** íbamos a cien kph; **to have nothing to — with** no tener nada que ver con; **that will — basta; that won't —** eso no sirve; **I'm —ing well** estoy bien; **this will have to —**

habrá que conformarse con esto; **—-it-yourself** hágalo usted mismo; V AUX **I feel as you —** pienso igual que tú; **how — you —?** ¿cómo estás? **— you hear me?** ¿me oyes? **yes, I —** sí; **— come again** vuelve por favor; N (hairstyle) peinado m; (party) fiesta f

DOA [**dead on arrival**] [díóé] ADJ muerto -ta antes de ingresar al hospital

docile [dásəl] ADJ dócil

dock [dak] N (pier) muelle m; (for landing) desembarcadero m, atracadero m; (water between piers) dique m, dársena f; **— worker** trabajador -ora portuario -ria mf; **dry —** dique seco m; VI/VT (a boat) atracar; (a space ship) acoplar[se]; (wages) descontar

doctor [dáktə] N (physician) médico -ca mf; (PhD, scholar) doctor -ora mf; (expert) especialista mf; VT (treat) atender; (cure) curar; (restore) restaurar; (counterfeit) alterar; **I —ed up this recipe** le hice unos retoques a esta receta

doctorate [dáktəɪt] N doctorado m

doctrine [dáktrɪn] N doctrina f

document¹ [dákjəmənt] N documento m

document² [dákjəmənt] VT documentar

documentary [dakjəméntəri] N documental m

documentation [dakjəmıntéʃən] N documentación f

dodder [dádə] VI (stumble along) tambalearse, titubear; (shake) temblequear

dodge [dadʒ] VT esquivar, sortear; VI (be evasive) dar rodeos; (move sideways) apartarse, echarse a un lado; N evasiva f

doe [do] N cierva f; (female of various animals) hembra f

dog [dɔg] N perro m, perra f; **—catcher** perrero -ra mf; **— collar** collar de perro m; **—fight** (dogs) pelea de perros f; (aircraft) combate aéreo m; (people) reyerta f; **—house** casilla de perro f; Sp caseta f; **to be in the —house** haber caído en desgracia, estar en capilla; **— paddle** natación estilo perrito m; **—sled** trineo para perros m; **— tag** placa de identificación f; **—wood** cornejo m; **to go to the —s** venirse abajo; ADJ **—-eared** sobado, muy gastado; **—gone** maldito; VT (follow) seguir la pista de; (harass) hostigar; **to—- paddle** nadar estilo perrito

doggy [dɔ́gi] N perrito -ta mf; **— bag** bolsa para las sobras f

dogma [dɔ́gmə] N dogma m

dogmatic [dɔgmǽDɪk] ADJ dogmático

doily [dɔ́ɪli] N mantelito m

doings [dúɪŋz] N actividades f pl

dole [doɫ] N (alms) limosna f; **to be on the —** estar cobrando el seguro de desempleo/paro; **to — out** repartir

doleful [dóɫfəɫ] ADJ apesadumbrado, triste

doll [daɫ] N (toy) muñeco -ca mf; (attractive female) muñeca f; **—house** casa de muñecas f; VI **to get —ed up** emperifollarse, empaquetarse

dollar [dálə] N dólar m; **— diplomacy** diplomacia del dólar f; **— sign** signo del dólar m

dolly [dáli] N (doll) muñeca f; (cart) carretilla f

dolphin [dɔ́lfɪn] N (mammal) delfín m; (fish) dorado m

dolt [doɫt] N zopenco -ca mf

domain [domén] N dominio m

dome [dom] N (roof) cúpula f, domo m; (head) coco m, pelada f

domestic [dəmɛ́stɪk] ADJ (appliance, pet, chore) doméstico; (devoted to homemaking) hogareño; (home-loving) casero; (of a country) interno, nacional; **— violence** violencia doméstica f; N doméstico -ca mf

domesticate [dəmɛ́stıket] VI/VT (animals) domesticar; (plants) aclimatar

domicile [dáməsaɪɫ] N domicilio m

dominant [dámənənt] ADJ dominante

dominate [dámənet] VI/VT dominar; VI señorear

domination [damənéʃən] N (act of dominating) dominación f; (rule) dominio m

domineer [damənír] VI/VT dominar, mandonear

domineering [damənírıŋ] ADJ tiránico, mandón

Dominica [dəmínıkə] N Dominica f

Dominican [dəmínıkən] ADJ & N (of Dominica) dominiqués -esa mf; (of the Dominican Republic) dominicano -na mf

Dominican Republic [dəmínıkənrɪpáblɪk] N República Dominicana f

dominion [dəmínjən] N dominio m, señorío m

domino [dáməno] N (game, costume) dominó m; (piece) ficha f

don [dɑn] N (title, form of address, mafia boss) don m; (lecturer) profesor -ora universitario -ria mf; VT ponerse, vestirse

donate [dónet] VI/VT donar

donation [donéʃən] N donación f

done [dʌn] see do

done [dʌn] ADJ terminado, acabado; **when you are —** cuando termines; **to be all —** estar muerto de cansancio; **the meat is well —** está bien asada la carne; **that sort of thing just isn't —** eso no se hace

donkey [dáŋki] N burro m, asno m, borrico m

donor [dónə] N donante mf, donador -ora mf

doodad [dúdæd] N (trinket) chuchería f; (device) chisme m, coso m

doohickey [dúhɪki] N chisme m, coso m

doom [dum] N perdición f; **—sday** día del juicio final m; VT condenar; **to be —ed to failure** estar condenado al fracaso

door [dɔr] N puerta f; **—bell** timbre m;

—keeper portero -ra *mf;* **—knob** pomo *m;*
—man portero *m;* **—mat** felpudo *m;* **—step**
umbral *m;* **—way** puerta *f,* portal *m;* **I**
showed him the — lo eché; ADJ **-to-—** de
puerta a puerta

dopamine [dópəmin] N dopamina *f*

dope [dop] N (narcotic) droga *f;* (stimulant)
estimulante *m;* (information) chismes *m pl;*
(moron) *fam* zopenco; VT dopar; **to —**
oneself up medicarse en exceso

dork [dɔrk] N *fam* idiota *mf,* tarambana *mf*

dorky [dɔ́rki] ADJ **that's a — dress** *fam* parece
una tonta con ese vestido

dormant [dɔ́rmənt] ADJ latente

dormitory [dɔ́rmɪtɔri] N residencia estudiantil *f*

DOS [Disk Operating System] [dɑs] N DOS *m*

dose [dos] N dosis *f;* VT dosificar

dossier [dɔ́sie] N expediente *m*

dot [dɑt] N punto *m;* (on a tie) pinta *f;* **—com**
punto com; **—matrix printer** impresora
de matriz de puntos *f;* **—ted eighth note**
corchea con puntillo *f;* **on the —** en punto;
VT marcar con puntos

dotage [dótɪdʒ] N chochez *f,* chochera *f;* **to be in**
one's — chochear, estar chocho

dote [dot] VI **to — on** estar chocho con

double [dʌ́bəl] ADJ doble; **— agent** doble agente
mf; **—barreled** de doble caño; **— bass**
contrabajo *m;* **— bed** cama doble *f;* **—-blind**
test prueba de doble incógnita *f;* **— bind**
dilema *m;* **— boiler** baño de María *m;* **—-**
breasted cruzado; **— chin** papada *f;* **—**
cross traición *f;* **— click** doble pulsación *f;* **—**
dealing duplicidad *f;* **— entry** entrada por
partida doble *f;* **— fault** doble falta *f;* **—**
indemnity doble indemnización *f;* **— play**
doble matanza *f;* **— sided** de dos caras; **—**
shift turno doble *m;* **— standard** trato
discriminatorio *m;* **— vision** doble visión *f;*
to do a — take quedar atónito; ADV **to sleep**
— dormir de a dos; N (in baseball) doble *m,*
doblete *m;* (in tennis) **—s** dobles *m pl,* juego
de dobles *m;* VI/VT duplicar[se]; (an effort)
redoblar[se]; (fold, be twice as old, challenge
a bid) doblar[se]; **to — up** (bend over)
doblarse; (crowd) amontonarse; **to —-check**
verificar; **to —-click** pulsar dos veces; **to —-**
cross traicionar; **to —-date** salir dos parejas
juntas; **to —-talk** salirse con evasivas; **this**
sofa —s as a bed este sofá sirve también de
cama

doubt [daʊt] VI/VT dudar; (not trust) desconfiar;
N duda *f;* **beyond a —** indudablemente; **in —**
en duda; **no —!** ¡sin duda!

doubtful [dáʊtfəl] ADJ dudoso

doubtless [dáʊtlɪs] ADV (certainly) sin duda;
(probably) probablemente

dough [do] N pasta *f,* masa *f;* (money) pasta *f,*
mosca *f;* **—nut** rosquilla *f;* *Mex* dona *f;* *Sp*
donut *m*

douse [daʊs] VI/VT empapar; (a flame) apagar
[con agua]

dove [dʌv] N paloma *f*

dove [dov] *see* dive

dowdy [dáʊdi] ADJ (article of clothing) pasado de
moda; (person) sin gracia

dowel [dáʊəl] N clavija *f*

down [daʊn] ADV abajo; **— and dirty** sucio; **—**
and out tirado; **to be — with** estar de
acuerdo con; **to come — with a cold** caer
con gripe, *Sp* cogerse un resfriado; **to fall —**
caerse; **to get — to work** aplicarse al trabajo;
to go/come — bajar; **to lie —** acostarse,
echarse; **to put someone —** denigrar a
alguien; **to turn — the volume** bajar el
volumen; **to water — a drink** rebajar una
bebida con agua; **to write —** anotar; **two**
blocks — dos calles más abajo; **slow —!**
¡anda más despacio! **the wind died —**
amainó el viento; **one — and two to go**
hicimos uno y nos quedan dos por hacer;
prices are — han bajado los precios; **the**
system is — se cayó el sistema; **they're —**
on me están mal conmigo; PREP **— the**
street calle abajo; ADJ (depressed) abatido; N
(turn for the worse) revés *m;* (feathers)
plumón *m;* VT (knock, shoot) derribar; (drink
quickly) despachar de un solo trago; (defeat)
vencer; (football play) oportunidad *f*

downcast [dáʊnkæst] ADJ abatido, cabizbajo

downfall [dáʊnfɔl] N ruina *f*

downgrade [dáʊngred] N declive *m,* pendiente
f; VT quitarle importancia a

downhill[1] [dáʊnhɪl] ADV cuesta abajo; **his**
health is going — su salud se deteriora

downhill[2] [dáʊnhɪl] ADJ **a — slope** una
pendiente; N bajada contra-reloj *f*

download [dáʊnlod] VT descargar; N descarga *f*

down payment [dáʊnpémənt] N entrega inicial
f, entrada *f*

downplay [dáʊnple] VT quitar la importancia a

downpour [dáʊnpɔr] N aguacero *m*

downright [dáʊnraɪt] ADJ absoluto; **—**
foolishness reverenda tontería *f;* **he was —**
angry echaba chispas

downshift [dáʊnʃɪft] VI rebajar [el cambio]

downside [dáʊnsaɪd] N inconveniente *m*

downsize [dáʊnsaɪz] VI (personnel) hacer
reducción; VT (an object or organization)
reducir el tamaño de; (one's lifestyle)
simplificar *f;* **he got —d** perdió el trabajo
cuando hicieron reducción de personal

downstairs[1] [dáʊnstérz] ADV abajo; (in the
apartment one floor lower) en el piso de abajo

downstairs[2] [dáʊnstɛrz] ADJ de abajo; N planta
baja *f*

downstream [dáʊnstrím] ADV río abajo

downtime [dáʊntaɪm] N (of a machine) tiempo

de inactividad *m*; (of a person) horas de ocio *f pl*

down-to-earth [dáʊntəə́θ] ADJ sensato, práctico

downtown [dáʊntáʊn] ADV (toward) al centro; (in) en el centro; ADJ del centro, céntrico; N centro *m*

downturn [dáʊntɜn] N tendencia a la baja *f*

down under [dáʊnʌ́ndə] ADV en/a Australia

downward [dáʊnwəd] ADJ descendente; — **mobility** descenso social *m*; —**s** hacia abajo

downwind [dáʊnwínd] ADV en la dirección del viento

downy [dáʊni] ADJ sedoso, suave

dowry [dáʊri] N dote *f*

doze [doz] VI dormitar; N siesta *f*

dozen [dázən] N docena *f*

drab [dræb] ADJ triste; N pardo *m*

draft [dræft] N (of air) corriente *f*; (drink) trago *m*; (bank) giro *m*; (outline) esbozo *m*; (military) conscripción *f*, quinta *f*; (of a ship) calado *m*; — **beer** cerveza de barril *f*; — **horse** caballo de tiro *m*; —**sman** dibujante *m*; VT (to sketch) esbozar; (to compose) redactar; (to select for military service) conscribir

drag [dræg] VI/VT (haul slowly) arrastrar[se]; (search a body of water) dragar; **don't — me into this** no me metas en esto; **to —- and-drop/release** arrastrar y soltar; **to — on and on** eternizarse; **to — out** estirar; N (dredge) draga *f*; (boring person) pesado -da *mf*; (hassle) lata *f*; (counterforce) resistencia *f*; (on a cigarette) pitada *f*; — **race** carrera de dragsters *f*; — **strip** pista de dragsters *f*

dragon [drǽgən] N dragón *m*; —**fly** libélula *f*

drain [dren] N (channel) desagüe *m*, sumidero *m*; (depletion of resources) sangría *f*, fuga *f*; —**pipe** desaguadero *m*, desagüe *m*; **to go down the —** irse por la borda; VI/VT (empty a sink) desagotar[se], desaguar[se]; (exhaust) agotar[se]; VT (wetlands) drenar, sanear; VI (a battery) descargarse

drainage [dréniʤ] N (act of draining) desagüe *m*, drenaje *m*; (system for draining) drenaje *m*; — **pipe** tubo de desagüe *m*

drake [drek] N pato [macho] *m*

drama [drámə] N drama *m*

dramatic [drəmǽDik] ADJ dramático

dramatically [drəmǽDikli] ADV (changing) de forma fundamental, fundamentalmente; (presenting) de manera dramática/teatral

dramatist [drámətist] N dramaturgo -ga *mf*

dramatize [drámətaiz] VI/VT dramatizar

drank [dræŋk] *see* drink

drape [drep] VI (hang in folds) colgar, drapear; VT (cover) cubrir; N cortina *f*

drapery [drépəri] N cortinado *m*, colgadura *f*

drastic [drǽstik] ADJ drástico

draw [drɔ] VT (a picture) dibujar; (lines, shapes) trazar; (a cart) tirar de; (a curtain) correr; (cards, blood, water, conclusion, strength) sacar; (a crowd) atraer; (comparison, distinction) hacer; (a sword) desenvainar; VI (of a boat) tener calado; (of a fireplace) tirar; (in sports, have the same score) empatar; (receive money) cobrar; (withdraw money) retirar, sacar; **to — aside** apartar[se]; **to — away** separar[se]; **to — a breath** aspirar, tomar aliento; **to — in** involucrar; **to — a blank** quedarse en blanco; **to — lots/ straws** echar a la suerte, sortear; **to — near** acercarse; **to — off** irse, retirarse; **to — on** (be based on) basarse en; (have recourse to) recurrir a; **to — out** (remove) sacar; (prolong) alargar, prolongar; **to — up** (approach) acercar[se]; (write) redactar; (shrink) encoger; N (in sports, tie game) empate *m*; (lot) número sorteado *m*; (attraction) atracción *f*; —**back** inconveniente *m*; —**bridge** puente levadizo *m*

drawer [drɔə] N cajón *m*; (small) gaveta *f*; —**s** calzones *m pl*

drawing [drɔ́iŋ] N (picture) dibujo *m*; (raffle) sorteo *m*; — **room** sala [de recibo] *f*

drawn [drɔn] ADJ demacrado; —**out** interminable

drawn [drɔn] *see* draw

dread [drɛd] N pavor *m*, terror *m*, espanto *m*; VT **I — going to the dentist** me aterra ir al dentista

dreadful [drɛ́dfəl] ADJ horrendo, espantoso, temible

dream [drim] N sueño *m* (also aspiration); (reverie) ensueño *m*, ensoñación *f*; (fancy) ilusión *f*; —**land** tierra del ensueño *f*; — **team** equipo de estrellas *m*; — **world** mundo de ensueño *m*; VI/VT soñar; **to — of** soñar con; **I wouldn't — of stealing** no se me ocurriría robar; **to — that** soñar que; **to — up** imaginar; ADJ **a — holiday** unas vacaciones perfectas

dreamer [drímə] N (impractical person) soñador -ora *mf*; (visionary) visionario -ria *mf*

dreamt [drɛmt] *see* dream

dreary [dríri] ADJ sombrío, deprimente

dredge [drɛʤ] N draga *f*; VT (a river) dragar; (facts) desenterrar, sacar a luz

dregs [drɛgz] N heces *f pl*, poso *m*; — **of society** escoria de la sociedad *f*

drench [drɛntʃ] VT empapar, calar; —**ed in blood** bañado en sangre

dress [drɛs] N (article of clothing for women) vestido *m*; (attire) ropa *f*; (formal) traje de etiqueta *m*, ropa de etiqueta *f*; (costume) vestimenta *f*; —**maker** modista *mf*; — **rehearsal** ensayo general *m*; — **shirt**

camisa para traje *f*; **what's the — code?**
¿cómo hay que ir vestido? VI/VT vestir; VT
(store window) arreglar; (slaughtered
animals) limpiar; (salad) aderezar; (hides)
adobar; (a wound) vendar; **to — down**
(scold) regañar; (wear casual clothes)
ponerse ropa informal; **to — up** (wear fine clothes)
vestirse de gala; (make more appealing)
embellecer

dresser [drésə-] N cómoda *f*; **she is a good —** se
viste con elegancia

dressing [drésɪŋ] N (act, result) vestir *m*; (for
salad) aderezo *m*; (for fowl) relleno *m*; (for
wounds) gasa *f*, vendaje *m*; **—-down** regaño
m; **— gown** bata *f*; **— room** (in a theater)
camerino *m*; (in a store) probador *m*; **— table**
tocador *m*

drew [dru] *see* draw

dribble [dríbəl] VI (trickle) gotear; (drool)
babear; VT (a ball) driblar, regatear; (liquid)
rociar; N (trickle) goteo *m*; (small quantity)
chorrito *m*; (of a ball) drible *m*, regate *m*

dried [draɪd] ADJ seco; **— fig** higo paso/seco *m*;
—-up (without water) seco; (wizened)
arrugado

drift [drɪft] N (direction) deriva *f*; (current)
corriente *f*; (meaning) sentido *m*, tenor *m*;
(pile) montón *m*, acumulación *f*; **—wood**
madera flotante *f*; **do you get my —?** ¿me
captas la onda? VI (float) flotar; (be adrift) ir a
la deriva; (wander) errar; **he —ed off** se
durmió; VI/VT (deviate) desviar[se];
(accumulate) amontonar[se], acumular[se]

drifter [dríftə-] N (wanderer) vagabundo -a *mf*;
(of a worker) itinerante *mf*

drill [drɪl] N (tool) taladro *m*; (dental) fresa *f*;
(training) ejercicios *m pl*; (procedure)
procedimiento *m*; (rehearsal) simulacro *m*;
(cloth) dril *m*; VI/VT (make a hole) taladrar,
perforar, barrenar; (train) entrenar[se],
adiestrar[se]; VI (train) hacer ejercicios;
(practice) practicar; VT hacer practicar

drink [drɪŋk] VI/VT (person) beber; (animal)
abrevar; (absorb, take in) absorber; **to — up**
apurar el trago; **to — to someone's health**
brindar por alguien; N bebida *f* (also
alcoholic); (a measure of beverage) trago *m*

drinkable [dríŋkəbəl] ADJ potable

drinking [dríŋkɪŋ] ADJ **— water** agua potable *f*;
he has a — problem tiene problemas con el
alcohol

drip [drɪp] N gotero *m*; (a bore) plasta *mf*; VI
gotear

drive [draɪv] VI/VT (a car) conducir, manejar; (an
animal) arrear; VI (go in a vehicle) ir en coche;
VT (move forth) impulsar, impeler; (convey)
llevar [en coche]; (force) forzar; (a nail)
clavar; (a ball) tirar, golpear; **to — a hard
bargain** regatear mucho; **to — away**

ahuyentar; **to — someone mad** volver loco
a alguien; **what are you driving at?** ¿qué
quieres decir con eso? N (ride) paseo [en coche]
m; (of an animal) arreo *m*; (urge) impulso *m*;
(of a computer) unidad *f*; (military offensive)
ofensiva *f*; (road) carretera *f*; (driveway)
camino *m*; (campaign) campaña *f*; (energy)
empuje *m*; (propulsion system) propulsión *f*;
(of a ball) tiro *m*; (in tennis and golf) drive *m*;
—-by shooting tiroteo desde un coche *m*; **—
-in** drive-in *m*, establecimiento en que el
cliente es atendido en el coche *m*; **—-in
movie theater** autocine *m*; **—way** camino
de entrada *m*, entrada de coches *f*; **front
wheel —** tracción delantera *f*

drivel [drívəl] N (saliva) baba *f*; (idiocy) tontería
f; VI babearse

driveling [drívəlɪŋ] ADJ baboso; **he's a — idiot**
es un oligofrénico

driven [drívən] *see* drive

driver [dráɪvə-] N (chauffeur) chofer *mf*,
conductor -ra *mf*; (of animals) arriero -ra *mf*;
(golf club) driver *m*; (in a computer)
controlador *m*

driving [dráɪvɪŋ] ADJ **— force** impulso *m*; **—-
rain** lluvia torrencial *f*; **— school**
autoescuela *f*

drizzle [drízəl] VI lloviznar; N llovizna *f*

drone [dron] N (male bee, idler) zángano *m*;
(remote-controlled vehicle) vehículo
teledirigido *f*; (drudge) esclavo *m*; (sound)
zumbido *m*; VI/VT (make a sound) zumbar;
(talk) hablar monótonamente

drool [drul] N baba *f*; VI babearse

droop [drup] VI (sag) colgarse; (flag)
languidecer; (wither) marchitarse; **his
shoulders —** tiene los hombros caídos;
—ing ears orejas gachas *f pl*

drop [drɑp] N (liquid quantity) gota *f*; (descent)
caída *f*; (incline) declive *m*; (in value) baja *f*;
(in prices) caída *f*; (lozenge) pastilla *f*; (of
mail, etc.) buzón *m*, punto de recolección *m*;
(of supplies) lanzamiento *m*; **—out** (student)
desertor -ora escolar *mf*; (marginalized
person) marginado -da *mf*; **— shot** dejada de
volea *f*; VI caer; (let fall) dejar caer, descargar;
(in golf) dropar; **to — a line** mandar unas
líneas; **to — from sight** desaparecer; **to —
in** caer de sorpresa; **to — out** (sports)
retirarse; (school) abandonar; **why don't
you — by?** ¿por qué no pasas por aquí? VI/VT
(a course) abandonar; (a curtain) bajar; ADJ
—-dead beautiful hermosísima

dropper [drɑpə-] N gotero *m*

drought [draut] N sequía *f*

drove [drov] N tropel *m*

drove [drov] *see* drive

drown [draun] VI/VT ahogar[se]

drowning [dráʊnɪŋ] N ahogamiento *m*

drowse [drauz] VI (be half-asleep) dormitar; (feel drowsy) estar amodorrado

drowsiness [dráuzinɪs] N modorra f, somnolencia f

drowsy [dráuzi] ADJ amodorrado, somnoliento; **to become** — amodorrarse

drudge [drʌdʒ] N esclavo del trabajo m, fregona f; VI trabajar como un esclavo

drug [drʌg] N (chemical substance, narcotic) droga f; (medicine) medicamento m; —**ged** drogado, endrogado; — **abuse** abuso de drogas m; —**addict** drogadicto -ta mf; —**store** (drugs) farmacia f; (non-drug items) droguería f, perfumería f; — **trafficker** narcotraficante mf; VT (stupefy with drugs) drogar; (mix with a drug) adulterar con droga

druggist [drʌ́gɪst] N farmacéutico -ca mf, droguero -ra mf

drum [drʌm] N (musical instrument) tambor m; (of ear) tímpano m; (receptacle for storing liquids) barril m; —**head** parche m; —**stick** (music) palillo de tambor m; (fowl) pata f; VI (play a drum) tocar el tambor; (beat rhythmically) tamborilear; **to** — **out** expulsar; **to** — **up** fomentar; **I'm trying to** — **this idea into his head** le estoy repitiendo esta idea con insistencia

drummer [drʌ́mə] N (classical) tambor m; (folk) tamborilero -ra mf; (rock & roll) baterista mf

drunk [drʌŋk] ADJ & N borracho -cha mf; fam mamado -da mf; **to get** — emborracharse

drunk [drʌŋk] see drink

drunkard [drʌ́ŋkəd] N borracho -cha mf, borrachín -ina mf

drunken [drʌ́ŋkən] ADJ borracho, embriagado

drunkenness [drʌ́ŋkənnɪs] N borrachera f, embriaguez f

dry [drai] ADJ seco; (sober) sobrio; (topic, book) árido, aburrido; — **land** tierra firme f; — **cleaner** (business) tintorería f; (owner of business) tintorero -ra mf; — **cleaning** limpieza en seco f; — **county** condado seco m; — **wit** humor agudo m; — **goods** géneros m pl; — **measure** medida para áridos f; — **run** prueba f; — **ice** hielo seco m; — **dock** dique seco m, varadero m; VI/VT (wet clothes) secar[se]; (leather) resecar[se]; **to** — **up** secarse, resecarse; **to** — **out** desintoxicar[se]

dryer [dráɪə] N (hair) secador m; (clothes) secadora f

dryness [dráɪnɪs] N (skin) sequedad f; (land, lecture) aridez f

dual [dúəl] ADJ (function) doble; (ownership) compartido

dub [dʌb] VT (translate a film) doblar; (give a nickname) apodar

dubious [dúbiəs] ADJ dudoso

duchess [dʌ́tʃɪs] N duquesa f

duck [dʌk] N (bird) pato m; (downward dodge)

agachada f; VI/VT (plunge under water) hundir[se]; (bend down) agachar[se]; VT (avoid) esquivar

duckling [dʌ́klɪŋ] N patito m

duct [dʌkt] N conducto m; — **tape** cinta aislante f

ductile [dʌ́ktl] ADJ dúctil

dud [dʌd] N (disappointing thing) chasco m; (useless person) inútil m; (unexploded bomb) bomba que no estalla f; —**s** (clothes) ropa f, fam trapos m pl; (belongings) pertenencias f pl

dude [dud] N (dandy) chulo m; (fellow) tipo m

due [du] ADJ (payable) pagadero; (immediately owed) vencido; (fitting, rightful) debido; (adequate) suficiente; — **date** fecha de vencimiento f; — **diligence** diligencia debida f; **in** — **time/course** a su debido tiempo; **the train is** — **at two o'clock** se supone que el tren llega a las dos; ADV — **east** hacia el este; N (punishment) merecido m; **give Mary her**—; **she's honest** tienes que reconocer que María es honrada; —**s** cuotas f pl

duel [dúəl] N duelo m; VI/VT batirse en/a duelo [con alguien]

duet [duɛ́t] N (played) dúo m; (sung) dueto m

dug [dʌg] see dig

dugout [dʌ́gaut] N (canoe) piragua f; (underground refuge) trinchera f

DUI [driving under the influence] [díjúái] N delito de conducir en estado de ebriedad m

duke [duk] N duque m; **to put up one's** —**s** levantar los puños; VT **to** — **it out** arreglarlo con los puños

dukedom [dúkədəm] N ducado m

dull [dʌl] ADJ (lackluster) opaco; (listless, muted) apagado; (boring) aburrido, soso, desanimado; (blunt) romo, desafilado; (sluggish, stupid) lento; (pain) sordo; VI/VT (a knife) desafilar[se]; (color) opacar[se]; (sound, impact) amortiguar[se]; (pain) aliviar[se]; (senses) embotar[se], entorpecer[se]

duly [dúli] ADV debidamente

dumb [dʌm] ADJ (mute) mudo; (dull) tonto; —**bell** (handweight) mancuerna f; (stupid person) bobo -ba mf; VT **to** — **down** simplificar demasiado

dumbness [dʌ́mnɪs] N (muteness) mudez f; (foolishness) estupidez f

dummy [dʌ́mi] N (figure) muñeco m; (fool) tonto -ta mf; (front) hombre de paja m; ADJ (fake) falso; **a** — **president** un títere

dump [dʌmp] VT (unload) descargar; (empty) botar; (transfer computer data) vaciar; (dismiss) echar, despedir; (discard waste) tirar la basura, descargar desechos; (flood a market) hacer dumping; (abandon) plantar; **to** — **on** (criticize) criticar; (unload problems) descargarse; N (place for waste) vertedero m, basural *m*, basurero *m*; (of weapons) depósito *m*; (act of discarding) vertido *m*; **—truck** camión volteador *m*, volquete *m*, *Am* volqueta *f*; **to be in the —s** estar deprimido, estar depre

dumping [dámpɪŋ] N vertido *m*

dunce [dʌns] N burro -rra *mf*, tonto -ta de capirote *mf*

dune [dun] N duna *f*, médano *m*

dung [dʌŋ] N boñiga *f*, bosta *f*; **—hill** estercolero *m*

dungeon [dʌ́ndʒən] N mazmorra *f*

dunk [dʌŋk] VT (a donut) remojar; (a basketball) volcar, enterrar; (a person) sumergir

duodenum [duədínəm] N duodeno *m*

dupe [dup] N (gullible person) ingenuo -nua *mf*, inocente *mf*; *Sp* primo -ma *mf*; (manipulated person) títere *m*; VT embaucar

duplex [dúpleks] N & ADJ dúplex *m*

duplicate[1] [dúplɪkɪt] ADJ & N duplicado *m*; **in —** por duplicado

duplicate[2] [dúplɪket] VT duplicar[se]

duplicity [duplísɪdi] N duplicidad *f*

durability [durəbílɪdi] N durabilidad *f*

durable [dúrəbəl] ADJ (long-lasting) duradero; (serviceable) sufrido

duration [duréʃən] N duración *f*

duress [durés] N coacción *f*

during [dúrɪŋ] PREP durante

dusk [dʌsk] N atardecer *m*, anochecer *m*; **at —** al atardecer

dusky [dʌ́ski] ADJ (dark) oscuro; (gloomy) sombrío

dust [dʌst] N polvo *m*; **—pan** pala *f*; **to bite the — (die)** *fam* espichar; (lose) morder el polvo de la derrota; **cloud of —** polvareda *f*; VI/VT (remove dust) quitar/sacudir el polvo [a]; VT (sprinkle with powder) espolvorear; VI (become dusty) empolvarse; **to — off** desempolvar

duster [dʌ́stə] N plumero *m*

dusty [dʌ́sti] ADJ polvoriento

Dutch [dʌtʃ] ADJ & N holandés -esa *mf*; (language) holandés *m*; **to go —** pagar a escote

Dutchman [dʌ́tʃmən] N holandés *m*

duty [dúdi] N deber *m*, obligación *f*; (tax on imports) derechos aduaneros *m pl*; (any tax) impuesto *m*; **to be on —** estar de guardia; **to be off —** no estar de guardia; ADJ **—-free** libre de impuestos

DVD [digital versatile disc] [dívidí] N DVD *m*

dwarf [dwɔrf] ADJ & N enano -na *mf*; VT hacer parecer pequeño

dwarfism [dwɔ́rfɪzəm] N enanismo *m*

dwell [dwɛl] VI morar, habitar; **to — on a subject** dilatarse en un asunto

dweller [dwɛ́lə] N habitante *mf*, morador -ora *mf*

dwelling [dwɛ́lɪŋ] N vivienda *f*, domicilio *m*

dwelt [dwɛlt] *see* dwell

DWI [**driving while intoxicated**] [dídʌbəljuáɪ] N delito de conducir en estado de ebriedad *m*

dwindle [dwíndl] VI/VT menguar, mermar

dye [daɪ] N tinte *m*, tintura *f*; VT teñir

dying [dáɪɪŋ] ADJ moribundo

dynamic [daɪnǽmɪk] ADJ dinámico; N dinámica *f*

dynamite [dáɪnəmaɪt] N dinamita *f*; VT dinamitar; ADJ fabuloso

dynamo [dáɪnəmo] N dínamo *m*

dynasty [dáɪnəsti] N dinastía *f*

dysentery [dísəntɛri] N disentería *f*

dysfunction [dɪsfʌ́ŋkʃən] N disfunción *f*

dyslexia [dɪsléksiə] N dislexia *f*

Ee

each [itʃ] ADJ cada; **— person** cada persona; PRON cada uno; **— receives a prize** cada uno recibe un premio; **they looked at — other** se miraron el uno al otro

eager [ígə] ADJ (enthusiastic) ansioso; (avid) ávido

eagerness [ígə-nɪs] N (enthusiasm) ansia *f*, afán *m*; (strong desire) avidez *f*

eagle [ígəl] N águila *f*; **—-eye** ojo de lince *m*

eaglet [íglɪt] N aguilucho *m*

ear [ir] N (outer organ) oreja *f*; (inner organ, sense of hearing, musical aptitude) oído *m*; (of corn) mazorca *f*; *Am* elote *m*; **—ache** dolor de oídos *m*; **—drops** gotas para los oídos *f pl*; **—drum** tímpano *m*; **—lobe** lóbulo de la oreja *m*; **— muff** orejera *f*; **—phone** audífono *m*, auricular *m*; **—plug** tapón del oído *m*; **—ring** pendiente *m*, zarcillo *m*, arete *m*; **by —** de oído; **within —shot** al alcance del oído; **he has the — of the governor** el gobernador le presta mucha atención; VT **to —mark** asignar

earful [írfʊl] N **I got an —** (scolding) me echó un rapapolvo; (gossip) me dio la lata

early [ə́li] ADJ temprano; **— detection** diagnóstico precoz *m*; **— man** hombre primitivo *m*; **— retirement** jubilación anticipada *f*; **— riser** madrugador -ora *mf*, mañanero -ra *mf*; **the — bird gets the worm** al que madruga, Dios lo ayuda

earn [ə́n] VI/VT (money, admiration, etc.) ganar; (salary) cobrar, ganar; (interest) devengar; **—ed run** carrera limpia *f*; **—ed run average** promedio de carreras limpias permitidas *m*; **to — a living** ganarse la vida

earnest [ə́nɪst] ADJ (sincere) serio, formal;

(grave) grave; **in** — en serio; **— money** señal f; *Mex* enganche *m*

earnestness [ɔ́:nɪstnɪs] N (sincerity) seriedad f, formalidad f; (gravity) gravedad f; **in all —** con toda sinceridad

earnings [ɔ́:nɪŋz] N (of a person) ingresos *m pl*; (of a business) ganancias f pl

earth [ɔθ] N tierra f; **—mover** excavadora f; **—quake** terremoto *m*, temblor de tierra *m*; **—worm** lombriz f; **the** — la Tierra; ADJ **—shaking** revolucionario

earthen [ɔ́:θən] ADJ (wall) de tierra; (pot) de barro; **—ware** vajilla de barro f, cerámica f

earthly [ɔ́:θli] ADJ terrenal; **— possessions** bienes terrenales *m pl*; **to be of no — use** no servir para nada

earthy [ɔ́:θi] ADJ natural; (person) campechano; (sense of humor, joke) basto; **— smell** olor a tierra *m*

ease [iz] N (facility) facilidad f; (unaffectedness) soltura f, desparpajo *m*; (comfort) comodidad f; (lack of worry) tranquilidad f; (fullness of a garment) holgura f; **at** — (military) en descanso; (comfortable) tranquilo, a gusto; **a life of** — una vida desahogada; **ill at** — incómodo; VT (make easier) facilitar; VI/VT (relieve pain) aliviar[se]; (release from tension) aflojar[se]; (relieve anxiety) tranquilizar[se]; **to — up** aflojar

easel [ízəl] N caballete *m*

east [ist] N este *m*, oriente *m*; ADJ del este, oriental; ADV **—of here** al este [de aquí]; **to go** — ir al / hacia al este; **—back** — en el este

Easter [ístə·] N Pascua f; **— egg** huevo de Pascua *m*; **— Sunday** Domingo de Pascua *m*

eastern [ístə·n] ADJ oriental, del este

eastward [ístwə·d] ADV & ADJ hacia el este

easy [ízi] ADJ (simple) fácil, sencillo; (compliant) fácil; (comfortable) cómodo; (informal) desenvuelto; (unworried) tranquilo; **— chair** poltrona f; **—going** calmoso; **— terms** facilidades de pago f pl; **— does it** despacito; **take it** — cálmate; **he's on — street** vive en la abundancia; **within — reach** al alcance de la mano; ADV **go — on me** sea bueno

eat [it] VI/VT comer[se]; VT (costs) absorber; **to — away** corroer, comer; **to — breakfast** desayunar[se]; **to — dinner** (midday) comer; (evening) cenar; **to — lunch** comer, almorzar; **to — one's heart out** morirse de envidia; **to — one's words** tragarse las palabras; **to — supper** cenar; **to — up** comerse todo; **what's —ing you?** ¿qué bicho te picó?

eaten [ítn̩] *see* eat

eating [íDɪŋ] N (act) comer *m*; (food) comida f; **— disorder** trastorno de la alimentación *m*; **— utensils** cubiertos *m pl*; **— apples** manzanas para comer f pl

eaves [ivz] N PL alero *m*; **to —drop** escuchar furtivamente

e-banking [íbæŋkɪŋ] N banca electrónica f

ebb [ɛb] N (flowing back) reflujo *m*; (decay) decadencia f; **— tide** reflujo *m*; **to be at a low** — estar en un punto bajo; VI (tide) bajar; (energy) decaer

ebony [ɛ́bəni] N ébano *m*

e-book [íbʊk] N libro electrónico *m*

e-business [íbɪznɪs] N comercio electrónico *m*

eccentric [ɛksɛ́ntrɪk] ADJ & N excéntrico -ca *mf*

ecclesiastic [ɪkliziǽstɪk] ADJ & N eclesiástico *m*

echelon [ɛ́ʃəlan] N (military formation) escalón *m*; (rank) nivel *m*, estrato *m*

echo [ɛ́ko] N eco *m*; VI hacer eco; **the gym —ed with laughter** el gimnasio resonó de risas; VT repetir

echocardiogram [ɛkokárdiəgræm] N ecocardiograma *m*

eclectic [ɪklɛ́ktɪk] ADJ ecléctico

eclipse [ɪklíps] N eclipse *m*; VT eclipsar

eco-friendly [ikofréndli] ADJ ecológico

ecological [ikəládʒɪkəl] ADJ ecológico

ecology [ɪkálədʒi] N ecología f

e-commerce [íkamə·s] N comercio electrónico *m*

economic [ɛkənámɪk] ADJ económico; N **—s** economía f

economical [ɛkənámɪkəl] ADJ económico

economist [ɪkánəmɪst] N economista *mf*

economize [ɪkánəmaɪz] VI economizar

economy [ɪkánəmi] N economía f (also thrift); ADJ **— car** coche económico *m*; **— class** clase turista f

ecosystem [íkosɪstəm] N ecosistema *m*

ecstasy [ɛ́kstəsi] N éxtasis *m* (also drug)

Ecuador [ɛ́kwədɔr] N Ecuador *m*

Ecuadorian [ɛkwədɔ́riən] ADJ & N ecuatoriano -na *mf*

ecumenical [ɛkjəménɪkəl] ADJ ecuménico

eczema [ɛ́gzəmə] N eccema *m*

eddy [ɛ́Di] N remolino *m*; VI arremolinarse

edge [ɛdʒ] N borde *m*, canto *m*; (of a knife) filo *m*; (of a block) arista f; **to be on** — estar nervioso; **her voice has an — to it** tiene la voz penetrante; **a competitive** — una ventaja sobre la competencia; VT (make an edge) hacerle el borde; (sharpen) afilar; (move sideways) meterse de costado; **to — out** ganar por un pelito; **to — up** aproximarse; ADV **—wise** de costado

edgy [ɛ́dʒi] ADJ nervioso

edible [ɛ́Dəbəl] ADJ & N comestible *m*

edict [íDɪkt] N edicto *m*, bando *m*

edifice [ɛ́Dəfɪs] N edificio *m*

edify [ɛ́Dəfaɪ] VT edificar

edit [ɛ́Dɪt] VT (revise, correct) corregir; (serve as editor) editar; (revise a film) montar; **to — out** eliminar; N corrección f

edition [ɪdíʃən] N edición f

editor [ɛ́DɪTɚ] N (director of a publication) redactor -ora *mf*; (compiler, radio or film worker) editor -ora *mf*; (proofreader) corrector -ora *mf*

editorial [ɛDɪTɔ́riəl] ADJ editorial; N editorial *f*

editorialize [ɛDɪTɔ́riəlaɪz] VI editorializar

educate [ɛ́dʒəket] VT educar

education [ɛdʒəkéʃən] N educación *f*, enseñanza *f*; (academic subject) pedagogía *f*; **school of — escuela normal** *f*

educational [ɛdʒəkéʃənl] ADJ educativo

educator [ɛ́dʒəkeDɚ] N educador -ora *mf*

EEG [electroencephalogram] [íídʒí] N electroencefalograma *m*

eel [il] N anguila *f*

eerie [íri] ADJ misterioso

effect [ɪfɛ́kt] N efecto *m*; **to go into —** entrar en vigencia, ponerse en operación; **in —** vigente, operativo; **I wrote a letter to that — escribí una carta en ese sentido; personal —s** efectos personales *m pl*; VT efectuar

effective [ɪfɛ́ktɪv] ADJ efectivo, eficaz; (a law) vigente; **— date** fecha de vigencia *f*

effectively [ɪfɛ́ktɪvli] ADV (well) eficazmente; (in fact) de hecho, en efecto

effectiveness [ɪfɛ́ktɪvnɪs] N efectividad *f*, eficacia *f*

effectual [ɪfɛ́ktʃuəl] ADJ eficaz

effeminate [ɪfɛ́mənɪt] ADJ afeminado

efficacy [ɛ́fɪkəsi] N eficacia *f*

efficiency [ɪfíʃənsi] N eficiencia *f*; **— apartment** estudio *m*

efficient [ɪfíʃənt] ADJ eficiente; (motor) económico

effigy [ɛ́fədʒi] N efigie *f*; **to burn in —** quemar en efigie

effort [ɛ́fɚt] N (exertion) esfuerzo *m*; (work of art) obra *f*; (campaign) campaña *f*

effrontery [ɪfrántəri] N descaro *m*

effusive [ɪfjúsɪv] ADJ efusivo

egg [ɛg] N huevo *m*; (female gamete) óvulo *m*; (fellow) tipo *m*; **—beater** batidor de huevos *m*; **—head** empollón -na *mf*; **—nog** rompopo *m*, rompope *m*, ponche de huevo *m*; **—plant** berenjena *f*; **—shell** cáscara de huevo *f*; **— white** clara de huevo *f*; **— yolk** yema de huevo *f*; **to have — on one's face** estar avergonzado, quedar mal; **to lay an —** (of a hen) poner un huevo; (fail) fracasar; **to walk on —shells** ir pisando huevos; ADJ **—-shaped** ovoide; VT **to — on** incitar

ego [ígo] N (self) yo *m*, ego *m*; (vanity) ego *m*; (self-esteem) amor propio *m*; **winning the prize was an — trip for him** ganar el premio le aceitó el ego

egocentric [igoséntrɪk] ADJ egocéntrico

egotism [ígətɪzəm] N egotismo *m*

Egypt [ídʒɪpt] N Egipto *m*

Egyptian [ɪdʒípʃən] ADJ & N egipcio -cia *mf*

eight [et] NUM ocho; **— hundred** ochocientos

eighteen [ettín] NUM dieciocho

eighth [etθ] ADJ, N & ADV octavo *m*; **— note** corchea *f*

eighty [éDi] NUM ochenta

either [íðɚ] ADJ & PRON **— will do** cualquiera de los dos está bien; **choose — suit** elige uno de los dos trajes; **choose —** elige uno [u otro] de los dos; **there were flowers on — side of the road** había flores a ambos lados de la carretera; ADV **if you don't, I won't —** si tú no lo haces, yo tampoco; **I'll go — by bus or by car** voy [o] en autobús o en auto

ejaculate [ɪdʒǽkjəlet] VI/VT eyacular; (exclaim) exclamar

eject [ɪdʒɛ́kt] VT (throw out) echar, expulsar; VI/ VT (throw from a plane) eyectar[se]

ejection [ɪdʒɛ́kʃən] N expulsión *f*

EKG [electrocardiogam] [íkédʒí] N electrocardiograma *m*

elaborate¹ [ɪlǽbɚɪt] ADJ (ornate) elaborado; (detailed) detallado

elaborate² [ɪlǽbɚet] VI/VT (create) elaborar; (develop) desarrollar

elapse [ɪlǽps] VI transcurrir, pasar

elastic [ɪlǽstɪk] ADJ elástico; N elástico *m*; (rubber band) goma elástica *f*

elasticity [ɪlæstísɪDi] N elasticidad *f*

elated [ɪléDɪD] ADJ eufórico

elbow [ɛ́lbo] N codo *m*; VI/VT codear, dar codazos; **to — one's way through** abrirse paso a codazos

elder [ɛ́ldɚ] ADJ (older) mayor; N (older person) mayor *mf*; (old person) anciano -na *mf*; (in a church) miembro del consejo de una iglesia *m*; **our —s** nuestros mayores *m pl*

elderly [ɛ́ldɚli] ADJ anciano

e-learning [ílɚnɪŋ] N educación en línea *f*

elect [ɪlɛ́kt] ADJ (elected) electo; (chosen by God) elegido; VI/VT elegir

election [ɪlɛ́kʃən] N elección *f*

elector [ɪlɛ́ktɚ] N elector -ora *mf*

electoral [ɪlɛ́ktɚəl] ADJ electoral

electric [ɪlɛ́ktrɪk] ADJ eléctrico; (exciting) electrizante; (excited) electrizado; **— chair** silla eléctrica *f*; **— eel** anguila eléctrica *f*; **— eye** célula fotoeléctrica *f*; **— meter** contador eléctrico *m*; **— storm** tormenta eléctrica *f*

electrical [ɪlɛ́ktrɪkəl] ADJ eléctrico; **— engineer** ingeniero -ra electricista *mf*; **— engineering** ingeniería eléctrica *f*; **— tape** cinta aislante *f*

electrician [ɪlɛktríʃən] N electricista *mf*

electricity [ɪlɛktrísɪDi] N electricidad *f*

electrify [ɪlɛ́ktrəfaɪ] VT (apply electricity) electrificar; (thrill) electrizar

electrocardiogram [ɪlɛktrokárDiəgræm] N electrocardiograma *m*

electrocute [ɪlɛ́ktrəkjut] VT electrocutar

electrode [ɪlɛ́ktrod] N electrodo *m*

electroencephalogram [ɪlɛktroɛnséfələgræm] N electroencefalograma *m*

electrolysis [ɪlɛktrálɪsɪs] N electrólisis *f*

electromagnet [ɪlɛktromǽgnɪt] N electroimán *m*

electromagnetic [ɪlɛktromægnéDɪk] ADJ electromagnético

electron [ɪléktran] N electrón *m*; — **microscope** microscopio electrónico *m*

electronic [ɪlɛktránɪk] ADJ electrónico; — **banking** banca electrónica *f*; — **mail** correo electrónico *m*; —**s** electrónica *f*; — **signature** firma electrónica *f*

elegance [élɪgəns] N elegancia *f*, gallardía *f*

elegant [élɪgənt] ADJ elegante, gallardo; (gift) de lujo

element [éləmənt] N elemento *m*; (component part) componente *m*, pieza *f*; (for heating) resistencia *f*; **the —s** los elementos

elemental [eləméntl] ADJ elemental; — **forces** fuerzas de la naturaleza *f pl*

elementary [eləméntri] ADJ elemental; — **school** escuela primaria *f*

elephant [éləfənt] N elefante -ta *mf*

elevate [éləvet] VT elevar

elevation [eləvéʃən] N (action of elevating, elevated place) elevación *f*; (altitude) altura *f*

elevator [éləveDɚ] N ascensor *m*; *Am* elevador *m*; (for grain) elevador *m*

eleven [ɪlévən] NUM once

elf [ɛlf] N elfo *m*; (mischievous person) pillo -lla *mf*

elicit [ɪlísɪt] VT provocar; **to — admiration** despertar admiración

eligibility [ɛlɪdʒəbílɪDi] N elegibilidad *f*

eligible [élɪdʒəbəl] ADJ elegible; **an — bachelor** un buen partido; **you are — for a scholarship** tienes derecho a solicitar una beca

eliminate [ɪlímənet] VT eliminar

elimination [ɪlɪmənéʃən] N eliminación *f*

elite [ɪlít] N elite *f*, élite *f*

elitist [ɪlíDɪst] ADJ & N elitista *mf*

elk [ɛlk] N alce *m*

elliptical [ɪlíptɪkəl] ADJ elíptico

elm [ɛlm] N olmo *m*

elongate [ɪlɔ́nget] VI/VT alargar[se]

elope [ɪlóp] VI fugarse para casarse a escondidas

eloquence [éləkwəns] N elocuencia *f*

eloquent [éləkwənt] ADJ elocuente

El Salvador [ɛlsǽlvədɔr] N El Salvador *m*

else [ɛls] ADJ & ADV **who — was there?** ¿quién más estaba? **someone —'s son** el hijo de otro; **somebody —** [algún] otro; **or —** si no; **leave town or —** vete del pueblo o sufre las consecuencias / o verás lo que es bueno; **nobody —** nadie más; **nothing —** nada más; **how —?** ¿de qué otra forma? ADV **—where** (location) en otra parte / en otro lado;

(movement) a otra parte / a otro sitio

elucidate [ɪlúsɪdet] VI/VT elucidar, dilucidar, esclarecer

elucidation [ɪlusɪdéʃən] N elucidación *f*, dilucidación *f*

elude [ɪlúd] VT eludir

elusive [ɪlúsɪv] ADJ (slippery) escurridizo; (evasive) esquivo; (difficult to understand) difícil de entender

emaciated [ɪméʃieDɪd] ADJ escuálido, descarnado

e-mail [ímɛl] N correo electrónico *m*; — **address** dirección de correo electrónico *f*

emanate [émənet] VI/VT emanar

emanation [ɛmənéʃən] N emanación *f*

emancipate [ɪmǽnsəpet] VT emancipar

emancipation [ɪmænsəpéʃən] N emancipación *f*

emasculate [ɪmǽskjəlet] VT castrar; (remove testicles) castrar, emascular

embalm [ɪmbám] VT (the body of a deceased person) preparar; (a mummy) embalsamar

embalming [ɪmbámɪŋ] N preparación del cuerpo *f*

embankment [ɪmbǽŋkmənt] N terraplén *m*

embargo [ɪmbárgo] N embargo *m*; VT imponer un embargo a/contra

embark [ɪmbárk] VI/VT embarcar[se]

embarrass [ɪmbǽrəs] VT (cause shame) hacerle pasar vergüenza a; (cause discomfit, financial difficulties) poner en aprietos; **—ed** avergonzado, en aprietos; **I'm —ed about my teeth** me dan vergüenza mis dientes; **I'm —ed to tell you** me da vergüenza decírtelo

embarrassing [ɪmbǽrəsɪŋ] ADJ (shameful) vergonzoso, penoso; (hindering) embarazoso

embarrassment [ɪmbǽrəsmənt] N (shame) vergüenza *f*, bochorno *m*, pena *f*; (act of embarrassing) vergüenza *f*; (financial difficulty) aprieto *m*; **he's an — to the company** hace quedar mal a la compañía; **we have an — of riches** nadamos en la abundancia

embassy [émbəsi] N embajada *f*

embattled [ɪmbǽdld] ADJ hostigado, agobiado

embed [ɪmbéd] VT incrustar

embedded [ɪmbéDɪd] ADJ incrustado

embellish [ɪmbélɪʃ] VT adornar, ornamentar

ember [émbɚ] N ascua *f*, brasa *f*

embezzle [ɪmbézəl] VT desfalcar, malversar

embezzlement [ɪmbézəlmənt] N desfalco *m*, peculado *m*, malversación *f*

embitter [ɪmbíDɚ] VT amargar

emblem [émbləm] N emblema *m*, divisa *f*

embody [ɪmbádi] VT (personify) personificar; (to provide with a body) encarnar

embolism [émbəlɪzəm] N embolia *f*

embrace [ɪmbrés] VI/VT (hug, adopt) abrazar[se]; (include) abarcar; N abrazo *m*

embroider [ɪmbrɔ́ɪdə] VI/VT bordar, recamar

embroidery [ɪmbrɔ́ɪdərɪ] N bordado *m*

embroil [ɪmbrɔ́ɪl] VT (involve in a conflict) meter en un lío; (throw into confusion) embrollar

embryo [émbrɪo] N embrión *m*

embryonic [embriánɪk] ADJ embriónico, embrionario

emerald [émɚəld] N esmeralda *f*

emerge [ɪmɝ́dʒ] VI (come into view) emerger; (arise, as a question, problem) surgir

emergency [ɪmɝ́dʒənsɪ] N emergencia *f*; — **brake** freno de emergencia *m*; — **exit** salida de emergencia *f*; — **room** urgencias *f pl*

emergent [ɪmɝ́dʒənt] ADJ emergente

emerging [ɪmɝ́dʒɪŋ] ADJ emergente

emigrant [émɪɡrənt] ADJ & N emigrante *mf*

emigrate [émɪɡret] VI emigrar

emigration [emɪɡréʃən] N emigración *f*

eminence [émənəns] N eminencia *f*

eminent [émənənt] ADJ eminente

emissary [émɪseri] N emisario -ria *mf*

emission [ɪmíʃən] N emisión *f*

emit [ɪmít] VT (light, sound) emitir; (smells) despedir; (sparks) echar

emoticon [ɪmóDɪkan] N emoticón *m*, emoticono *m*

emotion [ɪmóʃən] N emoción *f*

emotional [ɪmóʃən] ADJ (of the emotions) emocional; (arousing or expressing emotions) emotivo; (easily moved) sensible

empathy [émpəθi] N empatía *f*

emperor [émpərə] N emperador *m*; — **penguin** pingüino emperador *m*

emphasis [émfəsɪs] N énfasis *m*, hincapié *m*

emphasize [émfəsaɪz] VT enfatizar, hacer hincapié en, subrayar

emphatic [ɪmfǽDɪk] ADJ enfático

emphysema [emfɪsímə] N enfisema *m*

empire [émpaɪr] N imperio *m*

empirical [empírɪkəl] ADJ empírico

employ [ɪmplɔ́ɪ] VT emplear; (hire) emplear, ocupar; N empleo *m*; **to be in someone's —** trabajar a las órdenes de alguien

employee [ɪmplɔ́ɪ] N empleado -da *mf*

employer [ɪmplɔ́ɪə] N patrón -na *mf*; **—'s** patronal

employment [ɪmplɔ́ɪmənt] N empleo *m*; (occupation) ocupación *f*; — **bureau** agencia de empleo *f*; — **opportunities** oportunidades laborales *f pl*; **place of —** lugar de trabajo *m*

empower [ɪmpáʊə] VT (authorize) autorizar; (give strength) potenciar

empress [émprɪs] N emperatriz *f*

emptiness [émptɪnɪs] N vacío *m*

empty [émpti] ADJ (devoid of content) vacío; (devoid of activity) desocupado; **—-handed** con las manos vacías; VI/VT vaciar[se],

volcar[se]; (flow into) desembocar; N **to run on —** (of a car, person) quedarse sin combustible

emulate [émjəlet] VT emular (also computer term)

enable [inébəl] VT permitir

enact [ɪnǽkt] VT (a law) promulgar; (a role) desempeñar

enamel [ɪnǽml] N esmalte *m*; VT esmaltar

enamor [ɪnǽmə] VT enamorar; **to be —ed of** estar enamorado de

encamp [ɪnkǽmp] VI acampar

encephalitis [ɪnsefəláɪDɪs] N encefalitis *f*

enchant [ɪntʃǽnt] VT (bewitch) hechizar; (delight) encantar

enchanting [ɪntʃǽntɪŋ] ADJ encantador

enchantment [ɪntʃǽntmənt] N encantamiento *m*, encanto *m*, hechicería *f*

encircle [ɪnsɝ́kəl] VT cercar, ceñir

enclave [ánklev] N enclave *m*

enclose [ɪnklóz] VT (confine someone or something) encerrar; (fence in) cercar; (put in the same envelope) adjuntar, anexar

enclosure [ɪnklóʒə] N (wall or fence) cerca *f*; (enclosed area) cercado *m*, recinto *m*; (enclosed document) documento adjunto *m*; (act of enclosing) encierro *m*

encode [ɪnkód] VT codificar

encoding [ɪŋkóDɪŋ] N codificación *f*

encompass [ɪnkámpəs] VT (include) abarcar, englobar; (surround) circundar

encore [ánkɔr] N bis *m*; INTERJ ¡otra!

encounter [ɪnkáʊntə] VI/VT encontrar[se]; **they —ed the enemy army** se enfrentaron con el ejército enemigo; N (meeting, athletic event) encuentro *m*; (battle) enfrentamiento *m*

encourage [ɪnkɝ́ɪdʒ] VT (inspire with confidence) alentar, animar; (promote) fomentar, estimular

encouragement [ɪnkɝ́ɪdʒmənt] N (inspiration) aliento *m*, ánimo *m*; (promotion) estímulo *m*, fomento *m*

encouraging [ɪŋkɝ́ədʒɪŋ] ADJ alentador

encroach [ɪnkrótʃ] VT **to — upon** (liberties) cercenar; (territory) usurpar; (time) quitar

encrypt [ɪnkrípt] VT codificar, cifrar

encryption [ɪŋkrípʃən] N cifrado *m*

encumber [ɪnkámbə] VT (block) impedir; (burden) agobiar; (charge an account) gravar

encumbrance [ɪŋkámbrəns] N gravamen *m*

encyclopedia [ɪnsaɪkləpídɪə] N enciclopedia *f*

end [end] N (temporal) fin *m*, término *m*; (limit, boundary) final *m*, extremo *m*; (tip) cabo *m*; (aim) fin *m*; (in football) exterior *m*; — **key** tecla [de] fin *f*; **—-of-life care** cuidado terminal *m*; — **table** mesa pequeña *f*; — **zone** zona de ensayo *f*, zona de anotación *f*; **at the — of the movie** al final de la película; **the north — of town** el barrio norte; **no —**

electroencephalogram [ɪlɛktroɛnséfələgræm] N electroencefalograma *m*

electrolysis [ɪlɛktrálɪsɪs] N electrólisis *f*

electromagnet [ɪlɛktromǽgnɪt] N electroimán *m*

electromagnetic [ɪlɛktromægnéDɪK] ADJ electromagnético

electron [ɪlɛ́ktrɑn] N electrón *m*; — **microscope** microscopio electrónico *m*

electronic [ɪlɛktrɑ́nɪK] ADJ electrónico; — **banking** banca electrónica *f*; — **mail** correo electrónico *m*; —**s** electrónica *f*; — **signature** firma electrónica *f*

elegance [élɪgəns] N elegancia *f*, gallardía *f*

elegant [élɪgənt] ADJ elegante, gallardo; (gift) de lujo

element [éləmənt] N elemento *m*; (component part) componente *m*, pieza *f*; (for heating) resistencia *f*; **the —s** los elementos

elemental [ələméntl] ADJ elemental; — **forces** fuerzas de la naturaleza *f pl*

elementary [ələméntri] ADJ elemental; — **school** escuela primaria *f*

elephant [éləfənt] N elefante -ta *mf*

elevate [éləvet] VT elevar

elevation [ɛləvéʃən] N (action of elevating, elevated place) elevación *f*; (altitude) altura *f*

elevator [éləvebə-] N ascensor *m*; Am elevador *m*; (for grain) elevador *m*

eleven [ɪlɛ́vən] NUM once

elf [ɛlf] N elfo *m*; (mischievous person) pillo -lla *mf*

elicit [ɪlísɪt] VT provocar; **to — admiration** despertar admiración

eligibility [ɛlɪʤəbílɪDi] N elegibilidad *f*

eligible [élɪʤəbəl] ADJ elegible; **an — bachelor** un buen partido; **you are — for a scholarship** tienes derecho a solicitar una beca

eliminate [ɪlímənət] VT eliminar

elimination [ɪlɪmənéʃən] N eliminación *f*

elite [ɪlít] N elite *f*, élite *f*

elitist [ɪlíDɪst] ADJ & N elitista *mf*

elk [ɛlk] N alce *m*

elliptical [ɪlíptɪkəl] ADJ elíptico

elm [ɛlm] N olmo *m*

elongate [ɪlɔ́nget] VI/VT alargar[se]

elope [ɪlóp] VI fugarse para casarse a escondidas

eloquence [éləkwəns] N elocuencia *f*

eloquent [éləkwənt] ADJ elocuente

El Salvador [ɛlsǽlvɑdɔr] N El Salvador *m*

else [ɛls] ADJ & ADV **who — was there?** ¿quién más estaba? **someone —'s son** el hijo de otro; **somebody —** [algún] otro; **or —** si no; **leave town or —** vete del pueblo o sufre las consecuencias / o verás lo que es bueno; **nobody —** nadie más; **nothing —** nada más; **how —?** ¿de qué otra forma? ADV **—where** (location) en otra parte / en otro lado;

(movement) a otra parte / a otro sitio

elucidate [ɪlúsɪdet] VI/VT elucidar, dilucidar, esclarecer

elucidation [ɪlusɪdéʃən] N elucidación *f*, dilucidación *f*

elude [ɪlúd] VT eludir

elusive [ɪlúsɪv] ADJ (slippery) escurridizo; (evasive) esquivo; (difficult to understand) difícil de entender

emaciated [ɪméʃieɪDɪd] ADJ escuálido, descarnado

e-mail [ímel] N correo electrónico *m*; — **address** dirección de correo electrónico *f*

emanate [émənet] VI/VT emanar

emanation [ɛmənéʃən] N emanación *f*

emancipate [ɪmǽnsəpet] VT emancipar

emancipation [ɪmǽnsəpéʃən] N emancipación *f*

emasculate [ɪmǽskjəlet] VT castrar; (remove testicles) castrar, emascular

embalm [ɪmbám] VT (the body of a deceased person) preparar; (a mummy) embalsamar

embalming [ɪmbámɪŋ] N preparación del cuerpo *f*

embankment [ɪmbǽŋkmənt] N terraplén *m*

embargo [ɪmbárgo] N embargo *m*; VT imponer un embargo a/contra

embark [ɪmbárk] VI/VT embarcar[se]

embarrass [ɪmbǽrəs] VT (cause shame) hacerle pasar vergüenza a; (cause discomfit, financial difficulties) poner en aprietos; **—ed** avergonzado, en aprietos; **I'm —ed about my teeth** me dan vergüenza mis dientes; **I'm —ed to tell you** me da vergüenza decírtelo

embarrassing [ɪmbǽrəsɪŋ] ADJ (shameful) vergonzoso, penoso; (hindering) embarazoso

embarrassment [ɪmbǽrəsmənt] N (shame) vergüenza *f*, bochorno *m*, pena *f*; (act of embarrassing) vergüenza *f*; (financial difficulty) aprieto *m*; **he's an — to the company** hace quedar mal a la compañía; **we have an — of riches** nadamos en la abundancia

embassy [émbəsi] N embajada *f*

embattled [ɪmbǽtld] ADJ hostigado, agobiado

embed [ɪmbéd] VT incrustar

embedded [ɪmbéDɪd] ADJ incrustado

embellish [ɪmbélɪʃ] VT adornar, ornamentar

ember [émbə-] N ascua *f*, brasa *f*

embezzle [ɪmbézəl] VT desfalcar, malversar

embezzlement [ɪmbézəlmənt] N desfalco *m*, peculado *m*, malversación *f*

embitter [ɪmbíDə-] VT amargar

emblem [émbləm] N emblema *m*, divisa *f*

embody [ɪmbáDi] VT (personify) personificar; (to provide a body) encarnar

embolism [émbəlɪzəm] N embolia *f*

embrace [ɪmbrés] VI/VT (hug, adopt) abrazar[se]; (include) abarcar; N abrazo *m*

embroider [ɪmbrɔ́ɪdə·] vɪ/vᴛ bordar, recamar

embroidery [ɪmbrɔ́ɪdəri] ɴ bordado m

embroil [ɪmbrɔ́ɪl] vᴛ (involve in a conflict) meter en un lío; (throw into confusion) embrollar

embryo [émbrio] ɴ embrión m

embryonic [embriánɪk] ᴀᴅᴊ embriónico, embrionario

emerald [ém⭢əld] ɴ esmeralda f

emerge [ɪmɝ́dʒ] vɪ (come into view) emerger; (arise, as a question, problem) surgir

emergency [ɪmɝ́dʒənsi] ɴ emergencia f; — **brake** freno de emergencia m; — **exit** salida de emergencia f; — **room** urgencias f pl

emergent [ɪmɝ́dʒənt] ᴀᴅᴊ emergente

emerging [ɪmɝ́dʒɪŋ] ᴀᴅᴊ emergente

emigrant [émɪɡrənt] ᴀᴅᴊ & ɴ emigrante mf

emigrate [émɪɡret] vɪ emigrar

emigration [emɪɡréʃən] ɴ emigración f

eminence [émənəns] ɴ eminencia f

eminent [émənənt] ᴀᴅᴊ eminente

emissary [émɪseri] ɴ emisario -ria mf

emission [ɪmíʃən] ɴ emisión f

emit [ɪmít] vᴛ (light, sound) emitir; (smells) despedir; (sparks) echar

emoticon [ɪmóᴅɪkan] ɴ emoticón m, emoticono m

emotion [ɪmóʃən] ɴ emoción f

emotional [ɪmóʃənł] ᴀᴅᴊ (of the emotions) emocional; (arousing or expressing emotions) emotivo; (easily moved) sensible

empathy [émpəθi] ɴ empatía f

emperor [émpər⭢] ɴ emperador m; — **penguin** pingüino emperador m

emphasis [émfəsɪs] ɴ énfasis m, hincapié m

emphasize [émfəsaɪz] vᴛ enfatizar, hacer hincapié en, subrayar

emphatic [ɪmfǽᴅɪk] ᴀᴅᴊ enfático

emphysema [emfɪsímə] ɴ enfisema m

empire [émpaɪr] ɴ imperio m

empirical [empírɪkəl] ᴀᴅᴊ empírico

employ [ɪmplɔ́ɪ] vᴛ emplear; (hire) emplear, ocupar; ɴ empleo m; **to be in someone's —** trabajar a las órdenes de alguien

employee [ɪmplɔ́ɪ] ɴ empleado -da mf

employer [ɪmplɔ́ɪə·] ɴ patrón -na mf; **—s'** patronal

employment [ɪmplɔ́ɪmənt] ɴ empleo m; (occupation) ocupación f; — **bureau** agencia de empleo f; — **opportunities** oportunidades laborales f pl; **place of —** lugar de trabajo m

empower [ɪmpáʊə·] vᴛ (authorize) autorizar; (give strength) potenciar

empress [émprɪs] ɴ emperatriz f

emptiness [émptɪnɪs] ɴ vacío m

empty [émpti] ᴀᴅᴊ (devoid of content) vacío; (devoid of activity) desocupado; **—handed** con las manos vacías; vɪ/vᴛ vaciar[se],

volcar[se]; (flow into) desembocar; ɴ **to run on —** (of a car, person) quedarse sin combustible

emulate [émjəlet] vᴛ emular (also computer term)

enable [ɪnébəł] vᴛ permitir

enact [ɪnǽkt] vᴛ (a law) promulgar; (a role) desempeñar

enamel [ɪnǽməl] ɴ esmalte m; vᴛ esmaltar

enamor [ɪnǽmⵣ] vᴛ enamorar; **to be —ed of** estar enamorado de

encamp [ɪnkǽmp] vɪ acampar

encephalitis [ɪnsefəláɪᴅɪs] ɴ encefalitis f

enchant [ɪntʃǽnt] vᴛ (bewitch) hechizar; (delight) encantar

enchanting [ɪntʃǽntɪŋ] ᴀᴅᴊ encantador

enchantment [ɪntʃǽntmənt] ɴ encantamiento m, encanto m, hechicería f

encircle [ɪnsɝ́kəł] vᴛ cercar, ceñir

enclave [ánklev] ɴ enclave m

enclose [ɪnklóz] vᴛ (confine someone or something) encerrar; (fence in) cercar; (put in the same envelope) adjuntar, anexar

enclosure [ɪnklóʒⵣ] ɴ (wall or fence) cerca f; (enclosed area) cercado m, recinto m; (enclosed document) documento adjunto m; (act of enclosing) encierro m

encode [ɪŋkód] vᴛ codificar

encoding [ɪŋkódɪŋ] ɴ codificación f

encompass [ɪnkámpəs] vᴛ (include) abarcar, englobar; (surround) circundar

encore [ánkɔr] ɴ bis m; ɪɴᴛᴇʀᴊ ¡otra!

encounter [ɪnkáʊntⵣ] vɪ/vᴛ encontrar[se]; **they —ed the enemy army** se enfrentaron con el ejército enemigo; ɴ (meeting, athletic event) encuentro m; (battle) enfrentamiento m

encourage [ɪnkɝ́ɪdʒ] vᴛ (inspire with confidence) alentar, animar; (promote) fomentar, estimular

encouragement [ɪnkɝ́ɪdʒmənt] ɴ (inspiration) aliento m, ánimo m; (promotion) estímulo m, fomento m

encouraging [ɪŋkɝ́ədʒɪŋ] ᴀᴅᴊ alentador

encroach [ɪnkrótʃ] vᴛ **to — upon** (liberties) cercenar; (territory) usurpar; (time) quitar

encrypt [ɪnkrípt] vᴛ codificar, cifrar

encryption [ɪŋkrípʃən] ɴ cifrado m

encumber [ɪnkámbⵣ] vᴛ (block) impedir; (burden) agobiar; (charge an account) gravar

encumbrance [ɪŋkámbrəns] ɴ gravamen m

encyclopedia [ɪnsaɪkləpídiə] ɴ enciclopedia f

end [end] ɴ (temporal) fin m, término m; (limit, boundary) final m, extremo m; (tip) cabo m; (aim) fin m; (in football) exterior m; — **key** tecla [de] fin f; **—-of-life care** cuidado terminal m; — **table** mesa pequeña f; — **zone** zona de ensayo f, zona de anotación f; **at the — of the movie** al final de la película; **the north — of town** el barrio norte; **no —**

of things un sinfín de cosas; **at the — of the day** al fin y al cabo; **on —** de punta; **for days on —** día tras día; **to put an — to** poner fin a; VI/VT terminar; (a street) morir; **he —ed his life** puso fin a su vida; **a prayer —s the class** la clase termina con una oración; **a war to — all wars** una guerra que supera a todas las anteriores; ADV **— to —** uno tras otro

endanger [ɪndéndʒɚ] VT poner en peligro; **—ed species** especie en peligro de extinción f

endear [ɪndír] VI **to — oneself** congraciarse; **his humor —ed him to her** se ganó la simpatía de ella gracias a su humor

endearing [ɪndírɪŋ] ADJ entrañable

endeavor [ɪndévɚ] VT (try) tratar de, intentar, procurar; VI (strive) esforzarse por; N esfuerzo m

endemic [ɪndémɪk] ADJ endémico

ending [éndɪŋ] N final m; (of a story) desenlace m; (derivational, inflectional) terminación f; (inflectional) desinencia f

endless [éndlɪs] ADJ (having no end) interminable; (continuous) sin fin; (infinite) eterno

endocrine [éndəkrɪn] ADJ endocrino

endocrinology [endəkrɪnáləǰi] N endocrinología f

endoderm [éndodə͡m] N endodermo m

endorphin [ɪndɔ́rfɪn] N endorfina f

endorse [ɪndɔ́rs] VT (sign a check) endosar; (support) respaldar; (authorize a document) refrendar, visar

endorsement [ɪndɔ́rsmənt] N (signature) endoso m; (backing) respaldo m; (authorization) refrendo m

endorser [ɪndɔ́rsɚ] N (check signer) endosante mf; (supporter) partidario -ria mf; (authorizer) refrendario -ria mf

endow [ɪndáU] VT (grant funds) hacer un legado; (furnish powers) dotar

endowment [ɪndáUmənt] N (funds granted) legado m, dotación f; (power) dote f; **— annuity** anualidad dotal f; **— fund** fondo de un legado m

endurance [ɪndúrəns] N (stamina) resistencia f; (ability to bear pain) aguante m

endure [ɪndúr, ɪndǰúr] VT (undergo) sobrellevar, soportar, pasar; VI (live on) durar; (bear up) aguantar

enema [énəmə] N enema m, lavativa f

enemy [énəmi] N enemigo -ga mf

energetic [enɚdʒɛ́dɪk] ADJ enérgico

energy [énɚǰi] N energía f; **— policy** política energética f

enervate [énɚvet] VT enervar, debilitar

enforce [ɪnfɔ́rs] VT hacer cumplir

enforcement [ɪnfɔ́rsmənt] N **the sheriff is responsible for the — of the law** el

alguacil es responsable de hacer cumplir la ley

engage [ɪngéǰ] VT (hire) contratar; (attract) captar, atraer; (interlock) engranar; **to — the brake** poner el freno; **to — someone in conversation** trabar conversación con alguien; **to — in battle** trabar batalla; **to be —d in something** estar ocupado en algo; **to be —d to be married** estar comprometido [para casarse], estar prometido

engaged [ɪngéǰd] ADJ comprometido

engagement [ɪngéǰmənt] N (commitment) compromiso m; (betrothal) compromiso m, noviazgo m; (employment) empleo m; (battle) batalla f; (gear interlocking) engranaje m

engender [ɪndʒéndɚ] VT engendrar

engine [énǰɪn] N (machine) máquina f; (in a vehicle) motor m; (locomotive) locomotora f; **— block** bloque del motor m

engineer [enǰənír] N ingeniero -ra mf; (of locomotive) maquinista mf; VT (create) idear; (plot) maquinar

engineering [enǰənírɪŋ] N ingeniería f

English [ɪŋglɪʃ] ADJ inglés; N (spin) efecto m; **the —** los ingleses; **—man, —woman** inglés -esa mf

engrave [ɪngrév] VI/VT grabar

engraver [ɪngrévɚ] N grabador -ora mf

engraving [ɪngrévɪŋ] N grabado m

engross [ɪngrós] VT absorber

engrossed [ɪngróst] ADJ absorto

engulf [ɪngʌ́lf] VT (swallow) tragar; (overwhelm) abrumar

enhance [ɪnhǽns] VT (intensify) realzar; (improve) mejorar

enigma [ɪnígmə] N enigma m

enjoin [ɪndʒɔ́ɪn] VT instar; **to — from** prohibir

enjoy [ɪndʒɔ́ɪ] VI/VT (take pleasure) disfrutar [de], gozar [de]; (benefit from) gozar [de]; **—!** ¡que lo disfrutes! **to — oneself** divertirse; **to — the use of** usufructuar

enjoyable [ɪndʒɔ́ɪəbəl] ADJ (pleasant) agradable, gozoso; (fun) ameno

enjoyment [ɪndʒɔ́ɪmənt] N (act of enjoying) goce m, disfrute m; (right of use) usufructo m; (pleasure) placer m, gozo m

enlarge [ɪnlɑ́rǰ] VI/VT agrandar[se]; VT (blow up a photo) ampliar; VI **to — upon** explayarse sobre, extenderse sobre

enlargement [ɪnlɑ́rǰmənt] N (photo, building) ampliación f; (act of enlarging) agrandamiento m; (temporary swelling) dilatación f

enlighten [ɪnláɪtn̩] VT (morally) iluminar; (intellectually) explicar, ilustrar

enlightenment [ɪnláɪtn̩mənt] N (moral) iluminación f; (intellectual) explicación f; **the — la Ilustración**

enlist [ɪnlíst] VI/VT (for the army) alistar[se]; (for a campaign) conseguir el apoyo de

enlistment [ɪnlístmənt] N alistamiento m
enliven [ɪnláɪvən] VT animar, avivar
enmity [énmɪdi] N enemistad f
ennoble [ɪnnóbəl] VT ennoblecer
enormous [ɪnɔ́rməs] ADJ enorme, descomunal
enough [ɪnʌ́f] ADJ suficiente; ADV **he's tall —** tiene altura suficiente; N lo suficiente; **we have — to live comfortably** tenemos lo suficiente como para vivir cómodamente; **that is —** con eso basta; **more than —** bastante; INTERJ ¡basta!
enrage [ɪnréʤ] VT enfurecer
enrapture [ɪnrǽptʃə] VT embelesar
enrich [ɪnrítʃ] VT enriquecer
enrichment [ɪnrítʃmənt] N enriquecimiento m
enroll [ɪnról] VI/VT matricular[se], inscribir[se]
enrollment [ɪnrólmənt] N matrícula f, inscripción f; **what is your —?** ¿cuántos alumnos tienes matriculados?
ensemble [ɑnsámbəl] N conjunto m
ensign [énsɪn] N (naval rank) alférez de fragata mf; (flag) enseña f; (badge) insignia f
enslave [ɪnslév] VT esclavizar
ensnare [ɪnsnér] VT atrapar, coger en una trampa
ensue [ɪnsú] VI (follow) ocurrir después, suceder; (result from) resultar; **the ensuing events** los sucesos subsiguientes
ensure [ɪnʃúr] VT asegurar
entail [ɪntél] VT implicar, conllevar
entangle [ɪntǽŋgəl] VT enredar
enter [éntə] VT (go in) entrar en/a; (join) ingresar en/a; (write) escribir; (put data in a computer) dar entrada a; (put data in account books) asentar; (start negotiations) iniciar; VI/VT (register for a competition) inscribir[se]; VI salir / entrar a escena; **to — into** (make an agreement) concertar; (form part of) figurar en
enterprise [éntəpraɪz] N empresa f
enterprising [éntəpraɪzɪŋ] ADJ emprendedor
entertain [entətén] VI/VT (amuse) divertir, recrear; (host) invitar; **we — a lot** tenemos invitados muy a menudo; (consider) contemplar; (harbor) abrigar
entertainer [entəténə] N artista mf
entertaining [entəténɪŋ] ADJ (fun) divertido; (serving as pastime) entretenido; (pleasant) ameno
entertainment [entəténmənt] N (source of fun) diversión f; (pastime) entretenimiento m; (of guests) agasajo m
enthrall [ɪnθrɔ́l] VT (captivate) cautivar, hechizar; (make a slave of) esclavizar
enthusiasm [ɪnθúziæzəm] N entusiasmo m
enthusiast [ɪnθúzɪɪst] N entusiasta mf
enthusiastic [ɪnθuziǽstɪk] ADJ entusiasta; **I'm very — about the trip** estoy muy entusiasmado con el viaje

entice [ɪntáɪs] VI/VT (attract) atraer; (lure) tentar; (seduce) seducir
entire [ɪntáɪr] ADJ (unbroken) entero; (complete) completo; **the — crew** toda la tripulación, la tripulación entera
entirety [ɪntáɪrɪdi] N totalidad f
entitle [ɪntáɪdl] VT (give a title) titular, intitular; (give a right) dar derecho
entitlement [ɪntáɪdlmənt] N derecho m
entity [éntɪdi] N (institution) entidad f; (being) ente m, ser m
entomology [entəmálədʒi] N entomología f
entourage [ánturaʤ] N séquito m, cortejo m
entrails [éntrelz] N entrañas f pl
entrance¹ [éntrəns] N (act, point of entering) entrada f; (permission to enter) ingreso m; **— examination** examen de ingreso m
entrance² [ɪntrǽns] VT embelesar
entrant [éntrənt] N participante mf; **—s in the law profession** abogados recién recibidos m pl
entrap [ɪntrǽp] VT (ensnare) coger con una trampa; (deceive) embaucar
entreaty [ɪntrídi] N súplica f, ruego m
entrench [ɪntréntʃ] VI (establish) afianzar[se]; (dig trenches) atrincherar; **a deeply —ed habit** un hábito muy arraigado
entrepreneur [antrəprənúr] N empresario -ria mf
entrepreneurship [antrəprənúrʃɪp] N espíritu emprendedor m
entropy [éntrəpi] N entropía f
entrust [ɪntrʌ́st] VT confiar, encomendar
entry [éntri] N (act, point of entry) entrada f; (permission to enter) ingreso m; (record) anotación f; (contestant) participante mf; (dictionary definition) entrada f, artículo m; (computer) entrada f; (in bookkeeping) asiento m; **double — accounting** contabilidad por partida doble f; ADJ **—-level** que no requiere experiencia
enumerate [ɪnúməret] VT enumerar
enunciate [ɪnʌ́nsiet] VI/VT (pronounce) articular; (state a theory) enunciar; (proclaim) proclamar
envelop [ɪnvéləp] VT envolver
envelope [énvəlop] N sobre m
enviable [énviəbəl] ADJ envidiable
envious [énviəs] ADJ envidioso
environment [ɪnváɪənmənt] N ambiente m, medio ambiente m; (biological) medio ambiente m, ecología f; (in computers) entorno m; ADJ ambiental; (biological) medioambiental, ecológico
environmental [ɪnvaɪənméntl] ADJ ambiental; (biological) medioambiental, ecológico; **— impact study** estudio del impacto ambiental m
environmentalist [ɪnvaɪənméntlɪst] N

ecologista *mf*

envisage [ɪnvízɪdʒ] VT anticipar, prever

envision [ɪnvíʒən] VT imaginar

envoy [ánvɔɪ] N enviado -da *mf*

envy [énvi] N envidia *f*; VI/VT envidiar

enzyme [énzaɪm] N enzima *f*

ephemeral [ɪfémə.əl] ADJ efímero

epic [épɪk] ADJ épico; N (poem) epopeya *f*; (genre) épica *f*

epicenter [épɪsɛntə.] N epicentro *m*

epidemic [ɛpɪdémɪk] ADJ epidémico; N epidemia *f*

epidermis [ɛpɪdə́.mɪs] N epidermis *f*

epiglottis [épɪgladɪs] N epiglotis *f*

epilepsy [épələpsi] N epilepsia *f*

epileptic [ɛpəléptɪk] ADJ epiléptico

epilogue, epilog [épəlɔg] N epílogo *m*

epiphany [ɪpɪ́fəni] N epifanía *f*

episode [épɪsod] N episodio *m*

episodic [ɛpɪsádɪk] ADJ (sporadic) episódico; (serial) en episodios

epitaph [épɪtæf] N epitafio *m*

epitome [ɪpídəmi] N epítome *m*

epoch [épək] N época *f*; —**-making** trascendental

Epsom salt [épsəmsɔ́lt] N sal de Epsom *f*

equal [íkwəl] ADJ igual; — **rights** igualdad de derechos *f*; **an** — **contest** una competición pareja; **to be** — **to a task** ser capaz de cumplir una tarea; N igual *m*; — **sign** signo de igual *m*; VT igualar

equality [ɪkwálɪdi] N igualdad *f*

equalize [íkwəlaɪz] VT igualar; (electronically) ecualizar

equalizer [íkwəlaɪzə.] N (in soccer) gol del empate *m*

equally [íkwəli] ADV igualmente

equate [ɪkwét] VT equiparar

equation [ɪkwéʒən] N ecuación *f*

equator [ɪkwédə.] N ecuador *m*

Equatorial Guinea [ɛkwətɔ́riəłgíni] N Guinea Ecuatorial *f*

equidistant [ikwɪdístənt] ADJ equidistante

equilibrium [ikwəlíbriəm] N equilibrio *m*

equine [íkwaɪn] ADJ & N equino *m*

equinox [íkwənɑks] N equinoccio *m*

equip [ɪkwíp] VT equipar

equipment [ɪkwípmənt] N (supplies) equipo *m*; (act of equipping) equipamiento *m*

equitable [ékwɪdəbəl] ADJ equitativo, justo

equity [ékwɪdi] N equidad *f*, valor libre de hipoteca de una propiedad *m*; **equities** acciones *f pl*

equivalent [ɪkwívələnt] ADJ & N equivalente *m*

equivocal [ɪkwívəkəl] ADJ equívoco

era [írə] N era *f*

eradicate [ɪrǽdɪket] VT (extirpate) erradicar; (pull up by roots) arrancar

eradication [ɪrǽdɪkéʃən] N erradicación *f*

erase [ɪrés] VI/VT borrar[se]

eraser [ɪrésə.] N (pencil) goma de borrar *f*; (blackboard) borrador *m*

erasure [ɪréʃə.] N (act of erasing) borrado *m*; (smudge) borrón *m*

erect [ɪrékt] ADJ erecto; (of the body) erguido; VT erigir

ergonomic [ɜ.gənámɪk] ADJ ergonómico

ergonomics [ɜ.gənámɪks] N ergonomía *f*

Eritrea [ɛritríə] N Eritrea *f*

Eritrean [ɛritríən] ADJ & N eritreo -a *mf*

ermine [ɜ́.mɪn] N armiño *m*

erode [ɪród] VI/VT erosionar[se]

erogenous [ɪrádʒənəs] ADJ erógeno

erosion [ɪróʒən] N erosión *f*

err [ɛr] VI errar

errand [érənd] N mandado *m*, recado *m*; — **boy** mandadero *m*

errant [érənt] ADJ errante

erratic [ɪrǽdɪk] ADJ (unpredictable) irregular, errático; (eccentric) excéntrico; (wandering) errante

erroneous [ɪróniəs] ADJ erróneo, errado

error [érə.] N (also in baseball) error *m*; **to be in** — estar errado; — **message** mensaje de error *m*

erudite [érjədaɪt] ADJ erudito

erudition [erjədíʃən] N erudición *f*

erupt [ɪrápt] VI (volcano) hacer erupción; (angry person) estallar; (pimples) salir

eruption [ɪrápʃən] N erupción *f*

escalate [éskəlet] VI (prices) aumentar; (violence) intensificarse, aumentar

escalator [éskəledə.] N escalera mecánica *f*

escapade [éskəped] N (adventure) aventura *f*; (prank) travesura *f*

escape [ɪskép] N (of gas) escape *m*; (from reality) escape *m*, evasión *f*; (of prisoners) fuga *f*, evasión *f*; (means of escaping) escapatoria *f*; — **key** tecla de escape *f*; VI escapar[se], evadirse; VT (elude) eludir; **his name** —**s me** no me acuerdo de su nombre

escort[1] [éskɔrt] N (people who accompany) escolta *mf*; (male companion) acompañante *m*; (paid female companion) señorita de compañía *f*

escort[2] [ɪskɔ́rt] VT (protect) escoltar; (accompany) acompañar

escrow [éskro] N — **account** cuenta de depósito en garantía *f*; ADV LOC **in** — en custodia

escudo [ɪskúdo] N escudo *m*

Eskimo [éskəmo] N esquimal *mf*

esophagus [ɪsáfəgəs] N esófago *m*

esoteric [ɛsətérɪk] ADJ esotérico

especial [ɪspéʃəl] ADJ especial

especially [ɪspéʃəli] ADV (above all) especialmente; (mainly) sobre todo; **he's** — **tired today** hoy está más cansado que de costumbre

espionage [éspiənɑʒ] N espionaje *m*

esplanade [ésplənəd] N explanada *f*

espouse [ıspáuz] VT defender, abrazar

essay[1] [ése] N ensayo *m*

essay[2] [esé] VT ensayar

essence [ésəns] N esencia *f*; **time is of the —** el tiempo apremia

essential [ısénʃəl] ADJ esencial

establish [ıstǽblıʃ] VT (cause to be accepted, prove the validity of) establecer; (found) fundar

establishment [ıstǽblıʃmənt] N (action or fact) establecimiento *m*, conformación *f*; (authority) establishment *m*; (of a custom, system) implantación *f*; (of a regime) instauración *f*

estate [ıstét] N (piece of land) hacienda *f*; (possessions) bienes *m pl*; (property) propiedades *f pl*; (of a deceased person) testamentaria *f*; **— tax** impuesto de sucesión *m*

esteem [ıstím] VT (regard highly) estimar; (consider) considerar; N estima *f*

estimate[1] [éstəmet] VT estimar, evaluar; VI hacer una estimación

estimate[2] [éstəmıt] N (calculation) estimación *f*; (approximate charge) presupuesto *m*

estimation [estəméʃən] N (opinion) juicio *m*; (esteem) estima *f*; (estimate) estimación *f*; **in my —** a mi juicio

Estonia [estóniə] N Estonia *f*

Estonian [estóniən] ADJ & N estonio -nia *mf*

estrange [ıstréndʒ] VT (alienate) enajenar; **to become —d** separarse

estrogen [éstrədʒən] N estrógeno *m*

estuary [éstʃueri] N estuario *m*

et cetera, etc. [etsétrə] ADV etcétera, etc.

etch [etʃ] VI/VT (engrave) grabar; (outline) perfilar[se]

etching [étʃıŋ] N grabado *m*

eternal [ıtɜ́rnl] ADJ eterno

eternity [ıtɜ́rnıDi] N eternidad *f*

ethanol [éθənɑl] N etanol *m*

ether [íθə-] N éter *m*

ethernet [íθə-net] N ethernet *m*

ethical [éθıkəl] ADJ ético

ethics [éθıks] N ética *f*

Ethiopia [iθ[i]ópiə] N Etiopía *f*

Ethiopian [iθ[i]ópiən] ADJ & N etíope *mf*

ethnic [éθnık] ADJ étnico; (dances, clothes) tradicional; **— Chinese** de ascendencia china; **— cleansing** limpieza étnica *f*

ethnicity [eθnísıDi] N etnicidad *f*; (group) grupo étnico *m*

ethnography [eθnágrəfi] N etnografía *f*

ethnology [eθnálədʒi] N etnología *f*

ethyl alcohol [éθəlǽlkəhɑl] N alcohol etílico *m*

etiquette [édıkıt] N etiqueta *f*

etymology [eDəmálədʒi] N etimología *f*

EU [European Union] [íjú] N UE *f*

eucalyptus [jukəlíptəs] N eucalipto *m*

eulogy [júlədʒi] N (praise) elogio *m*; (at a funeral) panegírico *m*

eunuch [júnək] N eunuco *m*

euphemism [júfəmızəm] N eufemismo *m*

euphoria [jufɔ́riə] N euforia *f*

euro [júro] N euro *m*

Europe [júrəp] N Europa *f*

European [jurəpíən] ADJ & N europeo -a *mf*; **— Union** Unión Europea *f*; **— Union budget** presupuesto comunitario *m*

Eustachian tube [justéʃən] N trompa de Eustaquio *f*

euthanasia [juθənéʒə] N eutanasia *f*

evacuate [ıvǽkjuet] VI/VT (remove due to danger, defecate) evacuar; (empty a building) desalojar

evade [ıvéd] VT (taxes, responsibilities) evadir, burlar; (questions) eludir

evaluate [ıvǽljuet] VT (assess) evaluar; (appraise) avaluar, tasar

evaluation [ıvæljuéʃən] N evaluación *f*

evangelical [ıvændʒélıkəl] ADJ evangélico

evaporate [ıvǽpəret] VI/VT evaporar[se]; VI (vanish) esfumarse

evaporation [ıvæpəréʃən] N evaporación *f*

evasion [ıvéʒən] N (escape) evasión *f*; (subterfuge) evasiva *f*

evasive [ıvésıv] ADJ evasivo

eve [iv] N (day before) víspera *f*; (evening) atardecer *m*; **on the — of** en vísperas de

even [ívən] ADJ (flat) plano, llano; (smooth) liso; (parallel) paralelo; (without fluctuation) parejo; (equal) igual; (divisible by two) par; (placid) tranquilo; **—handed** imparcial; **—-tempered** apacible; **an — dozen** una docena exacta; **to be — with someone** estar a mano con alguien; **to get — with someone** desquitarse de alguien; ADV (still, yet) aun; (for extreme case) hasta, inclusive, incluso; **— if/though** aun cuando; **— my mother went** hasta mi madre fue; **— so** aun así; **it's — more expensive** es aun más caro; **not —** ni siquiera; VI/VT (make a surface even) nivelar[se]; (make accounts even) emparejar

evening [ívnıŋ] N tarde *f*; (dusk) atardecer *m*; **— gown** vestido de fiesta *m*, vestido de noche *m*; **— party** velada *f*; **— star** lucero de la tarde *m*; **good —!** ¡buenas noches!

event [ıvént] N (happening) hecho *m*, evento *m*; (of importance) acontecimiento *m*, suceso *m*; **in any —** en todo caso; **in the — of** en caso de

eventful [ıvéntfəl] ADJ agitado, movido

eventual [ıvéntʃuəl] ADJ (later) posterior; (final) final

eventuality [ıventʃuǽlıDi] N eventualidad *f*

eventually [ɪvéntʃuəlɪ] ADV a la larga

ever [évə] ADV alguna vez; **— more** para siempre; **— since** desde entonces; **have you — studied French?** ¿alguna vez has estudiado francés? **how did you — do this?** ¿cómo pudiste hacer esto? **for — and —** por/para siempre jamás; **hardly —** casi nunca; **if — si** si alguna vez; **more than —** más que nunca; **the best friend I — had** el mejor amigo que he tenido jamás; **for — more** para/por siempre jamás; ADJ **— green** [planta] perenne f; **— lasting** eterno

every [évrɪ] ADJ (each) cada; **— child is different** cada niño es diferente; (all) todo[s]; **— once in a while** de vez en cuando; **— other day** cada dos días, un día sí y otro no; **— where** (location) por/en todas partes; (direction) a todas partes; **we go — Friday** vamos todos los viernes; PRON **— body** todos -das mf pl, todo el mundo m; **— day** todos los días; **— one** todos -das mf pl, todo el mundo m; **— thing you are — thing to me** eres todo para mí; ADJ **— day** (of clothes) de diario, de todos los días; (of occurrences) cotidiano

evict [ɪvíkt] VT desalojar

evidence [évɪdəns] N evidencia f; (data in court) prueba f; **to be in —** ser evidente; VI/VT evidenciar[se], demostrar[se]

evident [évɪdənt] ADJ evidente

evil [ívəl] ADJ (wicked) malo, malvado; (harmful) maligno; N (force of nature) mal m; (human wickedness) maldad f; **— doer** malhechor -ora mf; **— eye** mal de ojo m; **the lesser of two — s** el mal menor

evocation [ɛvəkéʃən] N evocación f

evoke [ɪvók] VT (call up) evocar; (elicit) provocar

evolution [ɛvəlúʃən] N evolución f

evolutionary [ɛvəlúʃəneri] ADJ evolutivo

evolve [ɪválv] VI/VT desarrollar[se]; VI evolucionar

ewe [ju] N oveja f

ex [ɛks] N ex mf

exacerbate [ɪgzǽsəbet] VI/VT exacerbar

exact [ɪgzǽkt] ADJ exacto; VT exigir

exacting [ɪgzǽktɪŋ] ADJ exigente

exactly [ɪgzǽktlɪ] ADV exactamente, precisamente; **he's not — a genius** no es un genio ni mucho menos / no es ningún genio que digamos; **they arrived — at three** llegaron exactamente a las tres

exaggerate [ɪgzǽdʒəret] VT exagerar

exalt [ɪgzɔ́lt] VT exaltar

exam [ɪgzǽm] N examen m

examination [ɪgzǽmənéʃən] N examen m (also medical)

examine [ɪgzǽmɪn] VT (inspect) examinar; (analyze) analizar

example [ɪgzǽmpəl] N ejemplo m

exasperate [ɪgzǽspəret] VT exasperar

excavate [ékskəvet] VT excavar

excavator [ékskəvedə] N (person) excavador -ora mf; (machine) excavadora f

exceed [ɪksíd] VT (go beyond) exceder, rebasar; (be superior to) superar, sobrepasar

exceeding [ɪksíDɪŋ] N superación f

exceedingly [ɪksíDɪŋlɪ] ADV sumamente, extremadamente

excel [ɪksél] VI sobresalir, lucirse, descollar

excellence [éksələns] N excelencia f

excellent [éksələnt] ADJ excelente

except [ɪksépt] PREP excepto, menos; **all the students — Pam** todos los estudiantes menos Pam; CONJ excepto, salvo; **the cars are identical — that one is older** los coches son idénticos salvo que uno es más viejo; **we would go to the beach, — for the inclement weather** iríamos a la playa si no fuera por el mal tiempo; VT exceptuar

excepting [ɪkséptɪŋ] PREP exceptuando

exception [ɪksépʃən] N excepción f; **with the — of** con/a excepción de; **to take —** (object) objetar; (resent) ofenderse

exceptional [ɪksépʃənl] ADJ (unusual) excepcional; (gifted) superdotado; (handicapped) con necesidades especiales

excerpt[1] [éksəpt] N fragmento m

excerpt[2] [éksəpt, ɪksəpt] VT seleccionar fragmentos

excess [ékses] N exceso m, hartazgo m; **— baggage** exceso de equipaje m; **— profits tax** impuesto sobre ganancias excesivas m; **— weight** exceso de peso m; **in — of twenty pounds** más de veinte libras; **to drink to —** beber en exceso

excessive [ɪksésɪv] ADJ excesivo, desmedido

exchange [ɪkstʃéndʒ] VT (replace with something similar) cambiar; (give mutually) intercambiar; (trade political prisoners, books, CDs) canjear; (barter) permutar; **to — greetings** saludarse; N (replacement) cambio m; (interchange) intercambio m; (barter) permuta f; (of prisoners, books) canje m; (for stock trading) bolsa f; (for commodity trading) lonja f; (telephone) central de teléfonos f; **— student** estudiante de intercambio mf; **rate of —** tipo de cambio m, tasa de cambio f

excise [éksaɪz] N impuesto sobre bienes de consumo m

excite [ɪksáɪt] VT (agitate, arouse) excitar, alborotar; (enthuse) entusiasmar

excited [ɪksáɪDɪd] ADJ (agitated, aroused) excitado; (enthusiastic) entusiasmado, ilusionado; **to get —** (aroused) excitarse; (enthused) entusiasmarse

excitement [ɪksáɪtmənt] N (arousal) excitación f; (enthusiasm) entusiasmo m

exciting [ıksáıdıŋ] ADJ (stimulating) excitante; (thrilling) emocionante, apasionante

exclaim [ıksklém] VI exclamar

exclamation [ɛkskləméʃən] N exclamación f; — **point** signo de admiración m

exclude [ıksklúd] VT excluir

exclusion [ıksklúʒən] N exclusión f

exclusive [ıksklúsıv] ADJ exclusivo; — **of** sin incluir

excommunicate [ɛkskəmjúnıket] VT excomulgar

excrement [ékskrəmənt] N excremento m

excrescence [ıkskrésəns] N excrecencia f

excrete [ıkskrít] VI/VT excretar

excretion [ıkskríʃən] N excreción f

excruciating [ıkskrúʃiedıŋ] ADJ insoportable, atroz

excursion [ıkskɔ́ʒən] N excursión f

excusable [ıkskjúzəbəl] ADJ excusable, disculpable

excuse[1] [ıkskjúz] VT (release from a duty, seek exemption) excusar, eximir; (forgive) disculpar, perdonar; — **me!** (forgive me) disculpe; (let me pass) con permiso; (excuse me?) ¿cómo? ¿perdón? *Mex* ¿mande?

excuse[2] [ıkskjús] N excusa f, disculpa f; **it's a poor — for a car** no merece llamarse un coche

executable [ɛgzəkjúdəbəl] ADJ ejecutable

execute [éksıkjut] VT ejecutar (also computer term); (by firing squad) fusilar

execution [ɛksıkjúʃən] N ejecución f; (by firing squad) fusilamiento m; — **wall** paredón m

executioner [ɛksıkjúʃənə] N verdugo mf

executive [ıgzékjədıv] ADJ ejecutivo; N (person) ejecutivo -va mf; (branch of government) poder ejecutivo m

executor [ıgzékjədə] N albacea mf

exemplary [ıgzémpləri] ADJ ejemplar

exemplify [ıgzémpləfaı] VT ejemplificar

exempt [ıgzémpt] VT eximir, dispensar; ADJ exento, libre

exemption [ıgzémpʃən] N exención f, franquicia f

exercise [éksəsaız] N ejercicio m; —**s** ceremonia f; VT ejercer; VI hacer ejercicio; — **electrocardiogram** prueba de esfuerzo máximo f; **to be —d about something** estar disgustado por algo

exert [ıgzɔ́t] VT ejercer; **to — oneself** esforzarse, empeñarse

exertion [ıgzɔ́ʃən] N (use of powers, faculties) ejercicio m; (vigorous action) esfuerzo m, empeño m

exfoliation [ıksfoliéʃən] N exfoliación f

exhale [ɛkshél] VT exhalar; VI espirar

exhaust [ıgzɔ́st] VT agotar, desmadejar; (a topic) tratar exhaustivamente; N (from a car) escape m

exhausted [ıgzɔ́stıd] ADJ rendido, agotado

exhausting [ıgzɔ́stıŋ] ADJ agotador

exhaustion [ıgzɔ́stʃən] N (act or process of exhausting) agotamiento m; (weakness, tiredness) fatiga f

exhaustive [ıgzɔ́stıv] ADJ exhaustivo

exhibit [ıgzíbıt] VI/VT (manifest) exhibir; (put on view) exponer; N exposición f

exhibition [ɛksəbíʃən] N (manifestation, show of skills) exhibición f; (public display of objects) exposición f

exhibitionism [ɛksıbíʃənızəm] N exhibicionismo m

exhilarated [ıgzíləredıd] ADJ exultante

exhort [ıgzɔ́rt] VT exhortar

exhumation [ɛgzjuméʃən] N exhumación f

exile [égzaıl] N exilio m, destierro m; (person exiled) exiliado -da mf, desterrado -da mf; VT exiliar

exist [ıgzíst] VI existir

existence [ıgzístəns] N existencia f

existential [ɛgzısténʃəl] ADJ existencial

existing [ıgzístıŋ] ADJ existente

exit [égzıt] N salida f; VI/VT salir [de]; (theater) hacer mutis; — **interview** entrevista de salida f; — **strategy** estrategia de salida f; VI salir; **he —ed the building** salió del edificio

exodus [éksədəs] N éxodo m

exonerate [ıgzánəret] VT exonerar

exorbitant [ıgzɔ́rbıdənt] ADJ exorbitante

exorcise [éksɔrsaız] VT exorcisar

exorcism [éksɔrsızəm] N exorcismo m

exotic [ıgzádık] ADJ exótico

expand [ıkspǽnd] VI/VT expandir[se], ampliar[se]; (an equation, an idea) desarrollar[se]; (through heat) dilatar[se]; —**ed memory** memoria expandida f

expanse [ıkspǽns] N extensión f

expansion [ıkspǽnʃən] N expansión f; (of an equation, of an idea) desarrollo m; (through heat) dilatación f; — **slot** ranura para accesorios f

expansive [ıkspǽnsıv] ADJ expansivo

expatriate[1] [ɛkspétriet] VI/VT expatriar[se]

expatriate[2] [ɛkspétriıt] N expatriado -da mf

expect [ıkspékt] VT esperar; **we — guests** esperamos visita[s]; **I — you to be on time** cuento con que vengas puntualmente; **I'm —ed to work fifty hours a week** tengo que trabajar cincuenta horas por semana; **I — you're tired** estarás cansado; **she's —ing** está embarazada/encinta

expectation [ɛkspɛktéʃən] N (anticipation) expectación f; (expected thing) expectativa f; **he has great —s** tiene grandes expectativas

expectorant [ıkspéktə> ənt] ADJ & N expectorante m

expectorate [ıkspéktəret] VI/VT expectorar

expedient [ıkspídiənt] ADJ conveniente,

expeditivo

expedite [ɛ́kspɪdaɪt] VT (facilitate) agilizar; (deal with promptly) despachar

expedition [ɛkspɪdíʃən] N expedición f

expeditionary [ɛkspɪdíʃəneri] ADJ expedicionario

expel [ɪkspél] VT (discharge) expeler; (throw out) expulsar

expend [ɪkspénd] VT gastar, agotar

expenditure [ɪkspéndɪtʃə] N gasto m

expense [ɪkspéns] N gasto m; — **account** cuenta de gastos f; **they had fun at my** — se divirtieron a mi costa

expensive [ɪkspénsɪv] ADJ caro

experience [ɪkspírians] N experiencia f; VT experimentar; —**d** experimentado

experiment [ɪkspérəmənt] N experimento m; VI experimentar

experimental [ɪksperəméntl] ADJ experimental

experimentation [ɪksperɪməntéʃən] N experimentación f

expert [ɛkspət] N experto -ta mf; ADJ experto, idóneo, perito; — **system** sistema experto m

expertise [ɛkspətíz] N pericia f

expiration [ɛkspəréʃən] N (of a contract) vencimiento m, caducidad f; (breathing out) espiración f

expire [ɪkspáɪr] VI (die, terminate) expirar; (breathe out) espirar; (lapse) vencer, caducar

explain [ɪksplén] VT explicar; **he tried to** — **away his absence** trató de justificar su ausencia

explainable [ɪksplénəbəl] ADJ explicable

explanation [ɛksplənéʃən] N explicación f

explanatory [ɪksplǽnətɔri] ADJ explicativo

expletive [ɛkspliDɪv] N palabrota f

explicable [ɪksplíkəbəl] ADJ explicable

explicit [ɪksplísɪt] ADJ explícito

explode [ɪksplód] VI/VT estallar, hacer explosión, explotar; VT (a theory) hacer añicos; VI (population) dispararse

exploit¹ [ɛ́ksplɔɪt] N hazaña f, proeza f

exploit² [ɪksplɔ́ɪt] VT explotar

exploitation [ɛksplɔɪtéʃən] N explotación f

exploration [ɛkspləréʃən] N exploración f

exploratory [ɪksplɔ́rətɔri] ADJ exploratorio

explore [ɪksplɔ́r] VI/VT explorar; (a topic) bucear

explorer [ɪksplɔ́rə] N explorador -ora mf

explosion [ɪksplóʒən] N explosión f, estallido m

explosive [ɪksplósɪv] ADJ & N explosivo m

exponent [ɪkspónənt] N exponente m

export¹ [ɪkspórt] VI/VT exportar

export² [ɛ́ksport] N exportación f

exportation [ɛksportéʃən] N exportación f

exporter [ɪkspórdə] N exportador -ora mf

exporting [ɪkspórdɪŋ] N exportación f; — **firm** empresa exportadora f

expose [ɪkspóz] VT (to lay open to danger, exhibit, subject to light) exponer; (to make known) revelar; (to unmask) desenmascarar

exposition [ɛkspəzíʃən] N exposición f

exposure [ɪkspóʒə] N (to danger, to light, act of exposing) exposición f; (disclosure) revelación f; **to die of** — morir de frío

expound [ɪkspáund] VI/VT exponer, explicar

express [ɪksprés] VT expresar; (send by mail) enviar por correo expreso; (squeeze out) exprimir; ADJ (clearly indicated) expreso; — **delivery** envío rápido m; — **train** tren expreso m; ADV por expreso; N (train) expreso m

expression [ɪkspréʃən] N expresión f

expressive [ɪksprésɪv] ADJ expresivo

expressiveness [ɪksprésɪvnɪs] N expresividad f

expropriate [ɛkspróprieit] VT expropiar

expulsion [ɪkspʌ́lʃən] N expulsión f

exquisite [ɛkskwízɪt] ADJ exquisito, primoroso; (pain) penetrante

extant [ɛ́kstənt] ADJ existente

extemporaneous [ɪkstɛmpərénias] ADJ improvisado

extend [ɪksténd] VI/VT extender[se]; (a street) ampliar[se]; **he** —**ed his hand to her** le tendió la mano

extended [ɪksténdɪd] ADJ (extensive) extenso; (prolonged) prolongado; (folded out) extendido; — **coverage** cobertura extendida f; — **care facility** centro de atención médica prolongada m

extension [ɪksténʃən] N extensión f (also phone line); (of a deadline) prórroga f; (addition) anexo m, ampliación f; — **cord** extensión f

extensive [ɪksténsɪv] ADJ extenso; (agriculture) extensivo

extent [ɪkstént] N extensión f; **to a great** — en alto grado; **to such an** — **that** a tal grado que; **to the** — **that you are able** en la medida en que seas capaz; **to a certain** — hasta cierto punto

extenuate [ɪksténjuet] VT atenuar

exterior [ɪkstíria] ADJ & N exterior m

exterminate [ɪkstə́mənet] VT exterminar

extermination [ɪkstə́mənéʃən] N exterminio m, exterminación f

external [ɪkstə́nl] ADJ externo; (concerned with foreign countries) exterior

extinct [ɪkstíŋkt] ADJ extinto

extinguish [ɪkstíŋgwɪʃ] VT apagar, extinguir

extol [ɪkstól] VT ensalzar, enaltecer

extort [ɪkstɔ́rt] VT extorsionar

extortion [ɪkstɔ́rʃən] N extorsión f

extra [ɛ́kstrə] ADJ de más, adicional; **make some** — **cakes** haz unos pasteles de más / adicionales / extras; N extra m (including newspaper, actor); ADV extra; extrasensorial; (soccer) — **time** tiempo suplementario m, tiempo de descuento m; ADJ —**marital** extramarital; —**ordinary** extraordinario;

—sensory extrasensorial
extract¹ [ékstrækt] N (something extracted) extracto *m*; (passage from a book) fragmento *m*
extract² [ıkstrǽkt] VT extraer; (a secret) sonsacar
extraction [ıkstrǽkʃən] N extracción *f*
extradite [ékstrədaıt] VT extraditar
extradition [ɛkstrədíʃən] N extradición *f*
extraneous [ıkstrénıəs] ADJ superfluo
extrapolate [ıkstrǽpəlet] VI/VT extrapolar
extravagance [ıkstrǽvəgəns] N (unnecessary expense) despilfarro *m*, derroche *m*; (excess) exceso *m*; (oddity) extravagancia *f*
extravagant [ıkstrǽvəgənt] ADJ (shopper) gastador, derrochador; (price) exorbitante; (praise, demand) excesivo
extreme [ıkstrím] ADJ & N extremo *m*; **to go to —s** exagerar, llegar a extremos; **to the —** extremadamente, sumamente
extremely [ıkstrímli] ADV extremadamente, sumamente; **it's — cold** hace un frío que pela; **she's — intelligent** es inteligentísima
extremity [ıkstrémıDi] N extremidad *f*
extricate [ékstrıket] VT sacar; VI **to — oneself from** conseguir salir de
extrovert [ékstrəvət] N extrovertido -da *mf*
extroverted [ékstrəvəDıd] ADJ extrovertido
exuberant [ıgzúbəənt] ADJ exuberante
exude [ıgzúd] VI/VT (liquid) exudar; (cheerfulness, confidence) emanar
exult [ıgzʌ́lt] VI exultar
eye [aı] N ojo *m* (also of hurricane, needle, tools); (look) mirada *f*; **—ball** globo ocular *m*; **—brow** ceja *f*; **— chart** cartilla de examen de vista *f*; **— contact** contacto visual *m*; **—dropper** cuentagotas *m sg*; **— drops** colirio *m*, gotas oftálmicas *f pl*; **—glass** (of a telescope, microscope) ocular *m*; **—glasses** anteojos *m pl*, lentes *m pl*; **— injury** lesión ocular *f*; **—lash** pestaña *f*; **—lid** párpado *m*; **—liner** delineador *m*; **—-opener** revelación *f*; **—piece** ocular *m*; **—sight** vista *f*; **—sore** monstruosidad *f*; **— shadow** sombra para ojos *f*; **— socket** órbita *f*; **— strain** vista cansada *f*; **—tooth** colmillo *m*; **—witness** testigo ocular *mf*; **my —s are bad** tengo mala vista; **in the twinkling of an —** en un abrir y cerrar de ojos; **her dress caught his —** su vestido le llamó la atención; **to keep an — on** cuidar, vigilar; **to see — to —** estar de acuerdo; **in the —s of the law** ante la ley; **to give someone the —** hacerle ojito a alguien; **to have —s for someone** estar prendado de alguien; **to keep one's — open** tener cuidado; VT mirar
eyeful [áıfʊl] N **we got an —** vimos más que suficiente
e-zine [ízin] N revista electrónica *f*

Ff

fable [fébəl] N fábula *f*
fabric [fǽbrık] N tela *f*, tejido *m*; (wool) paño *m*; (of society) estructura *f*; **— softener** suavizante *m*
fabricate [fǽbrıket] VT (goods) fabricar; (a story) inventar
fabulous [fǽbjələs] ADJ fabuloso
facade [fəsád] N fachada *f*
face [fes] N (of head, coin, cube, facial expression) cara *f*; (of a building) frente *m*; (of a watch) esfera *f*; (of the Earth) faz *f*; **—cloth** toalla para la cara *f*; **—lift** lifting *m*; **— value** valor nominal *m*; **about—!** ¡media vuelta! **left—!** ¡a la izquierda! **on the — of it** aparentemente; **she put on a brave —** se comportó con entereza; **to make —s** hacer muecas; **to lose —** quedar mal; **to save —** quedar bien; **to show one's —** aparecerse; ADJ **—-to-—** cara a cara; ADV **in the — of** ante, frente a; VT (stand opposite to) encarar; (meet defiantly) enfrentar, enfrentarse con, afrontar; (look forward) mirar a/hacia; (to have the front toward) dar a/hacia; (to put on facing) ribetear; **to — down** intimidar; **to — the music** dar la cara; **to — with marble** revestir de mármol
faceless [féslıs] ADJ (anonymous) anónimo; (without a face) sin cara
facet [fǽsıt] N faceta *f*
facetious [fəsíʃəs] ADJ gracioso
facial [féʃəl] ADJ facial; N limpieza de cutis *f*
facilitate [fəsílıtet] VT facilitar
facility [fəsílıDi] N (skill) facilidad *f*; **facilities** (of a building) instalaciones *f pl*; (restroom) aseo *m*, servicio *m*
fact [fǽkt] N hecho *m*; **hard —s** datos concretos *m pl*; **is that a —!** ¡no me digas! **as a matter of —** de hecho; **in —** de hecho; **it's a — of life** así son las cosas
faction [fǽkʃən] N facción *f*
factor [fǽktə] N factor *m*; VT descomponer en factores; VI **to — in** tener en cuenta
factory [fǽktəri] N fábrica *f*
factual [fǽktʃuəl] ADJ (of facts) fáctico; (based on facts) objetivo; **— error** error de hecho *m*
faculty [fǽkəlti] N (ability) facultad *f*; (in a college) profesorado *m*, cuerpo docente *m*, claustro *m*
fad [fǽd] N moda pasajera *f*
fade [fed] VI/VT (cloth) decolorar[se], desteñir[se]; (color) deslavar[se]; VI (strength) disminuir; (lights) apagarse; (feelings, colors) desvanecerse

fail [feɪl] VI (of a plan, a person) fracasar; (faculties, organs, machinery, structure) fallar; (experiment, plan) fracasar, frustrarse; (health) decaer; (business) quebrar, hacer bancarrota; VI/VT (exam, student) suspender, reprobar; **he —ed to remember their anniversary** no se acordó de su aniversario; **don't — to come** no dejes de venir; **without —** sin falta

failure [féljə] N (of a plan, a person) fracaso *m*; (of organs) insuficiencia *f*; (of faculties) deterioro *m*; (of machinery) falla *f*, Sp fallo *m* (of business), quiebra *f*, bancarrota *f*; (in an exam) suspenso *m*; (to keep a promise, to reach a goal) incumplimiento *m*; **her — to respond puzzled me** su falta de respuesta me confundió

faint [feɪnt] ADJ (sound) débil; (light) tenue; (image) vago; **to feel —** sentirse mareado; **—-hearted** timorato, cobarde; N desmayo *m*, desfallecimiento *m*; VI desmayarse, desfallecer

faintness [féntnɪs] N (of sound) debilidad *f*; (of light) tenuidad *f*; (of an image) vaguedad *f*

fair [fer] ADJ (just) justo; (by the rules) limpio; (large) considerable; (of weather) bueno; (of sky) despejado; (of wind) propicio; (of complexion) blanco; **— market price** precio justo en el mercado *m*; **— play** juego limpio *m*; **— chance of success** buena probabilidad de éxito *f*; **the — sex** el sexo bello; **that's not —!** ¡no vale! ¡no es justo! ADV **to play —** jugar limpio; N feria *f*; **—ground** real de la feria *m*; **—way** calle *f*, fairway *m*

fairly [férli] ADV (justly) justamente; (moderately) medianamente; **— difficult** bastante difícil

fairness [férnɪs] N (justice) justicia *f*; (whiteness) blancura *f*

fairy [féri] N hada *f*; **— godmother** hada madrina *f*; **—land** país de las hadas *m*; **— tale** cuento de hadas *m*

faith [feθ] N fe *f*; (fidelity) fidelidad *f*; **— healing** curanderismo *m*; **in good —** de buena fe; **to have —** in someone tener confianza en alguien; **to keep —** cumplir con la palabra

faithful [féθfəl] ADJ fiel

faithfulness [féθfəlnɪs] N fidelidad *f*

faithless [féθlɪs] ADJ (disloyal) desleal, falso; (lacking in faith, fidelity) infiel

fake [fek] N (object) objeto falso *m*; (person who fakes) farsante *mf*; ADJ falso; **— pearls** perlas de fantasía *f pl*; N (in sports) amague *m*, finta *f*; VT (render false, counterfeit) falsificar; **to — a foul** tirarse; VI/VT (feign) fingir

falcon [fǽlkən] N halcón *m*

Falkland Islands [fɔ́kləndáɪləndz] N Islas Malvinas *f pl*

fall [fɔl] VI (drop) caer[se]; (slope downward) bajar; (be assigned to) tocar a, recaer sobre; **to**

— asleep dormirse; **to — back** retroceder; **to — back on** recurrir a; **to — behind** atrasarse, retrasarse; **to — down** (drop) caerse; (fail) fallar; **to — in with** asociarse con; **to — in love** enamorarse; **to — off** disminuir; **to — out with** reñir con; **to — through** quedar en la nada; **he —s for blondes** se enamora de las rubias; **you — for it** te dejas engañar; N (drop) caída *f*; (of a terrain) declive *m*; (season) otoño *m*; **— guy** cabeza de turco *mf*; **—ing out** desavenencia *f*, pique *m*; **—ing star** estrella fugaz *f*; **—s** catarata *f*, salto de agua *m*

fallacious [fəléʃəs] ADJ falaz

fallacy [fǽləsi] N (false notion) falacia *f*; (false argument) sofisma *m*

fallen [fɔ́lən] see fall

fallible [fǽləbəl] ADJ falible

Fallopian tubes [fəlópiəntúbz] ADJ trompas de Falopio *f pl*

fallout [fɔ́laut] N (particle-settling) precipitación radiactiva *f*; (consequences) repercusiones *f pl*

fallow [fǽlo] ADJ baldío, en barbecho; N barbecho *m*; VT dejar en barbecho

false [fɔls] ADJ falso; **to bear — witness** jurar en falso; **— advertising** publicidad engañosa *f*; **— alarm** falsa alarma *f*; **— arrest** detención ilegal *f*; **— pretense** estafa *f*; **— start** salida en falso *f*; **— step** paso en falso *m*; **— teeth** dentadura postiza *f*

falsehood [fɔ́lshud] N falsedad *f*, mentira *f*

falseness [fɔ́lsnɪs] N falsedad *f*

falsify [fɔ́lsəfaɪ] VT falsificar, falsear

falter [fɔ́ltə] VI (hesitate) vacilar, entrecortarse; (stutter) titubear

fame [fem] N fama *f*

famed [femd] ADJ afamado

familiar [fəmíljə] ADJ (generally known) familiar, conocido; (informal) familiar; (too friendly) confianzudo; (closely personal) íntimo; **to be — with a subject** conocer bien un tema

familiarity [fəmìljǽrɪDi] N familiaridad *f*

family [fǽmli] N familia *f*; **— doctor** médico general *m*; **— man** hombre de familia *m*; **— name** apellido *m*; **— planning** planificación familiar *f*; **— practice** medicina familiar *f*; **— room** cuarto de estar *m*; **— tree** árbol genealógico *m*; **— values** valores tradicionales *m pl*

famine [fǽmɪn] N (lack of food) hambruna *f*, hambre *f*; (scarcity) escasez *f*

famished [fǽmɪʃt] ADJ hambriento, muerto de hambre; **to be —** morirse de hambre

famous [féməs] ADJ famoso

fan [fæn] N (handheld) abanico *m*; (electrical) ventilador *m*; (for cleaning grain) aventadora *f*; (of sports) aficionado -da *mf*, hincha *mf*; (of a person) admirador -ora *mf*; **— belt** correa

del ventilador *f*; — **mail** correo de
admiradores *m*; VT (blow air) abanicar;
(enliven) avivar; **to — out** abrirse en abanico
fanatic [fənǽDɪk] ADJ & N fanático -ca *mf*
fanaticism [fənǽDɪsɪzəm] N fanatismo *m*
fanciful [fǽnsɪfəl] ADJ (whimsical) caprichoso;
(imaginary) imaginario; (given to fantasy)
fantasioso
fancy [fǽnsi] N fantasía *f*; (whim) capricho *m*; **to
strike one's —** gustarle a alguien; **to take a
— to** aficionarse a; **he took a — to his
teacher** se enamoró de su maestra; ADJ
(luxurious) de lujo; (elaborate) elaborado;
(strange) estrafalario; **— free**
despreocupado; **— work** bordado fino *m*; VT
imaginar[se]; **he fancies himself an artist**
se cree artista; **just — the idea!** ¡figúrate!
fanfare [fǽnfɛr] N fanfarria *f*; **with great —**
con bombo y platillo
fang [fæŋ] N colmillo *m*
fantasize [fǽntəsaɪz] VI fantasear
fantastic [fæntǽstɪk] ADJ fantástico
fantasy [fǽntəsi] N fantasía *f*
FAQ [frequently asked questions] [fæk] N
preguntas frecuentes *f pl*
far [fɑr] ADV lejos; — **and away** sin duda; —
and wide por todas partes; — **away/off**
lejos, lejano; — **be it from me to complain**
no es mi intención quejarme; — **more
money** mucho más dinero; — **off we could
see land** a lo lejos divisábamos tierra; **as —
as I know** que yo sepa; **as — as I'm
concerned** en lo que a mí respecta; **by —**
con mucho; **how — do I need to walk?**
¿cuánto tengo que caminar? **how — is the
church?** ¿a cuánto queda la iglesia? **so —**
hasta ahora; **we talked — into the night**
hablamos hasta entrada la noche; **we
traveled as — as Chicago** viajamos hasta
Chicago; ADJ lejano; **—fetched** (implausible)
inverosímil, peregrino; (forced) traído por los
cabellos; **—flung** remoto; **—off** distante;
—out radical, poco convencional; **—
reaching** de gran alcance; **—sighted** (with
defective vision) présbita, hipermétrope;
(seeing the future) con visión de futuro; **the
— corner** la esquina de más allá; **it is a —
cry from what you said** dista mucho de lo
que dijiste
farce [fɑrs] N farsa *f*
fare [fɛr] N (ticket) billete *m*; (ticket price) pasaje
m; (price of transport) tarifa *f*; (food) comida
f; (taxi patron) pasajero -ra *mf*; **—well**
despedida *f*; **to bid —well to** despedirse de;
—well! ¡adiós! VI **I —d well in the course**
me fue bien en el curso
farm [fɑrm] N (large) hacienda *f*; (small) granja *f*;
—hand labrador -ora *mf*, peón *m*; **—house**
alquería *f*, caserío *m*; **—land** tierra de cultivo

f; **— produce** productos agrícolas *m pl*;
—yard (enclosed) corral *m*; (open) patio *m*;
VI/VT cultivar; **to — out** (lease) dar en
arriendo; (distribute) repartir; (subcontract)
subcontratar
farmer [fɑrmɚ] N agricultor -ora *mf*; (small)
granjero -ra *mf*; (large) hacendado -da *mf*
farming [fɑrmɪŋ] N agricultura *f*; ADJ agrícola
mf
farther [fɑrðɚ] ADV más lejos; **it's an even —
distance** es una distancia mayor todavía;
the concept was extended — el concepto
se extendió más; **— on** más adelante; ADJ más
lejano
farthest [fɑrðɪst] ADJ el más lejano; ADV lo más
lejos
fascinate [fǽsənet] VI/VT fascinar, alucinar
fascinating [fǽsəneDɪŋ] ADJ fascinante
fascination [fæsənéʃən] N fascinación *f*
fascism [fǽʃɪzəm] N fascismo *m*
fascist [fǽʃɪst] N fascista *mf*
fashion [fǽʃən] N (style) moda *f*; (way) manera *f*,
modo *m*; **— plate** figurín *m*; **after a —** más o
menos; **to be in —** estar de moda; VT hacer;
(with metal) forjar; (with putty) moldear;
(character) formar
fashionable [fǽʃənəbəl] ADJ de moda
fast [fæst] ADJ (quick) rápido, veloz; (ahead, of a
watch) adelantado; (firm, permanent) firme;
(closed) atrancado; (loyal) fiel; (dissolute)
disipado; **—ball** recta *f*; **— break**
contraataque *m*; **— food** comida rápida *f*; **life
in the — lane** vida loca *f*; **— money** dinero
mal habido *m*; ADV (quickly) rápido,
rápidamente; (firmly) firmemente; **— asleep**
profundamente dormido; N ayuno *m*; VI
ayunar; VI/VT **to —-forward** avanzar
fasten [fǽsən] VT (with buckles, buttons, hooks)
abrochar[se], prender; (with ribbon, thread)
atar; (door) atrancar
fastener [fǽsənɚ] N cierre *m*
fastidious [fæstídiəs] ADJ (hard to please)
maniático; (painstaking) minucioso
fasting [fǽstɪŋ] N ayuno *m*
fat [fæt] ADJ gordo; — **cat** pez gordo *m*; — **cell**
célula adiposa *f*; — **chance** ¡ni soñar! **—head**
idiota *mf*; — **job** trabajo lucrativo *m*; —
profits pingües ganancias *f pl*; **to get —**
engordar; N (oily substance) grasa *f*; (animal
tissue) gordura *f*, sebo *m*; **the — of the land**
la abundancia de la tierra
fatal [fédl] ADJ letal
fatality [fətǽlɪDi] N víctima fatal *f*; **— rate**
índice de mortalidad *m*
fate [fet] N (lot) destino *m*, fatalidad *f*, hado *m*;
(outcome) suerte *f*; VT destinar
father [fɑðɚ] N padre *m*; — **figure** figura
paterna *f*; **—-in-law** suegro *m*; **—land** patria
f; VT engendrar

fatherhood [fáðə·hʊd] N paternidad f
fatherly [fáðə·li] ADV paternal
fathom [fæðəm] N braza f; VT (measure) sondear; (understand) comprender
fatigue [fətíg] N fatiga f; **—s** ropa de faena f; VI/VT fatigar[se], rendir[se]
fatness [fǽtnɪs] N gordura f
fatso [fætso] N pej gordinflón m, tonel m
fatten [fǽtn] VT engordar, cebar
fatty [fǽdi] ADJ adiposo, graso; **— acids** ácidos grasos m pl; N (insult for fat people) pej gordo -da mf
faucet [fɔ́sɪt] N grifo m, llave f
fault [fɔlt] N (defect, misdeed) falta f; (responsibility) culpa f; (geological) falla f; **—finder** crítico -ona mf; **no—** sin culpa; **careful to a—** demasiado cuidadoso; **to be at—** ser culpable; **to find—with** criticar a
faultless [fɔ́ltlɪs] ADJ perfecto
faulty [fɔ́lti] ADJ defectuoso; (grammar) vicioso
fauna [fɔ́nə] N fauna f
faux pas [fopá] N gaffe f, metedura de pata f
favor [févə·] N (kind act, goodwill) favor m, gracia f; (popularity) popularidad f; (party gift) sorpresa f; VT (give help, show preference) favorecer; (foster) propiciar; (approve of) estar a favor de; **they are —ed to win** son los favoritos; **she—s her mother** se parece a su madre; **he's out of—** ha caído en desgracia
favorable [févə·əbəl] ADJ favorable
favorite [févə·ɪt] ADJ & N preferido -da mf, favorito -ta mf, predilecto -ta mf
favoritism [févə·ɪtɪzəm] N favoritismo m
fawn [fɔn] N cervatillo m; VI **to—over** adular
fax [fæks] N fax m, facsímil m; VT faxear, enviar por fax
FBI [Federal Bureau of Investigation] [ɛ́fbíáɪ] N FBI m
fear [fɪr] N miedo m, temor m; **—of God** temor de Dios m; VI/VT (be afraid of) temer, tenerle miedo a; (suspect) temerse; **to—for** temer por
fearful [fɪ́rfəl] ADJ (causing fear) terrible, espantoso; (showing fear) temeroso, miedoso, medroso
fearless [fɪ́rlɪs] ADJ intrépido
fearlessness [fɪ́rlɪsnɪs] N intrepidez f
feasible [fízəbəl] ADJ factible
feast [fist] N (party, religious celebration) fiesta f; (abundant meal) festín m, banquete m; VI **to—on** darse un festín de; **to—one's eyes on** deleitarse la vista con
feat [fit] N (heroic act) hazaña f; (achievement) logro m
feather [féðə·] N pluma f; **a—in one's cap** un triunfo personal; **—weight** peso pluma m; **birds of a—flock together** Dios los cría y ellos se juntan; VI/VT (grow feathers, cover

with feathers) emplumar; (change blade angle) poner horizontal
feature [fitʃə·] N (characteristic) aspecto m, característica f; (newspaper article) reportaje m; (facial) facción f, fisonomía f, rasgo m; **—article** artículo principal m; **—film** largometraje m; VT (give prominence to) destacar; (depict) mostrar; **this film—s John Smith** esta película cuenta con la actuación de John Smith; **—that!** ¡imagínate! VI figurar
February [fébjueri] N febrero m
fecal [fíkəl] ADJ fecal
feces [físiz] N PL heces f pl
fed [fɛd] see feed
federal [fédə·əl] ADJ federal
federation [fɛdə·réʃən] N federación f
fee [fi] N (professional) honorarios m pl; (artist) cachet m; (admission) derecho de admisión m; **—s** (university) matrícula f
feeble [fíbəl] ADJ (person) débil, endeble; (sound, light) tenue; **—-minded** (retarded) pej retrasado; (stupid) tonto
feed [fid] VI/VT (supply with food, materials) alimentar[se]; (prompt lines) apuntar; (broadcast) transmitir; **he—s sugar cubes to his horse** le da terrones de azúcar a su caballo; **I fed him a lie** le dije una mentira; **to be fed up** estar harto, estar hasta la coronilla; VI **to—into** desembocar en; N (fodder) pienso m, cebo m; (transmission) transmisión f; **—back** (electronic, mechanical) retroalimentación f; (critical) respuesta f, reacción f
feeding [fídɪŋ] N alimentación f; **—ing frenzy** (of the press) escándalo periodístico m; (of sharks, etc.) carnicería f; **—tube** sonda de alimentación f
feel [fil] VI/VT (perceive, experience) sentir[se]; (examine with the hands) palpar; (suffer) sufrir; (have an opinion) creer; VI (grope, check out) tantear; (seem) parecer; **to— one's way** tantear el camino, andar a tientas; **I—for you** te compadezco; **it—s soft** está suave al tacto; **I—like a coffee** tengo ganas de tomar un café; **to—up to something** sentirse capaz de algo; N (feeling) sensación f; (sense) tacto m; (ability) don m; (groping) manoseo m, toqueteo m
feeler [filə·] N (of insects) antena f; (of snails) cuerno m; (person who feels) persona emotiva f; **to put out—s** tantear el terreno
feeling [filɪŋ] N (sense of touch) tacto m; (instance of physical perception) sensación f; (emotion) sentimiento m; (opinion) opinión f; (compassion) compasión f; **a—of sadness** un sentimiento de tristeza; **with—** con sentimiento; **to hurt someone's—s** herirle los sentimientos a alguien; ADJ sensible

feign [feɪn] VI/VT fingir, simular, aparentar

feisty [fáɪsti] ADJ (aggressive) pugnaz, belicoso; (energetic) vivaz

feline [fílaɪn] ADJ felino

fell [fɛl] VT (an animal) derribar; (a tree) talar; N (pelt) piel de animal f; **in one — swoop** de un golpe

fell [fɛl] see fall

fellow [félo] N (member) miembro m; (scholar) becario -ria mf; (man or boy) tipo m; **— citizen** conciudadano -na mf; **— man** prójimo m; **— student** compañero -ra de clase mf

fellowship [félosɪp] N (friendly relations) amistad f; (community of interest) confraternidad f; (scholarship) beca f

felony [féləni] N delito grave m

felt [fɛlt] N fieltro m; ADJ de fieltro

felt [fɛlt] see feel

female [fímel] N (animal) hembra f; (person) mujer f; ADJ (animal, fastener) hembra; (person) femenino

feminine [fémənɪn] ADJ femenino

femininity [femənínɪti] N feminidad f

feminism [fémənɪzəm] N feminismo m

feminist [fémɪnɪst] ADJ & N feminista mf

femur [fímɚ] N fémur m

fence [fɛns] N (barrier) cerca f, cerco m, valla f; (person who deals in stolen goods) Am reducidor -ora mf, Sp perista mf; (store for stolen goods) tienda de artículos robados f; **to be sitting on the —** estar indeciso; VT (enclose) cercar, vallar; **to — in** cercar; **to — off** dividir con una cerca; VI (sport) practicar esgrima

fencing [fénsɪŋ] N (dealing in stolen goods) tráfico en artículos robados m; (barrier) cerca f; (construction of barrier) cerco m; (sport) esgrima f

fender [féndɚ] N guardabarro[s] m sg, guardafango m; **— bender** choquecito m

ferment[1] [fɚment] N fermento m

ferment[2] [fɚmént] VI/VT fermentar[se]

fermentation [fɚmentésən] N fermentación f

fern [fɚn] N helecho m

ferocious [fərósəs] ADJ feroz, fiero

ferocity [fərásɪdi] N ferocidad f, fiereza f

ferret [férɪt] N hurón m; VI **to — out** hurgar

Ferris wheel [férɪshwil] N rueda gigante f

ferry [féri] N ferry m, transbordador m; **— boat** ferry m; VT transportar de una orilla a otra; VI viajar en ferry

fertile [fɚdl] ADJ fértil, fecundo

fertility [fɚtílɪdi] N fertilidad f

fertilization [fɚdlɪzéʃən] N fertilización f, fecundación f

fertilize [fɚdlaɪz] VT fertilizar; (female, egg) fecundar; (land) abonar

fertilizer [fɚdlaɪzɚ] N fertilizante m, abono m

fervent [fɚvənt] ADJ ferviente

fervor [fɚvɚ] N fervor m

fester [féstɚ] VI (form pus) supurar; (rankle) enconarse

festival [féstəvəl] N festival m

festive [féstɪv] ADJ festivo

festivity [festívɪdi] N festividad f

fetal [fidl] ADJ fetal; **— position** posición fetal f; **— monitoring** monitorización fetal f

fetch [fɛtʃ] VT buscar; Am ir a buscar; **the ring —ed a fancy price** nos dieron una buena suma por el anillo; VI/VT (dog) buscar

fetching [fétʃɪŋ] ADJ atractivo

fetish [fédɪʃ] N fetiche m

fetter [fédɚ] N grillete m; VT engrillar

fetus [fídəs] N feto m

feud [fjud] N enemistad hereditaria f; VI pelear

feudal [fjúdl] ADJ feudal

fever [fívɚ] N fiebre f, calentura f; **— blister** herpes febril m; **— pitch** punto álgido m

feverish [fívərɪʃ] ADJ (related to fever) febril; (having a fever) afiebrado, destemplado

few [fju] ADJ & PRON pocos; **—er than expected** menos de los que se esperaba; **a —** unos pocos, algunos; **the —** una minoría

fiancé [fiansé] N novio m, prometido m; **—e** novia f, prometida f

fiasco [fiǽsko] N fiasco m

fib [fɪb] N mentirilla f; VI decir mentirillas

fiber [fáɪbɚ] N (textile) fibra f; (animal, vegetable) hebra f; **—-optic** de fibra óptica; **—glass** fibra de vidrio f

fibrous [fáɪbrəs] ADJ fibroso

fickle [fíkəl] ADJ veleidoso, mudable

fiction [fíkʃən] N ficción f

fictional [fíkʃənl] ADJ novelesco

fictitious [fɪktíʃəs] ADJ ficticio

fiddle [fɪdl] N violín m; VI (play the violin) tocar el violín; **to — around** perder el tiempo; **to — with** juguetear con; **they like to — with the computer** siempre juguetean con la computadora

fidelity [fɪdélɪdi] N fidelidad f; **high —** alta fidelidad f

fidget [fíʤɪt] VI estar inquieto; **stop —ing!** ¡deja de moverte!

fiduciary [fɪdúʃieri] ADJ & N fiduciario -ria mf

field [fild] N (land, computers, heraldry, optics) campo m; (in sports) campo m; Am cancha f; (of oil) yacimiento m; (group of competitors) participantes mf pl; (of knowledge) campo m, terreno m; **— artillery** artillería de campaña f; **— day** (day for outdoor activity) día de campo m; (for military maneuvers) día de maniobras m; (unrestrained enjoyment) festín m; **— glasses** binoculares m pl; **— goal** gol de campo m; **— mouse** ratón de campo m; **— trip** (in school) paseo escolar m; (in science) viaje de estudio m; **— work** trabajo de campo *m*; VT (a baseball) atrapar, fildear; (questions) contestar

fielding [fíldɪŋ] N (of questions) contestación *f*; (of baseballs) fildeo *m*

fiend [find] N (devil) demonio *m*, diablo *m*; (fanatic) fanático -ca *mf*

fierce [firs] ADJ (animals) feroz, fiero; (illness) espantoso; (storms, etc.) furioso, espantoso; (competition, debate) intenso, encarnizado; (look) torvo

fierceness [fírsnɪs] N ferocidad *f*, bravura *f*

fiery [fáɪəri] ADJ (passionate) fogoso; (hot, causing burning sensation) ardiente

fife [faɪf] N pífano *m*

fifteen [fɪftín] NUM quince

fifth [fɪfθ] ADJ N quinto *m*; (measure of liquor) tres cuartos de un litro *m pl*

fifty [fɪfti] NUM cincuenta; ADV **to go —** — ir a medias; ADJ **a —-— chance** un cincuenta por ciento de probabilidades

fig [fɪg] N higo *m*; **— leaf** hoja de higuera *f*; **— tree** higuera *f*; **it's not worth a —** no vale ni un pepino/pito

fight [faɪt] N (combat) lucha *f*, combate *m*; **the — against AIDS** la lucha contra el SIDA; (argument) pelea *f*, riña *f*; VI/VT (combat) luchar [con], pelear [con]; VI (argue) pelear, reñir; **to — a duel** batirse a duelo; **to — back** (to hold back) contener; (resist) resistir; **to — it out** arreglarlo a los golpes; **to — off** rechazar; **to — one's way through** abrirse camino a la fuerza

fighter [fáɪDɚ] N (boxer) boxeador -ora *mf*; (someone who fights) luchador -ora *mf*; (dog, cock) animal de pelea/riña *m*; **— airplane** avión caza *m*

fighting [fáɪDɪŋ] N (fight) lucha *f*; ADJ combativo; **— chance** posibilidad remota *f*; **— words** palabras incendiarias *f pl*

figurative [fígjə→DɪV] ADJ (art) figurativo; (language) figurado

figure [fígjə→] N (number, amount) cifra *f*; (form, bodily shape, representation, dance move, syllogism) figura *f*; (character) personaje *m*; **—head** figurón de proa *m*; **— of speech** figura retórica *f*; **—s** (written symbols) números *m pl*; **— skating** patinaje artístico *m*; **to cut a poor —** dar una mala impresión; VI (appear) figurar; VI/VT (think) imaginar[se], figurar[se]; **to — in** tener en cuenta; **to — on** contar con; **to — out** (solve) resolver; (calculate) calcular; **it —s!** no me extraña, era de esperar; VT calcular

Fijian [fidʒiən] N fijiano -na *mf*

Fiji Islands [fidʒiáɪləndz] N Islas Fiji *f pl*

filament [fíləmənt] N filamento *m*

file [faɪl] N (documents) archivo *m*; (for computers) archivo *m*, fichero *m*; (official report) expediente *m*, legajo *m*; (line) fila *f*;

(tool) lima *f*; **— compression** compresión de archivos *f*; **— format** formato de archivo/ fichero *m*; **—name** nombre de archivo *m*; **— server** servidor *m*; **on —** archivado; **filing cabinet** fichero *m*, archivador *m*; VT (papers) archivar; (news story) entregar; (tax return, claim, etc.) presentar; **to — a suit** entablar una demanda, querellarse; VI (for a job) presentarse; (walk in a line) desfilar; VI/VT (smooth) limar

filial [fíliəl] ADJ filial

filiation [filiéʃən] N filiación *f*

filibuster [fíləbʌstɚ] VI/VT practicar obstrucción parlamentaria; N filibusterismo *m*, obstrucción *f*

filigree [fíligri] N filigrana *f*

fill [fɪl] VI/VT (glass, container) llenar[se]; (a hole, a pastry, land) rellenar; **the smell —ed the room** la habitación se llenó del olor; **the airline —ed the position** la compañía aérea llenó el cargo; **the new employee —ed the vacancy** el nuevo empleado ocupó el cargo vacante; VT (a tooth) empastar; (prescription, order) despachar; (a need) satisfacer; VI (sails) hinchar; **to — out** llenar; **to — in** (inform) informar; (fill out a form) llenar; (replace) sustituir; **to — up** llenarse hasta el tope

fillet¹ [fɪlé] N filete *m*; VT filetear

fillet² [fɪlɪt] N cinta *f*

filling [fílɪŋ] N (act) rellenado *m*; (filler) relleno *m*; (of a tooth) empaste *m*; **— station** estación de servicio *f*, gasolinera *f*

filly [fíli] N potranca *f*

film [fɪlm] N (video) película *f*, filme *m*; (celluloid) película *f*, cinta *f*; (thin coating) película *f*; **— industry** industria cinematográfica *f*; **—maker** cineasta *mf*; VI/ VT filmar, cinematografiar

filming [fílmɪŋ] N filmación *f*

filter [fíltɚ] N filtro *m*; VI/VT filtrar[se]

filtering [fíltə→ɪŋ] N filtración *f*

filth [fɪlθ] N (dirt, despicable person) mugre *f*, suciedad *f*; (moral impurity) porquería *f*; (vulgar material) obscenidades *f pl*

filthiness [fílθɪnɪs] N suciedad *f*

filthy [fílθi] ADJ (dirty) cochino, mugriento; (vile) puerco, cochino; *Sp* guarro; (obscene) obsceno; **— rich** riquísimo

filtration [fɪltréʃən] N filtración *f*

fin [fɪn] N aleta *f*

final [fáɪnl] ADJ (result, conclusion) final; (last) último; (conclusive) definitivo; **— score** resultado final *m*; **— stretch** recta final *f*; N (in sports) final *f*; (exam) examen final *m*

finalist [fáɪnlɪst] N finalista *mf*

finalize [fáɪnlaɪz] VT completar, ultimar

finally [fáɪnli] ADV (at last) finalmente, por fin; (lastly) finalmente, por último

finance [fáɪnæns] N finanza f; **—s** finanzas f pl; VI/VT (to fund) financiar; (to purchase on credit) comprar financiado

financial [fɪnǽnʃəl] ADJ financiero; **— disclosure** divulgación financiera f

financier [fɪnænsír] N financiero -ra mf

financing [fáɪnænsɪŋ] N financiamiento m; Am financiación f

find [faɪnd] VT hallar, encontrar; (discover) descubrir; (determine innocence or guilt) declarar; VI (determine officially) fallar; **to — fault with** criticar a, censurar a; **to — out** (discover) descubrir; (verify) averiguar; N hallazgo m

finding [fáɪndɪŋ] N fallo m; **—s** resultados m pl

fine [faɪn] ADJ (wine, sand, hair, precious metal) fino; (thread) delgado; (cloth) delicado; (artist, athlete) consumado; (manners) refinado; (good-looking person) atractivo, guapo; (weather) bueno; (distinction) sutil; **— arts** bellas artes f pl; **— print** letra pequeña f, letra chica f; **I'm —** estoy bien; **to feel —** sentirse muy bien de salud; **to have a — time** pasarlo bien; N multa f; VT multar; **to —-tune** (a receiver) sintonizar; (an engine) ajustar; (a plan) afinar

finery [fáɪnəri] N galas f pl

finesse [fɪnés] N (subtlety) sutileza f; (tact) diplomacia f; VI usar artimañas; VT conseguir por artimañas

finger [fíŋgɚ] N dedo m; **— food** canapé m, aperitivo m; **—nail** uña f; **—print** huella dactilar/digital f; **—tip** punta del dedo f; **at one's —tips** al alcance de la mano; **little — dedo** meñique m; **middle —** dedo del corazón m; **to give someone the —** hacerle un gesto obsceno a alguien; **I'll keep my —s crossed** cruzo los dedos; **to wrap someone around one's —** meterse a alguien en el bolsillo; **I can't put my — on it** no sabría decir lo que es; VT (play a guitar) tañer; (squeal on) delatar

finicky [fíniki] ADJ melindroso, dengoso

finish [fíniʃ] VI/VT (end) terminar[se], finalizar[se]; VT (polish) pulir; (varnish) barnizar; (kill) liquidar; **to — off** acabar con, rematar; **to — up** terminar; N (ending) final m; (decisive end) fin m; (polish, treatment) acabado m; (varnish) barniz m; (coat of paint) última mano f; **— line** meta f; **with a rough —** sin pulir

finished [fíniʃt] ADJ (doomed) acabado; (polished) pulido

finite [fáɪnaɪt] ADJ finito

Finland [fínlənd] N finlandia f

Finn [fɪn] N finlandés -esa mf, finés -esa mf

Finnish [fíniʃ] ADJ finlandés, finés

fir [fɚ] N abeto m

fire [faɪr] N (flame) fuego m; (conflagration) incendio m; (passion) ardor m; (for cigarettes, hearths) lumbre f; **— alarm** alarma contra incendios f; **—cracker** triquitraque m; **— drill** simulacro de incendio m; **— department** cuerpo de bomberos m; **— engine** coche de bomberos m, autobomba f; **— escape** escalera de incendios f; **— extinguisher** extinguidor [de incendios] m, extintor m; **— fighter** bombero -ra mf; **—fly** luciérnaga f; **— hydrant** boca de incendio f; **— insurance** seguro contra incendios m; **—man** (who extinguishes) bombero m; (who stokes) fogonero m; **—place** hogar m, chimenea f; **—proof** ininflamable, a prueba de incendio; **— sale** venta de liquidación f; **—side** hogar m; **— station** estación de bomberos f; **— trap** edificio sin medios de escape en caso de incendio m; **—wall** cortafuegos m sg; **—wood** leña f; **—works** fuegos artificiales m pl; **when he finds out, there will be —works** cuando se entere, se va a armar la gorda; **to be on —** estar quemándose; **to catch —** incendiarse, prenderse fuego; **to set — to** prender fuego a, incendiar; **under —** bajo fuego; **to play with —** jugar con fuego; **firing pin** percutor m; **firing squad** pelotón de fusilamiento m; VT (pottery) cocer; (an employee) despedir; (a projectile) lanzar; **to —-proof** hacer incombustible, ignifugar; VI/VT (a gun) disparar; VI **to — up** entusiasmar; **to — off** (gun) disparar; (letter) despachar

firm [fɚm] ADJ (solid, unwavering) firme; (fixed) fijo; (not fluctuating, as prices) estable; VI/VT **to — up** (finalize) concretar; (harden) endurecer; N firma f; **—ware** programas almacenados en circuitos integrados m pl

firmly [fɚmli] ADV con firmeza, firmemente

firmness [fɚmnɪs] N firmeza f

first [fɚst] ADJ primero; **— aid** primeros auxilios m pl; **— base** primera base f, inicial f; **— baseman** primera base mf, inicialista mf; **to get to — base** comenzar con éxito; **—born** primogénito -ta mf; **— chapter** capítulo primero m, primer capítulo m; **— class** primera clase f; **—-class** de primera clase; **— cousin** primo hermano; **—-degree** (burn) de primer grado; (murder) en primer grado; **— floor** (ground floor) planta baja f; **for the — time** por primera vez; **— half** primer tiempo m; **—hand** de primera mano; **— lady** primera dama f; **— name** nombre de pila m; **— person** primera persona f; **—-rate** de primera clase; ADV (before anything else) primero; **I'd die —** antes la muerte; **at —** al principio; **— off** al principio; N (first in series) primero -ra mf; (low gear) primera f

fiscal [fískəl] ADJ fiscal; **— period** año fiscal m

fish [fɪʃ] N (in water) pez m; (out of water)

pescado *m*; **— farm** piscifactoría *f*; **—hook** anzuelo *m*; **— market** pescadería *f*; **— story** patraña *f*; **like a — out of water** como sapo de otro pozo; **neither — nor fowl** ni chicha ni limonada; **I have other — to fry** tengo otras cosas mejores que hacer; VI/VT pescar; **to — out** sacar, rebuscar; **to — for compliments** buscar cumplidos; **to —tail** colear

fisherman [fíʃə-mən] N pescador *m*

fishery [fíʃəri] N (for breeding) piscifactoría *f*; (for fishing) pesquería *f*; (industry) industria pesquera *f*

fishing [fíʃɪŋ] N pesca *f*; **— pole/rod** caña de pescar *f*; **— tackle** aparejos de pescar *m pl*; **to go —** ir de pesca

fishy [fíʃi] ADJ (of smell, taste) a pescado; (suspicious) sospechoso

fissure [fíʃ] N fisura *f*

fist [fɪst] N puño *m*; **—fight** pelea a puñetazos *f*

fistula [fístʃələ] N fístula *f*

fit [fɪt] ADJ (suited) apto; (healthy) en buen estado físico; **are you — for driving?** ¿estás en condiciones de manejar? ADV **he didn't see — to greet her** no se dignó a saludarla; N (process of fitting) prueba *f*; (mechanical union) encaje *m*; (attack of a disease) ataque *m*; (sudden outburst) rapto *m*; (of anger, coughing) acceso *m*; **to throw a —** tener una pataleta; **by —s and starts** a trompicones; **that suit is a good —** ese traje le queda bien; VT (be suitable for) adecuarse a; (be in agreement with) cuadrar con, ajustarse a; (measure for clothes) tomarle las medidas a; (make suitable) capacitar, preparar; **to — in with** acomodarse a; **I tried to — you in** traté de incluirte; VI (conform to contours of a person) quedarle bien a alguien; (conform to the contours of a mechanism) encajar

fitness [fítnɪs] N (suitability) aptitud *f*; (health) buen estado físico *m*

fitting [fítɪŋ] ADJ apropiado; N ajuste *m*; (trying on) prueba *f*

five [faɪv] NUM cinco; **— hundred** quinientos

fix [fɪks] VT (repair, arrange) arreglar; (place permanently, determine) fijar; (prepare food) preparar; **to — up** arreglar, aviar; **to get an animal —ed** castrar a un animal; **I was —ing to call** estaba a punto de llamar; **I'll — you!** ¡ya te arreglo! N (predicament) apuro *m*, aprieto *m*; (temporary repair) arreglo provisorio *m*; (narcotic injection) chute *m*; **to get a — on** localizar

fixed [fɪkst] ADJ (stationary) fijo; (arranged in advance) arreglado; **— term** a plazo fijo; **—-rate mortgage** hipoteca de tasa fija *f*

fixture [fíkstʃə] N (bath, kitchen component) instalaciones *f pl*; **she's a permanent — in this office** está siempre en la oficina

fizzle [fízəl] VI (fail) fracasar; **to — [out]** (make a noise) apagarse chisporroteando; (interest) esfumarse

flabby [flǽbi] ADJ flácido/fláccido

flaccid [flǽsɪd] ADJ flácido/fláccido

flag [flæg] N (also in golf) bandera *f*; **—pole** mástil *m*; **—staff** mástil *m*; **—stone** losa *f*, baldosa *f*; VT (adorn with flags) embanderar; (mark with flags) marcar con banderas; (for attention) marcar, identificar; **to — [down]** hacer parar; VI (diminish) menguar

flagrant [flégrənt] ADV flagrante

flair [fler] N (aptitude) aptitud *f*, facilidad *f*; (style) estilo *m*

flak [flæk] N (antiartillery fire) fuego antiaéreo *m*; (criticism) crítica *f*

flake [flek] N (snow) copo *m*; (small thin piece) escama *f*; (eccentric person) chiflado -da *mf*; VI descascararse

flamboyant [flæmbóɪənt] ADJ (clothes) llamativo; (behavior) extravagante

flame [flem] N llama *f*; **— thrower** lanzallamas *m sg*; **old —** viejo amor *m*; VI llamear, flamear, encenderse

flaming [flémɪŋ] ADJ (emitting flames) llameante; (like a flame) flamígero; (ardent) ardiente; **— red** rojo encendido

flammable [flǽməbəl] ADJ inflamable

flank [flæŋk] N (of a bastion or army) flanco *m*; (of an animal) ijar *m*; VT flanquear

flannel [flǽnl] N franela *f*, lanilla *f*

flap [flæp] VI (wings) aletear; (flag) flamear; VT (wings) batir; (arms) sacudir; N (of a jacket, pocket) cartera *f*; (of a saddle, table) hoja *f*; (of an airplane) alerón *m*; (action of flapping) aleteo *m*

flare [fler] VI (burn unsteadily) llamear; (become wider) ensancharse; **to — up** (fire) avivarse; (activity, illness) recrudecer; VT (a skirt) levantar; (a flame) avivar; (a pipe) abocinar; (signal by flare) señalar con bengala; N (flaring light, burst of flame) llamarada *f*; (signal light) bengala *f*; (sudden emotional outburst) arranque *m*; (outward curvature) vuelo *m*; **—up** recrudecimiento *m*

flash [flæʃ] N (of light) destello *m*, ráfaga *f*; (of explosion) fogonazo *m*; (news, camera, vision, computer memory) flash *m*; **—back** flashback, escena retrospectiva *f*; **—bulb** flash *m*; **— flood** riada *f*; **—light** linterna *f*; **— of hope** rayo de esperanza *m*; **— of lightning** relampagueo *m*, rayo *m*; **in a —** en un instante; VI/VT (shine) destellar [sobre]; (expose oneself) exhibir[se]; VI (gleam) relucir, fulgurar, relampaguear; (appear) aparecer; VT (display) ostentar; **to — by** pasar como un relámpago

flashing [flǽʃɪŋ] ADJ destellante

flashy [flǽʃi] ADJ (colorful) llamativo;

(ostentatious) ostentoso; (tasteless) chillón, de mal gusto

flask [flæsk] N (glass container) frasco m; (in a laboratory) matraz m, redoma f; (for alcoholic beverages) petaca f

flat [flæt] ADJ (surface) plano; (land) llano; (skin) liso; (spatial orientation) horizontal, acostado; (city) arrasado, aplastado; (shoes, nose) chato; (tire) desinflado, pinchado; (color) apagado; (beer, tonic water) sin gas; (mood) soso; (paint) mate; (denial) terminante; (photo) sin contraste; (pitch) demasiado grave; (musical note) bemol; **—footed** con pie plano; **— rate** tarifa fija f; **— tax** impuesto de tasa única m; **trading was** — hubo poco movimiento bursátil; **to be — broke** estar completamente pelado; **to fall** — (of a body) caer de plano/redondo; (of a joke) caer mal; (of a plan) fracasar; N (shoe) zapato sin tacón m; (flat tire) desinflado m, pinchadura f, pinchazo m; (wooden box) caja para plantas f; (musical note) bemol m; **—iron** plancha f; **—out** ADV **—out** (directly) absolutamente; (at full speed) a toda velocidad; **in two minutes** — en dos minutos exactos

flatten [flǽtn] VI/VT (make flat) achatar[se], aplanar[se]; VT (knock down) tumbar, voltear; (raze) arrasar

flatter [flǽðə] VI/VT (manipulate) lisonjear, adular; (praise) halagar; **this picture —s you** esta foto te favorece; **I was —ed by his attentions** me halagaron sus atenciones

flatterer [flǽðərə] N lisonjero -ra mf, adulador -ora mf

flattering [flǽðə-ɪŋ] ADJ (comment) lisonjero, halagüeño; (person) adulón

flattery [flǽðəri] N lisonja f, adulación f, halago m

flatulence [flǽtʃələns] N flatulencia f

flaunt [flɔnt] VI/VT ostentar, lucir[se]

flavor [flévə] N (taste, quality) sabor m; (flavoring) condimento m; VT sazonar

flavorless [flévə-lɪs] ADJ insípido

flaw [flɔ] N (in character, in construction) defecto m; (in an argument) falla f

flawless [flɔ́lɪs] ADJ (logic) impecable; (behavior) intachable, irreprochable; (appearance) perfecto

flax [flæks] N lino m

flea [fli] N pulga f; **— collar** collar antipulgas m; **— market** Sp rastro m; Am mercado de [las] pulgas m

fled [flɛd] see flee

flee [fli] VI huir; VT huir de

fleece [flis] N vellón m; VT (shear) trasquilar, esquilar; (defraud) estafar; (in card games) pelar, desplumar

fleet [flit] N (of boats, buses) flota f; (of cars)

parque m; ADJ veloz

fleeting [flídɪŋ] ADJ fugaz, efímero, pasajero

flemish [flémɪʃ] ADJ & N flamenco -ca mf

flesh [flɛʃ] N carne f; (of a fruit) pulpa f; **— and blood** carne y hueso; **of my own — and blood** de mi propia sangre; **in the** — en persona; VI/VT **to — out** (a character) dar cuerpo a; (an argument) desarrollar

fleshy [flɛ́ʃi] ADJ (succulent) carnoso; (fat) metido en carnes

flew [flu] see fly

flexibility [flɛksəbílɪɾi] N flexibilidad f

flexible [flɛ́ksəbəl] ADJ flexible

flicker [flíkə] VI (stars) titilar; (candle) parpadear; N (of light) parpadeo m, titilación f; (of hope) rayo m

flier [flái ə] N (one who flies) volador -ora mf; (aviator) aviador -ora mf; (leaflet) volante m

flight [flaɪt] N (act of flying, trip) vuelo m; (trajectory) trayectoria f; (flock of birds) bandada f; (group of military aircraft) escuadrilla f; (escape) fuga f, huida f; **— attendant** auxiliar de vuelo mf; **— plan** plan de vuelo m; **— school** escuela de aviación f; **— recorder** caja negra f; **— simulator** simulador de vuelo m, registrador de vuelo m; **a — of fancy** una fantasía; **— of stairs** tramo de escalera m; **to put to** — poner en fuga; **to take** — darse a la fuga

flimsy [flímzi] ADJ (structure, argument) endeble; (excuse) flojo, pobre

flinch [flɪntʃ] VI pestañear

fling [flɪŋ] VT arrojar, lanzar; **she flung herself at the attacker** se le tiró arriba al atacante; **he flung himself into his work** se dedicó de lleno a su trabajo; **he flung open the door** abrió la puerta de golpe; N (act of flinging) lanzamiento m; (sexual affair) aventura f

flint [flɪnt] N pedernal m

flip [flɪp] VT (a coin) tirar; (a switch on) levantar; (a switch off) bajar; (a pancake) dar vuelta; VI (go head over heels) dar una voltereta; (get excited, go crazy) volverse loco; **to — through** hojear; **—-flop** (reversal of opinion) giro de 180 grados m; (backward somersault) voltereta para atrás f; (slipper) chancleta f; **— side** la otra cara de la moneda

flippant [flípənt] ADJ (frivolous) frívolo, displicente; (impudent) impertinente

flipper [flípə] N aleta f

flirt [flɜt] VI coquetear; N coqueto -ta mf

flirtation [flɜtéʃən] N coquetería f, coqueteo m

flit [flɪt] VI revolotear; **a smile —s across her face** una sonrisa le cruza la cara

float [flot] VI (rest on water, air, fluctuate freely) flotar; (in soup) sobrenadar; (drift) errar, ir a la deriva; **she —ed down the stairs** se deslizó por la escalera; VT (set afloat) poner a flote; (start a company, scheme) lanzar; (issue shares) emitir; (let fluctuate) dejar flotar; (try out an idea) proponer; N (thing that floats) flotador m; (on a line) corcho m, boya f; (in a parade) carro alegórico m, carroza f; (with soda) gaseosa con helado f

flock [flak] N (birds, children) bandada f; (sheep) rebaño m; (worshipers) grey f; (people) muchedumbre f; VI acudir en masa, afluir; **to — around someone** rodear a alguien; **to — together** andar juntos

flog [flag] VT azotar

flood [flʌd] N inundación f; (of tides) creciente f; **—gate** (of a dam) compuerta f; (of a canal lock) esclusa f; **— insurance** seguro contra inundaciones m; **—light** reflector m; **— of tears** torrente de lágrimas m; **the —** el Diluvio Universal; VI/VT inundar[se], anegar[se]; (car) ahogar[se], emborrachar[se]

floor [flɔr] N (surface of a room, vehicle) suelo m, piso m; (story) piso m; (of sea) fondo m; (for dancing) pista f; (minimum level) mínimo m; **to have the —** tener la palabra; VT (knock down) tumbar, derribar; (stun, surprise) asombrar; **— it!** ¡acelera! *Sp* ¡mete caña!

flooring [flɔrɪŋ] N revestimiento m

flop [flap] VI (flail) zarandearse; (fish) dar coletazos; (drop) dejarse caer; (fail) fracasar; **to — down** dejarse caer, desplomarse; **to — over** voltear[se] flojamente; N (failure) fracaso m; (sound) ruido sordo m

floppy [flápi] ADJ caído; **— disk** disquete m, floppy m

flora [flɔrə] N flora f

florist [flɔrɪst] N florista mf; **—'s shop** florería f

floss [flɔs] N (silk fibers) seda floja f; (for embroidery) hilo de seda m; (dental) hilo dental m; VI/VT pasar hilo dental [por]

flounder [fláʊndɚ] VI (in mud, etc.) andar/moverse con dificultades; (for an answer) quedarse sin saber qué decir, perder pie; N platija f

flour [flaʊr] N harina f

flourish [flɚɪʃ] VI (prosper) florecer, prosperar; VT (brandish) blandir; N (ornament, florid language, brandishing) floreo m; (of music) floritura f; (of a signature) rúbrica f; **in full —** en plena eclosión

flow [flo] VI (run) fluir, correr; (issue forth) surgir, brotar; (come and go) circular; (fall loosely) caer; (abound) abundar; (rise) crecer; **to — into** desembocar en, afluir a; N (of liquid) flujo m; (of electricity) corriente f; (of traffic, blood, air) circulación f; **—chart** diagrama de flujo m, organigrama m; **— of words** torrente de palabras m

flower [fláʊɚ] N flor f; (paragon) flor y nata f; **in — en** flor; **— bed** *Mex, Sp* arriate m; *RP*

cantero m; **—pot** maceta f, tiesto m; **— vase** florero m; VI florecer

flowery [fláʊɚi] ADJ (of a garden, language) florido; (of a pattern) floreado; (of a fragrance) floral

flowing [flóɪŋ] ADJ (liquid) fluyente; (clothing) suelto

flown [flon] see fly

flu [flu] N gripe f, *Am* gripa f

fluctuate [flʌktʃuet] VI fluctuar

fluctuation [flʌktʃuéʃən] N fluctuación f

fluency [flúənsi] N fluidez f

fluent [flúənt] ADJ fluido; **he is — in French** habla francés con fluidez/soltura

fluff [flʌf] VT mullir; (blunder) pifiar; N pelusa f; (blunder) pifia f; **this book is pure —** este libro es insustancial

fluffy [flʌfi] ADJ (airy) mullido; (covered with fluff) peludo

fluid [flúɪd] ADJ & N fluido m, líquido m; **— ounce** onza líquida [29.42 milliliters] f; **— retention** retención de líquido f

fluke [fluk] N (of whale) aleta f; (chance) chiripa f; **by a —** por chiripa

flung [flʌŋ] see fling

flunk [flʌŋk] VI/VT *Am* reprobar, *Sp* suspender; VI **to — out** *Am* salir reprobado, *Sp* salir suspendido

flunky [flʌŋki] N (lackey, servant) lacayo m; (yes-man) adulón m

fluorescent [flurésənt] ADJ fluorescente; **— light** tubo fluorescente m

fluoride [flɔraɪd] N (chemical) fluoruro m; (dental aid) flúor m

fluorine [flɔrin] N flúor m

flurry [flɚi] N (of snow) nevisca f; (of activity) frenesí m

flush [flʌʃ] N (rosy glow, heat) rubor m; (of anger) arranque m; (of youth, color) resplandor m; (of embarrassment) sonrojo m; (in poker) color m; **did you hear the — of the toilet?** ¿oíste el sonido de la cisterna? ADJ (well supplied, rich) forrado; (ruddy, reddish) rubicundo; (full) rebosante; **— with** a[l] ras de; **— against** pegado a; VI/VT (make or turn red) sonrojar[se], ruborizar[se]; (activate toilet) tirar la cadena; (rinse) baldear

fluster [flʌstɚ] VI/VT agitar[se], poner[se] nervioso

flute [flut] N (musical instrument) flauta f; (of a column) estría f; VT estriar

flutter [flʌɾɚ] VI (wings) aletear; (butterfly) revolotear; (flag) tremolar; (heart) palpitar; VT (agitate) agitar; N (of wings) aleteo m; (of excitement) agitación f; (of a fly) tremolar m; (of the heart) palpitación f

flux [flʌks] N flujo m; **a state of —** un estado de cambio continuo

fly [flaɪ] VI (through air) volar; (from danger)

huir; (flag) ondear; (kite) remontar; vt (aircraft) pilotar; (air cargo) transportar en avión; **to — away** volarse; **to — into a rage** montar en cólera; **to — off the handle** perder los estribos; **to — open [shut]** abrirse [cerrarse] de un golpe; **to — out of a room** salir disparado de un cuarto; **that idea won't —** esa idea no va a ser aceptada; **he flew the coop** se escapó; N (insect) mosca f; (over a zipper) bragueta f; **— ball** (in baseball) volea f, bombo m, elevado m, palomita f; **—catcher** papamoscas m sg; **—swatter** matamoscas m sg; **—wheel** volante m; **on the —** al vuelo

flying [fláɪɪŋ] ADJ (passing through the air) volador; (fluttering) ondeante; **with — colors** con distinción; **— saucer** platillo volador m; **N I hate —** no me gusta viajar en avión

foam [fom] N (suds, padding) espuma f; **— rubber** goma espuma f; vi hacer espuma; **to — at the mouth** echar espuma por la boca

focus [fókəs] N foco m; vi/vt (bring into or be in focus) enfocar[se]; (concentrate) centrarse; **to — on** fijarse en

fodder [fádə] N forraje m

foe [fo] N enemigo -ga mf

fog [fɑg] N niebla f; **to be in a —** estar confundido; **—horn** sirena de niebla f; vi/vt (confuse) ofuscar; (spray with insecticide) fumigar; (become faded) velar[se]; **to — up** (window) empañar[se]; (one's sight) nublar[se]; **the airport was —ged in** el aeropuerto estaba cerrado por niebla

foggy [fɑgi] ADJ (weather) brumoso, nebuloso; (window) empañado; (confused) confuso; (blurred, as a photograph) borroso

foil [fɔɪl] N (any metal) hoja de metal f; (aluminum) papel de aluminio m; (on mirrors) azogue m; (rapier) florete m; (thing contrasted) contraste m; vt frustrar

fold [fold] vi/vt (sheets) doblar[se]; (paper, folding chairs) plegar[se]; (wings, flag) replegar[se]; (in cards) abandonar; (close a business) cerrar[se]; (end a performance) bajar de cartel; **to — one's arms** cruzarse de brazos; N (pleat, hollow) pliegue m; (crease) doblez m; (enclosure) redil m, aprisco m; (sheep) rebaño m; (congregation) grey f; **to rejoin the —** volver al redil; **three —** tres veces

folder [fóldə] N (file) carpeta f; (instrument for folding) plegadera f

folding [fóldɪŋ] ADJ plegadizo, plegable; **— chair** silla plegable f; **— screen** biombo m; N doblado m

foliage [fóliɪdʒ] N follaje m, fronda f, ramaje m

folic acid [fólɪkæsɪd] N ácido fólico m

folio [fólio] N (page) folio m; (book) libro en folio m

folk [fok] N (people) gente f; (nation) pueblo m; ADJ popular; **— dance** baile folclórico/folklórico m; **—lore** folclore/folklore m; (traditional stories) leyendas tradicionales f pl; **— medicine** medicina tradicional f; **— music** música folclórica/folklórica f; **— song** canción tradicional f; **— tale** cuento folclórico/folklórico m; **old —s** los viejos; **—s** (relatives) parientes m pl; fam (parents) padres m pl, viejos m pl

folkloric [foklórɪk] ADJ folclórico/folklórico

follicle [fálɪkəl] N folículo m

folliculitis [fəlɪkjəláɪDɪs] N foliculitis f

follow [fálo] vi/vt seguir; vi (be a consequence) seguirse; (come next) ir a continuación; **to — suit** seguir el ejemplo, secundar; **to — through** llevar a cabo; **to — up [on]** (pursue) obtener más detalles [sobre]; (develop) desarrollar; N **—through** (in sports) acompañamiento m, continuación f; **—-up** seguimiento m

follower [fáloə] N seguidor -ora mf

following [fáloɪŋ] N seguidores -oras mf pl; **the —** lo siguiente; ADJ siguiente

foment [fomént] vt fomentar

fond [fɑnd] ADJ **I'm — of cats** soy amigo de los gatos, me encantan los gatos; **I'm — of Chinese food** me gusta la comida china; **I'm — of John** le tengo cariño a Juan; **— hopes** ilusión f; **to become — of** encariñarse de

fondle [fándl] vi/vt acariciar

fondness [fándnɪs] N (affection) cariño m, afecto m; (liking or weakness) afición f

font [fɑnt] N (of water) pila f; (of characters) tipo de letra m

food [fud] N comida f, alimento m; **— chain** cadena alimenticia f; **— poisoning** intoxicación por alimentos f; **— stamps** cupones para alimentos m pl; **—stuff** producto alimenticio m; **— for thought** algo para reflexionar

fool [ful] N (foolish person) tonto -ta mf, bobo -ba mf, necio -cia mf; (jester) bufón m; **—proof** (plan) infalible, a prueba de fallos; (device) a prueba de tontos; **to make a — of** hacer quedar como un tonto; **to play the —** hacer el tonto; **I'm a card-playing —** soy loco por los naipes; vi bromear; **to — around** tontear; vt engañar

foolish [fúlɪʃ] ADJ tonto, necio

foolishness [fúlɪʃnɪs] N tontería f, bobería f, sandez f

foot [fut] N pie m; (of an animal) pata f; **—-and-mouth disease** fiebre aftosa f; **—ball** (American) fútbol americano m; (soccer) fútbol m; (ball) balón [de fútbol] m, pelota [de fútbol] f; **— fault** falta de pie f; **—hill** pie de la montaña m; **—hold** punto de apoyo m;

—lights candilejas *f pl*; **—man** lacayo *m*; **—note** nota al pie de página *f*, llamada *f*; **—path** senda *f*; **—print** huella *f*, pisada *f*; **—race** carrera a pie *f*; **—soldier** soldado de infantería *m*; **—step** pisada *f*, paso *m*; **—print** huella *f*, pisada *f*; **—stool** taburete *m*; **—wear** calzado *m*; **—work** (in sports) juego de piernas *m*; **to follow in the —steps of** seguir los pasos de; **he has a —hold in the computer business** ha logrado establecerse en el negocio de la informática; **it'll take some pretty fancy —work to get out of this** va a ser difícil zafarse de esto; **on —** a pie; **to put one's— in it** meter la pata; VI **to — it** andar a pie; VT **to — the bill** pagar la cuenta

footing [fʊ́dɪŋ] N (basis) base *f*; (foothold) punto de apoyo *m*; **to be on a friendly — with** tener relaciones amistosas con; **to lose one's — perder pie

for [fɔr] PREP para, por; **this gift is — John** este regalo es para John; **we're headed — the beach** vamos para la playa; **this is a device — sorting letters** este es un aparato para clasificar cartas; **they gave me enough food — three people** me dieron comida [como] para tres personas; **she's studying — the bar** está estudiando para el examen de abogacía; **the party is planned — Saturday** la fiesta está organizada para el sábado; **he has a good eye — talent** tiene buen ojo para descubrir talento; **he works — IBM** trabaja para IBM; **smoking is bad — your health** fumar es perjudicial para la salud; **he's mature — his age** es maduro para su edad; **I've come — the money** he venido por el dinero; **she asked — you** preguntó por ti; **I walk to work — the exercise** voy al trabajo andando por el ejercicio; **we went to Spain — a month** fuimos a España por un mes; **she did it — the first time** lo hizo por primera vez; **my wife signed — me** mi esposa firmó por mí; **mothers feel love — their children** las madres sienten amor por sus hijos; **they fired him — arriving late** lo echaron por llegar tarde; **run — your life!** ¡corre por tu vida! **she took me — a fool** me tomó por tonto; **thanks — the help** gracias por la ayuda; **I paid ten dollars — the book** pagué diez dólares por el libro; **I'm — gun control** estoy por el control de armas; **— all her intelligence** a pesar de su inteligencia; **that's not — you to decide** a ti no te toca decidir esto; **as — him** en cuanto a él; **it's time — me to go** es hora de que me vaya; **to know — a fact** saber a ciencia cierta; CONJ porque, pues; **I wish to eat, — I'm hungry** quiero comer, pues tengo hambre

forage [fɔ́rɪdʒ] N (feed) forraje *m*; (searching) recolección *f*; VI (gather food) forrajear; VT (feed) dar forraje a; (collect) recolectar

foray [fɔ́re] N incursión *f*, correría *f*; VI (explore) incursionar; (maraud) saquear

forbade [fɔrbéd] *see* forbid

forbear [fɔrbér] VT abstenerse de; VI contenerse

forbid [fəbíd] VT prohibir

forbidden [fəbídn] ADJ prohibido

forbidden [fɔrbídn] *see* forbid

forbidding [fəbídɪŋ] ADJ (strict) severo; (daunting) imponente

force [fɔrs] N fuerza *f*; **— out** (baseball) out forzado *m*; **in —** (effective) en vigor, vigente; (in large numbers) en masa; **armed —s** fuerzas armadas *f pl*; VT (oblige, compel) obligar; (rape, break open) forzar; **she —d a laugh** soltó una risa forzada; **to — upon** imponer; **to — one's way** abrirse paso a la fuerza; **to — out** (from a place) echar a la fuerza; (in baseball) forzar out

forced [fɔrst] ADJ forzado, obligado; (of a landing) forzoso; **— page break** salto de página forzado *m*

forceful [fɔ́rsfəl] ADJ (of personality) fuerte; (of arguments) convincente, contundente; (of behavior) enérgico

forceps [fɔ́rsəps] N (in obstetrics) fórceps *m*; (in dentistry) tenazas *f pl*, gatillo *m*

forcible [fɔ́rsəbəl] ADJ (done by force) forzoso; (effective) convincente; **— entry** allanamiento de morada *m*

ford [fɔrd] N vado *m*; VT vadear

fore [fɔr] ADJ delantero; (of a ship) de proa; N **to come to the —** ponerse en evidencia; INTERJ (in golf) ¡cuidado!

forearm [fɔ́rɑrm] N antebrazo *m*

forebear [fɔ́rber] N antepasado -da *mf*

forebode [fɔrbód] VT (foretell) presagiar; (have a presentiment) presentir

foreboding [fɔrbódɪŋ] N (omen) presagio *m*; (presentiment) presentimiento *m*

forecast [fɔ́rkæst] N pronóstico *m*; VI/VT pronosticar

foreclose [fɔrklóz] VI ejecutar una hipoteca

foreclosure [fɔrklóʒə] N ejecución *f*

forefather [fɔ́rfɑðə] N antepasado *m*

forefront [fɔ́rfrʌnt] ADV LOC **at the —** a la cabeza, a la vanguardia

forego, forgo [fɔrgó] VT abstenerse de

foregone [fɔ́rgɔn] ADJ **it's a — conclusion** eso es de cajón

foreground [fɔ́rgraʊnd] N primer plano *m*

forehand [fɔ́rhænd] N (in tennis) derecha *f*, golpe de derecha *m*

forehead [fɔ́rɪd] N frente *f*

foreign [fɔ́rɪn] ADJ (from another country) extranjero; (not local) foráneo; (alien) ajeno; **— affairs** relaciones exteriores *f pl*; **— aid**

ayuda exterior f; — **body** cuerpo extraño m;
—**-born** nacido en el extranjero; —
currency divisa f; — **debt** deuda exterior f;
— **exchange** cambio de divisas m; —
exchange system sistema cambiario m; —
matter materia extraña f; — **policy** política
exterior f; — **trade** comercio exterior m

foreigner [fɔ́rənə] N extranjero -ra mf

foreman [fɔ́rmən] N (in a factory) capataz m,
sobrestante m; (of a jury) presidente m

foremost [fɔ́rmost] ADJ principal, preeminente

forensic [fərénzɪk] ADJ forense

forerunner [fɔ́rranə] N (precursor) precursor
-ora mf; (omen) presagio m; (harbinger)
mensajero -ra mf

foresaw [fɔrsɔ́] see foresee

foresee [fɔrsí] VT prever, prevenir

foreseeable [fɔrsíəbəl] ADJ previsible

foreseen [fɔrsín] see foresee

foresight [fɔ́rsaɪt] N previsión f

foreskin [fɔ́rskɪn] N prepucio m

forest [fɔ́rɪst] N (temperate) bosque m; (tropical)
selva f; — **fire** incendio forestal m; — **ranger**
guardabosque[s] m sg

forestall [fɔrstɔ́l] VT bloquear

forester [fɔ́rɪstə] N (forest ranger)
guardabosque[s] m sg

forestry [fɔ́rɪstri] N silvicultura f; — **division**
división forestal f

foretell [fɔrtél] VT predecir, vaticinar

foretold [fɔrtóld] see foretell

forever [fɔrévə] ADV para siempre; **I'm —
having to pick up after him** siempre
tengo que estar juntando sus cosas; **we can't
go on like this** — no podemos seguir así por
toda la vida

foreword [fɔ́rwəd] N prólogo m

forfeit [fɔ́rfɪt] VT perder; N (fine) multa f; (loss)
pérdida f

forfeiture [fɔ́rfɪtʃə] N confiscación f, pérdida f

forgave [fɔrgév] see forgive

forge [fɔrdʒ] N fragua f, forja f; VT (plans)
fraguar; (metal, agreement) forjar, fraguar;
VI/VT (signature, legal document) falsificar;
to — ahead abrirse paso

forgery [fɔ́rdʒəri] N falsificación f

forget [fəgét] VI/VT olvidar, olvidarse de; **I
forgot my keys** se me olvidaron las llaves;
to — oneself meter la pata; N —**-me-not**
nomeolvides mf

forgetful [fəgétfəl] ADJ olvidadizo; —**of**
negligente de

forgetfulness [fəgétfəlnɪs] N falta de memoria f

forgive [fəgív] VI/VT perdonar; (a debt)
perdonar, disculpar

forgiven [fəgívən] see forgive

forgiveness [fəgívnɪs] N perdón m

forgiving [fəgívɪŋ] ADJ clemente

forgo [fɔrgó] see forego

forgot [fɔrgát] see forget

forgotten [fɔrgátn] see forget

fork [fɔrk] N (for eating) tenedor m; (for hay)
horca f, trinche m; (for tuning) diapasón m;
(in a road) bifurcación f; —**lift** montacargas
de horquilla m sg; VI bifurcarse; **to — over**
soltar

forlorn [fɔrlɔ́rn] ADJ desamparado, abandonado

form [fɔrm] N forma f; (type) modalidad f;
(physical condition) condiciones físicas f pl;
(document to be filled in) formulario m; VI/VT
formar[se]

formal [fɔ́rməl] ADJ formal; — **attire** ropa de
etiqueta f; — **dance** baile de etiqueta m

formaldehyde [fɔrmældɪhaɪd] N formaldehído
m

formality [fɔrmælɪDi] N (conventionality)
formalidad f; (rigidity) formalismo m; (legal
step) trámite m

format [fɔ́rmæt] N formato m; VT formatear

formation [fɔrméʃən] N formación f

formative [fɔ́rmədɪv] ADJ formativo

formatting [fɔ́rmædɪŋ] N formateo m

former [fɔ́rmə] ADJ **the — capital** la antigua
capital; **my — husband** mi ex-marido; **the
— president** el ex-presidente; **in — times**
antiguamente; PRON aquel [aquella, etc.], ese
[esa, etc.]

formerly [fɔ́rməli] ADV antes, anteriormente

formidable [fɔ́rmɪdəbəl] ADJ formidable

formula [fɔ́rmjələ] N fórmula f, formulación f;
(for babies) preparado para biberón m

formulate [fɔ́rmjəlet] VT formular

formulation [fɔrmjəléʃən] N formulación f

fornicate [fɔ́rnɪket] VI fornicar

forsake [fɔrsék] VT abandonar, desamparar

forsaken [fɔrsékən] see forsake

forsook [fɔrsúk] see forsake

fort [fɔrt] N fuerte m, fortaleza f; **to hold [down]
the** — quedar de guardián

forth [fɔrθ] ADV (time) en adelante; (space) hacia
adelante; **to go** — irse; **and so** — etcétera, y
así sucesivamente

forthcoming [fɔrθkámɪŋ] ADJ (approaching)
venidero, próximo; (available) disponible;
(frank, friendly) abierto; (soon to be
published) de próxima aparición

forthright [fɔ́rθraɪt] ADJ directo

forthwith [fɔrθwíθ] ADV en seguida, al punto

fortification [fɔrdəfɪkéʃən] N fortificación f

fortify [fɔ́rdəfaɪ] VT (building, body) fortificar;
(food) enriquecer; (hair, mind) fortalecer;
(argument) reforzar

fortitude [fɔ́rdɪtud] N fortaleza f, entereza f

fortress [fɔ́rtrɪs] N fortaleza f

fortuitous [fɔrtúɪDəs] ADJ (coincidental)
fortuito; (lucky) afortunado

fortunate [fɔ́rtʃənɪt] ADJ afortunado

fortunately [fɔ́rtʃənɪtli] ADV afortunadamente

fortune [fɔ́rtʃən] N fortuna *f*; **— teller** adivino -na *mf*; **it cost me a —** me costó un dineral; **to tell someone's —** decirle la buenaventura a alguien

forty [fɔ́rɖi] NUM cuarenta; **— love** (in tennis) quince a nada

forum [fɔ́rəm] N foro *m*

forward [fɔ́rwəd] ADJ (toward the front) hacia adelante; (leading, in the front) delantero; (pushy) descarado; ADV adelante, en adelante; **to bring —** presentar; VT reexpedir; N (in sports) delantero -ra *mf*; (in basketball) alero -ra *mf*

fossil [fásəl] N fósil *m*; (old fogey) carcamal *m*, carca *mf*; **— fuel** combustible fósil *m*

foster [fɔ́stə] VT (promote) fomentar, promover; (bring up) criar; **— family** familia de acogida *f*

fought [fɔt] *see* fight

foul [faʊl] ADJ (dirty, illicit) sucio; (disgusting) asqueroso; (of a smell) fétido; (of weather) inclemente; (of winds) adverso; (morally offensive) vil; (of air) viciado; **—mouthed** mal hablado; **the police suspect — play** la policía sospecha que fue un crimen; N (in sports) falta *f*, faul *m*; **—-up** desastre *m*; VT (make dirty) ensuciar; (pollute) viciar; (tarnish) manchar; VI cometer una falta; **to — up** estropear

found [faʊnd] VT (establish) fundar; (build) cimentar

found [faʊnd] *see* find

foundation [faʊndéʃən] N (establishment, institution) fundación *f*; (of a building) cimiento *m*; (of an argument) fundamento *m*; (cosmetic) base *f*

founder [fáʊndə] N (establisher) fundador -ora *mf*; (smith) fundidor -ora *mf*; VI (sink) zozobrar, irse a pique; (fail) fracasar

foundry [fáʊndri] N fundición *f*

fountain [fáʊntn̩] N fuente *f*; **— pen** pluma fuente *f*

four [fɔr] NUM cuatro; **— hundred** cuatrocientos; **—score** ochenta; N **—-eyes** *fam* cuatro ojos *mf sg*; **—-letter word** palabrota *f*; **—some** grupo de cuatro *m*

fourteen [fɔrtín] NUM catorce

fourth [fɔrθ] ADJ cuarto; N cuarta parte *f*; **the Fourth of July** el cuatro de julio

fowl [faʊl] N (domestic) ave de corral *m*; (wild) ave *m*

fox [faks] N zorro *m*, zorra *f*; (crafty person) persona astuta *f*; (attractive person) guapetón -ona *mf*; **—hole** madriguera *f*; (military) trinchera *f*

foxy [fáksi] ADJ (crafty) zorro; (attractive) sexy

foyer [fɔ́ɪə] N vestíbulo *m*

fraction [frǽkʃən] N fracción *f*, quebrado *m*

fracture [frǽktʃə] N fractura *f*; VI/VT

fracturar[se]

fragile [frǽdʒəl] ADJ frágil

fragment[1] [frǽgmənt] N fragmento *m*

fragment[2] [frægmént] VI/VT fragmentar[se]

fragmentation [frægməntéʃən] N fragmentación *f*

fragrance [frégrəns] N fragancia *f*

fragrant [frégrənt] ADJ fragante

frail [freɪl] ADJ frágil, débil

frailty [frélti] N fragilidad *f*, debilidad *f*

frame [frem] N (of a building, airplane, furniture) armazón *m*; (of eyeglasses) montura *f*, armadura *f*; (of a car) chasis *m*; (of a person's body) estatura *f*; (of a picture, door) marco *m*; (for embroidery) bastidor *m*; (on a strip of film) imagen *f*; **— of mind** disposición *f*; **—work** (of a house, structure) armazón *m*; (of reference) marco *m*, esquema *m*; VT (a document) forjar; (a question, plan) formular; (a picture) enmarcar; (a person) tenderle una trampa

franc [fræŋk] N franco *m*

France [fræns] N Francia *f*

franchise [frǽntʃaɪz] N (license) concesión *f*, franquicia *f*; (voting privilege) derecho al voto *m*; VT conceder en franquicia, dar la concesión para

frank [fræŋk] ADJ franco, abierto; VT franquear; N salchicha alemana *f*

frankfurter [frǽŋkfɚɖə] N salchicha alemana *f*

frankness [frǽŋknɪs] N franqueza *f*

frantic [frǽntɪk] ADJ (wild) frenético; (desperate) desesperado

fraternal [frətɚ́n̩l] ADJ fraternal, fraterno

fraternity [frətɚ́nɪɖi] N (relationship) fraternidad *f*, confraternidad *f*; (student association) asociación estudiantil *f*

fraternize [frǽɖɚnaɪz] VI confraternizar, fraternizar

fraud [frɔd] N (deceit) fraude *m*; (impostor) farsante *mf*, impostor -ora *mf*

fraudulent [frɔ́dʒələnt] ADJ (of a business, etc.) fraudulento; (of a person) engañoso

fray [fre] N (fight) reyerta *f*, riña *f*; (harsh debate) refriega *f*; VI/VT (rub, wear out) desgastar[se], deshilachar[se]; (strain) crispar[se]

freak [frik] N (anomaly) anomalía *f*; (monster) monstruo *m*, anormal *mf*; (enthusiast) fanático -ca *mf*; (pervert) pervertido -da *mf*; ADJ (unusual) insólito; VI chiflar, flipar; **to — out** chiflar[se], flipar[se]

freakish [fríkɪʃ] ADJ insólito

freckle [frékəl] N peca *f*; VI/VT cubrir[se] de pecas

freckled [frékəld] ADJ pecoso

free [fri] ADJ (having liberty, unrestricted, loose, uncombined chemically, independent) libre; (unobstructed, unoccupied) libre, despejado; (without charge) gratis, gratuito; (generous) generoso; (unstinted) sin límites,

descontrolado; (frank) franco, abierto; —
and clear libre de gravámenes; — **and easy**
despreocupado; — **delivery** entrega gratuita
f; — **enterprise** empresa libre *f*; — **fall** caída
libre *f*; —**-for-all** rifirrafe *m*; — **kick** tiro
libre *m*; —**lance** freelance *m*; — **lunch/ride**
algo gratis *m*; — **market** mercado libre *m*; —
radical radical libre *m*; — **speech** libertad
de expresión *f*; — **spirit** espíritu fuerte *m*;
—**style** estilo libre *m*, crol *m*; —**thinker**
libre pensador -ora *mf*; — **throw** tiro libre *m*;
— **trade** libre comercio *m*; — **verse** verso
libre *m*; —**way** autopista *f*, autovía *f*; — **will**
libre albedrío *m*; **to give someone a —
hand** dar rienda suelta a alguien; **to set —**
poner en libertad; **sugar-—** sin azúcar; ADV
libremente; — **lance** por cuenta propia; **for
—** gratis; VT (liberate) liberar; (deliver, rid)
librar; (untie a knot) desenredar; (drain)
desatascar; **to —load** gorronear; **to — up**
(time) dejar libre
freebie [fríbi] N yapa *f*
freedom [frídəm] N libertad *f*; — **of speech**
libertad de expresión *f*; **we all want — from
fear** todos queremos vivir libres de miedo; **I
want — from having to go to work every
day** no quiero tener que ir a trabajar todos los
días
freeze [friz] VI/VT (food, water) congelar[se];
(accounts) bloquear[se], congelar[se]; **to —
dry** liofilizar; **he froze to death** murió
congelado; **my computer froze up** se me
colgó la computadora / el ordenador; VI (of
temperature) helar; N (action or state of being
frozen) congelación *f*; (cold snap) helada *f*
freezer [frízə-] N congelador *m*
freezing [frízɪŋ] ADJ helado; — **cold** frío glacial
m; — **point** punto de congelación *m*
freight [fret] N (load) carga *f*; (charge) flete *m*,
porte *m*; — **train** tren de carga *m*, tren de
mercancías *m*
freighter [frédə-] N buque de carga *m*
French [frɛntʃ] ADJ francés; — **dressing** salsa
francesa *f*; — **fries** *Am* papas fritas *f pl*; *Sp*
patatas fritas *f pl*; — **horn** corno francés *m*;
—**man** francés *m*; —**woman** francesa *f*; N
(language) francés; **the —** los franceses
frenzy [frénzi] N frenesí *m*; **he worked
himself into a —** se puso histérico
frequency [fríkwənsi] N frecuencia *f*
frequent [fríkwənt] ADJ frecuente; VT frecuentar
frequently [fríkwəntli] ADV con frecuencia, a
menudo; — **asked questions** preguntas
frecuentes *f pl*
fresh [frɛʃ] ADJ (pure, cool, not stale, not frozen,
not tired) fresco; (new) nuevo; (bold)
impertinente, atrevido; (healthy) lozano; —
paint pintura fresca *f*; — **water** agua dulce *f*;
ADV — **out of school** recién salido de la

escuela; **we're — out of ideas** se nos
acabaron las ideas
freshen [fréʃən] VI/VT refrescar[se]; **to — up**
arreglarse, lavarse
freshman [fréʃmən] N (student) estudiante de
primer año *mf*; (novice) novato -ta *mf*
freshness [fréʃnɪs] N (of food, of temperature)
frescor *m*, frescura *f*; (of skin, flowers, youth)
lozanía *f*; (of an idea) originalidad *f*;
(impudence) descaro *m*
fret [fret] VI/VT (worry) preocupar[se]; (irritate)
irritar[se]; N traste *m*
fretful [frétfəl] ADJ ansioso, inquieto
friar [fráɪə-] N fraile *m*
friction [fríkʃən] N fricción *f*, rozamiento *m*
Friday [fráɪde] N viernes *m*
fried [fraɪd] ADJ frito
friend [frɛnd] N amigo -ga *mf*
friendliness [fréndlinɪs] N afabilidad *f*,
simpatía *f*
friendly [fréndli] ADJ amistoso, simpático,
amigable; — **advice** consejo de amigo *m*;
user-— fácil de usar
friendship [fréndʃɪp] N amistad *f*
frigate [frígɪt] N fragata *f*
fright [fraɪt] N (fear) espanto *m*, susto *m*;
(grotesque thing or person) espantajo *m*,
esperpento *m*; **to take —** asustarse
frighten [fráɪtn̩] VI/VT espantar[se], asustar[se];
to — away ahuyentar, espantar
frightened [fráɪtn̩d] ADJ asustado, espantado;
to get — espantarse
frightful [fráɪtfəl] ADJ espantoso, pavoroso; **we
had a — time** lo pasamos horrible; **he's a —
flatterer** es un adulón espantoso
frigid [frɪdʒɪd] ADJ (of weather) gélido; (of
personal relations) frío
frill [frɪl] N (trimming) volante *m*; (something
superfluous) adorno *m*; **no-—s** sin lujos
fringe [frɪndʒ] N (of a rug) fleco *m*, orla *f*; (of a
city) periferia *f*; (of a political party) extremo
m; (of society) margen *m*; — **benefits**
prestaciones *f pl*, complementos *m pl*; VT
orlar, poner un fleco
Frisbee® [frízbi] N disco volador *m*
frisk [frɪsk] VI/VT (frolic) retozar, triscar;
(search) cachear
frisky [fríski] ADJ retozón
fritter [frídə-] VI/VT desmenuzar[se]; VI irse
gastando de poco a poco; **to — away**
malgastar; N buñuelo *m*, churro *m*
frivolity [frɪválɪdi] N frivolidad *f*
frivolous [frívələs] ADJ frívolo
fro [fro] ADV **to and —** de aquí para allá
frock [frɑk] N (dress) vestido *m*; (habit) hábito *m*
frog [frɑg] N (animal) rana *f*; (fastener) alamar *m*;
(of a hoof) ranilla *f*; (French person) *pej*
franchute -ta *mf*; **to have a — in one's
throat** tener gallos en la garganta; —**man**

hombre rana *m*

frolic [frálɪk] N retozo *m*; VI retozar

from [frəm, frʌm] PREP desde, de, por; — **here to there** desde aquí hasta allá; — **two to four** de las dos a las cuatro; — **what I can tell** por lo que yo veo; **four hours** — **now** de aquí a cuatro horas, dentro de cuatro horas; **different** — **the other one** diferente del otro; **to come** — **Minnesota** ser de Minesota; **death** — **starvation** muerte por inanición *f*

front [frʌnt] N frente *m*; (cover for illegal activity) pantalla *f*; — **runner** favorito -ta *mf*; — **wheel drive** tracción delantera *f*; **in** — **of** en frente de, delante de; ADJ delantero; VI/VT (face) dar a; (cover up) servir de pantalla

frontal [frántl] ADJ frontal

frontier [frʌntír] N frontera *f*; ADJ fronterizo; — **spirit** espíritu pionero *m*; — **town** pueblo fronterizo *m*

frost [frɔst] N helada *f*, escarcha *f*; VI/VT helar, escarchar; VT (a cake) bañar; (glass) esmerilar; (hair) hacer rayitos/reflejos; — **bite** necrosis por congelación *f*

frosting [frɔ́stɪŋ] N (of a cake) baño *m*; (for glass) esmerilado *m*; (of hair) rayos *m pl*, reflejos *m pl*

frosty [frɔ́sti] ADJ (cold, unfriendly) helado; (covered with frost) escarchado

froth [frɔθ] N espuma *f*; VI echar espuma; VT batir

frown [fraʊn] VI fruncir el ceño; **to** — **on** desaprobar; N ceño *m*

froze [froz] *see* freeze

frozen [frózən] ADJ congelado

frozen [frózən] *see* freeze

fructose [frúktos] N fructosa *f*

frugal [frúgəl] ADJ (economical) económico, ahorrativo; (meager) frugal

fruit [frut] N (food) fruta *f*; (plant part, product of labor) fruto *m*; — **cake** (food) torta de frutas secas *f*; (crazy person) *fam* chiflado -da *mf*

fruitful [frútfəl] ADJ fructífero

fruitless [frútlɪs] ADJ infructuoso

frumpy [frámpi] ADJ matrona

frustrate [frástret] VT frustrar; **to get** — **d** frustrar[se]

frustration [frʌstréʃən] N frustración *f*

fry [fraɪ] VI/VT (cook, also execute by electrocution) freír[se]; — **ing pan** sartén *f*; N (fried potato) papa/patata frita *f*; (gathering with fried food) fiesta con comida frita *f*; (young fish) alevín *m*; **small** — gente menuda *f*

fudge [fʌdʒ] N turrón blando de chocolate *m*; VI (cheat) hacer trampa; (avoid an issue) dar rodeos

fuel [fjúəl] N (combustible) combustible *m*,

carburante *m*; (topic) tema *m*; — **injection** inyección *f*; — **oil** fuel *m*; VT (a vehicle) llenar el tanque, cargar de combustible; (fire, debate) avivar

fugitive [fjúdʒɪDɪv] ADJ (fleeing) fugitivo; (transitory) fugaz; N fugitivo -va *mf*, prófugo -ga *mf*

fulfill [fʊlfɪ́l] VT (promise, order) cumplir; (need) satisfacer; **she doesn't feel** — **ed** no se siente realizada

fulfillment [fʊlfɪ́lmənt] N (of a promise, order) cumplimiento *m*; (of a need) satisfacción *f*; (of a person) realización *f*; (of a dream) culminación *f*

full [fʊl] ADJ (completely filled) lleno; (complete) completo; (a dress) amplio; (a person's figure) relleno; (sated) harto; — **blooded** de raza; — **blown** (of disease) declarado; (complete) auténtico; — **bodied** con cuerpo; — **fledged** verdadero; — **grown** adulto; — **house** full *m*; — **length** (movie) de largometraje; (mirror) de cuerpo entero; — **moon** luna llena *f*; — **name** nombre completo *m*; — **scale** (model) de tamaño natural; (war) total; (investigation) exhaustivo; — **service** de servicio completo; — **size** (bed) de matrimonio; (model) de tamaño natural; — **term** a término; — **time** tiempo completo *m*, de tiempo completo; **to pay in** — pagar el total de la deuda; VT **you know** — **well** sabes perfectamente; **it hit him** — **in the chest** le pegó en pleno pecho

fully [fʊ́li] ADV (entirely) completamente, plenamente; (at least) al menos

fumble [fámbəl] N pérdida de balón *f*; VI (search for) buscar a tientas; (move clumsily) andar a tientas; (blunder) meter la pata; (football) perder el balón; **he** — **d his way into the living room** entró a tientas a la sala

fume [fjum] VI (be angry) rabiar; (emit vapors, smoke) emitir humo; N — **s** gases *m pl*, vapores *m pl*, tufo *m*

fumigate [fjúmɪget] VT fumigar

fun [fʌn] N diversión *f*; **for** — por gusto; **to make** — **of** burlarse de; **to have** — divertirse; ADJ divertido

function [fáŋkʃən] N función *f*; — **key** tecla de función *f*; VI (work) funcionar; (serve) oficiar

functional [fáŋkʃənl] ADJ funcional

fund [fʌnd] N (of money) fondo *m*; (of knowledge) acervo *m*; — **raising** recaudación de fondos *f*; VT financiar

fundamental [fʌndəmɛ́ntl] ADJ fundamental; N fundamento *m*

fundamentalism [fʌndəmɛ́ntlɪzəm] N fundamentalismo *m*

fundamentally [fʌndəmɛ́ntli] ADV fundamentalmente

funding [fándɪŋ] N financiamiento *m*,

financiación f

funeral [fjúnəɚl] N funeral m, entierro m, exequias f pl; **— director** director -ora de pompas fúnebres mf; **— home** casa de pompas fúnebres f, funeraria f; **— service** funeral m; **it's your —** te estás cavando tu propia tumba; ADJ (march, procession) fúnebre; (pyre) funerario; (expenses) de entierro

funereal [fjuníriəł] ADJ lúgubre

fungible [fándʒibəł] ADJ fungible

fungicide [fándʒɪsaɪd] N fungicida m

fungus [fángəs] N hongo m

funky [fáŋki] ADJ (of music) funky; (strange) estrafalario, raro; (smelly) hediondo

funnel [fánł] N (for liquids) embudo m; (in a chimney) humero m; VT canalizar, encauzar

funny [fáni] ADJ (amusing) cómico, chistoso, gracioso; (strange) raro; **— farm** fam loquero m, loquería f; **that's not —** eso no tiene gracia; **don't get — with me** no te pases de listo; N **funnies** historietas f pl, tiras cómicas f pl; ADV raro

fur [fɚ] N (hair) pelo m; (coat) pelaje m; (hide) piel f; **— store** peletería f; VT forrar de piel

furious [fjúrias] ADJ (person) furioso, sañudo, rabioso; (fight, storm) feroz; (activity) febril

furlough [fɚlo] N licencia f, permiso m; VT dar licencia

furnace [fɚnɪs] N (for heating) caldera f; (in industry) horno m

furnish [fɚnɪʃ] VT (put in furniture) amueblar; (equip) equipar; (provide) proporcionar, suministrar, facilitar

furniture [fɚnɪtʃɚ] N muebles m pl, mobiliario m; **— store** mueblería f

furrow [fɚo] N surco m; VT (soil) arar; (face) fruncir

furry [fɚi] ADJ peludo

further [fɚðɚ] ADV **we want to go —** queremos ir más lejos; **I refuse to discuss this —** me niego a seguir discutiendo esto; (additionally) [lo que] es más; ADJ (more distant) más lejano; (additional) adicional; VT (promote) promover; ADV **—more** además

furthest [fɚðɪst] ADJ [el] más lejano, [el] más remoto; ADV más lejos

furtive [fɚDɪV] ADJ (stealthy) furtivo; (shifty) sospechoso

fury [fjúri] N furia f, furor m, saña f

fuse [fjuz] N (in an explosive) mecha f; (in a circuit) fusible m; **he has a short —** tiene pocas pulgas; **he blew a —** estalló; VT (to join) fusionar; VI/VT (to merge) fusionar[se]; (to blend metals) fundir[se]

fuselage [fjúsəlɑʒ] N fuselaje m

fusion [fjúʒən] N fusión f

fuss [fʌs] N (bustle) alboroto m, bulla f; (uproar) escándalo m; (argument) discusión f; VI

(worry about trifles) preocuparse por naderías; (complain) quejarse

fussiness [fásɪnɪs] N remilgo m, ñoñería f

fussy [fási] ADJ (particular) quisquilloso, remilgado; (whiny) quejica, cargoso

futile [fjúdl] ADJ inútil

futility [fjutílɪDi] N inutilidad f

future [fjútʃɚ] N futuro m, porvenir m; **—s** futuros m pl; ADJ futuro

fuzz [fʌz] N (fluff) pelusa f; (fine hair) vello fino m; (on the lip) bozo m

fuzzy [fázi] ADJ (fluffy) cubierto de pelusa; (hairy) velloso; (blurred) borroso; (muddled) confuso

FYI [for your information] [ɛfwáɪáɪ] ADV para su información

Gg

gab [gæb] VI parlotear, charlar; N parloteo m, charla f; **gift of —** labia f, facundia f

gable [gébəł] N hastial m; **— roof** tejado de dos aguas m; **— window** buhardilla f

Gabon, Gabun [gəbón] N Gabón m

Gabonese [gæbəníz] ADJ & N gabonés -esa mf

gad [gæd] VI **to — about** callejear

gadget [gædʒɪt] N coso m, chisme m

gaffe [gæf] N gaffe f, metedura de pata f

gag [gæg] VT (stop up mouth, silence) amordazar; (cause to choke) dar arcadas; VI tener arcadas; N (thing stuffed into mouth) mordaza f; (joke) gag m, burla f; **— order** orden de supresión de la libertad de expresión f

gaiety [géɪDi] N alegría f; **gaieties** festejos m pl

gain [gen] VT ganar; VI **to — on** irse acercando a; VI/VT (watch) adelantar; N (profit, act of gaining) ganancia f; (in weight) aumento m

gainful [génfəł] ADJ remunerado

gait [get] N marcha f, paso m

galaxy [gæləksi] N galaxia f

gale [geł] N ventarrón m, vendaval m; **—-force winds** vientos huracanados m pl; **— of laughter** risotada f

Galicia [gəlíʃə] N Galicia f

Galician [gəlíʃən] ADJ & N gallego -ga mf

gall [gɔł] N (bile, bitterness) hiel f; (impudence) morro m; (of a plant) agalla f; **— bladder** vesícula [biliar] f; **—nut** agalla f; **—stone** cálculo biliar m; VT (irritate) irritar

gallant[1] [gælənt] ADJ (brave) valiente; (attentive to women) galante

gallant[2] [gəlánt] N galán m

gallantry [gæləntri] N (courage) valentía f, bizarría f; (chivalrous attention) galantería f

gallery [gæləri] N (art, shopping) galería f;

(theater) paraíso *m*, gallinero *m*; (golf) público *m*

galley [gǽli] N (kitchen) cocina *f*; (boat) galera *f*; **— proof** galerada *f*

gallium [gǽliəm] N galio *m*

gallon [gǽlən] N galón [3.7853 liters] *m*

gallop [gǽləp] VI galopar; N galope *m*

gallows [gǽloz] N horca *f*, cadalso *m*

galore [gəlɔ́r] ADV en abundancia

galoshes [gəlάʃɪz] N chanclos *m pl*

galvanize [gǽlvənaɪz] VT (metals) galvanizar; (a crowd) electrizar

Gambia [gǽmbiə] N Gambia *f*

Gambian [gǽmbiən] N & ADJ gambiano -na *mf*

gamble [gǽmbəl] VI jugar; VT jugarse; **I'll — my whole fortune on this venture** voy a jugarme todo en este negocio; **to — away** perder en el juego; N (risk) riesgo *m*; (bet) apuesta *f*

gambler [gǽmblə·] N apostador -ora *mf*, tahúr *m*

gambling [gǽmblɪŋ] N juego [de apuestas] *m*

game [gem] N juego *m*; (match of chess, etc.) partida *f*; (sports match) partido *m*; (wild animals and their meat) caza *f*; **— console** consola de juegos *f*; **— plan** (deporte) plan de juego *m*; (negocios) estrategia *f*; **— point** punto de juego *m*; **— room** sala recreativa *f*; **— show** programa concurso *m*; **to be fair —** ser blanco legítimo; ADJ **I'm — for some tennis** me apunto para jugar al tenis; **he has a — knee** tiene la rodilla lisiada

gamut [gǽmət] N gama *f*

gander [gǽndə·] N ganso [macho] *m*; **to take a — at** echarle un vistazo a

gang [gǽŋ] N (of youths, thieves, etc.) pandilla *f*, gavilla *f*, banda *f*; (group of friends) grupo *m*; **—plank** pasarela *f*; **—way** (passage way) pasillo *m*; (on a ship) pasamano *m*; **—way!** ¡abran cancha! VI **to — up on** conspirar contra, conspirar en masa

gangrene [gǽŋgrin] N gangrena *f*; VI/VT gangrenar[se]

gangster [gǽŋstə·] N gángster *m*, maleante *m*

gap [gǽp] N (breach) brecha *f*, hueco *m*; (of memory) laguna *f*; (of time) intervalo *m*; **she has a — between her teeth** tiene los dientes separados; VT espaciar [correctamente]

gape [gep] VI mirar boquiabierto

garage [gəráʒ] N (for parking) garaje *m*; (for repairing) taller mecánico *m*; **— sale** venta de garaje *f*; VT estacionar en un garaje

garb [gɑrb] N vestimenta *f*, atavío *m*; VT vestir, ataviar

garbage [gárbɪʤ] N basura *f*; **— can** bote de basura *m*; **— disposal unit** trituradora *f*; **—man** basurero *m*; **— truck** camión de la basura *m*; **what a load of —!** ¡qué montón de mentiras!

garden [gárdn] N jardín *m*; **— of Eden** jardín del

Edén *m*; VI cultivar un jardín

gardener [gárdnə·] N jardinero -ra *mf*

gargle [gárgəl] VI hacer gárgaras; VT hacer gárgaras con; N (liquid) gargarismo *m*; (sound) gárgara *f*

garland [gárlənd] N guirnalda *f*

garlic [gárlɪk] N ajo *m*

garment [gármənt] N prenda *f*

garner [gárnə·] VT cosechar

garnet [gárnɪt] N granate *m*

garnish [gárnɪʃ] VT (decorate) decorar; (decorate food) aderezar, guarnecer; (withhold wages) retener; N (decoration) adorno *m*, decoración *f*

garret [gǽrɪt] N desván *m*, buhardilla *f*

garrison [gǽrɪsən] N guarnición *f*; VT guarnecer

garrulous [gǽrələs] ADJ locuaz, gárrulo

garter [gárdə·] N liga *f*; **— belt** liguero *m*, portaligas *m sg*; **— snake** culebra de jaretas *f*; VT sujetar con ligas

gas [gǽs] N (vapor) gas *m*; (fuel) gasolina *f*; (flatulence) gases *m pl*; **— chamber** cámara de gas *f*; **— mask** máscara de gas *f*; **— pedal** acelerador *m*; **— station** gasolinera *f*; **to step on the —** acelerar; **we had a —** lo pasamos bomba; VT asfixiar con gas, matar en la cámara de gas; **to — up** llenar el tanque

gaseous [gǽʃəs] ADJ gaseoso

gash [gǽʃ] N tajo *m*; VT hacer un tajo en

gasket [gǽskɪt] N junta de culata *f*

gasoline [gǽsəlin] N gasolina *f*, nafta *f*

gasp [gǽsp] N (cry) grito sofocado *m*; (pant) jadeo *m*, boqueada *f*; VI (cry out) dar un grito sofocado; (in surprise) quedar boquiabierto; (for breath) jadear, boquear

gastric [gǽstrɪk] ADJ gástrico; **— ulcer** úlcera gástrica *f*

gastritis [gæstráɪDɪs] N gastritis *f*

gastroenteritis [gæstroentəráɪDɪs] N gastroenteritis *f*

gastrointestinal [gæstrointéstɪnl] ADJ gastrointestinal; **— tract** tubo digestivo *m*

gastronomy [gæstránəmi] N gastronomía *f*

gate [get] N (to a garden) portón *m*; (to a city) puerta *f*; (at an airport) puerta de embarque *f*; **—way** (entrance, access) puerta [de entrada] *f*; (in computers) portal *m*

gather [gǽðə·] VT (bring together) reunir, allegar; (pick) recolectar; (deduce) deducir, colegir; (sew) fruncir; VI (come together) reunirse; (collect) juntarse; (contract into folds) fruncirse; **to — dust** juntar polvo/ tierra; **to — speed** acelerar; N frunce *m*

gathering [gǽðərɪŋ] N (meeting) asamblea *f*; (social) tertulia *f*; (assemblage of people) concurrencia *f*, reunión *f*; (act of gathering fruit, etc.) recolección *f*

gaudy [gɔ́di] ADJ (of bright color) chillón; (ostentatious) llamativo

gauge [geʤ] VT (measure) medir; (estimate) estimar; (calibrate) calibrar; N (measurement standard) medida f; (caliber) calibre m; (measuring device) medidor m; (track width) entrevía f

gaunt [gɔnt] ADJ demacrado

gauntlet [gɔ́ntlɪt] N (glove) guante m; (mailed glove) guantelete m; **to throw down the —** retar, desafiar; **to run the —** sufrir acosos

gauze [gɔz] N gasa f

gave [gev] see give

gavel [gǽvəl] N martillo m

gawk [gɔk] VT mirar boquiabierto

gawky [gɔ́ki] ADJ torpe, desgarbado

gay [ge] ADJ (happy) alegre, festivo; (homosexual) gay, homosexual; N fam gay m, homosexual m

gaze [gez] VI mirar fijamente, contemplar; N mirada fija f

gazelle [gəzɛ́l] N gacela f

gazette [gəzɛ́t] N gaceta f

gear [gir] N (equipment) equipo m; (cog) rueda dentada f; (assembly of cogs) engranaje m; (transmission speed) marcha f, cambio m; (personal property) pertenencias f pl; **—box** caja de cambios f; **—shift lever** palanca de cambios f; **to be in —** estar engranado; **to change —s** cambiar de marcha, poner el cambio; **to put into —** engranar; **to put out of —** desengranar; VI **to — up** prepararse

gearing [gírɪŋ] N engranaje m

gecko [gɛ́ko] N geco m

geek [gik] N persona que tiene exagerada pasión por la informática f

Geiger counter [gáɪgə-káʊntə-] N contador Geiger m

gel [ʤɛl] VI/VT cuajar[se]

gelatin [ʤɛ́lətn] N gelatina f

gem [ʤɛm] N (precious stone) gema f; (valuable person) joya f; **—stone** piedra preciosa f

gender [ʤɛ́ndə-] N género m; **— discrimination** discriminación de género f; **— gap** diferencias entre los sexos f pl; **— specific** propio de un solo sexo

gene [ʤin] N gen m; **— marker** marcador genético m; N **— pool** conjunto de genes de una población m; **— splicing** empalme genético m; **— therapy** terapia genética f

genealogy [ʤiniálədʒi] N genealogía f

general [ʤɛ́nə-əl] ADJ & N general m f; **in —** por lo general; **— practitioner** médico -ca general m f

generality [ʤɛnə-rélɪDi] N generalidad f

generalization [ʤɛnə-əlɪzéʃən] N generalización f

generalize [ʤɛ́nə-əlaɪz] VI/VT generalizar

generally [ʤɛ́nə-əli] ADV generalmente

generate [ʤɛ́nə-ret] VT generar

generation [ʤɛnə-réʃən] N generación f; **— gap**

brecha generacional f, abismo generacional m

generator [ʤɛ́nə-reDə-] N generador m

generic [ʤə-nɛ́rɪk] ADJ genérico; **— brand** marca genérica f

generosity [ʤɛnə-rásɪDi] N generosidad f, largueza f

generous [ʤɛ́nə-əs] ADJ generoso

genetic [ʤə-nɛ́Dɪk] ADJ genético; **— code** código genético m; **— engineering** ingeniería genética f; **— fingerprinting** identificación genética f; **— marker** marcador genético m; N **—s** genética f

genetically [ʤə-nɛ́Dɪkli] ADV **— modified** transgénico

genial [ʤíɲəl] ADJ afable, de buen genio

genital [ʤɛ́nɪdl] ADJ genital

genius [ʤíɲəs] N genio m

genocide [ʤɛ́nəsaɪd] N genocidio m

genome [ʤínom] N genoma m

genre [ʒánrə] N género m

genteel [ʤɛntíl] ADJ refinado

gentile [ʤɛ́ntaɪl] ADJ & N gentil m f

gentle [ʤɛ́ntl] ADJ (kindly) amable; (mild, slow, gradual) suave; (tame) manso

gentleman [ʤɛ́ntlmən] N caballero m

gentlemanly [ʤɛ́ntlmənli] ADJ caballeroso

gentleness [ʤɛ́ntlnɪs] N (kindness) amabilidad f; (mildness) suavidad f; (tameness) mansedumbre f

gently [ʤɛ́ntli] ADV (smoothly) suavemente; (tactfully) con mucho tacto

genuine [ʤɛ́njuɪn] ADJ genuino

genus [ʤínəs] N género m

geocentric [ʤiosɛ́ntrɪk] ADJ geocéntrico

geographical [ʤiəgrǽfɪkəl] ADJ geográfico

geography [ʤiágrəfi] N geografía f

geological [ʤiálɑʤɪkəl] ADJ geológico

geology [ʤiálədʒi] N geología f

geometric [ʤiəmétrɪk] ADJ geométrico

geometry [ʤiámɪtri] N geometría f

geophysics [ʤiofízɪks] N geofísica f

geopolitical [ʤiopəlíDɪkəl] ADJ geopolítico

Georgia [ʤɔ́rʤə] N Georgia f

Georgian [ʤɔ́rʤən] ADJ & N georgiano -na m f

geostationary [ʤiostéʃəneri] ADJ geoestacionario

geothermal [ʤioθɜ́-məl] ADJ geotérmico

geranium [ʤə-réniəm] N geranio m

geriatric [ʤɛriǽtrɪk] ADJ geriátrico; N **—s** geriatría f

germ [ʤɜ-m] N (microorganism) microbio m, germen m; (bud, embryo, rudiment) germen m; **— warfare** guerra biológica f

German [ʤɜ́-mən] ADJ & N alemán -na m f; **— measles** rubeola, rubéola f; **— shepherd** pastor alemán m

germane [ʤə-mén] ADJ pertinente, relacionado

Germanic [ʤə-mǽnɪk] ADJ germánico -ca

Germany [ʤɜ́-məni] N Alemania f

germinate [dʒɝ́mənet] VI germinar; VT hacer germinar

gerund [dʒérənd] N gerundio *m*

gestate [dʒéstet] VI/VT gestar[se]

gestation [dʒestéʃən] N gestación *f*

gesticulate [dʒestíkjəlet] VI gesticular

gesture [dʒéstʃə] N gesto *m*, ademán *m*; (token) muestra *f*; VI gesticular

gesundheit [gəzúnthaɪt] INTERJ (after a sneeze) ¡salud! *Sp* ¡Jesús!

get [gɛt] VT (receive, earn) recibir; (obtain) obtener; (reach by phone) comunicarse con; (hear, understand) entender; (seize) agarrar; *Sp* coger; (prevail) conseguir, lograr; (affect) afectar; (catch disease) pescar; *Sp* coger; **to — across** comunicar; **to — ahead** prosperar; **to — along [with]** llevarse bien [con]; **to — angry** enojarse; **to — around** (skirt) esquivar, evitar; (go out) salir mucho; **to — away** escapar[se]; **to — away with** quedar impune; **to — back** (return) volver; (recover something) recuperar; **to — back at** vengarse de; **to be —ting on in years** ponerse viejo; **to — by** (go past) pasar; (survive) ir tirando; **to — dark** oscurecer; **to — down** (lower oneself) bajar; (depress) deprimir; (swallow) tragar; **to — down to business / brass tacks** ir al grano; **to — going** ponerse en marcha; **to — in** (enter) entrar; (arrive) llegar; (a vehicle) subir a; **to — it** captar, entender; **to — married** casarse; **to — nowhere** no llegar a ningún lado; **to — off** (dismount, get down) bajar; (not receive punishment) salir impune; (leave work) salir; **to — off on** enloquecerse por; **to — off someone's back** dejar de fastidiar; **to — old** envejecer; **to — on** montarse a; **to — out** (take out) sacar; (exit) salir; **to — over** (recuperate) recuperarse, sobreponerse a; (forgive) olvidar; **to — ready** preparar[se]; **to — rich** enriquecerse; **to — rid of** deshacerse de; **to — sick** enfermarse; **to — somewhere** tener resultado; **to — through** (survive an ordeal) sobrevivir; (reach by phone, be understood) comunicarse; (complete) lograr terminar; **to — to someone** afectar a alguien; **to — together** reunirse; **to — up** (arise) levantarse; (prepare) montar; **I got him to do it** conseguí/logré que lo hiciera; **I have got to do it** tengo que hacerlo; **we got our house painted** nos pintaron la casa; **he got a year in jail** le dieron un año de cárcel; **we — to stay up late in summer** en el verano nos dejan quedarnos despiertos hasta tarde; **that —s my goat** eso me fastidia; N **—away** (escape) escape *m*; (vacation) escapada *f*; **— together** reunión *f*; **—up** disfraz *m*, atuendo *m*; **from the —-go** desde el principio

geyser [gáɪzə] N géiser *m*

Ghana [gánə] N Ghana *f*

Ghanaian [gániən] ADJ & N ghanés -esa *mf*

ghastly [gǽstli] ADJ (horrible) horrendo, espantoso; (cadaverous) cadavérico

ghetto [gɛ́do] N gueto *m*

ghost [gost] N fantasma *m*; **— town** pueblo fantasma *m*; **—writer** colaborador -ora anónimo -ma *mf*; **not a — of a chance** ni la menor posibilidad

ghostly [góstli] ADJ fantasmagórico

ghoul [guł] N fantasma *m*

giant [dʒáɪənt] N & ADJ gigante -ta *mf*

gibberish [dʒíbəɪʃ] N jerigonza *f*

gibbon [gíbən] N gibón *m*

Gibraltar [dʒɪbrɔ́ltə] N Gibraltar *m*

Gibraltarian [dʒɪbrɔltériən] ADJ & N gibraltareño -ña *mf*

giddy [gídi] ADJ (dizzy) mareado; (of heights) vertigoso; (of speed) vertiginoso

gift [gɪft] N (thing given, act of giving) regalo *m*, presente *m*; (special ability) don *m*; **— certificate** vale por un regalo *m*; **— tax** impuesto sobre las donaciones *m*; **—-wrap** envolver para regalo; VT regalar

gifted [gíftɪd] ADJ (artist) talentoso; (child) superdotado

gigabyte [gígəbaɪt] N gigabyte *m*

gigahertz [gígəhɝts] N gigahercio *m*

gigantic [dʒaɪgǽntɪk] ADJ gigantesco, gigante

giggle [gígəł] VI reír tontamente; N risita tonta *f*

gild [gɪłd] VT dorar

gill [gɪł] N agalla *f*

gilt [gɪłt] ADJ & N dorado *m*

gimmick [gímɪk] N treta *f*, estratagema *f*

gin [dʒɪn] N (liquor) ginebra *f*; **— rummy** gin rummy *m*

ginger [dʒíndʒə] N jengibre *m*; **— ale** ginger ale *m*; **—bread** pan de jengibre *m*

gingham [gíŋəm] N guingán *m*

gingivitis [dʒɪndʒəváɪdɪs] N gingivitis *f*

giraffe [dʒəræf] N jirafa *f*

gird [gɝd] VT ceñir; **to — oneself** prepararse

girder [gɝ́də] N viga *f*

girdle [gɝ́dł] N faja *f*; VT rodear

girl [gɝł] N (female child) niña *f*; (young female) muchacha *f*, joven *f*, chica *f*; (servant) muchacha *f*, chacha *f*; **—friend** novia *f*

girlhood [gɝ́łhʊd] N niñez *f*

girlish [gɝ́lɪʃ] ADJ de niña

girth [gɝθ] N (of things) circunferencia *f*; (of persons) contorno *m*; (of horses) cincha *f*; VT cinchar

gist [dʒɪst] N esencia *f*, lo esencial

GI [gastrointestinal] tract [dʒíáɪ] N tubo digestivo *m*

give [gɪv] VT dar; (a gift) regalar; (a party) organizar; (a name) poner; (a donation) donar; **I don't — a hoot** me importa un

comino; vi dar; (yield) ceder; (break)
romperse; **to — away** (a gift) regalar, donar;
(the bride) entregar; (a secret) revelar; **to —
back** devolver; **to — in** (acknowledge defeat)
rendirse; **to — off** emitir, despedir,
desprender; **to — out** (announce) anunciar;
(distribute) repartir; (become exhausted)
rendirse; (run out) acabarse; **to — over**
entregar; **to — up** (surrender) darse por
vencido; (stop) dejar [de]; **we'll work on
this two years, — or take a month** vamos
a trabajar en esto dos años, un mes más, un
mes menos; N elasticidad f; **— and take** toma
y daca m

given [gívən] ADJ (stated, fixed) dado;
(bestowed) regalado; **— name** nombre de
pila m; **— that she's not here** dado que ella
no está; **— to** propenso a; N premisa f

given [gívən] see give

giver [gívə] N dador -ora mf, donador -ora mf

gizmo [gízmo] N coso m, chisme m

glacial [gléʃəl] ADJ glacial

glacier [gléʃə] N glaciar m

glad [glæd] ADJ contento; **I'm — to see you** me
alegro de verte; **I'd be — to help** sería un
placer ayudarle

gladden [glǽdn] VT alegrar, regocijar, alborozar

gladiator [glǽDieDə] N gladiador m

glamorous [glǽmərəs] ADJ glamoroso,
encantador

glamour [glǽmə] N (charm) glamour f, encanto
m; (excitement) atractivo m

glance [glæns] VI echar un vistazo; **to — off**
rebotar con efecto; N (look) vistazo m;
(bounce) rebote oblicuo m

gland [glænd] N glándula f

glandular [glǽndʒələ] ADJ glandular

glare [glɛr] N (bright light) relumbre m; (stare)
mirada furiosa f; VI (shine) relumbrar; (stare
fiercely) lanzar una mirada hostil

glaring [glérɪŋ] ADJ (blinding) deslumbrante;
(obvious) evidente; (hostile) hostil

glass [glæs] N (substance) vidrio m; (window
pane) vidrio m, cristal m; (tumbler) vaso [de
vidrio] m; (mirror) espejo m; (glassware)
cristalería f; (magnifier) lupa f; **—blowing**
soplado de vidrio m; **— ceiling** techo de
cristal m; **— cutter** cortavidrio m; **—es**
anteojos m pl, lentes m pl, gafas f pl; **— eye** ojo
de vidrio m; **—maker** vidriero -ra mf;
—ware cristalería f

glassy [glǽsi] ADJ vidrioso

glaucoma [glɔkómə] N glaucoma m

glaze [glez] VT (windows) poner vidrios a;
(ceramics) vidriar; (food) glasear; (wood)
barnizar; VI vidriarse; N (pottery) vidriado m,
barniz m; (food) glaseado m

glazier [gléʒə] N vidriero -ra mf

gleam [glim] N reflejo m, brillo m; **a — of hope**

un rayo de esperanza; VI brillar, relucir

glean [glin] VT (grain) espigar; (information)
extraer, deducir

glee [gli] N regocijo m, júbilo m; **— club** coro m

glib [glɪb] ADJ (fluent) de mucha labia;
(superficial) simplista, superficial

glide [glaɪd] VI (slide) deslizarse; (fly) planear; N
(sliding movement) deslizamiento m; (flight)
planeo m

glider [gláɪdə] N planeador m

glimmer [glímə] N luz trémula f; **a — of hope**
un destello de esperanza; **the — of an idea** el
atisbo de una idea; VI guiñar, emitir una luz
trémula

glimpse [glɪmps] N (look) ojeada f, vistazo m;
(hint) atisbo m; VT ojear

glint [glɪnt] N destello m; VI destellar

glisten [glísən] VI brillar, relucir

glitch [glɪtʃ] N fallo m, problema técnico m

glitter [glíDə] VI destellar; N (light) destello m;
(showiness) brillo m; (sparkling powder)
brillantina f

gloat [glot] VI regodearse; N regodeo m

glob [glab] N pegote m

global [glóbəl] ADJ global, mundial; **— backup**
respaldo global m; **— positioning system**
sistema mundial de posicionamiento m; **—
warming** calentamiento global m

globalization [globəlizéʃən] N globalización f

globe [glob] N globo m; (map of the Earth) globo
terráqueo m

globule [glábjul] N glóbulo m

globulin [glábjəlɪn] N globulina f

gloom [glum] N (darkness) oscuridad f;
(melancholy) melancolía f, tristeza f

gloomy [glúmi] ADJ (dark, depressing) sombrío,
lúgubre, tenebroso; (melancholic)
melancólico, deprimido

glorify [glórəfaɪ] VT glorificar

glorious [glóriəs] ADJ (wonderful) magnífico,
excelente; (related to glory) glorioso

glory [glóri] N gloria f; VI **to — in** regocijarse con

gloss [glɔs] N (shine, cosmetic) brillo m;
(marginal note) glosa f; (in a dictionary)
acepción f; VT (polish) lustrar, dar brillo a;
(explain) glosar; **to — over** disfrazar,
encubrir

glossary [glósəri] N glosario m

glossy [glósi] ADJ lustroso; (paper) glaseado

glottal [glɑdl] ADJ (cancer) glótico; (phonetic)
glotal

glottis [glɑdɪs] N glotis f

glove [glʌv] N guante m; (baseball) guante m,
manopla f; **— compartment** guantera f

glow [glo] N incandescencia f; (of cheeks) rubor
m; (of emotion) calor m; VI resplandecer; (of
metal) estar al rojo vivo; (of cheeks)
ruborizarse; **to — with health** estar
rebosante de salud; **—worm** luciérnaga f

germinate [ʤэ́mənet] VI germinar; VT hacer germinar

gerund [ʤérənd] N gerundio *m*

gestate [ʤéstet] VI/VT gestar[se]

gestation [ʤestéʃən] N gestación *f*

gesticulate [ʤestíkjəlet] VI gesticular

gesture [ʤéstʃэ-] N gesto *m*, ademán *m*; (token) muestra *f*; VI gesticular

gesundheit [gazúnthaIt] INTERJ (after a sneeze) ¡salud! *Sp* ¡Jesús!

get [gɛt] VT (receive, earn) recibir; (obtain) obtener; (reach by phone) comunicarse con; (hear, understand) entender; (seize) agarrar; *Sp* coger; (prevail) conseguir, lograr; (affect) afectar; (catch disease) pescar; *Sp* coger; **to — across** comunicar; **to — ahead** prosperar; **to — along [with]** llevarse bien [con]; **to — angry** enojarse; **to — around** (skirt) esquivar, evitar; (go out) salir mucho; **to — away** escapar[se]; **to — away with** quedar impune; **to — back** (return) volver; (recover something) recuperar; **to — back at** vengarse de; **to be —ting on in years** ponerse viejo; **to — by** (go past) pasar; (survive) ir tirando; **to — dark** oscurecer; **to — down** (lower oneself) bajar; (depress) deprimir; (swallow) tragar; **to — down to business / brass tacks** ir al grano; **to — going** ponerse en marcha; **to — in** (enter) entrar; (arrive) llegar; (a vehicle) subir a; **to — it** captar, entender; **to — married** casarse; **to — nowhere** no llegar a ningún lado; **to — off** (dismount, get down) bajar; (not receive punishment) salir impune; (leave work) salir; **to — off on** enloquecerse por; **to — off someone's back** dejar de fastidiar; **to — old** envejecer; **to — on** montarse a; **to — out** (take out) sacar; (exit) salir; **to — over** (recuperate) recuperarse, sobreponerse a; (forgive) olvidar; **to — ready** preparar[se]; **to — rich** enriquecerse; **to — rid of** deshacerse de; **to — sick** enfermarse; **to — somewhere** tener resultado; **to — through** (survive an ordeal) sobrevivir; (reach by phone, be understood) comunicarse; (complete) lograr terminar; **to — to someone** afectar a alguien; **to — together** reunirse; **to — up** (arise) levantarse; (prepare) montar; **I got him to do it** conseguí/logré que lo hiciera; **I have got to do it** tengo que hacerlo; **we got our house painted** nos pintaron la casa; **he got a year in jail** le dieron un año de cárcel; **we — to stay up late in summer** en el verano nos dejan quedarnos despiertos hasta tarde; **that —s my goat** eso me fastidia; N **—away** (escape) escape *m*; (vacation) escapada *f*; **— together** reunión *f*; **—up** disfraz *m*, atuendo *m*; **from the —-go** desde el principio

geyser [gáIzэ-] N géiser *m*

Ghana [gánə] N Ghana *f*

Ghanaian [gúniən] ADJ & N ghanés -esa *mf*

ghastly [gǽstli] ADJ (horrible) horrendo, espantoso; (cadaverous) cadavérico

ghetto [gɛ́ɖo] N gueto *m*

ghost [gost] N fantasma *m*; **— town** pueblo fantasma *m*; **—writer** colaborador -ora anónimo -ma *mf*; **not a — of a chance** ni la menor posibilidad

ghostly [góstli] ADJ fantasmagórico

ghoul [gul] N fantasma *m*

giant [ʤáiənt] N & ADJ gigante -ta *mf*

gibberish [ʤíbэ-Iʃ] N jerigonza *f*

gibbon [gíbən] N gibón *m*

Gibraltar [ʤIbrɔ́ltэ-] N Gibraltar *m*

Gibraltarian [ʤIbrɔltériən] ADJ & N gibraltareño -ña *mf*

giddy [gídi] ADJ (dizzy) mareado; (of heights) vertigoso; (of speed) vertiginoso

gift [gIft] N (thing given, act of giving) regalo *m*, presente *m*; (special ability) don *m*; **— certificate** vale por un regalo *m*; **— tax** impuesto sobre las donaciones *m*; **—-wrap** envolver para regalo; VT regalar

gifted [gíftId] ADJ (artist) talentoso; (child) superdotado

gigabyte [gígəbaIt] N gigabyte *m*

gigahertz [gígəhэ-ts] N gigahercio *m*

gigantic [ʤaIgǽntIk] ADJ gigantesco, gigante

giggle [gígəl] VI reír tontamente; N risita tonta *f*

gild [gIld] VT dorar

gill [gIl] N agalla *f*

gilt [gIlt] ADJ & N dorado *m*

gimmick [gímIk] N treta *f*, estratagema *f*

gin [ʤIn] N (liquor) ginebra *f*; **— rummy** gin rummy *m*

ginger [ʤíndʒэ-] N jengibre *m*; **— ale** ginger ale *m*; **—bread** pan de jengibre *m*

gingham [gíɳəm] N guingán *m*

gingivitis [ʤIndʒəváIdIs] N gingivitis *f*

giraffe [ʤərǽf] N jirafa *f*

gird [gэ-d] VT ceñir; **to — oneself** prepararse

girder [gэ́-Dэ-] N viga *f*

girdle [gэ́-dl] N faja *f*; VT rodear

girl [gэ-l] N (female child) niña *f*; (young female) muchacha *f*, joven *f*, chica *f*; (servant) muchacha *f*, chacha *f*; **—friend** novia *f*

girlhood [gэ́-lhUd] N niñez *f*

girlish [gэ́-lIʃ] ADJ de niña

girth [gэ-θ] N (of things) circunferencia *f*; (of persons) contorno *m*; (of horses) cincha *f*; VT cinchar

gist [ʤIst] N esencia *f*, lo esencial

GI [gastrointestinal] tract [ʤíáI] N tubo digestivo *m*

give [gIv] VT dar; (a gift) regalar; (a party) organizar; (a name) poner; (a donation) donar; **I don't — a hoot** me importa un

comino; VI dar; (yield) ceder; (break)
romperse; **to — away** (a gift) regalar, donar;
(the bride) entregar; (a secret) revelar; **to —
back** devolver; **to — in** (acknowledge defeat)
rendirse; **to — off** emitir, despedir,
desprender; **to — out** (announce) anunciar;
(distribute) repartir; (become exhausted)
rendirse; (run out) acabarse; **to — over**
entregar; **to — up** (surrender) darse por
vencido; (stop) dejar [de]; **we'll work on
this two years, — or take a month** vamos
a trabajar en esto dos años, un mes más, un
mes menos; N elasticidad f; **— and take** toma
y daca m

given [gívən] *see* give

given [gívən] ADJ (stated, fixed) dado;
(bestowed) regalado; **— name** nombre de
pila m; **— that she's not here** dado que ella
no está; **— to** propenso a; N premisa f

given [gívən] *see* give

giver [gívə] N dador -ora mf, donador -ora mf

gizmo [gízmo] N coso m, chisme m

glacial [gléʃəl] ADJ glacial

glacier [gléʃə] N glaciar m

glad [glæd] ADJ contento; **I'm — to see you** me
alegro de verte; **I'd be — to help** sería un
placer ayudarte

gladden [glǽdn] VT alegrar, regocijar, alborozar

gladiator [glǽbieDə] N gladiador m

glamorous [glǽmə·əs] ADJ glamoroso,
encantador

glamour [glǽmə·] N (charm) glamour f, encanto
m; (excitement) atractivo m

glance [glæns] VI echar un vistazo; **to — off**
rebotar con efecto; N (look) vistazo m;
(bounce) rebote oblicuo m

gland [glænd] N glándula f

glandular [glǽndʒələ] ADJ glandular

glare [glɛr] N (bright light) relumbre m; (stare)
mirada furiosa f; VI (shine) relumbrar; (stare
fiercely) lanzar una mirada hostil

glaring [glérɪŋ] ADJ (blinding) deslumbrante;
(obvious) evidente; (hostile) hostil

glass [glæs] N (substance) vidrio m; (window
pane) vidrio m, cristal m; (tumbler) vaso [de
vidrio] m; (mirror) espejo m; (glassware)
cristalería f; (magnifier) lupa f; **—blowing**
soplado de vidrio m; **— ceiling** techo de
cristal m; **— cutter** cortavidrio m; **—es**
anteojos m pl, lentes m pl, gafas f pl; **— eye** ojo
de vidrio m; **—maker** vidriero -ra mf;
—ware cristalería f

glassy [glǽsi] ADJ vidrioso

glaucoma [glɔkómə] N glaucoma m

glaze [glez] VT (windows) poner vidrios a;
(ceramics) vidriar; (food) glasear; (wood)
barnizar; VI vidriarse; N (pottery) vidriado m,
barniz m; (food) glaseado m

glazier [glézə·] N vidriero -ra mf

gleam [glim] N reflejo m, brillo m; **a — of hope**

un rayo de esperanza; VI brillar, relucir

glean [glin] VT (grain) espigar; (information)
extraer, deducir

glee [gli] N regocijo m, júbilo m; **— club** coro m

glib [glɪb] ADJ (fluent) de mucha labia;
(superficial) simplista, superficial

glide [glaɪd] VI (slide) deslizarse; (fly) planear; N
(sliding movement) deslizamiento m; (flight)
planeo m

glider [gláɪDə] N planeador m

glimmer [glímə·] N luz trémula f; **a — of hope**
un destello de esperanza; **the — of an idea** el
atisbo de una idea; VI guiñar, emitir una luz
trémula

glimpse [glɪmps] N (look) ojeada f, vistazo m;
(hint) atisbo m; VT ojear

glint [glɪnt] N destello m; VI destellar

glisten [glísən] VI brillar, relucir

glitch [glɪtʃ] N fallo m, problema técnico m

glitter [glíDə·] VI destellar; N (light) destello m;
(showiness) brillo m; (sparkling powder)
brillantina f

gloat [glot] VI regodearse; N regodeo m

glob [glab] N pegote m

global [glóbəl] ADJ global, mundial; **— backup**
respaldo global m; **— positioning system**
sistema mundial de posicionamiento m; **—
warming** calentamiento global m

globalization [globəlɪzéʃən] N globalización f

globe [glob] N globo m; (map of the Earth) globo
terráqueo m

globule [glábjuł] N glóbulo m

globulin [glábjəlɪn] N globulina f

gloom [glum] N (darkness) oscuridad f;
(melancholy) melancolía f, tristeza f

gloomy [glúmi] ADJ (dark, depressing) sombrío,
lúgubre, tenebroso; (melancholic)
melancólico, deprimido

glorify [glórəfaɪ] VT glorificar

glorious [glóriəs] ADJ (wonderful) magnífico,
excelente; (related to glory) glorioso

glory [glóri] N gloria f; VI **to — in** regocijarse con

gloss [glɔs] N (shine, cosmetic) brillo m;
(marginal note) glosa f; (in a dictionary)
acepción f; VT (polish) lustrar, dar brillo a;
(explain) glosar; **to — over** disfrazar,
encubrir

glossary [glósəri] N glosario m

glossy [glósi] ADJ lustroso; (paper) glaseado

glottal [gládł] ADJ (cancer) glótico; (phonetic)
glotal

glottis [gládɪs] N glotis f

glove [glʌv] N guante m; (baseball) guante m,
manopla f; **— compartment** guantera f

glow [glo] N incandescencia f; (of cheeks) rubor
m; (of emotion) calor m; VI resplandecer; (of
metal) estar al rojo vivo; (of cheeks)
ruborizarse; **to — with health** estar
rebosante de salud; **—worm** luciérnaga f

glowing [glóɪŋ] ADJ (with light) incandescente; (colors) vivo; (with health) rebosante; (report) favorable

glucose [glúkos] N glucosa f

glue [glu] N cola f, pegamento m; VT (put glue on) engomar; (stick together) pegar; (stick wood together) encolar; **she's —d to the television** está pegada al televisor

glum [glʌm] ADJ tristón

glut [glʌt] VI/VT (with food) hartar[se]; VT (with products) saturar; N superabundancia f

gluten [glútn] N gluten m

glutton [glátn] N glotón -ona mf

gluttonous [glátnəs] ADJ glotón

gluttony [glátni] N glotonería f, gula f

glycerin [glísə-ɪn] N glicerina f

gnarled [nɑrɫd] ADJ (knotty) nudoso, sarmentoso; (twisted) retorcido

gnash [næʃ] VI/VT rechinar

gnat [næt] N jején m

gnaw [nɔ] VI/VT (bite, corrode) roer; (torment) remorder; **to — a hole** hacer un agujero a mordiscos

GNP [gross national product] [ʤiénpí] N PNB m

gnu [nu] N ñu m

go [go] VI (move) ir; (function) andar, marchar; **—ing price** precio vigente m; **to — against** oponerse a; **to — ahead** seguir adelante; **to — all out** dar todo de sí; **to — along** conformarse a; **to — around** (circumvent) dar la vuelta a; (circulate) circular; (be sufficient) alcanzar; **to — around with** andar con; **to — away** irse; **to — back** volver; **to — back on one's word** faltar a la palabra; **to — beyond** traspasar; **to — by** (pass) pasar; (be guided by) guiarse por; **to — by another name** usar otro nombre; **to — crazy** enloquecerse; **to — down** (descend) bajar; (fall) caer, estrellarse; (lose) perder; (be accepted) gustar; **to — for it** atreverse; **— for it!** ¡adelante! ¡atrévete! **to — in with** participar; **to — it alone** tirarse solo; **to — off** (explode) estallar; (happen) suceder; (leave) irse; **to — off on** regañar; **to — on** (happen) pasar; (continue) seguir; **to — out** (extinguish) apagarse; (socialize) salir; **to — over** (review) repasar, revisar; (read) leer; (cross) cruzar; **to — through** (suffer) sufrir; (examine) examinar; (be approved) ser aprobado; (spend) gastar; **to — through with** llevar a cabo; **to — to sleep** dormirse; **to — under** (go bankrupt) quebrar; (sink) hundirse; **to — up** (building) levantarse; (prices) subir; **pizza to —** pizza para llevar; **to let —** soltar[se]; **the car went for a good price** el coche se vendió a un buen precio; **he's smart, as dogs —** para ser perro, es inteligente; **that old couch has got to —**

hay que deshacerse de ese sofá viejo; **cows — "moo"** las vacas hacen "mu"; **they — straight for the pizza** se van derechito a la pizza; **she's —ing to buy a house** va a comprar una casa; **anything —es** todo vale; **what I say —es** lo que yo digo, vale; **don't — to any trouble** no te molestes; **— figure!** ¡vaya a saber uno! **I've got to — [to the bathroom]** tengo que ir [al baño]; N (energy) energía f; (attempt) intento m; **— ahead** visto bueno m; **—-between** intermediario -ria mf; **—-cart** kart m; **in one —** de una vez; **on the —** a las corridas; **at the first —** de primera; **they made a — of it** tuvieron éxito; **it's a —** ¡trato hecho! **from the word —** desde el vamos

goad [god] N aguijada f; VT aguijonear

goal [goɫ] N (objective) meta f; (score) gol m; **— area** área de penales f; **—keeper** portero -ra mf, arquero -ra mf; **— kick** saque de meta m, saque de puerta m; **— line** línea de meta f; **— post** palo m, poste m

goalie [góli] N guardameta mf

goat [got] N cabra f; **—herd** cabrero -ra mf; **he gets my —** me saca de quicio

goatee [gotí] N perilla f

gobble [gábəɫ] VI/VT (devour) engullir; VI (turkey) gluglutear; **to — up** engullir

gobbledygook [gábəɫdiguk] N jerigonza f

gobbler [gáblə-] N pavo m

goblet [gáblɪt] N copa f

goblin [gáblɪn] N duende m

god, God [gad] N dios m, Dios m; **— bless you!** (blessing) ¡que Dios te bendiga! (after a sneeze) ¡salud! ¡Jesús! **—child** ahijado -da mf; **—father** padrino m; **—forsaken** de mala muerte; **—-given** divino; **—mother** madrina f; **—send** bendición f; **—willing** si Dios quiere; **by —** por Dios; **my —!** ¡Dios mío!

goddess [gádɪs] N diosa f

godless [gádlɪs] ADJ impío

godly [gádli] ADJ piadoso

goggles [gágəɫz] N gafas protectoras f pl, antiparras f pl

going [góɪŋ] ADJ que marcha bien; **—s-on** tejemanejes m pl

goiter [gɔɪɾə-] N bocio m

gold [goɫd] N oro m; **— bullion** oro en lingotes m; **— digger** mujer cazafortunas f; **—finch** jilguero m; **—fish** pez dorado m; **— medal** medalla de oro f; **—smith** orfebre m; **a heart of —** un corazón de oro

golden [góɫdən] ADJ (made of gold) de oro, áureo; (of gold color) dorado; **— eagle** águila dorada f; **— parachute** paracaídas dorado m sg; **— retriever** golden retriever m; **— rule** regla de oro

golf [gaɫf] N golf m; **— bag** bolsa de golf f; **— ball** pelota de golf f; **— cart** coche/cochecito de golf *m*; — **club** (stick) palo de golf *m*; (place) club de golf *m*; — **course** campo de golf *m*

gonad [gónæd] N gónada *f*

gondola [gándələ] N (boat, basket under a balloon) góndola *f*; (cable car) cabina *f*

gone [gɔn] ADJ **my computer is —** desapareció mi computadora; **the candy is all —** se acabaron los dulces

gone [gɔn] *see* go

gong [gɔŋ] N batintín *m*, gong *m*

gonorrhea [gɑnəríə] N gonorrea *f*

good [gʊd] ADJ bueno; (valid) válido; — **faith** buena fe *f*; — **-for-nothing** inútil, zanguango; — **for two burritos** vale por dos burritos; — **-looking** guapo, apuesto; — **-natured** apacible, bonachón, de buen genio; — **will** buena voluntad *f*; **for —** para siempre; **a — hour** una hora larga; **a — many** muchos; **to have a — time** divertirse; **to make — cumplir; to smell —** oler bien; N (moral act, benefit) bien *m*; **for your own —** por tu propio bien; INTERJ ¡bien! — **afternoon** buenas tardes; **—bye** adiós; — **day** buenos días; — **evening** buenas noches; — **morning** buenos días; — **night** buenas noches; N **—s** mercancías *f pl*; **—s and services** bienes y servicios *m pl*; **to deliver the —s** cumplir lo prometido

goodly [gúdli] ADJ (considerable) considerable; (of fine appearance) de buen aspecto

goodness [gúdnɪs] N bondad *f*; (of food) calidad *f*; INTERJ ¡Dios mío!

goody [gúdi] N golosina *f*; — **—** santurrón -ona *mf*; INTERJ ¡qué bien!

goof [guf] VI pifiar; **to — off** perder el tiempo; **to — up** pifiarla; N pifia *f*

goofy [gúfi] ADJ (person) bobalicón; (idea) tonto

goose [gus] N (bird, fool) ganso -sa *mf*; **—berry** (berry) grosella espinosa *f*; (bush) grosellero *m*; **—bumps** carne de gallina *f*; — **egg** cero *m*; VT **to — someone** sorprender a alguien tocándole entre las nalgas

GOP [Grand Old Party] [ʤiópí] N Partido Republicano *m*

gopher [gófɚ] N ardilla de tierra *f*

gore [gɔr] N sangre derramada *f*; VT cornear

gorge [gɔrʤ] N (body part) garganta *f*; (ravine) garganta *f*, tajo *m*; VI **to — one's self [on]** atracarse [de], darse un atracón [de]

gorgeous [gɔrʤəs] ADJ (woman, outfit) precioso; (weather) espléndido

gorilla [gərílə] N gorila *mf*; (thug) matón *m*

gory [góri] ADJ (of a battle) sangriento; (of a surface) ensangrentado

gospel [gáspəl] N evangelio *m*; (music) gospel *m*; — **truth** pura verdad *f*

gossip [gásəp] N (rumor) chismorreo *m*, murmuración *f*, habladurías *f pl*; (person)

chismoso -sa *mf*; (woman) comadre *f*; **a piece of —** un chisme *m*; VI chismear, murmurar

gossipy [gásəpi] ADJ chismoso, lenguaraz

got [gut] *see* get

Gothic [gáθɪk] ADJ gótico; N (language) gótico *m*, godo *m*; (style) estilo gótico *m*

gotten [gatn] *see* get

gouge [gaʊʤ] N gubia *f*; VT (scoop) sacar con gubia; (overcharge) cobrar de más; **to — someone's eyes out** arrancarle los ojos a alguien

gourd [gɔrd] N calabaza *f*

gourmet [gɔrmé] N & ADJ gourmet *mf*; — **cheese** queso fino *m*

gout [gaʊt] N gota *f*

govern [gʌvɚn] VI/VT gobernar, regir; VT (in grammar) regir

governability [gʌvɚnəbílɪdi] N gobernabilidad *f*

governess [gʌvɚnɪs] N institutriz *f*

governing [gʌvɚnɪŋ] N gobernación *f*; — **principle** principio rector *m*

government [gʌvɚnmənt] N gobierno *m*; (in grammar) rección *f*; — **agency** agencia gubernamental *f*; — **-backed** respaldado por el gobierno

governmental [gʌvɚnméntl] ADJ gubernamental, gubernativo

governor [gʌvɚnɚ] N (leader) gobernador -ora *mf*; (of an engine) regulador *m*

gown [gaʊn] N (woman's dress) vestido *m*; (for sleeping) camisón *m*; (in hospital) bata *f*; (for graduation) toga *f*

grab [græb] VT agarrar, prender; **how does that idea — you?** ¿qué te parece esa idea? VI **to — at** tratar de agarrar; N agarrón *m*; **up for —s** a la rebatiña

grace [gres] N gracia *f*; (of movement) garbo *m*; (of expression) donaire *m*; **to say —** dar la oración; **to be in the good —s of someone** gozar del favor de alguien, disfrutar de la gracia de alguien; VT (adorn) adornar; (honor) honrar, agraciar

graceful [grésfəl] ADJ (of movement) grácil, garboso; (of behavior) donoso

gracefulness [grésfəlnɪs] N gracia *f*, donaire *m*

gracious [gréʃəs] ADJ (kind) gentil, cortés; (elegant) elegante; (merciful) misericordioso; **—!** ¡válgame Dios!

graciousness [gréʃəsnɪs] N gentileza *f*

gradation [gredéʃən] N gradación *f*

grade [gred] N (rank) grado *m*; (category) calidad *f*; (year in school) año *m*, curso *m*; (marks) nota *f*, calificación *f*; (slope) declive *m*; **to make the —** alcanzar el nivel deseado; — **point average** promedio de notas *m*; VT (classify) clasificar; (assign grades) calificar, corregir; (level) nivelar

gradual [græʤuəl] ADJ gradual

graduate[1] [græʤuɪt] N (advanced student)

estudiante de posgrado *mf*; (degree-holder) graduado -da *mf*, egresado -da *mf*; ADJ de posgrado; **— school** programa de posgrado *m*

graduate² [grǽʤuet] VI graduarse, titularse; VT (confer a degree) dar un diploma a; (mark a scale) graduar

graduation [græʤuéʃən] N graduación *f*

graffiti [grəfíbi] N grafiti *m*, pintada *f*

graft [græft] N (of plant, tissue) injerto *m*; (corruption) concusión *f*, corrupción *f*; VI/VT injertar[se]

grain [gren] N (cereal, seed) grano *m*, mies *f*; (photographic texture) grano *m*; (of gold) pepita *f*; (of wood, meat, stone) veta *f*; (texture) textura *f*; (small amount) pizca *f*; **against the** — a/al redopelo, a contrapelo

gram [græm] N gramo *m*

grammar [grǽmə] N gramática *f*

grammatical [grəmǽDɪkəl] ADJ gramatical

granary [grénəri] N granero *m*, troje *m*

grand [grænd] ADJ (splendid) grandioso, espléndido; (lofty) elevado; (impressive) impresionante; **—child** nieto -ta *mf*; **—children** nietos *m pl*; **—daughter** nieta *f*; **—father** abuelo *m*; **—fathered** eximido por la cláusula del abuelo; **— jury** jurado de acusación *m*; **—mother** abuela *f*; **—ma** abuelita *f*; **—pa** abuelito *m*; **—parent** abuelo *m*; **—parents** abuelos *m pl*; **— piano** piano de cola *m*; **—son** nieto *m*; **—stand** tribuna *f*; **a — old man** un gran señor; **the — total** el total

grandeur [grǽndʒə] N grandiosidad *f*

grandiose [grǽndios] ADJ (complex) complejo; (of speech) grandilocuente, rimbombante; (imposing) grandioso

granite [grǽnɪt] N granito *m*

grant [grænt] VT (give) conceder, otorgar, dispensar; (accept) admitir; (transfer) ceder; **to take for —ed** (an assumption) dar por sentado; (a person) no valorar; N (something granted) concesión *f*; (act of granting) concesión *f*, otorgamiento *m*; (subsidy, e.g., for scientists) subvención *f*

granular [grǽnjələ] ADJ granuloso

granulate [grǽnjəlet] VI/VT granular[se]

grape [grep] N uva *f*; **—fruit** pomelo *m*, toronja *f*; **—vine** vid *f*; (ornamental) parra *f*; **I heard it through the —vine** me lo contó un pajarito

graph [græf] N (curve) gráfica *f*; **— paper** papel cuadriculado *m*; VT grafiar

graphic [grǽfɪk] ADJ gráfico; **— design** diseño gráfico *m*; N gráfico *m*; **—s** gráfica *f*; **—s card** tarjeta gráfica *f*

graphite [grǽfaɪt] N grafito *m*

grapple [grǽpəl] VI/VT (hold) aferrar; (struggle) luchar, lidiar

grasp [græsp] VT (seize) agarrar, asir, aferrar; (understand) comprender; VI **to – at/for** tratar de agarrar; N (hold) agarre *m*, asidero *m*; (comprehension) comprensión *f*; **within one's** — al alcance; **to have a good – of a subject** dominar una materia

grass [græs] N (plant) hierba *f*; (lawn) césped *m*; (pasture) pasto *m*; (in tennis) césped *m*, hierba *f*; **—hopper** saltamontes *m sg*, saltón *m*; **—land** pradera *f*, pastizal *m*; **— roots** las bases *f pl*

grassy [grǽsi] ADJ herboso

grate [gret] N (of a fireplace) parrilla *f*; (partition, guard) reja *f*, verja *f*; VT (install a grate) enrejar; (mince) rallar; (rub teeth together) crujir, rechinar; VI **to — on** rechinar

grateful [grétfəl] ADJ agradecido

grater [gréDə] N rallador *m*

gratification [græDəfɪkéʃən] N gratificación *f*

gratify [grǽDəfaɪ] VT complacer, gratificar

grating [gréDɪŋ] N reja *f*, enrejado *m*, rejilla *f*; ADJ (discordant) rechinante; (irritating) irritante

gratitude [grǽDɪtud] N gratitud *f*

gratuitous [grətúɪDəs] ADJ gratuito

gratuity [grətúɪDi] N propina *f*

grave [grev] ADJ grave; N fosa *f*, sepultura *f*; **—digger** sepulturero *m*; **—stone** lápida *f*; **—yard** cementerio *m*; **—yard shift** turno de la noche *m*; **to have one foot in the —** *fam* estar por reventar

gravel [grǽvəl] N grava *f*; VT cubrir con grava

gravitation [grævɪtéʃən] N gravitación *f*

gravitational [grævɪtéʃənl] ADJ gravitatorio

gravity [grǽvɪDi] N gravedad *f* (also seriousness)

gravy [grévi] N jugo de carne *m*; **the rest is** — el resto es fácil

gray [gre] ADJ gris; (hair) canoso; (horse) rucio; **— area** zona gris *f*; **—-haired** cano, canoso; **— matter** materia gris *f*; N gris *m*; VI/VT agrisar; (hair) encanecer

grayish [gréɪʃ] ADJ grisáceo

graze [grez] VI/VT (feed) pacer, pastar, apacentar; (brush) rozar; N roce *m*

grease [gris] N grasa *f*; VT engrasar; **to — someone's palm** untarle la mano a alguien, engrasar a alguien

greasy [grísi, grízi] ADJ (covered with grease) grasiento; (impregnated with grease) grasoso; (hair) graso

great [gret] ADJ (large, numerous) grande; (good, excellent, considerable) gran; **—-aunt** tía abuela *f*; **—-grandchild** bisnieto -ta *mf*; **—-grandfather** bisabuelo *m*; **—-grandmother** bisabuela *f*; **—-grandchild** tataranieto -ta *mf*; **a — tree blocked the path** un árbol grande bloqueaba el camino; **she's a — friend** es una gran amiga; **a — while** un largo rato;

she's — at tennis juega muy bien al tenis; **a — deal of** mucho; ADV muy bien, excelente; **she did** — le fue muy bien; N **the —s** los/las grandes mf; **they occur in —er numbers** son más numerosos; **he's the —est** es el mejor; INTERJ ¡qué bien!

greatly [grétli] ADV **it's — improved** lo han mejorado mucho / está mucho mejor; **we're — interested** estamos muy interesados

greatness [grétnɪs] N grandeza f

Greece [gris] N Grecia f

greed [grid] N codicia f

greedy [grídi] ADJ (covetous) codicioso; (voracious) voraz; (eager) ávido

Greek [grik] ADJ & N griego -ga mf; **that's — to me** para mí es chino

green [grin] ADJ (green in color, verdant, unripe, inexperienced, nauseated, environmentally conscious) verde; **—back** dólar m; **— bean** Sp judía verde f; Mex ejote m; RP chaucha f; Carib habichuela; **— card** tarjeta verde f; **—horn** novato -ta mf; **—house** invernadero m; **—house effect** efecto invernadero m; **— light** luz verde f; **— pepper** pimiento verde m; N (color) verde m; (lawn) césped m; (pasture) prado m; (in golf) green m; (commons) ejido m; **—s** verduras de hoja verde f pl

greenish [gríniʃ] ADJ verdoso

greenness [grínnɪs] N verdor m

greet [grit] VT (say hello) saludar; (welcome) dar la bienvenida; (receive) recibir

greeting [grídɪŋ] N saludo m; **— card** tarjeta de felicitación f; **—s!** ¡saludos!

gregarious [grigériəs] ADJ (person) sociable; (animal) gregario

gremlin [grémlɪn] N duende m

Grenada [grənédə] N Granada f

grenade [grənéd] N granada f

Grenadian [grənédiən] ADJ & N granadino -na mf

grew [gru] see grow

greyhound [gréhaʊnd] N galgo m

griddle [grídl] N plancha f

gridlock [grídlɑk] N paralización f; VI paralizarse

grief [grif] N congoja f, pesar m, pesadumbre f; **to come to —** sufrir una desgracia; **to give someone —** meterse con alguien, jorobar a alguien; **good —!** ¡caramba! ADJ **—-stricken** acongojado, desconsolado

grievance [grívəns] N (complaint) queja f; (cause for complaint) motivo de queja m

grieve [griv] VI estar de duelo; **to — for/over** llorar, lamentar [la muerte de alguien]; **he's grieving over the loss of his dog** lamenta la muerte de su perro; VT **that —s me** eso me apena

grieved [grivd] ADJ apenado

grievous [grívəs] ADJ (painful) doloroso, penoso; (atrocious) grave, atroz; (sorrowful) dolido

grill [grɪl] N (metal grid, restaurant fixture) parrilla f; (food) parrillada f; VI/VT asar a la parrilla; (interrogate) interrogar

grille [grɪl] N parrilla f

grim [grɪm] ADJ (news, situation) desalentador; (war) cruento; (joke) macabro

grimace [grímɪs] N mueca f, mohín m; VI hacer muecas

grime [graɪm] N mugre f, suciedad f

grimy [gráimi] ADJ mugriento, sucio; **to make — percudir; to get —** percudirse

grin [grɪn] VI sonreír; N sonrisa f; **wipe that off your face** deja de reírte

grind [graɪnd] VI/VT (mill finely) moler; (mill coarsely) triturar; (make shiny) pulir; (rub harshly) rechinar; (study hard) estudiar mucho; Sp empollar; **to — to a halt** pararse con un chirrido; N (drudgery) trabajo pesado m; (overzealous student) empollón -ona mf; **—stone** muela f; **the daily —** la lucha diaria; **to keep one's nose to the —stone** matarse trabajando/estudiando

grinder [gráɪndə] N (for coffee, pepper) molinillo m; (for meat) picadora f; (for sharpening tools) afilador m

grip [grɪp] N (hold) agarre m; (control) control m; (handle) mango m; (on a baseball bat, golf club) agarre m, empuñadura f; **he had a firm — on the tool** tenía bien agarrada la herramienta; **get a — on yourself** contrólate, cálmate; VT (seize) agarrar, asir; (take hold, interest) atrapar

gripe [graɪp] VI quejarse, rezongar, renegar; N queja f

grisly [grízli] ADJ cruento, espantoso

gristle [grísəl] N cartílago m

grit [grɪt] N (sand) arena f; (pluck) firmeza f; **—s** sémola de maíz f; VT **to — one's teeth** apretar los dientes

gritty [gríɾi] ADJ (sandy) arenoso; (plucky) resuelto

grizzly [grízli] ADJ (grayish) grisáceo; **— bear** oso pardo m

groan [gron] N quejido m, gemido m; VI quejarse, gemir; (creak) crujir

grocer [grósə] N tendero -ra mf; Mex abarrotero -ra mf; Carib bodeguero -ra mf; RP almacenero -ra mf

grocery [grósəri] N tienda de comestibles f; Mex tienda de abarrotes f; Carib bodega f; RP almacén m; **groceries** comestibles m pl

groin [grɔɪn] N ingle f

groom [grum] N (in a wedding) novio m; (in a stable) mozo de cuadra m, caballerizo m; VT (a horse) almohazar; (prepare for a position) preparar; **to — oneself** arreglarse; **well-**

—ed bien arreglado

groove [gruv] N (narrow cut) estría *f*, ranura *f*; (on a record, road) surco *m*; (routine) rutina *f*; VT estriar, acanalar

grope [grop] VI (feel one's way) andar a tientas; (search) buscar a tientas; N toqueteo *m*

gross [gros] ADJ (before deductions) bruto; (flagrant) flagrante; (indecent) grosero; (overall) general; (disgusting) asqueroso; **— domestic product** producto interno bruto *m*; **— income** ingreso bruto *m*; **— pay** salario bruto *m*; N gruesa *f*; VT recaudar en bruto; **to — out** dar asco, asquear

grotesque [grotésk] ADJ grotesco

grotto [gráɖo] N gruta *f*

grouch [graʊtʃ] N cascarrabias *mf sg*, refunfuñón -ona *mf*, rezongón -ona *mf*; VI refunfuñar

grouchy [gráʊtʃi] ADJ cascarrabias, refunfuñón

ground [graʊnd] N (land, electrical cable) tierra *f*; (soil) suelo *m*; (basis) fundamento *m*; **— ball** (in baseball) roletazo *m*; **— floor** planta baja *f*; **—hog** marmota *f*; **—s** (reason) motivo *m*; (dregs) borra *f*, poso *m*; (tract of land) terreno *m*; **to gain/lose —** ganar/perder terreno; **to stand one's —** ponerse firme; **from the — up** de piso a techo; VT (a wire) conectar a tierra; (a ship) hacer encallar; (punish) poner en penitencia; **the 747 was —ed** se prohibió volar en el 747

ground [graʊnd] *see* grind

groundless [gráʊndlis] ADJ infundado

group [grup] N grupo *m*; **— discount** descuento por grupo *m*; **— therapy** terapia de grupo *f*; VI/VT agrupar[se]

grouper [grúpə·] N mero *m*

groupie [grúpi] N admiradora *f*

grouping [grúpɪŋ] N agrupamiento *m*

grove [grov] N arboleda *f*, plantío *m*; **orange —** naranjal *m*

grovel [grávəl] VI arrastrarse, humillarse

grow [gro] VI (naturally increase in size) crecer; (increase) aumentar, acrecentarse; (expand) desarrollarse; VT (crops) cultivar; (beard) dejarse crecer; **to — old** envejecer; **to — up** madurar; **Thai food —s on you** la comida tailandesa acaba gustándote

growing [gróɪŋ] N cultivo *m*; **— pains** (physical symptom) dolores del crecimiento *m pl*; (troubles) dificultades iniciales *f pl*; **he's a — boy** es un muchacho en crecimiento

growl [graʊl] VI gruñir; (of thunder) retumbar; (of stomach) rugir; N gruñido *m*

grown [gron] ADJ adulto; **— man** hombre hecho y derecho *m*; N **—-up** adulto *m*; ADJ **—-up** para adultos

grown [gron] *see* grow

growth [groθ] N (increase in size) crecimiento *m*; (increase in number) aumento *m*, acrecentamiento *m*; (tumor) bulto *m*;

(expansion) desarrollo *m*; **— hormone** hormona del crecimiento *f*; **a — industry** una industria en expansión

grudge [grʌdʒ] N resentimiento *m*

grueling [grúlɪŋ] ADJ arduo

gruesome [grúsəm] ADJ cruento, truculento

gruff [grʌf] ADJ (manner) bronco; (voice) ronco

grumble [grʌ́mbəl] VI/VT refunfuñar, rezongar; N refunfuño *m*, gruñido *m*

grumpy [grʌ́mpi] ADJ refunfuñón, gruñón, rezongón

grunt [grʌnt] VI/VT gruñir; N gruñido *m*

guarantee [gærəntí] N (promise, pledge) garantía *f*; (guaranty) fianza *f*; VT (promise, pledge) garantizar; (warrant) dar fianza, avalar; **—d loan** préstamo garantizado *m*

guarantor [gærəntɔ́r] N fiador -ora *mf*

guaranty [gǽrənti] N (guarantee) garantía *f*; (thing taken as security) fianza *f*; (guarantor) fiador -ora *mf*

guard [gard] VT custodiar; (watch over) vigilar; (protect) proteger; VI **to — against** guardarse de; N (person that guards) guardia *mf*, guarda *mf*; (of a machine) dispositivo protector *m*; **to be on —** estar alerta / estar en guardia; **— dog** perro guardián *m*; **—rail** baranda *f*, pasamano *m*

guardian [gárdiən] N guardián -ana *mf*; (legal) tutor -ora *mf*; **— angel** ángel de la guarda *m*

guardianship [gárdiənʃɪp] N tutela *f*

Guatemala [gwɑɖəmálə] N Guatemala *f*

Guatemalan [gwɑɖəmálən] ADJ & N guatemalteco -ca *mf*

guava [gwávə] N guayaba *f*

guerrilla [gərílə] N **— army** guerrilla *f*

guess [gɛs] VT (hazard, conjecture) adivinar; (suppose) suponer; N (conjecture) conjetura *f*; (supposition) suposición *f*; **I'll give you three —es** te doy tres oportunidades para adivinar

guest [gɛst] N (to a party, function) invitado -da *mf*; (at a restaurant) cliente *mf*; (overnight) huésped *mf*

guffaw [gəfɔ́] N carcajada *f*, risotada *f*

guidance [gáɪdns] N (act of guiding) dirección *f*; (counsel) orientación *f*; (in a missile) teledirección *f*

guide [gaɪd] VT (serve as a guide) guiar; (direct the course of) dirigir; (counsel) orientar; **—d missile** misil guiado *m*; N (person) guía *mf*; (publication, mechanism) guía *f*; **—book** guía *f*; **— dog** perro guía *m*; **—lines** directivas *f pl*, pautas *f pl*, directrices *f pl*

guild [gɪld] N gremio *m*, corporación *f*

guile [gaɪl] N astucia *f*

guilt [gɪlt] N culpa *f*; **— trip** manipulación por acusaciones falsas *f*

guiltless [gɪ́ltlɪs] ADJ inocente

guilty [gɪ́lti] ADJ culpable; **we find the**

defendant not — hallamos al acusado inocente

Guinea [gíni] N Guinea f; — **pig** conejillo de Indias m; —**-Bissau** Guinea-Bissau f

Guinean [gínɪən] ADJ & N guineano -na mf

guise [gaɪz] ADV LOC **under the** — of so/bajo pretexto de; **in the** — of a manera de

guitar [gɪtár] N guitarra f

gulf [gʌlf] N (body of water) golfo m; (abyss, gap) abismo m; — **Stream** Corriente del Golfo f

gull [gʌl] N (bird) gaviota f; (dupe) crédulo -la mf; Sp primo -ma mf

gullet [gʌlɪt] N gaznate m

gullible [gáləbəl] ADJ crédulo, ingenuo

gully [gʌli] N barranco m, barranca f; (gutter) alcantarilla f

gulp [gʌlp] VT tragar saliva; N trago m

gum [gʌm] N goma f; (for chewing) chicle m; —**s** encías f pl; VT **to** — **up** (ruin) jorobar; (stick) pegotear

gumption [gámpʃən] N (initiative) iniciativa f, arranque m; (courage) agallas f pl

gun [gʌn] N (firearm) arma de fuego f; (revolver) revólver m; (rifle) rifle m; (shotgun) escopeta f; (cannon) cañón m; (for painting, nailing) pistola f; VT (an engine) acelerar; —**boat** cañonero m; —**fire** tiroteo m; —**man** pistolero m; —**powder** pólvora f; —**shot** disparo m; —**shot wound** herida de bala f; **at** —**point** a mano armada; **to stick to one's** —**s** mantenerse firme; **don't jump the** — no te precipites; **to be under the** — estar bajo mucha presión; VT **to** — **down** matar a tiros; **to** — **for** andar a la caza de

gung-ho [ɡʌ́nhó] ADJ fanático, entusiasta

gunner [ɡánɚ] N (shooting artillery) artillero -ra mf; (shooting a machine gun) ametrallador -ora mf

gurgle [ɡɚ́ɡəl] VI (water) borbotar; (baby) gorjear; N (of water) borboteo m; (of a baby) gorjeo m

gush [ɡʌʃ] VI (liquids) chorrear, brotar; (talk effusively) hablar con efusividad

gust [ɡʌst] N ráfaga f; — **of wind** racha/ráfaga de viento f, ventolera f; VI soplar en ráfagas

gusto [ɡʌ́sto] N (pleasure) placer m; (enthusiasm) entusiasmo m

gut [ɡʌt] N tripa f; (belly) barriga f; — **feeling** corazonada f; —**s** (intestines) entrañas f pl; VT (eviscerate) destripar; (destroy the insides of) destrozar el interior de; (strip) desarmar

gutter [ɡʌ́dɚ] N (in the street) alcantarilla f; (on the roof) canaleta f, desagüe m; (squalor) miseria f

guy [ɡaɪ] N (man) tipo m; Sp tío m; **you** —**s** ustedes; Sp vosotros/vosotras; — **wire** cable m

Guyana [ɡaɪánə] N Guyana f

Guyanese [ɡaɪəníz] ADJ & N guyanés -esa mf

gym [dʒɪm] N gimnasio m

gymnasium [dʒɪmnéziəm] N gimnasio m

gymnastics [dʒɪmnǽstɪks] N gimnasia f

gynecologist [ɡaɪnəkálədʒɪst] N ginecólogo -ga mf

gynecology [ɡaɪnəkálədʒi] N ginecología f

gyp [dʒɪp] VT estafar, timar; N estafa f, timo m

gypsum [dʒípsəm] N yeso m

gypsy [dʒípsi] N & ADJ gitano -na mf

gyrate [dʒáɪret] VI girar

gyroscope [dʒáɪrəskop] N giroscopio m

Hh

habit [hǽbɪt] N (custom) hábito m, costumbre f; (clerical dress) hábito m; (vice) vicio m; —**-forming** adictivo

habitat [hǽbɪtæt] N hábitat m

habitual [həbítʃuəl] ADJ habitual

hack [hæk] N (cut) tajo m, machetazo m; (cough) tos seca f; (horse for hire) caballo de alquiler m; (nag) jamelgo m; (writer) escritor -ora mercenario -ria mf; —**saw** sierra para metales f; VI/VT tajar, cortar a machetazos; VI toser con tos seca

hacker [hǽkɚ] N pirata informático -ca mf

had [hæd] see have

hag [hæɡ] N (witch) bruja f; (ugly old woman) vieja fea f

haggard [hǽɡɚd] ADJ demacrado

haggle [hǽɡəl] VI regatear

hail [hel] N (precipitation) granizo m; (greeting) saludo m; (shout) llamada f; — **Mary** Ave María f; —**storm** granizada f; VI (precipitate) granizar; VT (greet) saludar; (call out) llamar; (acclaim) aclamar; **to** — **from** ser oriundo de

hair [her] N pelo m; (of the head only) cabello m; (of the body only) vello m; (on plants) pelusa f; —**brush** cepillo para el cabello m; —**cut** corte de pelo m; **to get a** —**cut** cortarse el pelo; —**do** peinado m; —**dresser** peluquero -ra mf, peinador -ora mf; —**follicle** folículo capilar m; —**line** nacimiento del pelo f; —**line fracture** fractura fina f; —**piece** postizo m; —**pin** horquilla f; —**-raising** horripilante, espeluznante; —**spray** fijador m

hairless [hérlɪs] ADJ (deprived of hair) pelado; (growing no hair) lampiño

hairy [héri] ADJ (including head) peludo; (body only) velludo

Haiti [hépi] N Haití m

Haitian [héʃən] ADJ & N haitiano -na mf

hake [hek] N merluza f

half [hæf] N mitad f; — **an apple** media

manzana *f*; ADJ medio; **—-baked** (not fully cooked) a medio cocer; (not fully developed) mal concebido; **—-breed** mestizo -za *mf*; **— brother** medio hermano *m*; **—-cocked** mal preparado; **he went off —-cocked** actuó precipitadamente; **—-cooked** a medio cocer; **—-dozen** media docena *f*; **—-hearted** desganado; **—-hour** media hora *f*; **—-life** vida media *f*; **—-moon** media luna *f*; **— note** blanca *f*; **—-open** entreabierto, entornado; **— past one** la una y media; **—-time** medio tiempo *m*, descanso *m*; **—-truth** verdad a medias *f*; **— volley** media volea *f*; **—way** a medio camino; **—way house** casa de rehabilitación *f*; **—way measures** medidas parciales *f pl*; **—way point** punto medio *m*; **—-wit** *pej* imbécil *mf*, papamoscas *mf*; **at —-mast** a media asta; **to do something —way** hacer algo a medias; **to go halves** ir a medias

halibut [hǽləbət] N hipogloso *m*

halitosis [hælɪtósɪs] N halitosis *f*

hall [hɔl] N (corridor) corredor *m*, pasillo *m*; (large room) salón *m*, sala *f*; (building) edificio *m*; **—mark** distintivo *m*; **—way** (corridor) corredor *m*, pasillo *m*; (entrance) zaguán *m*, vestíbulo *m*

Halloween [hæləwín] N víspera del día de Todos los Santos *f*, noche de brujas *f*

hallucinate [həlúsənet] VI alucinar

hallucination [həlusənéʃən] N alucinación *f*

hallucinogen [həlúsənədʒən] N alucinógeno *m*

halo [hélo] N halo *m*, aureola *f*

halogen [hǽlədʒən] ADJ halógeno

halt [hɔlt] N **to come to a —** detenerse; VI/VT parar, detener[se]; **—!** ¡alto!

halter [hɔ́ltə] N cabestro *m*

halting [hɔ́ltɪŋ] ADJ vacilante

halve [hæv] VT partir por la mitad

ham [hæm] N (meat) jamón *m*; (attention getter) payaso *m*; **—string** (human) ligamento de la corva *m*; (horse) tendón del jarrete *m*; **to — it up** sobreactuar, exagerar

hamburger [hǽmbɔgə] N (meat) carne picada de vaca/res *f*; (sandwich, patty) hamburguesa *f*

hamlet [hǽmlɪt] N aldea *f*, poblado *m*, caserío *m*

hammer [hǽmə] N martillo *m*; VI/VT martillar, amartillar; **to — out** (an agreement) forjar; (differences) negociar

hammock [hǽmək] N hamaca *f*

hamper [hǽmpə] N canasto *m*, cesto *m*; VT impedir, embarazar

hamster [hǽmstə] N hámster *m*

hand [hænd] N mano *f*; (of a clock) aguja *f*, manecilla *f*; (farm helper) peón *m*; **—bag** (purse) bolsa *f*, cartera *f*; (valise) maletín *m*; **—ball** (American game) pelota *f*, frontón *m*; (European game) balonmano *m*; (in soccer)

mano *f*; **—bill** volante *m*; **—cuffs** esposas *f pl*; **— grenade** granada de mano *f*, bomba de piña *f*; **—gun** revólver *m*; **— in —** [cogidos] de la mano; **—kerchief** pañuelo *m*; **—out** (notes) repartido *m*, ejemplario *m*; (alms) limosna *f*; **—saw** serrucho *m*; **—shake** apretón de manos *m*; **—stand** pino *m*, paro de manos *m*; **—work** trabajo manual *m*; **—writing** letra *f*; **at —** (within reach) al alcance; (about to happen) cerca; **in —** (under control) bajo control; (available) disponible, en mano; **on —** disponible, a mano; **on the other —** en cambio, por otra parte; **to have one's —s full** estar ocupadísimo; ADJ **—held** de mano; **—made** hecho a mano; **—-picked** cuidadosamente seleccionado; **—s-on** práctico; VT entregar, dar; **to —cuff** esposar; **to — down** (a thing) pasar; (a judgment) pronunciar; **to — in** entregar; **to — over** entregar

handful [hǽndfʊl] N manojo *m*, puñado *m*

handicap [hǽndikæp] N (physical disability) impedimento *m*, minusvalía *f*; (mental disability) retardo *m*; (disadvantage) desventaja *f*; (in golf) hándicap *m*; **— race** carrera de hándicap *f*; VT (hinder) perjudicar, handicapar; (injure) lisiar; **physically —ped** minusválido físico

handiwork [hǽndiwɔk] N labor *f*

handle [hǽndl] N (straight) mango *m*; (curved) asa *f*; (of a drawer) manija *f*; (of a knife) empuñadura *f*, puño *m*; **—bar** manubrio *m*; VT (manage) manejar; (touch) manipular, tocar; (deal in) comerciar en; **the car —s easily** el coche tiene buena maniobrabilidad

handling [hǽndlɪŋ] N (dealing) manejo *m*; (touching) manipulación *f*; (charge) porte *m*; (of a car) maniobrabilidad *f*; **— charges** cargos de tramitación *m pl*

handsome [hǽnsəm] ADJ guapo, bien parecido; **a — sum** una suma considerable

handy [hǽndi] ADJ (near) a [la] mano; (practical) práctico; (skillful) hábil, diestro; N **—man** hombre habilidoso *m*

hang [hæŋ] VI/VT colgar, suspender; VT (door) colocar; (one's head) inclinar; (a condemned person) ahorcar; VI pender; **— in there!** ¡ánimo! **to — around** quedarse por ahí, rondar; **to — on** (hold tight) agarrarse bien; (persevere) aguantar; (wait) esperar; **to — out** (be outside) estar fuera; (socialize with) andar [con]; **to — over** sobresalir; **to — paper on a wall** empapelar una pared; **to — up** colgar; **sentenced to —** condenado a la horca; N caída *f*; **— glider** ala delta *f*; **—man** verdugo *m*; **—nail** padrastro *m*, uña encarnada *f*, uñero *m*; **—out** sitio frecuentado *m*; **—over** resaca *f*; **—-up** complejo *m*; **to get the — of something** agarrarle la onda a algo

hangar [hǽŋə-] N hangar m

hanger [hǽŋə-] N colgadero m; (for clothes) percha f

hanging [hǽŋɪŋ] N muerte en la horca f; **—s** colgaduras f pl, tapiz m; ADJ colgante

hanky-panky [hǽŋkipǽŋki] N (deceit) tejemaneje m; (illicit sexual activity) aventuras f pl

haphazard [hæphǽzə-d] ADV a la buena de Dios; ADJ irregular

happen [hǽpən] VI suceder, pasar, acontecer; **I — to know** da la casualidad de que sé; **to — to pass by** acertar a pasar; **to — upon** encontrarse con, toparse con

happening [hǽpənɪŋ] N acontecimiento m, suceso m

happily [hǽpɪli] ADV (in a state of happiness) felizmente; (luckily) afortunadamente; **they lived — ever after** vivieron felices y comieron perdices

happiness [hǽpɪnɪs] N felicidad f, dicha f

happy [hǽpi] ADJ (satisfied) feliz, dichoso; (pleased) contento; (lucky) afortunado; **— ending** final feliz m; **to be — to** hacer algo de buena gana

harangue [hərǽŋ] N arenga f; VT arengar

harass [hərǽs] VT acosar, hostigar

harassment [hərǽsmənt] N acoso m, hostigamiento m

harbor [hárbə-] N (for ships) puerto m; (refuge) refugio m; **— authority** autoridad portuaria f; VT (refugees, criminals, suspicions) albergar; (hopes) abrigar

hard [hard] ADJ (firm) duro; (difficult) difícil; (arduous) arduo; **to play —ball** ser despiadado; **—-boiled egg** huevo duro m; **— cash** dinero contante y sonante m; **— coal** antracita f; **— copy** copia en papel f, copia impresa f; **— core** núcleo resistente m; **—-core** radical; **— disk** disco duro m; **— disk drive** unidad de disco duro f; **— feelings** resentimiento m; **— hat** casco m; **—-headed** testarudo; **—-hearted** duro de corazón; **— liquor** bebida alcohólica fuerte f; **— luck** mala suerte f; **— of hearing** medio sordo; **— page break** salto de página forzado m; **— palate** paladar óseo m; **—-pressed** en aprietos; **— return** salto de línea forzado m; **—ware** (metal articles) ferretería f; (computer) hardware m; **—ware store** ferretería f; **— wood** madera noble f; **— water** agua dura f; **— winter** invierno crudo m; **—-wired** programado; **—-working** trabajador; ADV (fall, push) con fuerza; (work) duro, con ahínco

harden [hárdn̩] VI/VT (make or become hard) endurecer[se]; (make or become experienced) curtir[se]

hardening [hárdn̩ɪŋ] N endurecimiento m

hardly [hárdli] ADV (scarcely) apenas, difícilmente; (at all) en absoluto; **— anyone** casi nadie; **— surprising** nada sorprendente

hardness [hárdnɪs] N dureza f

hardship [hárdʃɪp] N penuria f, penalidad f

hardy [hárdi] ADJ robusto

hare [hɛr] N liebre f; **—-brained** descabellado; **—lip** labio leporino m; **—-lipped** con labio leporino, labihendido

harem [hɛrəm] N harén m

harm [harm] N daño m, mal m, perjuicio m; VT (object) dañar; (person) hacer daño; (chances) perjudicar

harmful [hármfəl] ADJ perjudicial, dañino, nocivo

harmless [hármlɪs] ADJ inocuo, inofensivo

harmonic [harmánɪk] ADJ & N armónico m

harmonious [harmóniəs] ADJ armonioso

harmonize [hármənaɪz] VI/VT armonizar

harmony [hárməni] N armonía f

harness [hárnɪs] N arnés m, jaez m, guarnición f; VT (put on a harness) enjaezar; (utilize) aprovechar

harp [harp] N arpa f; VI (play the harp) tocar el arpa; (insist) machacar; **to — on** insistir sobre

harpoon [harpún] N arpón m; VT arponear

harpsichord [hárpsɪkɔrd] N clavicémbalo m

harrowing [hǽroɪŋ] ADJ angustioso; **— adventure** aventura espeluznante f

harry [hǽri] VT acosar, hostigar

harsh [harʃ] ADJ (words) duro; (surface) áspero; (character, discipline) severo, férreo; (winter) crudo, riguroso

harshness [hárʃnɪs] N (of words) dureza f; (of a surface) aspereza f; (of character, discipline) severidad f; (of a winter) rigor m

harvest [hárvɪst] N cosecha f; (of sugar) zafra f; VT cosechar

has [hæz] see have

hash [hæʃ] N guisado m, picadillo m

hashish [hæʃíʃ] N hachís m

hassle [hǽsəl] N rollo m, lío m; VT jorobar

haste [hest] N prisa f; **in —** de prisa; **to make —** darse prisa, apresurarse; Am apurarse

hasten [hésən] VI apresurarse; Am apurarse; VT acelerar, adelantar

hasty [hésti] ADJ apresurado, precipitado, presuroso; Am apurado; **to be —** precipitarse, apresurarse

hat [hæt] N sombrero m

hatch [hæʧ] VI/VT (chicks) empollar; (plot, scheme) fraguar, maquinar; N (chicks) nidada f; (opening) escotilla f; **— way** escotilla f

hatchet [hǽʧɪt] N hacha f; **— job** crítica feroz f; **— man** sicario m; **to bury the —** hacer las paces

hate [het] N odio m; VI/VT odiar; **I — to admit it** me molesta admitirlo; **I — eating leftovers**

detesto comer restos

hateful [hétfəl] ADJ odioso, aborrecible

hatred [hétrɪd] N odio *m*

haughtiness [hɔ́DɪNɪS] N altivez *f*, altanería *f*, soberbia *f*

haughty [hɔ́di] ADJ altivo, altanero, soberbio

haul [hɔɫ] VT (transport) transportar; (drag) arrastrar; (pull) jalar [de], tirar [de]; N (quantity transported) carga *f*; (tug) tirón *m*; (catch of fish) redada *f*; (stolen goods) botín *m*; **long —** distancia larga *f*

haunch [hɔntʃ] N anca *f*

haunt [hɔnt] VI/VT (frequent) frecuentar, rondar; (enchant) embrujar; **that idea —s me** me obsesiona esa idea; **—ed house** casa embrujada *f*; N (of animals, criminals) guarida *f*; (of people socializing) sitio frecuentado *m*

have [hæv] V AUX haber; VT tener; **to — to** tener que; **to — a baby** dar a luz; **to — a look at** echar una mirada a; **to — a suit made** mandarse hacer un traje; **— him come later** dile que venga más tarde; **what did she — on?** ¿qué tenía puesto? **we've been had** nos estafaron

haven [hévən] N abrigo *m*, refugio *m*

havoc [hǽvək] N estrago *m*; **to wreak —** hacer estragos

hawk [hɔk] N gavilán *m*; VT pregonar

hay [he] N heno *m*; **— fever** alergia al polen *f*; **—loft** henil *m*; **—seed** paleto -ta *mf*; **—stack** almiar *m*; **to look for a needle in a —stack** buscar una aguja en un pajar

hazard [hǽzə·d] N (chance) azar *m*; (danger) peligro *m*; VT arriesgar, aventurar

hazardous [hǽzə·Dəs] ADJ peligroso; **— substance** sustancia peligrosa *f*

haze [hez] N neblina *f*, calina *f*; VT atormentar [como parte de un rito de iniciación]

hazel [hézəl] N avellano *m*; **—nut** avellana *f*; ADJ de avellano

hazy [hézi] ADJ (weather) brumoso; (idea) confuso, vago

HDL [**high density lipoprotein**] [étʃdíél] N LAD *f*

he [hi] PRON él; **—-goat** macho cabrío *m*; **— who** el que, quien

head [hed] N (of body) cabeza *f*; (of bed) cabecera *f*; (chief) jefe -fa *mf*; **—ache** dolor de cabeza *m*; **— coach** entrenador -ora en jefe *mf*; **— cold** resfrío *m*; **—count** recuento de personas *m*; **—dress** tocado *m*, adorno para la cabeza *m*; **—gear** (hat) sombrero *m*; (helmet) casco *m*; (for a horse) cabezada *f*; **—hunter** cazatalentos *mf sg*; **—land** cabo *m*, promontorio *m*; **—light** faro delantero *m*; **—line** titular *m*; **—long** (head first) de cabeza; (hastily) precipitadamente; **— of** **hair** cabellera *f*; **— of state** mandatario -ria

mf; **—phone** audífono *m*, auricular *m*; **—quarters** (military) cuartel general *m*; (police) jefatura *f*; (corporation) oficina central *f*; **—rest** reposacabezas *m sg*; **—set** auriculares *m pl*; **—s or tails** cara o cruz; **I can't make —s or tails of it** esto no tiene ni pies ni cabeza; **— start** ventaja *f*; **—stone** lápida *f*; **—strong** testarudo; **—way** avance *m*; **—word** voz *f*; **to make —way** avanzar, progresar; **it went to his —** se le fue a la cabeza; **to be out of one's —** desvariar; **to come to a —** (a crisis) precipitarse; (an abscess) supurar; **to keep one's —** mantener la calma; VT (lead) encabezar; (steer) dirigir; (in soccer) cabecear; VI dirigirse; **to — up** liderar; **to — off** atajar; ADV **—-on** de frente, frontal

header [héDə·] N (in soccer) cabezazo *m*, pase de cabeza *m*; (in text) cabecera *f*, encabezado *m*

heading [hédɪŋ] N encabezamiento *m*

heal [hiɫ] VT curar; VI (get well) sanar, curarse; (form a scar) cicatrizarse

health [hɛlθ] N salud *f*; **— care** asistencia médica *f*; **— care system** sistema de asistencia de salud *m*; **— care provider** profesional de la salud *mf*; **— food** comida macrobiótica *f*; **— insurance** seguro de salud *m*

healthful [hélθfəl] ADJ saludable, sano

healthy [hélθi] ADJ sano, saludable

heap [hip] N montón *m*, pila *f*; VT amontonar, apilar; VI **to — up** amontonarse

hear [hir] VI/VT (perceive) oír; VT (listen) escuchar; **to — about/of someone/ something** oír hablar de alguien/algo; **to — from someone** tener noticias de alguien; **I won't — of your leaving** no quiero saber de que te vayas

heard [hɜ·d] *see* hear

hearer [hírə·] N oyente *mf*

hearing [hírɪŋ] N (sense) oído *m*; (trial) audiencia *f*; **within —** al alcance del oído; **— aid** audífono *m*; ADJ **—-impaired** sordo

hearsay [hírse] N testimonio de oídas *m*; **by —** de oídas

hearse [hɜ·s] N coche fúnebre *m*, carroza *f*

heart [hɑrt] N (organ) corazón *m*; (spirit) ánimo *m*; **—ache** angustia *f*; **— attack** ataque cardíaco *m*; **—beat** latido *m*; **I would do it in a —beat** lo haría sin pestañear; **—burn** acidez de estómago *f*; **— disease** enfermedad coronaria *f*; **— murmur** soplo cardíaco *m*; **at —** en realidad, en el fondo; **from the bottom of one's —** de corazón, con toda el alma; **to learn by —** aprender de memoria; **to take —** cobrar ánimo; **to take to —** tomar a pecho; ADJ **—broken** inconsolable; **—felt** sincero, sentido; **my —felt sympathy** mi más sentido pésame; **—-warming** reconfortante

hearten [hártn] VT animar

hearth [harθ] N hogar m

heartless [hártlɪs] ADJ despiadado, desalmado

hearty [hárbi] ADJ (cordial) cordial; (strong) fuerte; — **appetite** apetito saludable m; **a — laugh** una risa desbordante; — **meal** una comida abundante

heat [hit] N (warmth) calor m; (passion) ardor m; (estrus) celo m; (source of heat) calefacción f; (preliminary race) eliminatoria f; — **exchange** equilibrio térmico m; — **stroke** insolación f; VI/VT calentar[se]; **to — up** acalorarse

heater [híɾə] N calentador m

heating [híɾɪŋ] N calefacción f; — **pad** almohadilla eléctrica f

heave [hiv] VT (raise) levantar; (throw) arrojar, lanzar; (sigh) exhalar; (pull) jalar; VI (pant) jadear; (vomit) hacer arcadas; N (throw) lanzamiento m; (pull) tirón m

heaven [hévən] N cielo m

heavenly [hévənli] ADJ celestial; — **bodies** cuerpos celestes m pl; **it was —** estuvo divino

heavily [hévəli] ADV (fall) pesadamente; (drink) mucho; **he's breathing —** está jadeando; **he's — indebted** está muy endeudado / tiene muchas deudas

heaviness [hévɪnɪs] N pesadez f

heavy [hévi] ADJ (weighty) pesado; (thick) grueso, pesado; (dense) denso; (oppressive) opresivo; — **artillery** artillería pesada f; — **breathing** jadeos m pl; —-**duty** de servicio pesado; —-**handed** severo, autoritario; **with a — heart** abatido; — **rain** lluvia fuerte f; — **schedule** agenda cargada f; —**weight** peso pesado m; N villano -na mf

Hebrew [híbru] N & ADJ hebreo -a mf; (language) hebreo m

heck [hɛk] INTERJ ¡caramba! **what the — are you doing?** ¿qué demonios haces? **that was a — of a good game** fue un partidazo

hectare [hɛktɛr] N hectárea f

hectic [hɛktɪk] ADJ febril, agitado

hedge [hɛdʒ] N (row of bushes) seto m; (precaution) precaución f; — **fund** fondo especulativo m; —**hog** erizo m; VI/VT (a bet) cubrir[se]; VT (a question) evadir

hedonism [hídnɪzəm] N hedonismo m

heebie-jeebies [híbidʒíbiz] N **it gives me the —** me pone los pelos de punta

heed [hid] VT atender; N atención f, cuidado m; **to pay — to** prestar atención a

heel [hil] N (of foot or sock) talón m; (of shoe) tacón m; **to kick up one's —s** tirar la chancleta, soltarse el pelo; VT poner tacón a; VI/VT seguir de cerca

hegemony [hɪdʒémənɪ] N hegemonía f

heifer [héfə] N novilla f, vaquilla f

height [haɪt] N (of a building, mountain) altura f; (of a person) estatura f; (utmost point) colmo m

heighten [háɪtn] VI/VT (increase) aumentar[se]; (intensify) realzar

Heimlich maneuver [háɪmlɪkmənúvə] N maniobra de Heimlich f

heinous [hénəs] ADJ aborrecible

heir [ɛr] N heredero -ra mf; — **apparent** presunto heredero m, presunta heredera f; —**s and assigns** herederos y cesionarios m pl

heiress [érɪs] N heredera f

held [hɛld] see hold

helicopter [hélɪkɑptə] N helicóptero m

helium [híliəm] N helio m

helix [hílɪks] N hélice f

hell [hɛl] N infierno m

hello [həló] INTERJ ¡hola! (on the telephone) hola; Sp diga; Mex bueno

helm [hɛlm] N timón m

helmet [hélmɪt] N (for bikes, etc.) casco m; (armor) yelmo m

help [hɛlp] N (aid) ayuda f; (rescue) auxilio m; (remedy) remedio m; (employee) empleado -da mf; — **desk** servicio de ayuda al usuario m; INTERJ ¡auxilio! ¡socorro! VI/VT (aid) ayudar, asistir; (rescue) auxiliar, socorrer; — **yourself** sírvete; **he cannot — it** no puede evitarlo; **he cannot — but come** no puede menos que venir; **may I — you?** ¿en qué le puedo servir?

helper [hélpə] N ayudante mf, asistente mf

helpful [hélpfəl] ADJ (useful) útil; (willing to help) servicial

helping [hélpɪŋ] N porción f

helpless [hélplɪs] ADJ desamparado, desvalido

helplessness [hélplsnɪs] N desamparo m, desvalimiento m

hem [hɛm] N dobladillo m, Am ruedo m; VT hacer dobladillos en, orillar; **to — in** arrinconar; **to — and haw** vacilar

hematoma [himətómə] N hematoma m

hemisphere [hémɪsfɪr] N hemisferio m

hemlock [hémlɑk] N cicuta f

hemoglobin [híməglobɪn] N hemoglobina f

hemophilia [himəfíliə] N hemofilia f

hemorrhage [hémərɪdʒ] N hemorragia f

hemorrhoids [hémərɔɪdz] N hemorroides f pl

hemp [hɛmp] N cáñamo m

hen [hɛn] N (chicken) gallina f; (female bird) ave hembra f; ADJ —**pecked** dominado por su mujer

hence [hɛns] ADV de ahí; —**forth** de aquí en adelante, de hoy en adelante; **a week —** de aquí a una semana

hepatitis [hɛpətáɪdɪs] N hepatitis f

her [hɚ] PRON **I see —** la veo; **I talk to —** le hablo (a ella); **I went with —** fui con ella; POSS ADJ **this is — dog** este es su perro, este es el perro de ella

herald [hérəld] N heraldo *m*; VT anunciar, proclamar

herb [ɝb] N hierba *f*

herbal [ɝ́bəl] ADJ de hierbas; **— tea** tisana *f*

herbicide [hɝ́bɪsaɪd] N herbicida *m*

herbivore [hɝ́bəvɔr] N herbívoro *m*

herbivorous [hɝ·bívərəs] ADJ herbívoro

herd [hɝd] N (of animals) manada *f*; (of goats) hato *m*; (of sheep) rebaño *m*; (of horses, donkeys) recua *f*; **the common —** el populacho, la chusma; **—sman** pastor *m*; VT arrear; VI ir en manada

here [hir] ADV aquí, acá; **— it is** aquí está; **—after** en adelante; **the —after** el más allá; **—by** (in writing) por la presente; **I —by pronounce you husband and wife** los declaro marido y mujer; **—in** en el presente; **—'s to you!** ¡a tu salud! **—tofore** hasta ahora; **—with** (hereby) por la presente; (attached) adjunto; **come —!** ¡ven acá! **the — and now** el presente; **that is neither — nor there** eso no viene al caso

hereditary [hərédɪtɛri] ADJ hereditario

heredity [hərédɪti] N herencia *f*

heresy [hérɪsi] N herejía *f*

heretic [hérɪtɪk] N hereje *mf*

heritage [hérɪtɪʤ] N herencia *f*, patrimonio *m*

hermaphrodite [hə-mǽfrədaɪt] N hermafrodita *mf*

hermetic [hɝmédɪk] ADJ hermético

hermit [hɝ́mɪt] N ermitaño -ña *mf*; **— crab** ermitaño *m*

hernia [hɝ́niə] N hernia *f*; **—ted** herniado; **—ted disk** hernia de disco *f*

hero [híro] N (brave man) héroe *m*; (main character) protagonista *mf*

heroic [hɪróɪk] ADJ heroico

heroin [hérɔɪn] N heroína *f*

heroine [hérɔɪn] N heroína *f*

heroism [hérɔɪzəm] N heroísmo *m*

heron [hérən] N garza *f*

herpes [hɝ́piz] N herpes *m*

herring [hérɪŋ] N arenque *m*

hers [hɝz] PRON **this book is —** este libro es suyo / de ella; **these things are —** estas cosas son suyas; **— is bigger** el suyo / la suya es más grande; **a friend of —** un amigo suyo / de ella

herself [hɝsélf] PRON ella misma; **she's not — today** hoy no es la misma de siempre; **she was sitting by —** estaba sentada sola; **she — did it** lo hizo sola, lo hizo ella misma; **she talks to —** ella habla para sí, habla consigo misma; **she looked at — in the mirror** se miró en el espejo; **she bought — a house** se compró una casa

hesitant [hézɪtənt] ADJ vacilante

hesitate [hézɪtet] VI (pause) vacilar; (stutter) titubear; (doubt) dudar

hesitating [hézɪtedɪŋ] ADJ vacilante

hesitation [hɛzɪtéʃən] N (pause) vacilación *f*; (stammer) titubeo *m*; (doubt) duda *f*

heterogeneous [hɛdə·əʤínias] ADJ heterogéneo

heterosexual [hɛdərosékʃuəl] ADJ heterosexual

hexagon [héksəgan] N hexágono *m*

hey [he] INTERJ ¡oiga!

heyday [héde] N auge *m*

hi [haɪ] INTERJ hola; **say — to your sister for me** dale recuerdos a tu hermana de mi parte

hiatus [haɪéɾəs] N hiato *m*

hibernate [háɪbə·net] VI hibernar

hiccup, hiccough [híkʌp] N hipo *m*; VI hipar, tener hipo

hick [hɪk] N & ADJ paleto -ta *mf*

hickory [híkəri] N nogal americano *m*

hid, hidden [hɪd, hídn] *see* hide

hidden [hídn] ADJ (out of sight) oculto; (illegal) clandestino; **— agenda** intereses ocultos *m pl*

hide [haɪd] VI/VT ocultar[se], esconder[se]; **— and seek** escondite *m*, escondidas *f pl*; **—out** escondite *m*; N cuero *m*, piel *f*, pellejo *m*

hideous [hídiəs] ADJ horrendo, espantoso

hierarchy [háɪərɑrki] N jerarquía *f*

hieroglyphic [haɪrəglífɪk] ADJ & N jeroglífico *m*

high [haɪ] ADJ alto; (intoxicated) ebrio; (on drugs) volado; **— altitude sickness** enfermedad de altura *f*; **— and dry** (ship) en seco; (person) colgado; **— blood pressure** hipertensión *f*; **—brow** culto; **—class** de clase; **— contrast** alto contraste *m*; **— definition television** televisión de alta definición *f*; **— density** alta densidad *f*; **—er-up** superior; **—er education** educación superior *f*; **— explosive** explosivo de alta potencia *m*; **— fever** fiebre elevada *f*; **— fidelity** alta fidelidad *f*; **— finance** altas finanzas *f pl*; **—grade** de calidad superior; **—handed** arbitrario; **— jump** salto alto *m*; **—lands** tierras altas *f pl*; **—level** de alto nivel; **—light** lo más destacado; **—lighting** (on a computer) selección de texto *f*; **—lights** (in hair) claritos *m pl*, mechas *f pl*; **— minded** idealista; **—octane gasoline** súper *m*; **—-pitched** agudo; **— point** culminación *f*; **—-powered** de alta potencia; **—-pressure** estresante, intenso; **—-priced** caro; **—-quality** de alta calidad; **—-return** de alta rentabilidad; **—-rise** de muchos pisos; **—-risk** de alto riesgo; **—-risk behavior** conducta de alto riesgo *f*; **—-risk patient** paciente con alto riesgo *mf*; **— school** escuela secundaria *f*, colegio *m*; *Sp* instituto *m*; **— seas** alta mar *f*; **—-sounding** altisonante; **—-speed** de alta velocidad; **— spirits** buen ánimo *m*; **—-strung** nervioso; **—-tech** alta tecnología *f*; **— temperature** temperatura máxima *f*; **— tide** pleamar *f*; **—way** carretera f, ruta f; — **wind** ventarrón m; **in** — **gear** a toda marcha; **two feet** — dos pies de altura; **it is** — **time that** ya es hora de que; **to look** — **and low** buscar por todas partes; N flash m, subida f; VT **to** — **light** (emphasize) destacar, resaltar

highly [háili] ADV — **amusing** sumamente divertido; — **paid** muy bien pagado; — **qualified** altamente cualificado; **he spoke** — **of her** habló muy bien de ella

highness [háinis] N alteza f

hijack [háidʒæk] VT secuestrar [un vehículo]

hike [haik] N caminata f; **take a** —! ¡ve a freír espárragos! VI salir a caminar

hilarious [hilériəs] ADJ graciosísimo, para morirse de risa

hill [hił] N (elevated area) colina f, cerro m; (pile) montón m; —**billy** paleto -ta mf; —**side** ladera f; —**top** cumbre f, cima f

hillock [hílak] N otero m

hilly [híli] ADJ accidentada

hilt [hilt] N empuñadura f; **to the** — al máximo

him [him] PRON **I see** — lo veo; Sp le veo; **I talk to** — le hablo; **I went with** — fui con él

himself [himsélf] PRON él mismo; **he** — **wrote the letter** él mismo escribió la carta; **he's not** — **today** hoy no es el mismo de siempre; **he was sitting by** — estaba sentado solo; **he talks to** — él habla para sí, habla consigo mismo; **he looked at** — **in the mirror** se miró en el espejo; **he bought** — **a house** se compró una casa

hind [haind] ADJ trasero; —**most** último; **in** —**sight** a posteriori; N cierva f

hinder [híndɚ] VT impedir, entorpecer, estorbar

Hindi [híndi] N hindi m

hindrance [híndrəns] N obstáculo m, impedimento m, traba f

Hindu [híndu] ADJ & N hindú mf

hinge [hindʒ] N gozne m, quicio m; VT engoznar, poner goznes; VI **to** — **on** depender de

hint [hint] N (clue) indirecta f, pista f; (trace) dejo m; **to take the** — darse por enterado; VT insinuar

hip [hip] N cadera f; — **replacement** (operation) sustitución protésica de la cadera f; (prosthesis) prótesis de cadera f

Hippocratic oath [hipəkrǽdɪkóθ] N juramento hipocrático m

hippopotamus [hipəpάdəməs] N hipopótamo m

hire [hair] VT (engage for work) contratar; VI/VT (rent) alquilar[se]; — **and fire** contratar y despedir; **to** — **out** dar en alquiler, alquilar; N (engagement) contratación f; (employee) nuevo -va empleado -da mf; (rent) alquiler m

his [hiz] POSS ADJ **this is** — **dog** este es su perro / el perro de él; PRON **these things are** — estas cosas son suyas; — **is right here** el suyo / la suya está aquí; **a friend of** — un

amigo suyo / una amiga suya

Hispanic [hispǽnik] ADJ hispánico, hispano; N hispano -na mf

hiss [his] VI sisear; (to boo) silbar; N siseo m

histamine [hístəmin] N histamina f

historian [histɔ́rian] N historiador -ra mf

historic [histɔ́rik] ADJ histórico

historical [histɔ́rikəl] ADJ histórico

history [hístəri] N historia f

histrionics [histriániks] N histrionismo m

hit [hit] VT (a target) dar en; (a car) chocar con; (a key) pulsar, tocar; (a baseball) batear; **to** — **a homerun** batear un jonrón, pegar un cuadrangular; **to** — **it off** llevarse bien desde el principio; **to** — **the mark** acertar, dar en el blanco; **to** — **upon an idea** dar con una idea; **to** — **on a person** tratar de ligar con alguien; N (blow) golpe m; (success) éxito m; (dose) dosis f; **that was a** — **with me** me encantó; —**man** sicario m; —**s** (on a website) visitas f pl; ADJ —**and-run** que se da a la fuga después de atropellar a alguien; —**-or-miss** al azar

hitch [hitʃ] VT atar, amarrar; (pants) levantar; (yoke) uncir, enganchar; **to get** —**ed** casarse; **to** —**hike** Sp hacer autostop; Am hacer dedo; N (knot) nudo m; (difficulty) dificultad f; (period) período m

hither [híðɚ] ADV acá; — **and thither** acá y allá; —**to** hasta ahora

HIV [human immunodeficiency virus] [étʃáɪví] N VIH m

hive [haiv] N (shelter for bees) colmena f; (colony of bees) enjambre m; —**s** urticaria f

HMO [health maintenance organization] [étʃémó] N organización de mantenimiento de salud f

hoard [hɔrd] N reserva f; VI/VT acaparar

hoarse [hɔrs] ADJ ronco; (like alcoholics) aguardientoso

hoarseness [hɔ́rsnis] N ronquera f

hoax [hoks] N engaño m

hobble [hάbəl] VI (limp) cojear; VT (tie to impede walking) manear; (hinder) trabar; N cojera f; (rope) traba f, manea f

hobby [hάbi] N hobby m

hobo [hóbo] N vagabundo m

hockey [hάki] N hockey m

hodgepodge [hάdʒpadʒ] N mezcolanza f, batiburrillo m

hoe [ho] N azada f, azadón m; VI/VT limpiar con azadón

hog [hag] N puerco m, cerdo m, marrano m; Am chancho m; —**wash** pamplinas f pl; **to live high on the** — vivir en la abundancia; VT acaparar, adueñarse

hoist [hɔist] VT izar; N torno m, guinche m

hokey [hóki] ADJ sensiblero

hold [hołd] VT (bear) llevar, sujetar; (contain)

contener; (detain) detener; (decide legally,
sustain a note) sostener; (opine) opinar; **to —
back** detener; **to — down** sujetar; **to —
forth** perorar; **to — hands** tomarse de la
mano; **to — in place** sujetar; **to — a
meeting** celebrar una reunión; **to —
someone responsible** hacerle a uno
responsable; **to — someone to his word**
obligar a uno a cumplir con su palabra; **to —
oneself erect** ponerse derecho; **to — one's
own** defenderse; **to — one's tongue**
callarse, morderse la lengua; **— the pickles
on that burger!** una hamburguesa sin
pepinillos, por favor; VI (remain fast)
aguantar, resistir; (occupy a position) ocupar;
(be valid) ser válido; **to — off** mantener[se] a
distancia; **to — off doing something**
abstenerse de hacer algo; **to — liable**
responsabilizar; **to — on** (not let go)
agarrar[se], sujetar[se]; (stop) esperar;
(persist) persistir; **to — out** aguantar; **to —
still** quedarse/estarse quieto; **to — tight**
agarrarse; **to — to one's promise** cumplir
con la palabra; **to — up** (raise) alzar; (detain)
detener; (rob) atracar, asaltar; (persevere)
aguantar; **how much does it —**? ¿Qué
capacidad tiene? N (grip) agarro m; (thing to
grasp) asidero m; (dominion) dominio m;
(wrestling move) llave f; (in music) calderón
m; (of a ship) bodega f; **—up** golpe m, atraco
m; **to get — of** agarrar; **to take — of** Sp
coger, agarrar; **to have a good — on
something** agarrarse bien de algo
holder [hóldə] N (person) tenedor -ora mf,
poseedor -ora mf; (device) receptáculo m
holding [hóldɪŋ] N propiedad f; **— company**
holding m; **—s** (financial) valores en cartera m
pl; (of a library) fondos m pl
hole [hoł] N agujero m; (in a wall) boquete m; (of
an animal) madriguera f; (in the ground, in
golf) hoyo m; **to be in a —** hallarse/estar en
un apuro/aprieto; **—in-one** hoyo en uno m
holiday [hálɪde] N día de fiesta m; **—s** vacaciones
f pl
holiness [hólɪnɪs] N santidad f
holistic [holístɪk] ADJ holístico
Holland [háland] N Holanda f
hollow [hálo] ADJ (empty) hueco; (concave)
cóncavo; (sunken) hundido; (insincere) falso;
N (cavity) hueco m, concavidad f; (valley)
hondonada f, hondo m; VT **to — out** ahuecar,
vaciar
holly [háli] N acebo m
holocaust [hálǝkɔst] N holocausto m
holster [hólstǝ] N pistolera f, funda de pistola f
holy [hóli] ADJ santo, sagrado; **— Bible** Santa
Biblia f; **— cow/Moses/mackerel!** ¡que
increíble! Sp ¡jobar! **— Ghost** Espíritu Santo
m; **— Spirit** Espíritu Santo m; **— war** guerra

santa f; **— water** agua bendita f
homage [hámɪdʒ] N homenaje m; **to pay —**
rendir homenaje, honrar
home [hom] N casa f, hogar m; (for old people,
orphans) asilo m, hogar m; **—boy** amigo del
barrio m; **— economics** economía doméstica
f; **— delivery** entrega a domicilio f; **—
equity loan** préstamo garantizado por el
valor residual de la vivienda m; **— game**
partido en casa m; **—land** patria f; **—less** sin
techo; **— office** (headquarters) oficina
central f; (at home) oficina en el hogar f;
—owner propietario -ria de vivienda mf;
—owners' association asociación de
propietarios de vivienda f; **— page** página de
inicio f; **— plate** goma f, plato m; **— rule**
autonomía f; **— run** jonrón m, cuadrangular
m; **at —** en casa; **to be — sick** echar de
menos / extrañar [a la familia]; **—sickness**
morriña f, añoranza f; **— stretch** último
trecho m; **—work** tarea domiciliaria f, deber
m; ADJ doméstico; ADV (direction) a casa;
(location) en casa; **to strike —** dar en el
blanco; ADJ **—made** casero
homely [hómli] ADJ (ugly) feo; (familiar)
familiar, doméstico
homeopathic [homiɑpǽθɪk] ADJ homeopático
homeopathy [homiápǝθi] N homeopatía f
homestead [hómstɛd] N heredad f, casa de la
familia f
homeward [hómwǝd] ADV a casa; **— bound**
camino a casa
homicide [hámɪsaɪd] N homicidio m
homogeneous [homǝdʒíniǝs] ADJ homogéneo
homogenize [hǝmádʒǝnaɪz] VT homogeneizar
homonym [hámǝnɪm] N homónimo m
homophobia [homǝfóbiǝ] N homofobia f
homophobic [homǝfóbɪk] ADJ homofóbico
homosexual [homosékʃuǝł] ADJ & N
homosexual mf
Honduran [handúrǝn] ADJ & N hondureño -ña
mf
Honduras [handúrǝs] N Honduras f
hone [hon] VT afilar; **to — one's skills**
desarrollar las destrezas; N piedra de afilar f
honest [ánɪst] ADJ honrado, honesto; **I'll be —
with you** voy a ser franco contigo; **—!** ¡de
veras!
honesty [ánɪsti] N (integrity) honradez f,
honestidad f; (sincerity) franqueza f
honey [háni] N (sweet substance) miel f;
(endearment) querido -da mf; **—bee** abeja f;
—comb panal m; **—suckle** madreselva f
honeymoon [hánimun] N luna de miel f; VI
pasar la luna de miel
honk [haŋk] N (of a car) bocinazo m, pitazo m; (of
a goose) graznido m; VI/VT (car) tocar la
bocina; VI (goose) graznar
honor [ánǝ] N (respect, privilege) honor m;

(good reputation) honra f; **with —s** con honores; **your —** su señoría f; VT (revere) honrar; (accept invitation, check) aceptar; **to — a promise** cumplir [con] una promesa

honorable [ánə̄əbəl] ADJ honorable

honorary [ánɛrɛri] ADJ honorario

hood [hud] N (of a coat) capucha f, caperuza f; (of a car) capó m; *Am* tapa f; VT encapuchar

hoodlum [húdləm] N maleante mf, gamberro -rra mf

hoof [huf] N casco m, pezuña f; VI **to — it** ir andando

hook [huk] N (for lifting) gancho m, garfio m; (for fishing) anzuelo m; **— and eye** alamar m, macho y hembra m; **by — or by crook** por las buenas o por las malas; **—up** conexión f, enganche m; VT (snag) enganchar; (a dress) abrochar; **to — up** conectar, enganchar

hooked [hukt] ADJ (shaped like a hook) ganchudo; (addicted) enganchado

hooky [húki] N **to play —** hacer novillos

hooligan [húlɪgən] N *Sp* gamberro -rra mf, *Am* patotero -ra mf

hoop [hup] N (also in basketball) aro m

hoot [hut] VI/VT (of owl) ulular; (in derision) abuchear; N (of an owl) ululato m; (cry of derision) abucheo m; **I don't give a —** no me importa un comino; **it's a —** es para morirse de risa

hop [hɑp] VI saltar, brincar; **to — on** subirse a montar; (a short jump) saltito m, brinco m; (dance) bailongo m; **—s** lúpulo m

hope [hop] N esperanza f; VI/VT esperar; **to — for** esperar; **to — against —** esperar lo imposible

hopeful [hópfəl] ADJ (having hopes) esperanzado; (giving hopes) esperanzador, alentador

hopefully [hópfəli] ADV **— she'll come** ojalá [que] venga

hopeless [hóplɪs] ADJ (without hope) desesperanzado; (with no solution) irremediable; (unattainable) inalcanzable; **— cause** causa perdida f; **it is —** no tiene remedio; **the new secretary is — with numbers** el nuevo secretario es un desastre con los números

hopelessness [hóplɪsnɪs] N desesperanza f

horde [hɔrd] N (of people) horda f; (of animals) plaga f

horizon [həráɪzən] N horizonte m

horizontal [hɔrɪzántl] ADJ horizontal

hormone [hɔrmon] N hormona f; **— therapy** terapia hormonal f

horn [hɔrn] N (of an animal, substance) cuerno m, asta f; (of an automobile) bocina f, claxon m; (musical) corno m, trompa f; **— of plenty** cuerno de la abundancia m; **to toot one's own —** darse autobombo; VI **to — in** entrometerse

hornet [hɔ́rnɪt] N avispón m; **—'s nest** avispero m

horny [hɔ́rni] ADJ calloso

horoscope [hɔ́rəskop] N horóscopo m

horrendous [hɔréndəs] ADJ horrendo

horrible [hɔ́rəbəl] ADJ horrible

horrid [hɔ́rɪd] ADJ horrendo

horrify [hɔ́rəfaɪ] VT horrorizar

horror [hɔ́rə] N horror m

hors d'oeuvre [ɔrdə́v] N entremés m

horse [hɔrs] N caballo m; **—back** lomo de caballo m; **to ride —back** montar a caballo, cabalgar; **—fly** tábano m; **—laugh** carcajada f; **—man** jinete m; **—manship** equitación f; **—play** payasadas f pl; **—power** caballo de fuerza m; **— race** carrera de caballos f; **—radish** rábano picante m; **— sense** sentido común m; **—shoe** herradura f; **hold your —s!** ¡para el carro! VI **to — around** payasear

horticulture [hɔ́rdɪkʌltʃə] N horticultura f

hose [hoz] N (for legs) medias f pl; (for liquids) manguera f, manga f

hosiery [hóʒəri] N (stockings) medias f pl; (shop for stockings) calcetería f

hospice [háspɪs] N (inn) hospicio m; (hospital) hospital para enfermos terminales m

hospitable [haspɪɾábəl] ADJ hospitalario, acogedor

hospital [háspɪdl] N hospital m

hospitality [haspɪtǽlɪdi] N hospitalidad f

hospitalize [háspɪdlaɪz] VT internar

host [host] N (also computer) anfitrión m; (in a home or hotel, for a parasite) huésped m; (on television) presentador -ora mf; (army) hueste f; (multitude) multitud f, cúmulo m; (wafer) hostia f

hostage [hástɪdʒ] N rehén mf

hostel [hástl] N hostal m

hostelry [hástlri] N hostería f

hostess [hóstɪs] N anfitriona f

hostile [hástl] ADJ hostil; **— takeover** compra hostil f

hostility [hastílɪdi] N hostilidad f

hot [hat] ADJ (at high temperature) caliente; (sweltering) caluroso; (spicy) picante; (sexy) bueno; (stolen) robado; (recent) de último momento; (popular) popular; **— and heavy** apasionado, apasionadamente; **—bed** semillero m; **— dog** perro caliente m; **—headed** impetuoso, exaltado; **—house** invernadero m; **— potato** patata caliente f; **— seat** situación embarazosa f; **—shot** estrella f; **— tub** jacuzzi m; **it is — today** hace calor hoy; **— under the collar** enojado; VT **to —wire** hacerle un puente a

hotel [hotɛ́l] N hotel m; **—keeper** hotelero -ra mf

hound [haʊnd] N perro de caza m, sabueso m; VT

acosar, perseguir

hour [aʊr] N hora *f*; — **hand** horario *m*; **his finest** — su mejor momento *m*

hourly [áʊrli] ADV (on the hour) cada hora; (by the hour) por horas; — **wages** salario por hora *m*

house[1] [haʊs] N (residence) casa *f*; (legislature) cámara legislativa *f*; — **arrest** detención domiciliaria *f*; — **boat** casa flotante *f*; —**cleaning** limpieza de la casa *f*; —**hold** casa *f*, familia *f*; —**keeper** (in a house) ama de llaves *f*; (in a home) encargado -da de limpieza *mf*; —**keeping** mantenimiento del hogar *m*; —**top** techo *m*, tejado *m*; —**wife** ama de casa *f*; —**work** trabajo de casa *m*, quehaceres domésticos *m pl*; **in**— interno; **on the** — la casa paga; **to keep** — cuidar la casa; —**hold expenses** gastos del hogar *m pl*; ——**to**— puerta a puerta

house[2] [haʊz] VI/VT alojar

housing [háʊzɪŋ] N (place to live) vivienda *f*; (protective covering) caja *f*

hovel [hávəl] N (hut) choza *f*, cabaña *f*, tugurio *m*; (open shed) cobertizo *m*

hover [hávɚ] VI (bird) cernerse; (hang in air) estar suspendido; (linger) rondar; —**craft** aerodeslizador *m*

how [haʊ] ADV cómo; — **about your mom?** ¿y tu mamá? — **beautiful!** ¡qué hermoso! — **come?** ¿por qué? — **early [late, soon]?** ¿cuándo? ¿a qué hora? — **far is it?** ¿a qué distancia está? ¿cuánto dista de aquí? — **long?** ¿cuánto tiempo? — **many?** ¿cuántos? — **much is it?** ¿cuánto vale? — **old are you?** ¿cuántos años tienes? **no matter** — **much it rains** por mucho que llueva; **he knows** — **difficult it is** él sabe lo difícil que es

however [haʊévɚ] CONJ sin embargo, no obstante; ADV — **you want it** como quieras; — **difficult it may be** por muy difícil que sea; — **much it rains** por mucho que llueva

howl [haʊl] VI aullar; (wind) ulular; (with laughter) reír a carcajadas; N aullido *m*, alarido *m*

HQ [headquarters] [étʃkjú] N oficina central *f*, sede central *f*

HR [human resources] [étʃár] N recursos humanos *m pl*

HTML [HyperText Markup Language] [étʃtiéméł] N HTML *m*

hub [hʌb] N (center of wheel) cubo *m*; (center of activity) núcleo *m*; —**cap** tapacubos *m sg*

hubbub [hábʌb] N alboroto *m*, barullo *m*

huckster [hákstɚ] N (peddler) vendedor ambulante *m*; (promoter) mercachifle *m*

huddle [hádł] VI/VT (form a group) apiñar[se]; (curl up) acurrucar[se]; (consult) conferenciar; N tropel *m*; (group meeting for

consultation) reunión *f*; **to be in a** — estar agrupados; **to get in a** — agruparse

hue [hju] N matiz *m*

huff [hʌf] N **to get into a** — enojarse; VI **to** — **and puff** resoplar

hug [hʌg] VI/VT abrazar[se]; **to** — **the coast** costear; N abrazo *m*

huge [hjudʒ] ADJ enorme, fiero

hull [hʌl] N (of a ship, airplane) casco *m*; (of beans, peas) vaina *f*; (of fruits, nuts) cáscara *f*; VT (beans, peas) desvainar; (nuts) cascar

hum [hʌm] VI/VT (person) tararear; (insect, machine) zumbar; (place of activity) hervir; **to** — **to sleep** arrullar; N (of voice) tarareo *m*; (of insect, machine) zumbido *m*

human [hjúmən] ADJ & N humano *m*; — **being** ser humano *m*; — **immunodeficiency virus** virus de inmunodeficiencia humana *m*

humane [hjumén] ADJ humano, humanitario

humanism [hjúmənɪzəm] N humanismo *m*

humanitarian [hjumænɪtériən] ADJ humanitario

humanity [hjumǽnɪDi] N humanidad *f*; **humanities** humanidades *f pl*

humble [hámbəl] ADJ humilde; VT humillar

humid [hjúmɪd] ADJ húmedo

humidify [hjumíDəfaɪ] VT humidificar

humidity [hjumíDɪDi] N humedad *f*

humiliate [hjumíliet] VT humillar, vejar

humiliation [hjumɪliéʃən] N humillación *f*

humility [hjumílɪDi] N humildad *f*

hummingbird [hámɪŋbɚd] N colibrí *m*

humor [hjúmɚ] N humor *m*, humorismo *m*; **out of** — de mal humor, malhumorado; VT complacer a

humorous [hjúmɚəs] ADJ gracioso, chistoso

hump [hʌmp] N joroba *f*, giba *f*, corcova *f*; **we're over the** — ya pasamos lo peor; —**back** jorobado -da *mf*; —**back whale** ballena jorobada *f*, yubarta *f*

hunch [hʌntʃ] N presentimiento *m*, corazonada *f*; —**back** (person) jorobado -da *mf*; (hump) corcova *f*; VI encorvar

hundred [hándrɪd] NUM cien[to]; **a** — **people** cien personas; **a** — **and fifty people** ciento cincuenta personas; N cien/ciento *m*; —**s** centenares *m pl*, cientos *m pl*

hundredth [hándrɪdθ] ADJ centésimo

hung [hʌŋ] *see* hang 'ahorcar'

Hungarian [hʌŋgériən] ADJ & N húngaro -ra *mf*

Hungary [hʌŋgəri] N Hungría *f*

hunger [hángɚ] N hambre *f*; VI pasar hambre; **to** — **for** ansiar, anhelar

hungry [hángri] ADJ hambriento; **to be** — tener hambre; **to go** — pasar hambre

hunk [hʌŋk] N pedazo *m*, cacho *m*; **he's a real** — es un cacho de hombre, es un papacito

hunt [hʌnt] VI/VT (seek prey) cazar; **to** — **down** dar caza a; **to** — **for** buscar; N (activity of hunting caza *f*; (instance of hunting) cacería *f*; (search) búsqueda *f*

hunter [hántə] N (who captures game) cazador -ora *mf*; (seeker) buscador -ora *mf*; (dog) perro de caza *m*

hunting [hántiŋ] N caza *f*; — **knife** cuchillo de caza *m*

huntsman [hántsmən] N cazador *m*

hurdle [hə́dl] N (impediment) obstáculo *m*; (in races) valla *f*; VT saltar

hurl [hə̀l] VI/VT arrojar, lanzar, precipitar

hurrah [hərá] INTERJ ¡hurra!

hurricane [hə́ɪken] N huracán *m*

hurried [hə́ɪd] ADJ apresurado; *Am* apurado

hurry [hə́ɪ] VI darse prisa, apresurarse; *Am* apurarse; **to — in [out]** entrar [salir] de prisa; **to — up** apresurar[se], dar[se] prisa; *Am* apurar[se]; VT apresurar; *Am* apurar; N prisa *f*; *Am* apuro *m*; **to be in a —** tener prisa; *Am* estar apurado

hurt [hə̀t] VI/VT (to injure) lastimar[se], hacer[se] daño; (damage) dañar[se]; (harm) perjudicar[se]; **to — someone's feelings** lastimar/herir a alguien; VI (suffer pain) doler; **my tooth —s** me duele la muela / el diente; N (damage) daño *m*; (wound) herida *f*, lastimadura *f*; ADJ (physically) lastimado, herido; (emotionally) herido; **to get —** lastimarse

hurtful [hə́tfəl] ADJ hiriente

husband [házbənd] N marido *m*, esposo *m*; VT administrar

hush [hʌʃ] VI/VT aquietar[se], callar[se]; —! ¡chitón! ¡silencio! **to — up a scandal** encubrir un escándalo; N silencio *m*; **he gave her — money** compró su silencio

husk [hʌsk] N (shell) cáscara *f*; (pod) vaina *f*; (of corn) *Am* chala *f*; *Sp* farfolla *f*; VT (corn) quitar la chala/farfolla a; (beans, peas) desvainar

husky [háski] ADJ (build) ronco; (strong) recio; N (breed of dog) husky *m*, perro esquimal *m*

hustle [hásəl] VI (work energetically) afanarse; (swindle) estafar; VT (hurry along) empujar; N (bustle) ajetreo *m*; (scheme) timo *m*; — **and bustle** ajetreo *m*, trajín *m*

hut [hʌt] N choza *f*, cabaña *f*

hyacinth [háɪəsɪnθ] N jacinto *m*

hybrid [háɪbrɪd] ADJ híbrido

hybridization [haɪbrɪdɪzéʃən] N hibridación *f*

hydrate [háɪdret] N hidrato *m*; VI/VT hidratar[se]

hydraulic [haɪdrɔ́lɪk] ADJ hidráulico

hydrocarbon [háɪdrəkarbən] N hidrocarburo *m*

hydroelectric [haɪdroɪléktrɪk] ADJ hidroeléctrico

hydrogen [háɪdrədʒən] N hidrógeno *m*; — **bomb** bomba de hidrógeno *f*; — **peroxide** peróxido de hidrógeno *m*, agua oxigenada *f*

hydrophobia [haɪdrəfóbiə] N hidrofobia *f*

hydroplane [háɪdrəplen] N hidroavión *m*

hyena [haɪínə] N hiena *f*

hygiene [háɪdʒin] N higiene *f*

hygienic [haɪdʒénɪk] ADJ higiénico

hygienist [haɪdʒínɪst] N higienista *mf*

hymen [háɪmən] N himen *m*

hymn [hɪm] N himno *m*

hype [haɪp] N exageración *f*; VT promocionar [exageradamente]

hyper [háɪpə] ADJ hiperactivo

hyperactive [haɪpəǽktɪv] ADJ hiperactivo

hyperbaric chamber [haɪpəbǽrɪk tʃémbə] N cámara hiperbárica *f*

hyperdocument [haɪpədákjəmənt] N hiperdocumento *m*

hyperlink [háɪpəlɪŋk] N hiperenlace *m*, hipervínculo *m*

hypermedia [haɪpəmídiə] N hipermedia *m*

hypersensitive [haɪpəsénsɪtɪv] ADJ hipersensible

hypertension [haɪpəténʃən] N hipertensión *f*, presión arterial alta *f*

hyperventilate [haɪpəvéntlet] VI hiperventilar

hyphen [háɪfən] N guión *m*

hypnosis [hɪpnósɪs] N hipnosis *f*

hypnotherapy [hɪpnoθérəpi] N hipnoterapia *f*

hypnotize [hípnətaɪz] VT hipnotizar

hypoallergenic [haɪpoælədʒénɪk] ADJ hipoalérgico

hypochondriac [haɪpokándriæk] N hipocondríaco *mf*, hipocondriaco *mf*

hypocrisy [hɪpákrɪsi] N hipocresía *f*

hypocrite [hípəkrɪt] N hipócrita *mf*

hypocritical [hɪpəkrídɪkəl] ADJ hipócrita, doblado

hypodermic needle [haɪpədə́mɪk nídl] N aguja hipodérmica *f*

hypoglycemia [haɪpoglaɪsímiə] N hipoglucemia *f*

hypothesis [haɪpáθɪsɪs] N hipótesis *f*

hypothyroidism [haɪpoθáɪrɔɪdɪzəm] N hipotiroidismo *m*

hysterectomy [hɪstəréktəmi] N histerectomía *f*

hysterical [hɪstérɪkəl] ADJ (out of control) histérico; (funny) desternillante

Ii

I [aɪ] PRON yo

I-beam [áɪbim] N viga doble *f*

Iberian [aɪbíriən] ADJ ibérico

Ibero-American [aɪbiroəmérɪkən] ADJ iberoamericano -na

ibuprofen [aɪbjuprófɪn] N ibuprofeno *m*

ice [aɪs] N hielo *m*; — **age** periodo glaciar *m*; —**berg** iceberg *m*; —**box** nevera *f*;

refrigerador *m*; — **cream** helado *m*; — **cream cone** cucurucho de helado *m*; — **cream parlor** heladería *f*; — **hockey** hockey sobre hielo *m*; — **skates** patines de cuchilla *m pl*; — **water** agua helada *f*; **to break the** — romper el hielo; **on** — en suspenso; VI/VT (freeze) helar[se]; (cover with ice) cubrir[se] de hielo; VT (cover with icing) bañar; (insure a deal) cerrar; **to** —**-skate** patinar sobre hielo; —**d tea** té helado *m*

Iceland [áɪslənd] N Islandia *f*

Icelander [áɪsləndə] N islandés -esa *mf*

Icelandic [aɪslǽndɪk] ADJ islandés

icicle [áɪsɪkəl] N carámbano *m*

icing [áɪsɪŋ] N (frosting) baño *m*; (formation of ice) formación de hielo *f*

icon [áɪkɑn] N icono *m*, ícono *m* (also computer term)

ICU [intensive care unit] [áɪsíjú] N unidad de cuidados intensivos *f*

icy [áɪsi] ADJ helado

ID [identification card] [áɪdí] N tarjeta de identidad *m*

idea [aɪdíə] N idea *f*

ideal [aɪdíəl] N ideal *m*; ADJ ideal, idóneo

idealism [aɪdíəlɪzəm] N idealismo *m*

idealist [aɪdíəlɪst] N idealista *mf*

idealistic [aɪdíəlístɪk] ADJ idealista

identical [aɪdéntɪkəl] ADJ idéntico; — **twins** gemelos *m pl*, gemelas *f pl*

identification [aɪdɛntəfɪkéʃən] N identificación *f*; — **card** tarjeta de identidad *m*, cédula de identidad *f*

identify [aɪdéntəfaɪ] VI/VT identificar[se]

identity [aɪdéntɪDi] N identidad *f*; — **theft** robo de identidad *m*

ideological [aɪDiəládʒɪkəl] ADJ ideológico

ideology [aɪDiáləʤi] N ideología *f*

idiocy [ídiəsi] N idiotez *f*

idiom [ídiəm] N modismo *m*

idiosyncrasy [ɪDiosínkrəsi] N idiosincrasia *f*

idiot [ídiət] N idiota *mf*

idiotic [ɪDiádɪk] ADJ idiota

idle [áɪdl] ADJ (not active) ocioso; (lazy) perezoso, holgazán; (of a machine, worker) parado; (of an engine) en ralentí; (meaningless) vacío; VI (person) holgazanear; (motor) girar en vacío; VT (cause to be idle) dejar parado/desocupado

idleness [áɪdlnɪs] N (inactivity) ociosidad *f*, ocio *m*, holganza *f*; (sloth) pereza *f*

idler [áɪdlə] N holgazán -ana *mf*, zanguango -ga *mf*

idol [áɪdl] N ídolo *m*

idolatry [aɪdálətri] N idolatría *f*

idolize [áɪdlaɪz] VT idolatrar

idyll [áɪdl] N idilio *m*

if [ɪf] CONJ si; — **I were you** en tu lugar / yo que tú; — **only I had known** de haber sabido / ojalá hubiera sabido; **he's tall,** — **a bit**

stooped es alto, aunque un poco encorvado; N —**s** condiciones *f pl*; **no** —**s, ands, or buts** no hay pero que valga

igloo [íglu] N iglú *m*

ignite [ɪgnáɪt] VI/VT encender[se], prender fuego [a]

ignition [ɪgníʃən] N ignición *f*, encendido *m*; — **switch** llave de contacto *f*

ignoble [ɪgnóbəl] ADJ innoble

ignorance [ígnərəns] N ignorancia *f*

ignorant [ígnərənt] ADJ ignorante

ignore [ɪgnɔ́r] VT ignorar

ilk [ɪlk] N ralea *f*, calaña *f*

ill [ɪl] ADJ enfermo, malo; — **fortune** mala suerte *f*; — **nature** mal genio *m*, mala índole *f*; — **repute** mala fama *f*; — **will** mala voluntad *f*; N (sickness) enfermedad *f*; (calamity) calamidad *f*; ADJ —**-advised** imprudente; — **at ease** incómodo; —**-bred** maleducado; —**-fated** fatídico, funesto, desastrado; —**-gotten** mal adquirido; —**-humored** malhumorado; —**-mannered** maleducado, grosero; —**-natured** de mal genio; ADV **we can** — **afford to stop now** no podemos darnos el lujo de detenernos ahora

illegal [ɪlígəl] ADJ ilegal

illegitimate [ɪlɪʤídəmɪt] ADJ ilegítimo

illicit [ɪlísɪt] ADJ ilícito

illiteracy [ɪlídərəsi] N analfabetismo *m*

illiterate [ɪlídərɪt] ADJ & N analfabeto -ta *mf*

illness [íłnɪs] N enfermedad *f*

illuminate [ɪlúmənət] VI/VT iluminar[se]

illumination [ɪlumənéʃən] N iluminación *f*

illusion [ɪlúʒən] N ilusión *f*

illusory [ɪlúʒəri] ADJ ilusorio

illustrate [fləstret] VI/VT ilustrar

illustration [ɪləstréʃən] N ilustración *f*, estampa *f*

illustrator [fləstreDə] N ilustrador -ra *mf*, dibujante *mf*

illustrious [ɪlɑ́striəs] ADJ ilustre, eximio

image [ímɪʤ] N imagen *f*

imagery [ímɪʤri] N conjunto de imágenes *m*

imaginary [ɪmǽʤəneri] ADJ imaginario, fabuloso

imagination [ɪmæʤənéʃən] N imaginación *f*, fantasía *f*

imaginative [ɪmǽʤənəDɪv] ADJ imaginativo, fantasioso

imagine [ɪmǽʤɪn] VI/VT imaginar[se]; — **that!** ¡figúrate!

imbalance [ɪmbǽləns] N desequilibrio *m*

imbecile [ímbəsəl] N imbécil *mf*

imbibe [ɪmbáɪb] VI/VT beber

imbue [ɪmbjú] VT imbuir, infundir

IMF [International Monetary Fund] [áɪéméf] N FMI *m*

imitate [ímɪtet] VT imitar

imitation [ɪmɪtéʃən] N imitación *f*; — **leather**

imitación de cuero *f*

imitator [ímɪtɛɒ] N imitador -ora *mf*

immaculate [ɪmǽkjəlɪt] ADJ inmaculado

immaterial [ɪmətíriəł] ADJ inmaterial; **it is —
to me** me es indiferente

immature [ɪmətʃúr] ADJ inmaduro

immediate [ɪmídiɪt] ADJ inmediato

immediately [ɪmídiɪtli] ADV inmediatamente,
enseguida

immense [ɪméns] ADJ inmenso

immensity [ɪménsɪdi] N inmensidad *f*

immerse [ɪmɔ́rs] VT (submerge) sumergir;
(absorb) sumir

immersed [ɪmɔ́st] ADJ inmerso

immigrant [ímɪgrənt] ADJ & N inmigrante *mf*

immigrate [ímɪgret] VI inmigrar

immigration [ɪmɪgréʃən] N inmigración *f*

imminent [ímənənt] ADJ inminente

immobile [ɪmóbəł] ADJ inmóvil

immobilize [ɪmóbəlaɪz] VT inmovilizar

immodest [ɪmáDɪst] ADJ inmodesto

immodesty [ɪmáDɪsti] N inmodestia *f*

immoral [ɪmɔ́rəł] ADJ inmoral

immorality [ɪmɔrǽlɪdi] N inmoralidad *f*

immortal [ɪmɔ́rdl] ADJ & N inmortal *mf*

immortality [ɪmɔrtǽlɪdi] N inmortalidad *f*

immovable [ɪmúvəbəł] ADJ inamovible

immune [ɪmjún] ADJ inmune; **— system**
sistema inmune *m*

immunity [ɪmjúnɪdi] N inmunidad *f*

immunodeficiency [ɪmjənodɪfíʃənsi] N
inmunodeficiencia *f*

immutable [ɪmjúbəbəł] ADJ inmutable

impact [ímpækt] N impacto *m*; VI/VT repercutir
[sobre]; **—ed molar** muela impactada *f*

impair [ɪmpér] VT dañar, deteriorar,
menoscabar; **—ed** con las facultades
disminuidas

impairment [ɪmpérmənt] N daño *m*, deterioro
m, menoscabo *m*

impala [ɪmpálə] N impala *m*

impale [ɪmpéł] VT empalar

impart [ɪmpárt] VT (bestow knowledge)
impartir; (reveal) revelar

impartial [ɪmpárʃəł] ADJ imparcial

impartiality [ɪmpɑrʃiǽlɪdi] N imparcialidad *f*

impasse [ímpæs] N impasse *m*

impassioned [ɪmpǽʃənd] ADJ apasionado

impassive [ɪmpǽsɪv] ADJ impasible

impatience [ɪmpéʃəns] N impaciencia *f*

impatient [ɪmpéʃənt] ADJ impaciente

impeach [ɪmpítʃ] VT acusar formalmente; **to —
a person's honor** poner en tela de juicio el
honor de uno

impeachment [ɪmpítʃmənt] N impeachment *m*

impede [ɪmpíd] VT obstaculizar, estorbar, trabar

impediment [ɪmpédəmənt] N impedimento *m*,
obstáculo *m*; (of speech) defecto *m*

impel [ɪmpéł] VT impeler

impending [ɪmpéndɪŋ] ADJ inminente

impenetrable [ɪmpénɪtrəbəł] ADJ impenetrable

imperative [ɪmpérəDɪv] ADJ (like a command)
imperativo; (necessary) imperioso; N
(command, grammatical mood) imperativo
m; (obligation) obligación *f*

imperceptible [ɪmpəséptəbəł] ADJ
imperceptible

imperfect [ɪmpɔ́fɪkt] ADJ & N imperfecto *m*

imperial [ɪmpíriəł] ADJ imperial

imperialism [ɪmpíriəlɪzəm] N imperialismo *m*

imperil [ɪmpérəł] VT poner en peligro

imperious [ɪmpíriəs] ADJ imperioso

impersonal [ɪmpɔ́sənł] ADJ impersonal

impersonate [ɪmpɔ́sənet] VT (assume traits of)
hacerse pasar por; (mimic) imitar

impersonator [ɪmpɔ́sənɛɒ] N imitador -ora
mf

impertinence [ɪmpɔ́tn̩əns] N impertinencia *f*

impertinent [ɪmpɔ́tn̩ənt] ADJ impertinente

impervious [ɪmpɔ́viəs] ADJ impermeable; (to
reason) refractario

impetigo [ɪmpɪtáɪgo] N impétigo *m*

impetuous [ɪmpétʃuəs] ADJ impetuoso

impetus [ímpəDəs] N ímpetu *m*, empuje *m*

impious [ímpiəs] ADJ impío

implacable [ɪmplǽkəbəł] ADJ implacable

implant¹ [ɪmplǽnt] VT implantar

implant² [ímplænt] N implante *m*

implantation [ɪmplæntéʃən] N implantación *f*

implement¹ [ímpləmənt] N implemento *m*,
utensilio *m*

implement² [ímpləment] VT implementar,
instrumentar

implementation [ɪmpləmɪntéʃən] N
implementación *f*

implicate [ímplɪket] VT implicar, involucrar

implication [ɪmplɪkéʃən] N implicación *f*; **by —**
implícitamente

implicit [ɪmplísɪt] ADJ implícito

implore [ɪmplɔ́r] VI/VT implorar

imply [ɪmpláɪ] VT dar a entender

impolite [ɪmpəláɪt] ADJ descortés

import¹ [ɪmpɔ́rt] VT (bring in) importar

import² [ímpɔrt] N (act of importing, thing
imported) importación *f*; (significance)
significado *m*; **—export company**
compañía de importación y exportación *f*

importance [ɪmpɔ́rtn̩s] N importancia *f*,
relevancia *f*

important [ɪmpɔ́rtn̩t] ADJ importante,
relevante

impose [ɪmpóz] VT imponer; **to — [upon]**
abusar [de]

imposing [ɪmpózɪŋ] ADJ imponente,
impresionante

imposition [ɪmpəzíʃən] N (act of imposing,
burden) imposición *f*; (abuse) abuso *m*

impossibility [ɪmpɑsəbílɪdi] N imposibilidad *f*

impossible [ɪmpásəbəl] ADJ (not possible) imposible; (unbearable) insoportable; **to make—** imposibilitar

impostor [ɪmpástə·] N impostor -ora *mf*

impotence [ímpətəns] N impotencia *f*

impotent [ímpətənt] ADJ impotente

impoverish [ɪmpávə·ɪʃ] VT empobrecer

impregnate [ɪmprégnet] VT (cause to be permeated) impregnar; (make pregnant) fecundar, preñar

impress [ɪmprés] VT (make a mark by pressing) estampar; VI/VT (affect deeply) impresionar

impression [ɪmpréʃən] N impresión *f*; (feeling) impresión *f*, sensación *f*

impressive [ɪmprésɪv] ADJ impresionante

imprint¹ [ímprɪnt] N (indentation) impresión *f*, marca *f*; (printer's mark) pie de imprenta *m*

imprint² [ɪmprínt] VT (impress on) imprimir; (fix firmly in mind) grabar

imprison [ɪmprízən] VT (in jail) encarcelar; (anywhere) apresar

imprisonment [ɪmprízənmənt] N encarcelamiento *m*

improbable [ɪmprábəbəl] ADJ improbable

impromptu [ɪmprámptu] ADJ improvisado; **he gave the speech—** improvisó el discurso; N impromptu *m*

improper [ɪmprápə·] ADJ indecoroso, inconveniente

improve [ɪmprúv] VI/VT mejorar[se]; **to— upon** mejorar

improvement [ɪmprúvmənt] N (of a plan) mejora *f*; (in health) mejoría *f*

improvisation [ɪmprəvɪzéʃən] N improvisación *f*

improvise [ímprəvaɪz] VI/VT improvisar

imprudent [ɪmprúdnt] ADJ imprudente, desatinado

impudence [ímpjədəns] N impertinencia *f*, descaro *m*, desparpajo *m*

impudent [ímpjədənt] ADJ impertinente, descarado

impulse [ímpʌls] N impulso *m*; **to act on—** obrar impulsivamente

impulsive [ɪmpʌ́lsɪv] ADJ impulsivo

impunity [ɪmpjúnɪdi] N impunidad *f*

impure [ɪmpjúr] ADJ impuro

impurity [ɪmpjúrɪdi] N impureza *f*

in [ɪn] PREP en; (in tennis) buena, dentro; **— London** en Londres; **— haste** de prisa; **— the morning** por/en la mañana; **— writing** por escrito; **she was walking— the street** andaba por la calle; **to arrive— London** llegar a Londres; **the books— the box** los libros de la caja; **at two— the morning** a las dos de la mañana; **dressed— white** vestido de blanco; **the tallest— his class** el más alto de su clase; **to come— a week** venir dentro de una semana; ADV adentro, dentro; **is she— or out?** ¿está adentro o

afuera? **to be all—** estar rendido; **to be— with someone** estar bien con alguien; **to come—** entrar; **to have it— for someone** tenerle ojeriza a una persona; **to put— meter; the doctor is—** el doctor está; **hats are—** los sombreros están de moda; **—field** cuadro interior *m*; N **—patient** paciente internado -da *mf*; **—patient care** internación *f*; **—seam** entrepierna *f*; **—step** empeine *m*; ADJ **the— place to eat** el restaurante de moda; **an— joke** una broma para un grupo selecto

inability [ɪnəbílɪdi] N inhabilidad *f*, incapacidad *f*

inaccessible [ɪnæksésəbəl] ADJ inaccesible, inasequible

inaccurate [ɪnǽkjə·ɪt] ADJ (not precise) inexacto, impreciso; (wrong) incorrecto

inactive [ɪnǽktɪv] ADJ inactivo

inactivity [ɪnæktívɪdi] N inactividad *f*

inadequate [ɪnǽdɪkwɪt] ADJ (insufficient) insuficiente; (unacceptable) inaceptable

inadmissible [ɪnədmísəbəl] ADJ inadmisible

inadvertent [ɪnədvɔ́·tnt] ADJ (unintentional) involuntario; (careless) descuidado, negligente

inadvisable [ɪnədváɪzəbəl] ADJ desaconsejable

inane [ɪnén] ADJ necio

inanimate [ɪnǽnəmɪt] ADJ inanimado

inasmuch as [ɪnəzmátʃæz] CONJ puesto que

inattentive [ɪnəténtɪv] ADJ desatento

inaudible [ɪnɔ́dəbəl] ADJ inaudible

inaugurate [ɪnɔ́gjəret] VT (initiate) inaugurar; (induct into office) investir de un cargo

inauguration [ɪnɔgjəréʃən] N (initiation) inauguración *f*; (induction) investidura *f*

inboard [ínbɔrd] ADJ dentro del casco

inborn [ínbɔ́rn] ADJ innato

Inca [íŋkə] ADJ & N inca *mf*

incandescence [ɪŋkændésəns] N incandescencia *f*

incandescent [ɪnkændésənt] ADJ incandescente

incantation [ɪnkæntéʃən] N conjuro *m*

incapable [ɪnképəbəl] ADJ incapaz

incapacitate [ɪnkəpǽsɪtet] VT incapacitar

incarcerate [ɪnkársəret] VT encarcelar

incarnation [ɪnkarnéʃən] N encarnación *f*

incendiary [ɪnséndieri] ADJ & N incendiario -ria *mf*; **— bomb** bomba incendiaria *f*

incense¹ [ínsɛns] N incienso *m*

incense² [ɪnséns] VT encolerizar

incentive [ɪnséntɪv] N incentivo *m*, acicate *m*

inception [ɪnsépʃən] N comienzo *m*

incessant [ɪnsésənt] ADJ incesante

incest [ínsɛst] N incesto *m*

incestuous [ɪnséstʃuəs] ADJ incestuoso

inch [ɪntʃ] N pulgada [2.54 centímetros] *f*; **to be within an— of** estar a un punto de; VI avanzar poco a poco

incidence [ínsɪdəns] N incidencia f

incident [ínsɪdənt] N incidente m, lance m; (crime, accident) suceso m

incidental [ɪnsɪdéntl] ADJ (happening in accordance with) accesorio; **— music** música incidental f; N **—s** gastos menores m pl

incidentally [ɪnsɪdéntli] ADV a propósito

incinerate [ɪnsínəret] VT incinerar

incipient [ɪnsípiənt] ADJ incipiente, naciente

incision [ɪnsíʒən] N incisión f

incisive [ɪnsáɪsɪv] ADJ incisivo

incisor [ɪnsáɪzə˞] N (tooth) incisivo m

incite [ɪnsáɪt] VT incitar

inclement [ɪnklémənt] ADJ inclemente

inclination [ɪnklənéʃən] N (slope) inclinación f; (tendency) afición f, inclinación f

incline[1] [ɪnkláɪn] VI/VT inclinar[se]

incline[2] [ínklaɪn] N declive m, pendiente f

include [ɪnklúd] VT incluir

including [ɪŋklúdɪŋ] ADJ **it costs a thousand dollars, not — air travel** cuesta mil dólares, sin incluir el vuelo; **that whole week, — Saturday** toda esa semana, incluyendo el sábado / el sábado inclusive; **— you, there are four of us** incluyéndote a ti, somos cuatro

inclusion [ɪŋklúʒən] N (acceptance) inclusión f; (addition) incorporación f

inclusive [ɪnklúsɪv] ADJ inclusivo; **from Monday to Friday —** de lunes a viernes inclusive

incoherent [ɪnkohírənt] ADJ incoherente

income [ínkʌm] N Sp renta f; Am ingreso m; **— tax** Sp impuesto sobre la renta m; Am impuesto sobre ingresos m; **— tax return** declaración de impuestos sobre la renta / los ingresos f

incoming [ínkʌmɪŋ] ADJ entrante

incomparable [ɪnkámpərəbəl] ADJ incomparable, sin parangón

incompatible [ɪnkəmpǽɾəbəl] ADJ incompatible

incompetent [ɪnkámpɪtənt] ADJ incompetente

incomplete [ɪnkəmplít] ADJ incompleto

incomprehensible [ɪnkɑmprɪhénsəbəl] ADJ incomprensible

inconceivable [ɪnkənsívəbəl] ADJ inconcebible

inconclusive [ɪnkənklúsɪv] ADJ no concluyente

inconsiderate [ɪnkənsídə˞ɪt] ADJ desconsiderado

inconsistency [ɪnkənsístənsi] N (condition) inconsecuencia f; (instance) incoherencia f

inconsistent [ɪnkənsístənt] ADJ inconsecuente

inconspicuous [ɪnkənspíkjuəs] ADJ poco llamativo; **to be —** pasar inadvertido

inconstancy [ɪnkánstənsi] N inconstancia f

inconstant [ɪnkánstənt] ADJ inconstante

incontinent [ɪnkántənənt] ADJ incontinente

incontrovertible [ɪnkɑntrəvɝ́ɾəbəl] ADJ incontrovertible

inconvenience [ɪnkənvínjəns] N (state of being inconvenient) inconveniencia f; (thing that is inconvenient) molestia f, inconveniente m; VT incomodar, molestar

inconvenient [ɪnkənvínjənt] ADJ (bothersome) incómodo; (untimely) inoportuno

incorporate [ɪnkɔ́rpəret] VI/VT (include) incorporar[se]; (form a corporation) constituir[se] en sociedad

incorporation [ɪŋkɔrpəréʃən] N (inclusion) incorporación f; (integration) integración f

incorrect [ɪnkərékt] ADJ incorrecto

incorrigible [ɪnkɔ́rɪdʒəbəl] ADJ incorregible

increase[1] [ɪnkrís] VI/VT aumentar[se], incrementar[se]

increase[2] [ínkris] N aumento m, incremento m

increasingly [ɪnkrísɪŋli] ADV cada vez más

incredible [ɪnkrédəbəl] ADJ increíble

incredulous [ɪnkrédʒələs] ADJ incrédulo

increment [ínkrəmənt] N incremento m

incriminate [ɪnkrímənət] VT incriminar

incubator [íŋkjəbeɾə˞] N incubadora f

inculcate [ɪnkʌ́lket] VT inculcar

incumbent [ɪnkʌ́mbənt] ADJ **a duty — upon me** un deber que me incumbe; N titular m

incur [ɪnkɝ́] VT (an expense) incurrir en; (a debt) contraer

incurable [ɪnkjúrəbəl] ADJ incurable

indebted [ɪndɛ́ɾɪd] ADJ endeudado, en deuda

indebtedness [ɪndɛ́ɾɪdnɪs] N endeudamiento m, adeudo m

indecency [ɪndísənsi] N indecencia f

indecent [ɪndísənt] ADJ indecente; **— exposure** delito de exhibicionismo m

indecision [ɪndɪsíʒən] N indecisión f

indeed [ɪndíd] ADV de verdad; INTERJ (ironically) ¡no me digas! (sincerely) ¡tienes razón! ¡efectivamente!

indefensible [ɪndɪfénsəbəl] ADJ indefendible

indefinite [ɪndɛ́fənɪt] ADJ indefinido

indelible [ɪndɛ́ləbəl] ADJ indeleble

indelicate [ɪndɛ́lɪkɪt] ADJ (tactless) indelicado; (offensive) indecoroso

indemnify [ɪndɛ́mnəfaɪ] VT indemnizar

indemnity [ɪndɛ́mnɪɾi] N indemnización f

indent [ɪndɛ́nt] VI/VT sangrar

indentation [ɪndɛntéʃən] N (notch) muesca f; (blank space) sangría f

independence [ɪndɪpɛ́ndəns] N independencia f

independent [ɪndɪpɛ́ndənt] ADJ independiente, autónomo

indestructible [ɪndɪstrʌ́ktəbəl] ADJ indestructible

indeterminate [ɪndɪtɝ́mənɪt] ADJ indeterminado

index [índɛks] N índice m; **— card** ficha f; **— finger** índice m; VT (incorporate into an index) poner en el índice; (make the index) poner/hacer un índice; (adjust wages) indexar

indexing [índeksɪŋ] N indexación f

India [índiə] N India f

Indian [índiən] ADJ & N indio -a mf; **— Ocean** Océano Indico m

indicate [índɪket] VT indicar

indication [ɪndɪkéʃən] N indicación f

indicative [ɪndíkədɪv] ADJ & N indicativo m

indicator [índɪkedə-] N indicador m

indict [ɪndáɪt] VT acusar

indictment [ɪndáɪtmənt] N acusación f

indifference [ɪndífrəns] N indiferencia f

indifferent [ɪndífrənt] ADJ indiferente

indigenous [ɪndídʒənəs] ADJ (person) indígena; (plant, animal) autóctono

indigent [índɪdʒənt] ADJ & N indigente mf

indigestion [ɪndɪdʒéstʃən] N indigestión f

indignant [ɪndígnənt] ADJ indignado

indignation [ɪndɪgnéʃən] N indignación f

indignity [ɪndígnɪdi] N ultraje m, afrenta f

indigo [índɪgo] N índigo m, añil m; **— blue** azul añil m

indirect [ɪndɪrékt] ADJ indirecto; **— object** complemento/objeto indirecto m

indiscreet [ɪndɪskrít] ADJ indiscreto

indiscretion [ɪndɪskréʃən] N indiscreción f

indispensable [ɪndɪspénsəbəl] ADJ indispensable, imprescindible

indispose [ɪndɪspóz] VT indisponer

indisposed [ɪndɪspózd] ADJ indispuesto; **to become —** indisponerse

indistinct [ɪndɪstíŋkt] ADJ indistinto

individual [ɪndəvídʒuəl] ADJ individual; N individuo m, persona f; pej sujeto m, individuo m

individualism [ɪndəvídʒuəlɪzəm] N individualismo m

individualist [ɪndəvídʒuəlɪst] N individualista mf

individuality [ɪndəvɪdʒuǽlɪdi] N individualidad f

indivisible [ɪndəvízəbəl] ADJ indivisible

indoctrinate [ɪndáktrɪnet] VT adoctrinar

indolence [índələns] N indolencia f, desidia f

indolent [índələnt] ADJ indolente, haragán

indomitable [ɪndámɪdəbəl] ADJ indomable

Indonesia [ɪndəníʒə] N Indonesia f

Indonesian [ɪndəníʒən] ADJ & N indonesio -sia mf

indoor [índɔr] ADJ interior

indoors [ɪndɔ́rz] ADV dentro; **to go —** entrar, ir para adentro

induce [ɪndús] VT inducir

inducement [ɪndúsmənt] N aliciente m, incentivo m

induct [ɪndákt] VT (initiate) admitir, iniciar; (draft) reclutar

induction [ɪndákʃən] N (philosophical, electrical) inducción f; (into an organization) admisión f, iniciación f

indulge [ɪndʌ́ldʒ] VT mimar, consentir; VI **to — in** darse a, entregarse a; **to — oneself [in]** darse el gusto [de]

indulgence [ɪndʌ́ldʒəns] N (act or state of indulging, religious) indulgencia f; (thing indulged in) exceso m, lujo m

indulgent [ɪndʌ́ldʒənt] ADJ indulgente; (toward a child) complaciente

industrial [ɪndʌ́striəl] ADJ industrial

industrialist [ɪndʌ́striəlɪst] N industrial mf

industrialization [ɪndʌstriəlɪzéʃən] N industrialización f

industrious [ɪndʌ́striəs] ADJ (student) aplicado, diligente; (worker) industrioso

industry [índəstri] N (manufacturing) industria f; (hard work) diligencia f; **— standards** normas industriales f pl

inebriated [ɪníbrieDɪd] ADJ ebrio

inedible [ɪnéDəbəl] ADJ incomestible, incomible

ineffable [ɪnéfəbəl] ADJ inefable

ineffective [ɪnɪféktɪv] ADJ ineficaz, ineficiente

ineffectual [ɪnɪféktʃuəl] ADJ ineficaz

inefficient [ɪnɪfíʃənt] ADJ ineficiente

ineligible [ɪnélɪdʒəbəl] ADJ inelegible

inept [ɪnépt] ADJ inepto

inequality [ɪnɪkwálɪDi] N desigualdad f

inert [ɪnɝ́t] ADJ inerte

inertia [ɪnɝ́ʃə] N inercia f

inescapable [ɪnɪsképəbəl] ADJ inevitable, ineludible

inestimable [ɪnéstəməbəl] ADJ inestimable

inevitable [ɪnévɪDəbəl] ADJ inevitable

inexcusable [ɪnɪkskjúzəbəl] ADJ inexcusable

inexhaustible [ɪnɪgzɔ́stəbəl] ADJ inagotable

inexorable [ɪnéksəəbəl] ADJ inexorable

inexpensive [ɪnɪkspénsɪv] ADJ económico, barato

inexperienced [ɪnɪkspíriənst] ADJ no experimentado, inexperto

inexplicable [ɪnɪksplíkəbəl] ADJ inexplicable

infallible [ɪnfælləbəl] ADJ infalible

infamous [ínfəməs] ADJ infame, de mala fama

infamy [ínfəmi] N infamia f

infancy [ínfənsi] N primera infancia f

infant [ínfənt] N bebé mf

infantile [ínfəntaɪl] ADJ infantil

infantry [ínfəntri] N infantería f; **—man** infante m

infatuated [ɪnfǽtʃueDɪd] ADJ enamorado

infect [ɪnfékt] VT (cause disease) infectar; (spread a mood) contagiar

infection [ɪnfékʃən] N infección f

infectious [ɪnfékʃəs] ADJ (disease) infeccioso, contagioso; (mood) contagioso

infer [ɪnfɝ́] VT inferir, deducir

inference [ínfəəns] N inferencia f, deducción f

inferior [ɪnfíriə] ADJ inferior

inferiority [ɪnfirióriDi] N inferioridad f; **—**

complex complejo de inferioridad *m*
infernal [ɪnfɜ́nl̩] ADJ infernal
inferno [ɪnfɜ́no] N (fire) incendio *m*; (hot place) infierno *m*
infertility [ɪnfɚtílɪDi] N infertilidad *f*
infest [ɪnfɛ́st] VT infestar, plagar
infestation [ɪnfɛstéʃən] N infestación *f*
infiltrate [ɪnfíltret] VI/VT infiltrar[se]; **to — an organization** infiltrarse en una organización
infinite [ɪ́nfənɪt] ADJ & N infinito *m*
infinitive [ɪnfínɪDɪv] ADJ & N infinitivo *m*
infinity [ɪnfínɪDi] N (large number) infinidad *f*; (space) infinito *m*
infirm [ɪnfɜ́m] ADJ enfermizo, achacoso
infirmary [ɪnfɜ́məri] N enfermería *f*
infirmity [ɪnfɜ́mɪDi] N enfermedad *f*, achaque *m*
inflame [ɪnflém] VT (with infection) inflamar[se]; (with passion) enardecer[se]; (with fire) encender[se]
inflammation [ɪnfləméʃən] N inflamación *f*
inflate [ɪnflét] VI/VT (fill with air) inflar[se], hincharse; (exaggerate) exagerar
inflation [ɪnfléʃən] N (rise in prices) inflación *f*; (introduction of air) inflado *m*
inflexible [ɪnflɛ́ksəbəl] ADJ inflexible
inflict [ɪnflíkt] VT (impose on) infligir; **to — a blow** asestar un golpe
influence [ɪ́nfluəns] N influencia *f*, influjo *m*; VT influir en/sobre, incidir en; **— peddling** tráfico de influencias *m*
influential [ɪnfluénʃəl] ADJ influyente
influenza [ɪnfluénzə] N gripe *f*
influx [ɪ́nflʌks] N (of fluid, goods) entrada *f*; (of people) afluencia *f*
infomercial [ɪ́nfomɚʃəl] N infomercial *m*, publirreportaje *m*
inform [ɪnfɔ́rm] VI/VT (give knowledge) informar[se]; VT (inspire) inspirar; **to — against/on** delatar a, denunciar a
informal [ɪnfɔ́rməl] ADJ informal
informant [ɪnfɔ́rmənt] N informante *mf*
information [ɪnfɚméʃən] N (news, data, details, act of informing) información *f*; (details) informes *m pl*; **— superhighway** autopista de la información *f*
informative [ɪnfɔ́rməDɪv] ADJ informativo
informer [ɪnfɔ́rmɚ] N informante *mf*, delator -ora *mf*, *pej* soplón -ona *mf*
infotainment [ɪnfoténmənt] N entretenimiento informativo *m*
infraction [ɪnfrǽkʃən] N infracción *f*
infrared [ɪnfrəréd] ADJ & N infrarrojo *m*
infrastructure [ɪ́nfrəstrʌktʃɚ] N infraestructura *f*
infringe [ɪnfrínʤ] VT infringir; VI **to — upon** violar
infringement [ɪnfrínʤmənt] N infracción *f*, violación *f*

infuriate [ɪnfjúriet] VT enfurecer, sublevar
infuse [ɪnfjúz] VT infundir
ingenious [ɪnʤínjəs] ADJ ingenioso
ingenuity [ɪnʤənúɪDi] N ingenio *m*, inventiva *f*
ingenuous [ɪnʤénjuəs] ADJ ingenuo *f*
ingenuousness [ɪnʤénjuəsnɪs] N ingenuidad *f*
ingest [ɪnʤést] VI/VT ingerir
ingrate [ɪ́ngret] N ingrato -ta *mf*
ingratitude [ɪngrǽDɪtud] N ingratitud *f*
ingredient [ɪngrídiənt] N ingrediente *m*
ingrown [ɪ́ngron] ADJ encarnado
inhabit [ɪnhǽbɪt] VT habitar
inhabitant [ɪnhǽbɪtənt] N habitante *mf*
inhale [ɪnhél] VI/VT inhalar, aspirar
inherent [ɪnhérənt] ADJ inherente
inherit [ɪnhérɪt] VI/VT heredar
inheritance [ɪnhérɪDəns] N herencia *f*; **— tax** impuesto a la herencia *m*
inherited [ɪnhérɪDɪd] ADJ patrimonial
inhibit [ɪnhíbɪt] VT inhibir, cohibir
inhibiting [ɪnhíbɪDɪŋ] ADJ inhibidor
inhibition [ɪnɪbíʃən] N inhibición *f*, cohibición *f*
inhibitor [ɪnhíbɪDɚ] N inhibidor *m*
inhospitable [ɪnhaspíDəbəl] ADJ (person) inhospitalario; (place) inhóspito
inhuman [ɪnhjúmən] ADJ inhumano
inimitable [ɪnímɪDəbəl] ADJ inimitable
initial [ɪníʃəl] ADJ & N inicial *f*; VT firmar las iniciales
initialize [ɪníʃəlaɪz] VT inicializar
initially [ɪníʃəli] ADV al comienzo, inicialmente
initiate [ɪníʃiet] VT iniciar
initiative [ɪníʃəDɪv] N iniciativa *f*
inject [ɪnʤékt] VI/VT inyectar[se], pinchar[se]
injection [ɪnʤékʃən] N inyección *f*
injunction [ɪnʤʌ́ŋkʃən] N mandato judicial *m*, orden judicial *f*
injure [ɪ́nʤɚ] VI/VT herir[se]; (sports) lesionar[se]
injurious [ɪnʤúriəs] ADJ (harmful) perjudicial; (defamatory) injurioso
injury [ɪ́nʤəri] N herida *f*, lesión *f*; **— time** (soccer) descuento *m*
injustice [ɪnʤʌ́stɪs] N injusticia *f*
ink [ɪŋk] N tinta *f*; VT (mark with ink) entintar; (sign) firmar; **— cartridge** cartucho de tinta *m*; **—-jet printer** impresora de inyección de tinta *f*; **—pad** almohadilla *f*; **—well** tintero *m*
inkling [ɪ́ŋklɪŋ] N idea *f*
inlaid [ɪ́nled] ADJ incrustado; **— work** incrustación *f*
inland [ɪ́nlənd] ADJ interior; ADV tierra adentro
inlay[1] [ɪnlé] VT incrustar
inlay[2] [ɪ́nle] N incrustación *f*
inmate [ɪ́nmet] N (in a prison) preso -sa *mf*, recluso -sa *mf*; (in an asylum) internado -da *mf*; (in a hospital) paciente *mf*
inn [ɪn] N posada *f*, fonda *f*; **—keeper** posadero -ra *mf*, fondista *mf*

innate [ɪnét] ADJ innato

inner [ínɚ] ADJ (inside) interior; (intimate) íntimo; — **city** zona céntrica empobrecida f; — **ear** oído interno m; —**most** más recóndito; — **tube** cámara f

inning [ínɪŋ] N entrada f

innocence [ínəsəns] N (absence of guilt) inocencia f; (naiveté) candidez f, candor m

innocent [ínəsənt] ADJ & N inocente mf

innocuous [ɪnákjuəs] ADJ innocuo, inocuo

innovate [ínəvet] VI innovar

innovating [ínəvedɪŋ] ADJ innovador, renovador

innovation [ɪnəvéʃən] N innovación f

innovative [ínəvedɪv] ADJ innovador

innovator [ínəvedɚ] N innovador -ora mf

innuendo [ɪnjuéndo] N insinuación f

innumerable [ɪnúməəbəl] ADJ innumerables

inoculate [ɪnákjəlet] VI/VT inocular[se]

inoffensive [ɪnəfénsɪv] ADJ inofensivo

inoperable [ɪnápəəbəl] ADJ inoperable

inopportune [ɪnɑpətún] ADJ inoportuno

inordinate [ɪnɔ́rdṇɪt] ADJ desmesurado

inorganic [ɪnɔrgǽnɪk] ADJ inorgánico; — **chemistry** química inorgánica f

input [ínput] N (electric, computer) entrada f; (opinion) opinión f; VT ingresar/entrar datos

inquire [ɪŋkwáɪr] VI/VT inquirir, preguntar; **to — about/after** preguntar por; **to — into** indagar, investigar

inquiry [ɪŋkwəri] N (scientific) investigación f; (police) pesquisa f; **we made inquiries about hotels** hicimos averiguaciones acerca de hoteles

inquisition [ɪŋkwɪzíʃən] N inquisición f

inquisitive [ɪnkwízɪdɪv] ADJ (curious) inquisitivo, curioso; (asking many questions) preguntón

insane [ɪnsén] ADJ demente, loco; — **asylum** manicomio m

insanity [ɪnsǽnɪdi] N locura f, demencia f

insatiable [ɪnséʃəbəl] ADJ insaciable

inscribe [ɪnskráɪb] VT (mark) inscribir; (engrave) grabar; (dedicate) dedicar

inscription [ɪnskrípʃən] N (marks, engraving) inscripción f; (dedication) dedicatoria f

inscrutable [ɪnskrúəbəl] ADJ inescrutable

insect [ínsekt] N insecto m

insecticide [ɪnséktɪsaɪd] N insecticida m

insectivorous [ɪnsektívəəs] ADJ insectívoro

insecure [ɪnsɪkjúr] ADJ inseguro

insecurity [ɪnsɪkjúrɪdi] N inseguridad f

insemination [ɪnseminéʃən] N inseminación f

insensible [ɪnsénsəbəl] ADJ insensible

insensitive [ɪnsénsɪdɪv] ADJ insensible

inseparable [ɪnsépəəbəl] ADJ inseparable

insert¹ [ɪnsɚt] VT insertar, introducir; (into a text) intercalar

insert² [ínsɚt] N encarte m

insertion [ɪnsɚ́ʃən] N inserción f; (into a text) intercalación f

inside¹ [ɪnsáɪd] PREP dentro de; ADV dentro, adentro

inside² [ínsaɪd] N interior m; — **job** delito cometido por un empleado m; —**s** entrañas f pl; — **track** pista interior f; **to turn — out** volver del revés; **he passed me on the —** me pasó por la derecha; ADJ (interior) interior

insider [ɪnsáɪdɚ] N privilegiado -da mf; — **trading** abuso de información privilegiada m

insidious [ɪnsídiəs] ADJ insidioso

insight [ínsaɪt] N (intuition) perspicacia f; (discernment) discernimiento m

insignia [ɪnsígniə] N insignia f

insignificant [ɪnsɪgnífɪkənt] ADJ insignificante, menudo, nimio

insincere [ɪnsɪnsír] ADJ insincero

insinuate [ɪnsínjuet] VT insinuar

insinuation [ɪnsɪnjuéʃən] N insinuación f

insipid [ɪnsípɪd] ADJ insípido, soso

insist [ɪnsíst] VI/VT insistir; **to — on** insistir en

insistence [ɪnsístəns] N insistencia f

insistent [ɪnsístənt] ADJ insistente

insole [ínsol] N plantilla f

insolence [ínsələns] N insolencia f

insolent [ínsələnt] ADJ insolente, atrevido

insoluble [ɪnsáljəbəl] ADJ insoluble

insolvent [ɪnsálvənt] ADJ insolvente

insomnia [ɪnsámniə] N insomnio m

inspect [ɪnspékt] VT inspeccionar; **to — the troops** pasar revista a la tropa, revistar a la tropa

inspection [ɪnspékʃən] N inspección f; (of troops) revista f

inspector [ɪnspéktɚ] N inspector -ora mf

inspiration [ɪnspəréʃən] N inspiración f

inspire [ɪnspáɪr] VI/VT inspirar

instability [ɪnstəbílɪdi] N inestabilidad f

install [ɪnstɔ́l] VT instalar; N — **program** programa instalador m

installation [ɪnstəléʃən] N instalación f

installment [ɪnstɔ́lmənt] N (payment of debt) cuota f; (of a book) entrega f, fascículo m; **to pay in —s** pagar a plazos

instance [ínstəns] N ejemplo m; **for —** por ejemplo; **court of first —** tribunal de primera instancia m

instant [ínstənt] N instante m; **this —** ahora mismo; ADJ inmediato; — **coffee** café instantáneo m; — **messaging** mensajería instantánea f

instantaneous [ɪnstənténias] ADJ instantáneo

instead [ɪnstéd] ADV — **of** en lugar de, en vez de; **she didn't want a desk, so she ordered a chair** — no quería un escritorio, así que pidió una silla en su lugar

instigate [ínstɪget] VT instigar

instigator [ínstɪgeɪɾə·] N (of a crime) instigador -ora *mf*; (of an event) causante *mf*
instill [ɪnstíl] VT inculcar
instinct [ínstɪŋkt] N instinto *m*
instinctive [ɪnstíŋktɪv] ADJ instintivo
institute [ínstɪtut] N instituto *m*; VT instituir
institution [ɪnstɪtúʃən] N institución *f*
institutional [ɪnstɪtúʃənəɬ] ADJ institucional
instruct [ɪnstrʌ́kt] VT (teach) instruir; (command, advise) dar instrucciones; (command) mandar
instruction [ɪnstrʌ́kʃən] N instrucción *f*; **—s** (orders) órdenes *f pl*; (information) instrucciones *f pl*, indicaciones *f pl*
instructive [ɪnstrʌ́ktɪv] ADJ instructivo
instructor [ɪnstrʌ́ktə·] N (of skills) instructor -ora *mf*; (of knowledge) profesor -ora *mf*
instrument [ínstrəmənt] N instrumento *m*; **— panel** salpicadero *m*, tablero *m*
instrumental [ɪnstrəméntl] ADJ instrumental; **to be — in** ser fundamental para
insubordinate [ɪnsəbórdnɪt] ADJ insubordinado
insufferable [ɪnsʌ́fəʔəbəl] ADJ insufrible
insufficiency [ɪnsəfíʃənsi] N insuficiencia *f*
insufficient [ɪnsəfíʃənt] ADJ insuficiente
insulate [ínsəlet] VT aislar
insulation [ɪnsəléʃən] N aislamiento *m*
insulator [ínsəleɪɾə·] N (material) aislante *m*; (device) aislador *m*
insulin [ínsəlɪn] N insulina *f*; **— shock** choque insulínico *m*
insult[1] [ɪnsʌ́lt] VT insultar, injuriar
insult[2] [ínsʌlt] N insulto *m*, injuria *f*
insulting [ɪnsʌ́ltɪŋ] ADJ insultante, injurioso
insuperable [ɪnsúpə·əbəl] ADJ insuperable
insurable [ɪnʃúrəbəl] ADJ asegurable
insurance [ɪnʃúrəns] N seguro *m*; **— agent** agente de seguros *mf*; **— company** compañía de seguros *f*; **— policy** póliza de seguro *f*
insure [ɪnʃúr] VI/VT asegurar[se]
insurgent [ɪnsə́ʤənt] N alzado -da *mf*
insurmountable [ɪnsə·máʊntəbəl] ADJ insuperable
insurrection [ɪnsərékʃən] N insurrección *f*
intact [ɪntǽkt] ADJ intacto
intangible [ɪntǽnʤəbəl] ADJ intangible
integer [íntɪʤə·] N [número] entero *m*
integral [íntɪgrəl] ADJ (complete) integral; (forming part of) integrante; **— calculus** cálculo integral *m*; N integral *f*
integrate [íntɪgret] VT integrar; VI integrarse a
integration [ɪntɪgréʃən] N integración *f*
integrity [ɪntégrɪɾi] N integridad *f*
intellect [íntlekt] N intelecto *m*
intellectual [ɪntléktʃuəl] ADJ & N intelectual *mf*
intelligence [ɪntélɪʤəns] N inteligencia *f* (also secret information); **— quotient** coeficiente intelectual / de inteligencia *m*
intelligent [ɪntélɪʤənt] ADJ inteligente

intelligible [ɪntélɪʤəbəl] ADJ inteligible
intend [ɪnténd] VT pensar; **to — do something** pensar hacer algo; **a book —ed for children** un libro destinado/dirigido a los niños
intense [ɪnténs] ADJ intenso
intensify [ɪnténsɪfaɪ] VI/VT intensificar[se]
intensity [ɪnténsɪɾi] N intensidad *f*
intensive [ɪnténsɪv] ADJ intensivo; **— care unit** sala de cuidados intensivos *f*
intent [ɪntént] N intención *f*, propósito *m*; **to/ for all —s and purposes** en la práctica; ADJ atento; **— on** resuelto a
intention [ɪnténʃən] N intención *f*
intentional [ɪnténʃənəl] ADJ intencional; **— base on balls** base por bolas intencional *f*
intentionally [ɪnténʃənəli] ADV a propósito
inter [ɪntə́s] VT sepultar
interact [ɪntə·ǽkt] VI interactuar
interaction [ɪntə·ǽkʃən] N interacción *f*
interactive [ɪntə·ǽktɪv] ADJ interactivo
intercede [ɪntə·síd] VI interceder
intercept [ɪntə·sépt] VT interceptar
interception [ɪntə·sépʃən] N interceptación *f*
intercession [ɪntə·séʃən] N intercesión *f*
interchange[1] [íntə·tʃenʤ] N cambio *m*; (on road) enlace *m*; *Sp* intercambiador *m*
interchange[2] [ɪntə·tʃénʤ] VI/VT cambiar, intercambiar
intercourse [íntə·kɔrs] N comunicación *f*, trato *m*
interest [íntrɪst] N interés *m*; (financial) interés *m*, rédito *m*; (share in a business) participación *f*; **—-bearing** que devenga intereses; **—-free** libre de intereses, sin intereses; **— rate** tasa de interés *f*; **mining —s** los negocios mineros; VT interesar; **may I — you in a cookie?** ¿te puedo ofrecer una galleta?
interested [íntrɪstɪd] ADJ interesado; **— party** parte interesada *f*; **to be/become — in** interesarse en/por
interesting [íntrɪstɪŋ] ADJ interesante
interface [íntə·fes] N interface *mf*, interfaz *f*
interfere [ɪntə·fír] VI interferir; (meddle) entrometerse; **to — with** interferir en
interference [ɪntə·fírəns] N interferencia *f*, injerencia *f*
interferon [ɪntə·fírɑn] N interferón *m*
interim [íntə·ɪm] N ínterin *m*; ADJ (person) interino; (decision) provisional
interior [ɪntíriə·] ADJ & N interior *m*; **— decoration** decoración de interiores *f*; **— design** diseño de interiores *m*
interjection [ɪntə·ʤékʃən] N interjección *f*, exclamación *f*
interlace [ɪntə·lés] VI/VT entrelazar[se]
interlinear [ɪntə·línia·] ADJ interlineal
interlock [ɪntə·lák] VI/VT (gears) engranar[se];

(branches, etc.) entrelazar[se]; N interlock m

interlocking [ɪntə-lɑ́kɪŋ] ADJ (gears) engranado; (branches) entrelazado

interlude [ɪ́ntə-lud] N (interval) intervalo m; (musical) interludio m; (theatrical) entremés m

intermediary [ɪntə-mídɪeri] ADJ intermediario

intermediate [ɪntə-mídɪɪt] ADJ intermedio

interment [ɪntɚmənt] N entierro m

interminable [ɪntɚmənəbəl] ADJ interminable

intermingle [ɪntə-mɪ́ŋgəl] VI/VT entremezclar[se]

intermission [ɪntə-mɪ́ʃən] N entreacto m, intervalo m

intermittent [ɪntə-mɪ́tnt] ADJ intermitente

intern [ɪ́ntɚn] VT internar, confinar; N (prisoner, doctor) interno -na mf

internal [ɪntɚ́nl] ADJ interno, interior; —- **combustion engine** motor de combustión interna m; — **hard disk** disco duro interno m; — **revenue** rentas internas f pl; — **Revenue Service** Hacienda f

internalize [ɪntɚ́nəlaɪz] VT interiorizar, internalizar

international [ɪntə-nǽʃənl] ADJ internacional; — **law** derecho internacional m

Internet [ɪ́ntə-net] N internet m, red f, web f; — **access** acceso a internet m; — **access provider** proveedor de acceso a internet m; — **banking** banca por internet f; — **community** comunidad internauta f; — **user** internauta mf

internist [ɪntɚ́nɪst] N internista mf

internship [ɪ́ntə-nʃɪp] N (medical) internado m; (student) práctica f

interpersonal [ɪntə-pɚ́sənl] ADJ interpersonal

interpose [ɪntə-póz] VI/VT interponer[se]

interpret [ɪntɚ́prɪt] VI/VT interpretar

interpretation [ɪntɚprɪtéʃən] N interpretación f

interpreter [ɪntɚ́prɪDə-] N intérprete mf

interracial [ɪntə-réʃəl] ADJ interracial

interrelated [ɪntə-rɪléɪtɪd] ADJ interrelacionado

interrogate [ɪntɛ́rəget] VI/VT interrogar

interrogation [ɪntɛrəgéʃən] N interrogación f, interrogatorio m

interrogative [ɪntərágəDɪv] ADJ interrogativo; N palabra/oración interrogativa f

interrupt [ɪntərʌ́pt] VI/VT interrumpir

interruption [ɪntərʌ́pʃən] N interrupción f

intersect [ɪntə-sékt] VI/VT (math) intersecar[se]; (road) cruzar[se]

intersection [ɪntə-sékʃən] N (math) intersección f; (street) cruce m, intersección f

intersperse [ɪntə-spɚ́s] VT (scatter) esparcir; (intermingle) entremezclar, entreverar; (spice up) salpicar

interstate [ɪ́ntə-stet] ADJ interestatal; — **highway** autopista interestatal f

interstellar [ɪntə-stélə] ADJ interestelar

interstice [ɪntɚ́stɪs] N intersticio m

intertwine [ɪntə-twáɪn] VI/VT entrelazar[se]

interval [ɪ́ntə-vəl] N intervalo m

intervene [ɪntə-vín] VI intervenir; (mediate) interponerse, mediar

intervening [ɪntə-víníŋ] ADJ interventor

intervention [ɪntə-vénʃən] N intervención f; (mediation) mediación f

interview [ɪ́ntə-vju] N entrevista f; (for entertainment) Sp interviú f; VT entrevistar; VI entrevistarse

intestinal [ɪntéstənl] ADJ intestinal; — **flora** flora intestinal f; — **obstruction** obstrucción intestinal f

intestine [ɪntéstɪn] ADJ & N intestino m; **small** — intestino delgado m; **large** — intestino grueso m

intimacy [ɪ́ntəməsi] N intimidad f

intimate[1] [ɪ́ntəmɪt] ADJ íntimo, entrañable; (knowledge) profundo

intimate[2] [ɪ́ntəmet] VT insinuar, dar a entender

intimation [ɪntəméʃən] N insinuación f

intimidate [ɪntɪ́mɪdet] VT intimidar, acobardar

into [ɪntu] PREP **she came — the room** entró en/a la habitación; **he put it — the box** lo metió en la caja; **he translated it — German** lo tradujo al alemán; **he ran — a tree** chocó contra un árbol; **it fell — oblivion** cayó en el olvido; **he went — medicine** entró a medicina; **I'm really — pop music** me ha dado por la música pop

intolerable [ɪntálə-əbəl] ADJ intolerable

intolerance [ɪntálə-əns] N intolerancia f

intolerant [ɪntálə-ənt] ADJ intolerante

intonation [ɪntənéʃən] N entonación f

intoxicate [ɪntáksɪket] VI/VT embriagar (also exhilarate); (poison) intoxicar

intoxication [ɪntaksɪkéʃən] N (drunkenness) embriaguez f; (poisoning) intoxicación f

intransigent [ɪntrǽnzɪdʒənt] ADJ intransigente

intransitive [ɪntrǽnzɪDɪv] ADJ intransitivo

intrauterine device [ɪntrəjúDə-ɪndɪváɪs] N dispositivo intrauterino m

intravenous [ɪntrəvínəs] ADJ intravenoso; — **feeding** alimentación intravenosa f

intrepid [ɪntrépɪd] ADJ intrépido

intricate [ɪ́ntrɪkɪt] ADJ intrincado

intrigue[1] [ɪntríg] VI/VT intrigar

intrigue[2] [ɪ́ntrig] N intriga f

intrinsic [ɪntrɪ́nzɪk] ADJ intrínseco

introduce [ɪntrədús] VT (put in, bring) introducir; (make acquainted) presentar

introduction [ɪntrədʌ́kʃən] N (of a book) introducción f; (of a custom or system) introducción f, implantación f; (to a person) presentación f

introspection [ɪntrəspékʃən] N introspección f

introvert [ɪ́ntrəvɚt] N introvertido -da mf

introverted [ɪ́ntrəvɚDɪd] ADJ introvertido

intrude [Intrúd] VI/VT interrumpir; (penetrate, of rock) penetrar

intruder [Intrúdə] N intruso -sa *mf*

intrusion [Intrúʒən] N (interruption) interrupción *f*; (penetration) intrusión *f*

intrusive [Intrúsɪv] ADJ (rock) intrusivo; (people) entrometido

intubation [Intjubéʃən] N intubación *f*

intuition [Intuíʃən] N intuición *f*

intuitive [IntúIDIv] ADJ intuitivo

inundate [ínəndet] VT inundar

invade [Invéd] VI/VT invadir

invader [Invédə] N invasor -ora *mf*

invalid¹ [ínvəlɪd] ADJ & N (infirm) inválido -da *mf*

invalid² [Invǽlɪd] ADJ (not valid) nulo

invaluable [Invǽljuəbəl] ADJ invalorable, inestimable

invariable [Invériəbəl] ADJ invariable

invariably [Invériəbli] ADV siempre

invasion [Invéʒən] N invasión *f*

invasive [Invésɪv] ADJ invasivo

invent [Invént] VT inventar

invention [Invénʃən] N (act of inventing, thing invented) invención *f*, invento *m*; (falsehood) invención *f*

inventive [Invéntɪv] ADJ inventivo

inventor [Invéntə] N inventor -ora *mf*

inventory [ínvəntɔri] N inventario *m*; VT inventariar

inverse [Invɚs] ADJ & N inverso *m*

inversion [Invɚʒən] N inversión *f*

invert [Invɚt] VT invertir

invest [Invést] VI/VT (money) invertir; (a rank upon someone) investir

investigate [Invéstɪget] VI/VT investigar, indagar

investigation [Investɪgéʃən] N investigación *f*

investigator [Invéstɪgedə] N investigador -ora *mf*

investment [Invéstmənt] N (of money) inversión *f*; (of rank) investidura *f*; **— broker** corredor -ora de bolsa *mf*

investor [Invéstə] N inversionista *mf*, inversor -ora *mf*

invigorate [Invígəret] VT vigorizar

invincible [Invínsəbəl] ADJ invencible

invisible [Invízəbəl] ADJ invisible

invitation [Invɪtéʃən] N invitación *f*

invite¹ [Inváɪt] VI/VT invitar; **to — trouble** buscarse problemas

invite² [ínvaɪt] N *fam* invitación *f*

inviting [InváɪDIŋ] ADJ atractivo, seductor

in vitro fertilization [Invítrofɚdʒɪzéʃən] N fertilización in vitro *f*

invocation [Invəkéʃən] N invocación *f*

invoice [ínvɔɪs] N factura *f*; VT facturar

invoke [Invók] VT invocar

involuntary [Invúləntɛri] ADJ involuntario

involve [Inválv] VT (take, last) suponer; **how much time will this —?** ¿cuánto tiempo supone esto?; (consist of, entail) consistir en, involucrar; **what does your work —?** ¿en qué consiste tu trabajo?; (be in question) ser cuestión de; **national security is —d!** ¡es una cuestión de seguridad nacional!; (implicate) implicar; **they tried to — her** trataron de implicarla; (wrapped up in) estar metido; **he's very —d in the family business** está muy metido en el negocio familiar; (have a liaison) enredarse; **she got —d with a married man** se enredó con un hombre casado

involved [Inválvd] ADJ complicado, enrevesado

involvement [Inválvmənt] N (in a crime) implicación *f*; (in a project) participación *f*; (with a person) relación *f*

inward [ínwəd] ADV hacia dentro; ADJ interior

iodide [áɪədaɪd] N yoduro *m*

iodine [áɪədaɪn] N yodo *m*

ion [áɪən] N ión *m*

ionize [áɪənaɪz] VT ionizar

ipecac syrup [ípɪkæksírəp] N jarabe de ipecacuana *m*

IPO [initial public offering] [áɪpíó] N oferta pública inicial *f*

IQ [intelligence quotient] [áɪkjú] N coeficiente de inteligencia *m*

Iran [Irán] N Irán *m*

Iranian [Irénɪən] ADJ & N iraní *mf*

Iraq [Irǽk] N Irak *m*

Iraqi [Irǽki] ADJ & N iraquí *mf*

irascible [Irǽsəbəl] ADJ irascible

irate [aɪrét] ADJ airado

ire [aɪr] N ira *f*

Ireland [áɪrlənd] N Irlanda *f*

iridescent [Irɪdésənt] ADJ iridiscente, tornasolado

iridium [Irídɪəm] N iridio *m*

iris [áɪrɪs] N (part of eye) iris *m*; (plant, flower) lirio *m*; (rainbow) arco iris *m*

Irish [áɪrɪʃ] ADJ irlandés; N (language) irlandés *m*; **the —** los irlandeses

irk [ɚk] VT fastidiar; **—ed** fastidiado

irksome [ɚksəm] ADJ engorroso, molesto

iron [áɪən] N (element, golf club) hierro *m*; (appliance) plancha *f*; **in —s** en grilletes; **— deficiency anemia** anemia por deficiencia de hierro *f*; **—work** herrajes *m pl*; **—works** fundición *f*; ADJ férreo, de hierro; VI/VT planchar; **to — out a difficulty** allanar una dificultad

ironic [aɪránɪk] ADJ irónico

ironing [áɪənɪŋ] N planchado *m*

irony [áɪrəni] N ironía *f*; (mockery) ironía *f*, sorna *f*

irradiate [Irédiet] VT irradiar

irrational [Irǽʃənl] ADJ irracional

irrefutable [ɪrɪfjúːbəl] ADJ irrefutable

irregular [ɪrégjələ-] ADJ irregular

irregularity [ɪrégjəlǽrɪɾi] N irregularidad f

irrelevant [ɪrélə-vənt] ADJ no pertinente; **your age is —** tu edad no viene al caso

irreparable [ɪrépərəbəl] ADJ irreparable

irreplaceable [ɪrɪplésəbəl] ADJ irreemplazable

irreproachable [ɪrɪprótʃəbəl] ADJ irreprochable

irresistible [ɪrɪzístəbəl] ADJ irresistible

irresponsibility [ɪrɪspɑnsəbɪlɪɾi] N irresponsabilidad f

irresponsible [ɪrɪspánsəbəl] ADJ irresponsable

irretrievable [ɪrɪtrívəbəl] ADJ irrecuperable

irreverent [ɪrévə-ənt] ADJ irreverente

irreversible [ɪrɪvɜ́rsəbəl] ADJ irreversible

irrevocable [ɪrévəkəbəl] ADJ irrevocable

irrigate [ɪ́rɪget] VI/VT (a garden) irrigar, regar; (the eyes) irrigar

irrigation [ɪrɪgéʃən] N riego m, irrigación f; **— ditch** acequia f

irritable [ɪ́rɪɾəbəl] ADJ irritable, colérico

irritate [ɪ́rɪtet] VT irritar

irritating [ɪ́rɪteɾɪŋ] ADJ irritante

irritation [ɪrɪtéʃən] N irritación f

IRS [Internal Revenue Service] [áɪáːrés] N Hacienda f

is [ɪz] see be

Islam [ízlɑm] N islamismo m, islam m

Islamic [ɪzlámɪk] ADJ islámico

island [áɪlənd] N isla f

islander [áɪləndə-] N isleño -ña mf

isle [aɪl] N isla f

isobar [áɪsəbɑr] N isobara f

isolate [áɪsəlet] VT aislar

isolation [aɪsəléʃən] N aislamiento m, marginación f

isolationism [aɪsəléʃənɪzəm] N aislacionismo m

isometric [aɪsəmétrɪk] ADJ isométrico

isotope [áɪsətop] N isótopo m, isotopo m

Israel [ízriəl] N Israel m

Israeli [ɪzréli] ADJ & N israelí mf

issue [íʃu] N (of printed matter) tirada f; (of stock, bonds) emisión f; (copy of a magazine) número m, entrega f; (of a fluid) flujo m; (problem) problema m, tema m; (progeny) descendencia f; **he's got —s** es muy acomplejado; **to take — with** discrepar de; VT (written material) publicar; (a decree) promulgar; (a permit, document) expedir; (shares) emitir; (to flow) brotar; (to come out of) salir de; (to descend from) descender de

isthmus [ísməs] N istmo m

it [ɪt] PRON **— all started yesterday** todo empezó ayer; **— is necessary** es necesario; **— is raining** llueve, está lloviendo; **— is said that** se dice que; **— is two o'clock** son las dos; **— was broken** estaba roto; **who is —?** ¿quién es? **if — weren't five o'clock** si no fueran las cinco; **I saw —** lo/la vi; **he**

talked about — habló de eso; **what time is — ?** ¿qué hora es? **how is — going?** ¿qué tal? **I don't get —** no entiendo; **you're —!** ¡tú la quedas! / ¡tú la traes!

IT [information technology] [áɪtí] N informática f

Italian [ɪtǽljən] ADJ & N italiano -na mf

italic [ɪtǽlɪk] ADJ itálico; N **—s** letra bastardilla/ cursiva f

italicize [ɪtǽlɪsaɪz] VT poner en bastardilla/ cursiva

Italy [ɪdli] N Italia f

itch [ɪtʃ] VI/VT picar; **to be —ing to** tener ganas de; N (sensation) comezón f, picazón f; (longing) ansia f

itching [ɪ́tʃɪŋ] N comezón f, picazón f

itchy [ɪ́tʃi] ADJ que pica; **it feels —** me pica

item [áɪɾəm] N (piece of news) artículo m; (topic of gossip) tema de conversación m; (unit) ítem m; (couple) pareja f

itemize [áɪɾəmaɪz] VT (list) enumerar; (break down) desglosar; **—d invoice** factura detallada f

itinerant [aɪtínə-ənt] ADJ itinerante, ambulante

itinerary [aɪtínə-reri] N (schedule) itinerario m; (guidebook) guía de viajeros f

its [ɪts] POSS ADJ su/sus, de él, de ella, de ello

itself [ɪtséłf] PRON **this story wrote —** esta historia se escribió sola; **the bike was standing by —** la bici estaba parada sola; **the dog bit —** el perro se mordió [a sí mismo]; **the fox found — a hole** la zorra se encontró una guarida

IUD [intrauterine device] [áɪjúdí] N DIU m

IV [intravenous] [áɪví] ADJ intravenoso

Ivorian [aɪvórian] ADJ & N marfileño -ña mf

ivory [áɪvri] N marfil m; **— tower** torre de marfil f

Ivory Coast [áɪvrikóst] N Costa de Marfil f

ivy [áɪvi] N hiedra f

Jj

jab [dʒæb] VI/VT (hit) golpear; (hit with elbow) codear; N (blow) golpe m; (blow with elbow) codazo m; (in boxing) jab m, puñetazo directo m

jabber [dʒǽbə-] VI (unintelligibly) farfullar; (incessantly) charlotear; N (unintelligible) farfulla f; charloteo m

jack [dʒæk] N (tool) gato m; (card) sota f; (plug-in) hembra f, toma f; (flag) bandera de proa f; **—ass** asno m, burro m (also person); **—hammer** martillo neumático m; **—knife** navaja f; **— of all trades** hombre orquesta

m; **—pot** premio gordo *m*; **—rabbit** liebre
americana *f*; **you don't know** — no sabes ni
un comino; VT **to — up** (a car) alzar con gato;
(prices) subir
jackal [dʒǽkəl] N chacal *m*
jacket [dʒǽkɪt] N (clothing) chaqueta *f*; (of a
book) forro *m*; (of a potato) piel *f*
jade [dʒed] N jade *m*
jaded [dʒédɪd] ADJ (disenchanted) de vuelta;
(sated) hastiado
jagged [dʒǽgɪd] ADJ recortado, desigual
jaguar [dʒǽgwar] N jaguar *m*
jail [dʒel] N cárcel *f*; **—break** fuga *f*; VT
encarcelar
jailer [dʒélə] N carcelero -ra *mf*
jalopy [dʒəlápi] N cacharro *m*
jam [dʒæm] VT (stuff) embutir; (block) atestar;
(immobilize) trabar; (make unworkable)
obstruir, atascar, atorar; (stop radio signals)
interferir; VI (become stuck or unworkable)
atascarse; (crowd in) apiñarse; **to — on the
brakes** frenar de golpe; **to — one's fingers**
pillarse los dedos; N (jelly) mermelada *f*,
dulce *m*; (difficult situation) aprieto *m*;
(traffic) embotellamiento *m*; **— session**
jam *m*
Jamaica [dʒəmékə] N Jamaica *f*
Jamaican [dʒəmékən] ADJ & N jamaicano -na *mf*,
jamaiquino -na *mf*
janitor [dʒǽnɪdə] N conserje *m*
January [dʒǽnjueri] N enero *m*
Japan [dʒəpǽn] N Japón *m*
Japanese [dʒæpəníz] ADJ & N japonés -esa *mf*
jar [dʒar] VI/VT (shake) sacudir[se]; (clash) chocar;
to — one's nerves ponerle a uno los nervios
de punta; N (container) tarro *m*, frasco *m*,
pote *m*; (large earthen container) tinaja *f*;
(collision) choque *m*; (shake) sacudida *f*
jargon [dʒárgən] N jerga *f*
jasmine [dʒǽzmɪn] N jazmín *m*
jasper [dʒǽspə] N jaspe *m*
jaundice [dʒɔ́ndɪs] N ictericia *f*
jaundiced [dʒɔ́ndɪst] ADJ ictérico
jaunt [dʒɔnt] N excursión *f*; VI pasear
javelin [dʒǽvlɪn] N jabalina *f*
jaw [dʒɔ] N (of animal) quijada *f*; (of human)
mandíbula *f*; (of mammals) fauces *f pl*;
—bone mandíbula *f*, maxilar *m*
jay [dʒe] N arrendajo *m*
jazz [dʒæz] N jazz *m*; VI **to — up** animar
jealous [dʒéləs] ADJ (possessive) celoso; (envious)
envidioso; (protective) protector
jealousy [dʒéləsi] N celos *m pl*
jeans [dʒinz] N jeans *m pl*, vaqueros *m pl*
jeer [dʒir] VI/VT (mock) mofarse [de], burlarse
[de]; (boo) abuchear, befar; N (act of mockery)
mofa *f*, burla *f*; (boos) abucheo *m*, befa *f*
jelly [dʒéli] N jalea *f*; **—fish** medusa *f*
jeopardize [dʒépədaɪz] VT comprometer, poner

en peligro
jeopardy [dʒépədi] ADV LOC **in** — en peligro
jerk [dʒɚk] N (quick pull) tirón *m*; (muscular
contraction) espasmo *m*; (idiot) *pej* pelmazo
m; VI/VT tironear; **to — around** manipular
jerky [dʒɚki] ADJ espasmódico; N tasajo *m*
jersey [dʒɚzi] N jersey *m*
jest [dʒest] N broma *f*, chanza *f*; **in** — en broma;
VI bromear
jester [dʒéstə] N bufón *m*
Jesuit [dʒézuɪt] N jesuita *m*
jet [dʒet] N (stream) chorro *m*; (spout) surtidor *m*;
(stone) azabache *m*; **—[air]plane** avión a
reacción *m*; **— engine** motor a reacción *m*;
— lag jet lag *m*; **—liner** avión a reacción de
pasajeros *m*; **— propulsion** propulsión a
chorro *f*; **— set** jet *m*, jet-set *m*; **— stream** (of
air) corriente en chorro *f*; (of a jet) chorro *m*;
ADJ **—black** negro como el azabache; VI
(stream out) salir a chorros; (travel) volar en
avión a reacción; VT (spew out) lanzar a
chorros; (transport) transportar en avión a
reacción
jettison [dʒédɪsən] VT echar por la borda
Jew [dʒu] N judío -a *mf*
jewel [dʒúəl] N (ornament, prized person) joya *f*,
alhaja *f*; (stone) gema *f*; (watch jewel) rubí *m*;
— box joyero *m*
jeweler [dʒúələ] N joyero -ra *mf*; **—'s shop**
joyería *f*
jewelry [dʒúəlri] N joyas *f pl*, alhajas *f pl*; **— box**
alhajero *m*; **— store** joyería *f*
Jewish [dʒúɪʃ] ADJ judío
jiffy [dʒífi] ADV LOC **in a** — en un santiamén
jig [dʒɪg] N (dance) giga *f*; **—saw** sierra de vaivén
f; **—saw puzzle** rompecabezas *m sg*; VI
(dance) bailotear
jiggle [dʒígəl] VI/VT zangolotear[se],
zarandear[se]; N zangoloteo *m*, zarandeo *m*
jilt [dʒɪlt] VT dejar plantado
jingle [dʒíŋgəl] VI tintinear; VT agitar; N retintín
m; (short song) jingle *m*
jinx [dʒɪŋks] N persona que trae mala suerte *f*; VT
traer mala suerte
job [dʒab] N (task) tarea *f*; (position) trabajo *m*,
empleo *m*; (theft) golpe *m*; **to be out of a** —
estar sin trabajo; *Sp* estar en [el] paro; **by the
— a destajo; **to do a good** — hacer buen
trabajo; VI trabajar a destajo; **on-the-—
training** capacitación en el lugar de trabajo *f*
jobber [dʒábə] N (day-worker) trabajador -ora a
destajo *mf*; (wholesaler) vendedor -ora
mayorista *mf*
jobless [dʒáblɪs] ADJ sin trabajo; *Sp* en paro
jock [dʒak] N deportista *mf*; **— [strap]**
suspensorio *m*
jockey [dʒáki] N jockey *m*; VI **to — for position**
disputarse la posición
jocular [dʒákjələ] ADJ jocoso

jog [dʒag] VI (run) correr, trotar; VT (refresh) refrescar; N trote m; **to go for a —** salir a correr

jogging [dʒágɪŋ] N jogging m, footing m

join [dʒɔɪn] VI/VT juntar[se]; (pipes) acoplar[se], unir[se]; (bones) articular[se]; (a club) asociarse [a]; (the navy, etc.) alistarse [en]

joint [dʒɔɪnt] N (point of contact) juntura f, junta f; (connection between bones) articulación f, coyuntura f; (nodule on a plant) nudo m; (dive, bar) antro m; **out of —** descoyuntado; ADJ (shared) común; **— account** cuenta conjunta f; **— action** acción colectiva f; **— custody** custodia compartida f; **— owner** copropietario -ria mf; **— session** sesión plena f; **— venture** joint venture m

jointly [dʒɔɪntli] ADV conjuntamente

joke [dʒok] N broma f, chiste m; VI bromear

joker [dʒókə-] N (person who jokes) bromista mf, guasón -ona mf; (card) comodín m

jokingly [dʒókɪŋli] ADV en broma

jolly [dʒáli] ADJ jovial

jolt [dʒolt] N sacudida f; VT sacudir; **to — along** avanzar a los tumbos

Jordan [dʒórdn̩] N Jordania f

Jordanian [dʒɔrdénian] ADJ & N jordano -na mf

jostle [dʒásəl] VI/VT codear[se], dar empujones [a]; N empujón m

jot [dʒat] VT **to — down** apuntar; N pizca f

journal [dʒ$-nl] N (diary) diario m; (periodical) revista f; (logbook) cuaderno de bitácora m

journalism [dʒ$-nəlɪzəm] N periodismo m

journalist [dʒ$-nəlɪst] N periodista mf

journalistic [dʒ$-nəlístɪk] ADJ periodístico

journey [dʒ$-ni] N viaje m; VI viajar

joust [dʒaʊst] N justa f

jowl [dʒaʊl] N carrillo m, moflete m

joy [dʒɔɪ] N (delight) alegría f, regocijo m, alborozo m; (source of delight) deleite m; **—ride** paseo en coche robado m; **—stick** joystick m, palanca de mando f

joyful [dʒɔɪfəl] ADJ alborozado

joyous [dʒɔɪəs] ADJ jubiloso, alegre

jubilant [dʒúbələnt] ADJ jubiloso

jubilee [dʒúbəli] N jubileo m

Judaism [dʒúdiɪzəm] N judaísmo m

judge [dʒʌdʒ] N juez -eza mf; (in tennis) juez -eza de silla mf; **to be a good — of character** saber juzgar a la gente; VI/VT juzgar; (estimate) calcular

judgment [dʒʌdʒmənt] N juicio m; (in court) fallo m; **— day** día del juicio final m

judicial [dʒudíʃəl] ADJ judicial

judicious [dʒudíʃəs] ADJ juicioso, sensato

judo [dʒúdo] N judo m, yudo m

jug [dʒʌg] N (pitcher) jarro m, jarra f; (storage jar) pote m

juggle [dʒʌ́gəl] VI/VT hacer juegos malabares [con], hacer malabarismo [con]; **to — the accounts** manipular las cuentas

juggler [dʒʌ́glə-] N malabarista mf

jugular [dʒʌ́gjələ-] N yugular f

juice [dʒus] N jugo m; (fruit only) Sp zumo m

juicer [dʒúsə-] N exprimidor m

juicy [dʒúsi] ADJ jugoso; **a — story** un cuento sabroso

juke [dʒuk] N (in sports) amague m, finta f; **—box** juke-box m

July [dʒulái] N julio m

jumble [dʒʌ́mbəl] VI/VT revolver[se] m; N revoltijo m

jumbo [dʒʌ́mbo] ADJ jumbo, gigantesco; **— jet** jumbo m

jump [dʒʌmp] VI (spring) saltar; (increase, as temperature, prices) dar un salto; VT (capture in checkers) comer; (ride a horse over barrier) hacer saltar; (mug) asaltar; (cross a river, mountains, etc.) salvar; **to — at** abalanzarse sobre; **to — over** saltar; **to —-start** hacer un puente; **to — the track** descarrilarse; **to — to conclusions** hacer deducciones precipitadas; N salto m; (in prices) subida repentina f; **—rope** cuerda de saltar f; **— shot** tiro en suspensión m; **—suit** mono m

jumper [dʒʌ́mpə-] N (person who jumps) saltador -ora mf; (dress) jumper m; Sp pichi m; **— cable** puente m

jumpy [dʒʌ́mpi] ADJ nervioso, asustadizo

junction [dʒʌ́ŋkʃən] N (act or state of joining) unión f; (joining of two rivers) confluencia f; (of two railways) empalme m, entronque m; (of roads) cruce m

juncture [dʒʌ́ŋktʃə-] N (point where joined) juntura f; **at this —** en esta coyuntura

June [dʒun] N junio m

jungle [dʒʌ́ŋgəl] N selva f, jungla f; **the law of the —** la ley de la selva

junior [dʒúnjə-] ADJ (younger) menor; (more recent) más nuevo, de menos antigüedad; **— college** institución para los dos primeros años de la licenciatura f; **John Smith Jr.** John Smith, hijo; N estudiante del tercer año mf

juniper [dʒúnəpə-] N enebro m

junk [dʒʌŋk] N (useless articles) trastos viejos m pl; (metal) chatarra f; (Chinese boat) junco m; **— dealer** chatarrero -ra mf; **— food** comida basura f, porquerías f pl; **— mail** publicidad por correo f; **— e-mail** correo electrónico basura m; **—yard** chatarrería f; VT desechar, echar a la basura

junkie [dʒʌ́ŋki] N fam drogata mf, drogota mf

jurisdiction [dʒʊrɪsdíkʃən] N jurisdicción f

jurisprudence [dʒʊrɪsprúdn̩s] N jurisprudencia f

juror [dʒúrə-] N miembro de un jurado m, jurado -da mf

jury [dʒúri] N jurado m; **— box** banco de jurado m; VT **to —-rig** chapucear

just [dʒʌst] ADJ justo; ADV (exactly) exactamente,
precisamente; (only) solo; **— like that** *Am*
así nomás; **he — left** acaba de salir; **she is —
a little girl** no es más que una niña; **you'll
— have to wait** tendrás que esperar; **—
barely** apenas; **the meeting is — starting**
la reunión apenas comienza; **that is — what
I wanted to talk to you about**
precisamente de eso te quería hablar

justice [dʒʌstɪs] N (fairness) justicia *f*; (judge)
juez -eza *mf*; **to bring to —** enjuiciar; **the
painting doesn't do him —** el retrato no le
favorece

justification [dʒʌstəfɪkéʃən] N justificación *f*

justify [dʒʌstəfaɪ] VT justificar

jut [dʒʌt] VI sobresalir, proyectarse

juvenile [dʒúvənaɪl] ADJ juvenil; **— delinquent**
delincuente juvenil *mf*

juxtapose [dʒʌkstəpoz] VT yuxtaponer

Kk

kangaroo [kæŋgərú] N canguro *m*

karat, carat [kérət] N quilate *m*

kayak [káɪæk] N kayak *m*

Kazak, Kazakh [kəzæk] ADJ & N kazako -ka *mf*

Kazakhstan [kazákstan] N Kazajstán *m*

keel [kil] N quilla *f*; VI/VT volcar[se]; **to — over**
(ship) volcar[se]; (person) caer de cabeza,
desplomarse

keen [kin] ADJ (edge) afilado; (perception) fino;
(mind) agudo, penetrante

keenness [kínnɪs] N (of a blade) lo afilado; (of
perception) fineza *f*; (of mind) agudeza *f*

keep [kip] VI (continue) seguir; (not spoil)
aguantar; VT (retain) guardar; (maintain)
mantener; (employ) tener; (look after) cuidar;
to — a diary llevar un diario; **to — a secret**
guardar un secreto; **to — at it** persistir; **to —
away** mantener[se] alejado; **to — back** (stay
away) tener a raya; (restrain) contener; **to —
bad company** andar en mala compañía; **to
— from** (prevent) impedir; (protect)
proteger contra; **to — [on] talking** seguir
hablando; **to — the door open** mantener la
puerta abierta; **to — off the grass** no pisar el
césped; **to — up** (perform as well) seguir el
tren; (stay informed) mantenerse al tanto; **to
— one's hands off** no tocar; **to — someone
posted** mantener al corriente a alguien; **to —
quiet** estarse callado; **to — to the right**
mantenerse a la derecha; **to — track of** (do
accounts) llevar la cuenta de; (consider) no
perder de vista; **to — watch** vigilar; **he —s a
maid** tiene una criada; **she kept me on the

phone me [re]tuvo en el teléfono; N **for —s**
(forever) para siempre; (for real) en serio;
—sake recuerdo *m*

keeper [kípə-] N (of people) guardián *m*; (of
things) custodio *m*

keeping [kípɪŋ] N custodia *f*; **in — with** en
armonía con

keg [kɛg] N barril *m*

Kegel exercises [kégəl ɛksə-saɪzɪz] N ejercicios
de Kegel *m pl*

kennel [kénl] N residencia de perros *f*

Kenya [kénjə] N Kenia *f*

Kenyan [kénjən] ADJ & N keniata *mf*

kept [kɛpt] *see* keep

kernel [kɜ́nl] N (seed) semilla *f*, grano *m*;
(essence) meollo *m*

kerosene [kérəsin] N queroseno *m*

kestrel [késtrəl] N cernícalo *m*

ketchup [kétʃəp] N salsa de tomate *f*, cátsup *m*

kettle [kédl] N caldera *f*, hervidor *m*; (for tea)
tetera *f*; **—drum** tímpano *m*, timbal *m*;
that's another — of fish es harina de otro
costal

key [ki] N (for locks) llave *f*; (secret, book of
answers) clave *f*; (for winding) clavija *f*; (on
keyboard) tecla *f*; (island) cayo *m*; (music)
clave *f*; **—board** teclado *m*; **—hole** ojo de la
cerradura *m*; **— indicator** indicador clave *m*;
—note tónica *f*; **—note address** discurso de
apertura *m*; **—pad** teclado numérico *m*;
—ring llavero *m*; **— signature** armadura *f*;
—stone piedra angular *f*; **—stroke**
pulsación [de la tecla] *f*; **—word** palabra clave
f; **—word search** búsqueda por palabra
clave *f*; **to sing on —** cantar a tono; ADJ
clave; VT (scratch) rayar; **to be —ed up** estar
sobreexcitado

kg [kíləgræm] *see* kilogram

khaki [kǽki] N kaki *m*, caqui *m*

kick [kɪk] VI/VT (person) patear; (horse) dar coces
[a], cocear; VI (gun) dar un culatazo,
retroceder; **to — around** (discuss) discutir;
(to mistreat) dar por la cabeza; **to — at** dar
patadas; **to — out** echar a patadas; **to —start**
arrancar; **to — the bucket** estirar la pata; **to
— up a lot of dust** levantar una polvareda;
to — a habit dejar un vicio; N (by a person)
patada *f*, puntapié *m*; (by a soccer player)
patada *f*; (of a horse) coz *f*; *Am* patada *f*; (of a
gun) culatazo *m*; (in the air) pataleo *m*; **this
whisky has a —** este whisky es fuerte; **I get
a — out of swimming** me encanta nadar;
—back comisión ilegal *f*; *Mex* mordida *f*;
—off (football) saque de inicio *m*; (soccer)
saque inicial *m*; **—stand** soporte *m*

kid [kɪd] N (young goat) cabrito *m*, chivo *m*;
(leather) cabritilla *f*; (child) niño -ña *mf*;
(young person) chico -ca *mf*; **— stuff** juego de
niños *m*; VI bromear, embromar, tomar el

pelo
kidnap [kídnæp] VT secuestrar, raptar
kidnapper [kídnæpə-] N secuestrador -ora *mf*
kidnapping [kídnæpıŋ] N secuestro *m*, rapto *m*
kidney [kídni] N riñón *m*; — **bean** judía *f*; —
failure insuficiencia renal *f*; — **stone**
cálculo renal *m*
kill [kɪl] VI/VT matar; (drink completely)
terminar; (turn off) apagar; **that comedian
—s me** ese cómico me mata de risa; N (animal
killed) caza *f*; (slaughter) matanza *f*; —**joy**
aguafiestas *mf sg*
killer [kílə-] N asesino -na *mf*; — **bee** abeja
asesina *f*; — **whale** orca *f*; **a** — **game** un
partidazo
killing [kílıŋ] N (slaughter) matanza *f*; (murder)
asesinato *m*; (animal killed) caza *f*; **to make a**
— llenarse de oro
kilo [kílo] N kilo *m*, quilo *m*
kilobyte [kíləbaɪt] N kilobyte *m*
kilogram [kíləgræm] N kilogramo *m*
kilometer [kɪlámɪdə-] N kilómetro *m*
kilowatt [kíləwat] N kilovatio *m*; —**-hour**
kilovatio-hora *f*
kin [kɪn] N parentela *f*, parientes *m pl*; —**sman**
pariente *m*; —**swoman** parienta *f*; **next of**
— deudos *m pl*
kind [kaɪnd] ADJ (benevolent) bondadoso,
bueno; (words) amable; **to be — to animals**
ser cariñoso con los animales; —**hearted** de
buen corazón; — **of tired** algo cansado; N
clase *f*, tipo *m*, género *m*; **to pay in** —
(without money) pagar en especie; (retaliate)
pagar con la misma moneda
kindergarten [kíndə-gɑrtŋ] N jardín infantil /
de niños *m*; *Sp* parvulario *m*
kindle [kíndl] VT (fire) prender; (interest)
despertar, provocar; VI encenderse
kindling [kíndlıŋ] N leña ligera *f*, astillas *f pl*
kindly [káɪndli] ADJ bondadoso, bueno; ADV
(with kindness) amablemente; (please) por
favor; **we thank you** — le agradecemos
mucho; **not to take** — **to criticism** no
aceptar de buen grado las críticas
kindness [káɪndnıs] N (state) bondad *f*,
amabilidad *f*; (act) favor *m*
kindred [kíndrɪd] ADJ emparentado; — **spirits**
espíritus afines *m pl*, almas gemelas *f pl*
kinesiology [kənɪziάlədʒi] N quinesiología *f*
kinesthesia [kɪnɪsθíʒə] N cinestesia *f*
king [kɪŋ] N rey *m* (also in chess, cards); (in
checkers) dama *f*; —**fisher** martín pescador
m; —**pin** (in a mechanism) pivote central *m*;
(in bowling) bolo central *m*; (person) figura
central *f*; ADJ —**-sized** extra grande
kingdom [kíŋdəm] N reino *m*
kingly [kíŋli] ADJ real
kink [kɪŋk] N (bend) doblez *m*; (pain) tortícolis *f*
kinky [kíŋki] ADJ crespo

kinship [kínʃıp] N (family connection)
parentesco *m*; (likeness) afinidad *f*
kiosk [kíask] N quiosco *m*
Kiribati [kɪrəbάdi] N Kiribati *m*
kiss [kɪs] VI/VT besar[se]; N beso *m*
kit [kɪt] N (of tools) caja *f*; (of first aid) botiquín
m; (of sewing notions) costurero *m*
kitchen [kítʃın] N cocina *f*; —**ware** utensilios de
cocina *m pl*
kite [kaɪt] N (toy) cometa *f*; (bird) milano *m*
kitten [kítņ] N gatito *m*
kitty [kídi] N (young cat) gatito *m*, minino *m*;
(petty cash) caja chica *f*, fondo *m*
kleptomania [klɛptəméniə] N cleptomanía *f*
kleptomaniac [klɛptəméniæk] N cleptómano
-na *mf*
knack [næk] N buena mano *f*, maña *f*; **once you
get the** — una vez que le agarras la vuelta/
onda
knapsack [nǽpsæk] N mochila *f*
knave [nev] N pícaro *m*; (in cards) sota *f*
knead [nid] VT amasar, sobar
knee [ni] N rodilla *f*; —**cap** rótula *f*; —**-deep**
hasta las rodillas; —**-jerk liberal** liberal
fanático *m*; —**-jerk reaction** reacción
visceral *f*; VT dar un rodillazo
kneel [niɫ] VI arrodillarse
knell [nɛl] N doble *m*; VI doblar
knelt [nɛlt] *see* kneel
knew [nu] *see* know
knickknack [níknæk] N chuchería *f*, baratija *f*
knife [naɪf] N cuchillo *m*; (big) cuchilla *f*;
(folding) navaja *f*; (for carving) trinchante *m*;
VT acuchillar; **at** —**point** a punta de cuchillo
knight [naɪt] N caballero *m*; (in chess) caballo *m*;
— **errant** caballero andante *m*; VT armar
caballero
knighthood [náɪthʊd] N (all knights) caballería
f; (title) orden de la caballería *f*
knit [nɪt] VI/VT tejer; **to** — **one's brow** fruncir el
entrecejo / el ceño
knitting [nídıŋ] N tejido *m*; — **needle** aguja de
punto *f*
knob [nab] N (on a door) pomo *m*, perilla *f*,
tirador *m*; (protuberance) protuberancia *f*
knock [nak] VI (hit) golpear; (precombust)
golpetear; (call at the door) llamar, tocar; VT
(criticize) criticar; **to** — **a hole in the wall**
hacer un agujero en la pared a golpes; **to** —
down derribar, echar abajo, tumbar; **to** —
off (stop working) terminar; (reduce) rebajar;
(make fall) tirar; (kill) liquidar; — **it off!**
¡basta! **to** — **into** golpearse contra; **to** — **out**
noquear; **to** — **over** voltear, revolcar; N
(pounding) golpe *m*, toque *m*; (criticism)
crítica *f*; (in a motor) golpeteo *m*; —**out**
(boxing) nocaut *m*; (attractive person) bomba
f; ADJ —**-kneed** patizambo, zambo
knocker [nákə-] N llamador *m*, aldaba *f*

knoll [noɫ] N morro *m*, loma *f*

knot [nɑt] N nudo *m* (also in wood, unit of speed); (of people) grupo *m*; (swelling) chichón *m*; VI/VT anudar[se]

knotty [nádi] ADJ (full of knots) nudoso; (difficult) dificultoso, enredado

know [no] VI/VT (to have knowledge of, to know how to) saber; VT (to be acquainted with, have sexual intercourse with) conocer; (to recognize) reconocer; (distinguish) distinguir; **to — how to swim** saber nadar; **to — of** estar enterado de; N **to be in the —** estar al tanto; **— -how** pericia *f*; **— -it-all** sabelotodo *mf*

knowing [nóɪŋ] ADJ (complicitous) cómplice; (astute) astuto

knowingly [nóɪŋli] ADV a sabiendas

knowledge [nálɪʤ] N (awareness) conocimiento *m*; (information known) saber *m*, conocimientos *m pl*; **not to my —** no que yo sepa

known [non] ADJ **little —** poco conocido; **well — bien** conocido; **he's — for his cooking** se le conoce por su cocina; **the truth wasn't — until last year** no se supo la verdad hasta el año pasado

known [non] *see* know

knuckle [nákəɫ] N nudillo *m*; **—ball** bola de nudillos *f*; **—head** tarambana *mf*; VI **to — down** arremangarse, aplicarse con empeño; **to — under** someterse

Korea [kɔríə] N Corea *f*

Korean [kɔríən] ADJ & N coreano -na *mf*

kosher [kóʃə] ADJ kosher

Kuwait [kuwét] N Kuwait *m*

Kuwaiti [kuwébi] ADJ & N kuwaití *m*

Kyrgyzstan [kírgistan] N Kirguistán *m*

Ll

lab [læb] *see* laboratory

label [lébəɫ] N (sticker) etiqueta *f*, rótulo *m*; (characterization) calificativo *m*; (brand) marca *f*; (of recording companies) sello *m*; VT etiquetar, rotular

labor [lébə] N trabajo *m*, labor *f*; (body of workers) mano de obra *f*; (working class) clase obrera *f*; (uterine contractions) trabajo de parto *m*; **—-intensive** que requiere mucha mano de obra; **— pains** dolores de parto *m pl*; **— union** sindicato *m*; **to be in —** estar de parto; ADJ laboral; VI (work) trabajar; (dedicate oneself) afanarse; **to — under a disadvantage** sufrir una desventaja

laboratory [læbrətɔri] N laboratorio *m*

laborer [lébərə] N jornalero -ra *mf*; (unskilled)

peón -ona *mf*

laborious [ləbóriəs] ADJ (industrious) laborioso; (difficult) trabajoso

labrador [læbrədɔr] N (dog) labrador *m*

labyrinth [læbərɪnθ] N laberinto *m*

lace [les] N (cloth) encaje *m*; (cord) cordón *m*; VT (to adorn with lace) bordar con encaje; (to insert laces into) poner cordones a; (to spike) echar alcohol; VI atarse

lack [læk] N falta *f*, carencia *f*; VI/VT carecer de, faltarle a uno; **he —s courage** le falta valentía; **— luster** mediocre

lackey [læki] N lacayo *m*

lacking [lækɪŋ] ADJ (deficient) deficiente; **good bars are — in this town** faltan buenos bares en este pueblo; **— in** falto de, carente de

laconic [ləkánɪk] ADJ lacónico

lacquer [lékə] N laca *f*; VT lacar, laquear

lactation [læktéʃən] N lactancia *f*

lactic acid [læktɪkǽsɪd] N ácido láctico *m*

lactose [læktos] N lactosa *f*; **— intolerance** intolerancia a la lactosa *f*

ladder [lædə] N escalera *f*

laden [lédn] ADJ cargado

ladle [lédl] N cucharón *m*, cazo *m*; VT servir con cucharón

lady [lédi] N señora *f*, dama *f*; **—bug** mariquita *f*; **—like** muy fina; **—love** amada *f*; **ladies' room** *Sp* aseo de damas *m*, *Am* servicio de damas *m*

lag [læg] VI (fall behind) quedarse atrás, rezagarse; (flag) disminuir; N retardo *m*, retraso *m*

lagoon [ləgún] N laguna *f*

laid [led] *see* lay

laid-back [ledbǽk] ADJ apacible, tranquilo

lain [len] *see* lie 'estar situado'

lair [lɛr] N guarida *f*

lake [lek] N lago *m*

lamb [læm] N cordero *m*; (yearling) borrego *m*

lame [lem] ADJ cojo; *Am* rengo; **—brained** idiota; **— duck** funcionario -ria cesante *mf*; **— excuse** pretexto tonto *m*; VT dejar cojo

lament [ləmént] N lamento *m*; VI lamentar[se]; VT llorar

lamentable [ləméntəbəɫ] ADJ lamentable

lamentation [læməntéʃən] N lamentación *f*, lamento *m*

laminate [læmənet] VT laminar

lamp [læmp] N lámpara *f*; (on a street) farol *m*; **—post** farol *m*; **—shade** pantalla *f*

LAN [local area network] [læn] N red [de área] local *f*

lance [læns] N lanza *f*; (lancet) lanceta *f*; VT lancear; (a wound) abrir con una lanceta

lancet [lænsɪt] N lanceta *f*

land [lænd] N tierra *f*; (lot) terreno *m*; (country) país *m*, tierra *f*; **—fill** vertedero *m*; **— grant university** universidad con terrenos concedidos por el estado f; —**lady** casera f, propietaria f; —**lord** casero m, propietario m; —**mark** (marker) hito m, mojón m; (historical) hito m; —**mine** mina f; —**owner** hacendado -da mf; —**scape** (terrain) paisaje m; (in printing) orientación horizontal f; —**scape architecture** paisajismo m; —**slide** (mass of land) derrumbe m, desprendimiento m; (election) victoria aplastante f; — **use** ordenamiento territorial m; VI/VT (a ship) atracar; (an airplane) aterrizar; **you'll — in jail** terminarás en la cárcel; VT (a fish) Sp coger; Am pescar; (a job) conseguir

landing [lǽndɪŋ] N (of a ship) desembarco m; (of cargo) desembarque m; (of an airplane) aterrizaje m; (place) desembarcadero m; (on stairs) descansillo m; — **field** campo de aterrizaje m; — **gear** tren de aterrizaje m; — **strip** pista de aterrizaje f

lane [len] N (country road) sendero m; (road division) carril m; (for ships) ruta f

language [lǽŋgwɪdʒ] N lengua f, idioma m; (faculty of speech, computer code) lenguaje m

languid [lǽŋgwɪd] ADJ lánguido

languish [lǽŋgwɪʃ] VI languidecer

languor [lǽŋgɚ] N languidez f

lanky [lǽŋki] ADJ larguirucho, zancudo

lanolin [lǽnəlɪn] N lanolina f

lantern [lǽntɚn] N farol m; (of a lighthouse) faro m, linterna f

Laos [léas] N Laos m

Laotian [léoʃən] ADJ & N laosiano -na mf

lap [læp] N (part of body) regazo m; (part of a race) vuelta f; —**dog** perro faldero m; —**top computer** Am computadora portátil f, Sp ordenador portátil m; **to live in the — of luxury** vivir en la abundancia; VI/VT lamer

lapel [ləpɛ́l] N solapa f

lapidary [lǽpɪdɛri] ADJ & N lapidario -ria mf

lapse [læps] N (period of time) lapso m; (linguistic error) lapsus m; (defect in memory) fallo m; (fall) caída f; (termination) caducidad f; VI (fall) caer; (decline) decaer; (end) caducar, vencer

larceny [lársəni] N latrocinio m, hurto m

lard [lɑrd] N manteca f; VT enmantecar; (with bacon) mechar

large [lɑrdʒ] ADJ grande; —**-scale** a gran escala; **a — company** una gran compañía / una compañía grande; **at —** (not in jail) suelto, libre; N tamaño grande m

largely [lárdʒli] ADV (in the greatest number) en su mayoría; (to the greatest degree) en gran parte

lariat [lǽriət] N reata f

lark [lɑrk] N (bird) alondra f; (bit of fun) diversión f; **to go on a —** ir de jarana

larva [lárvə] N larva f

laryngeal [ləríndʒəl] ADJ laríngeo; — **angina** angina laríngea f

laryngitis [lærəndʒáɪDɪs] N laringitis f

larynx [lǽrɪŋks] N laringe f

lascivious [ləsívíəs] ADJ lascivo

laser [lézɚ] N láser m; — **beam** rayo láser m; — **printer** impresora láser f

lash [læʃ] N (blow with a whip, tail, etc.) azote m, latigazo m; (blow of waves) embate m; (part of eye) pestaña f; VT (whip) azotar; (tie) amarrar; **to — out at** fustigar

lasso [lǽso] N lazo m, reata f; VT lazar; Am enlazar

last [læst] ADJ (in a series) último; (definitive) final; —**-ditch** desesperado; — **minute** de último momento; — **name** apellido m; — **night** anoche; — **rites** extrema unción f, viático m; — **straw** colmo m; — **word** última palabra f; — **year** el año pasado; **next to the —** penúltimo; ADV último; **to arrive —** ser el último en llegar; **when — seen** cuando se lo vio por última vez; **at —** finalmente; N el último; (of a shoe) horma f; VI durar; (live on) perdurar

lasting [lǽstɪŋ] ADJ duradero, perdurable

lastly [lǽstli] ADV por último

latch [lætʃ] N pestillo m, picaporte m, cierre m; VI cerrar con el pestillo; **to — on** agarrarse de; **to — onto** pegarse a

late [let] ADJ (tardy) tardío; (hour) avanzada; (recent) reciente, último; (recently deceased) finado; — **afternoon** atardecer m; —**comer** rezagado -da mf; — **fee** recargo por mora m; ADV tarde; — **in the night** a una hora avanzada de la noche; — **into the night** hasta cualquier hora de la noche; — **in the week** a finales de la semana; **it is —** ya es tarde; **of —** últimamente; **to be —** llegar tarde; **to work —** trabajar hasta tarde; **the train was ten minutes —** el tren llegó con diez minutos de retraso

lately [létli] ADV últimamente

lateness [létnɪs] N tardanza f

latent [létnt] ADJ latente

later [létɚ] ADJ posterior; ADV más tarde, con posterioridad; **see you —** hasta luego; — **on** más tarde

lateral [lǽDɚəl] ADJ lateral

latest [léDɪst] ADJ último; **the — fashion** la última moda; **the — news** las últimas novedades; **at the —** a más tardar

latex [léDɛks] N látex m

lathe [leð] N torno m

lather [lǽðɚ] N (foam) espuma f; (sweat) sudor m; **he got into a —** se puso histérico; VT enjabonar; VI hacer espuma

Latin [lǽtn] ADJ latino; — **America** América Latina f, Latinoamérica f; — **American** latinoamericano -na mf; N (language) latín m

latitude [lǽɒɪtud] N latitud f; (freedom) flexibilidad f

latrine [lətrín] N letrina f

latter [lǽɒɚ] ADJ último; **in the — days of the Roman Republic** en los últimos días de la República Romana; **toward the — part of the week** a finales de la semana; **the —** este m, esta f

lattice [lǽɒɪs] N enrejado m, entramado m; (of a window) celosía f

Latvia [lǽtviə] N Letonia f

Latvian [lǽtviən] ADJ & N letón -ona mf

laud [lɔd] VT loar

laudable [lɔ́dəbəl] ADJ laudable, loable

laugh [læf] VI reír[se]; **to — at** reírse de; **to — loudly** reírse a carcajadas; **to — up/in one's sleeve** reírse para sus adentros; **she —ed in his face** se rió en su cara; N risa f; **we did it for —s** lo hicimos por diversión

laughable [lǽfəbəl] ADJ risible

laughingstock [lǽfɪŋstɑk] N hazmerreír m

laughter [lǽftɚ] N risa f

launch [lɔntʃ] VT (a boat) botar; (a rocket, new product) lanzar; (software) iniciar; **to — forth/out** lanzarse; N lancha f; (act of launching a boat) botadura f; (act of launching a rocket) lanzamiento m

launder [lɔ́ndɚ] VI/VT (clothes) lavar; (money) blanquear, lavar; (wash and iron clothes) lavar y planchar

Laundromat™ [lɔ́ndrəmæt] N lavadero automático m

laundry [lɔ́ndri] N (business establishment) lavandería f, lavadero m; (room in house) cuarto de lavado m, lavadero m; (clothes to be washed) ropa sucia f; (washed clothes) ropa limpia f

laurel [lɔ́rəl] N laurel m (also honor); **to rest on one's —s** dormirse sobre los laureles

lava [lávə] N lava f

lavatory [lǽvətɔri] N (basin) lavabo m; (bathroom) baño m, retrete m

lavender [lǽvəndɚ] N espliego m, lavanda f; ADJ lavanda

lavish [lǽvɪʃ] ADJ (generous) pródigo, espléndido; (abundant) abundante, copioso; VT prodigar; **to — praise upon** colmar de alabanzas a

law [lɔ] N ley f; (discipline) derecho m, jurisprudencia f; (police) policía f; **— and order** orden público m; **—breaker** infractor -ora mf, transgresor -ora mf; **—maker** legislador -ora mf; **— of diminishing returns** ley de [los] rendimientos decrecientes f; **— student** estudiante de derecho mf; **—suit** pleito m, litigio m; **to practice —** ejercer la abogacía; **to take the — into one's hands** hacer justicia por mano propia; ADJ **—-abiding** respetuoso de las leyes

lawful [lɔ́fəl] ADJ (in accordance with the law) legal; (allowed by law) lícito; (recognized by law) legítimo

lawless [lɔ́lɪs] ADJ (anarchic) anárquico; (illegal) ilegal

lawn [lɔn] N césped m, grama f; **— mower** cortadora de césped f

lawyer [lɔ́jɚ] N abogado -da mf

lax [læks] ADJ laxo

laxative [lǽksəDɪv] ADJ & N laxante m, purgante m

laxity [lǽksɪDi] N flojedad f, laxitud f

lay [le] VT colocar; (eggs) poner; (a cable) tender; **to — aside** (abandon) dejar de lado; (save) guardar; **to — a wager** apostar; **to — bare** poner al descubierto; **to — bricks** poner ladrillos; **to — down arms** rendir las armas; **to — down the law** imponerse; **to — hold of** asir, agarrar; **to — into** atacar; **to — off a workman** despedir temporalmente a un obrero; **to — one's head on a pillow** recostar la cabeza sobre una almohada; **to — open** exponer; **to — out a plan** trazar un plan; **to — up** almacenar; **to be laid up** estar en cama; **to — waste to** asolar; N situación f, orientación f; **—man** (nonexpert) lego m; (clergy) laico m; **—out** (despido temporal de un empleado m; **—out** diseño/trazado de página m; ADJ lego, laico

lay [le] see **lie** 'estar situado'

layer [léɚ] N capa f; (geological) estrato m; (hen) gallina ponedora f; **— cake** tarta de capas f

laziness [lézɪnɪs] N pereza f, holgazanería f, flojera f

lazy [lézi] ADJ perezoso, holgazán, flojo

LBO [leveraged buyout] [ɛ́lbíó] N compra apalancada f

LDL [low density lipoprotein] [ɛ́ldíɛ́l] N LBD f

lead¹ [lɛd] N (metal) plomo m; (graphite) mina f; **— poisoning** intoxicación con plomo f

lead² [lid] VT (guide) guiar; (guide a horse) llevar de la rienda; (induce, take) llevar, inducir; (be in charge, be first) encabezar, liderar; (direct) dirigir; (be superior to) estar a la cabeza de; **to — a life of ease** llevar una vida fácil; **to — the way** mostrar el camino; VI (provide passage to, result in) llevar a; (be first) estar a la cabeza; **to — astray** llevar por mal camino; N (first position) delantera f, primer lugar m; (clue) indicio m; (most important role) papel principal m, liderazgo m; **—off** comienzo; **— story** noticia principal f; **to take the —** (in sports) ponerse por delante en el marcador

leaden [lɛ́dn] ADJ (of lead) de plomo; (color) plomizo; (oppressive, slow) pesado

leader [lídɚ] N (in politics) líder mf, caudillo m; (in a race) líder mf; (in music) director -ora *mf*; (as a guide) guía *mf*

leadership [líːdəʃɪp] N dirección *f*, liderazgo *m*

leading [líːdɪŋ] ADJ (most important) principal; (arriving first) delantero; — **indicators** indicadores anticipados *m pl*; — **man** actor principal *m*

leaf [liːf] N hoja *f*; VI echar hojas; **to — through a book** hojear un libro

leafless [líːflɪs] ADJ sin hojas, deshojado

leaflet [líːflɪt] N (small leaf) foliolo *m*; (printed matter) volante *m*; (folded printed matter) pliego *m*

leafy [líːfi] ADJ (with foliage) frondoso; (in the form of leaves) de hoja

league [liːg] N (alliance) liga *f*; (unit of distance) legua *f*; VI/VT aliar[se]

leak [liːk] N (in a roof) gotera *f*; (in a boat, bucket, etc.) agujero *m*; (of information) filtración *f*; (of gas, steam, electricity) escape *m*, fuga *f*; VI (roof) gotear[se]; (boat) hacer agua; (gas) salirse, escaparse; (information) filtrarse; VT revelar información interna confidencial

leaky [líːki] ADJ (roof) que tiene goteras; (boat) que hace agua; (gas, electricity) que pierde

lean [liːn] VI/VT (incline) inclinar[se]; (support) apoyar[se], reclinar[se], recostar[se]; **to — on** presionar; ADJ magro; — **year** mal año *m*

leap [liːp] VI/VT saltar; **to — at a chance** aprovechar una oportunidad; **to — to mind** ocurrírsele a uno; N salto *m*; —**frog** pídola *f*; — **year** año bisiesto *m*

leapt [lɛpt] *see* leap

learn [lɜn] VI/VT aprender; (find out) enterarse de

learned [lɜ́nɪd] ADJ erudito, letrado

learner [lɜ́nə] N estudiante *mf*; (driver) aprendiz -iza *mf*

learning [lɜ́nɪŋ] N (result) erudición *f*, saber *m*; (process) aprendizaje *m*; — **disability** problema de aprendizaje *m*

learnt [lɜnt] *see* learn

lease [liːs] N (action) arrendamiento *m*; (contract) contrato de arrendamiento *m*; (period) período de arrendamiento *m*; **for —** se arrienda; **to have a new — on life** nacer de nuevo; VI/VT arrendar

leash [liːʃ] N traílla *f*, correa *f*

least [liːst] ADJ **he doesn't have the — chance** no tiene la más mínima posibilidad; **the — amount of money** la menor cantidad de dinero; — **common denominator** mínimo común denominador *m*; ADV menos; **the — important** el/la menos importante; **at —** al menos, por lo menos; N **I received the — of anyone** yo fui el que recibió menos de todos

leather [lɛ́ðə] N cuero *m*; ADJ de cuero; — **strap** correa *f*

leave [liːv] VT (a person, thing) dejar; (a place) salir de, irse de; VI salir, partir; **to — off**

(stop) parar de; (omit) omitir; **to — out** omitir; **I have two books left** me quedan dos libros; N permiso *m*; **to be on — estar de licencia; — of absence** licencia *f*; **to take — of** despedirse de

leaven [lɛ́vən] N levadura *f*; VT leudar

leavings [líːvɪŋz] N (leftovers) sobras *f pl*; (refuse) desperdicios *m pl*

Lebanese [lɛbəníːz] ADJ & N libanés -esa *mf*

Lebanon [lɛ́bənən] N Líbano *m*

lecherous [lɛ́tʃəəs] ADJ lujurioso

lecture [lɛ́ktʃə] N (presentation) conferencia *f*, disertación *f*; (sermon) sermón *m*; (long-winded speech) perorata *f*; VI (present) dar una conferencia, disertar; VT (scold) sermonear

lecturer [lɛ́ktʃəɾə] N conferenciante *mf*; (academic rank) profesor -ora *mf*

led [lɛd] *see* lead

LED [light-emitting diode] [ɛ́lídí] N LED *m*

ledge [lɛdʒ] N cornisa *f*

ledger [lɛ́dʒə] N libro mayor *m*

leech [liːtʃ] N sanguijuela *f*

leer [lɪr] VT (sideways) mirar de soslayo; (lecherously) mirar con lujuria; N (sideways) mirada de soslayo *f*; (lecherous) mirada lujuriosa *f*

leeway [líːwe] N margen de maniobra *m*; (of a ship) deriva *f*

left [lɛft] ADJ izquierdo; —**-click** presionar el botón izquierdo del ratón; —**-handed** zurdo; —**-handed compliment** alabanza irónica *f*; —**-handed tool** herramienta para zurdos *f*; — **justification** alineación a la izquierda *f*; —**-wing** de izquierdas; N izquierda *f*; **at / on/to/toward the —** a/hacia la izquierda; **to make a —** doblar/girar a la izquierda

left [lɛft] *see* leave

leftist [lɛ́ftɪst] N & ADJ izquierdista *mf*

leg [lɛg] N (human) pierna *f*; (animal, furniture) pata *f*; (wading bird) zanca *f*; (of a journey) etapa *f*; **to be on one's last —** estar en las últimas; **to pull someone's —** tomarle el pelo a alguien; **to stretch one's —s** estirar las piernas

legacy [lɛ́gəsi] N legado *m*

legal [líːgəl] ADJ (in accordance with the law) legal; (permitted by law) lícito; (recognized by law) legítimo; (having to do with the law) jurídico; — **age** mayoría de edad *f*; — **code** ordenamiento *m*; — **fees** honorarios del abogado *m pl*; — **holiday** día feriado *m*; — **procedure** procedimiento jurídico *m*; — **tender** moneda de curso legal *f*

legality [lɪgǽlɪɾi] N legalidad *f*

legalization [ligəlɪzéʃən] N legalización *f*

legalize [líːgəlaɪz] VT legalizar

legation [lɪgéʃən] N legación *f*

legend [lɛ́dʒənd] N leyenda *f* (also inscription);

(of a map) clave f

legendary [lédʒəndɛri] ADJ legendario

leggings [lέgɪŋz] N (ankle to knee) polainas f pl; (trousers) leggings m pl

legible [lédʒəbəl] ADJ legible

legion [lídʒən] N legión f

legionnaire [lidʒənér] N legionario m; —'**s disease** enfermedad del legionario f, legionelosis f

legislate [lédʒɪslet] VI/VT legislar

legislation [lɛdʒɪsléʃən] N legislación f

legislative [lédʒɪslɛDIV] ADJ legislativo

legislator [lédʒɪslɛDɚ] N legislador -ora mf

legislature [lédʒɪslɛtʃɚ] N legislatura f

legitimacy [lədʒídəməsi] N legitimidad f

legitimate [lɪdʒídəmɪt] ADJ legítimo

legitimize [lədʒídəmaɪz] VT legitimar

legume [légjum] N legumbre f

leisure [líʒɚ] N ocio m, holgura f; — **activities** actividades recreativas f pl; — **hours** horas de ocio f pl, tiempo libre m; **to be at** — estar desocupado; **do it at your** — hazlo cuando te convenga

leisurely [líʒɚli] ADJ lento, deliberado; ADV sin prisa

lemon [lɛmən] N limón m; ADJ de limón; — **tree** limonero m

lemonade [lɛmənéd] N limonada f

lend [lɛnd] VI/VT prestar; **to** — **a hand** dar una mano

lender [lɛndɚ] N (person who lends) prestador -ora mf; (professional) prestamista mf

length [lɛŋkθ] N (of an object, road) largo m, largura f, longitud f; (of a movie) duración f; (of a book) extensión f; **at** — (in detail) pormenorizadamente; (finally) finalmente; **by two** —**s** por dos cuerpos; **two meters in** — dos metros de largo; **to go to any** —**s** hacer lo imposible

lengthen [lɛŋkθən] VI/VT alargar[se]

lengthwise [lɛŋkθwaɪz] ADV & ADJ a lo largo

lengthy [lɛŋkθi] ADJ largo, prolongado

lenient [líniənt] ADJ indulgente

lens [lɛnz] N lente m; (of the eye) cristalino m

Lent [lɛnt] N Cuaresma f

lent [lɛnt] *see* lend

lentil [lɛntl] N lenteja f

Leon [león] N León m

Leonese [liəníz] ADJ leonés

leopard [lɛpɚd] N leopardo m

leprosy [lɛprəsi] N lepra f

lesbian [lɛzbiən] ADJ lesbiano; N lesbiana f

lesion [líʒən] N lesión f

Lesotho [ləsóto] N Lesoto m

less [lɛs] ADJ, ADV & PREP menos; **I have** — **than you do** tengo menos que tú; — **and** — cada vez menos

lessen [lɛsən] VI/VT disminuir, aminorar

lessening [lɛsənɪŋ] N disminución f

lesser [lɛsɚ] ADJ menor

lesson [lɛsən] N lección f

lest [lɛst] CONJ no sea que; — **you should think I'm teasing** para que no vayas a creer que estoy bromeando

let [lɛt] VT (permit) dejar, permitir; (rent) alquilar; — **him come** que venga; —'**s do it** hagámoslo; **to** — **be** dejar en paz; **to** — **down** (lower) bajar; (disappoint) decepcionar; **to** — **go** soltar; **to** — **in** dejar entrar; **to** — **know** hacer saber; **to** — **off** (not punish) dejar ir; (allow to get off) dejar bajar; **to** — **through** dejar pasar; **to** — **up** (permit to stand) dejar incorporarse; (cease) disminuir; N (in tennis) repetición f; —**down** desilusión f; —**up** tregua f

lethal [líθəl] ADJ letal

lethargic [ləθárdʒɪk] ADJ aletargado, letárgico

lethargy [lɛθɚdʒi] N letargo m; **to fall into a** — aletargarse

letter [lɛDɚ] N (of alphabet) letra f; (missive) carta f; — **carrier** cartero -ra mf; —**head** membrete m; —**head paper** papel membretado m; —-**spacing** espacio entre caracteres m; —**s** letras f pl; **the** — **of the law** la letra de la ley f; **to the** — al pie de la letra; VT grabar

lettuce [lɛDɪs] N lechuga f

leukemia [lukímiə] N leucemia f

levee [lévi] N dique m

level [lɛvəl] ADJ llano, plano; —-**headed** sensato; — **playing field** terreno de juego parejo m; — **with** a nivel de; **a** — **tablespoon** una cucharada al ras; N nivel m (also tool); **on the** — en serio; VT (make level) nivelar, igualar; (to demolish) arrasar, allanar; (to knock down a person) tumbar; (to aim criticism) dirigir; (to aim a gun) apuntar; **to** — **off** quedar paralelo al suelo; **to** — **with** hablar en serio con/a

lever [lévɚ] N palanca f

leverage [lévɚɪdʒ] N (influence) palanca f; (physical, financial) apalancamiento m

levity [lévɪDi] N ligereza f

levy [lévi] N (of taxes) recaudación f; (of troops) leva f; VT (taxes) recaudar; (troops) reclutar, hacer una leva de

lewd [lud] ADJ lascivo

lewdness [lúdnɪs] N lascivia f

lexical [lɛksɪkəl] ADJ léxico

lexicography [lɛksɪkágrəfi] N lexicografía f

lexicon [lɛksɪkɑn] N léxico m

liability [laɪəbílɪDi] N (disadvantage) desventaja f; (debit) pasivo m; (debts) deudas f pl; (responsibility) responsabilidad legal f; — **insurance** seguro contra daños a terceros m; **liabilities** obligaciones f pl

liable [láɪəbəl] ADJ responsable; — **to** propenso a; **she's** — **to get angry** es probable que se

enoje
liaison [liézɑn] N (connection) enlace *m*; (illicit love affair) aventura *f*

liar [láɪə-] N mentiroso -sa *mf*, embustero -ra *mf*

libel [láɪbəł] N libelo *m*, difamación *f*; VT difamar

liberal [líbə-əł] ADJ & N liberal *mf*

liberalism [líbə-əlɪzəm] N liberalismo *m*

liberality [lɪbə-rélɪDi] N (generosity) liberalidad *f*; (tolerance) tolerancia *f*

liberalization [lɪbə-əlɪzéʃən] N liberalización *f*

liberalize [líbə-əlaɪz] VI/VT liberalizar[se]

liberate [líbə-ret] VT (give freedom to) libertar, liberar; (release from obligation) librar; (give off) desprender

liberation [lɪbə-réʃən] N liberación *f*

liberator [líbə-reD-ə-] N libertador -ora *mf*

Liberia [laɪbírɪə] N Liberia *f*

Liberian [laɪbírɪən] ADJ & N liberiano -na *mf*

libertine [líbə-tin] ADJ & N libertino -na *mf*, calavera *m*

liberty [líbə-Dɪ] N libertad *f*; **at** — autorizado

libidinous [lɪbídŋəs] ADJ libidinoso

libido [lɪbíDo] N libido *f*

librarian [laɪbrériən] N bibliotecario -ria *mf*

library [láɪbreri] N biblioteca *f*

libretto [lɪbréDo] N libreto *m*

Libya [líbjə] N Libia *f*

Libyan [líbjən] ADJ & N libio -bia *mf*

license [láɪsəns] N (permission) permiso *m*; (driver's permit, poetic freedom) licencia *f*; — **plate** placa *f*, matrícula *f*; VT (issue license to) otorgar una licencia; (give permission) autorizar

licensing authority [láɪsənsɪŋ əθɔ́rɪDi] N autoridad para otorgar licencias *f*

licentious [laɪsénʃəs] ADJ licencioso

lick [lɪk] VT (touch with tongue) lamer (also waves); (thrash) dar una paliza; (defeat) derrotar; N lamida *f*, lengüetazo *m*; (blow) golpe *m*; **not to do a** — **of work** no mover un dedo

lickety-split [lɪkiDisplít] ADV en un santiamén

licking [líkɪŋ] N paliza *f*

licorice [líkə-ɪʃ] N regaliz *m*

lid [lɪd] N (of a container) tapadera *f*, tapa *f*; (of eye) párpado *m*; (on prices) tope *m*

lie [laɪ] N (falsehood) mentira *f*, embuste *m*; (orientation of an object) orientación *f*; — **detector** detector de mentiras *m*; **to give the** — **to** desmentir; VI mentir; **to** — **one's way out of a situation** salirse de una situación a mentiras; (be buried) yacer; (to be on a flat surface) estar; (to be situated) estar situado; (be horizontal) tumbarse, acostarse; **he's lying in bed** está acostado en la cama; **to** — **back** recostarse; **to** — **down** acostarse, tumbarse; **to** — **in wait** acechar

Liechtenstein [líktənstaɪn] N Liechtenstein *m*

Liechtensteiner [líktənstaɪnə-] N

liechtensteiniano -na *mf*

lien [lin] N gravamen *m*, carga *f*

lieu [lu] ADV LOC **in** — **of** en vez de

lieutenant [luténənt] N teniente *mf*; — **colonel** teniente coronel *mf*; — **governor** vicegobernador -ora *mf*

life [laɪf] N vida *f*; —**-and-death** de vida o muerte; — **boat** bote de salvamento *m*; — **cycle** ciclo vital *m*; — **expectancy** expectativa de vida *f*; —**guard** salvavidas *mf sg*; — **imprisonment** prisión perpetua *f*; — **insurance** seguro de vida *m*; — **jacket** salvavidas *m sg*; — **of the party** alma de la fiesta *f*; — **preserver** salvavidas *m sg*; — **raft** balsa salvavidas *f*; — **savings** ahorros de toda la vida *m pl*; —**span** duración de la vida *f*; —**style** estilo de vida *m*; —**-support system** (in space) equipo de vida *m*; (in a hospital) máquina corazón-pulmón *f*; —**time** vida *f*; (relative to life) vital; (for duration of life) vitalicio; ADJ —**like** natural, que parece vivo; —**long** de toda la vida; —**-sized** de tamaño natural

lifeless [láɪflɪs] ADJ (without living things) sin vida; (dead) muerto, sin vida; (fainted) desfallecido; (without liveliness) sin animación

lifer [láɪfə-] N (prisoner) condenado -da a cadena perpetua *mf*; (soldier) militar de carrera *m*

lift [lɪft] VT (hoist) levantar; (steal) robar; (plagiarize) copiar; VI (disperse) disiparse; (go up) elevarse; N (upward force) empuje *m*; (feeling) mejoría de ánimo *f*; (device for lifting) montacargas *m sg*; **to give someone a** — llevar en coche; *Mex* dar un aventón; —**off** despegue *m*

ligament [lígəmənt] N ligamento *m*

ligature [lígət͡ʃə-] N ligadura *f*

light [laɪt] N (luminescence) luz *f*; (device) luz *f*, lámpara *f*; (for traffic) semáforo *m*; (perspective) perspectiva *f*; (for cigarettes) fuego *m*; —**-emitting diode** diodo electroiluminiscente *m*; —**house** faro *m*; —**year** año luz *m*; ADJ (well-lighted) claro; (of little weight) ligero, leve; (of clothes) fresco; *Am* liviano; — **blue** azul claro *m*; —**-headed** mareado, —**hearted** alegre; — **rain** lluvia fina *f*; —**-skinned** de tez blanca; — **touch** mano delicada *f*; —**weight** de peso ligero; **to make** — **of** restar importancia a; VI/VT (turn on, ignite) encender[se], prender[se]; (provide light, brighten) iluminar[se]; (land on) posarse en; **to** — **up** (cigarette) prender, encender; (face) iluminarse; **to** — **upon** caer sobre

lighten [láɪtn̩] VI/VT (make / become lighter) aligerar[se], alivianar[se]; (brighten) iluminar[se]; — **up!** ¡no tomes las cosas a la tremenda!

lighter [láɪdə-] N encendedor m

lighting [láɪdɪŋ] N iluminación f; (in the street) alumbrado m

lightly [láɪtli] ADV (toast) ligeramente; (touch) levemente, suavemente; **I don't take your criticism** — no tomo tus críticas a la ligera

lightness [láɪtnɪs] N (little weight) ligereza f, levedad f; (brightness) claridad f

lightning [láɪtnɪŋ] N relámpago m; — **bug** luciérnaga f; — **rod** pararrayos m sg; **it happened at** — **speed** pasó como rayo; VI relampaguear

likable [láɪkəbəl] ADJ agradable, simpático

like [laɪk] ADV & PREP como; **to feel** — **going** tener ganas de ir; **to look** — **someone** parecerse a alguien; **it looks** — **rain** parece que va a llover; ADJ semejante, parecido; **in** — **manner** del mismo modo; —**-minded** del mismo parecer; N —**s** gustos m pl, preferencias f pl; VT gustarle a uno; **she** —**s dogs** le gustan los perros; **do whatever you** — haz lo que quieras; CONJ **he talked** — **he was crazy** hablaba como si estuviera loco; **she came** — **you predicted she would** vino, tal como tú pronosticaste; **I'm** —, **"you're crazy"** yo pensé/dije, "estás loco"; INTERJ **he was,** —, **way too old** era como que demasiado viejo

likelihood [láɪklihʊd] N probabilidad f; **in all** — **he came** lo más probable es que haya venido

likely [láɪkli] ADJ (probable) probable; (believable) creíble; (promising) prometedor; **John is** — **to win** es probable que gane Juan; ADV probablemente

liken [láɪkən] VT comparar

likeness [láɪknɪs] N (similarity) parecido m; (portrait) retrato m

likewise [láɪkwaɪz] ADV (the same thing) lo mismo; **we did** — hicimos lo mismo; (similarly) asimismo; (also) también

liking [láɪkɪŋ] N preferencia f, gusto m

lilac [láɪlək] N lila f; ADJ lila

lily [líli] N lirio m, azucena f; ADJ —**-white** (very white) blanquísimo; (pure) puro; (for whites only) exclusivamente para blancos

limb [lɪm] N (branch) rama f; (appendage) miembro m

limber [límbə-] ADJ flexible; VT hacer flexible; VI **to** — **up** estirarse

lime [laɪm] N (mineral) cal f; (fruit, color) lima f; —**light** candilejas f pl; **in the** —**light** en el candelero; —**stone** piedra caliza f; — **tree** limero m

limit [límɪt] N límite m; **to the** — al máximo; VT limitar

limitation [lɪmɪtéʃən] N limitación f

limitless [límɪtlɪs] ADJ ilimitado

limousine [líməzin] N limusina f

limp [lɪmp] N cojera f, renguera f; VI cojear,

renguear, renquear; ADJ (body) flácido; (plants) mustio

limpid [límpɪd] ADJ límpido

line [laɪn] N (bus route, telephone connection) línea f; (of words) renglón m, línea f; (row) raya f, hilera f; (cord) cuerda f; (persons waiting) cola f, fila f; (business) ramo m; (wrinkle) arruga f; (boundary) límite m; — **drive** (baseball) línea f; — **of credit** línea de crédito f; — **of scrimmage** línea de golpeo f; —**s** (in a play) parte f; —**sman** juez -eza de línea m f; —**up** hilera de personas f; (sports) alineación f; **drop me a** — escríbeme unas líneas; **out of** — irrespetuoso; **to get in** — hacer cola; VI/VT (border) alinear, bordear; (put in a lining) forrar; VI **to** — **up** alinear[se]; ADJ **off-** — fuera de línea; **on-** — en línea

lineage [línɪdʒ] N linaje m, estirpe f

linear [líniə-] ADJ lineal

lined [laɪnd] ADJ (with lines) rayado; (with a lining) forrado

linen [línɪn] N (fabric) lino m; (bedclothes) ropa blanca f

liner [láɪnə-] N (ocean) transatlántico m; (air) avión comercial m; (eye) delineador m

linger [líŋgə-] VI (stay) quedarse, demorarse; (persist) persistir; (saunter) rezagarse; (contemplate) detenerse; (delay death) aguantar

lingerie [lɑnʒəré] N lencería f

linguist [líŋgwɪst] N lingüista m f

linguistics [lɪŋgwístɪks] N lingüística f

liniment [línəmənt] N linimento m

lining [láɪnɪŋ] N forro m; **every cloud has a silver** — no hay mal que por bien no venga

link [lɪŋk] N (of a chain) eslabón m; (bond, tie) vínculo m; (rail, radio connection) enlace m; (computer) enlace m, vínculo m; VI/VT enlazar[se], conectar[se]; (on a computer) vincular

linnet [línɪt] N pardillo m

linoleum [lɪnóliəm] N linóleo m

linseed [línsid] N linaza f; — **oil** aceite de linaza m

lint [lɪnt] N pelusa f

lion [láɪən] N león m; —**'s share** la parte del león

lioness [láɪənɪs] N leona f

lip [lɪp] N labio m; (of a pitcher) borde m; — **balm** crema para labios f; —**stick** lápiz de labios m, carmín m; **don't give me no** —! no me contestes; VI **to** — **read** leer los labios

liposuction [láɪpəsʌkʃən] N liposucción f

liqueur [lɪkɜ́-] N licor m

liquid [líkwɪd] ADJ líquido; — **assets** activo líquido m; — **measure** medida para líquidos f; N líquido m

liquidate [líkwɪdet] VI/VT liquidar

liquidation [lɪkwɪdéʃən] N liquidación f

liquidity [lɪkwídɪdɪ] N liquidez f

liquor [líkə-] N bebida espirituosa f

lira [lírə] N lira f

lisp [lɪsp] N ceceo m; VI cecear

list [lɪst] N (series of items) lista f; (of a ship) escora f; **— price** precio de lista m; **— server** servidor de lista m; VT (make a list) hacer una lista de; VI (lean) escorar; **this chair —s for two hundred dollars** esta silla está a doscientos dólares

listen [lísən] VI/VT (hear) escuchar, oír; (heed) escuchar, prestar atención; **to — in** (on radio) sintonizar; (eavesdrop) escuchar a hurtadillas

listener [lísənə-] N oyente mf; **radio —** radioescucha mf, oyente mf

listing [lístɪŋ] N listado m

listless [lístlɪs] ADJ lánguido

lit [lɪt] ADJ (provided with light) iluminado; (tipsy) alegre, alumbrado

lit [lɪt] see light

literacy [lídə-əsi] N (action of making literate) alfabetización f; (rate) alfabetismo m

literal [lídə-əl] ADJ literal

literary [lídə-reri] ADJ literario

literate [lídə-ɪt] ADJ (who can read and write) alfabeto; (erudite) erudito, letrado; **he's barely —** apenas sabe leer y escribir

literature [lídə-ətʃə-] N literatura f; (handbills) impresos m pl, folletos m pl; **the scientific — la literatura científica**

lithium [líθiəm] N litio m; **—-ion battery** batería de iones de litio f

Lithuania [lɪθuéniə] N Lituania f

Lithuanian [lɪθuéniən] ADJ & N lituano -na mf

litigant [lídɪgənt] N litigante mf

litigation [lɪdɪgéʃən] N litigio m, pleito m

litter [lídə-] N (young animals) camada f, cría f; (stretcher) camilla f; (straw) cama de paja para animales f; (trash) basura f; (for cats) arena higiénica f; VI/VT (dirty) ensuciar; (strew) esparcir; VI (give birth) parir

little [lídl] ADJ (small) pequeño, chico; (not much) poco; **— brother** hermano menor m, hermanito m; **— finger** [dedo] meñique m; **— pig** puerquito m; **a — coffee** un poco de café; **a — while** un ratito, un poco; ADV & N poco; **— by —** poco a poco

livable [lívəbəl] ADJ funcional

live¹ [lɪv] VI/VT vivir; **to — together** convivir; **to — up to** cumplir; **to — it up** tirar la casa por la ventana; **long — the king!** ¡viva el rey! ADJ **all the — long day** todo el santo día

live² [laɪv] ADJ vivo; (ammunition) cargado; **— coal** ascua encendida f; **— oak** roble de Virginia m; **—stock** ganado m, ganadería f; **— wire** (electric) cable cargado m; (person) persona vivaz f; **before a — audience** en vivo; **—-in** con cama; ADV en vivo y en directo

livelihood [láɪvlihʊd] N sustento m

liveliness [láɪvlinɪs] N viveza f, animación f

lively [láɪvli] ADJ (party) animado; (person) vivaz, avispado; ADV con animación

liver [lívə-] N hígado m

livid [lívɪd] ADJ (pallid, bluish) lívido; (angry) furibundo

living [lívɪŋ] N (life) vida f; **— expenses** gastos de subsistencia m pl; **— room** sala f, living m; **— together** cohabitación f; **— wage** salario de subsistencia m; **— will** documento de instrucciones previas m, documento de voluntad anticipada m; **to earn/make a —** ganarse la vida; **the —** los vivos; ADJ vivo, viviente

lizard [lízə-d] N lagartija f

llama [lámə] N llama f

load [lod] N (supported mass) carga f; (weight) peso m; (ship cargo) cargamento m; **no — fund** fondo sin comisión de entrada m; **—s of** montones de; VI/VT cargar; **to — down** colmar; **to — oneself down** agobiarse

loaf [lof] N hogaza de pan f, pan m; VI holgar, holgazanear, haraganear

loafer [lófə-] N (idler) holgazán -ana mf, haragán -ana mf, gandul -la mf; (shoe) mocasín m

loan [lon] N préstamo m; (to a government) empréstito m; **— application** solicitud de préstamo f; **— guarantee** garantía de préstamo f; **— officer** funcionario -ria de préstamos mf; **— shark** usurero -ra mf; **—word** préstamo m; VI/VT prestar

loath [loθ] ADJ renuente; **to be — to** ser renuente a

loathe [loð] VT aborrecer

loathsome [lóðsəm] ADJ repugnante, abominable

lob [lɑb] VT tirar por lo alto; N (tennis) globo m

lobby [lábi] N (vestibule) vestíbulo m; (special interest) grupo de presión m, lobby m; VI/VT (influence) presionar

lobbyist [lábiɪst] N representante de un grupo de presión m

lobe [lob] N lóbulo m

lobotomy [ləbádəmi] N lobotomía f

lobster [lábstə-] N langosta f

local [lókəl] ADJ local; **— bus** (computer) vía de transmisión local f; **— printer** impresora local f; **— train** tren de cercanías m

localize [lókəlaɪz] VT localizar

locate [lóket] VI/VT (establish in a place) situar, ubicar; (find) localizar; VI (settle) radicarse, establecerse

location [lokéʃən] N (position) ubicación f, emplazamiento m; (finding) localización f; **on — en exteriores**

lock [lɑk] N (door) cerradura f; (canal) esclusa f; (firearms, wrestling) llave f; (of hair) mecha f, mechón m; **—jaw** tétanos m sg; **—-out** cierre patronal m; **—smith** cerrajero -ra mf; **to**

have a — on the award tener asegurado el premio; VI/VT cerrar con llave; (make immovable) trabar[se]; **to — in** encerrar; **to — out** dejar afuera; **to — up** (door) cerrar con llave; (animal) encerrar; (prisoner) encarcelar; (valuables) poner bajo llave

locker [lákə] N (for athletic equipment) casillero m; (for frozen food) cámara frigorífica f; **— room** vestuario m

locket [lákɪt] N relicario m, guardapelo m

locomotive [lokəmódɪv] N locomotora f

locust [lókəst] N langosta f; **— tree** algarrobo m

lodge [ladʒ] N (of fraternal organization) logia f; (cabin) cabaña f; (hotel) posada f, mesón m; VI/VT alojar[se], hospedar[se]; **to — a complaint** presentar una queja

lodger [ládʒə] N inquilino -na mf

lodging [ládʒɪŋ] N alojamiento m, hospedaje m, albergue m

loft [lɔft] N (attic) desván m; (for choir) coro m; (for hay) pajar m; VT tirar por lo alto

lofty [lɔ́fti] ADJ elevado, encumbrado

log [lag] N (wood) leño m, madero m, rollizo m; (ship record) cuaderno de bitácora m; (record of activity) diario m; (on a computer) registro m; (cabin) cabaña de troncos f; VI/VT (cut trees) cortar; **— -in name** nombre de acceso m; VT (write down) anotar; **to — in** ingresar al sistema; **to — off/out** finalizar una sesión; VT registrar una acción

logarithm [lágərɪðəm] N logaritmo m

logic [ládʒɪk] N lógica f; **— board** placa lógica f

logical [ládʒɪkəl] ADJ lógico

logically [ládʒɪkli] ADV lógicamente

logistics [lədʒístɪks] N logística f

loin [lɔɪn] N ijada f; (in animals) ijar m; (cut of meat) lomo m; **—s** entrañas f pl

loiter [lɔ́ɪtə] VI (idly) holgazanear; (with ill intent) merodear; **to — behind** rezagarse

loll [lɑl] VI arrellanarse

lollipop [lálɪpap] N Sp pirulí m; Mex paleta f; RP chupetín m

lone [lon] ADJ (solitary) solitario; (only) único

loneliness [lónlɪnɪs] N soledad f

lonely [lónli] ADJ solo

lonesome [lónsəm] ADJ solo

long [lɔŋ] ADJ largo; **a — way from home** lejos de casa; **to work — hours** trabajar muchas horas; **— distance** de larga distancia; **— division** división de más de una cifra f; **— -hand** letra manuscrita f; **— johns** calzoncillos largos m pl; **— jump** salto largo m; **— -lasting** duradero, perdurable; **— - lived** (batteries) duradero; (people) longevo; **— -range** (missiles) de largo alcance; (plans) a largo plazo; **— shoreman** estibador m; **— - suffering** sufrido; **— -term** a largo plazo; **— -term care** atención médica a largo plazo f; **— -time friend** viejo amigo; **— underwear**

calzoncillo largo m; **— -winded** verborrágico, palabrero; **it's a — shot** es muy improbable; **— ago** hace mucho tiempo; **— before** mucho antes; **— live . . . !** ¡viva . . . ! **all winter** — todo el invierno; **how — did he stay?** ¿cuánto tiempo se quedó? **not for** — no por mucho tiempo; **so — !** ¡hasta luego! **to be — in coming** tardar en venir; **three meters** — tres metros de largo; **will you be —?** ¿tardarás mucho? **the whole day** — todo el santo día; VI **to — for** anhelar

longer [lɔ́ŋgə] ADJ más largo; ADV más; **no —** ya no; **how much —?** ¿hasta cuándo?

longevity [lándʒévɪdi] N longevidad f

longing [lɔ́ŋɪŋ] N anhelo m; ADJ anhelante

longitude [lándʒɪtud] N longitud f

look [lʊk] VI (see) mirar; (seem) parecer; **it —s good on you** te queda bien, te luce; **to — after** atender, cuidar; **to — alike** parecerse; **to — down on someone** despreciar a alguien; **to — for** (search for) buscar; (anticipate) esperar; **I — forward to it** lo espero con ansia, me da mucha ilusión; **to — into** investigar; **she —s her age** aparenta la edad que tiene; **to — out** dar a, tener vista a; **to — out of** asomarse a; **— out!** ¡cuidado! **to — over** dar un vistazo a; **to — up** (upward) levantar la vista; (in a directory) buscar; **to — up to** admirar; N (gaze) mirada f; (examination) vistazo m; **— -alike** doble mf; **—out** (person) vigía mf; (place) mirador m, vigía f; **to be on the —out** estar alerta; **—s** aspecto m, pinta f; **good —s** belleza f

looking glass [lúkɪŋglæs] N espejo m

loom [lum] N telar m; VI (appear indistinctly) dibujarse; (threaten) cernerse

loon [lún] N (bird) somorgujo m; (person) chiflado -da mf

loony [lúni] ADJ chiflado

loop [lup] N (for fastening) presilla f; (in a rope) lazo m; (of a flight) rizo m; (electric) circuito cerrado m; (computer programming, ice-skating) bucle m; **—hole** escapatoria f; **in the —** al corriente, al tanto de lo que pasa; VI (make a loop) hacer un lazo; (curve around) serpentear; (loop the loop) rizar el rizo; VT enlazar

loose [lus] ADJ (free) suelto; (not tight) flojo; (approximate) libre; (unfettered) desatado; (immoral) disoluto; (promiscuous) fácil; **— cannon** mono con una metralleta m; **— change** suelto m, cambio m; **— end** cabo suelto m; **— -fitting** holgado; **— -jointed** de articulaciones flexibles; **— leaf** [de] hojas sueltas; **to let —** soltar; VT desatar, soltar

loosen [lúsən] VI/VT (untie) soltar[se], desatar; (make/become less tight/dense/strict) aflojar[se]

looseness [lúsnɪs] N (of skin) flojedad f; (of morals) relajamiento m; (of clothing) holgura f; (of soil) friabilidad f; (of translation) lo libre

loot [lut] N botín m; VI/VT saquear

lop [lap] VT (cut) cortar; (eliminate) eliminar; VI caer[se]; ADJ **—sided** (leaning to one side) ladeado; (unbalanced) desequilibrado; (listing) escorado

lope [lop] VI correr a pasos largos

loquacious [lokwéʃəs] ADJ locuaz

loquat [lókwɑt] N níspero m

lord [lɔrd] N señor m; (God) Señor m; (British title) lord m; **—'s Prayer** Padrenuestro m; **my —!** ¡Dios mío! VI **to — it over someone** tratarle a alguien con arrogancia

lordly [lɔ́rdli] ADJ (kingly) señorial; (haughty) altivo

lordship [lɔ́rdʃɪp] N (title) señoría f; (power) señorío m

lore [lɔr] N saber m

lose [luz] VI/VT perder; (a pursuer) dejar atrás; **to — sight of** perder de vista; **to — oneself in thought** ensimismarse

loser [lúzɚ] N perdedor -ora mf

loss [lɔs] N (destruction) pérdida f; (misplacement) pérdida f, extravío m; (sports) derrota f; **to be at a —** no saber qué hacer; **to sell at a —** vender con pérdida; **—es** bajas f pl

lost [lɔst] ADJ perdido; **— cause** caso perdido m; **— in thought** absorto; **to get —** perderse, extraviarse

lost [lɔst] *see* lose

lot [lɑt] N (parcel) lote m; (fate) suerte f, destino m; (piece of land) solar m, terreno m; **the — todo**; **a — of / —s of** mucho[s]; **a — of money** mucho dinero; **by —** al azar; **to draw —s** echar suertes; **to fall to one's —** caerle en suerte a uno; ADV **a — better** mucho mejor

lotion [lóʃən] N loción f

lottery [lɑ́dəri] N lotería f

loud [laʊd] ADJ (noisy) ruidoso; (strong) fuerte; (ostentatious) chillón; **—speaker** altavoz m, altoparlante m; **—mouth** bocazas mf sg; ADV fuerte, alto

Lou Gehrig's disease [lugérɪgz dɪzíz] N enfermedad de Lou Gehrig f

lounge [laʊndʒ] VI repantigarse, arrellanarse; N (waiting room) sala de espera f; (room in bar) salón m; (divan) diván m; **— chair** diván m

louse [laʊs] N piojo m

lousy [láʊzi] ADJ (infested with lice) piojoso; (contemptible) despreciable; (poorly done) pésimo

lout [laʊt] N bruto m

lovable [lávəbəl] ADJ adorable

love [lʌv] N (affection) amor m; (fondness) afición f; (in tennis) nada f; **— affair** aventura f, amorío m; **— at first sight** amor a primera

vista m, flechazo m; **— life** vida sentimental f; **— seat** confidente m; **books were her great —** los libros fueron su gran pasión; **to be in —** estar enamorado; **to fall in — with** enamorarse de; **to make — to** hacerle el amor a; VI/VT amar, querer; **I — to eat apples** me encanta comer manzanas

loveliness [lávlinɪs] N (beauty) hermosura f; (charm) encanto m

lovely [lávli] ADJ (beautiful) hermoso; (charming) encantador; (pleasant) ameno

lover [lávɚ] N (sexually involved) amante mf; (in love) enamorado -da mf, amante mf; (interested in) aficionado -da mf

loving [lávɪŋ] ADJ cariñoso, afectuoso

low [lo] ADJ (not high) bajo; (base) vil; (humble) humilde; (downcast) abatido; (deep in pitch) grave; **— beam** luces cortas f pl; **—brow** poco culto; **—-budget** de bajo presupuesto; **—-cal** de bajas calorías; **—cost** de bajo precio; **—down** verdad f; **—-end** de baja calidad; **— gear** primera marcha f; **—-grade** (inferior) inferior; (low) bajo; **—-income** de bajos ingresos; **—-key** tranquilo; **—land** tierra baja f; **—-level** de bajo nivel; **—life** canalla f; **—-quality** baja calidad f; **—-tech** sencillo; **— tide** bajamar f, marea baja f; **dress with a — neck** vestido escotado m; **to be — on something** estar escaso de algo; **to be in — spirits** estar abatido/desanimado; ADV bajo; **to buy —** comprar barato; N (sound of a cow) mugido m; VI mugir

lower [lóɚ] VI/VT bajar; (prices) rebajar; (flag, sail) arriar; ADJ más bajo, inferior; **—case** minúscula f; **— house** cámara de diputados f

lowliness [lólinɪs] N humildad f

lowly [lóli] ADJ humilde

loyal [lɔ́ɪəl] ADJ leal

loyalty [lɔ́ɪəlti] N lealtad f

LSD [**lysergic acid diethylamide**] [ɛ́lɛsdí] N LSD m

lubricant [lúbrɪkənt] ADJ & N lubricante m

lubricate [lúbrɪket] VI/VT lubricar

lucid [lúsɪd] ADJ lúcido

lucidity [lusídɪdi] N lucidez f

luck [lʌk] N suerte f; **in —** de suerte; **to be out of —** estar de mala suerte; VI **to — into** conseguir por un golpe de suerte; **to — out** tener suerte

luckily [lákəli] ADV afortunadamente

lucky [láki] ADJ afortunado; **— charm** amuleto de la suerte m; **to be —** tener suerte

lucrative [lúkrədɪv] ADJ lucrativo

ludicrous [lúdɪkrəs] ADJ ridículo

lug [lʌg] VT acarrear

luggage [lágɪdʒ] N equipaje m; **— rack** rejilla f

lukewarm [lúkwɔ́rm] ADJ (not warm or cold) tibio; (indifferent) indiferente

lull [lʌl] VT (put to sleep) arrullar; VI/VT (soothe)

calmar[se]; N (calm) calma f, tregua f; (sound) arrullo m

lullaby [lʌ́ləbaɪ] N canción de cuna f, nana f

lumbago [lʌmbégo] N lumbago m

lumbar [lʌ́mbɑr] ADJ lumbar

lumber [lʌ́mbɚ] N madera f; — **jack** leñador m; —**man** maderero m; — **mill** aserradero m; —**yard** almacén de maderas m; VI/VT (cut trees) talar; (move heavily) moverse pesadamente; (make a low noise) tronar

luminous [lúmənəs] ADJ luminoso

lump [lʌmp] N (in breast) bulto m; (in sauce) grumo m; (in throat) nudo m; (of coal) trozo m; (of food) plasta f; (on head) chichón m; (of sugar) terrón m; **to take one's —s** recibir palos; — **sum** pago global m; VT juntar; VI agrumarse

lumpectomy [lʌmpéktəmi] N tumorectomía f

lumpy [lʌ́mpi] ADJ grumoso

lunar [lúnɚ] ADJ lunar; — **eclipse** eclipse lunar m

lunatic [lúnətɪk] ADJ & N lunático -ca mf, loco -ca mf; — **fringe** extremistas mf pl

lunch [lʌntʃ] N comida f, almuerzo m; —**time** hora de comer/almorzar f; **out to —** (having lunch) almorzando; (crazy) en la luna; VI comer, almorzar

lung [lʌŋ] N pulmón m

lunge [lʌndʒ] N arremetida f; VI arremeter, abalanzarse; **to — at** arremeter contra, abalanzarse sobre

lupus [lúpəs] N lupus m

lurch [lɚtʃ] N tambaleo m; **to give a —** tambalearse; **to leave someone in the —** dejar a alguien en la estacada; VI tambalearse, dar barquinazos

lure [lur] N (thing that attracts) atractivo m, gancho m; (in hunting) señuelo m; (in fishing) cebo m; VT atraer, seducir

lurid [lúrɪd] ADJ (gruesome) sangriento; (shocking) escabroso

lurk [lɚk] VI (lie in wait) estar en acecho, acechar; (move furtively) moverse furtivamente

luscious [lʌ́ʃəs] ADJ (delicious) exquisito, delicioso; (sexy) voluptuoso

lust [lʌst] N (sexual desire) lujuria f, lascivia f; (craving) deseo m, ansia f; VI desear; **to — after** codiciar

luster [lʌ́stɚ] N lustre m, brillo m

lustful [lʌ́stfəl] ADJ lujurioso

lusty [lʌ́sti] ADJ (robust) robusto; (full of lust) lujurioso

Luxembourg [lʌ́ksəmbɚg] N Luxemburgo m

Luxembourger [lʌ́ksəmbɚgɚ] N luxemburgués -esa mf

Luxembourgian [lʌksəmbɚ́giən] ADJ luxemburgués

luxurious [lʌgʒúriəs] ADJ (characterized by luxury) lujoso; (luxuriant) exuberante

luxury [lʌ́gʒɚi] N lujo m; — **tax** impuesto suntuario m; ADJ de lujo

lye [laɪ] N lejía f

lying [láɪɪŋ] ADJ mentiroso

Lyme disease [láɪm dɪzíz] N enfermedad de Lyme f

lymph [lɪmf] N linfa f; — **node** nodo linfático m

lymphocyte [lɪ́mfəsaɪt] N linfocito m

lymphoma [lɪmfómə] N linfoma m

lynch [lɪntʃ] VT linchar

lynx [lɪŋks] N lince m

lyre [laɪr] N lira f

lyric [lírɪk] N poema lírico m; — **poetry** lírica f; —**s** letra f; ADJ lírico

lyrical [lírɪkəl] ADJ lírico

lyricism [lírɪsɪzəm] N lirismo m

Mm

ma'am [mæm] N señora f

Macao [məkáu] N Macao m

macaroni [mækəróni] N macarrones m pl

Macedonia [mæsɪdóniə] N Macedonia f

Macedonian [mæsɪdóniən] ADJ & N macedonio -nia mf

machine [məʃín] N máquina f; (of government) maquinaria f, aparato m; — **gun** (not portable) ametralladora f; (portable) metralleta f; — **language** lenguaje de máquina m, lenguaje máquina m; ADJ —-**made** hecho a máquina; VT trabajar a máquina

machinery [məʃínɚi] N maquinaria f

machinist [məʃínɪst] N maquinista mf, operario -ria mf

mackerel [mǽkɚəl] N caballa f

macro [mǽkro] N serie de instrucciones f

mad [mæd] ADJ (crazy) loco; (angry) rabioso, enojado; (hydrophobic) rabioso; — **cow disease** encefalopatía espongiforme bovina f, enfermedad de las vacas locas f; —**man** loco m; **to be — about someone** estar loco por alguien; **to drive —** enloquecer, volver loco; **to get —** enojarse; **to go —** volverse loco, enloquecerse; **like —** como loco

Madagascan [mædəgǽskən] ADJ & N malgache mf

Madagascar [mædəgǽskɑr] N Madagascar m

madam [mǽdəm] N (title) señora f

maddening [mǽdnɪŋ] ADJ enloquecedor

made [med] ADJ —-**to-measure** hecho a la medida; —-**to-order** hecho por encargo; —-**up** (invented) inventado, falso; (wearing makeup) maquillado; **to be — of** ser de; **to have something —** mandar hacer algo; **I'm**

a — man estoy hecho; **to have it** — estar hecho

made [med] *see* make

madness [mǽdnɪs] N (insanity) locura *f*; (anger) rabia *f*

Mafia [máfiǝ] N mafia *f*

mafioso [mafióso] N mafioso *m*

magazine [mǽgǝzin] N (publication) revista *f*; (room for ammunition) polvorín *m*; (part of gun) cargador *m*

magic [mǽdʒɪk] N magia *f*; ADJ mágico; — **bullet** panacea *f*; — **wand** varita mágica *f*

magical [mǽdʒɪkǝł] ADJ mágico

magician [mǝdʒíʃǝn] N (person adept at magic) mágico -ca *mf*; (person adept at finances) mago -ga *m*

magistrate [mǽdʒɪstret] N magistrado -da *mf*

magma [mǽgmǝ] N magma *m*

magnanimous [mægnǽnǝmǝs] ADJ magnánimo

magnate [mǽgnet] N magnate *m*

magnesia [mægnízǝ] N magnesia *f*

magnesium [mægníziǝm] N magnesio *m*

magnet [mǽgnɪt] N imán *m*

magnetic [mægnédɪk] ADJ magnético; — **pole** polo magnético *m*; — **resonance imaging** imagen por resonancia magnética *f*; — **tape** cinta magnetofónica *f*

magnetism [mǽgnǝtɪzǝm] N magnetismo *m*

magnetize [mǽgnǝtaɪz] VT magnetizar, imantar

magnificence [mægnífɪsǝns] N magnificencia *f*

magnificent [mægnífɪsǝnt] ADJ magnífico

magnify [mǽgnǝfaɪ] VT (to make larger) aumentar; (to make louder) amplificar; (to exaggerate) exagerar, magnificar

magnitude [mǽgnɪtud] N magnitud *f*

magnolia [mægnóljǝ] N (flower) magnolia *f*; (tree) magnolio *m*

magpie [mǽgpaɪ] N urraca *f* (also hoarder)

mahogany [mǝhágǝni] N caoba *f*

maid [med] N criada *f*, sirvienta *f*; (in hotel) camarera *f*; — **of honor** dama de honor *f*

maiden [médn] N *lit* doncella *f*, virgen *f*; — **voyage** primer viaje *m*; — **name** nombre de soltera *m*

mail [meł] N correo *m*; (electronic) mensaje *m*; (of metal) malla *f*; —**bag** cartera *f*; —**box** buzón *m*; —**man** cartero *m*; — **order** pedido por correo *m*; — **order business** negocio de ventas por correo *m*; VT echar al correo; —**ing list** lista de correo *f*

maim [mem] VT mutilar

main [men] ADJ principal; — **office** oficina central *f*; N (pipe) cañería principal *f*; (sea) alta mar *f*; —**frame** *Sp* ordenador central *m*, *Am* computadora central *f*; —**land** continente *m*; —**spring** muelle real *m*; —**stream** tendencia mayoritaria *f*; —**stream engineering** ingeniería conforme a la

corriente dominante *f*; —**stay** pilar *m*, puntal *m*; — **street** calle principal *f*

mainly [ménli] ADV principalmente, fundamentalmente

maintain [mentén] VT (repair, support) mantener; (assert) afirmar

maintenance [méntnǝns] N (repairs) mantenimiento *m*; (monetary support) manutención *f*; — **cost** costo de mantenimiento *m*

maize [mez] N maíz *m*

majestic [mǝdʒéstɪk] ADJ majestuoso

majesty [mǽdʒɪsti] N majestad *f*; **Your** — Su Majestad

major [médʒǝ] ADJ (greater) mayor, más grande; (large) grande; — **key** mayor *m*; N (military rank) comandante *m*; (field of study) especialidad *f*, carrera *f*; — **league** liga mayor *f*; VI especializarse

majority [mǝdʒɔ́rɪdi] N (greater number) mayoría *f*; (age) mayoría de edad *f*; — **ownership** propiedad mayoritaria *f*; **the** — el grueso

make [mek] VT (do) hacer; (create) fabricar; (cause) causar; (earn) ganar; (a speech) pronunciar; **to** — **a clean breast of** sacarse del pecho; **to** — **a decision** tomar una decisión; **to** — **a living** ganarse la vida; **to** — **a train** llegar a tiempo para tomar un tren; **to** — **a turn** girar, doblar; **to** — **away with** fugarse con; **to** — **believe** hacer de cuenta que; **to** — **out** (see) vislumbrar, divisar; (read) descifrar; (kiss) *Sp* morrear; *Am* besuquearse; **to** — **possible** posibilitar; **to** — **too much of** exagerar; **to** — **up** (a story) inventar; (after a quarrel) hacer las paces; (a loss) recuperar; (one's face) maquillarse; (one's mind) decidirse; **to** — **up for** compensar; **two plus two** — **s four** dos y dos son cuatro; **what do you** — **of that?** ¿cómo interpretas eso? **I'll** — **it up to you** te voy a compensar por eso; **you'll** — **a good teacher** vas a ser un buen profesor; N (brand) marca *f*; —**-up** (composition) composición *f*; (character) carácter *m*; (cosmetics) maquillaje *m*; ADJ —**shift** provisional

maker [mékǝ] N (creator) creador -ora *mf*, hacedor -ora *mf*; (manufacturer) fabricante *m*

makings [mékɪŋz] N (potential) potencial *m*; (ingredients) ingredientes *m pl*

maladjusted [mælǝdʒ́ʌstɪd] ADJ inadaptado

malady [mǽlǝdi] N mal *m*

malaise [mǝléz] N malestar *m*

malaria [mǝlériǝ] N malaria *f*, paludismo *m*

Malawi [mǝláwi] N Malawi *m*

Malawian [mǝláwiǝn] ADJ & N malawiano -na *mf*

Malaysia [mǝléʒǝ] N Malasia *f*

Malaysian [məléʒən] ADJ & N malasio -sia mf

malcontent [mǽlkəntent] ADJ & N descontento -ta mf

Maldives [mɔ́ldaɪvz] N Maldivas f pl

Maldivian [mɔ́ldívíən] ADJ & N maldivo -va mf

male [meł] ADJ (animal, plant) macho; (person) varón m; (trait) masculino; N (animal, plant) macho m; (person) varón m

malevolent [məlévələnt] ADJ malévolo

malformation [mæłfɔrméʃən] N malformación f

malfunction [mælfʌ́ŋkʃən] N funcionamiento defectuoso m; VI funcionar mal

Mali [máli] N Malí m

Malian [máliən] ADJ & N malí mf

malice [mǽlɪs] N malicia f; **with — aforethought** con premeditación y alevosía

malicious [məlíʃəs] ADJ malicioso

malign [məláɪn] VT calumniar, difamar

malignancy [məlíɡnənsi] N (quality) malignidad f; (tumor) tumor maligno m

malignant [məlíɡnənt] ADJ maligno

mall [mɔ́l] N (closed street) paseo m; (enclosed shopping area) galería f, centro comercial m

mallet [mǽlɪt] N mazo m

malnourished [mæłnɝ́rɪʃt] ADJ desnutrido

malnutrition [mæłnutríʃən] N desnutrición f

malpractice [mæłprǽktɪs] N negligencia f, mala práctica f

malt [mɔ́łt] N malta f; **—ed milk** leche malteada f

Malta [mɔ́łtə] N Malta f

Maltese [mɔ́łtíz] ADJ & N maltés -esa mf

mama, mamma [mámə] N mamá f; **—'s boy** nene de mamá m

mammal [mǽməł] N mamífero m

mammary [mǽməri] ADJ mamario

mammography [mæmáɡrəfi] N mamografía f

mammoth [mǽməθ] ADJ enorme; N mamut m

man [mæn] N hombre m; (servant) criado m; (in games) pieza f, ficha f; **— and wife** marido y mujer; **—hunt** persecución f; **—kind** humanidad f; **—-of-war** (ship) buque de guerra m; (jellyfish) medusa f; **—power** (for work) mano de obra f; **—slaughter** (accidental) homicidio culposo m, homicidio involuntario m; (unpremeditated) homicidio sin premeditación m; **—-to—defense** defensa al hombre f, defensa de asignación f, defensa individual f; **every — for himself** cada cual para sí; **to a —** unánimamente; ADJ **—-eating** que come carne humana; **—-made** (fiber) sintético; (lake) artificial; INTERJ ¡hombre! VT (a fort) guarnecer; (a ship) tripular; **to —handle** violentar

manage [mǽnɪdʒ] VT (succeed in) conseguir, lograr; (direct) dirigir, administrar, gestionar; (maneuver) manejar; VI **to — without help** arreglárselas sin ayuda

manageable [mǽnɪdʒəbəł] ADJ manejable;

(hair) dócil

managed [mǽnɪdʒd] ADJ **— care** plan de salud administrado m; **— funds** fondos administrados m pl

management [mǽnɪdʒmənt] N (act of managing) dirección f, gestión f; (persons controlling a business) gerencia f, patronal f, gestión f; (area of study) empresariales f pl

manager [mǽnɪdʒɚ] N (of a store) gerente -ta mf; (of a company) director -ora mf

mandate [mǽndet] N mandato m; VT decretar

mandatory [mǽndətɔri] ADJ obligatorio

mandolin [mǽndəlɪn] N mandolina f

mane [men] N (of a lion) melena f; (of a horse) crin f

maneuver [mənúvɚ] N maniobra f; VI/VT maniobrar

manganese [mǽŋɡəniz] N manganeso m

mange [mendʒ] N sarna f, roña f

manger [méndʒɚ] N pesebre m

mangle [mǽŋɡəł] VT (mutilate) magullar, mutilar; (ruin) estropear

mango [mǽŋɡo] N mango m

mangrove [mǽŋɡrov] N mangle m

mangy [méndʒi] ADJ sarnoso

manhood [mǽnhʊd] N virilidad f; (men collectively) hombres m pl; (adult age) edad adulta f

mania [méniə] N manía f

maniac [méniæk] N maníaco -ca mf, maniaco -ca mf

maniacal [mənáɪəkəł] ADJ maníaco

manic-depressive [mǽnɪkdɪprésɪv] ADJ maniaco-depresivo

manicure [mǽnɪkjʊr] N manicura f; VT manicurar

manifest [mǽnəfest] ADJ manifiesto; N (list of cargo) manifiesto m, hoja de ruta f; VT (show) manifestar, poner de manifiesto; (express) declarar

manifestation [mænəfestéʃən] N manifestación f

manifesto [mænɪfésto] N manifiesto m

manifold [mǽnəfołd] ADJ diverso; N (on a motor) colector m

manila [mənílə] N abacá m; **— envelope** sobre manila m

manioc [mǽniak] N mandioca f, yuca f

manipulate [mənípjəlet] VT manipular

manipulation [mənɪpjəléʃən] N manipulación f

manlike [mǽnlaɪk] ADJ (manly) varonil; (mannish) hombruna; (resembling a human) de hombre

manliness [mǽnlɪnɪs] N virilidad f

manly [mǽnli] ADJ varonil, viril

manner [mǽnɚ] N (way) manera f, modo m, forma f; (type) tipo m; (outward bearing) aire m, ademán m, porte m; **—s** modales m pl, crianza f; **in the — of** a la manera de

mannerism [mǽnərɪzəm] N peculiaridad *f*
mannish [mǽnɪʃ] ADJ hombruno, varonil
manor [mǽnə] N feudo *m*, solar *m*; — **house** casa solariega *f*
mansion [mǽnʃən] N mansión *f*
mantel [mǽntl] N repisa de chimenea *f*
mantle [mǽntl] N manto *m*
mantra [mǽntrə] N mantra *f*
manual [mǽnjuəl] ADJ & N manual *m*; — **labor** trabajo manual *m*
manufacture [mænjəfǽktʃə] VT fabricar, manufacturar; (clothes, shoes) confeccionar; N fabricación *f*, manufactura *f*; (of clothes, shoes) confección *f*
manufacturer [mænjəfǽktʃərə] N fabricante *m*; —**'s suggested retail price** precio sugerido por el fabricante *m*
manufacturing [mænjəfǽktʃəɪŋ] N fabricación *f*, manufactura *f*; ADJ fabril, manufacturero; — **empire** imperio industrial *m*
manure [mənúr] N estiércol *m*; VT estercolar, abonar
manuscript [mǽnjəskrɪpt] ADJ & N manuscrito *m*
many [méni] ADJ muchos; — **apples** muchas manzanas; — **came** vinieron muchos; — **a time** muchas veces; **a great** — muchísimos; **as** — **as** tantos como; **as** — **as five** hasta cinco; **how** —? ¿cuántos? **three books too** — tres libros de más; **too** — demasiados
map [mæp] N (geographical) mapa *m*; (of streets) plano *m*; VT trazar un mapa de; **to** — **out** planear
maple [mépəl] N Sp arce *m*; Am maple *m*; — **syrup** miel de arce/maple *f*
mar [mɑr] VT estropear
marathon [mǽrəθən] N maratón *mf*
marble [mɑ́rbl] N mármol *m*; (toy) canica *f*, bola *f*; **to play** —**s** jugar a las canicas; ADJ de mármol, marmóreo
march [mɑrtʃ] N marcha *f*; VI marchar; (leave) marcharse; **to** — **in** entrar; **to** — **out** marcharse; VT hacer marchar
March [mɑrtʃ] N marzo *m*
mare [mer] N yegua *f*
margarine [mɑ́rdʒəɪn] N margarina *f*
margin [mɑ́rdʒɪn] N margen *m*; — **of error** margen de error *m*; — **of safety** margen de seguridad *m*; **on** — comprado en cuenta de margen
marginal [mɑ́rdʒənl] ADJ marginal
marginalization [mɑrdʒənlɪzéʃən] N marginación *f*
marginalize [mɑ́rdʒənaɪz] VT marginar
marigold [mǽrɪɡold] N caléndula *f*, maravilla *f*
marijuana, marihuana [mærəwánə] N marihuana *f*, mariguana *f*
marinate [mǽrənet] VT marinar
marine [mərín] ADJ (of the sea) marino;

(maritime) marítimo; — **corps** infantería de marina *f*; N soldado de infantería de marina *m*
marionette [mæriənét] N marioneta *f*
marital [mǽrɪtl] ADJ conyugal, matrimonial; — **status** estado civil *m*
maritime [mǽrɪtaɪm] ADJ marítimo
mark [mɑrk] N marca *f*, seña *f*; (token) señal *f*; (indication) seña *f*; (grade) nota *f*, calificación *f*; (former German currency) marco *m*; —**down** rebaja de precio *f*; —**sman** tirador *m*; **he's a good** —**sman** tiene muy buena puntería / muy buen tino; —-**up** (amount above wholesale price) margen de ganancia *m*; **the halfway** — el punto medio, la mitad; **to hit the** — dar en el blanco; **on your** —, **get set, go!** ¡en sus marcas, listos y ya! ¡en sus marcas, listos, fuera! **to make one's** — distinguirse; **to miss the** — errar el tiro; **easy** — blanco fácil *m*; VT (write on) marcar; (indicate) señalar; (observe) observar, notar; (grade) calificar; —**ed for greatness** destinado a la grandeza; — **my words!** ¡ya verás! **to** — **down prices** rebajar los precios; **to** — **off** acotar, deslindar; **to** — **up prices** subir los precios
marker [mɑ́rkə] N marcador *m*
market [mɑ́rkɪt] N mercado *m*; — **analysis** análisis de mercado *m*; —**place** mercado *m*; — **price** precio de mercado *m*; — **share** sector del mercado *m*; **I'm in the** — **for** estoy buscando; VT comercializar, mercadear
marketable [mɑ́rkɪdəbəl] ADJ vendible
marketing [mɑ́rkɪdɪŋ] N (field of study) mercadotecnia *f*, marketing *m*; (selling) comercialización *f*
marmalade [mɑ́rməled] N mermelada de naranja *f*
maroon [mərún] ADJ & N bordó/bordeaux *m*; VT abandonar
marquis [mɑrkí] N marqués *m*
marquise [mɑrkíz] N marquesa *f*
marriage [mǽrɪdʒ] N matrimonio *m*; (combination) combinación *f*; — **license** licencia de matrimonio *f*
marriageable [mǽrɪdʒəbəl] ADJ casadero
married [mǽrid] ADJ (united in marriage) casado; (relation to marriage) conyugal; — **couple** matrimonio *m*; **to get** — casarse
marrow [mǽro] N (in the bones) médula *f*; (food) tuétano *m*; (essential part) meollo *m*
marry [mǽri] VT (to marry off) casar; (to get married) casarse con; VI casarse
marsh [mɑrʃ] N pantano *m*, ciénaga *f*
marshal [mɑ́rʃəl] N (military) mariscal *m*; (police chief) alguacil *m*; (of a parade) maestro de ceremonia, *m*; VT (facts, forces) reunir; (troops) formar
Marshallese [mɑrʃəlíz] ADJ & N marshalés -esa *mf*

Marshall Islands [márʃəláɪləndz] N Islas Marshall *f pl*

marshmallow [márʃmɛlo] N malvavisco *m*

marshy [márʃi] ADJ pantanoso, cenagoso

martial [márʃəl] ADJ marcial; **— arts** artes marciales *f pl*; **— law** ley marcial *f*

martin [mártn] N avión *m*

martini [mɑrtíni] N martini *m*

martyr [mártɚ] N mártir *m*; VT martirizar

martyrdom [mártɚdəm] N martirio *m*

marvel [márvəl] N maravilla *f*; VI maravillarse

marvelous [márvələs] ADJ maravilloso

Marxism [márksɪzəm] N marxismo *m*

mascara [mæskérə] N rímel *m*

mascot [mæskɑt] N mascota *f*

masculine [mæskjəlɪn] ADJ masculino

mash [mæʃ] VT aplastar, pisar; **—ed potatoes** puré de papas/patatas *m*; N (pulpy mass) puré *m*; (food for livestock) afrecho *m*; (malt) malta remojada *f*

mask [mæsk] N máscara *f*, careta *f*; VT enmascarar; **—ed ball** baile de máscaras *m*

masochism [mæsəkɪzəm] N masoquismo *m*

mason [mésən] N (builder) albañil *m*; (Freemason) masón *m*

masonry [mésənri] N (bricklaying) albañilería *f*; (fraternal order) masonería *f*

masquerade [mæskəréd] N mascarada *f*; VI **to — as** hacerse pasar por

mass [mæs] N masa *f*; (in church) misa *f*; **— communication** comunicación de masas *f*; **— marketing** comercialización masiva *f*; **— media** medios de comunicación [de masas] *m pl*; **— production** fabricación en masa *f*; **— storage** almacenamiento masivo *m*; **— transit** transporte público *m*; **— unemployment** desempleo/paro masivo *m*; **the —es** las masas *f pl*; VI/VT juntar[se] en masa; (troops) concentrar[se]

massacre [mæsəkɚ] N masacre *m*; VT masacrar

massage [məsáʒ] N masaje *m*; **— parlor** salón de masajes *m*; VT (give a massage) masajear; (change data) manipular

masseur [məsɚ] N masajista *m*

masseuse [məsús] N masajista *f*

massive [mǽsɪv] ADJ (severe) masivo; (solid) macizo; (large) enorme

mast [mæst] N mástil *m*, árbol *m*

mastectomy [mæstéktəmi] N mastectomía *f*

master [mǽstɚ] N (person in control) amo -a *mf*, señor -ora *mf*; (owner of slave or animal) amo -a *mf*; (best representative, skilled laborer) maestro *m*; (young boy) señorito *m*; (tape or disk) original *m*; **—'s degree** maestría *f*; ADJ (dominant) dominante; **— bedroom** dormitorio principal *m*; **— key** llave maestra *f*; **— mind** cerebro *m*; **— piece** obra maestra *f*; VT dominar; **to — mind** planificar y dirigir

masterful [mǽstɚfəl] ADJ magistral

masterly [mǽstɚli] ADJ magistral

mastery [mǽstɚi] N dominio *m*

mastiff [mǽstɪf] N mastín *m*, alano *m*

masturbate [mǽstɚbet] VI/VT masturbar[se]

mat [mæt] N (floor covering) estera *f*; (for wiping feet) felpudo *m*; (in gymnastics) colchoneta *f*; (of hair) maraña *f*; VI enmarañarse

match [mætʃ] N (pair) pareja *f*; (chess game) partida *f*; (tennis, golf game) partido *m*; (boxing encounter) combate *m*; (device for fire) fósforo *m*, cerilla *f*; **—ball** bola de partido *f*; **—box** cajita de fósforos *f*; **—maker** casamentero -ra *mf*; **—point** punto de partido *m*; **he has no —** no tiene igual; **he is a good —** es un buen partido; **the hat and coat are a good —** el abrigo y el sombrero hacen juego; VI/VT hacer juego [con]; VI (to correspond) estar de acuerdo; **the colors don't —** los colores no combinan; VT (equal) igualar; (come to correspond) poner de acuerdo; (form pairs) parear

matching [mætʃɪŋ] ADJ emparejados; **— colors** colores que combinan *m pl*; **— pair** pareja *f*; **— shoes** zapatos del mismo par *m pl*

matchless [mætʃlɪs] ADJ sin par

mate [met] N (one of a pair) pareja *f*; (friend) compañero -ra *mf*; (on a ship) oficial *m*; (in chess) mate *m*; VI/VT aparear[se]

material [mətíriəl] ADJ (made of matter) material; (pertinent) pertinente; N (substance) material *m*; (fabric) tejido *m*, género *m*

materialism [mətíriəlɪzəm] N materialismo *m*

materialize [mətíriəlaɪz] VI/VT materializar[se], plasmarse

maternal [mətɚnl] ADJ (motherly) maternal; (on mother's side of family) materno

maternity [mətɚnɪɾi] N maternidad *f*; **— leave** licencia por maternidad *f*

math [mæθ] N matemática[s] *f* [*pl*]

mathematical [mæθəmæɾɪkəl] ADJ matemático

mathematician [mæθəmətíʃən] N matemático -ca *mf*

mathematics [mæθəmǽɾɪks] N matemática[s] *f* [*pl*]

matinee [mæɾné] N matiné *f*

mating [méɾɪŋ] N (copulation) cópula *f*; (reproduction) reproducción *f*

matriarch [métriɑrk] N matriarca *f*

matriculate [mətríkjəlet] VI/VT matricular[se]

matriculation [mətríkjəléʃən] N matriculación *f*, matrícula *f*

matrilineal [mætrəlíniəl] ADJ matrilineal

matrimony [mætrəmoni] N matrimonio *m*

matrix [métrɪks] N matriz *f*

matron [métrən] N (married woman or widow) matrona *f*; (in a hospital) jefa de enfermeras *f*

matter [mǽɾɚ] N (substance, pus) materia *f*;

(affair) asunto *m*; (printed) impreso *m*; (reading) material de lectura *m*; **— for complaint** motivo de queja *m*; **a — of two minutes** cosa de dos minutos *f*; **as a — of fact** de hecho, precisamente; **it is of no —** no tiene importancia; **no — what you say** no importa lo que digas; **as a — of course** por rutina; **what is the —?** ¿qué pasa? VI importar; **it doesn't —** no importa

mattress [mǽtrɪs] N colchón *m*

maturation [mætʃəréʃən] N maduración *f*

mature [mətʃúr] ADJ maduro; **a — note** un pagaré vencido/pagadero *m*; **for — audiences** para adultos; VI/VT madurar[se]; (a savings bond) vencer[se]

maturing [mətʃúrɪŋ] N maduración *f*

maturity [mətʃúrɪdi] N madurez *f*; (of a debt) vencimiento *m*

maul [mɔl] VT atacar, herir gravemente

Mauritania [mɔrɪténiə] N Mauritania *f*

Mauritanian [mɔrɪténiən] ADJ & N mauritano -na *mf*

Mauritian [mɔríʃən] ADJ & N mauriciano -na *mf*

Mauritius [mɔríʃəs] N Mauricio *m*

maverick [mǽvərɪk] N cimarrón *m*; (person) inconformista *mf*, cimarrón -ona *mf*

maxim [mǽksɪm] N máxima *f*, sentencia *f*

maximize [mǽksəmaɪz] VT maximizar

maximum [mǽksəməm] ADJ & N máximo *m*

may [me] V AUX **— I sit down?** ¿puedo sentarme? **— you have a merry Christmas** que pases una feliz Navidad; **it — be that** puede ser que; **it — rain** puede [ser] que llueva, tal vez llueva; **she — have been late** puede [ser] que haya llegado tarde; **be that as it —** sea como fuere

May [me] N mayo *m*; **— Day** primero de mayo *m*; **—pole** mayo *m*

Maya [máɪə] N & ADJ maya *mf*

Mayan [máɪən] N & ADJ maya *mf*

maybe [mébi] ADV quizá[s], tal vez

mayonnaise [méənez] N mayonesa *f*, mahonesa *f*

mayor [méər] N alcalde *m*

mayoralty [méərəlti] N alcaldía *f*

maze [mez] N laberinto *m*

MBA [master of business administration] [émbié] N máster en administración de empresas *m*, maestría en administración de empresas *f*

MD [medicinae doctor] [émdí] N doctor -ora en medicina *mf*

me [mi] PRON **she sees —** me ve; **he talks to —** me habla; **he comes with —** viene conmigo; **he did it for —** lo hizo para mí

meadow [méɖo] N pradera *f*, prado *m*; **—lark** alondra *f*

meager [mígə] ADJ escaso, exiguo

meal [mił] N (repast) comida *f*; (flour) harina *f*;

—time hora de comer *f*

mean [min] ADJ (unkind) cruel; (petty) vil; (humble) humilde; (stingy) mezquino; (difficult) de mal genio; (middle) medio; **—-spirited** mezquino; **I make a — lasagna** me sale muy rica la lasagna; N (average) media *f*, promedio *m*; **—s** medios *m pl*; **the ends justify the —s** el fin justifica los medios; **a man of —s** un hombre adinerado; **by —s of** por medio de; **—s of transport** medios de transporte *m pl*; **—s test** prueba de ingresos *f*; **by all —s** (of course) por supuesto; (using all resources) por todos los medios; **by no —s** de ningún modo; VT (intend) querer, tener intenciones de; (signify) querer decir, significar; **he —s well** tiene buenas intenciones; **winning —s everything to them** lo que más les importa es ganar; **they are meant for each other** son el uno para el otro

meander [miǽndə] VI (be winding) serpentear; (to wander) vagar

meaning [mínɪŋ] N (sense) significado *m*, sentido *m*; (purpose) sentido *m*; ADJ **well-**bien intencionado

meaningful [mínɪŋfəl] ADJ (result, event) significativo, trascendente; (sentence) coherente

meaningless [mínɪŋlɪs] ADJ sin sentido

meanness [mínnɪs] N (cruelty) crueldad *f*; (pettiness) mezquindad *f*

meant [mɛnt] *see* mean

meantime [míntaɪm] ADV LOC **in the —** mientras tanto

meanwhile [mínhwaɪł] ADV mientras tanto

measles [mízəłz] N sarampión *m*

measurable [méʒərəbəł] ADJ medible, mensurable

measure [méʒə] N (dimension) medida *f*; (criterion) criterio *m*; (in musical bar) compás *m*; (bill) proyecto de ley *m*; **beyond —** sobremanera; **dry —** medida de áridos *f*; **in large —** en gran parte; **—s** medidas *f pl*; VI/VT medir; **to — up** compararse con; **measuring tape** cinta de medir *f*, metro *m*

measured [méʒəd] ADJ (rhythmical) acompasado; (moderate) moderado, mesurado

measurement [méʒəmənt] N (act of measuring) medición *f*; (dimension) medida *f*, dimensión *f*

meat [mit] N carne *f*; (essential point) meollo *m*; **—ball** albóndiga *f*; **—loaf** pan/pastel de carne *m*

meaty [mídi] ADJ (with meat) con mucha carne; (substantial) sustancioso

mechanic [mɪkǽnɪk] ADJ & N mecánico *m*; N **—s** mecánica *f*

mechanical [mɪkǽnɪkəł] ADJ mecánico

mechanism [mékənɪzəm] N mecanismo *m*

medal [médl] N medalla *f*; VI ganar una medalla

meddle [médl] VI entrometerse, inmiscuirse

meddler [médlə-] N entrometido -da *mf*

meddlesome [médlsəm] ADJ entrometido

media [mídɪə] N (communication) medios *m pl*, media *m pl*, medios de comunicación masiva *m pl*; (cables) cables del ordenador/ de la computadora *m pl*

median [mídɪən] ADJ mediano; N (middle value, line) mediana *f*

mediate [mídiet] VI/VT mediar

mediation [mɪdɪéʃən] N mediación *f*

mediator [mídɪeDə-] N mediador -ora *mf*

medical [médɪkəl] ADJ médico; — **chart** hoja clínica *f*; — **exam** examen médico *m*; — **examiner** médico -ca forense *mf*; — **history** historia clínica *f*; — **record** expediente médico *m*; — **school** facultad de medicina *f*

medicate [médɪket] VT medicar

medication [mɪdɪkéʃən] N medicación *f*

medicine [médɪsɪn] N (profession) medicina *f*; (drug) medicamento *m*, fármaco *m*; — **ball** balón medicinal *m*; — **cabinet** botiquín *m*; — **man** curandero *m*

medieval [mɪdívəl] ADJ medieval

mediocre [mɪdɪókə-] ADJ mediocre

mediocrity [mɪdɪákrɪDɪ] N mediocridad *f*

meditate [médɪtet] VI meditar

meditation [mɛdɪtéʃən] N meditación *f*, recogimiento *m*

Mediterranean [mɛdɪtərénɪən] ADJ mediterráneo

medium [mídɪəm] N (substance, agency) medio *m*; (person who contacts spirits) médium *mf*; — **of exchange** medio de cambio *m*; ADJ mediano; ADV término medio

medley [médlɪ] N (music) popurrí *m*; (mixture) mezcla *f*

meek [mik] ADJ manso

meekness [míknɪs] N mansedumbre *f*

meet [mit] VT (encounter) encontrarse con; (make acquaintance) conocer; (face in conflict) enfrentar; (satisfy) satisfacer; (pay) pagar; **to — a deadline** cumplir el plazo; **to — expenses** sufragar los gastos; **to — halfway** partir la diferencia; **to — a train** esperar un tren; **I will — you at the station** nos encontramos/vemos en la estación; **have you met my brother?** ¿conoces a mi hermano? **we were met with disapproval** se nos recibió con desaprobación; VI (encounter) encontrarse; (make acquaintance) conocerse; (have a meeting) reunirse; (cross) cruzarse; **to — in battle** trabar batalla; **to — with** (intentional) reunirse con; (unintentional) tropezar con; N encuentro deportivo *m*, competición *f*

meeting [mídɪŋ] N reunión *f*, junta *f*; (political) mitin *m*; (crossing of roads) cruce *m*

megabyte [mégəbaɪt] N megabyte *m*

megahertz [mégəhɜ-tz] N megahertz *m*, megahercio *m*

megalomania [mɛgəloménɪə] N megalomanía *f*

megaphone [mégəfon] N megáfono *m*, bocina *f*

melancholy [mélənkɑli] N melancolía *f*; ADJ melancólico

melanoma [mɛlənómə] N melanoma *m*

meld [mɛld] VT fusionar

melee [méle] N reyerta *f*, tumulto *m*

mellow [mélo] ADJ (soft) dulce, suave; (gentle) tranquilo; VI/VT suavizar[se]

melodic [məláDɪk] ADJ melódico

melodious [məlódɪəs] ADJ melodioso, melódico

melodrama [mélodramə] N melodrama *m*

melody [méləDɪ] N melodía *f*

melon [mélən] N melón *m*

melt [mɛlt] VI/VT (liquefy) derretir[se]; (dissolve) disolver[se]; —**ing pot** crisol *m*; N —**down** (fusion) catástrofe por fusión nuclear incontrolada *f*; (any developing disaster) catástrofe *f*

member [mémbə-] N miembro *m* (also body part)

membership [mémbə-ʃɪp] N (number) número de miembros/socios *m*; (state) calidad de miembro/socio *f*

membrane [mémbren] N membrana *f*

memento [məménto] N recuerdo *m*

memoir [mémwɑr] N memoria *f*; —**s** memorias *f pl*, autobiografía *f*

memorable [mémə-əbəl] ADJ memorable

memorandum [mɛmərǽndəm] N memorándum *m*

memorial [məmɔ́rɪəl] N (monument) monumento conmemorativo *m*; (petition) memorial *m*; ADJ conmemorativo

memorize [mémə-aɪz] VI/VT memorizar

memory [mémərɪ] N (faculty) memoria *f*; (recollection) recuerdo *m*; — **cache** caché de memoria *f*; — **map** mapa de memoria *m*

menace [ménɪs] N amenaza *f*; VI/VT amenazar

mend [mɛnd] VT remendar; **to — matters** enmendar la situación; **to — one's ways** enmendarse, reformarse; VI (sick person) mejorarse; (bones) soldarse; N remiendo *m*; **to be on the —** ir mejorando

menial [mínɪəl] ADJ (lowly) bajo; (job) servil; N criado -da *mf*

meningitis [mɛnɪndʒaɪDɪs] N meningitis *f*

menopause [ménəpoz] N menopausia *f*

menstruate [ménstruet] VI menstruar

menstruation [mɛnstruéʃən] N menstruación *f*

mental [méntl] ADJ mental; (insane) *fam* chiflado; — **health** salud mental *f*; — **illness** enfermedad mental *f*; — **retardation** retraso mental *m*

mentality [mɛntǽlɪɾi] N mentalidad f

mention [mɛ́nʃən] VT mencionar; **don't — it** no hay de qué; N mención f

mentor [mɛ́ntɔr] N mentor -ora mf

menu [mɛ́nju] N (list of dishes) carta f, menú m; (computer) menú m; **— bar** (computer) barra de menú f

meow [mjaʊ] INTERJ miau

mercantile [mɝ́kəntil] ADJ mercantil

mercenary [mɝ́səneri] ADJ mercenario

merchandise[1] [mɝ́tʃəndaɪs] N mercancía f, mercadería f

merchandise[2] [mɝ́tʃəndaɪz] VT comercializar

merchandising [mɝ́tʃəndaɪzɪŋ] N mercadeo m, comercialización f

merchant [mɝ́tʃənt] N (trader) comerciante m, mercader m; ADJ mercante; **— marine** marina mercante f

merciful [mɝ́sɪfəl] ADJ misericordioso

merciless [mɝ́sɪlɪs] ADJ despiadado

mercury [mɝ́kjəri] N mercurio m; (on a mirror) azogue m

mercy [mɝ́si] N (compassion) misericordia f, clemencia f, piedad f; **to be at the — of** estar a merced de; **— killing** eutanasia f

mere [mir] ADJ mero, simple; **a — trifle** una nonada

merely [mɝ́li] ADV (only) solo, solamente; (simply) simplemente

merge [mɝdʒ] VI/VT (forces) unir[se]; (colors) fundir[se]; (companies) fusionar[se]; (data files) fusionar; N fusión f

merger [mɝ́dʒɚ] N fusión f; **—s and acquisitions** fusiones y adquisiciones f pl

meridian [mərídiən] ADJ & N meridiano m

merit [mɛ́rɪt] N mérito m; **— pay** paga por mérito f; **— raise** aumento por mérito m; VT merecer

meritorious [mɛrɪtɔ́riəs] ADJ meritorio

mermaid [mɝ́med] N sirena f

merriment [mɛ́rimənt] N alegría f, algazara f

merry [mɛ́ri] ADJ alegre; **—-go-round** tiovivo m; **—maker** fiestero -ra mf, juerguista mf; **—making** fiesta f, juerga f; **to make —** divertirse; INTERJ **— Christmas** Feliz Navidad f, Felices Pascuas

mesa [mɛ́sə] N mesa f

mesh [mɛʃ] N (of metal) malla f; (of fiber) red f; (of gears) engranaje m; VI engranar

mesmerize [mɛ́zməraɪz] VI/VT hipnotizar

mess [mɛs] N (state of confusion) desorden m, desarreglo m; (disorderly person) desordenado -da mf, mugriento -ta mf; (confused person) desastre m; (difficult situation) lío m, jaleo m; (food for soldiers) rancho m; (cafeteria) cantina f; **— hall** cantina f; **to make a — of fish** plato de pescado m; **to make a — of** (a room) ensuciar, desordenar; (a project) estropear; VI/VT **to — around**

(waste time) perder el tiempo; (philander) correr detrás de las mujeres; **to — up** (a room) alborotar, desordenar; (clothes, hair) desarreglar; (a project) estropear; **to — with** meterse con

message [mɛ́sɪdʒ] N mensaje m, recado m; **I get the —** ya caí en cuenta

messenger [mɛ́səndʒɚ] N mensajero -ra mf

messy [mɛ́si] ADJ (chaotic) desordenado; (embarrassing) embarazoso

met [mɛt] see meet

metabolic [mɛɾəbálɪk] ADJ metabólico

metabolism [mətǽbəlɪzəm] N metabolismo m

metal [mɛ́dl] N metal m; **— detector** detector de metales m; ADJ de metal, metálico

metallic [mətǽlɪk] ADJ metálico

metallurgy [mɛ́dlɚdʒi] N metalurgia f

metamorphosis [mɛɾəmɔ́rfəsɪs] N metamorfosis f

metaphor [mɛ́ɾəfɔr] N metáfora f

metaphysical [mɛɾəfízɪkəl] ADJ metafísico

metaphysics [mɛɾəfízɪks] N metafísica f

metastasis [mətǽstəsɪs] N metástasis f

metastasize [mətǽstəsaɪz] VI metastatizar

meteor [mídiɚ] N meteoro m; **— shower** lluvia de meteoritos f

meteorite [mídiəraɪt] N meteorito m

meteorological [miɾiəráládʒɪkəl] ADJ meteorológico

meteorology [miɾiəráládʒi] N meteorología f

meter [mídɚ] N (unit of length) metro m; (measuring device) contador m, medidor m

methane [mɛ́θen] N metano m

method [mɛ́θəd] N método m

methodical [məθάdɪkəl] ADJ metódico

methodology [mɛθədáládʒi] N metodología f

meticulous [mətíkjələs] ADJ detallista

metric [mɛ́trɪk] ADJ métrico

metro [mɛ́tro] N metro m

metronome [mɛ́trənom] N metrónomo m

metropolis [mətrápəlɪs] N metrópoli f, urbe f

metropolitan [mɛtrəpálɪɾən] ADJ metropolitano

mettle [mɛ́dl] N temple m, valor m

mew [mju] N maullido m; VI maullar

Mexican [mɛ́ksɪkən] ADJ & N mexicano -na mf

Mexico [mɛ́ksɪko] N México m

mezzanine [mɛ́zənin] N entrepiso m, entresuelo m

mickey mouse [mɪ́kimáus] ADJ poco serio, informal

microbe [máɪkrob] N microbio m

microbiology [maɪkrobaɪáládʒi] N microbiología f

microcomputer [maɪkrokəmpjúɾɚ] N Am microcomputadora f; Sp microordenador m

microeconomics [maɪkroɛkənámɪks] N microeconomía f

microfiche [máɪkrofɪʃ] N microficha f

microfilm [máɪkrofɪlm] N microfilme *m*

micromanage [maɪkroménɪdʒ] VI/VT administrar con excesivo control

micron [máɪkrɑn] N micrón *m*, micrómetro *m*

Micronesia [maɪkroníʒə] N Micronesia *f*

Micronesian [maɪkrəníʒən] ADJ & N micronesio -sia *mf*

microorganism [maɪkroórgənɪzəm] N microorganismo *m*

microphone [máɪkrəfon] N micrófono *m*

microprocessor [maɪkroprásesə·] N microprocesador *m*

microscope [máɪkrəskop] N microscopio *m*

microscopic [maɪkrəskápɪk] ADJ microscópico

microsurgery [máɪkrosə́dʒəri] N microcirujía *f*

microwave [máɪkrowev] N microonda *f*; **— oven** [horno] microondas *m sg*

mid [mɪd] ADJ medio; **—air** en el aire; **—day** [del] mediodía *m*; **—field player** (soccer) centrocampista *m*; **—life** madurez *f*; **—life crisis** crisis de la edad madura *f*; **—night** [de] medianoche *f*; **—shipman** guardiamarina *m*; **in —stream** (of a river) en medio del río; (of a task) en plena actividad; **—summer** pleno verano *m*; **—term examination** examen a mitad del curso *m*; **—way** a medio camino, a mitad del camino; **—wife** partera *f*, comadre *f*

middle [mídl] ADJ (average) medio, mediano; (intermediate) intermedio; (central) central; **—-aged** de mediana edad; **— Ages** Edad Media *f*; **— class** clase media *f*, burguesía *f*; **—-class neighborhood** barrio de clase media; **— ear** oído medio *m*; **— finger** dedo mayor *m*, dedo del corazón *m*; **—man** intermediario *m*, revendedor *m*; **— management** administración intermedia *f*; **— name** segundo nombre *m*; **—-of-the-road** moderado; **—-sized** [de] tamaño mediano; N medio *m*; (waist) cintura *f*; **in the — of** en el medio de; **I'm in the — of something** estoy ocupado haciendo algo; **toward the — of the month** a mediados del mes

midget [mídʒɪt] N enano -na *mf*

MIDI [musical instrument digital interface] [mídi] N interfaz digital de instrumentos musicales

midst [mɪdst] ADV LOC medio *m*, centro *m*; **in the — of** en medio de, entre; **in our —** entre nosotros

mien [min] N porte *m*

might [maɪt] V AUX **it — be that** podría ser que; **he said it — rain tomorrow** dijo que tal vez lloviera mañana; **she — have been late** puede ser que haya llegado tarde; N poder *m*, poderío *m*

mighty [máɪdi] ADJ (strong) poderoso, potente; (large) imponente; ADV muy

migraine [máɪgren] N migraña *f*, jaqueca *f*

migrant [máɪgrənt] ADJ migratorio, migrante; N trabajador -ora itinerante *mf*, bracero -ra *mf*

migrate [máɪgret] VI (also computers) migrar

migration [maɪgréʃən] N migración *f*

migratory [máɪgrətɔri] ADJ migratorio

mild [maɪld] ADJ (gentle) suave; (moderate) moderado; (not serious) leve

mildew [míldu] N moho *m*

mildness [máɪldnɪs] N (gentleness) suavidad *f*; (lack of gravity) levedad *f*

mile [maɪl] N milla *f*; **—stone** hito *m*

mileage [máɪlɪdʒ] N (distance, odometer reading) millaje *m*, kilometraje *m*; **this car gets good —** este coche es económico; **what kind of — are you getting?** ¿cuántos kilómetros por litro hace tu coche?

milieu [mɪljú] N ambiente *m*

militance [mílɪtəns] N militancia *f*

militancy [mílɪtənsi] N militancia *f*

militant [mílɪtənt] ADJ & N (fanatic) militante *mf*; (combatant) combatiente *mf*

military [mílɪteri] ADJ militar; N **the —** (armed forces) el ejército; (military personnel) los militares

militia [mɑlíʃə] N milicia *f*

milk [mɪlk] N leche *f*; **— chocolate** chocolate con leche *m*; **—maid** lechera *f*; **—man** lechero *m*; **— shake** batido *m*; VT ordeñar; (exploit) exprimir; **he's —ing it for all it's worth** le está sacando todo el jugo

milky [mílki] ADJ (consistency) lechoso; (product) lácteo; **— Way** Vía Láctea *f*

mill [mɪl] N (building) molino *m*; (factory) fábrica *f*; (for sugar) trapiche *m*, ingenio *m*; (rotating tool) fresa *f*; (small grinder) molinillo *m*; **—stone** muela de molino *f*; **a —stone around your neck** una piedra al cuello; VT (grind grain) moler; (cut wood) aserrar; (cut grooves on coins) acordonar; (machine) fresar; **to — around** dar vueltas

millennium [mɑlíniəm] N milenio *m*

miller [mílə·] N (person who mills) molinero -ra *mf*; (machine for milling) fresadora *f*; (moth) mariposa nocturna *f*

milligram [mílɪgræm] N miligramo *m*

milliliter [mílɪlidə·] N mililitro *m*

millimeter [mílɪmidə·] N milímetro *m*

milliner [mílɪnə·] N sombrerero -ra *mf*

millinery [mílɪneri] N (shop) sombrerería *f*; (hats) sombreros de señora *m pl*

million [míljən] N millón *m*; **a — dollars** un millón de dólares

millionaire [mɪljənér] N millonario -ria *mf*

millionth [míljənθ] ADJ & N millonésimo *m*

mime [maɪm] N (actor) mimo *m*; (technique, performance) pantomima *f*; VI hacer la mímica

mimic [mímɪk] VT imitar, remedar; N mono -na

mf, remedador -ora *mf*

mince [mɪns] VT picar, desmenuzar; **not to —
words** no tener pelos en la lengua; **—meat**
picadillo *m*; **I'm going to make —meat of
you** te voy a hacer picadillo

mind [maɪnd] N (thinking process) mente *f*;
(person of intellect) inteligencia *f*; (opinion)
parecer *m*, opinión *f*; **— games**
manipulación psicológica *f*; **— over matter**
el espíritu sobre la materia; **—-set** actitud *f*,
forma de pensar *f*; **to be out of one's —**
estar loco; **to bear in —** tener en cuenta; **to
change one's —** cambiar de parecer /
opinión; **to give someone a piece of one's
—** cantarle a alguien las cuarenta; **I have a —
to** me dan ganas de; **to make up one's —**
decidirse; **to my —** a mi modo de ver; **to
speak one's —freely** hablar con toda
franqueza; **what do you have in —?** ¿qué
tienes en mente? **to call to —** recordar; **to
keep one's — on one's work** concentrarse
en el trabajo; ADJ **—-altering** alucinógeno;
VT (take care of) cuidar; (pay attention to)
atender a; (obey) obedecer; **I don't —** no
tengo inconveniente en ello; **— what you
say** cuidado con lo que dices; **to — one's
own business** no meterse en lo ajeno

mindful [máɪndfəl] ADJ atento

mine [maɪn] PRON **this book is —** este libro es
mío; **these things are —** estas cosas son
mías; **— is bigger** el mío / la mía es más
grande; **a friend of —** un amigo mío / una
amiga mía *f*; N mina *f* (also explosive device);
—field campo minado *m*; **— sweeper**
dragaminas *m sg*, barreminas *m sg*; VT (plant
explosives) minar; (dig out minerals) extraer;
(exploit an area for minerals) explotar; VI (lay
mines) sembrar minas; (dig a mine) cavar una
mina; **to — for** extraer

miner [máɪnɚ] N minero -ra *mf*

mineral [mínɚəl] ADJ & N mineral *m*; **— rights**
derechos mineros *m pl*; **— water** agua
mineral *f*

mingle [míŋgəl] VI mezclarse; (sounds)
confundirse; VT mezclar

miniature [mínɪətʃɚ] N miniatura *f*; ADJ en
miniatura

minicomputer [mɪnɪkəmpjúdɚ] N *Am*
minicomputadora *f*; *Sp* miniordenador *m*

minimal [mínəməl] ADJ mínimo

minimize [mínəmaɪz] VT minimizar

minimum [mínəməm] ADJ & N mínimo *m*; **—
wage** salario mínimo *m*

mining [máɪnɪŋ] N (exploitation of mines)
minería *f*; (act of mining) minado *m*; ADJ
minero; **open —** minería a cielo abierto *f*

miniskirt [mínɪskɚt] N minifalda *f*

minister [mínɪstɚ] N (official) ministro -tra *mf*;
(pastor) pastor -ora *mf*, clérigo *m*; VI **to — to**

atender a

ministerial [mɪnɪstíriəl] ADJ ministerial

ministry [mínɪstri] N (government agency)
ministerio *m*; (functions of pastor) clerecía *f*

minivan [mínɪvæn] N camioneta *f*

mink [mɪŋk] N visón *m*

minnow [míno] N pececillo *m*

minor [máɪnɚ] ADJ (smaller) menor, más
pequeño; (of secondary importance) menor;
— key tono menor *m*; **— league** liga menor
f; N (young person) menor de edad *mf*;
(musical interval) tono menor *m*; (subfield)
asignatura secundaria *f*; VI tener como
segunda especialización

minority [mənɔ́rɪdi] N (smaller part or group)
minoría *f*; (state of being underage)
minoridad *f*; (member of a minority)
miembro de una minoría *m*; ADJ minoritario;
— partner socio -cia minoritario -ria *mf*

mint [mɪnt] N (flavor) menta *f*, hierbabuena *f*;
(candy) pastilla de menta *f*; (money) casa de la
moneda *f*; VT acuñar

minus [máɪnəs] PREP **seven — four** siete menos
cuatro; **we came — my brother** vinimos
sin mi hermano; N signo de menos *m*; ADJ
negativo

minuscule [mínəskjul] ADJ minúsculo

minute[1] [mínɪt] N minuto *m*; **— hand** minutero
m; **—s** actas *f pl*

minute[2] [maɪnút] ADJ (small) diminuto;
(detailed) detallado, minucioso

miracle [mírəkəl] N milagro *m*

miraculous [mɪrǽkjələs] ADJ milagroso

mirage [mɪrɑ́ʒ] N espejismo *m*

mire [maɪr] N (mud) cieno *m*, fango *m*; (muddy
place) ciénaga *f*; VI/VT (bog down) atascar[se]
en el fango; (be or get covered with mud)
enlodar[se]

mirror [mírɚ] N espejo *m*; (large) luna *f*; **—
image** imagen especular *f*; VT reflejar

mirth [mɚθ] N risa *f*, hilaridad *f*

mirthful [mɚ́θfəl] ADJ risueño

miry [máɪri] ADJ cenagoso, fangoso

misanthropy [mɪsǽnθrəpi] N misantropía *f*

misappropriation [mɪsəpropriéʃən] N
malversación *f*

misbehave [mɪsbɪhév] VI portarse mal

miscalculate [mɪskǽlkjəlet] VI/VT (in math)
calcular mal; (in situations) equivocarse

miscarriage [mískærɪdʒ] N aborto espontáneo
m, malparto *m*; **— of justice** injusticia *f*

miscarry [mɪskǽri] VI (abort) abortar
espontáneamente; (fail) malograrse,
frustrarse

miscellaneous [mɪsəléniəs] ADJ diverso; (texts)
misceláneo; **— expenses** gastos varios *mf*

mischief [místʃɪf] N travesura *f*, diablura *f*,
picardía *f*; (serious prank) barrabasada *f*,
bellaquería *f*; **this will come to —** va a

suceder una desgracia

mischievous [místʃəvəs] ADJ travieso, pícaro

misconception [mɪskənsépʃən] N concepto erróneo m

misconduct¹ [mɪskándʌkt] N (bad behavior) mala conducta f; (malfeasance) mala administración f

misconduct² [mɪskəndákt] VT administrar mal; **to — oneself** portarse mal

miscue [mɪskjú] N pifia f; VI/VT pifiar

misdeed [mɪsdíd] N fechoría f

misdemeanor [mɪsdɪmínə˞] N delito menor m

miser [máɪzə˞] N avaro -ra mf, tacaño -ña mf

miserable [mízə˞əbəl] ADJ infeliz, desdichado; **a — day** un día asqueroso; **a — failure** un fracaso rotundo

miserly [máɪzə˞li] ADJ avariento, tacaño

misery [mízəri] N (wretchedness) desgracia f; (poverty) miseria f; (unhappiness) infelicidad f

misfit [mísfɪt] N inadaptado -da mf

misfortune [mɪsfɔ́rtʃən] N desgracia f, desdicha f, desventura f

misgivings [mɪsgívɪŋz] N aprensión f, recelo m

misguided [mɪsgáɪdɪd] ADJ mal aconsejado, poco feliz

mishap [míʃæp] N contratiempo m, percance m

misinform [mɪsɪnfɔ́rm] VT desinformar, dar información errónea

misjudge [mɪsdʒʌ́dʒ] VT juzgar mal

mislay [mɪslé] VT (keys, etc.) extraviar, perder; (a document) traspapelar; (lay wrong) colocar mal

mislead [mɪslíd] VT (in the wrong direction) guiar por mal camino; (into error) engañar, confundir

misleading [mɪslídɪŋ] ADJ engañoso

mismanage [mɪsmǽnɪdʒ] VT administrar mal

misogyny [mɪsádʒəni] N misoginia f

misplace [mɪsplés] VT (lose keys, etc.) extraviar; (lose a document) traspapelar; (place wrong) colocar mal; **she —d her trust** confió en la persona equivocada

misprint [mísprɪnt] N errata f, error de imprenta m

misrepresent [mɪsrɛprɪzént] VT distorsionar, tergiversar

misrepresentation [mɪsrɛprɪzentéʃən] N distorsión f, tergiversación f

miss [mɪs] VI (fail to hit) errar; (misfire) fallar; VT (fail to hit) errar, no acertar; (fail to be on time for) perder; (fail to attend) faltar a; (feel absence of) echar de menos; Am extrañar; **he just —ed being killed** por poco se mata; N (of a target) tiro errado m; (in a motor) falla f; (from class) falta f; (young woman) señorita f; **— Smith** la señorita Smith

misshapen [mɪsʃépən] ADJ deforme

missile [mísəl] N (projectile) proyectil m; (guided weapon) misil m

missing [mísɪŋ] ADJ (not present) ausente; (lost) perdido; **— link** eslabón perdido m; **one book is —** falta un libro

mission [míʃən] N misión f; **— statement** declaración de la misión f

missionary [míʃəneri] ADJ & N misionero -ra mf

misspell [mɪsspél] VT (written) escribir mal; (oral) deletrear mal

misstatement [mɪsstétmənt] N declaración errónea/falsa f

misstep [místɛp] N paso en falso m

mist [mɪst] N (of water droplets) neblina f, bruma f; (of perfume) rocío m; VI lloviznar; VT rociar

mistake [mɪsték] N error m, equivocación f; (orthographical) falta f; **to make a —** equivocarse; VI/VT equivocar[se]; **I — my sister for my mother** confundo a mi hermana con mi madre

mistaken [mɪstékən] ADJ equivocado; **to be —** estar equivocado, equivocarse; **unless I'm —** si no me equivoco

mistaken [mɪstékən] see mistake

mister [místə˞] N señor m

mistletoe [mísəlto] N muérdago m

mistook [mɪstúk] see mistake

mistreat [mɪstrít] VT maltratar

mistreatment [mɪstrítmənt] N maltrato m

mistress [místrɪs] N (of a household) señora f; (employing servants, animal owner) ama f; (lover) amante f

mistrial [mɪstráɪl] N proceso viciado de nulidad m

mistrust [mɪstrʌ́st] N desconfianza f; VT desconfiar de

mistrustful [mɪstrʌ́stfəl] ADJ desconfiado, receloso

misty [místi] ADJ (foggy) neblinoso, brumoso; (in tears) nublado; (blurry) empañado

misunderstand [mɪsʌndə˞stǽnd] VT comprender mal, malinterpretar

misunderstanding [mɪsʌndə˞stǽndɪŋ] N (confusion) malentendido m; (failure to understand) equivocación f, mala inteligencia f; (argument) desavenencia f

misuse¹ [mɪsjús] N (of drugs) abuso m; (of a word) mal uso m; (of funds) malversación f

misuse² [mɪsjúz] VT (drugs) abusar de; (a friend) maltratar; (a word) emplear mal; (funds) malversar

mite [maɪt] N ácaro m; ADV **a — greedy** un poquito codicioso

mitigate [mídɪget] VT mitigar

mitochondria [maɪdokándriə] N mitocondria f

mitten [mítn] N manopla f

mix [mɪks] VI/VT mezclar[se]; **to — up** confundir; N mezcla f; (for baking) preparado m; **—up** (confusion) confusión f; (fight) pelea *f*

mixed [mɪkst] ADJ mixto; — **bag** grupo heterogéneo *m*; — **doubles** dobles mixtos *m pl*; — **drink** cóctel *m*; — **-up** confundido

mixer [míksə] N (appliance) batidora *f*; (party) fiesta *f*; (soda) refresco *m*; (sound technician) mezclador -ora *mf*; (sound device) mezcladora *f*

mixture [míkstʃə] N mezcla *f*

moan [mon] N quejido *m*, gemido *m*; VI gemir, quejarse; VI/VT lamentar

moat [mot] N foso *m*

mob [mab] N (disorderly crowd) tumulto *m*, turba *f*; (crowd) muchedumbre *f*, populacho *m*; (mafia) mafia *f*; VT (attack) asaltar; (crowd) atestar

mobile [móbəl] ADJ móvil; (personnel) que tiene movilidad; — **home** casa prefabricada *f*; — **Internet** internet móvil *m*; — **phone** [teléfono] móvil *m*, [teléfono] celular *m*

mobility [mobílɪɾɪ] N movilidad *f*

mobilization [mobəlɪzéʃən] N movilización *f*

mobilize [móbəlaɪz] VI/VT movilizar[se]

moccasin [mákəsɪn] N mocasín *m* (also snake)

mock [mak] VI (ridicule) burlar[se]; VT (imitate) remedar; ADJ de práctica; — **battle** simulacro de batalla *m*; N — **-up** maqueta *f*, modelo *m*

mockery [mákəri] N (ridicule) burla *f*; (imitation) remedo *m*; (travesty) farsa *f*

mockingbird [mákɪŋbɚd] N sinsonte *m*

mode [mod] N modo *m*; — **of delivery** modo de entrega *m*; — **of payment** forma de pago *f*

model [mádl] N (guide) modelo *m*; (person) modelo *mf*, maniquí *mf*; ADJ modelo, ejemplar; — **school** escuela modelo *f*; VI/VT modelar; (display clothes) lucir

modem [módəm] N módem *m*

moderate[1] [mádəɹɪt] ADJ (not excessive) moderado, mesurado; (person) comedido; (weather) templado; (price) módico; N moderado -da *mf*

moderate[2] [mádəɹet] VI/VT moderar[se] (also preside at meetings)

moderation [mɑɾəɹéʃən] N moderación *f*, mesura *f*

modern [mádɚn] ADJ moderno; — **age** modernidad *f*

modernism [mádɚnɪzəm] N modernismo *m*

modernity [madɚnɪɾɪ] N modernismo *m*

modernization [maɾɚnɪzéʃən] N modernización *f*

modernize [máɾɚnaɪz] VI/VT modernizar[se], innovar

modernness [máɾɚnnɪs] N modernismo *m*

modest [mádɪst] ADJ (humble) modesto; (chaste) recatado, honesto

modesty [mádɪsti] N (humility) modestia *f*; (chastity) recato *m*, pudor *m*, honestidad *f*

modification [maɾəfɪkéʃən] N modificación *f*

modify [mádəfaɪ] VT modificar

modulate [mádʒəlet] VI/VT modular[se]

modulation [madʒəléʃən] N modulación *f*

module [mádʒul] N módulo *m*

mohair [móhɛr] N mohair *m*

moist [mɔɪst] ADJ húmedo

moisten [mɔ́ɪsən] VI/VT humedecer[se]

moisture [mɔ́ɪstʃə] N humedad *f*

moisturizer [mɔ́ɪstʃəɹáɪzɚ] N [crema] hidrante/humectante *f*

molar [mólɚ] ADJ molar; N muela *f*, molar *m*

molasses [məlǽsɪz] N melaza *f*

mold [mold] N (form) molde *m*; (fungi) moho *m*; (mettle) temple *m*; VT (shape) moldear, plasmar; (adapt) amoldar; (fuse) fundir; VI/VT (become moldy) enmohecer[se]

molder [móldɚ] VI/VT descomponerse; (paper) enmohecerse

molding [móldɪŋ] N (adornment) moldura *f*; (action of molding) moldeado *m*

Moldova [mɔ̀ldóvə] N Moldavia *f*

Moldovan [mɔ̀ldóvən] ADJ & N moldavo -va *mf*

moldy [móldi] ADJ mohoso

mole [mol] N (blemish) lunar *m*; (animal, spy) topo *m*; (breakwater) rompeolas *m sg*

molecular [məlékjələ] ADJ molecular

molecule [máltkjul] N molécula *f*

molest [məlést] VT abusar sexualmente de

mollify [máləfaɪ] VT apaciguar, aplacar

mollusk [máləsk] N molusco *m*

molt [molt] VI (birds) mudar la pluma; (snakes) mudar la piel; N muda *f*

molten [mótn̩] ADJ fundido

molybdenum [məlíbdənəm] N molibdeno *m*

mom [mam] N mamá *f*; — **and pop store** tienda familiar *f*

moment [mómənt] N momento *m*; **being a parent has its —s** ser padre/madre tiene sus momentos de recompensa

momentary [mómənteri] ADJ momentáneo

momentous [moméntəs] ADJ importante, trascendental

momentum [moméntəm] N (in physics) momento *m*; (in politics, sports) empuje *m*

mommy [mámi] N mami *f*

Monaco [mánəko] N Mónaco *m*

monarch [mánɚk] N monarca *mf*

monarchical [mənárkɪkəl] ADJ monárquico

monarchist [mánɚkɪst] N monárquico -ca *mf*

monarchy [mánɚki] N monarquía *f*

monastery [mánəsteri] N monasterio *m*

Monday [mánde] N lunes *m*

Monegasque [manɪgásk] ADJ & N monegasco -ca *mf*

monetary [mánɪteri] ADJ monetario

money [máni] N dinero *m*; — **-back guarantee** garantía de devolución de dinero *f*; — **belt** faltriquera en forma de cinturón *f*; —

changer cambista *mf*; — **laundering** lavado de dinero *m*; — **machine** cajero automático *m*; — **market** mercado de valores *m*; — **market account** cuenta de mercado monetario *f*; — **order** giro postal *m*; **to get one's —'s worth** sacar jugo al dinero; ADJ —**-grubbing** codicioso; —**-making** lucrativo, rentable

moneyed [mánid] ADJ adinerado

Mongolia [maŋgóliǝ] N Mongolia *f*

Mongolian [maŋgóliǝn] ADJ & N mongol -ola *mf*

mongoloid [máŋgǝlɔid] ADJ mongoloide

mongoose [máŋgus] N mangosta *f*

mongrel [máŋgrǝl] ADJ & N mestizo *m*

monitor [mánitǝ] N monitor *m*; (in a school) celador -ora *mf*; — **lizard** varano *m*; VT monitorear

monitoring [mánitǝ-iŋ] N monitoreo *m*, monitorización *f*

monk [mʌŋk] N monje *m*, religioso *m*

monkey [máŋki] N mono *m*, mico *m*; — **bars** jaula de los monos *f*; — **business** (mischief) picardía *f*; (trickery) chanchullo *m*; — **wrench** llave inglesa *f*; **to have a — on one's back** estar adicto; VI **to — around** bobear, payasear; **to — with** bobear con

monogamy [mǝnágǝmi] N monogamia *f*

monologue, monolog [mánǝlɔg] N monólogo *m*

mononucleosis [manonukliósis] N mononucleosis *f*

monopolize [mǝnápǝlaiz] VT monopolizar

monopoly [mǝnápǝli] N monopolio *m*

monotonous [mǝnátnǝs] ADJ monótono

monotony [mǝnátni] N monotonía *f*

monsignor [mansínjǝ] N monseñor *m*

monster [mánstǝ] N monstruo *m*; ADJ enorme, monstruo *inv*

monstrosity [manstrásidi] N monstruosidad *f*

monstrous [mánstrǝs] ADJ monstruoso

month [mʌnθ] N mes *m*

monthly [mánθli] ADJ mensual; — **installment** mensualidad *f*; N publicación mensual *f*, mensuario *m*; ADV mensualmente

monument [mánjǝmǝnt] N monumento *m*

monumental [manjǝméntǝl] ADJ monumental

moo [mu] N mugido *m*; VI mugir

mooch [mutʃ] VI/VT gorronear; N pedigüeño -ña *mf*

mood [mud] N (emotional state) humor *m*, vena *f*, ánimo *m*; (grammatical category) modo *m*; **to be in a good** — estar de buen humor; **to be in the** — tener ganas de

moody [múdi] ADJ (sullen) malhumorado; (changing) voluble

moon [mun] N luna *f*; —**beam** rayo de luna *m*; —**light** claro de la luna *m*, luz de la luna *f*; —**lighting** pluriempleo *m*; —**shine** bebida alcohólica destilada sin licencia *f*; **once in a blue** — de Pascuas a Ramos

moor [mʊr] VI/VT amarrar; N páramo *m*

Moor [mʊr] N moro -ra *mf*

Moorish [múriʃ] ADJ morisco, moro

moose [mus] N alce *m*

moot [mut] ADJ **it became a — point** dejó de tener importancia

mop [map] N (for floors) *Sp* fregona *f*, *Sp* mopa *f*; *Mex* trapeador *m*; (for dust) plumero *m*; (of hair) greña *f*; —**-up** (of an enemy) limpieza *f*; (of a task) remate *m*; VI/VT pasar la mopa [sobre]; *Am* trapear; **to — one's brow** enjugarse la frente; **to — up** (a spill) limpiar; (an enemy) acabar con; (a task) rematar

mope [mop] VI andar abatido

moped [móped] N ciclomotor *m*, scooter *m*

moral [mórǝl] ADJ moral; N moraleja *f*; —**s** moral *f*

morale [mǝrǽl] N moral *f*

moralist [mórǝlist] N moralista *mf*

morality [mǝrǽlidi] N moralidad *f*

moralize [mórǝlaiz] VI/VT moralizar

morbid [mórbid] ADJ mórbido, morboso

morbidity [mɔrbídidi] N (predisposition to illness) morbilidad *f*; (producing illness) morbosidad *f*

more [mɔr] ADJ & ADV más; — **and** — cada vez más; — **or less** más o menos; **there is no** — no hay más; —**over** además

morgue [mɔrg] N depósito de cadáveres *m*, morgue *f*

moribund [mórǝbǝnd] ADJ moribundo

morning [mórniŋ] N mañana *f*; — **glory** dondiego de día *m*; — **sickness** náuseas *f pl*; — **star** lucero del alba *m*; **good** —! ¡buenos días! **tomorrow** — mañana por la mañana; ADJ de la mañana, matutino

Moroccan [mǝrákǝn] ADJ & N marroquí *mf*

Morocco [mǝráko] N Marruecos *m*

moron [mórɑn] N imbécil *m*

morphine [mórfin] N morfina *f*

morsel [mórsǝl] N bocado *m*

mortal [mórdl] ADJ & N mortal *mf*; — **sin** pecado mortal *m*

mortality [mɔrtǽlidi] N (rate) mortalidad *f*; (toll) mortandad *f*

mortar [mórdǝ] N (for pounding) mortero *m* (also ballistics); (for bricks) argamasa *f*, mezcla *f*; —**board** birrete *m*

mortgage [mórgidʒ] N hipoteca *f*; VT hipotecar; ADJ hipotecario; —**-backed securities** valores respaldados por hipoteca *m pl*

mortgagor [mórgidʒǝ] N deudor -ora hipotecario -ria *mf*

mortification [mórdǝfikéʃǝn] N mortificación *f*

mortify [mórdǝfai] VI/VT mortificar[se]

mortuary [mórtʃueri] N mortuorio *m*

mosaic [mozéik] N mosaico *m*

Moslem [mázlǝm] ADJ & N musulmán -ana *mf*

mosque [mɔsk] N mezquita *f*

mosquito [məskíɒo] N mosquito *m*; **— net** mosquitero *m*

moss [mɔs] N musgo *m*

mossy [mɔ́si] ADJ musgoso

most [most] ADJ **— children are good** la mayoría de los niños son buenos; **— people** la mayoría de la gente; **the — money** más dinero *m*; **the — votes** el mayor número de votos; **for the — part** generalmente; PRON **the — that I can do** lo más que puedo hacer; **we ate the —** comimos más que nadie; **— of the guests are here** ha llegado la mayoría de los invitados; ADV **the — ambitious** el más ambicioso; **a — pleasant day** un día de lo más agradable

mostly [móstli] ADV generalmente

motel [motél] N motel *m*

moth [mɔθ] N (pest) polilla *f*; (nocturnal insect) mariposa nocturna *f*; **—ball** bolita de naftalina *f*; **—eaten** apolillado

mother [mʌ́ðə] N madre *f*; **—board** placa madre *f*; **— country** madre patria *f*; **—-in-law** suegra *f*; **—-of-pearl** madreperla *f*; **— tongue** lengua materna *f*; VT mimar a, cuidar de/a

motherhood [mʌ́ðəhʊd] N maternidad *f*

motherly [mʌ́ðəli] ADJ maternal

motif [motíf] N motivo *m*

motion [móʃən] N (movement) movimiento *m*; (signal) ademán *m*; (proposal) moción *f*; **— picture** película de cine *f*; **—-picture industry** industria cinematográfica *f*; **— sickness** mareo *m*; VI/VT hacer un ademán

motionless [móʃənlɪs] ADJ inmóvil

motivate [móɒəvet] VT motivar

motivation [moɒəvéʃən] N motivación *f*

motive [móɒɪv] N motivo *m*; ADJ motriz

motley [mátli] ADJ abigarrado

motor [móɒə] N motor *m*; **—bike** motocicleta pequeña *f*; **—boat** lancha a motor *f*; **—cycle** motocicleta *f*; **—cyclist** motociclista *mf*; **— home** casa rodante *f*, caravana *f*; **— scooter** scooter *m*; **— vehicle** vehículo motorizado *m*; VI pasear en coche

motorist [móɒərɪst] N automovilista *mf*

motto [máɒo] N lema *f*

mound [maʊnd] N montículo *m*; **burial —** túmulo *m*; **— of laundry** pila de ropa *f*

mount [maʊnt] VI/VT (get on) montar; VI (increase) subir; VT (assemble) armar; N (mountain) monte *m*; (getting on a horse) montar *f*; (animal for riding) montura *f*

mountain [maʊntn̩] N montaña *f*; **— bike** bicicleta de montaña *f*; **— climber** alpinista *mf*; **— climbing** alpinismo *m*, montañismo *m*; **— goat** cabra montés *f*; **— lion** puma *f*, gato montés *m*; **— range** (large) cordillera *f*; (small) sierra *f*; **—side** ladera [de una montaña] *f*; **—top** cumbre [de una montaña]

f; ADJ (animal, person) montañés; (thing) de montaña

mountaineer [maʊntnír] N alpinista *mf*

mountainous [maʊntnəs] ADJ montañoso

mourn [mɔrn] VI estar de duelo/luto; VT llorar; **to — for** llorar a

mourner [mɔ́rnə] N doliente *mf*

mournful [mɔ́rnfəl] ADJ lúgubre, triste

mourning [mɔ́rnɪŋ] N luto *m*, duelo *m*; **to be in —** estar de luto/duelo; ADJ de luto

mouse [maʊs] N ratón *m* (also computer); **— pad** alfombrilla [de ratón] *f*; **— port** puerto de ratón *m*; **—trap** ratonera *f*

mouth¹ [maʊθ] N boca *f*; (of a cave) abertura *f*; (of a river) desembocadura *f*; **—piece** (part of a trumpet) boquilla *f*; (spokesman) portavoz *mf*; **—-to-mouth resuscitation** respiración boca a boca *f*; **—wash** enjuague bucal *m*; ADJ **—watering** delicioso

mouth² [maʊð] VT articular silenciosamente una palabra; VI **to — off** contestar

mouthful [maʊθfʊl] N (of food) bocado *m*; (of liquid) bocanada *f*, buche *m*

movable [múvəbəl] ADJ movible, móvil

move [muv] VI (change position) mover[se] (also board games); (change residence) mudar[se] de casa; (sell) venderse; **to — away** (distance oneself) apartarse; (change residence) irse; **to — forward** avanzar; **to — on** seguir adelante; **to — out** mudarse de casa; VT (propose) proponer; (affect emotionally) conmover; N (act of changing position) movimiento *m*; (change of residence) mudanza *f*; (action toward a goal) paso *m*; (play, in games) jugada *f*; **get a — on there!** ¡date prisa! **he made the first —** dio el primer paso

movement [múvmənt] N (motion, part of a watch) movimiento *m*; (of troops) desplazamiento *m*; **to have a bowel —** mover el vientre

mover [múvə] N compañía de mudanzas *f*; **—s and shakers** la plana mayor

movie [múvi] N película *f*, filme *m*; **—s** cine *m*; **—making** cinematografía *f*

moving [múvɪŋ] ADJ (target) móvil; (car) en movimiento; (company) de mudanzas; (story) conmovedor; **— picture** película *f*; **— van** camión de mudanzas *m*

mow [mo] VT cortar; (harvest) segar

mower [móə] N (for lawns) cortadora de céspedes *f*, cortacésped *m*; (farm implement) segadora *f*; (farmworker) segador -ora *mf*

mown [mon] *see* mow

Mozambican [mozæmbíkən] ADJ & N mozambiqueño -ña *mf*

Mozambique [mozæmbík] N Mozambique *m*

Mozarabic [mozérəbɪk] ADJ mozárabe

Mr. [místə] N Sr. *m*

MRI [magnetic resonance imaging] [émárái] N IRM f

Mrs. [mísiz] N Sra. f

Ms. [miz] N Sra. f

much [matʃ] ADJ & ADV mucho; — **the same** casi lo mismo; — **like the others** muy parecido a los demás; **as — as** tanto como; **how — ?** ¿cuánto? **too —** demasiado; **very —** muchísimo; **to make — of** dar mucha importancia a; — **as I'd like, I won't do it** aunque me gustaría, no lo voy a hacer; **that's not — of a book** ese libro no es gran cosa; **she cried so** — lloró tanto; **they need water,** — **as they need sun** necesitan agua, del mismo modo que necesitan sol

muck [mʌk] N (manure) estiércol m; (mire) cieno m, lodo m; (filth) porquería f

mucous [mjúkəs] ADJ mucoso

mucus [mjúkəs] N mucosidad f

mud [mʌd] N lodo m, barro m; **—slinging** difamación f

muddle [mʌdl] VT (confuse) confundir; (make turbid) enturbiar; VI **to — along** ir tirando; **to — through** salir del paso; N (confusion) confusión f; (confused situation) embrollo m

muddy [mʌdi] ADJ (path) lodoso, barroso; (shoes) embarrado; (vague) confuso; VT (cover with mud) enlodar, embarrar; (make unclear) enturbiar

muff [mʌf] N manguito m; VT estropear

muffin [mʌfɪn] N mollete m

muffle [mʌfl] VT amortiguar

muffler [mʌflə] N (scarf) bufanda f; (exhaust device) silenciador m

mug [mʌg] N (ceramic) tazón m; (glass) jarra f; (face) jeta f; VT atracar

mugger [mʌgə] N asaltante mf; atracador -ora mf

muggy [mʌgi] ADJ bochornoso

mulatto [muládo] ADJ & N mulato -ta mf

mulberry [mʌlberi] N mora f; — **tree** moral m

mule [mjul] N mulo -la mf (also in drug trafficking)

mull [mʌl] VI/VT rumiar

multicultural [mʌltikʌltʃəɹəl] ADJ multicultural

multilateral [mʌltilædəɹəl] ADJ multilateral

multimedia [mʌltimídiə] N & ADJ INV multimedia m

multiple [mʌltəpəl] N múltiplo m; ADJ múltiple; **—-choice** de opción múltiple; — **personality disorder** trastorno de personalidad múltiple m; — **sclerosis** esclerosis múltiple f

multiplication [mʌltəplikéʃən] N multiplicación f; — **sign** signo de multiplicación m; — **table** tabla de multiplicar f

multiplicity [mʌltəplísɪdi] N multiplicidad f

multiply [mʌltəplaɪ] VI/VT multiplicar[se]

multiscreen [mʌltiskrin] ADJ multipantalla

multitasking [mʌltitæskɪŋ] N multitarea f

multitude [mʌltitud] N multitud f

multiuser [mʌltijúzə] N multiusuario -ria mf

multi-year [mʌltijír] ADJ multianual

mum [mʌm] ADJ callado; **to keep —** callarse la boca

mumble [mʌmbəl] VI/VT mascullar; N refunfuño m

mumbo jumbo [mámbodʒámbo] N jerigonza f

mummy [mámi] N momia f

mumps [mʌmps] N paperas f pl

munch [mʌntʃ] VT mascar

mundane [mʌndén] ADJ mundano

municipal [mjunísəpəl] ADJ municipal; — **council** concejo m

municipality [mjunɪsəpælɪDi] N municipio m, municipalidad m

munition [mjuníʃən] N munición f

mural [mjúrəl] ADJ & N mural m

murder [mɜ́də] N asesinato m, homicidio m; **to get away with** — salirse con la suya; **that exam was —** ese examen fue matador; VI/VT asesinar

murderer [mɜ́Dərə] N asesino mf, homicida mf

murderous [mɜ́Dəəs] ADJ asesino, homicida

murky [mɜ́ki] ADJ (of water, matter) turbio; (of sky) oscuro

murmur [mɜ́mə] N (noise) murmullo m, susurro m; (complaint) queja f; VI/VT (make noise) murmurar, susurrar; (complain) quejarse

muscle [mʌsəl] N músculo m; — **relaxant** relajante muscular m; — **strain** distensión muscular f; — **tone** tonicidad muscular f, tono muscular m

muscular [mʌskjələ] ADJ (relative to muscles) muscular; (endowed with muscles) musculoso; — **dystrophy** distrofia muscular f

muse [mjuz] VI meditar; VT cavilar; N musa f

museum [mjuzíəm] N museo m

mushroom [mʌ́ʃrum] N seta f, hongo m, champiñón m

mushy [mʌ́ʃi] ADJ (soft) fofo; (sentimental) sensiblero

music [mjúzik] N música f; — **stand** atril m; — **video** Am video musical m; Sp vídeo musical m

musical [mjúzikəl] ADJ (pertaining to music) musical; (fond of music) aficionado a la música, melómano; — **comedy** comedia musical f

musician [mjuzíʃən] N músico -ca mf

muskrat [mʌskræt] N ratón almizclero m

Muslim [mázləm] ADJ & N musulmán -ana mf

muslin [mázlin] N muselina f

muss [mʌs] VT revolver, alborotar; N revoltijo m

mussel [mʌ́səl] N mejillón *m*

must [mʌst] V AUX **you — arrive before nine** debes llegar antes de las nueve; **you really — eat at that restaurant** tienes que comer en ese restaurante; **you — be his son** debes [de] / has de ser su hijo; **they — have seen me** deben [de] haberme visto

mustache, moustache [mʌ́stæʃ] N bigote *m*; (large) mostacho *m*

mustard [mʌ́stɚd] N mostaza *f*; **— gas** gas mostaza *m*

muster [mʌ́stɚ] VT (troops) formar; (courage) juntar, reunir; VI (assemble for inspection) formar; (come together) reunirse; **to — out** dar de baja; **to — up one's courage** juntar valor; N revista *f*; **to pass —** ser aceptable

musty [mʌ́sti] ADJ (stale smelling) con olor a encierro/humedad; (antiquated) anticuado

mutant [mjútn̩t] ADJ & N mutante *mf*

mutation [mjutéʃən] N mutación *f*

mute [mjut] ADJ mudo; N (mute person) mudo -da *mf*; (for musical instruments) sordina *f*

mutilate [mjúdlet] VT mutilar

mutiny [mjútn̩i] N motín *m*; VI amotinarse

mutter [mʌ́dɚ] VI/VT refunfuñar, musitar; N refunfuño *m*

mutton [mʌ́tn̩] N carne de cordero *f*

mutual [mjútʃuəl] ADJ mutuo; **— fund** fondo mutuo/mutual *m*

muzzle [mʌ́zəl] N (snout) hocico *m*; (mouthguard) bozal *m*; (gun opening) boca *f*; VT (a dog) abozalar, poner bozal a; (critics) amordazar, silenciar

my [mai] POSS ADJ mi; **these are — friends** estos son mis amigos; **oh —!** ¡Dios mío! **— foot!** ¡ni lo pienses!

Myanmar [mjanmár] N Myanmar *m*

myocardial infarction [maɪoʊkárɖɪəɫɪnfárkʃən] N infarto del miocardio *m*

myopia [maɪópiə] N miopía *f*

myriad [míriəd] N miríada *f*, sinfín *m*; **— problems** un sinfín de problemas

myrtle [mɚ́dl̩] N mirto *m*, arrayán *m*

myself [maɪsɛ́lf] PRON **I — wrote the letters** yo mismo escribí las cartas; **I'm not — today** hoy no soy la misma de siempre; **I was sitting by —** estaba sentado solo; **I talk to —** hablo solo; **I looked at — in the mirror** me miré en el espejo; **I bought — a house** me compré una casa

mysterious [mɪstíriəs] ADJ misterioso

mystery [místəri] N misterio *m*

mystic [místɪk] ADJ & N místico -ca *mf*

mystical [místɪkəl] ADJ místico

myth [mɪθ] N mito *m*

mythic [míθɪk] ADJ mítico

mythical [míθɪkəl] ADJ mítico

mythological [mɪθəládʒɪkəl] ADJ mitológico

mythology [mɪθálədʒi] N mitología *f*

Nn

nab [næb] VT pescar; *Sp* coger

nag [næg] N (horse) jaca *f*, rocín *m*, penco *m*; (complainer) quejica *mf*; VI/VT regañar, criticar

nail [neɫ] N (for wood) clavo *m*; (of finger, toe) uña *f*; **—biter** situación angustiante *f*; **— file** lima *f*; **— polish** esmalte para uñas *m*; **to hit the — on the head** dar en el clavo; VT (fasten) clavar; (nab) pescar; *Sp* coger

naive [naív] ADJ ingenuo, cándido, bonachón

naiveté [naivté] N ingenuidad *f*

naked [nékɪd] ADJ desnudo

nakedness [nékɪdnɪs] N desnudez *f*

name [nem] N nombre *m*; **—brand** marca comercial *f*; **—plate** placa *f*; **—sake** tocayo *m*; **—tag** etiqueta de identificación *f*; **— of the game** lo esencial *m*; **to call someone —s** motejar a alguien; **to make a — for oneself** hacerse un nombre; **what is your —?** ¿cómo te llamas? VT nombrar; **— your price** haz una oferta

nameless [némlɪs] ADJ anónimo

namely [némli] ADV a saber, en concreto

Namibia [nəmíbiə] N Namibia *f*

Namibian [nəmíbiən] ADJ & N namibio -bia *mf*

nanny [nǽni] N niñera *f*

nanosecond [nǽnosekənd] N nanosegundo *m*

nanotechnology [nǽnotekná́lədʒi] N nanotecnología *f*

nap [næp] N (sleep) siesta *f*; (fibers) pelo *m*; **to take a —** echar/dormir una siesta; VI echar/dormir una siesta

napalm [népɑɫm] N napalm *m*

nape [nep] N nuca *f*

napkin [nǽpkɪn] N servilleta *f*

narcissism [nársɪsɪzəm] N narcisismo *m*

narcissus [narsísəs] N narciso *m*

narcolepsy [nárkəlɛpsi] N narcolepsia *f*

narcotic [narkádɪk] ADJ & N narcótico *m*, estupefaciente *m*

narcotrafficking [narkotrǽfɪkɪŋ] N narcotráfico *m*

narrate [næret] VI/VT narrar

narration [næréʃən] N narración *f*

narrative [nǽrədɪv] ADJ narrativo; N narrativa *f*

narrator [nǽrədɚ] N narrador -ora *mf*

narrow [nǽro] ADJ (of little width) estrecho, angosto; (limited in scope) limitado; (intolerant) intolerante; **to have a — escape** salvarse por poco; **— gauge** de vía angosta/estrecha; **—minded** intolerante; N **—s** desfiladero *m*, estrecho *m*, angostura *f*; VI/VT angostar[se], estrechar[se]; **to — down**

reducir

narrowness [nǽronɪs] N (quality of being narrow) estrechez f, angostura f

nasal [nézəł] ADJ nasal

nastiness [nǽstinɪs] N (filth) suciedad f; (stinkiness) asquerosidad f; (rudeness, obscenity) grosería f

nasturtium [nəstɔ́ʃəm] N capuchina f

nasty [nǽsti] ADJ (mess) sucio; (smell) asqueroso; (comment) hiriente; (accident) feo; (word) grosero; (disposition) malo

natal [nédḷ] ADJ natal

nation [néʃən] N nación f; ADJ — **wide** a escala nacional

national [nǽʃənḷ] ADJ nacional; — **park** parque nacional m; — **team** seleccionado nacional m; N ciudadano -na mf, nacional mf

nationalism [nǽʃənəlɪzəm] N nacionalismo m

nationalist [nǽʃənəlɪst] N & ADJ nacionalista MF

nationality [næʃənǽlɪDi] N nacionalidad f; **adjective of —** gentilicio m

nationalize [nǽʃənəlaɪz] VT nacionalizar

native [néDɪv] ADJ nativo; — **language** lengua nativa f; — **plants** flora nativa f; **my — Italy** mi Italia natal f; (innate) innato; N (person born in a place) natural m; (member of a tribal group) indígena mf, nativo -va mf; **he's a — of Italy** es oriundo de Italia

nativity [nətívɪDi] N nacimiento m; — **scene** pesebre m; **the —** la Natividad

NATO [North Atlantic Treaty Organization] [néDo] N OTAN f

natural [nǽtʃəəḷ] ADJ natural; (inborn) innato; — **childbirth** parto natural m; — **gas** gas natural m; — **resources** recursos naturales m pl; — **selection** selección natural f; N (musical sign) becuadro m; **he is a — for that job** tiene aptitud natural para ese puesto

naturalist [nǽtʃəəlɪst] N naturalista mf

naturalization [nætʃəəlizéʃən] N naturalización f

naturalize [nǽtʃəəlaɪz] VI/VT naturalizar[se]

naturally [nǽtʃəəli] ADV (of course) naturalmente; **I have — curly hair** tengo rizos naturales

naturalness [nǽtʃəəłnɪs] N naturalidad f

nature [nétʃə] N naturaleza f; (disposition) genio m, natural m

naught [nɔt] N (zero) cero m; (nothing) nada f

naughtiness [nɔ́Dinɪs] N travesuras f pl

naughty [nɔ́Di] ADJ (child) travieso, pícaro, pillo; — **word** picardía f

Nauru [naúru] N Nauru m

Nauruan [naúrʊən] ADJ & N nauruano -na mf

nausea [nɔ́ziə] N náuseas f pl, mareo m

nauseate [nɔ́ziet] VT dar náuseas; **to be — d** tener náuseas

nauseating [nɔ́zieDɪŋ] ADJ nauseabundo, nauseoso

nauseous [nɔ́ʃəs] ADJ (feeling nausea) mareado, nauseoso; (causing nausea) nauseabundo, nauseoso

nautical [nɔ́Dɪkəł] ADJ náutico

naval [névəł] ADJ naval; — **officer** oficial de marina m

Navarrese [nævəríz] ADJ & N navarro -rra mf

nave [nev] N nave f

navel [névəł] N ombligo m; — **orange** naranja de ombligo f

navigable [nǽvɪɡəbəł] ADJ navegable

navigate [nǽvɪɡet] VI/VT navegar

navigation [nævɪɡéʃən] N navegación f; (science) náutica f

navigator [nǽvɪɡeDə] N navegante m

navy [névi] N marina [de guerra] f, armada f; — **bean** judía blanca f; — **blue** azul marino m

nay [ne] N (refusal) no m; (negative vote) voto negativo m

Nazi [nátsi] N nazi mf

near [nɪr] ADV cerca; — **at hand** cerca, a la mano; **to come/go/draw —** acercarse; PREP cerca de; — **the end of the month** hacia fines del mes; **to be — death** estar a punto de morir; ADJ cercano, próximo; — **East** Cercano Oriente m, Oriente Próximo m; — **sighted** miope; **I had a — miss** por poco me sucede un accidente; VI/VT acercarse [a]

nearby [nírbáɪ] ADV cerca; ADJ cercano, próximo

nearly [nírli] ADV casi, cerca de; **I — did it** casi lo hago

nearness [nírnɪs] N cercanía f, proximidad f

neat [nit] ADJ (clean) limpio, pulcro; (ordered) ordenado; (cool) bueno

neatness [nítnɪs] N (cleanness) limpieza f, pulcritud f; (order) orden m

nebulous [nébjələs] ADJ nebuloso

nebulousness [nébjələsnɪs] N nubosidad f

necessary [nésɪseri] ADJ (needed) necesario; (involuntary) forzoso

necessitate [nəsésɪtet] VT requerir

necessity [nəsésɪDi] N necesidad f; **out of —** por necesidad

neck [nɛk] N (of a human) cuello m; (of an animal) pescuezo m; (of clothes) escote m; (throat) garganta f; — **and —** parejos; — **lace** collar m; — **line** escote m; — **of land** istmo m; — **tie** corbata f

necrology [nəkrálədʒi] N necrología f

necrosis [nəkrósɪs] N necrosis f

nectar [néktə] N néctar m

nectarine [nektərín] N nectarina f

need [nid] N (lack) necesidad f; (poverty) carencia f; **in —** en apriertos; **if — be** en caso de necesidad; VT necesitar, precisar; **you — to come at four** tienes que venir a las cuatro

needle [nídḷ] N aguja f; — **point** bordado m; — **work** (embroidery) bordado m; (sewing) costura f; VT pinchar

needless [nídlɪs] ADJ innecesario; — **to say** huelga decir

needy [nídi] ADJ necesitado, menesteroso

ne'er-do-well [nérduwɛl] N inútil *mf*

negate [nɪgét] VT negar

negation [nɪgéʃən] N negación *f*

negative [négəDIV] ADJ negativo; **the search proved** — la búsqueda no dio resultado; N negativa *f*; (photographic) negativo *m*; **this plan has one** — este plan tiene una contra; INTERJ ¡negativo!

neglect [nɪglékt] VT (fail to heed) postergar; (fail to care for) descuidar; (fail to carry out) desatender; **you're** —**ing your friends** tienes abandonados a tus amigos; **to** — **to** olvidarse de; N negligencia *f*, descuido *m*

neglectful [nɪgléktfəl] ADJ negligente, descuidado

negligence [néglɪdʒəns] N negligencia *f*

negligent [néglɪdʒənt] ADJ negligente, descuidado

negligible [néglɪdʒəbəl] ADJ despreciable, minúsculo

negotiate [nɪgóʃiet] VI/VT (a contract) negociar, gestionar; (an obstacle) salvar

negotiating [nɪgóʃieDɪŋ] ADJ negociador

negotiation [nɪgoʃiéʃən] N negociación *f*, gestión *f*

negotiator [nɪgóʃieDɚ] N negociador -ora *mf*

Negro [nígro] ADJ & N negro -gra *mf*

neigh [ne] N relincho *m*; VI relinchar

neighbor [nébɚ] N (person who lives near) vecino -na *mf*; (fellow human) prójimo -ma *mf*; ADJ vecino; VI **to** — **with** lindar con

neighborhood [nébɚhud] N vecindario *m*, barrio *m*; **in the** — **of a hundred dollars** alrededor de cien dólares

neighboring [nébɚɪŋ] ADJ vecino, colindante

neither [níðɚ] PRON ninguno de los dos, ni [el] uno ni [el] otro; — **of the two** ninguno de los dos; ADJ ninguno de los dos; — **one of us** ninguno de nosotros dos; CONJ ni; — **hot nor cold** ni caliente ni frío; — **will I** yo tampoco

nemesis [némɪsɪs] N némesis *f*

neologism [niáləjɪzəm] N neologismo *m*

neon [nían] N neón *m*

neonatal [nionédl] ADJ neonatal

Nepal [nəpɔ́l] N Nepal *m*

Nepali [nəpɔ́li] ADJ & N nepalés -esa *mf*, nepalí *mf*

nephew [néfju] N sobrino *m*

nephritis [nəfráɪDɪs] N nefritis *f*

nepotism [népətɪzəm] N nepotismo *m*

nerd [nɚd] N (technological adept) persona aficionada a las computadoras / los ordenadores *f*; (socially inept person) persona socialmente inepta *f*

nerve [nɚv] N (anatomy) nervio *m*; (courage) valor *m*; (impertinence) descaro *m*, morro *m*; — **cell** neurona *f*; — **gas** gas nervioso *m*; — **[w]racking** angustiante; **he gets on my** —**s** me saca de quicio

nervous [nɚ́vəs] ADJ nervioso; — **breakdown** ataque de nervios *m*

nervousness [nɚ́vəsnɪs] N nerviosismo *m*

nest [nɛst] N nido *m*; (brood) nidada *f*; — **egg** ahorros *m pl*; — **of thieves** guarida de ladrones *f*; VI/VT anidar; (fit together) encajarse

nestle [nɛ́səl] VI acurrucarse; VT apoyar, recostar

net [nɛt] N (fishing, network, tennis) red *f*; (in hair) redecilla *f*; —**work** red *f*; —**working** (social) relaciones profesionales *f pl*; (computer) diseño de redes y comunicaciones *m*; VT (catch a fish) pescar con red; (cover with a net) cubrir con una red; (catch a criminal) atrapar; (hit the tennis net) dar en la red; (make money after expenses) producir/ganar neto; ADJ neto; — **price** precio neto *m*; — **profit** ganancia neta *f*; — **assets** activo neto *m*; — **income** ingreso neto *m*; — **worth** patrimonio neto *m*

Netherlander [néðɚləndɚ] N holandés -esa *mf*

Netherlands [néðɚləndz] N Países Bajos *m pl*

nettle [nédl] N ortiga *f*

neural [nʊ́rəl] ADJ neural

neuralgia [nʊrǽldʒə] N neuralgia *f*

neurasthenia [nʊrəsθíniə] N neurastenia *f*

neurologist [nʊrálədʒɪst] N neurólogo -ga *mf*

neuron [nʊ́ran] N neurona *f*

neurosis [nʊrósɪs] N neurosis *f*

neurosurgeon [nʊ́rosɚdʒən] N neurocirujano -na *mf*

neurosurgery [nʊrosɚ́dʒɚi] N neurocirugía *f*

neurotic [nʊrɑ́Dɪk] ADJ & N neurótico -ca *mf*

neurotransmitter [nʊrotrǽnzmɪDɚ] N neurotransmisor *m*

neuter [nʊ́Dɚ] ADJ neutro; VT castrar

neutral [nʊ́trəl] ADJ neutral, imparcial; (of colors) neutro; N punto muerto *m*

neutrality [nʊtrǽlɪDi] N neutralidad *f*

neutralize [nʊ́trəlaɪz] VI/VT neutralizar[se]

neutron [nʊ́tran] N neutrón *m*; — **bomb** bomba de neutrones *f*

never [névɚ] ADV nunca, jamás; — **mind** no te preocupes; **this will** — **do** esto no va a funcionar; —**-ending** interminable

nevertheless [nevɚðəlés] ADV & CONJ sin embargo, no obstante

new [nu] ADJ (not old) nuevo; (fresh) otro; **a** — **sheet of paper** otra hoja de papel; — **age** [music]** [música] nueva era *f*; —**-born baby** recién nacido -da *mf*; —**comer** recién llegado -da *mf*; —**-fangled** moderno, recién inventado; —**found** nuevo; — **year** año nuevo *m*; — **Year's Eve** fin de año *m*; Sp nochevieja *f*

newly [núli] ADV recientemente; — **arrived** recién llegado; —**wed** recién casado

newness [núnis] N novedad *f*

news [nuz] N (item) noticias *f pl*; (latest gossip) novedades *f pl*; (newspaper) periódico *m*; **it is — to me** recién me entero; **— broadcast/ bulletin** noticiero *m*, noticiario *m*; **—cast** noticiero *m*, noticiario *m*, informativo *m*; **— clipping** recorte de diario *m*; **—letter** boletín informativo *m*; **—paper** periódico *m*, diario *m*; **—print** papel de periódico *m*; **—room** sala de redacción *f*; **—stand** quiosco *m*; **piece of —** noticia *f*; ADJ **—worthy** de interés periodístico

newt [nut] N tritón *m*

New Zealand [nuzíland] N Nueva Zelanda *f*

New Zealander [nuzíländə] N neozelandés -esa *mf*

next [nɛkst] ADJ (future) próximo, entrante; (following) siguiente; (contiguous) contiguo, de al lado; *Am* **—door** de al lado; **who's —?** ¿quién sigue? ADV después, luego; **— best** segundo en calidad; **when — we meet** cuando nos volvamos a ver; PREP **— of kin** familiares *m pl*; **— to** junto a, al lado de

nibble [níbəl] VI/VT (bite) mordiscar, mordisquear; (eat) picotear; (of fish) picar; N (bite) mordisco *m*; (act of nibbling) mordisqueo *m*

Nicaragua [nɪkərágwə] N Nicaragua *f*

Nicaraguan [nɪkərágwən] ADJ & N nicaragüense *mf*

nice [naɪs] ADJ (kind) amable, simpático; (agreeable) *Am* lindo, *Sp* majo; **it's — and hot** está bien calentito

nicety [náɪsɪdi] N (subtlety) sutileza *f*; (detail) detalle *m*

niche [nɪtʃ] N (also environmental) nicho *m*; **— marketing** mercadeo de nicho *m*; **I've found my —** he encontrado mi lugar

nick [nɪk] N (chip) muesca *f*; (cut) corte *m*; **in the — of time** justo a tiempo; VT (chip) hacer muescas; (cut) cortar; **—name** apodo *m*, mote *m*, sobrenombre *m*; **to —name** apodar

nickel [níkəl] N (metal) níquel *m*; (coin) moneda de cinco centavos *f*; **—-plated** niquelado

nicotine [níkətin] N nicotina *f*

niece [nis] N sobrina *f*

Niger [náɪdʒə] N Níger *m*

Nigeria [naɪdʒíriə] N Nigeria *f*

Nigerian [naɪdʒíriən] ADJ & N nigeriano -na *mf*

Nigerien [naɪdʒíriɛn] ADJ & N nigerino -na *mf*

niggardly [nígədli] ADJ mezquino

night [naɪt] N noche *f*; ADJ nocturno, de noche; **—club** club nocturno *m*; **—fall** anochecer *m*, atardecer *m*; **—gown** camisón *m*; **—life** vida nocturna *f*; *Sp* marcha *f*; **—light** lamparilla *f*; **—mare** pesadilla *f*; **— owl** trasnochador -ora *mf*; **—shift** turno de la noche *m*; **—stand** veladora *f*, mesilla de noche *f*; **—time** noche *f*; **—watchman** celador *m*

nightingale [náɪtɪŋgeł] N ruiseñor *m*

nightly [náɪtli] ADV todas las noches; ADJ nocturno

nihilism [náɪəlɪzəm] N nihilismo *m*

nil [nɪł] ADJ nulo

nimble [nímbəł] ADJ ágil

nincompoop [nínkəmpup] N *fam* tarambana *mf*, bobalicón -ona *mf*

nine [naɪn] NUM nueve; **— hundred** novecientos

nineteen [naɪntín] NUM diecinueve

ninety [náɪnti] NUM noventa

ninth [náɪnθ] ADJ & N noveno *m*

nip [nɪp] VT (pinch) pellizcar; (bite) mordiscar, mordisquear; (cause frostbite) helar; **to — in the bud** cortar de raíz; **to — off** despuntar; VI (drink in sips) dar sorbitos; N (pinch) pellizco *m*; (bite) mordisco *m*; (sip) traguito *m*, sorbito *m*; **it's going to be — and tuck** va a ser muy reñido

nipple [nípəł] N (on female breast) pezón *m*; (on male breast) tetilla *f*; (on bottle) tetina *f*

nitpick [nítpɪk] VI criticar detalles insignificantes

nitrate [náɪtret] N nitrato *m*

nitric acid [náɪtrɪkæsɪd] N ácido nítrico *m*

nitrogen [náɪtrədʒən] N nitrógeno *m*

nitroglycerin [naɪtroglísəɪn] N nitroglicerina *f*

nitty-gritty [nídɪgrídɪ] N **to get down to the — ** ir al grano

no [no] ADV no; **— longer** ya no; **— man's land** tierra de nadie *f*; **— matter how much** por mucho que; **— one** ninguno, nadie; **— smoking** se prohíbe fumar; **—where** (location) en ninguna parte / ningún lado; (direction) a ninguna parte / ningún lado; **he was a —-show** no se presentó; **a —-win situation** una situación insoluble; **there is — more** no hay más; ADJ ningun[o]; **I have — friends** no tengo amigos; **it's a —-brainer** la respuesta es obvia; **— friend of mine will go hungry** ningún amigo mío pasará hambre; **— of — use** inútil; N (refusal) no *m*; (negative vote) voto negativo *m*; ADJ **—-frills** básico, sin lujos

nobility [nobílɪdi] N nobleza *f*, hidalguía *f*

noble [nóbəł] ADJ & N noble *mf*; **—man** hidalgo *m*

nobody [nóbɑdi] PRON nadie, ninguno; N don nadie, pelagatos *mf sg*

nocturnal [nɑktɔ́ːnł] ADJ nocturno

nod [nɑd] VI/VT (signal affirmation) asentir con la cabeza; VI (doze) cabecear, dar cabezadas; **to — off** dormirse; N (as signal) inclinación de cabeza *f*, saludo con la cabeza *m*; (from sleepiness) cabezada *f*

node [nod] N (of cells) nódulo *m*; (in plants) nudo *m*; (in physics) nodo *m*

noise [nɔɪz] N ruido *m*; **— pollution**

contaminación sonora *f*; VI **it is being —d about that** corre el rumor que

noiseless [nóɪzlɪs] ADJ silencioso

noisy [nóɪzi] ADJ ruidoso

nomad [nómæd] N nómada *mf*

nomenclature [nómɪnklét͡ʃə-] N nomenclatura *f*

nominal [námən̩l] ADJ nominal

nominate [námənet] VT nominar

nomination [namənéʃən] N nominación *f*

nominee [naməní] N candidato -ta *mf*

nonchalant [nɑnʃəlánt] ADJ despreocupado

noncollectible [nankəléktəbəl] ADJ incobrable

noncommercial [nankəmɝ́ʃəl] ADJ no comercial

noncommissioned officer [nankəmíʃənd ɔ́fɪsə-] N suboficial *m*

nonconforming [nankənfɔ́rmɪŋ] ADJ no conforme

nonconformist [nankənfɔ́rmɪst] ADJ & N incomformista *mf*

none [nʌn] PRON ninguno; **I want — of that** no me quiero meter en eso; **that is — of your business** no es asunto tuyo; ADV **— too soon** al último momento; **—the less** sin embargo

nonentity [nanéntɪDi] N nulidad *f*

nonessential [nanɪsénʃəl] ADJ no esencial

nonexistent [nanɪgzístənt] ADJ inexistente

nonfiction [nanfíkʃən] N no ficción *f*

nongovernmental [nangʌvə-nméntl̩] ADJ no gubernamental

nonnegotiable [nannɪgóʃəbəl] ADJ no negociable

nonpartisan [nanpártɪzən] ADJ (neutral) imparcial; (not affiliated) sin afiliación política

nonperformance [nanpə-fɔ́rməns] N incumplimiento *m*

nonproductive [nanprədáktɪv] ADJ improductivo

nonprofit [nanpráfɪt] ADJ sin fines de lucro; N organización sin fines de lucro *f*

nonrefundable [nanrɪfándəbəl] ADJ no reembolsable

nonresident [nanrézɪdənt] ADJ & N no residente *mf*

nonsense [nánsens] N tonterías *f pl*, monsergas *f pl*, estupideces *f pl*; **to talk —** decir barbaridades/disparates

nonstop [nánstáp] ADJ sin escala, directo; ADV sin parar

nontaxable [nantǽksəbəl] ADJ no tributable

nonvoting [nanvóDɪŋ] ADJ sin derecho a voto

noodle [núdl̩] N fideo *m*, tallarín *m*

nook [nʊk] N rincón *m*

noon [nun] N mediodía *m*; **— hour** mediodía *m*, hora de comer; **—time** mediodía *m*

noose [nus] N soga *f*, lazo *m*; **with a — around his neck** con la soga al cuello; VT (catch with a rope) enlazar; (make a loop in) hacer un lazo corredizo en

nope [nop] ADV no

nor [nɔr] CONJ ni; **we have neither eggs — flour** no tenemos ni huevos ni harina

Nordic [nɔ́rdɪk] ADJ nórdico

norm [nɔrm] N norma *f*, normativa *f*

normal [nɔ́rml̩] ADJ normal; (perpendicular) normal; **to return to —** volver a la normalidad; (perpendicular line) línea perpendicular *f*

normalcy [nɔ́rml̩si] N normalidad *f*

normality [nɔrmǽlɪDi] N normalidad *f*

normalize [nɔ́rməlaɪz] VI/VT normalizar[se]

normally [nɔ́rml̩i] ADV (in a normal way) de manera normal, con toda normalidad *f*; (usually) normalmente

north [nɔrθ] N norte *m*; **—east** noreste, hacia el noreste; **—west** noroeste *m*, hacia el noroeste; ADJ (in the north) norte, norteño; (from the north) del norte; **— America** América del Norte *f*; **— American** norteamericano -na *mf*; **—eastern** del noreste; **— Korea** Corea del Norte *f*; **— Korean** norcoreano -na; **— Pole** Polo Norte *m*; **— wind** cierzo *m*, viento norte *m*; **the — entrance** la entrada norte; ADV al norte, hacia el norte

northern [nɔ́rðə-n] ADJ del norte; (from the north) norteño; (in the north) septentrional; **— lights** aurora boreal *f*

northerner [nɔ́rðə-nə-] N norteño -ña *mf*

northward [nɔ́rθwə-d] ADV hacia el norte

Norway [nɔ́rwe] N Noruega *f*

Norwegian [nɔrwídʒən] ADJ & N noruego -ga *mf*

nose [noz] N nariz *f*; (of an airplane) morro *m*; (of an animal) hocico *m*; (perspicacity) olfato *m*; **—bleed** hemorragia nasal *f*; **—dive** caída en picado *f*; **— job** rinoplastia *f*; **keep your — clean** no te metas en líos; **on the —** exactamente; **to pick one's —** hurgarse las narices; VI/VT (move forward) entrar de punta; (muzzle) hocicar; **to — around** husmear

nostalgia [nɑstǽldʒə] N nostalgia *f*

nostalgic [nɑstǽldʒɪk] ADJ nostálgico

nostrils [nástrəlz] N narices *f pl*, ventanillas de la nariz *f pl*

nosy, nosey [nózi] ADJ entrometido

not [nat] ADV no; **I'm — your friend** no soy tu amigo; **— at all** (no way) de ningún modo; (you're welcome) de nada; **— at all sure** nada seguro; **— even a word** ni una palabra

notable [nóDəbəl] ADJ notable, destacable

notably [nóDəbli] ADV notablemente

notarize [nóDəraɪz] VT notariar

notary [nóDəri] N notario -ria *mf*; **— public** notario -ria público -ca *mf*

notation [notéʃən] N (system of signs) notación

f; (act of writing) anotación *f;* (short note) anotación *f,* apunte *m*

notch [nɑtʃ] N (nick) muesca *f,* mella *f;* (degree) grado *m;* **a — above the rest** mejor que los demás; VT hacer una muesca; **he —ed another win** se anotó otra victoria

note [not] N (written) nota *f,* anotación *f;* (musical) nota *f;* (touch) toque *m;* (financial) pagaré *m;* (currency) billete *m;* **—book** cuaderno *m;* (small) libreta *f;* **—s** apuntes *m pl;* **of —** de renombre / de nota; **to take — of** notar; ADJ **—worthy** notable; VT (notice) notar; (write down) anotar, apuntar

noted [nódɪd] ADJ célebre

nothing [nɑ́θɪŋ] PRON nada; (score) cero, nada; N (insignificant person) don nadie *m;* (insignificant thing) nadería *f;* **— to it** no tiene ciencia; ADV **it was — like that** no fue así para nada; **we did it for —** (free) lo hicimos gratis; (fruitlessly) lo hicimos en balde

notice [nódɪs] N (information) aviso *m;* (warning) advertencia *f;* (attention) atención *f;* **a week's —** una semana de plazo; **to give — renunciar;** VT (hear of) hacer caso; VT (perceive) notar, advertir, percatarse [de]; (pay attention to) fijarse [en], reparar [en]

noticeable [nódɪsəbəl] ADJ perceptible, apreciable

noticeably [nódɪsəbli] ADV notablemente

notification [nodəfɪkéʃən] N notificación *f*

notify [nódəfaɪ] VT notificar

notion [nóʃən] N noción *f,* idea *f;* (whim) capricho *m;* **—s** mercería *f*

notorious [notóriəs] ADJ de mala fama; **he's a — liar** tiene fama de mentiroso

nougat [núgət] N turrón *m*

noun [naʊn] N sustantivo *m*

nourish [nɝ́ɪʃ] VT (a person) nutrir, alimentar; (a hope) abrigar

nourishing [nɝ́ɪʃɪŋ] ADJ nutritivo

nourishment [nɝ́ɪʃmənt] N (food) alimento *m;* (act of nourishing) alimentación *f*

novel [nάvəl] N novela *f;* ADJ novedoso

novelist [nάvəlɪst] N novelista *mf*

novelty [nάvəlti] N novedad *f;* **the — soon wore off** se pasó la novedad; **novelties** chucherías *f pl*

November [novémbɝ] N noviembre *m*

novice [nάvɪs] N novato -ta *mf,* pipiolo -la *mf;* (religious) novicio -cia *mf*

novocaine [nóvoken] N novocaína *f*

now [naʊ] ADV ahora; **— and then** de vez en cuando; **— that** ahora que; **he left just — salió hace poco, recién salió; —, —, calm down!** bueno, bueno, ¡cálmate!

nowadays [náʊədez] ADV hoy [en] día

noxious [nάkʃəs] ADJ nocivo

nuance [núɑns] N matiz *m*

nuclear [núkliɚ] ADJ nuclear; **— energy** energía nuclear *f;* **— family** familia nuclear *f;* **— fission** fisión nuclear *f;* **— fusion** fusión nuclear *f;* **— physics** física nuclear *f;* **— weapon** arma nuclear *f*

nucleus [núklias] N núcleo *m*

nude [nud] ADJ & N desnudo *m*

nudge [nʌdʒ] VI/VT codear; N golpe suave con el codo *m*

nugget [nʌ́gɪt] N (of gold) pepita *f;* (of chicken) pedacito *m;* (of wisdom) perla *f*

nuisance [núsəns] N molestia *f; Sp* pesadez *f;* (legal) perjuicio *m;* **you're such a —!** ¡qué pesado eres tú! **— tax** impuesto de consumo *m*

nuke [nuk] N arma nuclear *f;* VT (bomb) bombardear con armas nucleares; (cook) calentar en microondas

null [nʌl] ADJ nulo; **— and void** nulo

nullify [nʌ́ləfaɪ] VT anular

numb [nʌm] ADJ entumecido; **to get — entumecerse;** VT entumecer

number [nʌ́mbɝ] N número *m;* **— one** uno mismo *m;* **—-crunching** procesamiento de datos numéricos complejos *m;* VI (total) ascender a; **I — him among my friends** lo cuento entre mis amigos; VT numerar

numberless [nʌ́mbɝlɪs] ADJ sin número

numbskull, numskull [nʌ́mskʌl] N zopenco -ca *mf*

numeral [númɚəl] N número *m;* ADJ numeral

numerical [numérɪkəl] ADJ numérico

numerous [númɚəs] ADJ numeroso

nun [nʌn] N monja *f,* religiosa *f*

nuptial [nʌ́pʃəl] ADJ nupcial; N **—s** nupcias *f pl*

nurse [nɝs] N (for the sick) enfermero -ra *mf;* (for children) niñera *f;* VT (give milk) amamantar, lactar; (tend to a sick person) cuidar; **to — a grudge** guardar rencor; **to — a cup of coffee** tomar una taza de café a sorbitos; **to — a cold** cuidarse durante un resfrío; VI (drink milk) mamar

nursery [nɝ́sri] N (children's room) cuarto para niños *m;* (day-care center) guardería *f;* (place for growing plants) almáciga *f,* vivero *m,* plantel *m;* **— rhyme** canción infantil *f,* ronda *f;* **— school** preescolar *m; Sp* parvulario *m; Am* jardín infantil *m*

nursing [nɝ́sɪŋ] N (profession) enfermería *f;* (care) cuidado *m;* **— home** (for old people) hogar de ancianos *m;* (for sick people) casa de salud *f*

nurture [nɝ́tʃɚ] VT (rear) criar; (feed) nutrir, alimentar; (encourage) fomentar; N (rearing) crianza *f;* (feeding) alimentación *f*

nut [nʌt] N (fruit) fruto seco *m;* (device) tuerca *f;* (person) excéntrico -ca *mf;* **—cracker** cascanueces *m sg;* **—meg** nuez moscada *f;* **—s** ADJ crazy; **—s and bolts** los fundamentos;

—shell cáscara de fruto seco *f*; **in a —shell** en pocas palabras
nutrient [nútriənt] N nutriente *m*
nutrition [nutríʃən] N nutrición *f*, alimentación *f*
nutritious [nutríʃəs] ADJ nutritivo, alimenticio
nylon [náilɑn] N nilón *m*, nailon *m*

Oo

oak [ok] N roble *m*, encina *f*; **— grove** robledal *m*
oar [ɔr] N remo *m*; VI/VT remar, bogar; **—lock** tolete *m*
OAS [Organization of American States] [óéés] N OEA *f*
oasis [oésɪs] N oasis *m*
oat [ot] N avena *f*; **—meal** (flour) harina de avena *f*; (breakfast food) gachas de avena *f pl*; **—s** avena *f*
oath [oθ] N (pledge) juramento *m*; (curse) maldición *f*; (swear word) palabrota *f*, taco *m*; **to take an —** prestar juramento
obedience [obídiəns] N obediencia *f*
obedient [obídiənt] ADJ obediente
obese [obís] ADJ obeso
obesity [obísɪdi] N obesidad *f*
obey [obé] VI/VT obedecer
obituary [obítʃueri] N nota necrológica *f*, obituario *m*
object[1] [ábdʒɪkt] N objeto *m*; (of a verb) complemento *m*
object[2] [əbdʒékt] VI/VT objetar
objection [əbdʒékʃən] N objeción *f*
objectionable [əbdʒékʃənəbəl] ADJ objetable
objective [əbdʒéktɪv] ADJ objetivo; N objetivo *m*, finalidad *f*
objectivity [abdʒektívɪdi] N objetividad *f*
obligate [áblɪget] VT obligar
obligated [ábligeDid] ADJ obligado, comprometido
obligation [abligéʃən] N obligación *f*; **under no — to buy** sin compromiso de compra
obligatory [əblígətɔri] ADJ obligatorio, obligado
oblige [əbláidʒ] VT (make obliged) obligar; VI (do a favor for) complacer; VI (obey an order) obedecer; **much —d!** ¡muchas gracias! ¡muy agradecido!
obliging [əbláidʒɪŋ] ADJ complaciente; *Am* comedido
oblique [oblík] ADJ oblicuo
obliterate [əblídəret] VT (blot out) tachar; (destroy) arrasar, destruir
oblivion [əblíviən] N olvido *m*
oblivious [əblíviəs] ADJ inconsciente; **— to the danger** ajeno al peligro
obnoxious [əbnákʃəs] ADJ (remark, behavior) ofensivo; (person) odioso
oboe [óbo] N oboe *m*
obscene [əbsín] ADJ obsceno; **his salary is —** lo que gana es escandaloso
obscenity [əbsénɪdi] N obscenidad *f*
obscure [əbskjúr] ADJ oscuro; VT oscurecer
obscurity [əbskjúrɪdi] N oscuridad *f*
obsequious [əbsíkwiəs] ADJ obsequioso
observance [əbzɝvəns] N observancia *f*
observant [əbzɝvənt] ADJ observador
observation [abzɝvéʃən] N observación *f*
observatory [əbzɝvətɔri] N observatorio *m*
observe [əbzɝv] VT observar; (holidays, rituals) guardar
observer [əbzɝvə] N observador -ora *mf*; (of elections) interventor -ora *mf*
obsess [əbsés] VI/VT obsesionar[se]; **he's —ing over it** está obsesionado con eso
obsession [əbséʃən] N obsesión *f*
obsessive-compulsive [əbsésɪvkəmpÁłsɪv] ADJ obsesivo-compulsivo
obsolescence [absəlésəns] N desuso *m*
obsolete [absəlít] ADJ anticuado, desusado
obstacle [ábstəkəl] N obstáculo *m*
obstetrician [abstətríʃən] N obstetra *mf*
obstetrics [abstétrɪks] N obstetricia *f*
obstinacy [ábstənəsi] N obstinación *f*, terquedad *f*, porfía *f*
obstinate [ábstənɪt] ADJ obstinado, terco, recalcitrante; **to be —** obstinarse
obstruct [əbstrÁkt] VI/VT obstruir; (traffic) atascar, obstruir
obstruction [əbstrÁkʃən] N obstrucción *f*
obtain [əbtén] VT obtener, procurar; VI prevalecer
obtainable [əbténəbəl] ADJ conseguible
obviate [ábviet] VT obviar
obvious [ábviəs] ADJ obvio, evidente
obviously [ábviəsli] ADV & INTERJ evidentemente, obviamente
occasion [əkéʒən] N (moment) ocasión *f*; (chance) oportunidad *f*, ocasión *f*; (cause) motivo *m*; (event) acontecimiento *m*, ocasión *f*; VT ocasionar
occasional [əkéʒənl] ADJ ocasional
occasionally [əkéʒənli] ADV de vez en cuando, ocasionalmente
occidental [aksɪdéntl] ADJ & N occidental *mf*
occlusion [əklúʒən] N obstrucción *f*, oclusión *f*
occult [əkÁlt] ADJ oculto; N ocultismo *m*, ciencias ocultas *f pl*; VT ocultar
occupancy [ákjəpənsi] N ocupación *f*; **— rate** tasa de ocupación *f*
occupant [ákjəpənt] N ocupante *mf*
occupation [akjəpéʃən] N ocupación *f*
occupational [akjəpéʃənl] ADJ ocupacional; **— hazard/risk** riesgo ocupacional *m*; **— therapy** laborterapia *f*, terapia ocupacional *f*
occupy [ákjəpaɪ] VI/VT ocupar

occur [əkˈɜ˞] VI ocurrir, suceder; **it —red to me** se me ocurrió

occurrence [əkˈɜ˞əns] N suceso *m*, acontecimiento *m*

ocean [óʃən] N océano *m*

oceanic [oʃiǽnɪk] ADJ oceánico

oceanography [oʃənágrəfi] N oceanografía *f*

ocelot [ásəlat] N ocelote *m*

o'clock [əklák] ADV **it is one** — es la una; **it is two** — son las dos

octagon [áktəgan] N octágono *m*, octógono *m*

octane [ákten] N octano *m*

octave [áktɪv] N octava *f*

October [aktóbə˞] N octubre *m*

octopus [áktəpəs] N pulpo *m*

oculist [ákjəlɪst] N oculista *mf*

OD [overdose] [ódí] N sobredosis *f*; VI tomar una sobredosis

odd [ad] ADJ (unusual) extraño; (not even) impar, non; **—ball** excéntrico -ca *mf*; **— change** suelto *m*, cambio *m*; **— job** trabajo ocasional *m*; **— shoe** zapato sin compañero *m*; ADV **thirty—** treinta y tantos

oddity [ádɪti] N rareza *f*; (person) excéntrico -ca *mf*

odds [adz] N (probabilities) probabilidades *f pl*; **— and ends** cachivaches *m pl*; **the — are against me** llevo las de perder; **to be at —** estar en desacuerdo; ADJ **—on favorite** favorito *m*

ode [od] N oda *f*

odious [ódiəs] ADJ odioso

odor [ódə˞] N olor *m*; (bad) hedor *m*

odorless [ódə˞lɪs] ADJ inodoro

odorous [ódə˞əs] ADJ oloroso

of [ʌv] PREP de; **— course** por supuesto, desde luego; **a quarter — five** las cinco menos cuarto; **doctor — medicine** doctor -ora en medicina *mf*; **the smell — paint** el olor a pintura; **a friend — mine** un amigo mío

off [ɔf] ADV **— and on** de vez en cuando; **— the record** extraoficialmente; **ten cents —** rebaja de diez centavos *f*; **ten miles — a diez** millas de distancia; **to take a day —** tomarse un día libre; ADJ **— chance** posibilidad remota *f*; **—color** verde; **— season** temporada baja *f*; **— year** de producción decreciente; **our deal is —** se canceló nuestro plan; **prices are —** los precios han caído; **you're — by a mile** estás equivocadísimo; **he's a little —** está tocadito; **with his hat —** sin el sombrero; **the electricity is —** está apagada la electricidad; **to be — to war** haberse ido a la guerra; **to be well —** tener mucho dinero; PREP **— course** fuera de curso; **he drove — the road** se salió de la carretera; **I bought it — a gypsy** se lo compré a un gitano; **he's — playing golf** se fue a jugar al golf; VT

liquidar

off-duty [ɔfdúpi] ADJ **to be —** no estar de turno

offend [əfénd] VI/VT (insult) ofender, afrentar; (affect disagreeably) desagradar

offender [əféndə˞] N delincuente *mf*

offense¹ [əféns] N (sin, insult) ofensa *f*; (misdemeanor) delito *m*; **no — was meant** no te lo tomes a mal

offense² [áfɛns] N (in sports) ofensiva *f*

offensive [əfénsɪv] ADJ ofensivo; **— line** línea ofensiva *f*; **— series** serie ofensiva *f*, ataque *m*; N ofensiva *f*

offer [ɔ́fə˞] VT ofrecer; **to — to** ofrecerse a; N oferta *f*; **make an —** hacer una oferta

offering [ɔ́fə˞ɪŋ] N (thing given in worship) ofrenda *f*; (thing presented for sale) oferta *f*; (action of offering) ofrecimiento *m*

offhand [ɔ́fhǽnd] ADV **he remarked —** mencionó al descuido; ADJ **an — remark** un comentario descuidado

office [ɔ́fɪs] N (function) cargo *m*, función *f*; (place) oficina *f*, despacho *m*; (headquarters) oficinas *f pl*; **— boy** mandadero de oficina *m*; **— building** edificio para oficinas *m*; **— suite** (furniture) juego ofimático *m*; (rooms) suite *f*; (software) paquete de programas de productividad *m*; **through the —s of** por la intervención de

officer [ɔ́fɪsə˞] N (military) oficial *m*; (police) agente de policía *mf*; (of an organization) directivo -va *mf*

official [əfíʃəl] ADJ oficial; N funcionario -ria *mf*

officiate [əfíʃiet] VI oficiar; (in sports) arbitrar

officious [əfíʃəs] ADJ oficioso

off-key [ɔ́fkí] ADJ desafinado

off-limits [ɔ́flɪ́mɪts] ADV vedado, de acceso prohibido

off-line [ɔ́fláɪn] ADV fuera de línea

off-season [ɔ́fsizən] N temporada baja *f*; ADJ de temporada baja

offset¹ [ɔ́fsɛt] N offset *m*

offset² [ɔ́fsɛt, ɔ̀fsɛt] VT compensar

offshore [ɔ́fʃɔr] ADJ & ADV cerca de la costa; **— account** cuenta en un paraíso fiscal *f*; **— drilling** explotación petrolífera en el fondo del mar *f*

offside [ɔ́fsáɪd] ADV fuera de juego

offspring [ɔ́fsprɪŋ] N prole *m*

offstage [ɔ́fstéʤ] ADV & ADJ entre bastidores, fuera de escena

off-the-record [ɔ́fθə˞rékə˞d] ADJ oficioso

often [ɔ́fən] ADV a menudo; **how —?** ¿con qué frecuencia? ¿cada cuánto?

ogre [ógə˞] N ogro *m*

oh [o] INTERJ **— no!** ¡ay no! **— really?** ¿de veras? **— well** está bien, vale; **— yeah?** (not true) ¡qué va! (really?) ¿de veras?

ohm [om] N ohmio *m*

oil [ɔɪl] N (for cars, cooking) aceite *m*; (crude)

petróleo *m*; —**can** alcuza *f*, aceitera *f*; —**cloth** hule *m*, tela de hule *f*; —**factory** aceitera *f*; —**field** campo petrolífero *m*; —**industry** industria petrolera *f*; —**lamp** quinqué *m*; —**painting** pintura al óleo *f*, óleo *m*; —**pan** cárter *m*; —**pipeline** oleoducto *m*; —**rig** plataforma petrolífera *f*; —**slick** mancha de petróleo *f*; —**spill** vertido de petróleo *m*; —**tanker** barco petrolero *m*; —**well** pozo de petróleo *m*; ADJ —**-bearing** petrolífero; —**exporting** exportador de petróleo; —**producing** petrolífero; VT (apply oil) aceitar; (bribe) untar

oily [ˈɔɪli] ADJ (food) aceitoso; (liquid) oleoso; (hair) graso; (person) untuoso

oink [ɔɪŋk] V gruñir; N gruñido *m*

ointment [ˈɔɪntmənt] N ungüento *m*

OK/okay [okéˈ] ADJ bueno; **he's an —** guy es un buen tipo; **his work is just —** su trabajo no es nada del otro mundo; ADV bien; **it's —** (fine) está bien; (adequate) es regular; N **to give one's —** dar el visto bueno; VT dar el visto bueno, aprobar; INTERJ bien, *Sp* vale

okra [ˈokrə] N quingombó *m*

old [old] ADJ viejo; (objects only) antiguo; (wine) añejo; —**age** vejez *f*, ancianidad *f*; —**-boy network** red favoritista entre hombres *f*; —**-fashioned** (unfashionable) pasado de moda; (antiquated) anticuado; (morally prudish) chapado a la antigua; —**fogey** carcamal *m*, carca *f*; —**hat** pasado de moda; —**maid** solterona *f*; —**-time** antiguo, viejo; —**-timer** (longtime member) miembro de la vieja guardia *m*; (oldster) viejo *m*; —**wives' tale** superstición *f*; —**world** viejo mundo *m*; **days of —** antaño; **how — are you?** ¿cuántos años tienes? —**man** (husband) marido *m*; (father) *fam* viejo *m*; **I'm not — enough to drive** soy muy joven para conducir; **to be an — hand at** ser ducho en

olden [ˈoldn] ADJ **in — days** antaño

oldie [ˈoldi] N viejo éxito *m*

oleander [ˈoliændə] N adelfa *f*

olfactory [ɔlfǽktəri] ADJ olfatorio

olive [ˈɑlɪv] N (tree) olivo *m*; (fruit) aceituna *f*, oliva *f*; —**branch** ramo de olivo *m*; —**grove** olivar *m*; —**oil** aceite de oliva *m*; —**wood** madera de olivo *m*; ADJ verde oliva

Olympiad [olímpiæd] N Olimpiada *f*, Olimpíada *f*

Olympic [olímpɪk] ADJ olímpico; —**Games** Olimpiadas *f pl*, Olimpíadas *f pl*, Juegos Olímpicos *m pl*

Oman [omán] N Omán *m*

Omani [ománi] ADJ & N omaní *mf*

omelet [ˈɑmlɪt] N tortilla francesa *f*

omen [ˈomən] N agüero *m*, presagio *m*

ominous [ˈɑmənəs] ADJ (threatening) amenazador; (like an omen) agorero

omission [omíʃən] N omisión *f*

omit [omɪ́t] VT omitir

omnipotence [amnípətəns] N omnipotencia *f*

omnipotent [amnípətənt] ADJ omnipotente

omniscience [amníʃəns] N omnisciencia *f*

omniscient [amníʃənt] ADJ omnisciente

omnivorous [amnívəəs] ADJ omnívoro

on [an] PREP en, sobre, encima de; —**the table** en / sobre / encima de la mesa; —**all sides** por todos lados; —**arriving** al llegar; —**board** a bordo; —**call** de guardia; —**credit** al fiado; —**drugs** drogado; —**horseback** a caballo; —**Monday** el lunes; —**purpose** a propósito; —**-screen** en la pantalla; —**the house** la casa paga; —**time** a tiempo; **a book —stamps** un libro sobre sellos; **do you have any cigarettes — you?** ¿tienes cigarros? **drunk —beer** borracho de cerveza; **to talk —the phone** hablar por teléfono; ADJ —**line** en línea; —**line banking** banca en línea *f*; —**line help** ayuda en línea *f*; ADV —**and**— dale que dale; **his hat is —** lleva puesto el sombrero; **the light is —** está encendida la luz; **there's a war —** estamos en guerra; **you're —** (broadcasting) estás en el aire; (acceptance) te acepto la propuesta

once [wʌns] ADV (in the past, a single time) una vez; (if ever) si alguna vez; —**and for all** una vez por todas, definitivamente; —**in a while** de vez en cuando; —**upon a time** érase una vez; **at —** de inmediato, enseguida; **just this — —** sólo por esta vez; **cousin —removed** primo -ma segundo -da *mf*; CONJ una vez que, cuando; **to have a —-over** vistazo *m*

oncology [ankáˈləʤi] N oncología *f*

one [wʌn] NUM uno; —**book** un libro; —**hundred** cien; —**hundred and one** ciento uno; —**thousand** mil; —**-armed** manco; —**-armed bandit** tragaperras *mf sg*; —**-eyed** tuerto; —**John Smith** un tal John Smith; —**-man band** hombre orquesta *m*; —**on —** mano a mano; —**-sided fight** pelea desigual *f*; —**-upmanship** competitividad *f*; —**-way street** calle de sentido único *f*; **his — chance** su única oportunidad; **the — and only** el único; **this is —smart dog** es un perro muy listo; N & PRON uno *m*; —**at a time** de a uno; —**by —** uno por uno; **love — another** amaos los unos a los otros; **the — who** el/la que; **the green —** el verde; **this — —** este/esta

oneself [wʌnsélf] PRON **to be —** ser uno mismo; **to sit by —** estar sentado solo; **to talk to — —** hablar para sí; **to look at — in the mirror** mirarse en el espejo; **to buy — a house** comprarse una casa

ongoing [ˈángoɪŋ] ADJ continuo

onion [ˈʌnjən] N cebolla *f*; —**patch** cebollar *m*

onlooker [ánlʊkɚ] N espectador -ora *mf*, mirón -ona *mf*

only [ónli] ADJ único; ADV solo, solamente; **I — just caught the train** por poco pierdo el tren; CONJ solo que, pero

onomatopoeia [ɑnəmɑɽəpíə] N onomatopeya *f*

onset [ánset] N comienzo *m*

on-side kick [ɔ́nsaɪd kík] N patada lateral *f*

onto [ántu] PREP en, sobre, encima de; **she got — the plane late** subió tarde al avión; **he dropped it — the table** lo dejó caer en la mesa; **I'm — your plot** conozco tu plan

onward [ánwəd] ADV hacia adelante

onyx [ániks] N ónix *m*

oops [ʊps] INTERJ ¡huy!

ooze [uz] VI/VT rezumar[se]; N cieno *m*

opal [ópəl] N ópalo *m*

opaque [opék] ADJ opaco

OPEC [Organization of Petroleum Exporting Countries] [ópɛk] N OPEP *f*

open [ópən] VI/VT abrir[se]; **to — into** comunicarse con; **to — one's way** abrirse paso; **to — onto** dar a; **to — up** abrirse; ADJ abierto; **— and shut** claro, evidente; **— code** código abierto *m*; **— door policy** política de acceso libre *f*; **--ended** sin restricciones; **--heart surgery** cirujía de corazón abierto *f*; **--minded** de amplias miras; **--mouthed** boquiabierto; **— question** cuestión discutible *f*; **— season** temporada de caza *f*; **— source software** software de fuente abierta *m*; **— to criticism** expuesto a la crítica; N (outdoors) aire libre *m*; (tournament) abierto *m*

opener [ópənɚ] N abridor *m*; (in sports) primer partido *m*; **for —s** para empezar

opening [ópənɪŋ] N (open space) abertura *f*; (act of making or becoming open, ceremony) apertura *f*; (beginning) comienzo *m*; (clearing) claro *m*; (vacancy) vacante *m*, apertura *f*; (pretext) oportunidad *f*; **— bid** oferta de apertura *f*; **— ceremony** ceremonia de apertura *f*; **— night** estreno *m*; **at the —** a/en la apertura

openness [ópənnɪs] N franqueza *f*, transparencia *f*, apertura *f*

opera [ápərə] N ópera *f*; **— glasses** gemelos *m pl*; **— house** ópera *f*

operable [ápəəbəl] ADJ operable

operate [ápəret] VI (function) funcionar; (intervene surgically) operar; **to — on a person** operar a una persona; VT (run a machine) manejar; (administrate) dirigir; (make function) accionar

operating [ápəreɾɪŋ] N **— costs** costos de operación *m pl*; **— room** sala de operaciones *f*, quirófano *m*; **— system** sistema operativo *m*

operation [ɑpəréʃən] N (surgical intervention, mission, math function) operación *f*; (function) funcionamiento *m*; (use of a machine) manejo *m*; **to be in —** (law) estar vigente; (machine) estar funcionando

operative [ápəəɽɪv] ADJ (law) vigente; (contract provision) pertinente; (word) clave, operativo; N (machine worker) operario -ria *mf*; (spy) agente *mf*

operator [ápəreɽɚ] N (telephone, math) operador -ora *mf*; (machine) operario -ria *mf*; (stock) especulador -ora *mf*; **he's a smooth —** es un astuto

ophthalmologist [ɑfθəlmáləʤɪst] N oftalmólogo -ga *mf*

opiate [ópiət] N opiáceo *m*

opinion [əpínjən] N opinión *f*

opium [ópiəm] N opio *m*

opossum [əpásəm] N zarigüeya *f*

opponent [əpónənt] N opositor -ora *mf*, contrincante *mf*, adversario -ria *mf*, oponente *mf*

opportune [ɑpətún] ADJ oportuno

opportunistic [ɑpətunístɪk] ADJ oportunista, aprovechado

opportunity [ɑpətúnɪɽi] N oportunidad *f*, ocasión *f*

oppose [əpóz] VI/VT oponer[se]

opposing [əpózɪŋ] ADJ opuesto, contrario; **— thumb** pulgar oponible *m*

opposite [ápəzɪt] ADJ (contrary) opuesto, contrario; **— to** frente a; PREP frente a, en frente de; N contrario *m*, opuesto *m*; ADV en frente

opposition [ɑpəzíʃən] N oposición *f*; **they met with little —** encontraron poca resistencia

oppress [əprés] VT oprimir

oppression [əpréʃən] N opresión *f*

oppressive [əprésɪv] ADJ (regime) opresivo; (heat) bochornoso, sofocante

oppressor [əprésɚ] N opresor -ora *mf*

optic [áptɪk] ADJ óptico; **— s** óptica *f*

optical [áptɪkəl] ADJ óptico; **— character recognition** sistema de reconocimiento óptico de caracteres *m*; **— fiber** fibra óptica *f*; **— illusion** ilusión óptica *f*; **— resolution** resolución óptica *f*

optician [aptíʃən] N óptico -ca *mf*

optimal [áptəməl] ADJ óptimo

optimism [áptəmɪzəm] N optimismo *m*

optimist [áptəmɪst] N optimista *mf*

optimistic [aptəmístɪk] ADJ optimista

optimize [áptəmaɪz] VT optimizar

option [ápʃən] N opción *f* (also financial); (feature) extra *m*; **to leave one's —s open** no descartar posibilidades

optional [ápʃənəl] ADJ opcional, optativo

optometrist [aptámɪtrɪst] N optometrista *mf*

optometry [aptámɪtri] N optometría *f*

opulence [ápjələns] N opulencia *f*

opulent [ápjələnt] ADJ opulento

or [ɔr] CONJ o; **seven — eight** siete u ocho

OR [operating room] [óár] N quirófano *m*, sala de operaciones *f*

oracle [ɔ́rəkəl] N oráculo *m*

oral [ɔ́rəł] ADJ oral; (hygiene) bucal

orange [ɔ́rɪndʒ] N naranja *f*; **— blossom** azahar *m*; **— grove** naranjal *m*; **— tree** naranjo *m*; ADJ & N anaranjado *m*

orangutan [ərǽŋətæn] N orangután *m*

orator [ɔ́rəɖə-] N orador -ora *mf*

oratory [ɔ́rətɔri] N (skill in speaking) oratoria *f*; (place for prayer) oratorio *m*

orbit [ɔ́rbɪt] N órbita *f*; VI/VT orbitar

orbital [ɔ́rbɪdł] ADJ orbital

orbiter [ɔ́rbɪɖə-] N orbitador *m*

orchard [ɔ́rtʃə-d] N huerto *m*; (large) huerta *f*

orchestra [ɔ́rkɪstrə] N orquesta *f*

orchestrate [ɔ́rkɪstret] VT orquestar

orchid [ɔ́rkɪd] N orquídea *f*

ordain [ɔrdén] VT (as minister) ordenar; (with an edict) decretar

ordeal [ɔrdíł] N suplicio *m*, tortura *f*; **— by fire** ordalía de fuego *f*

order [ɔ́rɖə-] N (command) orden *f*, mandato *m*; (request, commission) pedido *m*; (sequence, obedience to law) orden *m*; **holy —s** órdenes sagradas *f pl*; **an apology is in —** corresponde una disculpa; **in — to** para; **in working —** en buen estado; **in — that** para que, a fin de que; **on —** encargado; **out of —** no funciona; **to put in —** ordenar; VI/VT (command, arrange) ordenar, mandar; (place an order) pedir

ordering [ɔ́rɖə-ɪŋ] N (putting in order) ordenación *f*, ordenamiento *m*

orderly [ɔ́rɖə-li] ADJ ordenado; N (military) ordenanza *m*; (hospital) camillero *m*

ordinal [ɔ́rdnəł] ADJ ordinal

ordinance [ɔ́rdnəns] N ordenanza *f*

ordinary [ɔ́rdnɛri] ADJ común, corriente, ordinario; **do it the — way** hazlo de la forma habitual

ordination [ɔrdnéʃən] N ordenación *f*

ore [ɔr] N mineral *m*

oregano [ərégəno] N orégano *m*

organ [ɔ́rgən] N órgano *m* (also musical instrument)

organic [ɔrgǽnɪk] ADJ orgánico; **— chemistry** química orgánica *f*

organism [ɔ́rgənɪzəm] N organismo *m*

organist [ɔ́rgənɪst] N organista *mf*

organization [ɔrgənɪzéʃən] N organización *f*, planificación *f*

organizational [ɔrgənɪzéʃənł] ADJ organizativo; **— chart** organigrama *m*

organize [ɔ́rgənaɪz] VI/VT organizar[se]

organized [ɔ́rgənaɪzd] ADJ organizado

organizer [ɔ́rgənaɪzə-] N organizador -ora *mf*

organizing [ɔ́rgənaɪzɪŋ] ADJ organizativo

orgy [ɔ́rdʒi] N orgía *f*

orient[1] [ɔ́riənt] N oriente *m*

orient[2] [ɔ́rient] VT orientar

oriental [ɔriéntł] ADJ & N oriental *mf*

orientate [ɔ́rientet] VT orientar

orientation [ɔrientéʃən] N (guidance) orientación *f*; (tendency, leaning) tendencia *f*

orifice [ɔ́rəfɪs] N orificio *m*

origin [ɔ́rədʒɪn] N origen *m*, procedencia *f*; (of a river) naciente *f*, nacimiento *m*

original [ərídʒənł] ADJ original, originario; N original *m*

originality [ərɪdʒənǽlɪɖi] N originalidad *f*

originate [ərídʒənet] VI/VT originar[se]

oriole [ɔ́riol] N oropéndola *f*

Orlon™ [ɔ́rlɑn] N orlón *m*

ornament[1] [ɔ́rnəmənt] N adorno *m*, ornamento *m*

ornament[2] [ɔ́rnəment] VT adornar, ornamentar

ornamental [ɔrnəméntł] ADJ ornamental

ornamentation [ɔrnəmɪntéʃən] N ornamentación *f*

ornate [ɔrnét] ADJ adornado en exceso; **— style** estilo rebuscado *m*

ornithology [ɔrnəθálədʒi] N ornitología *f*

orphan [ɔ́rfən] ADJ & N huérfano -na *mf*; VT dejar huérfano a

orphanage [ɔ́rfənɪdʒ] N orfanato *m*, hospicio *m*

orthodontics [ɔrθədántɪks] N ortodoncia *f*

orthodox [ɔ́rθədaks] ADJ ortodoxo

orthography [ɔrθágrəfi] N ortografía *f*

oscillate [ásəlet] VI oscilar; VT hacer oscilar

oscillation [asəléʃən] N oscilación *f*

osmosis [azmósɪs] N ósmosis *f*

osprey [áspre] N águila pescadora *f*

ossify [ásəfaɪ] VI osificarse

ostensible [asténsəbəł] ADJ supuesto

ostentation [astentéʃən] N ostentación *f*

ostentatious [astentéʃəs] ADJ ostentoso

osteoarthritis [astioarθráɪdɪs] N osteoartritis *f*

osteoporosis [astiopərósɪs] N osteoporosis *f*

ostracize [ástrəsaɪz] VT aislar

ostrich [ástrɪtʃ] N avestruz *m*

OTC [over-the-counter] [ótísí] ADJ extrabursátil

other [ʌ́ðə-] ADJ, PRON, & N otro -tra *mf*; **— than** Bob salvo Bob; **every — day** cada dos días, un día sí y otro no; **—wise** de otro modo; **—worldly** fantástico

otter [áɖə-] N nutria *f*

ouch [autʃ] INTERJ ¡ay!

ought [ɔt] V AUX **you — to sit down** deberías sentarte; **we — to get up early** deberíamos levantarnos más temprano

ounce [auns] N onza *f*

our [aur] POSS ADJ nuestro

ours [aurz] ADJ nuestro; **this book is —** este libro es nuestro; **these things are —** estas cosas son nuestras; PRON el nuestro / la nuestra; — **is bigger** el nuestro / la nuestra es más grande; **a friend of** — un amigo nuestro

ourselves [aʊrsélvz] PRON **we made the cake** — nosotros mismos hicimos la torta; **we were sitting by** — estábamos sentados solos; **we look at** — **in the mirror** nos miramos en el espejo; **we bought** — **a house** nos compramos una casa

oust [aʊst] VT echar, expulsar

out [aʊt] ADV (outside) fuera; ADJ (turned off, extinguished) apagado; (tennis) fuera; (baseball) out; —**-of-date** pasado de moda, anticuado; N (way out) escape m; (baseball) out m; PREP **she ran** — **the door** salió corriendo por la puerta; **they locked me** — me dejaron fuera; —**-and-** — **criminal** criminal empedernido m; —**-and-** — **refusal** una negativa rotunda; — **of bounds** (golf) fuera de límites; — **of commission/ order** fuera de servicio; — **of fashion** pasado de moda; — **of fear** por miedo; **he's really** — **of it** está ido, está despistado; — **of joint** dislocado; — **of money** sin dinero; — **of print/stock** agotado; — **of touch with** desconectado de; — **of tune** desentonado; — **of work** desempleado; — **to lunch** fam chiflado; **made** — **of** hecho de; **miniskirts are on the way** — las minifaldas se están dejando de usar; **I had it** — **with him** me peleé con él; **you were** — no estabas; **before the week is** — antes de que termine la semana; **the book is just** — acaba de publicarse el libro; **the secret is** — se ha divulgado el secreto; **we had some, but now we're** — teníamos, pero se nos acabó; **I'm** — **$10** perdí $10; INTERJ ¡fuera! VT (expel) expulsar; (expose) descubrir; VI **the truth will** — se descubrirá la verdad

outage [aʊtɪdʒ] N apagón m

outbreak [aʊtbrek] N (of pimples) erupción f; (of war) comienzo m; (of disease) brote m

outburst [aʊtbəst] N (emotional) arrebato m; (of tears) ataque m; (of violence) motín m, explosión f

outcast [aʊtkæst] ADJ & N marginado -da mf

outcome [aʊtkʌm] N resultado m, desenlace m

outcry [aʊtkraɪ] N clamor m, protesta f

outdated [aʊtdédɪd] ADJ anticuado

outdo [aʊtdú] VT superar

outdoor [aʊtdɔr] ADJ al aire libre; — **advertising** publicidad exterior f

outdoors [aʊtdɔ́rz] ADV al aire libre, afuera

outer [aʊdə] ADJ exterior; — **ear** oído externo m; — **space** espacio exterior m

outfield [aʊtfild] N jardín m

outfielder [aʊtfildə] N jardinero -ra mf

outfit [aʊtfɪt] N (gear) equipo m; (clothes)

conjunto m; (soldiers) unidad f; VI/VT equipar, habilitar

outfox [aʊtfáks] VT ser más listo que

outgoing[1] [aʊtɡoɪŋ] ADJ (leaving) saliente

outgoing[2] [aʊtɡóɪŋ] ADJ (extrovert) extrovertido

outgrow [aʊtɡró] VT **she will** — **her clothes** la ropa le quedará pequeña; **she will** — **her epilepsy** la epilepsia se le irá con la edad

outing [aʊdɪŋ] N excursión f, paseo m

outlandish [aʊtlændɪʃ] ADJ estrafalario

outlast [aʊtlǽst] VT (last longer than) durar más que; (live longer than) sobrevivir a

outlaw [aʊtlɔ] N bandido -da mf, forajido -da mf; VT prohibir

outlay[1] [aʊtle] N gasto m, desembolso m

outlay[2] [aʊtlé] VT gastar, desembolsar

outlet [aʊtlɪt] N (exit) salida f; (stream) desagüe m, emisario m; (store) tienda f; (electric connection) toma de corriente f; **she needs an** — **for her talent** necesita canalizar su talento

outline [aʊtlaɪn] N (abstract) bosquejo m, esbozo m, trazado m; (boundary) contorno m; VT (summarize) bosquejar, esbozar; (draw) delinear; (plan) trazar

outlook [aʊtlʊk] N perspectiva f, panorama m

outlying [aʊtlaɪŋ] ADJ (marginal) periférico; (distant) remoto

outpatient [aʊtpeʃənt] N paciente ambulatorio -ria mf, paciente externo -na mf

output [aʊtpʊt] N (production) rendimiento m; (computer information) salida f; — **device** dispositivo de salida m

outrage [aʊtredʒ] N (offense) ultraje m, agravio m, atropello m; (indignation) indignación f; VT (offend) ultrajar, agraviar; (enrage) indignar

outrageous [aʊtrédʒəs] ADJ (offensive) ultrajante; (exorbitant) exorbitante; (extravagant) extravagante

outreach[1] [aʊtritʃ] N extensión f

outreach[2] [aʊtrítʃ] VT exceder

outright[1] [aʊtráɪt] ADV completamente; **he bought it** — lo compró al contado; **he rejected it** — lo rechazó categóricamente

outright[2] [aʊtraɪt] ADJ — **denial** negativa rotunda f; — **lie** mentira descarada f

outset [aʊtset] N comienzo m, principio m

outshine [aʊtʃáɪn] VT eclipsar

outside[1] [aʊtsáɪd] ADV fuera, afuera; PREP fuera de

outside[2] [aʊtsaɪd] ADJ (external) exterior; (foreign) foráneo; N exterior m; — **chance** posibilidad remota f; — **interference** interferencia externa f; **in a week, at the** — en una semana, a lo sumo; **to close on the** — cerrar por fuera

outsider [aʊtsáɪdə] N forastero -ra mf

outskirts [aʊtskəts] N alrededores m pl, afueras

f pl

outsourcing [áʊtsɔrsɪŋ] N contratación externa *f*

outspoken [aʊtspókən] ADJ franco

outstanding [aʊtstǽndɪŋ] ADJ (excellent) sobresaliente, destacado; (pending) pendiente

outstretched [aʊtstrétʃt] ADJ extendido

outward [áʊtwəd] ADJ exterior, externo; — **appearances** apariencias *f pl*; ADV hacia fuera; — **bound** que sale

outweigh [aʊtwé] VT (weigh more) pesar más que; (be more important) sobreponerse a, valer más que

outwit [aʊtwít] VT ser más listo que

oval [óvəł] ADJ oval, ovalado; N óvalo *m*

ovarian [ovériən] ADJ ovárico

ovary [óvəri] N ovario *m*

ovation [ovéʃən] N ovación *f*

oven [ʌ́vn] N horno *m*

over [óvə-] PREP — **here** acá; — **in Japan** allá en Japón; — **many years** durante muchos años; — **the counter** (medicine) sin receta; (stocks) extrabursátil; — **the sea** al otro lado del mar; — **the hill** viejo; — **there** allá; **an umbrella** — **his head** un paraguas sobre la cabeza; **I heard it** — **the radio** lo oí por la radio; **he jumped** — **the fence** saltó por encima de la cerca; **he is** — **her in the hierarchy** él está por encima de ella en la jerarquía; **not** — **one year** no más de un año; **he hit him** — **the head with a rock** le golpeó en la cabeza con una piedra; **all** — **the city** por toda la ciudad; **I'm** — **it** (recovered) me he recuperado; (no longer interested) ya no me interesa; ADV — **again** de nuevo, otra vez; — **against** en contraste con; — **and** — una y otra vez; — **generous** demasiado generoso; **do it** — hazlo de nuevo, hazlo otra vez; **the world** — por todo el mundo; **it is** — **with** se acabó; INTERJ — **and out** cambio y fuera

overachiever [ovə-ətʃívə-] N (bookish) empollón -ona *mf*; (successful) persona muy exitosa *f*

overactive [ovə-ǽktɪv] ADJ hiperactivo, demasiado activo

overall [óvə-ół] ADJ global, total; N —**s** mono *m*, overol *m*

overbearing [ovə-bérɪŋ] ADJ mandón -ona, dominante

overboard [óvə-bɔrd] ADV (into the water) al agua; **she went** — **on her project** se le fue la mano con su proyecto

overcast [óvə-kæst] ADJ nublado, encapotado; **to become** — nublarse, encapotarse

overcharge[1] [ovə-tʃárdʒ] VI/VT cobrar demasiado, cobrar de más

overcharge[2] [óvə-tʃárdʒ] N cobro excesivo *m*

overcoat [óvə-kot] N sobretodo *m*, gabán *m*

overcome [ovə-kʌ́m] VI/VT (to get the better of)

superar; (to overwhelm) embargar; **to be** — **by weariness** estar agobiado

overcompensate [ovə-kámpInset] VI sobrecompensar

overcorrection [ovə-kərékʃən] N sobrecorrección *f*

overdose [óvə-dos] N sobredosis *f*; VI tomar una sobredosis

overdraft [óvə-dræft] N sobregiro *m*, descubierto *m*

overdraw [ovə-drɔ́] VI/VT sobregirar[se]

overdrawn [ovə-drɔ́n] ADJ en descubierto, sobregirado

overdrive [óvə-draɪv] N superdirecta *f*

overdue [ovə-dú] ADJ (borrowed item) atrasado; (bill) vencido

overeat [ovə-ít] VI comer en exceso

overestimate [ovə-éstɪmet] VT sobreestimar

overexcite [ovərɪksáɪt] VT sobreexcitar

overextended [ovə-ɪksténdɪd] ADJ sobreextendido

overflow[1] [ovə-fló] VI desbordar, rebosar

overflow[2] [óvə-flo] N desborde *m*

overgrown [ovə-grón] ADJ cubierto, crecido; — **boy** muchacho demasiado crecido para su edad *m*

overhang[1] [ovə-hǽn] VI (jut) proyectarse; (hang over) estar suspendido

overhang[2] [óvə-hæn] N saliente *m*

overhaul[1] [ovə-hɔ́ł] VT revisar

overhaul[2] [óvə-hɔł] N revisión *f*

overhead[1] [óvə-héd] N gastos generales *m pl*; ADJ elevado; — **projector** retroproyector *m*

overhead[2] [ovə-héd] ADV en lo alto

overhear [ovə-hír] VT oír por casualidad

overjoyed [ovə-dʒɔ́id] ADJ rebosante de alegría

overkill [óvə-kɪł] N exageración *f*

overland [óvə-lænd] ADV & ADJ por tierra

overlap[1] [ovə-lǽp] VI/VT solapar[se], superponer[se]

overlap[2] [óvə-læp] N traslapo *m*

overlay[1] [ovə-lé] VT cubrir; (with gold, etc.) incrustar

overlay[2] [óvə-le] N cubierta *f*; (with metal, wood) revestimiento *m*, chapa *f*

overload[1] [ovə-lód] VT sobrecargar, recargar, saturar

overload[2] [óvə-lod] N sobrecarga *f*

overlook[1] [ovə-lúk] VT (fail to mention) pasar por alto, omitir; (pardon) perdonar; (look from above) mirar desde arriba; (afford a view of) dar a, tener vista a

overlook[2] [óvə-lʊk] N mirador *m*

overly [óvə-li] ADV excesivamente

overnight[1] [óvə-naɪt] ADJ — **delivery** entrega al otro día *f*; — **guest** invitado -da a dormir *mf*

overnight[2] [ovə-náɪt] ADV **he succeeded** — tuvo éxito de la noche a la mañana

overpass [óvə-pæs] N paso elevado *m*

overpower [ovə-páʊə-] VT abrumar

overpowering [ovə-páʊə-ɪŋ] ADJ abrumador

overpriced [ovə-práɪst] ADJ demasiado caro

overproduction [ovə-prədákʃən] N superproducción f

overqualified [ovə-kwáləfaɪd] ADJ sobrecalificado

overreach [ovə-rítʃ] VI to — oneself abarcar demasiado

overreact [ovə-riǽkt] VI reaccionar exageradamente

override [ovə-ráɪd] VT anular

overrule [ovə-rúl] VT anular

overrun¹ [ovə-rán] VT (overflow) desbordar; (exceed) exceder; (invade) infestar

overrun² [óvə-rʌn] N exceso de costos m

overseas [ovə-síz] ADV (beyond the sea) en ultramar; (abroad) en el extranjero

oversee [ovə-sí] VI (workers) dirigir, supervisar; (accounts) fiscalizar

overseer [óvə-sir] N capataz -za mf, supervisor -ora mf

overshadow [ovə-ʃǽdo] VT eclipsar, opacar

overshoe [óvə-ʃu] N chanclo m

oversight [óvə-saɪt] N (mistake) descuido m; (act of overseeing workers) supervisión f; (act of overseeing accounts) fiscalización f

overstep [ovə-stép] VT excederse en

overstrike [óvə-straɪk] VT imprimir un carácter directamente encima de otro

overt [ovə́t] ADJ evidente

overtake [ovə-ték] VT (pass someone) pasar, rebasar; (befall) abatirse sobre

overtax [ovə-tǽks] VT (tax too much) gravar excesivamente; (demand too much) exigir demasiado

overthrow¹ [ovə-θró] VT derrocar, derribar

overthrow² [óvə-θro] N derrocamiento m

overtime [óvə-taɪm] N (in a game) prórroga f, tiempo suplementario m; (at work) horas extras f pl; to work — hacer horas extras

overture [óvə-tʃə] N (musical composition) obertura f; (initial move) propuesta f

overturn [ovə-tǽn] VI/VT volcar[se]; VT (a decision) anular; (a government) derrocar

overview [óvə-vju] N vista global f, panorama m

overweight¹ [ovə-wét] ADJ he's — pesa demasiado

overweight² [óvə-wet] N sobrepeso m

overwhelm [ovə-hwélm] VT abrumar, agobiar

overwhelming [ovə-hwélmɪŋ] ADJ (responsibility, task) abrumador, agobiante; (victory) arrollador

overwork¹ [ovə-wǽk] VI trabajar demasiado; VT hacer trabajar demasiado

overwork² [óvə-wǝk] N exceso de trabajo m

overwrite mode [óvə-raɪtmod] VT modo de reescritura m

ovulate [ávjəlet] VI ovular

ovulation [ɑvjəléʃən] N ovulación f

owe [o] VI/VT deber; (a sum) adeudar, deber

owing [óɪŋ] ADJ debido; — to debido a

owl [aʊl] N lechuza f, búho m

own [on] ADJ & PRON propio; — goal autogol m, gol en contra m; a house of his — una casa suya; to be on one's — ser independiente; to come into one's — conseguir lo que uno se merece; to hold one's — mantenerse firme; VT poseer; to — up [to] confesar

owner [ónə] N dueño -ña mf, propietario -ria mf; — financing financiamiento por el propietario m

ownership [ónə-ʃip] N propiedad f

ox [ɑks] N buey m

oxidation [ɑksɪdéʃən] N oxidación f

oxidize [áksɪdaɪz] VI/VT oxidar[se]

oxygen [áksɪdʒən] N oxígeno m; — tent cámara de oxígeno f

oyster [óɪstə] N ostra f; (large) ostión m

ozone [ózon] N ozono m; — layer capa de ozono f

Pp

pace [pes] N paso m; —maker marcapasos m sg; VT (traverse) ir y venir por; (set the tempo) marcar al paso; (measure) medir a pasos

pacific [pəsífɪk] ADJ pacífico; — Ocean Océano Pacífico m

pacification [pæsɪfɪkéʃən] N pacificación f

pacifier [pǽsəfaɪə] N chupete m

pacifism [pǽsəfɪzəm] N pacifismo m

pacify [pǽsəfaɪ] VT (a country) pacificar; (a person) apaciguar

pack [pæk] N (of wolves) manada f; (of dogs) jauría f; (of cigarettes) cajilla f, cajetilla f; (of cloth) compresa f; (of cards) baraja f; (of cyclists) pelotón m; — animal acémila f, bestia de carga f; —rat rata urraca f; (person who saves everything) urraca f; a — of lies una sarta de mentiras f; VT empacar, empaquetar; (carry a gun) portar; (crowd) atestar; (load) cargar; to — off despachar; to — one's bags hacer las maletas

package [pǽkɪdʒ] N paquete m (also organized vacation); — deal (agreement) acuerdo global m; (tourism, travel) paquete turístico m; VT (gift) empaquetar; (food) envasar

packaging [pǽkɪdʒɪŋ] N embalaje m, empaque m

packer [pǽkə] N empacador -ora mf, embalador -ora mf

packet [pǽkɪt] N paquete m

packing [pǽkɪŋ] N embalaje m

pact [pækt] N pacto m

pad [pæd] N (cushion) almohadilla f (also for ink); (block of paper) bloc m; (for aircraft) pista f; (for spacecraft) plataforma de lanzamiento f; VT (stuff with padding) acolchar; (add to dishonestly) rellenar

padding [pædɪŋ] N relleno m; (cotton) guata f; (of a speech) ripio m

paddle [pædl] N (for rowing) pala f, remo m; (for mixing, beating, ping-pong) paleta f; — **wheel** rueda de paleta f; VI (row) remar; VT hacer avanzar remando; (hit) dar una paletada

paddock [pædək] N (field) prado m; (enclosure at racetrack) paddock m

padlock [pædlak] N candado m; VT cerrar con candado

pagan [pégən] ADJ & N pagano -na mf

paganism [pégənɪzəm] N paganismo m

page [peʤ] N (sheet) hoja f, página f; (boy servant) paje m; (hotel employee) botones m sg; — **break** salto de página m; VT (number pages) paginar; (call) llamar por altavoz; Mex vocear; **to — through** hojear

pageant [pædʒənt] N (parade) desfile m; (show) espectáculo m

pager [péʤə-] N buscapersonas m sg

paid [ped] ADJ pagado; —-**up** liberado, totalmente pagada, pago

paid [ped] see pay

pail [pel] N balde m, cubeta f

pain [pen] N dolor m; (suffering) sufrimiento m; —**killer** analgésico m; **on — of** so pena de; **to take —s** esmerarse; **he's a —** es un chinche; ADJ —**staking** esmerado; VT (physical) doler; (mental) apenar

painful [pénfəl] ADJ (hurting) doloroso; (distressing) penoso; (difficult) arduo

painless [pénlɪs] ADJ sin dolor, indoloro

paint [pent] N (substance) pintura f; (spotted horse) pinto m; —**brush** (for art) pincel m; (for a house) brocha f; VI/VT pintar; **to — the town red** irse de juerga

painter [péntə-] N pintor -ora mf

painting [péntɪŋ] N pintura f

pair [per] N par m; (married couple) pareja f; **a — of scissors** unas tijeras, una tijera; VI/VT aparear[se], emparejar[se]; **to — off** aparearse

pajamas [pəʤáməz] N pijama/piyama mf

Pakistan [pǽkɪstæn] N Paquistán m

Pakistani [pækɪstǽni] ADJ & N paquistano -na mf

pal [pæl] N compañero -ra mf, compadre m, comadre f

palace [pǽlɪs] N palacio m

palate [pǽlɪt] N paladar m

palatial [pəléʃəl] ADJ suntuoso

Palau [pəláú] N Paláu m

pale [pel] ADJ pálido, macilento; N **beyond the — inaceptable**; VI palidecer

paleness [pélnɪs] N palidez f

paleontology [peliəntáləʤi] N paleontología f

Palestine [pǽlɪstaɪn] N Palestina f

Palestinian [pæləstíniən] ADJ palestino; N palestino -na mf

palette [pǽlɪt] N paleta f

palisade [pælɪséd] N empalizada f; —**s** acantilados m pl

pall [pɔl] VT (cover with a cloth) cubrir con un paño mortuorio; (satiate) hartar; VI (tire) cansar; N paño mortuorio m; —**bearer** portador del féretro m; **to cast a — on** empañar

palliative [pǽliəDɪv] N paliativo m

pallid [pǽlɪd] ADJ pálido

pallor [pǽlə-] N palidez f

palm [pɑm] N (part of hand) palma f; (tree) palmera f, palma f; — **Sunday** Domingo de Ramos m; —**top computer** Am computadora de mano f, Sp ordenador de mano m; VT (hide in palm) escamotear; **to — something off on someone** encajar algo a alguien

palpable [pǽlpəbəl] ADJ (perceptible) palpable; (tangible) tangible

palpitate [pǽlpɪtet] VI palpitar

palpitation [pælpɪtéʃən] N palpitación f

palsy [pɔ́lzi] N parálisis f

paltry [pɔ́ltri] ADJ miserable, despreciable

pamper [pǽmpə-] VT mimar, consentir

pamphlet [pǽmflɪt] N (informative) folleto m; (political) panfleto m

pan [pæn] N (for boiling) cazuela f, cacerola f, cazo m; (for frying) sartén f; (for baking) molde m; —**handle** mango de sartén m; —**handler** pordiosero -ra mf; VT criticar duramente; VI **to — for gold** extraer oro; **to — out** dar buen resultado; **to —handle** mendigar, pordiosear

panacea [pænəsíə] N panacea f

Panama [pǽnəmɑ] N Panamá f

Panamanian [pænəménian] ADJ & N panameño -ña mf

Pan-American [pænəmérɪkən] ADJ panamericano

pancake [pǽnkek] N panqueque m; **flat as a —** chato como una tabla

pancreas [pǽnkriəs] N páncreas m

panda [pǽndə] N panda m

pandemic [pændémɪk] ADJ pandémico m; N pandemia f

pander [pǽndə] VI consentir

pane [pen] N vidrio m, cristal m

panel [pǽnl] N (wall) revestimiento m; (group of experts) panel m; (of instruments) tablero m; VT revestir con paneles

paneling [pǽnlɪŋ] N (wall) panel m

pang [pæŋ] N (sharp pain, hunger) punzada f; (anguish) remordimientos m pl

panic [pǽnɪk] ADJ & N pánico *m*; ADJ → **stricken** sobrecogido de pánico

panorama [pænərǽmə] N panorama *m*

panoramic [pænərǽmɪk] ADJ panorámico

pansy [pǽnzi] N pensamiento *m*

pant [pænt] VI jadear

panther [pǽnθə-] N pantera *f*

panties [pǽntiz] N *Sp* bragas *f pl*; *Mex* pantaletas *f pl*; *RP* bombacha *f*

pantomime [pǽntəmaɪm] N pantomima *f*

pantry [pǽntri] N despensa *f*, alacena *f*

pants [pænts] N pantalones *m pl*, pantalón *m*

pantyhose [pǽntihoz] N panty *m*

papa [pápə] N papá *m*

papacy [pépəsi] N papado *m*

papal [pépəl] ADJ papal

papaya [pəpáɪə] N papaya *f*; *Cuba* fruta bomba *f*

paper [pépə-] N (material) papel *m*; (newspaper) periódico *m*; (assignment) trabajo *m*; (oral contribution) comunicación *f*; (written contribution) artículo *m*; **—back** libro en rústica *m*; **—clip** clip *m*, sujetapapeles *m sg*; **—cutter** guillotina *f*; **—feeder** alimentador de hojas *m*; **—money** papel moneda *m*; **—s** papeles *m pl*; **—shredder** trituradora *f*; **—weight** pisapapeles *m sg*; **—work** (forms) papeleo *m*; (procedures) trámites *m pl*; **on—** por escrito; VI/VT empapelar

paprika [pæpríka] N pimentón *m*, páprika *f*

pap smear [pép smir] N citología *f*

Papua New Guinea [pǽpjuəngíni] N Papúa Nueva Guinea *f*

Papua New Guinean [pǽpjuənugíniən] ADJ & N papú *mf*

par [pɑr] N (financial) paridad *f*; (in golf) par *m*; **—value** valor nominal *m*; **at —** a la par; **below —** bajo par; **to be on a — with** estar en pie de igualdad con; **to feel above —** sentirse mejor que lo normal; VT hacer el par

parachute [pǽrəʃut] N paracaídas *m sg*

parachuting [pǽrəʃudɪŋ] N paracaidismo *m*

parachutist [pǽrəʃudɪst] N paracaidista *mf*

parade [pəréd] N (procession) desfile *m*; (military review) parada *f*; **—ground** campo de maniobras *m*; VI desfilar; VT hacer ostentación de

paradigm [pǽrədaɪm] N paradigma *m*

paradise [pǽrədaɪs] N paraíso *m*

paradox [pǽrədaks] N paradoja *f*

paradoxical [pærədáksɪkəl] ADJ paradójico

paraffin [pǽrəfɪn] N parafina *f*

paragraph [pǽrəgræf] N párrafo *m*; VT dividir en párrafos

Paraguay [pǽrəgwaɪ] N Paraguay *m*

Paraguayan [pærəgwáɪən] ADJ & N paraguayo -ya *mf*

parakeet [pǽrəkit] N perico *m*, periquito *m*

parallel [pǽrəlɛl] ADJ & N paralelo *m*; (geometry) paralela *f*; **—port** puerto paralelo *m*; VT (run equidistant from) correr paralelo a; (compare) comparar

paralysis [pərǽləsɪs] N (of the body) parálisis *f*; (of a transportation system) paralización *f*

paralytic [pærəlídɪk] ADJ paralítico -ca

paralyze [pǽrəlaɪz] VT paralizar

paramedic [pærəmédɪk] ADJ & N paramédico -ca *mf*

parameter [pərǽmɪdə-] N parámetro *m*

paramilitary [pærəmílɪteri] ADJ & N paramilitar *mf*

paramount [pǽrəmaunt] ADJ supremo, sumo

paranoia [pærənɔ́ɪə] N paranoia *f*

paranoid [pǽrənɔɪd] ADJ & N paranoico -ca *mf*; **—delusion** delirio paranoico *m*

paranormal [pærənɔ́rməl] ADJ paranormal

paraphernalia [pærəfənéljə] N parafernalia *f*

paraphrase [pǽrəfrez] N paráfrasis *f*; VI/VT parafrasear

paraplegic [pærəplídʒɪk] ADJ N parapléjico -ca *mf*

parapsychology [pærəsaɪkáləʤi] N parapsicología *f*

parasite [pǽrəsaɪt] N parásito *m*

parasitic [pærəsídɪk] ADJ parasítico; **—disease** enfermedad parasitaria *f*

parasol [pǽrəsɔl] N parasol *m*, sombrilla *f*

paratroops [pǽrətrups] N tropas paracaidistas *f pl*

parcel [pɑ́rsəl] N (package) paquete *m*; (lot) partida *f*; (land) parcela *f*; **—post** paquete postal *m*; VT (land) parcelar; **to — out** repartir

parch [pɑrtʃ] VT secar; **I'm —ed** estoy muerto de sed

parchment [pɑ́rtʃmənt] N pergamino *m*

pardon [pɑ́rdn] N perdón *m*, gracia *f*; (legal) indulto *m*; **I beg your —** perdone; VT perdonar, disculpar; (legally) indultar

pare [per] VT mondar, pelar; **to — down expenditures** reducir gastos

parent [pérənt] N padre *m*, madre *f*; **—directory** directorio padre *m*; **—s** padres *m pl*

parental [pərént̩l] ADJ parental; **—control** control paternal *m*

parenthesis [pərénθəsɪs] N paréntesis *m*

parenting [pérəntɪŋ] N **—guide** guía para padres *f*; **—skill** habilidad para educar a los hijos *f*; **good —** buena crianza de los hijos *f*

pariah [pəráɪə] N paria *m*

parish [pǽrɪʃ] N parroquia *f*; **—priest** (cura) párroco *m*

parishioner [pəríʃənə-] N feligrés -esa *mf*, parroquiano -na *mf*

parity [pérɪdi] N paridad *f*

park [pɑrk] N parque *m*; (for baseball) estadio de béisbol *m*; VI/VT estacionar, aparcar

parking [pɑ́rkɪŋ] N estacionamiento *m*,

aparcamiento *m*; **— lot** estacionamiento *m*, aparcamiento *m*; **— place** lugar de estacionamiento/aparcamiento *m*

Parkinson's disease [párkɪnsənzdɪziz] N enfermedad de Parkinson *f*

parlance [párləns] N habla *f*

parley [párli] N (peace negotiation) parlamento *m*; (discussion) discusión *f*; VI parlamentar

parliament [párləmənt] N parlamento *m*

parliamentary [parləméntri] ADJ parlamentario

parlor [párlɚ] N sala *f*, salón *m*; **— game** juego de salón *m*; **beauty —** salón de belleza *m*

parochial [pərókiəl] ADJ (of a parish) parroquial; (provincial) pueblerino

parody [pǽrədi] N parodia *f*; VT parodiar

parole [pəról] N libertad condicional *f*; VT poner en libertad condicional

parrot [pǽrət] N loro *m*, papagayo *m*; VT repetir como loro

parry [pǽri] VT (a blow) parar; (a remark) eludir; N parada *f*

parse [pɑrs] VT analizar

parser [pársɚ] N analizador *m*

parsing [pársɪŋ] N análisis *m*

parsley [pársli] N perejil *m*

parsnip [pársnɪp] N chirivía *f*

parson [pársən] N pastor -ora *mf*

part [pɑrt] N (component) parte *f*; (role) papel *m*; (in hair) raya *f*; **— and parcel** parte esencial *f*; **— time** tiempo parcial *m*; **in foreign —s** en el extranjero; **spare —s** piezas de repuesto *f pl*, repuestos *m pl*; ADJ **—-time** a tiempo parcial; VI/VT (cut into parts) partir[se]; (divide into parts) dividir[se]; (separate, leave) separar[se]; **to — company** separarse; **to — one's hair** hacerse la raya; **to — with** desprenderse de

partake [pɑrték] VI **to — in** participar; **to — of** (share) compartir; (eat) comer

partial [párʃəl] ADJ parcial

participant [partísəpənt] ADJ & N participante *mf*, partícipe *mf*

participate [partísəpet] VI participar

participation [partɪsəpéʃən] N participación *f*

participle [párdɪsɪpəl] N participio *m*

particle [párdɪkəl] N partícula *f*; **— board** aglomerado *m*

particular [pətíkjələ] ADJ particular; (fussy) quisquilloso; N **in —** en particular; **—s** particulares *m pl*

parting [párdɪŋ] N (farewell) despedida *f*; (separation) separación *f*; **— of the ways** encrucijada *f*

partisan [párdɪzən] N (supporter) partidario -ria *mf*, partidista *mf*; (guerrilla) partisano -na *mf*; ADJ (of supporters) partidario, partidista; (of guerrillas) de partisanos

partition [partíʃən] N (distribution) reparto *m*; (division) división *f*, partición *f*; (wall) tabique *m*, mampara *f*; VT (distribute) repartir; (divide) dividir; (divide with a wall) tabicar

partly [pártli] ADV en parte

partner [pártnɚ] N (in business) socio -cia *mf*; (in an activity) compañero -ra *mf*; (in dancing, sports, marriage) pareja *f*

partnership [pártnɚʃɪp] N (business) sociedad *f*; (relationship) asociación *f*

partridge [pártrɪdʒ] N perdiz *f*

party [párdi] N (get-together) fiesta *f*; (political group) partido *m*; (group of people) partida *f*; (litigant) parte *f*; **— of four** mesa para cuatro *f*; **— animal** fiestero -ra *mf*, parrandero -ra *mf*; VI ir de juerga

pass [pæs] VI (to go by) pasar; **to — a kidney stone** expulsar un cálculo renal; **to — away** fallecer; **to — for** pasar por; **to — in review** pasar revista; **to — on** (die) fallecer; (approve) aceptar; (refuse) no querer; **to — out** desmayarse; **to — over** pasar por alto; **to — up an opportunity** dejar pasar una oportunidad; VT (a ball) pasar; (a law) aprobar; (an exam, test) aprobar; **to — judgment** juzgar; **to — oneself off as** hacerse pasar por; **— me the salt** pásame la sal, alcánzame la sal; N (road through mountains) paso *m*; (motion, permission) pase *m*; (for transportation) abono *m*; (over a surface) pasada *f*; (on an exam) aprobación *f*; (of a ball) pase *m*; **—key** llave maestra *f*; **—port** pasaporte *m*; **—word** contraseña *f*, clave de seguridad *f*; **—word protected** protegido por contraseña; **he made a — at her** trató de ligar con ella

passable [pǽsəbəl] ADJ (penetrable) transitable; (mediocre) pasable

passage [pǽsɪdʒ] N (fare, musical or textual phrase, alley) pasaje *m*; (passing of time) paso *m*, transcurso *m*; (hallway in a house) pasillo *m*; (secret pathway) pasadizo *m*; (crossing) travesía *f*; (approval of a bill) aprobación *f*; **—way** (corridor) corredor *m*, pasillo *m*; (alley) pasaje *m*

passenger [pǽsəndʒɚ] N pasajero -ra *mf*

passerby [pǽsɚbaɪ] N transeúnte *mf*, viandante *mf*

passing [pǽsɪŋ] N fallecimiento *m*; ADJ **each — day** cada día que pasa; **— grade** nota de aprobado *f*; **— fancy** capricho pasajero *m*; **— mention** mención al pasar *f*; **— shot** pasante *m*

passion [pǽʃən] N pasión *f*

passionate [pǽʃənɪt] ADJ apasionado

passive [pǽsɪv] ADJ pasivo; N pasiva *f*

past [pæst] ADJ pasado; **— due** en mora, vencido; **— participle** participio pasado *m*; **— perfect** pluscuamperfecto *m*; **— peformance** rendimiento previo *m*; **—**

precedents precedentes anteriores *m pl*; — **tense** tiempo pretérito *m*; **the — president** el expresidente; PREP — **hope** más allá de toda esperanza; — **noon** después de mediodía; **the house — the store** la casa pasando la tienda; **we went — the tower** pasamos al lado de la torre; **half — two** las dos y media; **a woman — forty** una mujer de más de cuarenta años; ADV **for some time —** desde hace algún tiempo; **they drove —** pasaron en coche; N (time) pasado *m*; (tense) pretérito *m*

pasta [pásta] N pasta *f*

paste [pest] N (soft material, puree) pasta *f*; (glue) engrudo *m*; —**board** cartón *m*; VT pegar

pastel [pæstél] ADJ & N pastel *m*

pasteurize [pǽstʃəraɪz] VT pasterizar/pasteurizar

pastime [pǽstaɪm] N pasatiempo *m*

pastor [pǽstə] N pastor -ora *mf*

pastoral [pǽstəəł] ADJ (literary) pastoril; (ecclesiastical) pastoral; N pastoral *f*; (literary work) égloga *f*

pastry [péstri] N (in general) pastelería *f*; (specific) pastel *m*; — **cook** pastelero -ra *mf*, repostero -ra *mf*; — **shop** pastelería *f*, repostería *f*

pasture [pǽstʃə] N (grassland) prado *m*; (grass) pasto *m*; (for horses) potrero *m*; VI/VT pastar, pacer, apacentar

pasty [pésti] ADJ pastoso

pat [pæt] ADJ banal; **down —** al dedillo; **to stand —** mantenerse firme; VI/VT dar palmaditas [a]; N palmadita *f*; N — **of butter** porción de mantequilla *f*

patch [pætʃ] N (piece of cloth to repair clothes) remiendo *m*, parche *m* (also for eye, computer); (spot or area, as of ice) tramo [con hielo] *m*; (plot) parcela *f*; VT (repair) remendar; — **up a quarrel** hacer las paces

patent [pátnt] ADJ (evident) patente; (protected by patent) patentado; — **leather** charol *m*; N patente *f*; — **pending** patente en trámite; VT patentar

paternal [patśnł] ADJ (fatherly) paternal; (of the father's lineage) paterno

paternity [patśnɪDi] N paternidad *f*; — **test** prueba de paternidad *f*

path [pæθ] N (walkway) senda *f*, sendero *m*; (on a computer) ruta *f*; (of a projectile, storm) trayectoria *f*; —**way** senda *f*, sendero *m*

pathetic [pəθéDɪk] ADJ (moving) patético; (contemptible) lamentable

pathogen [pǽθədʒən] N patógeno *m*

pathology [pæθáləʤi] N patología *f*

pathos [péθas] N patetismo *m*

patience [péʃəns] N paciencia *f*

patient [péʃənt] ADJ & N paciente *mf*

patiently [péʃəntli] ADJ con paciencia

patriarch [pétriark] N patriarca *m*

patriarchal [pétriárkəl] ADJ patriarcal

patrimonial [pætrɪmóniəł] ADJ patrimonial

patrimony [pǽtrəmoni] N patrimonio *m*

patriot [pétriət] N patriota *mf*

patriotic [pétriáDɪk] ADJ patriótico

patriotism [pétriətɪzəm] N patriotismo *m*

patrol [pətrół] VI/VT patrullar, rondar; N patrulla *f*, ronda *f*; — **car** patrullero *m*; —**man** patrullero *m*

patron [pétran] N (customer) cliente -ta *mf*; (benefactor) benefactor -ora *mf*, mecenas *mf*; (saint) patrono *m*

patronage [pétrənɪdʒ] N (support of an artist) mecenazgo *m*; (clientele) clientela *f*; (political) clientelismo *m*; **we appreciate your —** agradecemos su preferencia

patronize [pétrənaɪz] VT (be condescending) tratar con condescendencia; (do business with) frecuentar

patter [pǽDə] VI (strike lightly) golpetear; (chatter) parlotear; N (small blows) golpeteo *m*; (chatter) parloteo *m*

pattern [pǽDən] N (for sewing) molde *m*; (for drawing) plantilla *f*; (of behavior) patrón *m*; VI/VT **to — something after** modelar algo a imitación de, basarse en el modelo de; **to — oneself after** seguir el ejemplo de

paucity [pósɪDi] N escasez *f*

paunch [pontʃ] N panza *f*, barriga *f*

pause [pɔz] N pausa *f*; VI (while talking) hacer pausa; (while moving) detenerse

pave [pev] VT (with asphalt) pavimentar; (with bricks) enladrillar; (with flagstones) enlosar; **to — the way for** preparar el camino para

pavement [pévmənt] N (roadway) calzada *f*; (of asphalt) pavimento *m*; (of bricks) enladrillado *m*; (of flagstones) enlosado *m*

pavilion [pəvíljən] N pabellón *m*

paw [pɔ] N pata *f*; (with claws) garra *f*; VT (touch with paw) tocar con la pata; (touch with claws) dar zarpazos; (grope) manosear

pawn [pɔn] N (object left in deposit) prenda *f*; (chess piece) peón *m*; (puppet) títere *m*; —**broker** prestamista *mf*; —**shop** casa de empeños *f*, monte de piedad *m*; **in —** en prenda; VT empeñar, dejar en prenda

pay [pe] VT (remit) pagar; VI (be profitable) ser provechoso, convenir; (be worthwhile) valer la pena; **to — attention** prestar atención, fijarse en; **to — back** (return) restituir; (retaliate) vengarse; **to — a compliment** hacer un cumplido; **to — homage** rendir homenaje; **to — one's respects** saludar; **to — off a debt** cancelar una deuda, amortizar una deuda; **to — out** desembolsar, pagar; **to — a visit** hacer una visita; **to — through the nose** pagar demasiado; **I will — for**

your meal te pago la comida; N (payment) pago m; (wages) paga f, salario m; **—back** (payment) restitución f; (revenge) venganza f; **—check** cheque del sueldo m; **— cut** recorte salarial m; **—day** día de pago m; **— freeze** congelación salarial f; **—load** carga útil f; **—off** (pay) pago m; (reward) recompensa f; (bribe) soborno m; **— phone** teléfono público m; **— raise** aumento salarial / de sueldo m; **—roll** nómina f, planilla f; **— scale** escala salarial f; **to hit —dirt** encontrar una mina de oro

payable [péəbəl] ADJ pagadero

payee [peí] N tenedor -ora mf, beneficiario -ria mf

payment [pémənt] N pago m, abono m; **— in full** liquidación f; **car —s** cuotas del coche f pl

payola [peólə] N soborno m

PC [písí] N (personal computer) PC m; (political correctness) lo políticamente correcto; ADJ (politically correct) políticamente correcto

pea [pi] N guisante m; Am arveja f; **—nut** Sp cacahuete m; Mex cacahuate m; Am maní m; **—nut butter** Sp crema de cacahuete f; Mex crema de cacahuate f; Am manteca / mantequilla de maní f

peace [pis] N paz f; **— officer** oficial de policía m; **— of mind** serenidad f; **at —** en paz; **to keep the —** mantener el orden público; **to hold one's —** callar

peaceful [písfəl] ADJ pacífico, tranquilo

peach [pitʃ] N durazno m; Sp melocotón m; (nice thing or person) delicia f, monada f; **— tree** durazno m, duraznero m; Sp melocotonero m

peacock [píkak] N pavo real m, pavón m

peak [pik] N (of a mountain) pico m, cumbre f; (of production, of one's abilities) punto máximo m; (of one's career) punto culminante m; **— load** carga máxima f; **— season** temporada alta f; **— time** hora punta f

peal [pil] N (of bells) repique m; (of laughter) carcajada f; VI/VT repicar

pear [per] N pera f; **— tree** peral m

pearl [pɝl] N perla f; **— necklace** collar de perlas f

pearly [pɝli] ADJ (color) nacarado, perlado; (with pearls) perlado; **the — gates** las puertas del cielo

peasant [pézənt] ADJ & N campesino -na mf

peat [pit] N turba f

pebble [pébəl] N guijarro m, piedrecilla f; (smooth) canto m

pecan [pikán] N pacana f

peccary [pékəri] N pecarí/pécari m

peck [pek] VI/VT (strike with beak) picar; (eat bit by bit) picotear; (kiss) dar un besito; **—ing order** jerarquía f; **to — a hole** agujerear a picotazos; N (quick stroke) picotazo m; (kiss)

besito m; (measure) medida de áridos [9 litros] f; **you're in a — of trouble** estás metido en un lío

pectoral [péktəəl] ADJ & N pectoral m

peculiar [pɪkjúljə] ADJ peculiar, particular

peculiarity [pɪkjuljɛrɪDi] N peculiaridad f

pedagogical [pɛDəgágɪkəl] ADJ pedagógico

pedagogue [péDəgag] N pedagogo -ga mf

pedagogy [péDəgadʒi] N pedagogía f

pedal [pédl] N pedal m; VI/VT pedalear

pedant [pédn̩t] N pedante mf

pedantic [pədǽntɪk] ADJ pedante

peddle [pédl] VI/VT ir vendiendo de puerta en puerta; **to — gossip** repartir chismes

peddler [pédlə] N buhonero -ra mf, mercachifle m

pederast [pédərǽst] N pederasta m

pederasty [pédərǽsti] N pederastia f

pedestal [pédɪstl̩] N pedestal m

pedestrian [pədéstriən] N peatón -ona mf; ADJ pedestre

pediatrician [piDiətríʃən] N pediatra mf

pediatrics [piDiǽtrɪks] N pediatría f

pedigree [péDəgri] N (of persons) linaje m; (of animals) pedigrí m

pedophile [péDəfaɪl] N pedófilo -la mf

pedophilia [peDəfíliə] N pedofilia f

pee [pi] VI fam hacer pipí; N fam pipí m

peek [pik] VI atisbar; N atisbo m

peel [pil] VI/VT (fruit, tree) pelar[se], descortezar[se]; (paint) descascarar[se]; **to keep one's eyes —ed** mantener los ojos abiertos; N cáscara f

peeler [pílə] N pelador m

peep [pip] VI/VT (begin to appear) asomar[se]; VI (make sound of chicks) piar; **to — at** atisbar; N (look) atisbo m; (sound of chicks) pío m; **—hole** mirilla f

peer [pir] N par m (also nobleman); **— group** grupo paritario m; VI (look attentively) escudriñar; (peep out) asomar

peerless [pírlɪs] ADJ incomparable, sin par

peeve [piv] VT irritar; **to get —d** ponerse de mal humor; N cosa que irrita f

peevish [pívɪʃ] ADJ malhumorado

peg [pɛg] N percha f; (on violin) clavija f; **to take a person down a —** bajarle los humos a alguien; VT (fix with pegs) clavar, clavetear; (set a price) fijar

pejorative [pɪdʒɔ́rəDɪv] ADJ peyorativo, despectivo

pelican [pélɪkən] N pelícano m

pellet [pélɪt] N (ball) bola f, bolita f; (shot) perdigón m

pell-mell [pélmɛ́l] ADJ confuso, tumultuoso; ADV a troche y moche

pelt [pɛlt] N piel f, pellejo m; VI/VT acribillar; **to — with stones** apedrear

pelvis [pélvɪs] N pelvis f

pen [pɛn] N (fountain) pluma f; (ballpoint) bolígrafo m; (for pigs) pocilga f; (for sheep) redil m; (for cows) corral m; — **holder** mango de pluma m, portaplumas m sg; — **name** seudónimo m; VT (write) escribir; (shut in) acorralar, encerrar; — **computer** Am bolígrafo-computadora portátil f, Sp bolígrafo-ordenador portátil m

penal [pínl] ADJ penal

penalize [pínəlaɪz] VT penar; (in sports) penalizar

penalty [pénlti] N (punishment) pena f, castigo m; (forfeiture) multa f; (in sports) penalidad f, infracción f; — **area** (in soccer) área de penales f; — **kick** (in soccer) tiro de penalidad f, penalti m; — **shootout** (in soccer) definición por penales f; — **stroke** (in golf) golpe de penalidad m

penance [pénəns] N penitencia f

pencil [pénsəl] N (writing instrument) lápiz m; (beam of light) haz m; — **sharpener** sacapuntas m sg

pendant [péndənt] ADJ pendiente

pendent [péndənt] N colgante m; ADJ pendiente

pending [péndɪŋ] ADJ pendiente; PREP — **his arrival** hasta que llegue, mientras no llegue

pendulum [péndʒələm] N péndulo m

penetrate [pénɪtret] VT penetrar

penetrating [pénɪtredɪŋ] ADJ penetrante

penetration [penɪtréʃən] N penetración f

penguin [péŋgwɪn] N pingüino m

penicillin [penɪsílɪn] N penicilina f

peninsula [pənínsələ] N península f

penis [pínɪs] N pene m

penitent [pénɪtənt] ADJ & N penitente mf

penitentiary [penɪténʃəri] N penitenciaría f, penal m

penmanship [pénmənʃɪp] N escritura f, caligrafía f

pennant [pénənt] N banderín m, gallardete m

penniless [pénɪlɪs] ADJ pobre, sin dinero

penny [péni] N centavo m; —-**pincher** tacaño -ña mf; **to cost a pretty** — costar un dineral

pension [pénʃən] N (paid to a worker) jubilación f; (paid to a worker's survivors) pensión f; — **fund** caja de jubilaciones f; VT jubilar, pensionar

pensioner [pénʃənə] N pensionista mf

pensive [pénsɪv] ADJ pensativo

pent [pent] ADJ encerrado; —-**up** acumulado

pentagon [péntəgən] N pentágono m

penthouse [pénthaʊs] N penthouse m

penultimate [pɪnʌ́ltəmɪt] ADJ penúltimo

people [pípəl] N gente f; (national group) pueblo m; VT poblar

pep [pɛp] N energía f; VI **to — up** animar

pepper [pépə] N (black) pimienta f; (green) pimiento m; (plant, shaker) pimentero m; —-**mint** menta f; VT pimentar; **to — with bullets** acribillar a balazos

peptic ulcer [péptɪk ʌ́lsə] N úlcera péptica f

per [pə] PREP (for each) por; (according to) según; — **capita** per capita; —-**cent** por ciento; — **diem** Am viático m, Sp dieta f

percale [pəkél] N percal m

perceive [pəsív] VT percibir

percentage [pəséntɪdʒ] N porcentaje m

percentile [pəséntaɪl] N percentil m

perceptible [pəséptəbəl] ADJ perceptible

perception [pəsépʃən] N percepción f

perceptive [pəséptɪv] ADJ (pertaining to perception) perceptivo; (having keen perception) perspicaz

perch [pətʃ] N (rod for birds) percha f; (type of fish) perca f; VI (alight) posarse; VI/VT (set) encaramar[se]

percolate [pəkəlet] VI/VT filtrar[se]

percussion [pəkʌ́ʃən] N percusión f

perdition [pədíʃən] N perdición f

perennial [pəréniəl] ADJ perenne; — **plant** planta perenne f

perfect[1] [pəfɪkt] ADJ perfecto; **a — stranger** un completo desconocido

perfect[2] [pəfɛ́kt] VT perfeccionar

perfection [pəfɛ́kʃən] N perfección f

perfectionist [pəfɛ́kʃənɪst] N perfeccionista mf

perfectly [pɔ́fɪktli] ADV (completely) totalmente; (without error) a la perfección, perfectamente; **stand — still** no te muevas

perforate [pəfəret] VI/VT perforar[se]; VT calar

perforation [pəfəréʃən] N perforación f

perform [pəfɔ́rm] VT (a task) ejecutar, realizar; (a rite, ceremony) celebrar; (a contract) cumplir; (a play) representar; VI (give a performance) actuar; (play music) interpretar; (function) funcionar; (do well) rendir; **to — simultaneously** simultanear

performance [pəfɔ́rməns] N (of a task) ejecución f; (of a ceremony) celebración f; (of a contract) cumplimiento m; (of a device) desempeño m, rendimiento m; (of a play) representación f; (of an actor) actuación f; (of music) interpretación f; — **review** evaluación del rendimiento f

performer [pəfɔ́rmə] N (drama) artista mf, actor m, actriz f; (music) artista mf, intérprete mf

perfume[1] [pɔ́fjum] N perfume m

perfume[2] [pəfjúm] VT perfumar

perfumery [pəfjúməri] N (store) perfumería f; (collection) perfumes m pl

perhaps [pəhǽps] ADV tal vez, quizá[s], acaso

peril [pérəl] N peligro m

perilous [pérələs] ADJ peligroso

perimeter [pərímɪdə] N perímetro m

period [pɪ́riəd] N período m; (historical) época f; (punctuation) punto m; (menstruation) período m, regla f; **you can't go, —!** no puedes ir, y sanseacabó; **within a — of ten days** en el término de diez días

periodic [pɪriáDɪk] ADJ periódico; — **table** tabla periódica f

periodical [pɪriáDɪkəl] ADJ periódico; N revista f

peripheral [pərífərəl] ADJ & N periférico m; — **vision** visión periférica f

periphery [pərífəri] N periferia f

periscope [pérɪskop] N periscopio m

perish [pérɪʃ] VI perecer

perishable [pérɪʃəbəl] ADJ perecedero

peritonitis [perɪtn̩áɪDɪs] N peritonitis f

perjure [pɝdʒə] VI **to — oneself** perjurarse, jurar en falso

perjury [pɝdʒəri] N perjurio m

perks [pɝks] N beneficios adicionales m pl

permanence [pɝmənəns] N permanencia f

permanent [pɝmənənt] ADJ permanente; (of a position) titular

permeable [pɝmiəbəl] ADJ permeable

permeate [pɝmiet] VI/VT permear

permissible [pərmísəbəl] ADJ permisible, lícito

permission [pərmíʃən] N permiso m

permissive [pərmísɪv] ADJ permisivo

permit[1] [pərmít] VI/VT (allow) permitir; (make possible) posibilitar

permit[2] [pɝmɪt] N permiso m

permutation [pɝmjutéʃən] N permutación f

pernicious [pɝníʃəs] ADJ pernicioso

peroxide [pərúksaɪd] N peróxido m

perpendicular [pɝpɪndíkjələ] ADJ & N perpendicular f

perpetrate [pɝpɪtret] VT perpetrar

perpetual [pərpétʃuəl] ADJ perpetuo

perpetuate [pərpétʃuet] VT perpetuar

perplex [pərpléks] VT confundir, dejar perplejo; **—ed** perplejo

perplexity [pərpléksɪDi] N perplejidad f

persecute [pɝsɪkjut] VT perseguir

persecution [pɝsɪkjúʃən] N persecución f

persecutor [pɝsɪkjuDə] N perseguidor -ora mf

perseverance [pɝsəvírəns] N perseverancia f

persevere [pɝsəvír] VI perseverar, persistir

Persia [pɝʒə] N Persia f

Persian [pɝʒən] ADJ & N persa mf

persist [pərsíst] VI (continue, endure) persistir; (to be insistent) insistir

persistence [pərsístəns] N (endurance) persistencia f; (insistence) insistencia f

persistent [pərsístənt] ADJ (lasting) persistente; (insisting) insistente, machacón

person [pɝsən] N persona f

personable [pɝsənəbəl] ADJ agradable

personage [pɝsənɪdʒ] N personaje m

personal [pɝsənl] ADJ personal; — **computer** Sp ordenador personal m; Am computadora personal f; — **effects** efectos personales m pl; — **foul** falta personal f; — **identification number** número de identificación personal

m; — **pronoun** pronombre personal m; — **property** bienes muebles m pl; **to make a — appearance** presentarse en persona

personality [pɝsənǽlIDi] N personalidad f; — **disorder** trastorno de la personalidad m

personally [pɝsənəli] ADV personalmente; **don't take it** — no lo tomes a pecho / a mal

personify [pɝsánəfaɪ] VT personificar

personnel [pɝsənél] N personal m

perspective [pɝspéktɪv] N perspectiva f

perspicacious [pɝspɪkéʃəs] ADJ perspicaz

perspiration [pɝspəréʃən] N transpiración f

perspire [pəspáɪr] VI transpirar

persuade [pɝswéd] VT persuadir, convencer

persuasion [pɝswéʒən] N persuasión f; (belief) convicción f

persuasive [pɝswésɪv] ADJ persuasivo, convincente

pert [pɝt] ADJ (insolent) insolente; (lively) vivaz

pertain [pətén] VI atañer, corresponder

pertinent [pɝtnənt] ADJ pertinente

perturb [pətɝb] VT perturbar

Peru [pərú] N Perú m

perusal [pərúzəl] N lectura f

peruse [pərúz] VT (read carefully) leer con cuidado; (read carelessly) hojear

Peruvian [pərúvian] ADJ & N peruano -na mf

pervade [pəvéd] VT difundirse por

perverse [pəvɝs] ADJ perverso

perversion [pəvɝʒən] N perversión f

perversity [pəvɝsiDi] N perversidad f

pervert[1] [pəvɝt] VT pervertir; (misconstrue) desvirtuar

pervert[2] [pɝvɝt] N pervertido -da mf

peso [péso] N peso m

pessimism [pésəmɪzəm] N pesimismo m

pessimist [pésəmɪst] N pesimista mf

pest [pest] N (insect, disease) peste f, plaga f; (person) pesado -da mf

pester [péstə] VT molestar

pesticide [péstisaɪd] N pesticida m

pestilence [péstələns] N pestilencia f

pet [pet] N (animal) mascota f; (favorite) favorito -ta mf, preferido -da mf; ADJ predilecto; — **name** apodo cariñoso m; VT (caress) acariciar; (pat) dar palmaditas a

petal [pédl] N pétalo m

petition [pətíʃən] N petición f, solicitud f; VI/VT peticionar, solicitar

petrify [pétrəfaɪ] VI/VT petrificar[se]

petroleum [pətróliəm] N petróleo m; — **products** productos petrolíferos m pl; — **jelly** vaselina f

petticoat [pédikot] N enaguas f pl

petty [pédi] ADJ (trivial) trivial; (mean) mezquino; — **cash** caja chica f; — **larceny** ratería f; — **officer** suboficial de marina m

petunia [pɪtúnjə] N petunia f

pew [pju] N banco m / banca f de iglesia

pewter [pjúDə] N peltre m
peyote [peóɾi] N peyote m
phantom [fǽntəm] N fantasma m
pharmaceutical [farməsúDikəl] ADJ farmacéutico; N producto farmacéutico m, fármaco m
pharmacist [fárməsɪst] N farmacéutico -ca mf
pharmacology [farməkáləʤi] N farmacología f
pharmacy [fárməsi] N farmacia f
pharynx [fǽrɪŋks] N faringe f
phase [fez] N fase f; VI **to — out** retirar por etapas; **to — in** incorporar paulatinamente
pheasant [fézənt] N faisán m
phenomenon [fɪnámənən] N fenómeno m
philanthropy [fɪlǽnθrəpi] N filantropía f
philharmonic [fɪlharmánɪk] ADJ filarmónico; N filarmónica f
Philippine [fíləpin] ADJ & N filipino -na mf
Philippines [fíləpinz] N filipinas f pl
philosopher [fɪlásəfə] N filósofo -fa mf
philosophical [fɪləsáfɪkəl] ADJ filosófico
philosophy [fɪlásəfi] N filosofía f
phishing [fíʃɪŋ] N phishing m
phlegm [flɛm] N flema f
phobia [fóbiə] N fobia f
phone [fon] N teléfono m; **— card** tarjeta telefónica f; VI/VT telefonear
phonetic [fənéDɪk] ADJ fonético
phonetics [fənéDɪks] N fonética f
phonograph [fónəgræf] N fonógrafo m
phonology [fənáləʤi] N fonología f
phony [fóni] ADJ falso
phosphate [fásfet] N fosfato m
phosphorus [fásfəəs] N fósforo m
photo [fóɾo] N foto f; **— finish** final muy reñido m
photocopier [fóDəkapiə] N fotocopiadora f
photocopy [fóDəkapi] N fotocopia f; VI/VT fotocopiar
photoelectric [foDoɪléktrɪk] ADJ fotoeléctrico
photogenic [foDəʤénɪk] ADJ fotogénico
photograph [fóDəgræf] N fotografía f; VT fotografiar
photographer [fətágrəfə] N fotógrafo -fa mf
photography [fətágrəfi] N fotografía f
photon [fótan] N fotón m
photosynthesis [foDosínθəsɪs] N fotosíntesis f
phrase [frez] N frase f; VI/VT expresar; (musical) frasear
phylum [fáiləm] N filo m
physical [fízɪkəl] ADJ físico; **— education** educación física f; **— geography** geografía física f; **— science** ciencia física f; **— therapy** fisioterapia f
physician [fɪzíʃən] N médico -ca mf; **—'s assistant** ayudante médico -ca sanitario -ria mf
physicist [fízɪsɪst] N físico -ca mf
physics [fízɪks] N física f

physiological [fɪziəládʒɪkəl] ADJ fisiológico
physiology [fɪziáləʤi] N fisiología f
physique [fɪzík] N físico m
pianist [piǽnɪst] N pianista mf
piano [piǽno] N piano m; **— bench** banqueta de piano f; **— hammer** martinete m; **— player** pianista mf; **— stool** taburete de piano m
picaresque [pikərésk] ADJ picaresco
piccolo [píkəlo] N flautín m, pícolo m
pick [pɪk] VT (choose) escoger, elegir; (gather flowers) juntar; (play a guitar) puntear; (clean teeth) mondarse; (eat with the bill) picotear; (provoke a fight) armar, entablar; VI picar; **to — at** picotear; **to — apart** criticar; **to — a lock** violar una cerradura con ganzúa; **to — on** meterse con; **to — out** (choose) escoger; (distinguish) distinguir; **to — pockets** ratear; **to — up** (gather) recoger; (lift) levantar; (learn) aprender; (order) ordenar; (improve) mejorar; **to — up speed** acelerar la marcha; N (tool) pico m; (of a guitar) púa f; (act of selecting) selección f; (thing or person selected) elección f; (the best) lo selecto, lo mejor; **—ax[e]** zapapico m; **—lock** ganzúa f; **—pocket** ratero -ra mf, carterista mf; **—up** (taking on freight) recolección f; (improvement in business) recuperación f; (acceleration) aceleración f; **—up truck** camioneta f; ADJ **—-proof** a prueba de ladrones
picket [píkɪt] N piquete m (also union worker); **— fence** cerca de piquetes f; VT (fence) vallar; (block with workers) bloquear, Am piquetear
pickle [píkəl] N pepinillo en vinagre m, curtido m; **to be in a —** hallarse en un aprieto; VT encurtir, escabechar; **—d fish** pescado al/en escabeche m, pescado adobado m
picnic [píknɪk] N picnic m; **— area** merendero m; VI hacer un picnic
pictorial [pɪktóriəl] ADJ pictórico
picture [píktʃə] N (image) imagen f; (drawing) dibujo m; (photo) fotografía f; (situation) panorama m; (movie) película f; **— frame** marco m; **— gallery** galería de pinturas f; **— tube** tubo de imagen m; **she is the — of unhappiness** es la imagen de la infelicidad; VT (describe) describir; (imagine) imaginar
picturesque [pɪktʃərésk] ADJ pintoresco
pie [paɪ] N pastel m, tarta f; **— chart** diagrama de pastel m; **— graph** gráfica de pastel f; **— in the sky** castillos en el aire m pl; **it's as easy as —** es pan comido
piece [pis] N (of music, in a board game, of furniture) pieza f; (of wood, rock, pie) pedazo m, trozo m; **—meal** por partes; **— of advice** consejo m; **— of cake** pan comido m; **— of land** parcela f, terreno m; **— of one's mind** regaño m; **— of news** noticia f; **—work** trabajo a destajo m; **to go to —s**

descomponerse; VI **to — together**
(assemble) armar; (make sense of) atar cabos

pier [pir] N muelle m, embarcadero m;
(breakwater) rompeolas m sg

pierce [pirs] VI/VT (make a hole in) agujerear,
perforar; (penetrate) penetrar; (cause a sharp
pain) punzar

piercing [pírsɪŋ] ADJ (glance, sound)
penetrante; (pain) punzante; N perforación f

piety [páɪɪDi] N piedad f

pig [pɪg] N puerco m, cerdo m, cochino m; Sp
guarro m; **—-headed** testarudo, cabezón;
—-iron hierro en lingotes m; **— Latin**
jerigonza f; **—pen** pocilga f; **—tail** coleta f

pigeon [píʤən] N paloma f; (young) pichón m;
—hole casilla f; **— loft** palomar m; VT **to
—hole** encasillar

piggy [pígi] N cerdito m; **—bank** alcancía f; Sp
hucha f; ADV **—back** a hombros, a cuestas

pigment [pígmənt] N pigmento m

pike [paɪk] N (weapon) pica f; (fish) lucio m

pile [paɪl] N (ordered stack) pila f; (chaotic group)
montón m, amontonamiento m; (surface of a
carpet) pelo m; (post) pilote m; **— driver**
martinete m; **—s** almorranas f pl; **—-up**
accidente múltiple m; VI/VT apilar[se],
amontonar[se]

pilfer [pɪlfɚ] VI/VT ratear, sisar

pilferage [pɪlfɚɪʤ] N ratería f

pilgrim [pɪlgrəm] N peregrino -na mf, romero
-ra mf

pilgrimage [pɪlgrəmɪʤ] N peregrinación f,
romería f

pill [pɪl] N píldora f, pastilla f; (naughty child)
pesado -da mf

pillage [pílɪʤ] N pillaje m, saqueo m, rapiña f;
VI/VT pillar, saquear

pillar [pílɚ] N pilar m, columna f

pillow [pílo] N almohada f; **—case** funda f

pilot [páɪlət] N piloto mf (also test, light); (of a
boat) timonel m, piloto mf; VT pilotar,
comandar

pimple [pímpəl] N grano m, barro m

pin [pɪn] N (sewing implement) alfiler m;
(ornament) prendedor m; (rod) pasador m,
perno m; (bowling) bolo m; (electric) pata f,
clavija f; **—cushion** alfiletero m; **—wheel**
molinete m, remolino m; **to be on —s and
needles** estar en ascuas; VT (affix with pins)
prender; (in wrestling) inmovilizar; **to —
someone down** (hold down) inmovilizar;
(force to act) hacer que concrete detalles; **to
— one's hopes on** poner sus esperanzas en;
to —point localizar con precisión; **to — up**
sujetar con alfileres

PIN [**personal identification number**] [pɪn]
N PIN m

pincers [pínsɚz] N (of lobsters) pinzas f pl; (tool)
tenazas f pl

pinch [pɪntʃ] VT (squeeze with fingers) pellizcar;
(squeeze tightly, hamper) apretar; (steal)
birlar; (arrest) prender; VI (be too tight)
apretar; (economize) economizar; **—ed
nerve** nervio pellizcado m, nervio pinzado
m; N (act of pinching) pellizco m; (small
amount) pizca f; (trying circumstances)
aprieto m, apuro m; **— hitter** bateador -ora
emergente mf; **— runner** corredor
emergente m

pine [paɪn] N pino m; **—apple** piña f, ananá[s] m;
— cone piña f; **— grove** pinar m; **— nut**
piñón m; VI **to — away** languidecer; **to — for**
anhelar, suspirar por

pingpong [píŋpɑŋ] N ping-pong m, tenis de
mesa m

pinion [pínjən] N piñón m

pink [pɪŋk] N rosado m, rosa m; **—eye**
conjuntivitis f; **— slip** notificación de despido
f; **in the —** rebosante de salud; ADJ rosado,
rosa

pinnacle [pínəkəl] N pináculo m

pint [paɪnt] N pinta f; ADJ **—-sized** diminuto

pinto bean [píntobin] N judía pinta f

pioneer [paɪənír] N pionero -ra mf; VI ser el
primero en hacer algo; VT promover

pious [páɪəs] ADJ (religious) pío, piadoso;
(hypocritical) beato

pipe [paɪp] N (for smoking) pipa f; (for water)
tubo m, caño m; (of an organ) tubo m; (flute)
caramillo m, flauta f; **— dream** ilusiones f pl;
—line (for oil) oleoducto m; (for gas)
gasoducto m; (for water) tubería f; **in the
—line** en trámite; **— wrench** llave inglesa f;
VT (convey water) conducir por cañerías;
(make music) tocar la flauta; VI chillar; **to —
down** callarse

piping [páɪpɪŋ] N (many pipes) cañería f, tubería
f; (border on clothes) ribete m; (sound of
pipes) sonido de la gaita/flauta m; ADJ **— hot**
hirviendo

pipsqueak [pípskwik] N chisgarabís m,
mequetrefe m

piracy [páɪrəsi] N piratería f

pirate [páɪrɪt] N pirata mf; VT piratear

pistol [pístl] N pistola f, revólver m; VT **to —-
whip** dar culatazos

piston [pístn] N pistón m, émbolo m; **— ring**
segmento de compresión m; **— rod** eje del
pistón m

pit [pɪt] N (hole) hoyo m, pozo m; (in a garage,
theater) foso m; (trap) trampa f; (seed) hueso
m; (part of a racetrack) box m, paddock m;
(part of the stomach) boca f; **—fall** (trap)
trampa f; (difficulty) dificultad f; **this is the
—s** esto es lo peor; VI/VT (make holes)
picarse; VT **to — against** oponer, enfrentar

pitch [pɪtʃ] VT (throw) tirar, lanzar; (try to sell)
pregonar; **to — a tent** armar una tienda; VI

(plane, ship) cabecear; **to — in** colaborar; N (throw) tiro *m*, lanzamiento *m*; (in music) tono *m*; (in printing) espaciado *m*; (slope) grado de inclinación *m*; (tar) brea *f*, pez *f*; — **dark** oscuro como boca del lobo; —**fork** horca *f*, horquilla *f*

pitcher [pítʃə⋅] N (vessel) cántaro *m*, jarro *m*, jarra *f*; (in baseball) lanzador -ora *mf*; —**'s mound** montículo *m*

pith [pIθ] N (in plants, feathers) médula *f*; (essence) meollo *m*

pithy [píθi] ADJ sustancial

pitiful [pídIfəl] ADJ (deserving pity) lastimoso; (deserving contempt) despreciable

pitiless [pídIlIs] ADJ despiadado

pituitary [pitúrteri] ADJ pituitario; — **gland** glándula pituitaria *f*

pity [píɾi] N compasión *f*, lástima *f*; **what a —!** ¡qué lástima! VT compadecerse [de]

pivot [pívət] N pivote *m*; VI pivotar

pixel [píksəl] N píxel *m*

pizza [pítsə] N pizza *f*

placard [plǽkə⋅d] N cartel *m*

placate [pléket] VT apaciguar

place [ples] N (site) lugar *m*, sitio *m*; (position) puesto *m*; — **mat** mantel individual *m*; — **of birth** lugar de nacimiento *m*; — **of business** oficina *f*; — **of worship** templo *m*; — **setting** cubierto para una persona *m*; **in — of** en lugar de; **it is not my — to do it** no me corresponde a mí hacerlo; VT (put) colocar; (identify) situar, ubicar; **to — an order** hacer un pedido; **to — an ad** poner un anuncio; VI (in sports) clasificarse

placebo [pləsíbo] N placebo *m*

placement [plésmənt] N (in levels, categories) colocación *f*, posicionamiento *m*; (in space) emplazamiento *m*

placenta [pləséntə] N placenta *f*

placid [plǽsId] ADJ plácido

plagiarism [pléǰərIzəm] N plagio *m*

plague [pleg] N plaga *f*, peste *f*; VT atormentar, apestar

plaid [plæd] N tela escocesa *f*

plain [plen] ADJ (without embellishment) sencillo, llano; (clear) claro; (downright, unadulterated) puro; (ordinary) común; (unattractive) poco atractivo; **in — sight** en plena vista; —**clothesman** policía en traje de civil *m*; —**-Jane** sencillo; ADV completamente; N llano *m*, llanura *f*

plaintiff [pléntIf] N demandante *mf*, querellante *mf*

plan [plæn] N plan *m*; (drawing, sketch, map, outline) plano *m*; VI/VT planear, planificar; (diagram) hacer el plano de; —**ned parenthood** planificación familiar *f*

plane [plen] N (airplane) avión *m*; (surface) plano *m*; (tool) cepillo *m*; — **tree** plátano *m*; ADJ

plano; — **geometry** geometría plana *f*; VI (glide, hover) planear; VT (smooth) cepillar, planear

planet [plǽnIt] N planeta *m*

planetarium [plǽnItériəm] N planetario *m*

plank [plæŋk] N (board) tabla *f*, tablón *m*; (tenet) principio *m*, base *f*; VT entarimar

plankton [plǽŋktən] N plancton *m*

planning [plǽnIŋ] N planeamiento *m*, planificación *f*

plant [plænt] N (vegetation) planta *f*; (industrial installation) fábrica *f*, planta *f*; (mole, spy) topo *m*; VT (plants) plantar; (ideas) sembrar; (a spy, evidence) colocar

plantain [plǽnten] N plátano *m*

plantation [plæntéʃən] N plantación *f*

plaque [plæk] N placa *f*; (on teeth) sarro *m*, placa *f*

plasma [plǽzmə] N plasma *m*, gas ionizado *m*

plaster [plǽstə⋅] N (substance) yeso *m*; (preparation applied to body) emplasto *m*; — **of Paris** yeso *m*; VT (cover with plaster) revocar; (apply a preparation) emplastar; (cover with posters) cubrir, empapelar; (defeat) aplastar; **to — down one's hair** achatarse el pelo; **to get —ed** emborracharse

plastic [plǽstIk] ADJ plástico; — **surgery** cirugía plástica/estética *f*

plate [plet] N (for food) plato *m*; (for collections) bandeja *f*; (metal) plancha *f*, lámina *f*; (license) placa *f*; — **glass** vidrio cilindrado *m*; — **tectonics** tectónica de placas *f*; VT (apply metal covering) chapar, enchapar; (apply armor) blindar

plateau [plætó] N meseta *f*, macizo *m*

platform [plǽtfɔrm] N plataforma *f* (also in politics, computers); (railway) andén *m*; (mobile) tarima *f*, tinglado *m*

platinum [plǽtnəm] N platino *m*

platitude [plǽdItud] N lugar común *m*, perogrullada *f*

platter [plǽdə⋅] N fuente *f*

plausible [plɔ́zəbəl] ADJ plausible

play [ple] VT (game) jugar; (an opponent) jugar contra; (an instrument) tocar; (a drama) representar; (a role) desempeñar; (bet on) apostar; **to — a joke** gastar una broma; **to — cards** jugar a los naipes; **to — havoc** hacer estragos; **to — tennis** jugar al tenis; **to — the fool** hacerse el tonto; VI (divert oneself, gamble) jugar; (kid) bromear; (make music) tocar; **to — along** seguir la corriente; **to — down** minimizar; **to be all —ed out** estar agotado; N (recreational activity, looseness) juego *m*; (instance of playing) jugada *f*; (theater work) obra de teatro *f*; — **on words** juego de palabras *m*; —**boy** playboy *m*; —**ground** recreo *m*, patio *m*; —**ing card** naipe *m*; —**mate** compañero -ra de juego *mf*; —**off [game]** [partido de] desempate *m*; **the**

—**offs** las eliminatorias *f pl*; —**thing** juguete *m*

player [pléⱥ] N (one who plays, gambler) jugador -ora *mf*; (musician) músico -ca *mf*; (influential person) persona influyente *f*; (womanizer) mujeriego *m*; (actor) actor *m*, actriz *f*; (participant) participante *mf*; — **piano** pianola *f*

playful [pléfəl] ADJ juguetón

playwright [pléraıt] N dramaturgo -ga *mf*

plea [pli] N (entreaty) súplica *f*, ruego *m*; (allegation) alegato *m*; **to enter a — of guilty** declararse culpable

plead [plid] VI/VT (entreat) suplicar, rogar; (defend) abogar, defender; **to — guilty** declararse culpable

pleasant [plézənt] ADJ agradable, grato, placentero

pleasantry [plézəntri] N cortesía *f*

please [pliz] ADV por favor; VI/VT agradar, complacer; **as you —** como quieras; **to be —d to** tener el gusto de, tener gusto en; **to be —d with** estar satisfecho con

pleasing [plízɪŋ] ADJ agradable

pleasure [pléʒⱥ] N placer *m*, gusto *m*, agrado *m*; **— trip** viaje de placer *m*

pleat [plit] N pliegue *m*, tabla *f*; (wide) tabla *f*; VT plisar; (wide) tablear

pled [pled] *see* plead

pledge [pledʒ] N (promise) promesa *f*; (security deposit) prenda *f*; (in a fraternity) miembro provisorio *m*; **as a — of** en prenda de; VI/VT (promise) prometer; VT (give as a deposit) empeñar; **to — one's word** dar la palabra; **to — to secrecy** exigir promesa de discreción

plenary [plénəri] ADJ & N plenario *m*

plentiful [pléntıfəl] ADJ abundante, copioso

plenty [plénti] N abundancia *f*; **— of time** suficiente tiempo *m*; **that's —** con eso basta

pliable [pláıəbəl] ADJ (flexible) flexible; (docile) dócil

pliant [pláıənt] ADJ (flexible) flexible; (docile) dócil

pliers [pláıⱥz] N alicates *m pl*, tenazas *f pl*

plight [plaıt] N aprieto *m*

plod [plɑd] VI (walk) caminar trabajosamente; (work) trabajar laboriosamente

plop [plɑp] VI hacer plaf; VT dejar caer; N plaf *m*

plot [plɑt] N (storyline) trama *f*, argumento *m*; (conspiracy) complot *m*, conspiración *f*; (land) parcela *f*, era *f*; (floor plan) plano *m*; VI/VT (plan secretly) tramar, conspirar, maquinar; VT (make a graph) hacer un gráfico; **to — a course** trazar un curso

plotter [plɑ́tⱥ] N (one who plots) conspirador -ora *mf*; (device) trazador de gráficos *m*

plover [plóvⱥ] N chorlito *m*

plow [plaʊ] N arado *m*; —**share** reja de arado *f*; VI/VT arar; (uncultivated area) roturar; **to —**

through abrirse paso

plowing [pláʊɪŋ] N labranza *f*

pluck [plʌk] VT (a feather, flower) arrancar; (bird) desplumar; (guitar) puntear, pulsar; **to — out/off** desprender; **to — up courage** animarse, cobrar ánimo; N (act of plucking) tirón *m*; (courage) valor *m*

plug [plʌg] N (stopper) tapón *m*; (horse) *pej* penco *m*; (electric) enchufe *m*; (advertisement) mención favorable *f*; (tobacco) rollo *m*; —**-in** (electrical) enchufe *m*; (computer accessory) plug-in *m*; VT (close) tapar; (advertise) hacer una mención favorable de; VI **to — along** no parar; **to — in** enchufar; **to — up** tapar

plum [plʌm] N (fruit) ciruela *f*; **— tree** ciruelo *m*; **that job is a real —** ese trabajo es estupendo

plumage [plúmɪdʒ] N plumaje *m*

plumb [plʌm] N (lead weight) plomada *f*; **— bob** plomada *f*; **to be out of —** no estar a plomo; ADJ (perpendicular) a plomo; ADV (in a vertical direction) a plomo; (completely) completamente; VT (measure depth) sondear; (test for verticality) aplomar; (examine) examinar

plumber [plʌ́mⱥ] N plomero -ra *mf*; *Sp* fontanero -ra *mf*

plumbing [plʌ́mɪŋ] N (work and trade) plomería *f*; *Sp* fontanería *f*; (system of pipes) cañerías *f pl*

plume [plum] N penacho *m*; VT adornar con plumas

plummet [plʌ́mɪt] VI precipitarse; N plomada *f*

plump [plʌmp] ADJ rechoncho, regordete, rollizo; VI/VT **to — down** dejar[se] caer

plunder [plʌ́ndⱥ] N (act of plundering) pillaje *m*, saqueo *m*; (loot) botín *m*; VI/VT pillar, saquear

plunge [plʌndʒ] VI/VT (into water) zambullir[se], sumergir[se]; (into something solid) hundir[se]; VI (fall) precipitarse; (slope downward) bajar repentinamente; **to — headlong** echarse de cabeza; N zambullida *f*; (rush) salto *m*

plunger [plʌ́ndʒⱥ] N (for a toilet) desatascador *m*; (of a pump) émbolo *m*

pluperfect [plupⱥ́fɪkt] N pluscuamperfecto *m*

plural [plúrəl] ADJ & N plural *m*

plurality [plurǽlɪdi] N pluralidad *f*

plus [plʌs] PREP más; N (advantage) ventaja *f*; **two — three** dos más tres *m*; **on the — side** en el lado positivo; **— sign** signo de más *m*

plush [plʌʃ] N felpa *f*; ADJ (fabric) afelpado; (hotel) lujoso

plutonium [plutóniəm] N plutonio *m*

ply [plaı] VT (use) manejar; (assail with questions) acosar; (navigate a body of water) surcar; VI (travel regularly) recorrer con regularidad; (work steadily) aplicarse; **to — a trade** ejercer un oficio; N (layer of cloth, rubber) capa *f*; (layer of plywood) chapa *f*; —**wood**

madera compensada *f*, contrachapado *m*

pneumatic [numǽdɪk] ADJ neumático

pneumonia [numónjə] N pulmonía *f*

poach [potʃ] VT (eggs) escalfar; VI/VT (game) cazar furtivamente

pocket [pákɪt] N (in clothes) bolsillo *m*; (vein of ore) filón *m*; (on a pool table) tronera *f*; (of air) bache *m*; (of poverty) bolsa *f*; **—book** cartera *f*, Sp bolso *m*; **— book** libro de bolsillo *m*; **—knife** navaja *f*; **— of resistance** foco de resistencia *m*; VT meterse en el bolsillo; (appropriate) embolsar; (knock in a billiard ball) meter en la tronera

pod [pad] N (seed vessel) vaina *f*; (herd of cetaceans) manada *f*

podiatrist [pədáiətrist] N podólogo -ga *mf*

podiatry [pədáiətri] N podiatría *f*

podium [pódiəm] N podio *m*

poem [póəm] N poema *m*, poesía *f*

poet [póɪt] N poeta *mf*

poetic [poédɪk] ADJ poético; **— justice** justicia divina *f*; N **—s** poética *f*

poetry [pótri] N poesía *f*

poignant [póɪnjənt] ADJ conmovedor

poinsettia [pɔɪnsédɪə] N flor de Pascua *f*

point [pɔɪnt] N (place) punto *m*; (score, in sports) punto *m*, anotación *f*; (sharp end) punta *f*; **— after touchdown** punto extra *m*; **— guard** (basketball) base *mf*, conductor -ora *mf*, guardia *mf*; **— of origin** punto de origen *m*; **— of view** punto de vista *m*; **it is not to the —** no viene al caso; **I don't see the —** no le veo el sentido; **on the — of** a punto de; ADV **—-blank** a quemarropa; VT (direct finger at) apuntar con, señalar con; (indicate) señalar; **to — at** (with finger) señalar; (with a gun) apuntar hacia; **to — out** señalar, indicar; **to — up** enfatizar

pointed [pɔ́ɪntɪd] ADJ (having a point) puntiagudo; (piercing) agudo; **— arch** arco ojival *m*

pointer [pɔ́ɪntɚ] N (stick) puntero *m*; (on a scale) indicador *m*; (dog) perro de muestra *m*; (advice) consejo *m*

pointless [pɔ́ɪntlɪs] ADJ inútil

poise [pɔɪz] N (balance, steadiness) equilibrio *m*; (dignified bearing) aplomo *m*; **to be —d to** estar listo para; VI/VT equilibrar[se]

poison [pɔ́ɪzən] N veneno *m*, ponzoña *f*; **— ivy** hiedra venenosa *f*; VT envenenar, emponzoñar

poisoning [pɔ́ɪzənɪŋ] N (accidental) intoxicación *f*; (intentional) envenenamiento *m*

poisonous [pɔ́ɪzənəs] ADJ venenoso, ponzoñoso

poke [pok] VT (jab) clavar, pinchar; (stir a fire) atizar; (thrust out, as one's head) asomar; **to — out an eye** sacar un ojo; VI **to — along** andar perezosamente; **to — around** husmear; **to — fun at** burlarse de; **to — into**

meterse en; **to — out** (project) sobresalir; N pinchazo *m*

Poland [pólənd] N Polonia *f*

polar [pólɚ] ADJ polar; **— bear** oso polar *m*

polarity [pəlǽrɪdi] N polaridad *f*

polarization [polərɪzéʃən] N polarización *f*

polarize [pólɚaɪz] VI/VT polarizar[se]

pole [pol] N (long piece of wood, metal) poste *m*; (for a flag) asta *f*; (for vaulting) pértiga *f*, garrocha *f*; (earth's axis) polo *m*; (for skiing) bastón *m*; **— vault** salto con pértiga *m*

Pole [pol] N polaco -ca *mf*

polemic [pəlémɪk] ADJ polémico *m*; N polémica *f*

police [pəlís] N policía *f*; **— car** patrullero *m*; **— dog** perro policía *m*; **— force** cuerpo de policía *m*; **—man** policía *m*; **— officer** oficial de policía *m*, Am carabinero -ra *mf*; **— operation** Am operativo policial *m*; **— report** parte policial *m*; **— state** estado policíaco *m*; **— station** comisaría de policía *f*; **—woman** policía *f*; VT patrullar

policy [pálsi] N (procedure) política *f*; (for insurance) póliza *f*

polio [pólio] N polio *f*

Polish [pólɪʃ] ADJ & N polaco -ca *mf*

polish [pálɪʃ] N (sheen) lustre *m*, refinamiento *m*; (refinement) urbanidad *f*, cultura *f*; (substance for furniture) cera *f*; (substance for shoes) betún *m*; VT (a speech) pulir; (a metal) sacar brillo; (a car) encerar; (shoes) lustrar, embetunar; **to — off** despachar; **to — up** (metal) sacar brillo; (speech) pulir

polite [pəláɪt] ADJ cortés

politeness [pəláɪtnɪs] N cortesía *f*

politic [pálɪtɪk] ADJ diplomático, político

political [pəlídɪkəl] ADJ político; **— prisoner** preso -sa político -ca *mf*; **— science** ciencias políticas *f pl*

politically correct [pəlídɪklikɔrékt] ADJ políticamente correcto

politician [palɪtíʃən] N político -ca *mf*

politics [pálɪtɪks] N política *f*

polka [pólkə] N polca *f*; **— dot** lunar *m*

poll [pol] N (survey) encuesta *f*; **—s** (elections) comicios *m pl*; (voting place) urna *f*; VT (survey) encuestar; (receive votes) obtener; (record vote of) registrar

pollen [pálən] N polen *m*

pollinate [pálənet] VT polinizar

pollute [pəlút] VI/VT contaminar

pollution [pəlúʃən] N contaminación *f*

polo [pólo] N polo *m*

polyester [paliéstɚ] N poliéster *m*

polygamy [pəlígəmi] N poligamia *f*

polyglot [páliglat] ADJ & N políglota *mf*

polygraph [páligræf] N polígrafo *m*

polymer [páləmɚ] N polímero *m*

polyp [pálɪp] N pólipo *m*

polyunsaturated [paliʌnsǽtʃəreɪdɪd] ADJ

poliinsaturado

polyurethane [palijúrəθɛn] N poliuretano *m*

pomegranate [pámɪgrænɪt] N granada *f*; — **tree** granado *m*

pomp [pamp] N pompa *f*, boato *m*, aparato *m*

pompous [pámpəs] ADJ pomposo, aparatoso

pond [pand] N (natural) charca *f*; (artificial) estanque *m*; (for irrigation) balsa *f*

ponder [pándə·] VI meditar; VT considerar

ponderous [pándə·əs] ADJ enorme

pontoon [pantún] N (on a bridge) pontón *m*; (on an airplane) flotador *m*

pony [póni] N póney *m*; — **tail** colita *f*, cola de caballo *f*; VI **to — up** soltar

Ponzi scheme [pánzi skím] N timo en pirámide *m pl*

poodle [púdl] N caniche *m*

pool [puł] N (puddle of water, blood, etc.) charco *m*; (swimming place) piscina *f*, *Mex* alberca *f*; (association of competitors) pool *m*; (game) pool *m*, billar *m*; (bets) pozo *m*; — **table** billar *m*; — **hall** billar *m*; VI acumularse; VT combinar fondos

poop [pup] N (part of ship) popa *f*; (excrement) *fam* caca *f*; VI *fam* hacer caca

poor [pʊr] ADJ (lacking money) pobre; (deficient) malo; **I'm a — cook** no sé cocinar; —**house** asilo para los pobres *m*; — **little thing** pobrecito -ta *mf*; **the —** los pobres

pop [pap] VI (balloon) reventar, estallar; (eyes, cork) saltar; **to — in** entrar de paso; VT (make explode) hacer reventar; (take out cork) hacer saltar; (put) meter; (take, as pills) tomar; **to — a question** espetar una pregunta; **to — corn** hacer palomitas; N estallido *m*, detonación *f*; —**corn** palomitas *f pl*; — **music** música popular *f*; — **quiz** prueba sorpresa *f*; — **of a cork** taponazo *m*; —**-up menu** menú emergente *m*

pope [pop] N papa *m*

poplar [páplə·] N álamo *m*, chopo *m*; — **grove** alameda *f*

poppy [pápi] N amapola *f*

popular [pápjələ·] ADJ popular; **he's very — with the ladies** tiene mucho éxito con las mujeres

popularity [papjəlǽrɪDi] N popularidad *f*

populate [pápjəlet] VT poblar

population [papjəléʃən] N población *f*

populous [pápjələs] ADJ populoso

porcelain [pórsəlɪn] N porcelana *f*

porch [pórtʃ] N porche *m*

porcupine [pórkjəpaɪn] N puercoespín *m*

pore [pɔr] N poro *m*; VI **to — over a book** estudiar detenidamente un libro

pork [pork] N carne de cerdo *f*; — **chop** chuleta de cerdo *f*

porn [pɔrn] N porno *m*

pornography [pɔrnágrəfi] N pornografía *f*

porous [pórəs] ADJ poroso

porpoise [pórpəs] N marsopa *f*

port [port] N (harbor, computer) puerto *m*; (wine) oporto *m*; (left side of ship) babor *m*; — **city** ciudad portuaria *f*; —**hole** ojo de buey *m*; — **of entry** puerto de entrada *m*

portable [pórDəbł] ADJ portátil

portal [pórdl] N portal *m* (also of Internet)

portent [pórtɛnt] N (omen) presagio *m*, agüero *m*; (marvel, prodigy) portento *m*

portentous [portɛ́ntəs] ADJ (ominous) de mal agüero; (prodigious) portentoso

porter [pórDə·] N mozo -za *mf*

portfolio [portfólio] N cartera *f*

portion [pórʃən] N porción *f*; VI **to — out** repartir

portly [pórtli] ADJ grueso

portrait [pórtrɪt] N (likeness) retrato *m*; (printing orientation) orientación vertical *f*

portray [portré] VT (draw, describe) retratar; (in a drama) representar

portrayal [portréəł] N (portrait) retrato *m*; (act of portraying) representación *f*, caracterización *f*

Portugal [pórtʃəgəł] N Portugal *m*

Portuguese [pórtʃəgiz] ADJ & N portugués -esa *mf*

pose [poz] N (posture) pose *f*, postura *f*; (affected attitude) afectación *f*; VI (sit as a model) posar; (act affectedly) afectar una actitud; VT (to make sit as model) hacer posar; (to present) plantear; **to — as** hacerse pasar por

position [pəzíʃən] N (place) posición *f*; (job) puesto *m*, colocación *f*; (political stance) posicionamiento *m*; VI situar, colocar; **to — oneself** posicionarse

positive [pázɪDɪv] ADJ positivo; — **proof** prueba certera *f*; **I am —** estoy seguro

possess [pəzɛ́s] VT poseer

possessed [pəzɛ́st] ADJ (by a spirit) poseído; (by an idea) obsesionado

possession [pəzɛ́ʃən] N posesión *f*; **to take —** tomar posesión

possessive [pəzɛ́sɪv] ADJ & N posesivo *m*

possessor [pəzɛ́sə·] N poseedor -ora *f*

possibility [pasəbílɪDi] N posibilidad *f*

possible [pásəbł] ADJ posible, eventual

post [post] N (pole) poste *m*; (position) puesto *m*; (mail) correo *m*; —**card** tarjeta postal *f*; —**haste** a la brevedad; —**man** cartero *m*; —**mark** matasellos *m*; —**master** director de correos *m*; — **office** oficina de correos *f*, casa de correos *f*; —**-office box** apartado postal *m*; ADJ — **paid** porte pagado; — (affix) fijar; (announce) anunciar; (list) poner en lista; (place) apostar, situar; (mail) echar al correo; **keep me —ed** mantenme al tanto

postage [póstɪʤ] N franqueo *m*; — **meter** franqueadora *f*; — **stamp** *Sp* sello *m*; *Am* estampilla *f; Mex* timbre *m*

postal [póstl] ADJ postal; **to go —** perpetrar un ataque homicida, volverse loco

postdate [posdét] VT posfechar

poster [póstə-] N cartel *m,* póster *m,* afiche *m; — child* modelo perfecto *m*

posterior [pastíriə] ADJ posterior; N trasero *m*

posterity [pastéridi] N posteridad *f*

postgraduate [postgrǽdʒuɪt] ADJ de posgrado; N posgrado -da *mf*

posthumous [pástʃəməs] ADJ póstumo

postnasal [postnézəl] ADJ postnasal

postnatal [postnédl] ADJ posparto; **— care** cuidado posparto *m inv*

postpartum [postpárdəm] ADJ posparto *m*

postpone [postpón] VT posponer, aplazar

postponement [postpónmənt] N aplazamiento *m*

postscript [póstskrɪpt] N posdata *f*

postulate[1] [pástʃəlet] VT postular

postulate[2] [pástʃəlɪt] N postulado *m*

posture [pástʃə-] N (carriage, attitude) postura *f;* (affectation) afectación *f;* VI darse aires

postwar period [póstwár píriəd] N posguerra *f*

posy [pózi] N ramillete *m*

pot [pat] N (vessel) olla *f,* marmita *f;* (marijuana) marihuana *f; —hole* bache *m;* ADJ **— -bellied** panzudo, barrigón

potable [pódəbəl] ADJ potable

potassium [patǽsiam] N potasio *m*

potato [patédo] N *Sp* patata *f; Am* papa *f; —* **chip** patata/papa frita [a la inglesa] *f,* chip *m*

potency [pótnsi] N potencia *f*

potent [pótnt] ADJ potente

potentate [pótntet] N potentado -da *mf*

potential [paténʃəl] ADJ & N potencial *m*

potion [póʃən] N poción *f*

potter [pádə-] N alfarero -ra *mf*

pottery [pádəri] N (craft, shop) alfarería *f;* (objects) cerámica *f,* objetos de alfarería *m pl*

pouch [pautʃ] N bolsa *f;* (for mail) valija *f;* (for tobacco) petaca *f*

poultry [póltri] N aves de corral *f pl*

pounce [pauns] VI saltar; **to — upon/on** abalanzarse sobre; **to — on an opportunity** no dejar pasar una oportunidad; N salto *m*

pound [paund] N (unit of weight, British currency) libra *f;* (place for stray dogs) perrera *f;* VT (on a door) golpear; (seeds) machacar; (a military target) bombardear; VI (beat) latir con fuerza

pour [pɔr] VT verter; VI (leave en masse) salir en tropel; (rain) llover a cántaros; **to — out one's feelings** desahogarse

pout [paut] VI hacer pucheros; N puchero *m*

poverty [pávə-ɖi] N pobreza *f,* penuria *f;* ADJ **— - stricken** indigente

powder [páudə-] N polvo *m;* (for the face) polvos *m pl;* (for guns) pólvora *f; —* **compact**

polvera *f; —* **puff** borla *f;* **to take a —** poner pies en polvorosa; VI/VT (use powder) empolvar[se]; (pulverize) pulverizar[se]

power [páuə-] N (control, military might) poder *m,* poderío *m;* (in physics, in math) potencia *f;* (physical strength) fuerza *f;* (energy) energía *f; —* **of attorney** poder *m; —* **plant** central eléctrica *f; —-save mode* modo de ahorro de energía *m; —* **steering** dirección asistida *f; —* **supply** suministro de energía *m; —* **surge** sobrecarga de voltaje *f;* **in —** oficialista; **legislative —s** atribuciones legislativas *f pl;* VI **—ed by gas** movido por gas; **to — down** apagar; **to — on/up** encender

powerful [páuə-fəl] ADJ poderoso, potente

powerless [páuə-lɪs] ADJ impotente

PR [public relations] [piár] N relaciones públicas *f pl*

practical [prǽktɪkəl] ADJ práctico; **— joke** broma pesada *f,* chasco *m; —* **nurse** enfermero -ra sin título *mf*

practically [prǽktɪkli] ADV prácticamente

practice [prǽktɪs] N (repeated exercise) práctica *f;* (habit) costumbre *f;* (doctor's office) consultorio *m;* (lawyer's office) bufete *m;* VI/ VT practicar; VT (a profession) ejercer; **in —** en la práctica, prácticamente

practiced [prǽktɪst] ADJ experto, perito

practitioner [prǽktíʃənə-] N practicante *mf;* **general —** médico -ca general *mf*

pragmatic [prǽgmǽdɪk] ADJ pragmático

prairie [préri] N pradera *f,* llanura *f*

praise [prez] N alabanza *f,* elogio *m;* VT alabar, elogiar; **—worthy** loable, encomiable

prance [præns] VI cabriolar, hacer cabriolas; N cabriola *f*

prank [præŋk] N travesura *f,* chasco *m;* **to play —s** hacer travesuras

prawn [prɔn] N langostino *m; Sp* gamba pequeña *f*

pray [pre] VI/VT (religious) rezar, orar; (beg) rogar, suplicar

prayer [prɛr] N (devout petition to God) oración *f,* rezo *m;* (entreaty) ruego *m,* súplica *f*

praying mantis [préiŋmæntis] N mantis religiosa *f*

preach [pritʃ] VI/VT predicar; (moralize) sermonear

preacher [pritʃə-] N predicador -ora *mf*

preamble [príæmbəl] N preámbulo *m*

preapproved [priaprúvd] ADJ preaprobado

precancerous [prikǽnsə-əs] ADJ precanceroso

precarious [prikériəs] ADJ precario

precaution [prikóʃən] N precaución *f*

precautionary [prikóʃəneri] ADJ preventivo

precede [prisíd] VI/VT preceder

precedence [présɪdəns] N precedencia *f,* prioridad *f*

preceding [prisídɪŋ] ADJ precedente, anterior

precept [prísept] N precepto *m*

precinct [prísɪŋkt] N distrito *m*; (police station) comisaría *f*; **—s** límites *m pl*

precious [préʃəs] ADJ precioso; (overly refined) preciosista; **— little** muy poco; **— metal** metal precioso *m*; **— stone** piedra preciosa *f*

precipice [présəpɪs] N precipicio *m*, derrumbadero *m*

precipitate[1] [prɪsípɪtet] VI/VT precipitar[se]

precipitate[2] [prɪsípɪtɪt] ADJ & N precipitado *m*

precipitation [prɪsɪpɪtéʃən] N precipitación *f*

precipitous [prɪsípɪɾəs] ADJ (steep) escarpado; (hasty) precipitado

precise [prɪsáɪs] ADJ preciso, exacto

precisely [prɪsáɪsli] ADV & INT precisamente, exactamente

precision [prɪsíʒən] N precisión *f*, exactitud *f*; (of expression) propiedad *f*

preclude [prɪklúd] VT excluir; **that doesn't — our considering your application** esto no obsta para que tengamos en cuenta su solicitud

precocious [prɪkóʃəs] ADJ precoz

precursor [prɪkɔ́rsə-] N precursor *m*

predator [prédəɾə-] N depredador *m*

predatory [prédəɾɔri] ADJ (animal) depredador; (persona) rapaz

predecessor [prédɪsɛsə-] N predecesor -ora *mf*, antecesor -ora *mf*

predestine [pridéstɪn] VT predestinar

predetermined [priditə́-mɪnd] ADJ predeterminado

predicament [prɪdíkəmənt] N aprieto *m*

predicate[1] [prédɪkɪt] ADJ & N predicado *m*

predicate[2] [prédɪket] VT basar

predict [prɪdíkt] VT predecir

prediction [prɪdíkʃən] N predicción *f*, vaticinio *m*

predilection [predɪlékʃən] N predilección *f*

predispose [pridɪspóz] VI/VT predisponer

predisposition [pridɪspəzíʃən] N predisposición *f*

predominance [prɪdámənəns] N predominio *m*

predominant [prɪdámənənt] ADJ predominante

predominate [prɪdámənet] VI/VT predominar, preponderar

preeclampsia [priɪklǽmpsiə] N preeclampsia *f*

preexisting [priɡzístɪŋ] ADJ preexistente

preface [préfɪs] N prefacio *m*, prólogo *m*; VT hacer una introducción; (a book) prologar

prefer [prɪfɔ́-] VT preferir; **to — a claim** presentar una demanda

preferable [préfə-əbəl] ADJ preferible

preference [préfə-əns] N preferencia *f*

preferential [prefə-rénʃəl] ADJ preferente

preferred [prɪfɔ́-d] ADJ preferido; **— stocks** acciones preferentes *f pl*

prefix [prífɪks] N prefijo *m*; VT poner un prefijo

pregnancy [prégnənsi] N embarazo *m*; (of an animal) preñez *f*; **— test** prueba de embarazo *f*

pregnant [prégnənt] ADJ (person) embarazada, encinta; (animal) preñada; (full of meaning, rain) preñado, cargado

prehensile [prɪhénsəl] ADJ prensil

prehistoric [prihɪstórɪk] ADJ prehistórico

prejudge [pridʒʌ́dʒ] VT prejuzgar

prejudice [prédʒədɪs] N (bias) prejuicio *m*; (harm) perjuicio *m*; VT (cause bias against) predisponer en contra; (harm) perjudicar

preliminary [prɪlímənɛri] ADJ & N preliminar *m*

prelude [prélud] N preludio *m*; VI/VT preludiar

premarital [primǽrɪdl] ADJ prematrimonial

premature [primətʃúr] ADJ prematuro; **— birth** parto prematuro *m*

premeditated [priméditedɪd] ADJ premeditado

premenstrual [priménstruəl] ADJ premenstrual

premier [prɪmír] N primer ministro *m*; primera ministra *f*; ADJ principal

premiere [prɪmír] N estreno *m*, première *f*

premise [prémɪs] N premisa *f*; **—s** local *m*

premium [prímiəm] N (bonus) premio *m*; (insurance) prima *f*; (surcharge) recargo *m*; **at a —** muy escaso; ADJ superior

premonition [preməníʃən] N premonición *f*

prenatal [prinédl] ADJ prenatal; **— care** atención prenatal *f*, cuidado prenatal *m*

prenuptial [prinʌ́pʃəl] ADJ prenupcial; **— agreement** capitulaciones matrimoniales *f pl*

preoccupy [priákjəpaɪ] VT absorber

preowned [prióund] ADJ de segunda mano

prepacked [pripǽkt] ADJ preempacado

prepaid [pripéd] ADJ pagado de antemano; **to send —** enviar porte pagado

preparation [prepəréʃən] N (act of preparing) preparación *f*; (substance) preparado *m*; (for a trip) preparativos *m pl*

preparatory [prépə-ətɔri] ADJ preparatorio, preparativo

prepare [prɪpér] VI/VT preparar[se]

preponderance [prɪpándə-əns] N preponderancia *f*

preponderant [prɪpándə-ənt] ADJ preponderante

preposition [prepəzíʃən] N preposición *f*

preposterous [prɪpástə-əs] ADJ absurdo

prerecorded [prirɪkɔ́rdɪd] ADJ pregrabado

prerequisite [prirékwəzɪt] N prerequisito *m*

prerogative [prɪrágəɾɪv] N prerrogativa *f*

prescribe [prɪskráɪb] VT (order) prescribir; (medicine) recetar

prescription [prɪskrípʃən] N (order) prescripción *f*; (of medicine) receta *f*

presence [prézəns] N presencia *f*; **— of mind** aplomo *m*, presencia de ánimo *f*

present[1] [prézənt] N (time) presente *m*; (gift)

regalo *m*, presente *m*; **at —** ahora; **for the —** por ahora; ADJ (at a place) presente; (at this time) actual; **— company excepted** con perdón de los presentes; **— participle** gerundio *m*; **— perfect** pretérito perfecto *m*; **—-day** actual

present² [prɪzɛ́nt] VT presentar, entregar

presentable [prɪzɛ́ntəbəɬ] ADJ presentable

presentation [prɛzəntéʃən] N (act of presenting) presentación *f*, entrega *f*; (speech) ponencia *f*; (exposition) planteamiento *m*

presentiment [prɪzɛ́ntəmənt] N presentimiento *m*

presently [prɛ́zəntli] ADV (soon) pronto; (now) actualmente

preservation [prɛzə-véʃən] N preservación *f*, conservación *f*

preservative [prɪzɛ́-vədɪv] N conservante *m*

preserve [prɪzɛ́v] VI/VT (protect) preservar; (keep food fresh) conservar; N (for game) coto *m*; (for animals) reserva *f*; **—s** mermelada *f*, dulce *m*

preset [prisɛ́t] ADJ preestablecido

preside [prɪzáɪd] VI presidir; **to — over a meeting** presidir una reunión

presidency [prɛ́zɪDənsi] N presidencia *f*

president [prɛ́zɪDənt] N presidente -ta *mf*

presidential [prɛzɪdɛ́nʃəɬ] ADJ presidencial

press [prɛs] VI/VT (bear down, squeeze) apretar, oprimir; (a computer key) oprimir, presionar; (iron) planchar; (force) presionar; (extract juice) prensar; (put under pressure) apremiar; **to — on** avanzar; **to — one's point** insistir en un argumento; **to — through** abrirse paso; N (newspapers) prensa *f*; (printing machine) imprenta *f*; (crowding) empuje *m*; **— conference** conferencia de prensa *f*; **— corps** cuerpo de prensa *m*; **— release** comunicado de prensa *m*

pressing [prɛ́sɪŋ] ADJ apremiante, urgente

pressure [prɛ́ʃə-] N presión *f*; **— cooker** olla a presión *f*; **— gauge** manómetro *m*; **— group** grupo de presión *m*; VT apremiar, presionar

prestige [prɛstíʒ] N prestigio *m*

prestigious [prɛstíʤəs] ADJ prestigioso

presumably [prɪzúməbli] ADV **— he is already prepared** es de suponer que ya esté preparado

presume [prɪzúm] VI (be presumptuous) presumir; VT (suppose) suponer; (dare) atreverse a

presumption [prɪzʌ́mpʃən] N presunción *f*

presumptuous [prɪzʌ́mptʃuəs] ADJ presuntuoso, presumido

presuppose [prisəpóz] VT presuponer

pretax [pritǽks] ADJ antes de impuestos

preteen [pritín] ADJ & N preadolescente *mf*

pretend [prɪtɛ́nd] VI/VT (make believe) hacer de cuenta que; (feign) fingir; VT (claim)

pretender; **to — to the throne** pretender el trono

pretense [prítɛns] N (faked action or belief) engaño *m*; (false show) apariencia *f*; **under — of** so pretexto de

pretension [prɪtɛ́nʃən] N pretensión *f*; (pretext) pretexto *m*

pretentious [prɪtɛ́nʃəs] ADJ (full of pretension) pretencioso; (showy) ostentoso

pretext [prítɛkst] N pretexto *m*

pretrial [pritráɪɬ] ADJ anterior al juicio

pretty [prídi] ADJ bonito; (human only) *Sp* guapo; ADV bastante; **— well** bastante bien, francamente bien; VI/VT **to — up** embellecer

prevail [prɪvél] VI (win) prevalecer; (be widespread, dominant) preponderar, imperar; **to — on/upon** persuadir

prevailing [prɪvélɪŋ] ADJ (opinion) predominante; (feeling) reinante, imperante; **— winds** vientos predominantes

prevalent [prɛ́vələnt] ADJ prevaleciente, preponderante

prevent [prɪvɛ́nt] VT (keep from occurring) prevenir; VI/VT (impede) impedir

prevention [prɪvɛ́nʃən] N prevención *f*; (of a disease) prevención *f*, profilaxis *f*

preventive [prɪvɛ́ntɪv] ADJ preventivo, cautelar

preview [prívju] N preestreno *m*

previewing [prívjuwɪŋ] N previsualización *f*

previous [prívias] ADJ previo, anterior

previously [príviəsli] ADV previamente, anteriormente

prey [pre] N (animal) presa *f*; VI **to — on** (animals) alimentarse de; (people) explotar; **it —s upon my mind** me tiene preocupado

price [praɪs] N precio *m*; **at any —** a toda costa; **— control** control de precios *m*; **— fixing** fijación de precios *f*; **— index** índice de precios *m*; **— tag** etiqueta de precio *f*; VT (set price) poner precio a; (ask price) averiguar el precio de

priceless [práɪsl̩s] ADJ (without price) invalorable; (amusing) divertidísimo

pricey [práɪsi] ADJ caro

pricing [práɪsɪŋ] N fijación de precios *f*

prick [prɪk] N (puncture) pinchazo *m*; (sharp point) púa *f*; VI/VT pinchar, punzar; **to — up one's ears** parar las orejas

prickly [príkli] ADJ espinoso; **— heat** sarpullido causado por el calor *m*; **— pear** tuna *f*, nopal *m*

pride [praɪd] N orgullo *m*; (excessive) soberbia *f*; VI **to — oneself on** enorgullecerse de

priest [prist] N sacerdote *m*; (Catholic only) cura *m*

priesthood [prísthʊd] N sacerdocio *m*

prim [prɪm] ADJ remilgado

primarily [praɪmɛ́rɪli] ADV principalmente, más que nada

primary [práımeri] N elección primaria f; ADJ primario; (main) fundamental, principal; — **care** atención primaria f; — **colors** colores primarios m pl; — **election** elección primaria f; — **school** escuela primaria f

primate [práımet] N primate m

prime [praım] ADJ (principal) fundamental; (of a number) primo; (select) de primera; — **minister** primer ministro m, primera ministra f; N (number) número primo m; **to be in one's** — estar en la flor de la edad, estar en la plenitud de la vida; — **rate** tasa prima f; VT preparar; (a pump) cebar

primer[1] [prímə-] N (first book) manual elemental m

primer[2] [práımə-] N (pump part) cebador m

primitive [prímıtıv] ADJ & N primitivo -va mf

prince [prıns] N príncipe m

princely [prínsli] ADJ noble, principesco; **a — sum** una suma muy grande

princess [prínses] N princesa f

principal [prínsəpəl] ADJ principal; N (money invested) capital m; (giver of power of attorney) poderdante mf, mandante mf; (head of a school) director -ora mf

principle [prínsəpəl] N principio m

print [prınt] VI/VT imprimir; (write in block letters) escribir en letra de molde; **to — out** imprimir; N (type) letra de imprenta f; (of art) lámina f; (of photographs) copia f; (of finger) huella digital f; (on cloth) estampado m; **—out** versión impresa f; **in —** publicado, en venta; **out of —** agotado

printer [prínta-] N (person) impresor -ora mf, gráfico -ca mf; (machine) impresora f; — **driver** controlador de impresora m; — **feeder** alimentador de impresora m

printing [príntıŋ] N (art, trade) imprenta f; (process) impresión f, tipografía f; (block letters) letra de molde f, letra de imprenta f; — **press** imprenta f; **this book is in its second** — este libro está en su segunda tirada

prior [práıə-] ADJ previo; — **to** anterior a

priority [praıórıdı] N prioridad f; **having —** prioritario

prism [prízəm] N prisma m

prison [prízən] N prisión f, cárcel f, presidio m

prisoner [prízənə-] N (captive) prisionero -ra mf; (in jail) preso -sa mf, presidiario -ria mf; — **of war** prisionero -ra de guerra mf

pristine [prıstín] ADJ (immaculate) puro; (perfect) perfecto

privacy [práıvəsi] N privacidad f; — **statement** declaración sobre la privacidad f

private [práıvıt] ADJ (not public) privado; (individual) particular; — **enterprise** empresa privada f; — **eye** detective privado -da mf; — **parts** partes pudendas f pl; — **property** propiedad privada f; —**s** partes pudendas f pl; — **school** escuela privada f; — **sector** sector privado m; **a — citizen** un particular; **in —** en privado; N soldado raso m

privation [praıvéʃən] N privación f

privatization [praıvədızéʃən] N privatización f

privatize [práıvətaız] VT privatizar

privilege [prívəlıdʒ] N privilegio m

privileged [prívlıdʒd] ADJ privilegiado

privy [prívi] ADJ **to be — to** estar enterado de; N retrete m

prize [praız] N (reward) premio m; (booty) botín m; — **fight** pelea de boxeo profesional f; — **fighter** boxeador -ora mf, pugilista mf; VT apreciar

pro [pro] N profesional mf

probability [prabəbílıdi] N probabilidad f

probable [prábəbəl] ADJ probable

probate [próbet] N legalización de una validación testamentaria f

probation [probéʃən] N libertad condicional f

probationary [probéʃəneri] ADJ probatorio; — **period** período de prueba m

probe [prob] VI/VT (explore with a probe) sondear; (examine) examinar; N sonda f (also in space); (investigation) indagación f

problem [prábləm] N problema m; —**s** problemática f

procedure [prəsídʒə-] N procedimiento m; (legal) trámite m

proceed [prəsíd] VI (originate) proceder; (continue) proseguir, continuar; **to — against** demandar a; **to —** proceder a

proceeds [prósidz] N ganancia f, lo recaudado

proceedings [prəsídıŋz] N (events) acontecimientos m pl; (record of a conference) actas f pl, memoria f; (legal action) procedimiento m

process [práses] N proceso m; **in the — of** en vías de

processing [práses ıŋ] N (of applications) tramitación f; (of data, substances) procesamiento m; — **power** potencia procesadora f

procession [prəséʃən] N procesión f

processor [prásesə-] N procesador m

pro-choice [protʃóıs] ADJ pro-elección

proclaim [proklém] VT proclamar

proclamation [prakləméʃən] N proclamación f, proclama f

procrastinate [prəkrǽstənet] VI/VT dejar para último momento

procreate [prókriet] VI/VT procrear, engendrar

proctology [praktálədʒi] N proctología f

procure [prəkjúr] VT procurar, obtener

prod [prad] VT aguijonear; **they —ded me into going / to go** insistieron en que fuera

prodigal [prádıgəl] ADJ N pródigo -ga mf

prodigious [prədídʒəs] ADJ prodigioso

prodigy [prádədʒi] N prodigio m

produce[1] [pródus] N (vegetables) verduras f pl, hortalizas f pl

produce[2] [prədús] VI/VT producir; VT (present) presentar

producer [prədúsə·] N productor -ora mf; (of a movie) realizador -ora mf

product [prúpəkt] N producto m

production [prədákʃən] N producción f; (TV, radio) producción f, realización f; (exaggerated situation) teatro m

productive [prədáktiv] ADJ productivo

productivity [prɑpəktíviɖi] N productividad f

profane [prəfén] ADJ profano; (vulgar) grosero; VT profanar

profanity [prəfǽniɖi] N groserías f pl, palabrotas f pl

profess [prəfés] VI (publicly accept, take vows) profesar; VT (state) afirmar; (claim) pretender

profession [prəféʃən] N profesión f

professional [prəféʃənl] ADJ & N profesional f

professor [prəfésə·] N profesor -ora universitario -ria mf; (full) catedrático -ca mf

proffer [práfə·] VT ofrecer; N oferta f

proficiency [prəfíʃənsi] N competencia f

proficient [prəfíʃənt] ADJ competente

profile [prófail] N (contour) perfil m; **a high- case** un caso muy sonado

profit [práfit] N (gain) ganancia f; **— and loss** ganancias y pérdidas f pl; **— margin** margen de ganancia m; **— sharing** participación en las ganancias de una empresa f; **at a —** con ganancia; **to turn a —** dar ganancia; **not for —** sin fines de lucro; VI salir ganando; **to — from** (benefit) aprovechar, sacar provecho de; (use to get an advantage) aprovecharse de; VT servir

profitability [prɑfipəbíliɖi] N rentabilidad f

profitable [prúfiɖəbəl] ADJ (beneficial) provechoso; (lucrative) lucrativo, rentable

profound [prəfáund] ADJ profundo

profundity [prəfándiɖi] N profundidad f

profuse [prəfjús] ADJ profuso, pródigo

progesterone [prodʒéstəron] N progesterona f

prognosis [pragnósis] N pronóstico m

program [prógræm] N programa m; VI/VT programar

programmable [prógræmæbəl] ADJ programable

programmer [prógræmə·] N programador -ora mf

programming [prógræmɪŋ] N programación f; **— language** lenguaje de programación m

progress[1] [prágres] N progreso m

progress[2] [prəgrés] VI progresar

progression [prəgréʃən] N progresión f

progressive [prəgrésiv] ADJ (advancing) progresivo; ADJ & N (liberal) progresista mf, progresivo -va mf

prohibit [prohíbit] VT prohibir, vedar

prohibition [proəbíʃən] N prohibición f

project[1] [prádʒekt] N proyecto m

project[2] [prədʒékt] VI/VT (plan) proyectar[se]; VI (jut out) sobresalir

projectile [prədʒéktail] N proyectil m; ADJ arrojadizo

projection [prədʒékʃən] N (plan) proyección f; (jut) saliente f

projector [prədʒéktə·] N proyector m

proletariat [prolitériət] N proletariado m

pro-life [prolái] ADJ antiaborto

proliferation [prəlifəréʃən] N proliferación f

prolific [prəlífik] ADJ prolífico

prologue [prólɔg] N prólogo m

prolong [prəlɔ́ŋ] VT prolongar

prolongation [prolɔŋgéʃən] N prolongación f

promenade [pramənéd] N paseo m; (dance) baile m; VI/VT pasear[se]

prominent [prámənənt] ADJ prominente

promiscuous [prəmískjuəs] ADJ promiscuo, liviano

promise [prámis] N promesa f; **he showed —** prometía mucho; VI/VT prometer

promising [prámisɪŋ] ADJ prometedor

promissory [prámisɔri] ADJ promisorio; **— note** pagaré m

promontory [práməntɔri] N promontorio m

promote [prəmót] VT (foster) promover, fomentar; (advance in rank) ascender; (in school) pasar de año, promover; (advertise) promocionar

promoter [prəmóɖə·] N (fomenter) propulsor -ora mf; (organizer) promotor -ora mf

promotion [prəmóʃən] N (act of promoting) promoción f; (advance in rank) ascenso m

promotional [prəmóʃənl] ADJ promocional

prompt [prampt] ADJ (quick) rápido; (punctual) puntual; VT (cause) inducir; (in theater) apuntar; **to give someone a —** apuntarle a alguien

promptly [prámptli] ADV (soon) pronto; (punctually) puntualmente

promulgate [prámɪget] VT promulgar

prone [pron] ADJ (disposed) propenso, proclive; (face down) boca abajo; (prostrate) postrado

prong [prɔŋ] N púa f, diente m

pronoun [prónaun] N pronombre m

pronounce [prənáuns] VT (enunciate) pronunciar; (declare) declarar

pronounced [prənáunst] ADJ pronunciado

pronouncement [prənáunsmənt] N pronunciamiento m

pronunciation [prənʌnsiéʃən] N pronunciación f

proof [pruf] N (evidence, test, trial printing) prueba f; (of alcohol) graduación f, grado m; **— of purchase** comprobante de compra m; **—reader** corrector -ora de pruebas mf, revisor -ora de pruebas mf; **fifty —**

veinticinco por ciento de graduación alcohólica; **fire—** a prueba de incendios; **water—** impermeable; **bullet—** a prueba de balas

prop [prɑp] N (pole) puntal m; (in theater) accesorio m; (propeller) hélice f; (support) sostén m, apoyo m; (of a plant) tutor m; VT **to — against** apoyar en, sostener en; **to — up** apuntalar, sostener

propaganda [prɑpəgǽndə] N propaganda f

propagate [prɑ́pəget] VI/VT propagar[se]

propagation [prɑpəgéʃen] N propagación f

propane [própen] N propano m

propel [prəpɛ́l] VT propulsar, impulsar

propeller [prəpɛ́lɚ] N hélice f

propensity [prəpɛ́nsɪDi] N propensión f

proper [prɑ́pɚ] ADJ (appropriate) apropiado; (decorous) decoroso; (genuine) como Dios manda; (correct) correcto; (in math, grammar) propio; **to be — to** ser propio de

properly [prɑ́pɚli] ADV (appropriately) apropiadamente; (correctly) correctamente; (decorously) decorosamente

property [prɑ́pɚDi] N (characteristic) propiedad f; (real estate) propiedad f, finca f; (assets) bienes m pl; **— damage** daños materiales m pl

prophecy [prɑ́fɪsi] N profecía f

prophesy [prɑ́fɪsaɪ] VI/VT profetizar

prophet [prɑ́fɪt] N profeta -tisa mf

prophetic [prəfɛ́Dɪk] ADJ profético

propitious [prəpíʃəs] ADJ propicio

proponent [prəpónənt] N (person who proposes) proponente mf; (adherent) defensor -ora m

proportion [prəpórʃən] N proporción f; **out of —** desproporcionado; VT proporcionar; **well —ed** bien proporcionado

proportional [prəpórʃən] ADJ proporcional

proportionate [prəpórʃənɪt] ADJ proporcional

proposal [prəpózəl] N (suggestion) propuesta f; (of marriage, dishonest) proposición f

propose [prəpóz] VI/VT (suggest) proponer; VI (ask in marriage) declararse, hacer una propuesta de matrimonio; **to — to do something** proponerse hacer algo

proposition [prɑpəzíʃən] N proposición f; VT hacer proposiciones deshonestas

proprietor [prəpráɪɪDɚ] N propietario -ria mf

propriety [prəpráɪɪDi] N decoro m

propulsion [prəpʌ́lʃən] N propulsión f

prorate [prorét] VT prorratear

prosaic [prozéɪk] ADJ prosaico

prose [proz] N prosa f

prosecute [prɑ́sɪkjut] VI/VT (take to court) procesar, enjuiciar; VT (pursue) llevar adelante

prosecution [prɑsɪkjúʃən] N (act of prosecuting) procesamiento m; (officials who prosecute) ministerio público m, fiscalía f

prosecutor [prɑ́sɪkjuDɚ] N fiscal mf

proselytize [prɑ́səlɪtaɪz] VT convertir; VI buscar ganar prosélitos

prospect [prɑ́spɛkt] N (outlook, possibility) perspectiva f, expectativa f; (candidate) candidato -ta mf; (possible client) posible cliente -ta mf; VT prospectar; VI **to — for** buscar

prospective [prəspɛ́ktɪv] ADJ posible, potencial

prospector [prɑ́spɛktɚ] N prospector -ora mf

prosper [prɑ́spɚ] VI prosperar

prosperity [prɑspɛ́rɪDi] N prosperidad f, bonanza f

prosperous [prɑ́spərəs] ADJ próspero

prostate [prɑ́stet] N próstata f; **— gland** próstata f

prosthesis [prɑsθísɪs] N prótesis f

prostitute [prɑ́stɪtut] N prostituto -ta mf; VT prostituir

prostitution [prɑstɪtúʃən] N prostitución f

prostrate [prɑ́stret] VT postrar; ADJ (lying flat, overcome) postrado; (lying face down) boca abajo

protagonist [protǽgənɪst] N protagonista mf

protect [prətɛ́kt] VI/VT proteger, amparar

protection [prətɛ́kʃen] N protección f

protectionist [prətɛ́kʃənɪst] ADJ & N proteccionista mf

protective [prətɛ́ktɪv] ADJ protector

protector [prətɛ́ktɚ] N protector -ora mf

protectorate [prətɛ́ktərɪt] N protectorado m

protégé, protégée [próDəʒe] N protegido -da mf

protein [prótin] N proteína f

protest[1] [prótɛst] N protesta f, reclamación f

protest[2] [prətɛ́st] VI/VT protestar, reclamar

Protestant [prɑ́Dɪstənt] ADJ & N protestante mf

protestation [protɛstéʃən] N declaración f

protocol [próDəkɔl] N protocolo m

proton [prótɑn] N protón m

protoplasm [próDəplæzəm] N protoplasma m

prototype [próDətaɪp] N prototipo m

protozoan [proDəzóən] N protozoario m

protract [protrǽkt] VT prolongar

protrude [protrúd] VI sobresalir, proyectarse

protuberance [prətúbərəns] N protuberancia f

proud [praud] ADJ orgulloso; (haughty) soberbio; **to be — of** enorgullecerse de, ufanarse de

prove [pruv] VT (demonstrate, verify) probar, demostrar; VI resultar; **events have —d me right** los hechos me han dado la razón

proverb [prɑ́vɚb] N proverbio m, refrán m

provide [prəváɪd] VT (furnish) proveer, proporcionar; (supply) abastecer, aportar; (stipulate) estipular, prevenir; VI **to — for** (support) mantener; (stipulate) estipular; **to — with** proveer de, proporcionar; CONJ **—d [that]** con tal [de] que, siempre que

providence [práviɖəns] N providencia f

provider [prəvaíɖə·] N (supplier) proveedor -ora mf; (breadwinner) sostén m

province [právins] N (area) provincia f; (competence) competencia f

provincial [prəvínʃəl] ADJ (of a province) provincial; (rustic) provinciano, pueblerino; N provinciano -na mf

provision [prəvíʒən] N (act of providing, thing provided) provisión f, suministro m, prestación f; (precaution) medida f, precaución f; (clause) estipulación f, prevención f; —s provisiones f pl, víveres m pl, bastimentos m pl, suministros m

provisional [prəvíʒənəl] ADJ provisional

proviso [prəvaízo] N condición f, estipulación f

provocation [pravəkéʃən] N provocación f

provoke [prəvók] VT provocar

provost [próvost] N vicerrector -ora mf

prow [prau] N proa f

prowess [práuis] N valentía f

prowl [praul] VI/VT rondar en acecho

proximity [praksímiɖi] N proximidad f

proxy [práksi] N (person) apoderado -da mf; (power of attorney) poder m; **by** — por poder

prude [prud] N mojigato -ta mf, gazmoño -ña mf

prudence [prúdns] N prudencia f

prudent [prúdnt] ADJ prudente

prudery [prúdəri] N mojigatería f, gazmoñería f

prudish [prúdiʃ] ADJ mojigato, gazmoño

prune [prun] N ciruela pasa f; VI/VT podar

pry [prai] VT curiosear; **to** — **into** entrometerse; **to** — **open** abrir por la fuerza; **to** — **a secret out** extraer/arrancar un secreto

pseudonym [súdnɪm] N pseudónimo/ seudónimo m

psoriasis [sərájəsis] N psoriasis/soriasis f

psych [saik] VT — **out** intimidar psicológicamente

psychedelic [saikidélik] ADJ psicodélico/ sicodélico

psychiatrist [saikáiətrist] N psiquiatra/siquiatra mf

psychiatry [saikáiətri] N psiquiatría/siquiatría f

psychic [sáikik] ADJ psíquico/síquico; N médium mf, psíquico -ca / síquico -ca mf

psychoanalysis [saikoænəlaiz] N psicoanálisis/ sicoanálisis m

psychological [saikəládʒikəl] ADJ psicológico/ sicológico

psychologist [saikálədʒist] N psicólogo -ga / sicólogo -ga mf

psychology [saikálədʒi] N psicología/sicología f

psychopath [sáikəpæθ] N psicópata/sicópata mf

psychosis [saikósis] N psicosis/sicosis f

psychosomatic [saikosəmǽɖik] ADJ psicosomático/sicosomático

psychotherapy [saikoθérəpi] N psicoterapia/ sicoterapia f

psychotic [saikáɖik] ADJ psicótico/sicótico

puberty [pjúbə·ɖi] N pubertad f

pubic [pjúbik] ADJ púbico; — **hair** pelo púbico m

public [páblik] ADJ público; — **domain** dominio público m; — **health** salud pública f; — **relations** relaciones públicas f pl; — **school** escuela pública f; — **service** servicio público m; **to go** — proceder a la venta pública de acciones, salir a bolsa; N público m

publication [pablikéʃən] N publicación f

publicity [pablísiɖi] N publicidad f, propaganda f; — **campaign** campaña publicitaria f

publicize [páblisaiz] VT promocionar

publish [pábliʃ] VI/VT publicar, editar; —**ing house** [casa] editorial f

publisher [pábliʃə·] N editor -ora mf

puck [pʌk] N puck m

pucker [pákə·] VI/VT fruncir[se]; N frunce m

pudding [púdɪŋ] N budín m, pudín m

puddle [pádl] N charco m

pudendum [pjudéndəm] N partes pudendas f pl

Puerto Rican [pɔrɖəríkən] ADJ & N puertorriqueño -ña mf

Puerto Rico [pɔrɖəríko] N Puerto Rico m

puff [pʌf] N (air) resoplido m, soplo m; (smoke) bocanada f; (on a cigarette) pitada f, chupada f; (of a sleeve) bullón m; — **pastry** masa de hojaldre f; VI (blow) resoplar; (breathe hard) jadear; (smoke a cigarette) echar bocanadas; **to** — **up** hincharse; **to** — **up with pride** henchirse de orgullo

pug [pʌg] N dogo m; — **nose** nariz chata f

puke [pjuk] VI/VT vomitar, lanzar; N vómito m

pull [pul] VI/VT (tug) tirar, jalar; (extract) arrancar, extraer; (stretch) estirar; (injure) desgarrar; **to** — **apart** destrozar; **to** — **down** (demolish) demoler; (earn) sacar; **to** — **for** hinchar por; **to** — **off** conseguir; **to** — **oneself together** calmarse; **to** — **over** parar; **to** — **up** parar; **to** — **through** salvarse; **to** — **strings** mover palancas; **to** — **out** (leave a place) salir; (back out) retirarse; **the train** —**ed into the station** el tren entró a la estación; N (act of pulling) tirón m; (force) fuerza f; (influence) influencia f; (injury) desgarro m; —**-down menu** menú abatible m

pullet [púlit] N polla f

pulley [púli] N polea f, carrucha f

pulmonary [pálmənɛri] ADJ pulmonar

pulp [pʌlp] N (of paper, wood, fruit) pulpa f; (of grape, sugarcane, olive, etc.) bagazo m

pulpit [púlpit] N púlpito m

pulsar [pálsar] N púlsar m

pulsate [pálset] VI latir

pulse [pals] N pulso m; (single pulsation, act of pulsing) pulsación f

pulverize [pálvəraiz] VT pulverizar[se]

puma [pjúmə] N puma f

pumice [pʌ́mis] N piedra pómez f

pump [pʌmp] N bomba f; (shoe) zapatilla f, zapato escotado m; (for gasoline) surtidor m; VI/VT bombear; (inflate) inflar; **to — someone for information** sonsacar [información] a alguien

pumpkin [pʌ́mpkɪn] N calabaza f

pun [pʌn] N juego de palabras m, retruécano m; VI hacer juegos de palabras

punch [pʌntʃ] N (blow) puñetazo m; (drink) ponche m; (drill) sacabocados m sg; (force) fuerza f, empuje m; — **bowl** ponchera f; — **line** remate de un chiste m; VI/VT (hit) dar un puñetazo; VT (drive cattle) arriar; (make a hole) agujerear; **to — in/out** marcar tarjeta

punctual [pʌ́ŋktʃuəl] ADJ puntual

punctuality [pʌŋktʃuǽlɪDi] N puntualidad f

punctuate [pʌ́ŋktʃuet] VI/VT puntuar; (interrupt) interrumpir; (accentuate) salpicar

punctuation [pʌŋktʃuéʃən] N puntuación f

puncture [pʌ́ŋktʃɚ] VI/VT pinchar[se]; Mex ponchar[se]; **—d tire** neumático pinchado m; N (action of perforating) perforación f; (hole) pinchazo m; — **wound** herida perforada f

pundit [pʌ́ndɪt] N experto -ta mf

pungent [pʌ́ndʒənt] ADJ (acrid) acre; (sarcastic) mordaz

punish [pʌ́nɪʃ] VT castigar, penar

punishment [pʌ́nɪʃmənt] N castigo m

punitive [pjúnɪDɪv] ADJ punitivo; — **damages** daños punitivos m pl

punk [pʌŋk] N (inexperienced boy) mocoso m; (hoodlum) gamberro m; (rock) punk m; (punker) punkero -ra mf

punt [pʌnt] N (kick) patada de despeje f; (boat) balsa f; VI/VT despejar; VI andar en balsa

punter [pʌ́ntɚ] N despejador m

puny [pjúni] ADJ endeble

pupil [pjúpəl] N (student) escolar mf; (part of eye) pupila f, niña f

puppet [pʌ́pɪt] N títere m, monigote m; — **show** teatro de títeres m

puppy [pʌ́pi] N cachorro m

purchase [pɚ́tʃəs] VI/VT comprar, adquirir; N compra f; (hold) asidero m; — **order** orden de compra f; — **price** precio de compra m

purchaser [pɚ́tʃəsɚ] N comprador mf

purchasing [pɚ́tʃəsɪŋ] N compra f; — **agent** agente de compras mf; — **power** poder adquisitivo m

pure [pjʊr] ADJ puro; ADJ & N **—bred** purasangre m

puree [pjʊré] N puré m

purgative [pɚ́gəDɪv] ADJ & N purgante m

purgatory [pɚ́gətɔri] N purgatorio m

purge [pɚdʒ] VI/VT purgar[se]; N purga f

purify [pjúrəfaɪ] VI/VT purificar[se], depurar[se]

purist [pjúrɪst] N purista mf

puritanical [pjurɪtǽnɪkəl] ADJ puritano

purity [pjúriDi] N pureza f

purple [pɚ́pəl] N morado m, púrpura f; ADJ morado, púrpura

purport¹ [pɚ́pɔrt] N (meaning) significado m; (purpose) propósito m

purport² [pɚpɔ́rt] VT pretender

purpose [pɚ́pəs] N propósito m, objetivo m; **on — adrede, a propósito

purr [pɚ] N ronroneo m (also motors); VI ronronear

purse [pɚs] N bolso m, cartera f; VT **to — one's lips** fruncir los labios

pursuant [pɚsúənt] ADV LOC — **to** conforme a, de acuerdo con

pursue [pɚsú] VT (follow) perseguir; (strive) dedicarse a; (continue) continuar con; (practice a profession) ejercer

pursuer [pɚsúɚ] N perseguidor -ora mf

pursuit [pɚsút] N (chase) persecución f, seguimiento m, acoso m; (striving for) búsqueda f; (pastime) pasatiempo m; (practice) ejercicio m; **in — of** (chasing) detrás de; (striving for) en busca de

pus [pʌs] N pus m

push [pʊʃ] VI/VT (shove) empujar; VT (pressure) presionar, promover; (sell drugs) camellear; **to — a button** apretar un botón; VI (in childbirth) pujar; **to — aside/away** apartar; **to — forward** abrirse paso, avanzar; **to — open** abrir de un empujón; **to — through** hacer pasar; N empujón m; (military) ofensiva f; **—-up** lagartija f; ADJ **—-button** de botones

pusher [pʊ́ʃɚ] N camello mf

pushy [pʊ́ʃi] ADJ insistente

pussy [pʊ́si] N minino m, gatito m; — **willow** sauce m

put [pʊt] VT poner, colocar; **to — a question** plantear una pregunta; **to — across** expresar; **to — away** guardar; **to — down** (write down) apuntar; (suppress) sofocar; (attribute) atribuir; (humiliate) humillar; (make a down payment) hacer un depósito; (a pet) sacrificar; **to — into** meter; **to — into words** expresar, decir; **to — in writing** poner por escrito; **to — off** (postpone) aplazar, posponer; (perturb) desagradar; (dissuade) disuadir; **to — on** ponerse; **to — on airs** darse tono; **to — on weight** engordar; **to — out** (extinguish) apagar, extinguir; (annoy) molestar; **to — the blame** echar la culpa; **to — to sea** echar al mar; **to — to sleep** sacrificar; **to — up** (construct) levantar; (lodge) alojar; **to — up for sale** poner a la venta; **to — up with** aguantar; **I felt —-upon** sentí que se habían aprovechado de mí; N **— option** opción de venta f; **—-down** insulto m

putrid [pjútrɪd] ADJ putrefacto

putt [pʌt] VI/VT potear; N pat
putter [pʌ́Də] VI entretenerse; N (golf) putter *m*
putty [pʌ́Di] N masilla *f*; VT rellenar con masilla
puzzle [pʌ́zəl] N (jigsaw) rompecabezas *m sg*;
(riddle) acertijo *m*; (problem) enigma *m*;
(crossword) crucigrama *m*; VT dejar perplejo,
desconcertar; VI **to — out** desentrañar; **to —
over** meditar sobre; **to be —d** estar perplejo
pygmy [pɪ́gmi] N pigmeo -a *mf*
pylon [páɪlɑn] N pilón *m*
pyramid [pɪ́rəmɪd] N pirámide *f*
pyromania [paɪroméniə] N piromanía *f*
pyromaniac [paɪroméniæk] N pirómano -na *mf*
pyrotechnics [paɪrɑ́tɛknɪks] N pirotecnia *f*
python [páɪθɑn] N pitón *mf*

Qq

Qatar [kɑtɑ́r] N Qatar *m*
Qatari [kətɑ́ri] ADJ & N catarí *mf*
quack [kwæk] N (sound of duck) graznido *m*;
(charlatan) matasanos *mf*, charlatán -ana *mf*;
ADJ charlatán; VI graznar
quadrilateral [kwɑdrəlǽDəəl] ADJ & N
cuadrilátero *m*
quadriplegic [kwɑdrəplíʤɪk] ADJ & N
tetrapléjico -ca *mf*
quadruped [kwɑ́drəpɛd] ADJ & N cuadrúpedo *m*
quadruplet [kwɑdrúplɪt] N cuatrillizo -za *mf*
quagmire [kwǽgmaɪr] N (bog) cenagal *m*,
atascadero *m*; (crisis) atolladero *m*,
atascadero *m*
quail [kwel] N codorniz *f*
quaint [kwent] ADJ pintoresco
quake [kwek] N (instance of quaking) temblor *m*;
(earthquake) terremoto *m*; VI temblar
qualification [kwɑləfɪkéʃən] N (for a race)
clasificación *f*; (requirement) requisito *m*;
without — sin reservas
qualify [kwɑ́ləfaɪ] VT (characterize) calificar;
(moderate) moderar; (provide with
credentials) capacitar; VI (for a race)
clasificarse; (for a position) estar capacitado
qualifying [kwɑ́lɪfaɪɪŋ] ADJ calificativo
qualitative [kwɑ́lɪteDɪv] ADJ cualitativo
quality [kwɑ́lɪDi] N (characteristic) cualidad *f*;
(excellence) calidad *f*; **— control** control de
calidad *m*
qualm [kwɑm] N escrúpulo *m*
quantify [kwɑ́ntəfaɪ] VT cuantificar
quantitative [kwɑ́ntɪteDɪv] ADJ cuantitativo
quantity [kwɑ́ntɪDi] N cantidad *f*
quantum mechanics [kwɑ́ntəmmɪkǽnɪks] N
mecánica cuántica *f*
quarantine [kwɔ́rəntin] N cuarentena *f*; VT

poner en cuarentena
quarrel [kwɔ́rəl] N riña *f*, rencilla *f*; VI reñir,
pelear
quarrelsome [kwɔ́rəlsəm] ADJ pendenciero
quarry [kwɔ́ri] N (stone) cantera *f*; (game) presa
f; VT explotar
quart [kwɔrt] N cuarto de galón [0.9463 litros] *m*
quarter [kwɔ́rDə] N (one-fourth) cuarto *m*,
cuarta parte *f*; (coin) moneda de 25 centavos *f*;
(of a sporting match) tiempo *m*; (of a calendar
or school year) trimestre *m*; (district) barrio
m; **—back** mariscal de campo *m*; **—master
general** intendente *mf*; **— note** negra *f*; **—s**
alojamiento *m*; **from all —s** de todas partes;
to give no — to the enemy no dar cuartel al
enemigo; ADJ cuarto; VT (divide) cuartear,
dividir en cuartos; (execute) descuartizar;
(lodge troops) acuartelar, acantonar
quarterly [kwɔ́rDəli] ADV trimestralmente; ADJ
trimestral; N publicación trimestral *f*
quartet [kwɔrtét] N cuarteto *m*
quartz [kwɔrts] N cuarzo *m*
quasar [kwézɑr] N cuásar *m*, quásar *m*
quash [kwɑʃ] VT (a rebellion) sofocar; (a
decision) anular
quaver [kwévə] VI temblar; N temblor *m*; (in
music) trémolo *m*
queasy [kwízi] ADJ nauseoso
queen [kwin] N reina *f*
queer [kwir] ADJ (strange) raro; (eccentric)
excéntrico; **to feel —** sentirse raro; VT
comprometer
quell [kwɛl] VT (suppress) reprimir, sofocar;
(calm) calmar
quench [kwɛntʃ] VT (flames, thirst) apagar;
(passions) aplacar, apagar
query [kwíri] N (question) pregunta *f*; (question
mark) signo de interrogación *m*; (doubt) duda
f; VT (ask) preguntar; (question) expresar
dudas; (mark with a question mark) marcar
con signo de interrogación
quest [kwɛst] N búsqueda *f*
question [kwɛ́stʃən] N (thing asked) pregunta *f*;
(issue) cuestión *f*; **— mark** signo de
interrogación *m*; **beyond —** fuera de duda;
that is out of the — ¡ni pensarlo! VT (ask)
preguntar; (interrogate) interrogar; (call into
doubt) dudar, cuestionar
questionable [kwɛ́stʃənəbəl] ADJ (doubtful)
cuestionable, discutible; (morally dubious)
equívoco
questioner [kwɛ́stʃənə] N interrogador -ora *mf*
questioning [kwɛ́stʃənɪŋ] N interrogatorio *m*;
ADJ (asking) interrogador; (doubting)
cuestionador
questionnaire [kwɛstʃənér] N cuestionario *m*
queue [kju] N cola *f*, fila *f*; VT poner en la cola
quibble [kwíbəl] VI (split hairs) sutilizar; (evade)
evadir; (argue) andar en dimes y diretes; N

(hairsplitting) sutileza *f*; (evasion) evasiva *f*

quiche [kiʃ] N quiche *f*

quick [kwɪk] ADJ rápido, pronto; **—-tempered** irascible, geniudo; **—-witted** agudo; ADV rápido; N (flesh under nails) carne viva *f*; (the living) los vivos; **to cut to the —** herir en lo vivo; **—sand** arena movediza *f*; **—silver** mercurio *m*, azogue *m*

quicken [kwíkən] VI/VT (speed up) acelerar[se], aligerar[se]; (liven) avivar[se]

quickly [kwíkli] ADV rápido, deprisa, de prisa

quickness [kwíknɪs] N (speed) rapidez *f*; (of wit) agudeza *f*

quiet [kwáɪɪt] ADJ (not noisy) silencioso; (not talking) callado; (restrained) tranquilo; (peaceful, still) reposado; **be —!** ¡silencio! ¡cállate! N (freedom from noise) silencio *m*; (tranquillity) tranquilidad *f*, sosiego *m*; VT (make quiet) acallar; (make tranquil) sosegar, tranquilizar, serenar; VI **to — down** calmarse

quietly [kwáɪtli] ADV (talk) en voz baja; (walk) silenciosamente; **they — went about buying up shares** fueron comprando acciones sin llamar la atención

quill [kwɪl] N (feather) pluma *f*; (hollow base of feather) cañón *m*; (spine on a porcupine) púa *f*

quilt [kwɪlt] N colcha de retazos *f*; VI/VT hacer una colcha de retazos

quinine [kwáɪnaɪn] N quinina *f*

quip [kwɪp] N ocurrencia *f*; VI decir ocurrencias

quirk [kwɝk] N excentricidad *f*

quit [kwɪt] VT (a competition) abandonar; (a place) irse de, salir de; (a job) dejar; (a computer program) salir; **to call it —s** abandonar; **to — smoking** dejar de fumar; VI (withdraw) abandonar; (stop) parar; (resign) renunciar

quite [kwaɪt] ADV (very) bastante; (entirely) del todo, enteramente; **— a person** una persona admirable *f*; **— a lot** bastante; **it's — the fashion** está muy de moda

quiver [kwívɚ] VI temblar; N (shake) temblor *m*; (sheath for arrows) carcaj *m*, aljaba *f*

quiz [kwɪz] N (test) prueba *f*; (show) concurso *m*; VI (give a quiz) examinar, poner una prueba; (interrogate) interrogar

quota [kwóɒə] N cuota *f*

quotation [kwotéʃən] N cita *f*; (of a price) cotización *f*; **— marks** comillas *f pl*

quote [kwot] VI/VT (words) citar; (prices) cotizar; **to — from** citar a; VI (words) cita *f*; (of a price) cotización *f*; **in —s** entre comillas

quotient [kwóʃənt] N cociente *m*

Rr

R & D [**research and development**] [árndí] N ID *mf*

rabbi [ræbaɪ] N rabino *m*

rabbit [ræbɪt] N conejo *m*

rabble [ræbəɫ] N chusma *f*, plebe *f*, gentuza *f*

rabid [ræbɪd] ADJ rabioso

rabies [rébiz] N rabia *f*

raccoon [rækún] N mapache *m*

race [res] N (lineage) raza *f*; (competition) carrera *f*; **—horse** caballo de carreras *m*; **—track** (for runners) pista *f*; (for horses) hipódromo *m*; VI (participate in competition) correr, competir en una carrera; (hurry) ir corriendo; (of heart) latir rápido; (of a motor) acelerar; VT (a horse) hacer correr; (an engine) acelerar; **I'll — you** te echo una carrera

racer [résɚ] N corredor -ora *mf*; (horse) caballo de carreras *m*

racial [réʃəɫ] ADJ racial

racism [résɪzəm] N racismo *m*

rack [ræk] N (for clothes) perchero *m*; (for luggage) baca *f*; (for spices) especiero *m*; (for towels) toallero *m*; (for torture) potro de tormento *m*; **— and pinion** cremallera *f* y piñón *m*; VT **to be —ed with pain** estar transido de dolor; **to — one's brain** devanarse los sesos; **to — up** acumular

racket [rækɪt] N (sports) raqueta *f*; (noise of an impact) estrépito *m*, estruendo *m*; (noise of voices and movement) barahúnda *f*, batahola *f*; (swindle) estafa *f*; (extortion) extorsión *f*

racketeer [rækɪtír] N (swindler) trapacero -ra *mf*, estafador -ora *mf*; (extortionist) extorsionista *mf*; VI (swindle) estafar; (extort) extorsionar

radar [réɒɑr] N radar *m*

radial [rédiəɫ] ADJ radial

radiance [rédiəns] N resplandor *m*, fulgor *m*

radiant [rédiənt] ADJ radiante, resplandeciente

radiate [rédiet] VI/VT irradiar, radiar

radiation [rediéʃən] N radiación *f*; **— sickness** enfermedad por radiación *f*; **— therapy** radioterapia *f*

radiator [rédieɒɚ] N radiador *m*

radical [rædɪkəɫ] ADJ & N radical *mf*

radicalism [rædɪkəlɪzəm] N radicalismo *m*

radio [rédio] N (device, system of communication) radio *f*; **— announcer** locutor -ora *mf*; **— listener** radioescucha *mf*; **— station** radiodifusora *f*; **— telescope** radiotelescopio *m*; **— transmitter** radiotransmisor *m*; **by —** por radio; ADJ **—active** radiactivo, radioactivo; VT (broadcast) transmitir por radio; VI/VT (call) llamar por radio

radiologist [reɪdiálədʒɪst] N radiólogo -ga *mf*

radiology [reɪdiálədʒi] N radiología *f*

radish [rǽdɪʃ] N rábano *m*

radium [réɪdiəm] N radio *m*

radius [rédiəs] N radio *m*

radon [rédɑn] N radón *m*

raffle [rǽfəł] N rifa *f*, sorteo *m*; VI rifar, sortear

raft [ræft] N balsa *f*

rafter [rǽftɚ] N viga *f*

rag [ræg] N (piece of cloth) trapo *m*, guiñapo *m*; (on clothes) harapo *m*, andrajo *m*; — **doll** muñeca de trapo *f*

rage [reʤ] N ira *f*, rabia *f*, cólera *f*; **to be all the** — estar de moda; VI enfurecerse; **to** — **with anger** bramar de ira

ragged [rǽgɪd] ADJ (ill-clothed) andrajoso, harapiento, desharrapado; (voice) ronco, roto; (on an edge) irregular, desigual; **to be on the** — **edge** estar al borde

raid [red] N (military) incursión *f*; (by police) allanamiento *m*, redada *f*; (by air) bombardeo aéreo *m*; VI/VT hacer una incursión; VT (attack) atacar; (rob) asaltar; (carry out a police operation on) allanar

raider [rédɚ] N empresa tiburón *f*

rail [reł] N (of a railroad track) riel *m*, carril *m*; (on a balcony) baranda *f*, barandilla *f*; — **fence** barrera *f*; —**road** ferrocarril *m*; —**road company** empresa ferroviaria *f*; —**road crossing** cruce de ferrocarril *m*; —**road employee** ferroviario -ria *mf*; —**way** ferrocarril *m*; **by** — por ferrocarril; VT **to** —**road** (goods) transportar por ferrocarril; (laws) hacer aprobar apresuradamente; (a person) condenar injustamente

railing [rélɪŋ] N (barrier) baranda *f*; (on a bridge) pretil *m*; (on a stairway) pasamano *m*

rain [ren] N lluvia *f*; —**bow** arco iris *m*; —**coat** impermeable *m*; —**drop** gota de lluvia *f*; —**fall** precipitación *f*; — **forest** selva tropical *f*; — **gauge** pluviómetro *f*; —**storm** temporal de lluvia *f*; — **water** agua llovediza *f*; VI/VT llover; — **or shine** llueva o truene; **to** — **cats and dogs** llover a cántaros

rainy [réni] ADJ lluvioso

raise [rez] VI/VT (voice, hand, a house, spirits) levantar[se]; VT (an alarm) dar; (funds) recaudar, captar; (a salary) aumentar; (a flag) izar; (crops) cultivar; (animals, children) criar; (money) recabar, recaudar; **to** — **a question** plantear una pregunta; **to** — **a racket** armar un alboroto; N aumento *m*

raisin [rézɪn] N pasa [de uva] *f*

rake [rek] N rastrillo *m*; VI/VT rastrillar; **to** — **in money** amasar dinero

rally [rǽli] VI/VT (reorganize troops) reunir[se],

juntar[se]; (inspire) reanimar; VI (demonstrate) concentrarse; (recuperate) recuperarse; (reinvigorate) recobrar ánimo; (rise in value) repuntar; (in tennis) pelotear; **to** — **around someone** apoyar a alguien; N (demonstration) concentración *f*; (recovery) recuperación *f*; (rise in prices) subida *f*; (in tennis) peloteo *m*

RAM [random-access memory] [ræm] N RAM *m*

ram [ræm] N (male sheep) carnero *m*; (tool for battering) ariete *m*; (part of a ship) espolón *m*; VT chocar contra; **to** — **a boat** embestir un buque con el espolón

ramble [rǽmbəł] VI vagar; **to** — **on** divagar; N paseo *m*

ramp [ræmp] N rampa *f*

rampage [rǽmpeʤ] N **to go on a** — andar destrozando todo; VI andar destrozando todo

rampant [rǽmpənt] ADJ desenfrenado

ran [ræn] *see* run

ranch [ræntʃ] N hacienda *f*; *Mex* rancho *m*

rancid [rǽnsɪd] ADJ rancio

rancor [rǽŋkɚ] N rencor *m*

random [rǽndəm] ADJ aleatorio, azaroso; **at** — al azar; — **access memory** memoria de acceso directo *f*

randomize [rǽndəmaɪz] VT aleatorizar

rang [ræŋ] *see* ring

range [renʤ] N (of types) gama *f*; (of a gun) alcance *m*; (of variation) fluctuación *f*; (of mountains) cadena *f*; (for shooting) campo de tiro *m*; (of an aircraft) autonomía *f*; (grazing place) campo abierto *m*; (stove) cocina *f*, estufa *f*; — **finder** telémetro *m*; — **of vision** alcance visual *m*; VT (align) alinear; (of a gun) tener alcance; VI (vary) oscilar; (be found in an area) extenderse; **his children** — **in age between 2 and 10** sus hijos van en edad entre 2 y 10

ranger [rénʤɚ] N (in a park) guardabosque[s] *mf*; (soldier) guardia de asalto *m*

rank [ræŋk] N (in a hierarchy) rango *m*, grado *m*; (line) fila *f*; — **and file** (of an army) tropa *f sg*; **the** —**s** (soldiers) la tropa; (union members) bases *f pl*; **a sculptor of the first** — un escultor de primer orden; VT (arrange) poner en orden de importancia; VI (rate) figurar; **to** — **high** tener alto rango; **to** — **second** estar clasificado en el segundo lugar; ADJ (smelly) hediondo; (growing vigorously) exuberante

ranking [rǽŋkɪŋ] N ránking *m*

ransack [rǽnsæk] VT saquear, desvalijar

ransom [rǽnsəm] N rescate *m*; VT rescatar

rant [rænt] VI/VT despotricar

rap [ræp] VI/VT (strike) golpear; (chat) charlar; VI (in music) rapear, cantar rap; N (blow) golpe *m*; (accusation) cargo *m*; **to take the** — ser el cabeza de turco; — **music** música rap *f*

rapacious [rəpéʃəs] ADJ rapaz
rape [rep] N (violation) violación f; (statutory) estupro m; (plant) colza f; (grape pulp) orujo m; VT violar
rapid [ræpid] ADJ rápido; N —s rápidos m pl
rapidity [rəpíDITI] N rapidez f
rapport [rəpór] N relación f
rapt [ræpt] ADJ extasiado
rapture [ræptʃə] N éxtasis m, embeleso m; **to go into a** — arrobarse
rare [rer] ADJ (infrequent) raro, poco frecuente, extraño; (of gas, earth) raro; (thin, of air) enrarecido; (excellent) excepcional; (not well cooked) crudo; — **earths** tierras raras f pl
rarely [rérli] ADV raramente, raras veces
rarity [réridi] N rareza f; (of air) enrarecimiento m
rascal [ræskəl] N bribón m, bellaco m, pícaro m; Sp golfo m; **you little —!** ¡bandido! ¡sinvergüenza!
rash [ræʃ] ADJ (thoughtless) precipitado, temerario; N (on skin) sarpullido m
raspberry [ræzberi] N frambuesa f; — **bush** frambueso m
raspy [ræspi] ADJ ronco, áspero
rat [ræt] N rata f; **I smell a** — aquí hay gato encerrado; VT (one's hair) cardar; VI **to** — **on** delatar
ratchet [rætʃit] N trinquete m
rate [ret] N (charge) tarifa f; (unit charge for insurance) prima f; (pace) paso m, ritmo m; — **of exchange** tipo de cambio m; — **of interest** tasa de interés f; **at any** — en todo caso; **at this** — a este ritmo; **at the** — **of** a razón de; VT (estimate) valorar, estimar; (esteem) considerar; **he —s as the best** se le considera como el mejor; **he —s high** se le tiene en alta estima
rather [ræðə] ADV (somewhat) bastante; (more precisely) más bien; — **than** en vez de; **I would** — **die than** antes la muerte que; **I would** — **not go** prefiero no ir
ratification [rædɪfikéʃən] N ratificación f
ratify [ræDəfaɪ] VT ratificar
rating [réDɪŋ] N (act of adjudging) calificación f; (for credit) clasificación f; (TV quotient) rating televisivo m, índice de audiencia m
ratio [réʃio] N razón f, proporción f
ration [ræʃən] N ración f; VT racionar
rational [ræʃənl] ADJ racional
rationale [ræʃənǽl] N motivo m
rationalize [ræʃənlaɪz] VI/VT racionalizar
rationing [ræʃənɪŋ] N racionamiento m
rattle [rædl] VI (bang) golpetear; (move noisily) traquetear; **to** — **on** parlotear; VT hacer sonar, sacudir; **to** — **off** recitar; N (banging) golpeteo m; (movement) traqueteo m; (toy) sonaja f, sonajero m; (of a rattlesnake) cascabel m; (of death) estertor m; —**snake**

víbora de cascabel f
raucous [rókəs] ADJ (loud) estridente; (rowdy) escandaloso
ravage [rǽvɪdʒ] VI/VT asolar, arruinar; N estrago m
rave [rev] VI (rant) desvariar, delirar; VI/VT (roar) bramar; **to** — **about** deshacerse en elogios; N (theater review) crítica muy favorable f
raven [révən] N cuervo m; ADJ azabache
ravenous [rǽvənəs] ADJ voraz, famélico; **to be** — tener un hambre canina
ravine [rəvín] N quebrada f, barranco m, cañada f
raving [révɪŋ] ADJ delirante; (extraordinary) extraordinario; — **mad** loco de remate; N desvarío m
ravish [rǽvɪʃ] VT (kidnap) raptar, secuestrar; (rape) violar
raw [rɔ] ADJ (uncooked, unprocessed, damp and cold) crudo; (of vegetables) fresco, crudo; (unadorned) descarnado; — **flesh** carne viva f; — **material** materia prima f; — **sugar** azúcar bruto m; N —**hide** cuero crudo m
ray [re] N (beam) rayo m; (stingray) raya f
rayon [réan] N rayón m
raze [rez] VT arrasar, asolar
razor [rézə] N (device with blade) maquinilla de afeitar f, rasuradora f; (barber's tool) navaja f; (electric) rasuradora eléctrica f; — **blade** hoja de afeitar f; **safety** — navaja de seguridad f
reach [ritʃ] VI/VT (extend) alcanzar; **to** — **for** tratar de agarrar; Sp tratar de coger; **to** — **into** meter la mano en; VT (arrive at) llegar a; (contact) ponerse en contacto con; **to** — **out one's hand** alargar la mano; N alcance m; **beyond his** — fuera de su alcance; **within his** — a su alcance; **far** —**es** zona remota f
react [riækt] VI reaccionar
reaction [riækʃən] N reacción f
reactionary [riækʃəneri] ADJ & N reaccionario -ria mf
reactor [riæktə] N reactor m
read [rid] VI/VT leer; VT (interpret) interpretar; (give as a reading, indicate) decir, indicar, marcar; **it —s easily** es fácil de leer; N lectura f; — **protect** protección contra lectura f; —**/write file** archivo de lectura/ escritura m
readable [rídəbəl] ADJ (legible) legible; (nice to read) ameno
reader [rídə] N (person who reads) lector -ora mf; (schoolbook) libro de lectura m, cartilla f; (anthology) antología f
readership [rídəʃip] N lectores m pl
readily [rédli] ADV fácilmente
readiness [rédinis] N estado de preparación m; (willingness) buena disposición f; **to be in** — estar preparado, estar listo
reading [rídɪŋ] N lectura f; (interpretation) interpretación f; — **room** sala de lectura f

readjust [riəʤʌ́st] VI/VT (improve fit) reajustar; (acclimate) readaptar

readjustment [riəʤʌ́stmənt] N (fitting) reajuste m; (acclimation) readaptación f

ready [rédi] ADJ (prepared) listo, preparado, pronto; (willing) dispuesto; (available) disponible; (quick) rápido; —-**made** de confección

reaffirm [riəfɚ́m] VT reafirmar

reagent [riéʤənt] ADJ & N reactivo m

real [ril] ADJ real, verdadero; — **estate** bienes raíces m pl, bienes inmuebles m pl; — **time** tiempo real m

realism [ríəlizəm] N realismo m

realist [ríəlist] N realista mf

realistic [riəlístik] ADJ realista

reality [riǽliɾi] N realidad f; — **check** ajuste de perspectiva m

realization [riəlizéʃən] N (making real) realización f; (understanding) comprensión f

realize [ríəlaiz] VT (achieve) realizar; (comprehend) darse cuenta [de], comprobar, percatarse [de]

really [rili] ADV (extremely) realmente; (truly) verdaderamente; (as question) ¿de veras? ¿verdad? **he's not — a lawyer** en realidad, no es abogado / no es abogado de verdad; **it's — hot in Seville** hace mucho calor en Sevilla; **she's a — good colleague** es una colega superbuena / es una buenísima colega

realm [rɛlm] N (kingdom) reino m; (domain) terreno m, esfera f

realtor™ [ríəltɚ] N agente inmobiliario -ria mf

reap [rip] VI/VT (cut with sickle) segar; (harvest) cosechar; **to — a benefit** obtener beneficio, sacar provecho

reaper [rípɚ] N (person) segador -ora mf; (machine) segadora f; (death) la Parca, la Muerte

reappear [riəpír] VI reaparecer

rear [rir] ADJ trasero, posterior; —**guard** retaguardia f; N (space at the back) parte de atrás f, fondo m; (backside) trasero m, posaderas f pl; — **end** trasero m; —**view mirror** espejo retrovisor m; VT (raise) criar; VI (rise on back legs) encabritarse, empinarse

reason [rízən] N (faculty) razón f; (cause) motivo m, razón f; **by — of** por causa de; **it stands to —** es lógico; VT razonar; **to — out** resolver por medio de la razón; **to — with** hacer entrar en razón

reasonable [rízənəbəl] ADJ razonable; (in price) módico, moderado

reasoning [ríznɪŋ] N razonamiento m, raciocinio m; ADJ racional

reassert [riəsɚ́t] VT reafirmar

reassure [riəʃúr] VT tranquilizar

rebate [ríbet] N reembolso m, reintegro m; VT reembolsar, reintegrar

rebel[1] [rébəl] ADJ & N rebelde mf, insurrecto -ta mf

rebel[2] [rɪbɛ́l] VI rebelarse

rebellion [rɪbɛ́ljən] N rebelión f

rebellious [rɪbɛ́ljəs] ADJ rebelde, insurrecto

rebelliousness [rɪbɛ́ljəsnɪs] N rebeldía f

reboot [ribút] VT reiniciar

rebound[1] [ribáund] VI (bounce) rebotar; (catch a rebound) rebotear; (recover) recuperarse

rebound[2] [ríbaund] N (bounce) rebote m; (recovery) recuperación f; **on the —** de rebote

rebuff [rɪbʌ́f] N desaire m, repulsa f; VT desairar, rechazar

rebuild [ribíld] VI/VT reconstruir, reedificar; (car engine) reacondicionar

rebuke [rɪbjúk] VT reprender, reprochar; N reproche m, reprimenda f

recall[1] [rɪkɔ́l] VT (remember) recordar; (call back) retirar; (remove from office) destituir

recall[2] [ríkɔl] N (memory) memoria f; (of a diplomat, product) retirada f; (from office) destitución f

recapitulate [rikəpítʃəlet] VI/VT recapitular

recast [rikǽst] VT refundir

recede [rɪsíd] VI retroceder; (of hairline) tener entradas

receipt [rɪsít] N recibo m; **upon — of** el recibo de; —**s** entradas f pl, ingresos m pl

receivable [rɪsívəbəl] ADJ a cobrar

receive [rɪsív] VI/VT recibir; (suggestions) acoger, recibir; (a broadcast) captar, recibir

receiver [rɪsívɚ] N recibidor -ora mf; (of a telephone) auricular m; (of a television or radio, in football) receptor m; (in tennis) restador -ora mf; (of a bankrupt business) síndico m

recent [rísənt] ADJ reciente

receptacle [rɪsɛ́ptəkəl] N receptáculo m

reception [rɪsɛ́pʃən] N (hotel, social event, TV) recepción f; (act of receiving) recibimiento m, acogida f; — **room** recibidor m

recess [ríses] N (niche) nicho m; (pause) descanso m; (playtime) recreo m; **in the —es of** en lo más recóndito de; VI/VT (a meeting) interrumpir; VT (a wall) hacer un nicho en

recession [rɪsɛ́ʃən] N (act of receding) retroceso m; (economic) recesión f

recessive gene [rɪsɛ́sɪvʤin] N gen recesivo m

recidivism [rɪsídəvɪzəm] N reincidencia f

recipe [résəpi] N receta f

recipient [rɪsípiənt] N destinatario -ria mf

reciprocal [rɪsíprəkəl] ADJ recíproco

reciprocate [rɪsíprəket] VI/VT corresponder [a], Am reciprocar

recital [rɪsáɪɾl] N recital m

recitation [resɪtéʃən] N recitación f

recite [rɪsáɪt] VI/VT recitar

reckless [réklɪs] ADJ (driver) temerario,

imprudente; (speed) desenfrenado

recklessness [réklısnıs] N temeridad f, imprudencia f

reckon [rékən] VI/VT (calculate) calcular; (consider) considerar; (think) suponer

reckoning [rékənıŋ] N (computation) cálculo m; (settlement of accounts) ajuste de cuentas m; **the day of —** el día del juicio m

reclaim [rıklém] VT (win back, recover) recuperar; (make land usable) ganar, sanear

recline [rıkláın] VI/VT reclinar[se], recostar[se]

recluse [réklus] ADJ & N solitario -ria mf, ermitaño -ña mf

recognition [rekəgníʃən] N reconocimiento m

recognizable [rekəgnáızəbəl] ADJ reconocible

recognize [rékəgnaız] VT reconocer

recoil¹ [rıkóıl] VI (firearm) dar un culatazo; (move back) retroceder

recoil² [ríkoıl] N (of a gun) culatazo m; (move back) retroceso m

recollect [rekəlékt] VI/VT recordar

recollection [rekəlékʃən] N recuerdo m

recommend [rekəménd] VI/VT recomendar

recommendation [rekəmɛndéʃən] N recomendación f

recompense [rékəmpɛns] VI/VT recompensar; N recompensa f

reconcile [rékənsaıl] VT (persons) reconciliar; (statements) conciliar; **to — oneself to** resignarse a, conformarse con

reconciliation [rekənsıliéʃən] N reconciliación f

reconnoiter [rikənóıɖɚ] VT reconocer; VI hacer un reconocimiento

reconsider [rikənsíɖɚ] VI/VT reconsiderar

reconstruct [rikənstrákt] VT reconstruir

reconstruction [rikənstrákʃən] N reconstrucción f

record¹ [rékəd] N (account) registro m, asiento m; (account of a meeting) acta f; (of criminal acts) antecedentes m pl; (of past activities) historial m, hoja de servicios f; (phonographic) disco m; (best performance) récord m, plusmarca f; **— player** tocadiscos m sg; **off the —** extraoficialmente

record² [rıkórd] VI/VT (write down) registrar, apuntar; (cut a recording) grabar

recorder [rıkórɖɚ] N (archivist) archivero -ra mf; (sound device) grabadora f; (musical instrument) flauta dulce f

recording [rıkórdıŋ] N grabación f; **— company** grabadora f

recount¹ [rıkáunt] VT (tell) narrar, relatar

recount² [ríkaunt] VT (count again) recontar

recoup [rıkúp] VI/VT recuperar

recourse [ríkɔrs] N recurso m; **to have — to** recurrir a

recover [rıkávɚ] VI/VT recobrar[se], recuperar[se]; VI (lost health) restablecerse; VT (lost time, property) recuperar; (damages) obtener indemnización

recovery [rıkávəri] N (from an illness) recuperación f; (of investments) amortización f; (through a lawsuit) indemnización f; **— room** sala de recuperación f

recreation [rekriéʃən] N recreación f, recreo m, esparcimiento m

recreational [rekriéʃənəl] ADJ recreativo, de recreo; **— vehicle** caravana f

recriminate [rıkrímənet] VI/VT recriminar

recruit [rıkrút] N recluta mf; VI/VT reclutar

recruitment [rıkrútmənt] N reclutamiento m, recluta f

rectangle [réktæŋgəl] N rectángulo m

rectangular [rektǽŋgjələ-] ADJ rectangular

rectify [réktəfaı] VT rectificar

rector [réktɚ] N rector -ora mf

rectum [réktəm] N recto m

recuperate [rıkúpəret] VI/VT recuperar[se], recobrar[se]

recur [rıkɚ́] VI volver a ocurrir, repetirse

recurring [rıkɚ́ıŋ] ADJ recurrente

recycle [risáıkəl] VI/VT reciclar

recycling [risáıklıŋ] N reciclaje m

red [red] ADJ & N rojo m, colorado m; **— blood cell** glóbulo rojo m; **— card** tarjeta roja f; **—-handed** fam in fraganti; **—headed** pelirrojo; **—-hot** candente, al rojo vivo; **— light** luz roja f; **—neck** granjero -ra blanco -ca pobre mf; **— pepper** pimienta de cayena f; **— prawn** carabinero m; **— snapper** pargo m; **— tape** trámites m pl; **— wine** vino tinto m; **—wood** secoya/secuoya f; **in the —** en números rojos; **to see —** enfurecerse

redden [rédn] VI/VT enrojecer, ruborizar[se]

reddish [rédıʃ] ADJ rojizo, bermejo

redeem [rıdím] VT (deliver from sin) redimir; (pay off a mortgage) cancelar; (buy back from pawnshop) desempeñar; (exchange) canjear; (fulfill) cumplir

redemption [rıdémpʃən] N redención f; (of something pawned) desempeño m

redevelopment [ridıvéləpmənt] N remodelación f

redness [rédnıs] N rojez f; (inflammation) inflamación f

redress¹ [rídres] N reparación f, desagravio m

redress² [rıdrés] VT reparar, desagraviar

reduce [rıdús] VI/VT reducir[se]; **she was —d to tears** se echó a llorar

reduction [rıdákʃən] N reducción f

redundant [rıdándənt] ADJ (repetitive) redundante; (superfluous) superfluo

reed [rid] N caña f, junco m, carrizo m; (of a musical instrument) lengüeta f

reef [rif] N (underwater ridge) escollo m; (of coral) arrecife m

reek [rik] VI heder, apestar; N hedor m

reel [ril] N carrete m, bobina f; VT (on a spool)

bobinar; VI tambalearse; **to — off** recitar; **to
— in a fish** sacar un pez del agua
reelect [riilékt] VT reelegir
reelection [riilékʃən] N reelección f
reemployment [riimplɔ́imənt] N reinserción
laboral f
reestablish [riistǽbliʃ] VT restablecer
refer [rifɚ́] VI/VT referir; (direct to a source of
information) remitir; (direct to a doctor)
mandar; (mention) referirse a, aludir a
referee [refəri] N árbitro m; VT (a game) arbitrar;
(a submission) hacer el referato
reference [réfərəns] N (mention) referencia f;
— book libro de consulta m; **with — to** con
respecto a, respecto de
referendum [refəréndəm] N referéndum m
referral [rifɚ́əl] N **he gave me a — to a
specialist** me mandó con/a un especialista
refill[1] [rifíl] VI/VT rellenar
refill[2] [rifíl] N (for a pen) repuesto m; (for a
lighter) carga f; **may I have a —?** ¿me sirve
más?
refinance [rifáinæns] VI/VT refinanciar
refine [rifáin] VT (purify) refinar; (polish)
refinar, pulir
refined [rifáind] ADJ refinado
refinement [rifáinmənt] N (of manners)
refinamiento m, pulimento m; (of oil)
refinación f
refinery [rifáinəri] N (of oil) refinería f; (of
sugar) ingenio m
reflect [riflékt] VI/VT (mirror) reflejar; VI
(ponder) reflexionar; **to — poorly on**
desacreditar
reflection [riflékʃən] N (image) reflejo m;
(consideration) reflexión f; (unfavorable
observation) tacha f; **on —** pensándolo bien
reflector [rifléktɚ] N reflector m
reflex [rifleks] ADJ & N reflejo m
reflexive [rifléksiv] ADJ reflexivo
reflux [rifləks] N reflujo m
reform [rifɔ́rm] VI/VT reformar[se]; N reforma f
reformation [refɚméʃən] N reforma f
reformatory [rifɔ́rmətɔri] N reformatorio m
reformer [rifɔ́rmɚ] N reformador -ora mf,
reformista mf
refraction [rifrǽkʃən] N refracción f
refractory [rifrǽktəri] ADJ (not malleable)
refractario; (rebellious) rebelde
refrain [rifrén] VI abstenerse; N (of a song)
estribillo m
refresh [rifréʃ] VI/VT refrescar[se]; (computer
screen) actualizar, refrescar
refreshing [rifréʃiŋ] ADJ (drink) refrescante;
(sleep) reparador; (honesty) agradable
refreshment [rifréʃmənt] N (drink) refresco m;
(food) refrigerio m
refrigerate [rifrídʒəret] VT refrigerar
refrigeration [rifridʒɚréʃən] N refrigeración f

refrigerator [rifrídʒəredɚ] N frigorífico m,
nevera f, refrigerador m; RP heladera f
refuge [réfjudʒ] N refugio m; **to give —** dar
albergue
refugee [refjudʒí] N refugiado -da mf
refund[1] [rífʌnd] N reembolso m
refund[2] [rifʌ́nd] VT reembolsar
refurbish [rifɚ́biʃ] VT restaurar
refusal [rifjúzəl] N negativa f, rechazo m; **first
— option** f
refuse[1] [rifjúz] VI/VT (deny a request) negar[se]
[a]; **to — to** rehusarse a, negarse a; VT (decline
to accept) rechazar, no aceptar
refuse[2] [réfjus] N desechos m pl, desperdicios m
pl
refute [rifjút] VT refutar, rebatir
regain [rigén] VT (recover) recobrar; (get back
to) volver a
regal [rígəl] ADJ regio, real
regard [rigárd] VT (consider) considerar;
(esteem) estimar; N (consideration)
consideración f; (esteem) respeto m, estima f;
—s recuerdos m pl, saludos m pl; **as —s** en
cuanto a; **with — to** con respecto a
regarding [rigárdiŋ] PREP con respecto a
regardless [rigárdlis] ADV LOC **— of**
independientemente de
regenerate [ridʒénəret] VI/VT regenerar[se]
regent [rídʒənt] N regente -ta mf
reggae [régé] N reggae m
regime [riʒím] N régimen m
regiment [rédʒəmənt] N regimiento m
region [rídʒən] N región f
regional [rídʒənl] ADJ regional
register [rédʒistɚ] N (recording, range of voice)
registro m; (entry) asiento m; VI/VT (enter
into a list) registrar[se]; (enroll)
matricular[se], inscribir[se]; VT (indicate)
indicar, registrar; (a letter) certificar; VI
(appear) aparecer; **that didn't —** no cayó en
la cuenta
registered [rédʒistɚd] ADJ registrado; **— mail**
correo certificado m; **— nurse** enfermero -ra
titulado -da mf; **— trademark** marca
registrada f
registrar [rédʒistrar] N secretario -ria de
admisiones mf
registration [redʒistréʃən] N (of a car) matrícula
f; (of a student) inscripción f
regret [rigrét] VT (feel sorry) lamentar; (feel
rueful) arrepentirse de; N arrepentimiento m;
to send —s enviar sus excusas
regretful [rigrétfəl] ADJ lleno de
remordimientos
regrettable [rigrétəbəl] ADJ lamentable
regroup [rigrúp] VT reagrupar; VI reorganizarse
regular [régjələr] ADJ (symmetrical, uniform)
regular; (normal) normal; (habitual)
habitual; **a — fool** un verdadero necio; **a —**

guy un buen tipo; (habitual customer) parroquiano -na *mf*; (soldier) soldado de línea *m*

regularity [regjəlǽrɪɒi] N regularidad *f*

regulate [régjələt] VT (control) regular; (make regular) regularizar

regulation [regjəléʃən] N (act of regulating) regulación *f*; **—s** reglamento *m*, reglamentación *f*

regulator [régjəleɒəʳ] N regulador *m*

regurgitate [rɪgɝ́dʒɪtet] VI/VT regurgitar

rehabilitate [rihəbílɪtet] VI/VT rehabilitar[se]

rehabilitation [riəbɪlɪtéʃən] N rehabilitación *f*

rehearsal [rɪhɝ́səl] N ensayo *m*

rehearse [rɪhɝ́s] VI/VT ensayar

reign [ren] N reino *m*, reinado *m*; VI reinar

reimburse [riɪmbɝ́s] VI/VT reembolsar

reimbursement [riɪmbɝ́smənt] N reembolso *m*

rein [ren] N rienda *f* (also control); VI **to — in** dominar, refrenar

reincarnation [riɪnkɑrnéʃən] N reencarnación *f*

reindeer [réndɪr] N reno *m*

reinforce [riɪnfɔ́rs] VT reforzar

reinforcement [riɪnfɔ́rsmənt] N refuerzo *m*, reforzado *m*

reinsertion [riɪnsɝ́ʃən] N reinserción *f*

reinstate [riɪnstét] VT reinstaurar

reiterate [rɪíɒəret] VT reiterar

reject¹ [rɪdʒɛ́kt] VT rechazar

reject² [rɪdʒɛkt] N (thing) cosa rechazada *f*, desecho *m*; (person) rechazado -da *mf*

rejoice [rɪdʒɔ́ɪs] VI regocijarse

rejoicing [rɪdʒɔ́ɪsɪŋ] N regocijo *m*

rejoin [rɪdʒɔ́ɪn] VT (come again into a group) reincorporarse a; VI/VT (reunite) volver a unir[se]

rejuvenate [rɪdʒúvənet] VI/VT rejuvenecer

relapse¹ [rɪlǽps] VI (into bad health) recaer; (into crime) reincidir

relapse² [rɪlǽps] N (into bad health) recaída *f*, recidiva *f*; (into crime) reincidencia *f*

relate [rɪlét] VT (tell) relatar, narrar; (connect) relacionar; VI **to — to** relacionarse con

related [rɪlédɪd] ADJ (connected) relacionado; (kin) emparentado

relation [rɪléʃən] N (association) relación *f*; (act of narrating) narración *f*; (kinship) parentesco *m*; (relative) pariente -ta *mf*; **with — to** con respecto a

relationship [rɪléʃənʃɪp] N relación *f*

relative [rélətɪv] ADJ relativo; N pariente -ta *mf*, allegado -da *mf*; **— to** relativo a, referente a

relativity [relətívɪɒi] N relatividad *f*

relax [rɪlǽks] VI/VT relajar[se], distender[se]; VT (grip) aflojar

relaxation [rilækséʃən] N (recreation) esparcimiento *m*, recreo *m*; (loosening) relajamiento *m*, relajación *f*

relay¹ [ríle] N relevo *m*, posta *f*; (electrical) relé

m; **— race** carrera de relevos/postas *f*

relay² [rile, rɪlé] VT transmitir; **to — a broadcast** transmitir un programa

release [rɪlís] VT (let go) soltar; (free prisoners) librar, poner en libertad; (energy) liberar; (news) divulgar; (discharge from hospital) dar de alta; N (liberation) liberación *f*; (permission) permiso *m*; (of film) estreno *m*; (of gas) escape *m*; (of energy) desprendimiento *m*

relegate [rélɪget] VT relegar

relent [rɪlɛ́nt] VI aplacarse

relentless [rɪlɛ́ntlɪs] ADJ implacable

relevant [rélərvənt] ADJ pertinente

reliability [rɪlaɪəbílɪɒi] N fiabilidad *f*, confiabilidad *f*

reliable [rɪláɪəbəl] ADJ fiable, confiable; (a person) formal

reliance [rɪláɪəns] N (dependency) dependencia *f*; (trust) confianza *f*

relic [rélɪk] N reliquia *f*

relief [rɪlíf] N (ease) alivio *m*; (aid) ayuda *f*; (projection) relieve *m*; (soldier) relevo *m*; (in golf) alivio *m*; **in —** en relieve; **— map** mapa en relieve *m*

relieve [rɪlív] VT (alleviate) aliviar; (free) liberar; (replace) relevar; VI **to — oneself** orinar

reliever [rɪlívəʳ] N (baseball) relevista *mf*

religion [rɪlídʒən] N religión *f*

religious [rɪlídʒəs] ADJ religioso

relinquish [rɪlíŋkwɪʃ] VT (give up) renunciar; (let go) soltar

relish [rélɪʃ] VT (to like the taste) saborear, paladear; (enjoy) disfrutar; N (enjoyment) gusto *m*; (condiment) condimento de pepinillos en vinagre *m*

relocate [rilóket] VI/VT trasladar[se]

reluctance [rɪláktəns] N renuencia *f*

reluctant [rɪláktənt] ADJ renuente, reacio

rely [rɪláɪ] VI **to — on** (trust) confiar en; (depend on) depender de

REM [rapid eye movement] [áriém] N REM *m*, MOR *m pl*

remain [rɪmén] VI (continue to be) seguir siendo; (stay) quedar[se], permanecer; (to be left) quedar, restar; (to be left over) sobrar; N **—s** restos *m pl*

remainder [rɪméndəʳ] N (extra) sobrante, (other) restante

remake¹ [rɪmék] VT rehacer; (film) hacer de nuevo

remake² [rímek] N nueva versión *f*

remark [rɪmɑ́rk] VT (comment) comentar, observar; (notice) notar, observar; **to — on** comentar; N observación *f*, comentario *m*

remarkable [rɪmɑ́rkəbəl] ADJ notable

remedial [rɪmídɪəl] ADJ (rehabilitative) rehabilitador; (to improve skills) de recuperación

remedy [rémıdı] N (solution) remedio m; (cure) cura f; VT (solve) remediar, subsanar; (heal) curar

remember [rımémbə] VI/VT recordar, acordarse [de]; — **me to him** mándale saludos míos

remind [rımáınd] VT recordar

reminder [rımáındə] N (of a date, deadline) recordatorio m; (warning) advertencia f

reminiscence [remənísəns] N reminiscencia f, recuerdo m

remiss [rımís] ADJ negligente

remission [rımíʃən] N remisión f

remit [rımít] VI/VT remitir

remittance [rımítns] N remesa f, giro m

remnant [rémnənt] N (remainder) resto m; (of fabric) retazo m, retal m; (vestige) vestigio m

remodel [rimádl] VI/VT remodelar

remodeling [rimádlıŋ] N remodelación f

remorse [rımórs] N remordimiento m

remote [rımót] ADJ (far away) remoto, recóndito; (aloof) distante; (in kinship) lejano; — **access** acceso remoto m; — **control** control remoto m, mando a distancia m; — **login** acceso remoto m; — **server** servidor remoto m

removal [rımúvəł] N (dismissal) deposición f, alejamiento m; (elimination) eliminación f; (extirpation) extirpación f

remove [rımúv] VT (an obstacle) remover; (take away, take off) quitar; (dismiss) deponer; (eliminate) eliminar; (extirpate) extirpar; **to — from office** separar/apartar del cargo

remunerate [rımjúnəret] VT remunerar f, retribuir f

remuneration [rımjunəréʃən] N remuneración f, retribución f

renaissance [rénısns] N renacimiento m; — **architecture** arquitectura renacentista f

renal [rínl] ADJ renal; — **failure** insuficiencia renal f

rend [rend] VI/VT desgarrar[se], rajar[se]

render [réndə] VT (give) dar; (cause to become) dejar; (depict) representar; (translate) traducir; (give homage, account) rendir; (provide services, assistance) prestar; (melt down fat) derretir; (deliver a verdict) pronunciar; **to — useless** inutilizar

rendition [rendíʃən] N (translation) traducción f; (interpretation) interpretación f, versión f

renegade [rénıged] N renegado -da mf

renegotiate [rınıgóʃiet] VI/VT renegociar

renegue [rıníg] VI incumplir

renew [rınú] VT (vows, contract) renovar; (furniture) restaurar; (friendship, effort) reanudar; (a loan) prorrogar

renewable [rınúəbł] ADJ renovable

renewal [rınúəł] N (of vows, contract) renovación f; (of furniture) restauración f; (of a city) remodelación f; (of friendship, effort) reanudación f; (of loan) prórroga f

renounce [rınáuns] VT (give up) renunciar a; (repudiate) repudiar, renegar de

renovate [rénəvet] VT renovar

renown [rınáun] N renombre m

renowned [rınáund] ADJ renombrado

rent [rent] N (monthly payment) alquiler m, arrendamiento m; **for —** se alquila, se arrienda; (fissure) rajadura f, hendidura f; (tear) rasgadura f; VI/VT (lease) alquilar, arrendar

rent [rent] see rend

rental [réntł] ADJ de alquiler; — **agreement** contrato de alquiler m; N alquiler m, arrendamiento m

renter [réntə] N inquilino -na mf

renunciation [rınʌnsiéʃən] N renuncia f

reopen [riópən] VI/VT (doors) reabrir[se]; (negotiations) reanudar[se]

reorganization [riorgənizéʃən] N reorganización f

reorganize [riórgənaız] VI/VT reorganizar[se]

repaginate [ripǽdʒınet] VT repaginar

repair [rıpér] VT (fix) reparar, arreglar, componer; (shoes) remendar; **to — to** acudir a; N (fixing) reparación f; (of shoes) remiendo m, compostura f; **in good —** en buen estado; **—man** técnico en reparaciones m

reparation [repəréʃən] N reparación f, indemnización f

repay [rıpé] VT (return money, favor) devolver; (pay off) pagar

repayment [rıpémənt] N (of a sum) reembolso m; (of a loan) pago m

repeal [rıpíl] VT derogar, revocar, abrogar; N derogación f, revocación f, abrogación f

repeat[1] [rıpít] VI/VT repetir; N repetición f

repeat[2] [rıpít] N repetición f

repeated [rıpídıd] ADJ repetido

repel [rıpéł] VI/VT repeler; (an attack) rechazar

repellent [rıpéłənt] ADJ & N repelente m

repent [rıpént] VI/VT arrepentirse [de]

repentance [rıpéntəns] N arrepentimiento m

repentant [rıpéntənt] ADJ arrepentido, pesaroso

repercussion [repəkáʃən] N repercusión f; **to have —s** repercutir

repertoire [répətwar] N repertorio m

repetition [repıtíʃən] N repetición f

replace [rıplés] VT (place again) volver a colocar; (substitute for) sustituir, reemplazar; (provide a substitute for) reponer

replaceable [rıplésəbəł] ADJ reemplazable, sustituible

replacement [rıplésmənt] N (substitute, substitution) sustituto m, reemplazo m; (making up for) reposición f; — **parts** piezas de repuesto f pl

replenish [rıplénıʃ] VI/VT (supply) reabastecer;

(fill again) rellenar
replete [rɪplít] ADJ repleto
replica [réplɪkə] N réplica f
replicate [réplɪket] VT reproducir, replicar
replication [replɪkéʃən] N reproducción f, replicación f
reply [rɪpláɪ] VI replicar, contestar; N réplica f, contestación f
report [rɪpɔ́rt] VT (recount) relatar; (make a crime known, denounce) denunciar; (make an accident known) dar parte de; VI hacer un informe, informar; **to — for duty** presentarse; **to — on** hacer un informe sobre; **to — sick** dar parte de enfermo, reportarse enfermo; **it is —ed that** se dice que; N informe m, comunicado m; (rumor) rumor m; (loud noise) estallido m; **— card** boletín de calificaciones m
reportedly [rɪpɔ́rdɪdli] ADV según se informa
reporter [rɪpɔ́rdə] N (news) reportero -ra mf; (sports) cronista mf
repose [rɪpóz] VI/VT reposar, descansar; N reposo m, descanso m
repository [rɪpázɪtɔri] N (object) depósito m; (person) depositario -ria mf
repossess [ripəzés] VT retomar posesión de
represent [reprɪzént] VT representar
representation [reprɪzentéʃən] N representación f
representative [reprɪzéntədɪv] ADJ representativo; N representante mf
repress [rɪprés] VI/VT reprimir
repression [rɪpréʃən] N represión f
repressive [rɪprésɪv] ADJ represivo
reprieve [rɪprív] VT (pardon) indultar; (commute) conmutar; (delay) aplazar; N (pardon) indulto m; (commutation) conmutación f; (delay) aplazamiento m
reprimand [réprəmænd] N reprimenda f, regaño m; VT reprender, regañar
reprint[1] [riprínt] VI/VT reimprimir
reprint[2] [ríprɪnt] N (action, result) reimpresión f; (offprint) separata f
reprisal [rɪpráɪzəl] N represalia f
reproach [rɪpróʧ] VT reprochar; N reproche m
reproduce [riprədús] VI/VT reproducir[se]
reproduction [riprədákʃən] N reproducción f
reproof [rɪprúf] N reprobación f
reprove [rɪprúv] VT reprobar
reptile [réptaɪl] N reptil m
republic [rɪpáblɪk] N república f
republican [rɪpáblɪkən] ADJ & N republicano -na mf
repudiate [rɪpjúdiet] VT repudiar
repugnance [rɪpágnəns] N repugnancia f
repugnant [rɪpágnənt] ADJ repugnante
repulse [rɪpáls] VT repeler, rechazar; N repulsa f, rechazo m
repulsive [rɪpálsɪv] ADJ repulsivo

reputable [répjədəbəl] ADJ reputado
reputation [repjətéʃən] N reputación f, fama f
request [rɪkwést] N solicitud f, petición f, requerimiento m; **at the — of** a solicitud de, a instancias de; VT solicitar, pedir
require [rɪkwáɪr] VI/VT (need) requerir; (demand) exigir
requirement [rɪkwáɪrmənt] N (demand) requisito m; (need) necesidad f
requisite [rékwɪzɪt] ADJ requerido, necesario; N requisito m
requisition [rekwɪzíʃən] N (taking over) requisa f; (order) pedido m; VT (take over) requisar; (order) pedir
rerun [rírʌn] N refrito m
rescind [rɪsínd] VT rescindir
rescue [réskju] VT rescatar, salvar; N rescate m, salvamento m; **to go to the — of** acudir al socorro de, salir al quite de
research[1] [rísəʧ] N investigación f
research[2] [rísəʧ] VI/VT investigar
researcher [rísəʧə] N investigador -ora mf
resell [risél] VT revender
resemblance [rɪzémbləns] N semejanza f, parecido m
resemble [rɪzémbəl] VT semejar, asemejarse a, parecerse a
resent [rɪzént] VT resentirse de
resentful [rɪzéntfəl] ADJ resentido, rencoroso
resentment [rɪzéntmənt] N resentimiento m
reservation [rezəvéʃən] N reserva f; Am reservación f; **to have one's —s** tener reservas
reserve [rɪzɘ́v] VT reservar; N reserva f; (shyness) pudor m
reserved [rɪzɘ́vd] ADJ reservado
reservoir [rézəvwɑr] N (tank) depósito m, alberca f; (artificial lake) embalse m, represa f
reset [risét] VT (computer, machine) reiniciar; **— key** tecla de reinicio f
reside [rɪzáɪd] VI residir
residence [rézɪdəns] N residencia f
resident [rézɪdənt] ADJ & N residente mf; (of a neighborhood) vecino -na mf
residential [rezɪdénʃəl] ADJ residencial
residue [rézɪdu] N residuo m
resign [rɪzáɪn] VI/VT renunciar [a], dimitir [de]; **to — oneself to** resignarse a
resignation [rezɪgnéʃən] N (act of resigning an office) renuncia f, dimisión f; (accepting attitude) resignación f; **— letter** carta de renuncia f
resilience [rɪzíljəns] N (elasticity) elasticidad f; (adaptability) adaptabilidad f
resilient [rɪzíljənt] ADJ (elastic) elástico; (adaptable) adaptable
resin [rézɪn] N resina f
resist [rɪzíst] VT (a temptation) resistir; VI/VT (tyranny) resistirse [a]

resistance [rɪzístəns] N resistencia f
resistant [rɪzístənt] ADJ resistente
resolute [rézəlut] ADJ resuelto, decidido
resolution [rezəlúʃən] N resolución f
resolve [rɪzálv] VI/VT resolver[se]; **to — into**
convertirse en; **to — to** decidir, resolver; N
resolución f
resonance [rézənəns] N resonancia f
resonate [rézənet] VI/VT resonar
resort [rɪzɔ́rt] N (seaside) centro de veraneo m;
(for skiing) estación de esquí f; **as a last —**
como último recurso; VI **to — to** recurrir a
resound [rɪzáʊnd] VI/VT resonar; **—ing victory**
victoria contundente f
resource [rísɔrs] N recurso m
resourceful [rɪzɔ́rsfəl] ADJ ingenioso
respect [rɪspékt] VT respetar; N (esteem) respeto
m; (detail) aspecto m; **with — to** [con]
respecto a, respecto de
respectable [rɪspéktəbəl] ADJ respetable
respectful [rɪspéktfəl] ADJ respetuoso
respective [rɪspéktɪv] ADJ respectivo
respiration [respəréʃən] N respiración f
respiratory [réspəətɔri] ADJ respiratorio; **—
failure** insuficiencia respiratoria f
respite [réspɪt] N (pause) respiro f, tregua m;
(postponement) prórroga f
resplendent [rɪspléndənt] ADJ resplandeciente,
refulgente
respond [rɪspánd] VI/VT responder
respondent [rɪspándənt] N (to a lawsuit)
demandado -da mf; (to a poll) encuestado -da
mf
response [rɪspáns] N respuesta f
responsibility [rɪspansəbílɪɾi] N
responsabilidad f, reivindicación f
responsible [rɪspánsəbəl] ADJ responsable
rest [rest] N (repose) descanso m, reposo m;
(musical) pausa f; (support) apoyo m;
(remainder) resto m; **— home** (for
convalescents) casa de reposo f; (for the aged)
casa de ancianos f; **— room** servicio m; Sp
aseo m; **an object at —** un objeto en reposo;
VI/VT descansar, reposar; VT (one's gaze)
posar; (against a wall) reclinar; VI (stop)
parar; **to — on** depender de; **let it —** déjalo
en paz
restaurant [réstərənt] N restaurante m; Am
restorán m
restitution [restɪtúʃən] N restitución f
restless [réstlɪs] ADJ (worried) inquieto,
(fidgety) movedizo
restlessness [réstlɪsnɪs] N inquietud f,
desasosiego m
restoration [restəréʃən] N restauración f
restore [rɪstɔ́r] VT restaurar
restrain [rɪstrén] VT (hold back) refrenar,
contener, moderar; (bring under control)
reducir; **—ing order** medida cautelar f

restraint [rɪstrént] N (self-control) compostura
f, moderación f; (device) seguro m; **under —**
bajo control
restrict [rɪstríkt] VT restringir; (someone's
liberty) coartar
restriction [rɪstríkʃən] N restricción f
restructuring [ristráktʃəɪŋ] N reestructuración f
result [rɪzált] VI resultar; **to — from** resultar
de; **to — in** dar por resultado; N resultado m;
as a — de resultas, como resultado
resume [rɪzúm] VI/VT (take up again) reasumir,
volver a asumir; (continue) reanudar
résumé [rézume] N currículum m, historial
personal m
resurrection [rezərékʃən] N resurrección f
resuscitate [rɪsásɪtet] VI/VT resucitar
resuscitation [rɪsasɪtéʃən] N resucitación f
retail [rítel] N venta al por menor f; **— store**
tienda minorista f; **— trade** comercio
minorista m; VI/VT vender al por menor; **at —**
al por menor, al menudeo
retailer [rítelə·] N minorista mf, detallista mf
retain [rɪtén] VT (recall, confine, detain) retener;
(keep) conservar, quedarse con; (hire)
contratar
retainer [rɪténə·] N (device that holds back)
retén m; (payment) honorarios pagados por
adelantado m pl
retaliate [rɪtǽliet] VI vengarse
retaliation [rɪtæliéʃən] N venganza f
retard [rɪtárd] VI/VT retardar
retarded [rɪtárdɪd] ADJ retrasado
retention [rɪténʃən] N retención f
reticence [réɖɪsəns] N reserva f
retina [rétnə] N retina f
retinue [rétnu] N séquito m, comitiva f
retire [rɪtáɪr] VI/VT (stop working) retirar[se],
jubilar[se]; (withdraw) retirar[se]; (go to bed)
acostarse; (withdraw money, troops,
machines) retirar
retiree [rɪtairí] N jubilado -da mf
retirement [rɪtáɪrmənt] N retiro m, jubilación f;
— of debt retiro de deuda m
retort [rɪtɔ́rt] N (reply) réplica f; (vessel) retorta f
retouch [rɪtʌ́tʃ] VT retocar; N retoque m
retrace [ritrés] VT (mental steps) repasar; (one's
route) volver sobre
retract [rɪtrǽkt] VT (a statement) retractar;
(claws) retraer[se]; VI desdecirse, retractarse
retreat [rɪtrít] N (place of refuge, period of
meditation) retiro m, refugio m; (military)
retirada f, repliegue m; (bugle call) retreta f;
VI batirse en retirada, retroceder, replegarse
retrench [rɪtréntʃ] VI economizar
retrieval [rɪtrívəl] N recuperación f
retrieve [rɪtrív] VT (game animals) cobrar;
(something lost) recuperar
retriever [rɪtrívə·] N perro cobrador m
retro [rétro] ADJ retro

retroactive [rɛtroǽktɪv] ADJ retroactivo

retrospect [rétrəspɛkt] ADV LOC **in**— mirando para atrás

retrovirus [rétrovaɪrəs] N retrovirus *m*

return [rɪtɜ́n] VI (come back) volver, regresar; VT (put back) devolver, retornar; (deliver a verdict) fallar; **— to sender** devolver al remitente; N (to a place) vuelta *f*, regreso *m*; (of a thing) devolución *f*; (of profit) ganancia *f*; (on a typewriter) retorno de carro *m*; (on a computer) retroceso *m*, salto de línea *m*; — **address** señas del remitente *f pl*; — **game** revancha *f*; — **key** tecla de retorno *f*, tecla de retroceso *f*; — **of service** (tennis) resto *m*; — **ticket** billete de vuelta *m*; **by — mail** a vuelta de correo; **election —s** resultados electorales *m pl*; **in** — a cambio; **in — for** a cambio de; **income tax** — *Sp* declaración de la renta *f*; *Am* declaración de impuestos *f*

reunification [rijunɪfɪkéʃən] N reunificación *f*

reunion [rijúnjən] N reunión *f*

reunite [rijunáɪt] VI/VT reunir[se]

rev [rɛv] VI/VT acelerar en vacío

reveal [rɪvíł] VT revelar

revealing [rɪvíłɪŋ] ADJ revelador; (neckline) atrevido

revel [révəl] VI (enjoy) deleitarse, gozar; (party) parrandear; N parranda *f*

revelation [rɛvəléʃən] N revelación *f*; (book in Bible) Apocalipsis *m sg*

revelry [révəlri] N parranda *f*, jarana *f*

revenge [rɪvɛ́ndʒ] N venganza *f*, revancha *f*

revengeful [rɪvɛ́ndʒfəl] ADJ vengativo

revenue [révənu] N (of a government) rentas públicas *f pl*; (of a person) ingresos *m pl*; — **stamp** sello fiscal *m*

reverberate [rɪvɜ́bəret] VI reverberar; VT hacer reverberar

revere [rɪvír] VT reverenciar

reverence [révəəns] N reverencia *f*, veneración *f*; VT venerar

reverend [révəənd] ADJ & N reverendo -da *mf*

reverent [révəənt] ADJ reverente

reverie, revery [révəri] N ensueño *m*, ensoñación *f*

reverse [rɪvɜ́s] ADJ inverso, opuesto; **the — side** el revés; N (opposite) lo opuesto; (back of clothing, mishap) revés *m*; (back of a coin, medal) reverso *m*; (gear) marcha atrás *f*; (back of a piece of paper) dorso *m*; VI/VT invertir[se]; VT (a policy, a vehicle) dar marcha atrás; (a verdict) revocar

revert [rɪvɜ́t] VI revertir

review [rɪvjú] N (inspection of a military unit, periodical publication) revista *f*; (repetition of studied material) repaso *m*; (critique of a book, drama) reseña *f*, crítica *f*; (examination of a judicial case) revisión *f*; VI/VT (examine) repasar, revisar; VT (reexamine) revisar,

examinar; (inspect troops) pasar revista a; (write a critique of) reseñar

revile [rɪváł] VT vilipendiar, denostar

revise [rɪváɪz] VT corregir, enmendar

revision [rɪvíʒən] N (action of revising) corrección *f*; (revised version) versión corregida *f*

revitalize [rɪváɪdłaɪz] VT revitalizar

revival [rɪvávəł] N (of customs) retorno *m*; (of religious feeling) resurgimiento *m*, despertar *m*; (from unconsciousness) resucitación *f*; (of a play) reposición *f*, revisión *f*; (evangelical meeting) asamblea evangelística *f*

revive [rɪváɪv] VT (an unconscious person) reavivar, reanimar; (an apparently dead person) resucitar; (an old play) reponer; (a custom) restablecer; VI revivir, reanimarse; (be reestablished) restablecerse

revocation [rɛvəkéʃən] N revocación *f*

revoke [rɪvók] VT revocar

revolt [rɪvółt] N revuelta *f*, sublevación *f*; VI rebelarse, sublevarse; **it —s me** me da asco

revolting [rɪvółtɪŋ] ADJ repugnante, asqueroso

revolution [rɛvəlúʃən] N revolución *f*

revolutionary [rɛvəlúʃəneri] ADJ & N revolucionario -ria *mf*

revolve [rɪváłv] VI/VT girar

revolver [rɪváłvə] N revólver *m*

revolving credit [rɪváłvɪŋ] N crédito rotativo *m*

revue [rɪvjú] N revista *f*

revulsion [rɪvʌłʃən] N repugnancia *f*, asco *m*

reward [rɪwɔ́rd] N recompensa *f*; VT recompensar

rewind [riwáɪnd] VI/VT rebobinar

rewrite[1] [ríraɪt] VI/VT reescribir

rewrite[2] [ríraɪt] N corrección *f*

rhea [ríə] N ñandú *m*

rhetoric [rɛ́ɾəɪk] N retórica *f*

rheumatic [rumǽdɪk] ADJ reumático; — **fever** fiebre reumática *f*

rheumatism [rúmətɪzəm] N reumatismo *m*, reuma *m*

rheumatoid [rúmətɔɪd] ADJ reumatoide

Rh factor [árétʃfæktə] N factor Rh *m*

rhinoceros [raɪnásərəs] N rinoceronte *m*

rhinoplasty [ráɪnoplæsti] N rinoplastia *f*

rhinovirus [ráɪnováɪrəs] N rinovirus *m*

rhododendron [roɒdədéndrən] N rododendro *m*

rhubarb [rúbarb] N (vegetable) ruibarbo *m*; (brawl) reyerta *f*

rhyme [raɪm] N rima *f*; **without — or reason** sin ton ni son; VI/VT rimar

rhythm [ríðəm] N ritmo *m*

rhythmical [ríðmɪkəł] ADJ rítmico; (breathing) acompasado

rib [rɪb] N (of person, animal) costilla *f*; (of umbrella) varilla *f*; (in garment) canalé *m*, cordoncillo *m*; — **cage** caja torácica *f*; VT burlarse de

ribbon [ríbən] N (of cloth) cinta *f*; (of land) franja *f*, faja *f*

rice [rais] N arroz *m*; **— field** arrozal *m*

rich [ritʃ] ADJ rico; (tasty) sabroso; (buttery) mantecoso; (colorful) vivo; **— text format** formato de texto enriquecido *m*; N **—es** riquezas *f pl*

rickety [ríkɪɾi] ADJ (shaky) desvencijado; (affected with rickets) raquítico

ricochet [ríkəʃe] N rebote *m*; VI rebotar

rid [rɪd] VT librar, desembarazar; **to get — of** librarse de, deshacerse de

ridden [rídn] see ride

riddle [rídl] N (puzzle) acertijo *m*, adivinanza *f*; (something puzzling) enigma *m*; VI hablar en enigmas; VT acribillar, perforar; **to be —d with graft** estar plagado de corrupción

ride [raid] VI (on a horse) cabalgar, jinetear; (on a bicycle) montar; (in a vehicle) andar/viajar/ir en; **this car —s well** este coche anda bien; **his hopes are riding on that** tiene las esperanzas puestas en eso; **just let it —** déjalo tranquilo; VT (travel on horse, bicycle) montar; (travel on bus) andar en; (harass) hostigar; **to — away** irse; **to — by** pasar; **to — out** capear; **to — up** subirse; N (in a vehicle) paseo *m*, viaje *m*; (at an amusement park) aparato *m*; **to give someone a —** llevar/acercar en coche; **to go on a —** dar un paseo

rider [ráidə] N (on a horse) jinete *m*; (on a bicycle) ciclista *mf*; (on an insurance policy) cláusula añadida *f*; (law) anexo *m*

ridge [rɪdʒ] N (back of an animal) espinazo *m*, lomo *m*; (chain of hills) cadena *f*; (of a roof) caballete *m*; (of cloth) cordoncillo *m*

ridicule [rídɪkjul] N burla *f*, mofa *f*; VT ridiculizar, poner en ridículo

ridiculous [rɪdíkjələs] ADJ ridículo

riffraff [rífræf] N *pej* gentuza *f*, chusma *f*

rifle [ráifəl] N rifle *m*, fusil *m*; VT robar; **to — through** revolver

rift [rɪft] N (opening) grieta *f*, hendidura *f*; (disagreement) desavenencia *f*

rig [rɪg] VT (sails) aparejar, equipar; (an election) amañar; **to — up** armar; N (on a ship) aparejo *m*, equipo *m*; (apparatus) aparato *m*; (truck) camión *m*

rigging [rígɪŋ] N jarcia *f*

right [raɪt] ADJ (not left) derecho; (not wrong) correcto, acertado; (suitable) adecuado; **— angle** ángulo recto *m*; **—-hand** derecho; **—-hand man** brazo derecho *m*; **—-handed** diestro; **— justification** alineación a la derecha *f*; **—-to-life** antiaborto, pro vida; **— triangle** triángulo recto *m*; **—-wing** derechista, de derecha; **at the — moment** en el momento justo; **the — people** la gente indicada; **to be —** tener razón; **to be all —**

estar bien; **he's not in his — mind** no está en sus cabales; **to turn out —** salir bien; ADV (straight) derecho, directamente; (correctly) correctamente; (to the right) a la derecha; **— after** justo después de; **—-face** media vuelta a la derecha; **— now** ahora mismo, ahorita; **— there** allí mismo; **it is — where you left it** está exactamente donde lo dejaste; **to hit — in the eye** darle de lleno en el ojo; **— click** pulsación en el botón derecho del ratón *f*; N (just claim) derecho *m*; (moral good) bien *m*; (direction, political persuasion) derecha *f*; **— of way** prioridad *f*, preferencia *f*; **— to work** derecho al trabajo *m*; **make a — at the corner** gira/dobla a la derecha; **to the —** a la derecha; **to be in the —** tener razón; VI/VT (make upright) enderezar[se]; **to — click** pulsar el botón derecho del ratón; VT (correct) corregir

righteous [ráitʃəs] ADJ recto, justo; **— anger** rabia justificada *f*

righteousness [ráitʃəsnɪs] N rectitud *f*, superioridad moral *f*

rightful [ráitfəl] ADJ legítimo

rightist [ráidɪst] N derechista *mf*

rightly [ráitli] ADV con razón

rigid [rídʒɪd] ADJ rígido

rigidity [rɪdʒídɪti] N rigidez *f*

rigor [rígə] N rigor *m*

rigorous [rígəəs] ADJ riguroso

rim [rɪm] N (edge) borde *m*; (on a car) llanta *f*; Am rin *m*; (on a bicycle) aro *m*; (on a plate) filete *m*; (of glasses) montura *f*

rind [raind] N (cheese) corteza *f*; (fruit) cáscara *f*

ring [rɪŋ] N (on finger, of smoke) anillo *m*; (for women only) sortija *f*; (under the eyes) ojeras *f pl*; (in the nose) argolla *f*; (circle) círculo *m*, redondel *m*, ruedo *m*; (in a circus) pista *f*; (for bullfights) plaza de toros *f*; (for boxing) cuadrilátero *m*; (for gymnastics) anillas *f pl*; (of criminals) banda *f*; (undertone) tono *m*; (sound of telephone) timbrazo *m*, telefonazo *m*; (sound of bells) retintín *m*, repique *m*; **— finger** anular *m*; **— leader** cabecilla *mf*; **—worm** tiña *f*; VT (surround) cercar; (make doorbell sound) tocar; (make bell sound) tañer; VI (of ears) zumbar; (make sound of a doorbell) sonar; (make sound of a bell) repicar, repiquetear; **to — the nose of an animal** ponerle una argolla en la nariz a un animal; **to — the hour** dar la hora; **to — true** parecer verdad; **to — up the sale** marcar la venta

ringlet [ríŋlɪt] N (curl) rizo *m*, bucle *m*, sortija *f*; (small ring) sortija pequeña *f*

rink [rɪŋk] N pista de patinaje *f*

rinkydink [ríŋkidɪŋk] ADJ de pacotilla

rinse [rɪns] VI/VT enjuagar, aclarar; N enjuague *m*, aclarado *m*

riot [ráɪət] N (uprising) motín *m*, tumulto *m*; (excess) exceso *m*; **he's a —** es un cómico; VI amotinarse

riotous [ráɪəDəs] ADJ (wanton) desenfrenado; (funny) graciosísimo

rip [rɪp] VI/VT rasgar[se], rajar[se]; VT (something sewn) descoser; **to — away** desprender; **to — into** asaltar; **to — off** robar; **to — out a seam** descoser una costura; N rasgadura *f*, rajadura *f*; **— cord** cordón de apertura *m*; **—off** robo *m*

ripe [raɪp] ADJ maduro; **to be — for** estar preparado/listo para; **— old age** edad avanzada *f*

ripen [ráɪpən] VI/VT madurar[se], sazonar[se]

ripeness [ráɪpnɪs] N madurez *f*

ripening [ráɪpənɪŋ] N maduración *f*

ripple [rípəɫ] VI/VT (water) rizar[se]; (grass) agitar[se]; N ondulación *f*, rizo *m*

rise [raɪz] VI (go up) subir; (increase) aumentar; (get up, stand up) levantarse; (slope up) elevarse; (arise) surgir; (of mist) levantarse; (of the sun, moon) salir; (of dough) crecer, leudar; **to — up in rebellion** sublevarse, alzarse; **to — above** superar; **to — to the challenge** aceptar el desafío y triunfar; N (of prices, volume) subida *f*, aumento *m*; (of an empire, talent) surgimiento *m*; (slope upward) elevación *f*; **to get a — out of someone** provocar a alguien; **to give — to** ocasionar

risen [rízən] *see* rise

risk [rɪsk] N riesgo *m*; **— factors** factores de riesgo *m pl*; **at —** a riesgo; ADJ **—-free** sin riesgo; VT arriesgar, aventurar; **to — defeat** correr el riesgo de perder, exponerse a perder

risky [rískɪ] ADJ arriesgado, aventurado

risqué [rɪské] ADJ subido de tono, atrevido, picante

Ritalin hydrochloride [rídəlɪnhaɪdrəklóraɪd] N clorhidrato de Ritalina *m*

rite [raɪt] N rito *m*

ritual [rítʃuəɫ] ADJ & N ritual *m*

ritzy [rítsi] ADJ elegante

rival [ráɪvəɫ] ADJ & N rival *mf*; VT rivalizar con, competir con

rivalry [ráɪvəɫri] N rivalidad *f*

river [rívə] N río *m*; **—bank** orilla *f*, ribera *f*; **— transport** transporte fluvial *m*

rivet [rívɪt] N remache *m*; VT (put rivets) remachar; (fix) fijar, clavar

riveting [rívɪDɪŋ] N (action) remache *m*; ADJ (fascinating) fascinante

RNA [**ribonucleic acid**] [áréné] N ARN *m*

roach [rotʃ] N cucaracha *f*

road [rod] N (in the country) camino *m*; (highway) carretera *f*; **on the — to recovery** en vías de recuperación; **— map** mapa carretero *m*; **— rage** ira caminera *f*; **—side**

borde del camino *m*; **—way** camino *m*

roam [rom] VI/VT vagar [por], errar [por], rodar [por]; VI vagabundear

roar [ror] VI/VT rugir, bramar; **to — with laughter** reír a carcajadas; N rugido *m*, bramido *m*; **— of laughter** risotada *f*, carcajada *f*

roast [rost] VI/VT (meat, potatoes) asar[se]; (coffee, nuts) tostar, torrar; (criticize) criticar; N (meat) asado *m*; (party) barbacoa *f*; **— beef** rosbif *m*

rob [rab] VI/VT robar; **to — someone of something** robarle algo a alguien

robber [rábə] N ladrón -ona *mf*

robbery [rábəri] N robo *m*

robe [rob] N manto *m*, traje talar *m*, túnica *f*; (ceremonial dress) toga *f*; (bath wrap) bata *f*

robin [rábɪn] N petirrojo *m*

robot [róbat] N robot *m*

robotics [robáDɪks] N robótica *f*

robust [robást] ADJ (strong) robusto; (hearty) saludable; (solid) sólido

rock [rak] N roca *f*; (crag) peñasco *m*, peñón *m*; (diamond) diamante *m*; (music style) rock *m*; **— crystal** cristal de roca *m*; **— salt** sal de piedra *f*, sal gema/mineral *f*; **on the —** en las rocas; **to go on the —s** tropezar en un escollo; *Am* escollar; **to hit —-bottom** tocar fondo; VI/VT (move to and fro) mecer[se]; (stagger) sacudir, estremecer; **to — to sleep** arrullar

rocker [rákə] N (chair) mecedora *f*; (fan or performer of rock music) roquero -ra *mf*

rocket [rákɪt] N cohete *m*

rocketry [rákɪtri] N cohetería *f*

rocking [rákɪŋ] N **— chair** mecedora *f*; **— horse** caballito de madera *m*, caballito mecedor *m*

rocky [ráki] ADJ (with rocks) rocoso; (difficult) difícil

rod [rad] N (stick) vara *f*, varilla *f*; (in engine) vástago *m*; (measure of length) aproximadamente 5 metros *f*

rode [rod] *see* ride

rodent [ródənt] N roedor *m*

rodeo [ródɪo] N rodeo *m*

rogue [rog] N pícaro -ra *mf*, bribón -ona *mf*; ADJ solitario y bravo

roguish [rógɪʃ] ADJ (rascally) pícaro, bribón; (mischievous) travieso

role [roɫ] N (in a drama) papel *m*, rol *m*; **— model** modelo ejemplar *m*; **—-playing** improvisación *f*

roll [roɫ] VI (move on wheels, rotate) rodar; (rotate one's eyes) revolear; (sway) balancearse, bambolearse; (reverberate) retumbar; (flow as waves) ondular; VT (steel) aplanar; (cigarettes) liar; (a drum) redoblar; (one's r's) pronunciar la erre; **to — over in**

the snow revolcarse en la nieve; to — up arrollar, enrollar; to — around llegar; to — back reducir, rebajar; to — by pasar; to — out (products) lanzar; to — over (physically) volcar, darse vuelta; (investments) reinvertir; to get —ing ponerse en marcha; N (of paper, fabric, etc.) rollo m; (of coins) cartucho m; (of a ship) balanceo m; (of thunder) retumbo m; (of a drum) redoble m; (of members) lista f; (of waves) ondulación f; (of a typewriter) carro m; (of bread) bollo m, panecillo m; (of dice) tiro m; ADJ —-on de bolita

roller [róla] N (for painting, moving things) rodillo m; (hair) rulo m, rulero m; — coaster montaña rusa f; — skate patín de ruedas m

rolling [rólɪŋ] ADJ (countryside) ondulado; (wheel) rodante; — pin rodillo m, palote m

roly-poly [rólipóli] ADJ rechoncho

ROM [read-only memory] [ram] N ROM f, memoria de ROM f, memoria de sólo lectura f

Roman [rómən] ADJ & N romano -na mf; — numeral número romano m

romance [rómæns] N (love affair, story) romance m; (romantic atmosphere) romanticismo m; VT cortejar; ADJ (linguistic) romance, románico

romanesque [romənésk] ADJ románico

Romania [roméniə] N Rumania f

Romanian [roméniən] ADJ & N rumano -na mf

romantic [rómæntik] ADJ romántico

romanticism [rómæntəsizəm] N romanticismo m

romp [ramp] VI (frolic) retozar, brincar; (win easily) arrasar; N (frolic) retozo m; (victory) victoria fácil f

roof [ruf] N (ceiling) techo m, tejado m; (flat roof) azotea f; — of the mouth paladar m; to hit the — poner el grito en el cielo; VT techar

rookie [rúki] N novato -ta mf

room [rum] N (in building) cuarto m; (large) sala f; (in a hotel) habitación f; (space) lugar m, sitio m; — and board pensión completa f; —mate compañero -ra de cuarto mf; — service servicio a la habitación f; to take up — ocupar espacio; the whole — laughed todos los presentes se rieron; VI hospedarse, alojarse

roomy [rúmi] ADJ espacioso, amplio

roost [rust] N vara f; VI posarse [para dormir]

rooster [rústə] N gallo m

root [rut] N raíz f; — canal (part of tooth) canal radicular m, tratamiento de conducto m; — directory directorio de raíz m, directorio raíz m; to take — (a plant) echar raíces, prender; (an idea) arraigar[se]; VI (grow roots) arraigar[se], echar raíces; (dig) hozar; to — for animar; to — out/up (uproot) arrancar de raíz; (eradicate) erradicar

rope [rop] N (cord) soga f, cuerda f; (lasso) reata f,

lazo m; (on a ship) cabo m; (thick) maroma f; to be at the end of one's — no dar más; to know the —s conocer el paño, sabérselas todas; VT enlazar; to — off acordonar; to — someone in agarrar a alguien

Rorschach test [rórʃak test] N prueba de Rorschach f

rosary [rózəri] N rosario m

rose [roz] N rosa f; (color) rosa m; —bud capullo de rosa m, pimpollo de rosa m; —bush rosal m; ADJ —-colored de color rosa

rose [roz] see rise

rosemary [rózmɛri] N romero m

roseola [rozíələ] N roséola f

roster [róstə] N lista f

rostrum [rástrəm] N tribuna f

rosy [rózi] ADJ (pink) rosado, color de rosa; (of cheeks) sonrosado; — future porvenir halagüeño m

rot [rat] VI/VT pudrir[se]; N podredumbre f

rotary [ródəri] ADJ rotatorio, rotativo

rotate [rótet] VI/VT rotar

rotation [rotéʃən] N rotación f, giro m

rotor [ródə] N rotor m

rotten [rátn] ADJ (decomposing) podrido; (stinking) hediondo; (morally corrupt) corrupto; (despicable) odioso

rotund [rotánd] ADJ rollizo

rouge [ruʒ] N colorete m

rough [raf] ADJ (coarse) áspero, rugoso; (violent) violento; (rude) tosco; (approximate) aproximado; (bumpy) desigual, irregular; (rugged) agreste, bronco; (stormy) picado, revuelto; — diamond diamante en bruto m; — draft borrador m; — estimate aproximación f; — weather mal tiempo m; he had a — time le fue mal; VI to — it vivir sin lujos ni comodidades

roughly [ráfli] ADV (not smoothly) ásperamente; (rudely) groseramente, rudamente; (approximately) aproximadamente; to estimate — tantear

roughness [ráfnɪs] N (lack of smoothness) aspereza f; (rudeness) rudeza f; (unevenness) desigualdad f; the — of the sea lo picado del mar

roulette [rulét] N ruleta f

round [raund] ADJ redondo; — number número redondo m; — trip viaje de ida y vuelta m; N (of talks, drinks, dance) ronda f; (of cheese) rodaja f; (in cards, sports) vuelta f; (in boxing) round m, asalto m; (of golf) partido m, ronda f; (canon) canon m; — of ammunition carga de municiones f; — of applause aplauso m; —up (of cattle) rodeo m; (of criminals) redada f; to make the —s hacer la ronda; PREP & ADV —about indirecto; —-the-clock veinticuatro horas al día; all year — todo el año; to come —

pasar; **to go — a corner** doblar una esquina; vt (a corner) doblar; (an edge, a number) redondear; **to — off/out** redondear; **to — up** juntar, reunir; **to — up cattle** juntar el ganado

roundness [ráundnɪs] N redondez f

rouse [rauz] vi/vt (wake) despertar[se]; vt (instigate) incitar

rout [raut] N (defeat) derrota aplastante f; (flight) huida en desbandada f; vt (defeat) derrotar, destrozar; (cause to flee) poner en fuga

route [raut, rut] N ruta f, trayecto m, recorrido m; (of newspaper delivery) reparto m; vt dirigir

routine [rutín] N rutina f

rove [rov] vi/vt vagar [por], errar [por]

rover [róvə] N vagabundo -da mf

row[1] [rau] N (fight) riña f, pelea f, bronca f

row[2] [ro] N (line) fila f, hilera f, ringlera f; **four times in a —** cuatro veces seguidas; vi/vt (propel with oars) remar, bogar; **—boat** bote de remos m, barca f

rowdy [ráudi] ADJ (person) alborotador; (party) bullicioso; N camorrista mf

rower [ró-ə] N remero -ra mf

royal [rɔ́ɪəl] ADJ real; **— blue** azul marino m; **— flush** escalera real f

royalty [rɔ́ɪəlti] N (group) realeza f; (person) miembro de la realeza m; **royalties** derechos m pl, regalías f pl

RSVP [répondez s'il vous plaît] [árésvípí] LOC S.R.C.

rub [rʌb] vi/vt (apply friction) frotar[se]; (massage) friccionar; (spread on) aplicar frotando; (make sore) rozar; **to — off** quitar[se] frotando; **to — out** borrar; **to — shoulders with** codearse con; **to — the wrong way** peinar a contrapelo; **don't — it in!** ¡no me lo refriegues por la cara! N (act of rubbing) fricción f; (difficulty) dificultad f; (abraded area) roce m, frote m

rubber [rʌ́bə] N caucho m, goma f; **— band** goma elástica f; **—s** chanclos m pl; **— stamp** sello de goma m; **— tree** gomero m; vt **to — stamp** autorizar automáticamente

rubbing alcohol [rʌ́bɪŋ ǽlkəhɔ̀l] N alcohol para fricciones m

rubbish [rʌ́bɪʃ] N (trash) basura f; (nonsense) pamplinas f pl

rubble [rʌ́bəl] N (debris) escombros m pl; (stone fragments) ripios m pl, cascote m

rubella [rubélə] N rubéola/rubeola f, sarampión alemán m

rubric [rúbrɪk] N rúbrica f

ruby [rúbi] N rubí m

ruckus [rʌ́kəs] N barahúnda f, jaleo m

rudder [rʌ́də] N timón m

ruddy [rʌ́di] ADJ rubicundo

rude [rud] ADJ (impolite) grosero; (uncouth,

crude, simple) tosco; (harsh) rudo

rudeness [rúdnɪs] N (impoliteness) grosería f; (crudeness) tosquedad f; (harshness) rudeza f

rueful [rúfəl] ADJ (inspiring pity) triste; (repentant) arrepentido

ruffian [rʌ́fiən] N rufián m

ruffle [rʌ́fəl] vi/vt (gather cloth) fruncir[se]; (raise feathers) erizar[se]; (ripple water) agitar[se], rizar[se]; (muss hair) desgreñar[se]; (bother a person) molestar[se], fastidiar[se]; (frill on clothes) volante m; (gathering in cloth) frunce m, pliegue m; (ripples in water) ondulación f, rizo m

rug [rʌg] N alfombra f; (hairpiece) peluquín m

rugby [rʌ́gbi] N rugby m

rugged [rʌ́gɪd] ADJ (terrain) escarpado, áspero, fragoso; (face) recio; (manners) tosco; (way of life) duro; (man) robusto

ruin [rúɪn] N ruina f; **to go to —** arruinarse, venirse abajo; vi/vt arruinar[se], estropear[se]; (spoil) echar[se] a perder

ruinous [rúɪnəs] ADJ ruinoso

rule [rul] N (principle) regla f; (line separating newspaper columns) filete m; (government) mando m, gobierno m; **—s and regulations** reglamentos y disposiciones administrativas m pl; **the — of law** el imperio de la ley; **as a — of thumb** por regla general, a ojo de buen cubero; vi/vt (govern) reinar, gobernar; (decree) fallar, dictaminar, sentenciar; (put lines on paper) rayar, poner renglones; **to — out** excluir; **to — over** reinar, gobernar

ruler [rúlə] N (governor) gobernante mf; (measuring instrument) regla f

ruling [rúlɪŋ] N (decision) fallo m, sentencia f, dictamen m; (line on paper) renglón m; ADJ (governing) gobernante, reinante

rum [rʌm] N ron m

rumba [rʌ́mbə] N rumba f; vi rumbear

rumble [rʌ́mbəl] vi (as thunder) retumbar; (as a stomach) hacer ruido; (fight) pelear; N (roar) retumbo m; (growl) ruido m; (fight) pelea f

ruminate [rúmənet] vi rumiar

rummage [rʌ́mɪdʒ] vi/vt rebuscar, hurgar; N cachivaches m pl; **— sale** venta de beneficencia f

rumor [rúmə] N rumor m; vt murmurar; **it is —ed that** se rumorea que, corre la voz que

rump [rʌmp] N (of quadruped) anca f, grupa f; (of bird) rabadilla f; (of person) trasero m

run [rʌn] vi (person, tears, water) correr; (stockings, dyes) correrse; (machines) funcionar; (faucet) chorrear; (candidate) presentarse como candidato; (sore) supurar; vt (a mile, a risk) correr; (one object through another) pasar; (a business) manejar, dirigir; (a red light) comerse; (a news story) publicar; (a sum of money) costar; (a computer program) ejecutar; (a fever) tener; **— along**

now! ¡vete! **to — across someone** encontrarse con alguien; **to — after** perseguir; **to — around with** andar con; **to — away** fugarse, escaparse; **to — down** (stop working) dejar de funcionar; (capture) aprehender; (criticize) hablar mal de; (run over) atropellar; (tire) cansar; **to — dry** secarse; **to — into** (encounter) tropezarse con, encontrarse con; (collide) chocar con; **to — out** salir corriendo; **to — out of money** quedarse sin dinero; **to — over** (spill) derramarse; (run down) atropellar, arrollar; (move along a surface) deslizar por; **to — through** (stab) atravesar; (squander) despilfarrar; **to — up** acumular; **the play ran for three months** la obra estuvo en cartel durante tres meses; **it —s in the family** es un rasgo de familia; N (act of running) carrera *f*, corrida *f*; (point in baseball) carrera *f*, anotación *f*; (defect in stockings) carrera *f*, corrida *f*; (routine trip) recorrido *m*; (of newspapers) tirada *f*; (of a play) temporada en cartel *f*; (on a bank) pánico *m*, corrida *f*; **—away** fugitivo -va *mf*; **—away horse** caballo desbocado *m*; **— batted in** carrera impulsada *f*; **— of good luck** racha de buena suerte *f*; **— of the mill** del montón; **—way** (for planes) pista *f*; (for models) pasarela *f*; **to be on the —** estar huyendo; **in the long —** a la larga; **he gave me the —around** contestó con evasivas; **she gave us a —down** nos hizo un resumen; ADJ **—down** desvencijado

rung [rʌŋ] N (of a chair) barrote *m*; (of a ladder) peldaño *m*

rung [rʌŋ] *see* ring

runner [rʌnɚ] N (one who runs) corredor -ora *mf*; (on a table) tapete *m*; (on a sled) patín *m*; (on a skate) cuchilla *f*; (on a plant) estolón *m*; (of drugs, contraband) contrabandista *mf*; **— up** segundo -da *mf*

running [rʌnɪŋ] N (of a race) corrida *f*, carrera *f*; (of a business) manejo *m*, dirección *f*; (of water) flujo *m*; (of machines) funcionamiento *m*; (of a car) rodaje *m*; **to be out of the —** estar fuera de combate; **— board** estribo *m*; ADJ (sore) supurante; **— water** agua corriente *f*; **in — condition** en buen estado; **for ten days —** durante diez días seguidos

runt [rʌnt] N (animal) animal más pequeño de la camada *m*; (person) *pej* mequetrefe *m*

rupture [rʌptʃɚ] N (of relations, internal organ) ruptura *f*; (of a tire) rotura *f*; (hernia) hernia *f*; VI/VT romper[se], reventar[se]

rural [rʊrəl] ADJ rural

rush [rʌʃ] VI/VT (hurry) apresurar[se]; *Am* apurar[se]; VT (a parcel) llevar con prisa, llevar rápido; (an enemy) precipitarse, abalanzarse sobre; **to — by/past** pasar

corriendo; **to — out** salir corriendo; N (haste) prisa *f*; *Am* apuro *m*; (attack) acometida *f*; (hurried activity) bullicio *m*; (plant) junco *m*; **— hour** hora punta *f*; **— of air** ráfaga *f*; **— of people** tumulto *m*; **— of water** torrente *m*; **— order** pedido urgente *m*

Russia [rʌʃə] N Rusia *f*

Russian [rʌʃən] ADJ & N ruso -sa *mf*

rust [rʌst] N (oxidation) herrumbre *f*, orín *m*; (disease) tizón *m*; ADJ **—-colored** color herrumbre; **—-proof** inoxidable; VI/VT herrumbrar[se]

rustic [rʌstɪk] ADJ rústico; N campesino -na *mf*, paleto -ta *mf*

rusting [rʌstɪŋ] N oxidación *f*

rustle [rʌsəl] VI susurrar, crujir; VT hacer susurrar, hacer crujir; **to — cattle** robar ganado; N susurro *m*, crujido *m*

rusty [rʌsti] ADJ (oxidized) herrumbrado, oxidado; (rust-colored) color herrumbre; (out of practice) falto de práctica; **my German is —** se me ha olvidado el alemán

rut [rʌt] N (furrow) surco *m*; (of a wheel) rodada *f*; (routine) rutina *f*; (heat) celo *m*; **to be in a —** ser esclavo de la rutina; VI estar en celo

ruthless [rʊθlɪs] ADJ despiadado

ruthlessness [rʊθlɪsnɪs] N crueldad *f*

Rwanda [ruándə] N Ruanda *f*

Rwandan [ruándən] ADJ & N ruandés -esa *mf*

rye [raɪ] N centeno *m*; **— bread** pan de centeno *m*

Ss

saber [sébɚ] N sable *m*

sabotage [sæbətɑʒ] N sabotaje *m*; VT sabotear

sac [sæk] N bolsa *f*, saco *m*

saccharine [sækəɪn] ADJ empalagoso; N sacarina *f*

sack [sæk] N (bag) saco *m*, bolso *m*; (looting) saqueo *m*; (in football) captura *f*; **in the —** en la cama; VT (bag) embolsar, ensacar; (loot) saquear; (fire) despedir

sacrament [sækrəmənt] N sacramento *m*

sacred [sékrɪd] ADJ sagrado

sacrifice [sækrəfaɪs] N (also in baseball) sacrificio *m*; **at a —** con pérdida; VT sacrificar

sacrilege [sækrəlɪdʒ] N sacrilegio *m*

sacrilegious [sækrəlɪdʒəs] ADJ sacrílego

sacrum [sékrəm] N sacro *m*

sad [sæd] ADJ triste

sadden [sædn] VI/VT entristecer[se]; VT pesar

saddle [sædl] N (for horse) silla de montar *f*, montura *f*; (for bicycle) sillín *m*; **—bag** alforja *f*; **— horse** caballo de silla *m*; **— pad** carona *f*; **— tree** arzón *m*; VT ensillar; **to — up** ensillar; **to — someone with**

responsibilities cargar a alguien de responsabilidades

sadism [sédɪzəm] N sadismo *m*

sadistic [sədístɪk] ADJ sádico

sadness [sǽdnɪs] N tristeza *f*

safari [səfúri] N safari *m*

safe [sef] ADJ (secure) seguro, salvo; (trustworthy) digno de confianza; (careful) precavido, prudente; **— and sound** sano y salvo; **— deposit box** caja de seguridad *f*; **—guard** salvaguarda *f*; **—keeping** custodia *f*; **— mode** modo a prueba de fallos/errores *m*; N caja fuerte *f*; **—conduct** salvoconducto *m*; ADV (in baseball) safe; VT **to —guard** salvaguardar

safely [séfli] ADV (without danger) sin peligro; (without incident) sin percances; **I can — say** puedo decir con toda seguridad

safety [séfti] N seguridad *f*; **— belt** cinturón de seguridad *m*; **— device** mecanismo de seguridad *m*, seguro *m*; **— glass** vidrio inastillable *m*; **— net** red *f*; **— pin** imperdible *m*

saffron [sǽfrən] N (spice) azafrán *m*; (color) color azafrán *m*

sag [sæg] VI/VT (wall) combar[se], pandear[se]; VI (stock market, breast) caer; (spirits) decaer; (rope) aflojarse; (pants) abolsarse; **his shoulders —** tiene las espaldas caídas; N (of a wall) pandeo *m*, comba *f*; (in prices) caída *f*

sage [sedʒ] ADJ sabio; N (wise person) sabio -bia *mf*; (plant) salvia *f*

said [sed] *see* say

sail [sel] N (part of a boat) vela *f*; (trip) viaje en barco *m*; **—boat** velero *m*; **—fish** pez vela *m*; **under full —** a toda vela; **to set —** zarpar; VI/VT (travel by boat) navegar; (set sail) zarpar; **to — along** deslizarse, navegar; **to — along the coast** costear; **to — through an exam** aprobar un examen con facilidad

sailor [sélə] N marinero -ra *mf*

saint [sent] N santo -ta *mf*; **— John** San Juan

saintly [séntli] ADJ santo, piadoso

sake [sek] N **for the — of** por; **for my —** por mí; **for pity's —** por el amor de Dios; **for brevity's —** para ser breve; **for the — of argument** por vía de argumento; **art for art's —** el arte por el arte

salad [sǽləd] N ensalada *f*; **— dressing** aderezo *m*

salamander [sǽləmændə] N salamandra *f*

salary [sǽləri] N sueldo *m*, retribución *f*; **— bracket** categoría salarial *f*; **— range** escala de sueldos *f*, escala salarial *f*

sale [sel] N (act of selling) venta *f*; (special sales event) liquidación *f*, saldo *m*; **—s clerk** dependiente -ta *mf*; **—s force** personal de ventas *m*; **—sperson** dependiente -ta *mf*; **—s tax** impuesto sobre las ventas *m*; **for — en**

venta; **on —** con rebaja, rebajado

salient [séliənt] ADJ & N saliente *m*

saline [sélin] ADJ salino; **— solution** solución salina *f*

saliva [səláɪvə] N saliva *f*

sally [sǽli] N (sortie) salida *f*; (excursion) excursión *f*; VI salir, hacer una salida; **to — forth** salir

salmon [sǽmən] N salmón *m*

salmonella [sælmənélə] N salmonela *f*

salon [səlán] N salón *m*; (beauty parlor) salón de belleza *m*, peluquería *f*

saloon [səlún] N salón *m*, taberna *f*, bar *m*

salt [sɔlt] N sal *f*; (for smelling) sales *f pl*; **—cellar** salero *m*; **— lick** salegar *m*; **— mine** salina *f*; **—peter** salitre *m*; **—shaker** salero *m*; **—water** agua salada *f*; **old —** lobo de mar *m*; **the — of the earth** la sal de la tierra; VT salar; **to — away** ahorrar

salty [sɔlti] ADJ (food, water) salado; (soil, water) salobre

salutation [sæljətéʃən] N saludo *m*

salute [səlút] N saludo *m*; (of guns) salva *f*; VI/VT (greet) saludar; (acknowledge) reconocer

Salvadoran, Salvadorian [sælvədɔ́r[i]ən] ADJ & N salvadoreño -ña *mf*

salvage [sǽlvɪdʒ] N (recovery) salvamento *m*; (objects recovered) objetos salvados *m pl*; VT salvar

salvation [sælvéʃən] N salvación *f*

salve [sæv] N ungüento *m*, pomada *f*

salvo [sǽlvo] N salva *f*

same [sem] ADJ (identical) mismo; (similar) igual; **—day delivery** entrega el mismo día *f*; **it is all the —** to me me da igual, me da lo mismo; **the — to you** igualmente, me da lo — de todos modos

Samoa [səmóə] N Samoa *f*

Samoan [səmóən] ADJ & N samoano -na *mf*

sample [sǽmpəl] N muestra *f*; VT (try) probar; (take samples) muestrear

sampling [sǽmplɪŋ] N muestreo *m*

sanatorium [sænətóriəm] N sanatorio *m*

sanctify [sǽŋktəfaɪ] VT santificar

sanction [sǽŋkʃən] N sanción *f*; VT sancionar

sanctity [sǽŋktɪɾi] N santidad *f*

sanctuary [sǽŋktʃueri] N (church auditorium, place of refuge) santuario *m*; (game preserve) reserva *f*

sand [sænd] N arena *f*; **—box** arenero *m*; **— dollar** erizo de mar plano *m*; **—paper** papel de lija *m*; **to —paper** lijar; **—stone** arenisca *f*; **—storm** tormenta de arena *f*; **—trap** trampa de arena *f*; VT lijar, pulir

sandal [sǽndl] N sandalia *f*

sandwich [sǽndwɪtʃ] N bocadillo *m*, emparedado *m*; VT intercalar; **to be —ed between** quedar apretado entre

sandy [sǽndi] ADJ (full of sand) arenoso,

arenisco; (yellowish red) rubio

sane [sen] ADJ cuerdo

sang [sæŋ] *see* sing

sanitary [sǽnɪtɛri] ADJ sanitario; — **napkin** paño higiénico *m*

sanitation [sænɪtéʃən] N (sewers) saneamiento *m*; (hygiene) salubridad *f*

sanity [sǽnɪDi] N cordura *f*

sank [sæŋk] *see* sink

San Marinese [sænmærəníz] ADJ & N sanmarinense *mf*, sanmarinés -esa *mf*

San Marino [sænməríno] N San Marino *m*

Sanskrit [sǽnskrɪt] N sánscrito *f*

Santa Claus [sǽntəklɔz] N Papá Noel *m*, Santa Claus *m*

São Tomean [saʊtóméən] ADJ & N santotomense *mf*

São Tome and Principe [saʊtóméændprínsipe] N Santo Tomé y Príncipe *m*

sap [sæp] N (juice) savia *f*; (fool) tonto -ta *mf*; VT (exhaust) agotar

sapling [sǽplɪŋ] N (tree) árbol joven *m*; (person) jovenzuelo -la *mf*

sapphire [sǽfaɪr] N zafiro *m*

sarcasm [sárkæzəm] N sarcasmo *m*, socarronería *f*

sarcastic [sarkǽstɪk] ADJ sarcástico, socarrón

sarcoma [sarkómə] N sarcoma *m*

sarcophagus [sarkáfəgəs] N sarcófago *m*

sardine [sardín] N sardina *f*

sardonic [sardánɪk] ADJ sardónico

sash [sæʃ] N (around waist) faja *f*; (around shoulder) banda *f*; (on window) marco *m*, bastidor *m*

sassy [sǽsi] ADJ insolente

sat [sæt] *see* sit

satanic [sətǽnɪk] ADJ satánico

satchel [sǽtʃəl] N cartera *f*

satellite [sǽdlaɪt] N satélite *m*; — **dish** [antena] parabólica *f*

satiate [séʃiet] VT saciar, hartar

satin [sǽtn] N raso *m*, satén *m*

satire [sǽtaɪr] N sátira *f*

satirical [sətírɪkəl] ADJ satírico

satirize [sǽdəraɪz] VT satirizar

satisfaction [sædɪsfǽkʃən] N satisfacción *f*

satisfactory [sædɪsfǽktəri] ADJ satisfactorio

satisfied [sǽdɪsfaɪd] ADJ satisfecho

satisfy [sǽdɪsfaɪ] VI/VT satisfacer

saturate [sǽtʃəret] VI/VT (impregnate) saturar[se]; (soak) empapar[se]; —**d fat** grasa saturada *f*

Saturday [sǽdɚDe] N sábado *m*

sauce [sɔs] N salsa *f*; —**pan** cacerola *f*; VT aderezar con salsa

saucer [sɔsɚ] N platillo *m*

saucy [sɔsi] ADJ (insolent) fresco, descarado, insolente; (who talks back) respondón

Saudi Arabia [sóʊdiərébiə] N Arabia Saudí *f*,

Arabia Saudita *f*

Saudi Arabian [sóʊdiərébiən] ADJ & N saudí *mf*, saudita *mf*

saunter [sɔ́ntɚ] VI pasearse, deambular

sausage [sɔ́sɪdʒ] N (thick) chorizo *m*; (thin) salchicha *f*; (cured) longaniza *f*; —**-making** charcutería *f*

savage [sǽvɪdʒ] ADJ (uncivilized) salvaje; (furious) rabioso; (rugged) agreste; N salvaje *m*; VT hacer trizas de

savagery [sǽvɪdʒri] N salvajismo *m*, barbarie *f*

savannah [səvǽnə] N sabana *f*

save [sev] VT (a sinner, a person in danger) salvar; (furniture) salvaguardar, proteger; (money, time, energy) ahorrar, economizar; (data) guardar; VI (lay up money, be economical) ahorrar; (protect) salvaguardar; **to** — **from** librar de; — **as** (on a computer) almacenar como, guardar como; **to** — **one's eyes** cuidarse la vista; N (in baseball) salvado *m*; PREP salvo, menos

savings [sévɪŋz] N ahorros *m pl*; — **account** cuenta de ahorros *f*; — **bank** caja de ahorros *f*

savior [sévjɚ] N salvador -ora *mf*

savor [sévɚ] N (taste) sabor *m*; (trace) dejo *m*; VT saborear

savory [sévəri] ADJ (delicious) sabroso; (not sweet) salado

savvy [sǽvi] N astucia *f*; ADJ astuto

saw [sɔ] N sierra *f*; —**horse** caballete *m*; VI/VT aserrar[se]; —**dust** aserrín *m*, serrín *m*; —**mill** aserradero *m*

saw [sɔ] *see* see

sawn [sɔn] *see* saw

saxophone [sǽksəfon] N saxofón *m*

say [se] VT (something interesting) decir; (a prayer) rezar; VI (a clock) marcar; (a sign) rezar, decir; —! ¡oye! **that is to** — es decir; — **I bought it** supongamos que yo lo comprara; **it goes without** —**ing** huelga decir[lo]; **there's a lot to be said for** es muy recomendable; **when all is said and done** al fin y al cabo; **you can** — **that again** tú lo has dicho; N **the final** — la última palabra; **to have one's** — dar su opinión; ADV **you could earn,** —**, a million dollars** podrías ganar, pongamos, un millón de dólares

saying [séɪŋ] N dicho *m*, refrán *m*

scab [skæb] N (of a wound) costra *f*; (on plants) roña *f*; (strikebreaker) esquirol *m*, amarillo -lla *mf*; VI (wound) formar una costra; (break a strike) ser esquirol

scabby [skǽbi] ADJ (wound) costroso; (plant) roñoso

scaffold [skǽfəld] N (in construction) andamio *m*; (of a gallows) patíbulo *m*

scald [skɔld] VI/VT escaldar[se]; N escaldadura *f*

scale [skel] N (progression) escala *f*; (for weighing) balanza *f*; (heavy-duty) báscula *f*;

(on fish, reptiles, human skin) escama *f*; **pair of —s** balanza *f*; VT (climb) escalar; (remove scales) escamar; VI/VT (adjust proportionally) graduar, escalar; **to — down** rebajar proporcionalmente

scallion [skǽljən] N cebollino *m*

scallop [skǽləp] N (mollusk) vieira *f*; (of beef) escalope *m*; (of fabric) festón *m*; VT festonear

scalp [skælp] N cuero cabelludo *m*; VT (to skin) arrancar la cabellera; (to resell) revender

scalpel [skǽlpəl] N bisturí *m*

scalper [skǽlpə-] N revendedor -ora *mf*

scam [skæm] N timo *m*, estafa *f*

scamp [skæmp] N pícaro -ra *mf*, tunante -ta *mf*, pillo -lla *mf*

scamper [skǽmpə-] VI (run) escabullirse, escaparse; (caper) cabriolar

scan [skæn] VT (horizon) escudriñar, escrutar; (brain) hacer una tomografía; (page) echar un vistazo a; (verse) escandir; (digitalize for computer) escanear; N tomografía *f*

scandal [skǽndl] N escándalo *m*

scandalize [skǽndlaɪz] VT escandalizar

scandalous [skǽndləs] ADJ escandaloso

scanner [skǽnə-] N escáner *m*

scanning [skǽnɪŋ] N escaneado *m*

scant [skænt] ADJ escaso

scanty [skǽnti] ADJ (provisions) escaso; (skirt) muy corto; (bikini) breve

scapegoat [sképgot] N chivo expiatorio *m*, cabeza de turco *m*

scapula [skǽpjələ] N escápula *f*, omóplato *m*

scar [skɑr] N cicatriz *f*, lacra *f*; VT dejar una cicatriz

scarce [skɛrs] ADJ escaso; **to be —** escasear

scarcely [skɛ́rsli] ADV (barely) apenas; **he's — a genius** no es un genio ni mucho menos

scarcity [skɛ́rsɪdi] N escasez *f*, pobreza *f*, carestía *f*

scare [skɛr] VI/VT espantar[se], asustar[se]; **to — away** ahuyentar; **to — up** reunir; N susto *m*, sobresalto *m*; (of war, of a heart attack) amago *m*; **—crow** espantapájaros *m sg*

scared [skɛrd] ADJ asustado; **I'm — of spiders** tengo miedo de las arañas / las arañas me dan miedo

scarf [skɑrf] N (woolen) bufanda *f*; (silk, cotton) pañuelo *m*; VI **to — up** engullir

scarlet [skɑ́rlɪt] N escarlata *m*, grana *f*; **— fever** escarlatina *f*

scary [skɛ́ri] ADJ (causing fright) de miedo; (easily frightened) asustadizo

scat [skæt] INTERJ ¡fuera!

scatter [skǽdə-] VI/VT (seeds) esparcir[se], desparramar[se], desperdigar[se]; (crowd) dispersar[se]; **—brained** atolondrado; N **—brain** cabeza de chorlito *mf*

scattered [skǽdə-d] ADJ disperso

scavenge [skǽvɪndʒ] VT recoger, rescatar; VI hurgar

scenario [sɪnɛ́rio] N guión *m*; **worst-case —** el peor de los casos

scene [sin] N (act) escena *f*; (sphere of activity) ambiente *m*, ámbito *m*; **to make a —** montar una escena; **behind the —s** entre bastidores

scenery [sínəri] N (of a place) paisaje *m*; (on a stage) decorado *m*

scenic [sínɪk] ADJ panorámico

scent [sɛnt] N (smell) olor *m*; (fragrance) perfume *m*; (trace) pista *f*, rastro *m*; (sense of smell) olfato *m*; VI/VT (perceive through smell) olfatear; (intuit) presentir; (give fragrance to) perfumar

schedule [skédʒʊɫ] N (plan) calendario *m*; (timetable) horario *m*; (appendix) apéndice *m*; (list) lista *f*; **on —** al día, a la hora prevista; **ahead of —** adelantado; VT programar, fijar

scheme [skim] N (plan) plan *m*, proyecto *m*; (plot) ardid *m*, trama *f*; (of colors) combinación *f*; VI/VT maquinar, intrigar, tramar

schemer [skímə-] N maquinador -ora *mf*, intrigante *mf*

scheming [skímɪŋ] ADJ intrigante; N maquinación *f*

schizophrenia [skɪtsəfríniə] N esquizofrenia *f*

scholar [skɑ́lə-] N (student) alumno -na *mf*; (fellow) becario -ria *mf*; (erudite person) erudito -ta *mf*, estudioso -sa *mf*

scholarly [skɑ́lə-li] ADJ erudito

scholarship [skɑ́lə-ʃɪp] N (erudition) erudición *f*; (award) beca *f*

school [skuɫ] N (primary) escuela *f*, colegio *m*; (secondary) secundaria *f*; Sp instituto *m*; (university) universidad *f*; (of law, etc.) facultad *f*; (of language, driving) academia *f*; (of thought) escuela *f*; (of fish) banco *m*, cardumen *m*; **—boy** escolar *m*; **—girl** escolar *f*; **—house** escuela *f*; **—master** maestro -tra *mf*; **—mate** compañero -ra de escuela *mf*; **—room** aula *f*, sala de clase *f*; **—teacher** maestro -tra *mf*; **— year** año lectivo *m*; VT instruir, entrenar

schooling [skúlɪŋ] N instrucción *f*

schooner [skúnə-] N goleta *f*

sciatic nerve [saɪǽdɪknə-v] N nervio ciático *m*

science [sáɪəns] N ciencia *f*; **— fiction** ciencia ficción *f*

scientific [saɪəntífɪk] ADJ científico; **— method** método científico *m*

scientist [sáɪəntɪst] N científico -ca *mf*

scintillate [síntlet] VI (diamonds) centellear, destellar; (stars) titilar

scissor [sízə-z] VT cortar con tijera; N **—s** tijera *f*, tijeras *f pl*; **— kick** tijera *f*, tijereta *f*

sclerosis [sklərósɪs] N esclerosis *f*

scoff [skɑf] N mofa *f*, burla *f*; VI mofarse; **to — at** mofarse de, burlarse de

scold [skoʊld] VI/VT reprender, regañar, reñir; N regañón -ona *mf*

scolding [skóʊldɪŋ] N regaño *m*, reprimenda *f*

scoliosis [skoʊlióʊsɪs] N escoliosis *f*

scoop [skup] N (ladle) cucharón *m*; (spoon for ice cream) cuchara *f*; (shovel) pala *f*; (news item) primicia *f*; VT sacar con cuchara; (report first) adelantarse a; **to — in a good profit** sacar buena ganancia; **to — out** (water) achicar; (a hole) cavar; **to — up** recoger

scoot [skut] VI (go fast) correr; (go away) largarse

scooter [skúdɚ] N (with motor) scooter *m*; (toy) monopatín *m*, patinete *m*

scope [skoʊp] N (range) alcance *m*, ámbito *m*; (sphere) esfera *f*; VT observar

scorch [skɔrtʃ] VI/VT chamuscar[se], quemar[se]; N chamuscadura *f*; Am quemadura *f*

score [skɔr] N (partial result) tanteo *m*; (total result) resultado *m*, (on a test) calificación *f*; (scratch) arañazo *m*; (twenty) veintena *f*; (of music) partitura *f*; **—board** marcador *m*; **on that** — a ese respecto; **to keep** — llevar la cuenta; **to settle old —s** ajustar cuentas; **what is the —?** ¿cómo va el marcador? VT (grade) calificar; (orchestrate) orquestar; (scratch) arañar; VI/VT (make points) marcar, tantear; (hook up with someone) ligar; **to — a goal** marcar/meter un gol

scorn [skɔrn] N desdén *m*, menosprecio *m*; VI/VT desdeñar, menospreciar

scornful [skɔ́rnfəl] ADJ desdeñoso

scorpion [skɔ́rpiən] N escorpión *m*, alacrán *m*

Scotch [skɑtʃ] ADJ escocés; **— whisky** whisky escocés *m*

Scotland [skɑ́tlənd] N Escocia *f*

Scotsman [skɑ́tsmən] N escocés *m*

Scotswoman [skɑ́tswʊmən] N escocesa *f*

Scottish [skɑ́dɪʃ] ADJ escocés

scoundrel [skáʊndrəl] N bellaco *m*, infame *m*, truhán *m*

scour [skaʊr] VT (clean) fregar, restregar; (search an area) inspeccionar

scourge [skɝdʒ] N (affliction, means of affliction) azote *m*; VT azotar

scout [skaʊt] N (military) explorador -ora *mf*; (child explorer) explorador -ora *mf*, scout *mf*; (for talent) cazatalentos *mf sg*; **a good —** una buena persona; VI/VT explorar; VI **to — for** buscar

scowl [skaʊl] N ceño fruncido *m*; VI fruncir el ceño

scram [skræm] VI largarse

scramble [skræmbəl] VI (climb) subir a gatas; **to — for** pelearse por; (hurry) **to — up** subir a gatas; VT (eggs) revolver; (numbers) mezclar; **—d eggs** huevos revueltos *m pl*; N (difficult climb) subida difícil *f*; (struggle for possession) arrebatiña *f*

scrap [skræp] N (fragment) fragmento *m*,

pedacito *m*; (of truth) ápice *m*; (fight) riña *f*, reyerta *f*; **—book** álbum de recortes *m*; **— iron** chatarra *f*; **— paper** papel borrador *m*; **—s** sobras *f pl*, desperdicios *m pl*; VT (break apart) desguazar; (discard) desechar; VI (fight) pelearse, reñir

scrape [skreɪp] VI/VT (rub) raspar; (damage) arañar; **to — along** ir tirando, ir pasándola; **to — by** arreglárselas; **to — together** reunir; **to bow and —** ser muy servil; N (act of scraping) raspado *m*; (injury) raspón *m*, raspadura *f*; (sound) chirrido *m*; (fight) pelea *f*; (difficult situation) aprieto *m*

scraper [skréɪpɚ] N raspador *m*

scratch [skrætʃ] VI/VT (mark) arañar, rasguñar; (relieve itching) rascar[se]; (cancel from a race) retirar[se]; (cause itching) picar; VI (to dig, as a hen) escarbar; **to — out** (words) tachar; (eyes) sacar; N (injury) arañazo *m*, rasguño *m*; (sound) chirrido *m*; **to start from —** empezar de cero; **— test** examen dérmico de alergias *m*

scrawny [skróʊni] ADJ esmirriado

scream [skrim] N grito *m*, alarido *m*; **he's a —** es un payaso; VI/VT gritar

screech [skritʃ] N (of brakes) chirrido *m*; (of voice) chillido *m*; **— owl** lechuza *f*; VI (of brakes) chirriar; (of voice) chillar

screen [skrin] N (movie, computer) pantalla *f*; (divider) biombo *m*; (on window) mosquitero *m*; (sifter) tamiz *m*; **— door** puerta con mosquitero *f*; **—ing test** prueba de detección *f*; **—pass** pase pantalla *m*; **—play** guión *m*; **— saver** protector de pantalla *m*, salvapantallas *m sg*; **—writer** guionista *mf*; VT (conceal) tapar; (sift) tamizar; (project) proyectar; (select) seleccionar

screw [skru] N (device) tornillo *m*; (one turn) vuelta *f*; (propeller) hélice *f*; **—driver** destornillador *m* (also cocktail); VT atornillar; **to — on** enroscar; **to — up one's courage** cobrar ánimo; **to — around** perder tiempo

scribble [skríbəl] VI/VT garabatear, garrapatear; N garabato *m*

scrimp [skrɪmp] VI hacer economías

script [skrɪpt] N (writing) escritura *f*; (screenplay) guión *m*

scripture [skrɪ́ptʃɚ] N escritura sagrada *f*

scroll [skroʊl] N (roll) rollo *m*; (adornment) voluta *f*; VI **to — down** bajar el cursor

scrub [skrʌb] VI/VT (rub) fregar, restregar; **to — up** lavarse las manos; VT (cancel) cancelar; N (cleaning) friega *f*, fregada *f*; (bushes) maleza *f*; (rough terrain) breña *f*; **— pine** pino achaparrado *m*; **— team** equipo suplente *m*; **—woman** fregona *f*

scruple [skrúpəl] N escrúpulo *m*

scrupulous [skrúpjələs] ADJ escrupuloso

scrutinize [skrútnaɪz] VI/VT escrutar,

escudriñar

scrutiny [skrútn̩i] N escrutinio *m*, examen minucioso *m*

scuba [skúbə] N escafandra *f*; VI **to — -dive** bucear

scuff [skʌf] VT (shoes) rayar; (floor) marcar; N (on shoes) raya *f*; (on floor) marca *f*

scuffle [skʌ́fəł] N refriega *f*, riña *f*; VI (fight) pelear, reñir; (shuffle) arrastrar los pies

sculptor [skʌ́łptə] N escultor -ora *mf*

sculpture [skʌ́łptʃə] N escultura *f*; VI/VT esculpir

scum [skʌm] N (in a glass) capa de suciedad *f*; (on a pond) verdín *m*; (people) *pej* escoria *f*; (vile person) *pej* canalla *mf*; **—bag** *pej* canalla *mf*; VI cubrirse de espuma; VT espumar

scurrilous [skɜ́ələs] ADJ (coarse) grosero

scurry [skɜ́i] VI correr; **to — away/off** escabullirse

scurvy [skɜ́vi] N escorbuto *m*

scuttle [skʌ́dl̩] VI (run) correr; **to — away/off** escabullirse; VT (sink a ship) hundir; (abandon a plane) abandonar

scythe [saɪð] N guadaña *f*

sea [si] N mar *mf*; **— battle** batalla naval *f*; **—board** costa *f*, litoral *m*; **—coast** costa *f*, litoral *m*; **— cow** vaca marina *f*; **— current** corriente marina *f*; **—food** frutos del mar *m pl*; **— green** verdemar *m*; **—gull** gaviota *f*; **— horse** caballito de mar *m*; **— level** nivel del mar *m*; **— lion** léon marino *m*; **—man** marino *m*, marinero *m*; **—plane** hidroavión *m*; **—port** puerto de mar *m*; **— power** potencia naval *f*; **—shore** costa *f*; **—sickness** mareo *m*; **—side** costa *f*, litoral *m*; **— turtle** tortuga marina *f*; **— urchin** erizo de mar *m*; **—weed** alga [marina] *f*; **at —** (on the ocean) en el mar; (confused) perdido; **by —** por barco; **to put to —** hacerse a la mar; **on the high —s** en alta mar; ADJ marino; **—faring** marinero; **—sick** mareado; **to get —sick** marearse; **—worthy** marinero

seal [sił] N (stamp) sello *m*; (on a jar) precinto *m*; (animal) foca *f*; **to set one's —** sellar; VT (put a seal on) sellar; (close with a seal) precintar; **—ing wax** lacre *m*; **to — one's fate** determinar el destino de uno; **to — off** acordonar; **to — in** cerrar herméticamente; **to — with wax** lacrar

seam [sim] N (sewing) costura *f*; (in rock) grieta *f*; (in ore deposits) veta *f*; VT coser

seamstress [símstrɪs] N costurera *f*

seamy [sími] ADJ sórdido

sear [sir] VT chamuscar

search [sɜtʃ] VI/VT (an area) rastrear, requisar; (a suitcase) registrar; (a person) cachear; **— me!** ¡a mí que me registren! ¡yo que sé! **to — for** buscar; N (for something) búsqueda *f*; (of

baggage, ships) registro *m*; (of an area) rastreo *m*; **— and replace** buscar y reemplazar; **— engine** motor de búsqueda *m*, máquina de búsqueda *f*; **— function** función de búsqueda *f*; **—light** reflector *m*; **— warrant** orden de registro *m*; **in — of** en busca de

season [sízən] N (of the year) estación *f*; (period of time) temporada *f*, época *f*; (sports schedule) temporada *f*; **in —** en temporada/ época; **— ticket** billete de abono *m*; **open —** temporada de caza/pesca *f*; **out of —** fuera de temporada/época; VT (to spice) sazonar, aderezar; VI (wood) secarse; **a —ed pilot** un piloto experimentado

seasonal [sízənəł] ADJ estacional

seasoning [sízənɪŋ] N condimento *m*, aliño *m*

seat [sit] N (furniture) asiento *m*; (of bicycle) sillín *m*; (in parliament) escaño *m*; (of government) sede *f*; (in the theater) localidad *f*; (buttocks) asentaderas *f pl*; (of clothes) fondillos *m pl*; **to take a —** sentarse, tomar asiento; **— belt** cinturón de seguridad *m*; VT (cause to sit) sentar; (accommodate with seats) tener capacidad para; (place) colocar; **to — oneself** sentarse

seborrhea [sebəríə] N seborrea *f*

seclude [sɪklúd] VT aislar; **to — oneself from** recluirse de, aislarse de

secluded [sɪklúdɪd] ADJ apartado, aislado, recogido

seclusion [sɪklúʒən] N recogimiento *m*, aislamiento *m*

second [sékənd] ADJ segundo; **— base** segunda base *f*, intermedia *f*; **— baseman** segunda base *mf*, camarero -ra *mf*, intermediarista *mf*; **— child** segundón -ona *mf*; **— cousin** primo -ma segundo -da *mf*; **— fiddle** segundón -ona *mf*; **— floor** primer piso *m*; **— half** (sports) segundo tiempo *m*; **—hand** de segunda mano; **— lieutenant** subteniente *mf*; **— mortgage** segunda hipoteca *f*; **— nature** automático; **—-rate** mediocre, de segunda; **to get —s** repetir, servirse por segunda vez; **— serve** segundo servicio *m*; **on — thought** pensándolo bien; N (part of a minute) segundo *m*; (helper in a duel) padrino *m*; **—s** (inferior wares) artículos de segunda *m pl*; (additional helping) segunda ración *f*; **in a —** ahorita; **may I have —s?** ¿puedo repetir? VT (support) secundar, apoyar; (assist in duels) apadrinar; (support a motion) apoyar; **to —-guess** cuestionar

secondary [sékənderi] ADJ secundario; **— school** escuela secundaria *f*

secondly [sékəndli] ADV en segundo lugar

secrecy [síkrɪsi] N secreto *m*

secret [síkrɪt] ADJ & N secreto *m*

secretariat [sekrɪtǽriət] N secretaría *f*

secretary [sékrɪteri] N (assistant) secretario -ria *mf*; (government) ministro -tra *mf*; (furniture) escritorio *m*

secrete [sɪkrit] VT (discharge) secretar, segregar; (hide) ocultar

secretion [sɪkríʃən] N secreción *f*

secretive [síkrɪDɪv] ADJ hermético

sect [sɛkt] N secta *f*

section [sékʃən] N (component) sección *f*; (of a chapter) apartado *m*; (of a text) trozo *m*; (of a city) sector *m*; (incision) corte *m*; (of orange) gajo *m*; VT seccionar

sector [séktə-] N sector *m*

sectorial [sektóriəɫ] ADJ sectorial

secular [sékjələ-] ADJ secular; N (person) seglar *mf*, lego -ga *mf*

secure [sɪkjúr] ADJ (certain, safe) seguro; (firm) firme; VT (make certain, guarantee) asegurar, afianzar; (make firm) afirmar, cimentar; (obtain) obtener; (protect) proteger; (lock) cerrar con llave; (capture) capturar; (tie) amarrar

security [sɪkjúrɪDi] N (safety, freedom from worry) seguridad *f*; (guarantee) fianza *f*, garantía *f*; (guarantor) fiador -ora *mf*; — **deposit** depósito de garantía *m*; **securities** valores *m pl*

sedan [sɪdæn] N sedán *m*

sedate [sɪdét] ADJ sosegado, tranquilo; VT sedar

sedation [sɪdéʃən] N sedación *f*

sedative [sédəDɪv] ADJ & N calmante *m*, sedante *m*

sedentary [sédn̩teri] ADJ sedentario

sediment [sédəmənt] N sedimento *m*; (dregs) heces *f pl*

sedition [sɪdíʃən] N sedición *f*

seduce [sɪdús] VI/VT seducir [a]

seduction [sɪdákʃən] N seducción *f*

see [si] VI/VT (perceive, find out, meet, visit) ver; (understand) entender; (make sure) fijarse, asegurarse; (date) salir con; —**ing-eye dog** perro guía *m*; **let me —** a ver; **to —** to encargarse de, atender; **to — off** despedir; **to — through someone** calar a alguien; **to — about** ocuparse de; **to — out** acompañar a la puerta; N sede *f*

seed [sid] N (grains) semilla *f*; (in tennis) cabeza de serie *f*; **to go to —** echarse a perder; — **bed** semillero *m*; VI/VT (sow) sembrar; VT (remove seeds) despepitar, quitar las semillas; (player) clasificar; VI producir semillas

seedy [sídi] ADJ sórdido

seek [sik] VT (search for) buscar; (ask for) pedir; **to — after** buscar; **to — to** tratar de, esforzarse por

seem [sim] VI parecer; **they — to be here** parece que están aquí; **it —s to me** me parece

seemingly [símɪŋli] ADV aparentemente

seen [sin] *see* see

seep [sip] VI/VT rezumar[se]

seer [sir] N vidente *mf*

seesaw [sísɔ] N balancín *m*, subibaja *m*; VI oscilar

seethe [sið] VI bullir, hervir; **he was seething** hervía de rabia

segment [ségmənt] N segmento *m*

segregate [ségrɪget] VI/VT segregar

seismic [sáɪzmɪk] ADJ sísmico

seize [siz] VT (grab) asir, agarrar; (take possession) apoderarse de; (take advantage of) aprovecharse de; (confiscate) embargar, incautarse de, secuestrar; **to — upon** asir; VI **to — [up]** (mechanism, motor) agarrotarse; **to — upon** valerse de

seizure [síʒə-] N (of power) toma *f*; (of property) confiscación *f*; (of drugs, guns) incautación *f*, secuestro *m*; (epileptic) ataque *m*

seldom [séɫdəm] ADV rara vez, raramente

select [sɪlékt] ADJ selecto; VI/VT elegir, seleccionar

selection [sɪlékʃən] N selección *f*, elección *f*

selective [sɪléktɪv] ADJ selectivo

self [sɛɫf] N (ego) yo *m*; —**assurance** desenvoltura *f*; —**control** autocontrol *m*; —**defense** defensa propia *f*; (juridical term) legítima defensa *f*; —**denial** abnegación *f*; —**determination** autodeterminación *f*; —**discipline** autodisciplina *f*; —**esteem** autoestima *f*; —**government** autogobierno *m*; —**help** autoayuda *f*; —**image** autoimagen *f*; —**improvement** mejora personal *f*; —**interest** interés personal *m*; —**made man** hombre que debe su éxito a sus propios esfuerzos *m*; —**pity** autocompasión *f*; —**reliance** independencia *f*, autosuficiencia *f*; —**respect** amor propio *m*; —**sacrifice** sacrificio *m*; —**satisfaction** autosatisfacción *f*; **his better —** su lado bueno *m*; **his former —** lo que era antes; ADJ —**assured** desenvuelto; —**centered** egocéntrico; —**composed** tranquilo; —**confident** con confianza de sí mismo; —**conscious** (shy) cohibido; (with complexes) acomplejado; —**destructive** autodestructivo; —**employed** que trabaja por cuenta propia; —**evident** evidente; —**explanatory** claro, fácil de entender; —**propelled** autopropulsado; —**righteous** que afecta superioridad moral; —**satisfied** pagado de sí, satisfecho de sí; —**service** autoservicio; —**serving** interesado; —**sufficient** autosuficiente

selfish [séɫfɪʃ] ADJ egoísta

selfishness [séɫfɪʃnɪs] N egoísmo *m*

selfless [séɫflɪs] ADJ desinteresado, generoso

sell [sɛɫ] VI/VT vender[se]; **his books — well** se venden bien sus libros; **to be sold on** estar entusiasmado con; **to — off** liquidar; **to — out** (dispose of) liquidar; (betray) traicionar, vender; (run out) agotarse; N —**-off** (liquidation) liquidación *f*; (decline) baja *f*; —**out** traición *f*

seller [sέlɚ] N vendedor -ora *mf*

selling [sέlɪŋ] N venta *f*

semantics [sɪmǽntɪks] N semántica *f*

semblance [sέmbləns] N apariencia *f*

semester [səmέstɚ] N semestre *m*

semicircle [sέmɪsɚkəl] N semicírculo *m*

semicolon [sέmɪkolən] N punto y coma *m*

semiconductor [sɛmɪkəndʌ́ktɚ] N semiconductor *m*

semifinal [sέmifaɪnl] ADJ & N semifinal *f*

seminar [sέmənɑr] N seminario *m*

seminary [sέmənɛri] N seminario *m*

Semitic [səmɪ́tɪk] ADJ semítico

senate [sέnɪt] N senado *m*

senator [sέnətɚ] N senador -ora *mf*

send [sɛnd] VT enviar, mandar; **that sent chills down my spine** me dio escalofríos; **to — away** hacer salir; **to — back** devolver; **to — for** mandar buscar a; **to — in** remitir; **to — out for** encargar; **to — word** mandar decir

sender [sέndɚ] N remitente *m*

Senegal [sέnɪgɔl] N Senegal *m*

Senegalese [sɛnɪgəlíz] ADJ & N senegalés -esa *mf*

senile [sínaɪl] ADJ senil, chocho

senility [sɪnɪ́lɪdi] N senilidad *f*, chochera *f*, chochez *f*

senior [sínjɚ] ADJ (with more seniority) más antiguo; (in school) de cuarto año; (for the elderly) para ancianos; **John Smith —** John Smith padre; N (person of higher rank) superior *mf*; (fourth-year student) estudiante de cuarto año *mf*; (elderly person) persona de la tercera edad *f*; **to be somebody's —** ser mayor que alguien; **— citizen** persona de la tercera edad *f*; **— partner** socio -cia principal *mf*

seniority [sinjɔ́rɪdi] N antigüedad *f*

sensation [sɛnséʃən] N sensación *f*

sensational [sɛnséʃənl] ADJ sensacional

sense [sɛns] N (of humor, honor, direction) sentido *m*; (of pain, insecurity) sensación *f*; (meaning) significado *m*, sentido *m*; **— of hearing** sentido del oído *m*; **— of humor** sentido del humor *m*; **— of sight** sentido de la vista *m*; **— of smell** sentido del olfato *m*; **— of taste** sentido del gusto *m*; **— of touch** sentido del tacto *m*; **to make —** tener sentido; **to make — of something** entender algo; **in a —** en cierto sentido; **to take leave of one's —s** volverse loco; **to come to one's —s** (wake up) volver en sí; (be reasonable) recobrar el juicio; VT (perceive) percibir, sentir; (intuit) intuir

senseless [sέnslɪs] ADJ (meaningless) sin sentido; (unconscious) inconsciente

sensibility [sɛnsəbílɪdi] N sensibilidad *f*

sensible [sέnsəbəl] ADJ sensato, razonable, juicioso

sensitive [sέnsɪdɪv] ADJ (to emotions) sensible; (to stimuli) sensitivo

sensitivity [sɛnsɪtívɪdi] N sensibilidad *f*

sensitize [sέnsɪtaɪz] VT sensibilizar

sensor [sέnsɔr] N sensor *m*

sensory [sέnsəri] ADJ sensorial; **— overload** sobrecarga sensorial *f*

sensual [sέnʃuəl] ADJ sensual

sensuality [sɛnʃuǽlɪdi] N sensualidad *f*

sensuous [sέnʃuəs] ADJ sensual

sent [sɛnt] *see* send

sentence [sέntəns] N (to prison) sentencia *f*, condena *f*; (phrase) oración *f*; VT condenar, sentenciar

sentiment [sέntəmənt] N sentimiento *m*

sentimental [sɛntəmέntl] ADJ sentimental; (excessively) sensiblero

sentimentality [sɛntəmɛntǽlɪdi] N sentimentalismo *m*; (excessive) sensiblería *f*

sentinel [sέntnəl] N centinela *m*

sentry [sέntri] N centinela *m*; **— box** garita *f*

separate[1] [sέprɪt] ADJ (apart) separado

separate[2] [sέpəret] VI/VT separar[se]

separation [sɛpəréʃən] N separación *f*

Sephardi [səfárdi] N sefardí *mf*, sefardita *mf*

September [sɛptέmbɚ] N septiembre *m*, setiembre *m*

sequel [síkwəl] N continuación *f*

sequence [síkwəns] N secuencia *f*; (of events) serie *f*; **in —** en orden; VT secuenciar

Serb [sɚb] N (person) serbio -bia *mf*

Serbian [sɚ́biən] ADJ serbio; N (language) serbio *m*; (person) serbio -bia *mf*

serenade [sɛrənéd] N serenata *f*, ronda *f*; VI/VT dar [una] serenata [a], rondar [a]

serene [sərín] ADJ sereno

serenity [sərένɪdi] N serenidad *f*

sergeant [sárdʒənt] N sargento *m*

serial [síriəl] N (novel) novela por entregas *f*; ADJ (published in installments) por entregas; (murder) en serie; **— bus** bus en serie *m*; **— connector** conector en serie *m*; **— killer** asesino -na en serie *mf*; **— mouse** ratón en serie *m*; **— number** número de serie *m*; **— port** puerto serie/serial *m*; **— printer** impresora en serie *f*

series [síriz] N serie *f*

serious [síriəs] ADJ serio; (illness) grave

seriously [síriəsli] ADV (conduct) en serio; (injure) gravemente; **—, what do you want?** hablando en serio, ¿qué es lo que quieres?

seriousness [síriəsnɪs] N seriedad *f*; (of an illness) gravedad *f*

sermon [sɚ́mən] N sermón *m*

serpent [sɚ́pənt] N sierpe *f*, serpiente *f*

serrated [sέreɪdɪd] ADJ serrado

serum [sírəm] N suero *m*

servant [sɜ́ːvənt] N sirviente -ta *mf*, criado -da *mf*

serve [sɜ́ːv] VI/VT (in a restaurant, in a store) servir, atender; (in tennis) sacar; **to — a term in prison** cumplir una condena; **to — a warrant** entregar una orden judicial; **to — as** servir de; **to — notice** advertir; **to — one's purpose** resultarle útil a alguien; **it —s me right** me lo merezco; N (in tennis) saque *m*; **— and volley** saque y volea *m*

server [sɜ́ːvɚ] N (one who serves) servidor -ora *mf*; (in a restaurant) camarero -ra *mf*; (for pie) utensilio para servir *m*; (computer) servidor *m*; (tennis player) sacador -ora *mf*

service [sɜ́ːvɪs] N servicio *m*; (in tennis) saque *m*, servicio *m*; (of a warrant) entrega *f*; **— break** rotura de servicio *f*; **— entrance** entrada de servicio *f*; **—man** (soldier) militar *m*; (for repairs) reparador *m*; **— station** gasolinera *f*, estación de servicio *f*; **at your —** a su servicio; VT (a car) revisar; (an industry) atender, servir; (a debt) pagar; **in— training** capacitación para empleados; **out of —** (broken) averiado, fuera de servicio

serviceable [sɜ́ːvɪsəbəl] ADJ (practical) práctico; (durable) duradero

servile [sɜ́ːvaɪl] ADJ servil

servitude [sɜ́ːvɪtud] N servidumbre *f*

sesame [sésəmi] N sésamo *m*, ajonjolí *m*

session [séʃən] N (meeting) sesión *f*; (semester) semestre *m*; (of Congress) período de sesiones *m*

set [sɛt] VT (place) colocar; (fix) fijar, establecer; (sic) azuzar; (print) componer; VI (cement) fraguar; (jelly) cuajar; (sun) ponerse; (glue) endurecerse; **to — a bone** reducir un hueso dislocado; **to — a diamond** engastar un diamante; **to — an example** dar ejemplo; **to — a poem to music** ponerle música a un poema; **to — a precedent** establecer un precedente; **to — a trap** tender una trampa; **to — a watch** poner el reloj en hora; **to — about** disponerse a; **to — aside** (move an object) apartar; (money) ahorrar; (a claim) rechazar; (a verdict) anular; **to — back** (hinder, make earlier) atrasar; (cost) costar; (a clock) retrasar; **to — forth** exponer; **to — forth on a journey** ponerse en camino; **to — free** librar; **to — off** (make explode) hacer estallar; (start on a journey) ponerse en camino; (intensify) resaltar; **to — one's heart on** tener la esperanza puesta en; **to — one's mind on** resolverse a; **to — out for** partir para; **to — out to** proponerse; **to — right** rectificar; **to — the table** poner la mesa; **to — up** (assemble) armar; (set a trap for) tender; (establish) establecer; (a computer program) instalar; **to — upon someone** acometer a alguien; ADJ (fixed)

fijo; (ready) listo; (hard) duro; N (ensemble) juego *m*; (group) conjunto *m*; (TV) aparato *m*; (scenery) escenario *m*; (of tennis) set *m*, manga *f*; **—back** revés *m*; **— of teeth** dentadura *f*; **— point** punto de set/manga *m*; **—up** (arrangement) arreglo *m*; (assembly) montaje *m*; (installation) instalación *f*; (trap) tongo *m*, timo *m*; **—up program** programa de instalación *m*

setter [séɾɚ] N sétter *m*

setting [séɾɪŋ] N (act of putting down) colocación *f*; (jewel) engaste *m*; (in theater) escenario *m*; (of sun, moon) puesta *f*; (of dial) posición *f*; **— sun** sol poniente *m*

settle [sédl] VT (a territory) colonizar, poblar; (affairs) arreglar; (argument) zanjar; (lawsuit) arreglar; (an estate) liquidar; (a bill) saldar, solventar; (one's nerves) calmar; VI (end a dispute) llegar a un arreglo; (take up residence) establecerse; (alight) posarse; (sink to bottom) depositarse; **to — down** (get married) casarse; (mend one's ways) sentar cabeza; (take up residence) instalarse; (become calm) calmarse; **to — on a date** fijar/señalar una fecha; **to — for** conformarse con; **to — up** pagar

settlement [sédlmənt] N (community) colonia *f*, población *f*; (act of establishing) asentamiento *m*; (agreement) acuerdo *m*; (of a lawsuit) arreglo *m*; (of a bill) pago *m*, finiquito *m*; (final disposition) liquidación *f*

settler [sédlɚ] N colono -na *mf*, poblador -ora *mf*

settling [sédlɪŋ] N asentamiento *m*

seven [sévən] NUM siete *m*; **— hundred** setecientos

seventeen [sɛvəntín] NUM diecisiete

seventh [sévənθ] ADJ séptimo

seventy [sévənti] NUM setenta

sever [sévɚ] VT (an arm) cortar; (relations) romper

several [sévəɹəl] ADJ varios

severance pay [sévɚənspe] N indemnización por despido *f*

severe [səvír] ADJ (criticism, standards) severo; (winter, test) duro; (storm, heat) intenso; (illness) grave

severity [səvéɹɪɾi] N (of criticism, standards) severidad *f*; (of water, test) dureza *f*; (of storm, heat) intensidad *f*; (of illness) gravedad *f*

Sevillian [səvíljən] ADJ & N sevillano -na; **— dances** sevillanas *f pl*

sew [so] VI/VT coser

sewage [súɪdʒ] N aguas negras *f pl*; **— system** alcantarillado *m*

sewer [súɚ] N alcantarilla *f*, cloaca *f*, colector *m*

sewing [sóɪŋ] N costura *f*; **— machine** máquina de coser *f*

sewn [son] *see* sew

sex [sɛks] N sexo *m*; — **appeal** atractivo sexual *m*; — **symbol** símbolo sexual *m*; VT sexar

sexism [séksɪzəm] N sexismo *m*

sexist [séksɪst] ADJ & N sexista *mf*

sexton [sékstən] N sacristán *m*

sexual [sékʃuəl] ADJ sexual; — **assault** violación *f*; — **discrimination** discriminación sexual *f*; — **harassment** acoso sexual *m*

sexuality [sɛkʃuǽlɪɖi] N sexualidad *f*

sexy [séksi] ADJ sexy, morboso

Seychelles [seʃéɫ] N Seychelles *f pl*

shabby [ʃǽbi] ADJ (worn) gastado; (slovenly) andrajoso; (tawdry) sórdido; (mean) mezquino; **not too** — no está mal

shack [ʃæk] N casucha *f*, choza *f*

shackle [ʃǽkəl] N grillete *m*; —**s** cadenas *f pl*, grillos *m pl*; VT (put in chains) engrillar; (impede) estorbar

shad [ʃæd] N sábalo *m*

shade [ʃed] N (shadow) sombra *f*; (nuance) matiz *m*; (for windows) persiana *f*; (phantom) espectro *m*; (of a lamp) pantalla *f*; **a — longer** un poco más largo; **in the** — a la sombra; —**s** (sunglasses) *Am* lentes negros/oscuros *m pl*; *Sp* gafas de sol *f pl*; VT (protect from sun) sombrear, dar sombra

shadow [ʃǽdo] N (dark image, shade) sombra *f*; (phantom) espectro *m*; **in the — of** a la sombra de; **without a — of doubt** sin sombra de duda; VT (darken) sombrear; (make gloomy) ensombrecer; **to — someone** seguirle la pista a alguien

shady [ʃébi] ADJ sombreado, umbrío; — **character** sospechoso -sa *mf*; — **dealings** negocios turbios *m pl*

shaft [ʃæft] N (of a mine) pozo *m*; (of a feather) cañón *m*; (of an elevator) hueco *m*; (of an arrow) asta *f*

shaggy [ʃǽgi] ADJ peludo, lanudo

shake [ʃek] VI (tremble) temblar; VI/VT (move back and forth) sacudir[se]; (in order to mix) agitar[se]; (elude) deshacerse de; **to — hands** darse la mano; **to — one's head** menear la cabeza; **to — with cold** tiritar; **to — with fear** temblar de miedo; **to — off** (a cold, disappointment, etc.) deshacerse de; (depression) librarse de; **to — up** (a liquid) agitar; (a person) trastornar; N (violent) sacudida *f*; (of milk) batido *m*; **hand—** apretón de manos *m*; **the —s** escalofríos *m pl*; —**-up** reorganización *f*

shaken [ʃékən] *see* shake

shaky [ʃéki] ADJ (hand) tembloroso; (start) vacilante

shall [ʃæl] V AUX **I — come** vendré; — **I help you?** ¿te ayudo? **thou shalt not steal** no robarás

shallow [ʃǽlo] ADJ (plate) llano; (water) poco profundo; (breathing) superficial; (explanation) superficial, somero

shallowness [ʃǽlonɪs] N (of plate) lo llano; (of water) poca profundidad *f*; (of person) superficialidad *f*

sham [ʃæm] N (hoax) farsa *f*; (impostor) impostor -ora *mf*; — **battle** simulacro de batalla *m*

shambles [ʃǽmbəlz] N desorden *m*, caos *m*

shame [ʃem] N (embarrassment) vergüenza *f*; (dishonor) deshonra *f*; (pity) lástima *f*; — **on you!** ¡qué vergüenza! **to bring — upon** deshonrar; VT avergonzar

shameful [ʃémfəl] ADJ vergonzoso

shameless [ʃémlɪs] ADJ desvergonzado, descarado

shamelessness [ʃémlɪsnɪs] N desvergüenza *f*

shampoo [ʃæmpú] N (product) champú *m*; (act of washing) lavado del cabello *m*; VI/VT lavar con champú

shamrock [ʃǽmrɑk] N trébol *m*

shank [ʃæŋk] N (part of leg) canilla *f*, espinilla *f*; (cut of meat) pierna *f*, pata *f*

shanty [ʃǽnti] N casucha *f*; *Sp* chabola *f*; —**town** suburbio *m*

shape [ʃep] N (form) forma *f*; (condition) condición *f*; (silhouette) bulto *m*; **to be in bad** — andar mal; **to get in** — ponerse en forma; **to take** — configurarse; VT plasmar, dar forma a; **to — up** reformarse

shapeless [ʃéplɪs] ADJ informe

share [ʃer] N (portion) parte *f*, porción *f*; (stock) acción *f*; —**cropper** aparcero *m*; —**holder** accionista *mf*; VI/VT compartir; **to — in** participar en

shark [ʃɑrk] N (fish) tiburón *m*; (swindler) estafador -ora *mf*

sharp [ʃɑrp] ADJ (blade) afilado, filoso; (needle) puntiagudo; (curve) cerrado; (contrast) marcado, nítido; (smell) acre; (wind) cortante; (pain) punzante; (remark) mordaz, agudo; (mind) perspicaz; (musical note) sostenido; (dresser) elegante; (cheese) picante; (ear) fino; — **eye** vista aguzada *f*; —**shooter** tirador -ora de primera *mf*; —**-tongued** mordaz; —**-witted** agudo; N (in music) sostenido *m*

sharpen [ʃɑrpən] VI/VT (knife) afilar[se]; VT (pencil) sacar punta a; (skill) afinar

sharply [ʃɑrpli] ADV (contrast) marcadamente; (respond) bruscamente, con aspereza; (turn) bruscamente

sharpness [ʃɑrpnɪs] N (of a blade) lo afilado; (of a needle) lo puntiagudo; (of a curve) lo cerrado; (of a contrast) nitidez *f*; (of a smell) acritud *f*; (of pain) intensidad *f*; (of a remark) mordacidad *f*; (of a mind) perspicacia *f*, agudeza *f*; (of cheese) lo picante

shatter [ʃǽɖɚ] VI/VT (glass) astillar[se], hacer[se] añicos; (nerves) destrozar[se]; (health) quebrantar[se]; (hopes) frustrar

shave [ʃev] VI/VT (remove hair) afeitar[se], rasurar[se]; (cut thin slices) cepillar; (graze) rozar; **to — off** rapar; N afeitado *m*, rasurado *m*; **he had a close — se** salvó por poco

shaven [ʃévən] *see* shave

shaver [ʃévə] N afeitadora *f*

shavings [ʃévɪŋz] N virutas *f pl*

shawl [ʃɔl] N mantón *m*, chal *m*

she [ʃi] PRON ella; **— who** la que, quien; N **-- bear** osa *f*

sheaf [ʃif] N (of corn) gavilla *f*; (of arrows) haz *m*; (of paper) fajo *m*

shear [ʃir] VT esquilar, trasquilar; N **—s** (for sheep) tijeras para esquilar *f pl*; (for plants) tijeras para podar *f pl*; (for metal) cizallas *f pl*; (for hair) tijeras de peluquero *f pl*

shearing [ʃírɪŋ] N esquila *f*, esquileo *m*

sheath [ʃiθ] N (of sword, peas) vaina *f*; (of knife, umbrella) funda *f*

sheathe [ʃið] VT (a sword) envainar; (a knife) enfundar

shed [ʃɛd] N cobertizo *m*, tinglado *m*, *Am* galpón *m*; VT (tears) derramar; (light) arrojar; (leaves) perder; (skin, hair) mudar, perder; VI (be waterproof) ser impermeable; (lose hair) pelechar; (lose leaves) deshojarse; (lose skin) mudar la piel

sheen [ʃin] N brillo *m*

sheep [ʃip] N oveja *f*; **—dog** perro pastor *m*, ovejero *m*; **—skin** (hide) piel de oveja *f*; (leather) badana *f*; (parchment) pergamino *m*; (diploma) diploma *m*

sheepish [ʃípɪʃ] ADJ vergonzoso, tímido

sheer [ʃir] ADJ (absolute) puro, total; (fine) fino; (vertical) vertical, acantilado

sheet [ʃit] N (bedding) sábana *f*; (of ice) capa *f*; (of paper) hoja *f*; (of glass) lámina *f*; (of rain) cortina *f*; **— metal** chapa de metal *f*; **— music** música en hojas de partitura *f*

shelf [ʃɛlf] N estante *m*, repisa *f*, anaquel *m*; (of rock) saliente *f*

shell [ʃɛl] N (turtles, snail) caparazón *f*; (of mollusk) concha *f*; (of egg, nut) cáscara *f*; (of peas) vaina *f*; (of a ship) casco *m*; (of a building) armazón *m*; (of artillery) proyectil *m*; (of a rifle) cartucho *m*; **—fish** mariscos *m pl*; VT (nuts, eggs) pelar; (peas) desgranar; (military target) bombardear

shelter [ʃɛltə] N (refuge) refugio *m*, resguardo *m*, abrigo *m*; **to take —** refugiarse, guarecerse; VI/VT (take or give refuge) refugiar[se], resguardar[se], abrigar[se]

shelve [ʃɛlv] VT (place on a shelf) colocar en un estante; (defer) archivar

shepherd [ʃépəd] N pastor *m*; (dog) perro pastor *m*

sherbet [ʃɝbɪt] N sorbete *m*

sheriff [ʃérɪf] N alguacil *m*

sherry [ʃéri] N jerez *m*

shield [ʃild] N escudo *m*; VI/VT (protect) escudar[se]; VT (conceal) ocultar

shift [ʃift] VI/VT (gears) cambiar; **to — for oneself** arreglárselas solo; **to — the blame** echar la culpa a otro; N (of gears, of wind) cambio *m*; (dress) vestido suelto *m*; (of workers) turno *m*; **— key** tecla de [cambio a] mayúsculas *f*

shiftless [ʃíftlɪs] ADJ holgazán

shimmer [ʃímə] VI titilar; N titileo *m*

shin [ʃɪn] N espinilla *f*, canilla *f*; VI **to — up** trepar

shine [ʃain] VI brillar, relucir; VT (shoes) limpiar, lustrar; (furniture) lustrar; N brillo *m*, resplandor *m*; (of shoes) lustre *m*

shingle [ʃíngəl] N (on roof) teja *f*; (sign) chapa *f*; **—s** (skin disorder) culebrilla *f*, zona *f*; **to hang out one's —** abrir un consultorio; VT cubrir con tejas

shiny [ʃáini] ADJ (bright) brillante; (worn) brilloso

ship [ʃip] N (on water) buque *m*, navío *m*; (in air) avión *m*; **—builder** constructor -ora naval *m f*; **—mate** camarada de a bordo *m f*; **—wreck** naufragio *m*; **—yard** astillero *m*; ADJ **—shape** ordenado; VT transportar; **to — off** sacarse de encima; VI **to —wreck** naufragar

shipment [ʃípmənt] N cargamento *m*, remesa *f*

shipper [ʃípə] N (sender) expedidor -ora *m f*; (carrier) transportista *m f*

shipping [ʃípɪŋ] N envío *m*; **— charges** gastos de envío *m pl*; **— and handling** gastos de envío *m pl*

shirk [ʃɝk] VT evadir, esquivar, rehuir

shirt [ʃɝt] N camisa *f*; **in —sleeves** en mangas de camisa; **—tail** faldón *m*

shiver [ʃívə] VI (from cold) tiritar; (from cold, fear, etc.) temblar; N temblor *m*; **—s** escalofríos *m pl*

shoal [ʃol] N (sandbank) bajío *m*, banco de arena *m*; (school of fish) banco *m*, bandada *f*

shock [ʃak] N (impact, disturbance) choque *m*; (of electricity) sacudida *f*; (of wheat) hacina *f*; (physical convulsion) shock *m*, choque *m*; **— absorber** amortiguador *m*; **— of hair** guedeja *f*; **— therapy** terapia de electroshock *f*, terapia electroconvulsiva *f*; **— troops** tropas de choque *f pl*; **— wave** onda expansiva *f*; VT (bewilder) chocar, horrorizar; (discharge electricity) dar una descarga eléctrica; (make bundles of grain) hacinar, hacer gavillas de

shocking [ʃákɪŋ] ADJ chocante, escandaloso

shod [ʃad] *see* shoe

shoddy [ʃádi] ADJ chapucero

shoe [ʃu] N zapato *m*; (for brakes) zapata *f*; (for

horses) herradura *f*; **—horn** calzador *m*;
—lace cordón *m*; **—maker** zapatero -ra *mf*;
— polish betún *m*; **— repairman** zapatero
-ra remendón -ona *mf*; **— store** zapatería *f*;
—string cordón *m*; **to live on a —string**
vivir con poco dinero; **to tie one's —s** atarse
los zapatos; VT (a person) calzar; (a horse)
herrar

shone [ʃon] *see* shine

shoo-in [ʃúin] N favorito -ta *mf*

shook [ʃʊk] *see* shake

shoot [ʃut] VT (wound with a bullet) pegar un
tiro; (discharge a firearm) disparar; (film a
movie) rodar; (hit a soccer ball) chutar; VI
(discharge bullet, arrow) disparar, tirar; (be
discharged) dispararse; (hunt with a gun)
cazar; (germinate) brotar; (throw) lanzar;
(take a photo) fotografiar; (film) filmar; (try
to score, in soccer) chutar; (try to score, in
basketball) tirar; **to — at** disparar a, tirar a; **to
— at goal** patear al arco; **to — by** pasar
rápidamente; **to— down** (plane) derribar;
(argument) refutar; **to — forth** brotar; **to—
up** (grow) crecer rápidamente; (damage by
shooting) tirotear; (inject drugs) chutar; N
(new growth) yema *f*, retoño *m*, vástago *m*;
(filming) rodaje *m*

shooter [ʃúdɚ] N (of guns) tirador -ora *mf*; (of
balls, soccer) goleador -ora *mf*

shooting [ʃúdɪŋ] N (discharge of a gun) tiro *m*,
disparo *m*; (exchange of shots) tiroteo *m*;
(filming) filmación *f*; **— guard** escolta *mf*; **—
match** concurso de tiro *m*; **— pain** punzada
f; **— star** estrella fugaz *f*

shop [ʃap] N (store) tienda *f*; (artisan's place of
business, carpentry course) taller *m*;
(business) planta *f*; **—keeper** tendero -ra *mf*;
—lifter ladrón -ona de tiendas *mf*; **—lifting**
hurto en las tiendas *m*; **— window**
escaparate *m*, vitrina *f*; **to talk —** hablar de
negocios; VI ir de compras; **to — for** ir a
comprar; **to —lift** hurtar [en las tiendas]

shopper [ʃápɚ] N cliente -ta *mf*, comprador -ora
mf

shopping [ʃápɪŋ] N **to go —** ir de compras; **—
center** centro comercial *m*

shore [ʃɔr] N costa *f*, ribera *f*; (of a lake) orilla *f*;
VT **to — up** apuntalar

shorn [ʃɔrn] *see* shear

short [ʃɔrt] ADJ (not long in duration) corto,
breve; (not long in length) corto; (not tall)
bajo; (scanty) escaso; (curt) brusco; **— circuit**
cortocircuito *m*; **—comings** limitaciones *f pl*;
—cut atajo *m*, cortada *f*; **—fall** déficit *m*,
insuficiencia *f*; **—hand** taquigrafía *f*; **—
handed** escaso de personal; **—legged**
pernicorto; **—sighted** miope, corto de vista;
— stop torpedero -ra *mf*, campocorto *mf*; **—
story** cuento *m*; **—wave** onda corta *f*; **in the

— run/haul/term** a corto plazo; **for —** para
abreviar; **in —** en resumen, en suma; **in —
order** rápidamente; **to be — on** estar escaso
de, estar alcanzado de; **to be — on
something** faltarle a uno algo; **to cut —**
interrumpir; **I'm running — on sugar** se
me está acabando el azúcar; ADV **to stop —**
parar de repente, parar en seco; **to come up
—** quedarse corto; N (circuit) cortocircuito *m*;
—s short *m*, pantalón corto *m*; VI/VT (a
circuit) cortocircuitar[se]; (change) dar de
menos; **to —change** dar de menos; **to — out**
fundir

shortage [ʃɔrdɪʤ] N escasez *f*, penuria *f*

shorten [ʃɔrtn] VI/VT acortar[se]; VT recortar

shortening [ʃɔrtnɪŋ] N (lard) manteca *f*;
(abbreviation) acortamiento *m*

shortly [ʃɔrtli] ADJ (soon) en breve, pronto;
(curtly) bruscamente, secamente

shortness [ʃɔrtnɪs] N (of length, height)
cortedad *f*; (of time) brevedad *f*; (of breath)
falta *f*; (of a reply) brusquedad *f*

shot [ʃat] N (discharge) tiro *m*, disparo *m*;
(photograph) foto *f*; (pellet) perdigón *m*,
plomo *m*; (ball in shot-putting) bala *f*;
(injection) inyección *f*; (swallow) trago *m*;
(throw) tirada *f*; (in soccer) tiro *m*, disparo *m*;
—gun escopeta *f*; **— put** lanzamiento de bala
m; **not by a long —** ni con mucho; **he is a
good —** tiene buena puntería; **to take a —**
disparar; **to take a — at** intentar

shot [ʃat] *see* shoot

should [ʃʊd] V AUX **I — think so** ya lo creo; **you
— arrive before nine** deberías llegar antes
de las nueve; **you — eat less** tendrías que
comer menos; **you — have seen her**
tendrías que haberla visto; **were he to
come, I — be pleased** si viniera, me
alegraría

shoulder [ʃóldɚ] N (of a person, coat) hombro
m; (cut of meat) paletilla *f*; (of a road) arcén *m*;
— blade (person) homóplato *m*; (animal)
paletilla *f*; **— pad** hombrera *f*; **to turn a cold
— to** hacerle el vacío a; **the responsibility
is on your —s** tú tienes la responsabilidad;
VT (a load) cargar al hombro; (a task, an
expense) cargar con, asumir; (a door)
empujar con el hombro

shout [ʃaʊt] VI/VT gritar; N grito *m*

shove [ʃʌv] VI/VT empujar; **to — aside** echar a
un lado; **to — off** (go away) largarse; (push
off) desatracar; N empujón *m*, empellón *m*

shovel [ʃávəl] N pala *f*; VT echar con la pala

show [ʃo] VT (exhibit) mostrar, manifestar;
(prove) demostrar; (indicate) indicar, marcar;
(a film, a TV program) dar; VI (be visible)
verse, asomar; (make an appearance)
aparecerse; **— him in** hazle entrar; **to —case**
presentar; **to — mercy** tener piedad; **to —**

off hacer alarde, aparentar; **to — up** aparecer; **to — someone up** poner a alguien en evidencia; **to — the way** señalar el camino; N (exhibition) exposición f; (display) demostración f; (ostentation) ostentación f, alarde m; (performance) espectáculo m; (showing) función f; (on TV) programa m; (movie theater) cine m; **— business** farándula f; **—case** vitrina f; **—down** confrontación f; **—-off** fanfarrón -ona mf; **to go to the —** ir al cine; **for —** para impresionar

shower [ʃáuə] N (rain) aguacero m, chubasco m; (bath) ducha f; (for brides) fiesta para novias f; (of sparks, blows) lluvia f; VI (bathe) ducharse; (rain) llover; VT (with gifts) inundar; (with praise) colmar

shown [ʃon] see show

showy [ʃói] ADJ ostentoso; (attractive) vistoso

shrank [ʃræŋk] see shrink

shred [ʃred] N (of paper) tira f; (of evidence) pizca f; **to be in —s** estar hecho jirones; **to tear to —s** hacer trizas; VI/VT (documents) triturar; (vegetables) rallar

shrew [ʃru] N (animal) musaraña f; (woman) arpía f

shrewd [ʃrud] ADJ astuto, sagaz

shriek [ʃrik] VI/VT chillar; N chillido m

shrill [ʃrɪl] ADJ chillón

shrimp [ʃrɪmp] N (animal) camarón m; (small person) renacuajo m; VI pescar camarones

shrine [ʃraɪn] N (chapel) capilla f; (altar) altar m

shrink [ʃrɪŋk] VI/VT (in size) encoger; VI (in value) reducirse; **— from** retroceder; N (psychiatrist) fam loquero -ra mf; **—wrap** envoltura de plástico transparente f

shrinkage [ʃrɪ́ŋkɪʤ] N (of clothes) encogimiento m; (of value) reducción f

shrivel [ʃrɪ́vəl] VI/VT secar[se], marchitar[se]

shroud [ʃraud] N mortaja f; VT (to wrap for burial) amortajar; (to hide) cubrir

shrub [ʃrʌb] N arbusto m

shrug [ʃrʌg] VI encogerse de hombros; VT encogerse de; **to — off** minimizar, ignorar; N encogimiento de hombros m

shrunk [ʃrʌŋk] see shrink

shrunken [ʃrʌ́ŋkən] see shrink

shudder [ʃʌ́də] VI (from cold) tiritar; (from fear) temblar, estremecerse; N temblor m, estremecimiento m

shuffle [ʃʌ́fəl] VI/VT (cards) barajar; VT (mix) mezclar; VI (walk) arrastrar los pies; (dance) bailar arrastrando los pies; **to — along** ir arrastrando los pies; N (of cards) barajadura f; (of feet) arrastrapiés m sg

shun [ʃʌn] VT rehuir, evitar

shut [ʃʌt] VI/VT cerrar[se]; **to — down** cerrar; **to — off** cortar; **to — out** impedir la entrada de; **to — up** (close) cerrar bien; (lock up)

encerrar; (be quiet) callarse; N **—-down** cese de actividades m; **—-eye** sueño m; **—-in** enfermo -ma confinado -da a la casa mf

shutter [ʃʌ́də] N (of a window) postigo m, contraventana f; (of a camera) obturador m

shuttle [ʃʌ́dl] N (in loom) lanzadera f; (spaceship) transbordador espacial m; (airplane) puente aéreo m; (bus, train) servicio regular m; VI ir y venir; VT llevar y traer

shy [ʃaɪ] ADJ tímido, retraído; (wary) esquivo; (lacking) escaso; VI asustarse, respingar; **to — away** (start) asustarse, respingar; (avoid) esquivar

shyness [ʃáɪnɪs] N timidez f, retraimiento m

shyster [ʃáɪstə] N fam picapleitos m sg

sibling [sɪ́blɪŋ] N hermano m; hermana f; **—rivalry** rivalidad entre hermanos f

sic [sɪk] VT azuzar

sick [sɪk] ADJ (ill) enfermo; (deranged) enfermizo, morboso; (at heart) angustiado; **— and tired** harto; **to be — of** estar harto de; **to be — to one's stomach** tener náuseas; **to make —** (disgust) dar asco; (anger) dar rabia, enfermar; **— leave** licencia por enfermedad f

sicken [sɪ́kən] VI/VT (with illness) enfermar[se], poner[se] enfermo; (with disgust) dar asco; (with anger) dar rabia, enfermar

sickening [sɪ́kənɪŋ] ADJ repugnante

sickle [sɪ́kəl] N hoz f; **— cell anemia** anemia falciforme f

sickly [sɪ́kli] ADJ enfermizo, enclenque

sickness [sɪ́knɪs] N enfermedad f

side [saɪd] N lado m; (of a coin, piece of paper) cara f; (of a person) costado m; (of a hill) ladera f; (of beef) media res f; (of a boat) banda f; (team) equipo m; (garnish) acompañamiento m; **—arm** arma de mano f; **—bar** ladillo m; **—board** aparador m; **—burns** patillas f pl; **—-glance** mirada de soslayo/reojo f; **—arf** (illumination) luz lateral f; (detail) detalle incidental m; **—line** (in sports) banda f, línea de banda f; (in business) negocio suplementario m; **to sit on the —lines** no intervenir; **—walk** acera f; Carib andén m; Am vereda f; Mex banqueta f; **—wall** flanco m; **—ways** (walk) de costado; (glance) de soslayo; **— by —** uno al lado del otro; **by his —** a su lado; **by the — of** al lado de; **on all —s** por todos lados; ADJ (on the side) lateral; (secondary) secundario; VI **to —step** evitar, esquivar; **to —track** (a train) desviar; (attention) distraer; **to — with** ponerse del lado de

siding [sáɪdɪŋ] N revestimiento m

SIDS [sudden infant death syndrome] [sídz] N síndrome de muerte súbita infantil m

siege [siʤ] N sitio m, asedio m, cerco m; **to lay — to** sitiar

Sierra Leone [siéрəlión] N Sierra Leona f

sieve [siv] N tamiz m, cedazo m

sift [sift] VT cerner, tamizar; **to — through** revisar

sigh [sai] VI suspirar; N suspiro m

sight [sait] N (sense) vista f; (attraction) punto de interés m; (ridiculous thing or person) adefesio m, mamarracho m; (on a gun) mira f; **—seeing** turismo m; **in —** a la vista; **on —** en el acto; **he is out of —** ya no se ve; **at first —** a primera vista; **to catch — of** divisar; **to lose — of** perder de vista; **you're a — for sore eyes** dichosos los ojos que te ven; VT (a ship) avistar, divisar; (a gun) apuntar

sign [sain] N (gesture) seña f, señal f; (indication) muestra f, señal f, indicio m; (placard) letrero m; (omen) agüero m, presagio m; (astrological, mathematical) signo m; (on road) cartel m, letrero m; **— language** lenguaje de signos m; VI/VT (write name) firmar; (signal) hacer señas [de]; VT (hire) contratar; (use sign language) hablar por señas; **to — off on** aprobar; **to — over property** ceder una propiedad; **to — up** (in a club) anotarse; (in the army) alistarse

signal [sígnł] N señal f; VI/VT señalar, hacer señas [a]; ADJ notable

signature [sígnətʃə˞] N firma f

signer [sáinə˞] N firmante m f, signatario -ria m f

significance [sɪgnífɪkəns] N significación f

significant [sɪgnífɪkənt] ADJ significativo; **my — other** mi media naranja f

significantly [sɪgnífɪkəntli] ADV (considerably) apreciablemente, considerablemente; **he looked at me —** me dio una mirada significativa/expresiva

signify [sígnəfai] VT significar

silence [sáiləns] N silencio m; VT (child, fears) acallar; (criticism) silenciar, enmudecer

silencer [sáilənsə˞] N silenciador m

silent [sáilənt] ADJ (machine) silencioso; (person) callado, silencioso; **— agreement** acuerdo tácito m; **— film** película muda f

silhouette [siluét] N silueta f; VT **to be —d against** perfilarse contra

silicon [sílɪkən] N silicio m; **— chip** chip de silicio m

silk [sɪlk] N seda f; **— industry** industria sedera f; **—worm** gusano de seda m

silken [sílkən] ADJ (of silk) de seda; (like silk) sedoso

silky [sílki] ADJ sedoso

sill [sɪl] N alféizar m, antepecho m

silly [síli] ADJ necio, bobo, lelo

silo [sáilo] N silo m

silt [sɪlt] N cieno m, limo m

silver [sílvə˞] N (metal, color) plata f; (tableware) cubiertos de plata m pl; ADJ (of silver) de plata; (silver-colored) plateado; **— anniversary** las bodas de plata f pl; **—-plated** bañado en plata; **—-plating** plateado m; **—smith** platero -ra m f; **—ware** cubiertos de plata m pl; VT platear; (a mirror) azogar

similar [símələ˞] ADJ semejante, similar

similarity [sɪmɪlǽrɪdi] N semejanza f, similitud f

similarly [símɪlə˞li] ADV de manera similar; **—, a mile is longer than a kilometer** del mismo modo, una milla es más larga que un kilómetro; **they were — surprised** quedaron igualmente sorprendidos

simile [síməli] N símil m

simmer [símə˞] VI/VT hervir a fuego lento; **to — down** calmarse

simple [símpəl] ADJ (uncomplicated) simple, sencillo; (naive) simple; **—minded** simple, simplón

simpleton [símpəltən] N simplón -ona m f, mentecato -ta m f

simplicity [sɪmplísɪdi] N (lack of complication) sencillez f, simplicidad f; (naiveté) simpleza f

simplify [símpləfai] VI/VT simplificar

simplistic [sɪmplístɪk] ADJ simplista

simply [símpli] ADV (in a simple manner) con sencillez; (merely) simplemente; **it is — ridiculous** francamente, es ridículo

simulate [símjəlet] VI/VT simular

simulation [sɪmjəléʃən] N simulación f

simultaneous [saiməltǽniəs] ADJ simultáneo

sin [sɪn] N pecado m; VI pecar

since [sɪns] CONJ (continuously) desde que; (inasmuch as) puesto que, ya que; PREP (continuously) desde; (from a past time) a partir de; **we have been here — five** estamos aquí desde las cinco; ADV desde entonces; **ever —** desde entonces; **he died long —** murió hace mucho tiempo; **she has — agreed** después de eso consintió

sincere [sɪnsír] ADJ sincero

sincerity [sɪnsérɪdi] N sinceridad f

sine [sain] N seno m

sinew [sínju] N tendón m

sinewy [sínjui] ADJ (full of tendons) nervudo; (robust) membrudo; (chewy) estropajoso

sinful [sínfəl] ADJ (act) pecaminoso; (person) pecador

sing [sɪŋ] VI/VT cantar; N **—song** sonsonete m

Singapore [síŋəpɔr] N Singapur m

Singaporean [sɪŋəpɔ́riən] ADJ & N singapurense m f

singe [sɪndʒ] VT chamuscar, socarrar; N chamusquina f, socarrina f

singer [síŋə˞] N cantante m f; intérprete m f

single [síŋgəl] ADJ (only one) solo, único; (for one person) individual; (unmarried) soltero; **— bed** cama de una plaza f; **—-entry bookkeeping** teneduría por partida simple f; **—-family home** vivienda unifamiliar f; **—**

file fila india *f*; —**-handed** solo, sin ayuda; —**-minded** resuelto; —**-spacing** sencillo *m*; **every** — **one** cada uno; **not a** — **word** ni una sola palabra; *N* (bill) billete de uno *m*; (unmarried person) soltero -ra *mf*; (record) disco sencillo *m*; (in baseball) sencillo *m*; —**s** (in tennis) individuales *m pl*; *VT* **to** — **out** elegir

singular [síŋgjələ] *ADJ & N* singular *m*

sinister [sínɪstə] *ADJ* siniestro

sink [sɪŋk] *VI/VT* (ship) hundir[se]; *VT* (money) invertir; (a well) cavar; (a pipeline) enterrar; **it finally sank in** finalmente nos dimos cuenta de eso; **to** — **one's teeth into** clavar los dientes en; **to** — **to one's knees** caer de rodillas; **sunk in thought** absorto; **my heart sank** se me fue el alma al piso; **the sun was** —**ing** se iba poniendo el sol; *N* (in the kitchen) fregadero *m*; (in bathroom) lavabo *m*; (pond for sewage) pozo negro *m*; —**hole** socavón *m*, sumidero *m*

sinner [sínə] *N* pecador -ora *mf*

sinuous [sínjuəs] *ADJ* sinuoso

sinus [sáɪnəs] *N* seno *m*

sinusitis [saɪnəsáɪdɪs] *N* sinusitis *f*

sip [sɪp] *VI/VT* sorber; *N* sorbo *m*

siphon [sáɪfən] *N* sifón *m*; *VI/VT* (liquid) sacar con sifón; (money) desviar

sir [sɜ] *N* señor *m*

siren [sáɪrən] *N* sirena *f*

sirloin [sɜ́lɔɪn] *N* solomillo *m*

sister [sístə] *N* hermana *f*; —**-in-law** cuñada *f*; — **Mary** Sor María *f*

sit [sɪt] *VI* sentar[se]; (pose) posar; (be seated) estar sentado; (be located) estar situado; **to** — **down** sentarse; **to** — **in on a class** ir de oyente a una clase; **to** — **on** posponer; **to** — **out a dance** saltearse una pieza; **to** — **still** estarse quieto; **to** — **tight** mantenerse firme en su puesto; **to** — **up** incorporarse; **to** — **up all night** quedarse en vela; **to** — **well** caer bien; *N* —**-in** sentada *f*; —**-up** abdominal *m*

sitcom [sítkɑm] *N* comedia de situación *f*

site [saɪt] *N* (for construction) terreno *m*, solar *m*; (on the Internet) sitio *m*; — **license** licencia de sitio *f*; **on-** — **training** capacitación en el lugar de trabajo

sitter [sítə] *N* niñera *f*, *Sp* canguro *mf*

sitting [sídɪŋ] *N* sesión *f*; **in one** — de una sentada, de un tirón; *ADJ* — **duck** blanco fácil *m*; — **room** cuarto de estar *m*

situated [sítʃuedɪd] *ADJ* situado, ubicado

situation [sɪtʃuéʃən] *N* situación *f*

Sitz bath [síts bæθ] *N* baño de asiento *m*

six [sɪks] *NUM* seis; — **hundred** seiscientos; *N* —**-pack** paquete de seis *m*; —**-shooter** revólver de seis tiros *m*

sixteen [sɪkstín] *NUM* dieciséis

sixth [sɪksθ] *ADV & N* sexto *m*

sixty [síksti] *NUM* sesenta

size [saɪz] *N* tamaño *m*; (of clothing) talla *f*; *VT* clasificar según el tamaño; **to** — **up** juzgar

sizable, sizeable [sáɪzəbəl] *ADJ* de tamaño considerable

sizzle [sízəl] *VI* chisporrotear; *N* chisporroteo *m*

skate [sket] *N* patín *m*; —**board** monopatín *m*; *VI/VT* patinar

skein [sken] *N* madeja *f*

skeletal [skélɪdl] *ADJ* esquelético

skeleton [skélɪtən] *N* esqueleto *m*, osamenta *f*; (of a building) armazón *m*; — **key** llave maestra *f*

skeptic, sceptic [sképtɪk] *N* escéptico -ca *mf*

skeptical [sképtɪkəl] *ADJ* escéptico

skepticism [sképtɪsɪzəm] *N* escepticismo *m*

sketch [sketʃ] *N* (drawing) boceto *m*, croquis *m*; (outline) esbozo *m*, bosquejo *m*; (skit) sketch *m*; *VI/VT* (draw) dibujar; (outline) bosquejar

skew [skju] *VT* (cloth) sesgar; (data) tergiversar

skewer [skjúə] *N* brocheta *f*

ski [ski] *N* esquí *m*; — **jump** (sport) salto con esquís *m*; (course) pista de saltos *f*; — **lift** telesquí *m*; *VI/VT* esquiar [en]

skid [skɪd] *N* patinazo *m*; *VI* patinar

skiing [skíɪŋ] *N* esquí *m*

skill [skɪl] *N* destreza *f*, habilidad *f*, maña *f*

skilled [skɪld] *ADJ* diestro, habilidoso; — **worker** obrero -ra calificado -da *mf*

skillet [skílɪt] *N* sartén *f*

skillful, skilful [skílfəl] *ADJ* diestro, habilidoso

skim [skɪm] *VT* (milk) desnatar; (a broth) espumar; (pass near surface) rozar; *VI/VT* (read) leer por encima, repasar; **to** — **over** rozar; *N* — **milk** *Sp* leche desnatada *f*; *Am* leche descremada *f*

skimp [skɪmp] *VI* escatimar; **to** — **on** escatimar

skimpy [skímpi] *ADJ* (funds) escaso; (dress) corto; (bikini) pequeño

skin [skɪn] *N* piel *f* (also of animal, sausage, potato); (of the face) cutis *m*, tez *f*; (for carrying wine) pellejo *m*; (of boiled milk) nata *f*; (of grapes) hollejo *m*; —**-deep** superficial; —**-diving** natación submarina *f*; —**-flint** roña *mf*; —**-head** cabeza rapada *mf*; **to save one's** — salvar el pellejo; **to be saved by the** — **of one's teeth** salvarse por un pelo; *VT* (animal) despellejar, desollar; (fruit) pelar; (a person) quitarle a uno el dinero

skinny [skíni] *ADJ* flaco; **to** — **-dip** nadar desnudo

skip [skɪp] *VI* (jump) brincar, ir dando saltos; (omit) saltarse; (bounce) rebotar; *VT* (a page) saltar[se]; (class) faltar a; (a stone) hacer rebotar; **to** — **out** escaparse; *N* salto *m*, brinco *m*

skipper [skípə] *N* (captain) patrón -ona *mf*, capitán -ana *mf*; (jumper) saltador -ora *mf*

skirmish [skɜ́mɪʃ] *N* escaramuza *f*; *VI*

escaramuzar

skirt [skɜ˞t] N falda f; VT bordear; **to — an issue** evitar un tema

skit [skɪt] N sketch m

skull [skʌl] N cráneo m, calavera f; **— and crossbones** calavera f

skunk [skʌŋk] N mofeta f; Am zorrillo m

sky [skaɪ] N cielo m; **— blue** azul celeste m; **—diving** paracaidismo extremo m; **—high** muy alto; **—lark** alondra f; **—light** claraboya f; **—line** horizonte m; **—scraper** rascacielos m sg; VI **to—rocket** subir vertiginosamente

slab [slæb] N (of wood) trozo m; (of stone) losa f, laja f; (of meat) tajada f

slack [slæk] ADJ (not taut) flojo; (careless) descuidado; (sluggish) lento; **— season** temporada baja f; **to take up the —** llenar el vacío; **—s** pantalones m pl; VI holgazanear; **to — off** holgazanear

slag [slæg] N escoria f

slain [slen] see slay

slalom [slálom] N slalom m

slam [slæm] VI/VT cerrar[se] de un golpe; VI (hit) chocar; VT (throw down) hacer golpear; (criticize) criticar; **to — on the brakes** dar un frenazo; **to — the door** dar un portazo; N (blow) golpazo m; (criticism) crítica f; (of a door) portazo m; **—-dunk** (easy decision) éxito seguro m

slander [slǽndɚ] N calumnia f, difamación f; VT calumniar, difamar

slanderous [slǽndəəs] ADJ calumnioso, difamatorio

slang [slæŋ] N (jargon) jerga f; (argot) argot m

slant [slænt] N (orientation, bias) sesgo m; (of a roof) inclinación f; VI/VT (bias) sesgar; (slope) inclinar[se], ladear[se]

slap [slæp] N (to the body) palmada f; (to the face) bofetada f, torta f, cachetada f; (with a glove) guantada f; **—-happy** aturdido; **—-stick** de golpe y porrazo; **a — in the face** un desaire; **a — on the wrist** un tirón de orejas; **a — on the back** una palmadita en la espalda; VT abofetear; **to — down** reprimir

slash [slæʃ] VI/VT (cut) acuchillar; Am tajear; VT (whip) azotar; (reduce) reducir, rebajar; N (sweeping stroke, wound) cuchillada f, tajo m; (typographical sign) barra f

slat [slæt] N tablilla f

slate [slet] N (rock, roofing) pizarra f; (color) color pizarra m; (list of candidates) lista de candidatos f; VT empizarrar; **this building is —d for destruction** se ha programado la demolición de este edificio

slaughter [slɔ́dɚ] N matanza f; **—house** matadero m; VT (animals) matar; (people, opponents) masacrar

slave [slev] N esclavo -va mf; **—driver** capataz de

esclavos m; **— labor** (workers) mano de obra esclava f; (work) trabajo de esclavos m; VI trabajar como esclavo -va

slavery [slévəri] N esclavitud f

Slavic [slávɪk] ADJ eslavo

sleazy [slízi] ADJ (squalid) sórdido; (contemptible) despreciable

sled [slɛd] N trineo m

sledgehammer [slɛ́dʒhæmɚ] N almádena f

sleek [slik] ADJ (hair) lustroso; (sports car) elegante

sleep [slip] VI/VT dormir; **it —s three** tiene espacio para que duerman tres personas; **to — around** ser promiscuo; **to — in** dormir hasta tarde; **to — it off** dormir la mona; **to — something off** dormir para que desaparezca algo; **to — over** dormir en casa ajena; **to — together** acostarse juntos; **to — with** acostarse con; **to — on it** consultarlo con la almohada; N sueño m; **— apnea** apnea obstructiva del sueño f; **— disorder** trastorno del sueño m; **— mode** modo de dormir m; **—walker** sonámbulo -la mf; **to go to —** dormirse; **to put to —** (put to bed) dormir a; (euthanize) sacrificar

sleeper [slípɚ] N (one who sleeps) persona que duerme f; (beam) durmiente m; (on a train) coche cama m; (unexpected success) éxito inesperado m; (sofa bed) sofá-cama m

sleepily [slípɪli] ADV con somnolencia

sleepiness [slípinɪs] N sueño m, somnolencia f

sleeping [slípiŋ] N sueño m; ADJ dormido; **—bag** saco de dormir m; **— pill** píldora para dormir f, somnífero m; **— sickness** enfermedad del sueño f

sleepless [slíplɪs] ADJ (person) desvelado; (night) en blanco

sleepy [slípi] ADJ somnoliento, adormilado; **to be —** tener sueño

sleet [slit] N cellisca f; VI caer cellisca

sleeve [sliv] N manga f; **to have something up one's —** tener algo en la manga

sleigh [sle] N trineo m; **—bell** cascabel m; VI pasear en trineo

sleight of hand [sláɪd əvhǽnd] N prestidigitación f

slender [slɛ́ndɚ] ADJ delgado, esbelto

slept [slɛpt] see sleep

sleuth [sluθ] N sabueso -sa mf

slew [slu] see slay

slice [slaɪs] N (of bread, cheese) rebanada f; (of fruit) tajada f, raja f; (of meat) lonja f; (in tennis) cortado m, golpe cortado m; VT cortar, rebanar, tajar

slick [slɪk] ADJ (unctuous) untuoso; (sly) astuto; (slippery) resbaladizo

slicker [slíkɚ] N impermeable m

slid [slɪd] see slide

slide [slaɪd] VI/VT deslizar[se]; **to — in** cerrar[se] deslizando; **to — out** abrirse deslizando; **to let something —** dejar pasar algo; N deslizamiento m; (playground equipment) tobogán m; (of a trombone) vara corredora f; (photographic) diapositiva f; (for microscopes) portaobjeto m

slight [slaɪt] N desaire m; VT (snub) desairar; (neglect) descuidar; ADJ (slim) delgado; (delicate) delicado, tenue; (small in degree) leve, ligero

slightly [sláɪtli] ADV algo, un poco

slim [slɪm] ADJ delgado, esbelto; **a — chance** una posibilidad remota

slime [slaɪm] N (in rivers) limo m, fango m; (of snails) baba f; (despicable person) asqueroso -sa m/f

slimy [sláɪmi] ADJ (muddy) fangoso; (slobbery) baboso, gomoso; (despicable) asqueroso

sling [slɪŋ] N (weapon) honda f; (for arm) cabestrillo m; **—shot** (toy) tirachinas m sg, tirador m; (weapon) honda f; VT lanzar; **to — a rifle over one's shoulder** ponerse el rifle en bandolera

slink [slɪŋk] VI (move furtively) andar furtivamente; (move provocatively) caminar provocativamente; **to — away** escurrirse

slip [slɪp] VI (slide) deslizarse; (slide accidentally) resbalar[se]; (fail to engage) patinar; (deteriorate) empeorar; VT (make slip) hacer resbalar; (put) meter; **to — away** escaparse, escabullirse; **to — by** correr; **to — in** meter[se]; **to — one's dress on** ponerse el vestido; **to — out** (leave) salir inadvertido; (say inadvertently) escapársele a uno algo; **to — up** meter la pata; **to let an opportunity — by** dejar pasar una oportunidad; **it —ped my mind** se me olvidó; **it —ped off** se zafó; N (act of slipping) resbalón m, traspié m; (mistake) equivocación f; (pillow cover) funda f; (underskirt) viso m; (piece of paper) papeleta f, tira de papel f; (space for boats) embarcadero m; **— of the tongue** lapsus [linguae] m; **—knot** nudo corredizo m; **Freudian —** acto fallido m

slipper [slípɚ] N zapatilla f, pantufla f

slippery [slípɚi] ADJ resbaloso, resbaladizo; (evasive) evasivo, escurridizo

slipshod [slípʃad] ADJ chapucero

slit [slɪt] VT cortar a lo largo; **to — someone's throat** degollar a alguien; **to — into strips** cortar en tiras; N raja f, hendidura f

slither [slíðɚ] VI serpentear, culebrear; N serpenteo m, culebreo m

sliver [slívɚ] N astilla f; VI/VT astillar[se]

slob [slab] N (unkempt) dejado -da m/f; (uncouth) bruto -ta m/f

slobber [slábɚ] N baba f; VI/VT babosear, babear f

slogan [slógən] N eslogan m, lema m

slop [slap] VT (splash) salpicar; (feed) dar de comer; N (pigswill) bazofia f; (mud) fango m

slope [slop] VI/VT inclinar[se]; N vertiente f, declive m, cuesta f, cortado m; (in math) pendiente f

sloppiness [slápinɪs] N chapucería f

sloppy [slápi] ADJ (muddy) fangoso; (splashed) salpicado; (slovenly) cochino; (poorly done) chapucero

slot [slat] N (for coins, letters) ranura f; (in a computer) bahía f, ranura f; (place in a series) casilla f; (job) puesto m; **— machine** tragamonedas m/f sg, tragaperras m/f sg; VT hacer una ranura

sloth [slɔθ] N (vice) pereza f; (animal) perezoso m

slouch [slaʊtʃ] N (posture) encorvamiento m; (inept person) torpe m/f; (lazy person) holgazán -ana m/f; VI/VT (crouch) andar agachado, encorvar[se]; (shuffle) andar caído de hombros

Slovakia [slovákiə] N Eslovaquia f

Slovakian [slovákiən] ADJ & N eslovaco -ca m/f

Slovene [slovín] ADJ & N esloveno -na m/f

Slovenia [slovíniə] N Eslovenia f

slovenliness [slávənlinɪs] N (of a person) desaseo m, desaliño m; (of work) descuido m

slovenly [slávənli] ADJ (unclean) desaseado; (unkempt) desaliñado; (poorly done) descuidado

slow [slo] ADJ (not fast) lento, tardo; (running behind) atrasado; (sluggish) lerdo, torpe, pesado; **in — motion** en cámara lenta; ADV lentamente, despacio; VI/VT **to — down/up** andar más despacio, frenar; N **—down** (in business) disminución de actividades f; (in labor disputes) huelga de celo f

slowly [slóli] ADV despacio, lento, lentamente; **— but surely** lenta pero seguramente

slowness [slónɪs] N (of speed) lentitud f; (of intelligence) torpeza f

slug [slʌg] N (bullet) bala f; (coin) moneda falsa f; (animal) babosa f; (swallow) trago m; (blow with fist) puñetazo m; VT aporrear; **to — it out** agarrarse a puñetazos

sluggard [slʌgəd] N holgazán -ana m/f

sluggish [slʌgɪʃ] ADJ (slow) lento; (torpid) aletargado, torpe

sluggishness [slʌgɪʃnɪs] N torpeza f

sluice [slus] N (channel with a gate) esclusa f; (channel) canal m; **— gate** compuerta f

slum [slʌm] N barrio bajo m; **—s** tugurios m pl, **—lord** propietario de tugurio m; VI visitar los barrios bajos; **to — it** divertirse en lugares de poca categoría

slumber [slámbɚ] VI dormir; N sueño m; **— party** fiesta de niñas que se quedan a dormir f

slump [slʌmp] VI (a person) desplomarse; (prices, markets) bajar repentinamente; N (in prices) baja repentina *f*; (in the economy) ralentización *f*; (in sports) mala racha *f*

slung [slʌŋ] *see* sling

slunk [slʌŋk] *see* slink

slur [slɚ] VT (pronounce indistinctly) pronunciar mal; (connect notes) ligar; N (connection of notes) ligado *m*; (insult) insulto *m*

slush [slʌʃ] N (melted snow) nieve a medio derretir *f*; (sludge) nieve fangosa *f*; (mud) fango *m*; (refuse) desperdicios *m pl*; — **fund** (illicit fund) cuenta para fines ilícitos *f*; (petty cash) caja chica *f*

sly [slaɪ] ADJ astuto, taimado; **on the** — a escondidas

smack [smæk] N (taste) dejo *m*; *Sp* deje *m*; (kiss) beso ruidoso *m*; (loud eating) chasquido *m*; (slap) palmada *f*, sopapo *m*; (heroin) *fam* caballo *m*; VT (kiss) dar un beso ruidoso; (eat loudly) chascar, chasquear; (slap) dar una palmada; **to** — **of** tener un dejo de

small [smɔl] ADJ (not large) pequeño, chico; (of build) menudo; (narrow) estrecho; (lowercase) minúsculo; (petty) mezquino; — **caps** versalitas *f pl*, versalitas *f pl*; — **change** cambio suelto *m*; — **fry** gente menuda *f*; — **intestine** intestino delgado *m*; — **pox** viruela *f*; — **talk** cháchara *f*; **to feel** — avergonzarse; N (size) pequeño *m*; — **of the back** baja espalda *f*

smallness [smɔ́lnɪs] N pequeñez *f*

smart [smɑrt] ADJ (intelligent) listo, inteligente; (astute) astuto; (stylish) elegante; — **aleck/ alec** sabihondo -da *mf*; — **bomb** bomba inteligente *f*; — **card** tarjeta de circuito integrado *f*, tarjeta inteligente *f*; — **money** inversión inteligente *f*; — **remark** insolencia *f*; N (pain) escozor *m*; VI picar; **I'm —ing from his rude remarks** todavía me duelen sus groserías

smash [smæʃ] VT (destroy) estrellar, destrozar; (a rebellion) aplastar; **to** — **into** estrellarse contra; N (sound) estrépito *m*; (blow) choque violento *m*; (tennis shot) remate *m*; **a** — **hit** un exitazo

smear [smɪr] VT (daub) untar; (spot, vilify) manchar; (blur) correrse; (defeat) reventar; **to** — **with paint** pintorrear, pintarrajear; N (stain) mancha *f*; (culture) frotis *m*; — **campaign** campaña de difamación *f*

smell [smɛl] VI/VT oler; **to** — **of** oler a; **that —s** huele mal, apesta; **to** — **up** apestar; N (odor) olor *m*; (sense) olfato *m*; — **of** olor a

smelly [smɛ́li] ADJ hediondo, apestoso

smile [smaɪl] VI sonreír[se]; N sonrisa *f*

smiling [smáɪlɪŋ] ADJ risueño, sonriente

smirk [smɚk] N sonrisa suficiente *f*; VI sonreír con suficiencia

smith [smɪθ] N herrero -ra *mf*

smitten [smítn̩] *see* smite

smog [smɑg] N smog *m*

smoke [smok] N humo *m*; (cigarette) cigarro *m*, cigarrillo *m*; — **detector** detector de humo *m*, detector de incendios *m*; — **inhalation** inhalación de humo *f*; — **screen** cortina de humo *f*; — **stack** chimenea *f*; **to have a** — fumar; VI (put off smoke) echar humo; (go fast) volar; VT (tobacco) fumar; (ham, fish, glass) ahumar; **to** — **out** (drive out) ahuyentar con humo; (expose) poner al descubierto

smoker [smókɚ] N fumador -ora *mf*; (train car) vagón de fumar *m*

smoking [smókɪŋ] ADJ humeante; — **car** vagón de fumar *m*; — **gun** prueba irrefutable *f*; — **room** cuarto de fumar *m*; N (use of tobacco) tabaquismo *m*, fumar *m*

smoky [smóki] ADJ humoso

smolder, smoulder [smóldɚ] VI arder

smooth [smuð] ADJ (surface) liso; (skin) suave, terso; (tire) gastado; (sea) sereno, tranquilo; (manners) agradable, fino; (flatterer) zalamero; VT (make surface even) alisar; (make easy) allanar; **to** — **away** hacer desaparecer; **to** — **one's hair** atusarse el cabello; **to** — **over** limar asperezas

smoothness [smúðnɪs] N (of a surface) lisura *f*; (of skin) tersura *f*, suavidad *f*; (of sea) tranquilidad *f*; (of manners) fineza *f*; (of a flatterer) zalamería *f*

smote [smot] *see* smite

smother [smʌ́ðɚ] VT (stifle) ahogar[se], sofocar[se], asfixiar[se]; (envelop) cubrir; (overprotect) sobreproteger

smudge [smʌʤ] N borrón *m*, mancha *f*; VI/VT borronear[se], manchar[se]

smug [smʌg] ADJ suficiente, petulante

smuggle [smʌ́gəl] VI/VT contrabandear, hacer contrabando; **to** — **in** entrar de contrabando; **to** — **out** sacar de contrabando

smuggler [smʌ́glɚ] N contrabandista *mf*

smut [smʌt] N (soot) hollín *m*; (pornography) pornografía *f*; (parasite) tizón *m*

snack [snæk] N tentempié *m*, bocadillo *m*; — **bar** cafetería *f*, tizón *m*

snafu [snæfú] N relajo *m*

snag [snæg] N (branch) gancho *m*; (in fabric) enganchón *m*; (any obstacle) pega *f*, obstáculo *m*, contrariedad *f*; **to hit a** — tropezar con un obstáculo; VI/VT enganchar[se]; VT (a ball) agarrar

snail [snel] N caracol *m*; — **mail** correo regular *m*; —**'s pace** paso de tortuga *m*

snake [snek] N serpiente *f*; — **bite** mordedura de serpiente *f*; — **in the grass** víbora *f*; —**skin** piel de serpiente *f*; VI serpentear

snap [snæp] VI (make sound) chasquear, dar un chasquido; (lose control) estallar, perder los estribos; VT (take a photograph) sacar; VI/VT (break) quebrar[se]; **to — at** (try to bite) tirar un mordiscón; (speak harshly) ladrar; **to —one's fingers** chasquear los dedos, castañetear con los dedos; **to — out of** recuperarse de; **to — shut** cerrar[se] de golpe; **to — together** abrochar; **to — up** llevarse; N (sound) chasquido m; (fastener) broche m; (bite) tarascada f; **it's a —** es pan comido; **— judgment** decisión atolondrada f; **—dragon** dragón m; **—shot** instantánea, foto f

snappy [snǽpi] ADJ (biting) mordedor; (elegant) elegante; **make it —!** ¡date prisa!

snare [sner] N (trap) trampa f; **— drum** tambor con bordón m; VT atrapar

snarl [snarl] VI/VT (growl) regañar; (tangle) enmarañar[se], enredar[se]; N (growl) gruñido m; (tangle) maraña f, enredo m

snatch [snætʃ] VT (seize) arrebatar; (kidnap) secuestrar; VI **to — at** dar manotazos; N (act of snatching) arrebato m; (fragment) fragmento m

snazzy [snǽzi] ADJ llamativo

sneak [snik] VI andar furtivamente; **to — in** entrar a escondidas; **to — out** salir a hurtadillas; VT **to — something in** meter algo a escondidas; **to — something out** sacar a escondidas; **to — a cigarette** fumar a escondidas; N persona solapada f

sneakers [sníkɚz] N zapatillas [deportivas] f pl, tenis m pl

sneer [snir] VI (smile) sonreír con sorna; **to — at** mofarse de; N expresión de sorna f

sneeze [sniz] VI estornudar; **that's nothing to — at** no es nada desdeñable; N estornudo m

snicker [sníkɚ] VI reírse burlonamente; N risita burlona f

snide [snaid] ADJ malévolo

sniff [snɪf] VI/VT husmear, olfatear; **to — at** husmear; (ridicule) menospreciar; N (act of sniffing) husmeo m, olfateo m; (smell) bocanada f

sniffle [snífəl] VI (with a cold) sorberse los mocos; (when crying) gimotear; N (when crying) gimoteo m; **the —s** un resfrío

snip [snɪp] VT tijeretear; **to — off** cortar de un tijeretazo; N (act of snipping) tijeretada f, tijeretazo m; (piece cut off) pedacito m, recorte m; **— of conversation** retazo de conversación m

sniper [snáipɚ] N francotirador -ora mf

snitch [snɪtʃ] VI (tell on) chivar, chivatar; VT (rob) ratear; N soplón -ona mf, chivato -ta mf

snob [snab] N esnob mf

snoop [snup] VI fisgar, fisgonear; N fisgón -ona mf

snooze [snuz] VI dormitar; N siesta f; **to take a —** echar un sueñecito / un sueñito / una siesta

snore [snɔr] VI roncar; N ronquido m

snorkel [snɔ́rkəl] N esnórquel m

snort [snɔrt] VI resoplar, bufar; VI/VT (drugs) esnifar; N resoplido m, bufido m; (drink) trago m

snout [snaut] N hocico m, jeta f, morro m; (nose) fam napias f pl

snow [sno] N nieve f (also cocaine, heroin); **—ball** bola de nieve f; **—board** monopatín de nieve m; **—drift** ventisquero m; **—fall** nevada f; **—flake** copo de nieve m; **—man** muñeco de nieve m; **—mobile** motonieve f; **—plow** quitanieves m sg; **—shoe** raqueta f; **—storm** ventisca f; VI nevar; **the airport was —ed in** cerraron el aeropuerto por nieve; **to — under** (cover in snow) cubrir de nieve; (overwhelm) abrumar; **to —ball** aumentar rápidamente

snowy [snói] ADJ nevado; (white) níveo

snub [snʌb] VT volverle la cara a, desairar, despreciar; N desaire m, desprecio m; **—-nosed** chato; Am ñato

snuck [snʌk] see sneak

snuff [snʌf] VI **to — out** apagar, extinguir; N (tobacco product) rapé m; **to be up to —** dar la talla

snug [snʌg] ADJ (tight-fitting) ajustado; (comfortable) cómodo

so [so] ADV (in this way) así; (to this degree) tan; (so much) tanto; **— am I** yo también; **—-and-—** fulano [de tal]; **—-called** llamado; **— as to** para; **— far as I know** que yo sepa; **— many** tantos; **— much** tanto; **— — —** regular; **— much the better** tanto mejor; **— that** de modo que; **I was — a beauty queen!** ¡sí que fui reina de belleza! ¡hasta luego! **— and — forth** etcetera, y así sucesivamente; **I believe —** creo que sí; **is that —?** ¿en serio? ¡no me digas! **ten minutes or —** unos diez minutos; INTERJ (upon discovering a secret) ajajá; CONJ (in order that) de modo que; (consequently) así que, entonces

soak [sok] VI/VT (immerse) remojar[se]; (drench) empapar[se]; **to — through** colarse por; **to — up** absorber, embeber; **to be —ed through** estar empapado, estar calado hasta los huesos; N remojón m

soap [sop] N jabón m; (television show) telenovela f; **— bubble** pompa de jabón f; **—dish** jabonera f; VT enjabonar

soapy [sópi] ADJ jabonoso

soar [sɔr] VI/VT (airplane) elevar[se]; (kite) remontar[se]; (hopes) aumentar[se]; (prices) disparar[se]; (glider) planear[se]; VI (bird) volar

sob [sab] VI sollozar, hipar; N sollozo m, hipo m

sober [sóbɚ] ADJ (not drunk) sobrio; (temperate) moderado; (serious, subdued) serio, sobrio; VI **to — up** (get over drunkenness) despejarse; (become more serious) sentar cabeza

sobriety [səbráɪɪDi] N (not being drunk) sobriedad *f*; (moderation) moderación *f*; (seriousness) seriedad *f*

soccer [sáka·] N fútbol *m*, balompié *m*; — **ball** esférico *m*; — **field** campo de juego *m*, cancha *f*; — **player** futbolista *mf*; — **World Cup** Campeonato Mundial de Fútbol *m*

sociable [sóʃəbəl] ADJ sociable

social [sóʃəl] ADJ (of society) social; (friendly) sociable; — **climber** arribista *mf*; — **science** ciencias sociales *f pl*; — **security** seguridad social *f*; — **welfare** asistencia social *f*; — **work** asistencia social *f*; N reunión social *f*

socialism [sóʃəlɪzəm] N socialismo *m*

socialist [sóʃəlɪst] ADJ & N socialista *mf*

socialize [sóʃəlaɪz] VT socializar; VI salir, tener trato social

society [səsáɪɪDi] N sociedad *f*; (companionship) compañía *f*

socioeconomic [sosioekənámɪk] ADJ socioeconómico

sociology [sosiálədʒi] N sociología *f*

sociopath [sósiəpæθ] N sociópata *mf*

sock [sak] N (garment) calcetín *m*; (blow) puñetazo *m*, zumbido *m*; VT pegar, zumbar; **to — away** ahorrar

socket [sákɪt] N (of eye) cuenca *f*; (electrical outlet) enchufe *m*; (for bulb) portalámparas *m sg*, casquillo *m*

sod [sad] N (lawn) césped *m*; (piece) tepe *m*; VT cubrir de césped

soda [sóDə] N (drink) gaseosa *f*; (sodium hydroxide) soda *f*, sosa *f*; — **fountain** bar de bebidas sin alcohol *m*; — **pop** gaseosa *f*; — **water** agua con gas *f*

sodium [sóDiəm] N sodio *m*

sodomy [sáDəmi] N sodomía *f*

sofa [sófə] N sofá *m*; — **bed** sofá-cama *m*

soft [sɔft] ADJ (butter, bed, water, penalty) blando; (life) fácil, cómodo; (hair, skin) suave; (light) tenue; —**ball** softball *m*; —-**boiled eggs** huevos pasados por agua *m pl*; — **coal** carbón bituminoso *m*; — **drink** gaseosa *f*; — **page break** salto de página suave/ automático *m*; — **palate** velo del paladar *m*; — **return** salto de línea suave *m*; —**ware** software *m*

soften [sɔfən] VI/VT (butter) ablandar[se]; (skin) suavizar[se]; VT (a blow) amortiguar; (voice) bajar

softly [sɔftli] ADV (talk) en voz baja; (walk) sin hacer ruido

softness [sɔftnɪs] N (of butter) blandura *f*; (of hair, skin) suavidad *f*; (of light) tenuidad *f*

soggy [sági] ADJ (clothes) empapado; (day) húmedo

soil [sɔɪl] N suelo *m*, tierra *f*; VI/VT ensuciar[se], manchar[se]

solace [sálɪs] N consuelo *m*; VT consolar

solar [sólə·] ADJ solar; — **eclipse** eclipse de sol *m*; — **energy** energía solar *f*; — **plexus** plexo solar *m*; — **system** sistema solar *m*

sold [sołd] *see* sell

solder [sáDə·] VI/VT soldar[se]; N soldadura *f*; —**ing iron** soldador *m*

soldier [sółdʒə·] N (of low rank) soldado *m*; (of any rank) militar *m*

sole [soł] ADJ solo, único; N (of a foot) planta *f*; (of a shoe) suela *f*; (fish) lenguado *m*

solely [sółli] ADV solamente; **you are — responsible** eres el único responsable

solemn [sáləm] ADJ solemne

solemnity [səlémnɪDi] N solemnidad *f*

solenoid [sólənɔɪd] N solenoide *m*

solicit [səlísɪt] VT (aid) pedir; (a prostitute) ofrecerse; VI (sell) vender, ofrecer productos

solicitor [səlísɪDə·] N abogado *m*; — **general** subsecretario -ria de justicia *mf*

solicitous [səlísɪDəs] ADJ solícito

solid [sálɪd] ADJ (firm) sólido; (dense) denso; — **blue** azul liso *m*; — **geometry** geometría del espacio *f*; — **gold** oro puro *m*; — **line** línea continua *f*; —-**state** de estado sólido; **for one — hour** por una hora entera; N sólido *m*

solidarity [salɪdærɪDi] N solidaridad *f*

solidify [səlíDəfaɪ] VI/VT solidificar[se]

solidity [səlíDɪti] N solidez *f*

solitary [sálɪteri] ADJ solitario; **to be in — confinement** estar incomunicado

solitude [sálɪtud] N soledad *f*

solo [sólo] N (in music) solo *m*

soloist [sóloɪst] N solista *mf*

Solomon Islander [sáləmənáɪləndə·] N salomonense *mf*

Solomon Islands [sáləmənáɪləndz] N Islas Salomón *f pl*

solstice [sólstɪs] N solsticio *m*

soluble [sáljəbəl] ADJ soluble

solution [salúʃən] N solución *f*

solve [salv] VT resolver, solucionar

solvent [sálvənt] N solvente *m*, disolvente *m*

Somalia [somáljə] N Somalia *f*

Somalian [somáljən] ADJ & N somalí *mf*

somber [sámbə·] ADJ sombrío

some [sʌm] ADJ algún, alguno; **I worked for — time** trabajé por un rato; **that is — dog!** ¡menudo perro! PRON algunos; **and then —** y más todavía; ADV — **twenty people** unas veinte personas; **I like it —** me gusta un poco

somebody [sámbəDi] PRON alguien

someday [sámde] ADV algún día

somehow [sámhau] ADV de alguna manera; — **or other** de alguna manera u otra

someone [sámwʌn] PRON alguien, alguno

somersault [sáməsɔłt] N (on ground) voltereta *f*; (in air) salto mortal *m*; VI (on ground) dar una voltereta; (in air) dar un salto mortal

something [sʌ́mθiŋ] PRON algo *m*; **— else** otra cosa; **thirty—** (age) treinta y tantos; (person) treintañero -ra *mf*

sometime [sʌ́mtaim] ADV algún día, en algún momento; **—s** a veces, de vez en cuando

somewhat [sʌ́mhwɑt] ADV algo

somewhere [sʌ́mhwer] ADV en alguna parte; **— else** en alguna otra parte

son [sʌn] N hijo *m*; **—-in-law** yerno *m*; **— of a gun** *fam* hijo de su madre *m*

sonar [sónɑr] N sonar *m*

song [sɔŋ] N canción *f*; (of a bird) canto *m*; **— and dance** cuento chino *m*; **—writer** compositor -ora *mf*; **—bird** ave canora *f*, pájaro cantor *m*; **to buy something for a —** comprar algo muy barato

sonic barrier [sánikbǽria] N barrera del sonido *f*

sonnet [sánit] N soneto *m*

sonority [sənɔ́ridi] N sonoridad *f*

sonorous [sánəəs] ADJ sonoro

soon [sun] ADV pronto; **— after nine** poco después de las nueve; **as — as** tan pronto como, en cuanto; **see you —** hasta pronto; **how — do you want it?** ¿para cuándo lo necesitas? **he arrived —er** llegó antes; **—er or later** tarde o temprano; **I'd —er stay here** prefiero quedarme aquí

soot [sut] N hollín *m*, tizne *m*

soothe [suð] VT calmar, aliviar

soothsayer [súθseə] N agorero -ra *mf*

sooty [súdi] ADJ tiznado

sop [sɑp] VT empapar; **to — up** absorber; **to be —ping wet** estar empapado; N **—s** sopas *f pl*

sophisticated [səfístikeɪdɪd] ADJ sofisticado

sophomore [sáfəmɔr] N estudiante de segundo año *mf*

soprano [səprǽno] N soprano *m*

sorcerer [sɔ́rsərə] N brujo *m*, hechicero *m*

sorceress [sɔ́rsə-ɪs] N hechicera *f*

sordid [sɔ́rdɪd] ADJ sórdido, escabroso

sore [sɔr] ADJ (painful) dolorido, doloroso; (grieved) dolorido; (angry) enojado; **—head** cascarrabias *mf*; **my arm is —** me duele el brazo; **to have a — throat** tener dolor de garganta; N llaga *f*, úlcera *f*

soreness [sɔ́rnɪs] N dolor *m*

sorority [sərɔ́rɪdi] N asociación femenina de estudiantes *f*

sorrow [sáro] N (sadness) pena *f*, pesar *m*, pesadumbre *f*; (cause of sadness) disgusto *m*

sorrowful [sárəfəl] ADJ triste, pesaroso

sorry [sári] ADJ **I am —** lo siento; **I am — about that** lo lamento; **I am — for her** la compadezco; **—?** ¿Cómo? **you'll be —** te arrepentirás; **he was in — shape** estaba en un estado lamentable

sort [sɔrt] N clase *f*, tipo *m*; **— of tired** algo cansado; **all —s of** toda clase de; **out of —s** (depressed) de mal humor; (ill) indispuesto;

— key tecla de ordenación *f*; **— order** orden de clasificación *m*; VT (classify) clasificar; (put in order) ordenar; **to — out** separar, apartar; **to — out a problem** resolver un problema

SOS [ésoés] N SOS *m*

sought [sɔt] *see* seek

soul [sol] N alma *f*; **— music** música soul *f*; **not a —** nadie, ni un alma; **the — of tact** la imagen del tacto

sound [saund] N sonido *m*; (inlet) brazo de mar *m*; **— barrier** barrera del sonido *f*; **— card** tarjeta de sonido *f*; **—proof** a prueba de sonido; **—track** banda sonora *f*; **— wave** onda sonora *f*; ADJ (healthy) sano; (sane) cuerdo; (well founded) bien fundado, lógico; **— advice** buen consejo *m*; **— sleep** sueño profundo *m*; **a — beating** una buena paliza; **of — mind** en su sano juicio; **safe and —** sano y salvo; VI sonar; VT (an alarm) tocar; (a channel) sondar; (opinion) sondear; **to — out** tantear, sondear

soup [sup] N sopa *f*; **— dish** plato sopero *m*; **—spoon** cuchara sopera *f*; **— tureen** sopera *f*

sour [saur] ADJ (acidic) agrio, ácido; (peevish) agrio, avinagrado; **to go —** (milk) cortarse, agriarse; (a relationship) estropearse; **— cream** *Sp* nata agria *f*; *Am* crema agria *f*; **— milk** leche cortada *f*; **—puss** cascarrabias *mf*, avinagrado -da *mf*; VI/VT agriar[se], avinagrar[se]; (milk) cortar[se]

source [sɔrs] N fuente *f*, origen *m*; **— code** código fuente *m*

sourness [sáurnɪs] N acidez *f*

souse [saus] VI/VT (plunge) zambullir[se]; (soak) empapar[se]; N borracho -cha *mf*, esponja *f*

south [sauθ] N sur *m*, mediodía *f*; ADJ meridional, sureño; **— Africa** Sudáfrica *f*; **— African** sudafricano -na *mf*; **— America** América del Sur *f*, Sudamérica *f*; **— American** sudamericano -na *mf*; **—bound** con rumbo al sur; **—east** sureste, sudeste; **—eastern** sureste, sudeste; **— Korea** Corea del Sur *f*; **— Korean** surcoreano -na *mf*; **—paw** zurdo -da *mf*; **— pole** polo sur *m*; **—west** sudoeste, suroeste; **—western** sudoeste, suroeste; ADV hacia el sur

southern [sʌ́ðən] ADJ meridional, sureño

southerner [sʌ́ðənə] N sureño -ña *mf*, meridional *mf*, habitante del sur *mf*

southward [sáuθwəd] ADV hacia el sur, rumbo al sur

souvenir [suvənír] N recuerdo *m*

sovereign [sávə-ɪn] ADJ & N soberano -na *mf*

sovereignty [sávə-ɪnti] N soberanía *f*

sow¹ [sau] N puerca *f*

sow² [so] VI/VT sembrar

sown [son] *see* sow²

soy [sɔi] N *Sp* soja *f*; *Am* soya *f*; **—bean** *Sp* semilla

de soja *f*; *Am* semilla de soya *f*; — **sauce** *Sp*
salsa de soja *f*; *Am* salsa de soya *f*

spa [spɑ] N balneario *m*

space [spes] N espacio *m*; —**age** de la era
espacial; —**bar** barra espaciadora *f*; —**craft**
nave espacial *f*; —**ship** nave espacial *f*; —
shuttle transbordador espacial *m*; —
station estación espacial *f*; — **suit** traje
espacial *m*; VT espaciar; **to — out** distraerse

spacious [spéʃəs] ADJ espacioso, amplio

spade [sped] N (shovel) pala *f*; (in cards) pica *f*; **to
call a — a —** al pan, pan y al vino, vino

Spain [spen] N España *f*

spam [spæm] N correo electrónico basura *m*,
spam *m*

span [spæn] N (of hand) palmo *m*; (of time)
espacio *m*; (of attention) lapso *m*, período *m*;
(of bridge) tramo *m*; (of wing) envergadura *f*;
(of life) duración *f*; VT (time) abarcar; (a river)
atravesar, salvar

Spaniard [spǽnjəd] N español -ola *mf*

Spanish [spǽnɪʃ] ADJ (of Spain) español;
(Spanish-speaking) hispano; N (language)
español *m*; — **America** Hispanoamérica *f*

spank [spæŋk] VT dar nalgadas; N palmada *f*,
nalgada *f*

spanking [spǽŋkɪŋ] N zurra en las nalgas *f*; ADJ
— **new** flamante

spare [sper] VT (embarrassment) ahorrar, evitar;
(money) prestar; (an enemy) perdonar la vida
a; (a worker) prescindir de; — **me!** ¡ten
piedad de mí! **to — no expense** no escatimar
gastos; **to have time to —** tener tiempo de
sobra; ADJ (austere) austero; (extra) de sobra,
de más; — **cash** dinero disponible *m*; —
parts repuestos *m pl*; — **time** tiempo libre
m; N (part) repuesto *m*; (tire) neumático de
repuesto *m*

spark [spɑrk] N chispa *f*; — **plug** bujía *f*; VI
chispear, echar chispas; VT (a riot)
desencadenar; (interest, criticism) provocar

sparkle [spɑ́rkəl] VI (diamond) centellear;
(sparkler) chispear; (eyes) brillar; N (flashing)
brillo *m*, centelleo *m*; (spirit) viveza *f*,
animación *f*

sparkling [spɑ́rklɪŋ] ADJ (diamond)
centelleante; (eyes) brillante; — **water** agua
con gas *f*; — **wine** vino espumoso *m*

sparrow [spǽro] N gorrión *m*

sparse [spɑrs] ADJ escaso; (hair) ralo

spasm [spǽzəm] N espasmo *m*

spasmodic [spæzmɑ́dɪk] ADJ espasmódico

spastic [spǽstɪk] ADJ espástico

spat [spæt] N riña *f*

spat [spæt] *see* spit

spatial [spéʃəl] ADJ espacial

spatter [spǽtə] VI/VT salpicar; N salpicadura *f*

spatula [spǽtʃələ] N espátula *f*

spawn [spɔn] VI desovar; VT engendrar; N (of

fish) huevas *f pl*; (of frogs) huevos *m pl*

spay [spe] VT esterilizar, castrar

speak [spik] VI hablar; VT (a language) hablar;
(the truth) decir; (one's lines) recitar, decir;
so to — por decirlo así, valga la expresión; **to
— for** hablar en nombre de / a favor de; **to —
one's mind** hablar sin rodeos; **to — out
against** denunciar; **to — out for** defender;
to — up hablar fuerte

speaker [spíkə] N orador -ora *mf*; (at a
conference) conferenciante *mf*; (of a
language) hablante *mf*; — **of the House**
presidente -ta de la cámara de representantes
mf; —**phone** teléfono con parlante *m*

spear [spir] N (weapon) lanza *f*; (for fishing)
arpón *m*; (sprout) brote *m*; VT (a person,
animal) alancear, herir con lanza; (a fish)
arponear

spearmint [spírmɪnt] N mentaverde *f*

special [spéʃəl] ADJ especial; — **delivery**
entrega inmediata *f*; — **education** educación
especial *f*; — **effects** efectos especiales *m pl*;
— **interest [group]** grupo de presión *m*; N
(sale item) especialidad *f*; (TV program)
especial *m*

specialist [spéʃəlɪst] N especialista *mf*

specialization [spɛʃəlɪzéʃən] N especialización
f, especialidad *f*

specialize [spéʃəlaɪz] VI/VT especializar[se]

specially [spéʃəli] ADV especialmente,
específicamente

specialty [spéʃəlti] N especialidad *f*

species [spíʃiz] N especie *f*

specific [spɪsífɪk] ADJ específico, determinado;
— **gravity** peso específico *m*; N —**s** detalles *m
pl*

specifically [spɪsífɪkli] ADV concretamente,
específicamente

specify [spésəfaɪ] VI/VT especificar

specimen [spésəmən] N (representative)
espécimen *m*, ejemplar *m*; (sample) muestra *f*

speck [spɛk] N (small dot) mota *f*, manchita *f*;
(small amount) pizca *f*

speckle [spékəl] N manchita *f*, mota *f*; VT
salpicar, motear; —**d** moteado

spectacle [spéktəkəl] N espectáculo *m*; —**s** gafas
f pl, anteojos *m pl*; **to make a — of oneself**
dar un espectáculo, ponerse en ridículo

spectacular [spɛktækjələ] ADJ espectacular

spectator [spéktedə] N espectador -ora *mf*

spectrum [spéktrəm] N espectro *m*

speculate [spékjəlet] VI/VT especular

speculation [spɛkjəléʃən] N especulación *f*

speculative [spékjələdɪv] ADJ especulativo

speculator [spékjəledə] N especulador -ora *mf*

sped [spɛd] *see* speed

speech [spitʃ] N (faculty of speaking) habla *f*;
(formal) discurso *m*; (in a play) parlamento *m*;
— **defect** defecto de pronunciación *m*; —

recognition reconocimiento de habla *m*; — **synthesis** síntesis de habla *m*; **to make a —** pronunciar un discurso

speechless [spítʃlis] ADJ (dumb) mudo; (astonished) estupefacto

speed [spid] N (rapidity) velocidad *f*, rapidez *f*; (gear) velocidad *f*; (amphetamine) anfeta *f*; — **limit** límite de velocidad *m*; **at full —** a toda velocidad; VI (break speed limit) ir con exceso de velocidad; **to — by** pasar a toda velocidad; **to — off/away** irse a toda velocidad; **to — up** (a car, work) acelerar; (a delivery) hacer llegar a toda velocidad

speedometer [spidámɪɾə] N velocímetro *m*

speedy [spídi] ADJ veloz, rápido

spell [spɛl] N (charm) hechizo *m*, sortilegio *m*, conjuro *m*; (period) temporada *f*; (sickness) ataque *m*; **to put under a —** hechizar; ADJ **—bound** hechizado; VT (spoken) deletrear; (written) escribir; (represent) significar, representar; **to — check** comprobar la ortografía; **I —ed it out for him** se lo dije con todas las letras

spelling [spɛlɪŋ] N ortografía *f*; — **bee** concurso de ortografía *m*

spend [spɛnd] VT (money) gastar; (time) pasar; **—thrift** derrochador -ora *mf*, gastador -ora *mf*, pródigo -ga *mf*

spending [spɛndɪŋ] N gastos *m pl*; — **cut** recorte de gastos *m*; **to go on a —spree** salir a gastar dinero a lo loco

spent [spɛnt] *see* spend

sperm [spɚm] N esperma *mf*; — **whale** cachalote *m*

spermicide [spɚ́məsaɪd] N espermicida *m*

sphere [sfɪr] N esfera *f*; — **of influence** esfera de influencia *f*

spherical [sfɛ́rɪkəl] ADJ esférico

sphincter [sfɪ́ŋktɚ] N esfínter *m*

spice [spaɪs] N especia *f*; VT condimentar; **to — up** dar sal

spiciness [spáɪsɪnɪs] N lo picante

spick and span [spíkənspǽn] ADJ impecable

spicy [spáɪsi] ADJ picante

spider [spáɪdɚ] N araña *f*; — **monkey** mono araña *m*; **—'s web** telaraña *f*

spigot [spígət] N grifo *m*, espita *f*

spike [spaɪk] N (sprout) espiga *f*; (sharp object) púa *f*, pincho *m*; (on shoes) clavo *m*; **—s** zapatillas con clavos *f pl*; VT (impale) clavar; (add alcohol to) echar alcohol a; (hit a volleyball) picar

spill [spɪl] VI/VT volcar[se], derramar[se], verter[se]; VT (a rider) hacer caer; **to — the beans** descubrir el pastel; VI **to — over** (a liquid) desbordarse; (a conflict) extenderse; N (of water) derrame *m*; (of blood) derramamiento *m*; (fall) caída *f*

spilt [spɪlt] *see* spill

spin [spɪn] VT (wool) hilar; (a top, one's partner) hacer girar; VI dar vueltas, girar; **to — yarns** contar cuentos; N (turning) giro *m*, vuelta *f*; (of an airplane) barrena *f*; (political) sesgo *m*; **to take a —** dar una vuelta

spinach [spínɪtʃ] N espinaca *f*

spinal [spáɪnl] ADJ espinal, vertebral; — **column** columna vertebral *f*, espina dorsal *f*; — **cord** médula espinal *f*

spindle [spíndl] N (for weaving) huso *m*; (on machines) eje *m*

spine [spaɪn] N espina *f*, espinazo *m*

spinning [spínɪŋ] N (action) hilado *m*; (animation) hilandería *f*; — **machine** máquina de hilar *f*; — **mill** hilandería *f*; — **top** trompo *m*, peonza *f*; — **wheel** rueca *f*

spinster [spínstɚ] N solterona *f*

spiral [spáɪrəl] ADJ & N espiral *m*; — **notebook** cuaderno de espiral *m*; — **staircase** escalera de caracol *f*

spire [spaɪr] N aguja *f*, chapitel *m*

spirit [spírɪt] N (ghost) espíritu *m*; (animation) ánimo *m*, brío *m*; (alcohol) alcohol *m*; **low —s** abatimiento *m*; **to be in good —s** estar de buen humor; VT **to — away** llevar como por arte de magia

spirited [spírɪɾɪd] ADJ fogoso, brioso

spiritual [spírɪtʃuəl] ADJ & N espiritual *m*

spirituality [spɪrɪtʃuǽlɪdi] N espiritualidad *f*

spit [spɪt] VI/VT escupir; N (saliva) escupitajo *m*; (for roasting) asador *m*, espeto *m*, espetón *m*; (of sand) banco *m*

spite [spaɪt] N despecho *m*, inquina *f*; **in — of** a pesar de; **out of —** por despecho; VT contrariar

spiteful [spáɪtfəl] ADJ malicioso

splash [splæʃ] VI/VT salpicar; VI chapotear, chapalear; N salpicadura *f*, chapoteo *m*; **to make a —** hacer olas

splatter [splǽɾɚ] VI/VT salpicar; N salpicadura *f*

spleen [splin] N bazo *m*; (ill humor) mal humor *m*

splendid [spléndɪd] ADJ espléndido

splendor [spléndɚ] N esplendor *m*

splice [splaɪs] VT (tape, genes) empalmar, unir; N empalme *m*, unión *f*

splint [splɪnt] N tablilla *f*; VT entablillar

splinter [splíntɚ] N astilla *f*; VI/VT astillar[se]

split [splɪt] VI/VT (stone, wood) hender[se], rajar[se]; (candy bar) partir[se], dividir[se]; **to — hairs** hilar fino; **to — one's sides with laughter** desternillarse de risa; **to — the difference** partir la diferencia; ADJ (wood) partido, hendido; (a group) dividido; **—-level** en desnivel; **— personality** doble personalidad *f*; — **screen** pantalla dividida *f*; — **second** fracción de segundo *f*; N hendidura *f*, grieta *f*; (in a group) escisión *f*, división *f*

spoil [spɔɪl] VI (milk) cortar[se]; (food) echarse a perder; VT (vacation, performance) estropear, arruinar; (plans) desbaratar; (enjoyment) aguar; (child) malcriar, mimar demasiado; N **—s** botín m

spoiler [spɔ́ɪlə-] N alerón m

spoke [spok] N rayo m

spoke [spok] see speak

spoken [spókən] see speak

spokesperson [spókspə-sən] N portavoz mf, vocero -ra mf

sponge [spʌndʒ] N (animal, utensil) esponja f; (parasite) gorrón -ona mf; **— bath** baño de esponja m; **— cake** Am bizcochuelo m; Sp bizcocho m; VI **to — off** (clean) quitar con esponja; (take advantage of) gorronear; **to — up** absorber con una esponja

sponger [spʌ́ndʒə-] N gorrón -ona mf, parásito m

spongy [spʌ́ndʒi] ADJ esponjoso, esponjado

sponsor [spʌ́nsə-] N (of the arts) mecenas mf; (of sports, TV program) patrocinador -ora mf; (of a bill) proponente mf; VT (a child) apadrinar; (arts, sports, TV show) patrocinar; (bill) proponer

sponsorship [spʌ́nsə-ʃɪp] N patrocinio m

spontaneity [spɑntənéɪdi] N espontaneidad f

spontaneous [spɑnténiəs] ADJ espontáneo; **— abortion** aborto espontáneo m

spook [spuk] N (ghost) espectro m; (spy) espía mf

spool [spul] N carrete m, carretel m; VT (wool) devanar; (tape) enrollar

spoon [spun] N cuchara f; VT cucharear, poner con una cuchara; **to — -feed** dar de comer en la boca

spoonful [spúnfʊl] N cucharada f

spore [spor] N espora f

sport [spɔrt] N deporte m; **to be a good —** tener espíritu deportivo; **— utility vehicle** vehículo utilitario deportivo m; **—s car** coche deportivo m; **—s jacket** saco de sport m, americana f; **—sman** (hunter) cazador m; (in sports) hombre de espíritu deportivo m; **—smanship** espíritu deportivo m, deportividad f; **—swriter** cronista deportivo -va mf; ADJ deportivo; VT lucir

sporty [spórɖi] ADJ deportivo

spot [spɑt] N (stain) mancha f, mota f; (blemish) espinilla f; (insect bite) roncha f; (place) lugar m, paraje m; (difficult situation) aprieto m; **on the —** en el acto; **—-check** inspección al azar f; **—light** (in theater) foco m; (outdoors) reflector m; **to be in the —light** ser el centro de atención; **— remover** quitamanchas m sg; VI/VT (stain) manchar, ensuciar; VT (see in the distance) divisar; (notice) notar; (give advantage) dar como ventaja

spotless [spátlɪs] ADJ inmaculado

spotted [spáɾɪd] ADJ manchado, moteado

spouse [spaʊs] N cónyuge mf; **— abuse** abuso conyugal m

spout [spaʊt] VT (throw) arrojar chorros de; (talk) soltar tonterías; VI (flow out) salir a chorros; (talk) perorar; N (of a fountain) caño m; (of a gutter) canalón m; (of a teapot) pico m

sprain [spren] VT torcerse; N torcedura f

sprang [spræŋ] see spring

sprawl [sprɔl] VI (spread limbs) despatarrarse; (extend) extenderse; (fall) tumbarse; N postura despatarrada f

spray [spre] VI/VT rociar[se]; N (of liquid) rociada f; (foam) espuma f; (of flowers) ramillete m; **— can** aerosol m; **— paint** pintura en aerosol f

spread [spred] VI/VT (arms, newspaper) extender[se]; (butter) untar[se]; (map) desdoblar[se]; (legs) abrir[se]; (seeds) esparcir[se]; (news) difundir[se], diseminar[se]; (odor) difundir[se], expandirse; (rumor) propalar; (panic) sembrar; VT (panic, news) sembrar; N (of ideas) difusión f; (of opinion) diseminación f; (of disease) propagación f; (of nuclear weapons) proliferación f; (for a bed) cubrecama m; (for bread) pasta f; (of food) festín m; (ranch) hacienda f; **—sheet** (paper) planilla de cálculo f; (program) planilla electrónica f

spree [spri] N parranda f, farra f; **to go on a —** ir de parranda/farra; **to go on a shopping —** gastar dinero desenfrenadamente

spring [sprɪŋ] VI saltar; **to — at** abalanzarse sobre; **to — from** nacer de; **to — open** abrir[se] de golpe; **to — to mind** venir a la mente; **to — up** surgir; VT **to — a leak** (boat) hacer agua; (pipe) comenzar a gotear; **to — news** dar una noticia de sopetón; N (season) primavera f; (coil) muelle m, resorte m; (elasticity) elasticidad f; (jump) salto m; (water) manantial m, fuente f; **—board** trampolín m; **— fever** fiebre de primavera f; **— mattress** colchón de muelles m; **—time** primavera f; **— water** agua de manantial f; **he's no — chicken** no se cuece en el primer hervor

sprinkle [sprɪ́ŋkəl] VT (with sugar) espolvorear; (with droplets) salpicar, rociar; (rain) gotear, chispear

sprint [sprɪnt] VI (run) echarse una carrera; (run a competitive race) [e]sprintar; N (run) corrida corta f; (race) [e]sprint m

sprocket [sprákɪt] N piñón m, rueda dentada f

sprout [spraʊt] VI (leaf) brotar, salir; (plants) retoñar; (seeds) germinar; (houses) surgir; VT echar; **he —ed horns** le salieron cuernos; N retoño m, brote m, renuevo m

spruce [sprus] N picea f; VI **to — up** arreglarse

sprung [sprʌŋ] see spring

spun [spʌn] *see* spin

spunk [spʌŋk] N agallas *f pl*

spur [spɜ˞] N (on stirrups) espuela *f*; (stimulus) aguijón *m*; (of a rooster) espolón *m*; (of a mountain) estribación *f*; (of a railroad track) ramal *m*; **on the — of the moment** espontáneamente; VT espolear; **to — on** animar

spurious [spjúriəs] ADJ espurio

spurn [spɜ˞n] VT rechazar, desdeñar

spurt [spɜ˞t] VI salir a chorros; N (of water) chorro *m*; (of a runner) esfuerzo repentino *m*; **in —s** por rachas

sputter [spʌ́dɚ] VI (fire) chisporrotear; (person) refunfuñar; N (fire) chisporroteo *m*

sputum [spjúdəm] N esputo *m*

spy [spaɪ] N espía *mf*; **—glass** catalejo *m*; VI espiar; **to — on** espiar

squabble [skwɑ́bəl] VI reñir; N reyerta *f*

squad [skwɑd] N (of police) patrulla *f*; (for execution) pelotón *m*; (of athletes) equipo *m*; (for guarding) retén *m*; **— car** [coche] patrullero *m*

squadron [skwɑ́drən] N (in navy) escuadra *f*; (in army) escuadrón *m*

squalid [skwɑ́lɪd] ADJ escuálido

squall [skwɔl] N (rain) chubasco *m*, borrasca *f*; (sound) berrido *m*; VI berrear

squalor [skwɑ́lɚ] N miseria *f*, escualidez *f*

squander [skwɑ́ndɚ] VT despilfarrar, derrochar, disipar

squanderer [skwɑ́ndərɚ] N derrochador -ora *mf*

square [skwɛr] N (shape) cuadrado *m*; (on a pattern) cuadro *m*; (plaza) plaza *f*, Mex zócalo *m*; (tool in carpentry) escuadra *f*; (on chessboard) casilla *f*; **— brackets** corchetes *m pl*; **— dance** cuadrilla *f*; **— knot** nudo de rizo *m*; **— meal** comida completa *f*; **— root** raíz cuadrada *f*; **he is a —** es muy conservador; VT (make square) cuadrar; (draw squares on) cuadricular; (multiply by itself) elevar al cuadrado; **to — one's shoulders** erguirse; ADJ (in shape) cuadrado; (at ninety degrees) en ángulo recto; (tied) empatado; (frank) franco; **to be — with someone** estar a mano con alguien; ADV **right — between the eyes** justo entre los ojos

squash [skwɑʃ] N (gourd) calabaza *f*; (sport) squash *m*; VT (smash) aplastar, despachurrar

squat [skwɑt] VI (sit low) acuclillarse; (occupy) ocupar sin autorización; ADJ (sitting low) acuclillado; (thickset) rechoncho, achaparrado; N (nothing) nada; **he doesn't know—** no sabe un comino; **in a —** en cuclillas

squawk [skwɔk] VI (of chickens) cacarear; (complain) quejarse; N (of chickens) cacareo *m*; (complaint) quejido *m*

squeak [skwik] VI (door) rechinar, chirriar; (shoe) rechinar; (mouse) chillar; N (of door) rechinamiento *m*, chirrido *m*; (of shoe) rechinamiento *m*; (of mouse) chillido *m*

squeaky [skwíki] ADJ (door) chirriante; (shoes) rechinante

squeal [skwil] VI chillar; (complain) protestar; (snitch) chivatar, delatar; N chillido *m*

squeamish [skwímɪʃ] ADJ delicado

squeegee [skwídʒi] N escurridor de goma *m*, limpiavidrios *m sg*

squeeze [skwiz] VT apretar; (press very hard) estrujar; (an orange) estrujar, exprimir; (hug) abrazar; **to — into** meter[se] con dificultad en, encajar[se] en; **to — out** (an orange) exprimir; (a towel) escurrir; **to — through a crowd** abrirse paso entre la multitud; N (of hands) apretón *m*; (excessive squeeze) estrujón *m*; (hug) abrazo *m*; (lack) restricción *f*

squelch [skwɛltʃ] VT (revolt) aplastar, sofocar; (criticism) acallar

squid [skwɪd] N calamar *m*

squint [skwɪnt] VI (partially close eyes) entrecerrar los ojos; (look askance) mirar de soslayo; N (look with partially closed eyes) mirada con los ojos entrecerrados *f*; (side glance) mirada de soslayo *f*

squirm [skwɜ˞m] VI retorcerse; **to — out of a difficulty** zafarse de un aprieto

squirrel [skwɜ˞əl] N ardilla *f*

squirt [skwɜ˞t] VT echar un chisguete en; VI salir a chorritos; N chisguete *m*, chorrito *m*; **— gun** pistola lanzaagua *f*, pistola de agua *f*

Sri Lanka [srilɑ́ŋkə] N Sri Lanka *f*

Sri Lankan [srilɑ́ŋkən] ADJ & N cingalés -esa *mf*

stab [stæb] VI/VT apuñalar, acuchillar; **to — at** tirar puñaladas a; N (with a dagger) puñalada *f*; (with a knife) cuchillada *f*; (with a pocketknife) navajazo *m*; (of pain) punzada *f*, pinchazo *m*; **to take a — at** intentar; **— wound** cuchillada *f*

stability [stəbílɪdi] N estabilidad *f*

stabilization [stebəlɪzéʃən] N estabilización *f*

stable [stébəl] ADJ estable; N establo *m*, cuadra *f*; (for horses only) caballeriza *f*; VT poner en el establo

stack [stæk] N (ordered) pila *f*; (chaotic) montón *m*; (of a chimney) chimenea *f*; (in a library) estantería *f*; VT amontonar, apilar

stadium [stédiəm] N estadio *m*

staff [stæf] N (stick) cayado *m*; (of a flag) asta *f*; (personnel) personal *m*, plantel *m*; (of music) pentagrama *m*; **— of life** pan de cada día *m*; **— officer** oficial de estado mayor *m*; **editorial —** redacción *f*; **teaching —** cuerpo docente *m*; VT contratar personal para

stag [stæg] N (deer) venado *m*, ciervo *m*; (other animals) macho *m*; **— beetle** ciervo volante *m*; **— party** fiesta para hombres *f*

stage [stedʒ] N (showplace) escenario *m*; (for popular entertainment) tablado *m*; (theater) teatro *m*, las tablas *f pl*; (period) etapa *f*, estadio *m*; (distance) etapa *f*; —**coach** diligencia *f*; — **fright** miedo al escenario *m*, fiebre de candilejas *f*; —**hand** tramoyista *mf*; **by** —**s** por etapas; VT (a play) poner en escena; (an attack) organizar

stagger [stǽgɚ] VI (totter) tambalearse, dar tumbos; VT (hit hard) hacer tambalear; (overwhelm) dejar azorado; (alternate) escalonar; N tambaleo *m*

stagnant [stǽgnɪnt] ADJ estancado

stagnate [stǽgnet] VI estancarse

stagnation [stægnéʃən] N estancamiento *m*

staid [sted] ADJ envarado

stain [sten] N (spot) mancha *f*; (color) tinte *m*, tintura *f*; VI/VT (spot) manchar[se]; (color) teñir[se]; —**ed-glass window** vitral *m*

stainless [sténlɪs] ADJ sin mancha; — **steel** acero inoxidable *m*

stair [stɛr] N peldaño *m*, escalón *m*; —**case** escalera *f*; —**s** escalera *f*; —**way** escalera *f*

stake [stek] N (pole) estaca *f*; (investment) interés *m*; (bet) apuesta *f*; **at** — en juego; **to die at the** — morir en la hoguera; VT estacar; **to** — **out** vigilar

stalactite [stəlǽktaɪt] N estalactita *f*

stalagmite [stəlǽgmaɪt] N estalagmita *f*

stale [stel] ADJ (bread) duro; (air) viciado; (joke) viejo; —**mate** punto muerto *m*

stalk [stɔk] N tallo *m*; VT acechar

stall [stɔl] N (at a market) puesto *m*; (at a fair) caseta *f*, barraca *f*; (in a stable) compartimiento *m*; VI (airplane) entrar en pérdida; (talks) llegar a un punto muerto; (motor) pararse; **he is** —**ing** está arrastrando los pies; VT (airplane) hacer entrar en pérdida; (talks) paralizar; (motor) parar

stallion [stǽljən] N semental *m*

stamina [stǽmənə] N resistencia *f*, aguante *m*

stammer [stǽmɚ] VI balbucear; N balbuceo *m*

stamp [stæmp] VT (a letter) sellar; *Mex* timbrar; *Am* estampillar; (an official document) sellar, timbrar; (a coin) acuñar; VI (with foot) pisotear, patalear; (with hoof) piafar; **to** — **out** eliminar; N (on a letter) *Sp* sello *m*; *Mex* timbre *m*; *Am* estampilla *f*; (on an official document) sello *m*, timbre *m*; (instrument, character) sello *m*; (on the ground) pisotón *m*; (sound) paso *m*; — **tax** timbre *m*

stampede [stæmpíd] N estampida *f*; VI huir en estampida; VT hacer huir en estampida

stance [stæns] N posición *f*, postura *f*; (political) posicionamiento *m*

stanch, staunch [stɔntʃ] VT restañar; ADJ (strong) firme; (loyal) fiel

stand [stænd] VI (take a standing position) ponerse de pie, levantarse; *Am* parar[se]; (to be in a standing position) estar de pie; *Am* estar parado; (stop) detenerse; (withstand, tolerate) aguantar, tolerar, soportar; (remain valid) mantenerse; **to** — **aside** apartarse; **to** — **back** retroceder; **to** — **behind someone** respaldar a alguien; **to** — **by** (be uninvolved) mantenerse al margen; (be alert) estar alerta; (support) respaldar; **to** — **for** (denote) significar; (tolerate) tolerar; **to** — **one's ground** mantenerse firme; **to** — **out** destacarse, sobresalir; **to** — **up for** defender; **it** —**s to reason** es razonable; **it** —**s one meter tall** mide un metro de alto; **to** — **a chance of** tener posibilidad de; **where do you** — **on this issue?** ¿qué opinas al respecto? N (at a market) puesto *m*; (at a fair) caseta *f*; (of trees) bosque *m*; (opinion) posición *f*; (for music) atril *m*; (for taxis) parada *f*; —**by** recurso viejo *m*; —**by passenger** pasajero -ra en la lista de espera *mf*; —**off** empate *m*; —**point** punto de vista *m*; **to come to a** —**still** pararse; **to be at a** —**still** estar parado; ADJ —**alone** autónomo

standard [stǽndɚd] N (of behavior) norma *f*; (of living, performance) nivel *m*; (of weights) patrón *m*; (banner) estandarte *m*; **gold** — patrón oro *m*; —**bearer** portaestandarte *mf*; — **deviation** desviación estándar *f*; — **of living** nivel de vida *m*; — **time** hora oficial *f*; **to be up to** — satisfacer los requisitos; ADJ (normal) normal; (standardized) estándar

standardization [stændɚdɪzéʃən] N estandarización *f*

standardize [stǽndɚdaɪz] VT estandarizar, uniformar

standby [stǽndbaɪ] ADV **we're flying** — estamos volando standby

standing [stǽndɪŋ] N (position) posición *f*; (rank) rango *m*; (reputation) reputación *f*; ADJ (not seated) derecho, en pie; (permanent) permanente; (stagnant) estancado; — **order** pedido fijo *m*; — **ovation** ovación de pie *f*

stank [stæŋk] *see* stink

stanza [stǽnzə] N estrofa *f*

staple [stépəl] N (for paper) grapa *f*; (main product) producto principal *m*; (food) alimento básico *m*; ADJ (principal) principal; (basic) básico; VT engrapar

stapler [stéplɚ] N grapadora *f*

star [stɑr] N estrella *f* (also actor); (asterisk) asterisco *m*; —**fish** estrella de mar *f*; —**light** luz de las estrellas *f*; —**spangled** salpicado de estrellas; **a** — **student** un[a] estudiante sobresaliente; VT (act in) protagonizar; (put asterisk on) marcar con asterisco; (cover with stars) estrellar

starboard [stɑrbɚd] N estribor *m*; ADV a estribor

starch [stɑrtʃ] N almidón m (also food); VT almidonar

stardom [stɑrⅾəm] N estrellato m

stare [ster] VI/VT mirar fijamente; N mirada fija f

stark [stɑrk] ADJ (landscape) yermo; (truth) descarnado, desnudo; (contrast) marcado; ADV — **naked** en cueros; — **raving mad** loco de remate

starling [stɑrlɪŋ] N estornino m

starry [stɑri] ADJ estrellado

start [stɑrt] VI/VT (begin) comenzar, empezar; (a car) poner[se] en marcha, arrancar; VT (a fire) provocar; VI (jump) sobresaltarse; **to — off/ out/up** empezar; **don't get him —ed** no le des cuerda; N (beginning) comienzo m, principio m; (of a race) salida f; (nervous jump) sobresalto m; (nervous jump of a horse) respingo m; —**-up** compañía recién establecida f; —**-up funds** capital inicial m; — **button** botón de inicio m; — **menu** menú de inicio m

starter [stɑrⅾɚ] N (on an automobile) arranque m; (for a race) juez de salida mf; **for —s** para empezar

startle [stɑrdl] VI/VT asustar[se], sobresaltar[se]

startling [stɑrdlɪŋ] ADJ asombroso, sorprendente

starvation [stɑrvéʃən] N inanición f

starve [stɑrv] VI/VT hambrear; VI morirse de hambre; VT matar de hambre; (for affection) privar de cariño

starving [stɑrvɪŋ] ADJ hambriento, muerto de hambre

stash [stæʃ] VI **to — away** ir ahorrando; N alijo m

state [stet] N estado m; — **of the art** con los últimos avances; —**room** (on a ship) camarote m; (on a train) compartimiento m; —**-run company** compañía estatal f; —**sman** estadista m; —**swoman** estadista f; VT (declare) declarar, aseverar, manifestar; (describe) exponer

stately [stétli] ADJ majestuoso, imponente

statement [stétmənt] N (declaration) declaración f, aseveración f; (bill) estado de cuentas m

static [stæⅾɪk] ADJ estático; N interferencia f; — **electricity** electricidad estática f; **don't give me any** — no me compliques la vida

station [stéʃən] N estación f; (on the radio) emisora f; (on television) canal m; (social rank) condición f; — **wagon** camioneta f; VT (a sentry) apostar; (troops) estacionar

stationary [stéʃəneri] ADJ (not moving) estacionario; (stopped) detenido; (fixed) fijo

stationery [stéʃəneri] N (material) artículos de papelería m pl; (paper) papel de carta m

statistical [stətístɪkəl] ADJ estadístico

statistics [stətístɪks] N (science) estadística f; (data) estadísticas f pl

statue [stǽtʃu] N estatua f

stature [stǽtʃɚ] N (physical) estatura f; (moral) talla f

status [stǽⅾəs] N (prestige, rank) status m; (legal, financial) situación f; (marital) estado m; — **bar** (computer) barra de estado f; — **symbol** símbolo de status m

statute [stǽtʃut] N (bylaw) estatuto m; (law) ley f; — **of limitations** ley de prescripción f

statutory [stǽtʃətɔri] ADJ estatutario; — **rape** estupro m

stave [stev] N (of a barrel) duela f; VI **to — off** evitar

stay [ste] VI (remain) quedarse, permanecer; **to — away** mantenerse alejado; **to — in** quedarse en casa; **to — out of trouble** no meterse en líos; **to — up** quedarse levantado; VT **to — an execution** aplazar una ejecución; N (time spent) estancia f, estadía f, permanencia f; (support) sostén m, soporte m

stead [stɛd] N **in her** — en su lugar; **to stand one in good** — ser de provecho para uno

steadfast [stɛ́dfæst] ADJ fijo, firme

steadiness [stɛ́dinɪs] N (firmness) firmeza f; (of the hand) pulso m; (constancy) constancia f; (continuity) continuidad f

steady [stɛ́di] ADJ (not shaky) firme; (constant) constante; (continuous) continuo; — **boyfriend** novio formal m; — **customer** cliente -ta asiduo -dua mf; — **income** ingreso fijo m; VI/VT (an object) asegurar; (nerves) calmar

steak [stek] N bistec m, churrasco m

steal [stil] VT (a thing, a base) robar, hurtar; (a girlfriend) soplar; VI **to — away/out** escabullirse, escaparse; N (bargain) ganga f

stealth [stɛlθ] N sigilo m; **by —** furtivamente

stealthy [stɛ́lθi] ADJ furtivo

steam [stim] N (evaporated water) vapor m; (arising from an object) vaho m; — **engine** máquina de vapor f; — **roller** apisonadora f, aplanadora f; — **ship** [buque de] vapor m; — **shovel** excavadora f; VT (cook) cocer al vapor; VI (give off steam) echar vapor; **to get —ed up** (angry) indignarse; (covered with vapor) empañarse

steamer [stímɚ] N buque de vapor m

steed [stid] N corcel m

steel [stil] N acero m; — **blue** azul acero m; — **industry** siderurgia f; — **mill** acería f; — **wool** lana de acero f; VT acerar; **to — oneself** prepararse

steep [stip] ADJ (hill) empinado, escarpado, acantilado; (decline) marcado; (price) excesivo; VT (tea) infusionar; VI (tea) estar en infusión, infusionarse

steeple [stípəl] N (spire) aguja f, chapitel m; (bell tower) campanario m

steer [stir] N (young bovine) novillo m; (grown

bovine) buey *m*; VI/VT (a car) conducir, manejar; (a ship) gobernar, timonear; VI (turn) girar, doblar; **to — clear of** evitar; **to — a conversation** desviar una conversación; **the car —s easily** el coche es fácil de conducir; **—ing** dirección *f*; **—ing wheel** volante *m*

stellar [stélə] ADJ estelar

stem [stɛm] N (of a plant) tallo *m*; (of a leaf) pedúnculo *m*, rabo *m*; (of a glass) pie *m*; (of a pipe) cañón *m*; **— cell** célula estaminal/embrional *f*; VT detener, contener, estancar; **to — from** provenir de

stench [stɛntʃ] N hedor *m*, hediondez *f*, tufo *m*

stencil [sténsəl] N plantilla *f*, matriz *f*

stenographer [stənágrəfə] N taquígrafo -fa *mf*

step [stɛp] N (in walking, dancing) paso *m*; (on stairs) peldaño *m*, escalón *m*; (in music) tono *m*; **— by** paso a paso; **—ladder** escalera *f*; **to take —s** (walk) dar pasos; VI dar un paso; **— this way** pase por aquí; **to — aside** hacerse a un lado; **to — back** retroceder; **to — down** (descend) bajar; (resign) renunciar; **to — off** bajar; **to — off a distance** medir a pasos una distancia; **to — on** pisar, pisotear; **to — on the gas** pisar el acelerador; **to — out** salir; (act) tomar medidas; **to — up** subir; **in — with the music** al compás de la música

stepbrother [stépbrʌðə] N hermanastro *m*

stepdaughter [stépdɔðə] N hijastra *f*

stepfather [stépfɑðə] N padrastro *m*

stepmother [stépmʌðə] N madrastra *f*

steppe [stɛp] N estepa *f*

stepsister [stépsɪstə] N hermanastra *f*

stepson [stépsʌn] N hijastro *m*

stereo [stério] ADJ & N estéreo *m*

stereotype [stériotaɪp] N estereotipo *m*

sterile [stérəl] ADJ estéril

sterility [stərɪ́lɪti] N esterilidad *f*

sterilize [stérəlaɪz] VT esterilizar

stern [stɝn] ADJ austero, severo, adusto; N (of a ship) popa *f*

sternum [stɝnəm] N esternón *m*

steroid [stérɔɪd] N esteroide *m*

stethoscope [stéθəskop] N estetoscopio *m*

stew [stu] VI/VT (cook) estofar[se], guisar[se]; VI (worry) preocuparse; N estofado *m*, guiso *m*; **to be in a —** estar preocupado

steward [stúəd] N (manager) administrador *m*; (on a ship) camarero *m*; (on an airplane) auxiliar de vuelo *m*

stewardess [stúədɪs] N (on a ship) camarera *f*; (on an airplane) auxiliar de vuelo *f*, azafata *f*

stick [stɪk] N (of wood) palo *m*, vara *f*; (of firewood) raja *f*; (of dynamite) cartucho *m*; **— shift** palanca de cambios *f*; **—up** atraco *m*, asalto *m*; VI/VT (adhere) pegar[se], adherir[se]; VT (place) poner, meter; (stab) clavar,

pinchar; VI (become jammed) atascarse; **— 'em up!** ¡arriba las manos! **to — out** salir, sobresalir; **to — out one's head** asomar la cabeza; **to — out one's tongue** sacar la lengua; **to — to a job** persistir en una tarea; **to — up** (point up) estar parado de punta; **to — up for** defender; **to — someone up** asaltar/atracar a alguien

sticker [stíkə] N (thistle) abrojo *m*; (adhesive) etiqueta adhesiva *f*

sticky [stíki] ADJ pegajoso

stiff [stɪf] ADJ (leather, cardboard) tieso, duro; (drink) fuerte, cargado; (shirt) almidonado; (back) entumecido; (test) difícil; (breeze) fuerte; (personality) envarado; (climb) arduo; (price) alto; **to get —** entumecerse; N (cadaver) *fam* fiambre *m*

stiffen [stífən] VI/VT (leather) endurecer[se]; (back) entumecer[se]; (shirt) almidonar[se]; **to — up** agarrotar[se]

stiffness [stífnɪs] N (of leather) dureza *f*, tiesura *f*; (of one's back) entumecimiento *m*; (of one's personality) envaramiento *m*; (of resistance) firmeza *f*

stifle [stáɪfəl] VI/VT ahogar[se], sofocar[se]; **to — a yawn** contener un bostezo

stigma [stígmə] N estigma *m*

stigmatize [stígmətaɪz] VI/VT estigmatizar

still [stɪl] ADJ (not moving) quieto; (quiet) silencioso; **—born** nacido muerto; **— life** naturaleza muerta *f*; VT acallar; ADV todavía, aún; **he's — here** todavía está [aquí]; CONJ de todos modos, en todo caso; **—, it's a good buy** en todo caso, es una ganga; N (for distilling) alambique *m*; (quiet) silencio *m*

stillness [stílnɪs] N (not moving) quietud *f*; (silence) silencio *m*

stilt [stɪlt] N (for walking) zanco *m*; (support) pilote *m*

stilted [stíltɪd] ADJ (personality) envarado; (style) afectado

stimulant [stímjələnt] ADJ & N estimulante *m*

stimulate [stímjəlet] VT estimular

stimulation [stɪmjəléʃən] N estimulación *f*

stimulus [stímjələs] N estímulo *m*

sting [stɪŋ] VI/VT (insects, thorns) picar; (insects) aguijonear; VT (shampoo) hacer picar; (rain) azotar; (cheat) timar; N (pain) picadura *f*; (stinger) aguijón *m*; (confidence game) golpe *m*; **— of remorse** punzada de remordimiento *f*; **—ray** manta raya *f*

stinger [stíŋə] N aguijón *m*

stinginess [stíndʒinɪs] N tacañería *f*, mezquindad *f*

stingy [stíndʒi] ADJ mezquino, tacaño

stink [stɪŋk] VI (smell bad) heder, apestar; **to — of** heder a; **to — up** dar mal olor a; **your performance —s** tu actuación es un desastre; N hedor *m*

stipend [stáɪpɪnd] N (fellowship) beca f; (salary) estipendio m

stipulate [stípjəlet] VT estipular

stipulation [stɪpjəléʃən] N estipulación f

stir [stɜ˞] VI (move) bullir, rebullir; (awaken) despertar; VT (mix) revolver; (move emotionally) conmover; (stoke) atizar; **to — up** (trouble) provocar, suscitar; (an old grudge) remover; **to — -fry** saltear; **to — crazy** claustrofóbico; **to give something a — revolver** algo; **to cause a —** causar revuelo

stirring [stɜ˞ɪŋ] ADJ (moving) conmovedor

stirrup [stɜ˞rəp] N estribo m

stitch [stɪtʃ] N (in sewing) puntada f; (on a wound) punto m; **to be in —es** desternillarse de risa; VI/VT coser

St. Kitts and Nevis [sɛntkítsənnívɪs] N San Cristóbal y Nieves m

St. Lucia [sɛntlúʃə] N Santa Lucía f

St. Lucian [sɛntlúʃən] ADJ & N santalucense mf

stock [stɑk] N (selection) surtido m; (reserves) existencias f pl; (livestock) ganado m; (lineage) estirpe f; (shares) acciones f pl, valores m pl; (in grafting) patrón m; (broth) caldo m; **—broker** corredor -ora de bolsa mf, bolsista mf; **— company** sociedad anónima f; **— exchange** bolsa de valores f; **—holder** accionista mf; **— market** mercado de valores m, bolsa de valores f; **— market trends** tendencias bursátiles f pl; **— options** opciones f pl; **—pile** acopio m; **—room** depósito m; **— size** tamaño ordinario m; **—yard** corral m; **in —** en existencia; **out of —** agotado; VT (sell) vender; (fill shelves) abastecer; **to — up on** surtirse de, acumular; **to —pile** acopiar; ADJ (trite) trillado

stockade [stɑkéd] N (fence) estacada f, empalizada f; (prison) prisión militar f

stocking [stɑkɪŋ] N (hose) media f; (sock) calcetín m

stocky [stɑ́ki] ADJ robusto

stoic [stóɪk] ADJ & N estoico -ca mf

stoke [stok] VT (fire) atizar; (engine) alimentar

stole [stol] (fur) estola f

stole [stol] see steal

stolen [stólən] see steal

stomach [stʌ́mək] N (organ) estómago m; (belly) panza f, barriga f; **he has a big —** es barrigón; **to lie on one's —** estar panza abajo; VT (tolerate) aguantar

stomp [stɑmp] VI pisar fuerte; VT (crush) pisotear; (defeat) aplastar

stone [ston] N (rock, gem) piedra f; (in fruit) hueso m; (in kidneys) cálculo m; **within a —'s throw** a tiro de piedra; **— Age** Edad de Piedra f; ADJ **—-deaf** sordo como una tapia; VT (a person) lapidar; (a fruit) deshuesar; **to —wall** bloquear, ignorar

stony [stóni] ADJ (made of stone) pétreo;

(driveway) pedregoso; (silence) sepulcral

stood [stʊd] see stand

stool [stul] N (furniture) taburete m, banqueta f; (excrement) materia fecal f; **— pigeon** soplón -ona mf, chivato -ta mf

stoop [stup] VI (bend over) agacharse; (have bad posture) encorvarse; **to — to** rebajarse a; N (posture) encorvamiento m; (porch) entrada f, porche m; **to walk with a —** andar encorvado; ADJ **-shouldered** encorvado, cargado de espaldas

stop [stɑp] VI (halt) parar, detenerse; (malfunction) parar[se]; VT (halt) parar, detener; (cancel) cancelar; (suspend) suspender; (plug) tapar; **to — at nothing** no tener escrúpulos; **to — by/in** visitar; **to — from** impedir; **to — over at** hacer escala en; **to — short** parar en seco; **to — up** tapar, atascar; **it —ped raining** paró/dejó de llover; N parada f, detención f; (on organ) registro m; **—gap** arreglo provisorio m; **—light** semáforo m; **—over** escala f; **— sign** Sp stop m; Am señal de pare f; Mex alto m; **—volley** (tennis) dejada de volea f; **—watch** cronómetro m; **to bring to a —** parar; **to make a —** parar

stoppage [stɑ́pɪʤ] N interrupción f; (strike) huelga f

stopper [stɑ́pə˞] N tapón m

storage [stórɪʤ] N almacenaje m, almacenamiento m; (of electronic data) almacenamiento m; **— battery** acumulador m; **— device** dispositivo de almacenamiento m; **to keep in —** almacenar

store [stɔr] N (shop) tienda f, almacén m; (supply) reserva f, provisión f; **—house** (warehouse) almacén m, depósito m; (source) mina f, fuente f; **—keeper** tendero -ra mf, almacenista mf; **—room** almacén m, depósito m; **what is in — for us?** ¿qué nos espera? VT (commercial goods) almacenar; (personal effects) guardar; **to — up** acumular

stork [stɔrk] N cigüeña f

storm [stɔrm] N (on land) tormenta f; (at sea) tempestad f, temporal m; (of protest) ola f; **— troops** tropas de asalto f pl; VT (attack) tomar por asalto; VI **to — in/out** entrar/salir en tromba

stormy [stórmi] ADJ tormentoso, tempestuoso

story [stóri] N (tale) cuento m, historia f; (newspaper article) artículo m; (lie) mentira f; (information) información f; (plot) argumento m, trama f; (floor) piso m

stout [staʊt] ADJ (fat) corpulento; (robust) robusto, fornido; (strong) fuerte; (courageous) valiente

stove [stov] N (for heating) estufa f; (for cooking) cocina f; estufa f

stow [sto] VT (keep) guardar; (hide) esconder;

(put in cargo hold) estibar; **to — away on a ship** viajar de polizón

stowaway [stóəwe] N polizón -ona *mf*

straddle [strǽdl] VI/VT estar a horcajadas; VT (a fence) ponerse a horcajadas; (one's legs) abrir; (not take sides) no comprometerse

strafe [stref] VT ametrallar

straggle [strǽgəl] VI **to — along/behind** rezagarse; **to — in** entrar de a pocos

straight [stret] ADJ (not curved) recto; (not tilted) derecho; (in succession) seguido; (hair) lacio, liso; (teeth) parejo; (frank) franco; (heterosexual) heterosexual; **— A's** sobresaliente en todo; **—edge** regla *f*; **— face** cara seria *f*; **— flush** escalera de color *f*; ADJ **—forward** (honest) honesto; (simple) sencillo, campechano; (clear) claro; ADV **— ahead** todo derecho, todo recto; **for two hours** — dos horas seguidas; **to come — home** volver derecho a casa; **to leave — after lunch** irse justo después de comer; **to set a person —** aclararle algo a alguien; **tell me —** dímelo francamente; **he can't think —** no puede pensar con claridad; N (of a racetrack) recta *f*

straighten [strétn] VI/VT enderezar[se]; (situation) arreglar[se]; VT (hair) alisar, RP laciar; **to — out a child** enderezar a un niño

straightness [strétnɪs] N derechura *f*

strain [stren] VI (pull) tironear; (try hard) esforzarse; VT (exhaust) agotar; (hurt voice) forzar; (injure a joint) torcer; (injure a muscle) sufrir un tirón en; (hurt a relationship) crear una tirantez en; VI/VT (filter) colar[se]; N (effort) esfuerzo *m*; (injury) torcedura *f*; (pressure) presión *f*; (trouble in a relationship) tirantez *f*; (lineage) cepa *f*

strainer [strénɚ] N colador *m*

strait [stret] N estrecho *m*; **in dire —s** en aprietos; **—jacket** camisa de fuerza *f*, chaleco de fuerza *m*; ADJ **—laced** puritano

strand [strænd] VI/VT (a ship) encallar, varar; VT (a person) dejar plantado; **to be —ed** (boat) estar encallado; (person) quedar plantado; N (beach) costa *f*, playa *f*; (of rope) ramal *m*; (of thread) hebra *f*; (of hair) mechón *m*

strange [strendʒ] ADJ (bizarre) extraño, raro; (unknown) desconocido

strangeness [stréndʒnɪs] N (unusualness) lo extraño, rareza *f*; (unexpectedness) lo inesperado

stranger [stréndʒɚ] N (unknown person) extraño -ña *mf*, desconocido -da *mf*; (outsider) forastero -ra *mf*; **to be no — to something** tener experiencia con algo

strangle [strǽngəl] VI/VT estrangular[se]; VT (creativity) coartar; N **—hold** (in wrestling) llave al cuello *f*; (in markets) monopolio *m*

strap [stræp] N (leather band) correa *f*, tira *f*; (on

a dress) tirante *m*; VT atar con correa; **to — in** amarrar[se], abrochar[se]

stratagem [strǽdɪdʒəm] N estratagema *f*

strategic [strətíʤɪk] ADJ estratégico

strategy [strǽɪɵəʤi] N estrategia *f*

stratosphere [strǽɪɵəsfɪr] N estratosfera *f*

stratum [strǽɪɵəm] N estrato *m*

straw [strɔ] N paja *f* (also for drinking); **—berry** fresa *f*; **— man** testaferro *m*; **— vote** votación de prueba *f*; ADJ **—-colored** pajizo

stray [stre] VI (deviate, digress) desviarse; (get lost) perderse; (wander) vagar; (sin) descarriarse, perderse; ADJ extraviado, perdido; N perro/gato mostrenco *m*

streak [strik] N (line) raya *f*; (vein) vena *f*; (of luck) racha *f*; (of light) rayo *m*; VI (run naked) correr desnudo; (get discolored) aclararse

stream [strim] N (jet) chorro *m*; (river) río *m*; (brook) arroyo *m*; **—lined** (vehículo) aerodinámico; (business) racionalizado; VI (water) correr, fluir; (blood) derramar; **to — out** brotar, manar; **to — in** entrar a raudales

streaming [strímɪŋ] N corriente *f*, flujo *m*; **— audio** flujo continuo de datos de audio *m*; **— video** flujo continuo de datos de vídeo *m*

street [strit] N calle *f*; **—car** tranvía *f*; **—lamp** farol *m*, poste de alumbrado *m*; **— sweeper** barrendero -ra *mf*

strength [strɛŋθ] N fuerza *f*; (spiritual) firmeza *f*; **on the — of** en base a

strengthen [strɛŋθən] VI/VT fortalecer[se], reforzar[se]

strengthening [strɛŋθənɪŋ] N fortalecimiento *m*

strenuous [strɛ́njuəs] ADJ arduo

strep throat [strɛprót] N infección por estreptococo *f*

stress [strɛs] N (tension) tensión *f*; (strain) estrés *m*; (pressure) esfuerzo *m*; (emphasis) énfasis *m*; (accent) acento *m*; **— test** prueba de esfuerzo *f*; VT (emphasize) enfatizar; (accentuate) acentuar; (exert force) someter a un esfuerzo; (put under pressure) estresar; **to — out** estresarse

stressful [strɛ́sfəl] ADJ estresante

stretch [strɛtʃ] VI/VT (make or become longer) estirar[se], alargar[se]; (extend) extender[se]; (exaggerate) exagerar; **to — oneself** estirarse, desperezarse; **to — out** (lengthen) extender[se]; (lie) tumbarse, tenderse; N (act of stretching) desperezo *m*; (segment of road) trecho *m*, tramo *m*; (period of time) período *m*; (exaggeration) exageración *f*; **— mark** estría *f*

stretcher [strɛ́tʃɚ] N camilla *f*

strew [stru] VT esparcir

strewn [strun] *see* strew

stricken [stríkən] ADJ (with disease) aquejado; (by a flood) afectado; (with fear) aterrado

stricken [stríkən] *see* strike

strict [strɪkt] ADJ estricto; **in — confidence** en absoluta confianza

stridden [strídn] *see* stride

stride [straɪd] VI caminar a paso largo, dar zancadas; N (gait) paso *m*; (long step) zancada *f*, tranco *m*

strident [stráɪdənt] ADJ estridente

strife [straɪf] N conflictos *m pl*

strike [straɪk] VI/VT (hit) golpear, pegar; (stop work) hacer huelga [contra]; VT (find oil, etc.) dar con, encontrar; (occur to) ocurrírsele a uno; (cross out) tachar; (mark by chimes) dar; (light a match, etc.) encender; (make a coin) acuñar; **to — a compromise/deal** llegar a un acuerdo; **to — one's fancy** antojársele a uno; **to — out** (cross out) tachar; (set forth) encaminarse; (fail) fracasar; (in baseball) poncharse; **to — someone out** ponchar a alguien; **to — up a conversation** entablar conversación; **to — up a friendship** trabar amistad; **how does she — you?** ¿qué tal te parece? N (work stoppage) huelga *f*; (attack) ataque *m*; (finding of oil) descubrimiento *m*; (in baseball) strike *m*; **—breaker** esquirol *m*, rompehuelgas *m sg*; **—out** ponchado *m*, ponche *m*; **—through** tachado *m*; **— zone** zona de strike *f*; **called —** strike cantado *m*

striker [stráɪkɚ] N (person on strike) huelguista *mf*; (of a bell) badajo *m*; (in soccer) artillero -ra *mf*

striking [stráɪkɪŋ] ADJ (unusual, conspicuous) notable; (attractive) llamativo; (on strike) en huelga

string [strɪŋ] N (cord) cuerda *f*, cordel *m*; (of pearls, lies) sarta *f*; (of questions) serie *f*; (of data) secuencia *f*; (of beans) fibra *f*; (of garlic, peppers) ristra *f*; **— bean** habichuela *f*, judía verde *f*; **—s** (in an orchestra) cuerdas *f pl*; (on a tennis racket) cordaje *m*, encordado *m*; **no —s attached** sin condiciones; VT (beads) ensartar; (a musical instrument) encordar; **to — along** tener en ascuas; **to — out** extender[se], prolongar[se]; **to — up** colgar, ahorcar; **to be strung out** estar muy tenso

stringent [stríndʒənt] ADJ (law, need) riguroso; (time limit) estrecho, ajustado

strip [strɪp] VI/VT (make/get naked) desnudar[se]; VT (remove bark) descortezar; (remove leaves) deshojar; (remove sheets) deshacer; (remove varnish) quitar el barniz; (damage gears) estropear el engranaje; **to — search** registrar al desnudo; **to —-mine** explotar a cielo abierto; N (of a thing) tira *f*; (of land) faja *f*; **— mall** centro comercial *m*; **— search** registro al desnudo *m*

stripe [straɪp] N (band) raya *f*, lista *f*, banda *f*; (military insignia) galón *m*; (type) tipo *m*

striped [straɪpt, stráɪpɪd] ADJ listado, rayado

strive [straɪv] VI esforzarse por, luchar por

striven [strívən] *see* strive

strode [strod] *see* stride

stroke [strok] N (in golf, tennis, of luck, of genius) golpe *m*; (cerebral hemorrhage) derrame cerebral *m*; (movement in swimming) brazada *f*; (style in swimming) estilo *m*; (of a piston) carrera *f*; (of a painter's brush) pincelada *f*, trazo *m*; (of lightning) rayo *m*; **at the — of ten** al dar las diez; VT (pet) acariciar; (praise) halagar

stroll [strol] VI dar un paseo, pasearse; N paseo *m*, caminata *f*

stroller [strólɚ] N cochecito de bebé *m*

strong [strɔŋ] ADJ fuerte; (husky) recio; (eyesight, probability) bueno; (protest) enérgico; (views, faith, support) firme; (features, resemblance) marcado; (argument) sólido; **—hold** (fortress) fortaleza *f*; (center of activity) baluarte *m*; **—willed** (resolute) resuelto, decidido; (stubborn) terco; ADV **to be going —** seguir activo; VT **to —-arm** intimidar

strongly [strɔŋli] ADV (argue, object) enérgicamente; (pull) con fuerza

strove [strov] *see* strive

struck [strʌk] *see* strike

structural [strʌ́ktʃərəl] ADJ estructural

structure [strʌ́ktʃɚ] N (the way parts are arranged) estructura *f*; (thing constructed) construcción *f*; VT estructurar

structuring [strʌ́ktʃɚɪŋ] N estructuración *f*

struggle [strʌ́gəl] VI (with difficulties) luchar, bregar; (with an assailant) forcejear; **she —s in math** la pasa mal en matemáticas; N lucha *f*; (of ideas) pugna *f*, lucha *f*; (fight) contienda *f*, forcejeo *m*; **it's a —** da mucho trabajo

strung [strʌŋ] *see* string

strut [strʌt] VI pavonearse; N pavoneo *m*; (support) tirante *m*, puntal *m*; (shock absorber) amortiguador *m*

strychnine [stríknaɪn] N estricnina *f*

stub [stʌb] N talón *m*; VT **to — one's toe** dar[se] un tropezón, reventarse el dedo

stubble [stʌ́bəl] N (of a crop) rastrojo *m*; (of a beard) barba de unos días *f*

stubborn [stʌ́bɚn] ADJ terco, testarudo

stubbornness [stʌ́bɚnnɪs] N terquedad *f*, testarudez *f*

stucco [stʌ́ko] N estuco *m*; VT estucar

stuck [stʌk] ADJ (unable to move) atascado; (adhering) pegado; **to be — on someone** estar loco por alguien; **—-up** estirado, presumido

stuck [stʌk] *see* stick

stud [stʌd] N (knob) tachuela *f*, tachón *m*; (earring) arete *m*; (cufflink) gemelo *m*; (on shirtfront) botón *m*; (horse, man) semental *m*; (horse) garañón *m*; VT tachonar

student [stúdnt] N alumno -na *mf*; (secondary,

university) estudiante *mf*; — **body** alumnado *m*; ADJ estudiantil

studio [stúdio] N estudio *m*, taller *m*; — **apartment** estudio *m*

studious [stúdiəs] ADJ estudioso

study [stádi] N estudio *m*; VT estudiar

stuff [stʌf] N (material) materia *f*, material *m*; (things) trastos *m pl*, bártulos *m pl*; (cloth) paño *m*, tela *f*; (affair) cosa *f*; (junk) cachivaches *m pl*; VT (mattress) rellenar; (dead animal) embalsamar, disecar; **to — into** meter en; **I'm —ed** estoy lleno

stuffing [stáfɪŋ] N relleno *m*

stuffy [stáfi] ADJ (person) envarado; (air) viciado; (nose) tapado

stumble [stámbəł] VI (trip) tropezar, trastabillar, dar un traspié; (stutter) balbucear; **to — out** salir a tropezones; **to — upon** tropezar con; **stumbling block** obstáculo *m*; N tropezón *m*, tropiezo *m*, traspié *m*

stump [stʌmp] N (of a tree) tocón *m*, cepa *f*; (of a tooth) raigón *m*; (of a limb) muñón *m*; **to be on the —** hacer una campaña electoral; VT (baffle) dejar perplejo; (remove stumps) arrancar los tocones de; **to — the country** recorrer el país haciendo campaña

stun [stʌn] VT (shock, surprise) dejar atónito, pasmar; (render unconscious) dejar sin sentido; **— gun** pistola tranquilizante *f*

stung [stʌŋ] *see* sting

stunk [stʌŋk] *see* stink

stunning [stánɪŋ] ADJ (shocking) pasmoso; (beautiful) elegante, bellísimo

stunt [stʌnt] VT (stop growth) atrofiar; (do acrobatic tricks) hacer acrobacia; N (feat) acrobacia *f*; (for publicity) maniobra *f*; **—man** doble *m*; **—woman** doble *f*; **to pull a —** hacerse el listo

stupefy [stúpəfaɪ] VT (make lethargic) atontar, embrutecer; (astonish) dejar estupefacto, alelar

stupendous [stupéndəs] ADJ estupendo

stupid [stúpɪd] ADJ tonto, estúpido, majadero

stupidity [stupídɪdi] N tontería *f*, estupidez *f*, majadería *f*

stupor [stúpə] N estupor *m*

sturdy [stɚ́di] ADJ (person) fornido, fuerte; (construction) sólido, robusto

stutter [stádə] VI tartamudear, tartajear; VT decir tartamudeando; N (act of stuttering) tartamudeo *m*; (speech defect) tartamudez *f*

stutterer [stádərə] N tartamudo -da *mf*

stuttering [stádərɪŋ] ADJ tartamudo; N (act of stuttering) tartamudeo *m*; (speech defect) tartamudez *f*

St. Vincent and the Grenadines [sentvínsəntəndəgrénədinz] N San Vicente y las Granadinas *m*

sty [staɪ] N (for pigs) pocilga *f*; (in eye) orzuelo *m*

style [staɪł] N estilo *m*; (type) modelo *m*; **— sheet** página de estilo *f*; **out of —** fuera de moda; **like it's going out of —** como loco; VT (a book) intitular; (hair) peinar; **he —s himself Professor Smith** se hace llamar Profesor Smith

stylish [stáɪlɪʃ] ADJ elegante, de moda

stylistic [staɪlístɪk] ADJ estilístico

stylistics [staɪlístɪks] N estilística *f*

stymie, stymy [stáɪmi] VT obstaculizar

Styrofoam™ [stáɪrəfom] N poliestireno *m*

suave [swɑv] ADJ urbano, educado

subcommittee [sábkəmɪDi] N subcomité *m*

subconscious [sʌbkánʃəs] ADJ subconsciente

subcontract [sʌbkántrækt] VT subcontratar

subdivide [sʌbdɪváɪd] VT subdividir

subdivision [sábdɪvɪʒən] N subdivisión *f*; (of land) parcelación *f*

subdue [səbdú] VT (overcome, vanquish) sojuzgar, someter, rendir; (repress) reprimir; (attenuate) atenuar

subdued [səbdúd] ADJ (atmosphere) tranquilo; (mood) deprimido; (lighting, color) tenue

subject[1] [sábdʒɪkt] N (of a king) súbdito -ta *mf*; (of a sentence, in an experiment) sujeto *m*; (in school) asignatura *f*, materia *f*; **— matter** tema *m*; ADV LOC **— to** (changes, laws, conditions) sujeto a; (depression, earthquakes) propenso a

subject[2] [səbdʒékt] VT someter

subjection [səbdʒékʃən] N sometimiento *m*

subjective [səbdʒéktɪv] ADJ subjetivo

subjectivity [sabdʒektívɪDi] N subjetividad *f*

subjugate [sábdʒəget] VT subjuzgar, avasallar

subjunctive [səbdʒʌ́ŋktɪv] ADJ & N subjuntivo *m*

sublet [sáblét] VI/VT subarrendar

sublime [səbláɪm] ADJ sublime

submarine [sábmərɪn, sábmərin] ADJ submarino; N submarino *m*

submerge [səbmɚ́dʒ] VI/VT sumergir[se]

submerged [səbmɚ́dʒd] ADJ inmerso, sumergido

submission [səbmíʃən] N (humility) sumisión *f*; (subjugation) sometimiento *m*, sumisión *f*; (sending) entrega *f*, envío *m*

submissive [səbmísɪv] ADJ sumiso

submit [səbmít] VI/VT someter[se]; (to a judge) elevar[se]; **to — a report** presentar un informe

subordinate[1] [səbórdnɪt] ADJ & N subordinado -da *mf*, subalterno -na *mf*

subordinate[2] [səbórdnet] VT subordinar

subpar [sábpár] ADJ inferior

subpoena [səpínə] N citación *f*, orden de comparecencia *f*

subroutine [sábrutin] N subrutina *f*

subscribe [səbskráɪb] VI (underwrite, sign) suscribir; (receive a magazine) abonarse, suscribirse; (agree with) adherirse a

subscriber [səbskráɪbə·] N (to shares) suscriptor -ora *mf*; (to services) abonado -da *mf*; (to a magazine) suscriptor -ora *mf*, abonado -da *mf*; (to an idea) partidario -ria *mf*

subscript [sábskrɪpt] N subíndice *m*

subscription [səbskrípʃən] N suscripción *f*, abono *m*

subsequent [sábsɪkwənt] ADJ subsiguiente

subsequently [sábsɪkwəntli] N posteriormente, con posterioridad *f*

subservient [səbsə́·viənt] ADJ servil

subside [səbsáɪd] VI (sediment) hundirse; (water level) bajar; (volcano, storm, anger) calmarse, aquietarse

subsidiary [səbsídieri] ADJ subsidiario; N sucursal *f*, filial *f*

subsidize [sábsɪdaɪz] VT subvencionar, subsidiar

subsidy [sábsɪdi] N subvención *f*, subsidio *m*

substance [sábstəns] N sustancia *f*; — **abuse** abuso de sustancias *m*

substandard [sábstændə·d] ADJ de calidad inferior

substantial [səbstǽnʃəl] ADJ (changes) sustancial; (food, lecture) sustancioso; (furniture) sólido; (amount) considerable, importante; **to be in — agreement** estar básicamente de acuerdo

substantiate [səbstǽnʃiet] VT (verify) verificar; (prove) probar

substantive [sábstəntɪv] ADJ & N sustantivo *m*

substitute [sábstɪtut] VT sustituir, reemplazar; **I —d water for milk** usé agua en vez de leche, sustituí/reemplacé la leche por agua; VI **John—d for Mary** Juan sustituyó/ reemplazó a María; N (one who substitutes) sustituto *m*, reemplazo *m*; (teacher, athlete) suplente *mf*; (thing) sucedáneo *m*

substitution [sábstɪtúʃən] N sustitución *f*; **the — of water for milk** la sustitución de leche por agua

subterfuge [sábtə·fjuʤ] N subterfugio *m*

subterranean [sábtəréniən] ADJ subterráneo

subtitle [sábtaɪdl] N subtítulo *m*

subtle [sádl] ADJ sutil

subtlety [sádlti] N sutileza *f*

subtotal [sábtodl] N subtotal *m*

subtract [səbtrǽkt] VT (deduct) restar; (take away) sustraer

subtraction [səbtrǽkʃən] N sustracción *f*, resta *f*

suburb [sábə·b] N barrio residencial periférico *m*

suburban [səbə́·bən] ADJ (residential) residencial; (on the outskirts) periférico

subversive [səbvə́·sɪv] ADJ subversivo

subway [sábwe] N metropolitano *m*, metro *m*, subterráneo *m*

succeed [səksíd] VI (be successful) tener éxito; (manage) lograr; **to — to** heredar; VT (follow) suceder a

success [səksés] N éxito *m*

successful [səksésfəl] ADJ (person) exitoso; (effort) productivo, satisfactorio; **to be —** tener éxito

succession [səkséʃən] N sucesión *f*

successive [səksésɪv] ADJ sucesivo

successor [səksésə·] N sucesor -ora *mf*

succinct [səksíŋkt] ADJ sucinto, escueto

succor [sákə·] N socorro *m*; VT socorrer

succumb [sákʌm] VI sucumbir

such [sʌʧ] ADJ tal; — **as** tal como; **at — and — a place** en tal o cual lugar; **he's — an idiot!** ¡es tan idiota! **in — a case** en tal caso / en semejante caso; **there's no — thing** eso no existe; PRON **hobbies, pastimes, and —** hobbies, pasatiempos y cosas por el estilo; **a car — as yours** un coche como el tuyo; ADV **— nice neighbors** vecinos tan simpáticos

suck [sʌk] VI/VT chupar; (suckle) mamar; (vacuum, pump) aspirar; **to be —ed into** ser arrastrado a; VI; **to — in air** aspirar

sucker [sákə·] N (gullible person) primo -ma *mf*; (lollipop) *Sp* pirulí *m*; *Mex* paleta *f*; *RP* chupetín *m*

sucrose [súkros] N sacarosa *f*

suction [sákʃən] N succión *f*, aspiración *f*

Sudan [sudǽn] N Sudán *m*

Sudanese [sudníz] ADJ & N sudanés -esa *mf*

sudden [sádn] ADJ súbito, repentino, brusco; **— death** (also in sports) muerte súbita *f*; **— infant death syndrome** síndrome de muerte infantil súbita *m*; **all of a —** de repente, de improviso

suddenly [sádnli] ADV de repente, repentinamente

suddenness [sádnnɪs] N brusquedad *f*, lo repentino

suds [sʌdz] N espuma *f*

sue [su] VI/VT demandar, poner pleito; **to — for** pedir, suplicar; **to — for damages** demandar por daños y perjuicios

suede [swed] N gamuza *f*, ante *m*

suffer [sáfə·] VI/VT (feel pain) sufrir, padecer; VT (tolerate) tolerar

sufferer [sáfərə·] N paciente *mf*

suffering [sáfə·ɪŋ] N sufrimiento *m*, padecimiento *m*

suffice [səfáɪs] VI/VT bastar, ser suficiente

sufficient [səfíʃənt] ADJ suficiente, bastante

suffix [sáfɪks] N sufijo *m*

suffocate [sáfəket] VI/VT ahogar[se], sofocar[se]; (to die, kill) asfixiar[se]

suffocation [sáfəkéʃən] N ahogo *m*, sofoco *m*

suffrage [sáfrɪʤ] N sufragio *m*

sugar [ʃúgə·] N azúcar *m/f*; (endearment) cariño *m*; **— cane** caña de azúcar *f*; VT azucarar; **to — the pill** dorar la píldora

suggest [səgʤést] VT (propose) sugerir; (hint) insinuar; **—ed retail price** precio sugerido *m*

suggestion [səgʤéstʃən] N (proposal) sugerencia *f*; (in hypnosis) sugestión *f*

suggestive [səgʤéstɪv] ADJ insinuante; **to be — of** evocar

suicide [súɪsaɪd] N (act) suicidio *m*; (person) suicida *mf*; **to commit —** suicidarse

suit [sut] N (clothes) traje *m*; (in cards) palo *m*, color *m*; (lawsuit) demanda *f*, pleito *m*, querella *f*; — **case** maleta *f*, valija *f*; VT (adapt) adaptar, ajustar; (satisfy) satisfacer; (look good) quedarle bien a, sentarle bien a; (be convenient, appropriate) convenir, venir bien; — **yourself** haz lo que te parezca

suitable [súɾəbəl] ADJ (appropriate) apropiado; (apt) apto

suitably [súɾəbli] ADV como corresponde

suite [swit] N (series) serie *f*; (series of rooms, musical composition) suite *f*; (furniture) juego *m*; (software) paquete de programas de productividad *m*

suitor [súɾə·] N pretendiente *m*, galán *m*

sulfate, sulphate [sʌ́lfet] N sulfato *m*

sulfide, sulphide [sʌ́lfaɪd] N sulfuro *m*

sulfur, sulphur [sʌ́lfə·] N azufre *m*

sulfuric, sulphuric [sʌlfjúrɪk] ADJ sulfúrico

sulk [sʌlk] VI enfurruñarse; N **to be in a —** estar enfurruñado

sulky [sʌ́lki] ADJ malhumorado, enfurruñado

sullen [sʌ́lən] ADJ hosco, huraño

sully [sʌ́li] VT mancillar, ensuciar

sultry [sʌ́ltri] ADJ (hot) bochornoso, sofocante; (sensual) sensual

sum [sʌm] N suma *f*; **in —** en resumen; VI **to — up** resumir, recapitular

summarize [sʌ́məraɪz] VI/VT resumir

summary [sʌ́məri] N resumen *m*; ADJ sumario

summer [sʌ́mə·] N verano *m*, *lit* estío *m*; — **resort** balneario *m*, lugar de veraneo *m*; — **school** cursos de verano *m pl*; —**time** verano *m*; VI veranear

summit [sʌ́mɪt] N cumbre *f*, cima *f*

summon [sʌ́mən] VT (a witness) citar; (an employee, the police) llamar; N —**s** citación judicial *f*

sumptuous [sʌ́mptʃuəs] ADJ suntuoso

sun [sʌn] N sol *m*; **to —bathe** tomar el sol; —**beam** rayo de sol *m*; —**block** protector solar *m*; —**burn** quemadura de sol *f*; —**dial** reloj de sol *m*; —**down** puesta de[l] sol *f*; —**flower** girasol *m*; —**glasses** gafas de sol *f pl*, anteojos de sol *m pl*; —**lamp** lámpara solar *f*; —**light** luz del sol *f*; —**rise** salida de[l] sol *f*, amanecer *m*; —**screen** protector solar *m*; —**set** puesta de[l] sol *f*; —**shine** luz [del sol] *f*; —**spot** mancha solar *f*; —**stroke** insolación *f*; —**tan** bronceado *m*; —**up** salida del sol *f*; VI **to — oneself** tomar el sol; **to —burn** quemar[se] al sol

Sunday [sʌ́nde] N domingo *m*; — **school** escuela dominical *f*

sundry [sʌ́ndri] ADJ diversos

sung [sʌŋ] *see* sing

sunk [sʌŋk] *see* sink

sunny [sʌ́ni] ADJ (day, patio) soleado; (disposition) alegre

super [súpə·] N (of a building) conserje *m*, portero -ra *mf*; ADJ (wonderful) súper, bárbaro

superb [supə́·b] ADJ excelente

supercharger [súpə·tʃɑɾʤə·] N sobrealimentador *m*

supercomputer [súpə·kəmpjuɾə·] N *Am* supercomputadora *f*; *Sp* superordenador *m*

superego [supə·íɡo] N superego *m*, superyó *m*

superficial [supə·fíʃəl] ADJ superficial

superfluous [supə́·fluəs] ADJ superfluo

superhuman [supə·hjúmən] ADJ sobrehumano

superimpose [supə·ɪmpóz] VT superponer, sobreponer

superintendent [supə·ɪnténdənt] N (of work) superintendente *mf*, supervisor -ora *mf*; (of building) conserje *mf*, portero -ra *mf*

superior [supíriə·] ADJ & N superior *mf*

superiority [supɪrióriɾi] N superioridad *f*

superlative [supə́·ləɾɪv] ADJ & N superlativo *m*

supermarket [súpə·mɑrkɪt] N supermercado *m*, súper *m*

supernatural [supə·nǽtʃə·əl] ADJ sobrenatural

superpower [súpə·pauə·] N superpotencia *f*

superscript [súpə·skrɪpt] N superíndice *m*

supersede [supə·síd] VT reemplazar

supersonic [supə·sɑ́nɪk] ADJ supersónico

superstar [súpə·star] N superestrella *f*

superstition [supə·stíʃən] N superstición *f*

superstitious [supə·stíʃəs] ADJ supersticioso

superstore [súpə·stor] N hipermercado *m*

supervise [súpə·vaɪz] VI/VT supervisar, fiscalizar

supervision [supə·víʒən] N supervisión *f*, fiscalización *f*

supervisor [súpə·vaɪzə·] N supervisor -ora *mf*

supine [súpaɪn] ADJ supino

supper [sʌ́pə·] N cena *f*

supplant [səplǽnt] VT suplantar

supple [sʌ́pəl] ADJ (flexible) flexible, elástico; (agile) ágil, grácil

supplement[1] [sʌ́pləmənt] N (of a newspaper) suplemento *m*; (of a book) apéndice *m*; (of one's diet) complemento *m*

supplement[2] [sʌ́pləmɛnt] VT complementar, suplementar

supplemental [sʌpləmɛ́ntəl] ADJ suplementario

supplier [səpláɪə·] N abastecedor -ora *mf*, proveedor -ora *mf*

supply [səpláɪ] VT abastecer, suministrar; N (act of supplying) abastecimiento *m*; — **and demand** oferta y demanda *f*; **in short —**

escaso; **supplies** suministros *m pl*, provisiones *f pl*; **office supplies** artículos de oficina *m pl*; **military supplies** pertrechos *m pl*

support [səpórt] VT (keep from falling) sostener, soportar; (encourage) apoyar; (facilitate) potenciar; (corroborate) corroborar; (help with computers) soportar; **to be —ed by** fundamentarse en/sobre; N (of a structure) sostén *m*, soporte *m*; (of a family) sustento *m*; (of a candidate, idea) apoyo *m*; (of a theory) respaldo *m*; (for a computer) soporte *m*; **— group** grupo de apoyo *m*

supporter [səpórɖə-] N partidario -ria *mf*, simpatizante *mf*; (in sports) hincha *mf*

supportive [səpórɖɪv] ADJ solidario; **you've always been very — of us** siempre nos has apoyado

suppose [səpóz] VT suponer; **we are —d to go** tenemos que ir

supposedly [səpózɪdli] ADV supuestamente

supposition [sʌpəzíʃən] N suposición *f*, supuesto *m*

suppository [səpázɪtɔri] N supositorio *m*

suppress [səprés] VT (repress) reprimir; (eliminate) suprimir; (a revolt) sofocar

suppression [səpréʃən] N (repression) represión *f*; (elimination) supresión *f*; (of a revolt) sofocación *f*

supremacy [supréməsi] N supremacía *f*

supreme [suprím] ADJ supremo

surcharge [sɜ́tʃɑrdʒ] N recargo *m*, prima *f*

sure [ʃur] ADJ seguro; (judgment) certero; (hand) firme; **to make — of** asegurarse de; ADV **he — drinks a lot** es una esponja; **may I sit here? —!** ¡me puedo sentar? ¡cómo no!

surely [ʃúrli] ADV seguramente, ciertamente; **— you jest** no hablarás en serio; **he will — come** seguramente vendrá

surf [sɜ́f] N (breaking waves) rompientes *mf pl*; (foam) espuma *f*; (undertow) resaca *f*; **—board** tabla de surf *f*; VI/VT (on water) hacer surfing [en], surfear; (on the Internet) navegar, surfear

surface [sɜ́fɪs] N superficie *f*; (of a solid) cara *f*; VI (come to top) emerger; (turn up) salir a la luz; VT (a submarine) sacar a la superficie; (a road) revestir

surfeit [sɜ́fɪt] N (excess) exceso *m*; (feeling of fullness) hartazgo *m*; VI/VT hartar[se]

surfing [sɜ́fɪŋ] N (on water) surfing *m*; (on the Internet) navegación *f*

surge [sɜ́dʒ] N (of people, disgust) oleada *f*; (of waves) oleaje *m*; (of electricity) sobrecarga de voltaje *f*; **— protector** protector contra sobrecargas de voltaje *m*; VI (people) precipitarse; (current) subir

surgeon [sɜ́dʒən] N cirujano -na *mf*

surgery [sɜ́dʒəri] N cirujía *f*; (room) quirófano *m*

surgical [sɜ́dʒɪkəl] ADJ quirúrgico; **— dressing** vendaje quirúrgico *m*; **— instruments** instrumentos quirúrgicos *m pl*

Suriname, Surinam [súrɪnɑm] N Surinam *m*

Surinamese [surɪnɑmíz] ADJ & N surinamés -esa *mf*

surly [sɜ́li] ADJ malhumorado, hosco, arisco

surmise [sə-máɪz] VT conjeturar, suponer; N conjetura *f*, suposición *f*

surmount [sə-máunt] VT superar

surname [sɜ́nem] N apellido *m*

surpass [sə-pǽs] VT superar, sobrepujar

surpassing [sə-pǽsɪŋ] N superación *f*

surplus [sɜ́plʌs] N excedente *m*, sobrante *m*, sobra *f*; (of funds) superávit *m*

surprise [sə-práɪz] N sorpresa *f*; VT sorprender

surprising [sə-práɪzɪŋ] ADJ sorprendente

surprisingly [sə-práɪzɪŋli] ADV sorprendentemente; **not —** como era de esperar

surreal [sɔríəl] ADJ surrealista

surrealism [səríəlɪzəm] N surrealismo *m*

surrealist [səríəlɪst] N surrealista *mf*

surrealistic [sərɪəlístɪk] ADJ surrealista

surrender [səréndə-] VI (accept defeat) rendir[se], darse por vencido; (give oneself up) entregarse; VT entregar; N rendición *f*

surreptitious [sɜ-əptíʃəs] ADJ subrepticio

surrogate [sɜ́əgɪt] ADJ sustituto; **— mother** madre de alquiler *f*

surround [səráund] VT rodear, circundar; (a city) sitiar

surrounding [səráundɪŋ] ADJ circundante; N **—s** alrededores *m pl*, inmediaciones *f pl*, entorno *m*

surtax [sɜ́tæks] N sobretasa *f*

surveillance [sə-vélɑns] N vigilancia *f*

survey[1] [sə-vé] VT (evaluate) evaluar; (measure) medir; (contemplate) contemplar; (poll) encuestar

survey[2] [sɜ́ve] N (inspection) reconocimiento *m*, inspección *f*; (measure) medición *f*; (overview) panorama *m*; (poll) encuesta *f*, sondeo *m*; **— course** curso general *m*

surveyor [sə-véə-] N agrimensor -ora *mf*

survival [sə-váɪvəl] N supervivencia *f*, sobrevivencia *f*; (subsistence) subsistencia *f*; **the — of the fittest** la supervivencia del más apto

survive [sə-váɪv] VI/VT sobrevivir (also live longer than); (subsist) subsistir

surviving [sə-váɪvɪŋ] ADJ superviviente

survivor [sə-váɪvə-] N sobreviviente *mf*, superviviente *mf*

susceptible [səséptəbəl] ADJ susceptible; **to be — of proof** poderse demostrar; **to be — to pneumonia** ser propenso a la pulmonía

suspect[1] [sʌ́spɛkt] N sospechoso -sa *mf*

suspect[2] [səspɛ́kt] VT sospechar, recelar

suspend [səspénd] VT suspender

suspenders [səspéndəz] N tirantes *m pl*

suspense [səspéns] N (uncertainty) incertidumbre *f*; (in movie) suspenso *m*; *Sp* suspense *m*; **to keep in—** mantener en suspenso, tener en vilo

suspension [səspénʃən] N suspensión *f*; (of a ban) levantamiento *m*; **— bridge** puente colgante *m*

suspicion [səspíʃən] N sospecha *f*

suspicious [səspíʃəs] ADJ (causing suspicion) sospechoso; (experiencing suspicion) suspicaz, desconfiado

sustain [səstén] VT (weight) sostener, sustentar; (pretense, effort) mantener; (an injury) sufrir; (an objection) admitir; (a musical note) sostener

sustainable [səsténəbəł] ADJ sostenible, sustentable

sustenance [sástənəns] N sustento *m*, alimento *m*

suture [sútʃə] N sutura *f*

swab [swab] N bola de algodón *f*, *RP* hisopo *m*; VT pasar un hisopo sobre

swagger [swǽgə] VI (walk) pavonearse, contonearse; (boast) fanfarronear; N (walk) pavoneo *m*, contoneo *m*; (bluster) fanfarronería *f*

swallow [swálo] N (drink) trago *m*; (bird) golondrina *f*; VI/VT tragar; **to — up** consumir

swallowing [swáloɪŋ] N deglución *f*

swam [swæm] *see* swim

swamp [swamp] N pantano *m*, ciénaga *f*; **—land** cenagal *m*; VI/VT (flood) inundar[se]; (overwhelm) abrumar[se], agobiar[se]

swampy [swámpi] ADJ pantanoso, cenagoso

swan [swan] N cisne *m*; **— dive** salto del ángel *m*; **— song** canto de cisne *m*

swap [swap] VT cambiar, canjear; N cambio *m*, canje *m*

swarm [swɔrm] N enjambre *m*; VI (of bees) salir en enjambre; (of people, tourists) pulular, hormiguear; **to be —ing with** ser un hervidero de, abundar en

swarthy [swórði] ADJ trigueño, moreno

swat [swat] VT (a person) pegar; (flies) aplastar; **to — at** manotear; N manotazo *m*

sway [swe] VI/VT (move to and fro) balancear[se], bambolear[se]; (move hips) menear[se]; (influence) influir [en]; N (movement) balanceo *m*, vaivén *m*, bamboleo *m*; (influence) influencia *f*; **to hold — over** dominar

Swazi [swázi] N suazi *mf*

Swaziland [swázilænd] N Suazilandia *f*

swear [swer] VI/VT (vow) jurar; (use profanity) decir palabrotas; *Sp* soltar tacos; **to — in** (give oath) juramentar; (take oath) prestar juramento; **she —s by canned peaches**

para ella no hay nada como los duraznos enlatados; **to — off** renunciar a; **to — to** jurar por

sweat [swet] VI (perspire) sudar; (ooze) exudar, sudar; (worry) preocuparse; N sudor *m*; **— glands** glándulas sudoríparas *f pl*; **—shirt** sudadera *f*; **—suit** equipo deportivo *m*; *Sp* chándal *m*; **no —** no hay problema

sweater [swéðə] N suéter *m*, jersey *m*

sweating [swéðɪŋ] N sudor *m*, sudoración *f*, transpiración *f*

sweaty [swéði] ADJ sudoroso, sudado

Swede [swid] N sueco -ca *mf*

Sweden [swídn̩] N Suecia *f*

Swedish [swídɪʃ] ADJ sueco

sweep [swip] VI/VT (clean with broom, scan) barrer; (dredge) dragar; VT (touch) rozar; (search) rastrear; VI (spread) extenderse; **to — away** llevar, arrastrar; **to — down upon** caer sobre, asolar; **to — off** limpiar; **to — into** (enter majestically) entrar majestuosamente; (enter quickly) entrar rápidamente; **to — up** recoger; N (cleaning) barrida *f*; (extension) extensión *f*; (movement) barrido *m*; (search) rastreo *m*

sweeper [swípə] N (for cleaning) barredora *f*; (in soccer) líbero *m*

sweeping [swípɪŋ] ADJ (statement) [demasiado] general; (victory) aplastante

sweet [swit] ADJ (in flavor, personality) dulce; (in smell) bueno, fragante; **—-and-sour** agridulce; **—heart** querido -da *mf*; **— pea** *Sp* guisante de olor *m*; **— potato** batata *f*, boniato *m*; *Mex* camote *m*; **to have a — tooth** ser goloso; N dulce *m*, golosina *f*; **my — mi vida, mi alma; VT to —-talk** halagar

sweeten [swítn̩] VI/VT (a food) endulzar[se]; (an experience) dulcificar[se]

sweetener [swítnə] N endulzante *m*, edulcorante *m*

sweetness [swítnɪs] N (of personality) dulzura *f*; (of taste) dulzor *m*

swell [swel] VI/VT (limbs, with pride) hinchar[se], henchir[se]; VI (river) crecer; (population) crecer, engrosar[se]; VT (make grow) hacer crecer, hacer aumentar, engrosar; N (of ocean) oleaje *m*; ADJ regio, bárbaro

swelling [swélɪŋ] N hinchazón *f*

swelter [swéltə] VI sofocarse de calor

swept [swept] *see* sweep

swerve [swɚv] VI/VT (in a car) virar; (from a goal) desviar[se]; N viraje *m*

swift [swift] ADJ ligero, veloz, raudo; N vencejo *m*

swiftness [swíftnɪs] N velocidad *f*, rapidez *f*

swim [swim] VI/VT nadar; (float) flotar; **to — across** atravesar nadando; **my head is —ming** me da vueltas la cabeza; **I love**

—**ming** me encanta nadar; N *Mex* alberca *f*;
—**suit** traje de baño *m*; **to take a —** ir a
nadar, dar una nadada

swimmer [swímɚ] N nadador -ora *mf*; —**'s ear**
otitis externa *f*

swimming [swímɪŋ] N natación *f*; — **pool**
piscina *f*

swindle [swíndl̩] VT estafar; N estafa *f*,
trapacería *f*

swine [swaɪn] N puerco *m*, cerdo *m*; (person)
offensive puerco -ca *mf*, sinvergüenza *mf*

swing [swɪŋ] VI/VT (on a swing) columpiar[se];
(move to and fro) balancear[se],
bambolear[se]; (baseball, golf) dar un swing
[con]; VI (change) virar; **to — and miss**
abanicar; **to — around** dar vueltas; **to —
open** abrirse; VT (make turn) hacer girar;
(influence) influir sobre; **to — a deal**
concretar un negocio; **I can't — a new car**
no me puedo dar por el lujo de comprar un auto
nuevo; N (playground toy) columpio *m*;
(oscillation) balanceo *m*, vaivén *m*, bamboleo
m; (in golf, baseball, music) swing *m*;
(change) cambio *m*; — **and a miss** abanico
m; **in full** — en su apogeo; **to get into the
— of things** agarrarle la onda a algo, cogerle
el tranquillo a algo

swipe [swaɪp] VT (steal) afanar, sisar; (slide)
deslizar; **to — a card** pasar una tarjeta por un
lector; N (insult) insulto *m*; **to take a — at
someone** (physical) tirarle un manotazo a
alguien; (verbal) insultar

swirl [swɝl] VI/VT arremolinar[se]; (dancers)
girar; N remolino *m*; (smoke) espiral *f*

Swiss [swɪs] ADJ & N suizo -za *mf*; — **cheese**
queso suizo *m*

switch [swɪtʃ] N (change) cambio *m*; (electrical)
interruptor *m*, llave *f*; (stick for whipping)
varilla *f*; (on railways) agujas *f pl*; —**blade**
navaja automática *f*; —**board** centralita *f*;
—**man** guardagujas *m sg*; —**-hitter** (in
baseball) bateador -ora ambidiestro *mf*; VI/VT
cambiar [de]; (train cars) desviar; **to — off**
(current) cortar; (light, TV) apagar; **to — on**
encender, prender

Switzerland [swítsɚlənd] N Suiza *f*

swivel [swívəl] N pivote *m*; — **chair** silla
giratoria *f*

swollen [swólən] ADJ hinchado

swollen [swólən] *see* swell

swoon [swun] VI desvanecerse, desmayarse; **to
— over someone** morirse por alguien; N
vahído *m*

swoop [swup] VI **to — down upon** abalanzarse
sobre; N descenso súbito *m*; **at one fell —** de
un tirón

sword [sɔrd] N espada *f*; —**fish** pez espada *m*

swore [swɔr] *see* swear

sworn [swɔrn] *see* swear

swum [swʌm] *see* swim

swung [swʌŋ] *see* swing

sycamore [síkəmɔr] N sicomoro *m*

syllable [síləbəl] N sílaba *f*

syllabus [síləbəs] N programa [de estudios] *m*

syllogism [sílədʒɪzəm] N silogismo *m*

symbiosis [sɪmbióʊsɪs] N simbiosis *f*

symbol [símbəl] N símbolo *m*

symbolic [sɪmbɑ́lɪk] ADJ simbólico

symbolism [símbəlɪzəm] N simbolismo *m*

symbolize [símbəlaɪz] VT simbolizar

symmetrical [sɪmétrɪkəl] ADJ simétrico

symmetry [símɪtri] N simetría *f*

sympathetic [sɪmpəθɛ́θɪk] ADJ (compassionate)
compasivo; (understanding) comprensivo,
solidario; (favoring) favorable; (nervous
system) simpático

sympathize [símpəθaɪz] VI (be compassionate)
compadecer[se]; (be understanding)
comprender; (be in favor) favorecer; **to —
with** estar a favor de

sympathizer [símpəθaɪzɚ] N simpatizante *mf*

sympathizing [símpəθaɪzɪŋ] ADJ
simpatizante

sympathy [símpəθi] N (compassion) compasión
f; (understanding) comprensión *f*;
(condolence) condolencia *f*, pésame *m*; **to
extend one's —** dar el pésame

symphony [símfəni] N sinfonía *f*; — **orchestra**
orquesta sinfónica *f*

symposium [sɪmpóʊziəm] N simposio *m*

symptom [símptəm] N síntoma *m*

synagogue [sínəgɑg] N sinagoga *f*

synchronize [síŋkrənaɪz] VI/VT sincronizar[se]

synchronous [síŋkrənəs] ADJ sincrónico

syndicate¹ [síndɪkɪt] N sindicato *m*

syndicate² [síndɪket] VI/VT (form a syndicate)
sindicar[se]; VT (sell rights) vender los
derechos de

syndrome [síndrom] N síndrome *m*

synergy [sínɚdʒi] N sinergia *f*

synonym [sínənɪm] N sinónimo *m*

synonymous [sɪnɑ́nəməs] ADJ sinónimo

synopsis [sɪnɑ́psɪs] N sinopsis *f*

syntax [síntæks] N sintaxis *f*

synthesis [sínθəsɪs] N síntesis *f*

synthesize [sínθəsaɪz] VI/VT sintetizar

synthesizer [sínθəsaɪzɚ] N sintetizador *m*

synthetic [sɪnθɛ́θɪk] ADJ sintético

syphilis [sífəlɪs] N sifilis *f*

Syria [síriə] N Siria *f*

Syrian [síriən] ADJ & N sirio -ria *mf*

syringe [sərín dʒ] N jeringa *f*

syrup [sírəp] N (food) almíbar *m*, jarabe *m*;
(medicine) jarabe *m*

system [sístəm] N sistema *m*; — **crashes** caídas
del sistema *f pl*

systematic [sɪstəmǽθɪk] ADJ sistemático

systematize [sístəmətaɪz] VI/VT sistematizar

systemic [sɪstɛ́mɪk] ADJ sistémico

systolic [sɪstálɪk] ADJ sistólico

Tt

tab [tæb] N (on a keyboard) tabulador m; (on index cards) pestaña f, ceja f; (bill) cuenta f; — **key** tecla de tabulación f; VI tabular

table [tébəl] N (furniture) mesa f, (list) tabla f; — **lamp** lámpara de mesa f; — **of contents** tabla de contenido f, índice m; **at** — a la mesa; VT posponer indefinidamente, dar carpetazo a; —**cloth** mantel m; —**spoon** (spoon) cuchara grande f, (measurement) cucharada f; —**spoonful** cucharada f; — **tennis** tenis de mesa m; —**ware** vajilla f, servicio de mesa m

tablet [tǽblɪt] N (pill) pastilla f, tableta f; (paper) bloc m; (stone) tabla f, lápida f; (portable writing surface) tablilla f

tabloid [tǽblɔɪd] N (paper size) tabloide m; (type of press) prensa amarilla/sensacionalista f

taboo [tæbú] N tabú m

tabulate [tǽbjəlet] VT tabular

tachometer [tækámɪdɚ] N tacómetro m

tacit [tǽsɪt] ADJ tácito

taciturn [tǽsɪtɚn] ADJ taciturno

tack [tæk] N (nail) tachuela f; (stitch) hilván m; (heading of a boat) rumbo m; (course of action) táctica f; (equipment for a horse) arreos m pl; VT (to nail) clavar con tachuelas; (to stitch) hilvanar; **to** — **on** agregar; VI virar, cambiar de rumbo

tackle [tǽkəl] N (for fishing, hoisting) aparejo m; (in rugby, football) placaje m, parada f; (person) atajador m; VT (a problem) enfrentar, abordar; (a task) emprender; (a horse) poner arreos; VI/VT (rugby, American football) placar, atajar

tacky [tǽki] ADJ (in bad taste) de mal gusto, chabacano; Sp hortera; (sticky) pegajoso

tact [tækt] N tacto m

tactful [tǽktfəl] ADJ que tiene tacto

tactics [tǽktɪks] N táctica f

tactile [tǽktl] ADJ táctil

tactless [tǽktlɪs] ADJ falto de tacto

tag [tæg] N (label) etiqueta f; (question) coletilla f; (nickname) apodo m; **to play** — jugar al pillapilla; VT etiquetar; (in the game of tag) pillar; **to** — **along** acompañar

tail [tel] N cola f, rabo m; (of a shirt) faldón m; (pursuer) perseguidor -ora mf; —**bone** rabadilla f; — **end** (of a concert) final m; (of a procession) cola f; —**light** luz trasera f; —**pipe** tubo de escape m; —**s** (of a coin) cruz f; (of a tuxedo) frac m; —**spin** barrena f; **to** —**gate** seguir demasiado de cerca [a otro coche]

tailor [télɚ] N sastre m; — **shop** sastrería f; VT hacer a medida; (adapt) adaptar

taint [tent] N (stain) mancha f; (contamination) contaminación f; VI/VT (stain) manchar[se]; (contaminate) contaminar[se]

Taiwan [taɪwán] N Taiwán m

Taiwanese [taɪwaníz] ADJ & N taiwanés -esa mf

Tajik [tɑʤík] ADJ & N tayiko -ka mf

Tajikistan [tɑʤíkɪstɑn] N Tayikistán m

take [tek] VT (a load) llevar; (someone else's property) robar, llevarse; (one number from another) restar; (prisoner, medicine, measures, a course) tomar; (one of a set) elegir, coger; (a bribe) aceptar; (a prize) recibir; (advice) seguir; (a walk) dar; (a vacation) irse; (a trip) hacer; (a piece of news) recibir; (a photo) sacar; **to** — **a bath** bañarse; **to** — **after** parecerse a; **to** — **a look at** echar un vistazo a; **to** — **a notion to** ocurrírsele a uno; **to** — **apart** desarmar, desmontar; **to** — **aside** apartar; **to** — **away** (carry away) llevarse; (steal) sustraer; **to** — **back** devolver; **to** — **back one's words** retractarse; **to** — **by surprise** tomar desprevenido; **to** — **care of** (a person) cuidar de; (a matter) atender a; **to** — **charge of** encargarse de; **to** — **down in writing** anotar, apuntar; **to** — **effect** entrar en vigencia; **to** — **exercise** hacer ejercicio; **to** — **in** (include) incluir; (observe) observar; (deceive) embaucar; (provide shelter for) albergar; (make smaller) tomar, achicar; **to** — **leave** despedirse; **to** — **off** (remove) quitar[se]; (conduct) llevar; (discount) rebajar; (start flight) despegar; **to** — **offense** ofenderse; **to** — **office** asumir un cargo; **to** — **on** (accept) asumir; (hire) tomar, contratar; (acquire) adquirir; **to** — **out** (withdraw) sacar; (carry out [food], take on a date) llevar; **to** — **over** hacerse cargo [de]; **to** — **place** tener lugar; **to** — **revenge** vengarse; **to** — **stock** hacer un balance; **to** — **stock in** tener confianza en; **to** — **the floor** tomar la palabra; **to** — **to heart** tomar a pecho; **to** — **to one's heels** poner pies en polvorosa; **to** — **to task** reprender, regañar; **to** — **up a matter** tratar un asunto; **to** — **up again** retomar; **to** — **up space** ocupar espacio; **I** — **it that** supongo que; **it** —**s ten minutes** lleva diez minutos; **the vaccination didn't** — la vacuna no prendió; N (profits) ingresos m pl; (of fish) pesca f, captura f; (of a film production) toma f; (opinion) opinión f; (approach) enfoque m; —**off** (of an airplane) despegue m; (parody) parodia f; —**over** (of a government) toma de poder f; (of a company) adquisición f

taken [tékən] see take

talcum [tǽlkəm] N talco m; — **powder** polvo de

talco *m*

tale [teɪl] N (story) cuento *m*, relato *m*; (lie) mentira *f*

talent [tǽlənt] N talento *m*

talented [tǽləntɪd] ADJ talentoso

talk [tɔk] VI/VT hablar; (chat) charlar; VT (nonsense) decir; (a language) hablar; (politics) hablar de; **to — back** contestar con impertinencia; **to — down to** hablar con arrogancia a; **to — up** alabar, hacer propaganda; N (formal speech) charla *f*; (gossip) habladurías *f pl*; (lingo) habla *f*; **— of the town** la comidilla del pueblo *f*; **— show** programa de entrevistas

talkative [tɔ́kədɪv] ADJ hablador, parlanchín, charlatán

tall [tɔl] ADJ alto; **— order** misión imposible *f*; **— tale** cuento chino *m*, patraña *f*; **six feet —** de seis pies de altura; **how — are you?** ¿cuánto mides?

tallow [tǽlo] N sebo *m*

tally [tǽli] N (account) cuenta *f*; VT llevar la cuenta; **to — up** sumar; **to — with** concordar con

tambourine [tæmbərín] N pandereta *f*

tame [tem] ADJ (docile) manso, dócil; (domesticated) domesticado; (dull) aburrido; VT (make docile) amansar, domar; (domesticate) domesticar

tamper [tǽmpə] VI **to — with** (a jury) sobornar; (a lock) intentar forzar; (a document) alterar, amañar; ADJ **—proof** a prueba de alteración

tampon [tǽmpan] N tampón *m*

tan [tæn] VI/VT (cure) curtir[se]; (darken skin) broncear[se], tostar[se]; VT (cure) adobar; (spank) zurrar; N color tostado *m*; (of skin) bronceado *m*; ADJ (car) color tostado; (skin) bronceado, tostado

tandem [tǽndəm] N tándem *m*; **in — with** en colaboración con

tangent [tǽndʒənt] ADJ & N tangente *f*; **to go off on a —** salirse por la tangente

tangerine [tændʒərín] N mandarina *f*; *Am* tangerina *f*

tangible [tǽndʒəbəl] ADJ tangible

tangle [tǽŋgəl] VI/VT enredar[se], enmarañar[se]; N enredo *m*, maraña *f*; (in hair) nudo *m*, enredijo *m*

tank [tæŋk] N tanque *m* (also military), depósito *m*; VT guardar en un tanque; VI **to — up** (with gasoline) llenar el tanque; (with alcohol) emborracharse

tannery [tǽnəri] N curtiduría *f*, tenería *f*; *Am* curtiembre *f*

tantalize [tǽntlaɪz] VT atormentar con tentaciones

tantamount [tǽntəmaunt] ADJ **to be — to** equivaler a

tantrum [tǽntrəm] N berrinche *m*, perrera *f*, rabieta *f*

Tanzania [tænzəníə] N Tanzania *f*

Tanzanian [tænzéniən] ADJ & N tanzano -na *mf*

tap [tæp] N golpecito *m*; (repeated) golpeteo *m*; (with the hand) palmadita *f*; (faucet) llave *f*; *Sp* grifo *m*; **— dance** claqué *m*; **— water** agua de llave *f*; VI/VT (once) tocar; (repeatedly) golpetear; (with fingers) tamborilear; (utilize) explotar; (draw off liquid) extraer; **to — a tree** sangrar un árbol; **to — a telephone** intervenir un teléfono

tape [tep] N (adhesive, magnetic) cinta *f*; **— measure** cinta métrica *f*; **— recorder** grabadora *f*, grabador *m*; **— recording** grabación *f*; **—worm** lombriz *f*, solitaria *f*; VT (affix) atar con cinta; VI/VT (record) grabar; **to —-record** grabar

taper [tépə] N (diminished size) estrechamiento *m*; (candle) vela *f*, candela *f*; VI/VT afinar[se]; **to — off** (become smaller) afinar[se]; (diminish) ir disminuyendo

tapestry [tǽpɪstri] N (wall hanging) tapiz *m*; (art, industry) tapicería *f*

tapioca [tæpiókə] N tapioca *f*

tapir [tépər] N tapir *m*

tar [tar] N alquitrán *m*, brea *f*; VT alquitranar; **to — and feather** emplumar

tarantula [tərǽntʃələ] N tarántula *f*

tardy [tárdi] ADJ **to be —** llegar tarde

target [tárgɪt] N blanco *m*; **— practice** tiro al blanco *m*

tariff [tǽrɪf] N tarifa *f*, arancel *m*

tarnish [tárnɪʃ] VI/VT (metal) deslustrar[se], empañar; (reputation) manchar[se]

tart [tart] ADJ (fruit) agrio, ácido; (remark) mordaz; N (pie) tarta *f*

tartar [tárdə] N (in wine) tártaro *m*; (on teeth) sarro *m*; **— sauce** salsa tártara *f*

task [tæsk] N tarea *f*, labor *f*; **— force** fuerza de tarea *f*; **—master** tirano -na *mf*; **to take to —** reprender, regañar

tassel [tǽsəl] N borla *f*

taste [test] VT (perceive) sentir el gusto/sabor de; (try) probar; (try wine) catar; VI **to — of onion** saber a cebolla; **it —s sour** tiene un sabor agrio; N (sense, aesthetic judgment) gusto *m*; (flavor) sabor *m*; (small amount of food) bocadito *m*; (small amount of drink) sorbo *m*; **— bud** papila gustativa *f*

tasteless [téstlɪs] ADJ (with no taste) soso, desabrido; (in bad taste) de mal gusto

tasty [tésti] ADJ sabroso

tatter [tǽdə] N andrajo *m*, harapo *m*, pingajo *m*

tattered [tǽdəd] ADJ harapiento, andrajoso

tattle [tǽdl] VI acusar; **to — on** acusar a; N

—tale acusetas *mf sg*
tattoo [tætú] N tatuaje *m*; VI/VT tatuar[se]
taught [tɔt] *see* teach
taunt [tɔnt] VT provocar, burlarse de; N provocación *f*, pulla *f*
taut [tɔt] ADJ tenso, tirante
tavern [tǽvən] N taberna *f*, cantina *f*
tawdry [tɔ́dri] ADJ (affair) sórdido; (outfit) charro
tax [tæks] N impuesto *m*, contribución *f*, gravamen *m*; (burden) carga *f*; VT (a product) gravar; (a person) cobrarle impuestos a; (patience, resources) poner a prueba; — **attorney/lawyer** abogado -da tributarista *mf*; — **code** código impositivo *m*; —**-deductible** desgravable; — **deduction** deducción impositiva *f*; — **evasion** evasión de impuestos *f*; —**payer** contribuyente *mf*; — **return** declaración de impuestos *f*; — **shelter** abrigo impositivo *m*, refugio fiscal *m*; — **withholding** retención impositiva *f*; ADJ —**-exempt** no gravable, exento de impuestos; —**-free** libre de impuestos
taxable [tǽksəbət] ADJ imponible, tributable
taxation [tækséʃən] N (result of taxing) impuestos *m pl*; (act of taxing) imposición de contribuciones *f*
taxi [tǽksi] N taxi *m*; VI ir en taxi; (an airplane) rodar por la pista; —**cab** taxi *m*
taxidermy [tǽksɪdɚmi] N taxidermia *f*
taxonomy [tæksánəmi] N taxonomía *f*
tea [ti] N té *m*; — **bag** bolsita de té *f*; —**cup** taza de té *f*; —**kettle/pot** tetera *f*; — **party** té *m*; —**spoon** (spoon) cucharita *f*, cucharilla *f*; (measurement) cucharadita *f*; —**spoonful** cucharadita *f*; —**time** hora del té *f*
teach [titʃ] VI/VT enseñar; **to** — **a class** dar clase
teacher [títʃɚ] N (primary school) maestro -tra *mf*; (secondary school) profesor -ora *mf*; —**s college** [escuela] normal *f*
teaching [títʃɪŋ] N enseñanza *f*; —**s** enseñanzas *f pl*; — **activities** actividades pedagógicas *f pl*; — **profession** magisterio *m*
team [tim] N equipo *m*; (of yoked animals) yunta de bueyes *f*; (of horses) tiro *m*, enganche *m*; —**mate** compañero -ra de equipo *mf*; VI **to** — **up** unirse, formar un equipo
teamster [tímstɚ] N transportista *mf*, camionero -ra *mf*
tear¹ [tir] N lágrima *f*; —**drop** lágrima *f*; — **gas** gas lacrimógeno *m*; **to burst into** —**s** romper a llorar
tear² [tɛr] VI/VT (rip) rasgar[se]; (rip a hole) hacer[se] un siete; VT **to** — **along** ir a toda velocidad; **to** — **apart** (rip up) romper, destrozar; (separate) separar; **to** — **away** apartar[se]; **to** — **down** (a building) demoler, derribar; (a machine) desarmar, desmontar; (a person) denigrar; **to** — **one's hair** arrancarse los cabellos; N desgarrón *m*, desgarradura *f*, rasgón *m*
tearful [tírfəl] ADJ (look) lloroso; (farewell) triste
tease [tiz] VT (make fun of a person) molestar, fastidiar; (tantalize sexually) provocar; (comb wool, hair) cardar; **to** — **out** sacar; N provocadora *f*
teat [tit] N teta *f*
techie [tɛ́ki] N *fam* experto -ta en computación *mf*
technical [tɛ́knɪkəl] ADJ técnico; — **support** soporte técnico *m*
technician [tɛknɪ́ʃən] N técnico -ca *mf*, perito -ta *mf*
technique [tɛknɪ́k] N técnica *f*
technological [tɛknəládʒɪkəl] ADJ tecnológico
technology [tɛknálədʒi] N tecnología *f*, técnica *f*
tectonics [tɛktánɪks] N tectónica *f*
tedious [tídiəs] ADJ tedioso, aburrido
tedium [tídiəm] N hastío *m*
tee [ti] N (T-shirt) camiseta *f*; (golf ball support) tee *m*; (start of hole in golf) punto de salida *m*
teem [tim] VI **to** — **with** abundar en, estar lleno de
teen [tin] *see* teenager
teenager [tínedʒɚ] N adolescente *mf*
teens [tinz] N (teenage years) adolescencia *f*; (numbers 13–19) números de trece a diecinueve *m pl*
teethe [tið] VI **the baby is teething** al bebé le están saliendo los dientes
teetotaler [títódlɚ] N abstemio -mia *mf*
telecast [tɛ́ləkæst] N teledifusión *f*
telecommunication [tɛlɪkəmjunɪkéʃən] N telecomunicación *f*; —**s** telecomunicaciones *f pl*
telecommuting [tɛlɪkəmjúdɪŋ] N teletrabajo *m*
teleconference [tɛ́lɪkɑnfɚəns] N teleconferencia *f*
telegram [tɛ́ləgræm] N telegrama *m*
telegraph [tɛ́ləgræf] N telégrafo *m*; VI/VT telegrafiar
telegraphic [tɛləgrǽfɪk] ADJ telegráfico
telemarketing [tɛləmárkɪdɪŋ] N telemercadeo *m*, telemarketing *m*
telepathy [təlépəθi] N telepatía *f*
telephone [tɛ́ləfon] N teléfono *m*; — **book** guía telefónica *f*; — **booth** cabina telefónica *f*; — **number** número telefónico *m*; — **operator** telefonista *mf*; — **receiver** auricular *m*, tubo de teléfono *m*; VI/VT telefonear, llamar por teléfono
telescope [tɛ́lɪskop] N telescopio *m*; VI plegarse
televisable [tɛləvázəbəl] ADJ televisivo
televise [tɛ́ləvaɪz] VT televisar
television [tɛ́ləvɪʒən] N (medium) televisión *f*; (device) televisor *m*; — **program** programa televisivo *mf*; — **viewer** televidente *mf*
tell [tɛl] VI/VT (the truth) decir; (a story) contar;

to — apart distinguir; to — on someone acusar a alguien; to — someone off regañar a alguien; to — time decir la hora; I can't — if he's old or young no sé si es viejo o joven; his age is beginning to — se le comienza a notar la edad; ADJ a —tale sign una señal reveladora; he is a —tale es un acusica

teller [télə] N (narrator) narrador -ora *mf*; (in a bank) cajero -ra *mf*

temerity [təmériDi] N temeridad *f*

temp [temp] N empleado -da temporal *mf*

temper [témpə] N (hardness) temple *m*; (bad humor) mal genio *m*; **to keep one's** — mantener la calma; **to lose one's** — perder los estribos, encolerizarse; VT templar

temperament [témpəəmənt] N temperamento *m*, genio *m*, talante *m*

temperance [témpəəns] N (moderation) templanza *f*, temperancia *f*; (abstinence from alcohol) abstinencia de bebidas alcohólicas *f*

temperate [témpəɪt] ADJ (weather) templado; (opinions, habits) moderado

temperature [témpəətʃur] N temperatura *f*; **to have a** — tener fiebre

tempest [témpɪst] N tempestad *f*

tempestuous [tempéstʃuəs] ADJ tempestuoso

template [témplɪt] N plantilla *f*

temple [témpəl] N (church) templo *m*; (side of the forehead) sien *f*

temporal [témpəəl] ADJ temporal

temporary [témpəreri] ADJ temporal, eventual

tempt [tempt] VT tentar

temptation [temptéʃən] N tentación *f*

tempting [témptɪŋ] ADJ tentador

ten [ten] NUM diez; N —s **of candidates** decenas de candidatos *f pl*

tenacious [tənéʃəs] ADJ tenaz

tenacity [tənǽsɪDi] N tenacidad *f*

tenant [ténənt] N inquilino -na *mf*, arrendatario -ria *mf*

tend [tend] VT (care for) cuidar; **to — to** (take care of) ocuparse de; (lean toward) tender, inclinarse

tendency [téndənsi] N tendencia *f*

tender [téndə] ADJ tierno; (painful) sensible; N (offer) oferta *f*; (legal currency) curso legal *m*; (person who tends) cuidador -ora *mf*, vigilante *mf*; VT presentar, ofrecer

tenderness [téndəɪnɪs] N (of feeling) ternura *f*; (of meat) terneza *f*, ternura *f*; (sensitivity to pain) sensibilidad *f*

tendinitis [tendənáɪDɪs] N tendinitis *f*

tendon [téndən] N tendón *m*

tendril [téndrəl] N zarcillo *m*

tenement [ténəmənt] N casa de vecindad *f*

tenet [ténɪt] N principio *m*

tennis [ténɪs] N tenis *m*; — **court** cancha de tenis *f*, pista de tenis *f*; — **elbow** codo de tenista *m*; — **player** tenista *mf*; — **shoes** tenis *m pl*

tenor [ténə] N tenor *m*

tense [tens] ADJ tenso; N (grammatical) tiempo *m*

tension [ténʃən] N (stress) tensión *f*; (tautness) tirantez *f*

tent [tent] N (camping) tienda de campaña *f*; (circus) carpa *f*; VI acampar

tentacle [téntəkəl] N tentáculo *m*

tentative [téntəDɪv] ADJ tentativo

tenth [tenθ] ADJ & N décimo *m*

tenuous [ténjuəs] ADJ (light, color, cloth) tenue; (peace) frágil

tenure [ténjə] N (of professorship) titularidad *f*; (of an office) ocupación *f*

tepid [tépɪd] ADJ tibio

terabyte [térəbaɪt] N terabyte *m*

term [tɜm] N (word, mathematical expression) término *m*; (period) período *m*; (time in office) mandato *m*; (semester) semestre *m*; (trimester) trimestre *m*; (set date for payment) plazo *m*; — **life insurance** seguro de vida a término *m*; — **paper** trabajo final *m*; —s **conditiones** *f pl*; **at** — a término; **to be on good** —s estar en buenas relaciones; **not to be on speaking** —s no hablarse; **to come to** —s aceptar; VT denominar

terminal [tɜmən] ADJ terminal; N (of airport, computer) terminal *mf*; (electric) terminal *m*

terminate [tɜmənet] VI/VT terminar[se]

termination [tɜmənéʃən] N terminación *f*; (of an employee) despido *m*

terminology [tɜmənáləʤi] N terminología *f*

termite [tɜmaɪt] N termita *f*

terrace [térɪs] N terraza *f*, escalón *m*; VT poner terrazas en, escalonar

terrain [tərén] N terreno *m*

terrestrial [təréstriəl] ADJ terrestre

terrible [térəbəl] ADJ terrible, tremendo

terrier [tériə] N terrier *m*

terrific [tərífɪk] ADJ estupendo

terrify [térəfaɪ] VT aterrar, aterrorizar, espeluznar

territory [téritori] N territorio *m*

terror [térə] N terror *m*

terrorism [térəɪzəm] N terrorismo *m*

terrorist [térəɪst] N terrorista *mf*

terrorize [térəaɪz] VT aterrorizar

terse [tɜs] ADJ lacónico

test [test] N (trial, experiment) prueba *f*; (of intelligence, multiple choice) test *m*; (examination) examen *m*, prueba *f*; — **market** mercado de prueba *m*; — **pilot** piloto de pruebas *m*; — **tube** tubo de ensayo *m*, probeta *f*; —-**tube baby** bebé de probeta *m*; **to undergo a** — someterse a una prueba; **to take a** — dar un examen; **to give a** — poner un examen; **to put to the** — poner a prueba; VT (put to the test) probar, poner a prueba; (give an exam) poner una prueba, examinar; —**ing** pruebas *f pl*; **to** -**drive**

probar; VI **girls — better than boys** en los exámenes salen mejor las niñas que los niños

testament [téstəmənt] N testamento m; (testimony) testimonio m

testicle [téstɪkəl] N testículo m

testify [téstəfaɪ] VI (serve as witness) testificar; (confirm) dar fe

testimony [téstəmoni] N testimonio m

testosterone [tɛstástəron] N testosterona f

tetanus [tétnəs] N tétano[s] m

tetracycline [tetrəsáklɪn] N tetraciclina f

Teutonic [tutánɪk] ADJ teutónico

text [tɛkst] N texto m; —**book** libro de texto m; — **editor** editor de texto[s] m; — **message** mensaje de texto m; VT enviar mensajes de texto, RP textear

textile [tékstaɪl] ADJ textil; N textil m, tejido m; — **mill** fábrica de tejidos f

texture [tékstʃə] N textura f

Thai [taɪ] ADJ & N (person) tailandés -esa mf; (language) tailandés m

Thailand [táɪlænd] N Tailandia f

than [ðæn] CONJ que; **I have more — you** tengo más que tú; **more — once** más de una vez

thank [θæŋk] VT dar las gracias, agradecer; **to have oneself to — for** tener la culpa de; INTERJ — **heaven!** ¡gracias a Dios! — **you** gracias; —**-you letter** carta de agradecimiento f; N —**s** gracias f pl

thankful [θæŋkfəl] ADJ agradecido

thankfulness [θæŋkfəlnɪs] N gratitud f, agradecimiento m

thankless [θæŋklɪs] ADJ ingrato

thanksgiving [θæŋksgívɪŋ] N acción de gracias f; — **Day** día de acción de gracias m

that [ðæt] ADJ (something nearer the speaker) ese, esa; (something more remote from speaker) aquel, aquella; — **dog** ese/aquel perro m; — **one** (nearer) ese, esa; DEMON PRON (nearer to speaker) ese, esa; (more remote from speaker) aquel, aquella; (neuter) eso, aquello; — **is my daughter** esa/aquella es mi hija; — **was a nightmare** eso/aquello fue una pesadilla; REL PRON que; **the bike — disappeared** la bici que desapareció; **the pen — I was writing with** la lapicera con la que / la cual escribía; — **is** es decir; CONJ que; **she said — she would come** dijo que vendría; ADV tan; **it's not — far** no queda tan lejos; — **much** tanto; **she was — tall** era así de alta

thatch [θætʃ] N paja f; Am quincha f; VT techar con paja; Am quinchar; —**ed roof** techo de paja m; Am techo de quincha m

thaw [θɔ] VI/VT (food) descongelar[se]; (ice and snow) derretir[se]; (relations, refrigerator) deshelar[se]; N deshielo m

the [ðə, ði] DEF ART (singular) el m, la f; — **boy** el chico m; (plural) los m, las f; — **girls** las

chicas f pl; — **good thing about that** lo bueno de eso; ADV — **more I work, — less I accomplish** cuanto más trabajo, menos consigo

theater, theatre [θíəðə] N teatro m

theatrical [θiǽtrɪkəl] ADJ teatral

theft [θɛft] N hurto m, robo m

their [ðɛr] POSS ADJ **this is — dog** este es su perro, este es el perro de ellos

theirs [ðɛrz] PRON **this book is —** este libro es suyo, este libro es de ellos/ellas; **these things are —** estas cosas son suyas / de ellos / de ellas; — **is bigger** el suyo / la suya / el de ellos / la de ellos es más grande; **a friend of —** un amigo suyo, un amigo de ellos

them [ðɛm] PRON los m pl, las f pl; **I see —** los/las veo; **I talk to —** les hablo a ellos; **I went with —** fui con ellos/ellas

thematic [θɪmǽðɪk] ADJ temático

theme [θim] N (topic) tema m; (essay) ensayo m, redacción f; — **park** parque temático m; — **song** tema m

themselves [ðɛmsélvz] PRON **they — built their house** ellos mismos se construyeron la casa; **they are not —** today hoy no son los mismos de siempre; **they were sitting by —** estaban sentados solos; **they looked at — in the mirror** se miraron en el espejo; **they talk to —** hablan solos; **they bought — a yacht** se compraron un yate

then [ðɛn] ADV (at that time) entonces, en aquel tiempo; **it was cheaper —** era más barato en aquel tiempo; (after) luego, después; **from — on** a partir de entonces; **now and —** de vez en cuando; **until —** hasta entonces; **I ate, — I paid** comí, luego pagué; **now —** ahora bien; **are you sorry —?** ¿estás arrepentido pues? ADJ entonces; **the — president** el entonces presidente; CONJ entonces; **if not, — you should stay** si no, entonces deberías quedarte

theologian [θiəlódʒən] N teólogo -ga mf

theological [θiəládʒɪkəl] ADJ teológico

theology [θiáləʤi] N teología f

theoretical [θiərɛ́ðɪkəl] ADJ teórico

theory [θíəri] N teoría f; **in —** en teoría

therapeutic [θɛrəpjúðɪk] ADJ terapéutico

therapist [θɛ́rəpɪst] N terapeuta mf; (psychologist) psicólogo -ga mf

therapy [θɛ́rəpi] N terapia f

there [ðɛr] ADV ahí; Am allí; (more remote) allá; Sp allí; —**abouts** por ahí, más o menos; —**after** (later) después; (always subsequently) de allí en adelante; —**by** así, de ese modo; — **ensued a war** a continuación hubo una guerra; —**fore** por consiguiente, por lo tanto; —**in** en eso, allí; — **is/are** hay; — **goes the bus** ahí va el autobús; — —

bueno, bueno; **—of** de eso; **—on** (on that) encima; (later) luego, después; **—upon** (after) luego, después; (for this reason) por consiguiente; (upon that) encima; **—with** (with that) con eso; (after that) luego, en seguida; **who's —?** ¿quién es? **is Mary —?** ¿está María? **we got — at 5** llegamos a las 5

thermal [θɜ́ːməl] ADJ termal; **— energy** energía térmica f

thermal [θɜ́ːməl] ADJ térmico

thermodynamic [θɜːmodaɪnǽmɪk] ADJ termodinámico

thermometer [θəˈmɑ́mɪDə] N termómetro m

thermonuclear [θɜːmonúkliə] ADJ termonuclear

thermos [θɜ́ːməs] N termo m

thermostat [θɜ́ːməstæt] N termostato m

thesaurus [θɪsɔ́rəs] N (synonym dictionary) diccionario de sinónimos m; (large dictionary) diccionario m

these [ðiz] ADJ & PRON estos, estas

thesis [θíːsɪs] N tesis f

they [ðe] PRON ellos, ellas

thick [θɪk] ADJ (slice) grueso; (fog, soup) espeso; (accent) marcado; (wit) torpe; **one inch —** una pulgada de espesor; **— as thieves** como carne y uña; ADJ **—headed** estúpido; **—set** grueso; **—-skinned** insensible; N **the — of the fight** lo más reñido de la pelea; **through — and thin** pase lo que pase

thicken [θíkən] VI/VT espesar[se], trabar[se]; **the plot —s** la trama se complica

thicket [θíkɪt] N soto m, matorral m, boscaje m

thickness [θíknɪs] N (of paper, wood) espesor m, grosor m; (of soup) lo espeso; (of lips) lo grueso; (of a beard) lo tupido; (of hair) lo abundante

thief [θif] N ladrón -ona mf

thieve [θiv] VI/VT hurtar, robar

thigh [θaɪ] N muslo m

thimble [θímbəl] N dedal m

thin [θɪn] ADJ (ice, wire) delgado, fino; (person) flaco; (vegetation, beard, hair) ralo; (voice) tenue, fino; (air) enrarecido; (excuse) débil; (soup) aguado; VI/VT (paint, soup, sauce) diluir; (hair) entresacar; **to — out** (hair) ralear; (crowd) dispersarse

thing [θɪŋ] N cosa f; **there's no such —** eso no existe; **that is the — to do** eso es lo que hay que hacer; **the — about Mary** lo que pasa con María

thingamajig [θíŋəmədʒɪg] N chisme m, coso m

think [θɪŋk] VI/VT (reason) pensar, razonar; (believe) creer, opinar; **to — about** pensar en; **to — back** recordar; **to — it over/ through** pensarlo bien, reflexionar sobre; **I'm —ing of you** pienso en ti; **what do you — of Mary?** ¿qué piensas de María? **I thought of a plan** se me ocurrió un plan; **to**

— up an excuse inventar/elucubrar una excusa; **I don't — so** no creo; **who does he — he is?** ¿quién se cree que es? **to — well of** tener buena opinión de; **she —s nothing of spending $1000** no le importa nada gastar $1000

thinking [θíŋkɪŋ] N **current —** la opinión actual f; **to my way of —** a mi parecer; ADJ pensante

thinner [θínə] N disolvente m

thinness [θínnɪs] N (of ice, person) delgadez f, flacura f; (of hair) escasez f; (of air) enrarecimiento m; (of soup) fluidez f

third [θɜːd] ADJ tercer[o]; **— base** tercera base f, antesala f; **— baseman** tercero m, antesalista m; **— chapter** capítulo tercero m, tercer capítulo m; **— person** tercera persona f; **— rate** de poca categoría; **— World** Tercer Mundo m; ADV tercero; N tercio m; (gear, musical interval) tercera f; **the — of March** el tres de marzo

thirst [θɜːst] N sed f; VI tener sed; **to — for** tener sed de, estar sediento de

thirsty [θɜːsti] ADJ sediento; **to be —** tener sed

thirteen [θɜːtín] NUM trece

thirty [θɜːDi] NUM treinta; ADJ & N **—something** treintañero -ra mf

this [ðɪs] ADJ & PRON este m, esta f, esto (neuter); **— dog** este perro; **— is a disaster** esto es un desastre

thistle [θísəl] N cardo m

thong [θɔŋ] N (strip of leather) correa f; (garment) tanga mf; (shoe) chancleta f

thorax [θɔ́ræks] N tórax m

thorn [θɔrn] N (sharp growth) espina f; (plant) espino m

thorny [θɔ́rni] ADJ espinoso, escabroso

thorough [θɜ́ːo] ADJ (exhaustive) exhaustivo, minucioso, detenido; (conscientious) concienzudo; **—bred** ADJ de pura sangre; N purasangre m

those [ðoz] ADJ & PRON (nearer) esos m, esas f; PRON (more remote) aquellos m, aquellas f; **— of you** los de vosotros/ustedes; **— that/who** los/las que

though [ðo] CONJ aunque; **as —** como si; ADV sin embargo

thought [θɔt] N (act, product of thinking) pensamiento m; (idea) idea f; (opinion) opinión f; (concern) consideración f; **to be lost in —** estar abstraído; **to give it no —** no darle importancia; **the very —** la mera idea; **at the — of** ante la idea de; **on second —** pensándolo bien; **my —s are with you** te acompaño en el sentimiento

thought [θɔt] see think

thoughtful [θɔ́tfəl] ADJ (considerate) considerado, atento; (well thought out) bien pensado; (reflective) pensativo, reflexivo

thoughtfulness [θɔ́tfəlnɪs] N consideración f

thoughtless [θɔ́tlɪs] ADJ (inconsiderate) desconsiderado; (careless) descuidado; (not reflective) irreflexivo

thoughtlessness [θɔ́tlɪsnɪs] N (lack of consideration) desconsideración f; (carelessness) descuido m; (lack of reflection) falta de reflexión f

thousand [θáuzənd] NUM mil

thrash [θræʃ] VI/VT (whip, defeat) zurrar, vapulear, apalear; (thresh) trillar, desgranar; **to — around** revolverse, agitarse; **to — out a matter** ventilar un asunto

thread [θrɛd] N (in fabric) hilo m; (on a screw) rosca f; ADJ **—bare** raído; VT (a needle) enhebrar; (beads) ensartar; (a screw) enroscar; **to — one's way** abrirse paso

threat [θrɛt] N amenaza f

threaten [θrɛ́tn̩] VI/VT amenazar

threatening [θrɛ́tnɪŋ] ADJ amenazador, amenazante

three [θri] NUM tres; **— hundred** trescientos; ADJ **—dimensional** tridimensional; **—-point basket** triple m; **—-point play** jugada de tres puntos f

thresh [θrɛʃ] VT trillar

threshold [θrɛ́ʃhoᵘld] N umbral m

threw [θru] see throw

thrift [θrɪft] N economía f

thrifty [θrɪ́fti] ADJ económico, ahorrativo

thrill [θrɪl] VI/VT emocionar[se], ilusionar[se]; N emoción f, ilusión f

thrive [θraɪv] VI (person, economy) prosperar, florecer; (plants) crecer mucho

throat [θroᵘt] N garganta f

throb [θrɑb] VI latir, palpitar; N latido m, palpitación f

throes [θroᵘz] ADV LOC **in the — of war** en plena guerra; **in the — of death** agonizando

throne [θroᵘn] N trono m

throng [θrɔŋ] N muchedumbre f, turbamulta f; VI apiñarse, llegar en tropel

throttle [θrɑ́dl̩] N (of a motor) válvula reguladora / de aceleración f, regulador m; (of a motorcycle) puño giratorio del gas m; VT ahogar, estrangular

through [θru] PREP por, a través de; (as intermediary) por medio de; **Monday — Friday** de lunes a viernes; **all — the night** toda la noche; ADV (completely) de un lado a otro; (from beginning to end) de principio a fin, de cabo a rabo; **loyal — and —** leal a toda prueba; **he's an aristocrat — and —** es un aristócrata de pura cepa; **to carry —** llevar a cabo; ADJ (ticket, train) directo; **to be —** (with a task) haber terminado; (in a profession) estar acabado; **we're —!** (with a boyfriend) ¡se acabó entre nosotros!

throughout [θruáᵘt] PREP (all through) por

todo; (during) a lo largo de, durante; ADV (duration) de principio a fin; (space) por todas partes

throw [θroᵘ] VI/VT (a ball) tirar, lanzar; (a light, voice) arrojar; (a switch) conectar; (a pot on a wheel) modelar; (a punch) lanzar; (a wrestler) tumbar; (a game for a bribe) dejarse perder; (a rider) desmontar; (a party) dar, organizar; **that really threw me** eso me confundió; **to — away** (dispose of) tirar, arrojar; (squander) malgastar; **to — down** tirar al suelo; **to — in** añadir; **to — into gear** engranar; **to — in the clutch** embragar; **to — out** (garbage) tirar, arrojar; (unruly guest) echar; **to — up** vomitar, devolver; N (act or instance of throwing) tiro m; (of dice) tirada f; (shawl) chal m; (blanket) manta f; **—-in** (soccer) saque de banda m; ADJ **—away** desechable

thrown [θroᵘn] see throw

thrush [θrʌʃ] N tordo m, zorzal m

thrust [θrʌst] VT (stab) clavar; (shove) empujar; **to — oneself upon** meterse en; **to — a task upon someone** imponerle una tarea a alguien; **to — aside** echar a un lado; VI (push) dar un empujón; (stab at) lanzar una estocada; (push through) empujar para pasar; N (stab) estocada f; (force of a jet engine) empuje m; (shove) empujón m; (military assault) arremetida f, acometida f

thud [θʌd] N golpe sordo m; VI caer con un golpe sordo

thug [θʌg] N matón m

thumb [θʌm] N pulgar m; **—tack** chinche f, tachuela f; **under the — of** bajo la bota de; VT hojear; **to give a —s up** aprobar

thump [θʌmp] N golpe sordo m; VI hacer un ruido sordo

thunder [θʌ́ndɚ] N trueno m; **—bolt** rayo m; **—head** nubarrón m; **—storm** tormenta eléctrica f, tronada f; VI tronar

thunderous [θʌ́ndɚəs] ADJ atronador, estruendoso

Thursday [θɚ́zde] N jueves m

thus [ðʌs] ADV así; **— far** (space) hasta aquí; (time) hasta ahora

thwart [θwɔrt] VT frustrar

thyme [taɪm] N tomillo m

thyroid [θáɪrɔɪd] N tiroides m sg

Tibet [tɪbét] N Tíbet m

Tibetan [tɪbétn̩] ADJ & N tibetano -na mf

tic [tɪk] N tic m, manía f

tick [tɪk] N (sound of a clock) tic tac m; (cover of a pillow) funda f; (checkmark) marca f; (insect) garrapata f; VI hacer tic tac; **to — off** (check off) marcar; (anger) enojar

ticket [tɪ́kɪt] N billete m; Am boleto m; (slate of candidates) candidatura f; (summons) multa f; (tag) etiqueta f; **— office** taquilla f; VT (give passage) vender billetes; (give summons) multar

tickle [tíkəl] VT (poke) cosquillear, hacer cosquillas; (amuse) dar ilusión; VI picar; N picazón f, cosquilleo m

ticklish [tíklɪʃ] ADJ (prone to tickling) cosquilloso; (delicate) delicado

tidal [táɪdl] ADJ — **wave** (tsunami) tsunami m, maremoto m; (large wave) marejada f

tidbit [tídbɪt] N (snack) golosina f; (gossip) chisme jugoso m

tide [taɪd] N marea f; (of opinion) corriente f; —**water** (water) agua de marea f; (land) marisma f; VT to — **over** cubrir

tidy [táɪdi] ADJ (orderly) ordenado; (large) considerable; VI/VT arreglar; **to — oneself up** arreglarse

tie [taɪ] VI (fasten) atarse; (make same score) empatar; VT (fasten) atar; (make a knot) hacer un nudo en; (make same score as) empatar con; **to — a record** empatar una marca; **to — down** atar; **to — in** cuadrar; **to — one on** emborracharse; **to — tight** atar fuerte; **to — up** (bind) atar; (hinder) bloquear; (occupy) ocupar; (moor a ship) amarrar; N (cord) cuerda f; (relations) lazo m, vínculo m; (cravat) corbata f; (railway) durmiente m, traviesa f; (score) empate m; —-**break** (in sports) desempate m; (in tennis) muerte súbita f

tier [tir] N nivel m

tiger [táɪgə] N tigre m

tight [taɪt] ADJ (knot, nut) apretado, ajustado; (clothes) ceñido, ajustado; (control) firme, estricto; (race) reñido; (stingy) tacaño, mezquino; (drunk) borracho; — **end** (football) receptor cerrado m; —-**fisted** agarrado; —**rope** cuerda floja f; —**wad** tacaño -ña mf; **to be in a — spot** estar en un aprieto; ADV bien, herméticamente; **to hold on —** agarrarse bien

tighten [táɪtn] VI/VT (knot, nut, belt) apretar[se]; (control) estrechar[se]

tightness [táɪtnɪs] N (narrowness) estrechez f; (stinginess) tacañería f

tilde [tíldə] N tilde f

tile [taɪl] N (on a roof) teja f; (on a floor) baldosa f; (on a wall) azulejo m; — **roof** tejado m; VT (roof) tejar; (floor) embaldosar; (wall) azulejar

till [tɪl] PREP hasta; CONJ hasta que; VI/VT (plow) labrar, arar; N (cash drawer) caja f

tilt [tɪlt] VI/VT ladear[se], inclinar[se]; N (act or instance of tilting) ladeo m, inclinación f; (incline) declive m; (joust) justa f; **at full —** a toda velocidad

timber [tímbə] N (cut wood) madera [de construcción] f; (trees) árboles para madera m pl; (beam) viga f; — **line** límite de la vegetación arbórea m; — **wolf** lobo gris m

timbre [tímbə] N timbre m

time [taɪm] N (past, present, future) tiempo m; (on the clock) hora f; (occasion) vez f; (period) período m, momento m, época f; — **and-a-half pay** paga de tiempo y medio f; — **bomb** bomba de tiempo f; — **frame** plazo aproximado de tiempo m; —**keeper** cronometrador -ora mf; — **limit** límite de tiempo m; — **out** descanso m; —**piece** reloj m; —**share** tiempo compartido m; — **signature** compás m; —**table** horario m; — **zone** huso horario m; **at —s** a veces; **at the same —** a la vez, al mismo tiempo; **at this —** en este momento; **behind —** atrasado; **lunch—** hora del almuerzo f; **from — to —** de vez en cuando; **for the — being** por el momento; **in —** a tiempo; **in no —** en seguida; **it's about —** ya era hora; **on —** puntual; **to buy on —** comprar a plazo; — **after —** una vez tras otra; **to do —** cumplir una condena; **to have a good —** divertirse; **what — is it?** ¿qué hora es? VT (a race) cronometrar; (a test) fijar la duración de; (one's arrival) fijar la hora de; **to — an attack well** atacar en el momento oportuno

timeless [táɪmlɪs] ADJ eterno

timely [táɪmli] ADJ oportuno

timer [táɪmə] N (person) cronometrador -ora mf; (device) reloj m

timid [tímɪd] ADJ tímido, apocado

timidity [tɪmídɪɾi] N timidez f, apocamiento m

timing [táɪmɪŋ] N (measurement) cronometraje m; (synchronization) sincronización f; **that was good —** lo hiciste en el momento oportuno

timorous [tíməəs] ADJ timorato

tin [tɪn] N (metal) estaño m; (tin plate) hojalata f; — **can** lata f; —**foil** papel de estaño m, papel de aluminio m; VT estañar

tincture [tíŋktʃə] N tintura f

tinder [tíndə] N yesca f

tinge [tɪndʒ] VT (tint) teñir; (affect slightly) matizar; N (of color) tinte m, matiz m; (of taste) dejo m; (of irony) matiz m

tingle [tíŋgəl] VI sentir hormigueo, hormiguear; **to — with excitement** estremecerse de entusiasmo; N hormigueo m

tinker [tíŋkə] VI ocuparse, entretenerse; **to — with** hacer ajustes

tinkle [tíŋkəl] VT (ring lightly) tintinear; (urinate) fam hacer pipí; N tintineo m

tinnitus [tɪnáɪɾəs] N tinitus m

tinsel [tínsəl] N (Christmas trim) espumillón m, guirnalda f; (tawdry decoration) oropel m

tint [tɪnt] N (hue) matiz m; (for hair) tinte m, tintura f; (for glass) coloreado m; VT (hair) teñir; (glasses) colorear

tiny [táɪni] ADJ diminuto, chiquito

tip [tɪp] N (point) punta f; (gratuity) propina f;

(piece of advice) consejo m; VI/VT (tilt) inclinar[se], ladear[se]; (give a gratuity) dar propina [a]; **to — a person off** advertir a alguien; **to — one's hat** sacarse/quitarse el sombrero; **to — over** volcar[se]

tipsy [típsi] ADJ alegre

tiptoe [típto] N punta del pie f; **on —s** de puntillas; VI andar de puntillas

tirade [táired] N diatriba f

tire [taɪr] N neumático m; *Mex* llanta f; *Am* goma f; VI/VT cansar[se], fatigar[se]; **to — out** cansar, fatigar

tired [taɪrd] ADJ cansado, fatigado; **— out** agotado; **I'm — of your complaining** estoy harto de tus quejas

tireless [táirlis] ADJ incansable

tiresome [táirsəm] ADJ aburrido, pesado, plasta

tissue [tíʃu] N (cell aggregate) tejido m; (handkerchief) pañuelo de papel m; **— paper** papel tisú m

tit [tɪt] N paro m

titanic [taɪténɪk] ADJ titánico

titanium [taɪténiəm] N titanio m

tithe [taɪð] N diezmo m; VI pagar el diezmo

titillate [tídlet] VT (sexually) excitar; (interest) despertar interés

title [táɪdl̩] N título m; (of a painting) rótulo m; **— deed** título de propiedad m; **— page** portada f

TNT [tiéntí] N TNT m

to [tu] PREP **I gave it — you** te lo di a ti; **to count — ten** contar hasta diez; **I called — find out** llamé para averiguar; **— my surprise** para mi sorpresa; **a quarter — five** las cinco menos cuarto; **bills — be paid** cuentas por pagar; **things — do** cosas que hacer; **frightened — death** muerto de susto; **from house — house** de casa en casa; ADV **— and fro** de acá para allá; **to come —** volver en sí

toad [tod] N sapo m; **—stool** seta f, hongo no comestible m

toast [tost] VI/VT (brown) tostar[se]; VT (congratulate) brindar por; (bread) tostada f; (congratulation) brindis m

toaster [tóstə-] N tostadora f; **— oven** horno tostador m

tobacco [təbǽko] N tabaco m

today [tədé] ADV hoy; (nowadays) hoy día

toddler [tádlə-] N niño pequeño m, niña pequeña f

toe [to] N dedo del pie m; (of shoe, sock) punta f; **—nail** uña del dedo del pie f; VT (touch with toe) tocar con el dedo del pie; **to — the line** hacer buena letra, entrar en vereda

together [təgéðə-] ADV (in union) juntos; (at the same time) al mismo tiempo; **— with** junto con; **all —** todos juntos

Togo [tógo] N Togo m

Togolese [togəlíz] ADJ & N togolés -esa mf

toil [tɔɪl] VI trabajar, esforzarse, bregar; N trabajo m, esfuerzo m

toilet [tɔ́ɪlɪt] N (bowl) inodoro m; (lavatory) aseo m, lavabo m; **— paper** papel higiénico m; ADJ **—-trained** que ya no usa pañales

token [tókən] N (symbol) señal f; (keepsake) recuerdo m; (coinlike metal piece) ficha f; **— payment** pago nominal m; **as a — of friendship** en prenda de amistad

told [told] *see* tell

tolerance [tálə-əns] N tolerancia f

tolerant [tálə-ənt] ADJ tolerante

tolerate [tálə-et] VT tolerar

toll [tol] N (of bells) tañido m; (payment) peaje m; (charges) tarifa f; (of victims) balance m; **— bridge** puente de peaje m; **— road** carretera de peaje f; ADJ **—-free** libre de cargos; VI/VT tañer [a muerto]

tomato [toméɖo] N tomate m

tomb [tum] N tumba f, sepulcro m, sepultura f; **—stone** lápida f

tomcat [túmkæt] N gato macho m

tomorrow [tamóro] ADV & N mañana f; **— morning** mañana por la mañana f

ton [tʌn] N tonelada f

tone [ton] N (pitch) tono m; (of a voice, instrument) sonoridad f; (of a speech) tono m, tónica f; VI **to — down** moderar, matizar

toner [tónə-] N tóner m; **— cartridge** cartucho de tóner m

Tonga [tángə] N Tonga m

Tongan [tángən] ADJ & N tongano -na mf

tongs [tɔŋz] N tenazas f pl

tongue [tʌŋ] N (body part, language, of a flame) lengua f; (of a shoe) lengüeta f; **— depressor** depresor de lengua m; **— in cheek** irónicamente; **— twister** trabalenguas m sg; **on the tip of my —** en la punta de la lengua; **to hold one's —** callarse la boca; VI tocar con la lengua; **to —-lash** reprender; **to be —-tied** tener trabada la lengua

tonic [tánɪk] ADJ tónico; N (medicine) tónico m; (water, key note) tónica f; **— water** agua tónica f

tonight [tənáɪt] ADV esta noche

tonsil [tánsəl] N amígdala f

tonsillitis [tɑnsəláɪDɪs] N amigdalitis f, anginas f pl

too [tu] ADV (in addition) también; (excessively) demasiado; **— bad!** ¡qué lástima! **— many** demasiados; **— much** demasiado

took [tʊk] *see* take

tool [tul] N herramienta f; **—bar** barra de herramientas f; **—box/kit** caja de herramientas f; **—shed** cobertizo para herramientas m

toot [tut] VI/VT (horn) sonar; (whistle) pitar; (trumpet) tocar; **to — one's own horn** darse

autobombo; N (of horn, trumpet) toque m; (of
horn) bocinazo m; (of whistle) pitido m

tooth [tuθ] N (front) diente m; (back) muela f;
—**ache** dolor de muelas m; —**brush** cepillo
de dientes m; —**decay** caries [dental] f sg;
—**fairy** ratoncito Pérez m; —**mark** dentellada
f; —**paste** pasta dental f, pasta dentífrica f;
—**pick** mondadientes m sg, palillo de dientes
m; **to fight — and nail** luchar a brazo
partido; **to have a sweet —** ser goloso

toothed [tuθt] ADJ dentado

toothless [túθlɪs] ADJ desdentado

top [tɑp] N (of a mountain) cumbre f, cima f; (of a
page) parte superior f; (of a jar) tapa f; (of a
convertible) capota f; (of a table) superficie f;
(of a tree) copa f; (toy) trompo m, peonza f;
(blouse) blusa f; —**coat** abrigo m; —**dollar**
precio exorbitante m; —**hat** sombrero de
copa m; —**spin** liftado m; **at — speed** a
velocidad máxima; **to be — dog** ir a la
cabeza; **to be at the — of the class** ser el
mejor de la clase; **at the — of one's voice** a
voz en cuello; **filled up to the —** lleno hasta
el tope; **from — to bottom** de arriba abajo;
on — of encima de, arriba; **—flight** de
primera; —**heavy** desbalanceado; —**most**
superior; —**rated** de la más alta categoría;
—**secret** altamente confidencial; —
notch de primera; VT (a tree) desmochar; (a
list) encabezar; (a performance) superar; (a
level) exceder; **to — off** (an action) rematar;
(a tank) llenar hasta el tope; **that —s
everything!** ¡eso es el colmo!

topaz [tópæz] N topacio m

topic [tápɪk] N tema m, materia f, Am tópico m

topical [tápɪkəl] ADJ (of medicine) tópico;
(current) de actualidad

topless [táplɪs] ADJ topless; —**swimsuit**
monokini m

topple [tápəl] VT (knock over) derribar;
(overthrow) derrocar; VI (fall) volcarse; (lose
power) caer; **to — over** volcarse

topsy-turvy [tápsitɝvi] ADJ & ADV patas arriba

torch [tɔrtʃ] N antorcha f

tore [tɔr] see tear

torment[1] [tɔ́rment] N tormento m

torment[2] [tɔrmént] VT atormentar, martirizar

torn [tɔrn] see tear[2]

tornado [tɔrnédo] N tornado m

torpedo [tɔrpído] N torpedo m; —**boat**
torpedero m; VT torpedear

torpid [tɔ́rpɪd] ADJ torpe

torpor [tɔ́rpɚ] N letargo m, torpor m

torque [tɔrk] N par de torsión m

torrent [tɔ́rənt] N torrente m

torrential [tɔrénʃəl] ADJ torrencial

torrid [tɔ́rɪd] ADJ tórrido

torsion [tɔ́rʃən] N torsión f

torso [tɔ́rso] N torso m, tronco m

tortoise [tɔ́rtɪs] N tortuga f

tortuous [tɔ́rtʃuəs] ADJ tortuoso

torture [tɔ́rtʃɚ] N tortura f; VT torturar

torturous [tɔ́rtʃɚəs] ADJ torturante, torturador

toss [tɔs] VT (a ball, coin) tirar; (one's head)
echar; (a salad) revolver; **to — aside** echar a
un lado; VI (waves) cabecear; (a person in bed)
dar vueltas; N (of coin, ball) tiro m; (of head)
sacudida f

total [tódl] ADJ & N total m; —**amount** importe
total m, montante m; —**loss** pérdidas totales
f pl

totalitarian [totælɪtériən] ADJ totalitario

totter [tápɚ] VI tambalear[se], titubear

touch [tʌtʃ] VI/VT (have physical contact with)
tocar; (move deeply) conmover, enternecer;
(compare with) compararse con, igualar;
(affect) afectar; **to — down** aterrizar; **to —
off** provocar; **to — up** retocar; **to — upon**
mencionar; N (contact) contacto m, roce m,
toque m; (sense) tacto m; (knack) mano f;
(slight amount) poquito m; ; —**down**
anotación f; —**down pass** envío de
anotación m, pase de anotación m; —**screen**
pantalla táctil f; —**sensitive display**
pantalla táctil f; —**stone** piedra de toque f; **a
woman's —** un toque femenino; **finishing
—** toque final m; **to keep in —** mantenerse
en contacto; ADJ —**-and-go** precario; —
tone de botones

touching [tʌ́tʃɪŋ] ADJ conmovedor

touchy [tʌ́tʃi] ADJ hipersensible

tough [tʌf] ADJ (leather) fuerte, resistente;
(fighter) duro, fuerte; (steak) duro, correoso;
(situation) difícil; (neighborhood) bravo

toughen [tʌ́fən] VI/VT (leather) curtir[se]; (meat)
endurecer[se]; (person) endurecerse

toughness [tʌ́fnɪs] N (of leather) resistencia f;
(of a fighter, steak) dureza f; (of a situation)
dificultad f; (of a neighborhood) lo bravo

toupee [tupé] N peluquín m

tour [tur] N (professional, artistic) gira f;
(touristic) tour m, excursión f; (of a building)
visita f; VI/VT (artistic, political) hacer una
gira [por]; (touristic) hacer un tour

tourism [túrɪzəm] N turismo m

tourist [túrɪst] N turista mf; —**attraction**
atracción turística f; —**class** clase turista/
turística f

tournament [tɝ́nəmənt] N torneo m

tourniquet [tɝ́nɪkɪt] N torniquete m

tow [to] VT remolcar; N (pull) remolque m; (fiber)
estopa f; —**rope** cuerda de remolque f; —
truck remolque m, grúa f, Am guinche m; **in
— a** cuestas

toward, towards [təwɔ́rd[z]] PREP (in the
direction of) hacia; (for) para; —**four
o'clock** a eso de las cuatro; **to feel angry —**

estar enojado con

towel [táʊəl] N toalla f

tower [táʊə] N torre f; **— model** Am computadora torre f, Sp ordenador torre m; VI **to — over** elevarse sobre, dominar

towering [táʊə-ɪŋ] ADJ (tall) elevado, muy alto; (excessive) desmedido

town [taʊn] N (large) ciudad f; (small) pueblo m, localidad f; (downtown) centro m; **— hall** ayuntamiento m; **out of —** de viaje

toxic [táksɪk] ADJ tóxico; **— shock syndrome** síndrome de choque tóxico m

toxin [táksɪn] N toxina f

toy [tɔɪ] N juguete m; **— poodle** caniche enano m; VI **to — with** (fiddle with) juguetear con; (consider) considerar

trace [tres] N (path, mark, footprint) huella f; (mark) rastro m, traza f; (vestige) vestigio m; VT (a plan) trazar; (history) examinar; (an image) calcar; (a criminal) rastrear

trachea [trékiə] N tráquea f

tracheotomy [trekiáɾəmi] N traqueotomía f

track [træk] N (of a heel, animal) huella f; (of a wheel) rodada f; (for racing) pista f; (path) senda f, sendero m; (of a railroad) vía f; (on a record) surco m; (on a CD) tema m, pista f; (of study) orientación f; **— and field** atletismo m; **— meet** encuentro de atletismo m; **— record** trayectoria f; **to be off the —** estar descarrilado; **to keep — of** seguir el hilo de; VI/VT (a criminal) rastrear, seguir la pista de; (an aircraft, a student, progress) seguir; VI (wheels) estar alineado; (stylus) seguir los surcos; **to — down** perseguir; **to — in mud** traer lodo en los pies

tract [trækt] N (of land) terreno m; (political) octavilla f; (digestive) tubo m

traction [trǽkʃən] N tracción f

tractor [trǽktə] N tractor m; **—-trailer** tractocamión m

trade [tred] N (buying and selling) comercio m, trato m; (industry) industria f; (swap) canje m, cambio m; (manual labor) oficio m; (profession) profesión f; (people in a business) gremio m; **—-in** entrega como parte de pago f; **—-off** compensación f; **—mark** marca registrada f, marca de fábrica f; **— agreement** acuerdo comercial m; **— balance** balanza comercial f; **— barrier** barrera comercial f; **— name** (of product) nombre comercial m; (of company) razón social f; **— school** escuela industrial f; **— union** sindicato m; VI/VT (buy and sell) comerciar, negociar; (exchange) canjear; (traffic) traficar; **to — in** entregar

trader [trédə] N (dealer) comerciante mf; (at fairs) feriante mf; (of slaves) tratante mf

trading [trédɪŋ] N transacciones f pl, comercio m; **— partners** socios comerciales m pl

tradition [trədíʃən] N tradición f

traditional [trədíʃənəl] ADJ tradicional

traffic [trǽfɪk] N (of drugs) tráfico m; (of vehicles) tránsito m, tráfico m; **— accident** accidente de tránsito m; **— jam** atasco circulatorio m; **— light** semáforo m; VI traficar

tragedy [trǽdʒɪdi] N tragedia f

tragic [trǽdʒɪk] ADJ trágico

trail [trel] VI/VT (drag) arrastrar[se]; (follow in a race) ir detrás [de]; (track) seguir la pista [de], rastrear; VT (leave a trace) dejar una estela / un reguero de; VI **to — off** desvanecerse, apagarse; N (trace) rastro m, huella f; (path) trocha f, sendero m, senda f; (of smoke) estela f; (of blood) reguero m; **— bike** motocicleta de trail f

trailer [trélə] N (of a truck) remolque m; (of a film) sinopsis f, trailer m, avance m; (house) caravana f

train [tren] N (railroad) tren m; (part of a dress) cola f; **— of thought** hilo de pensamiento m; VI/VT (worker) capacitar[se]; (troops, athlete) adiestrar[se]; Am entrenar[se]; VT (an animal) amaestrar; (a child) educar, formar; (a cannon) apuntar; **to — on** (a camera, eye) enfocar

trainee [trení] N aprendiz -iza mf, practicante mf

trainer [trénə] N (of animals) amaestrador -ora mf; (of workers, troops, athletes) entrenador -ora mf

training [trénɪŋ] N (of animals) amaestramiento m; (of workers) capacitación f; (of troops, athletes) entrenamiento m, adiestramiento m; (of children) educación f

trait [tret] N rasgo m, seña f

traitor [trétə] N traidor -ora mf

trajectory [trədʒéktəri] N trayectoria f

tramp [træmp] VT (trample) pisar; VI andar con pasos pesados; (roam, as a hobo) vagabundear; N (hobo) vagabundo -da mf

trample [trǽmpəl] VT pisotear; **to — on/over** pisotear, atropellar; **to — out** apagar de un pisotón

trampoline [trǽmpəlín] N trampolín m, cama elástica f

trance [træns] N trance m

tranquil [trǽŋkwɪl] ADJ tranquilo

tranquilizer [trǽŋkwɪlaɪzə] N tranquilizante m

tranquillity [trǽŋkwɪlɪdi] N tranquilidad f

transact [trænzǽkt] VT llevar a cabo

transaction [trænzǽkʃən] N transacción f, negocio m; **—s** actas f pl

transatlantic [trænzɪtlǽntɪk] ADJ transatlántico

transcend [trænsénd] VI/VT trascender

transcendence [trænséndəns] N trascendencia f

transcendental [trænsəndéntl] ADJ trascendental, trascendente

transcribe [trænskráib] VT transcribir

transcript [trænskrɪpt] N transcripción f

transfer [trænsfɚ] VI/VT (on a bus, train) trasbordar; (a prisoner, worker) trasladar[se]; VT (loyalty, rights, money, data) transferir; (property) traspasar; N (on a bus, train) trasbordo m; (of loyalty, rights, money, data) transferencia f; (of a prisoner, worker) traslado m; (of property) traspaso m; — **of ownership** traspaso de propiedad m; — **rate** velocidad de transferencia f

transferable [trænsfɚəbəl] ADJ transferible

transfix [trænsfíks] VT (impale) traspasar, atravesar; (paralyze) paralizar

transform [trænsfɔ́rm] VI/VT transformar[se]

transformation [trænsfɚméʃən] N transformación f

transformer [trænsfɔ́rmɚ] N transformador m

transfusion [trænsfjúʒən] N transfusión f; **to give a —** dar una transfusión de sangre, poner sangre

transgress [trænzgrés] VT transgredir; **to — against** pecar contra; **to — the bounds of** traspasar los límites de

transgression [trænzgréʃən] N transgresión f, pecado m

transient [trǽnziənt] ADJ transeúnte, pasajero; N transeúnte mf, vagabundo -da mf

transistor [trænzístɚ] N transistor m

transit [trǽnzɪt] N tránsito m; **in —** en tránsito, de paso

transition [trænzíʃən] N transición f

transitive [trǽnzɪDɪv] ADJ transitivo

transitory [trǽnzɪtɔri] ADJ transitorio, pasajero

translate [trǽnzlet] VI/VT traducir

translation [trænzléʃən] N (rendering in different language) traducción f; (movement) translación f

translator [trǽnzleDɚ] N traductor -ora mf

transmission [trænzmíʃən] N transmisión f

transmit [trænzmít] VI/VT transmitir

transmitter [trænzmíDɚ] N transmisor m

transnational [trænznǽʃənəl] ADJ transnacional

transom [trǽnsəm] N travesaño m, montante m

transparency [trænzpérənsi] N transparencia f

transparent [trænzpérənt] ADJ transparente; **to be —** traslucirse

transpire [trænspáir] VI (happen) ocurrir; (become known) descubrirse; VI/VT (perspire) transpirar

transplant[1] [trænsplǽnt] VI/VT trasplantar

transplant[2] [trǽnsplænt] N trasplante m

transport[1] [trænspɔ́rt] VT transportar, acarrear

transport[2] [trǽnspɔrt] N (moving) transporte m, acarreo m; (airplane) avión de transporte m; (rapture) éxtasis m; (of freight) flete m

transportation [trænspɚtéʃən] N transporte m

transpose [trænspóz] VI/VT (letters) transponer;

(a song) transportar

transverse [trænzvɚ́s] ADJ transversal; (flute) transverso

trap [træp] N trampa f; (for hunting) trampa f, cepo m; (under a sink) sifón m; —**door** trampilla f; VI/VT (to capture animals) cazar con trampa, atrapar; VT (to pin) aprisionar

trapeze [træpíz] N trapecio m

trapezoid [trǽpəzɔid] N & ADJ trapezoide m

trash [træʃ] N basura f, desechos m pl; (people) pej gentuza f; —**can** cubo de basura m

trashy [trǽʃi] ADJ ordinario

trauma [trómə] N (physical) traumatismo m; (psychological) trauma m

traumatic [trəmǽDik] ADJ traumático

travel [trǽvəl] VI/VT viajar [por]; VI (sound waves) propagarse; (in basketball) caminar, hacer pasos; N viaje m; —**agency** agencia de viajes f; —**expenses** gastos de viaje m pl, gastos de desplazamiento m pl; —**s** viajes m pl

traveler [trǽvələ] N viajero -ra mf; —**'s check** cheque de viajero m

traverse [trəvɚ́s] VI/VT atravesar, cruzar; (skiing) bajar en diagonal; N (crossbar) travesaño m; (crossing) travesía f

travesty [trǽvisti] N farsa f

tray [tre] N bandeja f

treacherous [trétʃɚəs] ADJ traicionero, alevoso

treachery [trétʃɚri] N traición f, alevosía f

tread [trɛd] VI/VT (trample) pisar, pisotear; VI (walk) andar, caminar; N (step) paso m; (on tire) banda de rodadura/rodaje f; (on shoe) dibujo m; —**mill** cinta rodante f

treason [trízən] N traición f

treasure [tréʒɚ] N tesoro m; —**hunt** búsqueda del tesoro f; VT atesorar

treasurer [tréʒɚɚ] N tesorero -ra mf

treasury [tréʒɚri] N tesorería f, tesoro m; **secretary of the —** ministro -tra de hacienda mf

treat [trit] VI/VT (act toward, discuss in writing, give medical aid) tratar; **I —ed myself to ice cream** me di un festín de helado; N (pleasure) placer m; (gift) regalo m; **my —** yo invito

treatable [tríDəbəl] ADJ tratable

treatise [tríDɪs] N tratado m

treatment [trítmənt] N trato m, tratamiento m; (artistic handling) interpretación f

treaty [tríDi] N tratado m

treble [trébəl] ADJ (triple) triple; (of higher clef) de tiple; —**clef** clave de sol f; N tiple m; VI/VT triplicar

tree [tri] N árbol m; —**hugger** ecologista mf; —**top** copa de árbol f; **up a —** en aprietos

treeless [trílɪs] ADJ pelado, sin árboles

trek [trɛk] N expedición f; VI viajar con dificultad

tremble [trémbəl] VI temblar; N temblor m

tremendous [trɪméndəs] ADJ tremendo

tremor [trémɚ] N temblor *m*, sacudida *f*

tremulous [trémjələs] ADJ trémulo

trench [trentʃ] N (military) trinchera *f*; (for pipes) zanja *f*; (on sea floor) fosa *f*; — **coat** trinchera *f*, gabardina *f*

trend [trend] N tendencia *f*

trendy [tréndi] ADJ de moda

trespass [tréspæs] N (illegal entry) entrada ilegal *f*; (religious) deuda *f*; VI (enter illegally) entrar ilegalmente; **to — against** (violate) violar; (sin) pecar; **no —ing** prohibido el paso

triage [triáʒ] N triaje *m*, clasificación *f*

trial [tráɪəl] N (testing) ensayo *m*, prueba *f*; (attempt) tentativa *f*; (affliction) aflicción *f*; (in a court of law) juicio *m*, proceso *m*; — **balloon** globo sonda *m*; — **by fire** prueba de fuego *f*; — **flight** vuelo de prueba *m*; — **offer** oferta de prueba *f*; — **period** período de prueba *m*; — **run** ensayo *m*, prueba *f*; **by — and error** por ensayo y error

triangle [tráɪæŋgəl] N triángulo *m*

triangular [traɪǽŋgjələ˞] ADJ triangular

tribe [traɪb] N tribu *f*

tribulation [trɪbjəléʃən] N tribulación *f*

tribunal [traɪbjúnəl] N tribunal *m*

tributary [tríbjəteri] ADJ & N tributario *m*, afluente *m*

tribute [tríbjut] N (tax) tributo *m*; (testimonial) homenaje *m*

triceps [tráɪsɛps] N tríceps *m* sg

trick [trɪk] N (ruse) treta *f*, trampa *f*, trapisonda *f*; (magician's) truco *m*; (prank) broma *f*; (in cards) baza *f*; **to be up to one's old —s** hacer de las suyas; **to play a — on someone** gastarle una broma a alguien; VT hacer trampa, engañar; **to — someone into something** hacer que alguien haga algo por medio de artilugios

trickery [tríkəri] N engaños *m pl*, argucias *f pl*

trickle [tríkəl] VI gotear; **to — in [out]** llegar [irse] de a poco; N goteo *m*

trickster [tríkstə˞] N embustero -ra *mf*

tricky [tríki] ADJ (artful) mañoso; (difficult) complicado

tricycle [tráɪsɪkəl] N triciclo *m*

trifle [tráɪfəl] N (worthless thing) fruslería *f*, nadería *f*, bobada *f*; (cheap purchase) bagatela *f*; (small sum) miseria *f*; VI **to — with** jugar con; **to — away** perder

trigger [trígɚ] N gatillo *m*; VT desencadenar

trill [trɪl] VI/VT (birds) trinar; (musical instrument) tremolar; (the rsound) pronunciar con vibración; N (of birds, etc.) trino *m*; (of the rsound) vibración *f*

trillion [trɪ́ljən] N billón *m*

trilogy [trɪ́lədʒi] N trilogía *f*

trim [trɪm] VT (adorn) adornar, guarnecer; (an edge) bordear; (fingernails, hair, threads)

recortar; (hedge) podar; (airplane) equilibrar; (a wick) despabilar; ADJ (neat) cuidado; (slim) delgado; (fit) en buen estado físico; N (embellishment) adorno *m*; (of sails) orientación *f*; (cutting of hair) recorte *m*; (cutting of hedge) poda *f*; (of an airplane) equilibrio *m*

trimming [trɪ́mɪŋ] N (act of cutting) recorte *m*; (on a uniform) orla *f*, ribete *m*; —**s** (embellishments) adornos *m pl*; (food) guarniciones *f pl*; (parts cut off) recortes *m pl*

Trinidad and Tobago [trínɪdædəntəbégo] N Trinidad y Tobago *f*

Trinidadian [trɪnɪdádiən] ADJ & N trinitense *mf*

trinket [trɪ́ŋkɪt] N chuchería *f*, baratija *f*

trio [trío] N trío *m*

trip [trɪp] N (journey, drug-induced condition) viaje *m*; (experience) experiencia *f*; (accidental stumble) tropezón *m*; (making fall) zancadilla *f*; — **planner** planificador de rutas *m*; VT (cause to stumble) hacer una zancadilla a; (trip up) confundir; (release a catch) soltar; (blow a fuse) hacer saltar; VI (stumble) tropezar; (skip) andar con paso ligero; (make a mistake) equivocarse; (hallucinate) viajar; (blow a fuse) saltar

triphthong [trípθɔŋ] N triptongo *m*

triple [trípəl] ADJ & N (also in baseball) triple *m*; VI (in baseball) pegar un triple; VT (multiply by three) triplicar

triplet [trɪ́plɪt] N trillizo *m*

tripod [tráɪpɑd] N trípode *m*

trite [traɪt] ADJ trivial, trillado

triumph [tráɪəmf] N triunfo *m*; VI triunfar

triumphant [traɪʌ́mfənt] ADJ triunfante, triunfador

trivial [trɪ́viəl] ADJ trivial, baladí, fútil

trod [trɑd] *see* tread

trodden [trɑdn̩] *see* tread

trolley [trɑ́li] N (electric bus) trole *m*, trolebús *m*; (on tracks) tranvía *m*

trombone [trɑmbón] N trombón *m*

troop [trup] N (of scouts) tropa *f*; (of soldiers) escuadrón *m*; (of tourists) horda *f*; —**s** tropas *f pl*

trophy [trófi] N trofeo *m*

tropic [trɑ́pɪk] N trópico *m*

tropical [trɑ́pɪkəl] ADJ tropical

trot [trɑt] VI trotar; VT hacer trotar; **to — out** sacar a relucir; N trote *m*

trouble [trʌ́bəl] VT (afflict) aquejar; (make turbid) enturbiar; VI/VT (bother) molestar[se]; (disturb) preocupar[se]; **to — shoot** solucionar problemas; N (problem) problema *m*; (difficulty) dificultad *f*, sinsabor *m*; (disturbance) disturbio *m*; (effort) molestia *f*; (ailment) enfermedad *f*, trastorno *m*; (mechanical breakdown) avería *f*, desperfecto *m*; —**maker** agitador -ora *mf*, revoltoso -sa *mf*; —**shooter** solucionador -ora *mf*, localizador -ora de averías *mf*; **to be in —** estar en un aprieto; **it is not worth the —** no vale la pena; **to make —** causar problemas; **to take the —** tomarse la molestia; ADJ —**free** sin problemas

trough [trɔf] N (for food) pesebre *m*, comedero *m*; (for water) abrevadero *m*, bebedero *m*; (of weather, on ocean floor) depresión *f*

trousers [tráʊzəz] N pantalones *m pl*

trousseau [trúso] N ajuar *m*

trout [traʊt] N trucha *f*

trowel [tráʊəl] N (for mortar) llana *f*, paleta *f*; (for digging) desplantador *m*

truant [trúənt] N alumno -na que falta a clase sin permiso *mf*

truce [trus] N tregua *f*

truck [trʌk] N (vehicle) camión *m*; *Mex* troca *f*; (dealings) trato *m*; (vegetables) hortalizas *f pl*; — **driver** camionero -ra *mf*; *Mex* troquero -ra *mf*; VI/VT transportar en camión; *Mex* transportar en troca

trudge [trʌdʒ] VI andar con dificultad

true [tru] ADJ verdadero; (story) verídico; (copy, translation) fiel; (well) a plomo; (wheel) alineado, centrado; —**-blue** leal; —**-false test** prueba de verdadero o falso *f*; **his dream came —** su sueño se hizo realidad

truly [trúli] ADV (surprisingly) verdaderamente; (sincerely) sinceramente; (actually) en realidad, realmente; (accurately) fielmente; **very — yours** su seguro servidor, atentamente

trumpet [trʌ́mpɪt] N trompeta *f*; VI/VT (musician) trompetear; (elephant) barritar

trunk [trʌŋk] N (of tree, body) tronco *m*; (receptacle) baúl *m*; (of elephant) trompa *f*; (of a car) maletero *m*, *Mex* cajuela *f*; —**s** traje de baño *m*

trust [trʌst] N (confidence) confianza *f*; (charge) cargo *m*; (firm) trust *m*; (fund) fondo fideicomiso *m*; VI/VT (rely on) confiar en, fiarse de; VT (believe) creer; (hope) esperar

trustee [trʌstí] N (person holding property of another) fideicomisario -ria *mf*; (administrator) administrador -ora *mf*

trusteeship [trʌstíʃɪp] N (position of holding property) fideicomiso *m*; (administrative position) cargo de administrador *m*

trustful [trʌ́stfəl] ADJ confiado

trusting [trʌ́stɪŋ] ADJ confiado

trustworthy [trʌ́stwɜ˞ði] ADJ fidedigno, digno de confianza

trusty [trʌ́sti] ADJ leal

truth [truθ] N verdad *f*

truthful [trúθfəl] ADJ (account) verídico; (person) veraz

truthfulness [trúθfəlnɪs] N veracidad *f*

try [traɪ] VT (attempt) tratar de, intentar; (test, taste) probar; (strain) poner a prueba; (put on trial) procesar, enjuiciar; **to —** **on** probarse; **to —** one's luck probar fortuna; **to —** **and** tratar de; **to —** **out** (test) probar; (for a team) presentarse para; N intento *m*, tentativa *f*; —**out** prueba *f*

trying [tráɪɪŋ] ADJ penoso

tryst [trɪst] N cita romántica *f*

T-shirt [tíʃ˞t] N camiseta *f*

tub [tʌb] N (for bathing) bañera *f*; (for butter) envase *m*; (for washing) tina *f*

tuba [túbə] N tuba *f*

tube [tub] N tubo *m* (also electronic); (television) televisor *m*

tuberculosis [tʊbɝkjəlósɪs] N tuberculosis *f*

tubular [túbjələ˞] ADJ tubular

tuck [tʌk] VT (stick in) meter; (make fold) alforzar; **to —** in one's shirt meter la camisa dentro del pantalón; **to — into bed** arropar; **to — something under one's arm** meterse algo bajo el brazo; N alforza *f*

Tuesday [túzde] N martes *m*

tuft [tʌft] N (of feathers) penacho *m*; (of hair) mechón *m*, copete *m*; (of plants) mata *f*

tug [tʌg] VI/VT (pull) tirar, jalar; (drag) arrastrar; **to — at** tironear; N (pull) tirón *m*; (boat) remolcador *m*

tuition [tuíʃən] N matrícula *f*

tulip [túlɪp] N tulipán *m*

tumble [tʌ́mbəl] VI (fall) caer; (collapse) venirse abajo; (do handsprings, etc.) dar volteretas; **to — down** rodar; **to — dry** secar en la secadora; **to — over** tropezarse; N (fall) caída *f*; (gymnastic trick) voltereta *f*

tumbler [tʌ́mblə˞] N (glass) vaso *m*; (person) acróbata *mf*

tummy [tʌ́mi] N barriguita *f*

tumor [túmə˞] N tumor *m*

tumult [túmʌlt] N tumulto *m*

tumultuous [tumʌ́ltʃuəs] ADJ tumultuoso

tuna [túnə] N (fish) atún *m*, bonito *m*; (prickly pear) tuna *f*

tune [tun] N (melody) tonada *f*, aire *m*; (electronic adjustment) sintonía *f*; —**-up** afinación *f*; **to be in —** (in pitch) estar afinado; (adjusted) sintonizado; **to be out of —** estar desafinado; VT (engine) afinar; (musical instrument) afinar, templar; (radio) sintonizar; **to — in** sintonizar; **to — out** ignorar

tuner [túnə˞] N afinador -ora *mf*; (electronic) sintonizador *m*

tungsten [tʌ́ŋstən] N tungsteno *m*

tunic [túnɪk] N túnica *f*

Tunisia [tuníʒə] N Túnez *m*

Tunisian [tuníʒən] ADJ & N tunesino -na *mf*

tunnel [tʌ́nəl] N túnel *m*; (for traffic) viaducto *m*; — **vision** visión en túnel *f*; VI cavar; VT hacer un túnel

turban [tɚ́bən] N turbante *m*
turbine [tɚ́bɪn] N turbina *f*
turbocharger [tɚ́bòtʃɑɾdʒɚ] N turbocompresor *m*
turbojet [tɚ́bòdʒɛt] N turborreactor *m*
turbulence [tɚ́bjələns] N turbulencia *f*
turbulent [tɚ́bjələnt] ADJ turbulento
turf [tɚf] N (lawn) césped *m*; (peat) turba *f*; (track for horse races) pista *f*; (territory) territorio *m*; VT cubrir con césped
Turk [tɚk] N turco -ca *mf*
turkey [tɚ́ki] N pavo *m*; — **vulture** buitre pavo *m*
Turkey [tɚ́ki] N Turquía *f*
Turkish [tɚ́kɪʃ] ADJ turco; — **bath** baño turco *m*
Turkmen [tɚ́kmən] ADJ & N turcomano -na *mf*
Turkmenistan [tɚ̀kmɛnɪstǽn] N Turkmenistán *m*
turmoil [tɚ́mɔɪl] N confusión *f*, agitación *f*
turn [tɚn] VT (corner) doblar, dar vuelta; (wheel, key) girar, dar vuelta; (page) dar vuelta; (soil) labrar; (stomach) revolver; (ankle) torcer[se]; (a river) desviar; VI (change color) cambiar de color; (become) ponerse; (rotate) girar; (change direction) girar, dar la vuelta; **to — against** volverse en contra de; **to — around** dar la vuelta, girar; **to — away** (face) volver; (eyes) apartar; (person) rechazar; **to — back** (return) volver; (a clock) atrasar; **to — down** (offer, request) rechazar; (radio) bajar; **to — in** (hand in/over) entregar; (go to bed) acostarse; **to — inside out** dar vuelta al revés; **to — into** convertir[se] en; **to — off** (light) apagar; (faucet) cerrar; (a road) salir de; (person in general sense) disgustar; (person in sexual sense) quitarle las ganas a alguien; **to — on** (light) encender, prender; (faucet) abrir; (person) excitar; **to — out** (light) apagar; (people) expulsar; (product) producir; **to — out well** salir bien; **to — over** (car) volcar[se]; (engine) arrancar; (thought, idea, etc.) dar vueltas a; (criminal, weapon, etc.) entregar; **—table** plato giratorio *m*; **to — to** (have recourse to) acudir a, recurrir a; (become) volver[se]; **to — up** aparecer; **to — up one's nose** desdeñar; **to — up one's sleeves** arremangarse; **to — upside down** dar vuelta; N (rotation) vuelta *f*, revolución *f*; (change of direction) giro *m*, vuelta *f*; (change in condition) cambio *m*; (curve) recodo *m*, curva *f*; (opportunity) turno *m*; — **of mind** actitud *f*; **—off** (disgusting thing) asco *m*; (road exit) salida *f*; — **of phrase** giro *m*; **—out** concurrencia *f*; **—over** (of employees) renovación *f*; (of merchandise) volumen *m*; (in football) pérdida de balón *f*; (pastry) empanada *f*, pastelito *m*; (of a ball) pérdida *f*; **—pike** autopista *f*; **—stile** torniquete *m*, molinete *m*;

— **signal** intermitente *m*; **at every** — a cada paso; **bad** — mala pasada *f*; **good** — favor *m*; **his bad teeth are a —off** sus feos dientes me dan asco / me repugnan; **his foreign accent is a — -on** su acento extranjero me excita; **it's my** — me toca a mí; **to take** —s turnarse
turnip [tɚ́nɪp] N nabo *m*
turpentine [tɚ́pəntaɪn] N trementina *f*, aguarrás *m*
turquoise [tɚ́kɔɪz] N turquesa *f*
turret [tɚ́ɪt] N (small tower, gun tower) torreta *f*; (on a ship) torre *f*
turtle [tɚ́dl̩] N tortuga *f*; **—dove** tórtola *f*; **—neck** cuello vuelto *m*
tusk [tʌsk] N colmillo *m*
tutor [túdɚ] N profesor -ora particular *mf*; VI/VT dar clases particulares
tutorial [tutɔ́riəl] ADJ de tutoría; N (computer) tutorial *m*; (math, Spanish) cursillo *m*
Tuvalu [túvəlu] N Tuvalu *m*
Tuvaluan [tuvəlúən] ADJ & N tuvaluano -na *mf*
tuxedo [tʌksído] N esmoquin *m*
TV [**television**] [tívi] N *fam* tele *f*
twang [twæŋ] N (in music) tañido *m*; (of speech) nasalidad *f*; VI (vibrate) vibrar; VT hacer vibrar; VI/VT (speak nasally) ganguear
twangy [twǽŋi] ADJ gangoso
tweak [twik] VT (pinch) pellizcar; (adjust) ajustar; N (pinch) pellizco *m*; (adjustment) ajuste *m*
tweed [twid] N tweed *m*
tweezers [twízɚz] N pinzas *f pl*
twelve [twɛlv] NUM doce
twentieth [twɛntiɪθ] NUM vigésimo; **it's his — birthday** hoy cumple veinte años; **it's the — time I've told you** ya te lo dije veinte veces
twenty [twɛ́nti] NUM veinte; — **-five** veinticinco
twerp [twɚp] N idiota *mf*, papanatas *mf sg*
twice [twaɪs] ADV dos veces
twig [twig] N ramita *f*
twilight [twáɪlaɪt] N crepúsculo *m*, ocaso *m*; — **zone** zona gris *f*
twin [twin] ADJ & N (fraternal) mellizo -za *mf*; (identical) gemelo -la *mf*; — **bed** cama individual *f*
twine [twaɪn] N cuerda *f*; VI/VT (twist) enroscar[se]; (interlace) entrelazar[se]
twinge [twɪndʒ] N (of pain, remorse) punzada *f*
twinkle [twíŋkəl] VI (star) titilar, parpadear; (eyes) brillar; N (of stars) titileo *m*, parpadeo *m*; (of eyes) brillo *m*
twirl [twɚl] VI/VT girar, dar vueltas [a]; N giro *m*, vuelta *f*; (of ice cream) espiral *m*
twist [twɪst] VI/VT (wind, coil) torcer[se]; (distort) tergiversar[se]; (writhe) retorcer[se]; (coil) enroscar[se]; N (of an ankle) torcedura *f*; (distortion) tergiversación *f*; (in a road, coil)

vuelta *f*; (unforeseen event) vuelta de tuerca *f*

twister [twístə] N tornado *m*

twitch [twítʃ] VI/VT crispar[se], mover[se]; N (tic) tic *m*; (pang) punzada *f*; (tug) tirón *m*

twitter [twídə] VI gorjear; N gorjeo *m*

two [tu] NUM dos; **— hundred** doscientos; **—-point conversion** conversión de dos puntos *f*; **my — cents' worth** mi opinión *f*; **to put — and — together** atar cabos; ADJ **—-bit** de chicha y nabo; **—-edged** de doble filo; **—-faced** (with two faces) de dos caras; (hypocritical) hipócrita, falso; **—-fisted** pendenciero; **—-way** de dos sentidos

tycoon [taikún] N magnate *mf*

type [taip] N tipo *m*, índole *f*; **—face** tipo de letra *m*; **—script** texto escrito a máquina *m*; **—writer** máquina de escribir *f*; **—writing** mecanografía *f*; VI/VT (a letter) escribir a máquina, mecanografiar, digitar, teclear, tipiar, tipear; VT (blood) determinar el grupo sanguíneo; **to —set** componer; **to —write** escribir a máquina; ADJ **—written** escrito a máquina

typhoid [táifɔid] N tifoidea *f*; **— fever** fiebre tifoidea *f*, tifus *m*

typhoon [taifún] N tifón *m*

typhus [táifəs] N tifus *m*

typical [típikəl] ADJ típico

typist [táipist] N mecanógrafo -fa *mf*

typo [táipo] N error tipográfico *m*

typographical [taipəgrǽfikəl] ADJ tipográfico; **— error** error de imprenta *m*, errata *f*

typology [taipáləʤi] N tipología *f*

tyrannical [tɪrǽnikəl] ADJ tiránico

tyranny [tírəni] N tiranía *f*

tyrant [táirənt] N tirano -na *mf*

Uu

ubiquitous [jubíkwidəs] ADJ ubicuo

U-boat [júbot] N submarino alemán *m*

udder [ádə] N ubre *f*

UFO [**unidentified flying object**] [júéfó] N OVNI *m*

Uganda [jugǽndə] N Uganda *f*

Ugandan [jugǽndən] ADJ & N ugandés -esa *mf*

ugliness [áglinis] N fealdad *f*

ugly [ágli] ADJ feo; (incident) deplorable; (mood) de perros

uh-huh [ʌhʌ́] INTERJ *fam* sí

Ukraine [jukrén] N Ucrania *f*

Ukrainian [jukrénjən] ADJ & N ucraniano -na *mf*

ulcer [álsə] N úlcera *f*

ulcerate [álsəret] VI ulcerar

ulcerous [álsə-əs] ADJ ulceroso

ulna [álnə] N cúbito *m*

ulterior [ʌltíriə] ADJ ulterior; **— motive** segunda intención *f*

ultimate [áltəmit] ADJ (destination) último, final; (authority) final, máximo; (principle) fundamental; (vacation) perfecto; N súmmum *m*

ultimately [áltəmitli] ADV en última instancia

ultimatum [ʌltəmédəm] N ultimátum *m*

ultralight [áltrəlait] ADJ & N ultraligero *m*

ultramodern [ʌltrəmádə-n] ADJ ultramoderno

ultrasound [áltrəsaund] N ultrasonido *m*; **— imaging** imágenes por ultrasonido *f pl*

ultraviolet [ʌltrəváiəlit] ADJ & N ultravioleta *m*

umbilical cord [ʌmbílikəlkɔrd] N cordón umbilical *m*

umbrella [ʌmbrélə] N paraguas *m sg*

umpire [ámpair] N árbitro *m*; (in tennis) juez -eza de silla *mf*; VI/VT arbitrar

unable [ʌnébəl] ADJ **to be — to** no poder

unabridged [ʌnəbríʤd] ADJ íntegro

unaccented [ʌnǽksentid] ADJ sin acento

unacceptable [ʌnikséptəbəl] ADJ inaceptable, inadmisible

unaccustomed [ʌnəkástəmd] ADJ (not used to) no acostumbrado; (uncommon) insólito

unadjusted [ʌnəʤástid] ADJ no ajustado

unadulterated [ʌnədáltəredid] ADJ puro

unaffected [ʌnəféktid] ADJ (not affected) no afectado; (sincere) natural, sincero; (unpretentious) sin afectación

unaffiliated [ʌnəfílieid] ADJ no afiliado

unanimity [junənímidi] N unanimidad *f*

unanimous [junǽnəməs] ADJ unánime

unarmed [ʌnármd] ADJ desarmado

unassuming [ʌnəsúmiŋ] ADJ modesto, sin pretensiones

unattached [ʌnətǽtʃt] ADJ (piece of paper) suelto; (person) soltero

unauthorized [ʌnɔ́θəraizd] ADJ no autorizado

unavailable [ʌnəvéləbəl] ADJ no disponible

unavoidable [ʌnəvɔ́idəbəl] ADJ inevitable, ineludible

unaware [ʌnəwér] ADJ inconsciente; ADV **to be — of** ignorar; **—s** sin darse cuenta

unbalanced [ʌnbǽlənst] ADJ desequilibrado

unbearable [ʌnbérəbəl] ADJ inaguantable, insoportable

unbeatable [ʌnbídəbəl] ADJ imbatible

unbeaten [ʌnbítn] ADJ invicto

unbecoming [ʌnbikámiŋ] ADJ (behavior) impropio; (clothes) que no [le] luce

unbelief [ʌnbilíf] N incredulidad *f*, descreimiento *m*

unbelievable [ʌnbilívəbəl] ADJ increíble

unbeliever [ʌnbilívə] N descreído -da *mf*

unbending [ʌnbéndiŋ] ADJ inflexible

unbiased [ʌnbáiəst] ADJ imparcial

unbounded [ʌnbáundid] ADJ ilimitado

unbridled [ʌnbráɪdld] ADJ desenfrenado

unbroken [ʌnbrókən] ADJ (intact) intacto; (not tamed) indomado; (uninterrupted) ininterrumpido

unbuckle [ʌnbákəl] VT desabrochar

unbutton [ʌnbátn] VI/VT desabotonar, desabrochar

uncalled-for [ʌnkɔ́ldfɔr] ADJ injustificado

uncanny [ʌnkǽni] ADJ inexplicable, misterioso

uncertain [ʌnsɚ́tn] ADJ incierto

uncertainty [ʌnsɚ́tnti] N incertidumbre f

unchanged [ʌntʃéndʒd] ADJ inalterado

uncharitable [ʌntʃǽrɪdəbəl] ADJ duro, poco caritativo

uncivilized [ʌnsívəlaɪzd] ADJ incivilizado

uncle [ʌ́ŋkəl] N tío m; **to say —** darse por vencido

unclean [ʌnklín] ADJ (dirty) sucio; (impure) impuro

uncollectable [ʌnkəléktəbəl] ADJ incobrable

uncomfortable [ʌnkámfɚⱺbəl] ADJ incómodo

uncommon [ʌnkámən] ADJ (unusual) poco común; (extraordinary) extraordinario

uncompromising [ʌnkámprəmaɪzɪŋ] ADJ (intransigent) intransigente; (unfailing) incondicional

unconcerned [ʌnkənsɚ́nd] ADJ indiferente

unconditional [ʌnkəndíʃənəl] ADJ incondicional

unconfirmed [ʌnkənfɚ́md] ADJ no confirmado

unconscious [ʌnkánʃəs] ADJ inconsciente

unconstitutional [ʌnkənstɪtúʃənl] ADJ inconstitucional

uncontrollable [ʌnkəntróləbəl] ADJ (movement) incontrolable; (urge, laughter) incontenible

unconventional [ʌnkənvénʃənəl] ADJ poco convencional

uncouth [ʌnkúθ] ADJ tosco

uncover [ʌnkávɚ] VI/VT descubrir[se]; VI (remove bedcovers) destaparse

uncovered [ʌnkávɚd] ADJ descubierto

unctuous [ʌ́ŋktʃuəs] ADJ untuoso, zalamero

uncultivated [ʌnkʌ́ltəveɪdɪd] ADJ (person) inculto, no cultivado; (land) no cultivado

uncultured [ʌnkʌ́ltʃəd] ADJ inculto

undaunted [ʌndɔ́ntɪd] ADJ impávido, intrépido

undecided [ʌndɪsáɪdɪd] ADJ indeciso

undeclared [ʌndɪklérd] ADJ no declarado

undefined [ʌndɪfáɪnd] ADJ indefinido

undelete utility [ʌndɪlít jutíliɾi] N programa para recuperar datos borrados m

undeniable [ʌndɪnáɪəbəl] ADJ innegable, indudable

under [ʌ́ndɚ] PREP (below) bajo, debajo de, abajo de; (in a ranking) por debajo de; (less) menos de; **— the Democrats** durante el mandato de los Demócratas; **— a pseudonym** bajo un pseudónimo; **— cost** a menos del costo/coste,

por debajo del costo/coste; **— contract** bajo contrato; **— wraps** oculto; ADV (below) debajo, abajo; (less than) menos; **to be —** estar inconsciente

underage [ʌndɚéʤ] ADJ menor de edad; **— drinking** consumo de alcohol por menores de edad m

underarm [ʌ́ndɚɑrm] N axila f

underbrush [ʌ́ndɚbrʌʃ] N maleza f

undercharge [ʌndɚtʃɑ́rʤ] VI cobrar de menos

underclass [ʌ́ndɚklæs] N subproletariado m

undercover [ʌndɚkávɚ] ADJ clandestino, secreto

undercut [ʌndɚkát] VT (undermine) socavar; (sell for less) vender por menos que

underdeveloped [ʌndɚdɪvéləpt] ADJ subdesarrollado

underdog [ʌ́ndɚdɔg] N el de abajo m, la de abajo f

underemployed [ʌndɚɛmplɔ́ɪd] ADJ subempleado

underestimate [ʌndɚéstəmet] VT (person) subestimar; (price) subvaluar

underfed [ʌndɚféd] ADJ desnutrido

underfoot [ʌndɚfút] ADJ (beneath the feet) bajo los pies; (in the way) estorbando

undergird [ʌndɚgɚ́d] VT reforzar

undergo [ʌndɚgó] VT (an operation) someterse a; (a change) experimentar, sufrir

undergraduate [ʌndɚgrǽʤuɪt] N estudiante de pregrado mf; **— course** clase de pregrado f

underground[1] [ʌndɚgráund] ADV (under the earth) bajo tierra; (secretly) en secreto

underground[2] [ʌ́ndɚgraund] ADJ (under the earth) subterráneo; (secret) clandestino; N resistencia f, grupo clandestino m

underhanded [ʌndɚhǽndɪd] ADJ (secret) secreto, solapado; (illicit) ilícito

underlie [ʌndɚláɪ] VI/VT subyacer [a]

underline [ʌ́ndɚlaɪn] VT subrayar

underlying [ʌndɚláɪɪŋ] ADJ (inflation, racism) subyacente; (problems) de fondo

undermine [ʌndɚmáɪn] VT minar, menoscabar

underneath [ʌndɚníθ] PREP bajo, debajo de, abajo de; ADV debajo, abajo; N la parte inferior

undernourished [ʌndɚnɚ́ɪʃt] ADJ desnutrido

underpants [ʌ́ndɚpænts] N (for men) calzoncillos m pl; (for women) Sp bragas f pl; Mex pantaletas f pl; RP bombacha f

underrated [ʌndɚrédɪd] ADJ infravalorado

underscore [ʌndɚskɔ́r] N subrayado m; VT subrayar

undersecretary [ʌndɚsékrətɛri] N subsecretario -ria mf

undersell [ʌndɚsél] VT (to sell at a low price) malbaratar; (to sell cheaper) vender a menos precio

undershirt [ʌ́ndɚshɚt] N camiseta f

underside [ʌ́ndə-saɪd] N parte inferior f

undersigned [ʌ́ndə-sáɪnd] N abajo firmante mf, infrascrito -ta mf

underskirt [ʌ́ndə-skɝt] N enaguas f pl

understaffed [ʌ̀ndə-stǽft] ADJ falto de personal

understand [ʌ̀ndə-stǽnd] VI/VT comprender, entender; **I — you're leaving** tengo entendido que te vas; **to — about** saber de/ entender de

understandable [ʌ̀ndə-stǽndəbəl] ADJ comprensible

understanding [ʌ̀ndə-stǽndɪŋ] N (comprehension) comprensión f, entendimiento m; (tolerance) comprensión mutua f; (agreement) acuerdo m; ADJ comprensivo

understate [ʌ̀ndə-stét] VT minimizar

understood [ʌ̀ndə-stúd] ADJ entendido; (implicit) sobreentendido

understood [ʌ̀ndə-stúd] see understand

understudy [ʌ́ndə-stʌdi] N suplente mf, sobresaliente mf; VI/VT suplir [a], servir de sobresaliente [para]

undertake [ʌ̀ndə-ték] VT emprender, acometer; **to —** comprometerse a

undertaken [ʌ̀ndə-tékən] see undertake

undertaker [ʌ́ndə-tekə-] N director -ora de funeraria / pompas fúnebres mf, funerario -ria mf

undertaking [ʌ̀ndə-tékɪŋ] N empresa f

under-the-table [ʌ́ndə-ðətébəl] ADJ ilícito, bajo cuerda

undertone [ʌ́ndə-ton] N (low voice) voz baja f; (undercurrent) tónica f

undertook [ʌ̀ndə-tʊ́k] see undertake

undertow [ʌ́ndə-to] N resaca f

undervalued [ʌ̀ndə-vǽljud] ADJ infravalorado

underwater [ʌ̀ndə-wɔ́tə-, ʌ̀ndə-wɔ́tə-] ADJ submarino; ADV por debajo del agua

underwear [ʌ́ndə-wɛr] N ropa interior f

underweight [ʌ́ndə-wet] ADJ de peso insuficiente

underworld [ʌ́ndə-wɝ̀ld] N (of criminals) hampa f; (netherworld) el más allá

underwrite [ʌ́ndə-raɪt] VI/VT (finance) financiar; (sign) suscribir; (insure) asegurar

underwriter [ʌ́ndə-raɪtə-] N (insurance) asegurador -ora mf; (stock exchange) suscriptor -ora mf

undesirable [ʌ̀ndɪzáɪrəbəl] ADJ indeseable

undetermined [ʌ̀ndɪtɝ̀-mɪnd] ADJ indeterminado

undid [ʌ̀ndɪ́d] see undo

undisclosed [ʌ̀ndɪsklózd] ADJ no divulgado

undisturbed [ʌ̀ndɪstɝ́bd] ADJ (unworried, uninterrupted) tranquilo; (unspoiled) virgen

undivided [ʌ̀ndɪváɪdɪd] ADJ indiviso

undo [ʌ̀ndú] VT (reverse an action) deshacer, anular; (unfasten) desabrochar, desabotonar; (destroy) destruir; (loosen hair) soltar

undocumented [ʌ̀ndákjəmɛntɪd] ADJ indocumentado

undoing [ʌ̀ndúɪŋ] N (reversal) deshacer m; (destruction) destrucción f, perdición f; (of buttons) desabrochar m

undone [ʌ̀ndʌ́n] ADJ (unfinished) sin terminar; (ruined) perdido; (unfastened) desabrochado; **to come —** (clothing) desabrocharse; (person) desquiciarse

undoubtedly [ʌ̀ndáʊDɪdli] ADV indudablemente, sin duda

undress [ʌ̀ndrés] VI/VT desnudar[se], desvestir[se]

undue [ʌ̀ndú] ADJ (inappropriate) indebido; (excessive) excesivo

undulate [ʌ́ndʒəlet] VI/VT ondular

undying [ʌ̀ndáɪŋ] ADJ imperecedero, eterno

unearned [ʌnɝ́nd] N inmerecido; **— run** (baseball) carrera sucia f

unearth [ʌnɝ́θ] VT desenterrar

uneasiness [ʌnízinɪs] N (feeling) inquietud f, desasosiego m, desazón f; Sp grima f; (of peace) precariedad f; (of silence, situation) incomodidad f; (of sleep) agitación f

uneasy [ʌnízi] ADJ (feeling) inquieto; (peace) precario; (silence) incómodo; (situation) molesto; (sleep) agitado

uneducated [ʌnɛ́dʒəkeDɪd] ADJ inculto, ignorante

unemployable [ʌ̀nɪmplɔ́iəbəl] ADJ inempleable

unemployed [ʌ̀nɪmplɔ́id] ADJ (jobless) desocupado, desempleado, Sp parado; (unused) ocioso

unemployment [ʌ̀nɪmplɔ́imənt] N desocupación f, desempleo m, Sp paro m; **— compensation** seguro de paro m; Sp paro m; **— rate** Am tasa de desempleo f, Sp tasa de paro f

unending [ʌnɛ́ndɪŋ] ADJ interminable

unequal [ʌníkwəl] ADJ desigual; **to be — to a task** no ser capaz de cumplir una tarea

unequivocal [ʌ̀nɪkwívəkəl] ADJ inequívoco, tajante

unerase [ʌnɪrés] VT recuperar archivos borrados

unethical [ʌnɛ́θɪkəl] ADJ no ético

uneven [ʌnívən] ADJ (rough) irregular, accidentado; (inequitable) desigual; (not uniform) desparejo; (odd, of numbers) impar

uneventful [ʌnɪvɛ́ntfəl] ADJ sin incidente

unexpected [ʌ̀nɪkspɛ́ktɪd] ADJ inesperado

unexpressive [ʌ̀nɪksprésɪv] ADJ inexpresivo

unfailing [ʌnfélɪŋ] ADJ (inexhaustible) inagotable; (dependable) infalible

unfair [ʌnfér] ADJ (measure, price) injusto; (competition) injusto, desleal

unfaithful [ʌnféθfəl] ADJ infiel

unfamiliar [ʌnfəmíljə-] ADJ (unknown) poco

familiar, desconocido; (unacquainted) poco familiarizado

unfasten [ʌnfǽsən] VI/VT desabrochar[se], desprender[se]

unfavorable [ʌnfévəəbəl] ADJ desfavorable

unfeeling [ʌnfíliŋ] ADJ insensible

unfettered [ʌnfɛ́Dəd] ADJ (untied) desatado; (free) libre

unfinished [ʌnfíniʃt] ADJ (matter) inacabado, inconcluso; (business) pendiente; (wood) sin terminar, sin barnizar; (task) inconcluso, sin terminar

unfit [ʌnfít] ADJ (unsuitable) no apto; (incapable) incapaz

unfold [ʌnfóld] VT (open out) desdoblar, desplegar; VI (happen) desarrollarse; (reveal) revelarse

unforced error [ʌnfɔ́rst érə·] N (tennis) error no forzado m

unforeseen [ʌnfɔrsín] ADJ imprevisto

unforgettable [ʌnfə·gɛ́Dəbəl] ADJ inolvidable

unfortunate [ʌnfɔ́rtʃənit] ADJ desgraciado, desafortunado, desventurado

unfortunately [ʌnfɔ́rtʃənətli] ADV desafortunadamente, lamentablemente

unfounded [ʌnfáúndid] ADJ infundado

unfriendly [ʌnfréndli] ADJ (forces) hostil; (person) antipático

unfurl [ʌnfɔ̄l] VI/VT desplegar[se]

unfurnished [ʌnfɔ̄·niʃt] ADJ sin amueblar, desamueblado

ungainly [ʌngénli] ADJ (ungraceful) desgarbado, desmadejado; (clumsy) torpe

ungrateful [ʌngrétfəl] ADJ ingrato, desagradecido

unguarded [ʌngárDid] ADJ (incautious) descuidado, desprevenido; (unattended) sin vigilancia; (defenseless) indefenso; **an — moment** un momento de descuido

unhappiness [ʌnhǽpinis] N infelicidad f

unhappy [ʌnhǽpi] ADJ (sad) infeliz, desdichado, desgraciado; (dissatisfied) insatisfecho; (infelicitous) poco afortunado

unharmed [ʌnhármd] ADJ ileso

unhealthy [ʌnhɛ́lθi] ADJ (climate, food, lifestyle) malsano, insalubre; (complexion, obsession) enfermizo

unheard-of [ʌnhɔ̄·Dɑv] ADJ inaudito, desconocido

unhinge [ʌnhíndʒ] VT desquiciar

unholy [ʌnhóli] ADJ (noise) infernal; (alliance) nefasto

unhook [ʌnhúk] VT (disentangle) desenganchar; (undo) desabrochar

unhurt [ʌnhɔ̄·t] ADJ ileso

uniform [júnəfɔrm] ADJ & N uniforme m

uniformity [junəfɔ́rmiDi] N uniformidad f

unify [júnəfaɪ] VI/VT unificar[se]

unilateral [junəlǽDəəl] ADJ unilateral

unimportant [ʌnɪmpɔ́rtn̩t] ADJ insignificante, sin importancia

uninhabited [ʌnɪnhǽbɪDɪd] ADJ deshabitado

uninhibited [ʌnɪnhíbɪDɪd] ADJ desinhibido, desenfadado

uninspired [ʌnɪnspáɪrd] ADJ poco inspirado

uninstall [ʌnɪnstɔ́l] VT desinstalar

uninsured [ʌnɪnʃúrd] ADJ sin seguro médico

unintelligible [ʌnɪntélɪdʒəbəl] ADJ ininteligible

uninterrupted [ʌnɪntəáptɪd] ADJ ininterrumpido

union [júnjən] N unión f; (labor) sindicato m, gremio m; **— dues** cuotas sindicales f pl; **— labor** mano de obra sindicalizada/agremiada f; **— leader** dirigente sindical mf

unionize [júnjənaɪz] VI/VT sindicar[se], agremiar[se]

unique [juník] ADJ único, singular; **that feature is — to the South** ese rasgo es peculiar del sur

unisex [júnəseks] ADJ unisex

unison [júnəsən] ADV LOC **in —** al unísono

unit [júnɪt] N (part of a whole) unidad f; (part of a machine) módulo m

unitarian [junitériən] ADJ unitario

unitary [júnɪteri] ADJ unitario

unite [junáɪt] VI/VT unir[se]

United Arab Emirates [junáɪDɪdǽrəbémə·its] N Emiratos Árabes Unidos m pl

United Kingdom [junáɪDɪdkíŋdəm] N Reino Unido m

United States [junáɪDɪdstéts] N Estados Unidos m pl

unity [júnɪDi] N unidad f; (concord) unión f

universal [junəvɔ̄·səl] ADJ universal; **— donor** donante universal mf; **— joint** acoplamiento universal de cardán m

universe [júnəvəs] N universo m

university [junəvɔ̄·sɪDi] N universidad f; **— degree** título universitario m

unjust [ʌndʒást] ADJ injusto

unjustifiable [ʌndʒʌstəfáɪəbəl] ADJ injustificable

unkempt [ʌnkémpt] ADJ (uncombed) desgreñado, despeinado; (messy) desaliñado

unkind [ʌnkáɪnd] ADJ antipático, poco amable

unknown [ʌnnón] ADJ desconocido; **— quantity** incógnita f; **it is —** se ignora

unlawful [ʌnlɔ́fəl] ADJ ilegal

unleaded [ʌnléDɪd] ADJ sin plomo

unleash [ʌnlíʃ] VT desatar

unless [ənlés] CONJ a menos que, a no ser que

unlicensed [ʌnláɪsənst] ADJ (without permission) sin permiso, ilícito; (without credentials) no acreditado

unlike [ʌnláɪk] ADJ distinto, diferente; **he is — me** es diferente de mí; PREP a diferencia de; **how — you to forget!** ¡me extraña que te hayas olvidado!

unlikely [ʌnláikli] ADJ (improbable) improbable; (not realistic) inverosímil; (exotic) exótico; **I am — to come** es improbable que venga

unlimited [ʌnlímɪtɪd] ADJ ilimitado

unload [ʌnlód] VI/VT (take cargo from) descargar; VI (pour out one's feelings) desahogarse; (sell) liquidar

unlock [ʌnlák] VI/VT abrir con llave

unlucky [ʌnláki] ADJ (unfortunate) desafortunado; (ominous) aciago, funesto; **an — number** un número de mala suerte

unmanageable [ʌnmǽnɪdʒəbəl] ADJ (crisis, situation) inmanejable; (person) rebelde

unmanned [ʌnmǽnd] ADJ (deprived of courage) achicado; (with no crew) no tripulado

unmarked [ʌnmárkt] ADJ sin marcar

unmarried [ʌnmǽrid] ADJ soltero

unmask [ʌnmǽsk] VI/VT desenmascarar[se]

unmistakable [ʌnmɪstékəbəl] ADJ inconfundible

unmitigated [ʌnmídɪgeɪd] ADJ absoluto

unmoved [ʌnmúvd] ADJ (unflinching) impasible; (indifferent) indiferente

unnatural [ʌnnǽtʃəəl] ADJ (contrary to nature) no natural; (unloving) desnaturalizado; (monstrous) monstruoso; (affected) afectado

unnecessary [ʌnnǽsəseri] ADJ innecesario

unnoticed [ʌnnóDɪst] ADJ inadvertido, desapercibido

unobserved [ʌnəbzə́vd] ADJ inadvertido

unobtrusive [ʌnəbtrúsɪv] ADJ discreto

unoccupied [ʌnákjəpaid] ADJ (house) desocupado; (territory) no ocupado

unofficial [ʌnəfíʃəl] ADJ extraoficial, no oficial

unoriginal [ʌnəríʤənəl] ADJ poco original

unorthodox [ʌnɔ́rθədaks] ADJ heterodoxo

unpack [ʌnpǽk] VT (a suitcase) deshacer, desempacar; (a carton) desembalar

unpaid [ʌnpéd] ADJ (debt) impagado, por pagar; (work) no remunerado

unplayable [ʌnpléəbəl] ADJ (golf) injugable

unpleasant [ʌnplézənt] ADJ desagradable

unpleasantness [ʌnplézəntnɪs] N (quality or state of being unpleasant) lo desagradable; (unpleasant episode) desavenencia f, disgusto m

unplug [ʌnplág] VI/VT desenchufar

unpopular [ʌnpápjələ] ADJ (decision) impopular; **she was — in school** tenía pocos amigos en la escuela

unprecedented [ʌnprésɪdentɪd] ADJ sin precedente, inaudito

unpredictable [ʌnprɪdíktəbəl] ADJ impredecible, imprevisible

unpremeditated [ʌnpriméDɪteDɪd] ADJ impremeditado; (murder) sin premeditación

unprepared [ʌnprɪpérd] ADJ (surprised) desprevenido; (not ready) no preparado

unpretentious [ʌnprɪténʃəs] ADJ modesto, sin pretenciones

unprincipled [ʌnprínsəpəld] ADJ sin escrúpulos, falto de principios

unprintable [ʌnpríntəbəl] ADJ impublicable

unproductive [ʌnprədáktɪv] ADJ improductivo

unprofessional [ʌnprəféʃənəl] ADJ poco profesional

unprofitable [ʌnpráfɪDəbəl] ADJ no rentable

unpublished [ʌnpáblɪʃt] ADJ inédito, sin publicar

unpunished [ʌnpánɪʃt] ADJ impune

unqualified [ʌnkwáləfaɪd] ADJ (worker) Sp no cualificado; Am no calificado; (support) incondicional; (disaster) absoluto

unquestionable [ʌnkwéstʃənəbəl] ADJ incuestionable, indiscutible

unravel [ʌnrǽvəl] VI/VT (a rope) desenredar[se]; (a sweater) destejer[se]; (cloth) deshilachar[se]; (a plan) deshacer[se]; VT (a mystery) desentrañar

unreal [ʌnríəl] ADJ (not real) irreal; (unbelievable) increíble

unreasonable [ʌnrízənəbəl] ADJ (excessive) exagerado; (irrational) irracional, poco razonable

unrecognizable [ʌnrekəgnáizəbəl] ADJ irreconocible

unrefined [ʌnrɪfáɪnd] ADJ (oil, sugar) no refinado; (behavior) inculto, grosero

unrelated [ʌnrɪlédɪd] ADJ no relacionado

unreliable [ʌnrɪláiəbəl] ADJ (person) informal; (machine, information) Sp poco fiable; Am poco confiable

unreported [ʌnrɪpórDɪd] ADJ sin declarar

unrest [ʌnrést] N malestar m, agitación f

unrestricted [ʌnrɪstríktɪd] ADJ no restringido

unroll [ʌnról] VI/VT desenrollar[se]

unruly [ʌnrúli] ADJ (student) indisciplinado, revoltoso, díscolo; (country) ingobernable; (hair) rebelde

unsafe [ʌnséf] ADJ (risky) arriesgado; (dangerous) peligroso

unsanitary [ʌnsǽnɪteri] ADJ (behavior) antihigiénico, insalubre; (place, climate) insalubre

unsatisfactory [ʌnsæDɪsfǽktəri] ADJ no satisfactorio, insatisfactorio

unscrew [ʌnskrú] VT desatornillar, destornillar

unscrupulous [ʌnskrúpjələs] ADJ sin escrúpulos

unseasonable [ʌnsízənəbəl] ADJ impropio de la estación

unseat [ʌnsít] VT derribar

unsecured [ʌnsɪkjúrd] ADJ sin garantía

unseen [ʌnsín] ADJ invisible, oculto

unselfish [ʌnséɫfɪʃ] ADJ desinteresado

unselfishness [ʌnséɫfɪʃnɪs] N desinterés m

unsettled [ʌnsédld] ADJ (situation)

desordenado; (wilderness) sin colonizar; (case) pendiente; (weather) variable

unsightly [ʌnsáɪtli] ADJ feo, antiestético

unskilled [ʌnskɪ́ld] ADJ (not trained) inexperto; (not qualified) *Sp* no cualificado; *Am* no calificado

unsolicited [ʌnsəlísɪdɪd] ADJ no solicitado

unsophisticated [ʌnsəfístɪkeɪdɪd] ADJ sencillo, no sofisticado

unsound [ʌnsáund] ADJ (argument) erróneo, falso; (body) enfermizo; (mind) demente; (foundation) poco sólido; (investment) poco seguro

unspeakable [ʌnspíkəbəl] ADJ indecible

unspecified [ʌnspésɪfaɪd] ADJ no especificado

unsportsmanlike [ʌnspɔ́rtsmənlaɪk] ADJ antideportivo

unstable [ʌnstébəl] ADJ inestable

unsteady [ʌnstɛ́di] ADJ (walk) inseguro, inestable; (flame) tembloroso; (pulse) irregular

unsuccessful [ʌnsəksésfəl] ADJ sin éxito, infructuoso

unsuitable [ʌnsúdəbəl] ADJ (person) no apto; (place) inadecuado, inapropiado

unsuspected [ʌnsəspéktɪd] ADJ insospechado

untenable [ʌnténəbəl] ADJ insostenible

unthinkable [ʌnθíŋkəbəl] ADJ impensable

untidy [ʌntáɪdi] ADJ (dress) desaliñado, desastrado; (room) desordenado

untie [ʌntáɪ] VT desatar[se], destrabar[se]

until [əntíl] PREP hasta; CONJ hasta que

untimely [ʌntáɪmli] ADJ (ill-timed) inoportuno; (premature) prematuro

untiring [ʌntáɪrɪŋ] ADJ incansable, denodado

untold [ʌntóld] ADJ (riches) incalculable; (suffering) inaudito

untouched [ʌntátʃt] ADJ (not injured) ileso; (not affected) no afectado; **he left his dessert —** no tocó el postre

untrained [ʌntrénd] ADJ (worker) *Sp* no cualificado; *Am* no calificado; (animal) no amaestrado; (eye) inexperto

untried [ʌntráɪd] ADJ (untested) no probado, no ensayado; (not taken to trial) no juzgado

untrue [ʌntrú] ADJ (incorrect) falso; (unfaithful) infiel; (disloyal) desleal

untutored [ʌntúdə·d] ADJ (unschooled) sin instrucción; (unsophisticated) inculto

untwist [ʌntwíst] VT desenroscar

unused [ʌnjúzd] ADJ (no used) sin usar; (unaccustomed) no habituado

unusual [ʌnjúʒuəl] ADJ (infrequent) desacostumbrado, raro; (highly abnormal) inusitado, insólito

unvarnished [ʌnvárnɪʃt] ADJ (without varnish) sin barnizar; (straightforward) puro

unveil [ʌnvél] VT (remove a veil) quitar el velo a; (reveal) descubrir

unwarranted [ʌnwɔ́rəntɪd] ADJ injustificado

unwelcome [ʌnwɛ́lkəm] ADJ (untimely) inoportuno; (unpleasant) desagradable; (poorly received) mal recibido

unwholesome [ʌnhótsəm] ADJ malsano

unwieldy [ʌnwíldi] ADJ poco manejable, difícil de manejar

unwilling [ʌnwílɪŋ] ADJ **to be — to** no estar dispuesto a

unwise [ʌnwáɪz] ADJ imprudente

unwonted [ʌnwɔ́ntɪd] ADJ inusitado, inacostumbrado

unworthy [ʌnwə́ði] ADJ indigno

unwrap [ʌnrǽp] VT desenvolver

unwritten [ʌnrítn] ADJ no escrito; (agreement) de palabra

unzip [ʌnzíp] VT abrir la cremallera

up [ʌp] ADV (position) arriba; (direction) hacia arriba; **—-front** (paid in advance) inicial; (frank) franco; **— and down** de arriba para abajo; **— against** enfrentado con; **he's — for reelection** se presenta para la reelección; **I'm feeling —** me siento optimista; **I'm — for golf** tengo ganas de jugar al golf; **prices are —** los precios han subido; **that is — to you** queda en tus manos, es cosa tuya; **the children are already —** ya se levantaron los niños; **the moon is —** salió la luna; **the wheat is —** germinó el trigo; **time is —** se terminó el tiempo; **to be — on the news** estar al corriente de las noticias; **to be — to one's old tricks** hacer de las suyas; **what's —?** ¿qué pasa? **he — and went** agarró y se fue; PREP **— the current** contra la corriente; **— the river** río arriba; **— the street** calle arriba; **— to now** hasta ahora; N **—s and downs** altibajos *m pl*; VI; ADJ (assembled) armado; (finished) terminado, concluido; **—-and-coming** prometedor; **—-to-date** actualizado

upbeat [ʌ́pbit] ADJ optimista

upbringing [ʌ́pbrɪŋɪŋ] N crianza *f*

update [ʌpdét] VT actualizar; N actualización *f*

upend [ʌpénd] VI/VT (stand on end) poner[se] de punta; (defeat) derrotar

upgrade [ʌ́pgred] VT (facilities) mejorar; (computer) actualizar; N (facilities) mejora *f*; (computer) actualización *f*

upheaval [ʌphívəl] N trastorno *m*

upheld [ʌphéld] *see* uphold

uphill[1] [ʌ́phɪl] ADV cuesta arriba

uphill[2] [ʌ́phɪl] ADJ penoso, arduo

uphold [ʌphóld] VT sostener, apoyar; (legal decision) refrendar

upholster [ʌphóɫstə·] VT tapizar

upholstery [ʌphóɫstəri] N tapicería *f*

upkeep [ʌ́pkip] N mantenimiento *m*

uplift [ʌplíft] VT (physically) elevar; (spiritually)

edificar

upload [ʌ́plod] VT cargar, subir; N carga f

upon [əpán] PREP sobre, encima de; **— arriving** al llegar; **once — a time** érase una vez

upper [ʌ́pə·] ADJ (higher) superior; (high) alto; **to have the — hand** dominar, llevar la ventaja; N (of shoe) pala f; (of berth) litera superior f; **— class** clase alta f; **— crust** flor y nata f; **—case** mayúsculo; **—cut** (in boxing) gancho al mentón m; **—most** (highest) de más arriba; (most important) mayor; **— respiratory infection** infección respiratoria alta f; **—s** dentadura postiza superior f

uppity [ʌ́pɪɾi] ADJ presumido

upright [ʌ́praɪt] ADJ (posture) erecto, erguido; (position) vertical; (character) íntegro, recto, cabal; **— piano** piano vertical m; N (column) montante m; (piano) piano vertical m; (post) poste m

uprightness [ʌ́praɪtnɪs] N (physical) verticalidad f; (moral) rectitud f

uprising [ʌ́praɪzɪŋ] N alzamiento m, levantamiento m

uproar [ʌ́prɔr] N tumulto m, alboroto m, bulla f

uproarious [ʌprɔ́riəs] ADJ (tumultuous) tumultuoso; (funny) graciosísimo

uproot [ʌprút] VT arrancar de raíz, desarraigar

upscale [ʌ́pskel] ADJ de lujo

upset¹ [ʌpsɛ́t] VI/VT (overturn) volcar[se], tumbar; (distress) trastornar[se], perturbar[se], alterar[se]; VT (in sports) derrotar al favorito; ADJ (overturned) volcado; (ill) indispuesto; (distressed) disgustado, enojado

upset² [ʌ́psɛt] N (overturning) vuelco m; (unexpected defeat) derrota inesperada f; (emotional state) trastorno m, disgusto m; (illness) malestar m

upshot [ʌ́pʃɑt] N consecuencia f

upside [ʌ́psaɪd] N (upper part) parte superior f; (positive prospect) lo bueno; ADJ & ADV **— down** al revés, patas arriba

upstage [ʌpstédʒ] VT eclipsar

upstairs¹ [ʌpstérz] ADV (location) arriba, en el piso de arriba; (movement) [para] arriba

upstairs² [ʌ́pstɛrz] ADJ de arriba; N piso de arriba m

upstart [ʌ́pstɑrt] N advenedizo -za mf

uptake [ʌ́ptek] N **quick on the —** listo; **slow on the —** duro de entendederas

uptight [ʌptáɪt] ADJ (nervous) nervioso; (conventional) estreñido

up-to-the-minute [ʌ́ptəðəmínɪt] ADJ actualizado

upturn [ʌ́ptɜ·n] N (prices) aumento m, subida f; (markets) tendencia alcista f

upward [ʌ́pwəd] ADV (toward a higher place) hacia arriba; **— of** más de; ADJ ascendente; **—**

mobility ascenso social m; **— trend** tendencia al alza f

uranium [juréniəm] N uranio m

urban [ɝ́bən] ADJ urbano; **— blight** tugurización f; **— legend** leyenda urbana f; **— renewal** renovación urbana f; **— sprawl** expansión urbana f

urbanism [ɝ́bənɪzəm] N urbanismo m

urchin [ɝ́tʃɪn] N pilluelo -la mf, guaje -ja mf

urethra [jurḗθrə] N uretra f

urge [ɝdʒ] VT (exhort) exhortar, urgir; (beg) rogar; (propose) propugnar; **to — on** animar; N impulso m, gana f

urgency [ɝ́dʒənsi] N urgencia f

urgent [ɝ́dʒənt] ADJ urgente

urinal [júrənl] N urinario m, mingitorio m

urinalysis [jurənǽlɪsɪs] N análisis de orina m

urinary [júrəneri] ADJ urinario; **— tract** vías urinarias f pl

urinate [júrɪnet] VI/VT orinar

urine [júrɪn] N orina f

URL [Uniform Resource Locator] [juárɛ́l] N URL m

urn [ɝn] N urna f

urologist [juráɫədʒɪst] N urólogo -ga mf

Uruguay [júrəgwaɪ] N Uruguay m

Uruguayan [jurəgwáɪən] ADJ & N uruguayo -ya mf

us [ʌs] PRON nos; **she saw —** nos vio; **he came with —** vino con nosotros; **he gave it to —** nos lo dio [a nosotros]

USA [United States of America] [juésé] N EEUU m sg/pl

usable [júzəbəl] ADJ utilizable, aprovechable

usage [júsɪdʒ] N uso m, costumbre f

USB [Universal Serial Bus] [juésbí] N USB m; **— port** puerto USB m

use¹ [juz] VT usar, utilizar (also exploit); (consume) gastar; (take advantage of) aprovecharse de; VI **to — up** gastar, agotar

use² [jus] N (application) uso m; (utilization) empleo m, utilización f, aprovechamiento m; (usefulness) utilidad f; **it is of no —** es inútil; **out of —** en desuso; **to have no —** for no soportar; **to make — of** usar, utilizar; **to put to —** utilizar; **what is the — of it?** ¿para qué sirve?

used¹ [juzd] ADJ usado

used² [just] VI **to be — to** estar acostumbrado a; **it — to be green** antes era verde

useful [júsfəl] ADJ útil

usefulness [júsfənɪs] N utilidad f

useless [júslɪs] ADJ inútil, inservible

uselessness [júslɪsnɪs] N inutilidad f

user [júzə·] N usuario -ria mf; **—-friendly** fácil de utilizar; **— group** grupo de usuarios m; **—name** nombre del usuario m

usher [ʌ́ʃə·] N acomodador -ora mf; VT conducir, acompañar; **to — in** (a person) acompañar;

(an era) anunciar, marcar el comienzo de

usual [júʒuəl] ADJ (habitual) usual, habitual; (everyday) de todos los días; **as —** como siempre; **she wasn't her — self** no era la de siempre; **the — thing** lo normal; **more than —** más que de costumbre

usually [júʒuəli] ADV generalmente, normalmente; **he — doesn't mind** no suele importarle

usurp [jusɚp] VI/VT usurpar

usury [júʒəri] N usura f

utensil [juténsəl] N utensilio m, útil m

uterine [júɾə·ɪn] ADJ uterino

uterus [júɾəəs] N útero m

UTI [urinary tract infection] [jútiáɪ] N infección del tracto urinario f

utilitarian [jutɪlɪtériən] ADJ utilitario

utility [jutílɪti] N (usefulness) utilidad f; (public service) empresa de servicio público f, empresa de agua o electricidad f; **— furniture** muebles prácticos m pl; **— program** programa utilitario m; **— room** lavadero m

utilization [judlɪzéʃən] N utilización f

utilize [júdlaɪz] VT utilizar

utmost [Átmost] ADJ (extreme) sumo, extremo; (farthest) más distante; N máximo m; **he did his —** hizo cuanto pudo; **to the —** al máximo

utopia [jutópiə] N utopía f

utter [ÁDɚ] VT (emit) dar, proferir; (say) decir, pronunciar; (make circulate) poner en circulación; ADJ absoluto, completo

utterance [ÁDɚəns] N (of words) enunciado m; (of money) emisión f

uvula [júvjələ] N campanilla f, úvula f

Uzbek [Úzbɛk] ADJ & N uzbeko -ka mf

Uzbekistan [uzbékɪstæn] N Uzbekistán m

Vv

vacancy [vékənsi] N (job) vacante f; (room in hotel) habitación libre f; **no —** completo

vacant [vékənt] ADJ (position) vacante; (expression) vacío; (seat, room) libre

vacate [véket] VI/VT (a room) desalojar, desocupar; (a contract) anular; (a position) dejar vacante

vacation [vekéʃən] N vacaciones f pl; **on —** de vacaciones

vaccinate [væksənet] VI/VT vacunar

vaccination [væksənéʃən] N vacunación f

vaccine [væksín] N vacuna f

vacillate [væsəlet] VI vacilar

vacuum [vækjum] N vacío m; **— cleaner** aspiradora f; **— tube** tubo de vacío m; ADJ **— -**

packed envasado al vacío; VI/VT pasar la aspiradora

vagabond [vǽɡəbɑnd] ADJ & N vagabundo -da mf

vagina [vədʒáɪnə] N vagina f

vaginal [vǽdʒənl] ADJ vaginal; **— bleeding** hemorragia vaginal f; **— discharge** flujo vaginal m; **— itching** escozor vaginal m

vaginitis [vædʒɪnáɪdɪs] N vaginitis f

vagrancy [véɡrənsi] N vagancia f

vagrant [véɡrənt] ADJ & N vagabundo -da mf

vague [veɡ] ADJ vago, indistinto

vain [ven] ADJ (futile) vano, hueco; (proud of appearance) vanidoso; **in —** en vano

Valencian [vəlénsiən] ADJ & N valenciano -na

valentine [vǽləntaɪn] N (card) tarjeta del día de San Valentín f; (person) querido -da mf; **—'s Day** día de San Valentín m, día de los enamorados m

valet [vælé] N (manservant) criado m; (in a hotel) mozo de habitación m; (car parker) aparcacoches m sg

valiant [væljənt] ADJ valiente

valid [vælɪd] ADJ válido, valedero; **to be/ become —** tener efectividad

validity [vəlídɪti] N validez f

valise [vəlíz] N maleta f, valija f

valley [væli] N valle m

valor [vælɚ] N valor m, valentía f

valorize [væləraɪz] VT valorar

valorous [væləəs] ADJ valeroso, valiente

valuable [væljəbl] ADJ valioso, preciado; N **—s** objetos de valor m pl

valuation [væljuéʃən] N (value) valoración f; (appraisal) tasación f, valuación f

value [vælju] N valor m; VT valorar

valve [vælv] N válvula f; (on mollusks) valva f

vamp [væmp] N vampiresa f; VT seducir

vampire [væmpaɪr] N vampiro m

van [væn] N camioneta f

vandal [vændl] N vándalo m

vane [ven] N (for weather) veleta f; (of a fan, windmill) aspa f; (of propeller) paleta f

vanilla [vənílə] N vainilla f

vanish [vænɪʃ] VI desaparecer, esfumarse

vanity [vænɪDi] N vanidad f; **— table** tocador m

vanquish [vænkwɪʃ] VT vencer

vantage point [væntɪdʒpoɪnt] N mirador m

Vanuatu [vɑnuátu] N Vanuatu m

Vanuatuan [vɑnuátuən] ADJ & N vanuatuense mf

vapor [vépɚ] N vapor m, humo m

vaporize [vépəraɪz] VI/VT vaporizar[se]

variable [vériəbl] ADJ & N variable f; **— annuity** anualidad variable f

variance [vériəns] N discrepancia f, desacuerdo m; **to be at —** no concordar

variant [vériənt] N variante f, modalidad f

variation [veriéʃən] N variación f

varicose [værɪkos] ADJ varicoso; **— veins** Sp

varices *f pl*; *Am* várices *f pl*
varied [vérɪd] ADJ variado, vario
variegated [vériɪgeɪDɪd] ADJ variopinto
variety [vəráɪɪDi] N variedad *f*
various [vérias] ADJ vario
varnish [várnɪʃ] N barniz *m*, charol *m*; VT barnizar, charolar
varsity [vársɪDi] N equipo universitario *m*
vary [véri] VI/VT variar
vascular [véskjələ-] ADJ vascular
vase [ves] N jarrón *m*; (for flowers) florero *m*
vasectomy [vəséktəmi] N vasectomía *f*
Vaseline™ [vǽsəlín] N vaselina *f*
vast [væst] ADJ vasto, inmenso
vastly [vǽstli] ADV enormemente
vastness [vǽstnɪs] N inmensidad *f*
vat [væt] N tina *f*, barrica *f*
VAT [**value-added tax**] [víéti] N IVA *m*
Vatican City [vǽDɪkənsíDi] N Ciudad del Vaticano *f*
vaudeville [vɔ́dvɪl] N vodevil *m*
vault [vɔlt] N (arched structure) bóveda *f*; (burial chamber) panteón *m*; (place for valuables) cámara acorazada *f*; (jump) salto *m*; VT (cover with a vault) abovedar; VI/VT (jump) saltar
VCR [**videocassette recorder**] [vísiár] N *Am* video *m*; *Sp* vídeo *m*
veal [vil] N ternera *f*; — **cutlet** chuleta de ternera *f*
vector [vektə-] N vector *m*
veer [vɪr] VI/VT virar; N virada *f*
vegan [vígən] ADJ & N vegan *mf*
vegetable [véʤtəbəl] N (food) verdura *f*, hortaliza *f*; (plant, comatose person) vegetal *m*; — **garden** huerto *m*; (large) huerta *f*; — **kingdom** reino vegetal *m*; — **oil** aceite vegetal *m*
vegetarian [veʤɪtériən] ADJ & N vegetariano -na *mf*
vegetate [véʤɪtet] VI vegetar
vegetation [veʤɪtéʃən] N vegetación *f*
vegetative [véʤɪteDɪv] ADJ vegetativo
vehemence [víəməns] N vehemencia *f*
vehement [víəmənt] ADJ vehemente
vehicle [víɪkəl] N vehículo *m*
veil [vel] N velo *m*; VT velar
vein [ven] N (blood vessel, style) vena *f*; (small deposit of ore) veta *f*; (large deposit of ore) filón *m*
veined [vend] ADJ (marble) veteado; (leaf) nervado
velocity [vəlásɪDi] N velocidad *f*
velvet [vélvɪt] N terciopelo *m*; ADJ (of velvet) de terciopelo; (like velvet) aterciopelado
velvety [vélvɪDi] ADJ aterciopelado
vendetta [vendéDə] N vendetta *f*
vending machine [véndɪŋməʃin] N expendedor automático *m*, máquina expendedora *f*
vendor [véndə-] N vendedor -ora *mf*, proveedor

-ora *mf*; (in a stall) puestero -ra *mf*
veneer [vənír] N (layer of wood) chapa *f*; (outward appearance) barniz *m*; VT chapar, enchapar
venerable [vénəəbəl] ADJ venerable
venerate [vénəret] VT venerar
veneration [venəréʃən] N veneración *f*
venetian blind [vəníʃənbláɪnd] N veneciana *f*
Venezuela [venɪzwélə] N Venezuela *f*
Venezuelan [venɪzwélən] ADJ & N venezolano -na *mf*
vengeance [vénʤəns] N venganza *f*; **with a —** (violently) con furia; (energetically) con ganas
vengeful [vénʤfəl] ADJ vengativo
venison [vénəsən] N carne de venado *f*
venom [vénəm] N veneno *m*
venomous [vénəməs] ADJ venenoso
vent [vent] N (outlet for air) ventilación *f*; (opening of a volcano) chimenea *f*; **to give — to anger** desahogar la ira; VI/VT desahogar[se], descargar[se]
ventilate [véntlet] VI/VT ventilar[se]
ventilation [ventléʃən] N ventilación *f*
ventilator [véntlebə-] N ventilador *m*
ventricle [véntrɪkəl] N ventrículo *m*
venture [vénʧə-] N (adventure) aventura *f*; (business enterprise) empresa *f*; — **capital** capital de riesgo *m*; VI/VT aventurar[se], arriesgar[se]
venue [vénju] N lugar *m*
veranda [vərǽndə] N porche *m*, terraza *f*
verb [vɜb] N verbo *m*
verbal [vɜ́bəl] ADJ (linguistic, related to verbs) verbal; (not written) oral
verbatim [vɜ-bédəm] ADJ textual; ADV textualmente
verbiage [vɜ́biɪʤ] N palabrerío *m*
verbose [vɜ-bós] ADJ verboso
verdict [vɜ́dɪkt] N veredicto *m*
verdure [vɜ́ʤə-] ADJ *lit* verdura *f*
verge [vɜʤ] ADV LOC **on the — of** al borde de, a punto de; VI **to — on** rayar en, lindar con
verification [verɪfɪkéʃən] N verificación *f*, comprobación *f*
verify [vérɪfaɪ] VT verificar, constatar, comprobar
veritable [vérɪDəbəl] ADJ verdadero
vermillion [və-míljən] ADJ & N bermellón *m*
vermin [vɜ́mɪn] N bichos *m pl*
vermouth [və-múθ] N vermú *f*
vernacular [və-nǽkjələ-] ADJ vernáculo; N (plain language) lengua vernácula *f*
versatile [vɜ́sədl] ADJ versátil
verse [vɜs] N verso *m*; (stanza) estrofa *f*; (line of poem) verso *m*; (in Bible) versículo *m*
versed [vɜst] ADJ versado
version [vɜ́ʒən] N versión *f*
versus [vɜ́səs] PREP contra; (in sports) versus

vertebra [vɝ́ɾəbrə] N vértebra f
vertebrate [vɝ́ɾəbrɪt] ADJ vertebrado
vertical [vɝ́ɾɪkəl] ADJ vertical
vertigo [vɝ́ɾɪgo] N vértigo m
very [véri] ADV muy; — **many** muchísimos; —
much muchísimo; **it is — cold today** hace
mucho frío hoy; ADJ (same) mismo; (mere)
mero
vessel [vésəl] N (container) vasija f; (duct) vaso
m; (ship) nave f
vest [vest] N chaleco m; VT conferir; —**ed**
interests intereses creados m pl
vestibule [véstɪbjul] N vestíbulo m, zaguán m
vestige [véstɪdʒ] N vestigio m
vet [vet] N (veterinarian) veterinario -ria mf;
(veteran) veterano -na militar mf; VT evaluar
veteran [véɾəən] ADJ & N veterano -na mf
veterinarian [vɛɾəənériən] N veterinario -ria
mf
veterinary [véɾəəneri] ADJ veterinario; —
medicine veterinaria f
veto [víto] N veto m; VT vetar
vex [veks] VT molestar, irritar
via [váɪə, víə] PREP (by way of) vía; (by means of)
por
viability [vaɪəbɪ́liɾi] N viabilidad f
viable [váɪəbəl] ADJ viable
vial [váɪəl] N ampolla f, frasco m
vibrate [váɪbret] VI/VT vibrar
vibration [vaɪbréʃən] N vibración f
vibrator [váɪbreɾə] N vibrador m
vicarious [vaɪkériəs] ADJ indirecto
vice [vaɪs] N vicio m
vice president [váɪsprézɪdənt] N vicepresidente
-ta f
viceroy [váɪsrɔɪ] N virrey m
viceroyalty [vaɪsrɔ́ɪəlti] ADJ virreinato
vice versa [váɪsəvɝ́sə] ADV viceversa
vicinity [vɪsɪ́nɪɾi] N vecindad f, cercanías f pl,
aledaños m pl
vicious [víʃəs] ADJ (violent) violento,
sanguinario; (evil) maligno, perverso;
(malicious) malicioso; — **circle** círculo
vicioso m; — **dog** perro fiero m, perro
bravo m
vicissitude [vɪsɪ́sɪtud] N vicisitud f, peripecia f
victim [víktɪm] N víctima f
victimize [víktəmaɪz] VT (make victim)
victimizar; (dupe) estafar
victor [víktə] N vencedor -ora mf
victorious [vɪktóriəs] ADJ victorioso
victory [víktəri] N victoria f
video [vídio] N Am vídeo m; Sp vídeo m;
—**cassette** Am video m; Sp vídeo m;
—**cassette recorder** videocasete m;
—**conference** videoconferencia f; —
console videoconsola f; — **game** videojuego
m; — **portal** Am portal de videos m; Sp portal
de vídeos m; —**tape** Am cinta de video f; Sp

cinta de vídeo f; — **clip** videoclip m
vie [vaɪ] VI competir; **to — for power** disputarse
el poder
Vietnam [vietnám] N Vietnam m
Vietnamese [viitnəmíz] ADJ & N vietnamita mf
view [vju] N (field of vision) vista f; (opinion)
opinión f; (panorama) visión panorámica f;
—**point** punto de vista m; **in — of** en vista
de; **to be within — of** estar a la vista; **with a —
to** con el propósito de; VT (see) ver; (consider)
enfocar
viewer [vjúə] N telespectador -ora mf,
televidente mf
vigil [vídʒəl] N vigilia f, vela f; **to keep —** velar
vigilance [vídʒələns] N vigilancia f
vigilant [vídʒələnt] ADJ vigilante
vigor [vígə] N vigor m, pujanza f, dinamismo m
vigorous [vígəəs] ADJ vigoroso
vile [vaɪl] ADJ (evil) vil, ruin; (foul, bad) pésimo
villa [vílə] N quinta f, casa de campo f
village [vílɪdʒ] N aldea f, villa f
villager [vílɪdʒə] N aldeano -na mf
villain [vílən] N villano -na mf
villainous [vílənəs] ADJ vil, villano
villainy [víləni] N villanía f, vileza f
vindicate [víndɪket] VT reivindicar, vindicar
vindication [vɪndɪkéʃən] N reivindicación f,
vindicación f
vindictive [vɪndíktɪv] ADJ vengativo
vine [vaɪn] N (grapevine) vid f; (decorative) parra
f; (stem) sarmiento m; (climbing plant)
enredadera f
vinegar [vínɪgə] N vinagre m
vineyard [vínjəd] N viña f, viñedo m
vintage [víntɪdʒ] N (act or season of gathering
grapes) vendimia f; (harvest of grapes)
cosecha f; (year) año m; ADJ (wine) añejo;
(classic) excelente; (old) antiguo, de
colección; (typical) típico
vinyl [váɪnl] N vinilo m
viola [violə] N viola f
violate [váɪəlet] VT violar; (a law) violar,
quebrantar
violation [vaɪəléʃən] N violación f; (traffic)
infracción f
violence [váɪələns] N violencia f
violent [váɪələnt] ADJ violento
violet [váɪəlɪt] N (flower) violeta f; (color) violeta
m; ADJ violeta
violin [vaɪəlín] N violín m
violinist [vaɪəlínɪst] N violinista mf
VIP [**very important person**] [víáɪpí] N & ADJ
VIP m
viper [váɪpə] N víbora f
viral [váɪrəl] ADJ viral
virgin [vɝ́dʒɪn] ADJ & N virgen f; (uninitiated) no
iniciado -da mf; — **Islands** Islas Vírgenes f pl
virginal [vɝ́dʒənl] ADJ virginal
virile [vírəl] ADJ viril

virility [vərílıdi] N virilidad f
virology [vaıróladʒi] N virología f
virtual [vɔ́tʃuəl] ADJ virtual; **— community** comunidad virtual f; **— reality** realidad virtual f; **— stores** tiendas virtuales f pl
virtually [vɔ́tʃuəli] ADV (remotely) virtualmente; (almost) prácticamente
virtue [vɔ́tʃu] N virtud f
virtuosity [vɔtʃuósıdi] N virtuosismo m
virtuoso [vɔtʃuóso] ADJ & N virtuoso -sa mf
virtuous [vɔ́tʃuəs] ADJ virtuoso
virulent [vírələnt] ADJ virulento
virus [váırəs] N virus m; **—-free** libre de virus; **— protection software** programas de protección contra virus m pl
visa [vízə] N Am visa f; Sp visado m
vis-à-vis [vízəví] PREP con respecto a
visceral [vísərəl] ADJ visceral
viscous [vískəs] ADJ viscoso
vise [vaıs] N tornillo de banco m
visibility [vızıbílıdi] N visibilidad f
visible [vízəbəl] ADJ visible
Visigoth [vízıgɔθ] N visigodo -da mf
vision [víʒən] N (sense, apparition) visión f; (eyesight) vista f
visionary [víʒəneri] ADJ & N visionario -ria mf
visit [vízıt] VT visitar; (afflict) infligir; VI estar de visita; **to — with** charlar con; N (stay) visita f; (chat) charla f
visitation [vızıtéʃən] N (apparition) visitación f; (punishment) castigo m; (parental right) régimen de visita m
visiting [vízıdıŋ] ADJ (team) visitante
visitor [vízıdɚ] N visita f, visitante mf
visor [váızɚ] N visera f
vista [vístə] N (visual) vista f; (mental) perspectiva f
visual [víʒuəl] ADJ visual; **— recognition** reconocimiento visual m
visualize [víʒuəlaız] VT visualizar, imaginar
vital [váıdl] ADJ vital; **— signs** signos vitales m pl
vitality [vaıtǽlıdi] N vitalidad f
vitamin [váıdəmın] N vitamina f
vituperation [vaıtupəréʃən] N vituperación f, vituperio m
vivacious [vaıvéʃəs] ADJ vivaz, vivaracho
vivacity [vaıvǽsıdi] N vivacidad f
vivid [vívıd] ADJ vívido, vivo
vivisection [vívısekʃən] N vivisección f
vocabulary [vokǽbjəleri] N vocabulario m
vocal [vókəl] ADJ (musical) vocal; (outspoken) vociferante; **— cords** cuerdas vocales f pl
vocalic [vokǽlık] ADJ vocálico
vocation [vokéʃən] N vocación f
vociferous [vosífəəs] ADJ vociferante
vodka [vádkə] N vodka m
vogue [vog] N boga f, moda f; **in —** en boga, de moda
voice [vɔıs] N voz f; **—mail** correo de voz m,

contestador automático m; **— recognition** reconocimiento de voz m; **— synthesis** síntesis de voz f; VT expresar
voicing [vɔ́ısıŋ] N sonoridad f
void [vɔıd] ADJ (devoid, empty) vacío; (not binding) nulo, inválido; **— of** desprovisto de; N vacío m; VT (bowels) evacuar; (a check) anular; **—ed check** cheque anulado m
volatile [válədl] ADJ (liquid) volátil; (political situation) explosivo, conflictivo; (stock market) voluble; (temperament) cambiante
volcanic [valkǽnık] ADJ volcánico
volcano [valkéno] N volcán m
volition [volíʃən] N volición f; **of one's own —** por su propia voluntad
volley [váli] N (of firearms) descarga f; (of protests, arrows, stones) lluvia f; (of a tennis ball) volea f; **—ball** voleibol m, balonvolea m; VI/VT (shoot bullets) descargar; (hit tennis balls) volear
volt [volt] N voltio m
voltage [vóltıdʒ] N voltaje m
volume [váljəm] N volumen m, tomo m
voluminous [vəlúmınəs] ADJ voluminoso
voluntary [válənteri] ADJ voluntario
volunteer [valəntír] ADJ & N voluntario -ria mf; VI/VT (offer) ofrecer[se], brindar[se]; RP comedir[se]; VI (do volunteer work) trabajar de voluntario -ria
voluptuous [vəláptʃuəs] ADJ voluptuoso
vomit [vámıt] N vómito m; VI/VT vomitar
voodoo [vúdu] N vudú m
voracious [vɔréʃəs] ADJ voraz
vortex [vórteks] N vórtice m
vote [vot] N (right, ballot) voto m; (act of voting) votación f; VI votar; VT (a bill) aprobar; (a political party) votar a/por; **to — against** votar en contra; **to — in favor** votar a favor; **to — to do something** votar por hacer algo
voter [vódɚ] N votante mf
voting [vódıŋ] N votación f
vouch [vautʃ] VI **to — for** dar fe de, salir de fiador a, fiar a; VT **to — that** dar fe de que
voucher [váutʃɚ] N (receipt) comprobante m; (coupon) vale m; (person) fiador -ora f, garante mf
vow [vau] N voto m; **to take a —** prometer; VT jurar
vowel [váuəl] N vocal f
voyage [vɔııdʒ] N (long trip) viaje m; (trip by sea) travesía f; VI viajar
voyeur [vɔıɚ] N mirón -ona mf
VP [vice president] [vípí] N vice presidente -ta mf
vulgar [válgɚ] ADJ (rude) ordinario, grosero, soez; (popular, vernacular) vulgar
vulgarity [valgǽrıdi] N ordinariez f, vulgaridad f
vulnerable [válnəəbəl] ADJ vulnerable
vulture [váltʃɚ] N buitre m

Ww

wacky [wǽki] ADJ (person) chiflado; (idea) descabellado

wad [wad] N (for artillery, for filling) taco *m*; (ball) pelota *f*, pelotón *m*; (of money) rollo *m*, fajo *m*; (of cotton) bola *f*; VI/VT (a firearm) atacar; (a piece of paper) hacer una pelota [con]

waddle [wádl] VT anadear, andar como un pato; N anadeo *m*

wade [wed] VI andar por el agua; **to — through a book** leer con dificultad un libro

wafer [wéfɚ] N (cookie) oblea *f*; (in Catholic ritual) hostia *f*; (computer) lámina/oblea de silicio *f*

waffle [wáfəl] ADJ Sp gofre *m*; Am wafle *m*; — **iron** Sp plancha para hacer gofres *f*; Am waflera *f*

waft [wæft] VI flotar; VT llevar por el aire; N (of air) ráfaga *f*; (of odor) ola *f*

wag [wæg] VI/VT menear[se], mover[se]; **to — the tail** colear; N (movement) meneo *m*, movimiento *m*; (joker) bromista *mf*

wage [wedʒ] N salario *m*; — **earner** asalariado -da *mf*; (paid daily) jornalero -ra *mf*; —**s** salario *m*; (daily) jornal *m*; — **scale** escala salarial *f*; VT (war) hacer; (battle) librar

wager [wédʒɚ] N apuesta *f*; VI/VT apostar

wagon [wǽgən] N (horsedrawn) carro *m*; (covered) carreta *f*; (toy) carrito *m*; **to fix someone's** — vengarse de alguien; **to be on the** — abstenerse de bebidas alcohólicas

wail [wel] VI lamentar; N lamento *m*

waist [west] N cintura *f*; (of garment) talle *m*; —**band** pretina *f*; —**coat** chaleco *m*; —**line** talle *m*, cintura *f*

wait [wet] VI/VT esperar; **to — for** esperar; **to — on** servir; **to — tables** trabajar de camarero -ra; N espera *f*; **to lie in — for** estar en/al acecho de

waiter [wédɚ] N camarero *m*, mozo *m*, mesero *m*

waiting [wédɪŋ] N espera *f*; — **list** lista de espera *f*; — **room** sala de espera *f*

waitress [wétrɪs] N camarera *f*, moza *f*, mesera *f*

waive [wev] VT (rights) renunciar a; (a rule) hacer una excepción

waiver [wévɚ] N (of rights) renuncia *f*; (of rules) excepción *f*

wake [wek] VI/VT despertar[se]; **to — up** despertar[se]; N (at death) velatorio *m*; (of a ship) estela *f*, surco *m*; —**up call** (in a hotel) llamada del servicio despertador *f*; (to action) llamada de atención *f*; **in the — of** después de, detrás de

wakeful [wékfəl] ADJ (awake) despierto;

(insomniac) insomne

waken [wékən] VI/VT despertar[se]

Wales [welz] N Gales *m sg*

walk [wɔk] VI andar, caminar; (to a place) ir a pie; (go away) marcharse; (in baseball) sacar una base por bolas *f*; **to — back** volver a pie; **to — down** bajar a pie; **to — in** entrar caminando; **to — out** (to go out) salir caminando; (to abandon) dejar; (to strike) declararse en huelga; **to — up** subir a pie; VT (to cause to walk) hacer caminar; (to trace on foot) recorrer; **to — the streets** callejear; **to — someone** (baseball) darle una base por bolas; N (period of walking) paseo *m*, caminata *f*; (pace) paso *m*; (gait) andar *m*; — **of life** condición *f*; —**out** huelga *f*; **to take a —** pasear, dar un paseo

walker [wɔ́kɚ] N (device to aid walking) andador *m*; (one who walks) caminante *mf*; (in sports) marchista *mf*

walking [wɔ́kɪŋ] ADJ andante; — **papers** despido *m*; — **stick** bastón *m*

wall [wɔl] N (interior) pared *f*; (garden) muro *m*, tapia *f*; (fort) muralla *f*; (of silence) barrera *f*; —**paper** papel de empapelar *m*; —**flower** alhelí *m*; —**-to—** de pared a pared; **to have one's back to the** — estar entre la espada y la pared; **to drive someone up the** — sacar a alguien de quicio; **I was climbing the** —**s** me moría de aburrimiento; **she was a** —**flower** no la sacaban a bailar; VT **to** —**paper** empapelar

wallet [wálɪt] N cartera *f*, billetera *f*

wallow [wálo] VI (roll) revolcarse; (indulge oneself) regodearse

walnut [wɔ́lnʌt] N nuez *f*; — **tree** nogal *m*

walrus [wɔ́lrəs] N morsa *f*

waltz [wɔlts] N vals *m*; VI valsar

wand [wand] N (rod) vara *f*; (magic) varita *f*

wander [wándɚ] VI/VT vagar [por], errar [por]; **to — away** perderse; **my mind —s easily** me distraigo fácilmente

wanderer [wándərɚ] N vagabundo -da *mf*

wane [wen] VI menguar, flaquear; N **to be on the** — ir menguando

wannabe [wánəbi] N aspirante *mf*

want [want] VI/VT (desire) querer; **he —s judgment** le falta juicio; **he's —ed in Texas** se lo busca en Texas; N (desire) deseo *m*; (lack) falta *f*; (scarcity) escasez *f*; **to be in** — estar necesitado; — **ad** [anuncio] clasificado *m*

wanting [wántɪŋ] ADJ (lacking) falto; (deficient) deficiente

wanton [wántən] ADJ (immoderate) desenfrenado; (immoral) lascivo; (senseless, unprovoked) gratuito

war [wɔr] N guerra *f*; — **crime** crimen de guerra *m*; —**fare** guerra *f*; — **games** juegos de guerra *m pl*, simulacro de batalla *m*; **—head** ojiva *f*; **—ship** acorazado *m*; vi guerrear, hacer la guerra; **—like** bélico *f*

warble [wórbəl] vi gorjear; N gorjeo *m*

warbler [wórblə] N (European) curruca *f*; (American) arañero *m*

ward [wɔrd] N (district) distrito *m*; (of a hospital) pabellón *m*; (of a tutor) pupilo -la *mf*; vi **to — off** resguardarse de, conjurar

warden [wórdn] N (of prison) alcaide *m*

wardrobe [wórdrob] N (room) guardarropa *m*; (furniture) armario *m*, ropero *m*; (garments) vestuario *m*, guardarropa *m*

warehouse [wérhaʊs] N almacén *m*, depósito *m*

wares [wɛrz] N mercancías *f pl*

warm [wɔrm] ADJ (bath) caliente; (clothes) abrigado; (weather) caluroso; (colors, reception) cálido; **—-blooded** de sangre caliente; **—hearted** de buen corazón; **it is — today** hace calor hoy; N **—up** precalentamiento *m*; vi/vt calentar[se]; **to — over** recalentar; **to — up** calentar[se], templar[se]; **it —s my heart** me alegra el corazón; **she —ed to the idea** se entusiasmó con la idea

warmth [wɔrmθ] N calor *m*, tibieza *f*

warn [wɔrn] vi/vt (advise of danger) advertir; (urge to behave) amonestar

warning [wórnɪŋ] N (of danger) advertencia *f*; (of punishment) amonestación *f*

warp [wɔrp] N (yarn) urdimbre *f*; (curve) comba *f*, alabeo *m*; vi/vt (wood) combar[se], alabear[se]; (character) deformar[se]; **he has a —ed personality** tiene una personalidad retorcida

warrant [wórənt] N orden *f*; **a — for his arrest** una orden de arresto contra él; vt garantizar

warranty [wórənti] N garantía *f*; vt garantizar

warrior [wóriə] N guerrero -ra *mf*

wart [wɔrt] N verruga *f*

wary [wéri] ADJ cauteloso, cauto; **to be — of** desconfiar de

was [wɑz] *see* be

wash [wɑʃ] vi/vt lavar[se]; **to — out** (a bottle) lavar; (a substance) quitar lavando; (a creekbed) erosionar; **to — up** lavarse; **the bottle was —ed up on the shore** la botella fue traída por el mar; **he was —ed away by the waves** fue arrastrado por las olas; **his excuse won't —** su excusa no va a colar; N (act of washing) lavado *m*; (clothes to be washed) ropa para lavar *f*; (washed clothes) ropa lavada *f*; **—cloth** toallita para lavarse *f*; **—out** (erosion) derrubio *m*; (failure) fracaso *m*; **—room** lavabo *m*, lavatorio *m*; ADJ **—-and-wear** de lava y pon, de no planchar; **—ed-up** fracasado; **—ed-out** desteñido

washable [wáʃəbəl] ADJ lavable

washer [wáʃə] N (washing machine) lavadora *f*,

máquina de lavar *f*; (metal ring) arandela *f*; **—woman** lavandera *f*

washing [wáʃɪŋ] N lavado *m*; **— machine** lavadora *f*, máquina de lavar *f*

wasp [wɑsp] N avispa *f*

WASP [**White Anglo-Saxon Protestant**] [wɑsp] N persona blanca, anglosajona y protestante *f*

waste [west] vi/vt (squander resources) malgastar, desperdiciar; **to — away** consumirse; vt (squander time) perder; (murder) liquidar; N (of resources) desperdicio *m*, malgasto *m*, derroche *m*; (of time) pérdida *f*; (refuse) desperdicios *m pl*, desechos *m pl*; (liquid refuse) vertido *m*; **—land** tierra yerma *f*, páramo *m*; **— of time** pérdida de tiempo *f*; **—paper basket** papelera *f*; **— products** productos de desecho *m pl*; **— treatment** tratamiento de residuos *m*; **to go to —** desperdiciarse; **to lay — to** asolar

wasted [wéstɪd] ADJ (squandered) desperdiciado; (debilitated) consumido; (drunk) borracho

wasteful [wéstfəl] ADJ (person) despilfarrador, gastador; (method) antieconómico

watch [wɑtʃ] vi (look) mirar; (be careful) cuidarse; (be vigilant) vigilar; vt (view) mirar, ver; (observe) observar; (tend) cuidar; **— out for the cars!** ¡cuidado con los coches! **to — for** estar a la espera de; **to — over** proteger; N (timepiece) reloj *m*; (period of wakefulness) vela *f*, vigilia *f*; (vigilant guard) guardia *mf*; (duty shift) guardia *f*; (lookout) centinela *m*; **—band** pulsera *f*; **—dog** (type of dog) perro guardián *m*; (organization) organismo de control *m*; **—maker** relojero -ra *mf*; **—making** relojería *f*; **—man** vigilante *m*, sereno *m*; **—tower** atalaya *f*, torre de vigilancia *f*; **—word** (password) contraseña *f*; (motto) consigna *f*, lema *m*; **to be on the —** estar alerta; **to keep — on/ over** vigilar a

watchful [wátʃfəl] ADJ alerta, atento

water [wɔ́də] N agua *f*; **—bed** cama de agua *f*; **—bird** ave acuática *f*; **— buffalo** búfalo de agua *m*; **—color** acuarela *f*; **—cress** berro *m*; **—fall** (small) cascada *f*; (large) catarata *f*; **—front** muelles *m pl*; **—fountain** fuente *f*, *Mex, RP* bebedero *m*; **— heater** calentador de agua *m*; **— lily** nenúfar *m*; **—melon** sandía *f*; **— pistol** pistola de agua *f*; **— power** energía hidráulica *f*; **—shed** vertiente *f*; **— ski** esquí acuático *m*; **— softener** ablandador de agua *m*; **— sports** deportes acuáticos *m pl*; **—spout** (pipe) tubo de desagüe *m*; (tornado) tromba *f*; **— supply** abastecimiento de agua *m*; **— table** capa freática *f*; **—vapor** vapor de agua *m*; **—way** vía navegable *f*; **my — broke** se me rompieron las aguas, se me rompió la fuente; ADJ **—logged** empapado; **—proof** (fabric) impermeable; (watch) sumergible; **—tight** hermético; VT (irrigate) regar; (dilute) aguar; VI/VT (animals) abrevar; **—ed-down** (with water) aguado; (simplified) simplificado; (softened) suavizado; **to —proof** impermeabilizar; **to —-ski** hacer esquí acuático; **my eyes are —ing** me lloran los ojos; **it makes my mouth —** se me hace agua la boca

watery [wɔ́Dǝ-i] ADJ (watered-down) aguado; (like water) acuoso; (boggy) húmedo

watt [wɑt] N vatio *m*

wattage [wɑ́DIʤ] N vataje *m*

wave [wev] N (radio) onda *f*; (water, heat, fashion) ola *f*; (of disgust, of people) oleada *f*; (with the hand) saludo *m*; **—length** longitud de onda *f*; **on the same —length** en la misma onda, en sintonía; VI (flag) ondear; (hair) ondular[se]; VI (greet) saludar con la mano; **to — good-bye** decir adiós con la mano

waver [wévǝ-] VI (hesitate) vacilar, titubear; (falter) flaquear

wavy [wévi] ADJ ondeado, ondulado

wax [wæks] N cera *f*; (for seals) lacre *m*; **— paper** papel encerado *m*; VT (cover with wax) encerar; (defeat) derrotar; VI (moon) crecer; **to — poetic** ponerse poético

way [we] N (road) camino *m*; (manner) modo *m*, manera *f*; **—farer** caminante *mf*; **— in** entrada *f*; **— out** salida *f*; **—s** costumbres *f pl*; **—side** borde del camino *m*; **— through** paso *m*, pasaje *m*; **a long — off** muy lejos; **by — of London** por Londres; **by — of comparison** a modo de comparación; **by the —** a propósito; **in no —** de ningún modo; **on the — to** rumbo a; **to get out of the —** apartarse; **to go out of one's — to** desvivirse por; **to look the other —** hacer la vista gorda; **to lead the —** ir a la cabeza; **to be in a bad —** hallarse mal de salud; **to give —** (yield) ceder; (break) quebrarse; **to get one's —** salirse con la suya; **to make — for** abrir paso para; ADJ **—-out** estrafalario; VT **to —lay** (wait in ambush) estar al acecho de; (attack) asaltar; (stop) detener

wayward [wéwǝd] ADJ (disobedient) desobediente; (willful) porfiado

we [wi] PRON nosotros -as *mf*

weak [wik] ADJ débil; (deficient) flojo; **— force** fuerza débil *f*; **—-kneed** achicado; **— sister** (coward) cobarde *mf*; **— link** parte más delgada del hilo *f*

weaken [wíkǝn] VI/VT debilitar[se], quebrantar[se]

weakling [wíklIŋ] N alfeñique *m*

weakness [wíknIs] N debilidad *f*, flaqueza *f*; (deficiency) flojedad *f*

wealth [wɛlθ] N riqueza *f*

wealthy [wɛ́lθi] ADJ rico, adinerado, pudiente

wean [win] VT destetar; **to — oneself of** quitarse el vicio de

weapon [wépǝn] N arma *f*

wear [wɛr] VT (have on) llevar, tener puesto; (dress in habitually) usar; VI/VT (waste away) desgastar[se]; **to — away** gastar[se], desgastar[se]; **to — down** (a person) agotar; (a pencil) desgastar; **to — off** perder efecto; **to — on** prolongarse; **to — out** (make unfit) gastar[se], desgastar[se], sobar[se]; (expend) agotar; **it —s well** es duradero; N (use) gasto *m*; (clothes) ropa *f*; (durability) durabilidad *f*; (deterioration) desgaste *m*; **— and tear** desgaste *m*

weariness [wírinIs] N cansancio *m*, fatiga *f*

wearing [wɛ́rIŋ] ADJ (causing wear) desgastante; (causing fatigue) cansado

wearisome [wírisǝm] ADJ fastidioso

weary [wíri] ADJ cansado, fatigado; VI/VT cansar[se], fatigar[se]

weasel [wízǝl] N comadreja *f*

weather [wɛ́ðǝ-] N tiempo *m*; (storm) tempestad *f*; **—-beaten** desgastado/curtido por la intemperie; **— bureau** oficina meteorológica *f*; **— conditions** condiciones atmosféricas *f pl*; **—man** meteórologo *m*; **— report** parte meteorológico *m*; **—vane** veleta *f*; **it is fine —** hace buen tiempo; **to be under the —** estar enfermo; ADJ **—proof** resistente a la intemperie; VI/VT (a surface) gastar[se]; (skin) curtir; (crisis, storm) capear

weave [wiv] VT (cloth, basket) tejer, entretejer; (to put together) urdir, tramar; **to — together/into** entretejer, entrelazar; **to — one's way** zigzaguear; N tejido *m*

weaver [wívǝ-] N tejedor -ora *mf*

web [wɛb] N (of a spider) telaraña *f*; (of lies) sarta *f*; (membrane) membrana *f*; (Internet) web *f*; (animal) palmípedo *m*; **— browser** navegador [web] *m*; **—cast** transmisión por la web *f*; **—foot** pata palmada *f*; **— hosting** alojamiento web *m*; **—master** administrador -ora de un sitio web *mf*; **— page** página web *f*; **—site** sitio web *m*; VT; ADJ **—footed** palmípedo; VI/VT **to —cast** transmitir por la web

wed [wɛd] VI/VT casarse [con]; VT casar a

wedding [wɛ́DIŋ] N boda *f*, casamiento *m*; **— day** día de boda *m*; **— dress** traje de novia *m*; **— ring** anillo de boda *m*

wedge [wɛʤ] N cuña *f*; **to drive a — between** separar; VT acuñar, meter cuñas entre; **to be —d between** estar apretado entre

Wednesday [wɛ́nzde] N miércoles *m*

wee [wi] ADJ chiquito, pequeñito

weed [wid] N mala hierba *f*; (marijuana) hierba *f*; **—killer** herbicida *m*; VT deshierbar, escardar; **to — out** eliminar

week [wik] N semana f; **—day** día de semana m; **—end** fin de semana m; **a — from today** de aquí en una semana

weekly [wíkli] ADJ semanal; ADV semanalmente; N semanario m

weep [wip] VI llorar, lagrimear

weeping [wípiŋ] ADJ lloroso; **— willow** sauce llorón m; N llanto m

weevil [wívəl] N gorgojo m

weigh [we] VI/VT pesar; (consider) ponderar, sopesar, barajar; **to — anchor** levar anclas; **to — down** agobiar, abrumar; **to — on one's conscience** pesar en la conciencia de uno

weight [wet] N (heaviness, importance) peso m; (for clocks, scales, barbells) pesa f; **—lifting / —training** levantamiento de pesas m, halterofilia f; **—-watcher** persona a dieta f; **to put on —** engordar; **to lose —** adelgazar; VT (add weight) añadir peso; (in statistics) ponderar; **to — someone down** agobiarle a uno

weightless [wétlɪs] ADJ ingrávido

weighty [wédi] ADJ importante

weird [wird] ADJ (strange) extraño; (supernatural) misterioso

weirdo [wírdo] N bicho raro m, ente m

welcome [wélkəm] N bienvenida f; ADJ bienvenido; **— mat** alfombrilla f, felpudo m; **— rest** descanso agradable m; **you are —** no hay de qué, de nada; **you are — here** estás en tu casa; **you are — to use it** a tus órdenes; VT dar la bienvenida a, acoger

weld [wɛld] VI/VT soldar[se]; N soldadura f

welfare [wɛ́lfɛr] N (good fortune) bienestar m; (public assistance) asistencia social f; **— state** estado de bienestar m

well [wɛl] ADV bien; **— then** pues bien; **—-being** bienestar m; **—-nigh** casi, muy cerca de; **he is — over fifty** tiene mucho más de cincuenta años; **all is —** todo está bien; INTERJ ¡bueno! ADJ (healthy) bien de salud, sano; N (of water, oil) pozo m; (of staircase) caja f; **—spring** fuente f, manantial m; ADJ **—-bred** bien educado; **—-defined** bien definido; **—-done** (steak) bien cocido; (a task) bien hecho; **—-fed** bien alimentado; **—-founded** bien fundamentado; **—-groomed** bien arreglado, aseado; **—-heeled** adinerado; **—-informed** bien informado; **—-known** (of a fact) bien sabido; (of a person) bien conocido, notorio; **—-made** bien hecho; **—-meaning** bien intencionado; **—-off** adinerado, acomodado; **—-read** leído, educado; **—-rounded** completo; **—-spoken** bien hablado; **—-to-do** adinerado; VI **tears —ed up in his eyes** se le llenaron los ojos de lágrimas

wellness [wɛ́lnɪs] N (health) salud f; (health care) medicina preventiva f

welsh [wɛlʃ] VI **to — on** (a debt) no pagar; (a promise) no cumplir

Welsh [wɛlʃ] ADJ & N galés -esa mf

welt [wɛlt] N verdugón m

went [wɛnt] see go

wept [wɛpt] see weep

were [wɚ] see be

west [wɛst] N (cardinal point) oeste m; (hemisphere) occidente m; **— Berlin** Berlín occidental m; **— Indies** Antillas f pl; ADJ **— wind** viento del oeste m; ADV (direction) hacia el oeste; (location) al oeste

western [wɛ́stɚn] ADJ occidental, del oeste; N (movie genre) película del oeste f

westerner [wɛ́stɚnɚ] N occidental mf

westward [wɛ́stwɚd] ADV hacia el oeste; ADJ occidental

wet [wɛt] ADJ (drenched) mojado; (damp, rainy) húmedo; **— blanket** aguafiestas mf sg; **—land** humedal m; **— nurse** nodriza f; **— paint** pintura fresca f; **— suit** traje de buzo m; VI/VT (soak) mojar[se]; (dampen) humedecer[se]

wetness [wɛ́tnɪs] N humedad f

whack [hwæk] VI/VT (hit) golpear, pegar; (assassinate) fam liquidar; **to — off** (cut) cortar; N (blow) golpazo m; Sp vulg hostia f; **to take a — at** hacer un intento de; **out of —** descompuesto, averiado

whale [hwel] N ballena f; VI pescar ballenas

wharf [hwɔrf] N muelle m, embarcadero m

what [hwɑt] INTERR PRON & N qué; **— did you say?** ¿qué dijiste? **— for?** ¿para qué? **—'s the matter?** ¿qué pasa? **—'s the score?** ¿cómo va el marcador? **and —not** y demás; REL PRON lo que; **come — may** venga lo que venga; **anyplace —soever** en cualquier lugar; **so —?** ¿y qué? **take — you need** toma lo que necesites; ADJ qué; **— books did you want?** ¿qué libros querías? **take — books you need** toma los libros que necesites; INTERJ cómo, qué; **— happy children!** ¡qué niños más felices! **— luck!** ¡qué buena suerte!

whatever [hwɑtévɚ] PRON lo que; **do it, — happens** hazlo, pase lo que pase; **— you may think** pienses lo que pienses; **— do you mean?** ¿qué demonios quieres decir? **take — you need** toma lo que necesites; ADJ any **— person** una persona cualquiera / cualquier persona; **no money —** nada de dinero; INTERJ (anything) ¡lo que sea! (I give up) ¡lo que tú digas!

wheat [hwit] N trigo m; **— germ** germen de trigo m

wheel [hwil] N (disc) rueda f; (of cheese) horma f; (for pottery) torno m; (for steering a car) volante m; (for steering a ship) timón m;

—barrow carretilla *f*; **—base** batalla *f*, paso *m*; **—chair** silla de ruedas *f*; **—s** (car) *fam* coche *m*; VT (a round object) hacer rodar; (a person, bicycle, wheelchair) empujar; VI **to — out** sacar rodando; **to — in** entrar rodando; **to — around** girar sobre los talones

wheeze [hwiz] N resuello ruidoso *m*; VI resollar

when [hwɛn] ADV & CONJ cuando; INTERJ, ADV, & N cuándo

whenever [hwɛnévə] CONJ — **I see him** (each time) cada vez que lo veo; ADV (at a future time) — **I see him** cuando lo vea

where [hwɛr] ADV, N, & INTERR PRON dónde *m*; (direction) adónde; CONJ donde; (direction) adonde

whereabouts [hwɛrəbaʊts] N paradero *m*; INTERR ADV dónde

whereas [hwɛrǽz] CONJ mientras que; (in preambles) visto que, considerando que

whereby [hwɛrbáɪ] ADV por lo cual

wherefore [hwɛrfɔr] ADV por lo cual

wherein [hwɛrín] ADV en donde

whereof [hwɛrɑ́v] REL PRON de que; INTERR PRON de qué

whereupon [hwɛrəpán] ADV después de lo cual

wherever [hwɛrévə] ADV dondequiera que

wherewithal [hwɛrwɪðɔ̀l] N medios *m pl*, fondos *m pl*

whet [hwɛt] VT (stimulate) estimular; (sharpen) afilar; **—stone** piedra de afilar *f*

whether [hwɛðə] CONJ — **we like it or not** nos guste o no nos guste; **I doubt — we can do it** dudo [de] que lo podamos hacer; **he asked — I was coming** me preguntó si venía

which [hwɪtʃ] INTERR PRON cuál[es]; — **do you want?** ¿cuál[es] quieres? REL PRON que; **the apple, — I just bought** la manzana, que acabo de comprar; **the book of — I spoke** el libro del que / del cual hablé; **that — you don't know can hurt you** lo que no sabes puede hacerte daño; INTERR ADJ qué, cuál[es] de; — **house is it?** ¿qué casa es? ¿cuál de las casas es?

whichever [hwɪtʃévə] PRON & ADJ (no matter which) cualquiera [que]; — **you choose, you'll regret it later** elijas el que elijas, te arrepentirás después; (anyone that) el que / la que; **choose — you like** elije el que quieras

whiff [hwɪf] N (waft) soplo *m*; (odors, scandal) bocanada *f*, tufillo *m*; **to take a —** oler

while [hwaɪl] N rato *m*; **a short —** un ratito; **a short — ago** hace poco; CONJ (during) mientras; (whereas) mientras que; (even though) aunque; VT **to — away** pasar

whim [hwɪm] N capricho *m*, antojo *m*

whimper [hwímpə] VI/VT lloriquear, gimotear; N lloriqueo *m*, gimoteo *m*

whimsical [hwímzɪkəl] ADJ caprichoso, antojadizo

whine [hwaɪn] VI (whimper) gemir; (complain) quejarse; N (whimper) gemido *m*; (complaint) quejido *m*; **stop whining!** ¡deja de quejarte!

whiner [hwáɪnə] N llorón -ona *mf*, quejica *mf*

whiny [hwáɪni] ADJ quejoso, quejica

whip [hwɪp] N azote *m*, látigo *m*, rebenque *m*; VT (hit with a whip) azotar, fustigar; (spank) zurrar, dar una paliza; (beat to a froth) batir; (defeat) vencer; **to — out** sacar; **to — up** (prepare) preparar rápidamente; (incite) incitar

whipping [hwípɪŋ] N zurra *f*, paliza *f*; **— cream** crema para batir *f*

whir [hwɝ] VI zumbar; N zumbido *m*

whirl [hwɝl] VI girar; **to — around** arremolinarse; **my head —s** me da vueltas la cabeza; N (rotation) giro *m*; (of water) remolino *m*; **—pool** remolino *m*; **—pool bath** baño de remolino *m*; **—wind** torbellino *m*, remolino de viento *m*; **—wind tour** gira relámpago *f*; **my head is in a —** me da vueltas la cabeza; **to give it a —** probarlo

whisk [hwɪsk] VT (sweep) barrer; (beat) batir; **to — away** llevarse de prisa; VI **to — by** pasar rápidamente; N (broom) escobilla *f*; (beater) batidor *m*

whisker [hwískə] N (hair of beard) pelo de la barba *m*; (sideburn) patilla *f*; (of animals) bigote *m*

whiskey, whisky [hwíski] N whisky *m*

whisper [hwíspə] VI/VT (person) cuchichear, secretear; (leaves, water) susurrar; N (people) cuchicheo *m*; (leaves, water) susurro *m*; **to talk in a —** cuchichear

whistle [hwísəl] VI/VT silbar; (loud) chiflar; (in protest) rechiflar; VI (referee, train) pitar; **to — for someone** llamar a uno con un silbido; N (sound) silbido *m*; (loud sound) chiflido *m*; (of a referee) pitido *m*; (instrument) silbato *m*, pito *m*; **—-blower** acusador -ora *mf*

white [hwaɪt] ADJ (color, ethnicity) blanco; **— blood cell** glóbulo blanco *m*; **— bread** pan blanco *m*; **—caps** cabrillas *f pl*; **—-collar** administrativo, de cuello blanco; **— gold** oro blanco *m*; **— hair** cana *f*; **— lie** mentirilla *f*; **— noise** ruido blanco *m*; **—wash** (paint) lechada *f*; (cover-up) encubrimiento *m*; N blanco *m* (also ethnicity); (of egg) clara *f*; VT **to —wash** (paint) blanquear, enjalbegar; (cover up) encubrir

whiten [hwaɪtn̩] VI/VT blanquear[se], emblanquecer

whiteness [hwáɪtnɪs] N blancura *f*

whitish [hwáɪdɪʃ] ADJ blancuzco, blanquecino

whittle [hwíɾl̩] VI/VT tallar; **to — away** ir gastando; **to — down expenses** reducir los gastos

whiz [hwɪz] VI zumbar; **to — by** pasar zumbando; VT hacer zumbar; N (sound)

zumbido *m*; (ace) as *m*; — **kid** niño -ña
prodigio *mf*
who [hu] REL PRON quien[es]; INTERR PRON
quién[es]; **he** — el que
WHO [World Health Organization]
[dábətʃuétʃó] N OMS *f*
whoa [hwo] INTERJ (to express amazement) ¡jo!
(to stop a horse) ¡so!
whoever [huévə] REL PRON (whatever person)
quienquiera que, el/la que; INTERR PRON
(who) quién
whole [hoł] ADJ (complete) completo, íntegro;
(unbroken) entero; (uninjured) ileso; —
grain integral; —**hearted** sincero;
—**heartedly** de todo corazón; — **life
insurance** seguro de vida permanente *m*; —
milk leche entera *f*; — **note** redonda *f*; —
sale (in bulk) al por mayor; (massive)
masivo; —**sale slaughter** matanza *f*; —
wheat integral; **the** — **day** todo el día; **to go**
— **hog** tirar la casa por la ventana; N todo *m*;
(for amounts) totalidad *f*; —**sale** venta al por
mayor *f*, mayoreo *m*; —**saler** comerciante al
por mayor *mf*, mayorista *mf*, almacenista *mf*;
as a — en su totalidad; **on the** — en general;
ADV —**sale** al por mayor; VI/VT **to** —**sale**
vender al por mayor
wholesome [hółsəm] ADJ sano
whom [hum] REL PRON a quien[es]; **for/to/
with** — para/a/con quien; INTERR PRON a
quién[es]
whoop [hwup] N (shout) grito *m*; (gasp)
respiración convulsiva *f*; VI (person) gritar;
(owl) ulular; **to** — **it up** armar jaleo
whopper [hwápə] N (large thing) cosa enorme *f*;
(lie) mentira, trola *f*
whopping [hwápɪŋ] ADJ enorme
whose [huz] REL PRON cuyo; **the man** — **son is
here** el hombre cuyo hijo está aquí; INTERR
PRON de quién; — **book is this?** ¿de quién es
este libro?
why [hwaɪ] ADV & CONJ por qué; **that's the
reason** — **he left** es por eso que se fue; N
porqué *m*; INTERJ —, **of course!** ¡pero claro!
wick [wɪk] N mecha *f*, pabilo *m*
wicked [wɪkɪd] ADJ malvado, perverso
wickedness [wɪkɪdnɪs] N maldad *f*, perversidad *f*
wicker [wɪkə] N mimbre *m*; — **chair** silla de
mimbre *f*
wide [waɪd] ADJ (broad) ancho; (of great range)
amplio; (spacious) vasto, extenso; — **apart**
muy apartados; —**-awake** muy despierto,
despabilado; — **body** avión de fuselaje ancho
m; —**-eyed** ojiabierto, con los ojos bien
abiertos; — **of the mark** lejos del blanco; —
open abierto de par en par; — **receiver**
receptor abierto *m*; —**-spread** (over a wide
area) extendido; (among many people)
generalizado; **to open** — (a door) abrir de par

en par; (one's mouth) abrir bien; **two feet** —
dos pies de ancho
widely [waɪdli] ADV **it is** — **known that** es bien
sabido que; **he is a** — **known artist** es un
artista muy conocido; **he is** — **read** es muy
leído; — **different versions** versiones muy
diferentes
widen [waɪdn] VI/VT ensanchar[se], ampliar[se]
widow [wɪdo] N viuda *f*
widower [wɪdoə] N viudo *m*
width [wɪdθ] N ancho *m*, anchura *f*
wield [wiłd] VT (power) ejercer; (tool) manejar;
(weapon) blandir, esgrimir
wife [waɪf] N esposa *f*, señora *f*, Sp mujer *f*
wifi [wireless fidelity] [wáɪfaɪ] N wifi *f*
wig [wɪg] N peluca *f*
wiggle [wɪgəł] VI/VT (hips) menear[se]; (toes)
mover[se]; N (of hips) meneo *m*; (of toes)
movimiento *m*; — **room** flexibilidad *f*
wigwam [wɪgwam] N tienda indígena *f*
wild [waɪłd] ADJ (animal, savage) salvaje, bravío,
bronco; (plant) silvestre; (party)
desenfrenado; (conduct) alocado; (storm,
temperament) violento; (hair) desordenado;
(look) extraviado, desencajado; (enthusiasm)
delirante; — **boar** jabalí *m*; — **card** comodín
m; —**cat** gato montés *m*; —**-eyed** de mirada
extraviada, con los ojos desencajados; —**fire**
fuego arrasador *m*; —**flower** flor silvestre *f*;
— **goose chase** búsqueda inútil *f*; —**life**
fauna *f*; **I'm just** — **about Mary** estoy loco
por María; **not in your** —**est dreams** ni lo
pienses; **to drive someone** — volver loco a
alguien; **to talk** — decir disparates; N —**s**
regiones salvajes *f pl*
wilderness [wɪłdə·nɪs] N (near mountains)
monte *m*; (desert) desierto *m*; (jungle) jungla *f*
wile [waɪł] N artimaña *f*, treta *f*
will [wɪł] VT (use willpower) conseguir a fuerza
de voluntad; (bequeath) legar, dejar; V AUX **if
you** — si quieres; **she** — **come** va a venir,
vendrá; **this motorcycle** — **go 100 mph**
esta motocicleta puede hacer 100 millas por
hora; **in spite of everything, he** — **not
stop complaining** a pesar de todo, no deja
de quejarse; **she** — **just sit for hours
doing nothing** se pasa horas sentada sin
hacer nada; **that** — **do** basta; N (wish)
voluntad *f*; (testament) testamento *m*;
—**power** fuerza de voluntad *f*; **at** — a
discreción, a voluntad
willful [wɪłfəł] ADJ testarudo, porfiado
willies [wɪliz] N escalofríos *m pl*
willing [wɪłɪŋ] ADJ dispuesto, voluntarioso
willingly [wɪłɪŋli] ADV de buena gana,
gustosamente
willingness [wɪłɪŋnɪs] N buena voluntad *f*,
buena gana *f*
willow [wɪło] N sauce *m*

wilt [wɪlt] VI/VT (plant) marchitar[se]; VI (person) languidecer

wily [wáili] ADJ astuto, artero

wimp [wɪmp] N pelele *m*

win [wɪn] VI/VT ganar; VT (support, fame, affection) ganarse; (victory) alcanzar, conseguir; **to — out** ganar, triunfar; **to — over** conquistar; **a - — situation** una situación beneficiosa para ambas partes; N victoria *f*

wince [wɪns] VI hacer una mueca; N mueca *f*

winch [wɪntʃ] N cabrestante *m*, torno *m*, *Am* guinche *m*

wind[1] [wɪnd] N (air) viento *m*; (gas) gases *m pl*; **—bag** charlatán -ana *mf*; **—breaker**™ cazadora *f*; **—fall** ganancia inesperada *f*; **— instrument** instrumento de viento *m*; **—mill** molino de viento *m*; **—pipe** tráquea *f*; **— power** energía eólica *f*; **—shield** parabrisas *m sg*; **—shield wiper** limpiaparabrisas *m sg*; **—sock** manga de viento *f*; **—surfing** windsurf *m*; **— tunnel** túnel aerodinámico *m*; **to get — of** enterarse de; **to break —** ventosear; **to catch one's —** recobrar el aliento; ADJ **—ward** de barlovento; ADV **—ward** hacia/a barlovento

wind[2] [waɪnd] VT enrollar; (watch) dar cuerda a; VI (take a bending course) serpentear; **to — around** enrollarse; **to — down** (relax) tranquilizarse; (come to a conclusion) irse terminando; **to — up** (string) enrollar; (a clock) dar cuerda; (a project) completar; (in jail) acabar; N (turn) vuelta *f*; (bend) recodo *m*; **—up** conclusión *f*

winding [wáindɪŋ] ADJ sinuoso; **— staircase** escalera de caracol *f*

window [wíndo] N (in building, on screen) ventana *f*; (in building, large) ventanal *m*; (in car, plane) ventanilla *f*; (in a shop) escaparate *m*; *Am* vidriera *f*; **—pane** cristal *m*, vidrio *m*; **— shade** visillo *m*; **—sill** alféizar *m*

windy [wíndi] ADJ ventoso; **it is —** hace/hay viento

wine [waɪn] N vino *m*; **— cellar** bodega *f*; **—glass** copa *f*; **—grower** viticultor -ora *mf*, viñatero -ra *mf*; **— industry** industria vinícola *f*; **—skin** odre *m*; **— tasting** cata de vinos *f*

winery [wáinəri] N bodega *f*

wing [wɪŋ] N (of bird, plane, building, table) ala *f*; **— nut** tuerca [de] mariposa/palomilla *f*; **—span/—spread** envergadura *f*; **—tip** extremo del ala *m*; **in the —s** en los bastidores; **under one's —** al amparo de alguien; **to take — levantar vuelo**; VI volar; VT (wound slightly) herir en el ala/brazo; **to — it** improvisar

winger [wíŋə] N (in soccer) ala *mf*, extremo *mf*

wink [wɪŋk] VI/VT guiñar; **to — approval** guiñar en aprobación; **to — at** hacer la vista gorda; N guiño *m*, guiñada *f*; **I didn't sleep a — no pegué un ojo**

winner [wínə] N ganador -ora *mf*, triunfador -ora *mf*

winning [wínɪŋ] ADJ (successful) ganador, vencedor; (charming) atractivo; **—s** ganancias *f pl*

wino [wáino] N *pej* borracho -cha *mf*

winter [wíntə] N invierno *m*; **— weather** clima invernal *m*; VI invernar

wintry [wíntri] ADJ invernal

wipe [waɪp] VT (sweat, tears) enjugar; (wet surfaces) secar; (dry surface) limpiar; **to — away** enjugar; **to — off** limpiar; **to — out** aniquilar; **to — up** limpiar

wiper [wáipə] N limpiaparabrisas *m sg*

wire [waɪr] N (filament) alambre *m*; (telegram) telegrama *m*; **— fence** alambrado *m*; **— tap** intervención del teléfono *f*, pinchazo *m*; **— transfer** transferencia electrónica *f*; **— by** por telégrafo; VT (an appliance) alambrar; (a house) electrificar; VI/VT (a message) telegrafiar; (money) girar; **to — together** atar con alambre; **to —tap** intervenir un teléfono, pinchar un teléfono

wired [waɪrd] ADJ (installed) alambrado; (tied) atado con alambre; (electrified) electrificado; (enthusiastic) sobreexcitado

wireless [wáirlɪs] ADJ inalámbrico; **— Internet** internet inalámbrico *m*

wiring [wáiriŋ] N cableado *m*

wiry [wáiri] ADJ (skinny) nervudo; (like wire) crespo

wisdom [wízdəm] N (moral) sabiduría *f*; (scholarly) saber *m*; **— tooth** muela del juicio *f*

wise [waɪz] ADJ (discerning) sabio; (prudent) sensato, prudente; (erudite) erudito; **—crack** broma *f*, chiste *m*; **— guy** sabihondo *m*; **the Three — Men** los Tres Reyes Magos; N **in no — de ningún modo**; VI **to — up** avisparse

wish [wɪʃ] VT desear; **I — you were here** ojalá estuvieras aquí; **I — you the best** te deseo lo mejor; **to — for** pedir; **to — upon a star** pedir un deseo; N deseo *m*; **to make a —** pedir un deseo; **best —es** saludos

wishy-washy [wíʃiwaʃi] ADJ indeciso

wistful [wístfəl] ADJ (pensive) pensativo; (nostalgic) nostálgico

wit [wɪt] N (intelligence) agudeza *f*, ingenio *m*; (verbal humor) gracejo *m*, sal *f*, chispa *f*; (person) persona aguda *f*, persona ingeniosa *f*; **to be at one's —s' end** no saber qué más hacer; **to live by one's —s** vivir de su ingenio; **to lose one's —s** perder el juicio; **to use one's —s** valerse de su ingenio

witch [wɪtʃ] N bruja *f*; **—craft** brujería *f*; **— hunt** cacería de brujas *f*

with [wɪθ, wɪð] PREP con; **rice — chicken** arroz con pollo *m*; **the man — glasses** el hombre de gafas; **I left my son — Mary** dejé a mi hijo al cuidado de María; **to be — it** está al día; **— me** conmigo; **— you** contigo, con usted

withdraw [wɪðdrɔ́] VI/VT retirar[se]

withdrawal [wɪðdrɔ́əl] N (of troops) retirada *f*; (from public office) alejamiento *m*; (from a bank) *Am* retiro *m*; *Sp* retirada *f*; **[symptoms]** síndrome de abstinencia *m*

withdrawn [wɪðdrɔ́n] *see* withdraw

withdrew [wɪðdrú] *see* withdraw

wither [wɪðɚ] VI/VT (of a plant) marchitar[se]; (of a person) consumir[se]; **she —ed him with a look** lo fulminó con la mirada

withheld [wɪθhéld] *see* withhold

withhold [wɪθhóld] VT (approval) negar; (funds) retener; (truth) ocultar

withholding tax [wɪθhóldɪŋtæks] N impuesto deducido del salario *m*

within [wɪðín] PREP dentro de; **— five miles** a menos de cinco millas; ADV dentro, adentro

without [wɪðáʊt] PREP sin; **— my seeing him** sin que yo lo vea; ADV fuera, afuera

withstand [wɪθstǽnd] VI/VT resistir

withstood [wɪθstúd] *see* withstand

witness [wɪtnɪs] N (person) testigo *mf*; (testimony) testimonio *m*; **to bear —** atestiguar; VT (see) presenciar; (sign) firmar como testigo

witticism [wɪ́DISIZEM] N ocurrencia *f*

witty [wɪ́Di] ADJ ocurrente, dicharachero

wizard [wɪ́zɚd] N (sorcerer) mago *m*, brujo *m*, hechicero *m*; (computer expert) experto -ta *mf*; (genius) genio *m*

wobble [wɑ́bəl] N tambaleo *m*, bamboleo *m*; VI/VT tambalear[se], bombolear[se]

woe [wo] N aflicción *f*; **— is me!** ¡pobre de mí!

woeful [wófəl] ADJ lamentable

wok [wɑk] N wok *m*

woke [wok] *see* wake

woken [wókən] *see* wake

wolf [wʊlf] N lobo *m*; **— spider** araña lobo *f*

woman [wʊ́mən] N mujer *f*; *fam* tía *f*; **a —'s touch** un toque femenino; **women's lib[eration]** movimiento de liberación femenina *m*; **women's rights** derechos de la mujer *m pl*

womanhood [wʊ́mənhʊd] N (condition) condición de mujer *f*; (all women) las mujeres *f pl*

womanizer [wʊ́mənaɪzɚ] N mujeriego *m*

womankind [wʊ́mənkaɪnd] N las mujeres *f pl*

womanly [wʊ́mənli] ADJ femenino

womb [wum] N (uterus) útero *m*, matriz *f*; (insides of something) vientre *m*; (center) seno *m*

won [wʌn] *see* win

wonder [wʌ́ndɚ] VI/VT preguntarse; **to — at** admirarse de, maravillarse de; **I — what time it is** ¿qué hora será? N (marvel) maravilla *f*; (surprise) asombro *m*; (miracle) milagro *m*; **it's a — that** es asombroso que; **it's no — that** no es de extrañar que

wonderful [wʌ́ndɚfəl] ADJ maravilloso, estupendo

woo [wu] VT cortejar

wood [wʊd] N (material, also golf club) madera *f*; (firewood) leña *f*; **—cutter** leñador -ora *mf*; **—louse** cochinilla *f*; **—pecker** pájaro carpintero *m*; **—s** bosque *m*; **— shaving** viruta *f*; **—shed** leñera *f*; **—sman** leñador *m*; **—winds** maderas *f pl*; **—work** carpintería *f*, maderaje *m*; **to come out of the —work** salir de la nada

wooded [wʊ́dɪd] ADJ arbolado

wooden [wʊ́dn] ADJ (of wood) de madera; (lifeless) inexpresivo

woody [wʊ́di] ADJ (with trees) arbolado; (like wood) leñoso

woof [wʊf] N (of fabric) trama *f*; INTERJ (sound made by a dog) ¡guau!

wool [wʊl] N lana *f*; **— sweater** suéter de lana *m*

woolen [wʊ́lən] ADJ de lana; N **—s** (fabric) tejido de lana *m*; (clothes) ropa de lana *f*

woolly [wʊ́li] ADJ lanudo

word [wɚd] N (lexical unit) vocablo *m*, palabra *f*; (promise) palabra *f*; (news) noticia *f*, aviso *m*; (order) mandato *m*, orden *m*; **— for —** palabra por palabra; **— processing** procesamiento de textos *m*; *Sp* tratamiento de texto[s] *m*; **—s [of a song]** letra [de una canción] *f*; **— spacing** espaciado de palabras *m*; **— wrap** retorno de línea automático *m*; **I found out by — of mouth** me lo dijeron; **may I have a — with you?** ¿podemos hablar? **to eat one's —s** tragarse/comerse las palabras; VT (oral) expresar; (written) formular

wording [wɚ́dɪŋ] N formulación *f*

wordy [wɚ́di] ADJ verboso, prolijo

wore [wɔr] *see* wear

work [wɚk] N (effort) trabajo *m*; (employment) empleo *m*, trabajo *m*; (artistic product, fortification) obra *f*; **—book** cuaderno/libro de trabajo *m*; **—day** día laborable *m*; **— environment** entorno de trabajo *m*; **— flow** flujo de trabajo *m*; **—force** mano de obra *f*; **—load** cantidad/carga de trabajo *f*; **—man** obrero *m*; **— of art** obra de arte *f*; **—out** sesión de ejercicio *f*; **— permit** permiso de trabajo *m*; **— place** lugar de trabajo *m*; **— schedule** horario de trabajo *m*; **—sheet** planilla *f*, hoja de ejercicios *f*; **—shop** taller *m*; **—station** estación de trabajo *f*; **— stoppage** huelga *f*, paro laboral *m*; **—s** fábrica *f*; **the —s** todo; **—week**

semana de trabajo f; **he's hard at —** está trabajando duro; ADJ --**related** laboral; VI (labor) trabajar; (function) funcionar; VT (change) efectuar; (metal, land) trabajar; (a crowd) manipular; (employees) hacer trabajar; **to — in[to]** introducir; **to — loose** soltar[se], aflojar[se]; **to — on** (repair) arreglar; (improve) tratar de mejorar; **to — one's way through college** pagarse los estudios trabajando; **to — one's way up** ascender a fuerza de trabajo; **to — out** (a plan) urdir; (a problem) resolver; **he —s out every day** hace ejercicio todos los días; **to — overtime** trabajar horas extras; **it all —ed out** al final todo salió bien; **to be all —ed up** estar sobreexcitado; **to get —ed up** agitarse

workaholic [wɝkəhólɪk] N adicto -ta al trabajo mf

worker [wɝkɚ] N trabajador -ora mf; (in a factory) obrero -ra mf; (in an office) oficinista mf

working [wɝkɪŋ] N (act of someone who works, shaping of metals) trabajo m; (operation) funcionamiento m, operación f; (of a problem) cálculo m; (of a mine) explotación f; ADJ (class) obrero, trabajador; (majority) suficiente; **— class** clase obrera/trabajadora f; **— lunch** comida de trabajo f; **—man** obrero m

workmanship [wɝkmənʃɪp] N (skill) habilidad f, destreza f; (quality of work) confección f

world [wɝld] N mundo m; **— Bank** Banco Mundial m; **— Cup** Copa del Mundo f; **—view** cosmovisión f; **— war** guerra mundial f; **— Wide Web** web f, red [mundial electrónica] f; ADJ **—class** de categoría mundial; **—famous** de fama mundial; **—shaking** trascendental; **—wide** mundial

worldly [wɝldli] ADJ (mundane) mundano, temporal; (sophisticated) de mundo, corrido; (material) material

worm [wɝm] N gusano m; ADJ **—eaten** comido por los gusanos, carcomido; VT desparasitar, quitar las lombrices; **to — a secret out of someone** extraerle/sonsacarle un secreto a alguien; **to — oneself into** insinuarse en

worn [wɔrn] ADJ desgastado, usado

worn [wɔrn] see wear

worrisome [wɝisəm] ADJ preocupante, inquietante

worry [wɝi] VI/VT preocupar[se], inquietar[se]; VT (harass) hostigar; VI **to — with** juguetear con; N preocupación f, inquietud f, zozobra f; **—wart** preocupón -ona mf

worse [wɝs] ADJ & ADV peor; **— and —** cada vez peor; **— than ever** peor que nunca; **from bad to —** de mal en peor; **so much the —** tanto peor; **to be — off** estar peor que antes;

to change for the — empeorar[se]; **to get — empeorar[se]**

worship [wɝʃɪp] N (act of worshiping) adoración f; (ceremony) culto m; VT (revere) adorar, venerar; VI (attend services) asistir al culto

worshiper [wɝʃɪpɚ] N (one who worships) adorador -ora mf; **—s** fieles mf pl

worst [wɝst] ADJ & ADV **— one** el/la peor; **the — thing** lo peor; **—case scenario** el peor de los casos; VT derrotar

worth [wɝθ] ADJ **to be — a dollar** valer un dólar; **to be — hearing** ser digno de oírse; **to be —while** valer la pena; **it's — doing** vale la pena hacerlo; N valor m, valía f; **ten cents' — of** diez centavos de; **to get one's money's — out of** aprovechar al máximo

worthless [wɝθlɪs] ADJ (useless) inútil; (despicable) despreciable; **— check** cheque sin fondos m

worthy [wɝði] ADJ (meritorious) digno, meritorio; (esteemed) benemérito; **— cause** causa noble f; **— of praise** digno de elogio; N persona ilustre mf

would [wʊd] V AUX **I — do it if I could** lo haría si pudiera; **— you please open the door?** ¿podrías abrir la puerta por favor? **he said he — do it** dijo que lo haría; **as a child, I — play all the time** de niño, jugaba todo el tiempo; **— that she were alive!** ¡ojalá estuviera viva!

wound[1] [wund] N herida f; VI/VT herir; (with an arrow) flechar

wound[2] [waund] see wind

wove [wov] see weave

woven [wóvən] see weave

wow [waʊ] VT impresionar; INTERJ ¡huy!

wrangle [ræŋgəl] VI/VT (quarrel) discutir; (obtain) agenciarse de; VT (herd) juntar; Am rodear; N riña f, pendencia f

wrangler [ræŋglɚ] N vaquero -ra mf

wrap [ræp] VT envolver; **to — up** (a present) envolver; (a baby) arropar; (a task) terminar; (against the cold) abrigar[se]; **to be —ped in** estar envuelto en; **to be —ped up in** estar absorto en; N (coat) abrigo m; (shawl) chal m; **—up** (summary) resumen m; (end) final m; **keep under —s** mantener secreto

wrapper [ræpɚ] N envoltura f, envoltorio m

wrapping [ræpɪŋ] N envoltura f; **— paper** papel para envolver m

wrath [ræθ] N ira f, cólera f

wreak [rik] VT **to — havoc** hacer estragos

wreath [riθ] N corona f; **— of smoke** espiral de humo f

wreck [rɛk] N (building) ruina f; (car, plane) restos m pl; (a ship) pecio m; (shipwreck) naufragio m; (person) desastre m, ruina f; (accident) accidente m; VI tener un accidente; VT (a ship) naufragar; (a car, totally) destrozar; (a car, with minor damage) chocar; (a building) demoler

wreckage [rékɪʤ] N (of a building) escombros *m pl*; (of a car, plane) restos de un accidente *m pl*; (of a ship) pecio *m*

wrecker [rékɚ] N (tow truck) grúa *f*, camión de remolque *m*; (worker) obrero -ra de demolición *mf*

wrench [rentʃ] N (twist) torcedura *f*; (pull) tirón *m*; (tool) llave de tuercas *f*; VT torcer, retorcer; **to — off/out** arrancar de un tirón, arrebatar

wrest [rest] VT (pull) arrancar; (take away) arrebatar

wrestle [résəl] VI/VT luchar [con/contra]; N lucha *f*

wrestler [réslɚ] N luchador -ora *mf*

wrestling [réslɪŋ] N lucha libre *f*

wretch [retʃ] N miserable *mf*, infeliz *mf*

wretched [rétʃɪd] ADJ (unfortunate) desdichado, infeliz; (despicable) vil, miserable, arrastrado; (inferior) pésimo

wriggle [rígəl] VI culebrear, serpentear; **to — out of** escabullirse de; VT menear, retorcer

wring [rɪŋ] VT (twist) torcer, retorcer; (extract) arrancar; **to — one's hands** retorcerse las manos; **to — out** escurrir

wrinkle [ríŋkəl] N arruga *f*, surco *m*; (problem) problema *m*; VI/VT arrugar[se]

wrist [rɪst] N muñeca *f*; **—watch** reloj [de] pulsera *m*

writ [rɪt] N auto *m*, mandato *m*

write [raɪt] VI/VT escribir; (transfer data) grabar; **to — back** contestar; **to — down** apuntar; **to — off** cancelar; **to — out** escribir en forma completa; **to —-protect** proteger contra grabación; **to — up** hacer un reportaje sobre; **it's written all over his face** se le ve en la cara; **she —s for a living** es escritora; N —-**up** reportaje *m*; **— protection** protección contra grabación *f*

writer [ráɪdɚ] N escritor -ora *mf*, literato -ta *mf*

writhe [raɪð] VI retorcerse

writing [ráɪdɪŋ] N (act of writing) escritura *f*; (handwriting) letra *f*, escritura *f*; (style) estilo *m*; **— desk** escritorio *m*; **— paper** papel de escribir *m*; **—s** obra *f*; **to put in —** poner por escrito

written [rítn̩] *see* write

wrong [rɔŋ] ADJ (incorrect) incorrecto, equivocado; (improper) inapropiado; **what's — with you?** ¿qué te pasa? **you are —** estás equivocado; **in the — side of a fabric** el revés de una tela; **— side out** con lo de adentro para afuera; **to be on the — side of the road** ir a contramano / en sentido contrario; **that is the — book** ese no es el libro; **it is in the — place** está fuera de lugar; ADV mal; **to go —** salir mal; N (evil) mal *m*; (injustice)

injusticia *f*; **to be in the —** (not be right) estar equivocado; (be to blame) tener la culpa; **to do —** hacer mal; VT perjudicar

wrongful [rɔ́ŋfəl] ADJ injusto, injustificado

wrongly [rɔ́ŋli] ADV (reported) incorrectamente; (accused) injustamente

wrote [rot] *see* write

wrought [rɔt] ADJ forjado; **— iron** hierro forjado *m*

wrung [rʌŋ] *see* wring

wry [raɪ] ADJ (smile) torcido; (remark, humor) irónico; **to make a — face** torcer la cara

WTO [World Trade Organization] [dʌ́bəljutíó] N OMT *f*

WWW [World Wide Web] [dʌ́bəljudʌ́bəljudʌ́bəlju] N web *f*

Xx

xenophobia [zɛnəfóbiə] N xenofobia *f*

Xerox™ [zíraks] N fotocopia *f*; VI/VT fotocopiar

x-rated [éksreDɪd] ADJ pornográfico

x-ray [éksre] N rayos X *m pl*, radiografía *f*; VI/VT radiografiar

xylophone [záiləfon] N xilofón *m*, xilófono *m*

Yy

yacht [jɑt] N yate *m*; VI navegar en yate

y'all [jɔl] PRON *Am* ustedes *mf*; *Sp* vosotros -as *mf*

Yankee [jǽŋki] ADJ & N estadounidense del norte del país *mf*

yard [jɑrd] N (measure) yarda [0.9144m] *f*; (spar) verga *f*; (courtyard) patio *m*; (grassy area) jardín *m*; **—stick** (stick) vara de medida [de una yarda] *f*; (criterion) patrón *m*, norma *f*

yarn [jɑrn] N (material) hilo *m*; (story) cuento *m*

yawn [jɔn] VI bostezar; N bostezo *m*

yeah [jɛ́ə] ADV *fam* sí; *fam* **— right!** ¡de eso, nada! ¡qué va!

year [jir] N año *m*; **—book** anuario *m*; ADJ **—-end** de fin de año; **—-round** de todo el año; **—-to-date** del año hasta la fecha

yearling [jírlɪŋ] N animal de un año *m*; (of cows) añojo -ja *mf*

yearly [jírli] ADJ anual; ADV anualmente

yearn [jɚn] VI anhelar, suspirar por

yearning [jɚ́nɪŋ] N anhelo *m*

yeast [jist] N levadura *f*

yell [jɛl] VI/VT gritar; N grito *m*

yellow [jɛ́lo] ADJ (color) amarillo; (coward)

cobarde; **— card** (in soccer) tarjeta amarilla *f*; **— fever** fiebre amarilla *f*; **— jacket** avispa *f*; **— pages** páginas amarillas *f pl*; N amarillo *m*; VI/VT poner[se] amarillo, amarillear

yellowish [jélʊɪʃ] ADJ amarillento

yelp [jɛlp] VI gañir, aullar; N gañido *m*, aullido *m*

Yemen [jémən] N Yemen *m*

Yemeni [jémənɪ] ADJ & N yemení *mf*

yen [jɛn] N (currency of Japan) yen *m*; (desire) anhelo *m*; VI anhelar

yes [jɛs] ADV sí; **—no question** pregunta de sí o no *f*

yesterday [jéstəd̪e] ADV & N ayer *m*; **the day before —** anteayer

yet [jɛt] ADV & CONJ **are they here —?** ¿ya llegaron? **they aren't here —** todavía no llegan, aún no han llegado; **— another** otro más; **ugly — charming** feo pero encantador; **as —** todavía, aún

yield [jiłd] VI/VT (surrender, give in) ceder; (produce) rendir, redituar; **to — 5 percent** dar un cinco por ciento de interés; N (production) rendimiento *m*, producción *f*; (of stocks) rédito *m*

yodel [jódł] VI cantar a la tirolesa; N canto tirolés *m*

yoga [jógə] N yoga *m*

yogurt [jógət] N yogur *m*

yoke [jok] N (crossbar) yugo *m*; (pair of animals) yunta *f*; (on a shirt) canesú *m*; VT uncir

yolk [jok] N yema *f*

yonder [jándə] ADJ aquel; ADV (location) allá; (direction) hacia allá

yore [jɔr] N **in days of —** antaño

you [ju] SUBJ PRON (sg informal) tú; *RP, Central Am* vos; (sg formal) usted; (pl informal) *Sp* vosotros; *Am* ustedes; (pl formal) ustedes; **I see —** (sg informal) te veo; (sg formal) lo veo; (pl informal) *Sp* os veo; *Am* los veo; (pl formal) los veo; **I talk to —** (sg informal) te hablo; (sg formal) le hablo; (pl informal) *Sp* os hablo; *Am* les hablo; (pl formal) les hablo; **I went with —** (sg informal) fui contigo; (sg formal) fui con usted; (pl informal) *Sp* fui con vosotros; *Am* fui con ustedes; (pl formal) fui con ustedes; **it's for —** (sg informal) *RP, Central Am* es para vos; (sg formal) es para ti; (sg informal) *RP, Central Am* es para vos; (sg formal) es para usted; (pl informal) *Sp* es para vosotros; *Am* es para ustedes; (pl formal) es para ustedes; **this is how — make bread** así se hace el pan

young [jʌŋ] ADJ joven; **— man** joven *m*; **— people** gente joven *f*; **— woman** joven *f*; N (offspring) cría *f*

youngster [jʌ́ŋstə] N muchacho -cha *mf*, jovencito -ta *mf*

your [jɔr] POSS ADJ **this is — dog** (sg informal) este es tu perro; (sg formal) este es su perro;

(pl informal) *Sp* este es vuestro perro, *Am* este es su perro; (pl formal) este es su perro

yours [jɔrz] PRON **this book is —** (sg informal) este libro es tuyo; (sg formal) este libro es suyo / de usted; (pl informal) *Sp* este libro es vuestro; *Am* este libro es suyo / de ustedes; (pl formal) este libro es suyo / de ustedes; **— is bigger** (sg informal) el tuyo / la tuya es más grande; (sg formal) el suyo / el de usted / la suya / la de usted es más grande; (pl informal) *Sp* el vuestro / la vuestra es más grande; *Am* el suyo / el de ustedes es más grande; (pl formal) el suyo / el de ustedes es más grande; **a friend of —** (sg informal) un amigo tuyo; (sg formal) un amigo suyo / de usted; (pl informal) *Sp* un amigo vuestro; *Am* un amigo suyo / de ustedes; **— truly** atentamente

yourself [jɔrsélf] PRON **you — wrote the letter** (sg informal) tú mismo escribiste la carta; (sg formal) usted mismo escribió la carta; **you yourselves wrote the letter** (pl informal) *Sp* vosotros mismos escribisteis la carta; *Am* ustedes mismos escribieron la carta; (pl formal) ustedes mismos escribieron la carta; **you are not — today** (sg informal) hoy no eres el mismo de siempre; (sg formal) hoy no es el mismo de siempre; **you are not yourselves today** *Sp* hoy no sois los mismos de siempre; *Am* hoy no son los mismos de siempre; (pl formal) hoy no son los mismos de siempre; **you were sitting by —** (sg informal) tú estabas sentado solo; (sg formal) usted estaba sentado solo; **you were sitting by yourselves** (informal) *Sp* vosotros estabais sentados solos; *Am* ustedes estaban sentados solos; (pl formal) ustedes estaban sentados solos; **you look at — at the mirror** (sg informal) tú te miras en el espejo; (sg formal) usted se mira en el espejo; **you look at yourselves at the mirror** (pl informal) *Sp* vosotros os mirais en el espejo; *Am* ustedes se miran en el espejo; (pl formal) ustedes se miran en el espejo; **you bought — a house** (sg informal) te compraste una casa; (sg formal) usted se compró una casa; **you bought yourselves a house** (pl informal) *Sp* os comprasteis una casa; *Am* se compraron una casa; (pl formal) se compraron una casa

youth [juθ] N (person) joven *m*; (young age) juventud *m*

youthful [júθfəł] ADJ juvenil

yo-yo [jójo] N yo-yo *m*

yuan [juán] N yuan *m*

yucca [jákə] N yuca *f*

yuck [jʌk] INTERJ puaj, puaf

Yugoslavia [jugoslávia] N Yugoslavia *f*

Yugoslavian [jugoslávian] ADJ & N yugoslavo -va *mf*

Yuletide [júłtaɪd] N Navidad *f*

yummy [jʌ́mi] ADJ delicioso; INTERJ ¡qué rico!
yuppie [jʌ́pi] N yuppie *mf*

Zz

Zambia [zǽmbiə] N Zambia *f*
Zambian [zǽmbiən] ADJ & N zambiano -na *mf*
zany [zéni] ADJ loco, chiflado
zap [zæp] VT liquidar
zeal [zil] N celo *m*, fervor *m*
zealot [zélət] N fanático -ca *mf*
zealous [zéləs] ADJ celoso, fervoroso
zebra [zíbrə] N cebra *f*
zenith [zínɪθ] N cenit *m*
zephyr [zéfɚ] N céfiro *m*
zeppelin [zépəlɪn] N zepelín *m*, dirigible *m*
zero [zíro] NUM cero *m*; **there's — possibility
    that he'll come** las posibilidades de que
    venga son nulas
zest [zɛst] N entusiasmo *m*
zigzag [zígzæg] N zigzag *m*; ADJ & ADV en zigzag;
    VI zigzaguear, andar en zigzag; VT hacer
    zigzaguear
Zimbabwe [zɪmbábwe] N Zimbabue *m*
Zimbabwean [zɪmbábweən] ADJ & N zimbabuo
    -bua *mf*
zinc [zɪŋk] N cinc *m*, zinc *m*
zip [zɪp] VI/VT cerrar/abrir con cremallera; **to —
    by** pasar volando; **to — over** ir corriendo; N
    cero *m*; **— code** código postal *m*
zipper [zípɚ] N cremallera *f*, cierre [relámpago]
    m
zirconium [zɚkóniəm] N circonio *m*
zodiac [zódiæk] N zodíaco *m*
zombie [zámbi] N zombi *mf*
zone [zon] N zona *f*; **— defense** defensa en zonas
    f; VT dividir en zonas
zoning [zónɪŋ] N zonificación *f*
zoo [zu] N zoológico *m*; *Sp* zoo *m*; **—keeper**
    guardián -ana del zoológico *mf*
zoological [zoəládʒɪkəl] ADJ zoológico
zoology [zoáləʤi] N zoología *f*
zoom [zum] VI (make sound) zumbar; **to — in**
    ampliar una imagen; **to — off** salir
    zumbando; **to — out** achicar la imagen; N
    zumbido *m*; **— lens** teleobjetivo *m*, zoom *m*
zucchini [zukíni] N calabacín *m*
zygote [záɪgot] N cigoto *m*, zigoto *m*